Volume 1

A CONCORDANCE TO CONRAD'S *LORD JIM*

A CONCORDANCE TO CONRAD'S *LORD JIM*

Verbal Index, Word Frequency Table and Field of Reference

JAMES W. PARINS, ROBERT J. DILLIGAN AND TODD K. BENDER

Routledge
Taylor & Francis Group

LONDON AND NEW YORK

First published in 1976 by Garland Publishing Inc.

This edition first published in 2020
by Routledge
2 Park Square, Milton Park, Abingdon, Oxon OX14 4RN

and by Routledge
52 Vanderbilt Avenue, New York, NY 10017

Routledge is an imprint of the Taylor & Francis Group, an informa business

British Library Cataloguing in Publication Data
A catalogue record for this book is available from the British Library

ISBN: 978-0-367-44109-8 (Set)
ISBN: 978-1-00-302698-3 (Set) (ebk)
ISBN: 978-0-367-86084-4 (Volume 1) (hbk)
ISBN: 978-0-367-86094-3 (Volume 1) (pbk)
ISBN: 978-1-00-301685-4 (Volume 1) (ebk)

Publisher's Note
The publisher has gone to great lengths to ensure the quality of this reprint but points out that some imperfections in the original copies may be apparent.

Disclaimer
The publisher has made every effort to trace copyright holders and would welcome correspondence from those they have been unable to trace.

A Concordance to Conrad's *Lord Jim*

Verbal Index, Word Frequency Table and Field of Reference

James W. Parins
Robert J. Dilligan
Todd K. Bender

Garland Publishing, Inc., New York & London

1976

Library of Congress Cataloging in Publication Data

Parins, James W
    A concordance to Conrad's Lord Jim.

    (Garland reference library in the humanities ;
v. 10)
    1. Conrad, Joseph, 1857-1924. Lord Jim--Concord-
ances. I. Dilligan, Robert J., joint author.
II. Bender, Todd K., joint author. III. Conrad,
Joseph, 1857-1924. Lord Jim. IV. Title.
PR6005.04L75   823'.9'12   75-34972
ISBN 0-8240-9995-8

Printed in the United States of America

Contents

Preface

The complete works of Joseph Conrad are in the process of preparation for computer analysis in a multi-institutional project which has its administrative center at the University of Wisconsin—Madison. The verbal Index to *Lord Jim* follows the earlier *Concordance to Heart of Darkness* (Carbondale: Southern Illinois University Press, 1973) as a pilot or experimental publication testing ways to give easy and inexpensive access to scholars unable to work directly with our electronic data banks. The principles behind our work have been discussed in "Computer Assisted Editorial Work on Conrad," *Conradiana,* V (Number 3, 1973), 37-45, and "Computer Analysis of Conrad," *The Polish Review,* XX (Numbers 2-3, 1975), 123-132.

This publication falls into three parts: The Verbal Index, The Word Frequency Table, and The Field of Reference. A scholar interested in the full range of connotation for the word *heart* in Conrad would look first to the word frequency table to see how often the word in question occurs in *Lord Jim.* If the word is indeed part of the vocabulary of the novel, he then would turn to its alphabetical listing in the Verbal Index and find the line numbers in which it appears. Then turning to the field of reference, he could locate the lines cited and look at each occurrence of the word in context.

We feel that data provided by these tables is of basic importance to both the editor and the literary critic.

A simple index of an author's vocabulary is essential to find patterns of imagery, recurring words which tend to define his style, and to provide information for the lexicographer about the development of the language in his work. But such simple indexes can be broken down into more complex units for comparison and become more informative still. We can index the vocabulary of an early novel and compare it to a late work so as to see what words and images drop from the author's mind as he grows older, what new vocabulary enters. We can index one fictional time level of a novel and compare it to another so that as we see in *Heart of Darkness* there is a class of words which occurs as metaphoric in the fictional present frame on the Nellie, but recurs concretely in the Congo tale. For example, Marlow speaks in the fictional present about stepping into the *shoes* of his predecessor Fresleven metaphorically, but concretely he tears off his blood-stained *shoes* in the fictional past of the Congo. Such study shows how vocabulary resonates between present frame and past tale and creates an impression in the reader unobtrusively which can only be revealed through analytical indexes like those generated by modern technology. Or, we might index the speeches of one character to compare against another's so as to determine the characteristic vocabulary of Marlow as separate from that of other narrators. Or, instead of treating single words, we could study collocations of words much as psychologists practice word association tests, isolating sets of words which occur in close proximity in habitual patterns. Such study gives us access to the subconscious as well as the conscious level of the writer's mind. Or, we might want to

study the text in order to find orthographic differences between the author's English spelling and his American spelling of words, or the punctuation practices of a work set up by a printing house as opposed to the author's manuscript version of it.

Our overall objective is to build a model literary data bank; not merely to produce individual printed indexes or sets of analytic data, but to create a permanent electronic research tool. We must imagine the data bank as growing in two directions. On the horizontal plane, so to speak, we might imagine a linear growth as novel after novel is added in computer readable form: *Heart of Darkness,* plus *Lord Jim,* plus *Nostromo,* and so on. On the vertical plane, however, since no single edition of Conrad's work can be established as his pure and final intention, we must imagine the data bank growing by superimposing the 1924 Kent edition of *Lord Jim* on the 1921 Heinemann *Lord Jim,* plus the serial publication, plus manuscript versions, and so on. We can search in this data structure horizontally to compare the use of a word in early novels as compared to the use of that word in late novels. We can also search on the vertical axis to see how Conrad revised and altered his text as it passed through proof sheets, typescripts, early printed versions, and later revisions of the same work.

We believe that the "real" depository of information in our research is the electronic tape from which our printed indexes are generated. This tape is capable of many formulations. Any printed version of the data will be considerably less complex and flexible than the electronic form. What we are providing at this time for scholars unequipped to work directly with the electronic data is an index or partial summary of useful information derived from the full information in electronic storage. Such a publication is necessary because even in our own research work we find it necessary to print out long tables of information for visual analysis and because in most cases in the next decade scholars will work with our data without direct interactive connection to our electronic material. Our publication is, therefore, a compromise. We know that any printed version of the electronic data will be inherently less complete and less flexible than the electronic data bank, but we hope to provide the most useful information at the lowest cost to scholars who are unable at the present to work directly with the full electronic record.

When we work at an interactive terminal with our data and request a key-word-in-context concordance of a novel, we get in one column on our screen the word requested with a set of numbers identifying its locations in the text. We then can request each location to appear on the screen and we see the word in its contexts brought together for our comparison. The electronic screen creates for the nonce what is properly called a concordance. To create a printed concordance of this data, we would have to print the context of each word over and over, creating a bulky publication perhaps ten times the size of the initial text. Most concordances cut down on expensive bulk by "stopping" or omitting high frequency words, but this approach still leaves a bulk of about six times the length of the initial text and cuts out words which many modern linguists consider to be important to stylistic analysis. We have printed here the verbal index listing all the vocabulary of the author and a model of the field of reference to which it refers. The "Concordance" or comparisons of contexts must be made as on the interactive screen for the nonce by turning from the index to the field of reference. Many scholars seem to think that the perfect printed concordance to a work will be that which most closely

approximates handmade models developed in primitive times. We prefer to think of this series of publications as truly experimental. What kind of tabulation of information is most helpful to the textual scholar and the critic? How can we provide that information most inexpensively and clearly? We look forward to hearing from users how to improve, refine, make more economical these guides to our electronic data and we plan to modify our publications in the future to suit your requirements.

PART I

Index Verborum for
Conrad's *Lord Jim*

The following are parallel index columns (read top-to-bottom within each group).

A (CONT.) — 26.01

		26.01
26.09	26.14	26.15
26.15	26.20	26.22
26.23	26.26	26.29
27.01	27.01	27.03
27.05	27.05	27.07
27.16	27.27	27.29
27.30	28.02	28.06
28.06	28.07	28.08
28.09	28.12	28.20
28.24	29.03	29.04
29.04	29.10	29.15
29.19	29.23	29.23
29.27	30.02	30.04
30.05	30.07	30.25
30.29	31.01	31.02
31.03	31.09	31.14
32.01	32.05	32.05
32.10	33.06	33.14
33.18	33.22	33.24
33.27	33.28	33.30
34.07	34.09	34.13
34.14	34.23	34.24
35.02	35.13	35.18
35.20	35.21	35.23
35.24	35.25	35.26
36.05	36.06	36.07
36.07	36.17	36.20
36.21	36.25	37.02
37.04	37.06	37.23
38.04	38.11	38.11
38.12	38.14	38.20
38.25	38.29	38.29
39.01	39.01	39.02
39.02	39.03	40.04
40.06	40.13	40.15
41.06	41.10	41.10
41.15	41.16	41.17
41.27	42.06	42.07
42.08	42.13	42.18
42.21	42.26	42.28
43.05	43.10	43.10
43.22	43.32	43.35
43.37	43.37	43.38
43.39	44.03	44.04
44.06	44.08	44.20
44.25	44.27	45.09
45.21	45.22	45.26
45.30	46.04	46.07
46.15	46.20	46.20
46.22	46.23	46.24
46.24	46.24	46.25
46.25	47.02	47.11
47.13	47.21	47.21
47.22	47.22	47.25
47.26	47.30	48.11
48.16	48.16	48.17
48.19	48.20	48.21
49.08	49.10	49.13
49.23	49.27	49.27
50.03	50.04	50.04
50.06	50.09	50.12
50.29	50.30	51.05
51.09	51.10	52.06
52.09	52.10	52.11
52.12	52.21	52.22
52.22	53.07	53.09
53.10	53.20	53.24
54.09	54.11	54.14
54.21	54.22	54.24
55.06	55.09	55.11
55.12	55.15	55.18
55.18	55.22	55.25
55.28	55.29	55.30
56.04	56.05	56.05
56.06	56.07	56.07
56.09	56.09	56.10
56.12	56.12	56.23
56.26	56.29	57.01
57.02	57.04	57.04
57.08	57.12	57.16
57.24	58.01	58.03
58.06	58.18	58.18
58.18	58.18	58.19
58.23	58.28	59.01
58.29	58.30	59.01
59.05	59.05	59.06
59.08	59.08	59.09
59.14	59.16	59.17
59.19	59.26	59.27

'TWEEN / A

'TWEEN		101.20
A	1.03	1.04
1.05	1.07	1.08
1.14	1.20	2.02
2.05	2.06	2.08
2.08	2.09	2.10
2.11	2.12	2.12
2.16	2.16	2.17
2.18	2.19	2.21
2.24	2.26	3.07
3.08	3.08	3.12
3.14	3.25	3.28
4.05	4.06	4.06
4.09	4.11	4.13
4.15	4.17	4.19
4.22	4.25	4.30
5.01	5.01	5.06
5.11	5.11	5.12
5.12	5.16	5.19
5.19	5.22	5.26
5.28	6.09	6.09
6.16	6.17	6.19
6.21	6.22	6.25
6.29	7.03	7.04
7.08	7.11	7.17
7.26	7.28	7.28
7.28	8.06	8.06
8.11	8.14	8.14
8.15	8.15	8.18
8.21	8.22	8.25
8.27	9.05	9.08
10.14	10.16	10.18
11.04	11.06	11.08
11.09	11.19	11.20
11.21	12.03	12.09
12.17	12.18	12.18
12.19	12.25	12.27
12.27	12.28	13.06
13.09	13.13	13.21
13.25	13.29	14.11
14.11	14.20	14.22
14.25	14.27	14.28
14.29	14.30	15.01
15.05	15.06	15.06
15.10	15.13	15.14
15.14	15.15	15.18
16.18	16.23	15.24
16.24	17.01	17.02
17.07	17.07	17.08
17.12	17.12	17.13
17.14	17.15	17.17
17.18	17.18	17.19
17.22	18.01	18.01
18.02	18.03	18.07
18.09	18.09	18.10
18.11	19.01	19.06
19.07	19.08	19.09
19.10	19.11	19.15
19.16	19.16	19.16
19.17	20.03	20.15
23.18	20.22	20.23
20.23	20.24	20.24
20.25	20.25	20.29
21.03	21.04	21.06
21.07	21.07	21.08
21.09	21.10	21.11
21.13	21.14	21.15
21.16	21.18	21.19
21.22	21.22	21.26
22.12	22.19	22.23
22.24	22.27	22.28
22.28	22.28	22.30
23.02	23.08	23.08
23.16	24.02	24.03
24.14	24.14	24.15
24.16	24.17	24.20
25.06	25.10	25.15
25.15	25.16	25.17
25.17	25.19	25.21

A (CONT.) — 59.29

		59.29
60.02	60.07	60.09
60.09	60.09	60.13
60.19	60.22	60.23
60.30	61.03	61.09
61.12	61.14	61.16
61.18	61.24	62.09
62.11	62.14	62.25
62.27	62.29	62.29
63.09	63.16	63.19
63.24	63.29	64.06
64.08	64.11	64.12
64.14	64.22	64.26
65.01	65.03	65.05
65.07	65.08	65.09
65.15	66.09	66.20
67.07	67.09	67.13
67.14	67.14	67.21
67.21	67.22	67.26
68.05	68.06	68.06
68.18	68.26	68.27
68.28	69.08	69.09
69.13	69.25	69.25
69.25	69.29	70.05
70.06	70.06	70.12
70.13	70.16	70.17
70.18	70.20	70.32
70.34	70.38	70.41
70.41	71.03	71.07
71.09	71.11	71.27
71.28	71.28	72.06
72.22	72.23	72.29
73.11	73.12	73.16
73.22	73.27	73.27
74.05	74.14	74.15
74.17	74.19	74.20
74.22	74.23	75.06
75.08	75.08	75.12
75.13	75.21	75.30
76.13	76.20	76.24
76.27	77.09	77.10
77.13	77.20	77.29
78.02	78.04	78.05
78.09	78.13	78.14
78.17	78.20	78.29
79.02	79.12	79.15
79.19	79.23	79.24
79.25	79.29	80.04
80.07	80.09	80.12
80.13	80.16	80.25
80.26	80.27	81.02
81.03	81.04	81.08
81.10	81.12	81.16
81.22	81.23	82.01
82.03	82.05	82.06
82.12	83.05	83.06
83.08	83.09	83.09
83.10	83.13	83.15
83.16	83.21	83.25
83.26	83.26	83.28
83.29	84.01	84.05
84.06	84.17	84.17
84.21	84.23	84.24
84.25	85.01	85.03
85.03	85.09	85.10
85.11	85.28	85.30
86.05	86.20	86.25
86.26	87.04	87.07
87.07	87.08	87.12
87.19	87.21	87.21
87.25	87.28	87.30
88.04	88.08	88.10
88.15	88.16	88.20
88.27	88.27	88.28
89.03	89.03	89.11
89.13	89.19	89.25
89.26	89.29	90.04
90.05	90.13	90.21
90.26	90.29	91.07
91.09	91.14	92.04
92.21	92.22	92.23
92.24	93.05	93.09
93.14	93.18	93.19
93.21	93.22	93.23
93.24	93.25	94.03
94.06	94.13	94.15
95.01	95.01	95.05
95.08	95.10	95.14
95.21	95.23	96.17
96.19	96.22	96.23

A (CONT.) — 96.25

		96.25
96.25	96.26	96.29
97.01	97.02	97.05
97.10	97.10	97.12
97.13	97.21	97.24
98.01	98.27	98.30
99.01	99.04	99.06
99.07	99.11	99.12
99.13	99.17	99.26
99.28	99.28	99.30
100.01	100.18	100.27
100.28	100.30	101.03
101.07	101.12	101.19
101.29	102.11	102.15
102.16	102.21	102.25
102.27	102.27	102.28
102.29	103.15	103.16
103.24	104.19	104.23
104.24	104.30	105.04
105.05	105.10	105.29
106.02	106.02	106.06
106.14	107.05	107.06
107.08	107.10	107.16
107.22	108.07	108.12
108.13	108.15	108.23
109.03	109.06	109.11
109.12	109.13	109.17
109.20	109.21	109.28
110.04	110.05	110.11
110.23	110.27	110.29
111.01	111.02	111.06
111.12	111.13	111.13
111.14	111.16	111.28
112.01	112.02	112.03
112.04	112.06	112.07
112.15	112.21	112.24
112.25	113.07	113.09
113.14	113.16	113.22
113.22	113.23	113.23
113.24	113.27	113.29
114.11	114.15	114.20
114.21	114.22	114.28
115.01	115.02	115.07
115.12	115.21	115.22
115.23	116.01	116.02
116.05	116.10	116.18
116.21	116.22	116.25
116.26	116.27	117.04
117.09	117.24	118.01
118.02	118.04	118.07
118.17	118.21	118.23
118.23	118.25	118.26
119.05	119.08	119.09
119.11	119.16	119.17
119.18	119.18	119.28
120.03	120.04	120.25
121.01	121.02	121.07
121.07	121.12	122.05
122.12	122.12	122.17
122.23	123.02	123.03
123.04	123.04	123.10
123.11	123.11	123.13
123.15	123.19	123.22
123.23	123.24	124.05
124.10	124.22	124.26
124.30	125.02	125.03
125.08	125.11	125.21
125.23	125.29	125.29
125.29	126.01	126.08
126.08	126.15	126.16
126.21	126.22	126.25
126.29	127.02	127.05
127.06	127.12	127.14
127.29	128.02	128.05
128.07	128.08	128.08
128.09	128.24	128.29
129.07	129.07	129.08
129.14	129.26	129.29
129.29	130.19	130.20
131.05	131.06	131.09
131.14	131.18	131.19
131.24	132.05	132.05
132.06	132.07	132.13
132.24	132.25	133.03
133.04	133.05	133.08
133.09	133.13	133.13
133.27	134.03	134.04
134.07	134.13	134.17
134.19	134.21	134.26
134.29	135.03	135.04

A (CONT.)		135.04	A (CONT.)		175.21	A (CONT.)		210.20	A (CONT.)		243.22
135.05	135.05	135.08	175.22	175.24	175.25	210.24	210.25	210.29	243.25	243.28	243.29
136.04	136.10	136.10	175.25	176.01	176.13	211.01	211.01	211.07	243.29	243.30	244.02
136.14	136.14	136.20	176.23	176.24	176.26	211.09	211.12	211.17	244.05	244.08	244.09
136.22	137.03	137.10	176.30	177.01	177.06	211.17	211.18	211.19	244.30	245.08	245.26
137.10	137.13	138.08	177.07	178.06	178.07	211.20	211.28	212.09	245.27	245.29	245.30
138.11	138.24	138.28	178.23	178.24	178.25	212.11	212.15	212.15	246.07	246.09	246.10
138.28	138.29	139.01	178.27	179.10	179.10	212.16	212.23	212.25	246.12	246.15	246.23
139.06	139.06	139.07	179.24	179.24	180.07	213.02	213.05	213.07	246.27	246.28	247.01
139.14	139.16	139.17	180.08	180.18	180.19	213.15	213.22	214.03	247.02	247.07	247.08
139.24	139.25	139.26	180.19	180.30	180.30	214.27	214.28	214.29	247.15	247.18	248.05
139.26	139.27	139.28	181.07	181.10	181.11	215.01	215.02	215.03	248.08	248.09	248.15
139.30	139.30	140.02	181.21	181.21	182.05	215.05	215.06	215.07	248.17	248.20	248.24
140.06	140.17	140.20	182.11	182.13	182.17	215.22	215.24	215.27	249.08	249.11	249.21
140.22	140.22	140.24	182.18	182.18	182.30	215.29	215.29	215.30	249.24	249.26	249.27
140.26	140.28	140.28	183.02	183.04	183.06	215.30	216.12	216.14	249.28	249.29	250.01
140.28	141.06	141.07	183.12	183.14	183.14	216.20	216.22	216.24	250.10	250.11	250.14
141.13	141.19	141.26	183.15	183.18	183.26	216.30	217.01	217.01	250.15	250.15	250.19
141.28	142.11	142.14	183.29	183.29	184.07	217.04	217.05	217.06	250.20	250.20	250.24
142.16	142.20	143.06	184.09	184.10	184.13	217.07	217.14	217.18	250.29	251.04	251.08
143.06	143.08	143.09	184.14	184.15	185.08	217.22	217.24	217.25	251.09	251.09	251.10
143.10	143.10	143.30	185.08	185.11	185.14	217.26	217.28	217.30	251.20	251.23	251.25
144.20	144.21	144.23	185.22	185.22	185.23	218.04	218.05	218.07	252.02	252.04	252.05
144.23	145.01	145.04	185.28	186.15	186.15	218.15	218.21	219.01	252.13	252.14	252.18
145.08	145.08	145.09	186.23	187.03	187.21	219.04	219.09	219.28	252.22	252.25	252.29
145.09	145.13	145.13	187.30	188.04	188.06	220.03	220.07	220.08	253.13	253.15	253.20
145.13	145.14	145.24	188.26	188.29	188.30	220.10	220.11	220.12	253.27	253.28	253.28
145.27	145.29	145.30	189.06	189.12	189.13	220.14	220.14	220.22	253.30	254.02	254.06
145.30	146.06	146.16	189.14	189.15	189.15	220.26	222.03	222.06	254.06	254.12	254.13
146.23	147.01	147.14	189.17	189.19	190.02	222.10	222.14	222.21	254.14	254.16	254.23
147.17	147.18	147.20	190.07	190.10	190.14	223.09	223.21	223.25	254.28	254.28	254.29
147.22	147.27	147.28	190.15	190.19	191.11	223.25	223.30	224.06	254.30	255.04	255.05
148.02	148.03	148.04	191.11	191.15	191.18	224.07	224.07	224.08	255.07	255.10	255.10
148.09	148.16	149.01	191.24	191.26	191.28	224.12	224.14	224.16	255.14	255.15	255.26
149.02	149.09	149.11	191.28	191.29	191.29	224.18	224.20	224.22	255.30	256.06	256.09
149.11	149.16	149.19	191.30	192.01	192.06	224.22	224.26	224.27	256.15	256.21	256.23
149.24	149.25	149.26	192.07	192.08	192.09	224.33	225.10	225.17	256.26	257.05	257.07
150.01	150.19	150.26	192.09	192.11	192.16	225.17	225.20	225.22	257.15	257.18	258.03
150.26	150.30	151.02	192.20	192.26	193.02	225.23	226.02	226.03	258.07	258.11	258.12
151.21	151.27	152.18	193.05	193.05	193.06	226.04	226.06	226.12	258.14	258.19	258.19
152.18	152.20	152.22	193.13	193.13	193.16	226.14	226.15	226.16	258.28	259.01	259.04
152.27	153.03	153.07	193.17	193.20	193.29	226.19	226.27	226.29	259.07	259.10	259.13
153.10	153.16	153.27	194.11	194.12	194.13	227.01	227.03	227.04	259.21	259.26	259.26
153.30	154.05	154.09	194.16	194.16	194.22	227.06	227.07	227.09	259.27	259.28	260.20
154.15	155.03	155.08	194.24	194.25	194.26	227.11	227.14	227.18	260.25	260.26	260.26
155.09	155.11	155.15	194.27	195.01	195.02	227.20	227.21	228.01	261.08	261.11	261.14
155.16	155.21	155.22	195.02	195.08	195.09	228.10	228.13	228.22	261.17	261.25	261.30
155.23	156.01	156.02	195.21	196.04	196.06	228.28	229.05	229.07	262.01	262.01	262.04
156.13	156.16	156.16	196.06	196.08	196.09	229.09	229.15	229.21	262.15	262.21	262.22
156.19	156.29	156.30	196.10	196.10	196.12	229.21	229.23	229.26	262.24	262.26	262.30
156.30	157.02	157.02	196.13	196.17	196.18	229.29	229.29	230.02	263.04	263.08	263.09
157.03	157.03	157.04	196.20	196.21	196.25	230.08	230.08	230.17	263.12	263.13	263.14
157.05	157.17	157.22	196.29	196.30	197.01	230.18	230.22	230.23	263.15	263.15	263.28
157.23	157.26	157.27	197.02	197.02	197.04	230.26	230.29	231.06	263.30	264.01	264.10
157.28	158.03	158.07	197.06	197.12	197.13	231.07	231.08	231.09	264.25	264.27	266.03
158.07	158.17	158.19	197.16	198.02	198.07	231.18	231.20	231.22	266.04	266.05	266.06
158.24	158.25	158.27	198.10	198.12	198.18	231.25	231.28	231.30	266.11	266.20	267.02
158.28	159.11	159.14	198.18	198.23	198.25	232.07	232.09	232.15	267.05	267.09	267.15
159.15	159.17	159.18	199.03	199.04	199.07	232.16	232.19	232.22	267.26	268.06	268.15
159.21	160.12	160.15	199.14	199.15	199.15	232.25	232.27	232.30	268.15	268.17	268.25
160.25	160.26	160.28	199.15	199.17	199.18	233.05	233.06	233.10	268.29	268.30	269.05
151.02	162.07	162.07	199.20	199.22	199.24	233.20	233.24	233.27	269.07	269.07	269.09
162.08	162.16	162.24	199.30	200.01	200.01	233.28	234.04	234.05	269.13	269.14	269.15
163.01	163.12	163.20	200.02	200.03	200.05	234.10	234.11	234.12	269.20	269.27	269.30
165.01	165.01	165.07	200.14	200.18	200.18	234.16	234.20	234.21	270.02	270.12	270.13
165.07	165.08	165.15	200.24	201.04	201.04	234.23	234.25	234.26	270.18	270.18	270.18
165.17	165.18	165.19	201.06	201.09	201.10	234.27	235.09	235.10	271.01	271.11	271.14
165.19	165.21	166.05	201.10	201.11	201.12	235.17	235.24	235.25	271.23	271.24	272.19
166.08	166.11	166.21	201.26	201.29	201.30	235.26	236.04	236.07	272.23	272.30	273.03
166.26	166.29	167.01	202.01	202.06	202.18	236.08	236.08	236.10	273.07	273.09	273.11
167.03	167.06	167.08	202.21	202.22	203.08	236.12	236.12	236.15	273.16	273.18	273.20
167.09	167.11	167.15	203.10	203.11	203.15	236.18	236.22	236.24	273.22	273.24	273.26
167.20	167.22	167.24	203.19	203.23	203.26	236.24	236.25	235.25	274.03	274.06	274.21
167.29	168.14	168.15	203.28	203.29	204.02	236.27	236.27	236.29	274.23	274.28	275.22
168.15	168.17	168.18	204.06	204.08	204.14	236.30	237.05	237.06	276.05	276.09	276.10
168.22	168.24	169.01	204.23	204.26	204.29	237.09	237.21	237.22	276.14	276.18	276.21
169.02	169.04	169.07	205.06	205.08	205.18	237.22	237.25	237.26	277.01	277.09	277.10
169.12	169.13	169.17	205.19	205.22	205.25	237.27	238.06	238.11	277.12	277.17	277.19
169.30	170.01	170.03	205.28	205.29	206.01	238.15	238.20	239.07	277.27	278.04	278.07
170.08	170.10	170.11	206.02	206.03	207.04	239.10	239.11	239.18	279.05	279.06	279.11
170.14	170.16	170.19	207.05	207.06	207.07	239.20	239.21	240.07	279.11	279.12	279.12
170.28	171.05	171.08	207.13	207.14	207.15	240.09	240.09	240.11	279.17	279.21	280.01
171.11	171.12	171.15	207.25	208.04	208.10	240.13	240.20	240.27	280.02	280.04	280.06
171.17	171.17	171.24	208.15	208.16	208.17	240.30	241.01	241.06	280.08	280.09	280.18
172.03	172.06	172.13	208.23	209.02	209.07	241.07	241.08	241.09	280.19	280.22	280.27
172.14	172.20	172.24	209.10	209.10	209.12	241.11	241.17	241.19	280.28	281.02	281.04
172.24	173.09	173.14	209.12	209.14	209.15	241.25	241.27	242.10	281.10	281.14	281.19
174.01	174.03	174.10	209.18	209.22	209.23	242.11	242.15	242.25	281.27	282.07	282.08
174.19	175.03	175.05	209.30	210.02	210.12	242.29	242.30	243.02	282.10	282.13	282.16
175.13	175.15	175.17	210.15	210.16	210.18	243.08	243.10	243.15	282.18	282.20	283.03

A (CONT.)		283.04	A (CONT.)		321.02	A (CONT.)		360.14	A (CONT.)		396.14
283.07	283.09	283.11	321.14	321.26	321.28	360.17	360.20	360.20	396.16	396.19	396.19
283.15	283.17	283.19	321.30	322.01	322.01	360.21	360.26	361.02	396.29	397.03	397.05
283.23	283.25	283.26	322.03	322.03	322.04	361.08	361.09	361.10	397.07	397.20	397.24
285.03	285.05	285.06	322.04	322.07	322.07	361.13	361.30	362.10	397.25	398.03	398.09
285.07	285.11	285.18	322.08	322.20	322.23	362.13	362.13	362.13	398.10	398.22	398.25
285.23	286.02	286.04	322.29	323.03	323.09	362.16	362.20	362.23	399.02	399.03	399.21
286.07	286.08	286.19	323.10	323.12	323.13	363.10	363.14	364.01	399.21	399.27	399.29
286.23	286.25	286.26	323.15	323.15	323.22	364.01	364.21	364.27	400.24	400.25	401.03
286.26	286.27	286.29	323.25	323.28	323.28	365.01	365.04	365.07	401.08	401.09	401.19
287.03	287.10	287.11	323.29	324.09	324.16	365.08	365.11	365.14	401.19	401.29	402.07
287.11	287.15	287.16	324.18	324.19	324.23	365.15	365.16	365.17	402.07	402.14	402.18
287.17	287.17	287.18	324.30	325.08	325.08	365.21	365.22	365.29	402.20	403.01	403.04
287.21	288.02	288.09	325.09	325.12	325.14	366.01	366.09	366.20	403.05	403.05	403.17
238.25	288.25	288.26	325.15	325.20	325.25	366.22	366.23	366.27	403.18	403.25	403.27
288.28	289.02	289.06	325.25	326.03	326.05	367.03	367.09	367.14	404.03	404.06	404.07
289.07	289.22	289.23	327.04	327.07	327.11	367.17	367.17	367.19	404.15	404.17	404.18
289.25	289.27	290.08	327.13	327.14	327.15	367.20	367.21	367.22	404.23	404.26	405.02
290.10	290.14	290.18	327.19	327.24	328.11	367.23	367.23	367.27	405.02	405.09	405.11
290.21	290.22	290.27	328.15	328.16	328.18	367.29	368.02	368.03	405.14	405.30	406.01
290.28	290.29	291.01	329.01	329.08	329.11	368.07	368.08	368.13	406.07	406.07	407.05
291.03	291.26	292.03	330.08	330.09	330.12	368.14	368.18	368.19	407.05	407.15	407.21
292.04	292.06	292.09	330.12	330.13	330.17	368.25	369.03	369.24	408.24	408.28	408.29
292.10	292.11	292.14	330.20	330.23	330.24	369.24	369.25	369.26	408.29	409.02	409.02
292.15	292.24	292.29	330.26	331.09	331.12	369.28	369.29	370.01	409.09	409.12	409.12
293.11	293.13	293.16	332.09	332.12	332.15	370.01	370.03	370.08	409.14	409.23	409.24
293.25	293.26	293.26	332.16	332.18	332.20	370.09	370.17	370.19	409.26	409.27	409.30
293.28	293.28	293.30	332.22	332.23	332.25	370.21	370.21	370.30	410.02	410.04	410.06
294.01	294.02	294.08	332.26	333.03	333.05	370.30	371.02	371.03	410.06	410.08	410.09
294.10	294.12	294.16	333.08	333.13	333.20	371.04	371.04	371.05	410.13	410.22	410.23
294.18	295.06	295.08	333.22	333.25	333.26	371.05	371.05	371.06	410.26	410.28	410.30
295.13	295.17	295.17	334.02	334.03	334.06	371.07	371.09	371.09	411.09	411.18	411.23
296.02	296.04	296.06	334.06	334.16	334.18	371.12	371.12	371.13	411.30	412.10	412.13
297.03	297.07	297.08	334.18	335.06	335.08	371.14	371.18	371.20	412.18	412.28	413.02
297.10	297.12	297.17	335.13	336.11	336.12	371.23	371.25	371.29	413.11	413.12	413.25
297.18	297.20	298.01	336.14	336.18	336.20	372.02	372.14	372.19	413.26	414.01	414.04
298.06	298.16	298.30	337.03	337.11	337.13	373.02	373.04	373.05	414.12	414.20	414.21
299.01	299.18	299.22	337.15	337.18	337.25	373.07	373.09	373.12	414.30	415.12	415.15
299.24	299.25	300.02	337.30	338.06	338.10	373.17	373.19	374.01	415.16	415.16	415.17
300.06	300.07	300.16	338.12	338.15	338.15	374.02	374.04	374.05	416.05	416.11	416.14
300.20	300.21	300.25	338.19	338.27	339.07	374.10	374.11	374.12	415.19	416.22	417.02
300.26	300.27	301.07	339.19	339.21	339.22	374.23	375.01	375.08	417.04	417.05	417.06
301.29	302.02	302.09	339.22	339.25	339.27	375.09	375.10	375.15	417.07	417.07	417.09
302.17	302.17	302.21	339.28	340.09	340.10	375.17	375.24	375.26	417.11	417.21	417.21
302.23	302.25	302.26	340.18	340.22	340.22	376.01	376.01	376.03	417.23	417.25	417.27
302.27	303.03	303.24	340.24	340.25	340.28	376.04	376.06	376.17	417.27	417.28	418.20
304.10	304.28	304.29	341.02	341.03	341.04	376.20	376.22	376.24	418.22	418.26	418.27
304.30	305.01	305.03	341.10	341.15	341.22	376.29	377.02	377.09	419.08	419.12	419.21
305.04	305.08	305.08	342.06	342.07	342.12	377.23	377.23	377.24	420.08	420.09	420.10
306.04	306.07	306.08	342.16	342.18	342.24	378.03	378.17	378.18	420.13	420.18	420.23
306.08	306.09	306.15	342.25	342.26	342.27	378.18	378.24	378.28	420.23	420.23	420.26
306.24	307.04	307.06	342.28	342.29	343.02	378.28	379.10	379.10	421.01	421.02	421.05
307.08	307.09	307.17	343.07	343.07	343.10	379.21	379.25	379.27	421.10	421.13	421.17
307.21	307.22	307.23	343.11	343.13	343.15	379.30	380.07	380.14	422.15	422.15	422.25
307.26	307.26	307.27	344.02	344.10	344.16	381.04	381.16	381.19	423.05	423.08	423.09
307.28	307.30	308.04	344.28	344.30	345.07	381.20	382.02	382.07	423.13	423.23	424.05
308.05	308.08	308.19	345.16	345.21	345.23	382.10	382.15	382.16	424.06	424.06	424.07
308.28	309.03	309.03	345.24	345.27	346.01	382.24	383.08	383.16	424.07	424.12	424.13
309.04	309.04	309.08	346.02	346.08	346.09	383.20	383.24	383.25	425.01	425.01	425.03
309.08	309.19	309.20	346.10	347.02	347.22	384.13	384.14	384.23	425.03	425.06	425.21
309.27	310.04	310.10	347.24	348.03	348.04	384.27	384.30	385.02	425.24	426.01	426.01
310.11	310.21	310.23	348.06	348.13	348.15	385.09	385.19	385.22	426.04	426.06	426.07
310.24	310.29	311.03	348.18	348.26	348.27	385.30	386.01	386.03	426.13	426.18	426.19
311.08	311.08	311.09	348.29	348.30	348.30	386.15	386.17	386.17	426.21	426.25	426.25
311.11	311.13	311.14	349.10	349.15	349.18	386.17	386.18	386.22	426.26	426.27	426.27
311.17	311.28	312.01	349.24	349.25	349.25	386.25	387.08	387.13	427.01	427.02	427.04
312.05	312.05	312.10	350.05	350.06	350.09	387.16	387.22	387.27	427.06	427.08	427.10
312.17	312.27	312.30	350.12	350.14	350.29	387.30	387.30	388.01	427.22	427.28	427.28
313.04	313.08	313.10	351.05	351.11	351.16	388.07	388.08	388.09	428.08	428.13	428.20
313.11	313.13	313.18	351.17	351.18	351.22	388.10	388.18	388.25	428.22	428.26	429.01
313.21	313.22	313.23	351.25	351.26	352.03	388.29	388.29	389.03	429.13	429.25	429.27
313.24	313.24	313.25	352.17	352.17	352.18	389.03	389.05	389.07	429.30	430.06	430.06
313.25	313.26	313.30	353.04	353.10	353.13	389.18	389.18	389.24	430.16	430.18	431.23
314.01	314.02	314.09	353.23	353.23	353.25	389.25	389.26	390.12	431.23	432.03	432.03
314.15	314.19	314.19	354.01	354.02	354.03	390.13	390.15	390.22	432.09	432.11	432.13
314.21	314.22	314.23	355.10	355.10	355.15	390.24	390.25	390.26	432.15	432.20	432.21
314.27	315.04	315.10	355.21	355.23	355.24	390.27	390.28	391.01	433.09	434.06	434.08
315.12	315.15	315.16	355.24	355.24	356.01	391.08	391.12	391.15	434.09	434.21	434.21
315.25	316.05	316.08	356.01	356.02	356.07	391.21	391.25	392.10	434.22	434.24	434.29
316.10	316.20	316.25	356.09	356.10	356.11	392.12	392.17	392.18	435.08	435.11	435.13
316.27	316.27	317.01	356.13	356.14	356.22	392.23	392.30	393.01	435.14	435.15	435.21
317.02	317.03	317.17	356.26	356.30	357.03	393.04	393.07	393.08	435.24	436.07	436.11
318.03	318.07	318.10	357.06	357.13	357.13	393.13	394.02	394.03	435.13	436.17	436.19
318.11	318.12	318.14	357.20	357.22	357.27	394.05	394.08	394.09	436.21	436.21	436.23
318.15	318.16	318.18	358.05	358.08	358.14	394.10	394.11	394.11	436.25	437.01	437.11
319.02	319.04	319.08	358.16	358.18	358.20	394.13	394.22	394.22	437.13	437.13	437.14
319.11	319.18	319.19	358.21	358.30	359.03	394.23	395.06	395.06	437.19	437.21	437.22
319.21	319.21	319.23	359.04	359.07	359.07	395.11	395.21	395.23	437.27	438.02	438.03
319.27	319.28	319.29	359.08	359.23	359.29	396.03	396.06	396.13	438.10	438.15	438.16
320.01	320.14	320.17	360.01	360.11	360.12				438.20	438.21	438.22

A (CONT.)   438.25

```
438.27  438.30  439.04
439.05  439.09  439.12
439.15  439.21  439.25
439.27  440.01  440.01
440.05  440.06  440.07
440.07  440.08  440.13
440.16  440.24  440.26
440.26  441.02  441.02
441.03  441.10  441.13
441.16  441.27  441.28
441.28  442.03  442.06
442.13  442.14  442.17
442.19  442.26  443.04
443.06  443.09  443.13
443.15  443.17  443.17
443.18  443.22  443.26
444.02  444.03  444.03
444.04  444.08  444.17
444.18  444.21  444.23
445.01  445.04  445.04
445.05  445.08  445.09
445.10  445.14  445.20
445.21  446.08  446.08
447.01  447.03  447.05
447.16  447.24  448.07
448.14  448.17  448.19
448.26  448.30  449.07
449.09  449.16  449.17
449.26  450.01  450.03
450.04  450.06  450.07
450.08  450.09  450.13
450.21  451.03  451.03
451.04  451.05  451.09
451.10  451.13  451.25
452.01  452.02  452.03
452.07  452.08  452.09
452.10  452.13  452.15
452.18  452.19  452.22
452.26  453.04  453.07
453.08  453.15  454.03
454.05  454.08  454.09
454.19  454.28  454.30
455.01  455.01  455.04
455.05  455.19  455.26
456.04  456.18  456.22
457.03  457.05  457.07
457.10  457.12  457.14
457.15  457.20  457.20
458.02  458.05  458.13
458.15  458.17  458.20
459.05  459.06  459.10
459.17  459.21  459.24
459.27  459.28  459.29
460.07  460.10  460.17
460.20  461.05  461.05
461.06  461.12  461.24
462.04  462.06  462.10
462.15  462.16  462.17
462.22  462.28  462.29
463.03  463.06  463.09
463.14  463.15  463.21
463.21  464.08  464.09
464.11  464.11  464.15
464.17  464.19  464.21
464.29  465.04  465.05
465.17  465.19  465.20
465.24  465.25  465.27
466.04  466.09  466.13
466.15  466.21  466.22
466.24  466.25  466.26
467.14  467.14  467.17
467.18  467.22  467.28
467.29  467.29  468.06
468.07  468.12  468.16
469.02  469.04  469.05
469.06  469.16  469.17
470.19  470.20  470.23
470.24  471.08  471.15
471.19  471.21  471.21
471.22  471.23  471.28
471.28  471.29  471.30
471.30  472.04  472.10
472.24  472.27  473.02
473.03  473.08  473.10
473.13  473.21  473.21
473.25  473.29  473.30
474.12  474.24  474.29
475.11  475.14  475.16
475.17  475.20  475.22
```

A (CONT.)   475.23

```
475.25  475.26  476.04
476.05  476.09  476.10
477.19  477.19  477.19
478.04  478.08  478.09
478.19  478.24  478.28
478.29  479.02  479.07
479.07  479.08  479.10
479.15  479.22  479.22
479.25  479.26  479.28
480.04  480.07  480.18
480.27  481.13  481.13
481.14  481.22  482.02
482.06  482.07  482.08
482.15  482.15  482.16
482.17  482.28  483.10
483.15  483.21  483.25
483.25  484.11  484.13
484.21  484.25  484.27
485.04  486.02  486.05
486.13  487.06  487.21
487.24  488.05  488.06
488.09  488.12  488.17
489.02  489.14  489.16
489.18  489.20  489.26
489.29  489.29  489.30
490.09  490.15  490.17
490.18  490.19  491.05
491.07  491.14  491.18
492.02  492.05  492.17
492.20  492.22  492.23
492.25  493.02  493.02
493.12  493.25  493.30
494.01  494.06  494.08
494.10  494.18  494.19
494.20  494.24  495.01
495.05  495.13  495.18
495.25  495.27  495.28
495.28  496.01  496.01
496.02  496.06  496.08
496.11  497.02  497.04
497.08  497.10  497.17
497.19  497.20  497.21
497.24  498.04  498.11
498.12  498.15  498.16
498.25  498.26  498.27
498.29  499.08  499.21
499.26  499.29  500.02
500.08  500.09  500.02
500.23  500.24  500.25
500.26  500.27  501.08
501.11  501.16  501.16
501.18  501.19  501.19
501.20  501.26  501.26
501.27  501.28  501.30
502.02  502.03  502.04
502.12  502.12  502.25
502.26  503.09  503.11
504.05  504.10  504.17
504.18  505.12  505.20
505.23  505.27  505.28
506.10  506.12  506.18
506.19  506.24  506.27
507.10  507.19  508.13
508.14  508.16  508.20
508.21  508.29  509.02
509.08  509.13  509.15
509.17  509.20  509.21
509.27  510.01  510.02
510.05  510.06  510.08
510.14  510.17  510.25
511.04  511.21  511.24
512.04  512.09  512.10
512.21  512.24  512.29
512.29  513.07  513.17
513.23  513.29  514.02
514.06  514.11  514.14
514.15  514.17  514.22
515.04  515.06  515.10
515.17  515.19  515.29
516.02  516.03  516.12
516.17
```

A-A-A-ARM   140.28
A-HUNDRED-POUNDS-ROU
    92.04
A-QUIVER   204.02
ABACK   44.12   142.12
ABAFT   22.25
ABANDON   117.04   382.17
ABANDONED   190.15

ABANDONED (CONT.)
```
320.03  336.16  459.05
484.01
```
ABERRATIONS   266.11
  266.14
ABHORRENT   147.21
ABIDING   275.03   348.08
ABILITIES   268.30
ABILITY   1.15   2.21
```
  3.13   50.28   96.25
329.16  478.01
```
ABJECT   147.13   352.09
```
352.15  352.16  352.18
352.27  358.25  365.04
425.20  500.09
```
ABJECTLY   84.09   352.13
```
352.13  352.14  383.12
403.10
```
ABJECTNESS   352.07
  399.23
ABLE   57.27   65.18
```
 92.27  102.11  127.10
144.28  223.12  227.08
238.04  238.15  274.16
282.16  345.10  366.07
375.22  425.08  453.29
```
ABOARD   15.11   16.17
```
 74.22  290.19  377.18
475.30
```
ABOARD'   233.14
ABODE   430.09   508.17
ABODES   3.30
ABOMINABLE   63.15
```
 80.05   80.06   82.04
 86.18  178.28  356.27
```
ABOMINABLY   308.18
ABOMINATION   137.02
  147.09
ABOMINATIONS   142.18
ABOUT   1.18   5.23
```
  7.19   12.11   22.02
 26.26   29.28   30.03
 35.03   36.02   36.19
 37.13   40.24   42.07
 42.12   43.12   43.32
 46.27   47.26   49.27
 57.03   57.17   62.22
 71.20   74.09   74.28
 75.20   75.28   77.11
 79.01   81.01   86.04
 86.30   87.06   95.09
 95.13   98.15   98.19
101.22  105.06  110.03
113.04  113.21  116.02
119.01  120.03  120.26
121.04  123.02  129.08
129.21  130.29  131.06
133.03  134.24  137.08
140.17  144.25  145.30
146.27  149.08  149.10
153.25  155.16  157.07
158.16  158.27  165.27
165.29  166.26  168.25
172.16  175.18  177.05
177.20  179.03  180.25
181.16  182.01  186.01
189.13  193.11  194.14
197.12  200.26  201.06
201.08  202.02  203.06
210.01  213.06  213.11
213.24  213.24  223.26
228.17  233.09  233.30
234.19  234.22  235.01
238.23  239.24  240.17
242.14  242.22  243.15
247.23  248.20  249.26
253.20  253.20  253.21
266.09  267.10  267.22
269.09  270.12  270.24
272.24  273.01  273.18
274.10  275.10  275.11
276.20  278.08  279.09
279.18  283.22  286.14
287.18  288.22  289.12
289.15  299.23  301.21
305.05  306.07  306.15
310.07  311.07  311.10
312.07  315.06  315.07
315.20  319.03  324.24
329.17  330.10  330.19
```

ABOUT (CONT.)   337.27
```
339.29  340.16  342.21
343.02  344.29  345.27
350.03  357.27  359.26
360.15  361.07  363.22
367.06  367.30  372.17
374.28  377.03  382.29
383.22  384.25  390.12
392.05  398.19  399.09
410.26  412.10  422.02
422.02  435.04  435.09
435.16  439.18  444.18
447.03  451.26  452.27
461.14  467.17  467.26
472.23  474.02  474.08
490.12  491.06  505.01
509.20  510.14  510.28
```
ABOVE   5.22   21.11
```
 21.13   32.11   33.06
 36.27   37.07   41.16
 52.07   96.22  107.09
110.27  117.14  117.25
125.29  132.03  133.09
135.02  148.29  177.01
181.16  187.06  192.21
195.09  204.01  245.21
248.21  255.22  269.11
269.26  272.27  288.12
295.25  301.28  303.12
314.09  319.16  329.04
333.19  341.07  367.15
371.13  407.14  409.01
410.05  415.13  430.06
434.28  434.29  443.18
475.23  482.12  496.09
497.05  498.19  508.02
509.04  513.12
```
ABREAST   7.03   107.19
  167.10   443.14
ABRUPT   216.13   360.29
ABRUPTLY   38.30   113.05
```
125.23  139.15  174.05
377.01  391.08  460.02
```
ABSCONDED   56.02
ABSCONDING   78.21
  437.15
ABSCURE   515.28
ABSENCE   448.20   490.11
ABSENT   447.22
ABSENTLY   290.07   360.20
ABSIT   296.07
ABSOLUTE   123.18   219.10
  264.07   442.02
ABSOLUTELY   171.09
```
179.01  185.21  189.22
358.23  364.15  371.23
375.04  429.19  438.13
```
ABSOLUTION   116.30
ABSORBED   192.18   222.13
  408.02
ABSORPTION   252.24
ABSTENTION   126.10
ABSTRACT   1.16   2.22
```
  3.13  179.05  416.03
501.17
```
ABSURD   105.14   221.08
```
224.03  294.27  321.15
351.15  361.14  377.02
389.23
```
ABSURDITY   85.01
  114.26   147.09   239.08
ABSURDLY   56.02   288.22
ABUNDANTLY   347.21
ABUSE   141.18   330.16
  355.16
ABUSED   76.03   462.11
ABUSING   43.19   141.29
  141.30
ABUSIVE   25.16   232.04
ABYSS   11.24   18.06
  116.16   123.08   147.07
  262.16   325.11
ACCENT   285.18
ACCENTS   30.30   388.04
ACCENTUATED   302.18
ACCEPT   222.11
ACCEPTANCE   482.17
ACCEPTED   98.05   482.01
ACCEPTING   480.21
  488.13

ACCESS 283.17

ACCIDENT 6.18 13.27
61.15 61.26 62.27
64.05 67.21 76.13
115.20 117.21 194.07
194.11 286.12 286.15
394.24

ACCIDENTALLY 73.18
102.18 168.09 225.01

ACCIDENTS 11.07
286.15

ACCOMMODATED 183.30

ACCOMMODATION 151.22

ACCOMPANIED 279.16
335.15 408.11

ACCOMPANIMENT 432.10

ACCOMPANYING 453.11

ACCOMPLICE 112.04
437.19

ACCOMPLICES 349.05

ACCOMPLISH 117.27

ACCOMPLISHED 451.21
454.13

ACCOMPLISHMENT 500.10

ACCORD 30.19 120.29
214.04 246.18 349.06

ACCORDANCE 212.02

ACCORDING 42.16
82.17 148.27 218.15

ACCORDINGLY 290.21
372.26 478.07

ACCOST 42.18

ACCOSTING 490.08

ACCOUNT 54.03 81.29
113.20 176.18 247.17
251.12 271.03 304.22
458.05 501.14

ACCOUNTS 357.23 457.21

ACCUMULATED 138.06

ACCURACY 253.03

ACCURSED 53.27 138.11
431.20 505.13

ACCUSTOMED 506.21

ACH 241.17 258.09
259.17 428.19 433.21

ACHE 207.18

ACHIEVE 280.26

ACHIEVED 275.12 300.11
466.14

ACHIEVEMENT 8.28
13.26 332.11 334.24

ACHIEVEMENTS 23.14
100.17

ACHING 384.16

ACKNOWLEDGE 210.19

ACQUAINTANCE 42.14
93.09 169.30 273.19
288.19

ACQUAINTED 493.12

ACQUIRE 243.22

ACQUIRED 119.08 252.04
348.19 418.12

ACRIMONIOUSLY 93.03

ACROSS 17.16 31.14
38.07 43.17 45.24
47.01 49.25 56.04
93.29 94.17 100.15
104.21 120.06 134.29
146.17 167.23 168.23
175.29 197.29 201.05
231.14 238.17 239.21
249.10 250.07 263.12
306.05 320.04 323.15
351.01 357.05 367.11
378.05 387.30 390.29
397.06 397.10 408.24
417.17 441.05 441.23
445.25 448.30 449.12
466.01 470.12 477.09
480.23 500.01 503.03
510.17

ACT 11.17 38.02
48.18 74.07 77.04
84.09 180.14 203.14
239.11 293.03 294.13
297.20 371.01 383.08
395.16 395.17 449.19
465.25 489.10 499.27

ACTED 129.30 131.10
459.21

ACTION 54.16 186.06
186.08 215.17 299.24
322.06 363.12 364.13
365.04 375.25 425.13
448.24 478.15

ACTIONS 14.14 240.04
375.01

ACTIVE 170.02 227.17
249.21 454.26

ACTIVELY 28.26 85.06

ACTIVITIES 266.07

ACTIVITY 13.09 36.09
290.13 428.27 490.01

ACTORS 117.11

ACTS 280.18 352.12
425.21 488.14

ACTUAL 115.13 355.06

ACTUALITY 182.03

ACTUALLY 125.05 220.30
301.10 310.23 312.30
346.02 348.24 358.28

ACTUATED 351.26

ACUTE 68.25 171.13

ACUTELY 68.08

AD 261.29 413.07

ADANDONING 195.05

ADAPTING 259.14

ADD 95.19

ADDED 3.25 60.07
61.04 88.08 95.14
99.15 106.01 134.16
162.19 177.02 188.08
263.20 268.03 282.15
283.05 289.20 303.10
320.21 322.23 335.01
385.14 387.17 433.09

ADDING 395.12

ADDITION 99.05

ADDITIVE 72.03

ADDRESS 55.24 122.05
227.24 405.01

ADDRESSED 43.30
70.36 83.01 294.02
416.15

ADDRESSING 217.11
350.24

ADEN 42.05 118.11
164.12

ADEQUATE 339.19

ADJOURNED 66.02
82.24

ADJOURNMENT 77.28

ADMINISTER 310.17

ADMIRABLY 322.02

ADMIRAL 207.09 207.09

ADMIRATION 172.26
225.06 359.28

ADMIRE 177.17

ADMIRED 213.02 396.24
447.14

ADMIRING 163.14

ADMISSION 129.08

ADMIT 95.01 97.04
132.21 193.23 214.07
215.09 418.10 423.11
465.28

ADMITS 144.20 361.27
454.04

ADMITTANCE

ADMITTED 136.17 157.18
163.20 264.09 282.15
471.28 476.08 478.05

ADO 64.09

ADORATION 408.03

ADORNED 240.23

ADRIFT 75.29 108.21
495.13

ADVANCE 263.14 312.02
329.02 503.19

ADVANCED 1.02 44.21
158.02 233.28 469.05

ADVANCING 17.28
510.23

ADVANTAGE 2.22
113.19 187.12 187.13
281.11 438.10

ADVANTAGEOUS 373.01

ADVANTAGES 352.26
470.25

ADVENTURE 5.06
9.08 10.04 28.21

ADVENTURE (CONT.)
423.19

ADVENTURED 277.11

ADVENTURER 213.10
247.15

ADVENTURERS 276.20

ADVENTURES 11.03
114.21 156.17 251.08
285.13

ADVENTUROUS 24.02
184.04 251.29 341.16

ADVERSE 437.17

ADVICE 246.04 360.04
448.23 455.13 456.04
479.16

ADVISE 204.04 204.16
495.05

ADVISED 151.25 169.19
317.09 486.10

ADVISEDLY 131.07

ADVISER 247.15

ADVISERS 309.27

ADVISING 364.03

AFAR 62.27 94.16
397.07 416.20

AFFAIR 35.26 42.03
42.22 42.30 59.12
66.24 81.08 98.10
144.10 157.29 167.25
167.26 168.09 175.04
176.12 177.14 183.18
191.18 207.08 241.23
243.18 282.26 287.09
330.25 332.13 375.17
403.21 403.28 448.10

AFFAIRS 173.09 297.18
317.15 319.06 359.12
360.02 427.27 452.30
506.21

AFFECT 113.01 208.10

AFFECTED 92.23 369.04
403.11 450.02

AFFECTING 119.20
119.20

AFFECTION 271.23
340.07 348.23 387.09
412.19 421.18 487.23

AFFECTIONS 15.22
302.28 382.28

AFFIRM 275.11 419.10
485.11

AFFIRMED 84.30 90.04
97.06 165.11 268.01
357.17 391.16

AFFLICTED 12.20
56.05

AFFORD 188.13

AFFRONT 7.24

AFIELD 196.20

AFLOAT 123.19 182.10
445.25 463.16

AFRAID 15.05 29.21
29.26 29.29 50.01
72.20 86.05 87.25
104.23 105.23 105.24
105.25 110.09 114.07
151.23 160.06 160.07
172.12 177.27 178.03
204.10 219.03 219.22
273.16 275.15 301.06
303.21 308.18 308.26
308.27 308.28 316.16
316.18 321.03 321.03
328.30 382.23 388.24
391.11 409.20 438.14
468.09 468.09 470.29
474.11 482.25 500.27
501.21

AFRESH 51.25 124.10
252.03

AFT 15.17 15.25
21.09 71.29 72.26
72.28 101.21 132.07
145.06 150.03 151.11
294.03 295.24

AFTER 4.15 6.28
10.01 15.07 15.24
17.27 19.18 27.29
33.13 34.03 35.12
37.02 38.20 38.25

AFTER (CONT.) 41.07
41.15 41.23 41.26
43.13 43.21 46.20
52.30 55.28 56.10
56.12 56.17 56.23
58.07 58.22 59.14
60.19 63.08 65.07
65.16 69.14 69.29
69.30 72.10 72.11
72.21 75.29 77.28
79.21 80.10 82.23
86.25 91.13 95.21
96.06 98.02 99.19
100.02 108.28 118.17
121.07 121.11 128.03
131.28 133.02 133.22
136.16 141.29 142.28
144.25 146.18 148.02
152.11 153.21 159.02
160.16 161.02 162.16
163.21 164.09 165.09
167.13 167.22 174.01
175.22 176.10 177.25
182.02 183.14 183.29
184.11 184.23 185.04
187.17 188.28 188.28
190.02 193.03 196.12
197.09 199.16 201.11
202.10 208.15 209.21
214.02 214.07 214.25
220.26 223.24 224.07
226.25 229.30 231.30
233.15 234.02 235.29
240.09 242.02 242.23
244.19 244.26 245.29
248.02 248.06 251.14
254.08 255.19 258.11
266.03 267.23 269.19
270.20 274.12 277.27
282.16 283.16 283.20
287.06 289.22 294.16
299.22 300.23 301.27
302.08 303.19 321.06
322.29 322.30 323.13
333.30 336.19 340.14
342.09 342.14 342.15
343.26 349.25 351.24
351.27 352.02 359.03
365.15 367.27 369.02
374.09 375.20 377.06
378.01 381.19 382.12
382.13 385.14 387.22
394.03 400.20 400.24
402.10 403.15 406.04
407.06 412.22 413.26
419.11 419.11 419.24
421.01 422.21 425.12
426.10 431.05 431.22
432.18 433.09 435.19
436.30 438.25 442.17
447.08 450.14 450.21
451.16 452.11 453.07
456.21 457.06 460.29
461.05 465.08 466.24
471.08 473.11 477.07
481.13 482.26 484.15
484.25 489.02 489.11
490.07 492.04 492.22
495.25 495.28 499.13
499.25 500.02 500.23
500.24 500.29 501.25
502.13 506.09 508.14
512.21 512.26 513.01
515.15 516.08

AFTER-DECK 72.11

AFTER-DINNER 41.26

AFTERNOON 62.18
92.02 167.24 264.17
290.15 315.10 409.22
431.26 434.13 442.25
455.03 456.08 465.21
491.29 499.25

AFTERTHOUGHT 493.15

AFTERWARDS 3.20
11.21 32.01 76.11
83.27 98.07 134.12
152.20 164.06 168.02
182.17 183.10 198.22
215.01 227.01 251.01
251.23 262.20 293.24

AFTERWARDS (CONT.)		
297.02	308.10	316.07
338.26	360.09	372.01
438.27	453.27	456.30
465.11	466.10	466.13
468.18	483.12	499.16
501.23	502.18	503.11
503.17	508.10	510.06
AGAIN	10.23	12.05
30.29	31.11	34.29
36.30	38.15	46.14
52.26	55.26	56.04
62.07	63.28	75.29
82.25	85.19	85.23
88.11	89.28	95.22
100.01	102.29	104.01
105.16	109.24	113.05
113.25	121.12	122.03
122.18	126.27	127.23
128.10	134.28	136.05
137.16	140.07	142.09
143.05	152.28	153.16
156.05	162.17	171.18
173.04	174.19	181.30
182.22	189.02	218.04
218.10	221.03	226.01
232.21	233.23	256.03
257.09	257.22	259.21
259.24	261.28	264.13
289.24	294.04	299.11
303.16	310.15	312.19
313.11	320.23	357.05
357.30	360.24	362.17
364.10	368.07	368.21
372.23	376.02	385.29
387.15	391.14	391.21
400.14	403.03	403.22
413.06	414.02	414.14
421.01	422.01	424.11
426.10	431.26	440.30
445.17	460.26	462.23
466.24	473.07	480.09
481.18	489.02	497.01
498.12	499.16	507.04
509.08	511.05	514.19
AGAINST	1.18	4.30
6.22	21.14	29.14
40.18	50.11	59.30
60.17	83.29	87.19
102.17	106.15	108.05
115.13	115.24	124.19
126.24	129.27	141.22
157.02	159.20	172.22
181.29	186.19	200.28
212.05	220.19	236.29
251.10	254.21	289.11
295.05	295.21	312.11
359.19	385.26	386.06
394.04	401.14	405.27
408.04	409.05	431.12
444.08	456.11	458.16
463.15	481.28	488.03
488.25	495.29	511.01
514.27		
AGE	157.01	179.02
199.16	252.06	295.06
330.15	422.16	
AGED	52.15	227.02
516.18		
AGENCY	278.13	
AGENT	268.27	352.02
AGENT'S	42.23	207.04
366.18		
AGENTS	277.16	
AGES	119.15	322.13
AGGRAVATING		243.21
AGGRESSIVE		1.08
438.09		
AGGRIEVED		159.19
347.04		
AGIN	48.07	
AGITATE	169.16	
AGITATED	19.17	63.07
356.29		
AGITATION		117.08
224.15	374.29	
AGO	27.24	58.11
184.26	198.02	202.07
219.02	234.18	282.06
292.21	312.18	315.23

AGO (CONT.)		345.19
367.10	399.28	429.01
AGONIES	379.29	
AGONISING		370.24
AGONY	12.08	460.28
475.09		
AGREE	471.25	
AGREEABLE		174.20
AGREED	151.30	176.09
328.26	420.12	
AGUAINDT	48.12	
AGUAINDT'		48.15
48.16		
AH	46.13	64.28
99.27	100.06	109.18
110.11	130.12	157.21
171.20	175.21	176.22
177.24	180.09	181.02
188.25	199.12	287.05
387.21	389.02	405.05
405.06	413.03	430.21
472.22	511.08	511.29
AHA	81.11	119.04
255.15	377.20	
AHEAD	6.20	13.22
17.28	21.26	23.22
128.23	137.05	175.02
201.15	236.23	300.01
409.05	442.28	496.06
AHOY	236.19	236.19
AIM	186.15	222.08
255.25	459.28	501.02
501.02		
AIMED	261.11	
AIMING	32.07	
AIMLESS	194.29	420.26
AIMLESSLY		201.19
311.03		
AIN'T	29.10	29.12
29.20	30.08	75.22
79.29	143.13	143.22
145.08	205.28	231.04
237.24	237.26	238.09
AIR	6.08	15.05
20.15	22.08	24.26
27.06	28.29	29.19
30.11	31.15	46.27
49.27	53.28	61.28
63.09	65.14	84.03
85.05	85.25	118.19
124.06	129.24	139.25
146.13	149.19	150.11
158.19	162.07	163.17
170.19	171.06	191.23
205.09	208.05	210.09
220.06	231.06	260.28
271.10	294.15	311.23
341.14	349.06	365.12
370.16	376.27	387.24
397.18	408.18	408.26
422.26	440.15	453.12
460.25	463.08	482.19
490.01	493.11	498.23
504.06	512.11	
AIRILY	226.02	
AIRS	349.17	
AIRY	188.17	
AKIN	69.16	216.30
425.16		
ALABASTER		194.02
ALACRITY	365.28	510.24
ALARM	59.07	94.07
358.15	448.04	
ALARMED	224.29	394.08
ALARMING	298.24	
ALARMINGLY		61.10
ALARMS	366.29	
ALARUM	310.26	
ALAS	275.23	468.13
ALASKA	197.25	
ALCOHOL	146.03	
ALERT	37.21	148.26
359.28	418.05	453.01
459.07	493.26	
ALERTNESS		304.26
490.04		
ALEXANDER		281.03
ALI	317.10	324.27
331.16	332.13	336.01
336.19	359.10	373.22

ALI (CONT.)		383.05
ALI'S	323.17	363.18
363.20	368.12	383.04
484.07		
ALIGHTED	145.28	
ALIKE	103.05	352.15
ALIVE	44.13	101.16
143.19	183.16	197.24
312.12	344.11	388.28
421.26	489.08	
ALL	6.08	6.24
8.07	8.30	10.23
11.13	11.14	11.29
14.14	15.04	15.16
17.09	17.09	20.08
20.13	20.29	24.04
27.16	29.26	30.01
31.13	32.15	34.13
36.02	36.17	41.23
42.05	43.21	43.25
44.18	46.03	47.02
47.12	48.30	50.22
51.30	52.02	52.17
52.19	52.25	52.30
53.05	53.15	54.08
54.26	54.28	56.19
59.14	60.10	61.11
62.12	62.22	63.03
63.03	63.05	63.20
63.30	64.13	65.13
66.10	68.28	71.19
71.25	71.26	73.17
74.07	74.12	75.12
75.27	76.10	78.14
78.30	80.02	80.08
80.19	80.27	81.02
85.17	85.19	85.24
85.27	86.01	86.11
86.19	86.27	86.30
87.02	88.11	90.26
92.09	93.11	93.15
94.23	95.16	96.01
96.05	97.17	97.26
98.21	99.10	99.13
99.19	100.09	101.01
101.10	101.13	101.19
102.08	103.01	103.03
103.04	103.14	104.04
105.18	105.24	105.27
105.28	107.13	107.16
109.06	109.13	109.14
109.25	110.08	110.08
110.08	110.21	111.20
112.08	112.16	112.18
113.04	113.15	114.16
115.25	116.01	118.10
119.20	120.26	121.03
123.09	124.02	124.26
124.04	126.17	126.18
126.26	127.01	128.18
129.26	131.09	132.08
132.13	132.17	134.30
137.12	137.13	138.05
138.06	138.07	138.07
138.17	139.13	139.24
140.23	141.01	142.11
143.01	143.02	143.06
147.27	147.27	148.11
148.15	149.16	150.28
151.14	152.15	152.16
152.27	152.30	153.12
153.24	155.05	156.21
156.23	157.08	157.11
157.26	158.27	159.02
160.02	160.13	160.16
162.01	163.21	164.06
166.08	167.07	167.10
168.21	170.29	172.16
173.08	177.25	178.11
178.16	178.30	179.04
182.20	183.02	183.05
183.14	183.20	183.27
184.04	185.19	187.16
187.17	187.19	188.10
188.15	190.05	190.09
190.09	190.11	191.02
193.11	193.14	193.16
193.17	194.19	194.22
195.30	197.11	199.01
200.27	200.30	201.10

ALL (CONT.)		202.19
203.27	204.02	207.19
208.08	208.19	209.14
209.21	209.28	210.01
210.06	211.03	211.16
212.03	212.05	212.18
212.29	214.02	214.07
214.28	215.08	216.10
216.26	218.10	218.27
219.27	223.21	223.24
224.15	224.29	225.10
226.09	226.26	228.17
229.16	232.25	232.30
233.05	233.20	233.27
235.05	235.13	235.28
236.26	237.07	237.08
237.10	237.11	237.18
238.10	239.07	239.17
240.04	240.21	242.06
242.22	243.05	243.12
243.22	246.16	247.05
247.10	250.17	250.28
253.19	255.09	255.19
258.07	260.20	262.12
262.27	264.23	268.21
270.26	271.14	271.30
271.30	273.12	274.14
274.17	275.02	277.12
278.15	279.15	279.29
280.18	280.30	283.20
283.27	285.13	285.17
286.20	287.03	287.06
287.29	289.06	290.01
291.30	292.26	295.11
295.11	298.10	299.20
300.05	301.18	302.02
302.05	302.07	302.08
302.15	302.16	303.08
304.03	304.08	304.09
304.28	306.22	307.13
308.19	309.07	310.09
310.15	311.14	311.17
312.08	313.13	313.26
314.24	319.02	319.03
320.24	321.02	321.16
323.12	324.04	324.05
324.10	327.09	327.16
329.05	330.04	330.21
330.22	331.02	331.07
333.07	333.16	334.24
335.11	339.10	340.02
341.17	342.09	343.26
347.16	350.14	352.02
352.05	352.12	353.17
353.20	353.21	354.01
357.25	358.11	358.12
358.19	359.11	359.13
359.26	359.28	359.30
360.29	361.22	361.27
361.28	361.29	362.15
363.02	364.03	365.05
365.14	366.12	367.09
367.15	368.29	369.02
369.11	370.10	371.17
372.09	373.03	374.24
374.25	375.14	375.18
376.07	376.07	376.28
377.06	377.17	378.20
378.30	379.09	380.05
381.07	381.09	382.27
382.28	384.05	384.16
386.05	386.24	388.25
388.26	389.24	392.02
392.15	392.25	394.09
394.14	396.05	397.09
397.22	397.22	397.30
398.06	398.06	398.11
399.06	399.09	400.24
401.05	401.30	402.24
404.11	404.19	406.06
407.03	408.07	410.04
410.11	411.16	411.18
411.30	412.22	412.25
415.17	416.11	418.18
419.05	419.12	419.15
419.27	420.15	421.15
422.07	422.15	422.18
422.23	423.01	423.02
425.01	425.12	426.10
425.17	430.13	430.20

ALL (CONT.)   430.23
431.01 431.17 432.18
433.08 434.02 435.01
438.13 438.13 438.24
438.26 439.02 439.10
439.15 440.06 443.18
446.11 447.01 452.23
455.03 455.26 457.06
457.14 457.21 458.16
458.23 460.09 461.28
462.30 463.06 463.13
464.04 464.14 466.12
467.03 467.28 469.06
469.07 469.15 469.21
470.25 471.16 471.22
471.27 472.07 472.15
472.28 475.03 475.07
476.04 477.19 478.28
479.07 480.26 481.09
482.12 482.18 483.03
483.04 483.13 488.05
489.06 489.25 492.06
492.11 492.27 493.04
496.08 498.05 499.04
499.07 499.13 500.25
505.04 506.18 507.04
508.13 510.09 510.20
512.18 513.27 514.01
515.16 516.08 516.20
ALL-FIRED   286.20
ALL-FOURS   115.25
460.09
ALLANG   278.23 292.23
306.21 309.24 316.11
317.11 332.24 336.07
353.30 407.23 461.24
462.09
ALLANG'S 306.05 412.05
444.12 453.08
ALLEZ   178.17
ALLIANCES   458.24
ALLIES   453.28
ALLIGATOR   300.03
300.04
ALLMOTIONLESS   103.28
ALLOW   87.29   180.22
187.11 198.28 215.26
229.17 243.03 299.21
466.16
ALLOWANCE   14.22
109.02
ALLOWANCES   86.11
ALLOWED 40.14   46.12
170.18 225.11 250.09
281.12 337.03 349.17
486.08 491.06 499.08
ALLOY   53.25
ALLUDED 247.16
ALLUDING 90.23   245.01
ALLURING 515.22
ALLUSION 363.05
ALLUSIONS   168.04
268.14 350.27
ALLY   112.04 395.01
395.08
ALMIGHTY 343.24
ALMOST   22.09   44.01
44.19   56.29   76.30
77.01   79.09   87.20
108.13 137.21 172.30
202.04 224.29 225.09
240.16 252.24 286.24
303.15 308.09 333.01
346.06 348.24 357.13
357.25 364.17 369.26
370.09 376.06 381.05
382.22 400.19 421.27
426.20 434.19 449.24
458.28 462.09 468.20
475.06 480.15 488.15
495.14
ALOFT   4.23   365.17
ALONE   9.01   18.02
38.11   60.06   84.02
89.22   101.20 120.01
122.04 139.01 141.12
154.08 160.14 161.34
169.20 181.30 184.28
197.26 198.20 208.13
213.16 214.09 215.20

ALONE (CONT.)   226.21
227.11 230.30 244.11
254.17 255.27 259.05
261.19 294.23 302.10
313.05 313.06 320.29
329.20 334.19 334.28
336.23 351.06 369.23
378.10 385.25 387.01
389.16 397.17 400.06
410.25 416.05 418.08
423.18 428.17 452.13
455.30 468.10 468.11
470.02 482.14 482.28
483.05 495.13 510.13
513.24
ALONG   4.13   5.20
6.03   15.25   25.24
37.17   43.04   62.22
65.13   72.26   101.11
105.22 107.13 110.01
120.27 164.04 164.15
167.07 177.10 186.09
191.24 197.19 201.13
205.29 208.07 216.27
276.08 302.20 324.10
325.18 330.21 332.02
342.04 359.30 361.02
377.12 396.16 409.29
437.26 444.01 445.07
452.22 461.03 462.24
472.13 472.27 480.12
500.27
ALONGSIDE   6.30
15.10   132.05 133.26
138.15 164.25 182.22
183.13 300.28 495.10
496.11 498.04
ALOUD   16.25   96.11
104.18 151.11 157.11
187.21 193.09 204.22
334.12 442.13 455.30
506.06 514.16
ALPACA   428.21
ALREADY 34.06   110.09
122.24 127.22 148.04
156.11 186.20 221.04
224.08 225.25 237.17
255.27 294.10 294.14
297.18 298.06 319.27
327.01 332.14 336.15
367.13 386.02 408.22
415.14 431.13 435.24
446.13 457.23 458.25
461.28 462.05 467.24
485.25 503.07 512.24
ALSATIAN 240.20
ALSO   2.22   10.21
35.04   35.30   57.23
107.07 123.22 124.11
130.28 167.19 171.14
172.02 190.20 195.25
247.07 273.28 289.21
321.28 323.07 323.24
327.15 353.29 375.18
379.11 386.27 418.16
420.23 421.10 422.14
425.19 444.02 445.27
461.11 482.25 483.07
499.18 511.06
ALTER   71.17   152.04
ALTERATION   407.19
ALTERCATION   56.30
ALTERING 71.21
ALTERNATELY   22.13
ALTOGETHER   90.21
95.25   121.07 153.22
183.24 211.11 224.18
245.06 259.09 282.26
345.02 441.20 501.25
ALTRUISM 322.02

ALWAYS (CONT.)   239.18
241.16 246.10 260.14
282.14 295.01 300.04
325.29 338.23 369.03
377.26 377.30 379.14
381.23 413.07 419.19
423.09 430.12 433.12
435.07 474.26 486.14
495.03
AM   29.21   29.26
30.08   40.03   41.02
41.05   45.29   46.02
48.12   56.20   61.01
61.20   63.24   64.26
64.30   69.26   71.28
73.14   74.24   81.18
85.27   87.21   87.24
88.05   98.23   104.25
114.01 121.09 122.15
129.18 131.08 140.21
140.22 145.23 145.14
158.28 158.28 160.06
160.06 166.15 166.24
168.05 168.06 172.11
175.10 179.13 180.08
184.03 186.05 187.11
187.14 188.12 188.13
188.14 200.21 201.14
201.27 202.24 202.28
203.09 204.19 214.01
214.15 219.21 219.22
223.12 223.16 223.16
223.25 223.26 223.29
228.17 228.19 230.04
235.27 236.02 258.12
264.12 274.09 274.24
289.04 295.30 301.20
303.05 303.08 303.24
308.22 308.27 338.27
340.20 341.19 341.21
342.04 344.02 344.06
344.16 348.24 348.29
352.15 355.10 355.12
361.11 367.20 368.29
369.19 369.19 375.04
375.11 375.14 376.10
376.10 377.10 385.05
388.16 388.17 388.25
391.28 401.04 401.14
408.05 408.08 429.13
448.24 455.25 456.04
458.09 464.12 464.13
472.26 472.26 473.26
473.28 474.05 474.10
477.12 480.25 488.27
495.22 501.21 514.19
514.20
AMAZED   30.20   88.27
100.26 153.18 203.24
238.27 344.22 364.27
393.12
AMAZEMENT   173.07
314.10 380.08 431.01
482.16 500.24
AMAZING 77.20   114.05
253.13 275.21 298.14
304.28 310.18 324.14
332.05 345.22 392.23
395.27 422.27
AMAZINGLY   46.06
86.30
AMBER   199.19
AMBIENT 348.25
AMBITION 337.04 407.23
AMBITIONS   407.09
AMBUSH   255.09
AMBUSHES 449.12
AMERICAN 49.15
AMIABLE 26.19
AMIABLY 199.22 308.07
AMICABLE 352.28 451.29
AMID   293.08
AMID-SHIPS   293.08
AMIDSHIPS   17.29
126.01
AMMUNITION   440.05
461.24
AMONGST 26.09   29.19
80.28   82.27   118.10
139.11 183.26 192.17

AMONGST (CONT.)   201.12
213.23 252.06 260.23
262.13 264.03 264.26
286.20 293.09 317.09
320.19 325.14 329.05
332.27 334.07 351.10
353.23 355.19 357.30
364.07 364.08 384.28
387.27 389.11 410.10
423.07 426.26 427.24
447.24 450.04 451.24
463.30 468.24 482.08
492.29 494.17 502.13
502.15 506.09 506.15
512.04 516.13
AMOUNGST 83.22
AMOUNT   159.29
ANOINTED 240.01
AMPLE   30.10   170.11
315.02
AMUSED   28.17   78.02
134.20 228.08 361.15
481.23
AMUSEMENT   299.30
AMUSING 48.25   50.24
278.10 328.08
AMUSINGLY   348.16
AN   1.01   1.14
4.03   4.11   4.23
5.17   11.09   11.24
12.05   12.08   12.13
12.21   13.19   14.12
14.30   16.01   16.12
16.16   18.06   19.18
20.06   21.14   21.17
23.17   23.19   25.03
25.12   26.06   27.17
27.18   28.01   28.16
30.17   32.08   35.10
36.05   38.02   39.04
41.26   43.11   43.12
43.23   43.34   44.12
46.02   46.27   46.28
47.20   47.29   49.14
50.01   51.02   54.13
54.15   54.16   54.18
55.26   58.03   58.19
59.13   59.15   59.18
59.23   60.05   61.02
61.15   61.18   61.27
62.25   63.04   63.12
63.15   63.24   64.03
65.14   66.21   66.22
67.21   68.21   68.24
74.16   75.16   75.18
79.01   81.05   81.07
81.28   84.03   84.08
85.25   86.14   86.15
86.15   88.01   88.11
89.01   89.25   90.20
92.01   92.23   95.12
97.14   97.22   100.03
100.06 100.07 100.22
102.04 102.10 103.14
105.11 108.09 108.14
111.28 111.28 112.04
112.04 112.26 112.27
112.29 113.25 114.11
115.29 117.17 118.18
118.28 120.21 123.20
125.06 125.22 126.07
126.12 127.13 130.26
133.20 134.21 135.08
136.03 136.11 137.27
138.01 138.21 140.13
140.22 142.14 144.09
144.17 144.21 145.04
145.21 146.04 146.13
146.24 147.07 148.30
149.23 151.09 151.16
153.08 153.22 154.03
155.12 156.02 163.08
167.02 167.22 167.26
168.12 171.06 171.14
171.27 172.23 172.25
176.25 176.29 177.22
178.02 178.22 182.05
182.14 184.11 185.23
186.24 188.16 188.17
189.08 190.05 190.16

AN (CONT.)		190.22
191.27	192.19	192.29
193.09	193.19	194.29
196.12	197.06	198.16
198.17	199.11	199.14
199.18	202.26	205.02
205.09	207.02	207.23
208.05	209.12	209.17
210.09	211.06	211.08
211.25	212.01	213.10
216.13	216.17	220.05
220.20	222.07	222.15
223.05	223.27	224.03
224.21	226.03	228.20
230.12	232.04	233.15
235.03	237.05	239.11
239.14	240.13	240.21
240.23	241.23	243.21
243.30	245.02	245.14
246.20	246.25	246.26
247.22	248.02	248.04
249.21	250.06	250.08
252.08	252.12	252.27
253.10	255.30	257.24
258.01	258.04	258.30
260.05	262.16	262.30
264.01	266.18	266.22
268.14	268.20	271.03
271.23	273.08	273.25
276.03	276.07	276.13
277.18	277.19	278.01
278.03	278.09	278.12
279.07	279.26	280.10
282.05	285.10	285.18
286.20	286.27	288.10
288.29	289.07	290.23
293.03	293.21	295.26
298.25	299.16	300.02
300.09	301.29	304.11
306.15	307.12	308.01
309.19	311.24	314.16
315.12	316.21	319.14
320.06	321.12	322.01
322.07	323.12	324.18
325.14	325.17	328.02
329.24	329.29	330.05
330.05	331.16	332.05
336.13	336.20	337.14
339.24	339.26	340.03
341.10	341.11	343.01
345.01	345.01	345.02
345.20	348.02	348.23
349.06	351.02	351.28
352.27	355.06	355.23
356.25	358.21	359.21
360.29	361.26	365.04
366.05	366.19	367.16
368.05	370.02	370.07
370.24	371.21	373.01
374.20	376.22	377.27
378.17	378.18	378.26
383.17	383.24	385.17
386.08	386.20	387.19
388.22	389.08	390.17
390.23	390.25	391.29
392.11	392.13	393.12
393.16	395.02	395.14
397.23	399.09	399.12
399.24	399.28	400.12
405.23	406.02	407.08
408.06	408.22	408.23
408.30	409.10	412.19
412.21	412.24	417.29
418.05	418.08	418.24
420.08	420.09	420.21
420.27	420.30	421.10
423.06	423.16	423.20
423.27	423.29	425.21
426.06	426.09	427.05
427.11	427.13	429.01
433.07	434.25	436.16
436.29	437.03	437.12
437.14	437.17	438.17
440.04	440.30	441.10
442.02	443.24	444.06
445.15	445.19	446.02
448.11	451.02	451.26
451.29	452.29	453.11
454.06	454.07	455.01
455.24	455.24	455.25

AN (CONT.)		456.13
458.13	458.26	459.05
460.09	460.17	461.04
463.08	463.10	465.25
465.29	467.05	469.15
470.27	474.19	475.01
475.13	479.26	481.23
487.03	490.20	491.01
492.28	493.14	495.14
498.23	499.27	499.29
500.22	502.22	503.19
505.13	506.12	508.22
512.02	512.03	513.26
514.22	514.22	515.05
515.23	515.26	515.28
516.06	516.09	516.10
ANACHRONISM		197.07
214.26		
ANCHOR	1.19	6.05
6.17	166.07	244.23
293.21	438.03	441.01
ANCHORAGE		196.23
200.06	274.04	
ANCHORED	175.16	441.09
442.18	445.25	484.12
489.18		
ANCHORING		16.22
ANCHORING-GROUND		16.22
ANCHORS	47.21	
ANCIENT	201.19	297.18
AND	1.02	1.04
1.06	1.08	1.11
1.16	2.01	2.03
2.05	2.07	2.11
2.16	2.18	2.19
2.24	2.25	2.28
3.03	3.11	3.13
3.16	3.19	3.22
3.30	4.11	4.12
4.15	4.19	4.21
4.24	5.01	5.05
5.08	5.13	5.16
5.18	5.23	5.23
5.28	6.01	6.01
6.03	6.06	6.06
6.11	6.12	6.17
6.22	6.25	6.28
7.02	7.03	7.06
7.07	7.09	7.13
7.18	7.20	7.20
7.28	8.01	8.03
8.04	8.13	8.18
8.24	8.25	9.02
9.05	9.06	9.08
10.02	10.06	10.07
10.12	10.15	10.19
10.20	11.03	11.03
11.03	11.06	11.11
11.11	11.14	11.17
11.23	11.25	11.29
12.03	12.05	12.06
12.07	12.10	12.12
12.14	12.18	12.21
12.25	12.28	13.11
13.15	13.18	13.20
13.23	13.30	14.02
14.03	14.05	14.10
14.13	14.14	14.22
14.24	14.28	14.30
15.05	15.05	15.06
15.07	15.12	15.14
15.15	15.16	15.19
15.21	15.21	15.22
15.23	15.23	16.04
16.10	16.17	16.18
16.20	16.28	16.30
17.07	17.10	17.10
17.11	17.15	17.26
18.01	18.07	18.08
19.02	19.05	19.07
19.07	19.12	19.13
19.15	19.20	19.24
20.04	20.05	20.19
20.20	20.21	20.25
20.28	21.02	21.03
21.05	21.11	21.18
21.20	21.30	22.04
22.09	22.12	22.13
22.20	22.29	23.02
23.07	23.11	23.13

AND (CONT.)		23.18
23.22	23.27	23.28
24.03	24.06	24.09
24.10	24.12	24.15
24.18	24.19	24.22
24.26	24.29	25.08
25.21	25.24	25.27
26.06	26.07	26.08
26.17	27.05	27.06
27.09	27.15	27.16
27.25	27.28	28.03
28.13	28.14	28.17
29.01	29.06	29.14
29.17	29.20	29.22
29.27	29.30	30.03
30.04	30.05	30.10
30.11	30.13	30.14
30.18	30.19	30.20
30.24	30.28	31.03
31.10	31.12	31.15
32.07	32.11	32.12
32.21	32.22	33.03
33.07	33.07	33.15
33.19	33.27	33.30
34.02	34.05	34.14
34.19	34.23	34.25
34.28	34.30	35.02
35.05	35.08	35.18
35.19	35.22	35.27
35.30	36.01	36.04
36.08	36.11	36.13
36.18	36.21	36.22
36.23	36.25	36.29
37.02	37.05	37.06
37.10	37.15	37.16
37.19	37.21	37.24
37.26	37.26	37.29
38.10	38.21	38.23
38.26	38.29	38.30
39.04	39.07	40.02
40.08	40.10	40.19
41.01	41.03	41.09
41.11	41.14	41.17
41.19	41.20	41.23
41.24	41.25	42.08
42.15	42.16	42.27
42.29	43.06	43.09
43.19	43.20	43.21
43.24	43.29	43.35
44.02	44.06	44.08
44.13	44.14	44.17
44.19	44.21	44.21
44.25	44.26	44.30
45.01	45.07	45.08
45.15	45.23	45.26
45.27	45.30	46.02
46.07	46.09	46.13
46.16	46.19	46.24
46.25	47.02	47.03
47.09	47.12	47.13
47.17	47.18	47.25
47.28	48.08	48.08
48.19	48.24	48.29
49.06	49.15	49.16
49.17	49.22	49.24
49.29	49.30	50.01
50.14	50.15	50.17
50.19	50.23	50.25
51.02	51.03	51.04
51.12	51.15	51.17
51.20	51.21	51.25
52.01	52.06	52.08
52.09	52.10	52.12
52.16	52.18	52.18
52.27	53.01	53.03
53.04	53.05	53.07
53.10	53.11	53.14
53.15	53.16	53.18
53.21	53.21	53.26
54.03	54.05	54.10
54.11	54.20	54.23
54.26	54.28	55.01
55.02	55.04	55.05
55.07	55.08	55.08
55.13	55.15	55.18
55.21	55.24	55.26
55.27	56.02	56.05
56.13	56.16	56.25
56.25	56.25	56.29
57.01	57.17	57.20

AND (CONT.)		57.25
57.27	57.28	57.30
58.02	58.05	58.13
58.18	58.19	58.20
58.27	59.01	59.04
59.16	59.21	59.26
59.27	60.01	60.03
60.09	60.13	60.16
60.20	60.26	60.29
61.01	61.07	61.16
61.18	61.23	62.05
62.12	62.23	63.01
63.04	63.07	63.08
63.10	63.13	63.15
63.18	63.27	63.29
64.03	64.09	64.12
64.13	64.14	64.14
64.17	65.08	65.15
66.04	66.09	66.11
66.18	66.19	67.01
67.09	67.10	67.14
57.22	67.26	67.28
68.06	68.09	68.14
68.22	68.23	68.25
68.26	69.03	69.05
69.13	69.15	69.20
69.27	69.28	69.29
70.06	70.13	70.14
70.15	70.21	70.26
70.29	70.29	70.34
70.37	70.41	70.42
71.06	71.07	71.08
71.14	71.16	71.16
71.23	71.25	71.26
71.26	71.29	72.01
72.03	72.07	72.08
72.12	72.27	72.27
73.04	73.05	73.07
73.07	73.21	73.24
73.28	73.28	73.29
74.03	74.09	74.10
74.13	74.18	75.05
75.07	75.08	75.09
75.10	75.17	75.24
75.27	75.30	75.30
76.04	76.08	76.20
77.07	77.08	77.08
77.08	77.18	77.28
78.05	78.07	78.17
79.08	79.12	79.15
79.17	79.19	79.24
79.27	80.09	80.11
80.13	80.15	80.16
80.22	81.06	81.12
81.13	81.17	81.24
81.29	82.02	82.10
82.12	82.14	82.16
82.19	82.27	82.28
82.29	83.03	83.06
83.07	83.08	83.11
83.14	83.15	83.22
83.24	83.27	83.30
84.02	84.06	84.13
84.23	85.08	85.11
85.12	85.18	85.23
85.28	86.14	86.18
86.23	87.01	87.07
87.09	88.12	88.22
88.26	88.27	88.28
89.02	89.03	89.09
89.23	90.01	90.11
90.11	90.26	90.30
91.01	91.03	91.04
91.08	91.15	92.02
92.06	92.08	92.08
92.11	92.14	92.14
92.16	92.20	92.21
92.22	93.04	93.06
93.11	93.19	93.29
94.05	94.08	94.09
94.12	94.15	94.17
94.21	94.23	95.03
95.14	95.21	96.01
96.15	96.20	97.02
97.08	97.11	97.21
98.04	98.12	98.13
98.19	98.24	98.25
98.28	99.02	99.08
99.11	99.14	99.17
99.21	99.24	100.13

AND (CONT.)		100.27	AND (CONT.)		146.07	AND (CONT.)		193.03	AND (CONT.)		234.09
101.08	101.15	101.19	146.11	146.20	146.21	193.06	193.08	193.09	234.10	234.15	234.20
101.20	101.24	102.01	147.07	147.12	147.17	193.12	193.15	193.19	234.25	234.26	234.29
102.08	102.18	102.27	148.08	148.13	148.14	193.29	194.05	194.08	234.30	234.30	235.02
103.05	103.05	103.14	148.17	148.19	148.24	194.09	194.15	194.16	235.04	235.05	235.06
103.15	104.06	104.14	148.30	149.01	149.10	194.21	194.22	194.23	235.08	235.12	235.13
104.16	104.16	104.20	149.13	149.23	150.06	194.23	194.28	195.05	235.20	235.22	235.28
104.20	104.22	104.24	150.19	150.27	151.02	195.06	195.08	195.12	235.29	235.30	236.11
104.27	105.01	105.05	151.11	151.18	151.27	195.12	195.17	195.19	236.23	236.24	237.02
105.08	105.11	105.14	152.05	152.05	152.08	195.20	195.22	195.25	237.07	237.08	237.16
105.18	105.19	105.20	152.19	152.27	152.30	195.26	195.27	195.01	237.17	237.23	238.11
107.03	107.04	107.07	153.01	153.04	153.06	196.04	196.05	196.14	238.13	238.16	238.22
107.13	107.16	107.17	153.10	153.19	153.28	196.17	196.18	196.23	238.23	238.24	238.27
107.18	108.07	108.14	153.30	154.10	154.13	196.26	197.05	197.08	239.09	239.14	239.15
108.21	108.23	108.24	155.02	155.04	155.05	197.23	198.01	198.04	239.21	240.06	240.10
108.26	109.04	109.04	155.09	155.12	155.20	198.08	198.10	198.14	240.16	240.20	240.25
109.05	109.09	109.17	155.24	156.06	156.17	198.16	198.17	198.17	241.05	241.07	241.14
109.22	109.26	109.26	157.01	157.06	157.10	198.19	198.22	198.24	241.15	241.21	241.26
109.28	110.01	110.03	157.11	157.13	157.14	198.26	198.29	199.01	242.03	242.05	242.10
110.10	110.18	110.29	157.21	157.29	158.09	199.07	199.09	199.17	242.11	242.13	243.02
110.29	111.08	111.14	158.13	158.15	158.22	199.22	199.28	200.11	243.04	243.07	243.08
111.24	111.29	112.02	158.30	159.03	159.06	200.17	200.23	201.03	243.17	243.21	243.28
112.03	112.09	112.11	159.10	159.14	159.16	201.22	202.04	202.10	243.30	244.21	244.22
112.14	112.16	112.19	159.16	159.23	159.26	202.11	202.14	202.17	245.18	245.20	245.23
112.27	113.04	113.15	159.29	159.29	160.06	202.25	203.01	203.10	245.25	245.26	245.28
113.22	113.24	113.30	160.12	160.13	160.22	203.18	203.25	204.02	246.02	246.07	246.09
114.07	114.09	114.16	160.25	160.26	160.29	204.11	204.24	204.27	246.12	246.12	246.16
114.18	114.22	114.25	162.04	162.06	162.15	204.29	205.07	205.09	246.19	246.25	246.25
114.27	115.06	115.07	162.17	163.03	163.08	205.16	205.18	205.21	246.27	247.06	247.09
115.14	115.19	115.27	163.10	163.14	163.18	205.23	205.24	206.05	247.11	247.12	247.12
115.30	116.02	116.05	163.29	164.05	164.07	206.06	207.07	207.07	247.20	248.06	248.07
116.06	116.13	116.20	164.10	164.14	164.15	207.10	207.14	207.19	248.11	248.13	248.16
116.22	116.29	117.08	164.21	164.25	165.04	208.07	208.09	208.14	248.18	248.23	249.04
117.13	117.13	117.26	165.10	165.12	165.23	208.15	208.16	208.24	249.11	249.12	249.16
118.01	118.06	118.07	165.24	165.28	166.01	209.03	209.13	209.16	249.18	249.20	249.23
118.13	118.17	118.30	166.02	166.14	166.15	209.18	209.28	209.29	250.03	250.04	250.05
119.06	119.10	119.12	167.01	167.09	167.13	210.11	210.13	210.14	250.16	250.18	250.22
119.14	119.18	119.22	167.20	167.25	167.28	210.15	210.18	211.03	250.23	250.25	250.26
119.23	120.08	120.08	168.05	168.07	168.12	211.13	211.18	211.25	250.28	251.02	251.08
120.11	120.12	120.14	168.18	168.25	168.26	211.25	211.27	212.08	251.16	251.16	251.26
120.15	120.23	120.29	169.02	169.04	169.07	212.09	212.11	212.13	251.29	252.03	252.07
121.02	121.11	122.04	169.22	169.26	170.02	212.16	212.20	212.21	252.08	252.09	252.10
122.09	122.10	122.17	170.08	170.09	170.12	212.21	212.24	212.25	252.12	252.13	252.14
122.19	122.20	122.22	170.18	170.20	170.23	212.27	212.28	212.30	252.16	252.17	252.28
123.07	123.08	123.09	170.24	171.05	171.09	213.03	213.08	213.09	252.29	253.03	253.03
123.12	123.13	123.17	171.12	171.15	171.28	213.10	213.12	213.13	253.04	253.05	253.06
124.08	124.15	124.18	171.30	172.02	172.05	213.17	213.24	214.04	253.11	253.20	253.24
125.01	125.04	125.05	172.07	172.22	172.25	214.06	214.16	214.19	253.27	254.02	254.07
125.09	125.10	125.12	172.26	173.04	173.06	214.28	215.07	215.14	254.09	254.13	254.16
125.19	125.26	125.27	173.10	173.12	173.16	215.22	215.27	216.01	254.16	254.18	254.19
126.02	126.04	126.21	174.01	174.04	174.06	216.05	216.06	216.09	254.20	254.22	254.23
126.24	126.27	127.08	174.13	174.15	174.21	216.09	216.12	216.14	254.24	254.25	254.26
127.13	127.22	127.25	175.02	175.09	175.15	216.15	216.16	216.19	254.29	255.02	255.03
128.04	128.11	128.11	175.26	175.27	176.01	216.22	216.28	216.30	255.06	255.09	255.10
128.15	128.15	128.17	176.05	176.17	176.22	217.05	217.12	217.19	255.11	255.11	255.13
128.19	128.20	128.21	176.24	176.28	177.01	217.20	217.23	217.26	255.20	255.22	255.23
128.21	128.23	129.01	177.09	177.17	177.22	217.28	218.01	218.07	255.24	255.27	255.28
129.06	129.11	129.17	177.23	177.25	177.28	218.24	218.26	218.29	256.01	256.02	256.05
129.19	129.25	129.26	177.30	178.12	178.26	219.03	219.07	219.08	256.10	256.11	256.12
130.16	130.17	130.28	178.29	179.14	179.16	219.09	219.11	219.12	256.13	256.13	256.14
131.05	131.16	131.18	179.20	179.27	179.29	219.13	219.16	219.29	256.14	256.14	256.18
131.20	131.24	131.30	180.10	180.14	180.21	219.30	220.06	220.07	256.21	256.22	256.23
132.07	132.07	132.26	180.28	181.05	181.10	220.12	220.18	220.19	256.24	256.28	256.29
133.01	133.03	133.08	181.18	181.26	181.28	220.21	220.23	220.25	257.06	257.08	257.16
133.11	133.12	133.15	181.30	182.07	182.21	220.29	221.08	222.05	257.22	257.23	257.27
133.21	133.22	133.27	182.22	182.29	182.30	222.09	222.12	222.13	257.27	257.29	258.04
134.01	134.10	134.12	183.02	183.03	183.09	222.17	222.17	222.22	258.09	258.19	258.26
134.18	134.19	134.21	183.12	183.12	183.13	223.03	223.07	223.07	258.28	259.09	259.22
134.25	134.29	135.01	183.20	183.24	183.25	223.20	223.22	223.23	259.24	259.26	259.26
136.01	136.08	136.08	183.27	184.03	184.13	223.26	223.29	224.18	260.01	260.06	260.08
136.12	136.17	136.19	184.18	184.21	184.25	224.20	224.24	224.25	260.12	260.14	260.19
136.21	137.05	137.07	184.29	185.04	185.05	224.28	225.16	225.18	261.01	261.01	261.09
137.12	137.15	137.25	185.06	185.10	185.21	225.20	225.29	225.10	261.13	261.16	261.16
137.26	137.26	138.03	185.23	185.25	185.26	226.13	226.15	226.17	261.22	261.24	261.28
138.09	138.11	138.20	185.30	186.04	186.08	226.25	226.27	227.03	261.28	261.30	262.04
138.23	139.06	139.09	186.11	186.17	186.26	227.04	227.07	227.23	262.08	262.09	262.10
139.13	139.15	139.24	187.06	187.11	187.18	228.09	228.10	228.13	262.13	262.20	262.21
139.27	139.28	140.03	187.20	187.25	188.08	228.25	229.03	229.03	262.22	262.26	262.29
140.07	140.23	140.24	188.14	188.15	188.19	229.04	229.09	229.16	263.01	263.02	263.04
140.25	140.26	141.02	188.23	188.30	189.05	229.19	229.22	229.24	263.07	263.10	263.11
141.04	141.06	141.20	189.07	189.16	189.23	229.29	230.07	230.12	263.19	263.21	263.24
141.25	142.02	142.06	189.23	190.02	190.08	230.14	230.17	230.28	263.30	264.04	264.06
142.09	142.13	142.14	190.09	190.14	190.20	230.28	230.29	231.01	264.13	264.26	264.30
142.16	142.26	142.27	190.23	190.24	191.03	231.05	231.07	231.14	265.09	265.12	266.07
142.30	143.02	143.05	191.07	191.11	191.14	231.15	231.23	232.05	266.14	266.15	266.17
143.07	144.14	144.19	191.16	191.18	191.22	232.08	232.10	232.14	267.04	267.05	267.08
144.24	145.03	145.06	192.01	192.11	192.15	232.17	232.19	232.21	267.19	267.21	267.21
145.08	145.10	145.16	192.15	192.15	192.20	232.26	232.27	232.30	267.25	268.03	268.15
145.20	145.20	145.21	192.23	192.24	192.28	233.01	233.02	233.09	268.22	268.26	269.08
145.24	145.28	145.29	192.30	192.30	193.03	233.14	233.18	233.26	269.12	269.17	269.24

AND (CONT.)		269.30	AND (CONT.)		310.17	AND (CONT.)		352.23	AND (CONT.)		398.15
270.05	270.07	270.13	310.25	310.30	311.04	353.04	353.09	353.12	399.01	399.01	399.05
270.16	270.17	270.24	311.05	311.09	311.13	353.14	353.17	353.24	399.05	399.30	400.17
270.29	271.05	271.07	311.15	311.20	311.24	353.30	354.02	354.04	400.26	400.29	401.04
271.10	271.11	271.12	311.26	312.01	312.04	354.07	355.08	355.11	401.05	401.10	401.11
271.15	271.26	271.30	312.09	312.09	312.13	355.13	355.18	355.18	401.14	401.21	401.21
272.03	272.09	272.14	312.22	312.23	312.25	355.19	355.21	355.22	401.23	401.26	401.28
272.17	272.18	272.18	312.27	313.04	313.05	355.24	356.03	356.06	402.04	402.19	402.21
272.25	273.12	273.18	313.09	313.15	313.17	356.06	356.06	356.08	403.02	403.03	403.06
273.28	274.02	274.08	313.20	313.26	313.30	356.18	356.18	356.19	403.22	403.24	404.02
274.10	274.12	274.21	313.30	314.03	314.04	356.30	356.30	357.01	404.04	404.16	405.02
274.29	275.03	275.05	314.04	314.08	314.11	357.05	357.06	357.08	405.10	405.11	405.22
275.08	275.18	275.18	314.13	314.17	314.17	357.30	358.15	358.27	405.23	405.27	405.28
275.19	275.23	276.05	314.25	314.27	314.28	358.28	358.30	359.06	405.30	406.02	406.03
276.07	276.11	276.11	315.02	315.09	315.09	359.15	359.17	359.23	407.04	407.10	407.11
276.12	276.12	276.13	315.13	315.18	315.21	359.25	359.30	360.01	407.13	407.20	407.20
276.19	276.23	277.03	315.26	316.01	316.12	360.05	360.06	360.08	407.22	407.23	407.24
277.04	277.05	277.07	316.15	316.16	316.19	360.09	360.16	360.18	408.01	408.03	408.08
277.10	277.11	277.12	316.24	317.10	317.12	360.21	360.24	360.25	408.13	408.17	408.19
277.20	277.25	277.26	317.17	318.07	318.10	360.28	360.29	361.02	408.22	408.24	409.04
278.03	278.03	278.04	318.17	318.20	318.22	361.10	361.13	361.14	409.10	409.17	409.19
278.07	278.08	278.11	318.24	318.24	319.01	361.22	361.25	361.30	409.26	410.01	410.05
278.14	278.21	278.22	319.12	319.20	319.22	362.01	362.05	362.07	410.12	410.15	410.16
278.25	278.25	278.29	319.29	319.29	320.04	362.11	362.17	362.22	410.17	410.20	410.21
279.03	279.06	279.07	320.09	320.15	320.27	362.23	363.15	363.17	410.27	410.30	411.01
279.09	279.14	279.16	321.07	321.10	321.12	363.19	363.23	364.01	411.03	411.05	411.07
279.18	279.20	279.21	321.14	321.16	321.18	364.02	364.04	364.13	411.14	412.04	412.05
279.23	279.24	280.01	321.22	321.29	322.06	364.17	364.19	364.19	412.10	412.23	413.06
280.06	280.16	280.24	322.09	322.12	322.16	364.20	364.22	364.24	413.07	413.13	413.15
281.03	281.08	281.15	323.02	323.04	323.08	364.28	365.02	365.17	413.20	413.28	413.30
281.18	281.23	281.27	323.09	323.11	323.13	365.26	366.01	366.04	414.06	414.09	414.12
281.30	282.03	282.08	323.16	324.09	324.13	366.08	366.19	366.21	414.17	414.20	414.21
282.11	282.12	282.15	324.18	324.23	324.24	366.25	367.03	367.03	414.22	414.23	414.28
282.18	282.20	282.29	324.27	325.01	325.02	367.08	367.13	367.15	415.03	415.07	415.12
283.12	283.16	283.16	325.04	325.04	325.08	367.22	367.23	368.05	415.18	416.02	416.07
283.22	284.02	284.07	325.10	325.13	325.13	368.16	368.25	369.06	416.08	416.14	416.15
285.02	285.07	285.09	325.16	325.19	325.22	369.08	369.16	369.21	416.20	417.01	417.02
285.15	286.05	286.06	325.26	327.04	327.05	369.29	370.03	370.06	417.06	417.23	417.24
286.10	286.21	286.27	327.08	327.10	327.17	370.09	370.21	370.25	417.26	417.29	417.30
286.28	287.01	287.03	327.16	327.19	327.22	370.27	371.05	371.09	418.01	418.03	418.05
287.06	287.09	287.14	328.02	328.04	328.08	371.09	371.11	371.12	418.12	418.14	418.21
287.17	287.21	287.23	328.11	328.13	328.16	371.23	371.27	371.30	418.26	418.27	419.04
287.26	288.02	288.09	328.21	328.22	328.24	372.07	372.16	372.19	419.06	419.08	419.19
288.18	288.19	288.23	328.29	329.01	329.06	372.20	373.01	373.11	419.24	419.25	419.27
288.23	288.26	289.02	329.10	329.14	329.18	373.13	373.15	373.19	420.10	420.12	420.19
289.05	289.07	289.12	329.27	330.04	330.05	374.02	374.02	374.05	420.23	421.03	421.12
289.15	289.18	289.22	330.15	330.16	330.20	374.07	374.09	374.12	421.17	421.20	421.22
289.24	290.02	290.13	330.21	330.27	331.02	374.18	374.24	374.25	421.25	421.26	421.28
290.15	290.21	290.23	331.07	331.22	331.28	374.25	374.28	375.07	421.29	422.01	422.02
290.28	290.29	291.04	332.05	332.07	332.14	375.08	375.18	375.21	422.03	422.07	422.11
291.11	291.13	291.16	332.15	332.17	332.24	376.02	376.14	376.18	422.15	422.16	422.18
291.16	291.17	291.19	332.26	332.30	333.07	376.21	376.23	376.24	422.24	422.25	422.30
291.29	292.01	292.05	333.08	333.15	333.16	376.29	377.23	378.04	423.02	423.03	423.08
292.09	292.21	292.23	333.21	333.24	333.29	378.05	378.07	378.10	423.13	423.14	423.25
292.24	293.04	293.05	334.03	334.04	334.26	378.20	378.23	379.10	423.28	424.04	424.07
293.07	293.08	293.21	335.05	335.12	335.17	379.17	379.19	379.21	424.11	424.12	425.08
293.28	294.02	294.12	336.02	336.11	336.12	379.25	380.01	380.05	425.09	425.14	425.17
294.18	294.22	294.23	336.19	336.20	336.21	380.05	380.07	380.10	425.20	426.09	426.20
294.24	295.02	295.06	336.24	337.08	337.09	380.12	380.18	381.03	425.30	427.01	427.03
295.07	295.07	295.11	337.11	337.12	337.28	381.06	381.07	381.14	427.06	427.08	427.12
295.19	295.22	295.24	337.30	338.04	338.11	382.15	382.27	383.09	427.13	427.14	427.23
296.04	297.02	297.03	338.13	338.26	339.01	383.21	383.30	384.09	427.26	428.04	428.09
297.05	297.14	297.22	339.05	339.09	339.13	384.12	384.20	384.21	428.13	428.15	428.17
297.24	298.02	298.09	339.15	339.16	339.27	384.28	384.30	385.01	428.22	428.25	428.26
298.11	298.22	299.06	339.29	339.30	340.07	385.03	385.04	385.26	429.07	429.10	429.19
299.11	299.12	299.15	340.09	340.12	340.15	385.28	385.29	386.02	429.20	429.21	429.22
299.18	299.20	299.23	340.24	340.26	341.13	386.03	386.04	386.07	429.24	429.26	430.01
299.28	300.05	300.08	341.17	341.20	341.24	386.18	386.28	387.02	430.04	430.07	430.10
300.12	300.21	300.22	341.25	341.26	341.27	387.06	387.13	387.14	430.16	430.18	430.24
300.25	300.28	301.01	341.28	342.04	342.11	387.17	388.11	388.29	430.26	430.27	430.29
301.03	301.05	301.12	342.16	342.19	342.22	389.01	389.01	389.06	431.04	431.07	431.09
301.13	301.19	301.20	342.26	342.27	343.05	389.13	389.14	389.26	431.12	431.13	431.15
301.20	301.21	301.22	343.12	343.16	343.26	389.30	390.07	390.09	431.16	431.16	431.28
301.30	302.03	302.06	344.05	344.17	344.19	390.18	390.19	390.23	432.01	432.02	432.05
302.09	302.10	302.25	344.23	344.24	345.02	391.06	391.08	391.14	432.09	432.12	432.14
302.25	303.14	303.17	345.06	345.14	345.18	391.20	391.25	391.27	432.15	432.16	432.17
303.29	304.01	304.02	345.29	346.04	346.04	391.30	392.01	392.07	432.21	432.23	432.25
304.04	304.15	304.28	347.09	347.11	347.13	392.11	392.12	392.23	432.28	433.04	433.06
305.03	305.07	306.06	347.15	347.20	347.24	392.26	392.30	393.06	433.16	433.27	434.04
306.08	306.08	306.11	348.01	348.01	348.03	393.12	393.17	394.02	434.05	434.14	434.16
306.18	306.23	307.05	348.03	348.05	348.09	394.05	394.08	394.18	434.18	434.28	435.08
307.11	307.13	307.14	348.14	348.15	348.27	394.22	395.02	395.06	435.15	435.19	436.07
307.16	307.19	307.23	349.04	349.09	349.14	395.09	395.11	395.14	436.08	436.09	436.12
307.28	308.03	308.04	349.16	349.21	349.30	395.15	395.19	395.24	436.14	436.17	436.18
308.09	308.12	308.17	350.02	350.10	350.13	395.30	396.03	396.06	436.24	436.26	436.29
308.19	308.22	309.05	350.16	350.23	350.27	396.08	396.18	396.25	437.01	437.08	437.14
309.07	309.13	309.18	350.30	351.02	351.20	396.27	396.27	397.07	438.04	438.13	438.14
309.24	309.26	309.28	351.25	351.29	352.03	397.10	397.14	397.16	438.16	438.24	438.25
309.30	310.01	310.06	352.09	352.12	352.12	397.18	397.21	397.22	439.03	439.06	439.11
310.09	310.12	310.15	352.14	352.17	352.22	397.25	398.07	398.10	439.17	439.18	439.20

```
AND (CONT.)        439.27        AND (CONT.)        478.04        AND (CONT.)        516.10        ANTAGONISM          470.14
  439.28  440.01  440.05           478.07  478.09  478.19           516.17  516.19                 ANTAGONISTIC        111.28
  440.09  440.11  440.16           478.20  478.21  478.26         ANDTWENTY           319.26          278.22
  440.16  440.19  440.24           479.02  479.07  479.09         ANECDOTE   179.17                ANTARCTIC           215.05
  440.25  440.26  440.29           479.19  479.24  479.24         ANGEL       40.04                ANTE        44.16
  441.03  441.11  441.13           479.24  479.28  480.01         ANGELS     122.17                ANTE-ROOM            44.16
  441.14  441.17  441.21           480.02  480.07  480.15         ANGER       10.24   21.25         ANTHRACITE          208.18
  441.30  442.02  442.03           480.20  480.22  480.23           205.16  298.29  332.06         ANTICIPATE          383.26
  442.07  442.09  442.17           480.26  480.28  481.04           390.27  482.12  488.04         ANTICS     123.26
  442.22  442.24  442.25           481.07  481.14  482.03           507.13  510.04                 ANTIQUE    212.20
  442.29  443.08  443.15           482.04  482.08  482.12         ANGLE      101.11                ANTONIO     58.14   58.14
  443.17  443.19  443.25           482.12  482.15  482.18         ANGLE-IRON          101.11        ANTS       324.08  473.11
  443.29  444.08  444.10           482.27  483.05  483.06         ANGLES     366.17  420.10         ANXIETY     95.12   107.20
  444.17  444.23  444.27           483.06  483.09  483.11           80.14   130.26  141.09           210.17  216.29  348.07
  445.03  445.06  445.07           483.14  483.23  483.25         ANGRY       8.23    47.13           450.20  460.07  484.03
  445.09  445.11  445.12           483.27  483.29  483.30           62.28   85.01   85.30         ANXIOUS      3.06    15.02
  445.14  445.23  445.26           484.09  484.13  484.15           124.03  187.01  204.26           35.25   57.02   86.16
  445.29  446.05  446.07           484.16  484.22  484.23           283.06  293.01  361.15           86.17   90.11   105.04
  447.05  447.07  447.11           484.26  484.30  485.04           366.30  401.29  429.07           246.04  252.23  258.30
  447.13  447.14  447.21           485.06  485.12  485.14           446.06  509.12  512.07           329.15  332.10  336.24
  448.03  448.05  448.09           485.15  485.24  485.29         ANGUISH     12.05   32.21           337.27  342.24  359.21
  448.20  448.23  448.26           485.30  486.02  486.06           111.26  380.01  395.13           365.15  404.13  452.28
  449.03  449.08  449.10           486.12  486.14  487.09           427.13                           488.19
  449.11  449.13  449.13           487.12  487.17  487.22         ANGUISHING          138.02        ANXIOUSLY           108.01
  449.16  449.23  449.25           487.22  487.23  488.01           328.27                           209.04  241.13  308.20
  449.28  449.29  450.07           488.03  488.06  488.07         ANGULAR    416.15                ANY          1.18    8.14
  450.09  450.13  450.30           488.09  488.13  488.16         ANIMAL      45.08   88.30           12.09   28.26   33.16
  451.03  451.04  451.14           488.17  488.20  488.30           151.10  313.08                   38.18   40.07   41.30
  451.21  451.25  452.02           489.06  489.14  489.20         ANIMALS    192.11                   42.03   43.10   48.02
  452.10  452.11  452.16           489.21  489.24  490.04         ANIMATED   105.13  391.29           48.19   48.27   49.10
  452.17  452.19  452.26           490.08  490.09  490.13         ANIMATION           80.09           50.27   54.05   58.10
  453.07  453.09  453.13           490.16  490.18  490.18           139.20                           60.21   66.23   68.11
  453.15  453.17  453.20           490.22  490.23  490.27         ANIMOSITY           218.18          68.16   72.05   72.18
  453.24  453.26  453.30           490.29  491.02  491.08         ANKLES      49.16   453.13          81.09   82.20   85.22
  454.03  454.09  454.17           491.10  491.12  491.21         ANNAS      207.23                   85.29   86.28   95.28
  454.21  454.23  454.26           491.25  491.28  492.01         ANNEX      251.12                  100.30  103.10  103.12
  454.27  455.01  455.01           492.09  492.12  492.15         ANNIHILATE          11.13          113.21  127.03  129.10
  455.05  455.06  455.10           492.20  492.22  492.26         ANNIHILATION        117.18         132.21  136.18  138.12
  455.14  455.16  455.27           492.27  493.03  493.04           139.23                          138.18  139.03  144.28
  456.02  456.04  456.05           493.06  493.11  494.07         ANNOYANCE           145.01         147.08  150.07  150.18
  456.11  456.12  456.15           494.17  494.19  494.24         ANNOYANCES          361.22         153.13  153.26  159.29
  456.20  456.25  456.28           494.26  494.26  495.10         ANNOYED     86.12   242.28         160.01  162.12  164.17
  457.17  457.20  457.24           495.11  495.20  495.30           257.12  308.06  361.01          165.22  165.27  168.09
  458.02  458.05  458.15           496.06  496.10  496.10         ANOINTED    80.28                 169.25  172.07  173.15
  458.21  458.26  458.30           497.04  497.19  497.22         ANOTHER      3.05    3.11          175.25  186.07  186.25
  459.04  459.10  459.20           498.02  498.04  498.04           14.24   30.03   36.29          187.26  187.26  191.10
  459.25  459.28  459.30           498.07  498.09  498.12           37.26   67.30   78.10          197.23  198.28  199.09
  460.02  460.03  460.11           498.21  498.26  498.27           79.27   95.25   102.22         208.23  210.21  212.25
  460.12  460.15  460.26           499.04  499.14  499.26           111.30  113.08  128.05         217.18  218.02  220.01
  460.28  461.01  461.04           499.28  500.01  500.07           131.18  133.06  133.27         223.12  227.10  228.05
  461.06  461.11  461.15           500.07  500.12  500.14           134.07  137.11  138.19         235.07  236.09  238.15
  461.18  461.27  461.30           500.18  500.24  500.24           155.02  155.21  161.04         240.23  244.15  245.17
  462.07  462.10  462.14           500.26  501.01  501.05           181.24  197.27  200.17         252.21  266.01  268.26
  462.20  462.22  462.28           501.07  501.18  501.20           211.11  213.14  219.05         274.03  274.18  282.04
  462.30  463.18  463.28           501.24  501.25  502.03           224.18  229.10  235.06         288.15  288.29  288.30
  464.02  464.06  464.09           502.04  502.07  502.14           244.02  250.14  255.30         295.13  300.11  303.07
  464.10  464.11  464.14           502.15  502.17  502.20           256.20  259.01  268.27         304.05  308.22  311.06
  464.15  464.16  464.14           502.25  502.27  503.09           270.11  280.02  280.03         311.06  311.23  313.07
  464.17  464.26  464.29           503.13  503.16  503.18           281.14  287.06  321.06         331.08  331.10  345.04
  465.02  465.03  465.11           504.06  504.10  504.11           330.24  331.14  333.22         346.06  346.10  349.27
  465.13  465.15  465.16           504.14  504.17  504.20           336.02  340.08  343.12         352.24  353.03  354.10
  465.20  465.24  466.02           504.21  505.06  505.11           352.04  362.17  372.16         356.19  357.23  360.04
  466.05  466.06  466.09           505.11  505.14  505.17           375.04  375.20  389.09         369.18  376.04  377.22
  466.13  466.17  466.20           505.20  505.24  505.25           393.27  417.30  421.02         379.23  381.22  383.02
  466.21  466.24  466.25           505.27  505.30  506.02           428.05  441.13  460.01         388.04  392.12  396.12
  467.06  467.08  467.10           506.13  506.19  506.26           463.21  473.11  473.26         399.24  400.10  404.09
  467.11  467.19  467.20           506.27  506.29  507.03           483.17  489.01  491.10         405.01  407.19  412.14
  467.23  467.29  468.05           507.05  507.07  507.11           492.24  508.05                 422.13  424.08  428.01
  468.10  468.15  468.17           507.16  507.20  507.23         ANSWER      24.18   32.02         431.15  433.15  440.27
  468.21  468.21  468.24           507.23  507.30  508.05           36.15   36.24   36.29          445.18  445.22  449.09
  468.25  469.01  469.04           508.07  508.08  508.15           73.15   97.14   290.02         460.07  464.07  474.10
  469.08  469.10  469.12           508.18  508.20  509.01           292.10  381.12  388.15         474.13  479.06  485.22
  469.14  470.01  470.03           509.04  509.11  509.14           396.11  400.12  432.12         486.06  493.06  500.15
  470.06  470.12  470.18           509.24  509.24  509.28           464.27  485.20  486.06         507.28  508.21  513.06
  470.21  470.22  470.28           509.30  510.01  510.10           499.08  516.06                ANYBODY      1.09    7.06
  470.28  470.29  471.01           510.08  510.11  510.15         ANSWERED    36.25   37.26           7.25   55.27   62.01
  471.04  471.11  471.11           510.16  510.21  510.26           60.20   63.21   78.22          110.12  160.05  254.22
  471.17  471.23  471.26           510.28  511.06  511.07           188.29  204.17  258.06         266.08  267.11  281.01
  471.29  472.09  472.14           511.11  511.18  511.26           350.17  357.09  360.28         308.18  316.04  360.15
  472.16  472.17  473.04           511.27  512.04  512.05           361.12  395.27  413.23         370.21  491.04
  473.13  473.19  473.24           512.07  512.15  512.18           422.22  461.17  471.06        ANYHOW      25.24   26.30
  473.24  473.28  473.29           513.10  513.11  513.14           497.13  498.03  498.30           71.21   83.21   124.02
  473.30  474.06  474.12           513.20  513.24  513.28           505.03                         159.04  182.24  203.08
  474.16  474.18  474.20           513.29  513.29  514.05         ANSWERING           38.13         204.28  208.02  222.24
  474.23  474.26  474.27           514.06  514.08  514.16           233.19                         238.25  301.11  303.08
  475.01  475.04  475.08           514.18  514.20  514.25         ANSWERS     32.20   37.23         324.28  328.12  371.25
  475.17  475.24  475.25           514.27  514.28  514.30           75.21                          411.26  472.07
  475.27  476.02  476.10           515.07  515.07  515.10         ANT        112.27               ANYTHING     1.15    25.27
  476.11  476.11  477.07           515.16  515.17  515.19         ANT-HEAP   112.27                 28.09   29.21   33.12
  477.08  477.22  478.03           515.21  515.25  516.05                                          42.16   43.41   67.11
```

13

AS (CONT.)		45.25	AS (CONT.)		162.08	AS (CONT.)		264.25	AS (CONT.)		411.13
45.28	45.29	45.29	162.08	162.24	163.14	266.14	266.18	267.26	412.27	413.27	414.03
46.01	46.02	46.25	163.18	163.19	164.29	268.06	269.05	269.14	414.25	414.26	416.06
46.25	47.08	47.09	165.15	165.28	165.28	269.19	269.27	270.01	416.21	417.14	417.14
47.11	47.11	47.13	166.06	166.06	166.18	270.04	270.05	272.20	417.15	417.15	419.13
47.13	47.17	47.19	166.21	167.05	167.06	272.20	272.23	273.04	419.16	419.28	420.03
48.18	48.24	49.16	167.06	167.10	167.22	273.06	273.09	273.13	420.22	421.02	422.25
49.28	49.28	50.08	168.10	168.11	169.11	274.03	274.21	274.22	422.25	423.14	423.20
53.06	53.23	53.24	169.18	170.03	170.14	274.22	274.24	275.21	423.26	424.02	424.03
54.10	55.18	55.18	170.22	170.23	171.03	275.22	275.23	276.09	426.01	426.07	426.30
55.18	56.02	56.27	171.03	171.12	172.05	276.13	277.16	277.17	427.19	427.21	427.27
56.27	58.05	58.11	172.17	172.23	172.24	277.30	278.08	278.09	428.02	428.02	428.10
58.11	58.21	59.14	174.05	174.13	174.21	278.11	278.19	278.19	428.15	429.23	429.25
60.14	60.21	60.23	175.20	176.10	176.13	278.28	279.19	281.18	429.30	430.08	430.10
61.29	62.24	62.25	176.20	176.28	176.29	281.19	281.24	283.30	430.10	430.16	431.17
63.03	63.06	63.06	177.03	177.07	177.20	285.04	285.08	287.02	431.19	431.20	433.04
64.07	66.06	66.06	179.04	179.04	179.09	289.23	289.27	290.26	434.06	434.06	434.08
56.10	66.15	66.20	179.09	179.18	179.20	291.16	292.02	293.25	434.20	435.01	435.13
66.20	69.10	69.13	180.30	181.13	181.22	293.30	294.23	295.04	435.16	435.20	435.20
69.13	70.01	70.37	182.10	182.30	182.30	295.09	295.15	295.20	435.22	436.06	436.11
70.37	71.15	71.26	184.27	185.09	186.30	296.02	296.06	297.20	436.27	437.02	438.07
71.27	72.07	73.03	187.16	187.20	187.27	298.17	299.01	299.03	438.30	439.12	439.18
73.03	73.05	73.16	187.30	188.24	188.29	299.20	299.22	299.29	442.14	444.02	445.16
73.20	73.23	73.24	188.29	189.10	189.12	300.11	300.11	301.06	445.15	445.29	445.29
74.04	74.05	74.15	190.11	191.10	191.10	302.11	302.17	304.22	446.01	446.01	446.11
74.15	75.10	75.10	191.23	192.03	192.18	307.02	307.02	309.11	446.12	447.14	447.21
75.22	77.18	78.03	192.24	192.25	192.28	311.06	311.07	311.20	452.06	452.13	452.30
78.10	78.10	79.20	193.25	194.04	194.14	311.28	312.16	312.27	453.04	455.21	456.19
80.07	80.10	80.25	195.01	195.10	195.28	314.15	315.15	316.23	457.09	458.21	458.22
80.25	84.05	84.29	195.29	196.03	196.06	317.02	318.17	318.23	459.05	459.21	460.20
84.29	85.11	86.17	196.23	196.24	196.25	319.06	319.07	319.07	461.02	461.05	462.20
86.21	86.25	87.03	196.30	196.30	197.13	319.12	319.12	319.26	465.14	466.15	467.13
87.09	87.09	87.09	197.14	197.18	198.07	320.27	321.04	321.04	468.04	468.14	471.09
87.09	87.27	88.27	198.08	198.09	198.10	322.25	325.17	327.21	471.19	471.27	472.10
89.11	90.28	92.10	198.13	198.24	198.24	327.22	329.09	329.09	472.10	473.25	473.26
92.11	92.12	92.13	198.27	198.27	199.09	329.15	329.15	329.23	474.07	474.08	474.23
92.17	92.18	92.21	199.25	199.26	200.10	329.23	330.05	330.05	475.22	476.09	476.10
92.22	94.24	96.13	200.11	200.24	200.24	330.07	332.24	333.08	477.10	478.03	478.08
96.13	97.15	97.21	204.03	204.04	204.07	334.07	334.13	334.24	478.10	478.18	478.19
98.24	99.02	100.28	204.07	204.08	204.08	335.03	336.07	336.21	478.25	479.15	479.19
100.30	101.08	101.12	204.17	204.17	204.20	337.13	338.18	338.18	479.19	480.04	480.21
101.13	101.22	101.22	204.20	204.23	205.01	339.11	339.18	339.24	481.02	482.03	482.13
101.24	101.25	102.22	205.18	205.18	207.03	341.04	341.22	341.22	483.01	483.02	483.05
103.05	103.06	103.10	207.19	207.19	207.24	342.01	342.09	342.11	483.06	485.04	488.04
104.03	104.03	104.05	208.04	208.06	208.06	342.23	343.13	345.17	488.23	489.16	490.27
105.09	106.07	107.14	208.08	208.10	208.29	345.17	347.05	348.07	491.05	491.19	491.19
107.23	107.23	108.18	209.01	209.05	209.06	348.12	349.08	349.11	492.02	492.29	493.10
108.18	109.05	109.27	209.16	209.16	209.24	349.24	349.27	350.18	493.14	493.18	493.18
110.05	110.06	110.07	210.05	210.24	211.08	350.28	351.11	351.18	493.29	495.13	496.07
110.12	110.22	110.22	211.10	211.25	212.22	352.02	352.09	353.07	497.04	498.01	498.14
110.27	110.27	110.29	212.26	212.28	213.04	353.07	353.09	354.03	500.08	500.09	501.03
111.22	111.22	111.22	213.05	213.05	213.12	354.04	356.21	356.21	501.05	501.12	501.16
112.02	112.26	112.27	213.12	213.17	213.17	357.05	357.06	357.18	501.22	504.18	505.02
112.28	112.30	113.27	213.18	213.22	214.13	357.30	359.14	359.19	505.14	505.30	506.29
113.30	114.06	114.10	216.08	216.11	216.23	360.01	360.09	360.23	507.08	507.26	508.22
115.11	115.11	116.28	216.23	216.29	217.10	360.30	361.03	361.03	508.24	509.07	509.13
117.07	117.07	117.24	217.10	217.19	217.20	362.14	363.07	364.12	509.20	510.02	510.02
117.24	117.29	118.03	218.20	218.25	218.28	364.25	365.06	366.06	510.16	510.25	510.25
118.05	118.06	119.14	218.28	219.09	219.22	368.03	368.10	368.13	511.09	511.20	515.14
120.25	122.07	122.07	219.22	220.08	220.20	369.06	369.14	369.18	515.14		
123.14	124.03	124.15	222.20	222.21	222.23	370.22	371.10	371.16	ASCEND	292.13	292.16
124.23	125.05	125.23	224.08	224.23	225.02	372.06	372.11	372.17	ASCENDED	280.14	323.07
125.24	126.06	126.22	226.06	226.09	226.21	373.05	373.13	373.13	373.18	417.02	
127.30	127.30	129.19	226.27	227.12	227.23	374.19	374.22	375.08	ASCENDING		149.30
130.11	131.09	131.21	228.01	228.28	229.12	377.20	378.08	378.08	244.22	301.29	397.02
132.07	132.07	132.10	229.12	230.05	230.10	378.16	378.25	379.17	445.02		
132.24	132.29	133.03	230.19	230.19	230.27	379.18	379.24	380.06	ASCENT	324.01	
133.09	134.06	134.11	230.27	231.02	232.20	381.07	381.20	381.20	ASCERTAIN		33.16
134.26	134.30	135.07	234.04	234.20	237.04	383.05	383.22	384.11	166.29		
137.02	137.02	137.23	237.13	237.16	237.17	384.11	384.22	385.04	ASCERTAINED		162.23
138.02	138.02	138.03	237.21	237.21	239.10	385.04	385.09	385.10	372.01		
138.16	138.21	138.26	240.04	240.08	240.13	385.21	386.16	386.20	ASCERTAINING		167.13
139.02	140.08	140.12	241.01	241.02	241.10	386.21	387.06	391.25	ASH	23.27	
141.07	141.21	142.18	241.15	242.12	242.12	391.30	392.04	392.04	ASH-BUCKETS		23.27
143.03	143.20	144.11	242.16	242.20	242.21	392.06	392.17	392.17	392.04		
145.12	145.27	146.10	243.14	244.05	244.07	393.06	394.02	394.08	ASHAMED	62.04	362.15
147.06	147.09	147.11	244.14	245.02	245.03	394.15	395.17	395.21	400.27		
147.12	148.08	148.15	245.13	245.18	245.29	396.30	397.07	397.14	ASHES	80.04	279.24
149.08	149.17	150.01	246.07	246.09	247.17	397.24	398.09	398.21	292.25	333.29	468.24
150.04	150.10	150.18	247.23	247.24	248.08	399.11	399.11	399.15	ASHORE	52.19	52.28
150.18	151.20	151.21	250.01	251.05	251.16	399.15	400.12	400.22	98.25	198.04	244.20
151.24	152.23	153.25	252.25	252.28	252.29	400.25	400.25	400.26	343.05	438.24	439.15
153.26	154.06	154.07	254.04	254.11	254.11	401.25	401.25	402.02	475.15	493.16	504.13
154.08	155.10	155.20	254.14	255.24	255.24	402.02	402.04	402.13	ASHY	112.22	410.19
156.07	156.07	156.07	256.01	256.05	257.23	403.30	404.11	404.19	ASIA	81.03	
156.08	156.09	157.03	258.13	258.14	259.13	404.22	404.22	405.01	ASIDE	43.24	153.15
157.13	157.19	158.02	259.27	259.28	260.05	406.01	407.11	407.11	188.22	193.04	199.23
158.08	158.16	158.18	260.07	260.28	261.04	407.18	408.06	408.11	229.24	248.07	337.19
159.20	159.22	160.27	262.01	262.16	262.28	408.23	408.29	409.20	418.01	428.16	432.26
152.01	162.02	162.03	263.15	263.29	264.02	409.30	409.30	410.18	453.15	510.07	513.11
									ASK	30.05	40.12

ASK (CONT.) 48.26
52.07 98.15 177.06
185.29 200.16 228.25
234.14 238.18 259.02
261.03 272.27 273.20
274.25 303.07 341.11
344.13 359.21 376.04
376.11 378.27 379.06
382.09 473.19 473.20
474.13 478.14 486.15
496.03
ASKANCE 98.03
ASKANT 482.04
ASKED 33.17 47.23
62.03 63.17 67.28
77.05 78.19 84.12
96.20 96.26 104.23
110.14 141.09 141.11
148.02 151.23 154.06
157.30 160.24 162.21
163.05 164.06 177.26
188.28 197.10 199.24
202.27 217.01 223.25
230.22 234.07 234.19
258.04 282.18 283.04
289.01 290.07 290.30
294.11 301.04 301.13
301.22 303.03 303.17
338.19 361.07 364.30
365.26 367.26 372.23
382.11 387.03 388.14
392.15 393.08 402.23
414.03 419.23 428.07
428.11 428.24 433.10
433.23 441.21 461.22
467.16 467.25 471.05
474.04 479.10 479.20
480.20 486.11 488.22
489.09 491.07 495.25
502.21 506.03 507.12
507.17 508.12 511.14
ASKING 35.01 58.09
118.15 151.10 212.17
221.05 234.08 344.23
396.08
ASKS 235.13 237.15
237.19
ASLEEP 63.21 101.20
115.23 360.27 493.29
ASPECT 20.01 22.21
35.21 91.09 93.16
147.11 209.26 222.07
258.29 277.23 348.20
386.18 399.22 423.08
459.05 512.07
ASPIRATIONS 100.11
322.17
ASS 12.21 96.30
152.13 200.06 200.09
224.20 333.15
ASS' 310.16
ASS'S 197.12 218.15
ASSASSINATED 251.14
ASSASSINATION 358.02
ASSAULT 83.07 85.14
127.11 185.05 192.07
302.15
ASSAULT-AND-BATTERY
185.05
ASSEMBLE 447.19 505.28
ASSEMBLED 250.18
448.28 461.20 485.26
ASSENT 487.15
ASSENTED 467.01
ASSERT 289.05
ASSERTED 205.08
ASSERTION 1.07
289.06
ASSESSOR 33.18 34.09
37.05
ASSESSORS 33.05
67.10 67.13
ASSIDUOUSLY 314.25
ASSIST 125.12
ASSISTANCE 470.25
ASSISTANT 250.01
343.07
ASSOCIATED 13.16
68.30 225.09 232.05
ASSORTED 442.28

ASSUMED 146.13 223.04
294.12 399.22
ASSUMING 65.14 498.23
ASSUMPTION 97.27
479.26
ASSURANCE 19.04
138.17 261.21 378.17
404.19 470.22
ASSURANCES 215.14
ASSURE 113.19 193.12
213.05 296.01
ASSURED 86.03 107.19
140.16 288.06 308.16
320.12 347.24 353.24
360.02 366.30 392.17
415.01 474.20
ASSUREDLY 119.29
ASSURING 461.21
ASTERN 16.30 17.23
122.22 137.12 149.04
151.27
ASTHMA 425.09
ASTONISHED 78.23
202.23 443.05
ASTONISHING 343.01
ASTONISHMENT 369.29
ASTOUNDED 144.12
ASTOUNDING 423.19
423.20
ASTRAY 288.05 389.11
516.13
ASTRONOMER 266.18
ASTRONOMERS 266.08
266.23
ASUNDER 312.24
AT 1.03 1.09
1.09 3.10 4.11
4.17 4.26 6.05
6.12 6.17 6.26
7.22 8.07 10.12
11.08 11.19 11.24
12.09 12.13 13.06
13.07 14.04 14.19
14.20 16.01 16.06
16.14 17.02 17.17
17.22 17.24 18.10
19.20 21.19 22.16
22.23 23.01 23.11
23.30 25.15 25.18
26.10 26.16 27.29
28.06 28.23 30.20
30.21 31.06 31.13
32.07 32.12 33.04
33.21 34.10 34.18
34.28 36.09 38.01
38.05 38.12 38.19
38.23 39.05 40.20
42.01 42.22 42.23
43.14 43.28 44.06
44.22 45.07 45.07
45.27 45.28 46.22
47.12 47.24 48.02
48.08 48.26 49.26
51.08 52.06 52.13
52.19 52.19 53.13
54.07 54.23 54.27
54.29 55.19 55.22
56.13 57.17 58.29
60.14 61.03 61.09
61.11 62.07 62.12
62.25 62.30 62.30
65.03 65.10 67.24
68.04 68.11 68.11
69.10 69.11 69.28
71.05 71.10 71.13
71.15 71.25 71.29
72.04 72.06 72.09
72.19 72.26 73.12
74.29 75.05 75.10
75.19 76.07 77.21
78.15 78.22 79.03
79.05 80.08 81.28
82.05 82.26 83.18
83.26 84.03 84.10
84.14 84.14 84.23
85.01 85.17 85.18
86.12 86.28 87.02
87.23 87.26 88.11
88.14 88.24 88.25
88.26 89.03 89.05

AT (CONT.) 89.23
89.29 89.30 90.01
90.02 90.08 90.22
90.30 91.14 92.11
93.15 94.06 94.26
95.18 95.23 96.01
96.14 96.28 97.02
97.12 97.20 98.04
98.07 98.13 98.17
98.19 99.03 99.08
99.09 100.18 101.07
101.10 101.16 101.19
102.02 102.22 103.12
103.14 103.16 104.09
105.29 106.07 107.04
108.26 108.27 109.07
109.18 109.25 110.03
111.01 111.14 111.24
111.25 112.11 112.16
112.18 112.22 115.15
115.26 115.28 116.05
116.05 118.11 118.17
119.15 119.16 119.17
119.22 119.22 120.07
120.11 120.12 121.06
122.06 122.08 122.18
122.22 123.30 124.22
124.29 125.11 125.12
126.03 126.05 126.11
126.27 127.01 127.10
127.17 128.04 128.12
129.03 129.04 129.22
129.24 130.17 131.03
131.14 132.13 132.14
132.24 134.18 136.17
137.24 140.19 140.20
140.23 141.09 141.14
141.24 141.25 142.06
142.12 143.09 143.20
144.30 145.11 146.29
147.23 147.26 148.15
148.21 148.29 149.02
149.07 149.23 150.02
151.01 151.04 151.05
151.21 152.30 153.06
153.18 153.19 153.24
153.29 155.06 155.21
157.05 157.13 159.03
159.16 159.17 159.24
159.26 160.08 160.08
160.23 163.11 165.18
166.07 166.19 166.26
167.02 167.03 168.12
169.21 169.23 170.16
171.16 171.23 172.26
175.12 175.16 176.04
176.29 177.19 178.11
179.02 179.06 180.02
180.02 180.14 181.20
183.05 183.07 183.08
183.09 183.25 184.07
184.30 185.22 188.06
188.09 188.12 189.06
189.12 189.17 190.07
191.21 191.22 192.02
193.18 193.22 195.27
195.29 196.18 197.14
197.16 198.15 199.10
199.20 199.26 200.10
200.11 201.20 201.27
202.06 202.16 202.23
203.16 204.15 205.01
205.09 205.24 205.25
205.26 207.01 207.23
208.08 208.25 209.07
209.12 209.20 209.23
210.01 210.01 210.16
211.22 212.09 212.14
212.18 213.07 213.20
213.21 213.21 214.17
214.25 216.19 216.20
216.25 217.21 218.11
218.16 218.30 219.24
220.04 221.03 221.05
222.01 222.12 223.12
223.14 223.21 223.22
223.24 224.10 224.15
224.24 225.05 225.11
225.12 226.23 228.10
228.30 228.30 229.01

AT (CONT.) 229.22
229.23 230.22 230.26
231.05 232.19 232.28
234.13 234.20 234.24
235.11 235.13 235.16
235.27 236.14 236.18
236.22 237.08 237.13
237.20 237.26 238.22
239.01 239.22 241.09
241.19 241.30 242.03
242.14 242.27 243.01
244.01 244.02 244.23
244.25 244.29 245.05
245.09 246.13 246.14
246.24 248.22 249.18
249.23 250.10 251.16
251.18 252.05 252.25
253.01 253.02 253.30
254.01 254.04 254.17
254.24 255.05 255.26
255.28 256.05 256.08
256.15 256.16 257.09
257.21 258.11 258.26
260.04 261.11 261.16
261.26 262.02 262.02
262.17 262.21 263.22
263.27 264.17 264.24
267.21 267.25 268.26
269.06 269.22 272.14
274.18 274.19 275.09
277.15 279.21 280.25
281.04 281.15 281.18
284.02 286.05 287.19
288.17 288.27 288.27
290.12 290.13 290.24
291.18 291.24 292.30
293.01 293.05 294.06
294.18 297.06 297.12
298.10 298.30 299.09
300.23 300.27 303.05
303.29 304.02 304.03
304.11 304.12 304.12
304.12 304.13 304.14
304.14 304.23 306.13
306.16 306.23 307.18
308.03 308.03 308.07
308.25 309.17 310.08
310.09 311.05 311.11
311.16 313.23 313.25
313.26 314.07 316.18
317.03 319.28 320.19
320.24 321.01 321.05
321.10 322.09 322.16
324.04 324.08 324.27
325.10 326.03 327.24
328.08 328.10 328.13
329.07 329.09 329.22
330.17 330.26 331.05
332.26 333.05 333.09
336.08 336.09 336.22
337.26 338.05 339.10
339.12 339.26 340.02
340.05 341.09 341.24
342.17 342.19 343.02
343.28 345.25 348.02
348.08 350.14 350.22
350.24 352.27 352.30
353.10 353.19 353.20
355.04 355.21 355.22
355.23 357.21 357.30
358.26 358.30 359.13
359.26 360.04 360.09
360.10 361.01 362.02
362.05 362.07 362.12
363.09 365.17 365.20
365.28 366.17 366.20
370.12 370.17 370.19
371.07 372.03 372.17
373.11 374.15 375.30
377.04 377.11 378.08
379.23 381.17 382.05
382.14 382.29 384.03
384.04 384.06 386.29
387.20 388.01 388.07
388.17 389.24 389.30
390.07 390.09 390.21
391.28 392.22 393.20
394.09 395.27 396.11
396.29 397.09 399.15
400.06 401.17 401.30

```
AT (CONT.)          402.03
402.04  402.08  402.21
402.22  403.19  404.04
404.08  405.14  407.01
408.13  408.28  409.11
409.28  410.12  410.22
410.23  410.28  410.30
412.01  412.27  412.30
414.07  414.11  414.14
415.08  415.08  415.12
416.13  417.09  417.25
418.25  419.07  419.15
420.03  420.10  420.25
420.29  421.03  421.17
422.18  423.05  423.05
424.01  425.10  425.11
426.18  427.07  427.12
427.30  428.04  428.07
428.09  429.08  429.17
429.18  429.27  430.10
430.11  430.20  431.10
431.11  432.08  432.21
432.27  433.23  434.07
436.07  436.26  437.03
437.18  437.30  438.03
438.19  438.20  439.24
439.29  441.01  443.05
443.12  443.28  444.07
444.15  445.18  446.04
448.04  448.12  448.12
448.21  448.25  449.07
449.19  449.21  449.27
450.02  450.06  450.12
450.21  450.22  451.10
451.11  451.18  452.05
452.14  452.27  453.01
453.18  454.14  455.11
455.12  456.17  459.03
459.13  459.16  459.30
460.26  461.07  463.02
463.05  463.07  463.13
453.14  463.16  463.18
464.04  464.12  465.13
467.10  467.13  468.01
468.22  469.08  469.16
470.16  470.17  470.19
471.05  471.12  471.21
471.24  473.04  473.07
473.14  473.23  474.28
475.02  476.01  477.07
478.13  478.27  478.28
479.06  479.19  479.30
481.16  481.16  481.26
483.01  484.13  484.23
484.28  485.12  485.29
488.29  489.20  490.26
491.22  492.14  492.17
492.19  492.29  494.09
494.15  496.07  496.08
497.08  499.18  500.03
500.11  500.16  501.04
501.06  501.09  502.11
502.20  502.22  502.27
503.01  503.12  503.14
503.15  504.10  505.06
505.09  505.12  505.20
505.24  505.26  506.20
506.25  507.14  507.19
508.24  509.01  509.06
509.14  509.17  509.28
509.30  510.15  510.17
510.20  511.09  511.26
512.18  512.28  513.07
513.27  514.08  514.10
514.23  514.28  515.16
515.20  516.01  516.01
516.16  516.21
ATE        76.02
ATHWART    21.30             443.23
ATLANTIC   194.19
ATMOSPHERE         146.04
191.14  409.08
ATOMS      216.24
ATONED     372.11
ATROCIOUSLY        343.28
ATROCITY   465.25
ATTACHED   287.16   293.19
332.28
ATTACK     223.20   336.20   503.15
445.15  453.23  503.15

ATTAINING          478.24
ATTEMPT    201.24            420.02
445.19
ATTEMPTED          227.24
ATTEMPTING         148.12
ATTEMPTS   366.28
ATTEND     65.16             169.15
ATTENDANCE         78.07
311.11
ATTENDANT          45.02
308.01
ATTENDANTS         333.23
499.17  514.25
ATTENDED   40.01    66.04
66.11   327.16  490.01
ATTENDING          330.30
ATTENTION          94.20
119.11  194.30  199.02
210.09  267.26  337.25
350.26  455.17  492.08
ATTENTIVE          2.16
32.14   33.02   154.03
195.12  293.03  342.27
374.05  401.22  494.25
ATTENTIVELY        499.11
ATTIRE     452.18
ATTITUDE   82.13    112.28
132.09  172.07  174.02
286.27  404.18  458.14
512.29
ATTITUDES          181.06
ATTRACTION         69.06
ATTRACTIVE         69.05
ATTRIBUTE          501.21
ATTUNED    14.01
AU         176.04
AUBURN     238.14
AUCKLAND   200.01
AUDACIOUS          22.20
321.12  379.19  437.12
AUDACITY   348.05   507.20
AUDIBLE    32.18    391.09
AUDIBLY    38.24    176.09
AUDIENCE   33.09    66.09
67.03   119.20  279.10
336.11  416.02  461.26
AUDIENCE-HALL      336.11
461.26
AUGMENTED          25.01
AUSTERE    188.02   191.03
261.14  417.08
AUSTRALASIA        199.29
AUSTRALIAN         49.01
196.11  214.25  435.05
AUTHORISATION      448.17
AUTHORITIES        66.01
67.06   172.17  278.13
AUTHORITY          321.18
336.21  501.30
AUTOCRAT   488.18
AUTOMATIC          259.30
AUTOMATICALLY      373.06
AUTOUR     169.14
AUTRES     177.16
AVARICE    404.13
AVATAR     192.05
AVE        183.10
AVEC       177.16
AVERAGE    41.04
AVERSE     458.04
AVERSION   60.29    123.27
AVERTED    134.16   273.23
513.30
AVERTING   108.02
AVIDITY    9.07
AVOID      104.22   108.05
289.28  493.10
AVOIDED    243.16   244.06
262.28
AVOIDING   413.24
AVONDALE   98.09    162.13
165.12
AW         74.24    74.24
74.25   75.17
AWAITING   25.08
AWAKE      24.08    63.30
365.08  365.09  366.01
368.27  446.11  498.27
AWAKEN     69.24    166.14
350.25

AWAKENING          174.17
313.03
AWARE      38.18    68.09
82.14   84.04   103.01
103.17  172.14  195.01
208.19  233.10  270.14
273.08  278.19  300.18
338.27  341.19  347.03
399.07  449.05  454.18
456.12
AWASH      33.14
AWAY       3.22     5.11
6.08    6.27    11.16
16.20   23.18   29.16
34.25   37.29   38.20
41.07   49.11   49.18
49.21   51.10   52.26
57.14   57.24   61.13
67.04   74.07   79.10
79.14   79.21   80.07
80.18   80.26   83.25
88.01   89.20   90.01
90.03   96.12   98.20
100.01  100.08  100.14
102.07  105.09  108.14
109.30  120.17  122.20
131.01  139.15  141.15
142.02  143.28  144.13
160.08  163.11  165.10
168.02  177.10  183.11
187.22  188.07  189.18
191.05  196.03  198.17
199.06  201.23  216.14
219.17  220.09  224.02
224.05  233.04  233.25
237.19  239.09  243.27
245.24  256.10  256.16
260.02  261.05  269.02
269.26  278.29  278.30
291.21  301.28  311.19
321.15  329.30  331.28
338.01  361.16  361.29
369.13  371.01  372.18
379.28  381.18  382.11
383.05  385.04  388.09
392.19  393.22  393.27
398.08  399.19  405.03
407.13  408.29  412.02
412.22  414.13  416.10
416.10  417.22  427.04
427.14  431.19  432.11
439.01  440.12  440.19
440.22  445.15  447.04
455.16  456.07  457.08
457.24  460.01  463.02
463.17  463.20  465.28
467.17  468.23  480.14
481.02  481.15  482.24
483.20  483.21  484.30
490.02  492.04  494.27
497.12  500.03  502.09
515.19  516.02
AWE        6.13     7.22
140.05  191.21  298.02
303.14  387.17  389.25
431.01  509.13
AWE-STRICKEN       191.21
AWED       224.21   506.27
AWESTRUCK          306.05
513.11
AWFUL      36.08    45.17
50.03   54.15   74.18
97.28   107.10  109.26
109.26  116.27  121.08
133.14  133.20  137.27
144.23  145.04  151.16
155.12  163.03  183.16
185.06  189.08  189.11
200.29  207.23  228.16
231.11  273.21  331.16
340.14  341.25  355.06
368.05  375.07  389.23
392.11  396.07  400.16
420.27  430.26  444.06
452.05  460.28  475.22
501.15  501.20  503.01
508.25
AWFULLY    8.10     46.06
62.03   94.01   103.24
145.24  146.01  156.03

AWFULLY (CONT.)    186.27
191.13  285.17  308.21
330.19
AWHILE     514.18
AWKWARD    286.21
AWKWARDLY          178.04
AWNING     229.06
AWNINGS    17.30    20.03
34.02   117.14  127.28
131.25
AXE        180.20   193.15
AXES       170.30
AY         56.12    76.18
77.22   77.22   467.07
AZURE      475.13
B'GOSH     26.03    26.12
26.22   29.11   29.14
29.17   29.27   57.03
140.01
BABEL      5.07
BABIES     16.12
BABY       362.20   475.26
BACHELOR   227.02
BACK       2.30     4.11
7.18    10.11   11.23
15.15   20.25   21.05
23.23   25.12   30.13
33.22   34.17   34.28
37.04   39.07   43.22
44.06   45.08   46.29
49.24   51.08   52.11
53.09   55.04   56.13
57.20   62.13   62.18
65.18   72.13   83.04
83.14   83.19   83.29
96.22   99.23   100.24
101.19  103.13  107.04
110.09  116.19  118.29
120.10  120.23  124.01
125.10  126.05  126.09
126.23  128.03  133.26
134.05  135.07  136.20
137.10  138.11  138.14
138.15  140.02  145.06
145.16  145.18  145.28
151.01  152.08  154.11
155.06  163.13  164.24
164.25  166.17  171.11
172.22  174.19  181.25
182.22  184.30  196.03
205.17  205.26  207.14
210.03  211.16  211.23
212.28  215.15  216.21
217.14  218.10  221.06
226.13  226.18  227.24
233.05  233.30  244.18
246.12  249.18  253.24
254.15  254.26  255.07
255.26  255.30  257.24
265.16  289.08  290.06
290.07  299.30  310.20
312.18  314.05  314.18
320.13  321.15  327.24
329.19  331.01  333.28
336.04  343.10  347.22
349.14  355.23  357.05
359.04  363.06  367.04
369.25  371.29  372.03
372.20  377.04  379.15
385.26  386.22  386.26
388.26  394.04  399.11
401.10  401.14  407.07
407.13  408.12  411.22
415.08  417.19  432.19
434.13  443.30  451.22
453.17  459.14  460.25
460.29  461.06  463.12
466.14  469.09  470.01
473.22  476.01  481.19
482.21  485.09  490.23
493.12  493.21  495.19
496.08  500.06  500.16
503.12  504.22  508.19
510.15  511.01  512.14
512.25  513.02  514.12
BACK-WATER         493.12
BACK'     512.23
BACKBONE   109.13   363.16
BACKED     16.20    51.05
141.15  409.24  448.23
```

BACKED (CONT.) 469.21
498.11
BACKGROUND 216.11
339.21 352.20 415.05
BACKS 44.19 126.03
136.10 279.21 318.20
401.20 418.25
BACKSHOP 184.25
BACKWARDS 129.23
142.27 145.04 311.21
BACKWAY 495.23
BAD 26.02 28.22
48.21 101.17 138.02
144.11 198.07 198.30
201.12 237.27 263.19
263.19 343.16 476.03
489.05 502.03
BADE 499.03
BADLY 27.14 52.03
204.20 217.23 234.06
377.15 377.16 489.10
BAG 24.17 43.37
276.21 438.11 438.26
475.21
BAGGED 197.23
BAH 48.09 176.22
BAKER 183.01
BALANCE 253.05 395.02
BALANCED 501.14
BALD 76.24
BALE 145.15 299.23
496.04
BALES 81.05
BALK 332.20
BALL 155.05 204.01
247.04 388.01
BALLOON 55.16 496.01
BALLY 224.20 287.09
306.14 309.09 311.28
328.04 330.26 331.01
333.15 377.04
BALTIC 49.03
BALUSTRADE 83.03
96.21 129.04 163.13
188.23 350.02 394.04
BAMBOO 252.09 279.12
302.26 336.10 359.04
403.08 434.01 445.11
498.26
BAMBOOS 255.15 366.15
BANANAS 441.02 463.28
BAND 105.09 254.30
441.17 466.17 478.27
BANDAGE 61.16
BANDAGED 64.06
BANDSTAND 45.25
BANG 104.25 196.26
255.25 255.25 255.25
BANGED 26.06 45.14
BANISTER 361.04
BANK 71.19 300.08
300.18 312.26 373.17
375.27 382.12 445.08
451.11 459.14 463.06
465.18 469.03 480.11
484.02 484.24 489.15
497.19 503.17
BANKOK 240.14 240.29
243.27 426.22
BANKS 250.30 316.29
319.15 334.16 443.25
478.13 493.27 497.04
BAR 19.07 241.26
292.30
BAR-ROOM 241.26
BARE 12.30 15.14
20.07 21.27 37.20
62.22 64.14 70.14
73.17 127.20 153.12
192.16 192.20 209.12
315.04 329.21 334.14
359.05 362.02 370.06
372.08 397.04 425.10
427.01 438.19 444.21
BARED 20.25 24.12
83.15 515.08
BAREFOOTED 5.12
359.17 452.19
BAREHEADED 56.25
BARELY 69.29 391.09

BAREST 308.13
BARGAIN 205.05 304.20
BARGAINING 454.28
BARK 76.08 143.14
339.28 467.14
BARN 62.25 279.12
BARONET 435.13
BARQUE 47.20 194.13
436.16 440.30
BARRED 84.02 429.08
BARREL 22.16 364.01
BARREN 10.04 95.27
182.12
BARRICADE 313.22
BARRICADING 314.11
BARRIER 341.26
BARRING 310.05 320.16
BARS 254.27 366.23
370.05
BASE 24.22 339.27
357.20
BASED 50.25 418.22
BASH 63.25
BASHFULLY 282.13
BASHFULNESS 118.13
BASIS 454.24 458.20
471.27
BASS 6.26 102.25
BATAVIA 3.19 266.14
BATCH 118.10 229.25
BATH 358.04
BATH-HOUSE 358.04
BATHED 350.30
BATHING 480.13
BATHING-HUTS 480.13
BATRACHIAN 65.04
BATTENED 12.02
BATTER 124.27
BATTERED 11.23 60.16
243.17
BATTERY 83.07 185.05
328.19
BATTLE 106.06 180.20
449.16 458.07
BATTLE-AXE 180.20
BATTLING 106.15 437.17
BATU 294.06 297.13
442.18 443.12
BAULKED 442.11
BAVARIA 249.20
BAWLED 57.07
BAY 17.04 90.02
143.15 175.16 425.04
435.10 437.14 438.04
439.11 439.26

BE (CONT.) 129.08
129.12 130.09 131.11
133.17 133.22 134.30
136.02 137.01 137.08
138.02 138.16 139.04
140.26 141.21 143.04
144.23 144.24 150.05
151.13 152.15 152.15
152.17 153.01 153.20
156.02 156.08 155.28
157.20 158.13 158.14
159.03 159.05 159.06
163.02 164.21 165.09
166.10 168.19 169.25
170.24 172.24 174.13
174.16 177.08 178.13
178.19 179.25 180.29
182.13 182.27 186.08
191.06 191.08 191.12
191.21 191.22 191.25
196.18 196.24 199.27
202.12 203.09 204.10
205.22 208.13 209.08
211.19 212.15 216.04
218.03 221.08 223.04
224.27 226.02 227.12
228.07 228.24 228.26
229.20 230.08 230.30
231.06 231.09 232.02
232.08 232.13 233.14
236.12 238.28 239.11
239.19 240.26 241.18
242.01 245.22 250.08
254.15 256.11 258.14
259.17 259.17 259.20
259.24 259.24 259.26
259.26 259.28 260.10
260.21 261.03 261.19
262.18 263.12 266.21
267.27 267.30 269.11
270.10 270.13 270.26
271.02 272.24 273.11
273.12 274.05 274.09
274.12 274.16 274.22
274.25 274.30 275.05
275.09 275.11 275.13
275.15 275.17 277.21
277.30 280.23 281.12
281.13 281.15 281.21
282.25 282.26 283.01
283.06 283.10 283.13
283.25 283.27 283.29
287.13 288.20 288.25
290.04 290.10 290.24
291.17 292.09 292.14
293.19 298.22 299.17
300.30 302.07 304.18
304.23 307.01 307.16
308.16 309.08 309.22
312.18 316.03 316.11
318.13 325.03 325.05
327.11 329.19 331.08
331.13 335.04 337.04
337.15 337.20 337.22
339.10 339.18 340.17
341.14 341.23 343.25
345.29 346.01 346.05
346.09 346.11 347.11
349.03 349.15 352.26
353.02 354.05 355.13
355.14 356.16 356.27
358.03 368.03 358.07
358.29 359.22 361.15
361.21 364.15 365.05
365.06 366.07 366.25
369.03 369.14 374.16
376.03 376.08 377.13
378.14 378.24 383.07
384.04 384.21 385.06
389.03 390.24 391.02
391.19 391.20 392.24
394.16 394.17 395.09
398.12 399.30 399.30
400.15 400.27 401.01
402.01 402.23 403.15
403.21 403.23 403.26
404.08 405.12 412.02
412.29 412.30 413.24
414.02 415.04 419.02
419.20 419.23 419.27

BE (CONT.) 419.28
420.21 421.14 422.14
422.17 422.29 422.30
432.13 433.01 433.05
433.08 435.06 435.13
435.13 442.07 442.09
442.11 445.01 445.15
445.19 445.24 446.10
447.17 449.11 449.15
450.15 450.24 450.26
450.27 451.10 451.16
453.04 453.27 453.28
455.18 455.29 456.16
457.06 457.22 457.23
458.01 460.07 461.29
461.29 463.24 464.06
465.03 465.17 466.25
470.24 471.18 471.24
472.27 473.27 474.02
475.12 475.28 476.09
478.06 483.15 483.19
483.21 485.03 485.05
486.12 486.13 487.07
489.02 489.08 491.03
491.20 492.01 492.21
493.06 493.10 493.14
493.18 493.20 495.09
495.09 498.24 499.07
502.06 503.08 504.07
506.18 507.08 508.21
510.04 510.20 511.16
515.24
BE-WEAPONED 349.15
BEACH 409.23 411.29
413.29 414.23 435.22
439.04 475.14
BEACHCOMBER 455.02
456.27
BEACONS 417.04
BEAD 471.22
BEADY 232.08
BEAM 476.02
BEAMED 5.02 293.04
BEAR 10.06 69.03
111.01 141.02 231.26
291.08 344.26 351.22
358.26 398.01 400.04
425.13
BEARD 3.11 33.19
67.14 83.10 165.14
199.18 250.16 426.20
476.05
BEARDED 183.25 452.28
470.20
BEARDS 486.07 495.11
513.20
BEARING 93.19 129.09
214.28 222.06 240.20
273.21 315.18 322.04
470.22
BEARINGS 436.25
BEARS 269.08
BEAST 110.04 145.11
153.27 230.01 231.24
452.04 460.27
BEASTLY 160.15 286.02
309.08 343.27 354.11
BEASTS 293.16
BEAT 19.11 42.16
131.06 154.10 200.27
256.17 330.12 358.26
BEATEN 192.19 242.01
319.14 441.29
BEATING 65.18 85.03
85.04 277.19 390.12
483.23
BEATITUDE 100.18
BEATS 77.06
BEAUTIFUL 2.05
2.19 44.01 156.16
247.12 256.22 257.23
324.18 367.17
BEAUTY 253.02 264.07
367.19 381.02 434.04
BECALMED 232.29
BECAME 10.16 26.25
63.13 64.13 81.30
83.28 84.04 89.08
104.09 120.30 138.23

BECAME (CONT.)   149.04
202.04   217.03   224.18
233.10   234.03   240.08
245.03   251.02   251.06
256.24   258.10   259.08
300.18   306.17   336.06
338.07   338.30   353.21
364.16   403.28   404.22
405.08   435.16   452.24
454.18   496.06   502.21
BECAUSE   3.12   10.11
25.30   40.07   42.03
42.06   43.42   46.09
47.20   48.21   49.10
52.17   66.04   68.19
88.03   114.03   116.04
130.14   131.07   132.08
157.07   170.28   178.09
181.03   186.06   190.04
199.11   207.02   208.20
219.24   240.08   242.09
243.18   245.27   246.05
246.24   249.28   255.23
260.14   272.01   274.11
275.17   283.27   289.09
304.08   308.27   310.14
322.15   362.19   371.24
375.24   375.28   382.14
393.09   403.07   404.21
411.27   435.07   437.11
450.15   467.30   474.10
478.16   481.22   484.19
487.04   491.07   491.30
BECKON   43.24
BECKONED   151.06
BECOME   28.14   31.10
39.06   42.28   80.30
123.23   240.10   247.18
379.13   456.07   456.29
BECOMES   51.26   273.04
BECOMING   36.20   50.06
210.10   283.09
BED   53.16   57.08
59.02   61.30   141.12
193.04   210.29   273.26
314.16   314.17   350.08
471.15   473.03   506.01
506.08
BEDROOM   208.24
BEDROOMS   209.09
BEDS   4.10   62.21
BEDSTEAD   209.10
BEDSTEADS   61.14
62.19
BEEFY   475.04
BEEFY-FACED   475.04
BEEN   2.22   10.17
15.07   19.11   25.06
26.11   27.06   27.19
27.23   27.25   29.11
30.15   30.23   32.16
34.13   35.16   35.26
35.27   36.15   37.01
42.04   44.15   48.16
50.04   51.29   53.14
53.22   54.06   54.07
59.02   59.06   60.18
64.18   64.23   65.13
67.05   68.13   69.19
70.25   70.32   70.42
73.23   77.08   77.19
78.25   78.25   79.06
80.22   82.04   82.13
82.16   82.26   85.03
87.27   88.15   88.27
89.21   89.24   89.24
90.23   90.28   91.14
93.20   93.23   93.28
95.10   96.27   98.02
98.04   98.04   99.15
101.23   102.05   102.23
104.08   105.07   105.30
107.20   109.28   112.29
113.18   114.14   114.15
114.18   115.06   115.09
115.21   116.01   117.01
117.23   118.27   119.03
119.15   119.27   123.30
124.04   126.06   127.09
127.10   130.05   130.09

BEEN (CONT.)   130.22
131.01   133.09   134.06
134.12   140.14   140.17
142.18   142.28   145.27
146.06   147.08   148.10
148.17   149.08   150.04
150.08   150.24   154.05
155.18   157.06   158.03
158.09   158.27   159.05
160.09   160.18   160.22
164.16   164.23   165.03
165.07   165.30   166.07
166.10   166.22   167.10
168.27   168.28   169.09
170.14   170.24   171.13
172.18   174.08   175.01
176.25   179.05   182.20
182.23   182.30   183.10
183.18   185.15   186.30
187.15   187.27   188.24
190.13   192.19   193.03
193.25   194.08   194.14
195.29   195.30   196.12
196.15   199.06   202.08
202.20   205.01   208.08
208.07   209.06   210.26
212.01   212.02   213.04
213.22   214.18   216.23
217.19   218.14   219.02
219.19   219.23   224.20
227.08   227.19   227.23
228.14   229.13   230.03
231.03   231.24   232.05
232.21   232.29   233.29
234.21   235.04   236.26
237.06   237.19   238.15
240.06   240.07   241.11
242.19   242.29   243.07
244.05   245.16   246.28
246.28   247.02   247.04
248.09   249.16   249.20
251.22   252.22   255.01
257.28   261.05   261.15
262.09   265.04   266.17
267.03   267.13   267.19
267.26   268.06   268.14
268.18   272.12   277.26
279.02   280.15   280.30
281.21   281.22   281.28
282.16   285.02   285.03
285.12   286.01   286.11
286.19   288.13   288.15
289.10   290.16   290.17
292.25   292.30   293.24
293.30   294.30   295.10
295.28   297.14   298.19
298.20   300.15   300.19
301.01   301.03   301.23
301.24   303.10   303.21
303.22   304.23   306.10
307.05   310.14   312.17
314.15   314.19   316.08
316.09   317.02   323.19
323.19   324.01   327.03
329.12   330.10   331.07
331.17   331.18   332.14
332.18   332.21   332.24
333.17   335.03   336.23
340.16   340.22   340.29
341.30   342.10   343.22
345.20   346.02   350.13
351.21   352.15   352.24
352.27   357.10   359.10
359.29   360.09   360.14
360.30   361.24   362.03
362.14   363.14   363.16
363.20   363.21   365.22
367.28   368.04   368.12
369.18   370.12   370.13
370.18   374.05   374.24
375.06   375.21   378.11
379.03   380.03   381.11
387.06   388.13   388.14
388.24   390.03   393.14
394.03   395.17   396.17
396.18   397.15   397.24
398.09   398.28   399.07
399.14   401.03   401.29
404.12   404.19   405.21
406.01   410.26   411.13

BEEN (CONT.)   423.27
426.03   429.30   430.09
430.15   431.19   432.11
435.22   435.23   439.28
442.21   443.27   444.10
446.13   447.04   447.24
448.04   448.30   449.04
450.23   452.09   461.02
461.07   462.19   463.09
463.16   464.02   465.12
465.23   466.29   470.14
471.29   472.15   475.17
475.19   477.03   477.14
478.03   478.27   479.01
479.03   479.15   482.24
483.14   483.22   483.28
484.04   485.25   486.09
490.26   491.27   491.28
492.03   492.28   493.29
496.07   497.05   498.19
504.09   504.18   507.03
BEER   43.21   234.26
236.02   238.02   238.06
BEESWAX   307.07
BEETLE   50.01   251.13
351.05
BEETLES   247.10   248.21
332.20
BEFALLING   118.26
BEFORE   2.09   20.13
23.17   25.15   33.20
34.25   38.07   41.28
41.29   43.17   44.29
46.04   51.03   51.03
52.04   53.04   54.17
57.18   58.02   60.06
63.13   65.06   71.21
71.23   73.23   73.29
75.28   76.16   81.23
82.05   82.27   84.25
87.12   88.28   93.11
96.17   97.14   97.15
103.22   104.11   107.11
108.03   108.30   110.27
110.30   111.23   111.27
114.06   116.12   116.28
124.08   126.13   128.03
128.10   128.17   129.11
129.16   130.01   134.14
134.18   134.21   136.12
137.16   137.25   138.17
143.08   145.28   151.13
153.05   157.01   162.13
168.11   168.12   168.25
174.19   174.22   177.02
177.08   181.17   184.27
185.03   185.18   189.02
190.18   191.10   194.03
196.07   205.22   208.22
213.19   214.12   215.22
219.12   220.08   221.01
230.11   232.07   233.10
234.09   239.12   245.23
250.14   254.16   255.16
258.30   259.08   261.30
267.19   268.06   270.15
272.16   272.20   272.21
274.15   284.09   287.19
287.29   289.26   291.27
293.27   298.07   301.26
311.18   316.05   317.16
329.01   330.06   335.08
351.11   351.25   354.07
363.22   364.11   366.23
372.06   375.13   377.29
379.03   379.16   383.20
385.16   386.29   389.15
390.06   391.30   399.16
399.16   399.17   401.26
405.19   411.04   415.05
417.28   419.20   420.28
421.13   423.24   425.06
427.20   430.19   431.15
439.02   441.22   442.01
442.26   443.09   443.16
444.23   451.18   452.16
453.02   453.24   455.29
456.13   458.11   460.18
460.28   463.07   467.13
470.01   470.13   470.23

BEFORE (CONT.)   471.27
472.23   473.11   481.20
483.04   483.22   484.19
485.06   490.02   490.21
490.22   491.05   493.22
494.04   497.10   498.28
500.10   500.13   501.10
501.12   501.24   504.03
504.17   506.20   509.27
512.29   513.18   514.05
514.18
BEFOREHAND   5.08
101.05
BEFRINGED   475.13
BEG   472.05   474.16
478.12
BEGAN   43.01   54.04
54.23   57.12   59.10
75.05   78.05   82.25
83.16   84.08   90.11
94.26   95.22   96.28
97.29   105.16   107.07
108.19   113.05   122.03
131.25   132.06   133.03
137.16   140.23   142.09
144.29   145.07   153.04
153.10   163.20   168.21
176.03   177.17   179.22
188.03   188.20   193.08
195.13   195.23   204.05
212.09   220.24   223.17
224.27   230.19   231.15
231.25   233.09   235.01
235.15   238.24   256.17
257.07   257.26   259.21
264.13   287.03   287.24
289.23   289.27   304.02
307.14   311.27   323.10
328.23   336.03   337.06
342.16   354.05   368.29
374.28   376.02   377.01
381.17   390.26   393.23
399.01   400.14   403.02
404.24   405.03   410.22
414.08   439.29   443.22
443.30   454.12   461.29
467.19   467.20   473.07
485.17   492.15   492.26
499.01   505.15   505.28
506.05   510.09
BEGGAR   79.28   100.07
108.15   238.03   286.17
425.12   460.18   474.29
475.05
BEGGARLY   278.03
BEGGARS   109.19   115.22
117.22   131.26   139.09
183.27   328.03   411.12
BEGGED   150.23   164.25
254.20   281.09   283.01
454.20
BEGGING   109.05   120.12
150.05   353.09   480.29
BEGIN   43.32   108.22
141.18   185.27   218.30
226.15   328.30   355.16
458.04   474.04   478.20
BEGINNING   11.19
88.07   95.11   147.28
156.21   169.16   171.15
179.07   292.02   499.04
502.11   513.09
BEGINNINGS   159.22
227.17
BEGINS   77.14   255.13
330.16   425.01   435.01
BEGONE   49.15
BEGONE   399.21
BEGRUDGE   475.05
BEGUN   2.13   262.06
264.21   287.02
BEHALF   229.07
BEHAVED   81.04   209.01
BEHAVIOUR   47.26
78.01   118.09
BEHEADING   193.13
BEHELD   133.08   429.23
502.24   515.25
BEHIND   12.15   17.16
19.17   21.12   25.07

BLACK (CONT.)	132.24	BLINKING	118.21	343.08	BOARD (CONT.)		480.28	BODIES (CONT.)		255.28
137.13	143.05	143.06	365.23		502.05			266.23	275.17	301.03
146.08	148.30	170.10	BLISS	183.21	BOARDED	240.20	440.25	394.06	415.04	
175.21	190.06	208.17	BLISTER	299.29	BOARDING	168.28	203.02	BODILY	12.06	58.26
211.16	216.19	218.01	BLOCK	26.15	191.05	230.17		407.04		
238.11	242.11	269.23	299.25		BOARDS	7.19	236.17	BODY	22.19	24.05
292.06	302.23	318.20	BLOCK-TIN		299.25	BOAST	343.06	412.22	35.25	39.05	59.15
322.05	333.29	347.21	BLOCKADE	451.04		BOASTED	410.15	436.18	63.09	81.05	88.20
365.12	373.12	374.01	BLOCKS	110.23	131.24	479.16			97.16	131.15	158.19
376.30	385.04	395.21	442.29		BOASTFUL	310.02		160.30	170.17	175.23
397.05	399.04	410.04	BLOND	440.08		BOASTING	362.01	363.23	177.05	180.18	184.03
410.10	410.11	414.17	BLONDE	232.17		475.08			191.29	211.01	239.14
418.19	432.29	433.26	BLOOD	8.20	15.05	BOAT	5.16	6.27	246.29	266.05	266.20
440.20	441.13	444.28	24.04	89.10	205.09	8.02	8.05	8.09	294.14	307.09	318.05
446.01	449.29	462.29	219.11	262.29	277.19	8.15	8.17	14.11	322.23	332.02	351.06
479.19	497.05	512.05	304.17	358.29	372.14	92.01	98.01	109.20	371.06	371.16	372.15
BLACK-AND-WHITE		58.13	409.04	438.18	449.29	109.24	110.03	110.18	383.21	399.25	425.09
BLACKENED		249.06	462.05	464.20	479.26	110.20	115.14	115.18	425.18	436.28	448.07
316.29	323.16	330.18	512.02		BLOOD-AND-IRON		15.05	115.24	116.05	117.07	460.09	462.18	474.19
403.08	417.26	445.13	BLOOD-RED		372.14	117.22	120.10	122.12	475.26	480.07	506.30
465.10	470.20		512.02		125.14	126.03	126.10	508.27	509.17	509.23
BLACKMAILING		437.25	BLOOD-THIRSTY		449.29	126.23	128.02	129.23	510.06	514.08	
BLACKNESS		87.04	BLOOD-TO-WATER-TURNI			131.28	133.02	133.26	BOET'	257.02	
129.15	136.14	180.17	438.18		135.06	136.06	136.12	BOIL	205.09	
367.15			BLOODED	499.27		137.03	137.14	138.11	BOILER	64.27	
BLADE	253.06	272.02	BLOODSHED		461.30	138.28	139.10	142.05	BOILER-IRON		64.27
371.12	390.20	439.25	488.21	491.24	142.08	142.22	143.07	BOISTEROUSLY		92.09
496.01			BLOODTHIRSTY		485.02	143.30	144.15	144.16	260.24	498.03	
BLADES	21.13	234.17	BLOODY	479.02		146.16	146.20	147.01	BOLT	115.18	122.08
253.22	497.03		BLOOMIN'	29.26	143.11	147.22	148.09	148.15	125.11	133.01	332.26
BLAKE	230.04	230.14	BLOOMING	150.06	227.21	148.27	150.14	150.28	BOLTED	35.05	58.27
232.03	232.07	233.15	227.21	237.15	151.05	152.16	152.21	291.11	398.24	503.04
236.21			BLOSSOMS	193.05	397.13	153.01	159.29	163.01	BOLTING	317.15	
BLAKE'S	232.25	233.25	BLOT	420.29		165.06	166.00	167.15	BOMBASTIC		362.01
234.03	236.20		BLOTCHES	120.28		183.03	198.12	198.16	BOMBAY	3.18	
BLAME	241.24		BLOTTING	33.24	34.10	198.24	233.21	236.08	BONA	97.13	
BLAMED	199.30		149.03		236.16	236.25	242.11	BOND	156.27	479.28
BLAMELESSNESS		94.24	BLOTTING-PAD		33.24	244.24	245.23	291.14	BONDS	409.15	
BLAND	440.09		34.10		291.27	300.27	308.11	BONE	338.16	423.03
BLANK	59.07	67.28	BLOW	6.08	33.17	308.24	358.05	401.18	423.03		
133.20	192.11	212.18	87.07	89.26	108.25	408.17	408.25	413.11	BONES	33.19	202.18
466.07	494.24		109.21	111.10	159.10	413.28	414.05	414.13	272.28	277.13	311.14
BLANKET	426.21		368.03	503.05		442.21	442.26	443.08	328.30		
BLANKETS	12.07	20.07	BLOWED	25.22		443.13	443.25	443.29	BONFIRE	463.07	
BLASPHEMIES		405.28	BLOWING	102.24	104.08	444.16	445.20	449.11	BONSO	251.06	
BLAST	426.03		374.02		450.25	450.26	451.23	BONSO'	247.17	251.18
BLASTED	26.04	142.04	BLOWN	76.26	80.26	461.04	463.16	464.02	BONY	27.16	233.28
235.29			164.01	181.28	216.23	464.10	465.11	465.14	307.27		
BLATANT	227.22	335.11	257.21		466.02	473.28	480.07	BOOK	2.06	5.19
BLAZE	18.03	350.30	BLOWS	147.27	166.23	491.01	491.19	493.13	80.10	192.09	320.14
393.11	414.20		BLUBBERED		140.24	493.17	493.25	494.02	421.29	456.22	
BLAZED	32.23	99.29	BLUBBERING		217.26	494.18	494.27	495.01	BOOK-LINED		421.29
324.05	367.27	462.24	BLUE	17.11	33.21	495.08	495.14	496.05	BOOKS	252.16	286.09
469.03			46.24	67.17	89.09	497.02	499.22	501.27	290.27	353.17	
BLAZES	444.26		93.11	118.21	134.17	503.18			BOOM	293.08	294.22
BLEACHED	397.20		191.27	234.11	237.18	BOAT-CHOCK		115.18	BOOMED	5.29	
BLEACHING		277.13	272.19	292.04	297.07	BOAT-CLOAK		198.24	BOOMING	417.07	
BLEAK	62.25		299.08	347.21	409.05	BOAT-HOOK		8.02	BOON	2.18	
BLEAR	273.16		409.26	424.14	440.06	8.09	8.15	8.17	BOOT	72.11	375.26
BLEAR-EYED		273.16	453.14	460.21	150.19			BOOT-HEELS		72.11
BLEARED	204.14	410.24	BLUE-BLACK		347.21	BOAT-LOAD		242.11	BOOTS	83.06	189.21
BLEATED	133.06		BLUE-JACKETS		440.06	BOAT-SAIL		152.21	191.30	218.11	288.09
BLEATING	56.11		BLUENESS	413.02		BOAT-SAILING		233.21	395.22	506.01	
BLEIBT	256.04		BLUISH	193.07		BOAT-STRETCHER		109.24	BOOZER	65.10	
BLESS	79.13		BLUNDER	86.14		BOAT'S	137.08		BORDER	249.11	339.26
BLESSED	41.17	43.15	BLUNDERBUSS		324.18	BOATFALLS		131.23	BORE	260.02	298.04
51.02	197.03	199.29	BLUNDERED		313.25	BOATMEN	42.24	207.22	373.13	425.15	
215.07	295.13	310.15	BLUNDERING		86.14	291.13	300.21	505.18	BORED	67.19	69.15
350.13			BLUNT	196.14		BOATS	5.04	6.05	82.15	92.06	294.08
BLESSING	16.27	298.17	BLUR	151.17		101.23	103.19	104.16	BOREDOM	82.12	176.26
298.17	422.18		BLURRED	20.20	136.21	104.17	104.20	105.28	310.25		
BLEW	5.28	62.21	175.29	263.29	493.28	106.14	107.14	107.16	BORN	26.11	49.11
77.21	170.27	409.29	BLURT	99.16		108.20	108.27	108.27	152.25	179.23	198.14
430.03	445.14		BLURTED	134.14		109.19	124.14	124.28	249.20	260.26	278.26
BLIGHT	120.25	181.08	BLUSH	236.27		162.24	172.01	172.27	390.21		
317.03			BLUSHED	347.24	362.07	182.21	182.27	312.01	BORNE	63.19	147.02
BLIND	36.15	54.24	BLUSHING	170.24	305.03	332.25	439.04	441.07	215.28	219.16	378.02
55.13	116.27	216.15	BLUSTERING		216.24	444.11	444.24	445.17	510.07		
277.10	312.23	334.22	BLUNT	196.14		445.22	449.19	449.30	BORROWING		70.19
378.28	422.16	431.16	BOARD	2.03	15.09	450.15	484.11	489.17	BOSOM	170.13	225.13
432.14	437.19	452.06	17.29	58.07	76.11	502.18	504.05	505.29	346.12	356.29	
458.15	485.24	500.25	97.29	98.16	103.04	507.23			BOSS	203.21	
BLINDED	112.05	136.08	124.17	131.05	132.27	BOATSWAIN'S		72.25	BOSSE	178.14	
372.06			144.01	164.14	164.26	BOB	182.14	182.22	BOTH	26.20	33.19
BLINDFOLD		495.23	167.16	169.21	171.19	182.28	183.02		53.21	54.28	64.05
BLINDNESS		113.18	176.14	197.24	233.02	BOB'S	183.17		82.10	83.02	154.11
430.18			236.28	242.14	297.20	BOBBED	374.01		193.06	199.17	228.23
BLINDS	47.02		307.16	414.15	436.27	BOBBING	8.01	126.02	229.16	240.22	251.06
BLINK	364.19		437.27	438.22	439.16	BODIES	20.18	103.16	251.26	260.01	261.23
BLINKED	149.07	199.20	442.16	455.02	456.20	126.18	127.30	212.06	275.05	319.15	334.01

BOTH (CONT.)   344.21
  353.01 360.23 385.28
  395.02 395.03 405.06
  434.23 437.29 443.03
  443.25 444.01 471.26
  478.13 491.21 500.05
BOTHER 130.29 153.24
  165.29 329.16
BOTHERED 134.12 203.25
  208.28 232.22 405.09
  424.06
BOTTLE 27.01 43.23
  75.19 109.09 141.08
  145.25
BOTTLE-WASHERS 75.19
BOTTLES 2.09 58.03
  64.25
BOTTOM 7.19 11.24
  79.05 123.25 125.23
  139.08 147.23 176.04
  194.16 211.26 219.24
  236.17 378.26 396.29
  397.02 475.02
BOTTOMLESS 218.30
BOUGH 496.09
BOUGHS 333.15
BOUGHT 2.26 437.03
BOULDERS 198.18
BOUNCED 145.26
BOUND 7.03 92.01
  118.23 166.27 188.13
  194.13 212.28 218.09
  242.11 270.22 329.17
  410.20 502.02
BOUNDARY 151.18
BOUNDED 371.10
BOUNDLESS 417.14
BOUNDS 316.15 336.08
  361.27
BOUT 146.04
BOW 7.07 126.03
  126.11 131.02 143.18
  431.24 484.13
BOW-OW-OW-OW-OW 143.18
BOWED 125.27 175.14
  181.16 181.19 181.19
  185.07 205.26 263.17
  320.20 401.23 460.26
  466.18 490.22 515.10
BOWING 6.24
BOWL 28.06 257.09
  323.29
BOWMAN 7.27
BOWS 17.28 44.22
  128.20 136.06 136.19
  148.09 166.03 441.12
BOX 32.09 36.27
  41.16 54.29 55.10
  66.21 217.02 280.08
  291.30 299.03 301.15
BOXES 20.28 102.30
  167.05 248.18 291.04
  291.22
BOY 7.12 7.28
  21.04 47.11 52.16
  72.13 76.06 109.03
  134.26 198.08 201.28
  220.08 228.01 295.02
  313.25 383.16 395.27
  422.05
BOYHOOD 423.13
BOYISH 93.11 155.10
  233.19 281.27 325.09
  342.17 348.16 515.22
BOYS 5.21 6.15
  6.19 9.06 16.08
  26.02 51.30 100.24
  262.23 422.16
BRACED 181.28
BRACKET 370.08
BRAIN 77.19 104.15
  131.20 153.23 359.08
BRANCH 297.13
BRANCHED 263.04
BRANCHES 276.10 276.14
  432.06 459.29 491.15
  497.07 497.23
BRANDY 27.01 64.25
BRASS 21.12 22.10
  28.06 53.30 62.21

BRASS (CONT.) 170.12
  178.06 307.30 323.22
  323.23 330.10 330.15
  331.18 365.07 443.19
  467.15
BRAVE 178.13 178.13
  178.17 178.18 254.23
  376.12 379.21 388.08
  392.25 407.24 447.07
  483.19
BRAVEST 90.07
BRAWL 86.23
BRAWNY 58.12
BRAZEN 27.12 335.11
BRAZENLY 478.14
BREACH 191.15 316.12
BREACHED 297.11
BREAD 10.08 239.10
  245.16 271.01
BREADCRUMBS 287.22
BREADTH 25.12 125.24
  159.14 159.15
BREAK 131.26 139.25
  162.11 211.12 216.26
  220.19 224.28 309.27
  329.11 449.13
BREAKER 152.19
BREAKFAST 43.11
  46.10 190.01 199.10
  229.14 267.22 278.18
  353.03
BREAKFAST-TABLE 229.14
  278.18
BREAKING 26.09 166.21
  166.21
BREAKING-UP 26.09
BREAKS 217.08
BREAST 24.12 32.21
  33.27 104.28 114.27
  141.26 156.02 174.22
  177.04 178.06 192.20
  220.18 231.23 261.11
  261.16 264.13 276.19
  288.23 312.11 334.14
  337.12 358.27 374.07
  395.05 405.13 409.19
  430.15 469.19 509.09
  511.27
BREASTING 118.07
BREASTS 16.11 21.24
  410.20
BREASTWORK 444.23
BREATH 6.12 13.01
  25.09 48.07 63.24
  89.30 94.24 100.04
  124.05 126.11 131.20
  134.05 140.25 143.28
  176.22 210.05 211.04
  216.06 217.20 223.03
  257.24 304.17 313.27
  369.04 369.24 381.24
  387.19 391.06 393.22
  393.25 426.08 466.30
  480.05 494.15
BREATHE 271.13 307.21
  341.14 367.21 403.27
BREATHED 28.29 192.24
  374.17 391.25 409.07
BREATHING 102.01
  175.20 337.16 350.09
  422.26 450.13
BREATHLESS 6.26
  323.05 380.12 508.08
BREATHS 111.24
BRED 57.04 304.29
BREECH 442.29 480.27
BREECH-BLOCKS 442.29
BREECH-LOADERS 480.27
BREECHED 73.30
BREECHES 8.02 8.19
BREED 316.21
BREEDS 59.30
BREEZE 12.28 62.18
  140.01 149.19 232.30
  367.18 378.03 409.30
  442.27 445.14
BREEZES 442.17
BRICK 224.22
BRICKS 4.13
BRIDE 299.16 515.27

BRIDGE 19.23 25.18
  29.18 34.18 36.12
  70.28 71.22 72.13
  72.28 102.07 107.16
  109.07 109.18 110.01
  117.06 120.06 124.12
  125.30 167.08 167.21
  192.21
BRIDGE-LADDER 25.18
  34.18
BRIDGES 220.15
BRIDLE 254.06
BRIDLE-PATH 254.06
BRIEF 467.14
BRIEFLY 381.21
BRIEN 235.08 235.14
  235.21 235.23
BRIERLY 67.15 67.15
  67.16 68.20 70.25
  70.31 70.39 71.12
  71.25 73.11 75.18
  78.16 78.16 79.05
  79.22 80.08 80.26
  81.23 81.26 82.05
  82.10 82.15 95.04
  118.15 119.07 165.28
  192.25 195.23
BRIERLY'S 72.30
  75.23 76.28 95.08
  185.19 245.18 267.24
BRIERWOOD 325.07
BRIG 197.07 214.26
BRIG-RIGGED 197.07
  214.26
BRIGANTINE 290.14
  292.29 293.07 295.24
BRIGANTINE'S 291.30
BRIGHT 70.12 192.21
  203.17 228.09 260.03
  261.10 262.16 314.24
  330.30 469.03 498.28
BRIGHTENED 489.01
BRIGHTENING 282.19
BRIGHTNESS 224.14
BRILLIANCE 149.02
  191.24 214.03 216.21
  376.23
BRILLIANT 13.09
  175.25
BRILLIANTLY 340.23
BRIM 444.16
BRIM-FULL 444.16
BRING 35.14 138.18
  147.23 193.23 310.23
  355.12 436.12 461.04
  472.13 472.27
BRINGING 194.28 450.07
  453.08 508.19 510.02
BRINGS 339.05
BRINK 117.18 156.11
  211.17 258.15
BRISBANE 201.03 201.08
BRISK 226.02
BRISKLY 360.28
BRISTLED 205.15
BRITAIN 281.05
BRITISH 281.01
BROAD 5.02 6.04
  33.06 46.28 74.15
  82.28 170.13 226.20
  248.20 293.04 307.27
  384.10 421.05 432.23
  476.09 493.13
BROAD-BEAMED 5.02
BROAD-SHOULDERED 46.28
BROADCLOTH 399.04
BROKE 3.09 7.08
  63.11 81.12 96.30
  109.16 262.17 309.30
  374.22 387.26 398.24
  433.16 450.23 490.08
  504.19
BROKEN 12.18 21.10
  34.20 54.09 96.12
  125.04 134.04 135.01
  145.08 201.06 224.08
  225.17 243.02 272.28
  308.30 309.26 311.04
  353.14 361.04 366.15

BROKEN (CONT.) 368.23
  403.15 405.22 410.01
  416.02 416.23 452.19
  458.10 480.17 483.25
BROKEN-DOWN 201.06
BROKEN-RIMMED 452.19
BROKER'S 42.23
BRONZE 249.09 252.25
  371.15
BRONZED 59.03 93.13
BROODED 7.27 193.14
  293.30
BROODING 127.19 325.15
  333.06 334.15
BROOMSTICK 46.25
  55.09
BROTHER 2.08 20.14
  272.29 390.07 436.03
BROTHERS 240.15 241.13
  423.02 457.19
BROUGHT 2.23 12.29
  83.20 104.24 118.11
  166.03 166.25 172.20
  334.29 340.16 345.14
  392.05 404.01 404.06
  417.19 442.15 447.02
  448.30 454.05 454.22
  475.30 486.10 491.26
  508.27 509.11
BROW 30.27 109.15
  135.04 194.02 318.12
  409.24
BROWN 4.27 30.01
  30.01 61.16 118.24
  151.17 191.27 254.13
  314.23 314.28 319.14
  321.22 334.08 338.10
  339.25 353.23 410.18
  410.29 418.18 425.02
  425.24 426.07 426.15
  426.16 426.19 426.28
  427.19 435.02 435.24
  438.05 439.07 439.12
  440.11 440.12 440.22
  440.27 442.30 443.05
  444.06 444.30 445.15
  445.23 451.02 451.27
  452.12 452.23 453.14
  454.02 454.23 454.28
  455.08 455.15 455.23
  455.30 456.07 456.12
  456.17 456.21 456.30
  457.11 458.09 459.19
  460.13 461.03 463.11
  464.05 464.16 464.23
  464.27 466.28 467.12
  467.25 467.27 468.01
  468.07 468.14 468.21
  469.04 469.11 469.13
  469.23 470.02 470.05
  470.15 471.06 471.07
  471.10 471.12 475.15
  475.20 475.25 477.23
  478.03 478.16 479.17
  479.30 480.20 480.23
  481.06 481.18 481.21
  481.23 481.26 484.15
  485.09 488.10 488.18
  490.14 491.17 491.24
  492.01 492.05 492.08
  492.13 492.17 492.19
  492.25 493.02 493.09
  493.18 493.20 494.09
  494.13 494.26 494.29
  495.08 495.12 495.19
  495.22 495.26 496.02
  496.06 497.09 499.24
  500.05 500.17 501.01
  501.14 502.01 502.06
  502.11
BROWN'S 438.26 439.02
  439.05 439.27 440.03
  441.18 443.25 447.23
  452.30 453.16 457.01
  458.10 466.03 469.08
  491.14 492.29 493.13
  494.02 500.11 500.30
BRRRR 137.18
BRUSHED 193.03 207.14

BRUSHED (CONT.) 246.12
BRUSHWOOD 324.23
444.26
BRUSQUE 479.11
188.19
220.24
BRUTAL 6.11 8.24
116.16 242.24
BRUTALISED 15.04
BRUTALITY 12.07
54.24 106.16 187.10
BRUTALLY 21.23 36.24
219.23 393.10
BRUTE 72.20 99.06
224.27 368.05 418.20
BRUTES 63.25 124.26
436.09
BUBBLE 181.08
BUCCANEER 436.01
BUCCANEERS 13.20
BUCKETS 23.27
BUDGED 373.23
BUFFALO 85.15
BUFFALOES 367.10
BUFFETED 175.27
BUGGY 252.11
BUGIS 317.07 317.16
321.01 328.20 332.28
336.23 354.04 357.30
363.13 364.12 427.24
434.22 451.02 453.20
453.24 461.17 461.20
455.01 465.19 482.29
483.13 484.11 492.11
493.06 494.16 500.01
502.18 513.13
BUILDING 84.07 216.27
289.27 416.19
BUILDINGS 6.04
366.14 445.23 446.01
459.12
BUILT 1.02 366.19
443.14 498.19
BULGE 99.21
BULGED 101.11
BULGING 103.12
BULK 38.28 46.16
101.29 101.29 223.11
318.03 337.09
BULK-HEAD 101.29
BULK-LAMP 101.29
BULKHEAD 34.15 34.16
42.11 99.19 111.06
111.11 169.19 169.26
BULKHEAD'LL 34.22
BULKY 494.07
BULL 1.05 318.11
450.13 510.02
BULL'S 22.28
BULL'S-EYE 22.28
BULLET 49.19 254.19
372.03 390.20 501.09
BULLET-PROOF 254.19
BULLETS 212.26 255.06
451.13
BULLIED 57.05 112.06
129.06 438.08
BULLOCK 45.09 191.28
494.22 495.02 495.02
495.05
BULLOCK-CART 191.28
BULLOCKS 442.03
BULLY 436.03
BULLYING 205.30 499.26
BULWARKS 20.17 321.09
439.13
BUMP 133.26 133.27
BUMPS 207.13
BUNCH 128.05 193.05
373.02 410.07 410.13
441.02
BUNDLES 20.10
BUNGALOW 231.15
BUNGLER 189.20
BUNK 26.29 61.08
109.23 130.14 476.01
BUOY 158.11
BUOYANT 217.04
BUPRESTIDAE 247.09
BURDEN 242.20 270.18

BURDEN (CONT.) 398.01
BURDENED 166.19
BURIED 93.08 99.07
175.08 232.02 339.22
353.25 397.26
BURLESQUE 127.14
147.25
BURLY 83.19 181.25
BURN 33.01 80.04
276.18
BURNED 94.10 170.23
362.02 372.14
BURNING 32.09 100.20
374.10 412.22 455.07
489.22 493.28 498.11
498.28
BURNT 316.02
BURROWED 116.30
BURROWING 55.05
BURST 17.22 45.17
55.11 58.25 94.03
104.30 123.14 123.22
150.12 211.12 225.24
231.22 235.28 307.08
312.22 313.24 328.11
332.05 370.29 405.15
484.02 505.12
BURSTING 19.16 21.20
89.12 294.20 445.11
BURSTS 5.29 334.06
417.08
BURY 211.30 267.28
BURYING 312.12 376.29
BUSH 50.09 213.12
316.23 445.04 459.09
462.06 465.04 465.17
503.04
BUSH-FOLK 316.23
BUSHELS 247.18
BUSHES 129.02 297.05
323.11 327.06 329.06
396.28 461.03 466.10
491.21 498.12
BUSHY 246.16
BUSIED 310.25 375.26
453.18
BUSILY 257.08 314.27
454.27
BUSINESS 1.20 3.03
43.26 43.26 47.15
66.11 67.08 113.06
115.15 126.30 148.06
152.02 152.20 182.06
182.14 187.02 202.13
207.06 218.22 220.05
225.15 230.24 233.22
237.06 237.24 238.16
245.30 274.09 314.13
343.15 343.23 344.17
350.19 351.27 381.21
437.13 442.02 447.09
457.03 486.18
BUSTER 175.26 181.26
BUSY 75.16 110.02
116.07 184.02 200.21
232.16 234.26 260.11
BUSYBODY 426.22
BUT 1.15 2.01
3.05 3.08 3.14
3.16 4.07 4.14
8.08 10.09 10.21
12.01 12.04 13.18
14.20 15.03 24.19
25.29 26.13 26.28
28.09 28.10 28.25
28.28 28.29 30.03
31.06 34.15 34.30
37.25 38.09 38.14
40.09 41.22 43.26
43.42 44.26 44.30
45.04 45.16 46.11
48.02 50.04 50.07
50.24 50.30 51.02
51.29 52.01 52.13
53.24 53.27 55.12
56.06 56.12 56.28
57.13 57.15 58.16
59.01 59.19 60.06
61.13 61.22 62.06
64.28 65.02 65.14

BUT (CONT.) 66.24
68.15 68.30 69.06
70.07 70.35 70.36
73.10 73.14 74.20
75.10 75.15 75.22
77.09 79.04 80.29
81.03 81.10 81.20
81.26 84.13 84.22
85.08 86.02 86.08
87.03 88.05 88.20
89.20 89.30 90.09
90.16 92.09 95.07
95.14 96.14 96.16
97.18 97.26 98.10
98.30 99.29 101.06
102.09 103.20 104.09
105.21 105.25 105.30
106.03 108.25 111.05
111.16 112.25 113.18
113.20 113.26 113.30
116.25 118.27 120.02
121.06 121.13 124.02
124.10 124.18 125.03
125.16 126.12 127.08
127.17 129.12 131.10
132.14 132.20 133.28
137.04 137.08 139.09
140.01 140.13 141.13
141.15 142.23 145.03
146.26 148.07 149.26
150.17 153.12 156.18
157.26 158.01 159.27
159.28 160.01 160.13
160.17 160.22 164.08
164.22 166.17 166.25
167.04 167.18 168.07
168.20 171.24 172.15
173.09 174.05 174.09
174.16 176.01 176.20
176.26 177.02 177.14
178.03 178.11 179.06
179.25 180.27 181.12
181.14 182.27 183.21
183.28 184.03 184.26
185.13 186.12 186.14
186.29 187.17 187.24
188.07 188.16 190.11
190.20 191.12 191.17
194.24 195.02 195.11
196.18 196.19 196.22
196.29 198.20 199.08
200.10 200.21 200.24
201.24 202.21 203.09
204.20 205.11 207.08
207.18 207.24 208.02
208.27 208.30 209.03
209.05 210.03 210.19
212.10 214.07 214.11
214.17 215.06 215.16
216.03 219.01 220.04
221.06 222.01 222.14
222.24 223.09 223.15
224.14 225.11 226.21
228.13 228.17 228.22
229.21 229.27 230.10
232.25 233.10 233.23
238.16 239.13 239.23
241.02 241.24 242.01
242.19 242.30 243.05
243.25 244.04 245.15
247.05 248.02 248.20
249.27 249.30 251.05
251.22 252.01 252.06
252.15 252.23 253.02
253.13 255.01 255.26
256.04 258.15 259.01
259.11 259.22 261.13
262.03 262.30 263.01
263.22 263.31 264.11
264.16 264.27 266.08
267.30 268.15 268.24
268.29 269.02 269.05
269.15 270.21 271.01
271.05 271.20 271.25
271.30 272.06 272.07
272.14 273.08 273.28
274.24 275.12 275.14
277.16 277.27 278.09
278.15 280.02 281.04
281.25 282.01 282.25

BUT (CONT.) 283.04
284.01 286.13 286.22
287.19 287.28 288.30
289.03 289.20 291.02
291.24 292.13 292.17
293.29 294.07 295.18
296.01 298.12 298.17
298.28 299.26 300.05
300.06 300.24 301.04
302.11 303.03 304.15
304.30 306.20 308.17
309.05 309.19 309.23
310.05 310.08 312.05
313.02 314.07 314.10
315.15 315.17 315.25
316.04 316.13 316.27
318.04 319.06 320.06
320.23 321.07 321.28
322.02 323.19 323.23
324.05 325.01 326.03
327.08 330.22 331.13
331.23 332.01 332.27
334.28 337.07 337.23
337.30 340.12 341.03
341.21 342.08 342.26
342.30 344.09 345.09
346.01 347.08 348.29
349.03 349.26 351.08
351.19 352.16 353.02
353.17 353.22 353.25
353.28 354.03 355.02
356.17 357.16 357.23
357.25 358.10 359.08
359.12 359.28 362.21
364.15 365.22 367.08
368.15 368.29 368.30
370.04 370.23 370.29
374.02 375.05 375.14
375.30 377.17 377.24
379.12 379.20 380.09
381.13 382.26 383.06
383.09 383.26 384.01
384.25 385.05 386.22
387.21 387.22 389.03
389.13 394.19 394.24
395.30 396.05 398.01
399.10 399.22 399.28
400.02 400.16 400.29
402.09 402.30 403.12
403.17 403.27 405.14
407.01 407.18 408.07
410.21 412.01 412.27
412.30 413.08 416.11
417.18 419.06 420.02
421.26 422.06 422.22
423.06 423.08 423.24
423.28 424.06 425.05
426.05 426.11 427.10
427.17 428.28 429.17
432.26 433.02 433.14
435.06 436.02 436.09
437.06 437.12 438.03
438.14 439.05 442.13
442.16 444.07 444.21
445.21 446.09 447.09
449.04 451.18 452.12
453.02 453.21 454.30
455.07 458.02 458.23
463.05 463.22 467.28
471.15 471.28 472.03
472.26 473.07 473.21
473.26 476.09 477.12
478.25 479.01 480.05
481.16 482.10 482.25
482.30 483.04 483.07
483.16 484.30 485.25
486.09 487.10 487.12
488.07 488.14 488.18
489.13 490.03 490.19
491.14 491.23 492.14
492.20 493.05 493.28
494.11 495.16 495.30
497.17 497.24 500.02
500.09 500.28 501.05
501.26 503.02 503.17
504.09 504.22 505.04
505.27 506.05 506.06
506.18 506.26 508.17
509.13 510.25 511.21
511.29 512.20 512.23

```
BUT (CONT.)      513.06      BY (CONT.)           185.14    BY (CONT.)            456.24    CALLED (CONT.)      507.11
515.28                       186.13  188.02  188.02         456.26  456.27  457.01          509.18  510.29  512.15
BUTT      465.07             190.17  192.16  193.11         458.21  458.22  461.10          512.23  513.02
BUTTERFLIES      247.12      193.14  193.27  194.01         461.18  462.03  463.01    CALLING     13.17   144.27
249.01  253.23  260.24       194.19  195.16  201.25         464.03  464.19  465.26          184.06  214.25  231.13
265.17  516.22               205.16  205.21  205.26         465.29  467.08  467.08          291.11  355.08  396.12
BUTTERFLY      249.08        207.04  208.14  208.23         467.22  468.22  469.21          505.16
251.13  252.25  256.08       208.28  210.15  210.29         471.14  472.14  472.28    CALLOUS     47.24
258.04  259.21  264.27       211.18  211.24  212.29         473.28  475.28  476.11    CALLOUSNESS        93.21
267.13  428.18               214.09  217.27  222.07         477.03  478.07  478.20          505.04
BUTTERFLY-HUNTING            224.07  224.16  224.29         479.09  479.23  480.18    CALLS       72.14
267.13                       225.20  226.06  228.04         483.19  483.22  484.16    CALM        16.29   21.28
BUTTON      178.06           228.08  230.06  234.28         484.25  485.16  486.01          25.08   30.25   36.12
BUTTONED    37.18   170.10   234.30  234.30  239.07         488.12  488.12  489.01          59.04   59.10   63.13
BUTTONS     170.12           241.07  242.07  243.25         491.01  492.01  492.14          63.23   84.27   146.14
BUY         196.21  202.30   244.27  248.04  248.15         495.14  495.25  497.02          149.11  152.18  208.14
243.08  344.19  440.28       250.27  251.03  251.25         497.03  497.19  497.19          337.13  350.05  372.10
BUZZ        77.14   132.06   252.09  252.30  254.06         498.12  498.26  499.01          374.13  376.24  394.11
BY          2.08    2.14     260.12  261.06  261.16         499.18  501.23  501.28          427.08  440.15  442.15
4.27    7.09    10.17        261.16  262.16  263.05         502.06  505.03  505.05    CALMED      19.19   148.28
11.17   11.19   12.20        263.23  263.29  263.29         506.28  507.20  510.03          385.08  481.08
13.07   13.08   13.27        263.30  266.15  266.22         510.07  513.26              CALMING     158.25
14.29   14.30   15.01        268.30  269.13  269.28    BY-CHANNEL            497.02    CALMLY      108.18  176.21
15.12   15.28   15.28        270.27  273.16  274.06    BYE         52.20   220.09          344.04  494.10
15.30   16.26   17.01        274.14  275.10  276.04    237.25  291.11  413.26          CALMNESS    172.18  177.22
17.19   18.05   18.09        277.05  277.26  278.05    491.26                              385.17
19.23   20.15   20.28        278.13  279.01  279.16    BYSTANDERS            484.29    CAME        3.28    7.17
21.04   22.01   22.11        280.10  281.26  281.27    509.25  515.06                     15.29   16.04   16.16
22.20   23.24   23.25        284.03  286.12  287.25    C'EST       171.20                  25.16   27.03   32.21
25.25   26.04   28.17        289.01  289.14  290.05    CA          171.20  178.20          34.17   42.05   42.21
29.05   29.09   30.18        290.25  291.02  291.10    181.02                              50.21   54.21   56.24
32.16   33.15   33.28        292.15  292.26  293.16    CAB         205.18                  58.07   62.28   66.07
34.27   35.20   35.22        293.25  294.26  295.29    CAB-HORSE             205.18        70.10   70.19   71.22
36.24   36.25   38.27        297.11  298.01  298.18    CABBY       201.08                  74.22   77.29   81.03
39.03   40.16   40.19        299.16  299.17  299.22    CABIN       12.02   190.10          85.04   102.10  105.01
41.28   42.13   42.26        299.30  302.05  302.11    244.12  345.26  438.12              107.12  110.03  118.30
43.02   43.32   44.14        302.30  304.24  307.04    CABINET     247.12                  130.13  131.13  131.29
44.20   44.26   45.30        308.12  308.23  309.14    CABLE       2.06    42.05           133.05  140.02  140.30
47.15   49.03   50.17        310.04  310.08  310.08    274.04  439.25                      141.05  158.10  164.10
50.18   50.23   51.05        310.09  316.08  316.20    CABLES      323.27  347.09          167.16  167.23  183.21
51.16   52.01   52.03        317.03  319.08  319.16    441.30                              195.15  197.29  201.05
53.04   53.04   53.09        320.01  320.05  321.24    CABMAN      201.06                  215.03  217.07  220.06
53.16   53.21   54.15        324.21  327.05  327.12    CABOOSE     439.21                  222.01  222.20  224.17
54.16   56.06   56.23        328.15  329.07  331.04    CACKLING    42.06                   226.13  229.25  230.25
57.04   57.05   59.02        332.15  332.24  333.06    CAD         232.25                  233.05  233.26  235.05
59.16   59.16   60.08        333.10  335.04  335.16    CADAVRE     167.22  173.11          236.28  238.03  246.17
62.09   63.14   66.07        336.20  337.06  337.28    CAFE        167.25                  249.28  250.17  254.10
67.19   68.05   68.28        338.06  339.17  340.16    CAGE        293.16  390.13          258.02  259.07  263.31
70.35   71.04   72.03        340.17  340.30  341.17    CAIRO       105.03                  264.28  265.16  274.20
72.25   72.27   72.27        342.06  342.24  342.29    CALAMITIES            345.14        274.20  281.03  292.07
73.01   74.02   74.10        345.05  345.06  345.09    478.16                              293.21  294.22  297.20
74.19   76.13   79.17        345.21  345.27  346.07    CALAMITY    60.02   388.29          298.18  300.08  300.28
82.08   83.28   84.05        347.11  348.06  348.07    CALCULATED            95.08        306.17  311.27  312.28
85.17   87.17   87.23        348.10  350.11  351.26    358.12  442.30  467.03              316.17  320.28  324.21
88.16   89.10   89.26        352.07  352.19  353.28    CALCUTTA    3.18                    329.01  329.04  329.29
90.08   90.19   93.30        358.23  359.24  360.19    CALIBRE     324.18                  330.06  330.29  339.24
94.02   94.26   95.10        360.25  360.25  365.07    CALIFORNIA            245.06        342.04  359.13  359.18
95.16   96.09   96.23        366.15  368.07  368.21    CALL        16.01   26.24           360.10  361.01  362.11
96.30   97.27   97.28        370.01  370.12  370.14    33.29   59.18   62.29               364.26  369.24  375.28
98.18   99.10   99.30        378.11  379.20  380.07    70.24   71.20   80.13               379.11  384.26  385.21
100.24  101.04  102.03       381.17  382.07  382.25    81.10   81.10   85.29               386.26  389.20  389.21
102.03  102.05  102.12       383.25  384.07  388.11    95.24   126.27  145.09              401.13  403.09  404.10
102.24  103.24  103.28       388.12  389.08  389.14    148.18  157.11  182.07              404.23  405.09  416.13
104.26  105.05  107.01       390.04  390.17  390.30    185.19  192.05  200.25              416.14  419.04  422.29
109.05  109.23  110.18       391.17  391.21  391.29    214.01  230.05  271.24              428.04  428.30  431.14
111.02  114.04  114.05       392.05  392.21  394.07    272.08  290.20  312.04              432.21  438.01  438.22
114.25  115.28  116.03       395.16  395.16  395.22    317.08  320.17  358.01              440.01  443.13  443.20
116.10  116.10  116.20       397.15  398.27  400.16    369.27  376.09  378.19              445.14  451.26  453.08
117.17  117.22  118.25       400.25  400.25  401.05    389.04  389.18  392.18              454.27  456.12  457.20
119.08  121.14  125.21       403.10  403.13  405.09    396.06  409.12  418.17              459.22  461.06  462.22
125.22  125.23  127.06       405.22  406.01  407.05    437.30  455.20  458.18              463.14  466.04  469.02
128.09  128.12  128.30       408.25  409.18  409.24    486.17  505.06  516.01              473.17  473.20  473.22
129.07  129.17  130.11       409.30  411.01  411.01    CALLED      3.26    47.30           475.28  477.19  479.13
130.15  131.11  131.21       412.16  414.16  415.09    50.14   61.21   65.18               479.23  482.21  485.14
132.19  133.10  133.24       417.30  420.10  420.27    70.29   76.14   80.15               493.03  493.09  494.09
134.19  136.05  136.09       421.07  421.08  421.12    105.20  120.21  120.22              497.19  501.11  504.02
138.08  138.17  141.30       423.01  423.18  424.01    130.16  133.04  142.15              506.19  506.26  507.11
142.17  144.08  146.30       424.13  425.17  427.12    142.19  150.03  151.19              508.06  513.12  514.03
147.28  148.01  152.11       427.17  429.23  430.02    152.09  182.11  199.02              514.09  514.13  514.13
155.06  157.22  158.03       431.20  431.23  431.29    220.15  230.15  231.02              514.24
158.18  159.19  160.10       432.11  432.15  433.27    246.28  254.05  257.24        CAMP        192.09  316.25
160.26  162.04  166.07       434.03  434.24  434.25    268.10  281.03  285.10              322.28  323.18  451.04
167.01  167.11  167.20       435.23  436.10  436.17    285.14  285.22  295.02              455.11  468.24  491.14
167.22  167.24  168.21       436.19  438.21  439.01    297.24  316.24  342.06              493.14  493.16  498.01
168.27  169.11  170.30       441.18  442.27  443.17    342.11  356.13  361.04              498.15  500.01  500.13
171.13  171.29  172.15       444.11  445.22  448.02    361.17  361.25  365.08              503.14
172.18  173.01  175.27       448.06  448.16  448.18    368.18  402.03  420.17        CAMPED      323.03  493.16
175.27  175.29  179.07       449.14  451.01  451.07    422.30  425.02  435.02        CAMPONG     359.16  363.08
180.15  181.17  183.09       452.17  452.17  454.07    450.15  452.12  459.20              508.28  513.08
183.12  183.12  185.03       454.10  456.10  456.19    468.14  494.21  505.17        CAMPONGS    15.30
```

CAN 2.04 27.13
29.21 42.08 45.29
47.09 47.17 48.10
62.02 64.24 71.08
71.30 77.02 77.05
78.11 78.28 79.02
89.18 91.04 93.22
94.22 95.17 101.27
102.02 111.05 111.18
113.19 114.16 114.20
117.03 117.03 118.05
122.07 141.10 148.19
150.13 152.15 156.19
157.01 163.12 164.05
166.14 166.16 171.04
174.16 177.13 180.13
181.32 181.18 187.12
196.27 200.14 200.29
205.23 213.17 215.05
219.14 219.14 222.21
223.13 223.15 223.15
237.24 238.05 239.20
245.07 256.11 259.06
259.28 260.14 260.21
268.05 269.11 283.22
296.01 308.18 318.13
323.23 324.25 328.03
335.04 339.07 340.02
340.17 341.12 344.19
352.16 357.07 361.19
361.20 365.26 368.07
369.02 374.30 376.03
376.08 376.11 376.14
377.03 377.06 377.23
378.25 380.05 386.21
388.16 388.18 388.24
399.24 400.15 401.02
408.09 412.09 419.29
421.06 421.12 421.27
422.22 431.30 433.01
442.09 456.02 468.18
471.30 478.06 494.23
502.07 507.02 511.23
515.28
CAN'T 41.06 45.01
45.03 48.01 59.17
65.16 67.06 78.26
81.20 88.01 91.01
95.06 111.17 112.10
130.24 150.13 150.20
182.11 182.24 188.12
191.05 197.02 203.08
209.04 215.18 221.02
223.07 225.04 226.10
235.07 237.14 238.01
243.03 243.08 253.29
268.13 283.21 293.11
334.25 342.22 352.02
375.22 377.13 389.21
402.30 411.14 411.24
412.03 412.06 419.01
429.12 429.14 437.06
437.23 458.08
CANAL 151.14
CANALISED 432.02
CANCELLED 195.21
CANDELABRUM 263.22
CANDID 272.19
CANDLE 100.20 146.06
155.04 184.28 189.16
209.15 210.07 211.15
224.06 225.22 226.21
CANDLES 94.10 485.14
CANDLESTICK 263.04
CANE 38.28 201.01
343.10 394.05
CANE-CHAIR 38.28
CANNIBAL 197.30
CANNON 323.22 323.22
CANNOT 107.05 214.11
260.17 270.19 341.23
374.30 385.01 389.01
394.17 395.08 407.19
429.02 505.01
CANOE 280.04 298.09
298.14 299.20 300.05
300.17 300.28 363.08
393.01 401.22 410.10
410.12 450.08 489.20
493.20 496.04 497.15

CANOE (CONT.) 498.04
498.06 498.15 502.10
502.20 512.24 512.26
CANOES 15.26 443.04
451.05 456.09 480.09
484.09 503.13
CANOPY 191.28 250.21
CANTANKEROUS 198.05
CANTED 166.02
CANTERED 254.30
CANTING 126.20
CANTON 27.20
CANVAS 102.19 153.28
236.14 273.18 292.01
407.05 440.18 471.01
CANVASSER 182.14
CANVASSING 183.21
CAP 97.05 134.04
153.11 181.17 226.01
272.23 295.25 347.22
CAP'N 467.04
CAPABLE 93.13 98.21
182.12 272.12 342.08
CAPACITY 241.14 271.16
CAPE 435.10
CAPER 238.29
CAPERS 123.25
CAPITAL 146.08
CAPRICE 148.28
CAPRICIOUS 27.05
219.13
CAPS 318.20 451.14
CAPSIZE 194.15
CAPSIZED 300.05
CAPSTAN 323.28
CAPTAIN 1.19 2.15
7.11 7.15 11.20
26.21 29.08 33.15
34.17 34.27 36.11
43.26 45.03 45.12
47.30 54.03 56.11
56.11 64.18 67.17
70.30 70.31 71.12
71.24 72.17 72.22
72.30 73.11 73.27
74.21 74.24 74.26
75.14 75.23 76.03
76.06 76.18 77.04
77.16 80.24 98.12
199.12 199.13 200.16
200.28 201.07 201.16
202.02 202.14 205.03
205.29 233.16 233.29
234.23 234.27 235.08
235.14 235.21 235.23
236.10 236.19 236.29
238.05 238.17 243.06
453.18 468.15 471.07
475.20 493.08
CAPTAINS 3.04
CAPTIVATED 322.15
322.20
CAPTIVE 55.16 304.10
322.21 349.11
CAPTIVES 420.18
CAPTIVITY 277.03
328.07
CAPTOR 306.18
CAPTURE 253.28 399.28
438.23
CAPTURED 213.10 253.25
437.22
CAR 496.02
CARCASS 49.07 54.30
399.03
CARD 1.20 1.20
241.28
CARDS 12.25
CARE 11.25 27.21
46.03 47.26 53.28
54.05 64.20 76.05
79.24 81.02 86.27
128.15 132.28 144.29
147.06 150.30 151.30
169.28 194.08 228.26
229.21 235.22 237.28
272.08 295.12 346.04
392.14 438.26 439.03
456.13 478.07 479.14
482.20 484.04 484.08

CARED 7.24 22.21
66.10 177.20 240.24
247.20 358.20 381.10
400.06 440.11
CAREER 96.12 340.27
CAREERS 340.24
CAREFUL 107.21 254.15
266.03 276.24 294.29
351.21 491.20
CAREFULLY 73.01
256.03 299.24 410.21
421.11
CARELESS 37.06 193.09
273.05 273.23 424.04
CARELESSLY 121.09
163.27 178.18 351.15
CARELESSNESS
390.29
CARES 77.12 95.10
238.23 260.11 277.30
479.09
CARESS 367.21
CAREWORN 292.09
CARGO 17.30 21.10
81.04 182.05 194.13
200.22 442.06 442.22
501.28 502.02
CARGO-LAMP 21.10
CARGO-WORK 442.22
CARPET 417.13
CARPETED 319.29
CARPETS 21.01
CARRIAGE 56.11 322.03
510.14
CARRIE'S 421.23
CARRIED 8.17 23.17
52.24 56.30 100.10
108.08 156.24 217.15
247.01 250.15 260.05
263.06 267.20 274.26
313.29 324.11 327.23
350.07 351.09 361.26
363.20 368.21 379.03
390.28 392.18 420.07
436.26 454.24 475.26
508.28
CARRIES 212.25 488.03
501.16
CARRY 46.12 150.07
184.12 208.07 225.14
239.17 280.13 292.12
313.11 416.09 416.10
445.19 465.30 491.09
491.29
CARRYING 51.09 58.30
242.22 264.25 349.16
CART 191.28 197.03
CARTRIDGES 207.07
291.04 291.22
CARVED 443.15
CARVINGS 2.06
CASE 22.25 44.28
54.09 61.15 61.26
62.27 64.05 64.22
65.05 69.15 69.19
75.21 82.04 83.07
85.14 89.21 113.15
129.14 171.01 177.21
182.01 182.18 184.19
185.06 192.07 234.19
242.18 246.11 249.08
249.17 252.21 253.14
257.22 258.26 259.07
260.01 282.15 299.25
304.05 339.16 352.24
382.06 404.25 420.15
449.09 493.19
CASES 117.02 243.24
247.13 249.01 249.03
248.19
CASK 441.03
CASSIS 169.04
CAST 7.08 16.20
70.15 132.23 165.27
210.06 220.01 233.09
280.17 376.22 396.22
398.02 412.10 440.16
453.17 502.10 502.24
CAST-OFF 70.15
CASTAWAY 5.12

CASTAWAYS 56.23
98.05 106.13
CASTE 43.35 56.22
57.12 164.10 192.21
294.20 294.28 296.03
CASTE-MARK 192.21
CASTES 14.08 42.24
CASTING 241.19 414.21
475.15
CASTLE 229.07 230.10
CASUAL 67.09 240.28
280.16 310.09 366.05
CASUALLY 3.16 83.01
101.17 344.27
CASUALNESS 280.21
CASUALTIES 447.24
CASUARINA 432.06
CAT 360.11
CAT'S 293.09
CAT'S-PAWS 293.09
CATACOMBS 248.20
CATALOGUE 252.19
CATARACTS 297.04
CATASTROPHE 107.10
400.16 400.19
CATCH 89.28 134.02
148.22 158.01 203.20
207.25 235.19 255.23
265.08 279.29 287.13
319.01 364.20 369.03
415.17 512.12
CATCHING 22.13 30.19
140.24 201.25 253.23
488.05
CATTING 293.21
CATTLE 16.14 207.07
500.27
CAUGHT 6.22 8.02
17.23 78.04 85.14
94.13 108.06 109.04
120.17 122.12 124.03
150.25 151.02 195.17
195.27 207.21 254.25
291.29 320.06 334.03
379.17 393.22 395.25
432.19 445.04 471.30
505.05
CAUSE 27.22 48.24
59.22 132.15 140.15
194.11 315.29 325.30
433.05
CAUSED 81.28 94.05
210.15 282.03 450.09
CAUSES 40.17
CAUSING 292.27
CAUSTIC 322.16
CAUTION 63.15 341.08
CAUTIOUS 439.27 457.08
CAUTIOUSLY 120.06
350.10
CAVE 429.25
CAVERN 2.02 136.10
248.17 397.07
CAVERN-LIKE 2.02
CAVERNOUS 101.28
CE 167.21 169.14
171.04 173.08
CEASE 414.09 466.27
CEASED 31.13 84.06
86.12 104.07 165.29
170.27 179.30 186.20
217.29 513.18 514.04
CEASING 362.11
CEILING 33.06 248.19
319.30 370.09
CELEBES 250.07 250.08
285.17 315.20 316.10
316.17
CELEBRATE 516.02
CELEBRATED 436.02
CELEBRITY 86.25
CELL 38.11
CENSURE 478.09
CENT 72.02
CENTIPEDES 58.24
CENTRE 19.22 262.15
443.09
CENTRED 384.06 452.24
CENTUPLED 369.11
CENTURIES 4.07

```
CENTURY     276.16  277.27      CHANTING  198.14              CHEEKY         28.14            CHINA            14.11  181.07
CEREMONIES          399.05      CHAOS     386.25              CHEER     7.17  291.01           CHINAMAN         14.30   27.08
CEREMONY    181.21  186.17      CHAP       8.06    8.11         442.12                           354.03  440.09  455.01
  279.17    280.25              8.14      41.08   46.23       CHEERFULLY            99.20         456.28
CERTAIN      4.01   59.17       47.06     56.09   56.30         253.11                         CHINAMEN         14.07  242.11
  78.20     86.20   106.02      57.19     67.01   70.06       CHEERILY   1.19  233.13          CHINAMEN'S              504.08
  113.14    113.14  129.18      74.12     76.16   78.19         307.28  395.26                 CHINESE         252.12  315.05
  158.08    178.27  184.03      81.14     81.19   95.18       CHEERY     53.10  118.14         CHINS           446.04
  184.17    264.27  272.24      110.02    114.15  129.29        257.27  292.09  308.12         CHIP             46.25  107.05
  303.30    304.19  308.19      145.08    164.10  168.15        329.09                         CHIPPED         243.17
  351.17    371.23  374.21      183.07    200.18  201.09      CHEQUERED             277.28     CHIT            353.05
  382.07    383.06  408.05      202.06    202.19  203.03      CHERISH    92.15                 CHIVALROUS              432.25
  408.08    425.15  435.14      203.08    207.10  217.23      CHERISHED             156.25     CHOCK           115.18  125.14
  449.07    449.09  451.03      233.06    236.27  237.27        337.01  405.20                 CHOCKS          109.20
CERTAINLY           150.16      250.12    285.10  285.19      CHERISHING            422.20     CHOCOLATE               192.19
  184.05    204.17  209.05      324.14    324.25  362.14      CHEROOT    113.04  139.16        CHOCOLATE-COLOURED
  247.20    265.08  365.29      377.26    421.24  422.17      CHERRYWOOD            28.06        192.19
  365.30    392.25  468.14      457.05                        CHEST      58.13  159.11         CHOICE           68.01  323.07
CERTIFICATE         49.12       CHAP'S     72.19   286.11       196.13  368.04  370.19         CHOKE           104.11  124.08
  49.12     49.14   96.11       CHAPLET   397.20                375.13  479.04  510.01           374.07
CERTIFICATES        195.21      CHAPS      28.22   46.21        515.12                         CHOKED          188.11  220.21
CERTITUDE            9.07       54.03     325.04  465.28      CHESTER    196.11  199.23          426.10
  13.25     19.24   20.01       CHARACTER             79.05     199.26  200.15  201.24         CHOKING         425.08  514.24
  59.27     127.21  261.14      240.13    247.21  278.07        202.06  202.20  203.05         CHOPPED         466.09
  305.06                        356.26    453.30  455.14        203.07  204.06  204.15         CHOPPER         310.10  349.15
CERTITUDES          404.20      458.20    477.23                204.21  205.26  206.04         CHOPS           442.06
CET         173.11  173.21      CHARACTERISTIC        227.18    209.21  212.20  214.24         CHOSE           491.29
CHAFED      389.09              340.08    352.08                216.04  218.16                 CHROMO          192.08
CHAFF       126.13  231.16      CHARACTERISTICALLY            CHESTER'S             211.06     CHROMO-LITHOGRAPH
CHAFFED     105.05              280.27                          212.09  214.19                   192.08
CHAFFING    317.09              CHARACTERS            226.29   CHEWED     46.13  314.25         CHRONO           72.30
CHAIN        2.05   73.02       229.02                        CHEWING    330.03  427.02        CHRONO-          72.30
  234.11    297.08  409.30      CHARGE     14.11   51.19      CHICKEN    427.04                CHRONOMETER             68.05
CHAIN-HOOKS          2.05       76.12     87.19   172.16      CHIEF      10.16  14.25            69.22
CHAINED      6.23               203.21    257.07  328.20        16.15   26.26   26.28         CHUCK            30.07
CHAINS      22.15               404.09    438.02  442.23        27.06   29.10   43.33         CHUCKED          76.02
CHAIR       21.13   33.26       CHARGE'   195.07                52.05   54.11   64.21         CHUCKLING               475.09
  37.11     38.28   52.11       CHARGED    43.22   440.15       70.03   74.30   109.22        CHUMP            74.20  362.03
  58.18     75.23   94.21       509.15                          122.18  124.21  137.18        CHUMS           150.04  150.28
  96.22     99.07   110.07      CHARGING   1.05                 140.18  141.20  142.06        CHURCH           4.05
  111.23    124.08  128.30      CHARLEY    41.08   182.06       144.27  151.25  165.16        CHURCHES        417.03
  133.10    145.26  153.05      182.15                          182.28  190.04  235.01        CHURN            52.27
  154.12    158.20  188.14      CHARM      23.16   347.13       250.11  269.08  315.19        CIGAR            38.27   41.27
  195.23    209.02  221.01      348.03    381.03  389.08        317.16  447.19  449.01          139.12  266.04  394.08
  226.05    229.05  230.29      434.06    434.21  514.02        485.20  490.09  505.15        CIGAR-ENDS              38.27
  248.11    249.16  253.24      CHARMED   351.22              CHIEFS     442.09  461.20          139.12
  253.30    258.23  258.30      CHARMING   95.14   262.04       484.23  485.15  488.22        CIGARETTE               217.01
  314.02    315.11  318.22      CHARMS    327.12                498.20  499.07                  218.05  220.09
  320.05    324.12  333.18      CHART      22.24   23.26      CHIEFTAIN             324.15     CIGARS           2.10   41.16
  343.10    344.05  364.24      24.10     70.25   71.03       CHILD      21.08  27.01           58.08   94.09
  448.25    462.15  483.11      71.11     71.12   72.15         28.12   59.05   109.04        CINDER          192.27
  487.01    489.09  513.25      126.01    441.27                109.28  125.03  140.24        CINDER-TRACK            192.27
CHAIRS       2.09   12.26       CHART-ROOM            70.25     156.30  208.04  241.02        CIRCLE           16.23   19.09
  14.03     41.11   94.12       72.15     126.01                251.26  255.04  257.15          36.02  169.13  240.11
  105.09    209.11  394.05      CHARTER   230.11   233.24       257.20  303.07  313.11          241.09  260.03  261.10
CHALLENGED          150.23      CHARTERED             14.30     341.24  350.14  355.13          393.12
  498.13                        CHARTERERS            240.15    357.14  393.07  395.30        CIRCLED         262.15
CHAMBERS    301.10              CHARTS     71.11                403.04  403.05  403.07        CIRCLES          20.20  266.13
CHANCE      70.18   73.18       CHASE     463.18                404.01  406.07  406.07          267.12
  74.19     89.18   99.28       CHASED    198.17   409.30       415.15  427.06  433.17        CIRCLETS        180.16
  99.28     111.13  111.14      493.08                          467.29  468.12  493.03        CIRCLING        351.10
  117.25    122.20  123.18      CHASING   285.09              CHILD-               395.30     CIRCULAR         19.20  339.27
  130.19    150.26  161.04      CHASM     125.23   269.26     CHILD-LIKE            59.05     CIRCUMSCRIBED           279.01
  164.27    167.24  197.29      301.28    396.29              CHILD'S    177.24  331.10       CIRCUMSTANCES           147.14
  204.25    218.10  229.26      CHASMS    158.04              CHILD'S-PLAY          177.24      169.23  178.28  366.02
  229.27    236.29  281.27      CHAT      327.14              CHILDISH   134.22  379.01       CIRCUMSTANTIAL           40.09
  282.04    295.17  295.18      CHATTED    54.04                379.02                        CIRCUMVENTED            112.05
  308.14    308.15  324.26      CHATTER   228.03   294.27     CHILDLIKE             43.42     CISTERN          15.19
  383.27    394.22  395.08      CHATTERED             137.15    342.26  362.06               CITIZEN          49.15
  412.04    456.01  469.18      CHATTERING            137.09   CHILDRE    70.41               CIVIL            50.26   70.38
  478.23    491.23  497.10      CHEAP     196.20   199.24     CHILDREN   20.12  75.30           175.18  364.16  366.01
CHANCES     295.19  382.29      249.26    442.29                238.12  281.07  313.19          438.02  438.22
  383.01    463.17              CHEATED    76.30   159.20       364.05  448.03  450.04        CIVILISATION             13.23
CHANDELIER          430.06      CHEATING  163.09   457.09       466.15                          276.09  347.10
CHANDLER     1.20   2.08        CHECK      19.10   52.21      CHILDREN'S            307.17     CIVILITIES              352.14
CHANDLER'S           1.13       67.22     74.23   482.06      CHILL      162.07  184.29       CIVILITY        235.20
CHANDLERS           213.23      CHECKED    30.23   36.24        191.14  389.18  396.03        CLAD            318.05
  237.01                        87.11     94.25   111.02      CHILLED    430.08               CLAIM           210.21  270.18
CHANGE      166.07  172.07      131.19    134.15  220.25      CHILLIES   453.09                 379.14  379.23  389.10
  174.02    267.03  407.14      379.20    412.27  470.19      CHILLING   59.27  328.29          516.14
  441.10                        CHECKING   8.25    232.18     CHILLS     332.01               CLAIMING        403.23
CHANGED     81.12   88.04       294.18    418.03              CHILLY     215.05  452.10       CLAIMS          112.09  155.18
  153.10    157.19  181.14      CHEEK      33.19   187.07     CHIMED     78.19  253.23          263.30
  376.05    388.08  395.06      231.01    338.16  348.09      CHIMNEYS   4.29                 CLAMBER         279.10
  411.16    411.18  411.30      362.22    431.12              CHIN       20.22  24.17         CLAMBERED                6.19
  413.02    413.21  434.17      CHEEK-BONE            338.16    64.06   104.28  119.04          313.21  414.14  439.13
  495.30                        CHEEK-BONES           33.19     159.14  170.11  174.22          452.25
CHANNEL     417.05  497.02      CHEEKS     27.17   32.10        177.04  231.23  249.17        CLAMBERING              125.10
  500.16                        46.19     89.07   168.17        272.18  312.11  338.17          141.21  291.29  464.10
CHANTED     510.13              170.28    428.23  459.26        364.20  467.12  509.08          464.10
```

CLAMOROUS		103.25
CLANG	444.04	
CLANGS	21.20	
CLANKING	23.27	
CLAP	84.25	217.06
CLAPHAM	436.22	
CLAPPED	359.27	504.20
CLASH	443.17	
CLASHES	104.29	
CLASHING	263.30	
CLASPED	33.20	37.07
163.07	170.04	171.18
173.04	174.23	294.24
372.20	405.19	511.27
512.28		
CLASPING	16.10	
CLASPS	315.03	
CLASS	315.17	343.07
462.07		
CLASSING	252.16	
CLATTER	23.28	232.20
369.29		
CLATTERING		145.11
CLAW	151.24	
CLAWED	61.19	62.07
CLAWING	62.29	460.25
CLAWS	63.05	
CLAY	366.20	
CLAYED	471.01	
CLEAN	33.03	47.10
47.10	124.13	156.02
168.17	196.13	226.15
226.16	226.27	255.03
255.28	271.21	429.22
480.04		
CLEAN-FACED		47.10
CLEAN-LIMBED		47.10
CLEAN-SHAVED		33.03
168.17	196.13	
CLEANED	199.07	202.20
CLEANLY	479.03	
CLEAR	6.29	15.15
35.26	37.26	43.16
44.21	45.24	63.02
71.16	71.26	79.28
84.21	89.09	110.14
110.27	115.12	120.30
124.14	125.15	126.20
134.17	148.16	149.30
155.07	163.23	171.01
182.21	183.03	186.22
191.24	215.21	215.22
215.23	237.21	271.14
280.22	314.28	316.29
322.04	333.16	348.11
396.21	403.28	407.15
409.20	416.20	423.04
432.29	434.23	440.22
445.05	457.13	467.05
469.03	470.02	470.22
473.21	481.13	481.14
485.09	485.22	489.13
491.19	492.12	494.10
494.12	512.27	
CLEAR'	163.02	
CLEARED	17.04	78.27
159.24	165.10	172.28
350.10	370.16	394.11
396.14		
CLEARER	380.07	380.07
CLEARING	149.15	325.14
403.09	442.17	
CLEARINGS		16.02
CLEARLY	96.10	104.03
171.12	282.27	295.30
296.01	378.11	390.06
419.13	437.10	455.18
CLEARNESS		323.08
CLEAVAGE	269.14	
CLEAVING	21.27	31.11
102.13		
CLENCHED	220.02	
CLERK	1.13	1.14
2.15	2.21	3.14
3.20	43.33	56.22
182.10	236.13	268.18
CLERKS	1.18	2.20
252.13		
CLEVER	50.24	228.04
228.06	260.19	457.06
CLEVERER	178.12	
CLEVERLY	419.04	
CLEVERNESS		63.20
229.01	294.16	
CLICK	55.12	
CLICKED	260.01	430.06
CLICKING	431.08	
CLIFF	135.05	189.13
200.01	409.24	
CLIFFS	272.27	297.06
316.08		
CLIMATE	44.02	227.11
227.19		
CLIMB	218.23	260.27
CLIMBED	34.26	
CLIMBING	44.19	323.01
324.09	328.29	
CLINCH	205.05	
CLING	51.11	
CLINGING	387.05	487.23
CLINK	292.02	438.26
CLIPPED	432.04	
CLIPPING	348.16	
CLOAK	198.24	438.25
CLOAKS	363.23	
CLOCK	290.08	310.24
312.19	312.19	417.07
CLOSE	16.24	24.17
37.16	46.17	77.26
124.22	156.28	163.13
167.06	214.10	222.10
255.24	269.12	311.11
334.29	349.26	350.03
393.14	405.10	456.11
466.10	466.13	483.02
493.15	493.16	494.18
496.11		
CLOSED	20.23	24.08
31.07	127.28	145.20
226.19	279.30	286.21
287.05	297.14	469.24
507.16		
CLOSELY	417.26	
CLOSER	321.23	
CLOSING	116.17	156.05
216.28	232.07	507.06
CLOTH	191.19	191.20
287.22	371.14	
CLOTHES	28.03	70.19
143.04	149.06	288.24
314.04	469.06	470.30
CLOTHING	88.19	297.05
399.24		
CLOTHS	16.11	20.09
CLOUD	30.25	123.03
123.15	127.24	128.23
144.21	166.12	255.14
258.20	283.19	287.29
340.25	378.17	414.21
419.12	423.09	444.03
496.02	509.15	513.23
515.20		
CLOUDED	37.24	96.23
139.24		
CLOUDS	94.18	148.29
205.13	263.29	280.05
332.04		
CLOUDY	28.24	
CLOVER	230.03	
CLOWNS	126.16	
CLUB	229.23	
CLUBBED	30.15	
CLUMP	129.01	255.15
CLUMPS	94.11	444.30
CLUMSILY	234.10	452.26
CLUMSY	26.14	146.02
174.23		
CLUNG	62.18	108.15
202.16	515.09	
CLUSTERED		6.19
CLUSTERING		93.14
272.22		
CLUSTERS	279.28	
CLUTCH	124.22	129.24
178.02	189.15	212.13
325.08	393.14	
CLUTCHED	358.26	364.29
CLUTCHING		93.29
148.17	356.29	514.23
CO	245.28	268.24
COAL	141.07	208.18
396.21		
COAL-BLACK		396.21
COARSE	427.02	
COARSER	215.27	215.30
COAST	14.11	23.07
182.19	245.07	276.08
297.01	299.09	325.19
343.02	344.29	411.07
414.17	415.11	435.06
437.24	437.26	440.20
480.19	488.06	512.09
515.01		
COASTER	6.16	439.08
439.14		
COASTING	15.25	438.03
COAT	46.25	62.18
78.17	108.06	174.23
181.28	201.25	208.16
432.20	433.28	
COATS	37.19	
COAXING	330.24	
COAXINGLY		404.14
COBWEBS	134.12	
COCK	75.12	469.15
COCK-PIT	469.15	
COCKATOO	233.16	
COCKING	345.24	
COCKY	57.04	
COCOANUT	299.22	
COFFEE	21.15	94.08
97.03	104.25	139.11
267.28	307.30	308.28
396.19	412.05	
COFFEE-CUPS		104.25
139.11		
COFFEE-PLANTATION		
396.19		
COFFEE-POT		21.15
COGNAC	145.25	
COIF	61.12	
COILS	365.12	
COINCIDED		174.10
COINED	442.08	
COIR	439.24	
COL	144.30	
COL-	144.30	
COLD	100.30	115.30
116.24	137.13	141.02
143.03	143.03	143.04
155.20	193.16	275.22
301.30	312.10	328.29
331.30	361.09	430.09
438.17	464.20	468.24
477.11	490.03	499.27
509.26		
COLD-BLOODED		499.27
COLD-EYED		115.30
477.11		
COLD-SHOULDERED		490.03
COLD-SWEAT		438.17
COLDER	143.03	
COLDLY	80.11	
COLEOPTERA		248.23
COLIC	308.21	365.01
COLLAPSE	129.25	462.04
COLLAPSED		30.29
192.24	362.10	
COLLAPSING		220.16
COLLECT	45.18	57.12
343.04		
COLLECTED		15.22
410.27		
COLLECTING		246.02
250.03	256.27	316.09
COLLECTION		247.09
249.01	249.14	252.16
441.06		
COLLECTIONS		276.16
COLLECTOR		247.08
253.28		
COLLIDED	33.13	
COLLISION		6.20
34.15	182.18	488.20
COLLOQUY	118.18	
COLLUSION		395.13
COLONIES	268.19	
COLOSSAL	93.21	220.18
253.05	411.08	
COLOUR	187.07	191.26
COLOUR (CONT.)		196.14
248.19	292.05	296.04
407.04	410.09	418.19
COLOURED	188.10	192.19
282.12	318.06	469.04
469.24		
COLOURLESS		114.03
410.04	422.23	
COLOURS	397.14	469.10
COLUMNAR	497.22	
COLUMNS	94.13	146.08
COMBAT	240.07	
COMBATING		223.04
COMBED	238.13	
COMBINATION		178.27
348.05		
COMBINED	15.05	
COME	3.29	5.20
24.06	24.30	35.12
38.06	43.12	43.17
43.29	52.16	56.04
67.08	70.44	71.01
72.04	72.28	80.07
81.15	92.01	95.28
120.08	120.08	122.19
122.20	123.01	123.15
129.19	132.18	133.22
133.25	136.13	143.11
145.13	147.26	150.20
151.11	153.13	154.08
154.10	158.07	168.25
174.06	178.28	180.24
182.04	183.13	183.17
199.11	201.13	205.28
207.24	208.07	210.26
215.29	217.15	217.17
218.09	221.08	229.04
230.16	232.12	234.02
234.30	236.10	238.17
239.21	250.06	252.20
253.17	255.24	257.17
258.20	260.18	265.02
265.05	269.10	270.16
273.29	280.03	280.06
290.06	290.07	304.28
310.16	320.23	320.26
320.27	324.28	325.02
330.21	333.12	336.19
337.26	337.30	340.13
341.07	342.19	344.11
348.01	349.01	350.01
355.14	356.10	357.02
363.06	366.21	368.10
371.04	371.24	373.22
375.01	375.08	376.18
377.14	381.18	381.19
387.11	391.10	391.13
392.17	395.15	397.23
401.13	404.26	413.19
413.23	419.17	422.28
424.02	424.03	424.10
425.06	427.25	428.08
428.25	428.26	429.02
452.01	452.07	452.12
452.22	454.08	455.22
456.15	461.14	462.11
465.19	467.23	468.02
468.03	468.05	468.10
468.12	471.09	471.24
472.08	472.11	472.13
472.20	472.21	473.19
478.12	480.24	481.10
482.26	484.21	484.28
486.07	500.17	501.13
503.11	512.15	513.06
514.19	514.20	515.27
COMEDY	122.08	
COMER	336.18	
COMES	70.18	81.11
113.23	172.10	236.14
260.15	347.18	350.23
377.12	405.04	405.04
423.20	443.28	482.14
516.09		
COMFORTABLE		421.29
COMFORTING		165.24
COMIC	126.30	437.13
COMICAL	238.05	
COMING	11.08	15.23
22.05	29.05	36.23

COMING (CONT.) 36.23
 82.08 84.26 99.08
 145.11 165.25 168.03
 176.03 180.18 197.19
 198.25 202.22 213.01
 233.01 244.19 261.16
 262.02 273.22 279.20
 289.08 294.03 298.16
 330.17 301.06 309.16
 310.19 310.21 328.28
 338.20 368.23 372.03
 392.03 405.30 427.20
 449.30 451.01 457.12
 459.14 478.11 479.17
 493.24 498.09 503.06
 504.14 508.19
COMMAND 68.02 68.20
 70.43 73.26 154.07
 254.10 365.30 386.04
 448.05 450.25 451.12
 459.21 488.24 489.03
COMMANDED 14.30
 175.15 444.19 490.13
COMMANDER 2.07
 27.03 67.30 70.07
 166.28 169.19 438.30
COMMANDERS 3.29
COMMANDINGLY 21.05
COMMANDS 67.25
COMMEMORATION 68.08
COMMENCED 156.23
 403.10 451.10
COMMENT 223.02 387.16
 416.08
COMMENTED 107.24
 128.06 172.21 283.10
 367.04 455.30 495.22
COMMENTING 455.14
COMMERCE 48.26
COMMERCIAL 267.16
 268.19
COMMERCIALLY 268.25
COMMISERATION 314.13
COMMISSION 344.15
COMMISSIONERS 437.07
COMMIT 77.04 338.05
COMMITTED 69.14
 81.23 83.08 364.12
COMMON 30.18 35.26
 125.18 125.28 159.23
 193.20 194.18 240.07
 243.22 279.08 333.05
 340.27 341.02 364.09
 392.11 419.12 450.02
 479.25 479.26 479.27
 499.27 501.18
COMMONEST 50.05
 316.14
COMMONPLACE 149.25
 174.09 274.15 420.05
COMMOTION 44.06
 314.03
COMMUNICATING 171.29
 176.11
COMMUNICATION 62.09
COMMUNICATIONS 451.19
COMMUNION 185.07
 350.06
COMMUNITY 59.16
 191.16 317.18 321.01
 363.13
COMPANION 2.18
 35.06 83.24 288.02
 340.12
COMPANIONS 141.18
 502.04
COMPANIONSHIP 69.25
 208.20
COMPANY 48.19 48.22
 70.42 73.21 103.17
 174.04 191.29 200.07
 343.14 356.20 366.13
 437.28
COMPARE 112.14 335.02
COMPARING 293.15
COMPARISON 337.23
COMPARTMENT 166.04
COMPASS 22.16 71.25
COMPASSION 157.11
 211.21 430.22 465.04

COMPASSIONATE 432.25
COMPELLED 58.23
COMPETENCY 112.01
COMPETENT 74.04
COMPILED 292.15
COMPLACENT 69.08
COMPLACENTLY 277.22
COMPLAINING 130.05
 465.09
COMPLAININGLY 78.06
COMPLAINT 410.22
 466.26
COMPLAINTS 25.20
COMPLETE 42.18 117.14
 147.14 156.22 210.12
 212.21 214.04 290.29
 333.17 362.08 425.02
 492.23
COMPLETED 64.04
COMPLETELY 50.19
 112.26 137.21 147.15
 180.15 182.25 214.01
 216.01 232.13 245.03
 246.30 258.18 338.25
 348.18 388.01 398.06
 415.02 492.19
COMPLEX 436.10
COMPLEXION 89.06
 240.04 280.18 332.29
 347.20
COMPLICATED 35.21
 114.03 316.20
COMPLICATION 11.07
COMPLICATIONS 183.18
 352.05
COMPLIMENT 175.20
COMPLIMENTARY 306.18
COMPONENT 51.27
COMPORTED 232.20
COMPOSE 64.15
COMPOSED 33.09 93.19
COMPOSEDLY 289.24
 308.04
COMPOSITION 266.09
COMPOSURE 344.25
COMPOUND 26.05 350.12
 402.06
COMPREHEND 112.13
COMPRENDRE 169.06
COMPRESSED 466.19
COMPROMISED 249.22
COMRADE 285.14
 320.17 466.21
CON 131.30 399.30
CON- 131.30 399.30
CONCEAL 3.24 172.26
 399.22 399.24
CONCEALED 58.06
 172.29 328.22 345.27
 346.12 368.11 438.11
 459.06 514.09
CONCEALING 186.05
CONCEDE 40.05
CONCEDED 346.09
CONCEIT 61.28
CONCEITED 294.15
 459.25
CONCEIVABLE 223.05
 422.08
CONCEIVABLY 380.01
CONCEIVE 99.26 169.08
 178.18 190.15 375.22
 386.21
CONCEIVED 153.20
CONCENTRATED 17.24
 94.20 376.19
CONCENTRATION 176.19
CONCEPTION 86.04
 113.01 247.20 280.22
 379.06 386.14 386.28
 471.16
CONCERN 54.25 60.07
 146.23 332.01 497.14
CONCERNED 56.27
 59.14 100.13 191.01
 234.13 273.13 322.10
 384.23
CONCERNS 41.03
CONCESSION 404.07
CONCESSIONS 241.13

CONCEVEZ 169.06
CONCILIATE 309.21
 321.15
CONCISE 102.14
CONCLUDE 116.04
CONCLUDED 33.13
 140.13 223.06 284.06
 293.23 386.08 433.06
CONCLUSION 98.26
 240.27 382.05
CONCRETE 260.06
CONCURRED 383.11
CONDEMNATIONS 50.16
CONDEMNED 14.29
 184.14 185.08 242.24
CONDENSED 495.11
CONDENSING 26.05
CONDESCENDED 78.01
 281.23
CONDITION 219.10
 278.21 358.01
CONDITIONS 13.29
 184.01 239.03 267.06
 267.07 284.06 292.24
 303.30 457.17
CONDUCT 59.17 59.29
 73.25 147.16 240.01
 266.10 352.06 422.02
 422.08 451.07 457.10
 516.03
CONFERENCE 258.28
 453.15
CONFESS 178.23 187.11
 288.18
CONFESSED 64.08
 67.29 96.10 102.21
 114.17 116.28 117.30
 302.29 359.02 383.03
 419.07 463.11
CONFESSING 287.27
CONFESSIONS 41.06
CONFIDANT 379.25
 451.21
CONFIDANTE 340.12
 359.30
CONFIDE 246.04 399.08
CONFIDED 195.06 424.01
CONFIDENCE 23.19
 73.12 74.03 81.08
 86.18 187.19 207.12
 226.07 243.22 258.15
 276.02 282.21 297.22
 306.24 307.27 321.14
 328.18 337.14 377.12
 401.06 411.22 453.16
 470.11 507.04
CONFIDENCES 40.21
 40.21 127.09 247.23
 341.30 399.30
CONFIDENT 94.23
 114.12 303.01
CONFIDENTIAL 40.23
 62.09 230.24 405.11
 452.29 466.23
CONFIDENTIALLY 43.25
 202.20 426.23
CONFIDENTLY 283.05
 410.24
CONFINED 371.28
CONFINING 15.15
CONFIRMED 38.16
CONFLAGRATION 365.11
 445.05
CONFOUND 81.14 95.23
 157.06 158.21 283.23
 304.02 306.09 353.01
 377.19
CONFOUNDED 2.30
 5.24 36.18 42.20
 49.30 80.02 88.26
 96.30 105.26 113.16
 143.07 145.01 288.15
 330.09 342.21 393.06
 444.07 454.13 476.07
CONFOUNDEDLY 160.16
 214.20 396.07 457.06
CONFOUNDS 123.07
CONFRONTED 5.14
 87.05 149.05 180.15
 230.17 339.04 420.27

CONFRONTING 356.05
 478.09
CONFUSED 94.02 417.02
CONFUSEDLY 272.06
CONFUSING 302.06
CONFUSION 21.11
 102.30 188.10 210.14
 450.10 462.27
CONICAL 269.17 370.08
CONJECTURES 93.25
 429.07
CONJUNCTION 246.25
CONJUNCTIONS 392.05
CONNECTED 42.02
 91.08 192.07 342.30
CONNECTION 2.13
 149.13 177.13 184.24
 268.12 286.28
CONQUER 508.05
CONQUERED 96.24
 334.21
CONQUERING 206.05
CONQUEROR 515.28
CONQUERS 106.07
CONQUEST 276.01 349.11
CONQUESTS 304.08
CONSCIENCE 32.23
 84.21 157.11 191.02
 340.09 340.10 357.19
 376.02 409.21
CONSCIENTIOUSLY 421.30
CONSCIOUS 7.14
 86.20 138.23 418.27
CONSCIOUSLY 165.18
 271.16 398.11
CONSCIOUSNESS 210.08
 271.14
CONSECRATED 499.04
CONSENT 499.07
CONSENTED 487.11
CONSEQUENCE 41.09
 126.22 198.08 215.18
 423.21 454.11
CONSEQUENCES 67.09
 214.15 242.07 488.14
CONSIDER 208.10
CONSIDERABLE 252.04
CONSIDERABLY 490.03
CONSIDERATION 29.06
 176.10 281.11 356.16
 361.06 404.07
CONSIDERATIONS 86.19
CONSIDERED 68.12
 196.24 227.12 247.22
 268.29 308.16 353.04
 411.13 426.27
CONSIDERING 311.29
 404.21
CONSISTED 366.13
CONSISTS 1.17 113.08
 212.03
CONSOLATION 182.12
 287.30 430.27
CONSOLED 499.28
CONSOLING 191.25
 434.09
CONSPIRACY 117.09
 395.14
CONSTANCY 389.15
 516.07
CONSTANT 279.20
CONSTANTLY 5.03
 22.08 314.26 494.07
CONSTELLATIONS 123.06
CONSTERNATION 508.18
CONSTITUTED 67.06
CONSTITUTIONAL 305.01
CONSTRUCTION 90.17
 451.09
CONSULS 437.08
CONSULT 245.25 252.20
 454.27
CONSULTATION 258.29
 298.28 336.05
CONSULTED 319.05
CONSUMEDLY 67.19
CONTACT 141.05 207.25
CONTAGION 51.06
CONTAIN 352.29 397.30
CONTAINED 42.07

CONTAINED (CONT.)
416.14
CONTAINING 249.01
CONTEMNED 471.04
CONTEMPLATED 88.30
355.03 386.25
CONTEMPLATING 26.18
CONTEMPLATION 348.19
407.06 427.08 510.30
CONTEMPORARY 436.03
CONTEMPT 4.25 62.05
69.17 204.15 383.06
393.16 400.02 400.02
469.17
CONTEMPTIBLE 7.21
9.03
CONTEMPTUOUS 69.03
82.12 96.08 115.02
305.08 499.25
CONTEMPTUOUSLY 370.29
403.02
CONTENDED 180.22
418.20
CONTENT 23.30 384.21
CONTENTED 360.19
439.01
CONTENTS 241.11 290.26
CONTEST 242.16 469.16
477.15
CONTINUALLY 464.30
CONTINUED 17.04
25.20 85.23 90.25
132.28 170.20 179.08
283.15 294.08 344.04
357.28 375.24 404.28
411.29 433.15 481.10
CONTINUOUS 15.13
325.15
CONTINUOUSLY 21.27
335.16
CONTORTED 397.04
CONTORTION 54.19
CONTOUR 410.03
CONTRACT 393.12
CONTRACTED 144.17
356.06
CONTRACTION 138.28
CONTRACTOR 12.19
CONTRADICTING 367.07
CONTRADICTORY 101.04
CONTRARY 85.06 274.20
319.03
CONTRASTED 319.17
CONTRIVANCE 327.04
CONTRIVED 115.17
438.27
CONTROL 11.09 90.20
93.20 126.13 270.04
332.01 402.24 437.08
CONUNDRUM 330.06
CONVENIENCES 386.21
CONVENIENT 186.26
217.22
CONVENTION 97.25
112.16
CONVENTIONAL 304.23
CONVENTIONS 340.18
CONVERSATION 77.24
82.09 93.26 146.25
181.10 307.03 471.13
477.08 483.01
CONVERSATIONALLY 217.09
CONVERSATIONS 105.13
CONVERSE 38.10 78.01
107.07 422.22 456.05
CONVERSING 92.10
CONVERSION 475.18
CONVERTED 126.14
CONVEY 127.19 172.09
334.26
CONVEYANCE 54.30
CONVICTION 29.25
94.24 138.01 147.10
218.21 261.30 294.08
379.29 382.04 382.04
418.22
CONVINCED 245.03
245.10 322.24 340.21
492.20
CONVINCING 59.22

CONVINCING (CONT.)
264.01
CONVOLUTIONS 144.21
CONVULSIVE 145.24
158.17 210.03 313.03
CONVULSIVELY 374.01
COOKED 25.29 440.09
COOKING 167.05 366.05
453.19 484.14
COOKING-BOXES 167.05
COOKS 167.04
COOL 2.09 19.08
29.15 32.10 78.02
146.05 184.25 235.24
300.30 367.17 429.24
COOLIES 203.13 203.21
204.10
COOLLY 153.26 307.14
COON'S 460.06
COPRA 436.20
COPY 2.10
COQUET 175.22
CORAL 339.26 397.19
443.16
CORE 417.09
CORNELIUS 268.28
285.05 292.22 340.11
347.04 350.22 351.01
351.16 351.30 354.05
355.05 356.12 356.25
357.03 357.24 358.14
358.17 358.22 359.01
359.21 360.07 360.21
361.02 361.07 361.12
361.21 363.04 364.16
364.16 364.23 366.10
368.19 368.19 382.17
383.11 383.27 385.27
398.24 400.23 401.30
404.25 408.04 425.20
451.23 452.18 452.29
453.05 453.10 455.10
455.20 455.28 456.02
457.16 463.29 464.26
465.07 467.16 467.17
467.24 467.27 468.02
468.04 468.08 469.07
481.19 481.24 481.29
491.25 491.27 492.04
492.07 492.14 492.22
492.26 493.04 493.11
493.19 494.30 495.02
495.17 495.21 495.24
496.02 496.11 497.08
497.13 500.02 500.08
502.10
CORNELIUS'S 383.02
453.03 454.04 502.10
CORNER 55.30 58.19
74.14 146.09 165.20
191.18 248.14 248.14
289.07 302.19 351.13
355.20 366.16 369.22
370.09 386.01 402.09
422.24 427.02 479.02
504.10
CORNER-POSTS 366.16
CORNERED 125.08
CORNERS 20.08 224.05
353.14 480.01
CORPSE 21.07 132.25
168.27 173.10 294.11
296.02 474.22
CORPSES 194.18 333.30
458.30 502.15
CORRECTED 159.25
291.09
CORRECTION 72.02
CORRESPONDENCE 209.29
CORRESPONDENT 264.14
CORRESPONDING 252.17
CORRI 220.30
CORRI- 220.30
CORROSIVE 149.24
CORRUGATED 203.15
318.11
CORRUGATED-IRON 203.15
CORRUPTION 51.04
63.14
CORVETTE 441.13

COST 12.10 281.15
COSTERMONGER'S 184.14
COSTLY 240.25
COSTS 79.13 87.02
COSTUME 399.04
COSY 94.12
COTTAGES 4.02 252.09
COTTON 55.11 76.24
118.22 143.04 287.11
COTTON-POD 55.11
COUCH 250.20 250.23
385.26 427.07 476.06
498.25 501.07
COUGH 405.09
COUGHING 202.16 478.24
COULD 5.02 5.22
7.01 7.24 9.04
10.10 13.13 14.15
19.24 22.22 23.20
25.23 25.24 25.11
28.18 28.28 29.13
30.24 33.12 35.09
35.21 38.05 43.13
45.26 47.18 48.14
51.24 58.12 60.29
62.06 62.12 63.23
66.17 66.22 67.01
68.14 68.17 69.02
69.07 70.37 70.40
73.05 74.05 75.04
75.10 79.08 82.09
82.22 83.01 84.18
84.20 86.23 88.13
90.10 95.02 95.19
96.13 96.13 96.14
96.17 97.14 99.25
100.08 101.26 103.18
103.22 104.02 104.04
107.06 107.07 108.18
110.13 110.26 110.28
111.01 111.21 111.22
113.16 113.21 115.05
116.01 116.13 116.19
117.07 117.21 118.27
119.30 120.01 121.13
121.14 125.21 125.22
125.24 126.26 127.07
127.27 129.05 130.26
131.03 132.13 132.23
133.02 133.25 135.06
136.02 136.05 137.04
137.16 138.02 138.18
138.22 139.04 139.07
140.06 140.28 140.29
141.02 141.21 142.13
142.20 142.21 149.27
150.10 150.15 151.18
151.19 152.01 152.03
152.04 152.16 152.28
152.29 153.13 153.14
153.16 154.07 159.28
159.30 160.05 162.02
162.11 162.21 163.02
163.23 164.17 164.18
165.06 165.23 167.12
168.30 169.08 169.29
170.15 174.08 175.26
177.30 179.19 179.21
182.27 183.07 184.12
184.22 185.13 185.24
187.07 190.23 193.23
193.30 196.23 197.18
197.26 198.24 199.08
200.08 200.16 204.03
204.10 204.23 204.28
207.03 208.11 208.12
208.22 209.25 210.22
210.23 211.08 211.11
218.20 220.17 223.08
224.11 225.25 226.15
227.12 227.20 228.18
230.07 231.29 232.03
232.08 233.07 233.17
237.16 239.05 239.17
239.22 239.24 240.26
242.09 243.13 243.23
243.26 244.30 245.17
245.22 246.27 247.19
251.13 252.27 254.21
255.13 260.10 261.19

COULD (CONT.) 262.18
263.12 267.03 267.27
272.29 273.27 274.06
274.07 274.22 275.04
275.15 277.09 278.28
278.29 279.13 280.15
281.29 283.07 283.24
284.07 286.18 287.30
291.08 295.15 296.01
296.03 297.19 301.09
302.13 302.14 306.21
307.02 310.23 311.01
311.17 315.22 319.09
321.04 325.03 325.05
328.06 329.19 329.28
330.11 331.03 333.30
336.15 336.20 337.04
337.15 337.20 338.15
338.25 343.06 344.26
346.05 346.11 349.04
352.24 353.02 353.26
356.21 357.28 359.11
359.13 359.22 359.25
360.01 364.18 365.24
370.16 374.16 376.09
378.20 379.27 380.09
382.02 382.19 383.14
384.04 386.11 389.07
389.26 391.01 391.05
392.08 393.24 399.08
399.22 400.17 400.19
400.20 401.06 401.12
402.02 402.15 402.15
413.08 413.10 414.10
416.20 419.20 420.14
421.06 423.15 423.23
425.23 429.03 430.28
431.02 431.10 431.15
431.28 432.12 433.04
438.30 441.23 442.07
443.10 446.02 447.17
449.15 452.17 453.23
453.28 454.16 455.17
455.18 457.03 457.05
457.12 458.17 458.27
459.02 460.13 466.25
468.22 469.11 477.01
477.05 478.30 481.22
483.02 484.18 487.07
490.19 491.30 492.06
492.21 495.09 495.23
497.21 500.15 504.07
506.18 507.08 508.03
510.04 511.12 513.21
515.22
COULDN'T 26.29 43.41
45.18 54.01 68.11
68.16 70.30 74.11
81.26 90.12 105.23
114.14 115.03 116.20
127.17 128.15 128.15
139.04 140.08 140.10
140.16 143.16 143.16
144.09 150.24 152.25
152.30 157.20 167.17
181.12 186.22 190.14
207.11 218.22 230.01
231.26 231.29 236.26
237.07 242.23 281.28
301.05 306.06 311.26
312.04 314.07 345.16
352.29 353.21 354.07
354.09 367.07 369.15
370.26 387.04 396.12
396.15 400.04 401.08
403.18 426.02 438.12
452.15 454.15 475.09
476.09 481.25
COUNCIL 250.17 309.26
310.16 448.21 449.02
449.21 450.23 490.01
490.07 492.28 499.10
COUNCIL-HALL 250.17
COUNCIL-ROOM 310.16
COUNSELS 449.06
COUNT 239.05 272.02
419.01 472.12
COUNTENANCE 118.14
179.29 258.10
COUNTER 45.05 291.15

COUNTERFEIT 117.24
COUNTING 70.33
COUNTLESS 462.23
COUNTRY 13.28 15.02
49.11 91.09 119.13
240.18 241.12 250.10
250.30 251.02 251.27
254.18 263.28 276.15
277.28 278.26 283.27
295.13 285.24 310.19
310.21 316.11 316.28
317.11 319.11 322.29
331.04 336.01 337.27
338.22 344.12 345.07
345.15 353.08 383.30
417.16 418.06 454.02
454.12
COUNTRY-BORN 278.26
COUNTRY'S 185.01
193.28
COUNTRYMEN 462.13
COUNTRYSIDE 240.14
COUPLE 42.29 107.06
143.08 175.13 319.30
370.17 439.04 440.07
484.11
COUPLES 92.06
COURAGE 9.08 20.05
29.07 50.26 50.26
50.27 50.27 79.19
79.22 79.23 79.24
111.09 148.23 180.23
239.19 246.27 262.03
315.25 321.27 321.27
357.12 357.25 369.06
398.02 447.21 449.05
486.01
COURAGED 182.01
COURAGEOUS 391.18
COURAGEOUSLY 157.24
COURSE 3.05 3.17
4.15 8.20 23.04
26.02 30.24 40.09
41.25 62.01 64.28
65.11 70.27 71.17
71.21 72.01 75.01
77.24 81.25 82.09
98.10 113.06 130.04
131.03 132.30 137.04
147.09 151.03 158.24
158.26 159.30 163.27
165.12 165.01 166.01
166.29 167.18 170.25
185.22 191.05 198.20
200.06 204.07 211.28
214.16 214.30 225.07
227.17 228.15 230.07
230.10 235.21 241.05
241.30 252.04 267.30
268.05 275.02 278.06
282.01 283.11 286.02
289.30 295.14 308.08
308.14 315.27 320.22
331.02 331.03 332.10
334.27 341.19 342.29
351.25 353.26 355.02
365.30 374.27 374.30
384.13 395.12 403.05
403.27 432.02 437.18
440.28 449.01 454.17
454.25 457.13 458.09
461.19 482.01 482.29
503.01
COURT 32.08 32.23
33.09 37.18 40.15
66.08 78.07 82.08
83.02 84.06 85.13
85.29 87.18 90.27
91.03 104.02 112.01
118.18 119.17 127.08
130.02 165.13 165.29
191.08 192.13 194.03
194.05 195.19 199.11
250.14 344.28 462.02
COURT-ROOM 33.09
83.02 87.18 192.13
COURTED 333.08
COURTEOUS 90.19
322.08 454.26
COURTESY 263.14

COURTING 358.23
COURTYARD 64.17
192.06 279.19 306.06
308.11 310.07 312.16
342.15 350.22 350.29
367.09 369.16 390.29
450.03 451.25 487.06
505.01 508.06 513.13
COUSIN 81.18 183.22
COVER 329.13 466.12
500.12
COVERED 16.05 17.30
21.06 137.24 333.26
338.13 372.16 426.21
448.20 480.14 496.09
498.27 508.28
COVERING 20.24 25.03
117.15
COVERLET 63.07
COVERS 62.21 290.28
COVERTLY 114.10
COW 439.12 478.21
COWARD 120.20 120.20
120.21 143.26 144.27
179.24 472.27
COWARDICE 48.28
79.25 80.11 316.15
COWARDLY 355.05 472.24
COWED 395.10 468.25
COXSWAIN 44.17
CRACK 67.17 120.16
286.23 312.24 397.06
460.04
CRACKED 22.18 405.15
CRACKLING 445.10
CRACKS 279.13 279.30
CRAFT 6.03 27.28
51.23 51.24 53.06
54.02 156.09 156.28
159.19 175.17 175.21
194.15 252.14 427.29
434.15 438.04 440.19
440.26
CRAFTIEST 420.01
CRAFTY 27.08
CRAKEE 202.24
CRAMMED 132.20 323.24
CRAMPED 409.15
CRANE 26.29
CRANING 44.18 367.30
CRANKY 298.30
CRANNIES 15.19
CRASH 107.11 216.22
CRASHED 6.17
CRASHES 444.05
CRATE 370.02
CRAVEN 125.04 210.18
403.18
CRAVING 184.11 277.06
387.05 399.10
CRAWL 87.25 336.04
CRAWLED 372.26
CRAWLING 32.05
CRAZY 13.21 46.05
58.26 111.20 124.18
182.25 280.06 408.25
CREAK 369.28 440.02
CREAKING 294.22
CREAKINGS 350.09
CREASED 168.15 199.20
CREAPED 138.03 275.21
374.18 380.04 407.05
CREATING 33.30 162.24
CREATION 59.25
CREATIONS 25.09
CREATURE 36.05 241.06
280.02 399.13 436.12
CREATURES 68.03
302.24
CREDENTIAL 286.08
CREDIT 74.07 184.08
365.05
CREDITABLE 239.16
437.05
CREED 487.16
CREEK 309.04 311.19
312.03 444.14 445.08
445.18 449.12 450.24
456.10 459.05 459.17
461.03 464.07 464.18

CREEK (CONT.) 464.23
465.15 470.05 470.12
471.15 477.09 479.05
480.02 480.06 490.13
491.21 494.03
CREEP 79.16 152.27
245.19 267.24 386.15
CREEPERS 139.18 297.05
409.25
CREEPING 210.19 312.25
328.23 351.01 351.05
445.14 453.05 466.01
CREEPY 109.13
CREPT 76.09 152.22
153.11 391.12
CREPUSCULAR 262.01
262.14
CREVICE 36.07
CREVICES 15.19
CREW 44.18 105.15
190.11 214.27 292.27
293.14 324.27 435.17
439.01 439.05 439.14
502.05
CREWS 14.03
CRIED 49.15 65.16
88.10 130.25 135.06
137.11 139.19 145.14
152.01 158.21 183.24
202.24 204.05 221.02
223.19 224.22 231.28
233.03 287.23 293.18
303.16 328.14 334.12
370.24 371.04 373.16
377.19 377.20 377.26
398.17 389.25 393.09
393.20 395.26 409.17
419.24 464.11 464.27
467.05 481.06 484.30
505.05 505.09 505.23
506.06 508.02 511.02
511.05 511.22 511.29
513.01
CRIES 103.26 137.24
332.06 430.26 444.04
467.11 502.16 510.10
CRIME 50.04 95.24
191.15 316.04 478.10
CRIMINAL 50.05 186.14
CRIMINALS 50.06
CRIMSON 39.02 55.02
89.03 347.22 412.23
414.20 512.03
CRIMSONED 150.10
CRINGE 399.01
CRINGED 141.14
CRINGING 404.18
CRIPPLE 319.02
CRIPPLED 368.23
CRIPPLES 116.27 497.11
CRISIS 87.21
CRISPLY 203.05
CRITICAL 47.05 244.01
321.02
CRITICALLY 181.22
CRITICISED 242.27
CRITICISM 3.01
10.07 211.07
CROAKED 202.03
CROAKER 296.03
CROCKERY 92.23 104.29
CROCODILE 293.13
CRONIES 27.06
CROOKED 371.12 410.08
CROOKING 331.04
CROPPED 153.27 184.19
CROPS 331.01
CROSS 4.20 23.02
41.20 71.07 98.05
228.12 241.27
CROSS-EXAMINE 98.05
CROSS-EYED 241.27
CROSSED 16.22 17.04
33.27 104.27 142.24
142.26 220.29 258.17
351.29 364.10 395.05
441.12 484.16
CROSSING 15.26 64.17
199.16 320.13 410.16
439.20 445.26

CROSSLY 492.08
CROUCH 364.20
CROUCHED 136.19 498.16
514.08
CROUCHING 59.08
145.28 329.05 465.11
465.17
CROW 151.21 425.14
CROW-FOOTED 425.14
CROWD 9.06 14.18
18.03 57.12 80.18
102.23 127.29 167.14
240.28 334.05 434.11
440.03 472.13 509.07
509.28 514.16 515.13
CROWDED 7.30 25.06
44.15 131.05 169.13
448.09 469.08 484.17
CROWDING 266.05 302.20
483.30
CROWDS 106.16 263.29
CROWING 377.20
CROWN 131.17 290.29
CROWNED 38.26 434.04
CROWNING 114.23
CRUEL 98.06 98.07
145.21 241.07 251.28
339.22 356.11 388.28
390.12 400.16 405.22
429.05 485.02 488.09
505.24
CRUELTY 11.10 193.17
316.14 341.03 431.13
432.16
CRUMB 51.10 214.22
CRUMBLING 276.13
297.09 497.04
CRUMPLED 404.11
CRUNCH 189.20 189.20
CRUNCH-CRUNCH 189.20
CRUSH 87.23
CRUSHED 230.09 402.07
405.21
CRUSHING 189.15
CRUST 271.01
CRY 37.27 63.16
99.30 132.05 140.23
353.20 417.09 420.26
507.19 510.01
CRYING 133.03 450.05
451.30 465.08
CRYPTIC 78.25
CRYSTALLINE 263.13
CRYSTALS 430.05 431.07
CUBIC 241.11
CUCUMBER 29.15
CUDDY 76.26 291.05
291.23
CUDDY-TABLE 291.05
291.23
CUE 243.02 243.09
CUFFS 464.17
CULMINATING 137.27
216.22 312.23
CULTIVATED 254.06
CUMBERED 370.09
CUNNING 63.14 337.11
345.07 425.19 507.21
CUNNINGLY 327.04
CUP 42.13 97.03
213.15
CUPS 104.25 139.11
307.30
CUR 83.27 87.26
97.10 111.16
CURATE 203.24
CURE 259.06
CURED 259.11
CURIOSITY 49.21
59.18 91.10 154.14
273.03 404.04 483.26
CURIOUS 64.22 64.28
107.08 169.07 176.05
175.08 206.03 249.20
288.09 317.02 348.05
358.30 419.25 444.25
CURIOUSLY 16.09
90.30 174.24 481.26
CURLED 144.26 167.20
255.29 498.18

CURLY 89.08
CURRENCY 323.22
CURRENT 334.17 401.23
  443.23 494.11
CURRENTS 200.06
CURSE 15.02 122.01
  431.13 492.17
CURSED 110.20 110.20
  299.02 470.21
CURSES 464.17
CURSING 120.12 132.06
  501.01
CURT 36.25
CURTAIN 408.30
CURTAINS 62.20 417.10
CURTLY 205.01
CURVE 150.01 263.09
CURVED 145.20 365.13
  496.10
CURVES 27.15 334.16
CURVETED 414.01
CUSTOMARY 225.16
CUSTOMERS 237.01
CUSTOMS 277.23
CUT 4.27 26.15
  36.03 36.21 86.17
  90.18 98.29 107.13
  108.20 124.13 125.21
  147.15 160.16 171.01
  171.17 192.01 199.07
  204.20 276.22 282.02
  330.19 338.27 408.18
  343.22 396.18 408.18
  444.11 445.17 450.29
  458.18 470.19 491.16
CUT-THROATS 458.18
CUTAWAY 208.16
CUTTER 4.22 6.15
  7.01 7.17 7.28
  8.27 198.22 437.21
  437.27 438.29
CUTTING 5.10 444.03
  444.22
CYCLONE 512.09
CYNICAL 227.02
CYNICALLY 42.17
D 64.22 140.22
  361.12 361.12 464.06
  464.06 472.09 472.19
  472.19 473.29 473.29
D-D-DIE 361.12
D'ESTOMAC 179.11
D'HOTE 243.02
D'YE 192.05 233.17
  473.18
DAD' 95.08
DAGGER 224.06
DAGGERS 131.21
DAILY 2.14 10.08
  78.06 239.09 506.22
DAIN 320.15 321.19
  321.24 322.03 328.15
  328.21 329.06 332.07
  332.18 336.05 407.24
  447.05 447.17 448.12
  450.17 451.01 456.09
  461.12 478.15 486.17
  489.06 491.02 492.18
  493.07 498.24 498.27
  499.03 499.10 499.16
  501.06 503.02 504.04
  504.19 505.14 505.16
  508.27 509.16 514.07
DALE 43.12 97.30
DAM 103.14 122.15
DAM' 235.24 465.05
  476.03
DAMAGE 33.16 162.23
DAMAGED 191.26
DAMMAR 365.16
DAMN 30.16 75.03
  120.18 200.11
DAMNABLE 70.34
DAMNABLY 150.27 230.25
DAMNED 34.23 48.10
  75.19 189.04 208.29
  495.08
DAMNEDEST 361.20
DAMNEDLY 479.22
DAMNING 119.23

DAMP 25.19 37.03
  163.16 290.24 440.18
  445.09
DAMP-TIGHT 290.24
DANCE 47.18 104.25
  116.26 116.26 361.29
DANCED 468.20
DANCING 7.18
DANDIFIED 436.05
DANE 241.27 242.09
DANGER 11.02 11.27
  14.22 34.12 166.20
  195.06 273.27 281.15
  281.19 348.08 370.14
  382.15 384.01 386.16
  420.15 422.25
  450.02 464.07 477.20
  489.05
DANGEROUS 129.12
  196.23 209.06 225.23
  286.29 308.17 402.02
DANGEROUSLY 166.30
DANGERS 4.26 13.22
  114.18 294.29 338.21
  357.26 369.12 382.24
  421.26 454.10 506.30
DANS 173.21
DAPPER 292.03
DARE 74.27 95.18
  107.22 146.14 188.18
  238.24 388.06 400.08
  400.10 440.27 481.08
DARED 124.18 299.21
  329.10 336.13 370.27
  444.09 449.05
DAREN'T 183.13
DARES 219.04
DARING 94.21 462.11
DARK 13.23 19.09
  20.08 20.23 25.07
  31.07 32.13 37.13
  71.26 72.14 83.14
  92.19 108.09 109.07
  116.14 133.25 136.07
  137.03 137.22 141.26
  144.06 145.05 146.22
  147.29 149.03 155.06
  168.16 169.03 189.18
  191.30 194.18 198.25
  211.20 212.11 220.27
  220.28 223.09 248.18
  249.09 254.16 263.05
  279.27 290.28 292.07
  293.06 297.05 297.09
  302.15 307.28 315.04
  319.11 324.07 325.15
  329.06 332.29 351.02
  358.12 368.17 370.25
  371.05 373.18 374.20
  375.10 378.20 379.22
  380.18 386.25 387.11
  389.28 395.15 395.24
  397.09 397.20 398.30
  409.05 409.29 410.18
  414.21 415.04 415.05
  416.23 423.09 427.02
  429.17 432.16 436.25
  437.20 438.25 439.11
  444.24 445.20 446.10
  453.14 459.12 463.06
  464.08 465.30 467.21
  468.05 469.10 474.23
  475.14 479.13 482.01
  489.15 489.18 491.14
  497.21 506.23 513.09
DARK-BLUE 453.14
DARK-FACED 37.13
  92.19 279.27 371.05
DARK-SKINNED 415.04
DARKENED 24.28 89.10
  217.18 286.06 288.06
  397.12 412.23 415.17
  424.13 488.06
DARKENING 84.25
  123.03 127.23 376.26
DARKER 118.25
DARKLY 195.09 272.19
DARKNESS 7.02 112.21
  123.12 146.05 155.09
  166.12 184.29 216.21

DARKNESS (CONT.) 219.17
  312.24 369.23 378.01
  380.16 439.29 463.05
  485.14 487.06 496.07
DARTED 30.12 55.21
  93.29 100.09 125.08
  217.30 225.29 225.29
  342.16
DARTING 139.16 256.14
  337.09
DASH 101.10 285.23
DASHED 8.01 41.23
  109.08 125.09 187.14
  330.06
DASHEDEST 330.22
DASHES 36.04
DASHING 355.18
DATE 71.08 420.22
  421.12
DAUGHTER 251.25 269.05
  340.13 341.22 386.05
DAUGHTERS 46.05
  83.11 314.29
DAVIT 126.20 133.24
DAVITS 6.20 131.14
DAWN 149.07 224.08
  262.02 328.28 451.18
  467.11 468.23 493.22
DAWNED 44.26 310.28
  380.06
DAY 5.26 10.18
  12.26 13.04 26.08
  40.02 43.21 43.21
  43.21 43.32 51.26
  53.15 57.18 58.07
  58.22 60.11 62.13
  64.26 66.03 72.10
  73.17 82.08 82.23
  82.25 94.22 98.02
  112.19 114.23 149.11
  152.24 153.13 164.09
  164.09 172.21 175.25
  185.02 185.27 198.13
  200.27 201.12 218.09
  228.11 228.25 230.30
  232.05 234.16 236.07
  239.15 244.19 251.11
  257.11 269.19 270.20
  272.25 273.16 281.20
  288.03 293.28 303.23
  309.01 310.06 316.05
  322.23 322.25 322.25
  328.21 329.28 330.17
  330.24 331.06 331.10
  335.14 336.12 339.02
  344.27 346.06 353.10
  363.11 363.22 375.03
  376.16 385.04 394.18
  401.26 420.23 431.14
  431.14 433.22 436.01
  438.24 441.12 452.18
  456.09 458.03 458.03
  461.19 469.01 472.11
  481.11 488.03 489.08
  490.02 494.21 505.12
  505.13 511.21 512.08
DAY'S 119.20 330.23
  335.06 364.10
DAYLIGHT 127.30 167.04
  226.20 236.14 451.11
  483.22 497.19
DAYS 11.22 18.04
  22.23 26.01 38.08
  38.09 42.04 52.04
  59.03 64.24 69.30
  76.14 78.08 81.23
  91.14 98.16 99.07
  128.22 156.26 165.21
  244.09 251.26 267.14
  282.11 283.08 306.02
  337.07 353.03 361.24
  370.19 377.01 417.13
  420.23 421.13 426.28
  429.01 429.24 433.03
  434.10 435.15 436.15
  441.03 442.14 442.24
  475.12 503.11 513.18
  515.21 516.08
DAYS' 86.25 222.22
DAZED 11.23 34.19

DAZZLED 216.23 295.29
DAZZLING 191.27 216.16
DAZZLINGLY 371.15
DE 43.21 43.22
  169.06 169.14 170.16
  172.20 173.10 173.20
  173.22 182.09 182.10
  184.25 244.14 245.02
DEAD 17.13 24.15
  65.06 103.18 103.18
  119.12 130.01 131.04
  131.27 132.19 133.22
  152.18 153.23 163.09
  163.10 163.23 163.23
  167.20 169.14 176.05
  183.11 194.20 198.11
  212.07 247.18 255.23
  268.03 271.22 301.30
  342.03 355.16 358.01
  371.23 371.25 372.15
  373.09 388.28 391.04
  397.17 435.24 441.15
  446.13 459.27 460.04
  462.18 466.08 471.20
  471.26 472.02 473.12
  500.21 501.05 502.13
  505.22 514.10 515.18
DEAD-AND-GONE 119.12
DEADLIEST 117.20
  331.04 477.10
DEADLY 33.04 50.09
  110.29 115.20 352.05
  358.11 406.01 454.10
  479.23
DEAF 26.04 152.17
  199.22 232.21 431.16
  433.08 462.17
DEAL 9.01 75.14
  102.22 169.12 209.22
  243.16 252.05 281.13
DEALING 239.02 404.19
  461.16
DEALINGS 419.06
DEALS 212.26
DEALT 252.14 453.28
DEAN 95.09
DEAR 41.08 58.26
  100.24 126.17 140.25
  140.25 140.26 188.03
  205.28 220.08 226.08
  251.24 271.08 285.23
  295.02 328.09 333.16
  377.26 400.30 412.17
  421.19 422.09
DEARLY 374.29
DEATH 13.24 59.28
  74.10 98.07 102.04
  104.23 105.24 115.28
  119.02 119.26 127.15
  127.30 138.09 138.18
  138.26 147.03 152.07
  157.06 182.26 193.17
  194.28 215.10 247.11
  252.30 263.30 273.10
  273.11 273.26 277.01
  277.07 316.13 331.22
  340.17 358.23 372.11
  395.09 431.19 438.14
  442.03 449.09 458.12
  460.14 471.27 474.21
  475.28
DEATH-BED 273.26
DEATH-SENTENCE 193.17
DEATH'S 20.14
DEATHBED 499.28
DEATHBLOW 452.07
DEATHLIKE 362.08
DEBAUCHERIES 12.22
DEBILITATED 474.19
DEBT 77.08 280.29
DECAY 14.16 317.02
DECEASED 383.25
DECEITFUL 188.02
  355.24 405.25
DECEIVED 402.23 486.03
  487.05
DECEIVING 367.01
DECENCIES 88.18
DECENCY 80.29 81.07
  86.16 279.08

DECENT 41.16 49.02
52.15 60.21 81.03
232.24 273.22 394.16
400.27
DECENTLY 41.22 51.11
225.15 508.28
DECEPTION 93.22
117.02 366.27 418.16
DECEPTIVE 262.04
DECIDE 262.03 300.01
DECIDED 167.15 280.13
331.15 450.23 506.16
DECISION 97.07 112.07
DECISIVE 449.04 449.20
DECK 5.07 7.29
12.04 14.03 15.16
17.30 20.08 21.13
26.07 29.19 35.03
51.20 53.20 70.10
72.11 101.12 101.20
101.21 102.16 109.27
131.15 144.26 167.14
182.23 229.05 244.12
292.03 439.19
DECK-CHAIR 21.13
229.05
DECK-CHAIRS 14.03
DECK-WINCH 26.07
DECK' 244.04
DECKS 167.05
DECLAIM 355.22
DECLAIMING 464.28
DECLARATION 95.03
154.15 487.02
DECLARE 41.02 43.25
87.22 228.19 241.09
DECLARED 4.16 80.11
97.05 118.30 140.18
194.10 226.07 329.03
329.14 361.29 402.06
404.08 450.14 451.12
452.08 468.02 485.26
493.12 501.30
DECLARES 44.11 45.21
DECLARING 337.06
DECLINED 81.25
DECLINES 106.07
DECLINING 319.10
DECOMPOSED 63.13
DECORUM 88.19
DECOYED 112.05
DECREE 53.07 307.25
DECREPIT 20.13 366.06
DEEDS 23.12
DEEP 1.06 6.25
19.12 31.04 38.27
52.06 70.13 102.24
114.23 116.30 116.30
119.18 130.24 135.08
136.04 139.14 154.11
155.21 155.22 196.09
213.18 223.08 233.12
246.09 261.02 261.02
261.12 269.13 288.11
299.13 303.04 333.20
338.09 347.13 378.27
420.09 428.23 434.24
444.05 459.26 462.16
467.22 510.01
DEEP-ROOTED 130.24
DEEP-SET 261.12
DEEPENED 89.06
DEEPER 100.16 376.29
376.29
DEEPLY 305.05 345.29
355.03 390.08 409.07
DEER 251.20
DEER-HUNT 251.20
DEFEAT 7.14 399.27
453.24
DEFEATED 186.13 336.01
DEFECTION 453.25
DEFENCE 84.16 119.24
420.08 483.29 506.25
DEFENCELESS 278.27
355.04 383.24 441.29
DEFENCES 114.18 452.21
DEFEND 84.20 185.17
254.21 370.23 444.09
450.16 511.23

DEFENDANT 83.09
DEFENDERS 448.01
DEFENSIVE 148.26
DEFERENCE 24.19
205.30 432.25
DEFERENTIAL 506.25
DEFIANCE 279.08 288.27
289.06 499.29
DEFIED 361.28 458.30
506.18
DEFILED 49.03
DEFINE 245.14
DEFINED 69.05
DEFINITE 36.15 112.06
193.29 252.21
DEFINITELY 225.20
229.19
DEFORMITY 399.25
DEFY 62.01 138.18
277.01 430.27 506.11
DEFYING 167.27 252.28
DEGRADATION 127.14
222.09
DEGREE 17.05
DEGREES 71.17 72.04
DEJECTED 466.19
DEJECTEDLY 21.04
481.29
DELAY 290.17 309.22
453.07 454.22
DELAYED 497.17
DELIBERATE 35.30
38.16 105.08 176.23
246.23 319.05
DELIBERATELY 97.03
134.10 226.14 337.03
371.19 418.04 515.11
DELIBERATING 85.25
154.05 157.06
DELIBERATION 180.14
322.08 447.20
DELIBERATIONS 310.06
DELICACY 190.21 223.05
304.03 323.06
DELICATE 60.23 60.24
75.05 172.04 240.05
242.25 252.29 319.18
342.26 381.03
DELICATELY 33.24
193.01
DELIGHTED 274.23
396.01 490.05
DELIGHTFUL 286.26
DELIRIOUSLY 466.25
DELIRIUM 65.01
DELIVER 420.02 456.20
DELIVERED 172.16
179.04 445.16 449.09
466.11 499.06
DELIVERING 300.14
492.04
DELIVERY 294.09 307.04
DELUGE 136.14 220.26
DELUSION 86.04
DEMAND 186.24 272.07
306.14
DEMANDED 33.11 169.28
298.22 453.03 481.21
498.24
DEMANDING 454.04
DEMANDS 178.19
DEMEANOUR 82.11
87.01 172.29 294.12
454.03
DEMOCRATIC 113.17
DEMOLISH 85.09
DEMON 236.24 479.15
DEMONSTRATE 1.16
436.11
DEMONSTRATED 351.14
DEMONSTRATING 30.11
246.23
DEMONSTRATION 173.15
501.20
DEMORALISATION 399.26
DENIALS 328.08
DENN 257.03
DENSE 283.01 367.15
408.19 459.08

DENSER 129.15
DENUNCIATIONS 355.22
DENVER 231.13
DENY 87.01 88.21
88.23
DEPART 2.28 501.23
508.11
DEPARTED 28.11 55.28
56.01 278.01 294.14
462.12
DEPARTING 5.02
490.09 496.08 499.06
DEPEND 77.16
DEPENDANTS 252.10
279.23 306.05 315.21
DEPENDING 76.01
DEPENDS 401.05
DEPICT 48.14 116.13
DEPLORABLE 3.24
59.13 88.07 90.24
184.18
DEPLORABLY 64.05
DEPLORE 243.13
DEPOSIT 211.10
DEPOSITION 70.23
DEPRAVITY 422.11
DEPRESSED 94.23
191.13 299.20
DEPRESSION 398.25
DEPRIVE 80.17
DEPTH 497.05
DEPTHS 21.21 22.26
53.23 155.08 176.02
263.13 264.06 335.16
385.23 417.01 425.19
DEPUTED 310.16
DEPUTY 343.07
DEPUTY-ASSISTANT 343.07
DERANGE 179.10
DERELICT 194.12
DERISION 17.03 224.11
DERIVED 292.14 425.16
DESCEND 46.16
DESCENDED 13.13
18.11 64.14 175.30
280.04 298.21 301.30
374.13
DESCENDING 15.25
366.24
DESCENT 17.26 343.08
DESCRIBE 163.12 180.13
258.02
DESCRIBED 126.28
149.09 169.14 254.10
439.12
DESCRIBING 257.29
DESCRIPTION 117.21
378.16
DESCRIPTIVE 252.18
DESE 16.14
DESERT 106.14
DESERTED 64.12 135.02
300.24 316.28 340.30
435.14 443.04 459.11
DESERTER 440.07 459.21
467.01
DESERTION 280.19
357.21
DESERVE 223.18 473.13
473.14
DESERVING 268.29
DESIGN 407.04
DESIRABLE 122.12
DESIRE 12.09 15.28
57.07 60.03 95.23
106.06 106.08 156.23
185.13 213.08 257.12
275.07 277.01 278.30
283.15 399.08 469.17
483.06
DESIRED 230.10 246.04
256.26 266.17 270.13
292.16 317.05 385.27
458.28
DESIRES 501.18
DESIROUS 87.02
DESISTING 385.29
467.01
DESK 33.20 44.15
45.15 193.08 195.15

DESK (CONT.) 209.02
232.19 241.21 248.15
249.04 258.30 259.07
259.19 261.23
DESOLATE 76.08 262.13
513.24
DESPAIR 82.21 108.13
115.25 122.16 138.07
187.29 222.09 277.04
393.17 430.09
DESPAIRED 223.10
DESPAIRING 5.17
12.09 368.02 479.11
DESPAIRINGLY 505.02
DESPERADOES 436.15
452.28
DESPERATE 60.18
63.15 103.25 125.08
125.14 206.07 313.10
356.30 365.09 390.23
440.24 446.03 451.28
458.22 470.09 470.28
DESPERATELY 115.14
234.04 272.17 312.09
426.08
DESPERATION 313.22
DESPISE 68.17 235.18
DESPONDENCY 464.05
DESTINE 478.01
DESTINED 4.26 117.27
299.07 397.16
DESTINY 119.27 166.24
226.28 264.20 277.17
395.18 421.08 423.16
486.09 508.06
DESTITUTE 229.29
DESTITUTION 474.23
DESTROY 11.12
DESTROYED 261.21
449.15
DESTROYS 81.08
DESTRUCTION 30.27
212.26 252.28 503.09
DESTRUCTIVE 60.10
260.30 261.24 413.05
DETACH 440.18
DETACHED 99.10 295.24
371.07 414.21 493.11
DETACHING 175.12
DETACHMENT 179.07
489.26
DETAIL 38.23 91.08
103.30 185.11 372.09
440.23
DETAILED 392.23
DETAILS 59.13 281.07
363.02 409.22
DETAIN 428.27 456.23
DETAINED 195.27 332.24
DETECT 9.04 223.08
289.03 378.25 497.22
DETECTED 14.15 47.14
107.08 378.06
DETECTING 478.01
DETECTION 173.02
DETERMINATION 14.16
57.07 202.05 365.10
DETERMINED 456.06
DETESTABLE 35.25
DETONATION 159.11
DETONATIONS 445.11
DEUCE 287.13
DEUCEDLY 374.24
DEVASTATED 316.27
DEVASTATING 222.03
DEVASTATION 12.03
DEVELOP 190.10
DEVELOPMENT 44.27
DEVIATED 466.01
DEVICES 117.05
DEVIL 14.08 35.01
40.06 40.08 76.21
114.04 116.22 130.07
130.13 144.14 157.04
170.14 176.21 183.01
201.12 209.19 212.16
223.18 236.08 238.23
238.25 259.26 287.04
292.18 308.06 336.20
355.24 355.24 356.01

DEVIL (CONT.) 357.13
361.05 383.25 390.01
394.19 405.04 405.05
405.26 426.05 435.20
438.12 439.17 472.17
479.04
DEVIL'S 472.08
DEVILISH 205.11
DEVILISHLY 132.20
DEVILRY 194.29
DEVILS 25.23 489.08
DEVIOUS 40.16
DEVIOUSLY 399.20
DEVISE 321.11
DEVISED 321.12
DEVOID 112.26
DEVOTED 349.18 366.03
439.06
DEVOTION 2.17 5.18
12.24 333.01 358.24
432.17
DEVOURED 325.18
DEVOURING 25.15
276.14 511.07
DEVOUT 176.19
DEW 228.09 328.29
440.15 468.23
DEWY 331.30
DIABLE 179.03
DIABOLICAL 40.17
DIAGNOSED 258.26
DIAL 72.03
DIALECT 393.21
DIAMETER 240.11
DICE 394.23
DICK 436.06
DICTIONARY 292.15
DID 8.20 11.25
22.04 25.30 26.12
27.21 28.20 28.27
33.16 33.29 34.12
34.29 36.25 38.13
42.15 44.12 46.11
47.26 48.02 48.05
54.05 55.24 56.04
60.02 60.03 60.24
61.05 66.08 68.02
68.17 73.15 76.20
76.22 77.04 80.12
84.12 85.17 85.19
86.24 86.27 86.28
95.18 96.02 96.25
96.26 98.14 98.22
101.08 103.01 103.21
104.06 104.13 108.17
108.17 112.03 118.04
119.02 119.28 119.29
129.14 129.20 130.08
131.26 132.28 132.28
137.30 139.25 139.25
141.15 143.12 143.12
143.25 144.01 144.22
144.24 147.26 151.30
152.12 153.18 153.23
157.30 158.01 160.01
160.02 160.15 163.18
153.21 164.02 164.02
164.06 164.22 164.22
164.29 165.26 167.14
158.13 168.20 171.23
172.26 177.19 179.16
184.15 186.29 190.06
191.12 191.19 198.04
198.23 199.23 207.01
212.07 217.10 217.17
218.03 218.12 222.02
225.02 226.27 230.21
233.23 234.01 240.09
242.01 244.09 245.04
258.16 262.27 264.16
264.28 264.29 265.08
270.24 274.19 278.24
278.30 280.05 281.20
283.17 283.21 285.01
285.18 285.19 285.22
289.01 289.18 289.28
289.29 298.13 300.16
309.20 310.23 312.29
318.04 321.05 325.05
325.06 337.21 342.03

DID (CONT.) 347.16
353.06 353.15 356.22
359.02 359.20 359.22
360.01 360.16 364.21
365.10 366.05 368.20
371.24 373.08 374.14
376.17 381.15 381.19
382.09 383.15 385.02
385.13 385.15 387.18
387.22 391.09 392.27
394.14 394.19 395.03
395.04 400.20 401.17
403.14 403.26 403.27
414.13 425.06 426.09
428.10 430.24 430.30
440.27 446.06 456.30
466.26 470.24 470.28
473.19 473.19 474.07
475.05 477.18 481.10
481.16 484.08 484.28
488.10 488.14 488.18
492.09 493.05 496.03
500.29 502.29 503.05
503.10 506.04 507.09
510.24 512.25 513.07
514.05
DIDN'T 35.01 40.23
45.27 52.24 71.12
74.07 84.21 87.03
88.14 88.14 89.28
95.29 95.30 97.13
99.17 101.05 105.21
109.10 109.22 110.21
110.21 116.28 119.07
129.25 134.27 139.03
144.15 144.28 144.29
145.17 150.30 153.23
153.24 154.01 159.01
159.02 163.07 164.08
168.22 172.13 176.01
186.18 191.08 198.28
200.08 200.24 207.24
216.09 230.23 238.04
242.04 244.12 283.11
285.15 286.02 287.15
308.02 320.22 329.16
331.08 355.01 361.15
362.21 372.08 374.26
383.01 383.18 383.26
385.11 396.09 396.11
401.12 403.08 403.13
413.24 440.13 442.12
450.13 463.20 464.06
477.12 478.25 479.12
479.13 481.21 492.04
DIE 26.03 26.23
46.04 51.12 53.06
105.30 106.01 123.27
128.06 128.10 130.08
135.06 153.29 154.06
166.22 177.26 177.26
179.15 184.21 225.18
250.25 274.21 312.08
324.29 347.11 361.12
385.11 385.13 396.05
405.06 405.08 426.11
430.15 466.16
DIED 137.07 226.18
251.02 268.27 282.06
362.14 370.30 379.16
385.17 386.07 427.16
436.26 466.21 476.02
485.07 502.05
DIEU 170.27 174.07
DIFFERENCE 240.07
245.09 245.11 272.09
272.09 315.01 321.22
340.06 452.15 453.30
DIFFERENT 28.29
75.13 91.03 251.30
259.20 288.02 366.17
375.01 387.24 409.08
434.01 451.16
DIFFICULT 98.28
114.02 156.03 159.17
196.06 212.14 263.27
324.01 337.19 350.16
390.14 424.09 485.22
512.17
DIFFICULTIES 114.16

DIFFICULTIES (CONT.)
247.23 361.23
DIFFICULTY 38.19
176.11 179.24 189.10
192.29 208.03 246.05
309.25 317.12 318.24
338.28 361.08 449.01
485.18
DIFFUSED 269.22 376.21
DIGESTION 246.29
DIGGING 435.15
DIGNIFIED 57.13
337.05
DIGNITARY 311.10
DIGNITY 80.20 304.30
315.18 318.15 333.25
DILAPIDATED 452.24
DILATED 100.03 192.24
371.25
DILATING 393.11
DILATORY 449.06
DILIGENT 490.01
DIM 20.18 120.27
128.01 155.04 192.14
201.21 210.27 220.19
225.21 279.30 342.20
488.05
DIMINISHED 149.01
281.06 317.13
DIMLY 245.12 248.03
398.13 429.29 500.10
DIMNESS 248.24 262.05
DIMPLED 348.10
DIN 334.04 444.06
DINE 221.02
DINED 91.15
DINES 243.01
DINGY 55.04
DINING 92.02 92.09
146.06 211.14 248.03
448.22
DINING-HALL 146.06
DINING-ROOM 92.02
211.14 248.03 448.22
DINNER 38.25 41.08
41.08 41.26 285.02
488.30
DINNER-SERVICE 488.30
DIP 107.03
DIPLOMACY 457.02
463.29 490.02
DIPLOMATIC 449.20
DIPLOMATIST 451.21
DIPPED 128.20 390.24
401.20 414.06 496.01
DIRECTED 1.09 6.12
38.01 170.25 348.22
426.24 447.06 450.28
DIRECTING 35.23
232.17 324.10
DIRECTION 56.17
79.03 88.25 208.23
274.03 326.03 398.28
481.29 514.07
DIRECTIONS 451.16
DIRECTLY 13.13 51.13
75.04 83.27 99.14
120.11 133.17 145.03
233.14 264.11 300.06
340.05 386.23 425.23
488.21 490.29
DIRT 78.30 256.16
259.22 454.30
DIRTY 25.19 70.15
149.22 181.21 279.05
279.24 398.30 410.21
426.21 436.06 441.02
452.18 474.09 474.10
DIS 83.30 181.30
241.17
DIS- 83.30 181.30
DISABLED 11.19
DISADVANTAGES 69.01
DISAPPEAR 195.11
258.18 273.02 481.17
DISAPPEARANCE 280.26
DISAPPEARED 55.09
56.01 152.17 202.07
374.02 433.30 437.01
464.09

DISAPPEARING 18.05
351.12 470.04
DISAPPOINTED 179.18
355.14 370.11 429.10
DISAPPOINTING 482.01
DISAPPOINTMENT 74.29
89.15 177.02
DISASTER 105.29 134.22
147.26 182.18 209.22
384.27 418.12 434.16
478.09 506.17 506.18
DISASTROUS 191.04
448.10
DISBELIEVE 376.09
DISC 25.03 269.24
396.30
DISCERN 86.07
DISCERNED 510.05
DISCHARGE 500.23
500.29 501.09
DISCHARGED 443.19
DISCIPLINE 191.12
DISCLAIM 332.10
DISCLAIMING 287.20
DISCLOSE 358.02
DISCLOSED 63.06
66.17 180.14 398.22
446.01 509.19
DISCLOSING 369.29
DISCLOSURE 66.14
138.21
DISCOMFITURE 64.04
DISCOMFORT 112.15
DISCOMPOSED 195.28
505.20
DISCOMPOSING 44.23
298.23
DISCONCERTED 181.11
DISCONTENTED 481.22
DISCOUNT 65.03
DISCOURAGED 36.22
181.30
DISCOURAGING 82.19
456.16
DISCOVER 240.03 321.30
353.21 389.23
DISCOVERED 95.22
116.08 186.16 187.18
196.21 299.25 344.28
404.17 425.04
DISCOVERING 167.20
DISCOVERY 98.18
98.19 171.13 226.06
DISCREET 98.01 215.04
384.07
DISCREETLY 453.15
DISCRETION 88.17
88.17 120.05 215.08
278.14
DISCRIMINATING 113.09
DISCRIMINATION 177.18
DISCUSS 427.26
DISCUSSED 482.29
DISCUSSING 93.23
DISCUSSION 165.08
262.29 264.25 310.03
416.08
DISCUSSIONS 42.27
DISDAIN 14.23 88.08
147.29 166.18 187.24
351.16 438.09 463.13
DISEASE 12.21 54.15
DISEASED 475.28
DISEASES 277.03
DISEMBODIED 271.25
302.03 389.10 516.12
DISENCHANTING 10.12
DISENCHANTMENT 156.21
DISENGAGED 397.03
DISFIGURED 372.05
DISGRACE 80.27 215.20
235.17
DISGRACEFULLY 242.26
DISGUST 172.09 293.01
352.30 367.04 418.12
DISGUSTED 308.21
DISGUSTING 352.18
353.18
DISHES 267.16 488.30
DISHEVELLED 149.06

DISHEVELLED (CONT.)
514.09
DISHONOUR 127.15
DISJOINTED 137.29
DISLIKE 28.26
DISLIKED 453.20
DISMAL 27.30 128.08
386.18 429.07 497.11
DISMALLY 204.14
DISMAY 332.07 460.11
478.08 509.28
DISMAYED 163.05 242.19
DISMISS 376.04
DISMISSAL 14.06
DISMISSED 499.13
DISMOUNTED 256.12
DISMOUNTING 251.19
DISORDER 12.02 386.19
DISORDERED 394.05
504.16
DISPARAGEMENT 406.04
DISPASSIONATELY 9.03
171.26 404.20
DISPASSIONATENESS
302.02
DISPATCHED 309.17
451.16 461.12
DISPENSED 58.21
DISPIRITED 258.07
DISPLAY 8.21 56.07
94.02 172.23 189.08
224.30 294.16 318.15
352.28 365.29
DISPLAYED 1.06
54.27 123.26 304.25
392.20 410.02
DISPLAYING 252.29
DISPLEASED 183.25
DISPORT 55.23
DISPOSAL 386.29
DISPOSE 244.15 270.14
270.15
DISPOSED 129.10 155.07
268.27 327.04
DISPOSITION 67.15
322.07
DISPOSITIONS 180.06
180.07
DISPROPORTION 478.22
DISPUTE 111.28 112.07
387.22
DISPUTING 423.25
DISREGARD 195.03
232.13 351.28
DISREGARDED 292.19
400.30 423.07 441.16
DISREPUTABLE 86.22
112.09 306.20 335.10
DISSENT 95.26 178.09
DISSIMILAR 378.30
DISSOLVE 136.22
DISSOLVING 22.08
DISTANCE 5.05 17.23
17.27 46.22 60.14
54.04 72.05 125.16
125.16 125.17 127.17
129.14 137.07 138.12
260.13 279.22 281.04
291.28 318.18 323.25
333.05 355.22 361.05
388.12 408.24 411.02
422.06 441.12 459.16
452.25 462.25 513.07
DISTANCES 487.21
DISTANT 38.21 155.07
168.04 217.06 254.05
261.22 263.10 266.20
270.26 277.14 345.07
370.09 417.22 463.10
DISTENDED 55.15
DISTILLED 149.24
DISTINCT 32.19 33.08
55.08 59.19 104.14
146.10 155.15 162.06
193.09 195.03 212.20
216.19 323.08 348.03
391.01 417.25 420.18
434.06 464.22
DISTINCTION 14.03
92.15 98.24 100.02

DISTINCTION (CONT.)
247.07
DISTINCTIVE 270.06
DISTINCTLY 88.22
97.05 218.11 270.19
313.02 326.04 376.26
406.06 478.17
DISTINGUISH 139.04
380.16
DISTINGUISHABLE 434.02
DISTINGUISHED 319.24
321.19 333.10 352.10
436.02
DISTORTED 119.14
DISTRACTED 36.06
64.15 117.22 190.08
364.21
DISTRACTING 104.09
137.06
DISTRACTION 127.06
DISTRESS 57.27 68.04
103.26 167.03 170.09
210.18 217.07 345.09
390.09 429.04
DISTRESSED 62.27
108.07
DISTRESSFUL 431.29
DISTRESSING 184.06
DISTRIBUTING 185.04
DISTRIBUTION 451.13
DISTRICT 269.07
DISTRICTS 278.11
DISTRUST 454.25
DISTURBANCE 120.03
123.20 210.14 342.17
DISTURBED 51.16
77.17 132.07 162.04
251.02 283.04 365.06
366.05
DISTURBING 4.03
222.14 253.21
DITCH 420.09
DIVE 123.24 407.17
DIVERGING 19.15
DIVIDED 276.09 461.18
DIVIDERS 22.30 71.03
DIVIDING 29.02
DIVINE 23.19
DIVING 374.03 432.05
DIVORCE 330.01
DO 7.25 20.26
25.25 26.29 29.09
29.16 29.18 29.21
30.04 43.41 47.20
48.10 51.13 53.11
60.22 69.07 70.38
75.01 81.01 81.20
87.03 90.16 91.04
96.06 96.16 96.18
96.19 97.07 97.08
100.06 101.17 101.26
104.04 104.22 105.07
110.14 111.12 111.19
119.30 120.01 120.02
124.25 128.17 128.28
130.23 138.13 139.19
141.03 144.23 148.15
148.24 152.15 152.16
154.04 156.09 158.09
158.24 160.05 160.24
163.30 164.27 164.29
171.30 178.27 178.30
179.26 184.02 186.06
187.15 188.27 197.12
197.15 199.21 199.21
199.21 199.21 200.04
200.14 200.25 203.17
203.22 204.09 204.11
205.08 205.13 205.14
207.07 222.24 223.13
223.16 229.20 233.11
234.07 234.21 237.22
243.10 244.12 245.07
245.17 253.16 260.28
263.03 264.30 265.05
265.13 266.24 267.29
269.03 272.01 272.01
272.25 274.05 275.17
281.20 282.23 283.04
286.10 287.07 287.10

DO (CONT.) 287.12
290.23 294.11 298.27
301.22 308.07 308.22
308.26 309.21 311.01
314.15 320.25 321.05
328.03 338.02 343.30
345.28 346.10 347.08
353.28 357.08 357.28
361.20 365.24 367.04
376.07 381.07 383.04
383.15 386.11 387.03
388.16 390.15 391.11
391.11 391.28 394.15
399.12 401.02 401.07
402.09 407.17 411.28
415.10 420.05 422.13
429.02 433.01 433.21
446.12 455.26 456.02
457.08 460.13 464.24
464.25 464.25 467.07
468.03 468.18 469.13
472.17 472.20 473.13
473.16 477.01 481.07
481.23 484.06 492.09
492.30 494.23 506.02
511.10 511.13 513.15
DOCK 23.09 52.06
110.23
DOCTOR 12.21
DOCTORED 28.05
DOCUMENTARY 92.17
DODGE 212.21
DODGED 109.26
DODGES 96.03
DODGING 466.11
DOERS 486.08
DOES 52.25 78.28
79.14 79.20 97.04
155.13 157.16 171.04
177.26 179.15 180.23
233.08 266.04 340.29
341.03 382.21 390.14
400.10 402.27 402.28
455.22 464.24 493.01
507.15
DOESN'T 65.02 267.29
DOG 40.13 68.28
72.08 72.12 72.15
76.05 76.07 76.25
83.21 83.22 83.25
84.09 88.27 88.28
DOGGED 1.07 392.20
DOGS 83.23 181.07
188.29 216.04 350.27
463.25
DOING 14.13 14.21
29.26 50.13 57.13
63.16 143.10 150.18
202.29 223.16 223.29
229.02 282.29 354.10
395.24 428.07 437.24
457.03
DOLE 487.24
DOLEFULLY 77.21
DOLES 455.04
DOLLARS 30.05 273.20
353.05 358.16 358.21
383.18 383.18 383.24
402.18 438.11 454.09
DOMAIN 302.08
DOME 25.03
DOMESTIC 450.09 459.15
DOMESTICATED 92.06
DOMINATED 325.24
DOMINATING 214.04
DON'T 8.06 25.28
29.24 40.07 46.01
49.02 49.12 49.13
50.26 51.01 52.02
52.07 53.17 53.28
55.27 61.26 62.13
62.26 65.06 67.11
68.18 72.21 72.29
75.02 77.11 79.18
79.24 80.05 80.06
80.06 80.20 81.02
83.21 85.07 86.09
87.01 87.08 87.22
88.05 88.09 88.20

DON'T (CONT.) 88.21
88.23 91.03 91.05
94.22 97.08 97.10
97.17 98.05 99.12
109.29 109.29 110.16
111.11 122.13 124.01
128.15 129.11 129.13
130.20 130.25 141.09
145.05 148.18 150.14
154.13 155.13 155.14
156.01 156.05 158.20
159.18 165.02 168.19
169.17 177.12 180.04
180.05 181.16 183.30
185.12 185.13 185.17
188.04 188.07 189.03
190.17 197.14 197.21
198.06 198.07 200.20
201.09 201.15 203.04
205.13 205.14 205.27
208.01 210.21 214.01
215.16 218.18 219.21
219.22 220.01 223.13
225.23 226.08 228.26
231.06 231.11 234.12
237.21 238.03 241.24
249.30 253.27 265.06
266.01 268.05 269.02
272.05 272.08 282.17
290.04 295.14 295.27
300.30 303.22 303.25
314.07 314.20 325.06
325.28 326.01 328.09
338.04 339.09 339.16
342.12 344.07 344.16
350.23 356.15 361.10
374.15 374.23 374.26
375.24 376.24 377.07
378.18 378.29 384.24
386.23 391.14 391.21
394.18 394.20 399.26
401.04 401.07 402.23
412.17 415.10 418.07
426.12 433.20 436.18
451.05 472.01 472.11
472.19 472.21 472.27
473.12 473.20 474.05
476.07 477.01 481.03
481.04 491.23 497.01
497.12
DON'T-CARE-HANG 53.28
DON'T-YOU-TOUCH-ME
476.07
DONE 8.29 27.12
33.16 41.01 52.02
58.09 62.02 71.05
71.13 74.02 78.29
87.14 97.08 103.11
105.07 111.17 124.20
128.22 128.27 137.02
143.25 144.12 150.07
150.15 152.23 159.03
159.05 160.11 168.13
172.03 176.15 183.19
184.22 185.10 186.02
190.17 192.25 201.16
204.22 211.30 225.26
231.12 235.02 237.07
239.12 267.27 272.29
282.11 307.20 321.13
325.03 325.05 354.01
356.16 362.18 377.04
377.14 377.24 377.25
391.27 396.08 405.13
421.09 433.10 442.01
454.15 472.23 474.01
479.01 489.07 497.11
502.29 505.14
DONKEY 129.28 144.13
184.15
DONKEY-MAN 129.28
144.13
DONKEYMAN 194.27
DONKEYS 105.03 120.26
DONNERWETTER 153.29
DOOMED 56.26 103.16
339.13 399.29 503.09
DOOR 21.23 45.07
45.11 45.15 51.08
54.23 58.25 82.29

DOOR (CONT.)   83.10
83.19   84.10   175.23
181.25   195.25   209.12
211.02   211.15   214.14
216.28   220.30   221.08
226.12   226.19   228.13
228.28   232.15   233.06
233.25   234.03   238.04
248.06   255.24   264.24
283.16   283.23   287.23
288.13   309.27   342.17
366.20   369.23   369.28
370.22   385.27   386.06
427.04   428.04   429.08
429.19   483.02   505.10
507.11   507.19   514.29
DOOR-HANDLE   54.23
DOORS   216.26   232.06
DOORWAY 89.02   221.07
373.03   483.09   508.09
510.16
DOORWAYS 357.04   430.04
DOR   221.01
DORAMIN 285.11   285.19
286.10   307.08   313.28
313.28   315.15   317.11
318.01   320.02   324.11
333.17   337.01   337.26
338.07   353.30   357.27
369.09   369.09   407.20
420.11   443.14   448.28
450.11   450.22   451.01
451.06   453.20   462.13
465.27   482.27   483.04
483.10   484.16   484.28
486.15   487.08   498.30
505.02   509.20   509.27
513.24   514.04   514.18
515.03   515.14
DORAMIN'S   307.06
314.10   314.12   314.21
321.17   323.20   351.23
352.03   363.08   388.01
508.27   509.01   509.17
513.08
DORMANT 174.12
DOTTED   13.07
DOUBLE   24.17   396.20
444.27   461.16   466.11
DOUBLE-DEALING   461.16
DOUBLED 362.10   383.21
DOUBT   45.22   59.26
59.28   60.18   66.05
68.12   68.28   69.23
96.25   98.19   98.30
117.19   124.09   137.01
140.06   164.27   164.29
165.04   176.09   176.09
186.14   186.20   190.21
208.18   209.17   226.04
239.19   262.11   267.13
268.17   270.23   278.29
320.26   327.09   334.20
342.02   346.11   352.05
360.02   363.10   391.16
394.22   414.06   414.28
427.13   429.16   450.29
458.19   482.29   485.08
488.11
DOUBTED 38.14   140.09
DOUBTFUL 371.05   463.19
DOUBTFULLY   201.20
DOUBTING 388.05
DOUBTLESS   170.15
DOUBTS   98.11   258.07
239.06   508.19
DOUTE   170.15
DOVER   272.27
DOWN   4.25   6.06
12.03   12.18   15.17
19.19   20.21   23.27
24.30   25.10   26.06
29.20   30.14   31.10
31.10   34.21   34.24
34.28   35.05   37.04
37.12   43.33   45.23
47.18   55.13   58.26
59.02   61.02   62.29
63.10   63.17   64.16
67.08   71.02   71.13

DOWN (CONT.)   72.08
72.26   73.09   75.24
82.26   83.05   83.30
84.10   85.19   89.06
97.02   99.24   100.28
102.17   102.29   103.12
104.24   105.22   107.15
109.13   110.04   111.02
111.08   118.25   122.13
123.24   123.24   130.18
132.03   132.20   133.03
133.22   133.27   134.02
134.08   136.19   137.19
138.23   140.17   140.20
140.28   148.14   152.08
154.13   155.22   160.14
160.22   163.01   163.06
165.18   165.24   166.03
167.02   178.03   181.27
181.30   183.14   183.28
184.16   187.07   188.13
188.25   198.18   199.06
199.19   201.06   201.19
208.25   210.03   210.28
218.27   218.27   222.04
224.17   226.05   226.13
230.17   230.30   234.10
235.30   236.05   244.05
253.25   256.14   258.21
259.07   259.25   261.22
278.25   285.08   292.27
300.08   308.11   309.29
310.11   310.20   311.30
314.06   314.12   318.15
318.22   324.05   324.09
324.12   329.05   332.10
333.26   336.10   344.29
348.09   349.15   353.08
360.24   362.17   370.02
374.23   394.03   396.09
396.18   401.21   401.26
403.15   409.05   410.12
416.18   417.24   420.29
423.26   428.21   430.01
430.11   430.25   437.02
438.07   440.23   443.20
444.22   445.03   451.02
453.06   454.26   455.06
456.11   459.26   460.03
460.12   461.04   463.18
463.24   465.23   466.30
467.18   468.03   470.06
471.25   472.20   472.21
474.02   476.11   478.20
479.30   481.08   481.10
481.19   482.04   484.21
489.21   490.19   490.27
490.30   491.16   492.06
492.18   493.07   493.24
494.22   495.11   499.08
499.16   501.05   502.14
504.14   506.01   507.25
508.30   509.03   510.07
510.26   510.20   512.16
512.22   514.28
DOWN-RIVER   467.18
DOWN-STREAM   474.02
DOWNCAST 85.20   128.06
173.12   176.18   375.25
466.20
DOWNHILL 460.19
DOWNPOUR 220.13
DOWNRIGHT   157.27
DOWNWARD 246.09   296.06
DOWNWARDS   24.28
62.08   88.24   110.25
171.02
DOZE   29.03   300.16
DOZED   21.04
DOZEN   203.19   447.24
450.09
DOZING   463.30
DRAB   191.29   428.20
432.20
DRAG   199.23
DRAGGED 250.21   316.02
DRAINED 179.14
DRANK   42.13   97.02
152.19   178.18   238.05
308.08

DRAPED   20.24   38.26
192.16   409.25
DRAPERIES   37.14
430.04
DRAPERY 94.16   139.17
DRATTED 30.07   202.21
DRAUGHT 20.15   140.02
370.04   440.17
DRAW   287.30   321.23
387.19   461.01   482.02
DRAWING 22.24
DRAWING-PINS   22.24
DRAWING-ROOM   429.08
DRAWL   52.21   92.23
DRAWLING 343.17   387.30
DRAWN   17.18   20.30
23.03   23.24   23.25
129.08   293.20   365.15
384.04   409.28   471.22
473.02
DRAWN-UP 20.30
DRAWS   256.02   272.03
272.04
DREAD   385.23   385.23
DREAM   21.20   51.28
145.13   160.28   213.08
252.02   259.29   260.18
260.26   261.28   261.28
264.28   277.19   365.07
388.05   390.18   390.25
392.23   394.10   413.06
413.07   431.24   432.11
432.15
DREAMED 256.29   257.16
264.26   500.14
DREAMERS 13.21
DREAMILY 290.11   387.23
DREAMING 281.28   288.15
370.02
DREAMS   13.03   23.13
117.17   257.25   265.02
407.22   423.12
DREAMT   88.29
DREAMY   34.09
DREARY   149.06   369.25
DREGS   187.13
DRENCHED 441.06   468.23
DRESSED 93.02   511.20
DRESSER 64.06
DRESSING 42.10   43.33
DRESSING-DOWN   43.33
DREW   63.23   66.13
110.09   111.24   153.30
180.12   180.12   221.05
391.05   417.09   453.15
DRIED   375.27   399.02
410.18   453.09
DRIED-UP 399.02
DRIFT   34.05   443.30
DRIFTED 416.04   489.17
DRIFTING 401.27
DRILL   37.15   52.17
199.14
DRINK   26.18   29.13
37.02   69.27   109.01
109.11   152.19   177.28
213.18   222.17   225.10
225.16   235.24   235.25
235.26   238.02   238.07
242.02   273.15   274.05
302.25   308.02   360.20
DRINKING 54.23   145.04
412.04
DRINKING-BOUT   146.04
DRINKS   42.21   169.01
DRIP   224.03   224.03
DRIPPED 62.17
DRIPPING 329.06   496.10
DRIVE   143.21   181.26
235.11   284.07   317.10
321.08   355.19   378.02
386.13   388.09
DRIVEN   26.18   51.25
127.06   134.05   144.23
156.15   316.08   335.15
357.14   380.02   431.20
432.11   432.15   450.20
471.29   474.21
DRIVER   47.03   54.26
55.20   56.05
DRIVING 6.04   31.08

DRIVING (CONT.)   126.23
136.06   137.14   403.19
417.05
DRIZZLE 137.13   164.04
DROLE   172.20
DROLL   55.06   130.08
171.21   172.20   395.30
DRONED   493.03
DRONING 467.20
DROOPED 380.15   405.18
DROOPING 46.26   57.22
206.06   292.06
DROP   6.27   26.23
53.26   53.27   72.24
97.04   133.01   138.28
140.19   149.25   150.06
153.23   172.01   172.06
203.23   277.29   285.07
340.20   372.01   390.21
492.14
DROPPED 37.05   101.07
120.28   131.29   137.20
140.02   148.12   154.04
192.25   195.22   201.22
224.24   231.23   287.01
295.23   310.29   313.16
328.16   364.25   407.03
430.25   443.07   459.27
514.11   514.26
DROPPING 37.10   105.09
165.17   264.12   307.13
313.17   316.30   364.28
405.10   410.05   465.24
473.10
DROPS   497.07
DROVE   3.21   148.27
190.11   201.06   212.17
252.11   321.10   372.04
434.13   500.26
DROWN   136.24   138.14
DROWN-   136.24
DROWNED 52.01   74.25
104.12   136.08   139.10
182.17   243.07
DROWNING 108.15   138.15
211.20   375.09
DROWNS   260.29
DROWSED 408.17
DROWSILY 107.07   168.15
DRUG   158.17
DRUM   467.18   483.24
DRUMMED 33.23   37.05
DRUMMING 241.20   385.28
DRUMS   175.08   334.15
444.05
DRUNK   2.03   23.18
26.12   29.08   29.11
29.13   29.15   121.10
146.27   149.09   201.13
201.14   236.26   242.27
344.23
DRY   37.01   46.25
61.25   102.13   110.23
139.08   214.22   226.03
311.22   312.04   324.23
333.16   353.13   356.02
392.30   445.04   454.17
465.15
DUBASH   42.11
DUBIOUS 189.07   351.16
DUCKED   360.08   364.24
DUE   222.20   233.30
365.05
DUEL   435.21   477.10
DUFFER   47.20
DUG   280.06   298.30
498.07
DUG-OUT 280.06   298.30
498.07
DULCET   402.18
DULL   27.14   174.12
175.24   275.19   294.26
314.09   340.23   371.12
DULL-EYED   27.14
DULLNESS 11.30   174.14
340.26
DUMB   119.15   140.04
301.14   390.30   442.13
506.28
DUMBFOUNDED   134.19

```
DUMBLY      414.11  427.12     EAGER (CONT.)       35.16     EASY (CONT.)        245.02     EGSTROM'S           232.25
DUMP        203.12              56.25   145.21  186.16        245.13  290.03  303.30        233.12
DUMPY       55.18   202.15      193.24  371.26  391.03        322.04  334.15  339.17     EH          29.19   49.05
DUN         58.07               399.09  404.13  428.29        421.22  426.11  430.15        65.03   130.19  144.11
DUNDREARY           436.05  EAGERNESS           62.08         471.11  473.27                145.23  178.21  179.12
DUNDREARY-WHISKERED             258.05  281.27  468.21     EASY-CHAIRS         2.09          231.05  253.15  303.02
436.05                      EAR         56.05   75.05         12.26                         309.02  324.28  343.18
DUNGEON     369.30              75.21   75.21   124.24     EAT         46.11   78.30         343.27  344.03  344.10
DUNGEON-LIKE        369.30      162.02  165.14  197.30        222.17  239.15  306.07        344.13
DUNNAGE     75.27               198.19  205.04  246.22        332.27  357.02  458.03     EIGHT       15.08   15.20
DURING      57.24   77.27       508.03                        488.23  505.19                71.09   71.22   104.15
87.14   98.15   146.25      EARLY       52.16   58.29     EATABLES    43.37                 104.16  104.19  133.18
213.23  244.08  247.03          79.28   190.03  217.08     EATEN       2.03    14.28        133.21  138.07  251.14
299.27  337.02  339.24          247.03  254.07  339.24        103.12  122.24  239.15        427.20
350.14  379.30  385.24          364.22  435.15  442.25        360.23                     EIGHTEEN    73.07   319.28
393.03  393.10  427.16          489.28  491.17  498.17     EATING      37.01   172.10     EIGHTY      358.17  358.17
449.23  475.11  484.20          504.09                        234.28  287.02  499.20        358.21  383.18  383.18
491.29  508.22              EARN        245.16            EAVES       342.18                383.23  402.17
DURNED      26.05           EARNEST     105.08  215.14     EBB         401.27            EIN         241.21  241.22
DUSK        5.26    16.29   EARNESTLY           47.01     EBBED       218.01            EITHER      45.27   52.03
38.27   209.14  260.04          87.22   192.30  221.07     EBBING      415.13                77.18   82.21   96.02
261.05  261.14  267.18          258.22  281.10  342.20     EBONY       324.17  410.09        100.05  100.23  130.08
360.10  417.06  462.18          454.20  456.03  461.23     ECCENTRIC           59.10        153.24  160.07  168.14
492.03                          512.18                        240.13  315.09                190.10  215.23  229.16
DUSKY       322.05  347.24   EARNESTNESS         6.10     ECCENTRICITY        227.03        234.08  267.13  275.10
378.06                          229.20                        229.20                        306.07  331.11  354.10
DUST        16.05   37.01       10.24   328.08  393.24     ECHO        35.10   302.05        399.20  462.10  472.13
47.02   56.01   175.29          428.13  436.14            ECHOED      22.01             EJACULATIONS        405.29
263.29  376.21  376.30      EARNING     270.30            ECLIPSE     397.07            EJACULATORY         403.17
402.28  402.29  402.30      EARS        21.02   22.01     ECLIPSE-LIKE        397.07     EJECTED     46.14
495.10                          24.26   32.18   89.01     ECONOMY     26.24   209.15     ELABORATING         114.18
DUSTING     52.28               89.08   102.02  133.16     ECSTATIC    100.22            ELAPSED     513.18
DUSTY       20.28   191.30      139.23  148.22  170.06     EDDIED      37.12   370.02     ELASTICITY          90.21
DUTCH       249.29  268.15      174.12  203.30  210.27     EDDY        226.03                244.17
268.19  276.19  278.13          211.04  233.26  255.06     EDEN        435.10            ELATED      286.25  364.14
310.18  345.20  441.01          334.03  355.21  362.02     EDGE        10.19   24.16        368.06
441.13  448.17                  387.24  403.28  409.02        112.22  123.04  142.26     ELATION     225.01  285.07
DUTCH-      268.15              414.28  439.28  492.26        180.19  193.08  195.09        303.14  371.19  409.16
DUTIES      10.15   245.01   EARSHOT     356.28  480.14        211.15  262.16  300.02     ELBOW       21.02   89.30
DUTY        5.18    13.30    EARTH       6.11    8.24         364.29  368.24  373.18        108.07  109.12  124.29
46.01   70.37   71.04           13.01   19.04   20.29         414.07  445.07  464.30        145.25  207.23  296.05
74.02   107.22  113.27          24.30   30.23   43.16         500.11  506.07                303.12  311.11  362.21
195.04  351.26  353.28          68.20   76.19   90.04     EDGED       208.20                366.11  371.12  402.04
473.16  504.24                  118.01  139.03  139.09     EDIBLE      316.10                403.03  455.12  492.16
DWARFED     192.16  275.13      146.24  168.09  183.21     EDIFICATION         368.11        494.30  494.30  499.03
334.25                          190.19  200.05  208.09     EDIFICE     462.03                505.14
DWARFS      376.20  411.09      213.09  218.28  238.09     EDIFIED     191.09            ELBOWS      33.20   41.24
DWELL       348.26              238.28  247.14  255.02     EDUCATED    268.14                83.03   240.22  258.22
DWELLERS    389.17              255.28  270.29  272.02     EFFACING    376.28                261.23  273.19  318.21
DWELLING    271.25  447.22      273.15  275.06  275.09     EFFECT      9.05    49.23        470.20
DWELLINGS           462.30      302.19  311.21  312.24        55.07   56.21   111.26     ELDER       156.03  342.03
484.02                          332.01  341.06  356.02        133.18  158.25  166.11     ELDERLY     167.23  248.04
DWELLS      271.09              373.15  376.20  381.12        171.12  179.06  183.25        297.19  328.20
DWELT       35.24   149.26      389.11  390.24  396.26        195.17  232.24  260.05     ELECTED     3.24    315.23
486.04                          397.01  397.24  398.15        269.28  293.06  315.04        447.19
DYED        20.09               398.30  408.27  413.14        317.02  331.20  335.01     ELECTRIC    140.22  267.19
DYING       251.26  303.22      420.09  422.06  448.20        342.13  351.02  380.10     ELEMENT     127.13  260.30
417.22  422.03  422.09          462.23  465.10  474.09        443.09                        261.25  321.24  341.10
425.24  427.09  475.25          475.07  516.13            EFFECTED    290.25                352.11  413.05
479.05                      EARTHLY     204.21  266.08     EFFECTIVE           89.23     ELEMENTAL           11.08
DYSPEPSIA           241.07      266.21  267.04  341.08        97.26   147.27  173.06     ELEMENTS    95.15   264.23
E           64.03               480.10                        227.07                     ELEPHANT    337.11
EACH        3.19    4.30     EARTHQUAKE          508.22     EFFECTIVELY         209.22     ELEVATED    32.09   176.19
12.24   19.12   21.02       EARTHWORK           323.12     EFFECTS     173.01                462.28  498.19
21.08   22.09   38.28           323.30                     EFFICIENCY          180.19     ELEVEN      448.21
40.04   40.05   42.19       EASE        4.03    47.24         212.05                     ELIXIR      213.21
44.19   51.09   51.09           101.10  253.30  318.21     EFFICIENT           172.27     ELLIOT      45.03   45.26
54.07   85.13   87.05           512.16                        448.05                     ELONGATED           38.28
92.06   93.04   110.20      EASED       169.26            EFFIGY      26.14   89.01     ELOQUENT    275.15  303.03
113.15  115.13  115.26      EASIER      160.01  390.13     EFFLUVIA    310.12                304.30  363.15  374.16
115.28  117.26  126.24          400.03                     EFFORT      48.14   55.05     ELP         64.03
127.23  127.28  128.04      EASILY      44.30   101.27        61.01   106.11  141.23     ELSE        1.10    35.22
136.07  140.16  143.15          169.08  195.24  395.16        142.15  148.23  158.18        42.09   67.11   77.09
156.15  168.08  168.13      EASING      42.19                 258.02  312.24  333.23        90.20   138.09  140.11
178.01  178.21  178.22      EAST        3.11    13.07         396.04  408.23  514.22        163.28  175.25  211.05
181.06  181.20  226.28          15.24   27.49   68.14     EFFORTS     87.16   312.20        215.09  267.11  280.12
251.26  255.22  255.25          79.02   149.02  153.12        312.21  312.21  327.05        282.29  293.12  316.04
261.26  271.02  272.02          247.04  250.02  276.11        337.18  386.20  502.17        351.15  358.20  375.22
276.22  278.08  292.06          276.11  414.17  441.04     EFFUSIVELY          291.11        379.07  386.09  392.07
294.06  307.18  318.09      EASTERN     1.12    12.13     EGG         176.29                428.16  474.17  479.14
321.03  327.05  329.08          13.01   13.10   13.11     EGGS        410.26  412.06        481.14  491.04  510.27
348.12  358.06  386.15          14.02   32.08   67.26     EGOISM      186.05  305.08     ELSE'S      355.12  404.01
389.15  395.28  416.09          184.20  192.09  299.16        425.16  511.24  516.01     ELUCIDATED          177.27
416.24  419.28  420.11          345.03  515.26            EGOTISM     488.15            ELUDED      10.10
420.13  440.26  446.07      EASY        2.09    12.26     EGSTROM     230.04  230.14     ELUDING     494.08
453.17  470.12  470.13          14.05   14.09   14.12        232.04  232.15  233.19     ELUSIVE     219.13  264.08
474.03  484.13  485.15          29.01   29.05   32.05        233.27  234.08  235.25     EM          192.05  198.10
489.15  497.20  508.24          41.14   41.27   51.12        236.13  236.19  236.21        203.13
509.02                          52.25   130.08  179.25        237.03  237.27  238.13     EMACIATED           199.14
EAGER       7.29    27.30       204.08  212.01  214.11        238.21                     EMBARK      450.28
```

```
EMBARRASSED        170.24
EMBARRASSING       188.15
EMBER     412.24
EMBERS    333.29   463.27
  466.18
EMBEZZLE  356.18
EMBODIED  195.30   248.09
EMBODIMENT         361.22
EMBRACE   108.14   360.22
  383.23
EMBRACED  438.21
EMBRACING          254.08
EMBROIDERIES       318.06
EMBROIDERING       92.24
EMERALD   345.01   345.03
  345.17
EMERGE    364.27
EMERGED   17.22    325.28
  371.09   498.02
EMERGENCY          105.25
  167.18   447.20
EMERGING  168.02
EMIGRATING         278.27
EMINENTLY          173.16
  247.22
EMISSARIES         363.21
  368.12   477.15
EMIT      232.22
EMITTED   25.17    176.24
EMMA      254.09   268.11
EMOLUMENTS         266.21
EMOTION   9.04     12.01
  96.24    147.24   217.18
  237.03   253.27   256.25
  311.07   328.27   334.10
  360.22
EMOTIONAL          172.23
  392.02
EMOTIONS  66.16    106.11
  210.22   271.17   352.13
  385.20
EMPEROR   68.14
EMPHASIS  30.14    127.02
  257.05   301.21
EMPHATICALLY       195.13
EMPIRE    43.20
EMPLOY    75.18
EMPLOYED  278.16
EMPLOYER  2.23
EMPLOYERS          2.28
EMPLOYMENT         230.09
  240.15
EMPTINESS          149.28
EMPTY     41.27    47.01
  61.14    62.21    84.05
  92.22    140.13   160.28
  181.11   192.17   194.24
  204.02   204.02   211.06
  211.08   248.02   263.05
  290.27   300.07   300.28
  301.10   306.15   325.19
  334.03   366.11   370.02
  372.27   408.15   443.20
  448.25   456.27   460.10
  462.12   504.10
EMPTYING  97.03
EN        169.22   170.16
ENABLE    445.17
ENABLED   64.15    93.26
  244.17
ENABLES   4.04
ENCES     298.01
ENCHANTED          390.23
ENCHANTER'S        408.06
ENCLOSED  19.14    339.27
  420.04   423.11
ENCLOSING          318.10
ENCLOSURE          36.04
  306.11   313.30
ENCLOSURES         417.25
ENCOUNTER          85.02
  86.22    390.23   399.27
ENCOURAGED         217.09
  394.11   464.02
ENCOURAGEMENT      467.02
ENCOURAGING        113.25
  126.12   258.14   324.10
END       11.25    22.07
  22.22    23.06    23.29
  28.06    40.24    41.22

END (CONT.)        41.29
  41.29    41.30    42.27
  57.15    64.08    69.29
  71.05    73.24    74.14
  77.26    86.16    96.27
  116.19   117.25   117.29
  119.22   123.20   127.21
  136.13   142.05   147.28
  151.05   154.10   166.21
  168.12   170.17   178.11
  183.21   188.16   215.10
  218.05   219.30   225.26
  230.11   286.20   289.10
  293.21   301.03   303.10
  310.04   339.14   340.25
  347.09   351.28   354.02
  366.20   367.06   369.14
  372.17   391.20   397.23
  412.05   412.08   416.24
  426.06   426.10   429.27
  438.01   439.09   439.13
  439.29   451.11   459.13
  463.23   475.12   477.11
  493.26   497.16   499.11
  500.13   500.13   515.19
  516.23
ENDEAVOUR          260.28
  277.10   460.09
ENDEAVOURS         214.17
ENDED     44.10    156.24
  160.20   161.01   251.29
  340.27   351.18   384.05
  416.01   434.27
ENDING    86.22    488.20
ENDLESS   13.03    38.10
  317.07   483.27
ENDLESSNESS        356.10
ENDLICH   257.03
ENDOWED   340.23
ENDS      16.11    38.27
  139.12   166.24   430.13
  441.30   478.24   496.10
ENDURABLE          418.21
ENDURANCE          148.24
  210.20
ENDURING  418.21
ENEMIES   330.17
ENEMY     11.29    204.04
  254.28   257.13   395.09
  400.26
ENEMY'S   450.25   461.01
ENERGETIC          342.26
  478.15
ENERGY    13.19    17.10
  79.01    79.02    199.27
  293.23   396.25   396.27
  409.10   481.25
ENFIN     172.03
ENFOLDED  318.07
ENFUE     177.16
ENGAGED   396.13
ENGAGEMENT         14.07
ENGAGING  250.01   283.10
ENGINE    28.04    35.06
  125.06   129.28
ENGINE-ROOM        28.04
  35.06    125.06   129.28
ENGINEER  25.18    26.19
  27.06    28.30    29.05
  29.25    30.28    34.18
  35.04    35.10    54.11
  64.21    109.22   120.06
  122.14   122.18   125.03
  129.30   137.19   140.18
  141.20   151.25   165.16
  202.21   229.28
ENGINEERING        234.24
ENGINEERS          25.23
  98.13
ENGINES   30.23    35.02
  102.23
ENGLAND   310.24
ENGLISH   49.09    169.10
  170.26   276.19   285.16
  292.14   348.15   441.11
  451.30   491.30
ENGLISHMAN         455.24
  455.25   455.25
ENGLISHMEN         48.10
  48.30

ENIGMA    415.12
ENIGMATIC          419.30
ENIGMATICAL        352.22
ENJOINING          484.26
ENJOYED   11.13    122.06
  164.15   334.08   356.24
ENJOYMENT          244.01
  454.29
ENLARGE   172.12
ENLARGED  8.28     78.05
  227.06   307.15
ENLIGHTEN          456.14
ENLIGHTENED        86.08
ENLISTED  186.02
ENLIVENED          41.27
ENMESHED  454.10
ENORMOUS  44.08    58.13
  114.09   114.09   345.02
  497.05   512.03
ENOUGH    14.09    29.10
  36.12    40.10    40.23
  41.14    43.08    50.18
  50.29    51.22    56.02
  59.23    61.20    61.22
  61.23    68.10    68.29
  73.17    80.04    80.20
  86.07    89.19    97.27
  98.14    103.01   103.19
  107.22   108.11   108.23
  110.13   113.01   122.16
  125.05   128.05   131.27
  143.22   146.22   149.14
  152.09   152.14   157.10
  157.10   160.17   167.19
  169.10   170.24   179.11
  187.03   188.12   188.18
  190.15   194.08   194.25
  196.27   198.30   202.01
  205.27   207.11   209.24
  218.17   218.23   220.04
  229.14   238.02   238.10
  238.28   242.02   244.15
  249.28   255.16   260.19
  260.19   270.26   272.16
  280.27   281.06   283.14
  290.03   290.06   293.22
  313.27   316.18   331.13
  337.16   339.02   340.24
  341.10   344.26   351.07
  358.07   375.23   381.11
  384.29   389.24   393.09
  393.23   397.30   398.01
  398.04   398.28   400.09
  401.03   407.17   412.07
  423.29   426.26   435.11
  435.22   436.01   440.14
  440.29   442.23   445.16
  454.01   455.19   465.12
  472.03   477.18   478.27
  493.13   495.18   495.21
  511.15
ENRAGED   187.15   441.17
ENSIGN    167.02
ENSLAVED  32.16
ENSLAVING          10.12
ENSUED    87.15    160.25
  242.08
ENTENDU   178.23
ENTER     131.15   212.24
  307.09   429.25   445.18
ENTERED   248.01   299.06
  319.28   374.27   484.16
  485.05   497.02
ENTERING  10.02    12.28
  363.07
ENTERPRISE         92.19
  390.17   390.25   396.25
  437.05
ENTERPRISES        13.22
  273.05
ENTERPRISING       315.24
ENTERTAINER        264.18
ENTERTAINING       421.20
ENTHRONED          59.28
  462.14
ENTHUSIASM         29.25
  113.21   262.06   321.18
  396.27   436.23
ENTHUSIASMS        264.22

ENTHUSIASTICALLY   197.06
ENTICING  10.11
ENTIRELY  267.08   267.08
  333.26   448.20
ENTITLED  268.30   403.30
ENTOMOLOGIST       253.10
ENTOMOLOGISTS      252.17
ENTOMOLOGY         247.08
ENTRAILS  479.06
ENTRANCE  444.14
ENTREAT   353.10
ENTREATED          108.09
  150.23   226.09   385.06
  393.21   402.08   450.18
ENTREATING         221.07
  286.30
ENTRENCHED         444.23
ENTWINED  482.11
ENVELOP   283.18   348.25
ENVELOPE  217.11   219.10
  229.11   374.20   501.17
ENVELOPED          17.08
  146.03   409.03   459.01
ENVIABLE  69.09
ENVIED    69.07
ENVIOUSLY          241.19
ENVY      400.19
EPISODE   27.26    93.08
  117.12   119.19   173.22
  351.17   419.16
EPISODES  239.01   339.12
EPITHET   48.04
EPITHETS  141.24
EPOUVANTABLE       178.29
EQUABLY   421.24   422.26
EQUAL     20.13    295.05
  342.09   342.10   375.11
  375.14   380.03   415.02
  415.04   471.27   487.18
EQUALITY  341.20
EQUALLY   48.18    48.23
  239.07
EQUALS    471.27
EQUILIBRIUM        253.07
EQUIVALENT         356.23
ER        65.03    219.20
ERECT     141.13   325.07
  349.24   373.13   432.28
ERECTED   279.11
ERRAND    17.03    21.17
  125.06   452.02
ERRING    262.30   485.23
ERUPTION  258.19
ES        241.21   241.22
  257.04
ESCAPE    12.09    36.08
  96.04    118.03   139.29
  170.19   249.23   264.29
  265.01   305.04   311.07
  376.17   390.19   396.13
  431.25   450.29   454.05
  507.21   511.05
ESCAPED   64.10    195.04
  223.03   353.29   434.15
ESCAPES   8.26
ESCAPING  269.27
ESCORT    323.02
ESCORTED  263.05   308.12
ESPECIAL  316.07   410.15
ESPECIALLY         95.07
  266.14   280.30   282.05
  303.19   400.22   419.13
  449.17
ESPLANADE          45.25
  47.01    49.26    146.10
ESPOUSAL  340.07
ESSENCE   112.03   280.03
ESSENTIAL          66.14
  112.17
ESSEX     81.18    95.04
EST       179.24   394.21
ESTABLISHED        246.01
  251.17   316.24   418.23
  421.25   444.18
ESTABLISHMENT      168.30
  240.28   333.07   366.12
ESTIMATE  129.14
ESTUARY   297.13   410.02
ET        394.21
ETAT      173.10
```

ETC 185.30 185.30
ETERNAL 13.10 14.01
23.06 271.26 285.22
488.01 516.07
ETERNITY 24.29
ETHER 25.07
ETHICAL 418.24
EUROPE 243.09 247.19
252.18
EUROPEAN 321.28 469.06
EUROPEANS 37.14
EVASION 185.19
EVE 286.26
EVEN 3.23 15.20
28.22 41.29 47.06
74.03 87.01 89.09
89.29 96.28 101.09
101.23 118.14 127.08
131.02 143.30 146.28
147.10 157.13 164.07
165.16 175.18 177.08
178.29 179.09 179.21
185.26 186.01 191.09
193.09 193.19 194.23
208.19 209.18 211.29
214.16 215.30 216.04
218.12 223.16 227.11
232.12 240.10 242.28
243.29 245.04 245.22
257.16 267.19 270.20
271.05 271.07 271.08
273.29 274.07 274.16
278.27 278.30 281.02
281.06 281.12 281.18
289.09 289.10 295.20
295.20 302.12 302.16
307.01 307.21 309.28
315.02 339.14 347.20
349.16 350.17 357.16
358.17 364.05 369.07
383.05 383.30 384.01
390.21 392.28 395.02
399.17 399.29 403.24
433.04 471.29 472.04
480.13 482.16 488.08
492.13 492.28 495.09
497.10 501.15 507.21
513.22
EVENING 7.27 17.27
17.27 41.17 58.22
91.13 113.23 151.13
201.11 229.05 241.22
245.25 248.01 301.27
304.12 323.05 327.14
339.02 347.02 378.09
417.06 427.25 438.28
448.22 462.04 491.17
507.10 512.06
EVENINGS 349.20
EVENLY 21.26 195.07
351.07 433.15
EVENT 9.05 13.24
22.05 118.04 251.21
EVENTS 10.17 127.20
131.05 340.02 363.15
363.15 402.14 407.14
423.10 447.01 455.15
482.01 482.06
EVENTUALITY 85.05
EVER 10.16 18.06
24.21 38.15 42.04
42.15 47.12 55.28
57.06 65.11 70.08
77.22 81.03 95.10
96.03 100.29 103.06
105.29 110.30 114.14
116.18 127.03 128.21
141.22 153.26 174.18
176.17 183.20 197.29
198.28 201.29 202.17
202.25 214.24 215.02
218.20 223.10 229.19
237.29 246.06 266.01
268.09 270.19 283.02
297.09 297.23 299.10
300.11 318.02 319.07
320.16 331.15 344.20
358.16 359.16 369.15
389.15 392.09 395.15
396.24 398.16 407.12

EVER (CONT.) 412.08
416.12 417.16 421.15
422.29 480.29 486.09
486.10 500.14
EVER-UNDISCOVERED
417.16
EVERLASTING 19.04
135.08 136.04 232.10
295.08 297.10 299.14
304.12 422.12
EVERLASTINGLY 14.09
19.22 128.21
EVERY 13.04 17.20
20.08 21.17 24.04
26.08 41.20 41.21
42.20 42.22 43.23
45.23 50.09 51.26
51.27 51.28 53.08
58.17 76.02 94.26
100.15 101.06 107.02
111.05 111.24 114.23
114.25 117.22 127.26
139.08 139.09 147.24
149.13 152.10 172.20
194.04 198.26 199.28
201.24 202.12 203.01
213.15 222.12 223.05
226.23 232.05 236.07
239.15 241.09 243.01
244.03 244.19 251.13
252.11 253.05 253.06
259.26 279.07 281.17
293.29 303.23 303.23
308.25 310.02 322.21
322.23 330.17 330.26
334.27 335.13 341.28
345.28 347.04 348.06
350.15 352.30 353.05
353.14 353.24 358.01
375.03 378.02 384.04
390.19 402.03 404.22
409.13 420.14 426.30
432.01 438.04 449.24
450.01 455.17 459.06
462.02 472.11 474.27
480.04 482.24 488.28
493.25 495.12 499.23
509.05 511.21
EVERYBODY 42.02
119.21 242.15 242.21
243.06 265.08 289.19
289.19 382.30 468.11
468.17 482.23 484.08
485.05
EVERYBODY'S 402.29
EVERYTHING 2.04
24.22 27.13 35.26
35.28 103.04 115.08
139.13 162.01 174.18
178.25 196.17 207.10
289.19 312.05 329.27
331.15 342.05 351.03
351.19 359.24 369.14
372.12 375.16 392.07
397.21 403.26 405.17
405.17 405.17 445.15
446.09 454.16 455.27
457.12 478.04 480.21
495.04 507.02
EVERYWHERE 256.15
EV IDENCE 40.10 65.17
69.21 80.03 92.17
118.11 176.25 194.10
EVIDENT 85.12 107.20
159.27 179.08 263.22
437.07 488.10
EVIDENTLY 66.01
176.11 225.13 229.01
307.26 339.01 356.17
359.28 404.17 434.24
459.15 488.19
EVIL 118.26 195.30
226.25 262.25 262.25
279.06 425.15 449.15
486.08 486.09 501.15
505.12 514.01
EVIL-DOERS 486.08
EVIL-MINDED 449.15
EVOKED 105.26 389.14
423.01 516.06

EVOLVED 398.11
EVOLVING 28.08
EWIG 261.29
EWIGKEIT' 55.25
EX 360.30 455.02
456.27
EX- 360.30
EX-BEACHCOMBER 455.02
456.27
EXACT 27.22 63.23
70.01 132.15 194.11
253.04 378.16 451.17
478.02 513.20
EXACTING 16.13 20.07
EXACTIONS 10.07
EXACTLY 17.22 129.25
197.13 202.28 209.01
213.20 232.20 246.03
269.22 326.01 342.23
362.13 405.25
EXAGGERATED 129.16
193.20 223.05 281.19
449.26
EXALTATION 261.14
288.25
EXALTED 114.20 264.23
368.08 516.01
EXAMINATION 1.14
47.05 66.17 69.17
EXAMINE 98.05
EXAMINING 469.22
EXAMPLE 5.18 51.06
179.28 282.17
EXASPERATED 82.15
147.18 328.02 361.17
370.30 429.16 458.20
EXASPERATING 68.29
228.02 357.24
EXASPERATION 88.10
EXCAVATIONS 459.09
EXCEEDINGLY 192.04
356.24 410.11
EXCELLENCE 68.23
EXCELLENT 4.23
190.05 241.17 274.21
291.27 420.09 491.27
EXCEPT 119.21 184.17
369.12 384.08 388.06
421.18 438.10 496.03
500.21
EXCEPTION 90.06
272.01
EXCEPTIONAL 40.07
335.04
EXCEPTIONALLY 85.08
EXCESS 22.19 89.14
147.08
EXCESSIVE 333.01
394.10 432.16 432.17
EXCESSIVELY 308.05
515.21
EXCHANGE 82.24 244.09
307.07 319.07 324.19
384.28 396.02 403.30
EXCHANGED 169.24
285.20 294.24 484.20
498.04
EXCHANGING 54.08
105.02 126.25 244.26
371.02
EXCITABLE 8.10
EXCITED 145.23 192.28
300.25 310.03 359.15
361.18 428.09 457.16
EXCITEDLY 368.26
469.07
EXCITEMENT 119.10
130.06 256.21 286.07
300.06 314.03 333.27
341.16 374.23 385.09
391.17 424.13 446.11
483.26
EXCITING 138.20 291.15
EXCLAIM 196.25 328.02
477.05
EXCLAIMED 34.22
78.30 87.11 130.23
171.23 176.22 238.27
248.07 357.14 367.30
483.17 511.09

EXCLAIMING 144.09
EXCLAMATION 294.18
303.15 342.25 513.27
EXCUSABLE 281.08
EXCUSE 59.23 60.05
97.13
EXECUTING 311.07
EXECUTION 185.12
185.17 191.17 300.13
EXECUTIONER 307.29
308.12
EXEMPLE 181.02
EXERCISE 345.06
EXERCISES 347.11
EXERTED 295.09
EXERTION 41.12 121.15
130.06
EXERTIONS 117.13
126.14 261.01
EXHALATION 21.19
EXHAUST 28.16
EXHAUST-PIPE 28.16
EXHAUSTED 7.18
12.01 160.29 289.23
EXHIBIT 293.18
EXHIBITED 285.07
EXHIBITING 65.13
171.09
EXHORT 192.30
EXHORTED 364.02 461.15
EXIGEAIT 169.28
EXIGENCIES 112.10
EXILE 3.12 193.18
EXIST 263.26 264.14
273.06 348.25 352.01
408.06
EXISTED 268.09 274.12
283.30 284.03 294.26
379.07
EXISTENCE 10.05
12.08 13.24 14.17
25.14 35.18 50.24
78.03 111.29 114.20
119.29 219.10 247.04
251.30 263.28 268.01
346.02 353.27 375.03
386.14 390.03 398.08
398.17 398.21 438.15
508.02 516.09
EXISTS 112.20 274.13
EXORCISES 215.11
EXORCISM 60.17 390.26
EXPANDING 27.28
38.30
EXPANSE 149.17 262.01
319.10 325.11
EXPANSION 268.11
EXPECT 29.18 41.23
61.21 64.25 66.08
67.06 78.28 85.19
89.19 113.19 140.10
157.16 186.25 187.12
191.12 209.30 228.26
237.22 313.07 357.22
411.24 426.11 480.28
EXPECTANT 390.06
EXPECTATION 66.14
484.01
EXPECTATIONS 156.15
EXPECTED 25.29 54.24
55.09 89.18 101.23
132.30 190.07 195.10
211.05 232.23 274.25
356.15 441.19 445.15
470.18 499.23 507.29
EXPECTING 70.43
107.02 114.19 137.23
275.04 400.12 447.21
EXPEDIENCY 402.12
EXPEDIENT 188.09
456.21
EXPEDITION 242.12
EXPENSE 242.04 289.28
EXPENSE' 289.29
EXPERIENCE 32.03
60.26 119.05 153.20
182.16 298.13 389.05
479.26
EXPERIENCED 98.25
106.09 299.27 366.26

```
EXPERIENCES          183.23     EXTRAORDINARILY      261.04     EYES (CONT.)         244.13     FACE (CONT.)         431.10
EXPERIENCING         371.17       467.05                          253.14  254.01  256.01         433.20  441.23  452.27
EXPERIMENT            65.07     EXTRAORDINARY         54.18       256.10  256.14  257.06         460.11  466.08  470.21
  282.28  396.23                  65.10   86.03   99.22          259.27  260.15  261.12         471.18  473.03  474.30
EXPERIMENTS          396.24      119.23  132.22  138.21          264.15  272.19  279.06         482.03  485.11  490.23
EXPERT    177.22                 144.09  167.27  172.06          284.04  286.06  288.04         505.21  508.08  509.08
EXPIATION            184.11      172.21  174.11  256.23          288.06  290.08  291.21         512.05  512.18  514.09
EXPIRED   155.12  445.06         331.26  345.01  346.08          292.05  294.08  295.28         515.09  515.26
EXPIRING  113.03  361.13         361.26  366.02  388.22          302.13  303.01  303.24       FACED      37.13   46.23
  502.15                         448.11  515.23                  307.13  307.20  307.27          47.10   69.11   85.13
EXPLAIN    33.12   57.14       EXTRAVAGANT          191.03       311.04  312.15  314.18          92.19   93.04  129.29
   59.17   95.19   97.18         212.24                          314.26  314.29  318.12         181.06  185.03  264.24
   98.20  112.10  127.07       EXTRAVAGANTLY         70.11       322.05  324.16  325.09         273.17  279.27  299.12
  165.23  185.12  360.05         280.16  375.06                  329.23  332.29  337.09         311.09  371.05  394.05
  381.21  402.13  433.23       EXTREME    28.16   35.09          338.17  343.27  344.22         414.10  441.16  450.12
  485.22  490.02                 63.03  106.10  123.27           345.25  348.11  362.23         459.23  469.14  470.11
EXPLAINED             86.23      180.19  310.28  345.09          364.29  365.12  371.02         475.04  506.03  513.26
   90.02  118.25  129.30         379.21  454.07                  371.26  372.25  375.25       FACES      20.11   32.13
  134.25  267.29  285.06       EXTREMELY             36.22       378.24  379.04  380.16          32.13   32.14   32.14
  294.15  323.27  324.06         41.09   57.01   59.09           386.07  394.09  396.27          33.05  100.23  103.03
  345.21  370.11  385.17         87.02  138.30  179.18           402.29  402.29  403.01         105.11  120.29  137.14
  455.28  456.19  493.21         195.12  217.03  243.11          408.10  409.14  409.20         149.05  170.07  291.19
EXPLAINING           287.27       244.10  251.21  311.24         409.28  410.24  411.05         297.03  314.28  320.10
  332.12  385.24                 315.06  336.24  347.17          412.19  413.01  414.11         408.28  413.09  417.21
EXPLANATION           59.22      352.25  358.09                  418.05  419.14  423.04         434.12  469.10  485.29
  138.19  165.27  234.14       EXTREMITY            503.03       424.13  425.14  425.23         495.11  515.17
  238.20  378.18               EXTRICATE            338.28       426.18  430.20  431.07       FACETIOUSLY           62.16
EXPLANATORY           59.11     EXUBERANT            214.21       431.22  432.30  439.18       FACILITY   58.17
  417.29                        EXULTATION           425.10       452.30  455.09  460.05       FACING     56.16   79.19
EXPLODED   21.23  145.27         427.15  474.19                  460.19  460.24  465.20          82.02  145.06  240.02
  201.27  238.23               EXULTED     9.07  425.11          469.09  469.12  470.12         259.01  319.20  366.18
EXPLOIT   425.01               EYE        17.03   19.08          470.22  471.02  476.02         410.01  432.26
EXPLOITS  251.07                 22.28   24.08   35.22           480.01  480.05  480.15       FACT        3.08    3.09
EXPLOSION            371.28      46.09   54.06   55.26           481.18  482.09  482.09          3.16   42.07   42.08
EXPORT    448.18                 63.04   74.14   78.22           482.18  487.18  500.13          56.08   66.06   66.19
EXPOSE    308.07                 86.26  113.09  113.10           501.06  501.24  502.28          81.15  103.08  139.01
EXPOSED   297.17  455.08         144.20  155.08  165.20          504.17  505.11  509.06         158.24  165.15  165.25
  462.24                         166.16  169.05  171.27          509.22  511.07  515.05         239.20  269.15  271.20
EXPOSING  466.05                 179.26  184.09  193.07          516.12                         281.20  298.15  311.28
EXPOSTULATING         87.18      201.09  204.03  210.09        EYESIGHT   61.20  240.03         322.20  330.01  340.03
EXPOSURE  163.28  292.28         214.12  219.14  232.28        FABLE      41.28                 341.30  347.17  351.19
EXPOUNDED            169.27      235.20  235.26  237.16        FABRIC    462.01                 351.24  361.26  444.19
EXPRESS   207.11  262.18         255.13  293.14  304.11        FABULOUS  304.19                 452.13  459.06  503.04
  475.19                         322.10  378.06  397.14        FABULOUSLY           114.08     FACTION   315.29
EXPRESSED             51.24      402.10  421.05  423.27          345.16                       FACTITIOUS            425.18
  172.17  208.30  320.10         429.23  434.02  494.08        FACE        7.28   11.04       FACTORY     4.29
  354.08  404.12  470.14       EYE-WITNESS          423.27       20.03   21.03   23.20        FACTS      11.04   32.07
  475.22                        EYEBALLS            312.22       24.07   33.02   33.21          33.10   33.11   33.11
EXPRESSION            35.21     EYEBROWS  171.26  176.20         35.15   36.26   37.09          33.12   35.12   35.15
   79.01   86.08   88.03         180.04  246.16                  37.24   39.01   43.25          36.02   51.06   66.06
   90.22  102.14  105.11       EYED       27.14   76.23          48.20   50.29   54.19         127.16  177.23  382.06
  144.18  170.08  172.08         115.30  241.27  273.16          62.04   63.12   66.18         419.30
  178.15  180.13  244.03         475.12  477.11  499.16          69.09   84.24   85.24       FACULTY     3.25  116.22
  295.04  338.08  389.19         501.19                          88.03   88.22   93.12         213.07  267.06  267.07
  399.22  407.12  419.12       EYELID     43.24  343.27          95.17   96.23  100.28       FADED      93.04  118.22
  427.13  515.05               EYELIDS    20.23   37.05          102.19  108.01  108.09         149.02  217.30  387.13
EXPRESSIONS           28.25      128.18  149.07  171.02          108.24  111.25  114.07         421.29
  187.29  289.29                 176.20  180.12  199.20          114.28  118.24  120.15       FADING    417.21  494.27
EXPRESSIVE           272.15      328.16  509.19                  128.07  132.09  133.14       FAIL      147.05  155.15
  283.20  322.06  502.22       EYES        7.14    7.29          134.10  142.07  145.30       FAILED    100.13  251.12
EXPRESSIVELY         287.19       8.13   13.20   16.08           148.20  150.10  153.22         321.19  360.24  420.03
EXQUISITE             3.01       22.02   23.22   24.25           158.30  160.08  161.03         435.12  461.06
  243.19  249.10  374.20         27.19   31.05   32.12           170.23  172.08  175.05       FAILING   113.22  113.22
  434.03                         33.02   33.21   36.26           175.23  187.08  187.23       FAILINGS  267.04  487.22
EXTEND    446.05                 37.07   37.22   37.25           187.28  189.15  196.13       FAILS     147.04
EXTENDED   19.08   21.06         37.30   39.03   42.01           208.17  209.13  213.07       FAILURE    56.27   97.28
   33.23   39.05  261.11         53.21   58.13   61.07           214.23  216.05  216.15         214.15  434.21  449.19
  343.09  370.06  380.13         61.19   61.29   62.06           217.17  220.07  222.13         458.21  482.17
  414.18  463.04                 62.10   63.14   70.09           224.07  224.13  226.29       FAILURES  212.06
EXTENDING            233.28      73.03   74.11   75.09           238.11  238.22  239.21       FAINT       8.15   18.01
  350.21                         76.08   82.11   84.23           246.08  246.15  255.02          21.18   27.05   31.01
EXTENSIVE            252.08      85.20   85.23   86.29           256.05  257.07  257.19          31.13   86.06  107.09
  315.13                         88.24   89.09   91.01           261.15  261.27  263.16         132.04  137.10  151.16
EXTENT     30.11   60.15         93.12   95.18   97.15           270.29  271.03  271.08         151.17  157.22  164.09
  105.08  136.19  338.06         100.19  100.26  108.02          271.13  279.10  287.14         177.07  210.30  234.04
EXTENUATION          383.03      108.09  109.12  114.07          290.08  292.05  293.04         255.14  256.07  261.09
EXTERIOR  246.25  292.09         114.24  116.12  118.21          296.04  307.28  312.14         285.09  301.07  325.20
EXTERMINATE          449.30      124.08  125.27  127.21          314.24  318.08  322.05         334.06  342.25  350.09
EXTERNALS            113.10      127.29  128.07  128.10          330.18  331.29  332.29         361.02  374.03  378.02
  276.04  276.06                 128.14  134.17  137.25          336.10  338.08  338.24         378.24  382.02  384.30
EXTINCT   155.20  405.08         139.23  142.02  145.29          342.26  355.10  356.05         440.17
EXTINCTION           278.26      146.28  150.22  151.03          356.30  362.24  365.15       FAINTER   260.04
EXTINGUISHED         127.26      153.29  156.12  158.20          365.26  366.24  369.23       FAINTING    8.14
EXTORTED   32.19  278.03         162.05  163.05  167.08          371.27  372.05  377.11       FAINTLY     7.05   28.17
  442.07  448.27                 173.12  174.11  174.20          378.22  380.15  384.24         104.29  211.16  211.25
EXTORTING            278.24      176.18  187.05  192.03          388.29  391.04  396.15         216.10  257.23  307.22
EXTORTIONATE         404.05      192.22  195.08  202.04          397.06  399.10  399.20         362.05  384.10
EXTRA     341.11                 204.14  205.27  207.12          404.11  405.25  405.26       FAIR        8.11   36.26
EXTRA-TERRESTRIAL                215.13  216.23  219.11          412.22  424.12  426.19          89.05   93.15  112.07
  341.11                         224.13  232.08  241.03          427.02  429.28  430.13         130.30  150.25  195.12
```

39

FAIR (CONT.) 206.03
238.18 279.28 283.03
326.02 331.07 336.18
336.23 356.22 435.22
FAIRLY 64.09 73.30
74.26 77.14 129.18
153.20 284.09 311.21
344.01 404.27 408.25
444.23 473.12
FAIRNESS 125.07
FAIT 171.04
FAITH 15.12 15.21
17.03 20.07 21.18
50.25 51.05 191.16
214.10 272.04 275.07
408.01 419.08 420.16
422.02 422.08 453.05
463.14 465.03
FAITHFUL 2.16 74.08
350.16 408.04 412.29
412.30 420.14 482.13
500.09
FAITHFULLY 410.03
456.25 516.14
FAITHFULNESS 487.17
FALL 78.24 128.03
129.25 142.09 147.03
152.07 174.19 193.15
255.12 311.14 337.11
355.20 376.30 395.11
414.23 463.10 480.20
487.19
FALLEN 58.19 68.01
73.18 127.25 134.29
181.10 353.12 367.09
398.03 506.14 508.14
509.22 512.14 515.13
FALLING 7.01 11.19
12.18 18.05 101.29
102.03 112.22 121.01
125.14 149.26 153.01
198.15 204.08 222.03
279.09 313.19 315.07
373.12 396.30 417.06
462.26
FALLS 6.29 203.23
260.26 260.27
FALSE 47.15 90.13
133.18 190.21 251.14
364.19 433.16 433.19
511.10 512.30
FALSEHOOD 87.19
112.17
FALSER 293.13
FALTER 186.30
FALTERED 142.14
FALTERING 262.09
FAME 247.14 270.30
276.09 299.07 304.09
335.05 335.05 514.29
515.29
FAMILIAR 40.06 119.14
230.28 231.22 239.22
271.08 271.17 321.30
385.20 396.03 509.29
FAMILIARITY 230.01
298.02
FAMILIARLY 42.19
FAMILIARS 191.04
191.06
FAMILIES 20.27 315.21
FAMILY 4.14 16.06
95.11 298.11 319.28
330.27 421.22
FAMOUS 59.11 61.20
178.17 249.29 306.13
345.12 426.28 431.30
465.21
FAN 343.13
FANATICAL 333.01
FANCIED 95.07 196.07
246.13 391.02 421.16
FANCIFUL 100.10 189.09
210.10
FANCY 8.13 35.01
81.19 95.05 114.21
136.16 175.19 184.04
184.11 201.07 228.18
266.19 274.01 293.17
314.23 341.14 357.13

FANCY (CONT.) 378.25
400.18 407.05
FANNED 20.15
FANTASTIC 13.24
63.18 184.18
FAR 5.04 8.16
13.12 16.30 23.03
26.22 38.03 45.25
56.27 58.11 73.06
75.22 78.15 84.08
84.29 95.15 96.13
100.01 100.14 107.23
110.28 117.07 122.07
125.23 126.06 162.01
196.20 204.03 204.20
212.25 212.26 227.08
229.12 246.11 247.14
254.01 254.11 255.27
262.07 262.10 273.06
278.19 289.07 307.02
319.07 319.12 325.18
329.23 335.17 338.18
338.21 347.22 359.01
361.03 361.21 362.09
366.21 383.09 386.01
398.28 401.25 408.28
409.02 428.02 441.29
445.29 446.01 446.09
447.23 460.01 467.15
470.07 475.29 480.14
480.29 501.22 510.18
FAR-AWAY 100.01
FAR-OFF 409.02
FAR-REACHING 335.17
FARCE 126.16
FARE 93.03
FARTHER 3.11 274.03
437.11 513.06
FARTHEST 456.10
FARTHING 117.24
FASCINATE 55.08
FASCINATED 38.01
116.10 372.25 434.03
FASCINATION 14.20
32.16
FASHION 152.11 403.18
455.14
FASHIONED 319.21
FAST 101.19 223.08
415.13 449.10 482.06
492.15 505.28
FASTEN 194.21
FASTENED 150.22 207.04
284.04 315.03 323.27
348.12
FASTENS 341.02
FASTER 85.28 137.15
FAT 24.15 26.15
98.03 192.20 200.18
250.19 318.04 343.07
FATAL 69.01 129.08
508.06
FATALITY 280.17
FATALLY 103.13 351.18
FATE 60.10 76.29
103.17 166.18 166.22
168.11 191.22 212.25
214.29 215.12 283.26
294.27 310.06 326.01
337.26 339.05 340.27
341.02 392.11 400.01
418.11 420.27 423.01
458.25 473.13 477.10
485.10 509.14
FATED 295.30 397.27
FATEFUL 395.21
FATES 390.05
FATHER 3.30 11.29
21.03 45.25 52.15
73.27 76.20 231.28
319.27 340.15 340.22
355.08 355.15 387.18
387.19 421.12 423.02
FATHER'S 450.17
FATHERS 16.04 250.25
FATHOM 196.28 223.11
330.20
FATIGUE 11.11 160.27
175.04 300.16 488.25
FATIGUING 299.06

FATTENING 267.16
FATTEST 43.15
FAULT 75.06 113.06
199.28 288.09 353.18
FAVOUR 16.26 42.13
58.11 148.05 223.26
230.08 350.12 403.20
474.17
FAVOURED 41.02
FAVOURITE 73.27
207.15 422.15
FAWNING 230.28
FEAR 7.26 11.11
11.28 29.24 33.30
60.11 63.15 69.05
74.20 85.16 115.28
119.02 121.13 125.28
138.06 146.28 148.24
159.18 178.04 178.04
178.28 178.30 179.01
215.16 218.23 219.04
219.15 254.21 274.06
280.07 286.22 306.21
321.10 329.10 338.30
342.05 368.15 374.04
381.06 387.06 387.05
388.08 390.14 390.15
392.24 395.11 399.28
427.14 434.16 438.17
439.20 441.18 460.14
462.10 482.12 483.24
488.03 493.18 500.25
501.11 507.21 510.03
510.18
FEARED 379.20 381.07
451.06 456.15
FEARFUL 112.21 404.05
503.18
FEARING 234.19
FEARLESS 16.08 30.08
299.02 368.28 369.19
FEARLESSLY 288.18
FEARLESSNESS 304.21
FEARS 15.28 212.06
274.15 329.14 336.08
342.01 381.14 389.14
407.10
FEARSOME 55.07
FEASTED 455.09
FEASTING 92.09 105.13
FEATHER 27.05 80.25
FEATHERED 79.08
FEATHERS 409.30
FEATHERY 434.05
FEATURE 82.03 172.14
FEATURES 35.20 87.27
100.19 149.05 342.27
380.16
FECUND 408.27
FED 91.09
FEEBLE 211.12 386.03
392.30 445.21
FEEBLY 312.26 317.06
334.04 344.24 370.04
467.06 473.07
FEED 184.05 275.16
FEEDER 72.24
FEEL 40.07 51.15
70.34 74.12 78.14
80.06 101.17 107.02
126.09 153.02 184.22
218.20 219.22 228.01
228.11 271.30 272.01
295.15 303.23 375.05
375.14 391.24 401.01
412.08 412.10 438.20
463.14 477.21
FEELING 35.12 53.16
62.03 94.03 106.10
153.20 156.29 156.30
180.09 210.18 224.30
236.13 238.20 258.06
272.11 288.23 295.06
295.12 328.18 334.09
354.10 371.18 391.16
398.19 398.19 424.05
429.10 433.15 458.16
463.14 477.21
FEELINGS 88.03 98.15
112.12 162.03 166.14
215.24 274.10 342.01
356.28 402.25

FEELS 194.23 231.08
393.03 516.19
FEET 1.02 5.04
5.21 15.14 28.07
29.03 41.16 47.11
49.16 54.14 70.14
70.21 75.28 79.16
98.29 100.15 101.07
107.03 107.09 116.25
125.26 129.17 129.20
131.16 132.05 133.13
139.22 145.29 148.20
180.11 180.29 181.20
182.29 244.25 245.19
248.20 256.16 261.01
267.24 279.14 284.01
295.30 307.11 309.29
311.22 312.07 315.04
315.14 323.01 324.01
325.10 328.16 334.22
338.13 349.11 365.20
368.21 384.06 389.13
390.22 397.09 398.29
405.07 415.09 415.15
417.02 418.05 431.11
432.27 433.29 463.09
465.28 472.12 475.07
483.12 502.03 505.19
509.01 509.23 512.21
515.03
FEINT 147.28
FELICITOUS 350.28
FELICITY 213.14 213.14
FELL 33.06 45.14
73.03 84.07 101.07
101.13 104.28 108.09
109.21 119.16 120.25
128.10 145.04 164.20
164.30 195.21 209.15
211.16 216.15 218.08
220.13 236.06 254.26
261.16 289.20 307.19
309.05 311.04 312.14
325.17 365.12 370.23
373.18 380.13 384.06
386.07 397.09 417.30
433.26 439.19 460.04
460.25 462.18 470.01
485.04 498.08 500.21
501.05 501.11 505.25
512.22 514.27 515.18
FELLED 313.22 323.09
396.18 397.08 446.03
452.26 455.08 459.29
FELLOW 38.04 44.20
49.24 51.18 56.14
60.05 85.30 113.15
156.01 157.03 181.08
188.03 196.10 200.18
207.05 226.08 226.14
230.21 231.01 240.26
241.30 243.01 259.28
260.20 291.01 328.09
330.08 343.08 345.22
352.29 359.03 377.02
412.18 425.04 436.23
439.08 453.29 454.13
459.22 461.06 465.29
470.23 471.12 471.17
471.22 476.08 479.03
FELLOW'S 79.29 358.08
FELLOWS 8.15 30.09
40.05 48.26 67.12
67.23 80.19 99.15
160.07 275.16 318.19
381.09 472.06
FELLOWSHIP 155.19
156.28
FELT 7.10 8.23
8.30 12.03 22.21
24.03 36.22 37.04
44.29 45.21 47.17
82.22 98.29 99.21
108.14 108.21 109.13
112.04 128.19 128.28
134.30 140.28 146.21
152.06 152.23 156.07
156.29 160.25 164.28
177.09 177.20 186.18
187.01 188.14 193.21

FELT (CONT.) 200.27
201.12 216.05 216.07
216.09 224.11 226.27
228.13 244.09 245.09
256.19 272.06 272.06
291.10 299.20 305.05
308.05 309.10 311.22
311.23 312.25 322.24
328.29 357.26 368.05
369.05 376.17 382.20
385.21 391.27 393.03
393.14 398.16 412.18
430.28 495.13 502.26
FENCE 313.24 339.27
340.05 403.08 405.10
405.27 408.05
FENCES 367.09
FEROCIOUS 294.12
449.08 515.06
FEROCITY 190.10 333.11
345.10 458.19 499.28
FERRIES 5.03
FERRY 6.05
FERRY-BOATS 6.05
FESTAL 13.08
FESTIVE 65.07 504.06
FETCH 182.23 233.17
464.04
FETCHED 139.14
FETTERS 322.24
FEVER 55.09 153.23
251.27 361.09 476.03
FEVERISH 369.10
FEVERISHLY 427.10
FEW 13.18 19.15
19.16 19.16 19.17
20.18 27.07 31.09
33.27 36.17 42.27
43.38 45.30 46.15
48.17 51.10 56.12
58.23 60.19 78.29
81.23 83.05 91.14
92.23 111.24 123.19
149.14 154.09 166.08
168.24 174.16 175.03
188.26 193.05 217.05
228.28 247.18 260.05
266.15 266.16 267.17
271.16 271.29 275.11
279.21 307.06 331.27
341.18 366.24 386.01
389.20 389.27 396.17
404.26 417.27 421.13
423.11 425.06 435.15
437.22 442.14 443.04
444.21 449.24 452.16
453.07 454.08 459.06
463.28 465.27 477.22
478.09 480.27 484.21
500.28 503.12 504.23
512.21 514.17
FIBRE 10.19 409.13
FICKLE 288.02
FIDE 97.13
FIDELITY 2.26 59.16
271.28 482.14 482.15
FIELD 212.22 304.27
FIELDS 271.11 489.24
FIEND 2.26 236.18
FIENDISH 147.17
FIENDS 472.28
FIERCE 6.09 21.25
100.02 104.23 115.21
117.13 126.26 202.05
305.08 318.16 324.15
425.13 438.09 450.12
500.08 509.30
FIERCE-FACED 450.12
FIERCELY 33.08
FIERCENESS 380.03
391.12 392.20
FIERY 38.27 321.18
374.11 412.26 449.05
473.08
FIFTEEN 87.06 279.14
309.29 330.11
FIFTH 267.02
FIFTIETH 79.03
FIFTY 26.10 30.04
111.07

FIFTY-SEVEN 26.10
FIGHT 106.06 157.17
188.13 200.13 200.13
301.05 313.23 321.26
418.30 428.14 428.14
435.21 447.08 473.21
473.22 481.14 483.20
507.17 507.17 508.03
508.04 511.02 511.03
FIGHTING 75.12 115.24
128.02 183.06 188.14
210.04 210.05 220.22
328.21 333.11 426.30
458.04 461.18 483.16
484.23
FIGHTING-COCK 75.12
FIGHTS 315.29
FIGURATIVELY 51.20
289.08
FIGURE 24.20 26.21
76.28 162.07 170.15
192.16 211.18 237.12
279.27 319.21 325.25
338.27 339.21 362.09
368.23 372.16 380.14
385.10 408.07 415.11
430.05 469.10 469.20
482.18 506.24
FIGURED 23.03 272.26
FIGURES 71.09 212.19
224.16 264.04 437.15
469.04 498.01
FILE 24.16
FILL 24.25 24.26
74.10 299.07 315.30
334.02 366.29 473.18
FILLED 12.10 15.17
128.12 248.18 382.27
409.03 431.04 497.06
FILLING 15.18 166.04
508.18
FILLS 24.26
FILTH 310.12 313.13
FILTHY 28.25 143.17
306.06 355.02
FINAL 9.05 38.20
284.08 356.01
FINALITY 193.14 193.23
215.07
FINALLY 179.16 358.13
450.22 491.02 491.11
FINANCED 436.19
FINANCES 29.06
FIND 30.05 36.06
38.04 59.19 59.21
60.04 64.30 66.08
66.08 66.21 75.06
75.13 79.02 88.09
90.07 90.10 109.10
153.02 157.01 161.04
172.20 199.07 207.11
227.08 238.04 238.09
242.20 258.27 260.17
262.24 276.15 283.13
284.02 286.23 329.30
344.26 363.09 389.22
423.10 428.02 431.28
432.01 447.21 463.23
473.14 481.28 495.23
FINDING 36.05 314.04
332.26 375.07 375.15
465.13 478.04
FINDS 69.26 259.21
FINE 3.29 8.06
10.16 12.10 26.01
30.02 43.02 59.04
86.01 113.11 113.20
114.02 143.10 178.11
181.15 186.21 215.23
215.24 215.24 215.26
215.26 253.26 259.27
259.28 260.20 264.27
265.04 265.07 269.21
285.22 314.24 319.29
468.20
FINEM 261.29 413.07
FINER 337.05
FINES 185.04
FINEST 95.09
FINGER 26.26 33.24

FINGER (CONT.) 88.25
101.01 115.11 143.01
207.25 259.06 331.05
332.09 427.07
FINGER-TIP 101.01
FINGER-TIPS 33.24
FINGERING 442.29
FINGERS 22.12 34.10
37.07 39.01 109.15
110.25 134.11 136.01
145.20 170.04 171.09
173.05 177.29 218.06
238.14 238.21 239.05
256.30 258.23 259.18
282.13 393.15 460.26
512.17
FINIALS 443.15
FINIS 215.03 215.11
FINISH 90.15 176.01
510.21
FINISHED 116.21 176.23
217.11 258.21 284.09
431.06
FIR 4.11 432.08
FIR-TREES 4.11
FIRE 17.24 20.06
28.20 29.13 76.12
87.06 97.23 135.03
144.03 156.14 255.26
333.15 334.23 370.23
387.30 393.11 412.24
443.26 445.05 450.28
461.01 464.11 464.23
478.19 490.15 490.22
492.05 498.28 499.18
FIRE- 76.12
FIRE-SHIP 20.06
FIREARMS 440.04
FIRED 139.17 286.20
292.25 314.08 371.27
396.19 445.01 446.08
450.05 459.30 461.07
483.23 500.30
FIREMAN 208.16
FIRES 255.04 324.04
324.14 413.03 445.30
462.24 463.04 467.22
469.02 489.16 489.22
493.28 498.11 498.22
502.15
FIRESIDE 271.23
FIRING 5.30 143.27
198.26 443.23 444.06
464.17
FIRM 47.11 197.06
205.06 237.06 264.17
268.26 278.12 312.06
312.27 322.07 382.04
408.01 418.22 436.20
FIRMAMENT 115.08
FIRMLY 2.01 7.10
23.03 322.14 379.17
FIRMNESS 148.23
FIRST 2.01 4.08
4.22 14.19 24.20
27.29 30.15 35.12
39.04 42.01 42.09
42.15 43.14 43.30
45.07 47.08 52.09
58.30 63.26 70.06
72.10 75.05 77.28
82.28 88.06 88.26
98.02 98.04 102.08
111.10 119.22 120.05
121.06 123.02 123.21
128.23 131.13 132.12
134.01 134.01 134.04
136.17 137.24 138.04
139.29 142.12 148.09
158.10 160.08 162.24
163.30 165.10 171.10
185.26 187.02 194.04
196.30 200.02 205.22
209.07 210.25 224.24
229.07 229.11 229.13
233.14 236.04 235.11
236.20 241.29 242.30
243.03 249.24 251.29
252.05 258.26 269.10
269.23 276.20 281.20

FIRST (CONT.) 282.19
284.02 284.07 287.14
288.19 291.22 297.23
299.09 300.17 300.19
300.23 304.02 306.14
308.03 308.20 310.09
311.18 313.08 321.20
332.02 332.07 332.26
336.08 336.18 341.24
342.14 345.17 352.27
357.30 373.08 377.11
407.01 408.12 413.01
417.25 420.29 439.23
443.03 447.06 448.04
448.12 454.04 456.01
456.26 458.01 462.18
470.16 473.07 479.23
481.17 485.11 485.13
488.29 491.09 492.17
492.19 493.09 494.05
500.23 501.04 501.06
502.30 503.15 504.13
504.21 505.24
FIRST- 242.30
FIRST-RATE 70.06
196.30
FISH 5.14 306.09
357.06 360.12 360.13
360.15 453.09 500.09
FISHED 242.13
FISHER 297.12
FISHER-FOLK 297.12
FISHERMEN 360.12
411.12 412.01 414.25
FISHING 297.20 298.16
316.06 410.14 442.19
443.12
FISHY 153.28 207.13
479.21
FISHY' 98.10
FISSURE 269.13
FIST 55.18 57.11
87.28 110.10 130.17
159.10 220.02 287.08
355.10 371.13 500.07
505.26
FISTS 29.22 85.04
312.14 385.28
FIT 37.16 41.05
53.06 79.30 85.09
126.15 143.13 154.16
179.10 194.05 238.11
241.16 276.03 329.11
361.09 406.01 432.09
436.14 460.29 478.24
FITFUL 5.29
FITS 299.27 425.09
FITTED 47.27 97.05
127.09 168.21 272.23
423.28
FIVE 4.15 17.28
26.29 72.27 73.28
111.06 173.03 173.03
173.11 182.29 198.26
207.23 222.22 255.01
273.20 319.26 333.13
426.13 439.08 439.30
448.18
FIVE-AND-TWENTY 73.28
FIVE-ANDTWENTY 319.26
FIVE-POUND 426.13
FIVE-TON 26.29
FIX 203.25 214.11
485.18
FIXED 1.04 24.21
59.29 158.20 163.28
187.05 219.11 253.14
290.08 329.23 338.09
344.21 362.24 460.05
482.05
FIXEDLY 93.30 422.12
FIXING 307.19
FIXTURES 232.11
FLAG 367.23 441.01
FLAGSHIP 175.11
FLAKE 101.12
FLAME 17.03 18.09
155.21 210.07 224.05
257.21 276.19 316.01
322.05 324.23 367.21

FLAME (CONT.)		372.14	FLOATS	264.07	491.20	FOLDS (CONT.)		338.09	FOR (CONT.)		22.21
FLAMES	20.18	262.17	FLOOD	103.15	136.10	418.01	433.28	459.26	23.10	24.20	24.21
263.11	264.05	445.02	220.14	385.19	443.02	FOLIAGE	38.26	297.05	24.24	25.10	26.02
459.01	463.01	484.02	FLOODING	112.27		430.02	432.21	509.04	27.07	27.25	28.18
FLANKING	69.10		FLOOR	44.11	58.19	FOLK	297.12	316.23	28.30	29.11	29.14
FLANNEL	46.24	292.04	62.22	63.17	92.20	327.21	448.02	450.08	29.28	30.02	30.13
470.19			121.01	185.26	187.05	462.05			32.19	33.30	35.11
FLANNELETTE		44.10	209.12	235.12	248.19	FOLKLORE	460.27		35.18	35.29	35.29
FLAPPING	353.14		279.12	336.11	345.26	FOLLOW	219.14	261.27	38.04	38.08	38.09
FLARED	105.10	257.18	370.03	429.29	430.25	261.28	264.20	282.17	40.11	40.20	42.01
FLARES	493.28		FLOORING	359.05		307.03	369.17	413.06	42.04	42.19	42.21
FLARING	224.06		FLOORS	263.07		413.06	453.26	482.30	42.28	43.05	43.22
FLASH	39.02	63.19	FLOP	256.20		513.07			43.41	44.03	44.12
127.29	174.19	217.30	FLOPPED	300.05		FOLLOWED	3.16	16.19	44.14	44.23	45.16
378.22	464.11		FLOSS	60.23		30.17	34.27	72.10	46.03	46.10	46.17
FLASHED	77.19	108.22	FLOUNDERED		309.14	77.26	88.24	137.06	48.11	49.10	49.27
263.09	362.23	401.18	FLOUNDERING		103.24	208.04	251.30	262.09	50.14	50.15	50.22
414.06			FLOURISHES		55.18	264.15	303.04	350.27	50.23	51.22	52.02
FLAT	25.03	34.28	FLOURISHING		288.22	366.04	367.01	367.08	52.22	53.14	54.02
63.07	105.12	122.11	FLOUTED	471.04		373.11	402.05	411.05	54.08	55.17	56.03
140.17	170.28	224.16	FLOW	277.14		429.07	432.02	443.17	56.07	56.20	57.02
318.08	332.29	416.19	FLOWED	15.16	242.10	464.12	483.12	489.12	57.10	57.28	58.08
432.23	436.23	445.21	445.16	467.10		512.19	513.30		58.09	58.10	58.25
446.03	460.11	466.08	FLOWER	4.10	381.04	FOLLOWERS		251.10	59.01	59.03	59.06
490.15			FLOWER-BEDS		4.10	323.02	336.18	453.23	59.24	59.24	60.04
FLAT-FOOTED		436.23	FLOWERING		163.15	486.13	513.14		60.05	60.10	60.13
FLATTENED		55.12	FLOWERS	33.27	37.10	FOLLOWING		131.23	60.19	60.25	60.26
329.07			38.27	193.05	227.22	193.15	208.03	267.22	60.28	61.11	61.20
FLATTERED		70.38	339.29	339.30	382.01	319.15	351.11		64.02	64.24	67.04
FLATTERING		77.02	397.12	397.15		FOLLY	61.11	212.04	57.11	63.17	68.17
FLAVOUR	213.16		FLOWING	15.19	292.14	239.16			68.27	69.04	69.17
FLAXEN	263.16		347.21	378.21	467.09	FOND	306.23	374.26	70.03	70.16	70.40
PLEAS	84.11		482.07			FONDLY	183.19		71.29	72.23	73.15
FLED	45.15	55.30	FLOWN	56.08		FOOD	167.04	172.05	74.01	74.20	75.18
313.15	336.01	345.08	FLOWS	407.15		225.15	287.02	307.16	76.02	76.29	77.27
361.02	431.20	459.14	FLUENCY	293.02		307.17	339.01	440.25	78.04	78.05	78.16
489.27			FLUNG	12.29	24.07	441.24	442.23	453.04	78.29	79.11	79.24
FLEET	252.13	456.09	45.10	70.03	109.30	454.08	455.04	458.01	81.02	81.07	81.30
504.05	505.29		125.11	129.03	139.15	473.18	473.18	484.04	83.29	84.10	85.20
FLEETING	264.03		154.10	198.18	218.03	499.14	499.18		86.11	86.30	87.06
FLENSBORG		49.01	220.01	221.03	226.01	FOOL	2.30	53.08	87.12	87.28	88.06
FLESH	8.19	24.12	229.24	284.08	309.18	70.43	78.14	88.10	89.17	89.17	89.20
28.23	151.27	219.11	313.25	336.10	362.17	88.20	124.25	141.27	90.07	91.11	91.14
262.29	389.17	423.03	374.09	382.13	393.22	151.03	197.01	199.30	92.24	94.08	95.26
423.03			408.30	411.25	420.28	200.14	200.20	205.02	96.02	96.15	96.16
FLESHY	24.19	27.15	511.26			241.05	243.21	306.15	96.18	97.01	97.05
FLEW	36.01	128.19	FLURRY	115.16		329.29	331.12	332.16	97.14	98.14	99.14
134.04	290.12	352.30	FLUSHED	213.20	286.06	377.23	383.19	403.01	99.18	100.03	100.13
370.22	371.11	374.01	FLUSTER	73.13		425.24	455.26	457.18	101.23	102.29	103.06
408.25	495.10	508.17	FLUSTERED		57.13	468.06	468.07	493.02	103.19	103.26	105.10
FLEXIBLE	26.21		FLUTED	434.04		FOOLED	130.09	130.10	105.26	106.12	107.21
FLICKED	6.01	18.10	FLUTTER	145.21	155.21	130.11	458.01		107.24	109.05	111.07
FLICKER	123.10	263.11	155.22	225.18	273.18	FOOLHARDY		290.04	111.10	111.16	113.09
372.14	401.24	463.01	334.07	348.18	440.17	FOOLING	126.15	457.02	113.10	113.10	113.15
511.24			FLUTTERED		27.04	FOOLISH	26.25	169.24	113.23	113.25	113.30
FLICKERING		264.05	171.02			FOOLISHLY		264.26	114.16	114.28	115.24
FLICKERS	184.27	216.16	FLUTTERING		256.10	FOOLISHNESS		193.11	116.18	117.07	117.18
407.15			367.22	422.20		465.06			117.24	118.01	119.09
FLIES	64.02	123.05	PLY	25.27	35.04	FOOLS	64.19	90.27	119.15	119.17	120.08
123.07			76.26	89.03	137.04	FOOLSCAP	420.04		120.16	121.04	122.15
FLIGHT	58.24	157.23	203.18	225.28	256.09	FOOT	23.25	21.07	122.17	123.18	124.27
240.06	256.09	280.18	311.21	324.06	328.14	34.18	37.28	47.04	126.11	126.15	126.17
348.07	369.08	374.11	368.22	368.25	449.13	49.09	54.27	56.06	126.25	127.05	127.09
443.05			511.05			95.02	103.22	204.27	127.30	128.07	128.09
FLIMSY	410.07		FLY-BLOWN		76.26	221.06	283.19	313.05	128.22	130.06	130.26
FLINCH	289.18		FLYING	6.08	26.09	314.08	324.22	328.01	131.12	131.22	132.02
FLINCHED	8.30	110.04	47.22	115.28	167.02	331.09	393.07	409.25	133.16	133.27	134.13
FLINCHING		88.23	212.27	236.15	309.05	411.26	415.07	427.07	135.07	136.12	139.21
FLING	47.18	116.16	310.04	311.23	313.18	463.05	464.12	494.05	139.22	139.22	139.23
216.08	239.09	356.03	401.13	449.26	462.06	514.27			139.27	140.26	141.13
371.30	495.07	501.10	462.17			FOOTBALL		93.24	141.27	142.14	142.21
FLINGING	334.12		FOAM	17.17	19.15	FOOTED	425.14	436.23	144.04	144.05	144.13
FLINTLOCK		324.16	460.21	483.26	515.01	FOOTFALLS		226.18	144.20	145.01	146.15
513.25	514.23		FOAMING	16.24	120.15	288.07	417.12		146.25	147.08	147.18
FLITTED	37.19	368.18	FOAMY	25.16		FOOTHOLD	99.01		147.21	148.02	148.04
FLITTING	61.13	315.06	FOCUSED	147.19		FOOTING	385.22	479.19	148.05	148.18	149.09
342.24			FOES	212.29	400.25	FOOTREST	21.12		150.01	150.23	150.30
FLOAT	107.14	159.06	FOG	91.07	138.20	FOOTSTEPS		21.30	151.01	151.01	151.22
194.16	301.28		197.25	494.11	494.24	226.24	264.21	349.22	152.04	152.25	153.07
FLOATED	21.19	93.25	495.08	495.18	495.27	360.26	393.26	395.21	155.11	156.01	157.11
115.23	117.26	148.27	496.05	497.08	497.17	FOOTSTOOL		349.10	157.17	159.06	159.07
189.17	211.14	269.26	FOGS	194.20		FOR	1.18	2.06	160.01	160.09	160.13
331.28	414.05	414.21	FOILED	148.01	201.24	2.06	3.14	3.22	161.04	161.04	162.11
464.18	489.18	494.27	488.16			4.02	4.07	4.14	162.15	163.07	163.13
512.27			FOLD	24.16		4.16	4.18	6.16	163.21	164.03	164.14
FLOATING	5.04	23.08	FOLDED	410.21	491.18	7.03	7.24	8.15	165.08	165.27	166.24
24.27	33.14	98.01	FOLDING	490.17		8.17	8.24	8.26	168.13	169.01	169.09
111.02	147.07	165.20	FOLDING-STOOL		490.17	9.07	11.12	12.21	169.25	171.05	171.28
166.30	194.11	274.27	FOLDS	19.13	62.20	13.14	17.06	18.06	171.30	172.05	172.06
299.23			174.23	246.09	318.09	19.18	20.27	21.17	172.13	174.06	174.10

FOR (CONT.)

```
FOR (CONT.)          176.05   FOR (CONT.)          300.12   FOR (CONT.)          457.02
178.24   178.29   179.09     300.16   300.24   303.25     457.08   457.10   457.20
179.11   179.20   181.09     303.26   304.04   304.05     458.01   458.02   459.15
181.15   181.22   182.05     304.19   306.01   306.22     460.16   461.13   461.23
182.09   183.05   183.13     307.07   307.14   308.09     461.23   461.25   461.28
183.20   183.27   184.08     308.20   308.26   309.27     461.30   462.11   463.06
184.10   184.11   184.17     311.08   312.05   312.30     463.21   466.08   466.13
184.22   185.10   185.28     313.01   313.01   313.04     466.26   467.02   467.27
186.03   186.18   186.24     313.06   313.19   314.19     469.18   469.18   470.18
187.01   187.03   187.21     314.21   315.23   315.28     470.25   471.23   472.03
188.20   188.24   188.25     316.03   316.10   316.12     472.05   472.15   472.18
188.26   189.11   190.16     318.03   319.02   321.03     472.26   473.11   473.18
190.19   193.11   193.22     324.02   324.20   327.09     473.19   473.19   473.20
193.27   194.05   194.16     327.16   327.17   328.25     473.25   473.30   474.16
194.27   195.01   195.10     329.02   329.10   329.19     474.21   475.12   475.16
195.17   195.25   195.29     329.27   330.04   330.11     475.21   477.04   478.19
196.04   196.20   197.05     330.14   330.28   332.18     478.02   478.14   478.30
197.06   198.06   198.17     333.16   334.18   334.19     479.05   479.07   480.09
199.03   199.03   199.30     334.22   335.06   336.11     481.10   481.25   482.18
200.02   200.03   200.13     336.18   337.20   338.02     482.24   482.28   483.05
200.13   200.21   201.10     338.25   339.01   339.08     483.07   483.14   483.28
202.01   202.11   202.13     339.10   339.20   340.28     484.22   485.10   485.19
203.10   203.16   203.19     341.08   342.13   344.12     486.03   486.06   486.17
203.26   204.14   204.21     344.15   346.09   346.10     488.08   488.21   488.26
204.22   204.24   205.05     347.14   349.10   349.19     488.28   489.03   489.04
205.10   206.02   207.05     349.27   349.29   351.08     489.20   490.17   491.07
207.20   208.06   209.03     351.16   351.18   351.25     491.14   492.10   493.07
209.23   210.05   210.12     352.29   353.05   353.06     493.15   493.28   494.05
210.16   210.21   211.20     354.10   354.11   355.07     494.18   495.21   495.30
211.21   211.28   211.29     355.23   356.16   356.18     496.03   497.14   498.01
211.29   212.23   214.18     356.23   357.29   358.02     498.13   498.20   499.02
214.24   215.09   216.06     358.08   358.16   358.17     499.14   500.21   500.22
216.17   217.14   217.22     358.23   358.20   359.10     501.03   502.12   504.04
219.04   219.15   220.11     360.04   360.15   361.24     504.17   504.23   505.29
220.12   220.23   223.28     362.13   362.19   362.20     506.08   506.12   506.14
224.12   224.24   226.08     363.14   363.23   364.14     506.25   506.28   507.07
227.03   227.09   227.12     365.05   365.25   367.01     507.11   507.17   507.17
227.13   227.16   227.18     367.06   367.23   367.25     507.27   508.04   508.12
227.23   228.04   228.13     368.11   369.10   369.15     508.13   508.21   509.02
228.14   228.19   228.29     370.13   370.17   370.19     509.08   509.21   509.23
229.11   229.19   229.21     371.20   371.20   371.22     510.06   510.19   511.03
229.22   230.04   230.06     372.12   374.03   374.07     511.14   511.20   511.22
230.18   230.18   231.18     374.08   374.18   375.08     512.08   512.29   513.16
232.05   233.09   234.14     376.08   377.02   377.24     513.16   513.19   513.22
234.27   235.02   235.26     377.25   377.27   378.11     514.06   514.29   515.23
236.05   236.13   236.13     378.16   379.23   381.09     516.07
237.06   238.20   238.25     381.09   381.09   381.09
239.10   239.17   240.14     381.10   381.12   381.13
240.27   240.30   241.04     381.15   381.15   382.15
241.10   242.08   242.18     382.16   382.23   383.07
242.24   243.05   243.09     383.17   383.19   383.25
243.14   243.22   244.02     384.16   384.16   384.30
244.04   244.08   244.24     385.09   386.15   386.17
244.25   245.13   245.21     386.25   386.27   387.05
246.01   246.29   248.09     387.08   388.21   389.15
250.04   251.09   252.01     389.23   390.07   390.10
252.10   252.15   253.18     390.22   390.25   392.14
253.18   253.28   254.17     392.18   394.16   394.17
254.21   254.30   255.09     395.15   396.23   396.29
256.06   256.27   256.30     397.16   397.25   398.05
257.24   258.11   258.16     398.08   398.16   399.04
258.26   259.03   260.17     400.06   401.07   401.09
260.18   261.07   262.07     401.13   401.24   401.29
262.12   262.25   262.25     402.17   403.18   403.23
262.26   263.12   263.24     403.30   404.10   405.02
267.06   267.07   267.20     407.07   407.12   410.29
268.07   268.09   268.22     411.12   412.07   412.10
268.26   269.04   270.13     412.11   412.14   412.17
270.26   271.01   271.07     412.19   413.01   413.25
273.14   273.20   273.27     414.29   415.11   418.11
273.28   274.14   274.13     419.19   419.22   419.29
274.23   274.28   275.01     420.29   421.30   423.26
276.03   276.17   276.18     424.09   426.08   426.14
276.21   276.21   277.06     426.30   427.03   427.19
277.12   277.21   277.30     428.13   430.12   431.04
278.11   278.21   278.28     431.05   431.14   432.03
280.07   281.10   281.24     432.13   433.05   434.03
282.29   283.27   283.28     434.08   436.07   436.08
283.29   284.08   285.02     437.01   437.23   437.29
285.05   285.21   285.23     438.08   439.10   441.09
286.10   286.15   286.19     441.18   441.22   442.06
287.11   287.14   287.21     442.21   442.24   444.23
288.07   288.14   288.15     445.05   446.05   447.05
288.19   288.23   288.30     447.10   447.20   448.13
288.30   289.23   289.25     448.23   448.27   448.30
289.26   289.27   290.02     451.05   451.26   451.30
290.10   290.15   291.03     452.10   453.15   453.19
292.11   292.18   293.03     454.05   454.22   455.01
293.20   294.01   295.22     455.05   455.06   455.19
296.06   299.10   299.30     456.03   456.18   456.25
```

FORBADE 513.06

FORBID 353.19

FORBIDDING   512.05   139.16

FORCE 33.17   211.02   219.17   264.01   319.05   372.18   388.23   408.23   470.27   516.10

FORCED   68.29   131.08   225.14   352.06

FORCES   11.06   105.13   253.05   278.22   451.06   461.18   478.22

FORCIBLY   332.24   403.04   54.30

FORCING   1.19   223.19   485.10

FORE   4.24   101.20   132.06   166.04   293.08

FORE-'TWEEN-DECK   101.20

FORE-COMPARTMENT   166.04

FORE-TOP   4.24

FORE-TOPSAIL   293.08

FOREARM   393.15   432.23

FOREARMS   20.11   193.08

FOREBORE   90.05

FOREDECK   102.22

FOREFINGER   181.18   259.10   491.11   499.12

FOREFOOT   236.15   414.05

FOREFRONT   112.29

FOREGROUND   192.10   352.21

FOREHEAD   21.04   37.03   39.04   61.17   77.07   89.07   93.13   101.14   142.30   195.08   207.13   220.27   246.13   248.12   256.07   261.23   372.07   405.26   408.04   424.12   501.09   509.24   514.21

FOREHOLD   34.16

FOREIGN   68.07   169.01   397.13

FOREMOST   115.18   152.08   169.23   384.01   444.01

FOREPEAK   34.03   34.05   34.16

FORESEE   274.01

FORESEEN   165.25

FORESHORTENED   281.06

FORESIGHT   114.17   420.16

FOREST   3.23   254.07   269.11   276.06   300.19   319.11   325.24   330.23   341.27   376.21   449.13   473.09   500.11   512.04

FORESTALLING   116.22

FORESTS   16.01   214.05   241.14   297.08   299.13   304.13   325.11   331.29   334.15   338.18   349.05   392.15   409.05   417.15   445.07   469.14   480.17   508.26   514.30

FORETELLS   149.11

FORGED   390.20   441.22

FORGET   5.08   41.18   58.14   58.15   82.09   113.04   129.11   172.16   186.09   249.19   274.01   289.19   291.18   385.05   388.20   403.12   422.10

FORGETFUL   390.08

FORGETFULNESS   339.13   418.28

FORGETS   171.21   460.30

FORGETTING   286.04   377.05

FORGIVE   90.25   142.21   158.25   189.08   219.18   228.18   389.02   429.15   433.06   488.27   506.04   513.01

FORGIVEN   389.03   402.20   429.17   433.09

FORGIVENESS   413.10   432.13

FORGIVINGLY   180.04

FORGOT   38.03   114.24   261.20   261.20   290.18   465.13

FORGOTTEN   41.28   119.13   119.29   127.16   228.23   280.29   291.23   318.13   375.28   376.03   390.04   392.27   398.14   418.07   446.10   515.20

FORK   75.24   286.05   287.01

FORLORN   141.17   389.16   466.17

FORM   59.08   102.28   141.13   162.06   189.19   256.08   260.07   266.21   274.21   317.03   336.14   342.25   349.21   378.17   387.13   448.08   451.04   487.15   491.06

FORMAL   185.11   229.15

FORMALITY   211.06   211.09   250.27   294.30   320.09

FORMALLY   491.02

FORMED   104.14   315.27   379.08

FORMIDABLY   30.26

FORMING   213.03

FORMS   21.11   148.21   263.11   302.07   302.22   316.14   350.03   376.28   413.09   422.23   425.15   497.22

FORMULA   412.28   499.05

FORMULATED   122.04   186.22

FORSAKEN   57.08   166.16   214.22

FORSOOTH   40.21

FORSWEAR   276.23

FORT   167.21   420.06   420.22   447.20   448.04   450.06   451.22   457.14   457.15   461.22   463.07   483.13   483.23   483.30

43

FORT (CONT.) 484.17
488.23 489.03 489.13
491.28 503.01 504.11
FORTH 30.13 346.04
FORTHWITH 115.19
416.03
FORTIFIED 250.29
254.08 316.25
FORTITUDE 50.05
127.12 370.12
FORTMEN 504.22
FORTNIGHT 99.01
FORTUNATE 68.19
103.08
FORTUNATELY 35.28
425.07
FORTUNE 206.03 233.05
247.06 252.05 342.09
349.02 351.21 395.01
437.18 501.15
FORTY 196.28 203.12
204.10 269.09 279.18
292.04 345.19 421.30
494.14
FORWARD 1.04 15.16
16.07 20.15 30.18
33.15 34.03 34.21
37.09 52.26 84.02
84.13 89.16 102.05
136.06 141.14 141.21
145.26 148.13 167.05
180.21 249.16 255.12
258.22 291.15 292.07
293.15 302.24 351.09
360.10 363.24 371.30
459.22 460.02 500.08
506.07 509.21 511.25
515.15 515.18
FOSSIL 228.02
FOSTERED 24.01
FOSTERING 20.02
FOUGHT 59.01 138.22
216.06 485.30
FOUND 10.03 14.20
31.01 50.04 56.07
56.29 57.23 58.23
69.02 74.05 75.15
77.20 119.27 148.08
156.27 157.07 179.16
181.13 188.09 188.26
194.05 196.06 198.13
205.19 209.23 211.23
212.14 213.19 216.28
227.15 229.10 240.15
249.24 277.25 286.05
303.09 311.26 343.05
343.09 343.21 352.26
357.11 360.03 361.23
372.09 378.10 390.24
412.28 421.11 426.22
433.05 439.21 441.08
451.24 454.10 458.22
466.02 472.18 474.15
486.14 498.24
FOUNDATIONS 175.09
FOUNT 186.03
FOUR 22.24 26.26
28.07 43.03 64.25
65.08 70.26 71.09
73.07 73.10 75.30
80.12 97.30 107.17
117.12 128.02 149.28
189.23 209.10 248.20
250.04 254.30 290.13
291.19 311.19 319.26
363.03 365.27 366.14
366.16 411.09 421.22
508.28 510.07
FOUR-AND-TWENTY 65.08
189.23
FOUR-FINGER 26.26
FOUR-POSTER 209.10
FOURS 115.25 460.09
FOURTEEN 35.18 442.20
442.28 446.02 500.18
FOURTEEN-HUNDRED-TON
35.18
FOURTH 399.06
FOWLS 450.09
FRAGILE 253.03

FRAGMENT 39.03
FRAGMENTARILY 22.10
FRAGMENTARY 263.09
423.27
FRAGMENTS 195.18
462.27
FRAGRANCE 348.26
352.23
FRAIL 252.26 257.23
307.09 390.11
FRAME 36.26 288.28
288.29 419.20
FRAMES 289.15
FRAMEWORK 32.10
218.01
FRANK 89.21 93.16
278.17 281.17 315.25
FRANKLY 67.09 81.02
117.23 275.14 401.04
FRANKNESS 479.11
488.12
FRANTIC 291.19 502.17
FRAUD 26.28 426.08
FRAYED 417.30 422.20
FREE 28.10 29.10
49.16 82.03 108.24
147.08 200.03 239.10
250.19 251.01 271.06
347.23 351.14 422.25
474.18
FREE-HEARTED 29.10
FREED 294.25 374.19
FREEDOM 24.02 322.24
349.09 409.16
FREEING 115.24
FREELY 442.10
FREEWILL 471.25
FRENCH 164.11 166.26
167.23 175.11 177.15
184.23 437.04
FRENCHMAN 167.12
168.12 181.23
FRENCHMAN'S 193.27
FREQUENTED 240.28
FRESH 9.07 52.06
98.30 207.05 210.24
212.09 255.03 331.26
339.30 451.06
FRESHENED 5.27
140.02
FRESHNESS 41.17
227.19 373.17 409.03
FRETTING 49.15
FRIED 306.09
FRIEND 2.16 44.03
49.28 199.13 223.28
227.01 227.15 227.20
228.05 228.29 229.10
250.10 257.11 257.20
260.16 271.11 285.12
287.17 287.18 320.16
340.12 342.19 344.03
358.07 358.24 428.19
486.17 491.27 498.25
509.18 514.10 515.11
FRIEND'S 329.09 456.04
FRIENDLESS 222.10
FRIENDLINESS 408.02
FRIENDLY 60.20 68.11
150.27 150.28 280.30
367.19 449.22 452.04
FRIENDS 212.07 241.04
255.16 271.04 343.19
400.26 453.29 459.19
460.07 465.23 472.03
481.30
FRIENDSHIP 185.29
257.14 264.23 285.22
322.19 322.22 363.23
381.21
FRIENDSHIPS 271.19
304.09 321.21
FRIENDT 48.09
FRIGHT 111.20 123.25
191.11 216.30 341.11
375.24 435.24
FRIGHTEN 468.17
FRIGHTENED 45.09
159.03 191.10 209.05
236.17 286.24 313.10

FRIGHTENED (CONT.)
353.30 364.28 368.26
408.02 462.13 502.26
FRIGHTENING 345.09
FRIGHTFUL 429.12
429.16 512.07
FRIGHTFULLY 241.07
393.25
FRINGED 514.30
FRO 32.11 37.19
153.05 192.15 192.15
358.27 378.07 484.10
490.22 495.20 500.27
FROCKCOAT 170.11
FROM 1.04 1.11
2.05 3.13 3.22
3.28 3.29 4.24
5.10 9.06 11.17
12.19 15.23 15.23
15.26 15.29 15.30
15.30 16.20 17.29
18.01 18.10 19.06
20.15 21.06 22.06
22.23 24.01 25.17
26.21 27.02 28.08
28.11 28.23 29.03
30.15 32.12 33.06
33.11 33.17 34.16
36.03 37.24 39.08
41.24 42.05 42.23
42.23 42.24 42.24
43.05 43.11 43.28
43.36 44.16 45.13
47.19 48.05 48.22
48.23 48.27 48.27
48.28 49.08 49.17
49.18 49.21 50.06
50.07 50.09 50.21
54.29 55.28 58.10
58.24 59.12 60.16
61.15 62.27 65.18
67.04 68.07 72.14
75.20 76.13 80.24
83.02 86.26 89.14
89.14 89.18 90.03
90.03 90.04 92.23
93.23 94.07 94.14
96.04 97.23 98.06
98.07 98.16 98.29
99.10 100.14 100.28
102.07 108.06 108.28
110.01 115.27 116.24
117.07 118.11 121.11
123.05 123.29 124.21
124.28 125.21 125.24
126.07 127.25 129.01
131.07 131.15 133.09
136.04 139.05 139.29
141.19 141.24 142.05
142.23 143.15 143.27
146.08 147.02 147.15
147.28 148.30 150.01
150.03 152.19 152.26
153.12 153.28 159.10
163.11 165.07 166.09
166.27 168.03 173.05
175.13 180.18 181.01
182.04 182.27 183.12
186.06 187.13 190.07
190.18 191.05 191.16
192.04 197.27 198.16
200.28 202.07 207.05
209.30 210.06 210.13
211.01 211.01 211.14
211.15 213.19 215.11
217.01 218.25 221.01
222.09 224.05 225.08
227.04 229.10 230.02
230.16 232.05 233.06
233.25 234.16 235.02
237.19 237.21 239.18
242.16 243.24 243.27
245.24 246.11 246.12
246.17 248.19 249.04
249.25 251.20 251.27
254.01 254.08 255.20
256.04 257.06 258.20
259.06 261.15 263.06
263.28 268.13 268.20
269.02 269.09 269.16

FROM (CONT.) 269.19
269.27 270.16 272.04
273.22 275.22 276.06
278.04 278.04 278.06
278.13 279.22 280.05
280.12 281.01 281.03
283.18 288.01 291.21
292.14 292.26 292.28
294.13 294.25 295.01
295.16 295.27 297.17
298.29 299.07 301.08
307.16 308.01 309.17
310.16 311.12 311.22
312.05 313.04 313.07
313.09 315.20 316.14
317.15 318.18 322.25
323.03 323.06 323.13
324.07 324.19 325.28
329.29 331.13 331.22
332.22 333.02 333.28
334.04 334.23 335.12
338.17 338.20 338.29
340.15 340.19 344.15
345.07 345.22 346.04
347.22 348.15 349.27
357.16 357.16 357.22
358.05 359.11 360.07
360.07 361.05 364.26
367.18 369.11 369.13
369.24 369.27 371.13
372.13 372.26 374.19
375.30 376.04 376.22
378.14 378.29 379.11
381.24 382.03 382.06
384.04 385.03 385.06
385.18 386.07 387.29
388.09 389.09 390.08
391.05 391.12 391.21
392.03 392.15 394.10
396.30 397.04 397.07
398.25 402.05 404.28
405.04 405.16 405.17
407.13 403.15 410.10
412.24 414.30 415.06
415.13 417.01 417.29
417.29 418.14 419.29
421.12 421.15 421.20
422.15 425.16 427.04
431.17 431.19 432.11
433.28 435.08 435.10
435.14 436.03 436.22
440.07 440.13 440.19
440.26 441.04 441.29
441.30 443.18 443.25
444.12 444.19 444.20
445.27 448.03 448.16
448.28 449.12 451.28
452.11 453.13 454.11
455.07 455.23 455.25
456.10 457.15 458.03
458.09 459.03 459.16
459.24 459.28 461.07
462.25 463.25 464.18
469.19 470.07 470.30
471.23 472.08 474.23
474.23 476.05 477.05
477.17 478.13 480.06
480.30 482.07 482.08
482.21 483.23 488.01
489.01 491.17 492.10
492.13 492.16 493.23
493.25 496.12 497.08
499.20 500.13 500.25
501.24 502.13 504.14
506.11 506.30 507.19
508.16 509.23 509.26
510.01 510.18 513.03
513.12 514.13 514.23
514.25 516.02 516.12
FROM-UNDER 1.04
FROMA 48.28
FRONDS 13.05 509.03
FRONT 4.09 44.15
94.08 154.12 216.27
249.17 255.14 269.20
308.29 312.07 315.03
443.22 444.27 463.07
484.26
FRONTED 400.01
FRONTS 105.12 175.28

```
FROSTY        71.27            FUTURE (CONT.)        166.25    GAZE           22.03   63.12    GET (CONT.)            201.13
FROTHING     373.19              186.28  277.20  337.27          88.24  134.16  150.01      201.14  201.23  203.18
FROTHY         6.30              420.16                          159.01  201.22  374.09      205.24  218.10  225.15
FROWN        272.20           G            140.21  140.21        378.26  399.16  416.04      232.14  236.07  237.22
FROWNED      142.29  219.26   G-G-GLAD     140.21                432.27                      238.15  239.10  241.15
  224.20  362.05              GABASIDY     241.10             GAZED          49.25   54.13      248.12  254.16  255.18
FROWNS       293.06           GABLES       443.15                187.27  217.21  249.16      255.20  259.11  270.09
FROZEN       429.30           GAFF         167.02                257.20  315.11  338.14      271.12  278.29  278.30
FRUIT        314.01  444.30   GAGGED       212.29                407.21  423.03  455.16      282.19  285.06  286.23
  509.04                      GAIN         457.01             GAZING         30.20  171.23      288.16  289.13  289.14
FUDDLED      426.25           GAINED       478.19             GEAR           22.25  107.19      290.01  290.02  290.18
FULGOR        17.08           GAIT         288.10                439.10                      291.08  293.25  303.26
FULL          2.03    6.08    GAL          183.09           GELUNGEN       255.17               306.07  306.14  309.08
  7.18   21.24   23.12        GALE           5.26    6.09   GEM            342.07  345.01      310.26  311.30  312.01
  24.19   26.17   30.28          7.24    8.22   62.25       GENERAL        91.09  242.17       317.09  323.26  329.17
  33.23   34.06   41.03          210.16                        259.14  349.24  400.30         330.25  331.05  334.03
  47.22   49.23   56.26       GALES         11.03  194.21       453.25  484.03                 337.03  344.07  344.11
  61.04   62.15   63.01       GALLANT        4.20           GENERALLY              3.11        344.14  351.08  353.26
  81.04   92.04  100.27       GALLERY       64.11   94.08        4.20   76.14   85.09         356.21  356.27  365.18
  133.11  133.28  156.13         105.02  120.28  146.07        244.29  315.01  319.05         365.19  365.19  370.20
  168.16  176.28  184.08         184.28                        320.08                         383.19  385.28  398.05
  191.25  236.02  236.11      GALLOP        55.22           GENERATIONS            4.14        399.08  402.16  411.14
  239.12  257.15  262.16      GALLOWS      440.12              170.07  298.18  411.12          427.03  427.14  432.19
  269.19  275.01  278.08      GALVANIC      63.06           GENEROSITY            298.24       440.30  442.04  456.02
  300.27  312.26  314.12      GAME          53.08   97.25   GENEROUS        8.25   26.17       457.06  457.16  458.03
  338.08  351.01  356.05         130.30  238.09  242.03        214.20  240.26  262.07         468.01  468.19  472.18
  359.25  372.12  387.17         274.18  322.29  336.18        264.22  281.09  352.10         476.10  479.22  480.29
  402.02  423.06  429.22         357.07  472.02             GENEROUSLY            258.14       488.22  491.19  492.10
  443.05  443.16  444.13      GAMES        243.06  307.25   GENTLE         12.28  140.02       492.12  493.21  495.01
  444.16  459.19  465.23      GANG         150.26  324.06      170.19  233.12  241.06         495.03  497.10  502.17
  469.01  473.15  477.14         439.07  439.27  442.05        246.06  257.27  269.28      GETS           156.27  334.25
  478.29  479.30  491.22         497.11                        329.08  376.06  428.28         394.21
  513.13                      GANGWAYS      15.11           GENTLEMAN      52.22            GETTING        26.28   34.18
FULLNESS     340.30           GANZ         256.04              52.28   79.29  143.11          34.21   79.09   85.01
FULLY         66.11   76.20   GAP          309.14  432.20      145.09  158.27  158.28         109.08  109.19  141.15
  86.28  225.02  342.03       GAPING       372.05              231.07  231.08  279.05         164.19  184.02  237.20
  360.05  455.08  509.05      GARBAGE       58.29  279.14      292.12  294.05  294.10         307.15  309.19  310.03
  511.20                      GARBAGE-HEAP  58.29              404.10  404.22  426.15         317.14  372.12  437.09
FUMBLED      314.03           GARDEN       163.15  217.24      426.28  475.11  475.15         456.23  463.20
FUMES        397.18              231.15  252.08  427.21        475.21                      GEWISS         263.21
FUMING        49.16           GARDENS       13.04  431.29   GENTLEMANLY           10.13    GEWISSEN       257.04
FUN          300.04  363.10      431.30                     GENTLEMEN             437.09    GHARRY         47.02   54.23
  475.28                      GARLAND      339.28           GENTLY          6.24   19.19       55.17   55.30   56.03
FUNCTION     246.29           GARLANDED             13.07      32.11   52.14  119.18          56.17  284.07
FUNCTIONS            320.07      397.11                        128.21  129.26  132.26      GHARRY-WALLAH          55.17
FUNDAMENTAL           66.23   GARMENT      315.02              223.07  261.17  396.17      GHASTLY        189.07  308.21
FUNDAMENTALLY        352.09   GARRISON     333.13  448.08      411.01  439.29  440.19      GHOST          59.25   60.17
FUNERAL      211.29           GASP          12.06  313.28      509.03  514.19                 70.18   99.11  105.11
FUNK          58.20  117.23      320.19                     GENTS          475.29            111.14  124.26  133.16
  178.29  480.26              GASPED       216.06  224.09   GENUINE        53.24  177.13      201.30  206.02  239.11
FUNNEL        22.07              368.04  425.24                202.27  300.11                 239.20  240.01  248.09
FUNNIEST      86.18  240.09   GASPING      124.07  242.16   GENUINELY            387.04       301.30  389.09  425.07
FUNNY         72.29   76.13      312.21                     GEO            134.07             516.06
  93.01  122.16  127.14       GASPS        211.24  426.17   GEO-O-O-ORGE   134.07         GHOSTLY        380.14
  128.09  157.10  177.15      GATE          89.29  195.27   GEORGE         133.04  133.23  GHOSTS         37.21  188.02
  217.26  238.03  260.25         251.18  254.11  254.25        134.02  141.25  141.30         191.03  495.15
  285.17  289.28  330.07         254.27  300.25  301.20        144.25  150.30  150.30      GHOUL          194.17
  331.12  396.09                 311.30  314.11  332.10    GERMAN         15.01   16.14    GIDDINESS             299.28
FURIES        11.08              396.14  402.06  404.24        25.26   26.13   28.16     GIFT           13.03  375.15
FURIOUS        6.10   55.16      404.28  448.30  474.29        29.22   43.20                421.08  478.04  486.14
  60.25  216.24                  484.17  504.12  508.30    GERMANS        26.24          GIFTED         116.22  327.01
FURNACE       21.22              512.28                     GERMANY        195.20            379.12
FURNISH      420.12           GATES         70.03  504.21   GESTICULATING        307.10   GIFTS          175.04  304.25
FURNITURE                        507.16  508.09           GESTURE        56.16   63.18    GIG            291.24  295.23
  263.09                      GATEWAY       52.06   65.19      80.16  129.07  153.07     GIGANTIC        93.22
FURROWED     318.08           GATHER       404.26  414.24      171.10  222.21  287.20    GIRL            8.14  182.23
FURROWS      428.23           GATHERED     102.04  268.19      430.16  502.22               183.02  227.20  236.28
FURTHER       79.15  118.29      397.15                     GESTURES       30.10  212.22      268.09  268.15  340.15
  173.15  293.10  355.01      GATHERING            312.10      246.23  291.16  320.10        341.25  346.03  349.28
  400.08  455.04                 357.26  513.15           GET             2.04   13.15       355.04  355.17  357.13
FURTHERMORE          461.01   GAUDY         55.05              25.24   26.12   28.18         359.18  359.26  362.04
FURTIVE      136.20  210.09   GAUNT         61.16  378.04      30.02   30.04   35.03         362.21  364.21  365.16
FURY          28.15   52.28   GAVE           2.29   47.04      43.36   45.29   47.14         366.24  366.30  367.13
  141.28  220.15  232.10         73.13   73.22   74.27        49.18   50.14   50.15         367.25  368.21  368.26
  307.09  371.04  393.08         76.08   78.17   82.19        52.23   52.27   62.14         369.27  370.24  373.11
  444.08  510.01                 95.26  108.13  114.28        68.16   72.13   74.17         374.05  374.22  375.12
FUSED        132.01              121.06  125.09  125.12        76.20   83.30   96.12         378.21  383.28  386.08
FUSILLADE            297.17      130.26  151.16  171.10        96.14   96.17   98.30         395.20  395.26  403.30
  443.24                         180.18  190.02  195.28        108.13  108.26  108.27        404.09  405.20  408.02
FUSS          49.06   49.10      201.04  202.24  206.01        111.07  113.07  113.21        409.11  428.25  428.26
  198.28  237.11  412.06         217.01  218.04  230.04        115.05  115.17  117.07        429.27  432.22  432.28
FUSSINESS            319.19      233.26  234.20  237.25        122.09  124.25  125.02        436.22  448.21  450.11
FUSSING       71.20  301.17      238.10  254.25  257.05        125.24  143.25  144.15        450.18  475.16  484.21
FUSSY         56.28  310.15      278.06  288.09  301.08        148.16  150.11  152.27        489.04  504.14  504.24
  497.14                         308.09  315.12  337.28        153.23  156.18  162.23        506.26  507.19  507.24
FUTILE       148.03  389.23      358.10  421.04  425.07        163.23  167.12  169.01        509.12  510.16  510.25
FUTILELY      66.18              436.28  443.02  460.16        169.11  177.19  180.22        511.16  512.27  516.17
FUTILITY     181.09  239.08      466.08  487.11  489.24        180.25  181.26  187.25    GIRL'S          7.28   92.21
  347.12                         491.12  507.06  508.11        190.07  196.27  197.02        356.28  451.15  482.09
FUTURE        11.15   25.09   GAY          279.21              198.05  199.24  200.08    GIRLS          16.09   46.04
```

46

GOOD (CONT.)   155.12
155.13   160.18   169.12
179.29   184.22   186.27
188.12   191.11   196.25
196.30   197.11   199.12
200.03   200.22   201.30
202.22   203.04   203.09
203.22   204.06   204.21
204.30   213.12   214.16
220.08   220.09   225.26
226.25   228.03   237.16
237.22   237.25   238.15
243.15   246.08   246.29
252.05   257.11   257.30
259.03   260.17   263.19
268.15   285.15   287.17
289.29   291.11   301.12
303.18   308.04   308.22
309.02   311.09   320.17
322.30   324.20   330.08
330.09   330.12   338.10
344.01   344.18   348.15
349.02   351.21   354.10
358.07   362.18   363.10
364.23   364.26   369.06
384.29   393.09   393.23
400.09   401.03   401.24
411.23   413.26   417.25
421.16   424.09   438.03
439.03   447.23   453.05
453.12   456.13   462.06
466.28   472.02   473.25
474.13   477.18   481.06
483.08   483.21   491.26
492.25   497.24   499.05
499.21
GOOD-BYE   52.20   220.09
237.25   291.11   413.26
491.26
GOOD-HUMOUR   105.01
GOOD-HUMOURED   453.12
GOOD-HUMOUREDLY   301.12
GOOD-LOOKING   268.15
GOOD-NATURE   48.28
246.08
GOOD-NATURED   69.03
GOOD-NIGHT   364.23
364.26
GOOD-TEMPERED   228.03
GOODNESS   50.30   78.07
194.09   228.05   286.17
GOODS   303.30   353.22
356.20   501.26
GORGE   28.23
GORGEOUS   23.16   70.11
249.11   252.26   257.25
GOSH   25.25
GOSSIP   240.21   423.02
GOSSIPING   14.18
492.28
GOSSIPY   210.01
GOT   1.12   5.23
14.10   27.29   41.19
47.21   52.19   52.24
62.15   64.21   70.12
72.19   72.26   73.04
74.30   75.26   76.12
80.27   86.25   91.04
98.25   100.17   104.11
108.21   109.18   109.23
112.28   130.17   136.11
136.18   139.10   141.27
148.13   149.04   151.02
158.22   160.02   169.21
177.02   178.19   178.26
180.29   182.16   183.20
185.14   187.25   188.14
189.18   198.04   199.04
201.29   201.30   203.10
203.13   204.26   205.22
205.23   207.18   223.15
229.29   230.18   232.30
233.16   236.12   243.09
255.08   256.20   256.20
267.09   283.29   289.05
293.12   298.30   321.08
325.02   329.26   331.01
343.18   343.30   344.30
353.03   353.30   359.15
360.20   364.12   366.08

GOT (CONT.)   374.28
377.11   380.06   388.29
391.23   392.21   394.01
395.11   411.22   411.24
440.22   440.26   443.07
443.27   460.03   460.29
464.11   466.13   470.02
470.23   471.17   474.10
476.06   476.06   476.06
478.06   480.27   481.16
490.18   503.07
GOTT   122.15   125.01
133.30   260.21
GOTT-FOR-DAM   122.15
GOTTAM   49.06
GOUNDRY   241.17
GOVERNMENT   68.07
79.10   266.13   267.12
278.14   344.02   344.09
344.16   437.04   438.29
448.17
GOVERNOR   278.24   309.30
437.14
GOWN   16.18   373.12
378.21   433.25
GRABBED   8.04   109.09
312.09
GRACE   95.28   148.04
271.28   348.03   423.24
434.03
GRADUAL   376.26
GRADUALLY   222.04
226.18   277.29   281.26
310.03   329.03   380.06
403.29   496.05
GRANARY   311.04
GRANDEUR   249.09
GRANDFATHER   331.13
GRANDS   169.28
GRANGER   233.13   235.09
GRANITE   69.13
GRAPHICALLY   149.09
GRAPPLE   219.05   239.10
422.30
GRASP   49.17   116.16
196.03   219.14   271.22
304.25   393.05   422.21
431.03
GRASPED   250.22
GRASS   4.10   4.12
49.25   129.16   181.01
253.06   253.22   255.20
272.02   317.01   323.10
328.25   333.16   353.13
367.14   368.16   373.16
396.19   398.25   444.30
GRASS-PLOT   129.16
GRASS-PLOTS   4.10
49.25
GRASSY   490.15
GRATED   414.05
GRATEFUL   219.22   300.07
GRATIFIED   490.09
GRATIFY   341.04
GRATING   158.11
GRATIS   200.03
GRATITUDE   23.10
58.10   186.25   282.03
295.04   412.18
GRAVE   16.18   146.23
177.10   215.06   222.13
258.10   260.12   268.07
269.27   279.25   301.29
306.18   314.29   339.22
339.24   340.03   381.24
397.11   397.25   402.05
469.18   485.29
GRAVEL   189.21
GRAVELY   287.08
GRAVEN   226.28
GRAVES   16.04   260.23
262.06   262.13
GRAVEST   69.23
GRAVITY   28.07   287.16
GRAZE   171.17
GRAZING   192.11
GREASY   24.12   153.27
343.08
GREAT   5.22   5.29
18.03   19.23   21.11

GREAT (CONT.)   21.27
32.24   45.23   45.26
53.05   57.21   74.13
80.13   84.07   119.05
119.09   127.24   137.06
152.20   169.25   175.07
216.30   218.26   234.05
241.10   241.17   249.27
253.09   253.20   254.16
254.28   254.29   254.29
256.28   257.28   258.19
259.15   262.12   262.25
265.10   273.04   277.04
279.19   281.05   290.21
298.30   307.21   311.18
314.21   322.09   325.11
333.24   338.14   343.05
346.03   358.14   365.01
365.08   365.29   373.17
374.02   374.04   384.08
391.18   391.30   392.26
397.24   403.11   404.02
408.29   409.28   413.14
414.20   426.27   428.30
430.06   438.25   445.10
447.02   449.01   449.07
449.17   452.07   461.30
463.03   467.28   467.29
477.24   478.04   478.10
478.22   485.06   486.05
487.24   495.27   500.20
500.24   501.11   502.25
508.20   509.13   509.30
510.03   510.05
GREATER   7.24   149.02
150.02   155.09   267.03
267.21   328.05   389.26
456.18   488.07
GREATEST   141.22   169.28
185.25   209.15   216.21
314.02   335.06   393.24
401.22   436.16   475.10
478.16   483.06
GREATLY   79.03   90.22
256.26   257.12   310.13
333.10   362.12   396.01
407.23   516.18
GREATNESS   85.15
275.12   300.10   335.05
376.24   432.15   477.24
277.08
GREED   156.16
GREEDILY   217.12
GREEDY   436.09
GREEK'S   64.23
GREEN   4.12   55.04
70.13   191.26   199.15
290.29   297.05   319.11
343.11   344.01   475.13
GREEN-AND-GOLD   290.29
GREEN-AND-ORANGE   55.04
GREEN-HOUSES   4.12
GREEN-LINED   199.15
GREENISH   430.02   431.08
GREETED   7.17   427.22
GREETING   1.19   395.28
428.03   498.30
GREETINGS   244.26
320.09   373.21   484.24
GREW   14.23
GREY   7.29   27.10
46.26   54.10   70.05
74.23   118.23   171.16
175.04   180.16   205.15
302.22   307.19   315.07
325.13   338.15   421.27
432.24   434.09   470.20
494.01   514.09
GREY-HAIRED   421.27
432.24
GREY-HEADED   70.05
GREYBEARDS   157.05
GREYHOUND   14.28
GREYISH   417.27   420.04
GREYNESS   4.05   494.07
GRIEF   31.01   299.01
431.11   436.29   487.24
GRIEVANCE   172.13
GRIM   96.04   118.24
182.26   248.04   291.07
350.16   454.29   457.21

GRIMACE   144.17   356.14
GRIMACES   127.15
GRIMACING   358.25
GRIME   16.05
GRIMLY   142.19
GRIMY   4.30   279.10
GRIN   189.15   330.22
GRIND   495.28
GRINDING   131.13
GRINNED   54.07   426.15
GRINNING   92.24
GRIP   12.06   105.20
190.09   205.06   373.04
498.07   500.07
GRIPES   107.13
GRIPPED   7.10   365.23
GRIPPING   506.07
GROAN   189.17   343.24
369.25   464.18
GROANED   8.12
GROANS   405.30
GROG   57.28   64.24
GROG-SHOP   57.28
64.24
GROOMED   94.06
GROOVES   22.15
GROPED   141.05
GROPING   379.22
GROPINGLY   372.06
GROSSLY   186.11
GROTESQUE   55.07
397.28   406.02
GROUND   16.22   22.15
58.01   98.29   139.22
196.19   196.27   201.23
223.06   245.21   255.29
256.25   278.25   284.02
309.29   312.06   312.27
323.04   334.21   349.27
385.18   389.12   396.15
396.17   396.22   398.26
403.09   420.20   432.27
445.13   459.08   462.20
466.01   466.19   479.20
497.20   498.19   502.25
505.20   509.22   512.15
GROUNDING   465.06
GROUNDS   86.16   227.18
316.22   383.08   400.30
441.19
GROUP   46.22   47.03
125.27   192.08   435.17
462.29   469.09   469.24
515.04
GROUPED   408.08
GROUPS   444.29   504.08
GROVE   434.04
GROVELLED   383.20
GROVELLING   115.25
GROW   262.27   272.17
325.27   374.06   434.01
494.19   513.09
GROWING   13.05   84.26
114.26   244.16   317.12
374.03   397.05   398.25
508.01
GROWL   215.18   258.20
GROWLED   25.26   31.04
79.22   153.30   203.01
492.13
GROWLING   110.04
GROWLS   497.13
GROWN   52.01   60.28
286.27   337.08   379.04
387.11   397.16
GROWS   11.28
GROWTH   323.10
GRUB   202.08
GRUBBING   59.13
GRUDGE   298.04
GRUFF   188.29
GRUMPY   8.07
GRUNT   25.18   132.13
141.01   141.01   215.29
333.20   371.09
GRUNTED   200.26   217.04
495.24
GRUNTING   145.10
GUANO   196.22   197.28
200.12   203.30   205.19

```
GUANO (CONT.)        211.10    HAD (CONT.)            25.06    HAD (CONT.)           129.09    HAD (CONT.)           207.19
GUARANTEE            204.28    25.21   25.23   26.01          129.11  129.19  130.01          207.25  208.06  208.11
  453.05                      26.03   26.26   27.06          130.05  130.12  130.12          208.17  208.20  208.30
GUARD      173.09    437.27    27.12   27.19   27.23          130.15  130.22  130.27          209.18  209.23  209.30
  489.24  506.30              27.26   27.29   28.11          131.01  131.02  131.08          210.09  210.26  210.26
GUARDED    349.11              28.14   30.15   30.22          131.10  131.10  131.11          211.30  212.11  213.04
GUARDIAN   40.04     404.14    30.23   31.04   31.10          132.14  132.18  133.09          213.07  213.21  213.22
GUARDIANS           322.22    31.14   32.16   33.13          133.11  133.25  134.06          213.24  213.24  214.19
GUARDIANSHIP        349.18    33.13   33.18   33.27          134.12  134.15  134.26          215.28  216.23  217.11
  482.20                      34.20   35.12   35.16          134.27  134.28  135.02          217.19  217.25  218.02
GUARDING   349.05              35.20   35.26   35.27          135.07  136.03  136.04          218.13  219.01  219.02
GUESS      94.22     213.19    36.02   36.15   36.16          136.06  136.13  136.17          220.10  220.30  222.08
  228.15  268.06     355.03    36.24   37.01   37.05          137.04  137.20  137.24          222.14  224.01  224.08
  476.03                      37.09   38.06   38.08          138.01  138.16  139.01          224.10  224.19  224.23
GUESSED    460.06              38.09   38.09   38.14          139.08  139.10  140.01          225.01  225.08  225.10
GUEST      141.16    240.23    39.07   40.01   42.04          140.11  140.12  141.07          225.12  225.14  225.19
  264.17                      42.27   43.05   43.12          141.12  142.08  142.18          225.26  226.01  226.09
GUFFAW     215.30              43.17   43.29   44.14          143.22  143.23  144.02          226.26  227.13  227.15
GUIDED     447.18    451.07    44.20   45.15   45.21          144.02  144.08  144.12          227.19  227.23  227.23
GUIDING    288.03              45.26   46.17   46.21          144.26  145.16  145.17          228.02  228.04  228.09
GUILDER    43.22               47.14   47.15   48.04          145.21  145.27  146.05          228.14  228.24  229.01
GUILT      69.20     191.22    48.16   52.15   53.07          146.08  146.11  146.16          229.02  229.28  230.12
  215.20  479.27              53.13   54.06   55.23          146.19  147.08  147.16          230.16  230.19  231.01
GUILTY     185.09    185.09    55.28   56.03   56.08          147.22  148.08  148.10          231.02  231.09  231.12
  185.10  228.20     229.20    56.17   57.16   57.23          148.11  148.17  149.06          231.24  231.29  232.04
GUISE      364.05    474.29    57.23   57.30   57.30          149.08  149.17  150.04          232.21  233.09  233.24
GULF       61.29     421.05    58.17   58.30   59.02          150.08  150.08  150.19          234.21  235.02  235.04
GULLET     132.22              59.06   60.06   60.11          150.30  151.08  151.12          235.20  235.30  236.29
GULPED     97.09               60.25   60.27   60.28          152.09  152.17  152.18          237.06  238.01  239.12
GUM        307.06    454.09    63.01   65.13   67.20          152.24  153.11  153.21          239.15  239.15  240.11
GUMMED     92.16               67.21   67.25   67.27          153.30  154.01  154.05          241.11  241.13  242.02
GUN        28.20     217.07    67.28   68.01   68.04          154.08  155.02  155.04          242.02  242.05  242.06
  327.06  349.16     466.04    68.04   68.05   68.13          155.05  155.11  155.19          242.18  242.19  242.21
  468.16  483.23     510.14    70.02   70.25   70.32          155.23  156.15  157.06          242.26  243.16  243.28
  511.02                      70.34   70.42   71.13          157.07  157.08  157.09          244.05  244.17  244.17
GUN-CARRIAGE         510.14    71.14   71.20   72.06          157.19  158.02  158.03          245.01  245.03  245.15
GUNBOAT    12.17     164.11    73.05   73.16   73.18          158.05  158.06  158.27          245.15  245.24  245.29
  166.26  167.09     169.10    73.20   73.23   73.29          159.03  159.04  159.20          246.06  246.09  246.10
  441.11                      74.01   74.16   74.29          159.22  159.28  160.11          246.22  246.28  247.04
GUNPOWDER           448.15    75.01   75.04   75.11          160.22  160.27  160.29          247.13  247.17  247.19
GUNS       5.29      198.26    75.28   76.12   76.30          162.15  162.18  163.05          248.08  249.03  249.20
  323.23  327.23     328.12    77.02   77.08   77.19          163.06  163.24  164.02          249.21  250.06  250.13
  328.18  331.29     333.19    77.22   78.03   80.22          164.16  164.17  164.21          251.07  251.22  251.25
  359.14  420.10     420.12    80.25   81.14   81.22          164.23  164.26  165.03          251.25  251.28  252.03
  435.21  437.22     449.27    82.10   82.10   82.20          165.10  165.11  165.21          252.05  252.06  252.10
  454.21  478.10     504.07    82.26   83.01   83.20          165.24  165.25  165.30          252.12  252.20  253.27
GUNSHOT    171.12              84.06   85.04   86.04          166.07  166.10  166.11          254.12  255.01  255.02
GUNWALE    142.25    414.04    86.14   87.02   87.27          166.13  166.18  166.22          255.30  256.23  256.25
GUNWALES   152.21              87.30   88.15   88.16          166.28  167.03  167.10          256.26  256.29  256.30
GURGLED    220.21              88.27   88.28   89.12          167.26  167.30  168.11          257.11  257.12  257.13
GURGLING   28.24     217.27    89.20   89.21   89.24          168.13  168.25  168.27          257.14  257.15  257.16
  514.24                      89.29   91.13   92.01          168.28  169.09  169.15          257.16  257.24  258.26
GUSH       25.17               93.11   94.25   95.04          169.19  169.30  170.10          259.08  260.04  260.05
GUST       6.07      134.01    95.10   95.26   96.06          170.14  170.23  170.25          261.05  261.15  261.19
  136.17  145.17     508.16    96.24   96.27   96.28          170.29  171.13  172.18          261.21  261.21  262.03
GUSTAV     195.19              97.30   98.02   98.04          172.19  172.30  173.07          262.06  262.07  262.09
GUSTS      148.20    430.03    98.04   98.06   98.12          174.05  174.16  174.21          262.28  264.06  264.20
  431.07                      98.18   98.27   99.04          175.01  175.02  175.03          265.02  265.02  265.04
GUTTERS    149.09    218.27    99.06   99.16   99.18          175.17  176.12  176.13          266.06  266.17  267.01
H          64.03     361.12    100.11  100.12  100.13          176.14  176.15  176.18          267.05  267.13  267.18
  361.12                      100.21  100.25  100.28          176.23  177.16  177.18          267.19  267.23  267.26
H-E-ELP    64.03               101.01  101.09  101.23          178.07  179.04  179.05          268.06  268.09  268.12
H-H-HERE   361.12              101.30  102.05  104.06          180.01  180.06  181.05          268.14  268.18  268.23
HA         65.04     65.04     104.08  105.26  105.29          181.08  181.09  181.14          268.26  269.28  270.01
  120.21  120.21     120.21    107.16  107.20  108.04          181.22  182.02  182.03          270.02  270.03  270.07
  120.22  120.22     120.22    108.10  108.29  109.02          182.04  182.05  182.08          270.11  270.12  270.16
  120.22  130.07     130.07    109.03  109.04  109.23          192.15  182.20  182.23          270.19  270.20  272.12
  130.07  260.22     260.22    109.24  109.28  110.07          182.24  183.08  183.17          272.25  272.28  273.01
  260.22  405.15     405.15    110.17  111.09  111.10          183.19  183.20  184.05          273.07  273.08  273.15
  405.15  468.20     468.20    111.11  112.07  112.09          184.12  184.22  184.24          274.09  274.23  274.25
  468.20                      112.09  112.29  114.10          184.26  184.27  185.02          275.12  275.16  277.12
HABIT      48.27     149.12    114.14  114.15  114.18          185.09  185.25  186.02          277.25  277.26  277.30
  168.20  179.26     179.26    114.27  115.06  115.09          186.02  186.03  186.04          278.10  278.27  279.04
  329.26                      115.09  115.12  115.15          186.15  186.20  186.30          279.24  280.03  280.04
HABITUALLY          491.12    115.17  115.19  116.02          187.20  187.27  188.04          280.08  280.13  280.22
HAD        1.07      2.24      116.04  116.23  116.29          188.17  188.18  188.21          280.27  280.28  280.29
  3.05   3.07        3.13      117.10  117.22  117.23          188.22  188.24  188.26          280.30  281.13  281.22
  3.24   4.05        4.07      117.30  118.01  118.26          188.30  189.09  190.12          281.23  281.28  282.02
  4.13   4.16        4.21      118.27  119.08  119.15          190.13  190.14  191.21          282.05  282.06  282.10
  5.26   6.02        6.17      119.27  119.28  120.15          192.19  192.26  193.03          282.11  282.14  282.16
  6.18   8.17        8.22      120.23  120.24  122.24          193.16  193.17  193.25          282.19  283.15  283.30
  8.27   8.28        8.28      123.14  123.15  123.16          194.08  194.14  194.27          284.05  284.06  284.09
  8.29   10.06       10.23     123.29  123.30  124.04          195.10  195.22  195.28          285.02  285.03  285.04
  12.04  12.13       12.17     124.12  124.13  124.16          195.30  196.06  196.12          285.12  285.13  285.16
  13.19  13.27       13.28     124.16  124.16  124.20          196.15  196.19  196.21          285.19  285.20  285.23
  14.09  14.12       15.07     124.21  125.17  125.19          197.08  199.05  199.06          286.01  286.05  286.11
  15.22  16.01       19.11     125.30  126.05  126.06          201.09  201.23  201.24          286.13  286.13  286.17
  20.27  20.29       21.08     126.08  126.13  126.19          202.07  202.12  203.28          286.19  286.28  287.01
  21.24  23.15       24.05     127.01  127.10  127.22          204.18  205.01  207.02          287.08  287.27  289.10
  24.06  24.13       24.28     127.24  128.19  128.23          207.06  207.12  207.15
```

HAD (CONT.)   289.11

```
289.24   290.16   290.17
291.16   291.23   291.26
291.27   292.11   292.15
292.21   292.25   293.18
293.24   293.30   294.26
294.28   294.30   295.05
295.10   295.20   295.23
296.03   297.14   297.15
297.22   297.23   298.04
298.07   298.09   298.09
298.12   298.19   298.19
298.20   299.19   299.26
300.03   301.01   301.10
301.23   301.27   302.14
303.09   303.10   303.27
304.04   304.07   304.10
304.22   304.25   304.25
304.28   305.02   305.06
306.13   307.05   307.20
309.04   309.11   309.18
310.01   310.13   310.14
311.29   312.02   312.17
313.16   313.27   314.05
314.06   314.15   314.22
314.23   315.03   315.23
316.07   316.15   316.22
316.24   317.02   317.13
318.02   319.07   319.25
320.16   320.25   320.25
320.26   320.27   320.30
321.08   321.11   321.13
321.14   321.15   321.27
321.28   322.03   322.15
322.19   323.02   323.03
323.19   323.19   323.20
323.27   323.27   324.01
324.02   324.03   324.06
324.09   324.11   324.26
324.27   324.28   326.02
327.01   327.03   327.14
327.23   328.18   328.20
329.12   329.14   329.20
329.24   329.26   329.29
330.14   331.06   331.17
331.21   331.30   332.09
332.14   332.21   332.23
332.24   332.25   332.28
333.06   333.10   333.11
333.16   333.17   334.13
334.29   335.03   336.08
336.23   337.07   337.08
337.14   337.20   337.29
338.20   338.21   338.22
339.01   340.04   340.09
340.11   340.13   340.16
340.20   340.22   342.14
343.01   343.04   343.15
343.22   344.12   344.30
345.05   345.08   345.14
345.20   346.02   347.14
347.18   348.13   348.14
348.14   348.19   348.23
349.01   349.29   350.11
350.13   350.13   351.16
351.19   351.21   351.23
351.27   352.01   352.03
352.04   352.27   353.10
353.12   353.12   353.19
353.25   353.28   354.06
354.08   355.07   356.15
357.10   357.18   357.21
357.27   358.22   359.03
359.10   359.29   360.03
360.09   360.18   360.24
360.30   361.23   361.24
362.14   362.14   363.13
363.16   363.18   363.20
363.21   364.07   364.12
364.13   364.25   365.22
366.01   366.13   366.20
366.21   366.29   366.29
367.01   367.03   367.09
368.03   368.04   368.10
368.12   369.05   369.18
370.05   370.12   370.13
370.18   370.20   370.22
371.01   372.02   372.11
373.03   374.05   375.12
375.15   375.18   376.21
```

HAD (CONT.)   378.01

```
378.08   378.11   379.03
379.04   379.05   379.05
379.06   379.15   379.17
379.18   379.18   380.02
380.04   381.03   381.18
381.22   382.11   382.12
382.13   382.17   382.20
382.26   382.27   382.27
383.04   383.06   383.27
383.27   384.03   384.11
384.23   385.12   385.16
385.21   385.25   386.13
386.17   386.25   386.29
387.06   387.09   387.11
387.11   387.12   387.15
388.24   389.02   389.24
389.25   389.28   390.02
390.03   390.04   391.12
391.27   391.28   392.06
392.07   392.08   392.20
392.27   393.14   394.03
394.14   395.03   395.10
395.11   395.12   395.15
395.17   395.20   395.21
396.17   396.18   396.19
396.24   397.01   397.15
397.24   398.06   398.16
398.09   398.15   398.16
399.06   399.07   399.11
399.14   400.05   400.06
400.07   401.26   401.27
401.29   401.30   402.03
402.04   403.11   404.01
404.12   404.19   405.13
405.20   405.21   406.01
407.11   407.12   408.12
408.21   408.29   408.30
410.25   410.27   411.13
411.20   412.19   412.27
413.02   413.15   414.14
414.16   414.25   414.26
415.01   415.05   415.14
416.01   416.02   416.08
417.28   418.10   418.14
418.25   419.06   419.07
419.17   419.19   419.19
419.25   420.04   420.07
420.12   420.24   421.01
421.03   421.05   421.09
421.15   421.15   421.23
421.24   421.30   422.04
422.16   422.17   422.28
423.22   423.26   425.11
425.13   426.04   426.14
426.22   426.13   426.27
427.17   427.23   427.27
427.29   428.22   429.30
430.09   430.10   430.30
431.06   431.15   431.19
431.20   431.27   432.10
432.11   434.15   434.17
434.20   434.23   435.12
435.19   436.22   437.02
437.05   437.30   438.08
438.09   438.17   439.17
439.28   440.28   441.25
441.30   443.12   443.14
443.26   444.10   444.12
444.15   445.16   445.17
446.12   446.13   447.04
447.06   447.10   447.24
448.04   448.08   448.12
448.15   448.16   448.21
448.29   448.30   449.08
449.16   450.14   450.23
451.19   451.25   452.09
453.22   453.30   454.08
454.10   454.19   454.28
455.11   456.05   458.01
458.06   458.25   458.28
458.29   459.14   460.17
461.09   461.12   461.14
461.14   461.19   461.24
461.24   462.19   463.15
463.15   463.21   464.02
465.10   465.12   465.21
465.23   465.25   466.01
466.28   466.29   469.08
470.05   470.17   470.18
```

HAD (CONT.)   470.23

```
470.25   471.03   471.09
471.21   471.22   471.24
471.29   472.05   474.01
474.30   474.30   475.01
475.02   475.17   475.19
475.25   475.25   477.13
477.16   478.03   478.04
478.11   478.15   478.18
478.19   478.26   478.26
479.01   479.01   479.03
479.05   479.15   479.20
480.04   481.17   482.10
482.24   482.27   483.10
483.14   483.22   483.24
483.25   483.28   484.04
484.08   484.19   484.21
484.21   484.22   485.07
485.10   485.20   485.24
485.25   485.30   486.03
486.10   488.22   489.07
489.27   489.29   489.30
491.16   491.17   491.26
491.27   491.28   492.10
492.12   492.16   492.17
492.28   494.10   495.04
496.07   497.05   497.16
497.17   497.18   498.19
499.13   500.03   501.04
501.12   502.03   502.07
502.09   502.11   502.19
503.03   503.04   503.07
503.19   504.05   504.09
504.18   504.22   505.14
506.11   506.13   506.16
507.03   507.04   507.07
507.08   507.26   507.28
508.14   508.15   508.29
509.11   510.16   510.27
512.04   512.20   512.25
513.18   514.26   514.29
515.13   515.14   515.15
515.27
```

```
HADN'T            79.12    82.04
 90.24   126.29   128.22
130.09   150.07   150.29
151.06   152.24   156.23
160.09   163.05   163.24
176.13   202.29   219.23
309.22   332.17   351.28
362.20   426.05   435.23
478.12
HAFT             333.04
HAG              299.02   366.05
369.25
HAGGARD          129.29   347.10
468.25
HAI               76.15
HAI-PHONG                  76.15
HAIL             396.03   466.09
HAILED            62.27   167.12
HAIR              16.09    21.05
 74.23    89.08    93.15
116.10   133.10   149.06
159.15   159.17   171.16
175.04   193.02   207.14
232.08   238.22   241.03
246.11   254.13   272.23
279.08   279.28   307.19
315.07   338.15   347.21
353.09   356.04   358.26
373.12   390.19   433.26
508.07   512.14   514.09
HAIR'S           159.14
HAIR'S-BREADTH             159.14
HAIRED           421.27   432.24
HAIRLESS         246.08
HAIRS             27.10   196.15
HAIRY            460.26
HAJI             449.07   450.05
HALF              5.13     7.18
 14.08    16.23    24.08
 25.29    33.08    34.06
 42.24    42.25    43.35
 50.01    50.12    55.09
 56.22    57.04    57.12
 57.24    57.25    70.40
 72.26    76.01    83.12
```

HALF (CONT.)   92.03

```
103.19   108.30   119.28
134.13   136.08   137.23
138.02   138.02   138.11
145.28   148.20   150.26
156.07   156.07   158.07
164.10   168.16   174.12
176.09   187.21   188.10
194.01   200.02   203.19
236.03   236.16   237.26
264.08   273.23   279.23
290.29   291.28   294.20
294.28   295.03   296.03
299.22   313.14   313.29
313.29   316.21   317.08
321.13   323.04   328.04
329.02   330.28   330.29
353.11   355.23   361.17
367.03   385.10   398.11
414.10   414.25   428.27
435.24   447.24   452.29
455.30   467.21   472.29
477.20   477.21   480.08
483.27   510.29
HALF-AVERTED               273.23
HALF-BRED                   57.04
HALF-BREED                 316.21
HALF-CASTE                  43.35
 56.22    57.12   164.10
294.20   294.28   296.03
HALF-CASTES                 14.08
 42.24
HALF-CROWN                 290.29
HALF-HEARTED               428.27
HALF-HOUR                  329.02
HALF-LIGHT                  33.08
HALF-LOST                  385.10
HALF-NAKED                 414.25
HALF-PAST                   72.26
236.03
HALF-PAY          76.01
HALF-RESENTFUL             477.20
HALF-RESIGNED              477.21
HALF-SUBMERGED             414.10
HALF-UTTERED               295.03
HALF-WAY         323.04   510.29
HALFCASTE                  292.03
HALFCONSUMED               333.29
HALFHEARTED                147.18
HALFTRANSPARENT             25.02
HALL             146.06   250.17
279.11   279.30   336.11
461.26
HALLO             76.05   236.21
395.26   395.26
HALT             288.10
HALT'            257.03
HALTER            50.17   293.26
HALTING           3.19
HALTING-PLACES              3.19
HALVES           269.18
HAMMER            66.21   125.01
125.01   125.02   125.10
125.13   125.19
HAMMERING                   89.16
HAMMERS          166.23
HAMMOCK          366.09
HAMS             372.20
HAND              7.12    20.23
 22.12    37.12    39.01
 53.07    53.10    62.29
 71.03    93.30    99.22
101.13   101.14   103.22
103.29   104.24   108.08
108.21   109.12   109.15
110.11   110.24   112.12
117.18   119.14   125.10
125.29   133.09   133.12
133.24   134.10   137.10
141.05   141.26   143.11
148.11   153.05   171.08
171.12   173.03   177.30
180.21   181.19   181.27
187.24   188.22   189.15
203.19   205.21   209.03
210.28   219.12   219.14
224.23   225.14   226.17
228.08   231.21   233.04
233.28   235.30   247.26
249.07   254.11   254.25
```

HAND (CONT.)		255.18
256.13	256.18	257.17
259.25	261.11	261.15
261.26	264.30	270.02
274.14	278.02	279.02
282.27	286.05	287.06
287.21	290.22	291.17
294.18	299.17	306.16
308.05	310.05	320.03
324.22	329.08	333.04
333.14	333.14	338.13
343.12	346.11	348.10
350.22	353.24	356.26
365.21	369.22	373.04
379.18	386.04	391.23
392.10	398.21	401.09
402.11	402.16	408.29
410.29	414.13	420.06
421.02	424.05	427.11
430.24	431.12	432.22
433.18	447.09	457.14
458.12	458.26	460.21
461.19	466.10	467.12
476.05	479.23	480.20
481.02	485.10	485.16
487.10	491.10	496.12
499.13	506.27	509.02
509.26	512.25	515.14
515.18	516.21	
HAND-LAMP		125.29
HAND-TO-HAND		333.14
HANDED	111.21	419.03
454.14	457.10	
HANDEN	257.03	
HANDFUL	356.02	454.09
HANDING	168.21	499.01
HANDKERCHIEF		76.24
118.22		
HANDKERCHIEFS		52.13
410.21		
HANDLE	54.23	199.18
202.17		
HANDLED	131.11	236.25
HANDLING	21.23	
HANDS	21.01	26.20
31.07	33.20	46.29
49.24	51.30	54.29
64.05	65.15	105.18
109.10	120.13	124.29
126.16	127.05	130.15
145.21	154.11	163.07
171.18	171.24	173.05
174.23	183.04	184.26
189.11	190.09	193.06
199.17	200.23	214.27
216.24	225.30	230.20
233.02	239.06	239.10
243.26	246.22	251.13
260.01	261.01	265.11
271.21	288.11	294.24
307.11	308.01	312.09
313.17	323.01	331.02
332.08	340.04	353.01
355.17	357.12	358.27
359.27	372.06	372.21
372.27	380.19	383.22
388.19	405.19	413.28
426.02	453.14	460.03
462.03	462.12	480.25
483.11	484.29	488.29
490.23	500.06	504.07
504.20	506.07	506.13
511.20	512.13	512.28
513.03		
HANDSOME	16.17	
HANDWRITING		229.25
249.06	416.16	417.28
HANDY	41.17	208.27
273.11	330.29	
HANG	41.12	45.08
51.07	53.28	76.15
80.29	94.15	111.12
150.30	181.07	203.26
229.21	240.29	273.07
287.09	289.30	295.14
303.06	321.15	355.02
362.10	374.25	377.05
435.11	494.19	
HANGED	50.15	59.01
78.22	79.22	283.10

HANGING	26.20	99.24
116.10	195.14	234.10
255.14	365.22	405.19
428.12	460.19	
HANGS	28.20	322.12
509.15		
HANKER	86.24	
HAPHAZARD		417.03
465.05		
HAPPEN	22.22	78.28
103.27	109.17	117.21
134.28	157.16	304.07
309.23	329.18	423.22
423.23	488.26	510.19
HAPPENED	3.10	23.22
30.22	34.13	56.19
57.16	134.27	137.20
146.19	148.02	148.07
172.24	230.30	242.18
273.11	273.12	289.17
375.16	420.28	423.24
441.26	465.17	493.05
501.04		
HAPPENS	41.30	114.30
HAPPINESS		213.11
213.13	391.03	507.28
HAPPY	28.14	312.17
312.28	368.06	
HARASSED	160.29	
HARBOUR	2.10	2.14
42.22	43.03	44.18
70.22	80.23	146.09
172.25	229.06	234.24
HARBOURED		38.29
HARD	14.05	40.18
57.25	64.23	69.13
75.09	75.21	94.01
141.02	148.17	156.04
181.29	199.02	209.14
209.18	219.09	231.09
231.20	272.22	281.22
299.25	324.04	349.12
358.26	376.10	378.13
391.25	393.04	430.21
431.07	433.23	466.22
479.22		
HARDENED	142.17	
HARDER	13.29	303.22
HARDEST	59.29	
HARDLY	27.26	31.02
164.05	173.17	186.22
366.07	484.18	512.10
HARDSHIPS		478.25
HARDWOOD	366.16	
HARM	150.08	150.08
150.09	150.12	150.14
153.13	484.28	486.06
HARM'S	451.08	
HARMLESS	101.07	493.01
HARMONY	253.03	
HARP	63.10	
HARP-STRING		63.10
HARROW	40.24	
HARROWING		103.30
440.24		
HARSH	21.21	24.15
44.25		
HARSHLY	146.26	421.21
HARVEST	42.21	
HAS	2.08	2.22
11.13	11.27	40.04
40.05	43.10	50.03
51.13	51.29	52.18
52.29	52.30	53.04
64.23	78.27	90.16
95.16	106.08	113.06
113.18	168.04	168.07
172.03	178.19	186.08
202.19	232.29	232.30
234.02	237.19	241.14
243.15	269.03	270.27
272.02	274.17	278.01
279.02	289.05	302.02
303.24	332.08	341.13
343.18	343.30	352.20
375.06	377.07	378.19
388.13	388.18	388.29
392.22	396.09	398.20
402.19	402.20	420.28
423.24	424.01	430.11

HAS (CONT.)		467.23
482.18	487.05	493.01
514.01	516.18	
HASN'T	70.18	
HASTE	46.16	70.20
165.26	206.08	220.10
351.13	367.12	379.19
HASTENED	406.03	456.28
HASTILY	134.25	158.29
291.01	310.30	396.16
404.06	421.21	459.18
513.11		
HASTY	163.17	261.08
HAT	1.11	44.21
47.18	52.07	70.15
188.20	188.26	206.01
242.15	255.06	255.19
399.02	428.22	432.24
452.20	511.21	
HATCH	34.03	102.16
105.16	107.02	
HATCHED	130.21	
HATCHES	456.29	
HATCHWAY	5.24	12.18
102.20	103.28	
HATCHWAYS		15.17
HATE	142.20	147.10
149.24	169.22	388.28
402.02	407.10	425.20
HATED	11.14	126.30
142.22	307.02	400.22
400.23	453.21	470.15
470.18		
HATEFUL	361.22	
HATH	514.01	514.15
HATRED	147.19	
HATS	37.17	
HAUGHTILY		363.22
HAUGHTY	337.09	
HAULED	62.30	108.23
493.17		
HAULING	183.08	
HAUNT	99.12	
HAUNTED	187.28	194.19
239.13	384.29	495.14
HAUNTING	215.12	302.01
HAVE	1.15	2.26
13.25	14.08	26.11
27.25	34.13	35.09
40.08	40.23	41.01
41.03	43.34	44.03
45.23	45.28	46.02
46.10	52.02	53.09
53.14	53.14	53.15
53.19	53.22	54.07
58.09	59.19	60.18
60.27	62.02	64.20
67.01	67.05	67.16
67.29	68.14	68.28
69.05	69.19	71.05
73.16	75.13	77.17
78.25	79.06	79.08
80.19	81.04	82.13
82.16	82.20	83.24
85.02	88.13	90.23
90.28	91.06	93.08
93.20	93.23	93.28
97.08	98.08	99.15
103.11	105.30	107.12
111.01	111.04	111.09
111.15	111.15	111.17
111.18	111.19	113.12
114.20	115.21	115.30
117.01	117.24	119.03
119.26	120.13	121.11
121.14	127.09	127.16
127.26	128.08	128.26
129.09	129.17	137.04
137.26	138.01	138.09
138.27	139.07	140.06
140.14	140.16	141.04
141.08	141.27	142.13
142.28	143.23	143.24
144.02	145.14	145.18
146.19	147.20	150.15
151.09	151.24	155.18
158.08	158.10	158.14
158.26	158.28	159.04
159.05	159.07	160.05

HAVE (CONT.)		160.10
160.18	160.20	160.20
161.01	163.20	164.08
164.18	164.24	164.24
164.25	164.26	164.28
165.03	165.07	165.19
166.11	166.12	166.15
168.20	169.30	170.10
172.19	173.22	174.08
176.25	178.14	178.16
178.26	179.12	180.05
185.15	186.28	188.06
188.09	188.18	188.20
190.17	191.19	191.20
198.30	199.06	199.25
200.16	201.04	201.16
202.26	203.18	204.22
204.26	207.04	208.07
208.22	208.28	210.23
210.29	210.29	211.22
212.01	212.01	214.18
214.21	214.24	214.30
215.28	215.28	216.01
217.01	217.24	218.14
224.11	225.04	226.07
227.10	227.12	227.20
228.22	228.23	228.25
228.27	229.17	229.19
230.03	230.18	231.12
231.29	233.04	235.22
235.24	236.26	237.07
238.17	239.01	239.12
239.21	240.06	240.07
242.06	243.07	246.14
246.27	247.02	247.19
247.20	249.12	250.08
250.25	251.22	252.02
252.22	252.22	254.20
257.28	258.13	265.04
266.01	266.23	267.03
267.12	269.01	270.04
270.11	271.06	271.08
271.16	272.13	272.23
273.14	274.14	274.24
275.03	275.18	275.20
278.06	278.12	280.04
280.15	281.21	283.30
284.02	287.18	292.16
292.20	292.30	295.28
296.01	300.15	301.02
301.03	301.09	301.24
302.05	303.21	303.21
312.08	312.29	314.18
314.21	315.06	321.19
324.26	325.01	325.28
325.29	328.14	329.28
330.02	331.18	332.19
334.08	335.07	337.25
339.08	340.26	341.30
342.10	342.11	344.09
347.12	351.18	352.02
352.05	352.15	352.19
352.24	354.08	356.24
357.11	357.20	358.05
360.14	361.06	361.10
361.16	362.03	362.18
363.03	367.28	368.11
368.21	370.16	374.24
375.28	376.03	376.25
377.17	377.25	379.08
380.01	381.11	383.02
383.13	384.18	385.18
386.24	387.08	389.08
389.15	389.17	389.26
390.10	390.14	396.07
398.03	398.08	398.18
399.12	399.13	400.09
401.02	401.03	401.05
402.16	402.17	404.20
405.20	407.17	408.19
411.16	411.20	411.21
411.22	418.08	419.03
419.15	421.13	421.21
422.23	423.30	426.02
426.03	428.08	429.17
430.15	431.17	433.10
434.17	435.03	435.04
435.22	437.05	437.10
437.16	442.10	442.15
447.01	449.03	450.20

HAVE (CONT.)		453.29	HE (CONT.)		28.16	HE (CONT.)		75.11	HE (CONT.)		110.06
454.15	454.19	454.21	28.18	28.25	28.27	75.18	75.26	76.03	110.10	110.12	110.14
455.26	456.03	458.09	28.29	28.29	29.01	76.04	76.05	77.02	110.16	110.24	110.26
459.02	461.02	463.08	30.10	30.13	30.15	77.04	77.07	77.08	111.24	111.26	111.26
463.17	463.19	470.14	30.16	30.16	32.03	77.09	77.10	77.21	111.27	112.03	112.17
470.16	472.04	472.09	32.08	33.18	34.08	77.29	77.29	78.01	112.22	112.25	112.29
472.15	474.02	474.08	34.19	34.19	34.20	78.05	78.12	78.13	113.12	113.25	113.30
474.15	474.21	477.03	34.21	34.24	34.26	78.16	78.19	78.23	114.03	114.05	114.05
480.27	481.03	481.08	34.29	34.29	35.01	78.26	78.26	78.28	114.07	114.12	114.13
481.13	481.25	483.07	35.01	35.04	35.07	78.30	79.12	79.14	114.14	114.15	114.17
485.09	486.14	491.23	35.07	35.08	35.08	79.20	79.20	79.29	114.18	114.20	114.24
492.03	492.10	493.14	35.09	35.12	35.25	79.30	79.30	80.01	114.28	115.03	115.06
493.20	493.29	499.14	35.28	35.28	36.12	80.07	80.14	80.16	115.06	115.09	116.01
500.15	500.18	504.19	36.12	36.14	36.14	80.19	81.12	81.14	116.01	116.02	116.04
505.04	507.16	507.18	36.15	36.16	36.20	81.23	82.15	82.17	116.19	116.21	116.21
515.22	516.05		36.22	36.22	36.23	82.17	82.19	84.01	116.28	116.29	117.06
HAVEN'T	40.02	40.09	36.24	36.25	36.27	84.03	84.18	84.21	117.07	118.15	118.16
51.21	68.12	84.29	36.28	37.01	37.02	85.06	85.07	85.08	118.27	118.28	118.29
112.10	185.14	205.19	37.11	37.28	37.30	85.09	85.18	85.22	119.02	119.04	119.05
221.04	227.14	229.13	38.05	38.06	38.07	85.25	85.28	86.03	119.06	119.06	119.08
237.20	238.14	309.02	38.08	38.09	38.12	86.05	86.13	86.27	119.10	119.30	119.30
322.27	377.14	404.28	38.14	38.14	38.15	86.28	86.29	87.06	120.01	120.01	120.03
474.10	507.25		40.01	40.10	40.11	87.09	87.15	87.21	120.10	120.13	120.14
HAVING	2.22	4.22	42.13	43.19	43.26	87.23	87.25	87.27	120.17	120.20	120.21
10.16	23.30	92.13	43.28	43.30	43.41	87.28	87.29	87.30	120.22	120.23	121.06
102.23	113.09	121.06	44.04	44.05	44.07	88.02	88.06	88.08	121.08	121.12	121.13
132.12	173.16	175.01	44.11	44.11	44.12	88.11	88.21	88.25	121.14	122.03	122.03
202.08	209.14	214.28	44.23	44.28	44.28	88.28	88.30	89.12	122.04	122.04	122.06
227.08	228.10	234.25	44.29	45.04	45.12	89.13	89.15	89.16	122.23	124.07	124.08
250.05	300.19	316.09	45.12	45.15	45.16	89.18	89.19	89.20	124.13	124.14	124.15
340.29	344.19	353.23	45.17	45.21	45.21	89.21	89.24	90.01	124.20	124.20	124.21
392.21	398.28	403.25	45.21	45.27	45.27	90.03	90.04	90.07	124.23	124.29	125.04
439.15	442.21	461.07	45.28	46.04	46.07	90.08	90.11	90.18	125.08	125.09	125.13
466.14	475.07	511.16	46.10	46.11	46.17	90.23	90.24	90.25	125.15	125.16	125.16
HAVOC	458.29		46.19	47.01	47.08	91.02	91.06	91.11	125.17	125.17	125.20
HAWK	219.28	249.26	47.10	47.12	47.15	91.13	91.15	93.07	125.23	125.24	126.06
316.27	360.15		47.24	47.24	47.24	93.17	93.18	93.18	126.28	126.29	127.01
HAWSERS	169.21	170.30	48.01	48.02	48.03	93.28	94.03	94.22	127.05	127.07	127.16
HAYES	436.04		48.05	48.06	48.13	94.26	95.02	95.06	127.18	127.20	127.21
HAZARD	13.30	395.01	48.14	49.06	49.14	95.16	95.19	95.20	127.22	127.23	127.27
HAZARDS	422.11		49.15	49.18	49.28	95.22	95.24	95.25	127.28	127.28	128.01
HAZE	297.10	325.20	50.21	50.22	50.22	95.29	95.30	96.01	128.06	128.11	128.13
HAZED	474.02		51.14	51.18	52.17	96.02	96.05	96.06	128.14	129.03	129.04
HAZILY	299.28		52.30	53.01	53.02	96.08	96.09	96.10	129.11	129.16	129.19
HAZY	5.04	28.08	53.04	53.06	53.23	96.13	96.13	96.14	129.20	129.22	129.25
58.04	85.04	167.01	53.27	53.28	53.29	96.15	96.16	96.20	129.25	129.30	130.03
182.19			54.11	54.14	54.17	96.22	96.24	96.26	130.08	130.09	130.12
HE	1.01	1.02	54.22	55.09	55.17	96.28	97.02	97.05	130.10	130.15	130.17
1.10	1.12	1.13	55.19	55.23	55.28	97.06	97.09	97.11	130.20	130.25	130.26
1.15	2.08	2.15	56.01	56.03	56.07	97.13	97.14	97.28	130.28	130.29	130.30
2.23	2.27	2.29	56.08	56.15	56.15	98.16	98.16	98.17	131.02	131.03	131.08
3.04	3.05	3.05	56.24	56.28	57.02	98.18	98.22	98.25	131.10	131.27	132.03
3.09	3.10	3.11	57.03	57.03	57.05	98.25	98.26	98.27	132.04	132.07	132.08
3.12	3.15	3.17	57.07	57.10	57.26	98.29	98.30	99.01	132.09	132.16	132.21
3.24	3.28	4.17	58.04	58.07	58.08	99.06	99.06	99.09	132.23	132.26	132.27
4.19	4.20	4.21	58.12	58.17	58.23	99.13	99.14	99.20	132.28	132.29	132.30
4.23	4.25	5.02	58.25	58.30	59.02	99.25	99.26	99.27	133.08	133.12	133.15
5.08	5.09	5.14	59.09	60.20	60.28	99.27	99.29	100.01	133.19	134.10	134.12
5.21	5.23	5.24	60.29	61.04	61.05	100.06	100.07	100.08	134.13	134.14	134.15
6.13	6.13	6.15	61.09	62.03	62.04	100.11	100.12	100.12	134.16	134.24	134.27
6.22	6.27	6.28	62.05	62.07	62.16	100.13	100.14	100.16	134.28	134.29	135.01
6.29	7.23	7.23	62.30	63.02	63.08	100.17	100.20	100.21	135.02	135.06	136.01
7.24	7.25	7.26	63.15	63.17	63.22	100.26	100.28	100.30	136.03	136.04	136.05
7.30	8.07	8.07	63.23	63.28	63.28	101.01	101.03	101.08	136.09	136.17	136.19
8.10	8.12	8.16	64.23	65.02	65.02	101.09	101.10	101.14	136.20	136.23	136.23
8.17	8.23	8.26	65.06	65.07	65.16	101.18	102.05	102.07	137.01	137.18	137.24
8.27	8.28	8.30	65.16	67.19	67.20	102.11	102.14	102.15	137.28	137.30	138.09
9.01	9.02	9.04	67.22	67.25	67.26	102.18	102.21	102.22	138.15	138.21	138.22
9.07	10.01	10.04	67.27	67.29	68.03	102.27	102.30	103.10	138.23	138.24	138.28
10.05	10.06	10.10	68.08	68.12	68.16	103.15	103.22	103.23	139.02	139.02	139.04
10.13	10.15	10.23	69.13	69.18	69.20	103.27	103.28	103.29	139.10	139.14	139.19
11.13	11.25	12.02	69.28	70.02	70.10	103.30	104.01	104.02	139.20	139.21	140.01
12.04	12.10	12.13	70.11	70.19	70.26	104.13	104.12	104.13	140.11	140.23	140.24
12.14	13.13	13.13	70.27	70.32	70.34	104.23	104.24	104.27	140.26	141.09	141.11
13.16	14.09	14.20	70.35	70.38	70.41	105.08	105.20	105.21	141.17	141.24	141.24
14.25	15.04	16.17	70.43	71.02	71.06	105.23	105.23	105.24	141.29	142.01	142.06
16.26	22.21	22.21	71.11	71.13	71.13	105.25	105.29	105.30	142.13	142.14	142.18
22.23	23.12	23.20	71.14	71.16	71.20	106.01	107.01	107.06	142.19	142.23	142.25
23.20	23.21	23.22	71.28	72.08	72.09	107.07	107.08	107.12	142.29	143.01	144.11
23.23	23.29	24.02	72.12	72.14	72.17	107.19	107.20	107.22	144.28	144.30	145.04
24.09	24.13	24.14	72.20	72.21	72.22	107.22	107.24	108.04	145.15	145.16	145.17
25.15	25.17	25.22	72.23	72.23	72.25	108.04	108.08	108.10	145.20	145.23	145.26
25.23	25.28	25.29	72.27	72.29	73.06	108.13	108.16	108.17	145.28	146.02	146.13
25.30	25.30	26.01	73.13	73.15	73.16	108.17	108.18	108.21	146.18	146.26	147.19
26.03	26.10	26.11	73.18	73.19	73.19	108.22	108.27	108.28	147.20	148.06	148.08
26.12	26.19	26.25	73.20	73.22	73.24	108.29	108.30	109.01	148.10	148.17	149.09
26.30	27.06	27.19	73.26	73.29	74.01	109.02	109.04	109.07	149.10	150.10	150.12
27.21	27.23	27.29	74.01	74.03	74.04	109.10	109.12	109.16	150.25	151.21	151.23
27.29	28.01	28.01	74.06	74.16	74.25	109.28	109.28	109.30			
28.03	28.09	28.11	74.28	75.01	75.06						

HE (CONT.)		151.24	HE (CONT.)		197.10	HE (CONT.)		238.26	HE (CONT.)		282.20
151.26	152.01	152.05	197.11	197.19	197.24	238.27	239.16	240.08	282.29	282.30	283.02
152.14	152.15	152.15	197.26	197.28	197.29	240.09	240.14	240.19	283.02	283.04	283.10
153.04	153.09	153.21	197.30	198.13	198.15	241.04	241.05	241.09	283.11	283.13	283.13
153.24	153.30	154.01	198.27	198.28	198.29	241.10	241.14	241.15	283.15	283.15	283.17
154.03	154.07	154.08	199.01	199.03	199.19	241.16	242.02	242.09	283.19	283.21	283.29
154.09	154.10	154.12	199.21	200.04	200.08	242.16	242.17	242.19	283.30	283.30	284.02
154.13	154.16	155.01	200.15	200.21	200.26	242.21	242.23	242.24	284.03	284.05	284.06
155.03	155.13	155.15	201.07	201.10	201.15	242.26	242.29	242.29	284.07	284.08	285.01
156.30	157.06	157.07	201.18	201.18	201.18	243.01	243.10	243.15	285.01	285.04	285.06
157.08	157.08	157.18	201.19	201.21	201.21	243.16	243.20	243.29	285.07	285.13	285.16
157.19	157.20	157.24	201.21	201.21	202.11	244.03	244.05	244.06	285.18	285.22	286.04
158.01	158.02	158.14	202.12	202.14	202.23	244.17	244.24	244.27	286.05	286.09	286.13
158.15	158.17	158.20	202.24	202.27	203.01	244.29	244.29	245.01	286.22	286.24	286.25
158.21	158.26	158.29	203.02	203.05	203.07	245.01	245.03	245.08	287.01	287.01	287.05
159.09	159.10	159.13	203.08	203.11	203.24	245.10	245.11	245.12	287.07	287.09	287.13
159.15	159.20	159.22	204.09	204.11	204.16	245.12	246.05	246.13	287.15	287.16	287.18
159.25	159.26	160.22	204.18	204.19	204.19	246.14	246.19	247.01	287.19	287.20	287.23
160.23	160.24	161.01	204.20	204.21	204.22	247.04	247.06	247.16	287.27	288.13	288.18
162.05	162.14	162.16	204.26	204.27	204.29	248.08	248.12	249.07	288.21	288.30	289.01
162.19	162.21	163.03	205.01	205.03	205.05	249.16	249.18	249.20	289.07	289.08	289.13
163.04	163.05	163.07	205.08	205.11	205.15	249.23	249.25	249.28	289.18	289.20	289.23
163.09	163.11	163.13	205.21	205.28	205.29	250.06	250.15	250.17	289.26	289.28	289.30
163.17	163.18	163.21	207.12	207.15	207.15	250.21	250.24	250.26	290.01	290.02	290.07
163.23	163.27	163.29	207.18	207.24	208.01	251.05	251.13	251.22	290.11	290.15	290.18
164.20	165.01	166.28	208.02	208.04	208.06	251.23	251.24	251.25	290.19	290.21	290.25
168.13	168.14	168.18	208.11	208.11	208.12	251.27	252.03	252.03	291.01	291.09	291.10
168.20	168.26	168.28	208.14	208.18	208.22	252.05	252.07	252.10	291.15	291.16	291.23
169.02	169.07	169.14	208.27	208.29	209.01	252.11	252.12	252.13	292.08	292.11	292.12
169.17	169.19	169.27	209.13	209.17	209.25	252.15	252.22	252.24	292.16	292.17	292.19
170.01	170.02	170.03	210.02	210.04	210.05	252.27	253.01	253.13	292.21	293.02	293.04
170.04	170.09	170.13	211.02	211.03	211.05	253.14	253.17	253.19	293.10	293.12	293.15
170.17	170.19	170.25	211.16	211.24	212.07	253.19	253.24	253.25	293.17	293.17	293.18
170.27	171.01	171.05	212.27	213.04	213.06	254.02	254.04	254.07	293.21	293.23	293.24
171.08	171.18	171.21	213.10	213.18	213.21	254.10	254.15	255.13	293.27	293.30	294.03
171.25	171.28	172.08	213.23	214.08	215.19	256.02	257.01	257.05	294.05	294.07	294.08
172.12	172.13	172.14	215.21	215.21	215.22	257.07	257.14	257.18	294.12	294.15	295.02
172.14	172.15	172.17	215.25	216.03	216.06	257.20	257.22	257.26	295.09	295.10	295.11
172.17	172.21	172.26	216.08	216.10	216.22	258.04	258.09	258.11	295.20	296.06	297.21
173.04	173.07	173.13	216.23	216.27	216.29	258.13	258.13	258.17	297.22	297.23	297.24
173.14	173.17	174.02	217.01	217.03	217.05	258.21	258.25	258.26	298.04	298.14	298.27
174.07	174.21	175.12	217.08	217.11	217.13	259.04	259.08	259.13	299.01	299.04	299.06
175.16	175.17	175.19	217.13	217.15	217.19	259.15	259.18	259.20	299.09	299.17	299.19
175.20	175.22	175.24	217.20	217.28	218.04	259.22	259.23	259.24	299.19	299.21	299.24
175.30	176.01	176.03	218.07	218.08	218.11	259.24	259.25	259.26	299.26	299.27	299.28
176.09	176.13	176.14	218.12	218.13	218.16	259.27	259.27	259.28	299.30	300.01	300.03
176.14	176.15	176.16	218.21	218.24	218.25	259.30	260.02	260.10	300.07	300.10	300.12
176.19	176.21	176.23	218.28	218.29	219.24	260.27	260.28	261.05	300.16	300.17	300.18
176.26	176.29	177.02	219.26	219.27	220.02	261.08	261.17	261.18	300.23	300.25	
177.06	177.10	177.18	220.04	220.05	220.08	261.19	261.20	261.20	301.06	301.08	301.10
177.19	177.25	177.27	220.08	220.09	220.12	261.22	261.25	262.07	301.12	301.20	301.22
178.01	178.03	178.05	220.24	220.26	220.26	262.08	262.11	262.14	301.26	302.14	302.29
178.09	178.14	178.17	220.29	221.03	221.05	262.22	262.25	262.30	302.29	302.30	303.03
178.20	178.22	179.03	222.01	222.20	223.07	263.03	263.13	263.18	303.03	303.07	303.09
179.05	179.06	179.08	223.13	223.17	223.19	263.18	263.20	263.20	303.10	303.11	303.15
179.14	179.15	179.16	223.23	224.01	224.09	263.21	264.09	264.13	303.16	304.01	304.07
179.20	179.23	180.04	224.10	224.15	224.18	264.14	264.15	264.20	304.11	304.25	304.25
180.07	180.12	180.20	224.19	224.21	224.22	264.24	264.30	265.03	304.29	305.02	305.05
180.21	180.29	181.08	224.22	224.23	224.25	265.07	265.07	265.11	305.07	306.02	306.17
181.13	181.14	181.14	224.27	225.03	225.05	265.16	265.16	266.21	306.22	306.22	307.01
181.16	181.17	181.22	225.12	225.24	225.29	267.05	267.05	267.08	307.02	307.10	307.15
182.08	183.10	183.19	226.05	226.07	226.09	267.13	267.14	267.17	307.29	307.30	308.04
183.19	183.20	183.23	226.12	226.17	226.26	267.23	267.25	267.27	308.09	308.13	308.14
183.23	183.26	184.07	226.27	227.17	227.17	267.31	267.31	268.02	308.15	308.15	308.23
184.12	184.12	184.13	227.19	227.20	227.22	268.03	268.09	268.12	308.27	309.22	310.04
184.15	184.15	185.09	228.02	228.03	228.08	269.02	269.06	269.20	310.07	310.10	310.13
185.09	186.02	186.02	228.11	229.14	229.21	270.01	270.02	270.16	310.14	310.14	310.25
185.03	186.04	186.14	230.03	230.14	230.16	272.04	272.06	272.06	310.29	310.29	311.01
186.16	186.19	186.23	230.20	230.22	230.23	272.11	272.11	272.12	311.02	311.02	311.05
186.27	186.29	187.04	230.23	230.24	230.26	272.12	272.13	272.14	311.07	311.08	311.09
187.06	187.13	187.16	230.29	231.05	231.07	272.15	272.17	272.30	311.12	311.15	311.16
187.20	187.21	187.23	231.15	231.16	231.19	273.07	273.07	273.08	311.17	311.17	311.19
187.26	187.27	187.27	231.20	231.21	231.22	273.13	273.14	274.01	311.22	311.25	311.26
188.02	188.04	188.05	231.25	231.28	232.01	274.02	274.07	274.08	311.27	311.27	312.02
188.09	188.12	188.18	232.21	232.21	232.25	274.09	274.12	274.13	312.02	312.05	312.08
188.19	188.21	188.21	232.28	233.01	233.02	274.19	274.20	274.22	312.08	312.12	312.13
188.22	188.24	188.26	233.03	233.05	233.07	274.26	275.12	278.06	312.15	312.15	312.18
188.29	189.04	189.06	233.11	233.20	233.26	278.08	278.10	278.10	312.18	312.20	312.25
189.09	189.18	189.19	234.01	234.07	234.15	278.15	278.15	278.16	312.26	312.29	312.29
189.21	189.23	190.05	234.15	234.20	234.28	278.17	278.19	278.20	312.29	312.30	313.02
190.06	190.07	191.17	235.02	235.03	235.04	279.03	279.05	279.10	313.03	313.04	313.05
192.24	192.26	193.03	235.10	235.11	235.19	279.16	280.01	280.04	313.11	313.13	313.18
193.04	195.11	195.11	235.25	235.30	235.13	280.05	280.13	280.14	313.18	313.18	313.20
195.12	195.14	195.28	236.02	236.04	236.06	280.28	280.29	280.30	313.27	313.28	314.03
195.29	196.01	196.02	236.11	236.24	236.26	281.14	281.22	281.27	314.07	314.10	314.14
196.03	196.04	196.05	236.28	237.04	237.07	281.28	281.28	281.29	314.21	315.16	315.19
196.06	196.07	196.11	237.13	237.13	237.15	281.29	281.30	282.02	316.15	316.16	316.18
196.12	196.15	196.19	237.16	237.25	237.26	282.02	282.04	282.05	316.26	316.27	317.12
196.21	196.21	196.25	237.30	238.04	238.10	282.10	282.12	282.13	318.04	318.04	318.14
197.04	197.05	197.09	238.11	238.19	238.25	282.16	282.17	282.20	318.15	318.16	318.18

HE (CONT.)		318.22	HE (CONT.)		364.12	HE (CONT.)		411.01	HE (CONT.)		463.22
318.23	319.05	319.20	364.14	364.15	364.17	411.16	411.18	411.21	463.23	463.26	464.03
319.25	319.26	319.28	364.18	364.22	364.25	411.25	411.26	411.30	464.06	464.09	464.11
320.02	320.14	320.19	364.29	365.05	365.10	412.10	412.26	412.27	465.10	465.12	465.13
320.21	320.23	320.24	365.15	365.20	365.23	412.29	412.30	413.03	465.19	466.01	466.03
320.30	321.01	321.03	365.24	365.24	365.27	413.07	413.10	413.14	466.03	466.06	466.08
321.08	321.08	321.10	365.29	365.30	366.04	413.18	413.20	413.22	466.10	466.12	466.21
321.11	321.12	321.13	366.26	366.28	366.28	413.24	413.25	413.26	455.23	466.24	466.27
321.15	321.18	321.25	366.29	366.30	366.30	414.08	414.12	414.29	467.16	467.23	467.28
321.26	321.28	322.06	367.01	367.03	367.04	415.01	415.01	415.06	467.28	468.02	468.05
322.13	322.13	322.15	367.08	367.16	367.18	415.15	416.21	417.09	468.06	468.07	468.08
322.28	323.13	323.20	367.26	367.30	368.03	417.23	417.25	417.28	468.09	468.11	468.12
323.26	323.26	323.27	368.03	368.04	368.04	418.03	418.10	419.07	468.13	468.14	468.20
324.02	324.03	324.05	368.04	368.05	368.15	419.16	419.20	419.23	469.13	469.14	469.16
324.07	324.08	324.13	368.16	368.18	368.29	420.01	420.04	420.07	470.02	470.16	470.17
324.21	324.22	324.26	369.05	369.05	369.07	420.17	420.21	420.24	470.18	470.21	470.23
324.28	325.07	325.23	369.07	369.10	369.12	420.24	420.28	420.28	470.25	470.26	470.27
325.25	325.29	327.18	369.16	369.17	369.19	421.01	421.04	421.05	470.28	471.03	471.09
328.10	328.11	328.14	369.22	369.26	369.28	421.06	421.07	421.09	471.19	471.20	471.24
328.19	328.26	328.27	370.06	370.11	370.11	421.13	421.13	421.15	471.30	472.10	473.01
328.29	328.30	328.30	370.13	370.14	370.16	421.15	421.19	421.20	473.07	473.13	473.23
329.03	329.09	329.14	370.18	370.20	370.20	421.30	422.04	422.04	473.29	474.01	474.24
329.14	329.15	329.16	370.22	371.01	371.02	422.09	422.22	422.27	474.25	474.30	474.30
329.17	329.22	329.23	371.03	371.04	371.17	422.27	423.30	424.01	475.01	475.02	475.08
329.24	329.25	329.29	371.17	371.19	371.19	424.02	424.03	424.10	475.30	476.05	476.06
329.30	330.02	330.06	371.20	371.21	371.23	425.07	425.07	425.11	476.08	476.08	477.01
331.06	331.16	331.20	371.24	371.25	371.27	425.11	425.12	425.24	477.02	477.03	477.04
331.27	331.30	332.10	371.29	371.29	372.01	426.01	426.01	426.02	477.05	477.07	477.07
332.12	332.16	332.25	372.01	372.08	372.09	426.04	426.05	426.06	477.12	477.16	477.17
333.02	333.03	333.09	372.14	372.17	373.07	426.10	426.15	426.17	478.05	478.05	478.07
333.22	333.24	333.25	373.07	373.10	373.11	426.19	426.29	427.10	478.10	478.11	478.14
333.30	334.12	334.18	373.23	374.14	374.14	427.12	427.13	427.16	478.18	478.19	478.19
334.27	335.03	336.06	374.15	374.15	374.22	428.07	428.10	428.12	478.24	478.25	478.28
336.10	336.15	336.21	374.28	375.13	375.15	428.14	428.14	428.14	479.09	479.10	479.10
336.21	337.03	337.06	375.17	375.20	375.24	428.15	428.19	428.22	479.11	479.17	479.18
337.06	337.08	337.10	376.02	376.06	376.16	428.26	428.28	428.29	479.20	479.20	479.21
337.13	337.13	337.15	376.18	377.01	377.10	429.04	429.06	429.08	481.02	481.02	481.07
337.25	337.28	337.30	377.20	377.21	377.29	429.09	429.09	429.12	481.09	481.14	481.16
338.19	338.21	338.23	379.13	381.10	382.08	429.18	429.18	430.11	481.17	481.18	481.19
338.30	340.09	342.08	382.12	382.14	382.16	430.17	430.20	431.09	481.20	481.21	481.28
342.09	342.09	342.10	382.16	382.18	382.18	431.10	431.15	431.16	481.30	482.01	482.03
342.11	342.11	342.16	382.19	382.20	382.26	431.17	431.18	431.20	482.04	482.17	482.19
342.20	343.13	343.14	383.01	383.02	383.04	431.20	432.11	432.24	482.24	482.29	483.02
343.16	343.17	343.21	383.12	383.12	383.14	432.30	433.01	433.13	483.09	483.12	483.17
343.23	343.26	343.28	383.15	383.20	383.22	433.16	433.17	433.19	484.18	484.20	485.04
343.29	343.30	344.04	383.26	384.11	384.12	433.22	434.20	434.23	485.10	485.10	485.17
344.12	344.21	344.23	385.27	386.30	386.30	434.29	435.05	435.06	485.26	485.29	486.02
344.24	345.08	345.24	387.01	387.21	387.24	435.07	435.12	435.14	486.04	486.05	486.09
345.25	345.29	345.30	387.25	387.25	387.26	435.17	435.18	435.19	486.11	486.11	486.15
346.02	346.07	346.09	388.02	388.13	388.13	435.19	435.20	436.09	487.11	488.04	488.10
347.07	347.16	347.17	388.15	388.19	388.24	436.10	436.12	436.16	488.18	488.22	488.23
349.03	349.08	349.11	388.24	388.30	388.30	436.20	436.26	436.28	488.25	488.26	488.28
349.25	349.26	350.11	389.01	390.02	390.02	436.30	437.02	437.02	488.28	489.01	489.04
350.15	350.19	350.22	391.06	391.07	391.10	437.03	437.05	437.06	489.05	489.11	489.29
350.24	351.03	351.07	392.17	392.25	392.26	437.10	437.12	437.16	490.03	490.06	490.08
351.08	351.10	351.14	392.26	393.09	393.18	437.19	437.22	437.24	490.19	490.20	490.20
351.21	351.23	351.26	394.02	394.04	394.14	437.25	438.07	438.07	490.26	490.27	491.08
351.27	351.27	351.28	395.21	395.23	395.25	438.08	438.13	438.17	491.12	491.30	492.16
351.29	352.02	352.04	395.26	396.09	396.12	438.27	439.01	439.02	492.17	492.21	492.24
352.06	352.09	352.13	396.19	396.23	398.24	439.21	439.24	439.26	492.30	493.01	493.01
352.19	352.21	352.26	398.29	399.01	399.08	440.13	440.28	441.19	493.02	493.03	493.04
352.27	352.30	353.04	399.09	399.13	399.14	441.23	441.25	441.26	493.06	493.14	493.19
353.05	353.07	353.15	399.15	399.18	399.19	441.30	442.04	442.10	493.21	494.05	495.03
353.18	353.25	354.08	400.04	400.07	400.07	442.10	442.18	444.10	495.03	495.04	495.13
355.01	355.01	355.03	400.14	400.16	400.17	444.13	444.14	444.18	495.25	496.07	495.11
355.07	355.08	355.09	400.17	401.01	401.06	446.01	447.10	447.12	497.18	498.03	498.04
355.16	355.18	355.21	401.08	401.08	401.11	447.14	447.14	448.15	498.08	498.08	498.13
356.01	356.15	356.21	401.11	401.12	401.24	449.01	449.05	449.14	498.13	498.24	499.12
357.10	357.14	357.17	401.28	402.02	402.02	449.21	450.13	450.21	499.13	499.13	499.30
357.17	357.18	357.21	402.03	402.04	402.06	451.23	452.02	452.03	500.17	501.03	501.05
357.23	357.26	357.28	402.08	402.12	402.15	452.03	452.07	452.13	501.11	501.11	502.01
357.29	358.03	358.10	402.18	402.19	402.20	453.01	453.03	453.03	502.04	502.07	502.15
358.07	358.17	358.22	402.21	402.24	402.25	453.14	453.21	453.24	502.16	502.18	502.19
358.26	358.30	359.02	402.25	402.27	402.27	454.01	454.07	454.12	502.23	502.23	502.24
359.03	359.09	359.11	402.28	402.28	402.29	454.18	454.19	455.03	502.26	502.26	502.27
359.13	359.13	359.15	402.30	403.01	403.03	455.22	455.22	455.24	502.29	504.14	504.18
359.16	359.18	359.22	403.09	403.09	403.11	455.24	455.26	455.29	505.03	505.03	505.09
359.22	359.24	359.25	403.13	403.16	403.19	456.06	456.14	456.15	505.10	505.12	505.22
359.29	360.02	360.03	403.19	403.23	403.24	456.16	456.19	456.22	505.24	505.28	505.30
360.04	360.09	360.10	403.29	404.01	404.06	457.03	457.05	457.11	506.01	506.03	506.05
360.12	360.18	360.19	404.08	404.18	404.19	457.15	457.17	457.22	506.11	506.16	506.19
360.25	360.28	361.03	404.20	404.21	404.23	458.04	458.22	458.24	506.20	506.24	506.26
361.06	361.15	361.16	404.26	404.27	404.29	458.28	459.02	459.15	506.27	507.03	507.05
361.19	361.23	361.23	404.30	404.30	405.01	459.19	459.23	459.26	507.08	507.11	507.12
361.27	361.27	361.27	405.03	405.04	405.04	459.27	460.20	460.20	507.14	507.17	507.18
361.29	362.02	362.06	405.06	405.09	405.09	460.25	460.28	461.12	507.22	507.28	507.29
362.07	362.11	362.12	405.11	405.12	405.14	461.14	461.15	461.19	507.29	507.30	508.04
362.15	362.15	362.16	405.20	405.23	405.26	461.21	462.15	463.12	508.06	508.09	508.11
362.19	363.06	363.14	406.01	406.03	408.10	463.15	463.16	463.16	508.13	509.07	509.13
363.16	363.17	364.04	408.12	409.18	410.28	463.19	463.20	463.21	509.16	509.17	509.27

```
511.01   511.03   511.04
511.05   511.08   511.16
511.20   511.24   512.20
512.25   513.01   513.04
513.29   514.01   514.01
514.02   514.03   514.06
514.11   514.13   514.13
514.14   514.15   514.16
514.19   514.24   514.26
515.09   515.18   515.19
515.22   515.25   516.02
516.04   516.05   516.08
516.11   516.16   516.19
516.20   516.21
HE'S        75.03    78.29
197.11   199.04   202.08
203.04   403.04   455.24
HEAD         1.04     4.22
6.24     8.01    16.06
15.11    20.24    21.06
24.09    25.18    27.16
27.16    30.15    32.12
33.26    37.20    44.07
44.21    45.13    47.07
48.08    49.09    49.20
52.04    54.17    55.15
56.13    59.03    59.05
62.17    63.04    63.26
64.06    64.27    64.28
70.17    70.38    76.24
77.14    82.28    89.11
89.26    99.27   101.29
102.27  104.19   107.12
109.22  110.04   110.27
111.02  116.11   116.18
116.26  119.07   122.05
124.01  124.23   124.27
127.05  128.26   129.22
131.17  132.03   134.05
134.08  137.20   141.25
142.03  148.29   151.26
152.12  153.06   153.12
153.25  153.28   155.01
155.10  163.03   163.29
165.05  166.01   166.06
167.01  167.17   169.05
171.17  173.12   175.19
181.27  184.16   185.01
186.23  189.09   191.07
192.20  193.01   193.02
193.30  198.10   199.15
200.28  202.04   203.03
204.01  207.13   207.18
208.15  210.28   216.13
217.02  223.14   224.01
225.28  226.01   226.13
228.12  230.17   237.16
241.08  250.18   255.07
255.12  256.19   256.24
259.18  259.13   262.20
264.12  264.16   265.03
283.18  287.20   287.25
288.12  288.18   295.26
297.19  303.11   307.18
307.23  311.15   312.14
313.05  315.23   318.07
318.23  320.20
331.08  332.17   333.07
333.20  336.06   338.13
338.26  343.12   345.30
347.23  348.22   349.10
349.14  349.23   350.04
355.17  358.29   362.05
364.14  365.13   371.05
371.05  371.07   371.14
371.30  373.09   373.23
374.27  377.05   380.19
384.15  386.03   390.16
393.26  396.16   401.23
402.09  403.11   405.18
405.23  407.18   409.18
410.16  411.15   415.06
415.14  420.30   428.12
428.22  429.28   430.06
431.12  433.03   442.09
443.11  448.25   448.28
450.21  452.20   454.07
456.26  460.01   460.19
463.15  473.04   474.02
```

HEAD (CONT.)   481.12

```
481.20   482.28   487.09
490.22   496.09   502.20
506.14   506.20   507.01
509.04   509.23   511.08
511.20   512.14   512.20
514.05   514.08   514.15
514.17   515.08
HEAD-CLOTHS         16.11
HEAD-MAN   297.19   333.07
410.16   443.11
HEAD-MEN   250.18   336.06
442.09   448.28
HEADACHE   179.10
HEADED      16.21    28.12
57.20    70.05   124.18
280.11   420.06
HEADKERCHIEF        318.07
HEADLAND   276.10
HEADLONG  100.10   220.18
287.26   380.10   504.13
HEADS       20.10    20.30
33.07    37.13    37.29
51.26    52.14    70.33
108.05   126.17   137.22
149.05   151.04   165.12
191.30   193.12   255.22
262.23   291.18   316.05
318.21   327.08   339.29
367.16   374.01   409.01
410.20   423.17   434.05
466.19   485.26   509.15
513.28
HEADWAY    414.24
HEALTH    241.16   299.26
460.06
HEALTHY     77.12
HEAP        21.14    26.06
30.29    30.29    58.29
112.27   202.18   256.16
259.22   259.23   312.10
370.08   371.03   454.30
HEAPS       64.02   279.14
366.15   459.09   463.27
466.18
HEAR        42.11    42.15
53.10    55.24    63.22
76.03    86.02   112.11
127.27   128.11   128.11
133.02   137.23   139.06
142.20   143.19   146.12
151.11   151.19   151.23
152.28   164.17   174.18
207.24   211.05   227.06
232.03   233.17   242.05
252.21   255.06   295.27
298.05   307.24   343.18
350.09   359.21   364.18
368.16   369.21   382.22
388.30   393.21   393.24
411.01   416.12   419.26
424.10   426.12   429.18
430.30   430.30   431.10
431.10   446.08   464.24
464.25   464.28
473.18   474.05   499.19
507.10
HEARD        5.22     6.29
34.04    35.03    36.17
42.22    44.06    45.23
45.24    57.09    67.16
70.27    72.06    72.11
72.16    73.20    75.07
78.08    80.16    84.22
88.06    88.11    92.21
95.19    98.25    99.04
105.29   110.07   120.24
121.06   124.16   125.13
130.01   131.02   132.03
132.04   132.12   133.17
133.26   134.06   137.08
137.26   138.27   141.17
141.21   141.25   145.09
145.16   149.23   150.05
152.12   154.01   155.01
164.01   164.02   164.21
167.09   188.25   189.20
210.25   210.29   214.24
217.06   217.13   231.12
232.08   233.12   241.05
```

HEARD (CONT.)   242.05

```
250.12   253.10   254.27
258.17   260.09   266.02
266.06   282.06   291.12
293.24   295.26   300.25
318.18   319.07   322.27
322.28   335.16   339.08
342.13   344.08   345.22
350.20   360.18   360.25
362.06   368.24   369.26
376.01   385.12   387.14
396.02   398.07   402.20
403.21   404.29   406.06
431.01   431.21   435.04
437.03   441.25   451.28
454.04   464.10   466.25
467.14   471.09   475.19
483.02   487.07   490.08
494.09   498.08   507.19
514.02   514.16
HEARERS    485.26
HEARING    59.11    72.18
84.30   164.07   243.14
275.13   298.06   340.20
499.13
HEART        2.13    11.06
17.09    26.16    43.43
70.21    93.06    99.18
100.18  100.22   100.22
101.01  114.25   121.08
130.05  130.21   131.21
138.05  139.03   159.09
178.08  187.01   187.06
187.09  197.10   197.17
203.07  211.06   211.12
212.08  214.14   227.09
227.16  256.16   257.15
260.15  294.25   304.15
317.18  364.15   368.15
374.06  382.26   384.16
389.25  390.16   390.26
391.23  392.07   392.10
396.03  397.30   403.17
405.22  408.14   415.12
423.06  463.02   464.19
470.21  483.05   506.23
507.25  515.20   516.17
HEART-RENDING       187.06
187.09  464.19
HEARTED     29.10   384.26
428.27
HEARTHSTONE         270.27
HEARTHSTONES        270.26
HEARTILY  211.28
HEARTLESS           229.16
HEARTS       5.17    16.29
24.23  156.09   429.03
479.29  482.07   487.10
507.22  508.18   510.03
HEARTY     53.17
HEAT      155.23   204.03
289.18  343.24   343.25
408.16  430.13
HEATED    328.28
HEATHEN   427.07
HEAVE     131.19   210.04
337.13  405.30
HEAVED    170.13
HEAVEN     18.10    29.22
150.01  173.07   275.05
275.08  472.29
HEAVEN'S  422.17
HEAVENLY  266.05   266.20
266.23
HEAVENS    79.17   128.30
130.11  144.08   160.10
266.22  277.05   289.14
365.07  512.07
HEAVIER   114.26   131.18
177.05  201.22
HEAVILY    22.06    22.15
181.17  186.19   224.27
249.22  421.01   441.14
512.22  515.09
HEAVING     6.06    55.03
HEAVY      18.04    20.27
21.09    29.22    33.22
53.09    53.15   109.21
126.10  131.14   145.09
145.17  148.16   156.27
```

HEAVY (CONT.)   162.08

```
171.02   175.04   180.12
193.13   210.16   211.27
216.13   220.13   232.16
250.15   291.03   294.22
307.26   318.09   319.20
332.04   342.17   372.19
390.26   395.22   397.09
397.18   408.29   417.10
444.29   450.12   487.08
493.30   502.20
HECTOR     71.18
HEDGED    378.03
HEEL      153.21   367.03
403.02   481.14
HEELS      72.09    72.11
220.29   300.22   332.17
333.04   349.13   378.08
402.22   411.03   489.20
HEIGHT    133.11   136.05
150.02   409.28
HEIGHTENED          179.06
HEINOUS   228.18
HEIR      299.18
HELD        7.03     8.08
8.19    12.21    17.06
18.08    32.08    36.27
38.10    49.22    54.28
59.15    66.03    75.10
84.04    99.19    99.20
105.22  110.24   117.17
129.04  181.17   182.25
211.03  264.13   333.24
371.13  371.16   371.20
371.22  384.21   422.23
443.08  448.21   481.02
494.15  500.05   509.27
HELL       94.03   130.21
190.19  412.03   426.01
HELM      118.29   119.25
294.03
HELMET    469.06   470.30
HELMSMEN  118.09
HELP       40.22    41.23
64.02    68.17    73.09
81.26    96.15   103.26
103.27  117.03   120.08
120.09  122.19   122.20
144.09  150.24   164.03
169.29  204.03   204.18
222.11  222.14   223.06
223.12  243.23   282.10
283.07  289.21   291.06
291.08  298.08   306.21
313.07  319.01   333.24
341.23  354.01   359.26
367.02  367.07   442.16
457.04  457.07   475.09
HELPED    140.06   225.04
442.25  512.16   514.25
HELPER    112.04
HELPING   188.22
HELPLESS  126.24   134.21
369.07
HELPLESSLY          339.23
HELPLESSNESS        102.10
381.05  452.14
HELTER    309.27
HELTER-SKELTER      309.27
HEMISPHERE          112.20
HEMISPHERES         45.20
HEN       502.26
HENCE     123.25
HENCEFORTH           92.13
226.10  482.06
HER         1.19     2.04
2.06     2.07     2.07
6.23     6.25     6.26
6.28     7.03     7.04
7.07     7.09     7.19
15.09    17.02    17.03
17.05    17.16    17.24
17.28    18.08    18.10
18.11    21.27    25.04
29.30    30.03    30.24
52.21    61.02    61.09
61.22    66.07    71.02
83.14    83.16    83.18
92.22   110.27   123.20
123.21  123.22   126.22
```

HER (CONT.)

HER (CONT.)		127.26
128.20	131.30	134.04
137.19	166.01	166.02
166.03	166.05	166.08
166.08	166.17	166.21
166.22	166.28	167.02
172.28	175.17	182.29
183.09	183.11	183.13
190.14	198.12	214.11
234.17	235.04	235.05
250.19	251.02	254.13
254.13	254.21	254.23
268.17	290.16	291.15
292.01	292.02	292.03
293.07	293.08	297.16
314.14	314.15	314.17
314.17	314.22	314.29
314.29	314.29	315.02
315.04	315.06	315.06
315.07	315.11	315.14
315.14	319.20	319.20
330.12	330.15	330.16
338.13	338.13	338.17
340.10	340.13	340.15
340.21	340.26	342.06
342.11	342.22	346.06
346.07	346.12	346.19
347.20	347.21	347.23
347.23	348.02	348.04
348.09	348.10	348.11
348.13	348.14	348.17
348.21	348.21	348.22
348.22	348.22	349.05
349.10	349.11	349.30
350.03	350.03	355.06
355.08	355.10	355.17
355.17	355.18	355.19
355.20	355.21	355.22
356.04	356.05	356.29
356.29	357.08	357.12
357.15	357.17	359.20
359.21	359.27	359.28
359.30	359.30	360.04
360.05	362.04	362.22
362.23	365.25	366.04
366.24	366.25	367.01
367.08	368.23	368.25
369.03	369.12	369.13
369.17	370.06	370.25
373.12	373.13	374.29
375.06	375.07	378.21
378.22	378.22	378.24
379.11	379.03	379.11
379.11	379.15	379.15
379.15	379.18	379.28
380.02	380.03	380.09
380.16	380.19	380.19
381.01	381.02	381.02
381.04	381.05	381.06
381.07	381.14	382.01
382.03	382.14	382.14
382.17	382.18	382.26
392.27	382.28	383.30
384.01	384.05	384.11
384.12	384.14	385.07
385.10	385.14	385.15
385.25	385.26	386.02
386.03	386.03	386.05
386.06	386.07	386.10
387.07	387.17	387.19
388.12	388.19	388.23
389.07	389.19	389.29
390.06	390.09	390.11
391.03	391.05	391.05
392.06	392.08	392.13
392.17	393.07	393.15
393.15	393.22	393.25
394.14	395.13	395.15
395.16	395.29	395.29
404.01	405.24	405.24
405.25	405.26	408.02
408.13	413.29	413.30
414.02	429.09	429.14
429.15	429.28	429.29
429.29	430.04	430.06
430.11	430.13	430.14
430.24	431.02	431.04
431.04	431.06	431.22
431.23	431.26	431.27
432.11	432.12	432.22

HER (CONT.)

HER (CONT.)		432.24
433.02	433.03	433.05
433.10	433.18	433.20
433.25	433.26	434.18
436.25	436.26	436.28
437.02	438.30	441.22
448.09	448.11	450.20
454.30	465.14	475.18
475.26	475.30	476.01
477.11	482.10	482.11
482.11	482.12	482.12
482.12	484.26	484.27
484.30	485.03	488.08
488.24	488.29	489.02
501.29	503.16	504.17
504.20	504.21	505.03
505.04	506.30	507.28
508.30	511.04	511.07
511.25	511.26	511.26
512.12	512.13	512.14
512.14	512.16	512.17
512.18	512.18	512.21
512.22	512.27	514.09
HERALD	464.29	
HERALDED	298.18	
HERD	302.24	500.27
HERE	20.19	25.21
462.18		
28.01	29.30	36.11
41.09	41.19	41.25
43.07	45.09	45.10
61.02	63.25	64.22
70.44	71.01	76.04
76.05	76.19	77.13
81.15	96.28	102.27
106.08	111.22	128.29
143.10	143.23	158.22
164.10	165.03	166.15
168.06	170.21	182.06
182.15	188.26	192.15
200.17	200.29	208.14
208.21	213.06	217.05
223.23	225.29	231.03
232.24	233.08	233.17
233.30	234.17	234.22
234.25	235.11	235.22
235.27	236.11	238.02
243.08	243.16	253.20
254.07	255.24	256.29
258.02	258.13	263.02
263.07	287.05	301.20
302.25	303.02	308.22
323.13	323.16	324.05
325.13	343.29	350.23
354.01	361.11	361.12
370.28	375.07	375.21
375.29	377.22	377.30
383.26	388.05	394.08
400.10	401.03	401.13
401.13	401.15	402.27
402.28	405.03	405.04
405.05	420.04	421.17
423.01	423.11	423.26
428.26	428.28	428.29
428.30	445.03	452.09
455.10	455.21	455.27
456.04	462.28	467.02
468.01	468.03	468.05
471.10	472.11	472.18
472.20	473.15	473.18
473.20	474.10	478.12
481.10	481.25	482.04
486.02	492.13	493.03
493.08	495.07	495.18
504.06	506.03	507.25
512.15	513.10	
HERE'	166.15	376.05
HERE'S	162.02	238.07
342.18		
HEREAFTER		467.04
HERMITS	283.09	283.10
HERO	5.19	7.29
59.01	213.05	306.22
HEROES		251.07
HEROIC	23.17	28.21
100.11	120.05	276.03
277.05	299.26	
HEROICS		184.10
HEROISM	8.22	126.09
147.09	239.11	
HERSELF	357.16	364.22

HERSELF (CONT.)

HERSELF (CONT.)		384.02
387.08	431.09	510.17
HESITATE	36.09	258.15
258.16	381.16	457.12
460.02		
HESITATED		141.14
HESITATING		434.22
452.21	506.10	
HESITATION		85.11
190.02	276.23	419.15
489.11		
HESITATIONS		189.08
HEY	87.26	139.19
139.24	201.07	201.16
203.20	236.18	236.18
236.19	236.19	236.20
236.20	236.21	377.18
472.19		
HIDDEN	23.15	40.19
50.10	194.01	321.14
322.11	347.13	429.28
443.30		
HIDE	3.08	157.05
347.16		
HIDEOUS		87.30
HIDING	183.04	461.02
462.18		
HIDINGS		292.28
HIGH	5.16	7.07
16.27	20.17	21.25
23.11	27.04	32.11
36.04	45.29	71.27
83.16	104.30	105.01
115.10	132.03	136.21
146.09	147.22	166.02
191.19	192.14	201.01
239.07	250.20	256.09
264.13	295.25	302.17
305.01	319.30	323.15
325.22	331.09	338.15
340.22	353.23	369.26
372.03	395.30	396.04
408.15	408.16	410.03
410.09	437.07	443.28
445.20	448.06	462.30
465.15	497.23	510.12
HIGH-MINDED		115.10
239.07		
HIGH-PITCHED		83.16
369.26		
HIGH-SPIRITED		448.06
HIGH'		114.14
HIGHBORN		279.02
HIGHER	52.11	86.20
135.05	186.15	300.20
312.06		
HIGHEST	173.02	251.19
416.19		
HIGHLY		490.05
HOLIDAY		13.09
HILL	4.05	12.28
16.24	135.04	191.20
269.17	323.14	323.21
324.12	325.23	327.23
329.18	332.03	333.28
336.10	359.15	396.20
417.17	445.20	449.10
450.27	452.11	453.06
459.17	461.27	463.05
464.12	464.14	464.25
465.03	465.08	466.17
481.17	483.17	485.20
HILLOCK		459.03
HILLS	14.27	94.17
269.12	269.22	301.28
316.26	319.16	338.18
HILLSIDE	324.08	333.18
HIM	1.20	2.01
3.16	3.22	3.26
6.12	6.12	6.13
6.16	6.21	7.04
7.23	7.30	8.06
8.12	8.19	8.24
10.10	11.08	11.10
12.06	12.06	12.09
22.22	23.17	23.29
26.07	26.23	26.26
27.26	28.28	32.13
32.21	33.04	33.11
34.28	34.28	34.29

HIM (CONT.)

HIM (CONT.)		34.30
35.01	35.03	36.02
36.03	36.09	36.14
36.28	38.01	38.08
38.17	38.19	38.23
40.08	40.09	43.18
43.28	43.34	43.39
43.41	44.04	44.29
45.06	45.08	46.06
46.13	46.14	46.21
46.27	47.12	47.14
47.23	49.18	49.29
52.16	52.30	54.02
54.17	54.20	55.19
55.25	55.26	55.28
56.03	57.09	57.18
57.24	58.02	58.02
58.09	58.17	58.29
58.30	60.24	60.25
60.26	60.26	62.17
62.26	63.11	63.21
63.23	64.19	65.10
67.03	67.04	67.20
67.28	68.05	68.10
68.11	69.07	69.10
69.15	69.21	70.16
70.36	71.08	71.21
72.06	72.11	72.21
73.05	73.09	73.15
73.20	74.18	74.27
74.28	76.14	77.27
78.09	78.15	78.24
78.28	79.07	79.11
79.16	79.21	80.11
81.14	81.17	82.20
82.22	83.02	83.13
83.24	84.17	84.24
85.30	86.02	86.03
86.11	87.02	87.12
88.17	89.05	89.28
90.01	90.12	90.13
90.18	90.29	90.30
91.05	91.12	93.28
94.25	95.19	95.23
95.27	96.27	96.28
97.15	99.04	99.14
100.15	100.24	101.27
102.02	102.07	102.11
102.17	102.19	103.07
105.27	107.04	107.07
108.10	108.18	108.26
108.28	108.30	109.03
109.08	109.23	109.27
109.30	112.11	114.06
114.10	114.11	115.02
115.04	115.09	115.11
116.06	116.23	116.24
117.01	118.16	119.16
120.17	120.18	120.18
124.09	124.09	124.11
124.12	124.17	124.22
125.07	125.18	126.05
126.06	127.22	127.29
129.11	130.13	131.06
131.12	131.13	132.14
132.15	132.18	133.01
133.08	133.10	133.12
134.18	134.26	135.02
136.24	139.02	140.28
141.26	143.16	144.07
144.26	145.02	145.02
145.12	145.14	146.27
147.18	148.08	148.19
149.05	149.23	151.25
152.04	152.14	153.19
154.01	154.01	155.06
155.11	155.15	155.23
156.06	157.07	157.12
157.13	159.20	164.15
164.17	171.10	174.04
174.21	174.22	175.02
175.03	175.15	176.12
177.06	179.20	179.21
181.17	181.26	181.27
182.03	182.11	182.15
183.12	183.22	184.02
184.06	184.08	184.23
184.27	185.11	185.18
186.01	186.28	186.29
188.24	189.09	189.12

HIM (CONT.)		191.04	HIM (CONT.)		319.25	HIM (CONT.)		479.05	HIMSELF (CONT.)		427.29
195.11	195.17	195.27	320.03	320.06	320.06	479.16	481.18	481.21	438.07	438.12	439.01
196.07	198.01	198.13	320.26	320.28	321.20	481.26	481.28	482.10	444.08	447.16	448.29
198.17	198.19	198.20	322.14	322.14	324.12	482.23	482.25	482.30	451.13	454.10	454.23
198.23	198.24	198.29	324.23	324.25	324.30	484.18	484.19	484.25	455.11	457.22	458.18
199.02	199.05	199.10	325.22	326.02	327.01	484.26	485.21	486.02	458.23	458.28	459.16
199.23	199.25	199.26	329.04	329.14	329.19	487.18	487.21	487.23	459.27	463.14	463.23
200.10	200.22	200.23	329.20	329.20	330.16	488.05	488.09	488.16	465.13	466.02	466.05
201.11	201.16	203.11	330.18	330.20	331.01	488.23	488.29	489.01	466.08	457.08	471.21
203.11	203.20	203.21	331.07	331.22	332.19	490.05	490.17	490.24	472.07	473.08	474.26
204.06	204.13	204.16	333.07	333.08	334.05	490.27	491.06	491.29	477.04	477.18	478.08
204.24	204.29	205.06	334.13	334.29	335.03	492.09	492.14	492.18	479.11	479.30	481.03
205.08	205.13	205.14	339.01	343.09	344.08	492.21	493.04	493.06	483.15	488.27	490.05
207.20	208.07	208.20	344.11	344.11	344.19	493.10	497.17	498.03	492.14	492.19	493.12
208.21	208.22	208.24	344.22	348.17	348.20	498.09	499.01	499.03	500.04	502.11	502.24
208.30	209.19	211.21	348.26	349.06	349.23	499.26	499.28	500.07	505.13	515.29	516.14
211.22	211.30	211.30	350.20	353.01	353.06	500.10	501.03	501.10	516.19		
212.11	213.02	213.06	353.11	353.16	353.19	501.11	502.21	504.18	HIND	70.11	
213.12	213.19	214.02	353.26	354.08	355.02	505.05	505.05	505.20	HINDERED	87.17	
214.03	214.13	214.19	355.08	356.05	356.13	505.28	506.18	506.23	HINDRANCE		116.13
216.19	216.28	217.06	356.16	356.19	356.22	506.26	506.30	507.06	HINGE	24.18	
217.21	218.03	219.15	357.12	357.27	357.28	507.07	507.09	507.10	HINGES	366.21	
219.17	220.11	221.07	358.02	358.05	358.10	507.14	507.27	508.07	HINT	59.06	60.09
222.08	222.11	222.23	358.12	359.13	359.20	509.01	510.17	510.21	209.07	213.07	301.07
223.03	225.08	225.11	360.01	360.22	361.05	511.07	511.09	511.26	322.09	344.06	353.18
225.20	226.02	227.13	361.25	361.29	362.06	511.27	512.20	512.26	395.13		
227.24	228.01	228.01	362.07	362.18	363.09	513.06	513.07	513.30	HINTED	148.05	281.08
228.08	228.09	228.10	364.19	364.27	365.08	514.05	514.25	514.29	506.25		
228.10	228.19	228.26	367.01	367.30	368.30	515.09	515.28		HINTS	73.24	212.06
228.28	230.13	231.05	369.04	369.10	369.17	HIMMEL	260.21		360.01	370.14	497.22
231.29	233.17	233.23	371.07	371.10	371.24	HIMSELF	1.09	5.08			
234.01	235.02	236.05	372.02	372.06	373.06	5.10	9.04	10.22	HIPPED	217.23	
237.17	237.18	237.23	374.07	374.08	375.16	13.27	14.08	22.18	HIRSUTE	240.20	
238.04	238.17	238.28	375.30	376.17	376.25	27.22	28.22	29.01	HIS	1.06	1.06
239.17	240.02	240.17	381.10	381.15	381.23	29.02	36.16	38.03	1.12	1.16	2.01
241.01	241.04	241.12	382.09	382.11	382.18	38.11	38.22	43.20	2.23	2.28	2.30
241.20	242.20	243.14	382.20	382.23	382.24	43.30	44.30	45.28	3.01	3.06	3.21
243.20	243.23	243.27	383.15	383.17	385.06	47.05	49.19	55.24	3.24	3.26	4.16
243.27	244.01	244.11	387.03	388.09	389.02	56.29	58.23	58.27	4.24	5.04	5.09
244.14	244.15	244.18	390.01	390.02	391.12	62.08	64.07	68.13	5.21	6.12	7.10
244.20	245.05	245.15	391.14	391.15	391.18	70.39	71.14	73.12	7.14	7.22	8.01
245.19	246.05	246.21	391.19	391.22	392.18	73.19	77.03	79.06	8.02	8.08	8.13
246.24	247.03	247.22	392.24	392.27	392.27	79.13	83.22	85.26	8.16	8.19	8.19
250.01	250.02	250.13	392.28	394.15	396.09	88.01	89.20	89.21	8.29	9.07	10.03
250.15	250.22	251.28	399.11	399.15	399.28	90.08	91.06	95.22	10.13	10.15	10.19
252.02	252.06	253.18	400.19	400.21	400.23	95.30	98.19	99.10	10.19	10.20	10.21
254.11	256.03	256.10	400.22	400.22	401.09	100.07	100.08	104.13	11.10	11.11	11.11
256.12	256.15	256.20	400.28	400.30	401.10	104.27	114.15	114.24	11.11	11.17	11.18
256.29	256.30	258.13	401.10	402.08	402.16	115.07	116.13	116.28	11.20	11.23	11.25
259.01	260.05	261.22	402.17	402.21	403.13	120.23	125.11	125.21	11.26	12.02	12.12
263.23	263.24	265.16	404.04	404.05	404.17	128.13	130.10	131.10	12.14	12.18	12.22
267.02	267.04	267.24	404.29	405.14	405.19	132.29	132.30	134.15	13.16	15.02	16.15
267.28	268.09	268.23	408.09	408.09	410.30	136.17	137.29	139.20	16.18	16.19	16.27
269.06	269.21	270.08	411.01	414.10	415.18	142.25	145.01	145.15	17.21	17.24	17.26
270.09	270.14	270.15	416.10	416.13	418.09	157.03	172.23	174.03	21.03	21.03	21.04
270.19	270.20	270.22	418.11	419.13	419.15	175.14	177.03	179.04	21.05	21.30	22.01
272.24	273.09	273.28	419.17	419.20	419.22	184.13	184.16	186.03	22.02	22.18	22.22
274.06	274.12	274.14	419.26	420.12	421.20	189.18	190.20	203.01	23.11	23.13	23.18
274.14	274.26	278.04	421.21	421.27	423.04	208.28	215.23	216.09	23.22	23.29	24.02
279.17	280.03	280.08	425.06	425.23	426.03	220.25	228.04	230.29	24.05	24.05	24.06
280.12	280.24	280.24	426.05	426.10	426.22	232.15	232.20	239.03	24.09	24.10	24.11
281.09	281.16	281.18	427.11	427.15	427.23	243.29	253.21	253.24	24.12	24.13	24.13
282.02	282.04	282.14	427.27	428.01	428.07	259.27	262.19	263.24	24.16	24.18	24.18
282.27	283.01	283.07	428.16	428.27	429.07	268.29	281.23	283.03	24.21	25.14	25.20
283.07	283.16	283.18	429.15	430.15	431.14	284.04	289.27	293.18	26.08	26.16	26.17
283.25	283.26	285.14	430.19	431.05	431.14	293.25	295.09	298.09	26.18	26.29	27.02
285.20	286.07	286.10	432.22	433.06	433.12	299.21	300.24	301.11	27.10	27.22	27.23
286.30	287.15	288.21	433.24	435.05	435.13	310.26	311.09	311.15	27.24	27.28	28.02
288.30	289.10	289.11	435.21	436.02	436.30	311.22	311.23	311.27	28.03	28.10	28.11
289.25	289.26	290.01	437.22	437.28	438.09	312.12	312.25	314.05	28.12	28.23	29.02
290.23	291.29	292.16	440.30	442.11	442.12	316.04	316.19	316.24	29.03	29.06	29.06
294.17	295.02	295.21	442.14	447.10	450.18	316.25	320.20	321.03	30.11	30.12	30.17
295.22	295.24	295.30	450.19	451.26	453.22	324.02	324.08	324.11	32.11	32.17	32.18
295.30	297.24	298.05	454.20	455.20	455.27	332.28	333.10	333.25	32.20	32.21	33.20
298.06	298.08	300.14	455.08	456.01	456.14	334.19	334.23	336.10	33.21	33.22	33.23
300.26	301.09	301.16	456.29	457.11	457.16	336.15	337.06	343.23	33.24	33.26	33.27
302.13	302.14	303.27	457.16	458.06	458.07	344.12	344.25	349.17	33.27	33.28	34.10
303.29	304.06	304.10	458.30	459.20	459.24	350.17	352.29	356.18	34.20	34.25	34.26
304.10	304.15	304.16	461.07	461.13	461.16	357.11	358.06	358.14	34.27	34.28	35.12
304.19	304.28	305.04	463.14	465.15	467.17	358.27	360.03	360.19	35.29	35.30	36.01
305.06	308.03	308.07	467.30	468.01	468.14	361.23	361.28	362.12	36.03	36.09	36.21
309.17	309.18	309.21	468.16	468.17	468.22	362.16	362.17	364.13	36.27	36.28	36.30
310.13	310.17	310.24	469.07	469.14	469.20	371.22	372.10	382.25	37.03	37.03	37.04
310.29	311.19	312.07	470.06	470.10	470.18	382.28	383.05	383.13	37.05	37.09	37.11
312.12	312.22	312.28	470.23	471.19	471.22	386.15	394.20	399.01	37.11	37.11	37.22
313.09	313.11	313.25	472.02	472.04	472.05	399.09	402.06	402.19	37.24	37.28	37.29
314.06	314.06	314.23	472.08	473.06	473.14	402.25	403.29	404.06	38.11	38.16	38.16
315.18	315.23	317.06	474.04	474.21	475.05	404.29	412.27	415.15	38.19	39.06	39.08
317.08	317.14	318.22	475.30	477.06	477.16	418.03	419.06	419.29	42.01	42.16	43.18
319.01	319.02	319.03	477.19	478.13	478.23	420.02	420.21	424.01	43.24	43.29	43.32
									43.33	43.42	44.06

HIS (CONT.)		44.07	HIS (CONT.)		107.03	HIS (CONT.)		176.20	HIS (CONT.)		242.25
44.07	44.15	44.21	107.12	107.22	108.06	176.20	176.22	176.23	242.27	243.12	243.12
44.21	45.13	45.14	108.07	108.08	108.14	176.26	176.27	177.04	243.19	243.21	244.11
45.15	45.16	45.18	108.24	109.04	109.10	177.04	177.04	177.05	244.16	244.18	244.24
45.19	46.05	46.09	109.12	109.15	109.23	177.07	177.21	177.27	245.01	245.16	245.23
46.15	46.18	46.19	110.06	110.07	110.15	177.28	177.29	178.01	245.27	246.02	246.02
46.23	46.29	46.29	110.24	111.25	111.29	178.05	178.07	178.08	246.04	246.08	246.11
46.29	47.04	47.04	111.30	112.11	112.28	179.07	179.14	179.14	246.18	246.20	246.22
47.05	47.07	47.11	112.30	113.03	113.08	179.21	179.22	179.30	246.22	247.01	247.02
47.20	47.21	48.06	114.19	114.23	114.24	180.04	180.09	180.11	247.03	247.06	247.06
48.07	48.08	49.07	114.24	114.26	115.05	180.12	180.20	180.29	247.09	247.09	247.12
49.16	49.16	49.19	115.11	116.10	116.12	181.14	181.17	181.19	247.14	247.21	248.01
49.24	49.28	50.20	116.18	116.19	116.24	181.25	181.27	181.27	248.11	248.12	248.13
50.21	50.23	51.19	116.25	116.26	117.03	181.27	181.28	181.29	248.15	249.07	249.17
52.16	52.29	52.29	117.04	118.13	118.24	183.03	183.06	183.22	249.18	249.19	249.23
53.01	53.09	53.25	118.24	118.30	119.01	183.23	184.01	184.03	249.25	249.30	250.07
53.28	54.14	54.17	119.04	119.07	120.07	184.09	184.10	184.11	250.21	250.21	250.29
54.18	54.19	54.21	120.10	120.11	121.12	184.16	184.30	185.01	251.12	251.17	251.18
54.26	54.27	54.29	121.15	122.05	124.13	185.01	185.07	185.22	251.20	251.29	252.07
54.30	55.13	55.15	124.15	124.23	124.24	185.24	186.14	186.18	252.10	252.11	252.16
56.07	56.10	56.13	124.29	125.16	125.16	186.21	187.01	187.05	252.16	252.19	253.14
56.26	56.30	57.07	125.17	125.26	125.27	187.07	187.08	187.14	253.24	253.25	253.30
57.07	57.07	57.11	126.09	126.10	127.05	187.24	187.28	188.20	254.03	254.04	254.08
57.13	57.14	57.20	127.05	127.09	127.12	188.25	188.26	189.09	254.09	254.09	254.12
57.20	57.23	57.27	127.14	127.17	127.19	189.15	189.19	189.21	255.12	255.14	255.30
57.30	58.03	58.05	127.21	127.28	128.10	190.07	190.10	191.02	256.01	256.02	256.05
58.12	58.20	59.02	129.03	129.20	129.21	191.02	191.04	191.07	256.07	257.06	257.08
59.03	59.07	59.12	129.22	129.27	130.14	191.13	191.17	191.22	257.19	257.24	257.25
60.08	60.11	60.26	130.15	130.15	130.17	191.22	192.03	192.21	257.27	258.09	258.18
60.27	61.06	61.10	131.04	131.07	131.15	192.22	192.25	193.07	258.21	258.21	258.22
62.08	62.26	63.09	131.16	131.16	131.17	193.08	193.27	194.01	258.23	258.23	258.30
63.11	63.12	64.05	131.20	131.20	131.20	195.23	195.26	195.27	259.13	259.18	259.23
64.06	64.29	65.03	132.03	132.05	132.11	195.29	196.02	196.03	259.25	259.27	260.06
65.17	67.07	67.20	132.12	132.15	132.20	196.05	196.11	196.15	260.09	261.04	261.08
67.22	67.29	68.09	132.22	132.23	133.10	196.17	196.19	197.23	261.10	261.12	261.13
68.09	68.15	69.03	133.11	133.11	133.13	197.29	197.30	198.29	261.15	261.23	261.27
69.08	69.12	69.17	133.14	133.14	133.14	199.01	199.03	199.19	261.29	262.06	262.20
69.19	69.30	70.04	134.10	134.10	134.11	199.20	200.23	201.18	263.15	263.17	263.31
70.05	70.07	70.07	134.16	134.17	134.30	201.22	202.03	202.04	264.12	264.12	264.15
70.09	70.14	70.17	134.30	136.01	136.15	202.14	202.15	202.16	264.20	264.30	265.03
70.21	70.23	70.40	137.10	137.16	137.25	203.03	203.24	203.29	265.06	265.12	265.15
71.01	71.05	71.09	137.29	138.03	138.05	203.30	204.09	204.09	265.17	266.21	267.04
71.11	72.09	72.11	138.05	138.16	138.29	204.14	204.27	205.05	267.06	267.07	267.13
72.16	73.09	73.11	138.30	139.03	139.11	205.07	205.10	205.15	267.14	267.16	267.28
73.13	73.24	73.28	139.15	139.21	139.22	205.16	205.17	205.26	268.13	268.22	268.30
73.30	74.02	74.07	139.22	139.23	140.22	205.27	206.06	206.07	270.04	270.09	270.17
74.07	74.09	74.10	140.24	141.05	141.17	207.11	207.13	207.13	270.17	272.04	272.05
74.14	74.23	74.30	141.17	141.25	142.01	207.14	207.19	207.23	272.10	272.16	272.19
75.03	75.04	75.12	142.03	142.16	142.26	208.08	208.13	208.15	272.22	273.10	273.18
76.04	76.20	76.24	142.30	142.30	143.17	209.13	210.03	210.03	274.25	274.28	278.02
76.27	76.29	76.30	144.16	144.18	144.29	210.05	211.16	211.22	278.05	278.12	278.14
77.03	77.06	77.07	145.11	145.18	145.20	211.23	211.24	211.29	279.08	279.09	279.27
77.11	77.19	77.21	145.21	145.25	145.27	212.20	212.28	213.04	279.28	280.07	280.09
77.26	77.30	78.03	145.29	146.30	147.19	213.06	213.08	213.08	280.18	280.26	280.30
78.27	79.04	79.08	147.22	148.11	148.19	213.21	214.02	214.05	281.01	281.08	281.20
79.12	79.18	80.10	148.20	148.22	148.29	214.09	214.09	214.12	281.21	281.21	281.25
80.16	81.09	81.16	149.13	150.02	150.10	214.15	214.20	214.26	281.25	282.03	282.09
81.19	81.23	81.24	150.11	150.22	151.01	214.29	215.14	215.19	282.10	282.12	282.13
82.02	82.02	82.03	151.22	153.05	153.06	215.23	215.24	215.24	282.28	283.26	284.01
82.06	82.28	82.28	153.06	153.08	153.14	216.06	217.13	217.17	284.02	284.04	284.08
83.04	83.11	83.12	153.16	153.21	153.27	217.19	218.06	218.29	285.04	285.07	285.10
83.26	84.16	84.24	153.28	154.10	154.11	220.02	220.06	220.23	286.01	286.04	286.06
85.22	85.23	86.13	154.11	155.01	155.04	220.26	220.29	221.06	286.10	286.13	286.16
86.29	86.30	87.24	155.06	155.10	156.13	222.05	222.05	222.08	286.24	287.01	287.03
87.28	88.03	88.06	157.08	157.14	158.02	222.16	222.21	223.03	287.05	287.06	287.08
88.14	88.16	88.17	158.04	158.30	159.09	223.11	223.14	224.01	287.09	287.20	287.20
88.23	88.24	89.05	159.10	159.10	159.13	224.07	224.10	224.11	287.25	287.29	287.29
89.07	89.07	89.08	159.14	160.27	162.03	224.17	224.20	224.26	288.05	288.06	288.07
89.08	89.09	89.10	162.04	163.03	163.04	224.28	225.13	225.14	288.09	288.10	288.11
89.11	89.14	89.25	163.07	163.12	163.28	225.16	225.30	225.30	288.11	288.12	288.18
89.30	91.01	93.06	163.29	164.30	165.14	226.01	226.01	226.13	288.22	288.23	288.24
93.07	93.29	95.01	165.16	165.18	165.20	226.18	227.15	227.18	289.04	289.20	290.05
95.05	95.07	95.24	165.21	166.29	167.13	227.19	228.07	228.08	290.08	290.16	290.18
95.28	96.03	96.15	168.16	168.17	168.21	228.12	230.30	231.16	290.20	290.22	290.26
96.23	96.25	97.15	169.05	169.19	170.03	231.21	231.23	231.23	291.02	291.12	291.12
97.23	97.23	97.29	170.04	170.11	170.12	231.28	232.09	232.18	291.13	291.16	291.17
98.15	98.24	98.29	170.17	170.18	170.28	232.28	233.03	233.07	291.30	292.05	292.07
99.05	99.08	99.10	171.02	171.02	171.05	233.17	233.19	234.09	292.08	292.14	292.21
99.23	99.24	99.27	171.08	171.12	171.17	234.10	235.11	235.26	292.25	292.27	293.02
99.27	100.03	100.08	171.18	171.18	171.21	235.30	236.01	236.05	293.04	293.06	293.10
100.09	100.19	100.19	171.24	171.26	172.07	237.07	237.14	237.16	293.14	293.15	293.22
100.26	101.01	101.04	172.08	172.22	172.26	237.16	238.21	238.22	294.08	294.09	294.16
101.07	101.14	101.14	172.29	173.05	173.05	238.26	238.26	238.28	294.21	294.27	294.29
102.02	102.06	102.07	173.05	173.07	173.12	239.02	239.03	239.17	295.04	295.21	295.21
102.10	102.19	102.21	173.13	173.16	173.17	239.19	240.01	240.01	295.25	295.26	295.29
103.11	103.17	103.22	174.06	174.07	174.22	240.11	240.17	240.26	296.06	297.22	297.24
103.29	104.15	104.22	174.22	174.23	174.23	241.03	241.03	241.08	298.08	298.11	298.11
104.24	104.27	104.28	174.24	174.24	175.12	241.15	241.20	241.21	298.11	298.23	298.24
104.28	105.06	105.22	175.18	175.19	175.23	241.28	242.20	242.22	299.03	299.04	299.07
105.22	105.26	106.10	176.02	176.16	176.18				299.15	299.16	299.19

HIS (CONT.)

		299.23
299.30	300.09	300.12
300.17	300.20	300.21
300.28	300.29	301.07
301.11	301.26	302.13
303.01	303.11	304.08
304.14	304.17	304.21
304.25	304.26	304.27
305.02	305.02	306.18
306.21	306.22	306.24
306.24	307.10	307.11
307.12	307.16	307.16
307.18	307.18	307.20
307.23	308.05	308.23
308.28	309.14	309.15
309.25	309.30	310.04
310.05	310.13	310.27
310.28	311.04	311.07
311.11	311.12	311.14
311.15	311.21	311.26
311.26	312.09	312.11
312.11	312.14	312.14
312.14	312.15	312.15
312.22	312.25	313.06
313.12	314.05	314.12
315.18	316.07	316.11
316.13	316.14	316.15
316.19	317.10	317.13
318.02	318.03	318.13
318.16	318.21	318.22
318.23	319.01	319.03
319.06	319.22	320.02
320.03	320.05	320.30
321.08	321.12	321.13
321.18	321.25	322.16
322.15	322.16	322.16
322.20	322.23	323.10
323.20	323.30	324.03
324.12	324.15	324.16
324.27	325.08	325.08
325.09	325.10	325.23
325.26	326.01	326.03
327.24	328.01	328.06
328.07	328.08	328.15
328.16	328.16	328.30
329.07	329.08	329.15
329.21	329.23	329.27
329.29	330.01	330.14
330.17	330.18	331.04
331.13	331.14	331.20
331.26	332.02	332.16
332.19	332.29	332.29
332.29	333.01	333.02
333.04	333.05	333.06
333.07	333.11	333.18
333.20	333.21	333.23
333.23	333.28	334.03
334.12	334.14	334.21
334.22	334.24	334.26
334.28	334.29	334.30
335.01	335.01	335.01
335.05	335.13	336.08
336.11	336.14	336.17
336.19	336.21	337.02
337.05	337.07	337.07
337.08	337.12	337.16
337.17	337.21	337.22
337.26	338.08	338.12
338.20	338.22	338.23
339.06	340.04	340.07
340.09	342.09	342.10
342.14	342.23	343.10
343.12	343.12	343.15
343.21	343.27	344.20
344.21	344.22	345.06
345.09	345.25	345.30
346.07	346.08	347.05
347.06	347.08	347.16
348.16	348.18	348.20
349.02	349.09	349.10
349.13	349.14	349.19
349.19	349.20	350.03
350.04	350.20	350.21
350.24	350.25	351.04
351.08	351.15	351.19
351.20	351.20	351.30
351.25	351.29	351.30
352.06	352.08	352.11
352.12	352.14	352.14
352.15	352.17	352.19

HIS (CONT.)

		352.20
352.24	353.09	353.12
353.15	353.17	353.18
353.20	354.06	354.09
356.17	356.21	356.23
356.25	356.27	357.07
357.19	357.29	358.02
358.07	358.20	358.23
358.25	358.26	358.26
358.27	358.28	359.04
359.08	359.09	359.19
359.25	360.05	360.06
360.07	360.18	360.24
360.25	361.18	361.23
361.24	361.30	362.02
362.03	362.11	364.10
364.14	364.15	364.18
364.20	364.24	364.25
365.03	365.09	365.12
365.20	365.21	365.21
365.28	366.03	366.28
366.29	367.02	367.03
367.30	368.14	368.20
368.22	369.12	369.16
369.20	369.20	369.23
369.26	369.29	370.12
370.22	370.23	370.29
371.11	371.13	371.13
371.14	371.15	371.15
371.19	371.30	371.30
372.04	372.05	372.05
372.07	372.16	372.20
372.20	372.20	372.21
373.09	373.09	374.06
374.07	374.08	374.09
374.15	375.13	375.17
375.18	375.26	376.05
378.08	378.09	382.26
382.29	383.01	383.21
383.22	383.30	384.06
384.24	388.06	388.30
389.06	390.03	391.23
392.07	392.10	392.10
392.10	394.01	394.04
394.07	395.05	395.05
395.16	395.22	396.24
396.25	396.25	396.26
396.26	396.27	398.26
398.29	399.02	399.04
399.08	399.10	399.10
399.20	399.20	399.23
400.06	400.19	400.25
400.26	401.23	402.05
402.10	402.13	402.22
402.25	403.10	403.11
403.12	403.17	403.20
404.11	404.13	404.18
404.19	404.21	405.08
405.13	405.18	405.18
405.21	405.22	405.23
405.26	407.20	408.01
408.01	408.01	408.04
409.15	409.18	409.19
409.19	409.21	410.17
410.24	410.26	410.28
411.14	411.25	411.26
412.12	412.16	413.01
413.16	413.21	413.24
414.07	414.11	414.13
414.29	414.30	415.08
415.08	415.09	415.13
415.14	416.01	416.02
416.03	416.10	416.18
416.20	417.01	417.11
417.12	417.13	418.09
418.11	420.07	420.08
420.13	420.16	420.16
420.24	420.27	421.08
421.09	421.11	421.12
421.16	421.19	421.28
422.01	422.05	422.09
422.11	422.20	423.03
423.03	423.12	424.04
424.04	424.05	424.08
424.11	424.11	425.07
425.09	425.12	425.13
426.04	426.18	426.19
426.20	426.21	426.30
427.15	427.15	428.03
428.03	428.12	428.20

HIS (CONT.)

		428.21
428.22	428.23	430.19
431.11	431.12	431.12
431.21	432.23	432.24
432.27	432.27	432.28
433.05	433.18	434.19
434.27	436.01	436.03
436.06	436.08	436.11
436.15	436.27	436.29
436.30	437.10	437.11
437.17	437.18	437.21
438.05	438.05	438.07
438.11	438.14	438.15
438.27	439.03	439.06
439.14	440.11	442.12
443.01	444.10	444.10
445.01	445.18	445.19
447.09	448.29	449.05
449.16	450.07	450.08
450.16	450.17	450.21
451.07	451.08	451.08
451.12	451.22	451.23
451.25	451.28	452.14
452.18	452.20	452.23
452.27	453.20	454.07
454.18	454.21	454.27
454.29	455.03	455.05
455.09	455.12	455.13
455.14	455.19	456.06
456.07	456.08	456.11
456.19	456.22	457.14
457.23	458.11	458.12
458.14	458.15	458.25
459.01	459.19	459.20
459.23	459.25	459.26
460.01	460.03	460.05
460.07	460.09	460.19
460.19	460.21	460.24
460.28	460.29	461.11
461.17	461.22	462.09
462.11	462.14	462.16
463.12	463.12	463.13
463.13	463.15	463.15
463.17	463.26	465.12
465.23	465.24	465.26
466.04	466.04	465.08
466.10	466.11	466.15
466.30	467.03	467.12
467.12	468.10	468.11
468.22	468.23	469.08
469.16	469.19	469.22
469.23	470.06	470.09
470.21	470.22	470.22
470.26	471.03	471.06
471.25	472.03	473.03
473.03	473.04	473.09
473.23	474.01	474.19
474.22	475.02	475.07
475.08	475.10	475.15
475.27	476.01	476.04
476.06	476.10	477.04
477.13	477.17	477.20
477.23	478.05	478.18
478.24	478.27	478.28
479.04	479.06	479.16
479.21	480.01	480.02
480.01	480.20	481.02
481.12	481.14	481.18
481.19	481.20	481.20
481.30	482.03	482.05
482.11	482.15	482.19
482.21	482.21	483.02
483.08	483.11	483.11
483.12	483.12	484.15
484.17	484.18	484.20
485.08	485.09	485.10
485.10	485.11	485.18
485.20	485.21	485.26
485.27	485.28	485.28
486.01	486.06	486.10
487.01	487.08	487.15
487.16	487.18	487.22
487.22	488.02	488.08
488.14	488.16	488.25
489.09	489.12	489.20
489.24	489.28	490.01
490.04	490.07	490.17
490.21	490.23	490.23
490.23	490.24	490.25
490.26	490.29	490.30

HIS (CONT.)

		491.06
491.09	491.10	491.11
491.13	492.14	492.15
492.26	493.16	493.20
494.05	494.26	495.19
496.03	496.04	496.09
496.12	497.09	497.11
497.14	497.17	498.07
498.08	498.14	498.14
498.15	498.25	498.28
498.30	499.03	499.12
499.17	499.17	499.24
499.28	499.30	500.06
500.06	500.09	501.06
501.09	501.10	501.14
501.18	502.01	502.01
502.03	502.04	502.07
502.20	502.22	502.28
502.28	505.08	505.11
505.13	505.13	505.15
505.18	505.19	505.19
505.21	505.25	505.26
506.01	506.06	506.07
506.13	506.14	506.15
506.15	506.19	506.21
506.22	506.24	506.27
507.01	507.03	508.01
508.01	508.02	508.03
508.05	508.10	508.30
509.04	509.05	509.06
509.08	509.08	509.19
509.22	510.04	510.04
510.15	510.18	510.24
510.30	511.01	511.08
511.19	511.19	511.20
511.27	512.01	512.15
512.20	513.04	513.06
513.25	513.26	514.05
514.10	514.15	514.21
514.23	514.24	514.25
514.27	515.03	515.04
515.04	515.10	515.11
515.11	515.14	515.18
515.18	515.22	515.24
515.27	516.01	516.03
515.07	516.09	516.14
516.21	516.21	

HISS		17.14	19.16
	134.01	170.19	374.12
HISSED	136.14		
HISSING	137.06	171.25	
HISTORIC	325.23		
HISTORY	249.19	252.19	
	268.16	297.19	437.19
HIT	120.18	120.18	
	145.08	464.12	464.13
HITCHED	104.27		
HIVA	437.03		
HIVE	132.07		
HOARSE	151.21	318.17	
HOBART	203.16		
HOBBLED	366.08		
HOD	113.10		
HOGSHEAD	44.09		
HOISTING	324.06		
HOLD	6.12	6.22	
	22.13	23.28	48.06
	52.21	52.27	90.06
	108.06	108.21	112.28
	120.17	158.10	169.11
	177.19	181.26	183.20
	201.25	219.04	238.10
	238.28	241.15	254.25
	255.18	267.09	277.09
	293.12	309.19	337.22
	343.30	345.01	356.04
	364.20	370.20	379.17
	398.05	402.03	411.24
	437.09	454.30	456.27
	457.07	495.06	503.07
	511.29		
HOLDING	37.16	69.18	
	101.11	117.10	148.10
	196.27	209.04	217.19
	223.08	256.13	263.21
	308.04	346.07	365.16
	370.07	372.27	380.18
	412.08		
HOLDING-GROUND			196.27
HOLDS		81.06	271.07

HOLDS (CONT.) 389.10
395.02
HOLE 34.07 135.08
136.04 191.18 217.25
225.18 293.26 338.14
359.07 370.26 474.14
479.23
HOLE-AND-CORNER 191.18
HOLES 3.07
HOLIDAY 4.16 286.26
HOLIDAYS 399.04
HOLLERING 62.26
HOLLOW 21.08 131.29
374.07 426.01 445.09
451.29
HOLLOWED 323.28
HOLLOWS 27.16 118.24
HOLY 23.05 197.27
205.01
HOLY- 197.27
HOME 13.15 13.29
14.25 27.11 46.02
52.03 53.02 62.25
79.11 92.11 95.02
95.16 96.14 99.02
99.12 156.27 164.13
168.22 223.20 250.05
250.05 270.13 270.16
270.25 270.25 271.02
271.07 272.11 272.16
277.15 330.20 338.20
342.12 404.11 404.23
404.29 414.02 416.13
419.23 421.15 422.18
432.08 435.08 435.14
441.08 452.30 455.11
476.07
HOME-LIKE 342.12
HOME-PORT 27.11
HOMELESS 222.10
HOMELY 315.08
HOMERIC 328.11
HOMES 483.28 508.11
HOMEWARD 166.27
HOMICIDAL 459.24
HONEST 50.25 178.22
387.09 421.20
HONESTLY 32.03 190.14
307.17
HONESTY 282.08
HONEY 404.22
HONEYED 310.17
HONG 229.06
HONG- 229.06
HONOLULU 48.12 55.22
HONOUR 54.02 67.19
97.11 180.27 180.27
180.28 181.01 184.14
203.17 213.10 213.13
276.01 330.14 330.29
387.26 418.13 516.11
HONOURABLE 356.23
383.11 383.13 402.03
402.17 402.23 402.26
402.30 403.01 403.14
404.03
HONOURED 405.01
HOOK 8.02 8.09
8.15 8.17 132.06
150.19
HOOKED 206.06
HOOKER 29.27
HOOKS 2.05 286.18
HOP 43.36 225.18
HOPE 5.05 11.11
15.12 16.07 59.10
89.22 106.07 116.17
116.30 124.01 148.04
186.22 191.08 193.15
194.23 215.16 231.08
252.21 304.06 337.01
413.19 417.14 454.05
507.29
HOPED 59.20 59.24
60.16 80.15 183.19
286.16 329.25 403.11
483.15 483.18
HOPEFUL 180.10 419.25
439.28
HOPELESS 11.23 38.19

HOPELESS (CONT.) 82.18
160.26 193.02 209.27
211.18 216.12 241.30
245.18 259.09 359.11
381.16 389.18
HOPELESSLY 124.17
126.06 175.03 214.22
288.05
HOPES 13.22 15.21
117.17 407.10 422.09
452.23 470.16 475.17
HORDE 458.17
HORIZON 13.12 19.09
22.03 22.17 26.16
110.27 123.03 149.15
262.01 409.08 409.27
414.19
HORIZONS 417.14
HORN 27.08
HORN-RIMMED 27.08
HORRIBLE 58.23 81.20
142.15 189.19 189.20
247.10 312.10 344.25
405.28 508.18
HORRIBLY 186.29 426.15
HORRID 294.01 351.06
HORRIFIED 191.21
HORROR 13.29 35.14
53.23 63.11 66.15
138.07 148.06 222.21
357.15 386.12 438.19
509.28
HORRORS 105.27 442.15
474.23
HORSE 27.17 182.30
197.07 205.18 254.12
254.26 255.23 255.27
256.04 256.13 256.17
HORSE-POWER 197.07
HORSESHOE 33.19
HOSE 72.26
HOSPITAL 12.14 12.27
57.10 57.17
HOSPITALS 187.22
HOST 113.26 420.21
HOSTILE 141.21
HOT 18.04 25.09
37.15 70.20 116.25
124.05 141.07 170.23
215.04 306.22 310.30
333.13 359.15 417.15
437.09
HOT-TEMPERED 215.04
HOTEL 49.27 92.03
199.11 208.03 240.19
241.23 426.23
HOTEL-KEEPER 426.23
HOTELS 202.30
HOTLY 78.12
HOTTEST 429.24
HOUND 47.30 48.03
304.29
HOUNDS 497.12
HOUR 41.26 43.13
168.12 198.17 329.02
330.05 355.23 399.28
417.07 417.18 454.06
456.13 491.01 507.26
HOUR'S 152.24 452.29
503.19
HOURS 148.18 148.25
148.26 159.06 171.07
171.22 176.14 176.14
199.30 279.07 298.07
328.23 363.04 370.17
425.06 479.06 493.22
HOURS' 173.20
HOURSE 510.27
HOUSE 91.14 128.29
184.29 215.12 227.11
227.23 228.10 243.20
245.27 248.03 250.29
251.09 252.07 254.08
254.19 254.21 268.19
269.06 269.20 269.21
279.04 279.15 284.08
289.27 293.27 301.26
303.29 307.06 342.25
346.04 350.12 353.12
353.28 355.19 356.03

HOUSE (CONT.) 357.20
358.04 363.06 366.19
378.10 384.24 398.26
406.06 420.08 427.22
427.24 428.03 429.06
429.20 432.19 450.11
459.06 475.14 484.19
485.06 489.29 491.28
504.15 505.06 510.15
516.18
HOUSE' 245.27
HOUSEHOLD 338.21
366.06 510.09
HOUSEHOLDER 327.13
HOUSEHOLDS 314.30
316.06
HOUSES 4.12 175.28
269.10 300.19 302.20
303.05 304.12 311.18
313.08 313.21 319.15
334.01 336.04 373.20
407.02 443.03 443.07
444.28 445.28 450.23
463.25 466.14 469.05
480.03 480.12 481.18
482.27 492.11 495.06
504.04 504.22
HOVE 280.24
HOVEL 58.04 426.29
473.04
HOVELS 410.07 410.14
HOVERED 37.09 249.08
260.07 348.17 368.23
410.05
HOVERING 247.12 383.22
475.12
HOW 4.19 9.01
11.22 14.10 14.12
23.09 25.30 49.28
53.25 66.07 66.24
70.39 73.06 78.07
86.04 88.02 91.12
95.29 107.01 109.11
118.05 123.01 132.23
144.14 146.01 156.06
156.06 157.30 158.06
164.05 164.18 164.27
164.28 168.25 168.27
169.08 171.21 172.14
174.08 174.11 182.21
183.30 193.18 193.21
198.06 199.21 199.21
200.08 209.09 212.14
213.14 218.02 219.06
231.08 231.24 233.07
233.07 234.21 243.29
250.12 254.02 254.10
258.13 258.27 259.11
259.11 259.16 259.17
260.21 261.03 264.20
265.01 265.01 265.05
272.05 272.08 274.01
274.06 278.29 279.16
280.14 281.25 281.28
287.16 293.11 295.19
299.25 304.22 305.04
305.05 309.08 309.10
309.13 314.20 314.30
321.26 323.27 324.21
325.02 328.28 328.30
329.22 331.27 340.13
340.15 341.12 342.22
347.08 351.30 359.01
363.15 372.22 378.19
383.14 388.16 388.17
388.24 389.19 389.20
389.20 390.14 390.15
393.13 402.15 412.21
423.30 425.15 447.07
474.24 474.25 476.06
493.17 508.12
HOWEVER 12.12 44.02
46.10 58.06 66.22
71.05 97.13 184.24
190.24 208.18 228.06
243.18 266.16 266.22
280.05 291.09 299.19
327.15 338.29 339.20
341.18 360.16 366.18

HOWEVER (CONT.) 381.14
400.28 419.05 437.25
443.11 463.20 483.17
502.09 503.11
HOWL 61.24 64.03
64.11
HOWLED 133.06 133.29
151.09
HOWLING 144.25
HOWLS 142.04
HUDDLED 224.04
HUDDLING 463.26
HUFF 82.05
HUGE 318.06 338.10
HUGGING 240.17
HULL 19.21 21.25
31.08 131.19
HULLABALOO 300.09
HUM 18.01 105.12
463.09
HUMAN 11.28 17.30
66.05 66.16 69.02
72.18 103.25 113.16
117.16 138.08 166.13
165.17 235.17 264.04
268.01 302.27 313.13
321.23 340.08 366.07
397.29 398.07
HUMANE 2.19
HUMBLE 117.30 264.21
274.29 279.23
HUMBLED 412.16
HUMBLEST 270.27
HUMBUG 224.13
HUMILIATED 224.11
HUMILIATION 89.14
HUMILITY 405.03 434.20
HUMMED 467.22
HUMMING 6.25 31.15
HUMOROUS 248.13 258.05
262.26
HUMOUR 105.01 151.25
HUMOURED 453.12
HUMOUREDLY 301.12
HUMOURING 2.24
2.25
HUMP 178.14
HUNCHED 129.26
HUNDRED 5.07 15.08
15.21 30.04 35.18
41.15 48.28 69.01
79.26 79.27 81.13
92.04 101.19 104.15
104.16 104.19 133.19
133.21 138.07 229.27
230.02 237.05 276.10
311.19 315.22 323.01
323.14 324.01 347.08
358.16 439.08 448.18
460.15 460.22 460.22
463.25 472.21 479.14
HUNDREDS 117.15 167.08
313.06
HUNDREDTH 229.27
HUNG 20.19 24.09
24.11 34.02 34.26
55.15 56.13 73.01
87.06 163.03 188.27
199.19 248.21 273.08
291.25 316.26 332.15
361.03 393.25 397.17
399.09 426.20 428.21
430.25 433.28 437.16
467.16 483.24 512.13
HUNGER 277.03 441.17
471.11
HUNGRILY 22.03 442.28
HUNGRY 45.22 239.14
306.10 310.14 441.06
470.28
HUNT 84.10 251.20
HUNTED 313.08 336.03
441.18 452.04
HUNTING 196.19 267.13
HUNTING-GROUND 196.19
HURL 288.27
HURRICANE 5.11
5.28 80.26 214.29
HURRICANES 196.29
200.11

HURRIED	165.21	190.01	
	294.25	333.23	342.23
	391.13	395.09	504.23
HURRIEDLY			84.10
	90.12	184.26	195.10
	384.23	506.02	
HURRY	63.28	65.16	
	141.16	226.12	238.06
	290.21	362.16	
HURT	66.07	134.19	
	145.24	226.09	273.14
	424.06		
HUSBAND	315.11	421.23	
	475.18		
HUSH	92.22	508.14	
HUSKILY	364.26	385.29	
HUSKY	174.06		
HUT	351.14	366.19	
	427.05	448.19	462.28
	474.22		
HUTS	15.29	387.28	
	420.19	480.13	
HYAENA'	293.11		
HYAENAS	293.12		
HYPOTHESIS			82.21
HYSTERICALLY			140.21
I	8.01	8.01	
	8.03	8.03	8.03
	8.06	8.15	29.08
	29.13	29.15	29.15
	29.16	29.17	29.17
	29.21	29.24	29.26
	30.04	30.05	30.08
	33.29	33.29	34.01
	34.01	34.03	34.04
	34.06	34.12	34.12
	34.14	34.17	34.17
	34.21	34.27	34.30
	35.03	36.13	36.16
	36.17	36.19	36.25
	40.01	40.02	40.03
	40.03	40.06	40.07
	40.08	40.08	40.08
	40.08	40.09	40.21
	40.23	41.01	41.02
	41.02	41.02	41.03
	41.05	42.06	42.10
	42.10	42.14	43.02
	43.03	43.04	43.06
	43.06	43.13	43.17
	43.28	43.39	43.39
	43.40	44.03	44.03
	44.05	45.01	45.02
	45.23	45.23	45.29
	45.29	46.01	46.02
	46.02	46.03	46.04
	46.12	46.15	47.13
	47.14	47.16	47.17
	47.18	47.19	47.23
	47.26	48.01	48.02
	48.03	48.05	48.10
	48.12	48.14	48.15
	48.16	48.20	48.23
	49.01	49.11	49.12
	49.14	49.14	49.29
	50.01	50.02	50.19
	50.20	50.20	50.26
	50.27	51.21	51.21
	51.21	51.22	51.29
	52.02	52.02	52.03
	52.04	52.10	53.12
	53.14	53.14	53.15
	53.17	53.18	53.18
	53.19	54.01	54.01
	54.01	54.05	54.08
	54.08	54.19	54.24
	55.09	55.24	55.26
	55.27	56.04	56.11
	56.11	56.20	57.09
	57.14	57.16	57.18
	57.23	57.23	58.11
	58.16	59.02	59.10
	59.12	59.17	59.19
	59.19	59.20	59.20
	59.23	59.24	60.02
	60.03	60.04	60.05
	50.11	60.12	60.15
	60.18	60.22	60.23
	50.24	60.25	60.25
	61.01	61.02	61.02

I (CONT.)

		61.11
61.20	61.21	61.27
61.28	62.01	62.01
62.03	62.06	62.06
62.07	62.12	62.14
62.14	62.23	63.10
63.21	63.24	63.25
64.04	64.08	64.12
64.14	64.16	64.19
64.21	64.26	64.27
64.30	65.05	65.11
65.13	65.15	65.16
65.18	66.06	67.11
67.28	68.09	68.10
68.12	68.15	68.17
68.18	68.18	68.19
68.30	68.30	69.02
69.02	69.05	69.07
69.10	69.15	69.21
69.26	70.29	70.30
70.31	70.36	70.37
70.39	70.42	70.43
71.02	71.06	71.08
71.19	71.20	71.28
72.06	72.07	72.11
72.16	72.29	73.04
73.05	73.05	73.10
73.14	73.14	73.20
73.23	73.26	73.28
74.11	74.19	74.24
74.26	74.27	74.29
75.02	75.04	75.04
75.07	75.08	75.10
75.11	75.15	75.21
75.21	75.22	75.24
75.26	76.02	76.19
77.13	77.17	77.18
77.22	77.26	77.30
78.08	78.08	78.12
78.14	78.15	78.22
78.22	78.23	79.03
79.04	79.06	79.17
79.18	79.19	79.24
79.26	79.26	80.10
80.14	80.14	80.15
80.15	80.15	80.26
81.02	81.11	81.14
81.15	81.17	81.17
81.18	81.20	81.22
81.25	81.27	81.30
82.04	82.08	82.09
82.10	82.10	82.14
82.17	82.20	82.21
82.22	82.28	82.29
83.01	83.08	83.12
83.21	83.28	84.01
84.04	84.04	84.14
84.14	84.16	84.20
84.22	84.22	84.29
84.29	84.30	84.30
85.02	85.03	85.04
85.04	85.10	85.11
85.14	85.21	85.21
85.27	85.28	86.01
86.03	86.04	86.05
86.06	86.08	86.09
86.11	86.14	86.15
86.20	86.24	87.01
87.01	87.03	87.03
87.07	87.08	87.08
87.10	87.10	87.11
87.13	87.16	87.17
87.20	87.20	87.22
87.22	87.22	87.24
87.26	87.29	88.01
88.02	88.02	88.04
88.05	88.05	88.10
88.14	88.14	88.20
88.23	88.23	88.29
89.05	89.13	89.28
89.29	89.30	90.02
90.02	90.05	90.07
90.09	90.09	90.11
90.12	90.12	90.14
90.15	90.22	90.28
90.30	91.01	91.03
91.04	91.05	91.05
91.12	91.13	93.07
93.11	94.01	94.01
94.08	94.20	94.21

I (CONT.)

		94.22
94.22	95.06	95.17
95.18	95.19	95.19
95.20	95.23	95.25
95.26	95.29	95.30
96.01	96.05	96.20
96.01	96.26	96.27
96.27	96.30	97.04
97.06	97.14	97.17
97.17	97.18	97.19
98.14	98.17	98.23
98.28	98.30	99.03
99.12	99.16	99.17
99.18	99.18	99.19
99.21	99.21	99.23
100.05	100.08	100.24
100.29	101.03	101.05
101.10	101.11	101.16
101.17	101.18	101.23
101.24	101.26	101.27
102.02	102.04	102.06
102.12	103.30	104.03
104.03	104.04	104.05
104.05	104.06	104.06
104.06	104.11	104.11
104.11	104.22	104.22
104.25	104.26	104.26
105.30	107.05	107.22
107.23	108.01	108.18
108.18	108.20	108.21
108.23	108.26	108.26
108.27	108.28	108.29
108.30	109.03	109.05
109.08	109.10	109.11
109.18	109.18	109.20
109.24	109.26	109.29
109.30	110.04	110.05
110.07	110.09	110.09
110.14	110.16	110.16
110.21	110.21	110.21
110.26	110.28	111.01
111.04	111.05	111.07
111.21	111.22	112.04
112.05	112.10	112.13
112.14	112.15	112.15
112.23	113.12	113.16
113.19	113.20	113.29
113.30	114.01	114.06
114.08	114.09	114.10
114.27	114.27	114.28
114.30	115.02	116.03
116.06	116.06	116.28
116.29	117.23	117.23
118.04	118.15	120.13
120.15	120.16	120.16
120.18	120.18	120.24
121.04	121.09	122.01
122.07	122.15	123.30
124.01	124.03	124.04
124.04	124.05	126.30
126.30	127.01	127.08
127.10	127.16	127.17
127.18	128.08	128.09
128.10	128.14	128.15
128.15	128.15	128.19
129.04	129.06	129.07
129.10	129.11	129.13
129.14	129.17	129.18
130.01	130.04	130.09
130.11	130.19	130.21
130.23	130.25	130.26
130.30	131.07	131.08
132.11	132.12	132.13
132.24	132.27	132.28
132.29	132.30	133.02
133.08	133.16	133.23
133.24	133.26	134.06
134.06	134.15	134.19
134.23	134.24	134.24
135.06	135.06	135.07
136.16	137.19	137.19
138.04	138.10	138.18
139.03	139.09	139.12
139.29	140.21	140.22
140.28	140.28	140.29
141.02	141.02	141.03
141.03	141.03	141.07
141.08	141.10	141.15
142.13	142.20	142.24
142.27	143.05	143.19

I (CONT.)

		143.21
143.23	143.23	144.01
144.04	144.04	144.07
144.08	144.09	144.12
144.14	144.14	144.15
144.16	144.22	144.22
144.22	144.24	144.25
144.26	144.29	144.30
145.02	145.03	145.03
145.05	145.06	145.06
145.09	145.12	145.13
145.14	145.17	145.18
145.18	145.22	145.23
145.25	146.14	146.14
146.14	146.15	146.16
148.18	146.21	146.21
146.30	148.01	148.03
148.06	148.13	149.23
149.27	150.04	150.07
150.12	150.15	150.16
150.16	150.16	150.17
150.17	150.24	150.26
151.06	151.07	151.08
151.08	151.09	151.10
151.10	151.19	151.19
151.20	151.23	151.26
151.29	151.30	152.02
152.04	152.06	152.06
152.07	152.09	152.10
152.11	152.12	152.16
152.17	152.19	152.21
152.23	152.23	152.24
152.25	152.28	152.30
153.02	153.09	153.09
153.11	153.13	153.13
153.18	153.19	153.20
153.23	153.23	153.24
153.25	153.30	154.01
154.01	154.02	154.06
154.07	154.08	154.14
155.02	155.05	155.23
156.08	157.12	157.13
157.15	157.18	157.21
157.24	157.30	158.01
158.01	158.02	158.05
158.05	158.05	158.08
158.09	158.13	158.14
158.15	158.21	158.24
158.24	158.26	158.28
158.28	158.28	158.29
159.01	159.02	159.03
159.04	159.04	159.07
159.13	159.17	159.18
159.18	159.19	159.26
159.28	159.28	159.29
160.02	160.03	160.03
160.04	160.06	160.06
160.06	160.06	160.07
160.08	160.09	160.10
150.13	160.13	160.13
160.14	160.16	160.19
160.19	160.25	162.10
162.10	162.11	162.18
162.18	162.20	162.21
163.05	163.05	163.06
163.10	163.12	163.12
163.20	163.20	163.22
153.23	163.24	163.24
163.25	163.27	163.30
164.01	164.01	164.02
164.02	164.03	164.04
164.05	164.06	164.07
164.08	164.08	164.08
164.14	164.15	164.16
164.17	164.18	164.18
164.19	164.21	164.24
164.24	164.25	164.26
164.28	164.29	165.05
166.15	166.24	167.22
167.23	167.26	168.05
168.06	168.11	168.20
168.22	168.23	168.25
169.08	169.29	170.15
170.23	171.10	171.14
171.18	171.21	171.23
172.02	172.09	172.11
172.12	174.04	174.20
174.21	174.21	174.22
175.10	175.14	175.15

I (CONT.)		175.18	I (CONT.)		209.04	I (CONT.)		237.27	I (CONT.)		285.19
175.30	176.07	176.11	209.05	209.05	209.11	237.30	237.30	238.01	285.22	286.01	286.29
176.23	177.02	177.05	209.15	209.18	209.19	238.03	238.05	238.05	287.15	288.18	288.19
177.12	177.13	177.17	209.27	209.28	210.01	238.07	238.19	238.20	288.30	289.01	289.02
177.20	177.20	177.20	210.09	210.13	210.17	238.24	238.24	238.27	289.03	289.09	289.09
177.26	177.29	178.09	210.20	210.22	210.23	239.01	239.05	239.21	289.09	289.10	289.15
178.09	178.13	178.16	210.24	210.25	210.27	239.23	240.03	240.30	289.16	289.16	289.21
178.21	179.12	179.12	211.03	211.05	211.22	241.05	241.12	241.20	290.04	290.10	290.11
179.16	179.17	179.20	211.23	211.28	212.09	241.24	241.24	242.01	290.13	290.17	290.19
180.03	180.04	180.05	212.11	212.12	212.14	243.03	243.03	243.04	290.23	290.27	290.30
180.38	180.08	180.13	212.17	212.17	212.23	243.08	243.15	243.23	291.02	291.05	291.07
180.15	180.22	181.02	212.27	213.01	213.05	243.25	243.26	243.27	291.09	291.12	291.14
181.03	181.03	181.05	213.11	213.14	213.19	244.06	244.09	244.14	291.18	291.22	291.24
181.11	181.16	181.19	213.24	214.01	214.01	244.20	244.29	244.30	291.27	291.29	292.02
181.25	181.30	182.03	214.06	214.06	214.07	244.30	245.04	245.04	292.17	293.17	293.24
182.04	182.05	182.08	214.11	214.12	214.15	245.05	245.07	245.09	294.01	294.11	294.17
182.24	183.18	183.30	214.19	214.20	214.23	245.11	245.15	245.20	294.23	295.02	295.02
184.01	184.03	184.08	214.24	215.14	215.14	245.24	246.03	246.04	295.12	295.13	295.14
184.08	184.21	184.22	215.16	215.17	215.17	246.06	246.18	246.24	295.15	295.16	295.20
184.23	184.27	185.09	215.18	215.21	216.04	247.05	247.07	247.21	295.20	295.20	295.24
185.11	185.12	185.13	216.05	216.07	216.09	248.01	248.04	249.14	295.26	295.27	295.28
185.13	185.14	185.17	216.18	217.01	217.01	249.17	249.29	249.30	295.30	296.01	296.03
185.19	185.25	185.26	217.02	217.03	217.04	250.12	250.25	250.25	297.01	297.15	297.19
185.27	185.29	185.30	217.06	217.10	217.10	251.10	252.20	252.23	298.05	298.05	300.15
186.05	186.06	186.11	217.13	217.15	217.17	252.23	253.11	253.23	300.15	300.16	300.30
186.16	186.16	186.17	217.21	218.02	218.02	253.25	253.27	253.30	301.02	301.04	301.05
186.18	186.20	186.23	218.03	218.12	218.17	254.22	254.22	254.23	301.05	301.06	301.08
186.24	186.25	186.28	218.20	218.30	219.01	254.24	254.26	254.27	301.12	301.14	301.18
187.01	187.03	187.03	219.17	219.18	219.21	254.30	255.05	255.09	301.18	301.19	301.20
187.06	187.09	187.10	219.21	219.21	219.22	255.10	255.12	255.13	301.23	303.05	303.06
187.11	187.14	187.14	219.22	219.26	219.29	255.15	255.18	255.23	303.06	303.08	303.09
187.15	187.18	187.25	219.30	220.03	220.23	255.24	255.26	255.26	303.10	303.10	303.17
187.26	188.03	188.06	220.24	220.28	221.01	255.27	256.03	256.05	303.18	303.20	303.23
188.07	188.07	188.07	221.02	221.02	221.02	256.06	256.10	256.10	303.23	303.24	303.27
188.10	188.12	188.12	221.04	221.05	221.07	256.10	256.11	256.12	304.03	304.06	304.18
188.13	188.13	188.14	222.01	222.11	222.11	256.15	256.17	256.20	304.21	304.22	304.24
188.16	188.17	188.18	222.12	222.14	222.17	256.20	256.21	256.21	306.01	306.06	306.07
188.20	188.25	188.28	222.18	223.03	223.04	256.23	256.25	256.25	306.13	306.19	306.19
188.30	189.01	189.02	223.06	223.08	223.10	256.28	256.29	255.30	306.20	307.02	307.28
189.03	189.10	189.11	223.11	223.12	223.12	257.11	257.12	257.13	308.02	308.05	308.06
189.11	189.13	189.20	223.12	223.13	223.15	257.13	257.14	257.15	308.08	308.19	308.19
190.01	190.13	190.14	223.15	223.15	223.15	257.16	257.28	258.01	308.21	308.22	308.24
190.17	190.17	190.20	223.16	223.16	223.19	258.02	258.06	258.12	308.24	308.27	309.01
190.23	191.05	191.07	223.20	223.22	223.22	258.15	258.20	258.25	309.04	309.06	309.07
191.08	191.12	191.23	223.24	223.25	223.26	258.27	258.30	259.10	309.10	309.10	309.11
193.12	193.18	193.19	223.28	223.29	224.11	260.16	260.29	261.06	309.11	309.29	312.07
193.21	193.22	193.24	224.11	224.14	224.19	262.17	263.20	264.02	312.07	314.15	314.18
194.06	194.12	195.01	224.25	224.25	224.26	264.09	264.12	264.14	314.19	314.20	315.05
195.10	195.10	195.17	224.27	224.28	224.29	264.16	264.19	264.25	316.21	318.02	319.07
195.25	195.26	195.27	224.29	225.01	225.02	265.01	265.02	265.04	320.05	320.05	320.06
195.28	195.30	196.01	225.03	225.08	225.10	265.06	265.07	265.15	320.16	320.17	320.18
196.03	196.07	196.07	225.11	225.14	225.19	266.01	266.17	266.18	320.18	320.22	320.24
196.10	196.10	196.16	225.27	226.01	226.02	267.01	267.12	267.12	320.24	321.04	321.28
197.01	197.03	197.05	226.09	226.14	226.16	267.23	267.26	267.29	322.14	322.14	322.15
197.10	197.16	197.17	226.22	226.22	226.25	268.01	268.05	268.05	322.18	322.24	322.25
197.18	197.18	197.19	226.27	227.05	227.10	268.13	268.14	268.19	322.27	323.15	325.03
199.05	199.07	199.08	227.12	227.14	228.09	269.02	269.04	269.05	325.06	325.09	325.22
199.09	199.09	199.10	228.11	228.13	228.14	269.05	269.21	270.07	325.28	326.01	326.04
199.24	199.25	199.30	228.15	228.17	228.18	270.11	270.11	270.12	327.14	328.09	328.09
200.01	200.04	200.09	228.19	228.19	228.25	270.13	270.14	270.15	328.11	329.10	329.10
200.10	200.13	200.16	228.25	228.26	228.27	270.16	270.19	270.19	329.12	329.14	329.22
200.19	200.20	200.21	228.29	229.01	229.02	270.20	270.21	270.22	329.28	330.03	334.09
200.22	200.24	200.24	229.02	229.07	229.09	270.24	270.25	270.25	334.13	334.25	334.27
200.25	200.27	201.03	229.09	229.10	229.11	271.22	271.30	272.05	337.19	337.23	337.24
201.05	201.07	201.08	229.12	229.13	229.19	272.06	272.08	272.23	337.28	338.04	338.15
201.12	201.13	201.13	229.20	229.21	229.24	272.24	272.25	272.25	338.25	338.25	338.27
201.13	201.14	201.15	229.25	230.01	230.04	272.26	272.27	272.29	338.27	338.30	339.01
201.15	201.23	201.23	230.06	230.09	230.10	272.30	273.01	273.11	339.03	339.07	339.16
201.26	201.27	201.30	230.12	230.19	230.20	273.12	273.13	273.15	339.24	340.02	340.03
202.05	202.09	202.10	230.22	230.25	231.02	273.27	273.28	274.06	340.20	340.25	340.28
202.24	202.26	202.26	231.02	231.05	231.08	274.06	274.08	274.09	341.11	341.14	341.18
202.26	202.28	202.29	231.07	231.08	231.08	274.14	274.16	274.22	341.19	341.21	341.23
203.03	203.04	203.04	231.09	231.11	231.12	274.23	274.24	274.24	341.30	342.04	342.13
203.05	203.06	203.09	231.12	231.16	231.19	274.25	275.03	275.09	342.14	342.22	342.23
203.14	203.15	203.17	231.24	231.26	231.26	275.11	275.14	275.15	342.29	342.30	343.04
203.24	203.25	203.28	231.27	231.28	231.29	275.15	275.17	278.06	343.05	343.09	343.18
203.28	204.04	204.05	231.30	232.01	232.01	279.04	279.17	279.24	343.22	344.02	344.06
204.06	204.12	204.13	233.01	233.03	233.07	280.08	280.22	280.26	344.06	344.09	344.13
204.17	204.19	204.20	233.07	233.09	233.10	280.28	281.09	281.10	344.16	344.18	344.20
204.26	204.28	204.29	233.12	233.23	233.24	281.17	281.18	281.24	344.22	344.25	344.28
204.30	205.01	205.08	233.24	233.26	234.06	281.20	281.24	281.24	345.05	345.22	347.02
205.10	205.13	205.14	234.07	234.13	234.19	281.29	282.02	282.04	347.18	347.19	348.01
205.18	205.19	205.25	234.21	235.18	235.20	282.11	282.14	282.15	348.28	348.28	348.29
205.28	207.01	207.02	235.21	235.22	235.26	282.16	282.17	282.23	349.01	349.04	349.23
207.03	207.04	207.09	235.26	235.27	236.02	282.27	283.01	283.01	349.28	349.30	350.08
207.19	207.20	207.21	236.03	236.04	236.06	283.05	283.06	283.07	350.10	350.14	350.20
207.25	208.01	208.02	236.13	236.28	237.09	283.12	283.12	283.14	350.23	350.24	351.07
208.07	208.08	208.12	237.11	237.14	237.15	283.15	283.17	283.21	352.02	352.05	352.15
208.18	208.20	208.21	237.16	237.17	237.19	283.21	283.22	283.24	353.02	353.03	353.03
208.24	208.30	209.02	237.23	237.24	237.25	283.24	284.06	284.09	353.10	353.19	353.20

I (CONT.) [353.24]

353.27	353.28	353.28
353.29	354.04	354.07
354.09	354.10	355.07
355.10	355.12	355.14
356.15	357.07	357.24
361.07	361.10	361.10
361.11	361.16	362.05
362.14	362.21	362.22
363.01	363.05	363.16
367.05	367.05	367.07
367.20	367.29	368.01
368.29	369.03	369.12
359.13	369.19	369.19
370.17	370.18	373.22
374.15	374.26	374.29
374.29	374.30	375.04
375.11	375.11	375.12
375.14	375.14	375.14
375.22	375.28	375.28
375.30	375.30	375.30
376.03	376.03	376.09
376.10	376.11	376.11
376.17	376.17	376.24
376.25	377.02	377.03
377.03	377.03	377.05
377.06	377.07	377.09
377.10	377.14	377.16
377.19	377.23	377.26
378.03	378.09	378.18
378.20	379.06	379.18
379.22	379.24	379.27
379.27	380.05	380.07
381.01	381.08	381.11
381.15	381.15	381.17
381.17	381.19	381.21
381.22	382.02	382.09
382.23	383.02	383.08
383.14	383.17	383.19
383.26	383.26	383.27
384.24	385.02	385.04
385.05	385.11	385.11
385.12	385.13	385.21
386.17	386.22	386.24
386.25	386.29	387.03
387.14	387.21	387.26
387.26	388.01	388.03
388.05	388.07	388.09
388.12	388.14	388.15
388.16	388.16	388.17
388.18	388.21	388.24
388.25	388.28	389.02
389.03	389.07	389.12
389.16	389.16	389.21
389.30	390.08	390.10
390.15	390.26	390.30
391.05	391.07	391.13
391.14	391.14	391.16
391.19	391.24	391.27
391.27	391.28	391.28
391.29	392.06	392.08
392.15	392.17	392.18
392.19	392.20	392.20
392.29	393.03	393.06
393.08	393.09	393.10
393.13	393.14	393.21
393.23	393.24	393.25
393.27	394.15	394.17
394.17	394.18	395.10
395.10	395.11	395.12
395.17	395.20	395.25
396.02	396.09	396.11
396.11	396.12	396.13
396.15	396.15	396.24
396.28	397.21	397.25
398.03	398.03	398.04
398.04	398.06	398.06
398.09	398.12	398.15
398.16	398.18	398.18
398.18	398.26	399.06
399.07	399.17	399.26
399.28	399.29	400.05
400.06	400.08	400.10
400.29	401.01	401.01
401.02	401.04	401.05
401.07	401.07	401.09
401.12	401.13	401.13
401.14	401.16	401.27
401.30	402.08	402.09
402.16	402.17	402.19

I (CONT.) [402.20]

402.23	403.01	403.06
403.12	403.18	403.21
403.26	403.27	404.04
404.05	404.05	404.16
404.17	404.20	404.24
404.25	404.27	405.05
405.08	405.13	406.03
406.05	406.06	407.11
407.12	407.16	407.17
407.18	407.19	408.05
408.08	409.07	409.07
409.12	409.13	409.17
409.17	409.22	411.17
411.20	411.21	411.21
411.22	411.23	411.23
412.02	412.04	412.05
412.06	412.07	412.09
412.13	412.16	412.17
412.18	412.22	412.29
412.29	413.04	413.17
413.17	413.19	413.19
413.22	413.23	413.28
414.03	414.04	414.04
414.08	414.10	414.13
414.14	414.22	414.26
415.02	415.03	415.05
415.10	415.18	418.07
418.10	418.17	419.10
419.15	419.16	419.19
419.22	419.23	419.25
420.06	421.02	421.06
421.10	423.04	423.26
423.26	423.30	424.10
424.11	425.04	425.06
425.13	425.14	425.14
425.23	425.23	426.07
426.09	426.11	426.11
426.12	426.13	426.14
426.21	427.14	427.16
427.17	427.21	427.23
427.23	427.30	428.03
428.04	428.05	428.07
428.09	428.09	428.11
428.16	428.24	428.27
429.03	429.06	429.10
429.11	429.13	429.16
429.26	429.26	430.08
430.10	430.18	430.19
430.24	430.25	430.30
431.01	431.05	431.11
431.18	431.19	431.24
431.26	431.27	431.28
431.28	432.01	432.19
432.19	432.21	432.26
433.04	433.05	433.06
433.09	433.10	433.12
433.23	433.25	434.03
434.07	434.13	436.18
437.06	437.23	438.28
442.11	448.24	451.05
455.25	456.03	456.04
458.08	458.08	458.09
459.02	460.23	464.12
464.13	470.07	470.15
471.18	471.19	471.21
471.25	471.27	471.28
471.28	472.02	472.03
472.05	472.09	472.22
472.26	472.26	473.06
473.06	473.14	473.14
473.17	473.17	473.22
473.24	473.24	473.26
473.28	473.29	474.01
474.04	474.05	474.05
474.11	474.13	475.05
475.09	475.28	475.29
476.03	476.03	477.01
477.06	477.12	477.20
479.16	480.25	480.26
480.26	480.28	480.29
481.03	481.03	481.08
481.22	481.25	483.03
483.04	483.06	483.07
485.14	486.14	486.18
488.04	488.27	491.09
491.23	492.06	494.16
494.22	495.04	495.04
495.06	495.16	495.16

I (CONT.) [495.22]

497.01	501.21	502.07
502.21	502.23	505.09
506.15	506.18	507.05
507.18	507.25	511.10
511.14	511.16	511.29
512.07	512.08	513.15
514.19	514.20	516.04
516.05	516.07	

I'		158.15	
I'D		187.19	
I'LL		64.01	81.12
	88.09	105.25	143.04
	200.02	200.25	201.14
	203.11	203.18	226.10
	226.11	233.20	245.07
	288.14	288.14	288.17
	301.16	301.23	419.25
	493.20	494.21	497.09
I'M		203.12	213.05
	288.14		
I'VE		29.11	45.30
	48.19	66.10	70.08
	70.41	71.12	75.14
	87.14	88.05	88.11
	91.04	99.12	105.07
	167.30	182.30	187.15
	187.25	199.11	201.26
	202.20	203.10	203.13
	219.30	223.25	224.20
	225.27	229.23	243.05
	243.09	274.13	288.13
	288.15	299.03	301.27
	306.10	322.27	322.29
	334.24	344.08	375.20
	377.11	377.24	398.27
	402.13	408.11	411.18
	411.24	411.29	421.17
	423.28	435.01	464.11
	474.06	495.17	
ICE		19.08	
ICEBERGS		194.20	
ICED		94.07	
ICH'S		257.03	
ICICLES		430.07	
IDEA		14.25	16.01
	23.21	88.01	91.08
	97.23	103.08	120.05
	153.15	172.09	188.17
	199.12	203.22	215.10
	215.19	222.07	223.08
	226.01	228.09	228.27
	272.16	311.01	312.20
	316.13	321.08	323.20
	329.28	336.22	359.25
	425.11	441.18	443.08
	457.14	460.17	482.05
IDEAL		147.16	516.03
IDEALISED			215.25
IDEALIST		209.23	
IDEAS		51.07	51.07
	69.24	262.07	418.22
IDEE		241.21	241.22
IDENTITY		97.24	
IDIOT		141.22	330.27
IDIOTIC		90.18	
IDIOTS		201.05	
IDLE		122.17	
IDLY		22.23	171.28
	359.05		
IDOLISED		320.06	
IDYLLIC		375.17	
IF		5.24	7.05
	11.24	17.03	17.20
	18.05	18.09	20.26
	21.23	22.01	22.20
	25.23	29.15	30.10
	30.27	31.04	32.14
	33.11	33.15	40.05
	41.29	45.30	45.12
	47.16	49.16	50.02
	51.01	51.11	54.06
	57.06	57.08	59.18
	62.06	64.07	64.26
	67.28	69.21	73.05
	73.19	74.06	76.19
	77.07	77.18	78.03
	78.22	79.20	79.24
	79.27	79.29	80.07
	80.10	81.11	81.18

IF (CONT.) [82.16]

84.05	84.14	87.08
94.24	96.01	97.15
98.06	100.05	100.25
100.30	101.23	110.12
110.23	111.10	112.07
112.30	113.27	117.29
119.14	119.27	120.15
122.13	123.14	123.17
126.06	128.28	129.13
129.21	130.09	130.12
130.12	130.14	132.24
133.03	133.09	134.06
135.07	137.23	138.15
138.16	141.03	141.07
141.21	143.20	143.23
144.02	144.11	145.27
147.06	148.18	149.17
150.01	150.18	151.08
151.24	152.10	152.23
153.10	155.10	155.20
157.19	158.16	158.18
158.27	159.04	160.06
160.09	162.03	163.14
163.25	164.23	165.02
165.30	166.18	166.21
167.10	168.08	171.12
173.07	174.05	176.10
177.03	178.22	179.20
181.13	182.01	185.13
185.23	186.01	187.14
187.16	187.20	190.06
191.01	191.02	192.18
192.28	193.30	195.29
196.06	196.26	197.14
199.09	200.04	201.27
201.28	203.13	204.23
205.20	207.24	208.20
209.05	210.23	212.08
212.12	212.22	212.28
213.19	214.19	215.21
215.26	216.08	216.11
218.17	218.20	218.21
219.09	219.22	220.20
223.29	224.08	224.28
226.06	226.14	226.27
228.17	229.03	230.07
231.02	231.12	234.20
237.06	237.13	237.27
238.06	238.08	238.18
241.14	243.06	243.14
243.19	243.21	243.29
247.03	250.08	253.18
256.01	257.23	258.15
259.09	260.05	260.27
262.16	265.04	269.06
269.27	272.20	272.20
272.25	273.14	274.03
274.27	275.04	276.09
281.22	281.29	282.04
282.25	284.05	287.13
289.21	289.23	290.05
292.19	295.15	296.06
297.19	298.04	301.01
301.06	304.19	304.22
308.22	309.11	311.07
314.15	317.02	318.17
318.23	321.05	322.15
322.19	323.23	324.26
324.29	325.17	329.30
332.17	337.15	339.14
341.04	342.23	343.29
343.30	344.11	347.07
348.07	349.27	351.11
353.03	353.09	354.08
356.12	357.10	357.18
358.20	359.19	360.24
360.30	362.14	364.25
365.03	368.03	368.10
368.12	368.29	369.13
369.18	370.17	371.16
372.11	374.19	376.03
376.09	376.11	377.05
379.13	381.21	384.01
387.06	387.18	389.14
391.30	392.04	392.07
394.08	397.07	397.24
399.08	400.12	401.01
401.09	403.25	404.03
407.11	408.06	408.23

IF (CONT.) — 408.29

409.20 410.18 412.02
412.27 414.04 416.06
420.03 421.02 423.14
425.14 426.02 426.07
426.13 426.14 428.10
429.23 430.08 430.17
431.19 431.20 435.11
435.23 436.11 437.23
446.11 446.12 447.21
452.03 462.20 471.09
471.19 472.01 474.07
474.13 475.29 477.13
479.15 480.04 480.25
481.02 483.21 486.07
488.18 489.06 493.05
493.29 494.20 495.03
497.04 501.05 504.18
506.29 508.24 509.07
509.20 510.16

IGNOMINOUSLY — 336.15
IGNORANCE — 117.15
379.01 381.02 381.08
389.19 390.12 488.03
IGNORANT 103.04 216.01
IGNORED 50.12 68.15
124.29 223.03 283.27
ILL 207.03 268.30
355.07 436.26 458.21
478.08 479.09 486.10
ILL-LUCK 207.03 458.21
478.08 479.09
ILL-USAGE — 355.07
ILL-USED 268.30
ILLEGAL 209.17
ILLUMINATED — 369.30
ILLUMINATING — 105.10
144.19
ILLUMINED — 22.14
246.08
ILLUSION 131.09 132.23
156.20 156.21 159.21
225.10 272.08 376.23
392.21 398.11 398.23
475.06
ILLUSIONS — 155.19
219.01 275.18 398.11
ILLUSIVE 494.01
ILLUSORY 418.15 441.20
ILLUSTRATED — 331.20
ILLUSTRATION — 32.06
ILLUSTRIOUS — 270.29
IM 61.25 260.21
IMAGE 78.21 214.12
252.27 299.11 410.08
416.06
IMAGES 220.16 459.03
IMAGINARY — 23.13
154.09
IMAGINATION — 10.03
11.29 105.26 138.04
138.16 164.04 164.16
214.21 272.21 272.24
273.29 340.01 345.04
347.12 382.01 423.15
IMAGINATIONS — 275.16
IMAGINATIVE — 100.07
116.11 191.04 209.27
267.07 274.02 274.02
IMAGINE 78.12 87.04
98.28 148.19 149.27
155.17 182.11 184.13
187.12 193.21 228.19
229.21 293.11 294.16
324.26 329.13 339.08
352.16 363.01 389.21
407.19 457.05 459.02
IMAGINED 82.17 103.27
188.16 312.02 503.08
507.29
IMAGININGS — 190.06
IMAGINATIVE — 267.06
IMBECILE 28.07 278.02
321.16
IMBECILITY — 46.27
60.15 368.07 368.08
368.09
IMBIBE 240.24
IMCOMPREHENSIBLE — 464.22
IMITATED 294.13

IMMACULATE — 1.11
476.07
IMMATERIAL — 162.05
260.11 323.08
IMMEASURABLY — 453.09
IMMEDIATE — 166.25
298.28 448.23 505.29
IMMEDIATELY — 56.29
242.08 287.10 308.10
451.14 499.15
IMMENSE 22.07 55.03
80.24 90.20 196.13
199.26 232.17 314.16
318.03 319.14 319.20
324.16 331.21 334.11
334.11 334.17 334.20
334.20 407.16 408.22
408.30 412.25 423.06
429.21 446.02 453.02
487.03 512.02 513.24
516.10
IMMENSELY — 286.16
364.09 378.26 381.01
463.10
IMMENSITY — 18.09
69.16 123.11 138.26
147.08 148.30 160.29
411.06 433.08 475.01
IMMERSE 261.25 413.05
IMMIGRANTS — 315.20
IMMINENT 102.04
IMMOBILISE — 408.09
IMMOBILITY — 30.26
117.14 132.16 148.26
171.06 173.17 174.07
176.27 192.22 210.08
247.11 302.18 319.23
362.11 386.10 390.06
IMMORAL 58.16
IMMORALITY — 186.13
IMMORTAL 183.28
IMMOVABLE — 272.17
299.12 332.03
IMMOVABLY — 179.04
333.18 485.18
IMPACT 113.14
IMPALED 50.01
IMPALING 133.19
IMPALPABLE — 222.15
262.05 262.14 376.30
IMPART 240.23
IMPARTING — 419.15
455.12
IMPASSABLE — 279.01
IMPASSIBLE — 33.03
IMPASSIONED — 87.18
348.27 448.26
IMPASSIVE — 175.18
318.14 337.01
IMPATIENCE — 54.24
188.04 202.23 457.21
468.21
IMPATIENT 28.18
185.27 328.27
IMPATIENTLY — 428.12
IMPECCABLE — 409.10
419.21 487.18
IMPELLED 191.07 408.17
500.07
IMPENDING — 408.21
IMPENETRABLE — 91.01
106.05 154.06 279.26
449.23
IMPENITENCE — 293.17
IMPENITENT — 273.26
IMPERCEPTIBLE — 25.05
495.14
IMPERCEPTIBLY — 84.26
385.19
IMPERFECT — 11.27
365.04
IMPERFECTLY — 89.25
368.17
IMPERISHABLE — 226.29
263.31
IMPERTURBABLE — 177.21
178.15 386.08
IMPETUOSITY — 123.14
180.30
IMPETUOUSLY — 62.19

IMPETUOUSLY (CONT.)
361.01
IMPETUS 372.04
IMPLACABLE — 395.18
IMPLEMENTS — 2.10
IMPLICITLY — 154.16
329.20
IMPLIED 95.12
IMPLORED 16.27
IMPLY 67.11 81.27
187.24 272.25 350.19
IMPORT 69.23
IMPORTANCE — 35.27
56.28 60.27 80.13
98.23 112.27 266.08
281.08 287.16 294.21
383.10 447.02 498.23
502.30
IMPORTANT — 118.18
124.11 307.12 452.02
490.20 491.08
IMPOSE 457.17
IMPOSED 457.09
IMPOSING 248.02 250.16
318.04 324.25 337.08
IMPOSINGLY — 315.15
IMPOSSIBILITY — 378.15
IMPOSSIBLE — 59.24
66.07 69.26 100.16
112.07 169.06 169.09
173.01 180.26 218.15
239.20 240.05 245.21
268.08 277.08 283.06
315.01 330.19 357.15
380.15 382.19 389.29
416.09 419.13 420.24
474.24 507.30 511.12
511.12
IMPOTENCE — 389.30
IMPRECATION — 122.06
156.26
IMPREGNABLE — 323.17
IMPRESSED — 191.09
214.06 277.26 286.24
306.20 461.10
IMPRESSION — 90.13
214.08 288.10 291.25
334.26 348.03 367.02
380.05 392.23 416.10
IMPRESSIONS — 56.22
92.12 348.30
IMPRESSIVE — 279.26
IMPRESSIVELY — 108.16
143.01 357.09
IMPRISONED — 36.05
149.28 226.03 349.08
IMPRISONMENT — 185.05
438.17
IMPROPER 288.29
IMPROVING — 92.18
307.03
IMPROVISED — 323.28
462.15
IMPRUDENCE — 423.16
IMPUDENCE — 48.09
82.12 93.21
IMPUDENT 82.16 273.23
IMPULSE 70.05 88.16
102.08 138.13 138.23
185.18 192.29 277.19
288.04 356.27 370.29
IMPULSES 17.09 26.17
IMPULSIVE — 280.18
506.12
IMPULSIVENESS — 283.11
IMPUNITY 293.17 464.03
IN 1.08 1.10
1.11 1.14 1.16
1.17 2.14 2.19
2.21 3.03 3.12
3.13 3.15 3.17
3.18 3.18 3.18
3.18 3.19 3.19
4.02 4.04 4.10
4.21 4.22 4.24
4.26 4.27 5.05
5.06 5.07 5.09
5.11 5.13 5.16
5.19 5.29 5.30
6.04 6.07 6.09

IN (CONT.) — 6.10

6.10 6.12 6.16
6.25 6.30 7.01
7.04 7.14 8.02
8.02 8.12 9.04
9.07 9.08 10.09
10.15 10.18 10.23
10.24 11.02 11.25
11.30 12.03 12.16
12.22 12.23 12.25
12.26 13.02 13.17
13.21 13.23 14.12
14.13 14.14 14.14
14.14 14.15 14.20
14.21 14.23 15.12
15.13 15.25 15.26
15.29 16.11 16.18
16.23 16.29 17.03
17.08 17.20 18.06
18.08 19.05 19.16
19.22 20.08 20.09
20.09 20.18 20.20
20.24 20.29 21.08
21.21 21.30 22.08
22.11 22.14 22.15
22.19 23.08 23.19
24.05 24.06 24.11
24.13 24.14 24.20
24.21 24.23 24.23
24.24 24.25 24.25
24.26 25.02 25.08
25.22 26.14 27.05
27.11 27.11 27.20
27.20 27.20 27.23
27.26 27.28 27.30
28.02 28.06 29.04
29.12 29.26 30.11
30.12 30.24 30.26
30.30 31.04 31.05
31.09 32.01 32.08
32.09 32.10 32.15
32.17 32.18 32.20
33.08 33.22 33.25
33.25 33.28 34.04
34.13 34.15 34.23
34.27 35.17 35.25
35.27 36.06 36.09
37.11 37.13 37.15
37.18 37.22 38.07
38.11 38.12 38.21
38.23 38.26 38.27
39.02 39.05 40.07
40.11 40.15 41.04
41.09 41.11 41.19
41.22 42.03 42.06
42.09 42.10 42.13
42.20 42.21 42.22
42.30 43.02 43.12
43.15 43.18 43.18
43.21 43.21 43.29
43.30 43.37 43.42
44.07 44.09 44.10
44.11 44.15 44.25
45.12 45.17 45.20
46.09 46.15 46.16
46.24 46.24 46.29
47.22 48.12 48.12
48.13 48.15 48.18
49.11 49.24 50.04
50.04 50.06 50.08
50.09 50.29 51.10
51.16 51.19 51.22
51.24 51.28 52.17
52.21 53.08 53.08
53.12 53.16 53.23
53.25 54.11 54.13
54.22 55.09 55.10
55.11 55.14 55.24
55.25 55.30 56.08
56.10 56.16 56.19
56.29 57.01 57.16
57.19 57.20 57.24
57.27 58.01 58.01
58.03 58.18 58.19
58.24 58.29 59.07
59.10 59.29 60.02
60.11 60.22 60.23
60.28 61.08 61.09
61.13 61.14 61.15
62.08 62.24 62.25

IN (CONT.)		62.27	IN (CONT.)		127.15	IN (CONT.)		203.08	IN (CONT.)		266.16
63.09	63.11	63.19	127.21	128.05	128.25	203.16	203.29	203.30	266.18	267.09	267.12
63.26	63.29	64.02	128.26	129.01	129.15	204.03	204.09	205.10	267.13	267.14	267.17
64.04	64.07	64.08	129.22	130.02	130.15	205.12	205.21	207.01	267.18	267.28	268.01
64.14	64.23	64.29	130.21	131.19	131.25	207.04	208.03	208.16	268.02	268.10	268.12
65.01	65.05	65.15	131.29	131.30	132.09	208.22	208.26	209.01	268.18	268.19	268.21
65.18	66.09	66.10	132.09	132.09	132.22	209.06	209.09	210.10	268.24	269.17	269.20
67.20	67.22	67.25	133.14	133.14	133.14	210.13	210.19	210.22	269.21	269.27	270.02
67.27	67.29	68.04	133.19	134.26	135.03	210.27	210.30	211.19	270.03	270.18	270.22
68.07	68.15	68.20	136.14	136.19	137.03	211.20	212.02	212.03	270.28	271.10	271.10
58.30	69.05	69.21	137.03	137.17	137.22	212.16	212.22	213.06	271.10	271.11	271.22
69.26	70.01	70.07	137.29	138.04	138.08	213.12	213.15	214.02	272.10	272.16	272.22
70.09	70.10	70.12	138.28	139.03	139.09	214.03	214.04	214.09	273.06	273.07	273.25
70.19	70.21	70.22	139.23	140.29	141.05	214.30	215.06	215.07	273.30	274.03	274.04
70.25	70.29	70.38	141.13	141.17	141.26	215.18	216.06	216.07	274.21	274.23	274.26
70.42	70.44	70.44	142.11	142.20	142.21	216.27	217.12	217.24	274.29	275.13	275.13
71.01	71.02	71.03	143.05	143.12	144.11	217.25	217.30	218.21	275.19	275.21	276.16
71.10	71.23	71.27	145.13	145.13	145.30	218.29	219.03	219.26	276.19	277.01	277.06
72.15	72.18	72.24	146.04	146.06	146.07	220.01	220.08	220.11	277.10	277.18	277.19
73.09	73.12	73.13	146.16	146.19	146.20	220.19	220.22	221.06	277.22	277.22	277.23
73.21	73.23	73.25	146.23	147.01	147.07	221.07	221.08	222.01	277.24	277.25	278.10
73.30	74.13	74.13	147.12	147.22	148.09	222.18	223.09	223.26	278.11	278.11	278.18
74.18	74.22	74.23	148.11	148.23	149.09	224.04	224.05	224.06	278.22	279.07	279.09
74.23	74.25	75.06	149.13	149.19	149.21	224.10	224.21	224.22	279.11	279.18	279.19
75.07	75.18	75.23	149.22	149.29	150.02	225.21	226.02	226.03	279.21	279.23	279.26
75.25	76.15	76.20	150.11	150.28	151.13	226.05	226.12	226.16	279.26	279.27	279.30
76.29	77.08	77.29	151.26	152.16	153.05	226.20	226.25	226.25	280.04	280.06	280.28
77.29	78.07	78.09	153.10	153.26	153.30	226.29	227.09	227.11	281.21	282.10	282.13
78.09	78.19	78.22	154.04	154.06	154.12	227.11	227.15	227.18	282.18	282.20	282.24
78.29	79.05	79.11	155.03	155.03	155.07	227.19	227.23	228.10	283.02	283.04	283.08
79.12	79.19	80.23	155.10	156.01	156.08	228.14	228.24	229.05	283.09	283.17	283.24
80.26	80.28	81.05	156.09	156.14	156.19	229.06	229.07	229.18	283.29	285.04	285.07
81.12	81.18	81.30	156.20	157.03	157.09	229.26	229.29	230.03	285.12	285.17	286.05
82.03	82.05	82.29	157.11	157.12	157.23	230.08	230.15	230.16	286.09	286.09	286.23
83.11	83.15	83.16	158.07	158.10	158.19	230.26	231.13	231.16	286.27	286.28	286.28
83.22	83.23	83.28	158.24	158.30	159.02	231.25	232.03	232.04	287.28	288.10	288.19
34.05	84.06	84.07	159.06	159.11	159.18	232.19	232.20	232.27	288.25	288.26	289.02
84.09	84.10	84.15	159.29	160.07	160.15	233.01	233.02	233.15	289.06	289.22	290.01
84.17	84.18	84.27	160.18	160.18	162.04	233.19	233.21	233.26	290.16	290.21	290.22
84.29	85.02	85.05	162.07	162.21	163.01	234.04	234.13	234.17	290.27	290.28	291.08
85.13	85.15	85.24	163.12	163.15	163.25	234.25	234.30	235.06	291.15	291.17	291.26
86.08	86.09	86.19	165.13	165.19	165.20	235.10	235.18	235.23	292.04	292.16	292.25
86.22	86.27	86.29	165.23	166.03	166.08	235.25	235.30	236.09	292.28	293.26	293.28
87.05	87.17	87.21	166.08	166.12	166.18	236.10	236.14	236.24	294.02	294.07	294.10
88.03	88.10	88.22	166.21	167.05	167.08	236.25	237.05	237.08	294.27	295.01	295.05
89.21	89.22	89.23	167.24	167.24	167.26	237.09	237.12	237.14	295.06	295.23	296.02
89.25	90.27	91.03	167.29	168.15	168.26	237.16	237.29	238.06	297.00	297.09	297.15
91.07	91.13	92.02	168.30	169.10	169.22	238.07	238.16	238.22	297.16	298.02	298.11
92.05	92.07	92.22	169.30	170.03	170.15	240.12	240.14	240.17	298.11	298.28	299.03
92.23	93.10	93.25	171.01	172.06	172.07	240.29	241.14	241.19	299.13	299.14	299.19
34.03	94.07	94.10	172.08	172.25	172.27	241.23	241.29	242.15	299.20	300.04	300.06
94.13	94.21	94.23	173.03	173.07	173.19	242.18	242.23	242.25	300.10	301.08	301.11
94.26	94.26	95.04	173.21	174.19	175.16	243.12	243.17	243.20	301.20	301.22	302.01
95.16	95.24	95.24	175.18	175.19	176.11	243.23	243.23	243.27	302.13	302.21	302.25
95.28	96.18	96.22	176.12	176.23	176.25	243.30	244.03	244.11	303.02	303.04	303.10
96.25	96.30	97.17	176.26	177.13	177.15	244.12	244.15	244.21	303.15	304.04	304.06
98.01	98.10	98.26	177.22	178.16	178.18	244.23	245.14	245.25	304.07	304.27	304.28
99.02	99.05	99.07	180.05	180.09	180.25	246.01	246.18	246.25	304.30	305.02	306.16
99.13	99.23	100.06	181.09	182.07	182.18	247.01	247.04	247.05	306.24	307.25	307.26
100.08	100.19	101.03	182.28	182.29	183.15	247.11	247.19	248.01	308.05	308.05	308.23
101.12	101.20	101.27	183.21	183.22	183.23	248.05	248.08	248.11	309.01	309.09	309.10
102.01	102.14	102.28	184.02	184.06	184.16	248.13	248.14	248.20	309.14	310.05	310.10
103.11	103.15	103.24	184.24	184.27	184.28	248.23	249.02	249.08	310.11	310.17	310.26
103.29	104.15	104.23	185.05	185.07	185.15	249.12	249.16	249.20	310.27	311.11	311.24
105.01	105.03	105.06	185.18	185.19	185.21	249.21	249.25	250.02	311.26	312.07	312.10
105.17	106.02	106.04	185.23	185.24	185.25	250.07	250.07	250.10	312.22	312.24	313.12
106.10	106.14	106.14	185.29	185.30	186.01	250.19	250.24	250.29	313.16	313.21	313.23
107.23	108.01	108.08	186.08	186.10	186.18	250.30	251.02	251.08	313.30	314.02	314.02
108.12	108.24	109.07	186.21	187.16	187.19	251.19	252.04	252.11	314.04	314.17	314.26
109.11	109.14	109.29	187.30	188.10	188.17	252.14	252.18	252.26	314.30	315.03	315.10
110.21	110.23	111.02	188.27	188.29	188.30	252.26	253.07	253.23	315.10	315.12	315.19
111.06	111.06	111.13	189.18	190.10	191.14	253.24	253.30	254.07	316.06	316.11	316.20
111.20	111.25	111.28	191.15	191.29	191.30	254.10	254.13	254.14	316.23	316.25	317.04
112.06	112.08	112.16	192.01	192.02	192.06	254.30	255.01	255.06	317.08	317.17	318.05
112.21	112.25	112.29	192.07	192.09	192.10	255.10	255.14	256.18	318.07	318.19	319.08
113.09	113.15	113.29	192.14	192.18	192.22	256.29	256.30	257.01	319.09	319.10	319.20
114.02	114.08	114.26	192.23	192.26	193.04	257.03	257.04	257.08	319.22	319.25	320.01
115.01	115.16	115.17	193.06	193.09	193.20	257.16	257.27	258.19	320.10	320.11	320.14
115.23	115.25	116.09	193.28	194.04	194.16	258.30	258.30	259.14	320.18	320.18	320.29
116.12	116.21	116.26	194.17	194.19	194.24	259.20	259.28	260.01	321.02	321.10	321.20
116.30	117.11	117.14	195.02	195.03	195.05	260.09	261.01	261.05	321.22	321.27	322.06
120.04	120.15	120.24	195.25	196.04	196.17	261.09	261.10	261.14	322.06	322.20	322.21
122.05	122.05	122.13	196.26	196.28	197.14	261.22	261.24	261.25	322.28	323.04	323.08
122.16	123.06	123.10	197.15	197.23	197.28	262.06	262.06	262.10	324.06	324.12	324.13
123.17	123.17	123.26	197.29	198.23	199.11	262.15	263.02	263.10	324.19	325.08	325.09
124.07	124.10	124.26	199.14	199.16	199.20	263.14	263.27	263.30	325.20	325.22	325.26
124.30	125.07	125.10	199.29	200.01	200.18	264.02	264.08	264.21	326.01	326.05	327.07
125.18	125.28	126.16	200.18	200.22	201.03	264.22	264.22	264.23	327.09	327.11	327.22
126.20	126.23	126.25	201.08	201.10	201.27	264.28	265.02	266.03	328.01	328.07	328.17
127.05	127.11	127.14	202.08	202.11	203.02	266.05	266.13	266.13	328.21	328.22	328.23

IN (CONT.)   328.24

329.03	329.29	330.14
330.17	330.24	330.26
331.04	331.21	331.21
332.02	332.04	332.17
332.21	333.01	333.18
333.27	334.03	334.06
334.16	334.18	334.23
334.25	334.27	334.29
336.05	337.05	337.07
337.14	337.21	337.23
337.30	338.09	338.19
338.22	339.03	339.13
339.16	339.20	339.22
340.07	340.20	340.27
340.30	341.18	341.20
342.07	342.14	342.19
343.03	343.04	343.10
343.12	343.18	343.21
343.26	344.04	344.20
344.30	345.08	345.08
345.13	345.18	345.18
346.02	346.08	347.05
347.17	348.18	348.21
348.21	348.25	348.26
349.01	349.24	350.05
350.07	350.12	350.17
350.30	351.01	351.17
351.24	351.26	352.03
352.03	352.17	352.20
352.20	352.24	352.26
353.03	353.12	353.22
353.27	354.01	355.10
355.18	356.01	356.05
356.10	356.16	356.19
356.28	357.15	358.01
358.02	358.04	358.12
358.15	359.01	359.06
359.07	359.08	359.19
359.21	360.10	360.12
350.14	360.24	361.09
3b1.10	361.11	361.13
351.23	361.26	361.26
361.30	362.03	362.10
362.16	362.21	363.04
363.10	363.21	363.22
363.24	364.03	364.05
364.15	364.17	365.01
365.03	365.12	365.12
365.14	365.17	365.23
365.24	366.02	366.04
366.22	367.04	367.09
367.11	367.13	367.14
367.24	367.29	368.09
368.18	368.23	369.12
369.15	369.22	369.23
370.02	370.04	370.24
370.25	370.25	371.01
371.03	371.04	371.06
371.28	372.13	372.15
373.02	373.04	373.07
373.12	374.04	374.07
374.29	375.09	375.15
375.26	376.01	376.06
377.14	378.02	378.03
378.16	379.01	379.19
379.22	379.24	380.14
380.17	380.19	381.11
381.20	381.22	382.02
382.07	382.08	382.13
382.23	383.03	383.04
383.10	383.20	384.01
384.05	384.07	384.22
384.26	385.09	385.09
385.15	385.19	385.22
385.27	385.28	385.30
385.30	385.30	385.30
386.08	386.15	386.19
386.24	387.24	387.26
388.02	388.04	388.08
388.11	388.30	389.17
389.17	389.19	389.22
389.26	389.28	390.11
390.24	390.27	391.01
391.02	391.15	391.23
392.02	392.09	393.01
393.08	393.20	394.06
394.23	395.06	395.12
395.15	395.22	395.23
395.24	396.11	396.13

IN (CONT.)   396.21

397.01	397.07	397.12
397.16	397.17	397.22
397.26	397.28	397.28
398.09	398.17	398.22
398.25	398.28	398.30
399.03	399.06	399.08
399.27	400.29	401.06
401.16	401.17	401.22
401.30	402.13	402.18
403.17	403.20	403.29
403.30	404.07	404.18
404.20	404.25	404.27
405.25	405.27	405.27
405.28	405.28	407.07
407.08	407.10	407.12
407.15	408.01	408.02
408.25	409.07	409.08
409.12	409.25	410.02
410.04	410.17	410.18
410.21	411.04	411.12
411.18	411.22	412.09
412.12	412.20	413.05
413.10	413.18	414.04
414.09	414.11	414.20
415.03	415.11	415.17
416.04	416.14	416.15
416.18	416.19	417.08
417.15	417.28	418.09
418.19	418.22	418.23
418.26	418.30	419.01
419.12	419.15	420.15
420.16	420.21	420.24
421.11	421.17	421.18
421.28	422.11	422.19
423.10	423.14	423.23
424.01	424.02	424.03
424.04	424.04	425.19
426.05	426.17	426.22
426.29	427.02	427.08
427.08	427.10	427.24
427.24	427.25	428.05
428.16	428.17	428.30
429.04	429.05	429.07
429.17	429.19	429.26
429.29	430.03	430.05
430.14	431.07	431.08
431.21	431.27	431.30
432.20	433.07	433.17
433.28	434.10	434.11
434.14	434.15	434.21
434.23	435.07	435.11
435.15	435.17	435.17
435.19	436.08	436.15
436.23	437.05	437.13
437.14	437.17	437.17
437.28	438.01	438.02
438.04	438.04	438.10
438.11	438.16	438.25
438.26	439.05	439.06
439.14	439.15	439.21
439.26	439.29	439.30
440.06	440.17	440.22
441.09	441.12	441.15
441.20	441.26	441.28
442.01	442.17	442.23
443.01	443.05	443.09
443.21	443.22	443.23
443.27	443.29	443.29
443.30	444.02	444.06
444.16	444.19	444.24
445.09	445.22	445.26
447.04	447.16	447.20
447.21	448.05	448.07
448.08	448.14	448.20
448.21	448.22	448.22
449.09	450.03	450.07
450.08	450.11	450.12
450.15	450.17	450.18
450.20	451.16	451.24
451.30	452.18	452.22
452.24	452.25	453.12
453.13	454.06	454.07
454.11	454.17	454.25
454.24	454.30	455.03
455.11	455.14	456.05
456.05	456.06	457.12
457.17	458.09	458.10
458.15	458.22	458.25
458.26	458.28	459.01

IN (CONT.)   459.21

460.03	460.09	460.10
460.28	461.02	461.19
461.20	461.25	461.26
462.15	462.16	462.17
462.23	462.27	462.28
463.01	463.03	463.14
463.20	463.23	463.23
464.02	464.07	464.08
464.20	464.28	465.02
465.09	465.11	465.12
465.16	465.17	465.20
465.22	465.23	465.25
465.27	465.30	466.12
467.05	467.12	467.15
467.21	468.04	468.25
469.04	469.05	469.06
469.10	469.19	470.15
470.19	470.21	470.23
470.28	470.29	471.02
471.03	471.05	471.18
471.24	471.28	471.30
472.08	472.14	472.29
473.03	473.27	473.29
474.11	474.18	474.22
474.29	475.06	475.08
475.28	476.01	476.06
476.10	477.04	477.16
477.23	478.01	478.05
478.15	478.18	478.21
478.21	478.24	478.29
478.29	479.02	479.04
479.13	479.16	479.21
480.03	480.08	480.10
480.17	480.26	480.27
480.28	481.02	481.22
481.27	481.29	482.15
482.22	483.09	483.11
483.18	483.29	483.30
484.07	484.12	484.14
484.27	485.11	485.21
485.22	486.05	486.17
486.17	487.04	487.06
487.11	487.15	487.18
487.24	488.07	488.13
488.16	488.20	488.24
488.28	489.02	489.05
489.17	489.20	489.24
489.28	490.09	490.10
490.12	491.17	491.27
492.03	492.23	492.27
492.28	492.28	493.15
493.19	493.25	493.29
494.07	494.26	494.29
494.30	495.13	495.27
496.02	497.18	497.20
497.21	498.06	498.16
498.20	499.08	499.15
500.06	500.12	500.26
501.01	501.08	501.09
501.15	501.27	501.29
502.09	503.02	503.11
503.14	503.16	504.07
504.08	504.13	504.24
505.05	505.16	505.21
505.27	506.14	506.16
506.17	506.22	506.26
506.28	507.22	507.27
508.05	508.13	508.17
508.21	508.24	508.24
508.28	509.24	509.26
510.11	510.16	510.20
510.28	511.24	512.11
512.24	512.24	512.26
512.29	513.20	513.25
514.07	514.19	515.08
515.09	515.21	515.24
516.18		

IN-   145.30

INABILITY   48.06
    95.01
INACCESSIBLE   21.28
    211.10   332.13   430.14
INADEQUATE   2.29
    48.29   247.02
INANIMATE   54.13
INANITION   225.19
INARTICULATE   89.25
INAUDIBLE   387.19
INBORN   50.28

INCALCULABLE   174.14
INCANDESCENT   204.01
INCANTATIONS   327.12
INCAPABLE   89.13
    172.23   384.19
INCARNATION   24.22
    192.05   307.12   447.12
INCENSE   397.19
INCERTITUDE   66.05
    379.21   387.05   387.06
INCESSANTLY   34.10
    232.09   432.07
INCH   1.01   356.25
INCHES   31.09   175.13
    249.10
INCHI   356.13
INCIDENT   112.26   173.21
    194.25   241.25   243.12
    326.02
INCIDENTAL   113.09
INCIDENTS   105.29
INCISIVE   260.11
INCISIVELY   159.25
    188.05
INCITED   316.22   398.20
INCLINED   33.26   110.25
    170.17   317.08   382.30
INCLUDES   471.16
INCOGNITO   3.07
    3.09   3.26
INCOHERENT   38.10
INCOMMODED   310.12
INCOMPLETE   416.06
    425.05
INCOMPLETENESS   416.07
INCOMPREHENSIBLE   103.06
    205.02   219.06   392.04
    395.14   430.17   450.01
INCOMPREHENSIBLY   268.04
INCONCEIVABLE   112.13
    270.06   300.24   302.03
    379.09   379.14   385.17
    488.15
INCONSOLABLE   219.13
INCONSOLABLY   274.28
INCONTINENTLY   498.07
INCONVENIENCE   234.05
INCONVENIENCES   78.06
INCORRIGIBLE   267.15
INCREASED   216.18
INCREASING   7.21
    408.24   463.08
INCREDIBLE   473.08
INCREDIBLY   437.12
INCREDULOUS   380.08
    468.07
INDECISION   67.24
    462.10
INDEED   56.06   68.13
    87.30   126.06   136.03
    167.26   170.22   172.29
    175.02   184.17   186.30
    239.16   246.11   258.28
    271.15   277.11   278.28
    280.29   302.14   303.27
    311.01   336.21   338.11
    345.15   346.10   356.09
    392.22   394.18   398.13
    401.02   465.21
INDEFINABLE   11.05
    397.14
INDEFINITE   69.04
    138.26   226.04   260.09
    268.22   384.09
INDEFINITENESS   156.16
INDEPENDENTLY   178.01
INDESCRIBABLE   320.11
INDIAN   172.25   441.23
    501.28
INDICATED   323.29
INDIFFERENCE   11.26
    130.04   146.13   176.26
    381.12   430.25   492.23
INDIFFERENT   27.18
    60.19   276.07   399.17
    440.12   455.16   487.22
INDIGESTION   179.10
INDIGNANT   204.17
    350.25   488.17
INDIGNATION   42.26

INDIGNATION (CONT.)
61.03 81.29 87.15
223.19 368.02
INDIGNATIONS 352.14
INDIRECTLY 190.20
INDISCREET 293.24
INDISCRETION 338.07
INDISCRETIONS 101.04
INDISSOLUBLY 369.18
INDISTINCT 125.27
225.22 295.26 349.21
362.09
INDISTINGUISHABLE
316.13
INDIVIDUAL 46.24
54.10 57.22 97.22
112.29 193.26 227.10
340.06 495.12
INDIVIDUALITY 80.17
INDIVIDUALS 92.08
INDOLENT 113.23
INDOMITABLE 68.24
220.06 499.29
INDOORS 362.16 431.28
INDUCE 458.17 461.21
INDUCED 77.02 86.10
185.18 324.03 338.05
483.19
INDUCEMENTS 180.02
INDULGE 59.10
INDULGED 12.21
INDULGENCE 169.18
INDULGENT 246.26
262.26
INDULGENTLY 177.25
INDUSTRIOUS 210.10
INDUSTRIOUSLY 374.04
INDUSTRY 115.21 351.06
INEFFABLE 61.28
INEFFICIENT 7.22
INERT 172.07 516.18
INEVITABLE 480.22
INEVITABLY 3.16
INEXPERIENCED 260.28
INEXPLICABLE 118.04
190.12 222.15 282.03
360.22 391.29 395.14
421.07
INEXPRESSIBLE 351.02
434.24
INEXPRESSIBLY 76.27
153.18 406.02
INEXPUGNABLE 387.08
INFAMOUS 58.04 126.26
405.23
INFANTRY 191.29
INFECTED 244.06
INFECTIOUS 251.27
INFER 98.17
INFERIOR 308.01
INFERIORITY 68.15
INFERNAL 36.18 40.20
53.25 80.01 120.20
120.21 123.30 131.11
132.19 201.26 213.23
324.27 331.01 472.13
473.16 473.26 474.14
478.12
INFERNALLY 230.28
INFIDEL 383.05
INFIDELS 364.04
INFINITE 13.02 181.05
204.15 351.15 384.15
393.02
INFINITELY 31.02
105.14 173.06 193.13
278.09 308.16 381.08
383.09 414.18
INFINITY 393.16
INFLAMED 425.16
INFLATED 464.29
INFLEXIBLE 115.29
277.07 431.02 507.30
INFLEXIBLY 283.16
298.22 349.11 462.14
INFLICTS 341.04
INFLUENCE 281.12
281.13 317.13 328.06
333.09 392.01
INFLUENCED 270.12

INFLUENCES 392.03
INFORM 173.18
INFORMANTS 345.11
358.06
INFORMATION 35.11
40.23 49.23 278.08
423.27 425.05 461.14
INFORMED 167.22 333.21
492.18
ING 50.01 137.01
INGLORIOUS 59.16
INGRATITUDE 2.27
INHABITANTS 379.10
443.10 459.13 483.14
INHERITED 250.27
INHUMAN 514.24
INIQUITIES 60.28
INITIAL 226.28
INJECTED 332.30
INJUNS 235.16
INJUSTICE 100.06
INK 71.10 185.25
420.29
INKSTAND 33.28
INLAID 339.26
INLAND 299.08 445.30
489.22
INNATE 94.24 399.23
INNER 10.18 15.18
88.19 100.09 114.24
266.13 342.28
INNERMOST 304.16
331.23 342.01
INNOCENCE 70.21
213.12
INNOCENT 92.21 114.09
168.24 246.20 255.03
473.16
INNUMERABLE 114.01
251.07 273.05
INOFFENSIVE 243.21
INQUIRE 67.06 229.14
INQUIRED 26.13 105.08
154.14 455.23
INQUIRING 262.21
INQUIRY 32.07 40.01
40.12 42.01 47.29
57.18 65.17 66.02
66.22 69.12 69.18
69.29 77.28 78.05
82.01 82.24 93.28
96.06 112.01 118.12
136.18 273.01 345.20
INQUISITIVE 337.10
INQUISITIVELY 97.12
218.16
INSANITY 357.25
INSCRIBED 68.21
INSCRIPTION 68.07
INSCRUTABLE 331.25
379.01 434.25 454.03
515.20 516.16
INSECT 81.28 267.27
352.17
INSECTS 247.18 250.03
INSECURE 30.26 251.21
INSECURITY 278.20
317.07 508.22
INSENSIBLE 345.29
INSEPARABLE 111.29
270.23 333.02
INSIDE 15.08 43.11
55.29 64.27 66.22
104.18 306.11 311.29
333.14 428.11 439.11
450.10 476.11 477.12
484.17 508.11
INSIGNIFICANT 112.24
226.24 276.13 358.21
383.24 402.01 412.21
INSINUATED 205.25
INSINUATINGLY 383.21
404.24
INSIST 332.12 456.03
INSISTED 178.10 223.15
355.08 382.17 388.15
487.05
INSISTENCE 108.12
122.23 298.23 369.10
INSOLENCE 82.21

INSOLENCE (CONT.)
289.07
INSOLENT 289.03 289.04
INSOLUBLE 377.27
488.09
INSPIRATION 389.22
425.21
INSPIRE 60.29 321.13
INSPIRED 261.05 261.21
INSPIRER 271.12
INSPIRING 409.16
INSTANCE 43.31 67.04
113.15 157.17 176.05
179.12 193.27 210.16
240.14 244.02 246.29
273.14 278.12 287.28
378.16 412.15
INSTANCES 190.23
INSTANT 19.18 30.17
100.03 100.15 107.21
144.21 163.08 257.24
422.11 440.04 510.08
INSTANTANEOUS 56.21
INSTANTANEOUSLY 300.18
INSTANTLY 62.01
63.12 123.21 125.10
311.16 345.08 459.20
464.14 478.18
INSTEAD 35.02 170.11
262.23 330.30 331.18
INSTINCT 45.08 50.25
INSTINCTIVE 274.10
280.13
INSTINCTIVELY 83.17
300.22
INSTINCTS 97.28
INSTITUTIONS 43.19
480.10
INSTRUCTED 289.25
290.16
INSTRUCTIONS 73.22
284.08
INSTRUCTIVE 48.24
66.20
INSTRUCTORS 6.18
INSTRUMENTS 277.17
INSUFFERABLY 294.15
INSULTING 88.29
300.09
INSURANCE 182.14
200.07
INSURGENTS 437.23
INTANGIBLE 387.13
INTELLECTUAL 304.26
INTELLIGENCE 51.17
322.09 336.09 448.12
499.20
INTELLIGENT 38.02
103.02 246.07 307.27
308.12 315.24 322.17
407.24 447.07
INTELLIGENTLY 92.11
INTELLIGIBLE 157.12
423.29
INTELLIGIBLY 211.11
INTEND 220.01 222.17
361.10 387.22
INTENDED 124.13 492.21
INTENSE 54.28 84.27
118.12 189.05 252.23
273.10 333.27 347.20
350.30 364.09 369.29
407.11 409.26 425.16
425.20
INTENSELY 89.08
269.23 357.11
INTENSITY 273.09
275.20 348.23 391.09
INTENT 371.26
INTENTION 11.05
82.20 95.26 101.06
114.11 127.12 149.23
159.27 221.05 239.08
275.03 293.18 303.28
381.18 420.07 436.10
451.12 475.19
INTENTIONS 57.14
141.22 186.12 281.09
379.25
INTENTLY 249.17 362.24

INTER 245.30
INTER-ISLAND 245.30
INTERCEDE 403.20
INTERCOURSE 277.28
295.01 461.26
INTERESSANT 173.11
INTEREST 65.14 66.05
66.13 243.30 281.26
294.27 325.30 349.02
363.01 418.08 484.11
INTERESTED 37.25
52.17 65.05 67.02
86.07 113.07 176.12
191.09 229.13 267.26
385.08
INTERESTING 61.17
173.10 176.30 190.22
216.03 274.27
INTERFERED 450.26
INTERFERENCE 283.28
INTERIOR 241.14 250.07
250.08 316.23 369.30
447.05
INTERJECTED 158.13
169.18
INTERLACED 397.12
INTERLOCUTOR 78.03
INTERMINABLE 64.03
INTERMINABLY 427.25
INTERNALLY 294.07
INTERNATIONAL 193.26
437.08
INTERPOSITION 280.11
INTERPRET 56.20
419.29
INTERPRETER 118.16
118.17 451.26
INTERROGATIVELY 60.30
429.09
INTERROGATORIES 310.18
INTERRUPT 154.01
344.08 344.16
INTERRUPTED 78.13
173.17 180.11 217.27
245.08 282.23 283.17
343.23 369.30 413.20
477.04 486.02
INTERRUPTING 137.28
439.22
INTERRUPTIONS 310.05
INTERSPERSED 459.08
INTERVAL 162.16
INTERVALS 37.22
128.12 153.07 248.22
324.04 510.11
INTERVIEWS 337.03
484.15
INTIMACY 295.07
INTIMATE 219.06 223.27
448.16
INTO 3.23 8.16
8.27 12.29 13.14
15.19 17.26 18.05
18.06 19.20 22.03
27.09 30.29 36.14
39.02 39.07 47.07
47.21 50.13 51.26
52.28 54.30 55.20
55.25 56.08 56.21
58.28 59.13 61.07
64.10 64.12 67.07
69.18 69.21 69.24
74.21 77.19 78.24
80.18 82.08 89.02
89.12 93.12 94.08
95.21 100.09 100.10
100.16 102.09 102.29
105.02 105.09 107.12
109.09 109.10 112.06
113.03 113.20 115.02
115.10 116.24 118.24
119.01 119.18 123.08
123.24 126.04 126.14
126.22 127.20 129.08
129.26 130.10 130.11
133.01 134.05 134.13
135.08 135.08 136.03
137.07 137.14 138.25
144.15 144.16 144.17
144.21 149.24 149.26

INTO (CONT.) 154.11
155.08 157.14 163.04
163.08 164.20 169.05
170.06 174.19 175.25
176.02 181.06 182.21
187.22 189.09 190.15
192.25 195.03 195.15
199.05 202.18 205.03
208.24 211.27 212.13
212.21 212.25 214.27
218.27 219.17 220.30
224.13 224.15 225.13
225.14 225.18 225.30
228.12 230.26 231.22
234.02 238.26 243.08
244.18 248.17 250.17
257.17 260.03 260.04
260.26 260.27 260.27
265.11 266.20 267.02
267.20 269.10 269.23
270.07 277.18 279.02
280.19 284.06 288.11
289.07 290.12 300.05
300.13 302.21 306.17
309.18 310.02 312.01
312.15 312.23 313.24
313.26 314.16 315.05
316.02 316.30 317.18
321.09 325.17 328.11
329.11 329.26 331.23
332.05 332.23 333.25
335.15 341.09 345.20
355.19 356.03 359.12
359.23 363.17 365.21
367.09 369.17 370.29
372.25 374.10 376.20
380.02 385.01 386.22
387.24 388.23 389.25
390.18 391.13 393.16
395.29 396.03 398.03
398.18 402.28 402.29
402.30 405.10 407.17
411.14 414.28 419.03
426.20 427.20 431.29
433.20 434.18 434.20
437.19 438.23 440.21
440.27 442.20 442.27
444.08 444.28 448.04
449.13 451.09 451.23
456.27 459.11 460.14
461.05 462.04 463.02
463.05 463.08 464.10
464.15 466.07 470.10
470.10 472.22 473.08
473.09 474.14 482.15
482.26 484.04 491.10
491.10 491.25 494.03
495.07 495.28 497.04
498.21 500.28 500.30
502.18 503.04 504.02
508.03 508.06 508.27
510.03 510.26 514.03
INTOLERABLE 3.21
244.16 283.03 311.02
380.01
INTOLERABLY 104.09
170.22
INTONATION 86.10
348.17 390.28
INTONING 510.13
INTOXICATED 213.20
INTOXICATING 100.04
213.17
INTREPID 44.26
INTREPIDITY 246.26
INTRIGUE 255.07
INTRIGUED 168.27
317.06 458.26
INTRIGUES 167.21
INTRODUCE 175.13
310.02
INTRODUCED 250.13
INTRODUCTION 185.23
285.10 403.16
INTRUDER 153.08
INTRUDERS 450.20
INTUITION 86.14
INVADED 89.07
INVADERS 446.03 461.22
INVADERS' 449.25

INVADING 367.13
INVALID 60.17 61.18
193.03
INVARIABLY 225.09
315.14
INVASION 513.17
INVERTED 410.08
INVEST 171.05
INVESTED 182.13
INVESTIGATE 198.23
INVESTIGATED 438.23
INVESTIGATION 164.12
359.12 438.23
INVINCIBLE 22.21
349.07 390.11 392.13
392.26 420.21 447.11
INVIOLABLE 421.28
INVISIBLE 35.23
49.17 111.28 117.18
153.08 189.04 208.30
212.29 260.08 288.10
322.29 427.11 480.05
494.29 495.29 495.29
INVITATION 91.15
INVITE 435.21
INVOKED 16.26
INVOKES 422.17
INVOLUNTARILY 133.16
INVOLVED 56.29 112.30
INVOLVING 243.20
INVULNERABLE 51.05
447.17
INVULNERABLY 216.01
INWARD 51.03 263.23
277.18
IRON 15.05 20.06
61.14 64.27 66.21
73.08 73.10 99.22
101.11 101.24 102.02
103.03 111.03 118.05
140.18 175.04 203.15
203.19 306.16 323.21
370.08 441.09
IRON-GREY 175.04
IRONGREY 196.14
IRONIC 322.07 408.01
IRONICALLY 89.24
IRONY 130.24 351.20
IRRATIONAL 58.20
147.23
IRREGULAR 248.22
443.24 480.17
IRREGULARITIES 266.10
266.14
IRREGULARLY 269.17
IRRELEVANT 36.20
IRREMEDIABLE 41.21
386.12 399.23
IRREPRESSIBLE 184.19
IRREPROACHABLE 186.11
IRRESISTIBLE 264.01
376.27 379.12 392.04
IRRESISTIBLY 191.06
337.10
IRRESOLUTE 99.11
IRRESPONSIBLE 271.06
IRRESPONSIVE 292.26
297.17 433.08
IRRETRIEVABLY 364.12
IRRITABLY 61.26
IRRITATED 130.23
172.15 471.02
IRRITATING 28.19
IRRITATION 77.30
114.29 210.18 222.19
328.07
IS 2.03 2.07
2.09 2.13 2.15
2.19 2.19 2.23
3.13 8.05 8.09
10.09 10.11 11.01
11.03 11.14 13.06
25.09 29.24 40.10
41.26 41.29 41.29
43.26 44.29 45.03
45.30 46.03 47.24
47.24 48.09 49.21
49.28 50.07 50.13
50.25 51.16 51.27

IS (CONT.) 52.17
52.28 53.12 56.06
57.10 59.25 59.29
59.30 60.15 64.29
65.08 65.17 67.07
70.32 72.02 72.05
76.05 77.25 78.11
79.19 79.23 80.01
80.05 80.06 80.19
80.27 81.06 81.15
82.07 86.17 87.14
88.18 88.19 94.03
96.02 97.16 98.28
101.04 102.12 106.03
106.03 111.13 114.30
118.09 123.09 124.26
125.20 132.27 141.10
147.01 147.06 148.25
150.25 155.14 156.01
156.03 156.13 156.14
156.20 156.21 156.27
156.30 157.04 159.17
160.04 163.11 168.06
170.08 170.21 171.19
171.21 173.02 174.13
176.05 176.29 177.03
177.09 177.12 178.02
178.05 178.11 178.12
178.13 178.20 178.23
178.24 178.28 178.28
178.30 179.03 179.11
179.23 179.23 179.24
180.28 180.28 181.02
181.15 184.21 187.03
187.04 187.04 187.16
187.17 188.26 190.24
191.10 191.11 191.15
193.18 193.22 194.19
197.28 198.11 199.28
200.10 200.11 202.02
202.22 202.30 203.04
204.07 204.07 204.19
204.21 204.23 204.29
207.17 209.17 210.15
212.15 213.15 213.16
214.08 214.23 214.30
215.04 215.07 215.08
215.09 215.12 215.15
215.16 215.20 215.22
218.25 218.26 219.05
219.09 219.27 220.23
220.28 222.20 223.24
224.09 224.25 225.09
225.19 228.09 228.15
228.17 228.21 228.22
228.27 229.14 229.15
229.20 229.21 229.27
231.04 232.30 235.17
237.10 237.18 238.25
239.13 239.20 240.13
241.16 241.16 242.29
242.30 243.24 244.03
244.28 246.30 250.24
253.02 253.04 253.05
253.13 253.13 253.17
253.17 253.18 253.28
255.17 256.04 257.28
257.29 258.25 259.05
259.11 259.15 260.16
260.25 260.26 260.30
261.07 261.24 261.24
263.18 263.19 263.20
263.23 263.24 264.09
265.09 267.31 267.31
268.03 268.08 269.05
269.07 269.15 269.16
269.29 270.23 271.22
271.26 272.03 272.09
272.10 273.01 273.05
273.12 273.15 274.13
274.23 274.30 275.02
275.06 275.14 275.17
278.01 279.01 279.15
280.21 281.02 282.23
282.30 287.17 288.16
289.04 289.04 289.06
289.07 289.16 289.17
290.10 293.29 295.16
297.02 297.12 299.05
301.24 302.01 302.04

IS (CONT.) 302.05
302.05 302.08 303.16
304.21 305.07 306.01
308.17 308.22 308.30
309.04 309.28 314.30
319.27 319.27 320.07
320.11 320.15 320.27
320.29 320.30 325.30
327.10 327.11 336.08
339.07 339.15 339.17
339.19 339.20 340.01
340.07 340.18 340.28
341.08 341.21 345.17
345.19 345.26 345.28
347.19 348.29 351.04
352.21 358.30 360.02
360.28 365.02 367.19
368.07 373.09 375.03
375.06 375.10 375.23
376.05 376.12 376.12
376.12 376.12 377.02
377.13 377.25 378.13
378.27 378.28 379.09
379.28 380.04 380.05
380.09 382.04 382.29
384.19 384.22 386.20
386.28 387.24 387.21
387.24 387.25 387.25
387.26 388.02 388.15
388.19 388.22 388.22
388.27 388.27 388.28
388.28 388.28 390.17
390.20 391.20 391.22
391.27 393.09 393.18
393.23 394.22 394.24
395.08 395.09 397.30
397.30 398.01 398.19
400.08 400.16 401.11
402.27 403.01 404.30
405.24 408.01 409.17
411.11 411.27 413.18
418.28 418.29 419.05
419.07 419.11 419.13
419.14 420.01 420.06
420.22 420.23 421.12
421.18 422.07 422.07
422.14 422.19 423.12
423.13 423.20 423.20
423.25 423.29 428.11
428.19 428.26 428.29
428.29 430.23 432.14
432.17 435.08 435.14
436.27 437.02 437.07
437.25 437.27 440.24
449.04 451.07 455.22
455.23 455.24 455.26
455.26 456.01 458.20
461.08 467.03 467.09
467.28 468.01 468.06
468.07 468.09 468.11
472.01 472.18 472.18
473.25 474.06 474.09
474.16 474.24 477.20
480.26 482.10 482.11
482.14 482.16 483.03
485.01 485.02 485.24
487.04 487.12 488.10
490.28 491.08 493.02
493.07 493.04 499.05
501.16 501.21 501.26
503.04 503.10 503.15
505.09 505.12 505.22
506.08 506.19 507.12
507.21 507.29 511.03
511.03 511.05 516.04
516.05 516.08 516.16
516.17 516.20
ISLAND 15.26 15.27
196.22 198.03 203.11
204.28 205.19 220.20
245.30 252.14 499.30
500.16
ISLANDER 439.06 439.13
439.22 461.04 464.03
ISLANDS 252.06 297.09
410.01 435.17
ISLE 206.03
ISLES 281.01
ISLET 214.22 276.13
325.14 475.13

ISLETS	13.08	16.21
410.27		
ISN'T	8.10	77.11
121.04	130.09	137.28
144.23	202.13	203.22
204.20	223.02	223.21
225.25	228.15	236.03
304.03	306.06	330.07
342.08	375.07	
ISOLATED	17.29	276.13
388.02	411.09	445.30
ISOLATION		147.13
214.09	302.19	334.27
334.30		
ISSUE	84.18	
ISSUED	28.24	.462.16
ISSUES	111.30	
ISSUING	314.13	
IST	241.21	241.22
IT	1.08	1.08
1.08	1.16	2.19
3.06	4.06	5.26
6.13	6.21	7.23
7.23	8.02	8.16
8.19	8.21	9.03
9.03	11.03	11.06
11.22	12.11	13.02
14.09	23.01	23.18
25.10	25.12	25.14
25.21	26.29	26.29
27.25	27.26	29.20
30.08	31.10	32.05
32.17	32.17	32.18
33.17	35.03	35.27
36.03	36.08	36.17
38.02	38.25	41.07
41.14	41.23	41.30
42.06	42.07	42.22
43.30	43.43	44.25
44.26	44.28	45.23
45.24	46.09	47.19
48.16	49.08	49.12
49.14	49.22	49.29
50.02	50.07	51.26
51.27	52.03	52.09
52.25	53.02	53.12
53.22	54.01	54.09
55.12	56.02	56.08
56.19	56.25	57.16
57.26	58.04	58.16
58.16	59.06	59.18
59.29	59.30	60.03
60.04	60.09	63.22
66.03	66.04	66.07
66.12	66.18	66.20
67.07	67.27	69.26
69.27	69.27	69.28
70.05	70.09	70.18
70.24	70.25	70.37
71.26	72.07	72.23
72.24	72.25	72.30
72.30	73.03	73.05
74.01	74.11	74.26
74.27	75.01	75.04
75.15	75.25	76.03
77.06	77.16	77.17
77.26	77.28	78.08
78.09	78.11	78.11
78.17	78.23	79.04
79.10	79.13	79.14
79.19	79.25	80.19
80.29	81.20	81.27
82.02	82.04	82.07
82.18	84.17	85.02
85.03	86.04	86.13
86.29	87.04	87.14
87.25	87.30	88.08
88.10	88.21	89.01
89.26	90.15	90.18
90.28	91.04	91.10
93.09	94.01	94.03
95.13	95.16	95.24
95.29	96.02	96.14
96.16	97.12	97.12
97.16	97.21	98.04
98.08	98.08	98.20
98.28	99.19	99.20
99.21	100.18	100.22
101.04	101.08	101.08
101.09	101.10	101.10

IT (CONT.) ... 101.16

101.22	102.26	103.06
103.07	103.08	103.21
103.28	103.29	104.01
104.04	104.21	106.03
106.07	106.13	107.11
108.22	108.23	109.10
109.22	110.07	110.07
110.08	110.08	111.12
111.12	112.01	112.12
112.23	113.12	114.08
114.08	114.09	114.21
114.30	115.16	115.21
115.30	116.01	116.02
116.03	116.23	117.29
118.17	118.30	119.03
119.30	120.03	120.25
121.04	122.04	122.16
123.16	123.28	123.29
124.02	124.09	124.09
124.10	125.05	125.07
125.20	126.27	126.28
128.01	128.03	128.09
128.16	128.25	129.06
129.22	130.07	130.09
130.11	131.09	132.10
132.17	132.28	133.25
134.16	134.23	134.24
134.27	134.28	135.07
136.07	136.09	136.11
136.12	136.22	136.23
137.25	137.28	137.30
138.10	138.19	138.20
138.21	139.03	139.13
139.16	139.19	139.24
139.27	140.06	140.15
140.17	141.07	141.15
142.22	142.22	142.23
143.01	143.11	143.17
143.18	143.19	143.19
143.20	143.23	144.05
144.06	144.23	145.17
146.16	146.21	147.06
147.24	147.27	148.13
148.16	148.18	150.12
150.14	150.18	150.20
150.20	150.29	151.16
152.02	152.04	152.10
152.11	152.11	152.18
153.01	153.16	153.18
154.08	154.13	155.13
155.14	155.15	155.24
156.01	156.02	156.03
157.10	157.15	157.16
157.18	157.24	157.26
157.26	157.27	158.08
158.22	159.07	159.08
159.17	160.01	160.04
160.04	160.07	160.09
160.12	160.14	160.16
160.18	160.20	160.20
161.03	162.18	163.09
163.12	163.25	164.18
164.18	164.21	164.29
164.29	165.09	165.24
165.29	166.09	166.14
166.22	167.18	167.28
168.01	168.04	168.06
168.07	168.21	168.25
168.26	168.28	169.09
169.20	169.20	170.14
171.10	171.21	171.25
171.30	172.03	172.06
172.10	172.16	172.17
172.18	172.29	173.06
174.13	174.13	175.02
175.02	175.18	175.25
176.05	176.13	176.25
177.03	177.03	177.12
177.26	178.05	178.20
178.20	179.15	179.18
179.24	179.25	179.27
181.04	181.10	181.12
181.16	182.02	182.13
183.01	183.05	183.21
183.22	184.05	184.06
184.07	184.07	184.10
184.15	185.02	185.19
186.23	187.04	187.04
187.05	187.09	187.10

IT (CONT.) ... 187.16

187.17	187.20	187.23
187.26	187.26	188.09
188.13	188.14	188.16
188.17	188.26	189.01
189.09	189.11	190.03
193.07	193.12	193.18
193.22	193.25	193.25
194.15	194.27	195.02
195.04	196.03	196.06
196.23	196.24	197.01
197.09	197.16	198.04
198.30	199.06	199.07
199.09	199.28	200.04
200.10	200.11	200.11
200.25	200.25	200.29
201.10	201.10	202.28
202.30	203.06	203.07
203.22	203.26	204.12
204.23	205.21	205.23
205.23	205.25	207.04
207.06	208.13	208.28
208.30	209.13	209.16
209.18	209.20	209.23
209.24	209.24	210.05
211.19	211.23	211.27
212.01	212.07	212.14
213.12	213.15	213.17
213.21	214.01	214.17
214.18	214.23	215.09
215.20	215.28	216.07
216.09	217.15	217.18
217.20	217.24	217.25
218.10	218.12	218.13
218.14	218.14	218.19
218.25	218.25	219.01
219.05	219.09	219.14
219.15	219.30	220.01
220.23	220.28	221.01
222.02	222.02	222.08
223.03	223.21	224.03
224.09	224.14	224.23
224.24	225.02	225.07
225.07	225.21	226.02
226.26	227.13	227.14
228.05	228.12	228.15
228.17	228.18	228.21
228.22	228.24	228.27
229.06	229.06	229.11
229.26	229.27	230.08
230.23	231.04	231.05
231.10	231.11	231.13
231.19	231.29	232.13
232.13	232.28	233.08
233.20	234.22	235.17
235.26	235.27	236.03
236.05	236.11	237.04
237.10	237.18	239.12
239.13	239.20	239.21
239.21	240.05	240.06
240.06	240.16	240.27
241.02	241.11	241.25
241.25	241.27	242.08
242.16	242.22	243.05
243.13	243.28	245.02
245.09	245.10	245.11
245.13	245.27	246.07
246.09	246.15	246.28
246.30	247.05	249.27
249.28	249.30	251.11
251.22	253.16	253.28
254.05	254.14	254.17
254.25	255.03	255.05
255.07	255.09	256.02
256.07	256.11	257.01
258.16	258.27	259.02
259.03	259.13	259.22
260.02	260.04	260.16
261.17	261.24	261.24
262.02	262.04	262.09
262.17	262.22	263.15
263.23	263.24	263.27
264.02	265.03	266.04
266.06	266.12	266.15
266.24	267.21	267.29
267.30	268.07	268.22
269.04	269.26	269.29
270.06	270.10	270.13
270.21	271.01	271.21
271.22	271.26	271.30

IT (CONT.) ... 272.03

272.09	273.08	273.13
273.14	273.29	273.30
274.05	274.13	274.17
274.23	275.14	275.17
276.02	276.03	276.06
277.04	277.05	277.05
277.08	277.20	277.22
277.30	277.30	278.01
278.14	278.16	280.21
280.21	281.02	281.20
281.30	282.01	282.05
282.23	282.25	282.29
283.06	283.12	283.13
283.22	283.22	283.23
283.25	283.26	283.29
284.03	285.15	285.16
285.18	285.22	286.03
286.28	287.02	287.05
287.06	287.08	287.12
287.14	287.17	287.17
288.01	288.16	289.04
289.05	289.16	289.17
289.21	289.26	290.02
290.03	290.10	290.14
291.05	291.18	294.04
294.23	295.18	295.21
295.28	296.03	297.01
298.05	298.25	299.01
299.03	299.22	300.04
301.04	301.11	301.22
301.24	302.02	302.04
302.07	302.17	303.10
303.16	303.21	303.21
303.27	303.28	304.03
304.05	304.15	304.18
304.20	304.20	304.21
304.22	304.22	306.02
306.06	306.08	306.08
306.20	307.07	308.09
308.13	308.24	308.27
309.08	309.13	309.19
309.20	309.21	309.21
309.28	310.13	310.26
311.06	311.20	311.25
312.03	312.04	312.12
312.14	312.25	312.29
313.09	314.30	318.16
319.05	319.09	320.07
320.22	320.23	320.26
320.27	320.29	321.09
321.10	322.25	322.28
322.30	323.12	323.19
324.19	324.30	325.03
325.04	325.05	325.17
326.01	326.06	327.02
328.05	328.07	328.17
329.02	329.24	330.03
330.07	330.19	330.21
330.22	331.03	331.07
331.09	331.14	331.17
331.18	331.21	331.21
332.09	332.16	332.17
332.21	332.26	333.17
334.07	334.11	334.11
334.20	335.11	335.14
335.15	336.05	336.08
337.19	337.29	338.19
339.07	339.18	339.19
339.24	340.09	341.03
341.06	341.08	341.13
341.14	342.05	342.08
342.21	342.30	342.30
343.15	343.19	344.05
344.07	345.05	345.15
345.18	345.21	345.21
345.28	346.09	347.17
347.18	348.15	348.23
348.24	348.29	349.08
350.15	350.18	351.17
351.19	351.20	351.22
352.11	352.25	352.26
353.08	353.11	353.18
353.20	353.26	354.01
354.05	354.07	354.09
354.11	354.12	355.05
356.03	356.09	356.12
356.22	357.15	357.17
357.18	357.18	358.07
358.20	358.30	359.09

IT (CONT.) — 359.10

359.14	359.20	359.25
359.26	359.29	360.13
360.17	360.28	363.09
364.06	364.17	365.02
365.02	365.03	365.06
365.06	365.23	365.29
365.29	366.11	366.19
366.20	366.27	367.02
367.13	367.17	367.18
367.26	368.03	368.07
368.11	369.07	369.13
370.16	371.10	371.20
371.22	371.24	374.14
374.25	375.06	375.07
375.10	375.11	375.17
376.04	376.05	376.10
376.12	377.04	377.06
377.07	377.20	377.24
378.13	378.13	378.14
378.19	378.19	378.27
378.28	378.29	379.24
379.28	380.04	380.05
380.06	380.15	381.09
381.22	382.04	382.04
382.05	382.06	382.11
382.19	382.29	383.06
383.27	383.30	384.10
384.22	384.30	385.03
335.05	385.07	386.13
386.20	386.22	387.02
387.07	387.11	387.16
387.21	388.15	388.22
388.22	388.26	388.27
388.28	388.28	388.28
388.28	388.29	388.30
388.30	389.03	389.05
389.13	389.26	389.29
390.17	390.27	390.27
391.27	392.04	392.06
392.08	392.10	392.11
392.27	392.27	393.02
393.16	394.16	394.21
394.24	395.08	395.15
395.17	395.19	396.01
396.03	396.05	396.07
396.29	397.03	397.06
397.18	397.24	397.30
398.02	398.10	398.16
398.17	398.19	398.21
398.24	398.28	399.05
399.27	400.01	400.03
400.20	400.22	401.05
402.14	403.13	403.14
403.20	404.12	405.15
406.02	407.07	407.17
408.23	408.29	409.23
411.14	412.02	412.03
412.11	414.29	414.29
414.29	415.04	415.10
416.10	416.13	416.14
416.18	418.01	418.01
418.28	419.02	419.13
419.14	420.01	420.06
420.08	420.23	421.04
421.11	421.12	421.13
421.14	421.15	421.18
421.22	422.21	422.27
422.27	423.12	423.14
423.14	423.20	423.24
423.26	423.30	424.02
424.03	425.01	425.15
426.14	426.24	426.27
426.30	428.08	428.19
429.15	429.15	429.30
430.15	430.18	430.18
430.19	430.20	430.23
430.24	430.25	430.25
431.01	434.07	434.10
434.16	434.17	434.18
435.01	435.13	435.13
435.14	436.21	436.25
436.27	437.06	438.12
439.12	439.17	439.25
440.24	443.11	443.16
444.16	445.10	446.02
447.05	448.11	448.18
449.04	449.20	450.23
451.26	452.15	453.22
454.05	454.15	455.28

IT (CONT.) — 456.21

456.25	457.18	458.30
459.03	459.03	461.08
461.23	461.28	461.29
462.07	463.11	463.13
463.19	464.04	464.11
464.24	465.12	465.14
467.07	468.04	469.20
471.29	472.09	472.09
472.18	472.18	473.26
474.05	474.06	474.09
474.13	474.20	474.24
474.28	474.30	475.01
475.22	477.20	478.27
479.01	479.01	479.12
479.15	480.21	482.14
483.16	483.20	484.07
484.27	485.24	486.05
486.12	486.13	487.12
488.10	488.21	490.28
491.12	491.24	491.26
492.10	493.10	493.22
494.09	494.19	494.20
495.03	495.12	496.01
497.03	497.12	498.15
499.24	499.27	499.28
500.18	501.18	501.19
502.09	503.10	503.15
505.05	505.23	506.08
506.14	506.17	506.28
507.04	507.06	507.29
508.28	509.24	509.27
509.30	510.07	510.26
511.09	511.12	512.08
512.16	513.04	513.09
514.11	514.15	515.23
516.19		

IT'S — 11.21   30.01

41.14	60.01	62.11
91.03	99.22	110.11
113.07	113.22	113.22
132.22	142.03	174.11
174.13	179.08	183.27
195.30	196.26	196.29
198.11	204.08	204.12
204.24	204.25	205.19
213.05	220.27	228.28
229.16	234.08	235.16
235.17	238.15	238.18
241.17	286.08	301.23
304.03	314.30	320.11
329.12	330.22	331.26
413.27	424.09	471.11
474.13		

ITALIAN — 47.20

ITALIAN'S — 64.24

ITAM — 332.21   349.12

349.17	350.11	378.05
378.08	401.20	408.03
428.06	428.10	428.25
434.14	434.19	483.01
483.10	483.15	485.13
487.01	489.01	489.12
489.17	489.21	490.16
490.18	490.25	490.29
491.05	491.13	491.13
497.16	498.01	498.23
499.01	499.05	499.12
499.14	499.18	500.20
501.03	501.10	501.24
502.13	502.19	502.21
502.29	503.19	504.01
504.11	504.12	504.16
504.23	505.02	505.08
505.09	505.15	505.18
505.23	506.04	506.09
506.25	507.11	507.13
507.15	507.18	507.20
509.11	510.18	510.23
511.17	511.25	512.06
512.12	512.16	512.19
512.23	512.25	513.03
513.07		

ITAM'S — 399.18   482.09

ITS — 8.22   13.08

13.09	13.29	17.02
19.08	19.11	19.22
22.07	23.06	23.15
23.15	31.08	31.09
31.11	31.12	34.05

ITS (CONT.) — 39.07

49.07	54.25	54.30
60.11	63.12	66.04
66.23	68.27	73.01
77.01	84.18	89.02
90.24	97.27	97.28
98.21	98.23	102.24
112.09	112.10	123.07
140.03	157.08	159.23
163.16	168.07	174.09
182.02	185.19	188.25
191.14	191.15	194.27
196.22	214.30	225.21
230.06	249.04	260.02
260.07	262.05	262.14
266.07	266.09	266.10
266.11	266.14	269.22
270.26	271.09	271.10
271.10	271.10	271.10
271.11	271.11	271.12
271.13	271.13	271.25
271.27	271.27	271.28
272.02	272.03	272.03
276.11	276.12	276.12
277.07	280.01	281.07
283.27	289.05	289.05
298.07	299.10	301.29
302.03	317.03	327.07
331.15	333.23	335.09
335.09	335.11	337.05
339.20	347.14	352.22
352.23	352.23	367.09
367.19	379.10	379.23
379.24	379.25	379.26
386.17	389.19	390.11
390.16	390.17	393.12
396.20	396.22	396.30
397.02	397.06	397.06
397.28	397.28	398.15
398.21	398.22	407.04
407.04	407.04	407.08
410.08	412.25	414.11
414.18	416.07	418.15
418.16	418.25	418.26
418.26	421.26	421.27
423.25	432.14	432.15
432.15	438.26	442.26
461.15	461.16	480.10
483.06	497.06	509.23
509.23		

ITSELF — 4.17   20.26

23.20	24.21	24.28
36.05	36.08	101.14
113.02	115.05	180.24
181.12	183.30	195.02
215.19	215.29	243.24
246.30	264.07	271.25
289.05	299.15	332.04
339.24	341.06	371.06
390.11	395.11	397.03
398.07	409.01	416.07
432.14	440.19	450.26
452.08	457.09	508.06

JA — 259.14   259.14

260.19

JAB — 8.15   309.08

JABBERING — 42.12

JACKET — 24.07   248.05

254.12

JACKETS — 440.06

JAGGED — 297.07   466.06

JAILER — 349.19

JAMES — 185.30   195.20

231.02   231.02   276.20

JAMES' — 421.19   422.09

JAMMED — 55.14   115.18

167.07

JAMS — 65.06

JANE — 342.12

JANISSARY — 349.15

JAPAN — 14.12

JAR — 131.15

JARGON — 25.16   143.17

JARRED — 311.14

JAUNTY — 46.27   273.21

JAVA — 441.05   502.02

JAVANESE — 248.05   291.19

JAW — 24.18   364.28

JAWS — 307.13   313.18

JEALOUS — 322.22   349.04

JEALOUS (CONT.) — 515.29

JEALOUSIES — 321.16

JEALOUSLY — 349.03

JEALOUSY — 190.08

JEE — 238.27

JEERED — 330.17

JEERING — 127.12   438.16

JEERINGLY — 491.26

JERK — 44.21   54.23

108.13   145.24   371.30

JERKED — 118.29   196.02

225.30   426.19

JERKS — 63.06

JERKY — 217.27   224.15

350.18

JETS — 443.21

JETTY — 15.10   232.07

JEWEL — 342.07   342.10

342.19	342.18	345.21
345.24	346.12	347.17
353.20	413.14	413.16
448.05	488.22	

JEWEL'S — 484.04

JEWELLED — 315.03

JIB — 413.30

JIB-SHEET — 413.30

JIFFY — 201.10

JIM — 2.24   3.04

3.20	3.26	3.27
4.14	6.01	7.10
7.13	7.21	8.21
11.19	12.01	13.03
14.18	19.23	21.30
22.16	23.09	24.18
25.11	26.15	28.17
30.18	32.01	33.21
33.29	37.26	38.02
38.19	38.23	41.15
47.08	51.13	65.06
79.10	81.22	82.02
82.16	82.26	84.01
84.12	85.18	95.06
95.17	98.15	105.16
119.21	119.29	120.14
122.18	122.22	123.28
125.07	125.12	140.23
150.04	151.29	165.08
178.07	182.08	184.22
191.01	194.29	195.10
195.26	196.12	197.09
202.07	203.28	207.01
207.21	227.16	227.19
228.06	230.02	231.18
232.24	233.03	233.18
234.25	235.29	236.30
239.23	240.29	241.24
242.13	244.04	266.24
267.23	269.01	269.28
272.05	275.04	279.17
279.25	281.03	281.12
286.13	292.10	294.17
294.23	297.24	298.04
302.11	307.02	307.14
307.19	307.20	308.02
308.13	316.17	316.23
317.15	320.12	322.13
322.19	322.20	323.09
324.15	327.23	328.01
329.08	332.07	332.09
333.02	333.06	333.12
333.28	336.05	337.20
340.04	342.04	342.06
345.23	347.14	347.24
348.15	349.27	349.30
350.17	351.18	352.26
352.30	356.08	356.24
357.01	357.07	357.09
358.19	358.20	358.25
359.02	360.08	360.16
361.01	361.04	361.09
361.14	363.07	363.08
363.11	364.09	364.22
364.27	364.30	366.26
367.13	368.13	370.29
371.10	371.17	372.08
372.22	372.23	373.01
373.16	373.22	374.04
376.14	378.08	379.23
379.28	379.30	381.10
381.18	382.03	383.07

JIM (CONT.) 383.29
384.22 390.01 391.05
396.01 396.08 400.05
400.26 400.29 400.29
401.23 401.29 403.20
406.05 408.01 408.11
410.24 410.29 411.11
414.03 414.07 414.22
419.06 425.10 427.27
428.08 428.11 444.15
447.04 447.15 448.13
451.16 455.18 455.19
455.19 455.21 455.22
468.13 470.03 470.08
470.16 471.05 471.08
474.25 475.04 477.22
478.06 478.25 478.30
479.10 479.20 480.01
480.02 480.20 480.22
481.01 481.12 481.17
482.08 482.26 484.15
485.04 486.17 487.05
487.14 488.14 488.18
489.24 490.05 490.14
490.17 491.04 491.06
491.18 491.29 494.03
494.09 494.21 505.11
505.22 506.11 507.13
507.23 510.14 510.20
510.25 510.29 512.12
512.17 512.24 513.01
513.11 513.23 513.27
514.05 514.09 514.18
514.28 515.07 515.13
JIM-JAMS 65.06
JIM-MYTH 345.23
JIM'S 3.30 37.22
69.15 83.19 93.06
124.29 177.14 182.01
183.30 210.22 215.15
227.06 228.30 229.07
229.25 242.04 247.23
252.20 262.28 263.28
269.20 276.05 291.24
296.05 298.16 310.06
316.05 322.17 328.18
332.22 332.28 336.22
337.14 339.05 347.01
349.16 351.15 365.02
365.06 366.11 372.08
387.28 388.12 390.27
395.21 399.16 402.06
427.24 437.19 447.04
447.10 447.20 448.06
448.20 448.22 448.25
450.10 450.18 450.19
453.24 455.13 462.03
470.30 477.12 483.21
489.26 490.12 491.28
499.06 513.03
JIMMY 233.13 237.11
JINGLED 108.25
JOB 2.17 2.28
30.07 170.14 198.07
203.11 229.30 231.09
331.11 456.23
JOCULAR 105.03
JOHNNIE 285.05
JOHNNIES 205.04
JOHNNY 197.24
JOIN 328.21 484.23
JOINED 140.03 199.16
251.04 421.14
JOINTED 246.19 459.22
JOINTS 22.18
JOKE 78.04 130.20
131.12 132.19 147.17
200.16 237.15 293.30
330.30 331.14 465.24
JOKER 203.01
JOKES 42.27 54.08
200.15
JOKING 92.10 331.17
JOKINGLY 489.05
JOLLIFICATION 439.15
JOLLITY 2.18
JOLLY 26.04 29.27
43.14 114.11 152.02
191.11 217.22 286.17
286.21 287.23 353.04
JONES 70.44 71.01
72.15 72.28 74.25
75.03 75.17 76.12
76.23 77.05 77.16
77.20
JONGH 43.22 182.09
182.11 244.14 245.02
JONGH'S 43.21 184.25
JOSTLED 6.15 462.08
JOSTLING 126.24 302.22
JOURNEY 16.27 218.30
298.08 299.27 330.23
335.07 343.02 408.12
490.21 497.17
JOURNEYS 250.07 256.28
349.13
JOVE 40.19 42.26
50.17 53.22 114.05
116.20 132.19 193.11
193.27 218.20 224.09
225.04 231.11 244.27
284.03 287.07 288.16
288.16 290.13 295.15
303.06 303.15 306.10
320.18 324.30 328.13
331.08 332.17 370.18
375.10 377.01 384.22
401.05 412.02
JOVIAL 27.07 364.17
JOY 271.13 352.29
465.13 467.27
JOYED 452.02
JOYOUS 342.16
JU 137.17 137.17
JU-JU-ST 137.17
JUBILATING 477.08
JUDGE 112.03 122.08
271.12 309.30 400.25
421.21
JUDGED 171.25 188.30
283.28 456.21 462.07
500.17
JUDGING 227.04
JUDICIALLY 294.04
JUDICIOUS 420.16
JUDY 75.08
JUMBLED 6.03 191.25
462.27
JUMP 29.16 72.21
95.01 133.23 133.23
133.23 134.02 134.03
134.08 138.10 143.22
143.26 206.01 235.13
237.25 255.11 280.19
284.06 356.08 373.23
473.28 506.12
JUMPED 45.05 69.28
74.16 96.20 101.15
134.15 135.07 136.03
145.03 148.09 150.16
150.16 150.17 151.06
158.17 159.25 159.26
163.05 188.06 309.29
359.17 364.23 371.11
444.15 465.13 466.05
469.23 470.05 500.28
501.07 504.13
JUMPING 141.19 287.24
473.25
JUMPING-OFF 473.25
JUMPS 75.11 255.06
368.24
JUNGLE 3.23 15.24
335.08 336.04 367.12
445.08 458.29 489.29
JUST 3.04 3.20
6.20 8.01 13.15
34.12 42.19 43.10
43.29 46.01 47.07
50.28 60.21 62.05
70.44 71.21 73.12
81.07 81.13 83.10
83.18 86.06 86.10
86.17 88.04 92.11
104.05 104.20 105.23
109.21 114.06 114.10
117.10 123.16 128.17
128.20 128.29 130.11
132.08 136.07 136.20
140.17 140.30 146.21
JUST (CONT.) 148.08
151.09 154.02 156.07
162.13 174.13 183.09
194.15 196.07 197.05
197.14 198.29 199.08
200.03 200.21 203.10
204.22 217.04 217.25
222.03 224.23 231.12
233.11 236.03 237.01
237.12 251.16 266.18
273.09 280.12 286.14
292.02 301.07 301.12
308.26 313.16 313.27
314.19 330.13 341.10
344.05 344.08 357.08
357.12 363.07 372.08
376.12 377.22 394.16
400.18 407.11 412.18
413.27 414.03 421.18
441.26 459.18 468.06
468.16 475.22 476.01
479.18 481.05 493.10
501.08 505.14 512.26
JUSTE 176.04
JUSTICE 281.20 394.24
418.26
JUSTIFIED 86.28
123.17 165.26
KALASHEE 105.17
KALEIDOSCOPE 191.26
KANAKAS 436.17 475.29
KASSIM 301.16 449.20
450.14 451.18 451.25
453.11 453.20 454.11
454.18 454.20 454.26
456.12 456.24 458.01
458.27 461.09 489.30
KASSIM'S 457.02 463.29
KEEL 23.24 122.11
KEEN 3.21 304.29
KEENLY 283.15
KEEP 7.05 7.05
29.14 70.38 73.17
73.26 79.23 98.11
102.06 107.21 108.29
117.25 123.19 128.14
136.12 152.21 159.21
171.27 183.03 184.02
196.06 215.05 237.28
238.08 256.01 256.05
256.17 259.23 260.14
261.02 262.29 269.06
281.10 283.22 304.05
316.18 349.12 353.06
357.04 385.27 395.15
401.22 407.17 412.12
442.24 451.08 461.17
474.05 515.03
KEEPER 240.19 426.23
434.29
KEEPERS 439.16
KEEPING 17.20 23.21
58.20 79.11 81.24
231.09 253.14 293.14
333.05 402.18 412.20
446.11 460.05 483.01
497.18
KEEPS 214.10 354.03
KEGS 448.18
KELP 198.13
KEPT 2.13 3.12
5.17 36.11 90.11
103.13 105.17 109.07
115.27 124.30 125.16
125.16 125.17 130.12
141.18 142.23 143.19
144.03 144.27 169.01
174.04 184.01 184.08
207.15 209.05 210.29
219.15 227.19 237.01
285.02 291.17 324.09
353.07 356.20 369.08
385.28 399.11 413.25
431.08 448.15 449.24
462.10 462.13 465.10
489.23 497.24 498.13
499.21
KETTLES 136.15
KEY 58.18 448.21
KICK 236.21 256.03
KICK (CONT.) 426.07
502.12
KICKED 27.24 148.13
474.17 475.28
KICKING 286.20 313.20
502.25
KIDNAP 435.17
KIDNAPPED 439.06
KIDNEY 437.10
KILL 93.02 115.27
145.03 153.16 194.17
336.19 357.12 364.03
390.15 401.07 426.11
450.28 455.27 456.01
468.17 481.21 492.09
KILLED 17.08 145.02
145.02 286.01 309.22
316.03 354.06 382.12
447.17 450.07 479.03
482.25 504.19
KILLING 130.10 194.27
244.28 245.04 478.30
485.03
KIND 1.07 12.19
36.03 40.11 40.12
40.16 42.16 44.06
50.27 51.15 51.16
51.18 53.19 64.23
64.25 66.16 68.27
77.09 79.19 79.25
81.07 85.10 91.02
112.30 113.08 114.17
128.16 149.11 155.24
156.19 168.21 187.04
194.16 214.09 225.16
227.10 230.23 246.24
280.02 280.28 289.10
294.16 306.04 313.06
330.07 334.28 358.09
374.25 400.24 404.16
418.15 418.20 442.01
454.14 477.10
KIND' 96.27
KINDLINESS 37.08
KINDLY 87.13 231.16
403.12 498.30
KINDNESS 111.20 205.08
212.01
KINDRED 271.04
KINDS 13.17 80.27
279.15 434.01
KING 242.13 455.27
KINSMEN 338.22
KISS 320.02
KISSED 58.01 120.13
KITCHEN 267.16
KNEADING 25.19
KNEE 47.04 307.18
431.12 459.28 509.02
KNEELING 198.13
KNEES 21.03 37.17
52.29 102.21 133.11
200.09 203.29 280.07
323.02 324.17 355.20
383.22 428.21 439.19
460.03 473.03 483.11
512.22 512.27 513.26
514.23
KNEW 7.23 9.02
10.05 34.07 34.14
47.13 50.20 66.12
73.04 75.02 95.06
107.22 130.04 132.16
134.24 138.06 139.29
148.03 152.03 156.08
160.13 162.18 168.08
168.25 169.10 182.15
195.10 197.05 237.28
244.30 247.05 247.21
258.13 267.10 272.30
274.08 279.03 286.01
287.18 300.17 311.02
321.25 329.23 340.19
343.14 379.09 387.20
392.24 393.13 418.15
447.07 457.15 468.13
473.06 484.05 486.01
490.20 492.24
KNID 50.23
KNIFE 20.26 75.24

KNIFE (CONT.)   124.15
286.05   287.01   439.21
439.24
KNIGHT   384.27
KNOCK   34.28   128.25
140.28   198.10   218.22
KNOCKABOUT   126.15
KNOCKED   102.19   110.01
124.09   145.25   198.19
243.15   314.06   332.15
435.04
KNOCKING   45.11   51.08
129.21   133.02   149.08
364.24   495.27
KNOCKS   72.27
KNOLL   444.18   444.21
445.03   445.09   456.13
469.11   480.16   491.14
KNOT   68.02   452.27
469.04
KNOTS   498.16
KNOTTY   238.14
KNOW   9.01   27.30
29.09   29.24   35.16
40.08   41.02   42.02
42.28   43.41   44.03
48.11   51.21   53.18
54.08   55.27   57.09
62.16   63.01   63.25
65.07   67.23   68.10
68.18   69.27   70.32
74.29   76.15   76.22
77.11   78.22   79.18
81.16   83.21   84.14
84.29   85.07   86.01
86.09   87.03   87.22
94.21   94.22   95.29
95.30   96.02   96.10
96.29   97.07   101.05
103.01   105.17   106.13
108.17   109.02   112.14
118.04   119.06   121.05
123.01   124.01   125.17
129.13   130.25   131.03
134.27   137.25   143.05
144.15   144.24   145.05
149.12   150.15   152.10
155.14   156.01   156.05
157.15   159.30   160.13
163.22   163.30   164.28
168.19   172.10   176.13
177.12   179.19   181.03
182.03   183.30   189.03
190.17   197.20   197.21
198.06   200.20   201.15
202.05   203.01   203.15
204.20   205.14   205.20
209.09   210.17   213.09
213.22   214.01   218.12
219.21   225.27   228.17
229.13   230.07   230.27
230.27   231.07   231.08
231.11   231.19   231.27
234.07   234.22   236.08
237.30   238.03   239.12
241.24   242.16   243.02
243.15   244.12   244.14
247.21   253.28   253.29
253.23   265.01   265.05
265.06   268.05   270.24
272.05   272.06   273.21
275.10   278.10   295.20
295.27   301.01   301.22
303.25   310.22   314.07
314.20   314.30   319.07
324.20   325.28   326.01
334.27   335.11   338.02
338.05   338.11   339.17
341.13   342.12   342.21
344.18   344.21   350.10
351.23   355.01   356.15
357.08   359.22   361.05
361.15   361.19   367.04
368.27   368.28   370.17
374.23   374.27   376.14
376.24   377.03   377.06
378.19   383.02   383.14
384.21   384.24   386.23
388.17   389.20   391.22
391.24   391.25   392.28

KNOW (CONT.)   393.08
394.15   394.18   394.21
398.04   399.26   400.15
401.08   402.15   403.14
415.10   419.02   419.16
420.13   425.14   426.12
428.10   429.20   435.12
436.18   448.13   454.01
465.28   467.30   470.15
471.10   473.17   473.17
473.30   474.06   474.11
474.13   475.29   475.30
481.03   481.04   483.03
483.05   483.06   483.07
488.14   490.26   492.07
492.25   493.17   495.16
503.05   506.18   507.14
507.16   510.24   512.08
513.15   516.05
KNOWING   47.12   67.05
77.12   79.20   101.21
180.23   211.04   231.06
452.06   453.17
KNOWINGLY   62.30
119.04   173.13   197.09
266.13
KNOWLEDGE   4.01
8.29   10.14   55.29
60.08   77.25   96.04
102.03   116.03   118.26
119.08   156.24   240.24
261.06   270.23   301.23
387.10   397.27   477.11
479.28   487.04   500.15
KNOWN   3.17   10.03
11.13   43.34   48.19
57.30   66.19   75.18
79.07   87.03   124.16
143.23   158.28   159.05
164.08   174.17   178.17
229.02   240.08   240.10
240.13   240.18   242.21
246.06   247.18   264.20
266.15   267.11   275.20
301.09   318.16   336.08
379.05   436.05   483.22
491.07   491.30
KNOWS   50.30   78.07
89.15   128.16   130.07
132.17   139.02   157.27
179.02   194.09   198.21
220.04   265.07   265.08
292.18   324.21   397.29
402.25   405.04   405.05
405.07   429.14   442.08
467.28   507.20   516.16
KNUCKLES   110.06   139.11
348.10
KONG   229.06
KORAN   510.13
KOSMOS   253.07
KRING   294.06   297.13
442.18   443.12
KRIS   310.04
KRISS   333.05   349.15
371.12   372.01
KRISS'   315.23
KRISSES   309.18
L'   173.10
L'EAU   169.04
L'HOMME   179.24
L'OEIL   171.28
LABELLED   92.13
LABORIOUS   351.04
LABOUR   393.25
LABOURING   118.12
126.02   299.10
LACE   287.11   506.01
LACED   191.30   395.22
LACHEZ   178.26
LACHRYMOSE   403.10
125.29
LACKADAISICAL   56.05
LACKED   340.26
LAD   199.28
LADDER   25.18   34.18
34.26   35.05   72.08
102.20   109.20
LADDERS   5.22
LADY   485.16
LADY'S   182.17

LADY'S-MAID   182.17
LAID   7.11   45.30
127.30   132.17   158.10
229.07   255.09   258.21
261.17   333.25   504.18
509.01   510.07
LAME   116.26   241.08
455.01
LAMENESS   12.12
LAMENTABLE   241.26
LAMENTATION   508.15
LAMENTATIONS   217.27
510.12
LAMP   21.10   22.28
34.04   101.11   101.29
103.29   108.08   108.24
125.29   248.16   260.03
261.10   417.11   417.19
434.27
LAMPS   34.02
LANCE   349.16
LAND   114.16   129.01
139.08   203.26   214.23
271.09   271.25   272.04
272.26   273.04   299.06
300.22   304.14   305.07
312.02   322.21   325.10
325.17   331.24   335.12
336.07   337.29   338.03
349.04   407.22   442.16
444.18   456.19   457.23
463.03   464.30   469.21
486.04   488.28   494.04
503.08   508.21
LANDED   43.10   46.21
58.26   110.23   129.17
134.28   311.13   342.14
372.07   409.23   410.17
444.17   470.10   499.30
LANDING   6.06   64.12
311.30   484.22   489.12
500.03   512.19
LANDING-   311.30
LANDING-STAGE   484.22
489.12   512.19
LANDING-STAGES   5.05
LANDMARKS   385.20
LANDS   322.12
LANDSCAPE   325.16
LANE   489.18   513.29
LANGUAGE   108.11   195.18
419.29   485.21
LANGUID   28.26   39.01
60.21   99.04   289.23
512.10
LANGUOR   12.30   24.03
LANK   410.23
LANKY   440.06   459.22
LANTERN   416.22
LANYARD   34.05
LANYARDS   107.13
LAP   280.09   299.04
426.21   514.27
LAPA   465.26
LAPEL   78.17
LAPSE   39.07
LARGE   14.03   16.18
43.09   44.10   46.18
92.08   95.10   135.03
168.18   233.28   235.09
245.30   252.14   314.01
314.24   319.28   343.11
345.17   350.29   409.20
420.25   436.07   440.05
449.27
LARGER   43.09
LARGISH   441.28
LASCAR   105.21
LASCARS   80.03   119.25
LASHED   22.28   55.21
125.29
LAST   16.17   19.20
23.01   26.01   28.19
52.19   72.16   72.17
73.13   74.06   74.17
75.10   77.20   77.24
77.27   78.08   81.18
81.26   85.18   87.26
88.24   88.27   89.30
93.01   93.24   97.04

LAST (CONT.)   99.29
100.18   101.01   103.30
106.06   106.07   109.18
115.16   119.16   122.22
123.22   129.19   131.04
131.14   132.14   132.27
136.22   145.17   148.29
149.19   151.01   155.24
159.23   160.23   173.02
176.30   177.29   180.14
183.07   184.27   185.08
188.12   189.17   201.04
201.27   202.09   214.03
216.17   217.11   222.01
225.13   225.25   229.20
232.06   235.05   243.17
251.16   256.15   257.05
260.04   262.17   270.20
274.29   275.04   275.06
275.07   275.11   278.19
281.21   281.22   285.21
287.28   288.17   288.19
292.21   294.25   298.19
320.19   321.10   323.01
323.30   328.08   337.18
337.26   339.03   353.10
353.16   353.19   357.21
358.30   360.10   362.07
363.18   370.19   374.15
376.16   383.10   385.24
388.18   392.22   393.20
396.01   398.10   400.06
401.24   407.07   410.30
412.27   416.06   416.12
417.30   419.07   419.15
419.16   419.19   419.22
421.14   421.19   423.05
423.10   423.24   426.28
437.18   439.03   443.01
448.10   450.14   455.15
463.14   463.28   466.12
467.10   469.01   471.05
479.30   481.01   488.02
488.05   489.25   490.26
498.14   499.10   500.29
502.08   509.06   511.22
511.24   515.25
LASTED   58.21   139.27
159.07
LASTING   214.08
LASTS   494.11
LATE   7.11   75.14
82.08   91.13   99.09
141.15   188.17   201.28
248.01   252.07   281.01
306.18   306.24   309.21
319.25   349.20   353.18
353.20   402.05   516.19
LATELY   182.04   196.21
350.13   398.06   465.19
LATER   2.18   38.21
251.05   267.14   279.05
307.29   309.03   342.30
350.07   363.04   416.14
436.20   437.12   453.10
464.09   489.05   501.27
507.10
LATEST   499.19
LATITUDE   213.16
LATITUDES   71.27
LATTER   351.30   436.01
LATTER-DAY   436.01
LAUGH   79.15   83.26
92.21   97.02   114.27
121.03   130.20   183.24
183.28   189.16   203.24
218.04   231.22   238.01
264.10   303.23   306.19
328.02   361.17   370.30
378.30   484.25   511.18
LAUGHABLE   293.11
LAUGHED   88.13   96.28
140.21   142.23   146.26
201.19   254.22   260.24
301.21   362.06   365.27
403.01
LAUGHING   128.06   235.08
235.16   235.16   235.28
402.22   405.13   511.21

LAUGHTER 120.24 328.12
364.19 485.02
LAUNCH 44.18
LAUNCHED 156.10
LAUT 441.02
LAW 66.04 83.11
96.09 146.28 185.01
211.30 298.11 394.22
394.23 410.17
LAWLESS 435.08
LAWS 419.08
LAY 12.02 15.09
23.07 71.02 75.24
101.25 185.18 200.07
239.20 251.13 255.03
312.26 314.19 325.16
328.24 332.07 336.11
349.19 359.03 360.24
412.24 414.17 445.20
452.10 455.06 466.13
476.01 484.11 490.18
490.27 493.30 498.04
499.16 501.05 502.27
LAYING 4.08 59.24
416.18 418.01
LAZILY 343.13 459.23
LE 178.20
LEAD 34.24 128.24
153.02 211.27 236.24
288.05 322.19 390.22
408.13 421.02 466.09
486.18
LEADER 16.16 322.20
322.20 458.17
LEADING 220.30 250.22
256.12 333.21 396.14
429.06 516.17
LEAF 2.06 226.03
256.21 329.01 343.11
LEAK 502.03
LEAN 14.28 16.07
27.15 59.03 350.02
410.18 511.25
LEANED 6.30 104.21
109.12 139.10 201.21
220.26 258.22 287.20
366.17 394.04 405.26
508.08 509.20
LEANING 21.14 195.22
207.21 269.18 291.15
364.01 408.04 410.27
431.06 489.09 506.07
510.14
LEAP 58.25 69.21
102.09 128.30 142.17
212.13 309.02 309.04
470.09 470.09
LEAPED 5.21 83.25
108.27 216.21 221.01
261.04 263.08 300.23
309.01 309.14 365.20
439.18 466.12 503.16
LEAPING 7.07 7.13
300.21
LEAPS 409.16
LEARN 164.01 427.18
LEARNED 4.19 53.05
58.16 246.19 247.08
247.19 258.29 264.18
285.16 307.29 322.25
348.14 434.02
LEARNEDLY 266.09
LEAST 53.13 53.26
53.26 53.27 65.18
86.08 97.20 98.07
111.14 118.08 119.18
123.19 125.04 142.29
142.29 146.29 152.30
165.18 180.02 196.24
209.20 213.20 219.01
255.05 275.09 290.24
308.25 351.17 370.17
381.11 381.18 385.16
470.29
LEATHER 192.02 254.13
290.22
LEATHERY 43.25 459.26
LEAVE 3.09 51.19
82.27 118.28 119.02
126.21 150.12 169.20

LEAVE (CONT.) 182.25
189.06 244.26 245.05
303.19 303.20 303.25
308.10 309.06 320.09
328.19 338.02 357.20
381.23 382.18 383.29
383.30 385.06 385.25
387.01 395.08 410.25
429.15 430.12 468.10
468.11 473.29 480.19
508.11 511.11 511.13
516.20 516.21
LEAVE-TAKINGS 320.09
LEAVED 94.11
LEAVES 4.06 271.22
317.01 339.29 434.05
496.09 509.10
LEAVING 69.30 74.04
90.13 229.14 254.09
276.11 290.15 303.18
348.02 360.21 407.19
413.11 419.22 427.15
431.27 451.22 481.30
483.26 507.23
LECTED 145.01
LECTURE 44.05 307.04
LED 13.18 14.05
67.04 114.20 205.20
246.10 263.04 274.14
331.22 336.20 353.27
355.06 498.24 500.01
LEDGE 16.24
LEERED 62.30 205.07
343.28
LEERY 475.22
LEERY-EYED 475.22
LEEWARD 166.09 294.23
LEFT 4.12 7.26
12.14 16.01 17.16
19.17 24.08 33.18
33.23 34.20 34.26
40.03 41.24 51.15
56.25 70.20 72.25
73.06 74.01 75.26
76.03 91.13 122.04
134.30 140.12 141.20
142.08 163.08 173.09
173.19 175.01 175.03
182.23 184.24 199.10
208.21 211.29 218.28
226.21 234.02 234.15
238.26 241.20 251.27
252.07 254.14 255.15
256.14 267.04 269.05
270.15 277.13 278.02
300.19 300.20 308.05
313.15 318.24 339.28
351.23 354.04 356.29
366.03 373.19 375.12
392.22 395.20 398.16
401.21 401.26 415.17
426.19 430.01 436.30
439.02 439.16 451.11
462.19 464.02 466.02
472.12 478.20 479.17
483.29 488.06 489.30
491.13 496.06 513.29
514.06 515.10 515.16
LEG 8.08 8.12
8.13 8.16 12.18
108.14 221.03 250.21
256.02 309.30 414.03
464.08 480.03
LEGAL 50.07 347.05
LEGEND 213.03 327.01
LEGGED 22.25 301.15
378.04
LEGGINGS 471.01
LEGION 58.24
LEGITIMATE 77.01
LEGS 8.05 21.01
26.21 49.07 63.08
70.11 73.04 83.23
99.24 105.04 108.05
110.01 132.11 132.18
152.06 159.13 176.01
181.29 196.05 230.30
253.25 256.24 258.17
258.21 311.26 351.05
360.24 372.21 383.23

LEGS (CONT.) 394.01
426.21 427.01
LEISURE 38.04 100.12
126.09
LEISURELY 22.19
206.04 397.03 459.19
LEMON 292.05
LEMON-PEEL 292.05
LEND 110.11 246.21
LENDER 83.08
LENDS 330.15
LENGTH 14.20 30.28
31.09 33.23 38.23
120.27 167.28 175.19
198.16 239.02 243.19
246.24 281.02 312.26
313.14 336.15 365.17
403.24 410.28 433.02
449.08 479.30
LENGTHS 245.23
LENIENT 180.08
LENT 280.08
LES 169.28 177.16
LESS 15.08 31.02
53.16 56.19 67.24
69.02 69.30 115.04
130.11 146.14 148.25
182.12 196.28 205.24
209.27 215.08 228.11
229.29 268.22 270.21
277.15 296.02 345.19
396.26 399.28 411.28
413.08 439.30 441.22
442.17 454.06
LESSLY 37.01
LESSON 384.04 458.05
501.19
LESSONS 186.10
LEST 114.27 129.07
229.17 271.21 404.05
LET 6.29 8.04
25.15 26.22 27.30
30.10 41.12 42.17
45.06 45.10 49.18
51.18 62.26 63.08
64.19 79.16 85.29
89.22 91.06 95.24
103.15 108.18 108.26
113.14 128.16 128.17
131.22 131.22 131.22
133.12 138.21 152.04
152.07 152.14 178.25
191.04 196.02 198.30
199.05 202.28 203.20
219.17 220.01 223.06
228.28 231.29 235.11
245.19 255.24 256.17
264.28 265.01 267.24
269.05 274.01 290.01
293.15 314.06 324.27
340.20 344.11 355.14
360.16 361.23 368.06
369.17 369.25 371.24
376.17 377.30 385.30
385.30 385.30 399.28
400.14 409.13 435.12
438.26 439.26 457.16
464.23 466.17 471.25
471.26 472.14 473.24
475.23 478.12 480.20
483.03 485.01 485.03
486.12 486.15 487.03
487.12 491.20 492.14
498.06 500.18 502.11
509.30 513.11
LET'S 72.01 234.15
358.17 395.07
LETS 40.11 78.23
LETTER 73.30 185.27
190.07 210.01 223.24
227.15 229.01 229.10
229.24 285.05 319.14
417.29 417.30 418.08
421.10 421.10 421.11
421.19 422.20 434.26
LETTERS 73.20 208.25
210.22 232.19 248.24
441.27 448.16
LETTING 22.13 58.22
183.02 413.01 426.06

LETTING (CONT.) 426.09
LEVEL 19.09 22.29
30.20 41.16 170.20
259.11 323.04 324.13
397.06 444.02
LEVUKA 455.02
LEVYING 277.07
LIABLE 12.08
246.21
LIAR 361.25 377.23
LIBERATED 387.28
420.17
LIBERTIES 471.20
LIBERTY 59.01 98.17
356.17 442.03 442.04
LICKED 442.06
LICKING 187.13
LID 259.30 299.25
LIE 50.10 61.03
157.26 157.28 160.03
162.08 165.15 229.23
237.29 277.13 328.05
346.09 390.24 393.19
440.29
LIED 165.16 395.07
474.25 474.25
LIES 57.04 98.24
181.09 347.10 487.15
LIEUTENANT 167.23
175.10 177.17 184.23
241.29 242.30 243.04
LIFE 5.06 5.09
10.12 11.18 23.06
23.14 26.08 29.01
29.12 41.26 43.09
44.03 48.18 51.16
53.13 58.26 67.20
69.07 69.24 73.14
74.07 76.30 81.09
84.19 85.03 104.04
105.08 112.03 113.03
114.24 116.19 118.07
120.20 120.24 124.14
126.17 127.26 128.08
128.25 132.02 139.21
143.05 143.20 149.30
150.23 156.20 157.08
158.03 158.11 159.23
150.17 168.13 173.21
174.11 174.14 180.26
180.28 182.02 183.13
183.17 184.01 191.10
195.30 197.29 212.02
214.05 214.06 215.12
215.15 220.23 225.15
236.26 237.29 239.04
244.01 246.10 247.01
247.06 247.21 252.03
256.06 257.24 262.06
263.30 264.21 272.03
272.05 273.10 274.04
275.20 278.07 278.21
280.30 283.03 285.23
286.12 299.15 299.19
301.06 304.13 304.13
313.19 319.25 326.03
329.03 329.29 331.23
333.16 336.21 340.11
341.01 344.20 349.19
351.22 355.06 356.25
357.19 358.20 366.28
372.21 375.06 383.25
384.05 401.13 403.25
404.19 407.08 407.15
409.09 418.17 422.02
422.08 426.30 429.05
429.05 430.13 434.07
435.08 438.14 442.03
452.24 462.02 469.17
470.09 470.10 471.04
471.16 472.06 474.11
475.21 479.07 479.07
479.13 479.21 480.05
481.27 482.10 486.05
488.02 488.28 502.28
507.18 508.13 516.18
LIFE-BOATS 124.14
LIFE-BUOY 158.11
LIFE'S 218.17 384.27
LIFELESS 17.18 247.16
252.29 302.25 459.12

LIFETIME 50.12

LIFT 45.13 95.18
216.13 386.02 494.11
514.05

LIFT' 122.10

LIFTED 7.07 29.22
54.17 99.26 102.27
109.27 128.20 131.18
141.24 163.29 199.03
203.03 204.14 224.01
259.04 264.30 384.11
384.12 384.21 405.23
408.29 480.20

LIFTING 48.07 115.11
171.08 171.26 202.03
349.22 473.04 481.12
483.08 498.10 514.10
515.11

LIGHT 4.15 5.09
10.18 17.22 20.20
22.11 22.27 26.14
33.05 33.08 39.01
57.20 77.19 82.29
100.20 101.28 102.18
108.08 108.25 112.19
112.22 114.26 126.01
135.03 136.21 140.19
143.06 149.18 152.30
152.30 155.09 155.22
159.29 165.17 165.22
187.06 198.15 211.15
212.28 214.04 216.20
224.08 225.22 226.26
246.07 248.22 260.04
261.09 261.20 262.04
262.15 264.04 264.13
266.11 267.19 267.19
269.22 275.20 295.25
302.01 312.27 319.10
319.18 324.14 325.14
325.17 326.05 350.30
365.24 367.14 368.17
368.24 368.25 368.27
370.05 373.13 373.18
376.22 382.15 384.07
384.26 384.30 386.28
397.08 407.09 407.14
409.01 415.17 417.11
433.27 459.17 488.06
489.16 494.01 505.27
514.03 515.08

LIGHT-HEADED 57.20
LIGHT-HEARTED 384.26
LIGHTED 13.08 140.20
216.10 248.15 324.04
341.16 444.26 463.24
457.22

LIGHTHOUSE 17.01
416.22 434.29

LIGHTHOUSE-KEEPER
434.29

LIGHTING 266.04

LIGHTLY 110.06 170.04
189.01 303.12 331.28
359.27 366.10 369.22
405.19 409.29 432.07

LIGHTNESS 364.15
434.05

LIGHTNING 123.10
144.20 217.30 439.18

LIGHTS 41.20 94.16
137.13 140.09 140.10
146.05 146.19 164.22
164.22 165.06 166.08
263.06 395.23 445.24
445.25 445.27 467.20

LIKE 2.02 2.08
2.16 2.16 4.30
5.01 5.29 7.28
8.14 13.09 13.26
14.28 15.18 15.19
15.20 17.17 18.11
19.06 19.08 20.01
21.07 23.07 23.10
24.17 25.16 26.06
26.14 27.01 27.05
27.16 28.16 28.19
29.19 29.30 30.07
32.22 34.24 35.10
35.24 36.03 36.18

LIKE (CONT.) 36.21
37.21 38.11 38.11
40.07 41.26 45.09
46.01 47.17 48.11
49.08 49.13 50.01
51.01 51.12 51.15
52.27 55.07 55.15
56.09 58.28 59.01
59.05 59.05 59.18
59.26 59.27 60.09
61.18 61.24 62.07
62.10 62.28 63.09
64.02 64.11 67.27
70.17 70.23 70.44
72.29 73.11 73.27
74.11 75.12 75.25
78.14 81.04 84.17
84.24 89.03 89.25
91.06 93.05 93.09
94.15 94.17 97.18
97.19 99.11 100.29
101.07 101.15 102.25
103.14 107.04 108.15
110.04 110.24 110.25
111.13 112.20 113.15
115.29 116.18 120.16
120.25 121.02 121.03
123.04 123.11 124.03
125.03 125.08 126.13
126.21 127.06 128.02
129.12 131.06 132.07
134.04 134.23 135.03
135.05 136.09 136.15
136.22 138.29 139.17
140.17 140.20 140.22
140.24 142.27 143.08
144.20 144.24 145.14
146.22 149.22 149.25
150.26 151.09 151.27
153.30 155.13 155.16
155.17 157.17 157.23
157.25 159.11 162.06
163.02 163.09 165.17
168.18 169.17 170.08
170.20 179.09 180.16
180.19 181.07 182.26
183.06 183.09 183.26
184.14 185.08 187.21
189.02 191.26 192.08
194.02 194.22 194.23
198.20 203.01 205.12
208.17 209.02 211.17
211.27 217.07 219.28
220.07 223.09 224.15
225.17 225.22 226.05
227.21 227.22 231.28
232.11 233.05 234.12
235.20 236.03 236.07
236.24 236.25 236.27
237.09 237.26 238.25
242.01 243.10 245.05
246.14 246.28 248.17
249.12 253.10 255.04
255.30 256.06 256.21
260.26 261.11 262.23
264.07 265.09 267.29
269.13 270.18 270.26
271.02 271.12 272.23
276.18 279.12 280.02
280.12 283.08 283.19
286.04 286.08 286.25
287.11 288.02 289.09
294.14 295.08 297.04
297.10 299.15 302.05
301.29 301.30 302.05
302.23 302.27 304.29
306.15 307.17 309.09
309.19 310.20 310.29
311.13 313.08 314.19
316.27 318.11 318.15
319.04 319.13 319.19
319.21 320.14 321.26
321.29 322.04 322.22
324.08 324.09 324.18
324.30 325.12 325.14
325.25 326.04 327.07
328.05 329.01 330.20
331.29 332.16 332.20
333.02 337.13 338.10
339.19 341.03 342.12

LIKE (CONT.) 342.28
344.07 345.12 348.17
348.26 348.27 349.15
349.18 350.06 352.07
357.14 360.11 361.08
362.20 362.20 365.07
366.12 367.23 369.30
375.07 376.29 377.03
377.17 380.14 380.18
383.16 384.27 385.14
385.19 387.13 387.16
387.21 390.12 390.22
392.13 393.07 393.12
396.01 396.06 397.03
397.07 397.18 397.20
398.11 398.25 401.18
402.07 403.05 405.07
405.24 405.24 407.05
409.14 409.27 412.24
416.11 416.24 417.04
417.11 418.04 418.19
425.21 426.04 426.06
427.06 429.01 429.15
430.06 430.18 433.13
433.14 434.28 436.01
436.03 439.11 450.13
456.02 457.07 457.19
460.27 462.17 463.24
464.15 464.20 468.06
468.12 468.18 468.19
468.19 470.24 471.28
472.07 473.10 475.24
475.26 479.04 479.28
482.07 483.25 492.07
494.19 495.05 495.18
495.24 496.01 497.19
499.29 500.18 500.27
501.22 502.26 505.24
508.16 509.15 509.21
511.18 512.02 514.22
515.02 515.26 516.06
516.12

LIKED 4.20 50.20
68.09 147.20 151.24
152.02 202.11 211.22
231.17 231.19 254.23

LIKELIHOOD 86.21

LIKELY 29.20 33.17
188.29 189.10 198.09
214.23 242.12 308.27
360.15 385.05 435.20
492.01

LIKES 269.06
LIKEWISE 394.22
LIKING 227.17 314.21
318.14 390.19 397.04

LIMB 20.24 24.04
149.15 172.13 292.28

LIMBED 47.10
LIMBS 104.05 162.08
312.25 409.15 460.08

LIMIT 411.27
LIMITS 411.08
LINE 5.12 22.02
23.03 23.25 29.02
43.12 52.21 62.23
67.17 78.24 93.14
97.30 110.26 149.15
183.23 196.07 229.13
240.01 302.22 323.15
324.11 352.06 421.02
424.12 444.27 457.10
462.30

LINED 123.05 199.15
319.29 421.29

LINEN 113.11 113.20
LINES 347.15 378.21
418.03 462.26

LING 64.01
LINGER 434.08
LINGERED 220.10
LINGERING 341.04
388.04

LINK 322.23 373.07
LINKS 22.14
LION 45.22
LIP 37.29 81.10
196.15 203.25 224.20
514.14 514.14

LIPPED 318.10

LIPS 37.04 39.08
54.21 84.29 89.11
93.04 103.22 138.29
144.17 151.04 151.08
163.04 167.10 170.18
171.24 176.23 179.22
195.14 197.30 198.29
213.21 233.08 261.13
272.18 284.04 292.07
294.19 314.24 325.08
329.10 335.18 339.23
343.09 348.12 380.09
381.17 433.10 460.22
465.24 466.20 470.14
496.03 504.17 515.18

LIQUEUR 139.12 141.06
LIQUEUR-GLASS 141.06
LIQUEUR-GLASSES 139.12
LIQUID 29.13 168.16
LIQUIDATED 209.28
LIQUOR 28.10 29.12
LIQUORS 240.25
LISTEN 45.01 45.03
102.28 134.26 155.12
348.11 452.21 467.25
479.05 505.14

LISTENED 44.23 94.20
132.24 164.09 167.16
176.16 322.29 337.24
359.27 363.02 392.12
410.29 449.22 455.16
467.17 499.10

LISTENER 38.29
LISTENERS 364.07
416.12 494.25

LISTENING 75.20
225.26 235.10 263.15
328.15 359.06 376.25
414.29 431.01 459.01
466.20 485.29

LIT 209.15 248.03
263.03 485.14 490.15

LITERALLY 85.03
131.28

LITERATURE 4.16
5.09

LITHOGRAPH 192.08
LITTER 58.19 353.23
370.03 468.24

LITTLE 4.05 4.19
5.03 8.10 12.25
16.09 24.03 27.01
29.23 34.13 41.23
43.24 43.34 44.26
44.26 45.04 46.22
46.23 47.13 49.02
49.10 51.09 52.08
52.10 53.03 53.05
53.11 53.18 55.01
55.10 55.29 56.09
56.23 57.04 57.19
58.26 60.01 71.28
74.22 75.12 83.26
85.01 85.28 88.04
89.11 90.26 93.05
94.10 95.05 97.21
99.04 104.19 104.21
109.06 109.28 110.02
114.15 115.11 122.14
125.03 125.29 127.09
128.22 128.29 133.08
133.13 142.02 142.10
142.27 142.29 145.07
158.19 159.18 161.02
164.10 166.05 166.29
170.28 171.08 171.15
171.24 173.09 175.17
175.21 176.01 180.07
182.14 190.01 190.19
196.06 199.05 199.22
200.15 206.01 207.05
208.04 215.27 217.18
218.04 222.23 223.30
227.06 228.16 229.15
229.28 230.01 231.24
232.07 232.25 235.24
238.12 245.08 249.03
252.03 253.15 254.09
254.23 255.04 255.07
255.10 259.01 259.13

LITTLE (CONT.) 259.22
270.12 272.09 272.10
274.11 279.05 282.07
286.29 287.15 287.29
292.03 292.06 296.04
297.15 304.22 307.24
311.03 313.19 313.20
319.18 323.25 324.15
328.02 328.17 330.13
330.13 331.05 332.16
332.27 334.07 337.09
338.01 338.12 340.19
342.26 343.02 344.28
345.23 347.19 348.10
355.10 358.16 359.23
362.04 362.23 364.18
367.17 368.24 371.04
371.13 372.02 373.04
375.18 382.16 382.16
384.15 388.09 394.02
395.10 396.14 399.02
399.02 400.16 401.29
403.04 403.05 403.05
404.11 404.24 405.09
406.07 406.07 407.20
411.02 412.21 420.19
422.01 424.05 424.06
424.06 427.06 432.22
434.23 438.04 438.26
440.26 441.02 443.19
444.18 445.14 448.07
449.22 451.25 464.15
466.18 468.12 468.13
471.08 473.23 482.03
490.17 490.19 493.02
497.17 498.11 498.18
502.16 504.05 509.20
509.21 515.05
LIVE 4.04 5.08
13.21 43.39 51.11
53.06 69.26 143.13
160.14 163.06 163.24
167.29 178.26 202.11
215.04 223.02 227.13
259.12 290.05 302.05
354.04 357.30 361.11
375.22 398.17 414.04
474.28 477.18 505.23
LIVED 11.22 17.29
38.15 144.19 188.02
227.10 239.12 252.15
261.19 275.23 295.07
348.18 392.17 456.03
474.06 481.25 495.17
502.06 506.22
LIVELY 146.16 283.14
292.04
LIVER 67.08 165.19
LIVERPOOL 183.22
LIVERY 248.05
LIVES 12.25 13.19
14.06 29.29 68.04
95.15 138.27 147.02
175.08 195.06 273.05
273.25 275.01 277.12
291.25 331.17 341.28
376.13 389.28 392.02
408.08 414.28 418.27
419.01 473.16 474.03
485.25 486.13 507.07
507.18
LIVID 123.11 476.05
LIVING 1.12 4.13
43.10 72.18 99.13
121.14 133.21 176.07
277.15 287.28 287.28
302.27 330.10 370.18
391.04 397.26 398.08
426.26 450.01 452.09
465.02 473.10 478.20
483.29 486.05 516.02
LOAD 226.04 242.11
281.23 497.05
LOADED 16.19 182.05
200.08 244.24 301.01
365.22 401.09
LOADERS 480.27
LOADING 43.18 254.20
LOAFER 42.20 243.22
273.17 475.22

LOAFING 426.25
LOAN 185.22 185.22
273.20
LOATHED 126.30
LOATHSOME 277.02
352.17
LOATHSOMENESS 352.17
LOCAL 14.27
LOCALITIES 455.12
LOCALITY 27.22 343.06
LOCATE 461.02
LOCK 58.12 233.04
259.30 338.15
LOCKED 133.12 136.01
438.19
LOCKS 263.16 279.09
324.18
LODGED 466.06
LODGING 164.14
LODGMENT 443.09
LOF' 257.14
LOFTY 32.10 186.15
246.12 264.03 279.01
408.20 416.19 498.12
LOG 21.16 71.24
71.29 72.02 72.23
73.06 204.08 300.02
314.19 323.28 469.23
470.03
LOGGED 33.14
LOGIC 65.01 90.17
423.14 423.25
LOGS 240.18 448.19
478.29
LOINS 371.14
LOLLING 101.10 495.19
LONDON 249.12
LONE 20.30 92.08
LONELINESS 208.13
219.09 335.01 369.11
488.07 507.06 508.01
LONELY 5.12 18.07
53.16 149.29 192.06
211.17 271.06 271.23
280.17 339.22 341.28
375.09 384.14 435.18
LONG 2.14 16.09
20.16 27.16 28.07
37.18 38.15 43.21
45.24 46.24 48.20
52.18 53.15 54.10
57.22 58.06 61.14
62.13 63.24 64.10
73.17 75.10 78.08
94.13 99.07 105.04
107.01 107.05 107.16
123.24 128.12 140.14
140.17 146.07 148.16
153.07 162.16 164.18
167.22 184.26 184.28
185.03 191.10 193.06
193.06 194.21 196.04
202.07 206.06 207.14
218.17 220.10 228.22
238.02 246.08 246.22
249.02 255.16 256.28
257.07 258.16 259.04
263.16 281.04 286.26
290.05 293.16 293.20
297.14 300.07 301.15
309.09 311.28 312.06
314.20 315.07 323.13
330.10 330.12 330.12
331.11 335.08 344.26
351.25 354.07 356.21
364.01 367.10 373.16
374.09 374.11 379.30
392.17 394.05 398.04
398.25 401.01 401.22
403.18 407.06 415.05
421.19 426.18 430.03
432.03 433.27 434.08
438.24 439.21 441.23
442.21 443.13 444.03
444.16 444.17 445.20
445.28 448.26 454.27
455.30 460.17 461.24
463.18 465.21 466.25
470.23 481.13 482.28
485.15 494.02 495.01

LONG (CONT.) 495.18
495.20 496.05 498.21
501.27 505.23 506.20
508.12 509.02 510.08
513.20
LONG-BOAT 442.21
443.13 444.15 445.20
494.02 495.01 496.05
501.27
LONG-DRAWN 293.20
LONG-LEGGED 301.15
LONG-STEMMED 257.07
LONGED 59.12 200.22
300.12 312.18
LONGER 38.18 60.29
118.01 123.19 127.27
158.06 170.02 211.24
226.23 260.11 274.03
357.22 398.09 423.05
452.03 488.04
LONGEST 350.20
LONGICORNS 247.10
LONGING 11.12
LONGINGS 215.24
LONGISH 243.28
LOOK 13.14 15.15
16.14 41.10 42.17
45.09 45.10 46.20
47.10 47.16 50.17
50.28 56.23 57.25
61.07 61.09 61.30
62.06 62.12 70.20
74.27 81.28 82.19
83.26 85.24 94.07
100.01 100.18 100.29
105.19 111.01 111.22
112.15 122.21 122.21
125.15 126.05 126.09
127.01 132.21 137.12
142.06 142.24 145.30
152.22 152.27 167.14
169.21 178.05 188.20
195.28 197.16 199.26
200.10 200.11 203.09
208.15 215.14 223.24
237.23 238.11 245.05
250.23 253.02 253.02
254.01 255.23 256.04
259.08 271.16 271.18
279.25 286.14 303.04
318.04 338.02 339.11
341.12 343.29 344.12
348.06 351.27 353.13
367.30 369.16 377.11
384.03 384.04 385.02
399.10 401.03 402.08
404.04 412.11 412.18
414.14 419.15 420.03
420.29 426.24 427.12
429.23 433.20 434.07
446.04 459.30 461.13
464.13 464.13 467.30
469.07 469.07 470.24
473.04 477.02 478.27
498.13 512.23 512.25
513.19
LOOK-OUT 105.19 498.13
LOOKED 4.25 7.13
13.03 30.21 33.04
37.29 38.19 46.26
47.08 49.28 53.23
56.02 59.04 63.10
69.10 71.06 75.07
78.15 83.18 85.09
85.18 85.19 89.05
89.16 90.08 90.30
95.20 96.21 97.11
98.02 110.03 118.02
118.14 119.22 122.22
129.04 132.28 134.13
134.24 141.09 141.14
149.08 151.03 153.19
154.13 157.13 160.07
163.04 168.18 170.01
181.22 192.02 193.18
195.10 195.29 197.09
201.19 204.15 205.01
216.19 218.16 218.24
220.04 220.08 222.12
225.05 230.22 231.05

LOOKED (CONT.) 233.03
234.20 245.29 246.14
252.24 256.05 257.09
262.21 267.25 283.02
287.11 302.11 304.11
306.15 308.03 318.04
319.26 328.10 329.07
331.13 371.07 394.09
396.30 398.15 399.15
409.17 414.11 416.17
421.17 428.10 429.18
430.07 430.20 452.27
459.03 469.14 469.16
471.19 477.10 481.26
485.29 500.14 505.20
506.02 507.13 510.15
512.18 514.06 514.10
LOOKING 25.11 32.12
33.21 43.28 47.12
48.08 54.29 56.25
60.13 65.10 71.13
87.28 88.22 92.06
93.12 101.16 102.22
103.16 117.13 120.19
123.16 134.18 156.11
158.30 169.03 172.23
176.16 183.09 186.27
188.06 192.08 192.25
196.12 196.20 200.21
208.01 223.14 225.11
226.17 229.24 229.30
244.02 247.11 253.01
258.11 261.26 263.22
268.15 290.12 291.13
299.30 307.23 339.23
363.09 372.24 375.30
377.29 382.14 386.06
410.30 412.30 416.21
430.11 431.09 433.23
450.12 459.10 463.12
468.21 479.19 483.11
490.27 492.13 496.07
502.19 504.04 506.06
508.24 509.03 509.21
510.17 515.08
LOOKS 14.14 38.05
51.19 53.19 71.14
71.25 125.08 134.23
204.12 237.13 243.30
269.13 281.06 330.08
475.24 515.02
LOOM 445.30 467.22
LOOMED 135.05 225.21
261.09 274.27 441.14
494.09 500.10
LOOMS 463.03
LOOPED 234.11
LOOPHOLE 454.05
LOOSE 16.11 25.15
28.02 81.01 116.29
129.21 197.23 246.19
292.01 293.15 324.27
412.03 417.27 423.15
433.26 459.22 478.13
LOOSE-JOINTED 246.19
459.22
LOOSENED 93.06
LOOSENS 40.19
LOOT 455.10 492.11
495.05
LOQUACIOUS 434.19
LORD 3.27 73.10
197.26 198.21 237.26
333.02 349.11 350.12
414.28 455.22 480.11
482.15 498.25 513.04
LORD'S 298.03 410.15
509.18
LOSE 90.12 190.09
243.26 287.07 372.09
375.10 484.09 485.25
LOSER 301.25
LOSING 72.05 106.06
219.04 219.15 385.22
402.24 440.04
LOSS 60.19 84.23
124.19 251.28 416.05
LOSSES 421.24 485.28
485.28
LOST 24.28 38.12

LOST (CONT.) 100.12
106.14 112.24 126.29
132.05 153.11 157.15
165.06 166.12 187.19
196.07 198.30 221.07
244.17 251.23 256.11
265.02 298.21 299.09
330.19 330.24 378.28
385.10 386.24 398.14
399.03 415.05 415.18
427.08 429.07 433.07
436.25 436.30 485.25
507.04 510.20 511.03
LOT 2.24 43.05
67.26 73.22 80.28
83.28 113.23 118.23
119.11 124.26 125.05
131.24 173.08 240.27
245.30 266.05 300.26
321.14 323.22 324.28
330.24 334.06 353.25
360.01 410.26 443.22
475.14 480.28
LOTH 70.29
LOTS 8.20 277.25
324.23 401.05
LOUD 1.06 22.01
32.17 145.04 264.10
282.20 330.17 365.09
395.23 406.05 446.08
466.22 485.06 489.19
490.09 511.18
LOUDER 164.19 288.08
393.05
LOUDLY 364.07 471.07
LOUNGE 14.16 357.01
LOUNGED 12.26 499.19
LOVE 10.09 20.02
24.23 68.26 147.10
183.18 264.23 271.05
271.18 275.07 276.01
276.19 304.09 305.07
322.22 339.06 339.10
341.09 345.30 352.15
352.17 367.19 368.07
374.29 375.17 387.07
405.21 418.13 422.19
470.11 474.22 482.13
486.05 514.29 516.01
LOVE' 257.14
LOVED 11.13 14.02
23.13 68.28 184.12
213.02 302.30 349.03
400.22 429.09 486.04
488.08 506.26
LOVELY 200.30 367.20
LOVER 213.09 379.11
LOVERS 214.11
LOW 18.02 19.05
19.16 22.24 27.03
27.05 34.30 77.07
84.12 104.24 113.29
122.08 125.09 132.17
146.04 148.22 149.04
151.17 158.01 162.22
166.03 188.28 210.25
234.11 248.07 289.22
297.06 300.21 303.15
307.19 312.03 320.11
337.17 364.07 365.26
369.30 371.09 373.13
405.03 408.24 409.24
412.23 417.21 444.15
445.01 445.13 457.18
459.08 493.02 493.30
494.04 494.08 494.18
497.13 501.02 501.02
LOWER 5.07 6.27
7.29 8.27 101.12
149.15 177.04 264.11
387.18 448.03
LOWERED 34.04 55.02
163.01 257.06 259.30
272.18 293.22 396.16
LOWERING 85.08 158.20
514.21
LOWLANDS 432.01
LUCID 11.26 374.21
LUCK 7.15 14.10

LUCK (CONT.) 98.06
189.05 207.03 238.07
288.17 295.16 320.18
320.18 329.26 375.14
394.23 414.30 414.30
415.01 415.03 436.29
438.07 442.14 458.21
473.26 474.16 478.08
479.09
LUCKILY 170.19
LUCKY 67.23 242.08
249.28 353.04 447.23
LUGGAGE 16.19 92.15
LUGUBRIOUS 44.25
LUMINOUS 17.15 18.09
496.06
LUMP 34.24 55.18
208.17 445.21 476.04
LUMPILY 199.19
LUMPS 339.26 390.22
397.19
LUNATIC 141.19 201.04
236.12 292.15
LUNGS 24.26 150.11
409.03
LURCH 183.15 473.29
LURCHED 137.14
LURED 155.08
LURID 63.19 370.01
474.26
LURKED 59.07
LURKS 24.23 112.16
147.23
LUST 458.06
LUSTRE 25.02
LUSTRELESS 148.30
469.09
LUSTROUS 149.01
LUSTY 20.13
LUXURIATING 434.07
445.08
LYING 166.01 200.30
255.29 279.15 291.04
300.02 313.03 329.07
343.09 358.10 359.15
411.03 433.18 438.03
444.02 446.03 448.01
462.19 465.15 466.08
479.04 492.06 498.25
509.19
M 71.09 185.28
M' 281.03 304.05
324.21
MA 173.22 178.14
MACASSAR 440.23
MACHINE 55.01 193.29
MACHINERY 229.30
MACHINES 193.30
MAD 47.29 76.13
77.09 77.10 122.19
128.02 142.22 153.09
153.14 201.14 204.20
238.01 253.15 286.29
309.24 325.01 344.23
388.25 430.23 474.22
488.16 511.10 515.05
MADAGASCAR 207.05
441.19 480.29
MADDENED 124.02 124.09
MADE 1.05 4.01
6.12 6.21 10.04
11.01 14.09 20.27
21.09 22.20 23.18
26.04 26.07 26.08
29.12 30.10 32.24
33.01 35.20 36.09
36.15 36.28 45.08
46.22 49.19 53.27
53.29 56.15 58.25
60.08 61.02 61.05
63.19 67.20 70.32
71.14 74.10 74.12
74.19 74.27 80.09
80.16 82.29 84.01
87.06 87.07 87.16
89.24 96.05 96.29
98.18 99.16 101.16
102.25 104.25 108.25
108.30 112.13 112.15
114.28 118.25 124.10

MADE (CONT.) 128.14
134.11 137.03 139.02
139.16 142.14 142.22
147.05 147.13 152.20
157.25 158.19 160.05
160.12 162.19 164.14
168.07 171.13 171.24
172.01 172.14 173.06
176.11 177.12 177.18
178.09 179.12 181.10
181.13 183.20 183.24
190.19 192.28 195.16
195.25 197.03 197.13
197.16 198.28 205.09
206.03 207.18 207.20
208.02 208.30 211.27
212.29 212.30 214.21
215.19 216.13 217.13
220.12 227.14 229.09
230.23 231.19 235.04
235.12 237.23 237.30
239.08 241.04 243.05
243.18 244.21 244.30
245.24 246.21 249.25
251.28 256.24 256.22
259.08 264.11 265.04
270.01 272.14 273.09
277.01 277.04 277.05
277.05 278.16 283.22
290.18 291.27 292.18
292.21 292.24 293.16
293.19 295.05 298.01
300.09 304.04 304.10
304.10 304.16 306.07
307.22 309.27 312.20
314.15 318.12 322.28
324.02 332.25 333.06
333.22 334.06 339.27
344.09 347.02 348.23
351.07 353.04 353.09
353.11 353.20 354.06
354.09 355.02 358.05
360.22 363.04 364.13
365.29 367.14 369.16
372.22 373.24 374.08
375.02 375.05 376.08
377.09 377.13 380.08
381.08 381.16 382.07
382.10 384.10 387.08
388.01 388.07 389.28
397.05 400.03 400.05
403.13 404.22 411.08
413.16 416.08 417.12
420.01 430.02 430.16
431.16 431.24 434.18
437.06 437.28 438.05
439.09 442.09 442.13
444.06 445.05 445.22
448.26 451.09 451.14
452.15 452.20 455.11
455.29 460.01 471.09
471.11 477.14 478.14
478.28 479.16 483.22
485.08 485.24 486.16
487.17 488.16 490.29
491.06 492.16 493.01
493.04 497.20 498.25
502.17 502.22 502.25
504.11 505.27 506.27
507.09 510.25 511.04
514.22 515.03
MADLY 312.13 484.26
504.01
MADMAN 291.26
MADNESS 117.08 147.04
148.15 153.15 425.16
431.13
MAGAZINE 448.19
MAGIC 10.05 132.24
187.30
MAGICIAN 86.29
MAGICIAN'S 408.09
MAGICIANS 389.16
MAGISTRATE 33.03
33.25 37.08 67.10
67.12 69.11 185.04
193.01 194.01 195.21
MAGISTRATE'S 40.15
195.01
MAGNA 394.21

MAGNANIMOUS 319.22
407.20
MAGNIFICENCE 226.24
277.26
MAGNIFICENT 156.14
259.21 295.17 295.18
295.18 306.19 324.17
MAGNIFIED 277.16
MAGNITUDE 98.22
267.03 510.03
MAHOGANY 196.14 429.27
MAID 182.17
MAIDEN 384.28
MAIDS 93.02
MAIL 92.01 233.17
441.07
MAIL-BOAT 92.01
MAIL-BOATS 441.07
MAILBOAT 347.09
MAIMING 436.13
MAIN 167.02 270.10
293.08 303.27 499.22
MAIN-BOOM 293.08
MAINLY 332.13 383.07
458.09
MAINMAST 73.08
MAINSAIL 292.01 294.24
413.30
MAINTAINED 242.26
418.30
MAIZE 313.24
MAIZE-PATCH 313.24
MAJESTICALLY 320.04
MAJESTY'S 198.12
MAJORITY 13.26 174.15
279.22 339.09
MAKE 2.04 12.06
29.10 29.13 33.30
35.25 40.22 41.07
41.18 43.26 44.24
48.15 49.06 49.10
49.10 57.27 58.12
60.30 61.25 70.23
79.28 86.11 86.24
102.08 103.23 107.06
118.02 121.12 122.16
123.20 128.04 128.05
129.07 139.28 140.30
143.16 149.14 150.29
151.30 152.03 153.14
154.14 156.02 160.01
167.03 167.17 171.10
173.19 176.27 179.09
179.29 180.26 182.24
186.24 189.04 189.10
190.22 198.06 200.03
203.21 205.23 209.25
212.15 213.17 223.28
228.01 233.20 236.23
237.07 239.24 242.03
245.09 245.10 249.23
257.15 258.14 260.17
261.02 272.30 282.24
283.03 283.24 285.23
289.28 295.19 303.30
310.24 312.22 315.05
320.02 320.20 328.01
342.16 344.10 344.17
349.10 349.23 350.16
353.15 356.07 359.05
359.29 361.29 368.14
383.15 389.29 390.18
391.11 393.02 399.17
403.18 404.06 412.05
418.26 420.18 423.29
426.05 426.09 432.12
438.22 441.18 444.17
452.17 455.05 455.17
456.19 467.03 467.29
474.28 477.06 484.18
503.12 507.10
MAKER 117.04
MAKES 117.19 174.14
212.05 215.10 239.14
256.02 263.23 263.24
273.10 374.21 386.15
430.22
MAKING 35.02 47.06
47.22 70.34 99.14
111.20 120.03 171.02

MAKING (CONT.) 199.27
201.02 201.02 207.23
222.21 232.18 253.20
257.28 300.26 306.04
309.25 330.25 336.02
362.14 396.13 397.18
400.28 414.29 420.07
459.25 467.26 472.24
483.20 485.21 494.01
514.14
MALABAR 49.26 91.14
184.29 202.08
MALACCA 268.18 340.14
455.26
MALAITA 437.01
MALAY 247.15 268.09
268.15 318.03 332.22
427.22 428.05 434.14
488.22 492.02 509.11
MALAYS 3.23 22.08
31.05 117.09 278.26
315.26 356.13
MALE 94.06
MALEDICTION 115.07
MALEVOLENT 27.14
35.24 194.26 247.11
357.06
MALICE 11.09 419.02
MALICIOUS 40.11
425.10 474.20
MALIGNANT 473.05
MAN 4.25 6.15
10.18 11.07 11.21
26.15 26.23 33.22
37.23 37.30 38.07
38.18 41.03 42.17
43.10 43.15 43.26
45.04 45.13 45.22
46.02 48.11 48.18
49.13 49.27 50.03
53.07 57.15 57.30
60.21 64.18 65.11
66.09 66.18 67.18
68.01 68.20 68.27
69.05 69.17 69.25
70.17 70.32 73.11
74.17 74.19 79.23
80.04 81.04 81.08
83.17 83.25 85.29
86.25 87.29 88.15
88.21 89.25 90.04
90.04 95.01 95.09
96.03 98.20 100.30
103.11 103.17 108.03
108.16 109.17 113.11
113.12 117.03 119.05
122.19 122.21 122.21
125.09 126.21 127.06
129.28 130.05 130.28
131.04 132.19 133.22
134.21 137.16 138.29
139.09 144.13 144.23
145.13 150.18 151.02
153.26 156.03 156.30
165.18 167.20 168.18
168.21 169.14 172.24
176.05 177.09 177.18
178.12 178.22 179.23
180.01 180.05 185.08
185.23 186.12 187.04
187.21 189.13 190.05
190.15 190.19 192.20
194.24 195.15 196.02
196.09 196.12 196.17
197.13 197.22 197.27
197.28 199.03 199.12
200.01 201.05 201.14
202.03 203.15 204.12
204.26 209.22 211.08
211.20 212.29 213.14
220.01 220.10 220.17
222.06 222.11 223.25
224.18 226.20 227.12
231.20 232.07 234.12
235.07 235.09 235.15
235.29 236.07 236.20
236.25 238.15 239.21
242.25 242.29 243.07
245.17 246.10 246.26
247.01 249.29 250.09

MAN (CONT.) 250.15
252.20 253.12 253.13
253.17 256.01 258.08
258.12 258.15 259.22
260.26 260.26 267.10
268.20 269.01 270.18
272.03 273.24 279.06
282.10 285.04 286.14
286.28 288.25 288.30
293.01 294.02 296.01
297.19 297.21 297.23
298.09 298.19 298.29
300.11 303.07 307.15
307.26 310.20 310.22
314.01 319.21 319.27
321.03 321.26 332.21
333.07 336.13 338.04
340.28 340.28 344.30
345.05 346.03 346.05
352.08 355.11 356.15
358.18 361.08 371.09
371.21 371.23 371.25
371.30 372.04 372.11
372.18 372.24 373.09
376.04 377.12 382.13
383.07 383.25 386.21
388.04 390.20 392.12
394.09 397.15 400.25
400.27 402.01 403.26
404.02 409.14 410.16
410.22 416.11 416.17
420.13 420.27 425.02
426.01 426.04 426.25
427.09 429.01 429.13
429.24 431.23 433.27
434.22 435.01 435.11
435.23 436.11 438.15
438.20 438.27 439.07
440.07 443.11 447.16
447.22 449.02 452.08
452.09 453.26 455.18
455.23 456.24 457.04
457.10 457.11 457.18
457.23 458.11 458.26
459.10 459.30 460.11
460.27 462.02 462.17
462.19 464.08 464.13
465.08 465.17 465.20
465.22 466.03 466.21
467.05 467.28 468.16
469.05 469.21 470.01
470.17 470.24 471.20
473.02 475.18 475.24
478.08 479.01 479.09
479.22 480.08 482.24
482.30 484.06 488.15
489.06 493.08 493.25
495.13 500.23 501.16
505.29 509.01 509.05
513.21 514.21 514.28
515.16
MAN-BEAST 460.27
MAN-OF-WAR 440.07
MAN-OFWAR 172.24
MAN' 295.03
MAN'S 59.25 67.07
81.16 186.07 205.04
205.30 219.05 228.03
244.03 255.26 273.09
346.12 400.03 449.03
455.20 456.14 460.08
MANAGE 41.21 228.18
233.14 244.30 286.22
341.09 472.28
MANAGEABLE 208.04
MANAGED 44.20 83.30
98.30 127.18 128.25
171.05 172.08 176.27
240.29 249.23 352.01
352.04 363.16 383.13
443.12 451.19 490.03
MANAGEMENT 255.11
MANAGER 234.23 235.01
235.13 268.23
MANE 255.12
MANFULLY 50.11
MANGY 40.14 353.13
MANIAC 109.27
MANIACAL 122.23
MANIFEST 151.02

MANIFESTATION 208.05
MANIFESTATIONS 272.13
319.04
MANILA 437.14
MANILLA 70.16
MANKIND 68.02 147.16
191.16 228.14 266.06
276.12 299.12 304.13
325.25 341.20 397.27
398.10 418.18 419.06
432.14 436.07 458.16
471.17
MANKIND'S 113.01
MANLY 93.20 240.20
MANNED 6.27 291.24
436.16 442.27 489.27
MANNER 1.06 55.11
58.02 75.06 85.12
124.10 172.27 215.06
222.05 224.27 225.21
230.26 232.16 233.15
239.02 241.02 304.29
306.24 307.28 317.17
322.08 348.04 422.03
422.08 424.05 447.08
458.27 501.26
MANNERISMS 310.01
MANNERS 70.40
MANOEUVRE 169.26
MANSIONS 4.04
MANTELPIECE 181.07
MANTLING 187.07
MANY 3.07 3.28
9.08 10.04 11.02
11.22 14.19 32.12
37.21 38.09 38.21
48.21 58.11 63.27
70.33 80.30 89.10
101.22 104.07 105.12
113.12 119.08 128.10
147.12 159.08 166.23
173.21 202.13 211.12
232.05 239.04 245.15
252.11 259.20 265.01
265.02 265.05 266.05
270.03 275.10 278.05
278.11 279.19 282.06
286.06 292.22 293.13
298.17 298.18 308.25
327.03 327.05 335.06
338.21 339.08 340.20
356.14 356.19 361.12
369.02 369.02 370.13
370.14 372.23 396.24
417.26 422.04 422.21
422.28 444.26 449.28
449.30 452.06 454.21
455.03 456.03 462.01
462.06 463.10 472.12
475.12 480.05 481.25
481.27 483.18 483.19
484.07 485.22 486.03
487.08 489.16 494.25
495.05 495.17 498.11
498.16 498.17 503.02
504.20 508.20 509.09
509.13 513.18
MANY-SIDED 9.08
MARBLE 162.09 168.23
185.03 381.20
MARBLE-FACED 185.03
MARCH 322.28 373.10
MARCHED 226.17 490.12
MARCHES 218.27
MARCHING 51.15 191.30
349.12
MARIANI 57.29 58.06
58.21
MARIANI'S 57.28
58.27
MARIN 170.16
MARINE 4.18 164.13
172.25 198.18
MARINS 173.10
MARITAL 190.22 342.12
347.01
MARITIME 194.17
MARK 71.14 130.28
192.21 238.08 357.03
MARKED 23.02 71.06

MARKED (CONT.) 73.07
172.07 188.25 332.18
352.07
MARKEDLY 352.10 481.08
MARKET 363.21 504.09
MARKET-PLACE 363.21
504.09
MARKINGS 252.27
MARLOW 38.22 41.12
70.30 72.17 72.22
73.28 74.26 77.05
80.05 81.13 113.03
113.28 113.29 139.15
236.29 266.02 394.01
394.09 394.13 395.05
396.08 396.10 400.12
401.01 416.01 417.29
418.02 434.26 435.03
MARLOW'S 39.05 416.15
MARRIAGE 268.17 356.17
MARRIED 46.04 92.05
190.13 436.22
MARROW 62.23
MARRY 340.14
MARSH 408.27
MARSHY 451.29
MARTIAL 449.11
MARVEL 423.23
MARVELLED 90.22
298.10 404.16
MARVELLOUS 19.01
249.18 253.01
MASK 144.18 338.10
MASS 21.18 28.23
55.06 129.15 167.08
323.12 440.20 513.28
MASSACRE 501.19
MASSES 94.18 269.23
302.23 384.08
MASSIVE 168.14 180.18
210.06 246.12 410.01
MASSIVELY 314.02
MAST 6.22 96.17
293.08
MASTER 41.15 43.31
45.02 45.11 45.20
137.16 138.29 195.19
248.07 292.03 299.17
304.10 341.03 363.24
421.09 451.23 482.21
483.02 483.08 483.13
485.13 489.12 490.17
490.21 490.24 490.25
490.26 491.09 505.08
505.13 505.25 505.25
506.06 510.19 510.24
511.19 512.15 513.06
MASTER'S 96.17 333.04
450.16 485.16 489.20
MASTERED 382.26 390.04
400.06 413.15 418.11
MASTERING 337.26
MASTERPIECE 253.08
253.11 253.13
MASTERS 43.36 390.25
MASTHEAD 136.21 140.18
165.17 236.16
MASTICATING 338.16
MASTIFFS 63.04
MASTS 5.11 21.27
441.12
MAT 83.10 102.27
307.10 359.04 360.25
410.07 490.18
MATCH 93.24 140.20
165.17 182.26 257.18
257.21
MATCHED 27.14
MATCHES 105.10
MATE 10.16 14.26
16.15 47.21 52.05
52.22 70.06 70.29
71.23 72.25 77.11
86.26 98.12 107.23
142.04 182.28 190.05
195.20 222.23 238.19
475.27
MATERIAL 65.17 66.06
147.11 175.07 222.07
263.31 438.10

MATERIALS   203.17

276.03

MATHERSON   76.13

76.14

MATRIMONIAL   46.08

MATS   20.07   20.28

280.01   319.29   353.14

370.08   371.03   371.10

372.26   386.01   455.05

498.27

MATTED   426.20   476.04

MATTER   28.27   38.13

69.22   80.12   97.02

111.07   158.24   159.09

163.07   163.18   165.08

165.15   166.30   177.15

178.08   180.09   199.08

204.05   222.24   233.08

235.14   235.14   235.15

235.16   266.04   269.14

281.20   286.15   301.13

302.08   304.24   310.12

311.28   348.25   351.18

364.30   371.24   376.19

377.10   381.22   400.04

400.20   400.21   402.14

403.16   407.15   428.24

452.13   459.05   484.03

491.05   506.12

MATTER-OF-FACT   158.24

MATTERED 146.25   272.11

400.05

MATTERS 70.37   114.03

215.20   244.07   353.29

360.17   478.02

MATTRESS 58.18

MATURE   176.10   177.22

295.10

MATURED 157.19   311.08

359.09

MATURING 84.27

MAUL 111.10

MAXIMUM 207.17

MAY   36.08   43.06

46.12   50.10   50.15

53.02   53.07   58.17

59.18   64.19   71.16

72.04   75.21   77.16

81.08   87.04   88.13

90.25   113.17   113.30

130.09   153.10   166.10

167.26   174.13   177.08

178.03   180.22   180.29

182.19   185.19   188.06

193.21   196.18   197.14

210.17   212.14   213.18

214.01   215.21   217.01

224.26   228.23   228.24

239.11   246.18   250.08

270.13   271.14   271.24

274.05   274.16   277.30

291.05   291.08   320.05

321.28   322.15   329.13

352.25   355.03   363.01

365.06   375.08   378.25

379.08   419.10   420.03

422.22   433.30   435.14

444.03   455.21   455.29

471.20   474.12   475.28

495.07   505.22   507.21

512.08   515.24

MAYBE   50.12   73.11

106.09   183.11   209.25

454.09   509.23

MAZE   13.21   417.04

MAZES   482.19

ME   8.07   8.09

11.21   26.27   29.13

29.18   30.01   30.03

30.08   34.19   34.25

34.25   36.14   38.05

40.05   40.11   40.17

40.20   40.23   43.04

43.24   43.27   43.41

44.22   45.29   46.17

46.20   47.15   47.30

48.01   48.04   48.08

48.12   49.05   49.07

49.13   49.21   49.22

51.29   52.06   52.08

ME (CONT.)   52.21

53.11   57.10   58.06

59.14   60.14   60.28

61.05   61.08   61.21

61.27   62.08   62.13

62.30   63.20   64.01

64.02   64.11   64.13

64.15   64.18   65.16

67.04   68.17   69.12

70.21   70.29   71.15

72.07   72.14   72.23

73.04   73.04   73.22

73.22   74.01   74.05

74.06   74.12   75.19

76.04   76.05   77.06

77.10   77.21   77.29

78.08   78.13   79.18

80.12   80.16   80.17

80.18   81.28   82.06

82.19   83.01   83.17

84.03   84.12   84.13

84.14   84.16   85.02

85.06   85.17   85.24

85.29   86.02   86.10

86.24   87.12   87.13

87.14   87.15   87.23

89.17   89.22   90.03

90.08   90.15   90.25

91.06   91.13   91.15

93.11   93.26   95.08

96.11   96.26   97.01

97.12   98.27   99.14

100.06   100.14   100.26

102.07   104.01   104.21

105.14   107.19   108.15

108.19   108.22   108.28

109.05   109.22   110.03

110.20   110.27   111.16

111.19   111.27   111.27

112.13   112.23   112.28

113.19   114.06   114.12

116.04   116.28   117.19

118.03   120.17   120.21

120.22   121.07   124.02

125.08   125.17   126.28

127.02   127.08   127.20

127.28   129.05   129.07

129.11   129.17   130.23

130.26   132.08   133.01

133.05   133.19   133.28

134.09   134.17   134.18

136.09   136.22   137.17

137.30   138.10   138.24

139.14   140.30   141.09

141.29   141.29   141.30

142.15   142.19   142.21

142.23   143.08   143.19

143.21   143.30   144.03

144.28   144.30   145.11

145.29   146.02   149.14

149.23   150.03   150.05

150.07   150.19   150.24

151.04   151.06   151.11

151.16   151.24   151.25

152.04   152.06   152.09

153.14   153.16   153.17

153.29   154.01   154.04

154.16   155.01   155.10

155.13   155.14   157.01

157.02   158.20   158.21

158.22   158.25   158.30

159.20   159.20   159.25

160.01   160.05   160.23

160.27   161.02   163.11

163.17   163.21   164.11

164.26   164.27   165.03

165.04   165.13   168.22

168.26   170.14   170.18

170.22   171.10   172.05

173.18   174.10   176.02

176.12   176.16   177.12

178.21   179.02   179.11

180.12   180.15   180.22

181.15   181.16   183.04

184.28   185.18   186.19

187.09   187.10   187.11

187.20   188.06   189.04

189.06   189.09   189.18

190.04   190.13   190.21

192.02   193.24   194.30

ME (CONT.)   195.05

195.26   195.28   195.29

196.09   197.16   197.28

199.03   199.08   199.10

199.20   201.04   201.06

201.20   202.30   203.06

203.19   204.13   204.15

204.18   204.22   205.01

205.07   205.17   205.26

207.19   207.24   208.03

208.04   208.06   209.08

209.20   209.30   211.29

214.18   215.21   215.26

216.13   216.28   217.09

217.10   217.14   218.16

218.21   218.22   218.25

219.15   219.16   219.23

219.28   220.04   221.03

223.06   223.14   224.10

224.12   225.04   225.05

225.23   225.26   225.26

226.05   226.07   226.09

226.11   226.21   227.04

227.13   227.14   228.13

228.22   228.29   229.11

229.17   229.17   230.12

230.17   230.22   230.26

231.09   231.13   231.16

231.17   231.19   231.22

231.25   232.24   233.05

233.27   234.09   234.20

236.01   236.23   236.24

237.11   237.13   237.26

237.28   237.30   238.10

242.30   243.18   244.06

244.29   245.08   245.18

245.19   248.13   249.07

249.14   253.01   253.16

254.15   254.17   254.20

254.28   255.03   255.05

255.09   255.28   257.09

258.02   258.10   258.11

258.17   258.22   258.26

261.03   261.12   261.26

261.30   262.21   263.22

263.24   264.01   264.11

264.15   264.24   265.03

267.25   269.03   270.01

270.12   270.16   270.21

271.01   272.23   272.27

273.14   273.28   274.01

274.12   274.13   278.07

278.18   280.10   280.22

282.02   282.03   282.21

282.24   283.23   286.05

286.24   287.19   287.24

287.29   289.01   289.09

289.21   289.24   290.12

291.11   293.05   293.10

294.03   294.18   295.09

295.16   295.27   295.27

295.27   295.28   297.21

298.04   299.19   301.03

301.08   301.17   301.18

301.26   302.29   303.16

303.17   303.19   306.02

308.07   308.16   308.25

308.26   308.27   308.28

310.14   312.15   314.15

314.16   314.18   320.12

320.24   321.03   322.15

322.18   322.28   323.26

324.30   325.29   328.10

328.26   329.09   329.23

333.28   334.13   337.03

337.24   338.05   338.08

338.19   339.05   339.20

340.19   342.19   343.01

343.28   344.11   344.15

344.21   345.21   345.25

347.18   350.05   350.24

350.28   352.27   352.30

353.04   353.06   353.07

353.11   354.06   355.01

355.11   356.08   357.09

358.08   358.25   359.02

360.02   361.19   362.05

365.30   366.26   366.30

367.17   368.06   369.05

369.13   370.11   370.18

ME (CONT.)   371.17

374.14   374.22   374.26

375.07   375.20   375.24

376.08   376.09   376.16

376.17   377.05   377.14

377.17   377.21   377.25

377.30   378.14   378.23

378.29   379.09   380.06

380.08   381.05   381.16

382.09   383.03   383.13

383.21   384.07   385.07

385.21   385.21   385.30

385.30   385.30   386.13

387.01   387.02   388.27

389.01   390.06   391.06

391.08   391.11   393.06

393.14   393.20   393.21

394.16   395.22   396.13

398.05   398.19   398.20

398.29   399.05   399.08

399.09   399.28   400.07

401.02   401.05   401.07

401.25   401.28   401.29

402.03   402.05   402.08

402.19   403.19   403.29

405.01   405.05   405.10

405.14   405.16   405.17

406.04   408.11   409.11

412.09   412.09   412.17

412.20   412.30   413.13

413.16   413.18   413.20

414.12   415.01   415.11

419.24   424.01   426.04

426.06   426.07   426.09

426.11   426.18   426.24

426.29   427.12   427.23

427.27   428.08   429.01

429.06   429.13   429.18

429.19   430.10   430.11

430.20   431.03   431.04

431.10   431.15   431.17

431.19   432.06   432.07

432.26   433.02   433.03

433.07   433.22   434.14

438.07   440.22   442.10

452.13   455.29   458.11

460.13   460.20   460.26

463.11   465.09   465.09

468.14   471.13   471.19

471.23   471.30   472.24

472.25   473.01   473.04

473.17   473.24   473.25

474.12   474.25   475.08

476.05   476.07   477.06

477.07   477.08   478.06

478.17   479.17   479.18

479.19   481.05   481.07

485.01   488.04   493.01

493.03   494.17   495.12

495.15   500.20   502.07

502.19   502.22   502.24

502.27   506.05   507.26

509.13   509.16   511.11

511.14   511.24   512.06

513.01   516.09

MEAGRE   20.24   63.07

MEAL   99.09   172.24

MEAL-TIMES   99.09

MEALS   228.11   353.03

MEAN   26.22   40.08

46.23   50.02   50.26

50.27   61.05   66.06

67.11   76.27   84.14

85.03   85.17   91.03

97.04   100.25   102.12

108.11   143.08   154.04

158.05   159.19   164.19

179.17   191.14   191.17

203.14   204.06   210.17

215.16   231.24   272.25

275.17   295.14   309.11

309.20   340.28   353.06

355.05   357.16   370.18

383.15   403.13   452.25

464.24   468.03   468.13

MEANING 63.19   74.05

74.06   90.25   171.03

177.28   211.25   291.07

303.04   308.03   341.29

375.15   407.05   418.18

MEANING (CONT.) 481.09
MEANINGS 291.10
MEANNESS 147.25
MEANS 11.10 11.12
11.15 44.14 50.24
79.09 116.03 173.01
223.30 225.14 228.05
250.27 272.10 286.11
289.02 321.11 339.17
342.06 479.23
MEANT 3.08 86.02
90.02 96.15 110.17
115.03 138.15 148.06
148.07 150.29 158.14
158.15 177.06 188.07
236.05 239.15 267.01
287.17 289.14 289.14
293.17 293.30 356.14
361.06 490.14 494.26
510.24 513.16
MEANTIME 80.22 117.10
251.11 286.18 300.12
323.03 329.26 357.25
439.27 444.24 450.10
456.08 457.24 497.16
MEANWHILE 310.07
MEASLY 30.04
MEASURE 188.30 226.16
352.03
MEASURED 153.04 232.26
335.04 514.07
MEASURES 162.23 172.02
MEAT 55.19 176.29
350.28
MECHANICALLY 311.20
MECHANISM 89.04
MEDDLE 81.25
MEDICAL 169.03 258.29
MEDICAL-LOOKING 169.03
MEDICALLY 65.11
MEDICINE 12.22
MEDIEVAL 209.02
MEDITATE 157.07
MEDITATED 159.13
287.08 320.20
MEDITATING 187.16
MEDITATION 29.03
46.18 54.26 192.18
MEDITATIONS 432.10
MEDITATIVE 323.13
387.16
MEEK 68.10
MEEKLY 85.22
MEERACLE 11.21
MEET 42.14 106.04
114.14 118.06 236.09
240.26 271.09 271.25
304.06 321.29 370.16
396.09 413.21 470.06
508.30
MEETING 15.27 84.17
168.01 279.04 384.28
MEETINGS 273.24
MEIN 125.01 133.29
257.04
MEINEN 257.03
MELANCHOLY 339.21
398.10
MELANESIA 436.24
475.16
MELLIFLUOUS 436.04
MELLOWED 260.12
MELT 389.12
MELTED 143.03 248.17
MELTS 2.11 219.11
MEMBER 59.15
MEMORABLE 402.14
MEMORIES 11.15 15.22
167.28 384.06 434.11
434.12 507.02
MEMORY 24.21 27.26
41.04 61.01 76.27
87.16 156.24 168.07
171.19 212.05 294.01
340.07 397.14 398.09
398.18 407.07 474.27
499.29
MEN 3.03 3.22
5.17 7.19 8.30
10.07 11.29 13.16

MEN (CONT.) 13.26
14.21 15.21 16.06
16.07 17.25 20.04
20.11 20.30 21.23
24.24 25.05 27.28
28.20 28.27 31.06
33.07 35.11 35.15
40.18 41.09 41.25
43.03 50.23 51.05
59.15 68.11 69.22
80.12 81.06 82.25
87.09 99.03 103.03
105.01 105.19 106.04
106.14 107.06 108.19
111.08 113.12 113.19
113.23 115.08 118.06
119.01 119.09 125.19
128.02 129.23 131.24
146.22 147.07 147.12
147.15 148.01 149.28
159.05 167.30 168.08
175.06 175.27 176.07
178.17 188.08 198.05
214.06 229.18 235.19
239.11 239.14 246.06
250.18 254.18 255.29
262.12 263.11 263.29
271.18 273.02 277.09
278.15 279.27 285.11
291.16 293.21 295.19
300.27 313.16 313.27
315.22 315.24 316.02
316.17 317.10 318.02
324.07 327.05 327.20
329.04 334.22 335.04
335.18 336.06 337.30
340.23 345.18 352.10
363.13 365.27 373.05
387.15 394.24 402.07
407.14 410.11 410.16
414.08 416.04 421.21
422.24 427.25 437.08
442.09 442.12 443.22
443.26 444.10 444.13
446.06 447.19 448.28
449.08 449.17 449.28
450.16 450.20 451.18
452.06 452.23 453.08
453.16 454.01 454.02
454.20 454.21 455.03
455.05 456.08 459.06
461.08 461.23 461.28
463.12 463.26 465.01
465.02 467.02 468.23
469.08 469.16 471.14
471.26 472.07 473.27
475.03 477.17 477.24
478.29 480.06 482.07
482.22 483.20 484.14
484.24 485.19 485.23
486.07 487.19 488.04
489.09 489.23 490.07
490.12 491.16 491.20
491.22 492.02 492.30
494.14 494.26 497.09
498.02 498.06 498.16
499.06 499.19 499.30
500.11 500.15 500.26
500.30 501.12 503.16
504.06 508.08 508.23
508.28 509.09 510.07
510.13 513.20
MEN-OF-WAR 437.08
MEN' 447.08
MEN'S 12.17 16.28
57.19 181.09 276.01
327.10 461.13 501.24
507.04 507.22 509.14
510.03
MENACE 7.20 7.22
9.02 116.08 477.19
MENACING 210.15 361.30
MENACINGLY 220.05
511.22
MENAGEMENTS 169.29
MENAM 242.10
MENDING 312.19 312.19
MENT 179.10
MENTAL 240.03 311.06
392.01

MENTION 235.05 237.12
282.11 353.20
MENTIONED 138.24
243.14 267.23 268.12
301.27
MENTIONING 401.30
MENTIONS 71.23
MERCANTILE 4.18
266.16
MERCHANT 3.29 175.15
182.28 245.26 247.15
282.01 315.17
MERCHANT-SHIPS 3.29
MERCHANTS 240.16
436.20
MERCI 168.23 170.27
171.21
MERCIES 421.27
MERCIFUL 59.22 101.03
340.17
MERCILESS 340.18
MERCILESSLY 88.15
MERCY 27.23 117.30
310.09 355.04
MERE 28.03 121.14
177.24 185.11 214.15
241.11 243.30 277.08
322.11 334.25 382.26
385.09 386.11 423.05
MERELY 113.16 195.02
245.16 280.26 318.04
389.23 436.09 454.05
MEREST 167.24
MERGED 138.25
MERIDIAN 79.03
MERIT 210.20 210.21
MERITED 281.29
MERITORIOUS 383.09
MERITS 68.09 68.25
MERRIMENT 120.26
MERRY 128.08
MESH 118.25
MESS 47.21
MESSAGE 42.05 418.02
419.21 419.28 461.12
465.30 491.08
MESSAGES 461.22
MESSENGER 254.03
456.18
MESSENGER'S 499.02
MESSENGERS 449.23
451.15 505.30
MET 37.30 42.01
48.03 64.16 65.11
81.17 82.18 82.19
90.30 113.12 113.13
168.09 197.08 230.14
233.26 343.01 470.07
474.03 481.19 504.14
513.10
METAL 53.25
METALLIC 21.20
METAPHOR 48.12
METAPHORICALLY 280.24
METER 73.01
METHOD 64.29
METHODICAL 333.10
METICULOUS 35.13
METIER 178.20
MICE 493.18
MID 365.12
MID-AIR 365.12
MIDDAY 484.14
MIDDLE 33.25 44.10
52.15 61.09 61.14
70.26 73.21 74.24
129.15 142.30 149.22
196.26 217.12 227.02
293.26 369.15 370.03
378.03 393.01 427.10
428.18 484.12 489.14
505.01
MIDDLE-AGED 52.15
227.02
MIDNIGHT 159.17 185.02
242.14
MIDST 4.10 4.26
12.03 70.02 86.19
92.07 116.09 141.17
168.26 210.10 279.26

MIDST (CONT.) 314.02
364.04 385.22 469.11
MIDSTREAM 443.29
MIEN 90.05 206.05
MIGHT 3.27 11.02
27.25 34.12 43.34
51.04 54.07 82.13
82.16 82.20 90.23
90.28 93.20 93.23
98.08 104.05 105.30
106.15 119.03 126.19
138.27 146.19 153.20
159.07 160.09 164.08
165.19 172.19 176.25
180.06 180.30 218.14
225.18 235.07 236.04
238.17 240.06 240.07
243.07 270.11 273.29
277.14 280.04 280.23
299.14 320.29 329.18
342.11 343.25 346.09
349.28 351.18 379.23
380.01 389.08 391.26
423.16 428.08 437.05
450.30 452.07 461.02
463.08 467.13 470.16
488.26 492.03 492.10
493.29 510.19
MIGHTIER 419.08
MIGHTY 75.16 253.06
269.14 276.14 299.18
312.23 319.04 333.23
510.02
MIGRATING 192.03
MILD 200.24 423.01
436.23
MILDEST 48.04 435.09
MILDLY 202.27
MILE 21.17 138.11
165.07
MILES 55.23 71.15
71.30 73.07 76.01
168.02 199.24 230.02
236.09 237.05 240.12
252.08 254.05 255.01
269.09 276.06 276.10
281.05 313.06 327.17
329.30 343.02 347.09
439.04 446.05 451.03
MILES' 294.07
MILITARY 50.26
MILK 24.05
MILL 227.04 229.30
230.26
MILLION 112.25
MILLIONS 62.09 62.10
63.30 69.01
MIND 4.03 5.09
8.05 11.06 25.30
30.06 36.01 36.09
44.03 45.27 46.03
51.08 63.19 75.03
82.01 82.06 92.22
93.25 95.03 99.16
109.24 114.13 114.27
118.09 119.01 124.13
126.27 127.19 128.14
129.13 142.19 159.26
162.19 163.28 170.28
179.09 181.15 197.03
214.19 220.16 225.23
226.11 237.05 237.30
239.24 240.08 240.25
245.24 283.11 286.27
288.28 288.29 289.15
309.25 321.28 354.06
354.09 359.20 360.18
367.03 369.16 376.04
384.17 386.11 386.21
389.29 392.10 396.19
400.05 407.11 418.17
420.24 423.13 438.05
452.13 456.06 458.25
462.10 478.18 485.08
497.12
MINDANAO 437.24
MINDED 115.10 239.07
449.15
MINDS 42.20 115.20

MINDS (CONT.) 167.29
275.15 276.04 321.09
449.18 461.28 479.28
508.23 513.22
MINE 61.07 61.29
62.07 62.10 78.20
79.16 93.12 100.23
113.07 130.22 136.16
145.27 150.22 177.13
196.25 196.30 199.13
254.28 265.15 290.23
292.10 402.10 474.06
474.16 511.30
MINGLED 131.30 134.20
210.17 211.13 302.22
405.29 417.05 509.09
MINIATURE 247.10
MINIMISE 98.23
MINIMISED 461.15
MINIMUM 207.16
MINISTERED 8.22
57.30
MINOR 60.28
MINUTE 34.23 41.20
116.02 119.18 128.28
131.04 139.30 158.07
158.07 201.25 232.06
249.06 255.10 313.01
426.30
MINUTES 28.19 35.19
63.28 70.26 107.05
111.06 118.08 123.19
136.13 173.03 173.11
198.27 225.13 333.14
342.14 439.30 449.24
MIRACLE 60.03 60.13
332.16 389.27
MIRACULOUS 60.15
172.30
MIRROR 187.30 410.13
MIRRORS 263.10
MIRTHLESS 220.03
MISANTHROPIC 252.15
MISAPPREHEND 282.23
MISBEGOTTEN 241.28
MISCHIEF 194.21
MISDEEDS 436.06 475.02
MISERABLE 43.35
109.27 189.14 270.17
278.04 294.28 310.21
336.03 352.25 353.27
405.29 410.14 414.27
460.28 473.03
MISERIES 397.28
MISFORTUNE 27.27
137.27 268.07 342.10
MISFORTUNES 295.21
403.11
MISHAP 67.21
MISLEADING 91.12
302.06
MISS 215.14 255.26
391.22
MISSED 99.28 99.29
100.02 130.19 192.09
218.14
MISSED' 99.30
MISSILE 131.01
MISSING 73.08 109.21
114.01 121.07 194.14
229.12 353.17 509.08
MISSION 56.26 475.14
490.30 491.13
MISSION-HOUSE 475.14
MISSIONARIES 475.04
MISSIONARY 436.21
MIST 6.04 59.26
135.04 145.13 151.17
155.03 162.02 236.15
270.18 274.26 441.15
452.10 493.30 494.29
497.06 497.23 498.10
498.18 499.21
MISTAKE 43.13 60.13
67.21 71.30 84.22
86.13 87.30 90.22
95.13 96.25 97.01
129.06 140.10 227.14
272.30 324.29 348.29
363.17 492.02

MISTAKEN 81.19 477.13
MISTER 52.22 62.26
74.25 74.25 75.17
233.18
MISTRUST 67.24 275.14
488.10 488.18
MISTRUSTED 273.28
389.05 433.12
MISTRUSTFUL 357.06
399.21 452.27
MISTRUSTFULLY 221.06
MISTRUSTS 321.17
MISTS 156.05 157.13
255.02
MISTY 219.07 297.03
441.03
MISUNDERSTANDING 488.19
MIXED 112.12 263.16
MIXTURE 169.07 298.01
MIZZEN 6.22
MIZZEN-MAST 6.22
MOAN 396.06
MOANED 35.07 359.23
MOANING 35.10 344.24
368.25 467.06
MOANS 465.10 466.22
MOB 6.19 169.17
500.26
MOCKING 224.14 302.07
MODE 182.11 240.07
MODERATE 174.06 403.22
MODEST 457.17
MODESTLY 227.21
MOHAMMED 247.17 251.06
251.17 254.03 255.08
285.24 285.24
MOHAMMED'S 251.23
MOLUCCAS' 245.29
MOMENT 7.03 24.21
52.22 56.22 71.08
74.02 83.29 90.10
95.21 96.22 97.05
102.29 103.12 107.02
107.11 115.16 120.14
122.17 127.05 128.07
129.19 129.22 132.15
138.04 140.19 142.14
151.02 155.10 163.12
171.05 174.10 180.02
189.06 195.02 195.06
204.15 210.12 211.23
216.20 217.04 219.02
220.07 229.21 230.16
232.06 263.12 263.27
280.25 283.05 292.11
295.06 302.17 302.18
306.16 308.05 309.03
326.04 334.03 338.29
371.08 379.24 384.04
384.18 386.17 386.22
392.01 395.25 396.29
398.22 401.08 428.13
434.22 436.23 448.27
449.20 450.03 451.05
463.21 464.09 466.26
469.01 471.30 488.01
494.19 499.23 500.03
500.17 503.15 506.10
506.16 515.24
MOMENT'S 393.10 492.20
MOMENTARILY 248.09
MOMENTARY 113.13
285.06 484.01
MOMENTOUS 112.02
113.01
MOMENTS 11.26 46.15
69.06 140.05 166.09
174.17 268.11 359.11
374.19 385.24 386.16
389.22 392.03 516.11
MON 174.07
MONDE 173.08
MONEY 2.24 69.27
79.13 83.08 84.19
96.12 186.26 199.05
202.19 222.20 223.17
223.21 235.04 252.03
270.30 344.20 353.16
353.25 357.23 403.21

MONEY (CONT.) 403.30
404.15 421.24 440.28
442.08 455.05 492.10
MONEY-LENDER 83.08
MONGERING 266.11
MONGRELS 143.09
MONKEYS 300.08
MONOPOLY 316.12
MONOSYLLABLE 3.25
MONOTONE 365.18 386.08
MONOTONOUS 325.16
MONOTONY 10.05
MONSIEUR 180.27 181.03
181.15 181.24
MONSIEUR' 181.24
MONSOON 217.08
MONSTER 88.28 378.28
MONSTERS 247.10
MONSTROUS 46.16
387.07 399.25
MONTAGUE 68.20
MONTH 30.05 32.01
185.28 215.01 251.09
289.25 308.25 311.08
501.27
MONTHS 43.17 194.16
203.16 227.01 240.30
278.20 292.21 427.20
MONTHS' 2.12 233.24
MONUMENTAL 175.09
318.05
MOOD 101.03 288.02
398.04
MOODILY 90.26 119.21
MOODY 123.28 488.28
MOON 19.05 24.27
112.20 269.19 270.05
301.28 302.02 396.22
396.28 402.11 489.14
MOONBEANS 302.16
MOONLIGHT 302.12
397.12 408.05
MOOR 47.22
MOORED 480.12
MOORINGS 6.23
MOP 307.12
MOPPING 76.24
MORAL 48.22 48.22
97.24 186.13 331.20
MORALITY 44.05 185.17
185.17 267.20 418.24
421.22 488.13
MORE 3.05 8.29
10.11 12.11 14.19
15.08 25.01 25.29
26.07 26.10 27.25
31.02 34.06 42.29
47.13 48.20 48.25
50.03 50.04 50.12
53.30 54.05 55.27
58.09 59.14 59.27
63.27 64.09 67.26
69.02 69.08 70.40
70.43 71.11 71.15
72.01 74.11 75.17
76.10 81.27 82.06
84.18 88.18 89.01
92.03 93.10 97.26
100.06 101.20 101.21
110.05 110.30 110.30
121.13 123.03 125.20
126.05 130.10 130.25
132.16 136.02 138.12
141.08 142.12 147.14
147.15 148.25 150.15
150.25 156.20 156.22
156.22 157.09 157.30
158.15 162.10 163.02
163.03 164.17 165.07
166.16 169.04 170.21
171.13 173.04 173.06
174.09 176.08 176.16
176.30 178.12 179.18
180.26 182.02 182.12
184.11 186.07 186.15
192.13 197.22 197.23
202.16 205.24 215.06
215.08 216.09 216.09
219.19 223.13 223.16

MORE (CONT.) 223.16
224.11 225.27 227.02
227.09 227.16 228.13
228.29 229.18 229.29
230.20 231.03 231.27
236.10 236.24 237.08
239.04 240.25 243.13
245.17 249.10 249.13
250.04 255.26 256.04
262.18 262.27 267.10
267.11 268.10 268.21
268.21 270.13 270.22
270.24 272.24 273.10
273.10 273.24 274.07
278.10 280.15 280.16
280.16 280.16 281.16
282.11 283.02 286.19
294.28 295.05 295.10
298.24 299.05 304.24
307.24 308.16 309.22
311.20 312.02 313.09
313.14 315.25 322.25
327.20 328.05 330.05
339.03 341.01 344.19
345.03 347.02 349.30
357.18 358.12 359.16
360.03 364.17 372.23
372.24 372.26 374.21
374.29 376.11 376.18
379.01 382.07 384.13
386.09 386.09 386.16
388.02 388.03 388.07
389.27 390.14 392.26
394.15 399.24 403.04
404.14 405.01 406.07
411.25 412.14 416.13
417.13 417.14 417.18
417.18 419.27 419.30
420.02 421.04 427.17
430.26 431.16 433.03
435.10 436.01 441.22
445.29 447.05 448.30
449.06 449.28 449.30
450.10 450.30 452.11
452.16 453.22 460.07
460.12 465.16 467.29
469.16 469.18 473.17
475.11 477.01 477.05
480.27 482.02 485.18
485.25 487.09 488.07
491.01 491.05 493.06
503.06 504.20 507.26
509.21 512.10 516.08
MOREOVER 43.16 136.08
204.19 228.27 298.10
447.15
MORIBUND 386.01
MORNING 17.20 42.10
43.02 46.11 52.17
53.04 58.29 70.10
70.36 79.29 85.18
166.26 182.19 190.03
193.18 199.12 200.22
204.30 231.20 232.30
243.03 252.11 253.26
254.07 263.02 264.27
267.22 278.18 285.01
331.30 339.25 350.21
353.01 360.14 363.04
367.11 407.01 451.27
454.25 489.28 491.20
498.17 503.14
MORNINGS 46.07
MOROSE 126.28 333.03
MORROW 52.03 64.19
79.28 185.02 186.09
200.26 223.01 265.13
303.02 369.01 391.19
398.15 412.03 462.02
MORT 169.14
MORTAL 111.05 389.07
438.16
MORTALITY 212.04
MORTIFICATION 47.19
MORTIS 475.06
MOSLEMS 364.06
MOSQUE 443.14 443.22
MOSQUITO 209.11 350.08
MOSQUITO-NET 209.11
350.08

MOSSY 4.05
MOST 16.27 45.19 / 49.21 59.25 64.30 / 65.10 68.26 80.09 / 85.10 107.21 114.20 / 116.09 138.22 166.16 / 168.04 169.15 169.30 / 176.12 198.11 204.25 / 214.22 215.04 230.24 / 242.04 244.04 246.01 / 246.05 268.16 271.06 / 274.18 280.22 281.09 / 297.22 307.01 308.27 / 317.05 318.01 319.24 / 320.01 321.02 324.01 / 324.25 327.19 327.22 / 339.10 345.11 345.22 / 346.08 348.16 352.16 / 352.28 353.27 400.08 / 402.07 404.13 405.22 / 423.19 425.05 436.15 / 436.19 436.27 450.28 / 456.07 458.23 477.24 / 487.13 489.28 500.05 / 500.29 504.21 505.23
MOSTLY 210.05 222.02 / 339.15 342.05 387.28 / 397.26 482.09
MOTE 376.20
MOTHER 52.11 183.06 / 251.25 268.11 338.23 / 341.22 348.13 355.23 / 379.15 385.14 385.16 / 385.25 389.02 405.24 / 405.25 422.18 508.29 / 514.08
MOTHER'S 20.03 320.05
MOTHERLY 314.22 319.19 / 338.12 407.21
MOTION 25.05 132.22 / 338.16 410.06
MOTIONED 414.13
MOTIONLESS 6.04 / 22.09 26.13 38.26 / 115.22 174.24 212.12 / 226.06 244.23 318.05 / 336.11 359.18 395.20 / 407.08 432.29 445.28 / 469.05 489.18
MOTIONS 134.11 270.05
MOTIVE 60.12 270.11 / 280.28
MOTIVES 422.13
MOTTO 207.17
MOUND 21.10 339.25 / 371.08 397.20
MOUNTAIN 315.16 444.03 / 467.14 494.19
MOUNTAINS 220.17 / 279.01 319.13
MOUNTED 68.22 323.20 / 324.17 359.14 420.10
MOUNTING 328.17
MOURNED 510.10
MOURNFUL 37.06 76.07 / 397.02 432.09
MOURNFULLY 165.02 / 261.18
MOURNING 485.28 485.28
MOUSTACHE 15.06 / 129.30 202.15 205.15 / 292.06 473.23
MOUSTACHES 46.26 / 54.10 57.22 59.04
MOUTH 36.30 54.18 / 102.13 128.19 187.18 / 238.26 279.06 291.07 / 292.13 292.25 294.05 / 297.07 297.12 309.03 / 312.15 318.11 347.06 / 372.02 401.25 427.08 / 442.19 449.27 456.20 / 460.28 473.15 490.13 / 491.22
MOUTHFUL 76.02
MOUTHPIECE 179.05
MOUTHS 63.05 75.20
MOVE 5.03 38.30 / 54.04 110.21 128.20 / 128.29 128.29 129.20

MOVE (CONT.) 177.30 / 179.22 195.24 219.04 / 311.26 407.14 445.22 / 460.08 482.06 506.04
MOVED 25.04 28.02 / 32.11 72.09 87.08 / 89.01 105.09 116.12 / 132.12 139.28 141.03 / 144.07 151.04 154.14 / 155.03 187.24 191.22 / 193.04 259.25 367.08 / 390.09 413.11 433.24 / 433.29 436.10 459.19 / 460.12 500.22 509.07 / 514.06 514.14
MOVEMENT 47.06 56.15 / 84.06 94.05 126.29 / 188.04 209.03 209.07 / 209.16 220.13 248.11 / 249.22 279.20 299.21 / 314.26 334.13 360.29 / 380.12 381.19 386.03 / 388.07 394.07 397.02 / 486.16 510.25
MOVEMENTS 133.14 / 148.21 189.07 192.28 / 260.09 264.15 293.14 / 319.04 347.23 348.21 / 397.22 411.05 484.09
MOVES 378.27
MOVING 19.21 36.11 / 139.01 145.12 205.02 / 324.07 324.22 351.06 / 373.06 378.07 397.10 / 399.19 441.07 445.26 / 450.06 480.09 494.06 / 494.23 504.07
MR 6.21 70.44 / 71.01 72.15 72.28 / 183.08 185.30 231.01 / 231.02 231.13 285.04 / 285.12 285.13 285.15 / 286.11 286.12 286.14 / 286.18 289.24 292.15 / 292.22 292.23 303.20 / 320.17 353.06 353.15 / 358.24 383.15 404.25
MUCH 1.09 2.25 / 25.30 27.25 36.29 / 41.04 43.09 43.23 / 47.24 53.25 56.19 / 67.10 67.24 70.37 / 72.06 74.10 77.18 / 77.23 84.13 84.17 / 95.29 109.11 114.22 / 115.11 117.24 118.22 / 128.22 129.12 136.16 / 137.05 143.10 148.03 / 150.17 156.06 156.11 / 157.30 158.06 159.07 / 163.21 165.08 167.19 / 168.27 169.24 172.14 / 174.18 176.07 177.01 / 179.09 180.25 181.15 / 181.21 185.21 186.18 / 189.02 191.09 197.10 / 198.23 201.29 203.09 / 204.12 205.12 208.02 / 209.09 209.16 211.06 / 212.02 212.07 213.10 / 214.14 215.19 217.17 / 218.13 218.14 218.19 / 228.04 228.20 228.21 / 229.22 230.27 235.07 / 237.21 241.24 242.28 / 246.14 258.28 261.19 / 270.04 270.24 272.05 / 274.10 283.22 287.16 / 293.22 304.21 306.09 / 324.26 330.13 331.10 / 333.09 339.19 341.22 / 341.30 342.05 342.22 / 351.24 356.14 357.17 / 373.05 381.15 382.15 / 382.21 383.03 383.10 / 384.25 388.21 399.11 / 400.28 402.01 404.30 / 419.11 422.19 424.01 / 427.19 429.02 429.09 / 438.04 447.10 453.21

MUCH (CONT.) 455.10 / 461.10 461.30 462.12 / 467.04 468.17 474.24 / 474.25 475.17 477.12 / 477.23 482.10 485.12 / 489.10 489.19 497.14 / 507.12 507.13 507.21
MUCH-DISAPPOINTED 356.14
MUCHED 463.27
MUD 52.20 259.23 / 279.24 293.26 309.09 / 309.15 312.13 314.04 / 356.02 356.03 366.19 / 375.27 407.16 408.26 / 445.21 480.08
MUD-FLAT 445.21
MUD-HOLE 293.26
MUD-STAINS 279.24
MUDBANK 311.25
MUDDLE 77.19 189.07
MUDDY 300.01 309.03 / 313.04 441.05 445.07 / 471.15
MUFFLED 16.10 20.09 / 30.30 94.03 159.11 / 224.22 433.07 438.25 / 453.13 467.17 494.24
MUGS 306.12
MULATTO 440.08
MULISH 224.26
MULTITUDE 4.27 / 103.05 167.10 191.21 / 410.09 412.21 417.21 / 463.09
MULTITUDES 341.19 / 392.15
MULTITUDINOUS 460.10
MUMBLE 27.30 90.18 / 96.29 141.01 141.01
MUMBLED 36.16 74.28 / 87.29 125.01 146.02 / 149.14 163.26 187.21 / 217.28 342.20 428.12 / 429.06 492.08 493.01 / 495.17
MUMBLING 366.08 368.25 / 439.20
MUR- 513.30
MUR- 513.30
MURDER 204.18 380.02 / 459.04
MURDERED 383.07
MURDERERS 368.12
MURDERING 144.27
MURMUR 15.14 18.02 / 83.05 119.18 165.14 / 318.17 367.29 376.17 / 377.09 381.16 391.01 / 409.02 412.13 467.23 / 486.02 494.08 498.17 / 509.27 514.14
MURMURED 65.15 99.20 / 113.27 130.19 137.28 / 145.22 162.10 176.10 / 187.14 231.30 258.09 / 284.03 306.02 320.24 / 334.09 381.23 388.03 / 393.03 413.17 429.12 / 432.30 507.14
MURMURING 140.03 / 150.24 279.21
MURMURS 148.22 350.04 / 448.27 485.06
MURS 514.01
MUSCLE 87.08
MUSCLES 144.16
MUSED 204.22 267.31 / 413.20
MUSING 493.11
MUSKETS 461.25 494.14 / 498.20
MUSLIMS 485.01
MUST 1.15 26.11 / 34.07 42.02 45.02 / 48.18 51.11 51.25 / 60.18 67.16 69.19 / 79.06 79.30 80.29 / 93.28 94.01 98.22 / 103.10 103.13 105.17

MUST (CONT.) 111.13 / 111.18 114.20 115.21 / 115.30 116.20 125.07 / 134.30 137.30 138.10 / 150.20 158.23 169.30 / 182.03 183.10 184.08 / 185.15 186.28 197.13 / 199.09 201.13 201.14 / 203.14 204.26 205.02 / 209.19 214.07 214.24 / 217.24 218.10 223.01 / 223.06 225.03 232.02 / 233.01 233.14 234.06 / 244.29 246.13 252.02 / 265.13 271.02 271.13 / 271.24 275.09 275.20 / 277.20 295.28 300.15 / 303.23 308.24 314.18 / 320.30 321.04 325.01 / 327.11 334.08 340.26 / 341.14 341.29 342.10 / 345.29 351.23 352.02 / 357.02 360.13 362.03 / 365.05 374.24 375.12 / 386.23 391.24 391.24 / 395.10 398.03 404.20 / 412.07 412.09 418.30 / 421.02 421.13 421.14 / 423.11 424.02 424.03 / 433.06 435.04 437.10 / 448.13 457.06 459.02 / 465.28 468.11 470.14
MUSTARD 209.11
MUSTARD-SEED 208.11
MUSTER 315.22
MUSTERED 125.05
MUSTN'T 121.03 187.25
MUTE 83.23 116.27 / 166.11 271.11 357.05 / 373.06 399.21 423.09 / 500.09
MUTELY 181.07 217.21 / 451.24
MUTINIES 5.15
MUTINY 190.12
MUTTER 188.29 232.14 / 282.18 338.26 417.02 / 497.08
MUTTERED 121.09 134.23 / 149.10 157.20 159.15 / 161.01 186.27 217.03 / 218.17 220.26 308.02 / 350.26 363.06 363.10 / 369.20 405.13 411.18 / 465.06 467.07
MUTTERING 110.10 / 132.04 145.15 241.21 / 466.25 495.15
MUTTERS 28.24 110.21 / 391.13
MUTUAL 454.24
MUZZLE 89.02 323.24 / 372.25
MY 8.01 8.04 / 8.08 8.12 8.13 / 29.12 34.22 38.06 / 40.24 41.01 41.03 / 41.08 42.01 42.10 / 42.11 43.40 43.43 / 45.29 46.01 46.03 / 46.04 47.08 47.18 / 48.06 48.09 48.21 / 48.30 49.12 51.22 / 51.30 52.04 52.07 / 52.09 55.29 57.21 / 58.08 60.04 60.12 / 60.15 61.03 61.08 / 61.11 61.17 61.19 / 61.19 61.20 61.25 / 62.04 62.12 62.13 / 62.17 62.17 62.18 / 62.30 63.08 63.14 / 63.19 63.20 64.04 / 64.15 68.13 68.23 / 68.24 68.25 68.25 / 69.03 70.28 70.33 / 73.25 74.08 74.11 / 74.20 74.28 75.09 / 75.09 75.09 75.10

MY (CONT.)		75.16
75.24	75.26	75.27
75.28	76.01	77.13
77.24	78.09	78.17
78.22	80.17	81.16
81.18	81.30	82.11
82.17	82.30	83.24
84.02	84.16	84.19
84.19	84.23	84.29
85.02	85.12	85.13
85.16	86.12	87.27
88.03	88.03	88.22
88.25	90.14	90.14
90.17	90.21	90.30
91.15	93.16	93.25
93.30	93.30	94.21
95.03	95.08	95.18
95.02	96.22	97.11
99.16	99.21	99.28
100.24	101.11	101.13
101.19	104.05	104.18
105.16	108.01	108.01
108.02	108.21	108.24
109.07	109.09	109.09
109.13	109.21	109.22
109.29	110.09	111.25
112.12	113.06	113.08
114.06	114.25	114.26
115.01	116.30	118.09
120.13	120.15	120.24
124.01	124.08	126.15
128.07	128.14	128.14
128.18	128.19	128.26
129.04	130.29	131.01
133.16	133.20	133.24
134.04	134.05	134.05
134.06	137.20	140.27
140.27	141.16	142.03
142.06	142.24	143.04
143.05	143.20	144.01
145.26	149.13	149.26
151.08	151.22	151.26
152.06	152.08	152.12
152.22	153.05	153.11
153.12	153.25	154.03
154.12	154.15	156.01
157.13	158.10	158.19
159.05	159.09	159.22
160.29	160.30	162.05
162.08	162.11	162.19
163.04	163.30	164.27
165.05	165.14	169.29
170.15	170.23	171.13
171.19	171.30	172.10
173.21	174.20	175.14
175.30	177.02	178.14
179.02	179.12	182.07
182.09	182.10	183.28
184.08	185.13	185.15
185.16	185.17	185.21
185.26	186.02	186.05
186.06	186.09	186.12
187.17	187.18	188.03
188.10	188.11	188.14
188.22	188.30	189.15
190.01	190.02	190.03
190.04	191.08	193.11
194.30	196.02	197.03
197.18	197.20	197.30
198.08	199.05	199.28
199.28	200.09	200.22
200.28	201.08	201.25
201.28	203.08	203.11
203.16	204.04	205.09
205.19	207.04	207.17
207.18	207.25	207.25
208.14	208.19	208.24
209.01	209.02	209.07
209.28	210.09	210.10
210.11	210.26	210.28
210.28	211.04	211.04
211.15	211.21	211.26
212.18	213.24	214.03
214.12	214.14	214.17
214.18	215.13	215.17
216.05	216.07	216.13
216.22	216.29	217.02
218.11	218.18	218.28
220.01	220.05	221.01
222.07	222.11	223.18

MY (CONT.)		223.20
224.13	224.23	225.27
225.28	226.05	226.08
226.17	227.01	227.05
227.09	227.10	227.15
227.20	228.05	228.19
228.29	229.01	229.06
229.10	229.22	229.25
230.08	230.10	230.11
231.21	233.23	233.26
235.20	236.06	236.13
236.15	236.26	237.27
237.28	237.30	238.08
239.05	239.24	240.03
242.14	243.01	243.04
243.22	243.26	243.27
244.04	244.10	245.24
246.05	247.17	247.23
247.24	249.13	249.14
249.19	250.24	251.06
251.24	253.30	254.18
254.25	254.26	255.06
255.06	255.07	255.08
255.11	255.12	255.15
255.16	255.18	255.18
255.27	256.04	256.10
256.13	256.13	256.14
256.16	256.17	256.17
256.19	256.19	256.24
256.24	256.29	256.30
257.07	257.11	257.12
257.15	257.16	257.17
260.16	261.11	261.16
261.17	264.11	264.15
264.24	265.02	265.12
268.10	268.11	269.29
270.20	272.29	273.28
273.30	274.10	274.15
274.24	275.11	275.14
282.11	282.21	282.26
284.04	287.14	287.20
290.19	291.07	291.21
291.24	294.19	294.25
295.05	295.23	295.28
297.15	301.06	301.15
302.11	302.13	303.11
303.17	303.22	303.24
303.28	304.07	306.12
306.16	307.24	308.23
308.23	309.01	309.04
309.06	309.06	320.19
323.01	324.28	325.05
325.30	328.09	329.03
329.10	329.11	336.22
338.12	338.26	339.03
340.01	340.20	342.15
343.01	343.04	343.05
344.09	345.11	349.01
349.22	350.01	350.08
350.14	353.01	353.09
353.28	354.01	362.24
363.06	365.01	369.21
370.19	373.21	374.27
375.14	375.21	376.02
376.04	376.16	377.05
377.12	377.26	378.06
379.17	379.28	379.30
380.02	380.04	380.09
381.17	382.04	382.04
383.22	383.23	385.14
385.16	385.22	386.11
386.14	386.23	386.24
386.29	387.18	387.24
387.25	389.02	389.13
389.29	389.30	390.07
390.07	390.09	390.10
390.26	392.01	393.05
393.15	393.22	393.26
394.17	396.03	396.15
396.27	397.09	397.10
397.10	398.09	398.17
399.07	399.11	399.16
399.27	399.27	400.05
400.30	401.10	401.13
401.14	401.27	402.04
402.09	402.10	402.30
403.02	403.03	403.27
404.28	407.03	407.10
407.18	408.10	408.12
409.13	409.14	409.18

MY (CONT.)		411.08
411.22	411.27	412.04
412.08	412.17	412.20
412.22	413.15	414.03
420.17	423.13	423.13
425.05	425.23	426.03
426.14	428.19	428.29
429.08	430.07	431.10
431.10	431.11	431.11
431.12	431.24	432.10
432.29	433.07	433.17
434.03	437.25	449.04
451.06	471.05	472.06
472.06	473.26	473.27
474.11	474.18	480.29
481.05	483.03	483.05
485.13	485.16	486.17
487.04	491.27	514.17
516.11	516.12	
MYSELF	29.16	40.22
40.24	43.06	47.16
47.23	48.14	48.17
52.04	64.08	69.06
71.29	74.19	80.15
81.20	82.08	91.13
96.30	97.18	101.18
101.27	109.11	114.28
122.01	124.03	129.08
141.11	151.10	153.02
153.24	156.08	160.14
160.26	161.04	162.10
170.15	185.10	187.20
188.11	193.23	194.12
197.04	199.07	211.23
212.10	212.17	214.07
219.18	223.23	223.28
224.12	225.11	228.11
228.27	231.26	234.25
235.22	237.09	238.06
243.05	243.13	253.26
256.26	256.30	265.06
270.14	270.24	272.26
274.25	288.20	291.09
295.12	309.08	315.06
330.21	338.05	338.28
341.11	341.23	344.23
353.04	354.11	367.05
373.22	378.10	379.06
381.09	383.19	385.21
391.16	394.15	398.18
400.09	401.06	401.09
411.22	420.25	429.11
MYSTERIES		53.05
MYSTERIOUS		12.20
13.19	21.24	42.04
42.06	42.30	49.17
49.20	54.16	115.17
119.24	142.10	155.09
166.13	172.30	209.26
222.15	226.04	229.18
230.25	248.08	344.30
381.14	387.27	392.05
395.13	482.17	
MYSTERIOUSLY		17.26
84.27	248.24	260.10
343.29		
MYSTERY	60.09	82.06
112.28	170.09	214.29
264.09	302.04	322.12
335.18	340.18	349.07
354.02	377.27	377.29
379.26	423.06	434.25
488.09		
MYSTIC		321.24
MYTH		345.23
N		472.09
NA	171.20	171.20
257.29	263.01	
NAB		237.06
NAIL		365.22
NAILED		462.20
NAIVE	89.19	287.16
NAIVENESS		228.08
352.23		
NAKED	5.13	20.25
21.08	23.08	24.11
42.07	42.08	42.25
54.06	62.24	198.13
279.23	318.19	371.15

NAKED (CONT.)		372.16
410.19	414.25	427.06
469.12		
NAKHODA	315.17	338.29
363.11	451.12	486.16
498.30	509.06	509.29
NAME	3.05	25.09
45.19	81.07	141.25
141.30	196.11	198.01
201.04	205.10	213.04
230.06	230.07	233.11
233.18	241.29	243.21
243.24	247.14	249.30
262.28	266.15	268.28
269.08	270.22	276.15
282.12	286.01	342.13
342.29	356.23	378.19
411.23	418.23	420.23
426.13	441.26	450.19
455.19	455.20	465.26
472.09	498.14	502.01
NAME'S	426.14	471.06
NAMELESS		263.01
NAMELY		345.01
NAMES	50.14	85.29
119.12	119.12	119.13
119.13	126.26	130.16
142.15	199.02	278.07
361.25		
NAPE	55.02	116.25
NARRATED	7.30	98.17
142.13	254.02	
NARRATING		365.27
NARRATIVE		137.29
185.15	416.02	435.03
477.04		
NARROW	8.26	31.14
32.15	139.30	180.16
248.17	269.15	279.11
444.14	497.02	500.16
NARROWLY	63.21	186.28
NASTY	75.06	169.04
242.02		
NATION		465.02
NATIONS		277.23
NATIVE	14.03	15.02
40.14	83.23	118.10
191.29	191.30	195.19
207.22	241.06	249.13
250.14	252.14	269.07
269.21	278.09	344.28
393.21	427.29	437.26
439.16	440.26	441.28
472.03		
NATIVE-RULED		269.07
NATIVES	37.13	42.24
80.02	251.11	285.08
426.26	435.18	457.07
NATUR'		235.17
NATURAL	74.29	88.16
97.27	109.26	126.22
138.22	157.10	246.28
259.02	317.02	320.27
327.22	381.06	399.11
404.14	458.19	
NATURALISE		247.07
250.01	250.05	
NATURALISTS		264.19
NATURALLY		13.16
65.16	100.13	122.10
222.06	242.23	244.08
395.15	428.02	
NATURE	20.01	48.28
51.04	58.15	86.15
98.15	106.15	112.12
115.20	167.18	214.10
215.27	225.12	242.07
242.20	245.14	246.08
246.26	253.04	253.08
334.29	335.14	336.13
352.12	379.25	399.23
451.28	501.21	
NATURED		69.03
NATURELLEMENT		170.26
NATURES		434.17
NAUGHTY		183.06
NAUSEOUS		158.16
NAUTICAL	33.05	67.10
76.11		
NAVAL		169.02

NAVIGABLE 250.30
NAVIGATED 194.08
NAVIGATION 4.21
  27.27
NAVY 14.13 241.29
  280.09
NAY 86.21 358.09
NAZARENE 350.23 502.14
NE 179.24 180.24
NEAR 23.29 37.09
  57.28 62.22 72.25
  81.09 85.03 131.18
  165.13 178.06 197.02
  222.21 223.10 337.26
  353.07 398.27 403.16
  406.06 425.04 432.03
  450.01 467.11 472.01
  489.29 498.22
NEARER 24.30 87.07
  146.11 261.17 264.06
  319.17 336.14 376.18
  382.10
NEAREST 105.21 170.26
  341.07 450.24 459.04
NEARLY 8.03 8.05
  52.23 74.19 102.19
  107.19 164.29 200.09
  246.16 269.24 281.21
  292.29 297.01 309.24
  342.15 377.11 400.07
  400.18 400.18 400.19
  443.30 450.07 470.05
  477.05
NEAT 1.10 71.09
  339.26
NEATLY 193.02
NEATNESS 470.30
NECESSARILY 67.03
NECESSARY 11.14
  88.18 210.23 375.03
  375.04 391.30 462.07
NECESSITY 1.08
  48.21 48.27 115.13
  179.26 289.05 363.12
  384.17 418.26 442.02
  454.07 457.08
NECK 43.35 55.02
  116.25 120.18 185.07
  254.12 255.14 263.17
  287.09 293.25 367.30
  453.13 511.28 515.10
NECKS 44.19
NEED 1.14 208.07
  219.06 237.11 384.15
  384.15 390.01 392.10
  392.14 413.17
NEEDED 117.30 381.10
NEEDN'T 201.23 308.02
NEGATIVELY 165.05
NEGLECT 207.03
NEGLECTED 276.12
  502.10
NEGLIGENTLY 343.16
  394.12
NEGLIGIBLE 68.18
NEGOTIATING 197.05
NEGOTIATION 454.24
NEGOTIATIONS 251.14
  454.18
NEIGHBOURHOOD 254.30
  347.05
NEIGHBOURING 12.19
  94.06
NEIGHBOURS' 367.10
NEIL 281.03 304.05
  324.21
NEITHER 76.21 77.22
  84.19 100.29 130.10
  133.25 153.15 186.24
  191.12 205.24 232.22
  266.23 271.06 280.22
  324.22 352.20 357.22
  360.18 381.10 391.04
  392.17 395.04 400.10
  403.27 421.05
NELYUS 356.13
NENN' 257.04
NERVE 358.13 438.18
NERVE-SHAKING 438.18
NERVES 51.18 361.24

NERVOUS 124.30 189.16
  492.02
NERVOUSLY 388.10
  428.24
NEST 49.03 79.08
  342.29
NESTLED 512.03
NESTS 316.10
NET 209.11 350.08
NETWORK 158.03
NEUTRALITY 444.25
NEVER 2.08 29.11
  38.08 44.03 55.26
  56.04 58.14 58.15
  58.16 60.06 65.05
  67.20 67.21 67.21
  67.22 68.27 69.05
  70.31 70.36 71.11
  72.06 75.07 77.08
  81.15 84.23 85.02
  88.15 88.28 90.01
  90.02 95.02 95.12
  95.17 95.19 100.23
  113.21 118.30 119.22
  120.24 121.12 130.04
  134.28 136.05 136.18
  140.08 142.19 143.04
  147.16 168.11 174.16
  174.21 183.16 184.16
  184.22 197.12 197.15
  197.16 219.18 223.25
  224.19 226.11 236.25
  239.24 247.16 251.05
  251.12 253.10 259.23
  259.28 261.19 266.06
  272.11 272.12 274.30
  275.06 279.25 280.29
  281.06 282.06 283.30
  284.03 285.03 290.02
  290.10 290.11 291.18
  292.13 295.30 299.19
  311.16 318.13 318.16
  320.06 325.01 325.27
  329.24 329.25 329.25
  329.29 346.04 349.28
  353.02 360.03 369.05
  374.27 376.08 376.09
  376.14 382.10 386.30
  388.09 388.19 389.02
  389.03 391.13 391.20
  392.18 392.19 392.19
  394.19 398.27 404.26
  404.29 405.03 412.07
  412.14 413.23 417.28
  422.09 422.12 422.21
  422.29 422.30 424.08
  424.10 424.10 429.23
  431.18 431.18 435.12
  438.01 460.06 460.30
  466.26 475.27 481.18
  481.24 481.24 481.28
  482.04 486.03 487.05
  487.19 487.21 488.27
  493.18 507.08 507.08
  511.13 513.01 513.02
  513.21
NEVERTHELESS 2.26
  7.26 174.15 185.10
  245.02 359.08 399.14
NEW 15.01 16.15
  28.15 53.24 56.17
  74.24 90.29 92.12
  113.03 123.25 123.26
  153.19 153.22 166.19
  169.30 184.01 184.06
  230.11 239.03 243.09
  267.05 267.08 289.27
  309.02 310.24 323.10
  326.03 337.21 359.25
  437.30 453.21 453.28
  481.30
NEWCOMER 452.25
NEWCOMERS 454.01
NEWLY 396.14
NEWS 168.22 214.28
  214.29 234.14 257.30
  278.19 286.19 333.20
  338.10 421.23 422.15
  426.14 456.15 498.05
  499.04 499.05 503.01

NEXT 6.07 7.15
  41.03 53.04 56.22
  70.43 82.08 82.25
  83.07 113.11 113.11
  120.14 131.04 131.27
  166.26 178.12 194.06
  195.04 220.07 224.22
  233.24 243.08 285.01
  344.27 369.01 371.08
  385.04 395.25 407.01
  413.22 437.03 438.28
  472.26 505.03
NICE 46.06 70.06
  121.04 241.01 242.29
NICEST 240.25
NICHT 260.29
NICKEL 310.24
NIGGERS 109.30 236.17
  236.22
NIGHT 26.08 26.30
  28.11 29.19 36.06
  71.27 72.10 76.04
  94.14 96.21 97.16
  99.09 100.09 102.25
  105.18 124.05 126.04
  129.03 136.18 137.24
  138.08 139.26 142.11
  146.05 148.11 148.20
  155.06 157.09 157.23
  159.12 160.09 162.08
  163.15 166.02 168.05
  184.30 185.07 187.02
  188.23 189.19 192.26
  216.11 216.16 221.03
  225.25 243.01 254.02
  255.01 262.03 263.02
  266.06 285.03 287.26
  293.28 298.28 310.06
  324.04 324.08 328.04
  336.12 349.29 350.06
  350.15 358.02 358.14
  359.09 362.19 363.05
  364.23 364.26 367.17
  367.20 368.01 368.30
  369.01 369.01 369.02
  374.12 374.17 376.27
  381.20 382.12 383.27
  385.03 385.20 387.10
  388.02 402.14 414.19
  415.08 427.16 440.21
  441.01 447.01 460.16
  462.21 464.15 466.15
  484.20 489.03 489.13
  489.16 489.19 489.27
  490.07 490.21 496.08
  511.10 515.02
NIGHT-GLASSES 76.04
NIGHT-WATCHES 210.30
NIGHTS 18.11 215.18
  369.02 374.17
NIMBLER 313.15
NINE 43.17 166.26
  254.05
NINETY 197.07
NIP 26.26
NIPPERS 45.14
NO 3.14 3.10
  8.18 9.04 12.11
  25.09 29.08 29.08
  33.29 33.30 34.15
  36.15 36.24 38.09
  38.17 40.21 42.13
  42.27 43.13 45.22
  46.25 47.06 47.15
  49.05 50.23 52.11
  52.19 54.03 56.15
  56.16 56.16 57.05
  57.26 59.14 60.13
  60.25 60.26 60.27
  60.29 61.12 61.28
  62.06 62.10 64.20
  65.04 66.05 66.05
  68.28 69.07 69.15
  69.22 71.30 72.05
  72.07 73.24 74.20
  76.19 77.12 78.13
  79.23 80.19 80.30
  81.27 82.22 85.24
  86.04 86.29 87.29

NO (CONT.) 88.23
  89.01 90.03 91.08
  91.10 93.10 95.13
  95.23 95.26 95.26
  96.03 96.05 96.12
  96.12 96.27 97.06
  97.06 98.19 98.30
  99.17 99.18 100.11
  103.20 103.20 103.21
  103.26 104.20 104.26
  105.07 105.23 109.08
  109.24 110.05 113.06
  113.10 113.18 113.30
  114.27 117.01 117.02
  117.03 117.19 118.27
  120.02 121.06 121.13
  121.13 123.03 123.09
  123.09 123.09 124.09
  124.17 125.06 126.01
  126.05 126.08 126.11
  126.19 127.27 128.24
  129.05 129.07 132.16
  135.07 137.01 137.13
  140.09 142.05 145.02
  146.20 146.23 146.26
  146.27 146.28 146.28
  146.28 150.08 150.09
  150.12 150.14 151.07
  156.08 156.19 156.20
  159.13 160.03 160.10
  161.03 163.10 164.03
  164.07 164.07 164.16
  165.22 165.26 167.12
  170.02 170.21 171.25
  173.04 176.09 176.09
  176.11 178.12 178.12
  179.15 179.15 179.28
  180.13 181.02 181.03
  185.17 186.14 188.07
  188.17 189.05 190.21
  191.17 191.18 191.19
  191.21 191.22 194.10
  196.02 196.27 197.11
  201.28 201.28 202.01
  202.02 202.03 202.03
  203.04 204.13 204.21
  205.28 208.02 208.05
  208.11 209.01 209.17
  209.30 211.24 212.23
  212.29 212.30 213.09
  213.09 218.04 218.23
  219.01 219.14 219.14
  219.20 220.17 221.07
  222.14 225.26 226.01
  226.22 228.12 229.12
  230.23 233.11 234.07
  234.08 234.27 235.16
  237.11 238.24 241.05
  242.19 243.09 243.10
  244.30 245.10 247.19
  249.13 250.05 253.18
  254.20 255.17 256.04
  260.11 260.29 261.13
  262.11 262.18 266.07
  266.17 267.12 268.17
  270.08 271.08 271.08
  272.23 272.28 273.01
  273.17 274.07 275.18
  276.05 278.29 281.11
  282.09 282.11 282.21
  282.25 282.29 286.15
  286.19 286.20 286.22
  289.26 289.01 289.10
  290.17 291.02 291.06
  293.18 296.01 298.04
  298.25 300.04 303.22
  304.24 306.22 307.15
  307.22 307.24 308.09
  313.06 313.07 313.07
  316.15 320.26 324.29
  327.09 328.10 329.14
  329.19 329.28 330.30
  331.02 331.14 331.17
  331.30 334.20 336.08
  336.13 337.20 338.06
  338.06 338.21 338.22
  338.23 339.17 340.12
  340.21 342.02 342.21
  343.15 343.23 344.09

NO (CONT.) 344.13
344.17 346.11 349.08
350.19 352.05 354.02
355.15 360.02 360.28
361.09 363.05 363.10
363.17 369.08 369.11
372.22 375.10 376.18
377.10 378.19 379.06
380.09 381.18 382.10
384.12 384.22 386.04
386.04 388.15 390.14
391.04 391.04 391.05
391.15 391.15 391.16
392.09 394.22 395.23
396.15 397.15 399.22
400.14 400.26 403.04
404.14 406.06 407.15
408.09 411.23 412.03
412.05 412.06 414.12
414.26 414.28 415.15
417.12 417.13 417.14
417.18 417.18 418.29
419.06 419.15 419.26
419.28 420.22 422.19
423.05 423.25 428.12
428.28 429.16 431.17
431.24 432.12 432.13
433.17 433.17 433.17
433.18 433.19 440.17
440.28 440.29 440.29
441.21 443.02 445.21
450.17 450.29 452.03
452.15 452.16 453.29
455.30 456.01 457.11
457.18 458.19 460.12
454.23 465.03 465.04
465.04 465.04 465.16
467.02 467.29 467.30
472.26 473.12 474.04
474.06 477.11 478.10
480.26 482.29 482.30
483.07 485.08 486.16
487.09 488.04 488.11
489.04 491.23 492.08
492.21 495.25 500.14
506.04 507.18 508.21
509.24 510.27 511.05
511.14 516.08
NO-ACCOUNT 54.03
NO' 84.14
NOBLE 63.13 65.10
224.09 254.29 315.09
352.19 397.29
NOBLE-LOOKING 65.10
NOBODIES 54.12
NOBODY 79.21 88.28
111.12 111.15 111.18
113.26 137.03 139.18
140.06 146.24 159.30
165.15 169.10 173.09
236.29 243.13 266.16
277.30 303.24 307.21
319.06 325.02 370.28
388.05 388.06 393.23
393.23 400.12 405.07
461.08 484.05 500.14
NOD 123.21 202.06
NODDED 48.06 99.25
108.01 154.07 203.12
231.27 287.19 362.04
363.09 429.10 468.04
NODDING 77.21 237.26
259.16
NOISE 31.01 31.13
33.30 34.11 45.22
84.06 89.25 92.20
103.02 104.08 107.08
120.25 137.06 139.28
143.21 144.29 148.07
169.12 216.14 218.02
253.20 276.07 283.22
316.01 332.05 362.15
367.23 463.04 464.15
457.03 467.26 467.29
487.08
NOISELESS 37.20
349.22
NOISELESSLY 24.06
62.22 260.08
NOISES 131.29 133.29

NOISILY 124.19 432.05
NOISOME 476.06
NOISY 9.06 235.09
NOMADIC 93.02
NONCHALANTLY 493.09
NONDESCRIPT 59.08
440.10
NONE 61.21 73.19
180.02 202.13 344.01
413.08 440.10
NONPLUSSED 126.25
NONSENSE 85.22 188.03
202.01 342.21 384.22
384.25
NOON 5.27 17.24
23.01
NOR 27.22 76.21
77.22 84.19 100.29
130.10 133.26 186.24
190.24 205.24 215.17
232.23 266.23 280.22
324.22 352.20 357.23
357.23 359.20 360.18
381.10 391.04 392.18
421.05 424.11
NORMAL 278.21
NORTH 15.23 71.18
151.15 194.19 196.18
276.10 308.29 332.23
411.07 441.04
NORTH-EAST 441.04
NORTH-WEST 151.15
NORTHWARD 152.18
229.09
NORWEGIAN 194.13
NOSE 15.06 45.14
57.12 72.10 77.21
83.16 142.03 192.22
306.12 311.13 413.29
NOSE-NIPPERS 45.14
NOSTRILS 100.03 145.30
192.23 318.10 323.06
371.26
NOT 1.14 3.06
3.08 7.26 8.10
8.19 8.27 10.10
10.21 11.01 11.25
11.27 12.04 15.04
22.04 23.20 25.30
26.21 26.29 26.30
27.21 28.20 28.27
28.28 29.21 29.26
30.24 33.29 34.12
34.29 35.26 38.01
38.13 41.05 41.22
42.26 43.38 43.40
44.13 46.02 46.11
47.06 47.26 48.16
49.11 49.18 50.04
50.13 51.16 54.06
54.06 55.24 56.08
57.03 57.05 57.25
59.06 60.24 60.25
62.02 65.18 66.02
66.08 66.09 66.12
66.22 66.23 67.10
67.30 68.02 68.14
68.17 68.19 68.20
68.21 68.24 70.05
70.27 70.33 73.15
74.03 76.20 76.22
77.10 79.14 80.12
81.04 81.18 82.09
82.13 82.14 82.15
82.16 82.17 84.13
85.05 85.08 85.21
86.08 86.23 86.24
86.27 87.21 87.24
90.04 90.12 94.20
95.05 95.18 95.24
96.02 96.10 96.16
96.25 96.28 97.01
97.04 97.17 97.17
97.20 98.06 98.15
98.22 99.17 99.18
99.25 101.03 101.08
101.09 102.11 103.01
103.21 104.02 104.06
104.13 104.26 104.26
105.23 105.24 106.03

NOT (CONT.) 106.09
107.05 107.06 107.07
108.29 111.11 111.15
111.21 111.27 112.03
113.09 117.23 118.02
118.04 118.08 118.28
119.03 119.28 119.29
120.27 123.10 124.05
124.18 125.21 125.22
127.07 127.08 127.10
127.16 129.10 129.12
129.20 130.08 130.28
130.30 131.02 131.03
131.10 132.13 132.21
132.28 133.27 136.16
136.16 137.01 137.04
137.30 138.02 138.02
138.14 139.06 139.06
139.07 139.25 139.25
139.30 140.06 140.14
141.16 142.21 143.06
143.06 143.30 144.11
145.23 146.28 147.26
150.10 151.06 152.12
153.13 153.14 153.23
155.24 156.07 156.07
157.16 157.17 157.18
157.21 157.26 157.28
158.01 158.05 158.09
158.27 159.07 159.15
159.28 160.01 160.02
160.06 160.10 160.19
163.18 163.20 163.23
163.23 164.06 164.22
164.23 165.01 165.01
165.03 165.07 165.16
165.18 165.26 167.09
167.14 168.04 168.13
169.24 169.29 172.06
172.26 174.05 176.15
176.15 177.01 177.26
177.30 178.20 178.30
179.15 179.16 179.18
180.23 180.26 181.13
183.24 184.21 184.24
184.26 186.02 186.29
187.01 187.09 187.22
188.12 188.29 189.23
190.06 190.17 190.24
191.04 193.23 193.25
194.06 196.18 197.01
198.04 198.10 198.23
203.23 203.27 204.17
207.01 207.03 208.02
208.07 208.20 208.27
208.30 209.09 210.19
212.16 213.19 213.21
214.08 214.19 214.23
215.02 215.03 215.21
215.22 215.22 215.28
217.16 217.17 218.03
218.12 218.23 219.04
220.12 221.08 224.11
224.14 225.02 225.10
225.23 226.28 227.08
227.22 227.23 228.04
228.04 229.20 231.12
233.08 233.23 235.07
239.13 239.17 239.23
241.12 242.01 242.12
243.23 243.26 244.09
245.01 245.04 245.11
245.13 245.22 246.03
246.18 246.28 247.20
248.19 249.27 251.22
252.15 253.13 253.17
253.18 254.18 255.16
255.17 258.16 259.11
260.14 260.17 260.18
260.19 262.03 262.27
264.16 264.28 265.07
265.08 266.04 267.03
267.18 268.25 269.29
270.19 270.24 271.24
272.01 272.01 272.12
272.15 272.25 272.29
273.08 274.16 274.19
274.19 274.24 274.27
274.30 275.01 275.09
275.10 275.14 275.15

NOT (CONT.) 275.17
277.16 278.27 278.30
280.02 280.03 281.12
281.20 281.22 282.02
282.23 282.24 283.01
283.06 283.07 283.28
285.01 285.18 285.23
286.17 286.18 288.28
288.29 289.16 289.18
291.10 295.13 295.14
298.13 301.01 301.09
302.12 303.03 303.05
303.05 304.19 304.21
304.30 306.09 306.21
308.28 310.13 313.08
316.17 317.04 317.13
318.04 319.25 319.27
320.30 321.05 322.13
325.05 328.11 329.10
330.11 330.13 331.03
331.06 335.10 335.11
335.11 337.21 337.22
338.02 338.30 340.02
340.23 340.29 341.03
341.30 342.21 342.05
342.30 343.16 343.22
344.10 344.26 345.28
347.16 349.04 352.24
353.06 353.11 355.07
355.13 356.22 357.10
357.15 359.02 359.20
359.22 359.25 360.17
361.10 361.16 362.13
362.13 364.22 365.30
366.21 367.05 368.08
368.15 368.20 369.24
369.24 370.21 370.21
370.27 371.24 373.22
374.14 375.28 375.29
376.05 376.09 376.11
376.17 377.16 381.15
382.06 382.17 382.19
382.21 384.13 385.05
385.12 385.13 385.15
387.03 387.09 387.10
387.21 387.22 389.26
390.20 390.20 390.20
391.18 391.28 392.27
392.28 393.09 394.14
394.15 394.24 395.10
396.11 397.16 398.28
399.14 400.10 400.21
401.08 401.30 403.14
403.25 403.26 405.01
405.12 406.05 408.08
410.25 411.26 413.17
414.14 414.30 418.10
419.07 421.21 426.06
426.14 427.30 428.10
428.14 428.14 429.11
430.17 430.24 431.03
431.15 431.18 431.18
431.28 432.14 433.14
433.19 433.21 435.06
435.20 437.12 438.02
438.14 438.26 438.30
440.27 441.19 446.06
447.10 447.12 448.29
449.05 450.26 452.06
455.14 455.19 456.12
456.14 456.30 457.04
457.05 457.18 458.04
460.17 466.15 468.09
468.09 470.07 470.17
470.24 470.28 470.28
471.09 471.21 472.01
472.05 472.26 473.28
475.05 477.06 477.14
477.18 479.02 479.04
479.09 479.19 480.24
481.16 482.25 484.08
484.19 484.28 485.02
486.19 488.10 488.14
488.18 488.20 489.07
490.19 490.25 491.04
492.01 492.09 492.30
493.05 494.24 495.09
495.18 496.03 500.22
501.12 501.18 501.21
502.29 503.05 503.06

NOT (CONT.)   503.07
503.10 506.04 506.08
506.14 506.23 507.09
508.03 509.12 510.18
510.24 511.12 511.16
512.25 513.15 514.05
515.21 516.06
NOTE   47.25 223.19
229.15 269.30 302.07
307.01 348.28 350.05
388.10 426.13 466.23
491.30
NOTE'   171.11
NOTED   127.23 371.17
376.25
NOTEPAPER   210.24
NOTEZ   170.29
NOTHING 1.07   3.04
7.24   10.11 12.01
13.15 22.22 23.20
42.09 49.20 50.03
51.13 53.02 53.30
52.03 66.16 67.23
67.27 70.35 71.06
72.08 75.01 76.21
78.28 84.20 89.20
90.10 90.16 96.16
97.26 98.27 101.22
103.18 104.04 111.22
112.14 114.13 115.04
116.12 118.20 119.30
120.01 120.02 124.16
124.16 125.18 125.19
134.24 136.02 137.07
137.26 139.05 139.06
140.01 140.13 141.03
143.07 143.29 143.29
146.24 148.06 148.07
151.07 152.03 159.02
160.21 161.01 162.20
164.17 164.21 165.09
169.04 172.29 174.08
176.30 178.08 179.20
180.25 181.04 184.05
196.06 186.30 188.16
200.03 203.05 203.28
204.08 205.10 210.01
212.10 212.27 218.20
228.02 230.20 238.16
253.02 257.12 258.06
262.30 269.03 269.15
280.15 281.16 284.01
295.15 299.05 302.12
302.14 308.09 308.14
319.02 321.08 321.11
335.02 337.04 337.23
345.10 353.06 353.07
353.22 353.26 357.22
357.28 358.12 358.19
361.19 370.21 377.07
379.05 379.05 379.20
382.02 382.25 383.06
384.08 384.25 390.13
390.14 390.30 391.02
391.03 391.07 391.27
394.13 394.15 396.25
400.04 400.20 401.01
402.26 402.26 403.12
411.27 412.08 414.12
419.10 419.26 419.27
421.04 421.18 422.19
422.28 427.17 430.28
433.04 438.10 446.12
453.10 454.30 471.24
479.18 479.21 481.01
492.12 492.22 494.02
495.09 495.30 508.04
511.03 511.03 511.23
NOTICE 103.02 167.26
211.07 285.19 298.13
347.08 403.06 420.05
428.28 501.15
NOTICEABLE   81.27
NOTICED 46.20 77.30
85.10 93.07 109.03
123.16 140.11 313.18
367.18 371.25 393.11
515.07
NOTION   58.30 59.19
64.20 95.08 97.24

MOTION (CONT.)   143.02
163.21 180.19 184.09
185.14 201.26 201.26
270.08 280.12 280.28
312.28 337.24 359.12
366.01
NOTIONS 46.01 51.11
379.08
NOTORIOUS   42.04
54.12 197.21 202.15
205.16 240.10
NOTWITHSTANDING 215.13
292.08 333.12 365.09
463.13
NOW   5.28   7.20
7.22   11.03 12.04
13.28 22.12 25.17
25.30 36.23 38.29
46.03 48.20 49.02
52.01 53.01 59.23
63.16 65.14 71.12
74.03 79.04 79.25
80.07 80.23 81.13
81.17 82.07 82.10
85.02 87.24 87.26
92.20 95.02 104.03
108.21 118.06 119.03
120.01 121.13 128.28
129.06 131.18 142.16
146.14 150.27 151.15
153.01 159.01 175.10
179.22 183.03 184.13
188.14 188.23 191.11
193.19 196.01 197.24
200.21 202.29 214.02
219.03 224.27 225.03
226.10 226.15 227.10
230.04 232.21 232.30
234.18 235.27 237.08
244.16 246.14 268.01
268.03 268.26 272.12
274.16 278.01 288.23
303.19 305.03 310.15
337.07 343.16 347.18
356.06 356.30 357.01
358.20 367.03 367.20
367.22 368.27 368.28
369.27 370.19 370.23
370.28 375.21 382.04
383.06 385.08 385.29
391.28 392.13 396.26
398.19 401.02 401.28
404.02 421.03 424.06
426.12 427.03 428.24
442.02 446.07 454.11
457.23 466.22 466.22
473.23 474.25 477.09
477.22 479.04 479.12
481.05 481.30 484.08
485.19 487.21 492.12
498.10 500.07 506.13
516.04 516.08
NOW'   218.05
NOW'S   52.24
NOWADAYS 65.03
NOWHERE 172.11 189.22
NUDITY 191.27
NUISANCE 232.14 330.23
NUKA   437.03
NUKA-   437.03
NUMBER 102.16 105.15
119.09 168.22 420.23
NUMBERS 341.21
NUMBNESS 162.11
NUMEROUS 417.03
NURSE   340.24
NURSED 347.04
NURSING 61.12 280.09
299.04 362.22 407.22
NUT   314.23 330.04
NUT-BROWN   314.23
O   134.07 134.07
248.02 342.18 368.19
483.04 485.01
O'   215.18 235.08
235.14 235.21 235.23
O'CLOCK 26.27 166.26
290.13 360.14 448.22
OAR   136.11 145.11
145.18 158.11 461.04
OCEAN   5.16   5.30

OAR (CONT.)   497.03
OAR-BLADES   497.03
OAR'S   198.16
OARS   1.17   7.08
141.24 413.12 414.06
443.07 443.26 495.27
OARS'   245.23
OB   276.24
OB-   276.24
OBEDIENCE   271.29
277.18 482.20
OBEDIENT 45.06 208.05
386.05
OBEDIENTLY   411.02
OBESE   192.19
OBEY   271.04
OBEYED 373.06 448.06
489.25
OBJECT   44.14 57.06
65.08 66.21 66.23
194.27 257.25 265.19
300.01 303.27 310.21
314.19 350.25 457.01
459.15
OBJECTS 292.18
OBLIGATION   58.16
OBLIGATORY   192.10
OBLIGING 43.34 234.09
OBLIQUE 351.10
OBLIQUELY   16.22
OBLITERATING   385.20
OBLIVION 398.18
OBLONG 249.05 366.19
OBSCENE 24.11
OBSCURE 59.15 112.24
112.30 159.27 173.22
185.15 264.08 270.29
291.10 398.15 501.20
OBSCURELY   166.22
357.26
OBSCURITY   123.08
211.17 212.13 385.10
OBSEQUIOUS   402.10
OBSERVE 180.01 420.22
OBSERVED 101.17 106.09
175.24 253.11 256.06
303.09 349.01 493.09
OBSERVER 374.05
OBSERVING   469.11
OBSTACLE 125.22 208.24
222.15
OBSTINACY   428.28
482.02 508.01
OBSTINATE   59.25
OBSTINATELY   161.02
OBTAIN   60.16 96.13
100.14 337.15 441.21
450.25
OBTAINED 213.21 345.05
448.16 455.04
OBTRUDES 215.19
OBTUSENESS   115.01
OBVIOUS 49.22 90.06
165.24 167.19 198.09
382.29
OBVIOUSLY   2.29
239.22 378.14
OCCASION 112.23 282.21
286.12 294.30 306.03
307.03 329.24 347.03
375.20 383.12 396.02
441.13
OCCASIONS   184.19
333.03
OCCULT 176.27 302.12
327.09
OCCUPATION   2.20
41.10 76.16 327.18
OCCUPIED 266.03 310.27
360.17 450.24
OCCUPY 490.06
OCCUPYING   35.17
OCCUR   488.20
OCCURRED 103.07 126.28
209.20 337.24 378.29
428.08 453.22 506.17
OCCURRENCE   59.13
90.24 193.20
OCCURRING   194.30
OCEAN   5.16   5.30

OCEAN (CONT.)   18.04
101.30 103.13 118.03
150.03 204.02 211.18
212.11 297.03 325.19
441.24 501.28
OCEANS 14.01 215.05
OCTAGON 94.10
ODD   260.05
ODIOUS 24.19 49.29
86.15 220.22
ODIOUSLY 343.10
ODOUR   146.03
OF   1.03   1.05
1.07   1.20   2.03
2.05   2.06   2.07
2.10   2.11   2.12
2.12   2.15   2.17
2.17   2.18   2.22
2.24   2.26   3.04
3.05   3.14   3.17
3.19   3.21   3.23
3.25   3.29   3.30
4.01   4.02   4.03
4.03   4.05   4.06
4.08   4.09   4.10
4.12   4.13   4.15
4.15   4.18   4.25
4.26   4.27   4.28
4.29   5.05   5.06
5.06   5.07   5.09
5.14   5.17   5.18
5.26   5.28   5.29
6.02   6.08   6.10
6.11   6.18   6.19
6.20   6.22   6.26
7.02   7.04   7.11
7.13   7.14   7.18
7.20   7.22   7.23
7.26   7.27   7.29
8.08   8.14   8.20
8.20   8.21   8.23
8.24   9.02   9.03
9.04   9.05   9.06
9.08   10.01 10.04
10.05 10.07 10.07
10.08 10.09 10.15
10.16 10.17 10.18
10.18 10.19 10.19
10.20 10.21 10.24
10.24 11.03 11.04
11.05 11.06 11.07
11.09 11.10 11.11
11.17 11.19 11.20
11.24 11.24 11.28
11.29 11.29 11.30
12.02 12.03 12.05
12.08 12.08 12.17
12.19 12.22 12.24
12.30 12.30 13.01
13.02 13.03 13.04
13.05 13.05 13.10
13.11 13.16 13.17
13.20 13.20 13.22
13.22 13.23 13.24
13.25 13.28 13.29
13.30 13.30 14.02
14.04 14.05 14.06
14.07 14.10 14.10
14.11 14.11 14.16
14.21 14.21 14.22
14.25 14.26 15.01
15.03 15.05 15.09
15.12 15.14 15.15
15.18 15.24 16.01
16.02 16.03 16.04
16.06 15.08 16.11
16.12 16.16 16.19
16.22 16.23 16.24
16.26 16.26 16.28
16.30 16.30 17.03
17.03 17.03 17.08
17.10 17.11 17.16
17.17 17.18 17.19
17.21 17.22 17.23
17.24 17.25 17.28
18.02 18.03 18.03
18.04 18.06 18.07
19.03 19.04 19.07
19.08 19.09 19.11
19.11 19.12 19.13

OF (CONT.)		19.15	OF (CONT.)		43.40	OF (CONF.)		70.21	OF (CONT.)		101.18
19.18	19.19	19.20	44.06	44.10	44.15	70.27	70.32	70.34	101.20	101.25	101.28
19.21	19.24	20.01	44.18	44.21	44.27	70.37	71.01	71.03	101.28	101.29	101.30
20.02	20.02	20.03	45.07	45.08	45.11	71.05	71.10	71.18	102.01	102.04	102.06
20.04	20.05	20.06	45.19	45.26	46.01	71.28	72.18	72.24	102.09	102.10	102.13
20.06	20.15	20.16	46.08	46.18	46.27	73.13	73.22	73.24	102.19	102.30	103.02
20.18	20.20	20.22	47.05	47.08	47.14	73.24	73.26	74.07	103.03	103.08	103.17
21.02	21.07	21.08	47.20	47.21	47.22	74.14	74.14	74.18	103.18	103.19	103.25
21.10	21.11	21.12	47.26	47.29	47.30	74.21	75.01	75.08	103.26	104.05	104.13
21.13	21.13	21.14	48.14	48.16	48.17	75.23	76.05	76.12	104.21	104.23	104.29
21.14	21.15	21.17	48.21	48.22	48.26	76.23	76.25	76.26	104.30	105.03	105.11
21.18	21.19	21.21	49.03	49.04	49.08	76.27	76.27	75.29	105.12	105.12	105.13
21.22	21.22	21.25	49.19	49.22	49.23	77.01	77.03	77.09	105.15	105.16	105.19
21.25	21.26	21.28	49.25	49.26	49.27	77.18	77.19	77.20	105.21	105.24	105.25
21.29	22.02	22.04	50.05	50.08	50.13	77.23	77.24	77.24	105.27	105.29	105.30
22.06	22.10	22.11	50.18	50.22	50.23	77.26	77.27	77.30	106.02	106.05	106.06
22.13	22.15	22.15	50.25	50.27	50.30	78.02	78.03	78.06	106.08	106.08	106.10
22.19	22.20	22.21	51.04	51.04	51.06	78.10	78.11	78.13	106.11	106.11	106.15
22.22	22.26	22.26	51.06	51.07	51.08	78.16	78.17	78.20	106.16	107.04	107.06
22.27	22.29	22.30	51.09	51.10	51.14	78.20	78.21	78.27	107.08	107.11	107.13
23.04	23.04	23.05	51.16	51.16	51.17	79.01	79.02	79.02	107.18	107.19	108.02
23.05	23.08	23.11	51.17	51.17	51.18	79.02	79.04	79.06	108.03	108.06	108.08
23.12	23.13	23.14	51.19	51.20	51.23	79.07	79.09	79.15	108.11	108.12	108.13
23.16	23.19	23.23	51.23	51.27	51.28	79.19	79.23	79.23	108.13	108.21	109.05
23.29	24.02	24.07	52.11	52.27	53.01	79.25	79.25	80.11	109.08	109.11	109.15
24.11	24.15	24.16	53.02	53.06	53.17	80.12	80.17	80.18	109.19	109.23	109.30
24.16	24.18	24.19	53.19	53.20	53.23	80.20	80.20	80.23	110.09	110.22	110.25
24.22	24.27	24.29	53.26	54.02	54.09	80.24	81.03	81.05	110.26	111.03	111.05
25.01	25.02	25.03	54.09	54.16	54.19	81.05	81.07	81.16	111.05	111.14	111.26
25.05	25.07	25.08	54.24	54.25	54.27	81.22	81.22	81.24	111.29	111.30	112.01
25.09	25.12	25.13	54.28	55.02	55.03	81.25	81.26	81.29	112.01	112.03	112.05
25.16	25.18	25.20	55.04	55.05	55.06	82.02	82.04	82.06	112.07	112.12	112.14
25.21	25.22	25.23	55.07	55.11	55.12	82.06	82.09	82.11	112.15	112.17	112.19
26.02	26.09	26.14	55.18	55.18	55.23	82.12	82.20	82.22	112.19	112.20	112.26
26.15	26.15	26.15	55.26	55.27	55.28	82.23	82.24	82.29	112.26	112.27	112.28
26.17	26.23	26.28	56.01	56.07	56.14	83.03	83.04	83.06	112.28	112.30	113.02
27.01	27.02	27.03	56.18	56.21	56.24	83.06	83.07	83.12	113.06	113.07	113.08
27.04	27.05	27.09	56.26	57.04	57.06	83.14	83.28	84.03	113.10	113.11	113.17
27.10	27.12	27.13	57.11	57.18	58.02	84.09	84.15	84.16	113.18	113.23	114.01
27.15	27.17	27.18	58.03	58.03	58.08	84.25	84.27	85.01	114.11	114.12	114.17
27.22	27.24	27.26	58.15	58.19	58.20	85.05	85.10	85.12	114.21	114.23	114.23
27.27	27.28	28.06	58.22	58.24	59.05	85.13	85.15	85.20	114.26	114.29	115.05
28.07	28.08	28.09	59.06	59.07	59.08	85.22	85.25	85.26	115.10	115.13	115.18
28.10	28.12	28.13	59.09	59.11	59.11	86.06	86.07	86.10	115.19	115.20	115.20
28.14	28.15	28.19	59.12	59.13	59.15	86.15	86.15	86.16	115.22	115.23	115.24
28.21	28.23	28.24	59.15	59.16	59.17	86.19	86.20	86.20	115.28	116.03	116.03
28.27	29.01	29.02	59.23	59.24	59.25	86.22	86.26	86.27	116.08	116.09	116.14
29.06	29.06	29.21	59.25	59.27	59.28	87.10	87.13	87.16	116.15	116.15	116.16
29.25	29.26	29.28	59.29	60.02	60.05	87.19	87.21	87.24	116.18	116.19	116.22
29.29	30.02	30.03	60.07	60.08	60.09	87.25	88.03	88.07	116.24	116.25	116.26
30.08	30.11	30.14	60.09	60.12	60.14	88.08	88.17	88.17	116.26	115.27	116.30
30.17	30.20	30.22	60.15	60.17	60.19	88.18	88.19	88.25	117.01	117.02	117.06
30.27	30.30	31.01	60.23	60.26	61.01	88.29	89.03	89.05	117.08	117.09	117.12
31.01	31.05	31.11	61.04	61.06	61.08	89.06	89.08	89.09	117.15	117.15	117.18
31.12	31.13	31.14	61.12	61.13	61.14	89.10	89.12	89.13	117.20	117.21	117.26
31.15	32.03	32.04	61.14	61.21	61.25	89.14	89.19	89.22	117.28	118.06	118.07
32.08	32.10	32.13	61.28	61.29	62.01	89.30	90.07	90.09	118.08	118.09	118.10
32.13	32.13	32.14	62.04	62.09	62.10	90.10	90.13	90.13	118.12	118.16	118.23
32.16	32.22	32.24	62.15	62.19	62.20	90.14	90.14	90.16	118.25	118.26	119.02
33.03	33.05	33.06	62.21	62.24	63.01	90.17	90.20	90.21	119.05	119.08	119.10
33.07	33.08	33.10	63.04	63.06	63.07	90.29	91.02	91.06	119.11	119.12	119.13
33.17	33.28	33.30	63.12	63.14	63.14	91.07	91.09	91.09	119.14	119.19	119.19
34.02	34.05	34.06	63.15	63.18	63.20	91.11	92.03	92.04	119.22	119.24	119.24
34.12	34.18	34.24	63.26	63.27	63.30	92.07	92.12	92.16	119.25	120.05	120.05
35.02	35.10	35.11	64.07	64.08	64.10	92.18	92.22	92.24	120.10	120.17	120.28
35.12	35.14	35.15	64.16	64.20	64.20	93.01	93.03	93.08	120.29	120.30	121.01
35.21	35.23	35.27	64.21	64.22	64.25	93.09	93.14	93.17	121.06	121.08	121.15
36.02	36.03	36.04	64.25	64.28	64.29	93.18	93.18	93.20	122.06	122.07	122.08
36.09	36.17	36.21	65.01	65.05	65.08	93.21	93.21	93.21	122.12	123.01	123.02
36.26	36.26	37.02	65.11	65.14	65.14	93.22	93.25	93.26	123.03	123.04	123.08
37.07	37.11	37.11	65.15	65.15	66.01	93.30	94.02	94.11	123.10	123.12	123.20
37.12	37.22	37.27	66.04	66.14	66.15	94.12	94.12	94.16	123.20	123.22	123.25
37.30	38.01	38.02	66.16	66.17	66.19	94.18	94.24	95.07	124.01	124.05	124.10
38.16	38.17	38.19	66.24	67.07	67.07	95.10	95.11	95.15	124.13	124.14	124.17
38.21	38.28	39.01	67.13	67.14	67.16	95.15	95.25	95.25	124.19	124.26	124.26
39.01	39.03	39.04	67.16	67.17	67.17	95.26	95.27	95.27	125.05	125.13	125.14
39.07	40.04	40.05	67.23	67.23	67.24	95.28	95.29	96.04	125.24	125.28	126.03
40.09	40.11	40.12	67.25	67.27	68.01	96.09	96.23	96.30	126.10	126.12	126.15
40.15	40.16	40.20	68.06	68.08	68.09	97.16	97.22	97.23	126.18	126.19	126.20
41.01	41.03	41.06	68.09	68.14	68.16	97.24	97.25	97.25	126.30	127.09	127.12
41.15	41.16	41.17	68.20	68.21	68.21	97.27	97.28	98.01	127.14	127.14	127.15
41.18	41.23	41.25	68.22	68.23	68.24	98.09	98.10	98.13	127.17	127.19	127.20
41.26	41.28	42.09	68.25	68.25	68.26	98.15	98.21	98.23	127.23	127.24	127.26
42.13	42.16	42.19	68.27	69.01	69.03	98.26	98.28	99.04	127.29	127.30	128.02
42.21	42.22	42.27	69.04	69.07	69.08	99.08	99.08	99.15	128.09	128.16	128.24
42.28	42.29	43.03	69.09	69.16	69.17	99.29	100.02	100.04	128.27	129.02	129.10
43.08	43.09	43.11	69.19	69.20	69.22	100.11	100.15	100.17	129.12	129.15	129.15
43.14	43.16	43.20	69.23	69.23	69.29	100.18	100.18	100.20	129.18	129.23	129.27
43.23	43.33	43.37	70.02	70.03	70.14	100.27	101.01	101.08	130.01	130.04	130.05
43.37	43.38	43.40	70.17	70.18	70.21	101.12	101.13	101.13	130.06	130.14	130.28

OF (CONT.)		131.02	OF (CONT.)		167.27	OF (CONT.)		196.14	OF (CONT.)		231.26
131.03	131.05	131.09	167.27	167.28	167.29	196.24	196.26	196.28	232.09	232.10	232.11
131.12	131.14	131.16	167.30	167.30	168.01	197.01	197.07	197.12	232.15	233.15	233.17
131.17	131.24	131.28	168.02	168.04	168.08	198.03	198.04	198.07	233.20	233.21	233.27
131.29	132.04	132.05	168.09	168.12	168.16	198.12	198.20	198.21	234.03	234.04	234.14
132.12	132.13	132.14	168.21	168.22	168.26	198.22	199.13	199.14	234.17	234.22	234.23
132.15	132.15	132.17	168.28	169.01	169.02	199.18	199.27	199.29	234.26	234.29	235.01
132.19	132.21	132.21	169.07	169.11	169.12	200.02	200.06	200.15	235.04	235.08	235.19
132.23	132.24	132.30	169.25	169.25	170.01	200.20	200.23	200.25	235.20	235.21	236.01
133.10	133.13	133.17	170.05	170.05	170.07	200.30	201.02	201.03	236.09	236.11	236.12
133.18	133.20	133.28	170.09	170.11	170.14	201.04	201.12	201.18	236.15	237.11	238.02
134.01	134.01	134.06	170.16	170.17	170.29	201.25	201.30	202.04	238.19	238.22	239.02
134.20	134.21	135.04	171.01	171.06	171.12	202.12	202.17	202.18	239.03	239.04	239.05
136.13	136.21	137.04	171.12	171.14	171.16	202.23	202.25	202.27	239.08	239.11	239.19
137.18	137.25	137.27	171.16	171.17	171.17	203.23	203.28	203.30	239.20	239.23	240.01
138.03	138.06	138.07	171.26	172.08	172.09	204.01	204.07	204.10	240.04	240.05	240.07
138.10	138.18	138.19	172.11	172.23	172.24	205.12	205.23	205.30	240.11	240.12	240.19
138.24	138.25	138.25	172.27	172.27	172.28	205.30	206.02	206.04	240.20	240.21	240.22
138.29	139.02	139.08	172.30	173.01	173.02	206.05	207.01	207.06	240.23	241.05	241.06
139.17	139.19	139.21	173.09	173.14	173.14	207.08	207.09	207.12	241.08	241.10	241.11
139.22	139.23	140.05	173.19	173.21	174.02	207.16	207.17	207.19	241.15	241.19	241.26
140.06	140.15	140.19	174.04	174.07	174.10	207.21	207.21	207.25	241.27	241.30	242.04
140.29	141.11	141.17	174.16	174.17	174.17	208.05	208.17	208.19	242.06	242.07	242.11
141.28	141.30	142.05	174.23	174.24	175.04	208.29	209.03	209.07	242.13	242.13	242.20
142.17	142.18	142.26	175.05	175.06	175.07	209.10	209.15	209.18	242.28	243.12	243.19
142.30	143.08	143.10	175.07	175.09	175.10	209.19	209.26	209.28	243.21	243.22	243.26
143.12	143.14	143.17	175.11	175.13	175.14	210.07	210.07	210.08	243.27	244.02	244.03
143.28	144.06	144.07	175.19	175.28	175.29	210.09	210.10	210.11	244.15	244.17	244.21
144.18	144.20	144.21	176.02	176.04	176.18	210.14	210.16	210.16	244.25	245.02	245.06
145.15	145.24	145.29	176.18	176.24	176.26	210.21	210.21	210.24	245.14	245.22	245.28
145.30	146.02	146.03	176.26	176.28	176.29	210.27	210.30	211.07	245.30	246.01	246.05
146.04	146.05	146.09	177.06	177.13	177.15	211.09	211.12	211.13	246.07	246.09	246.23
146.13	146.16	146.27	177.18	177.19	177.22	211.15	211.17	211.18	246.24	246.27	246.29
146.30	147.03	147.04	177.23	177.26	177.26	211.21	211.26	211.26	246.30	247.01	247.03
147.06	147.07	147.08	177.27	177.29	178.01	212.02	212.03	212.04	247.05	247.06	247.07
147.09	147.11	147.14	178.09	178.11	178.16	212.04	212.04	212.05	247.09	247.12	247.13
147.16	147.16	147.17	178.21	178.22	178.24	212.06	212.07	212.11	247.13	247.14	247.15
147.19	147.24	147.25	178.28	179.01	179.04	212.19	212.20	212.22	247.18	247.18	247.21
147.29	147.30	148.01	179.05	179.07	179.10	212.29	213.03	213.05	248.05	248.05	248.14
148.04	148.05	148.05	179.15	179.19	179.26	213.07	213.08	213.08	248.16	248.18	248.21
148.09	148.10	148.15	179.28	180.02	180.11	213.13	213.15	213.18	248.22	249.01	249.03
148.16	148.17	148.20	180.14	180.17	180.19	213.22	214.03	214.05	249.05	249.11	249.14
148.21	148.23	148.24	180.24	181.04	181.09	214.06	214.09	214.12	249.17	249.21	249.22
148.26	148.28	149.11	181.11	181.18	181.21	214.14	214.15	214.16	249.26	250.01	250.07
149.12	149.15	149.15	181.26	181.28	182.06	214.17	214.18	214.21	250.11	250.11	250.16
149.16	149.17	149.18	182.07	182.08	182.11	214.22	214.23	214.27	250.27	250.30	251.04
149.19	149.20	149.24	182.12	182.12	182.13	214.29	214.29	215.02	251.04	251.07	251.10
149.25	149.26	149.28	182.14	182.18	182.21	215.03	215.04	215.06	251.11	251.14	251.18
149.29	149.30	149.30	183.03	183.04	183.11	215.07	215.10	215.12	251.26	251.29	252.01
150.01	150.06	150.11	183.17	183.18	183.18	215.12	215.13	215.19	252.04	252.07	252.08
150.24	150.29	151.03	183.20	183.22	183.29	215.25	216.11	216.12	252.10	252.13	252.19
151.05	151.05	151.07	183.29	184.01	184.04	216.16	216.18	216.20	252.20	252.25	252.27
151.14	151.17	151.18	184.09	184.10	184.20	216.20	216.21	216.25	253.05	253.06	253.08
151.22	151.27	152.10	184.23	184.27	184.28	216.27	217.06	217.07	253.12	253.22	254.07
152.20	152.22	152.25	184.29	184.30	185.05	217.12	217.26	217.28	254.12	254.25	254.27
152.26	152.28	152.29	185.11	185.13	185.14	217.28	217.30	218.01	254.28	255.02	255.07
152.29	153.08	153.15	185.16	185.19	185.22	218.05	218.10	218.15	255.14	255.14	255.15
153.20	153.27	154.01	185.28	185.29	186.04	218.21	218.23	218.26	255.18	255.19	255.29
154.12	154.15	155.05	186.05	186.10	186.12	218.27	218.28	219.02	256.06	256.08	256.08
155.08	155.16	155.17	186.13	186.17	186.21	219.02	219.04	219.08	256.16	256.26	256.27
155.18	155.19	155.21	186.23	186.23	186.25	219.09	219.10	219.10	256.29	257.01	257.05
155.22	155.23	155.23	186.27	187.04	187.08	219.15	220.06	220.10	257.09	257.14	257.25
155.24	156.02	156.09	187.13	187.14	187.23	220.11	220.11	220.14	258.07	258.15	258.19
156.09	156.12	156.13	187.26	187.26	187.29	220.15	220.16	220.16	258.23	258.23	258.29
156.13	156.15	156.16	187.29	187.29	188.01	220.17	220.22	221.04	259.15	259.18	259.22
156.18	156.19	156.20	188.04	188.14	188.18	221.05	222.06	222.07	259.23	260.03	260.07
156.20	156.25	156.26	189.06	189.07	189.08	222.07	222.08	222.14	260.03	260.06	260.07
156.28	156.29	157.02	189.14	189.21	190.04	222.16	222.21	222.23	260.23	261.01	261.06
157.03	157.04	157.04	190.06	190.11	190.11	223.05	223.09	223.10	261.08	261.10	261.10
157.12	157.15	157.22	190.14	190.16	190.21	223.13	223.19	223.21	261.14	261.27	261.29
157.23	157.28	157.29	190.22	191.04	191.05	223.25	223.27	224.05	262.01	262.02	262.05
157.29	158.03	158.10	191.06	191.13	191.15	224.06	224.08	224.09	262.14	262.16	262.23
158.19	158.23	158.24	191.15	191.16	191.17	224.16	224.26	224.30	262.29	263.08	263.09
158.26	159.15	159.19	191.23	191.25	191.25	225.03	225.07	225.08	263.09	263.10	263.11
159.21	159.22	159.23	191.27	191.29	192.01	225.12	225.15	225.16	263.11	263.13	263.29
159.23	159.28	159.29	192.06	192.09	192.09	225.19	225.21	225.22	263.29	263.30	264.03
159.30	160.17	160.27	192.10	192.17	192.21	225.26	225.28	226.02	264.04	264.09	264.16
160.28	162.02	162.04	193.01	193.02	193.04	226.03	226.04	226.11	264.18	264.19	264.20
162.06	162.07	162.09	193.05	193.07	193.08	226.19	226.26	225.28	264.23	264.24	264.27
162.11	163.15	163.27	193.14	193.15	193.15	226.29	227.05	227.07	265.07	265.08	266.01
165.05	165.06	165.07	193.16	193.17	193.17	227.10	227.17	227.17	266.02	266.04	266.06
165.11	165.12	165.14	193.19	193.20	194.01	227.22	228.02	228.07	266.06	266.07	266.07
165.15	165.16	165.20	194.07	194.11	194.13	228.09	228.15	228.20	266.10	266.11	266.11
165.22	166.04	166.05	194.15	194.17	194.20	229.01	229.04	229.05	266.22	267.02	267.05
166.11	166.12	166.13	194.24	194.26	194.27	229.07	229.15	229.20	267.06	267.07	267.09
166.14	166.16	166.16	194.28	194.29	195.01	229.28	229.30	229.30	267.15	267.16	267.18
166.18	166.20	166.23	195.03	195.06	195.08	230.01	230.03	230.07	267.20	267.22	267.29
166.28	166.29	167.03	195.09	195.15	195.18	230.10	230.10	230.11	268.05	268.11	268.11
167.08	167.10	167.18	195.20	195.23	195.30	230.12	230.15	230.23	268.24	269.04	269.07
167.18	167.18	167.25	196.02	196.13	196.14	230.28	231.10	231.10	269.11	269.12	269.14

OF (CONT.)		269.14	OF (CONT.)		298.27	OF (CONT.)		328.06	OF (CONT.)		353.13
269.16	269.20	269.26	298.29	299.07	299.08	328.07	328.08	328.12	353.14	353.21	353.23
269.30	270.05	270.07	299.09	299.12	299.14	328.18	328.20	328.24	353.25	353.26	353.26
270.09	270.09	270.14	299.17	299.18	299.22	328.25	328.28	329.18	353.29	354.02	354.09
270.14	270.15	270.20	299.23	299.25	299.27	329.27	330.02	330.07	354.12	355.02	355.04
270.22	270.23	270.27	299.29	300.02	300.04	330.14	330.24	330.25	355.06	356.02	356.02
270.29	271.01	271.02	300.08	300.14	300.18	330.26	330.28	330.30	356.03	356.03	356.11
271.07	271.16	271.17	300.19	300.20	300.21	331.02	331.03	331.05	356.12	356.17	356.20
271.28	271.29	272.02	300.22	300.26	300.27	331.14	331.15	331.18	356.23	356.25	356.26
272.07	272.10	272.12	301.03	301.06	301.07	331.20	331.23	331.24	356.27	357.03	357.13
272.15	272.16	272.19	301.14	301.18	301.30	331.25	331.25	331.26	357.23	357.25	357.25
272.22	272.26	272.27	302.02	302.02	302.03	331.27	331.29	331.29	357.26	358.01	358.01
272.30	273.03	273.04	302.07	302.08	302.12	332.01	332.02	332.03	358.05	358.09	358.11
273.04	273.05	273.08	302.13	302.15	302.17	332.05	332.06	332.06	358.13	358.14	358.19
273.11	273.16	273.18	302.18	302.19	302.19	332.06	332.06	332.09	358.24	358.25	359.11
273.19	273.20	273.21	302.22	302.23	302.24	332.10	332.20	332.20	359.14	359.16	359.20
273.25	273.25	273.29	302.27	302.28	302.28	332.25	332.25	332.26	359.25	359.30	360.01
273.30	274.04	274.04	303.02	303.10	303.18	333.04	333.07	333.08	360.20	360.20	360.23
274.08	274.12	274.18	303.19	303.21	303.28	333.09	333.11	333.13	361.09	361.13	361.22
274.26	275.02	275.07	303.29	304.11	304.13	333.15	333.19	333.25	362.08	362.15	362.19
275.07	275.20	275.20	304.13	304.14	304.14	333.26	334.01	334.02	363.05	363.12	363.13
275.21	275.22	276.01	304.17	304.18	304.19	334.04	334.05	334.06	363.18	363.23	363.24
276.02	276.02	276.04	304.20	304.21	304.22	334.06	334.07	334.08	364.01	364.01	364.04
276.06	276.07	276.07	304.24	304.25	304.27	334.09	334.14	334.16	364.05	364.06	364.06
276.08	276.09	276.10	305.03	305.06	305.08	334.21	334.22	334.22	364.15	364.18	364.20
276.14	276.15	276.16	306.03	306.04	306.05	334.24	334.26	334.27	364.24	364.29	365.03
276.19	276.19	276.20	306.08	306.11	306.13	334.28	334.29	335.01	365.04	365.07	365.11
276.21	276.23	277.01	306.14	306.20	306.22	335.03	335.05	335.09	365.12	365.13	365.28
277.09	277.16	277.17	306.23	307.04	307.06	335.10	335.12	335.13	365.29	365.30	366.01
277.19	277.23	277.23	307.11	307.12	307.23	335.14	335.14	335.18	366.02	366.06	366.09
277.24	277.25	277.27	307.24	307.27	307.30	336.04	336.07	336.09	366.11	366.12	366.14
277.28	277.29	278.06	308.01	308.08	308.14	336.09	336.11	336.13	366.14	366.15	366.16
278.07	278.08	278.08	308.15	308.18	308.20	336.16	336.22	336.23	366.19	366.20	366.22
278.23	278.23	278.24	308.21	308.26	308.27	337.01	337.02	337.02	366.23	366.27	366.28
278.26	278.27	279.02	308.28	308.29	308.30	337.04	337.05	337.11	366.29	366.29	367.16
279.03	279.04	279.08	309.03	309.04	309.15	337.12	337.13	337.17	367.18	367.21	367.27
279.11	279.13	279.14	309.19	309.25	309.30	337.18	337.25	337.27	368.02	368.09	368.11
279.15	279.17	279.27	310.01	310.09	310.11	338.07	338.12	338.15	368.13	368.13	368.17
279.28	279.30	280.01	310.12	310.21	310.24	338.16	338.18	338.28	368.18	368.24	368.30
280.01	280.02	280.02	310.25	310.28	311.01	339.02	339.05	339.06	369.01	369.01	369.02
280.07	280.09	280.11	311.03	311.05	311.07	339.09	339.10	339.11	369.03	369.04	369.07
280.18	280.18	280.19	311.16	311.18	311.28	339.12	339.12	339.14	369.08	369.14	369.15
280.21	280.23	280.28	311.28	312.01	312.07	339.21	339.22	339.26	369.18	370.01	370.03
281.02	281.04	281.05	312.11	312.28	313.03	339.26	339.28	339.29	370.03	370.05	370.07
281.07	281.11	281.13	313.06	313.06	313.10	339.29	340.01	340.03	370.08	370.14	370.15
281.14	281.15	281.19	313.13	313.14	313.22	340.06	340.07	340.09	370.15	370.17	370.20
281.20	281.28	282.01	313.26	313.29	314.02	340.11	340.15	340.18	370.21	371.01	371.02
282.05	282.06	282.08	314.08	314.09	314.10	340.23	340.30	341.08	371.03	371.03	371.12
282.13	282.19	283.09	314.12	314.28	315.05	341.15	341.16	341.17	371.18	371.18	371.20
283.11	283.12	283.17	315.09	315.13	315.16	341.19	341.19	341.20	371.21	371.22	371.27
283.19	284.01	284.08	315.18	315.19	315.24	341.20	341.20	341.21	372.03	372.04	372.08
285.09	285.11	285.17	315.27	315.29	315.29	341.22	341.26	341.27	372.09	372.11	372.12
285.21	285.23	286.02	315.30	316.01	316.04	341.30	342.01	342.07	372.23	372.25	373.04
286.07	286.08	286.09	316.06	316.08	316.09	342.08	342.24	342.28	373.16	373.18	373.20
286.11	286.20	286.26	316.12	316.13	316.14	342.28	342.29	342.29	373.21	373.23	374.04
286.26	286.27	286.30	316.16	316.16	316.25	343.03	343.06	343.08	374.07	374.10	374.17
287.11	287.14	287.25	316.26	316.26	316.29	343.11	343.11	343.15	374.18	374.25	374.26
287.25	287.26	288.01	317.01	317.01	317.02	343.17	343.19	343.20	374.27	374.30	375.01
288.07	288.09	288.10	317.03	317.06	317.11	343.23	343.27	343.30	375.15	375.17	375.19
288.10	288.16	288.16	317.14	317.16	317.17	344.01	344.01	344.03	375.23	375.26	375.27
288.21	288.24	288.28	317.18	318.01	318.02	344.07	344.11	344.27	376.19	376.20	376.24
288.29	289.06	289.15	318.10	318.15	318.20	344.28	345.01	345.02	376.26	376.26	376.27
289.28	289.30	290.08	319.02	319.04	319.10	345.06	345.07	345.11	376.30	377.05	377.06
290.14	290.23	290.25	319.11	319.12	319.13	345.11	345.13	345.13	377.11	377.14	377.22
290.26	290.27	291.04	319.14	319.15	319.15	345.16	345.17	345.20	378.02	378.03	378.05
291.07	291.14	291.19	319.19	319.21	319.21	345.22	345.23	345.24	378.07	378.17	378.17
291.20	291.22	291.29	319.23	319.28	319.30	345.26	345.27	345.30	378.21	378.22	378.22
291.30	292.04	292.05	320.09	320.22	321.09	346.02	347.01	347.04	378.23	378.26	379.06
292.07	292.09	292.10	321.10	321.14	321.16	347.05	347.06	347.07	379.08	379.10	379.13
292.13	292.19	293.01	321.17	321.21	321.23	347.09	347.10	347.12	379.16	379.17	379.24
293.02	293.04	293.06	321.24	321.24	321.27	347.14	347.14	347.15	379.25	379.25	379.28
293.12	293.13	293.14	321.30	322.01	322.02	347.17	347.19	347.20	379.29	380.03	380.10
293.16	293.20	293.22	322.02	322.07	322.08	347.21	348.03	348.04	380.11	380.11	380.12
293.26	293.28	293.30	322.09	322.12	322.13	348.05	348.07	348.08	380.15	380.16	381.04
294.05	294.08	294.10	322.14	322.19	322.23	348.10	348.15	348.18	381.06	381.12	381.14
294.13	294.14	294.15	322.24	322.25	322.25	348.19	348.25	348.30	381.16	381.24	382.06
294.16	294.23	294.27	322.30	322.30	323.04	348.30	348.30	349.02	382.24	382.28	382.29
294.29	294.30	295.04	323.05	323.07	323.09	349.04	349.06	349.07	383.03	383.08	383.11
295.06	295.08	295.08	323.10	323.11	323.12	349.07	349.09	349.10	383.20	384.05	384.08
295.10	295.12	295.14	323.15	323.17	323.21	349.13	349.17	350.01	384.09	384.13	384.15
295.23	295.25	295.27	323.22	323.28	323.30	350.06	350.06	350.12	384.17	384.18	384.19
295.27	295.28	295.29	323.30	324.01	324.14	350.19	350.26	350.27	384.24	384.27	385.02
296.02	296.04	297.01	324.14	324.16	324.23	350.30	351.02	351.02	385.15	385.19	385.20
297.04	297.05	297.07	324.23	325.09	325.11	351.03	351.05	351.13	385.22	385.23	385.26
297.07	297.08	297.10	325.12	325.13	325.14	351.14	351.17	351.18	386.03	386.10	386.13
297.12	297.12	297.13	325.15	325.21	325.23	351.20	351.21	351.25	386.14	386.14	386.14
297.18	297.19	297.21	325.23	325.27	325.30	351.26	351.29	352.08	386.15	386.16	386.17
297.22	297.24	298.02	327.05	327.10	327.10	352.10	352.11	352.16	386.18	386.20	386.21
298.05	298.06	298.13	327.13	327.17	327.18	352.21	352.23	352.23	386.25	386.28	387.07
298.17	298.21	298.25	327.20	327.20	327.21	352.28	353.08	353.12	387.08	387.09	387.13

OF (CONT.)		387.17	OF (CONT.)		422.06	OF (CONT.)		450.08	OF (CONT.)		482.14
387.17	387.25	387.28	422.06	422.08	422.09	450.11	450.25	450.29	482.16	482.17	482.19
388.05	388.23	389.08	422.15	422.20	422.23	450.29	450.30	451.02	482.19	482.20	482.20
389.09	389.11	389.17	422.24	422.25	422.26	451.06	451.08	451.10	482.25	482.25	482.26
389.18	389.22	390.08	423.02	423.03	423.03	451.11	451.13	451.22	482.28	483.10	483.16
390.13	390.21	390.22	423.06	423.06	423.10	451.25	451.28	452.01	483.19	483.23	483.26
390.27	390.29	391.03	423.12	423.13	423.16	452.05	452.06	452.11	483.27	483.28	483.28
391.09	391.10	391.12	423.17	423.19	423.21	452.13	452.14	452.18	483.30	484.01	484.09
391.16	392.01	392.05	423.24	423.29	424.07	452.24	452.28	452.30	484.10	484.11	484.12
392.12	392.13	392.16	424.08	424.09	425.01	453.05	453.06	453.07	484.13	484.13	484.17
392.20	392.21	392.23	425.03	425.09	425.10	453.08	453.12	453.21	484.29	484.29	485.06
392.30	393.01	393.01	425.13	425.15	425.19	453.25	453.26	453.30	485.11	485.21	485.26
393.03	393.05	393.12	425.24	426.06	426.10	454.01	454.05	454.08	487.06	487.08	487.09
393.14	393.16	393.25	426.18	426.25	426.28	454.09	454.11	454.12	487.13	487.15	487.16
394.05	394.06	394.09	426.30	427.04	427.07	454.14	454.18	454.20	487.18	487.19	487.24
394.10	394.23	394.24	427.09	427.10	427.13	454.25	454.28	454.29	487.24	488.01	488.02
395.01	395.02	395.04	427.14	427.22	427.29	454.30	455.02	455.04	488.02	488.04	488.08
395.12	395.13	395.14	427.30	428.04	428.18	455.04	455.05	455.08	488.13	488.14	488.15
395.18	395.18	395.20	428.18	428.21	428.27	455.09	455.13	455.15	488.17	488.23	488.25
395.25	395.29	396.14	428.28	429.05	429.05	455.18	455.23	456.06	488.30	489.03	489.06
396.21	396.28	396.29	429.08	429.22	429.22	456.08	456.09	456.12	489.07	489.14	489.16
397.02	397.04	397.05	429.23	429.27	429.30	456.20	456.22	456.29	489.16	489.23	489.23
397.08	397.11	397.16	430.02	430.04	430.06	457.03	457.07	457.10	489.26	489.26	489.28
397.19	397.19	397.20	430.09	430.13	430.29	457.13	457.14	457.22	490.01	490.02	490.10
397.26	397.27	397.27	431.02	431.03	431.13	458.01	458.06	458.08	490.13	490.16	491.05
398.05	398.08	398.08	431.23	431.23	431.23	458.09	458.11	458.12	491.16	491.16	491.18
398.10	398.12	398.14	431.27	431.30	432.01	458.13	458.15	458.16	491.21	491.22	492.02
398.14	398.17	398.22	432.02	432.06	432.07	458.17	458.17	458.18	492.02	492.11	492.18
398.26	399.03	399.07	432.08	432.15	432.16	458.20	458.23	458.25	492.23	492.24	492.27
399.07	399.23	399.24	432.17	432.17	432.20	458.28	459.04	459.06	493.26	493.27	494.01
399.25	399.27	399.27	432.21	432.24	433.02	459.07	459.08	459.09	494.02	494.04	494.08
399.29	399.30	400.08	433.27	434.01	434.04	459.11	459.13	459.14	494.09	494.16	494.24
400.10	400.15	400.17	434.06	434.09	434.10	459.15	459.17	459.18	494.25	494.29	495.01
400.24	400.25	400.26	434.12	434.12	434.16	459.19	459.21	459.29	495.05	495.13	495.15
400.28	401.06	401.11	434.16	434.21	434.24	460.04	460.07	460.11	495.23	495.28	496.01
401.12	401.18	401.23	434.25	434.28	434.30	460.14	460.17	460.17	496.08	496.10	497.06
401.25	402.02	402.05	435.03	435.05	435.07	460.19	460.24	460.27	497.14	497.16	497.21
402.06	402.07	402.09	435.09	435.13	435.16	461.08	461.19	461.25	497.22	497.22	498.02
402.10	402.14	402.14	435.17	436.06	436.11	462.01	462.02	462.06	498.02	498.07	498.08
402.20	403.05	403.09	436.13	436.15	436.15	462.09	462.18	462.21	498.10	498.14	498.17
403.21	403.24	403.26	436.17	436.18	436.20	462.23	462.24	462.26	498.18	498.23	498.25
403.27	403.28	404.07	436.21	436.23	436.28	462.27	462.29	462.29	498.26	498.26	498.26
404.09	404.15	404.16	436.29	437.03	437.04	462.30	463.03	463.03	498.29	499.02	499.07
404.18	404.28	405.02	437.08	437.10	437.11	463.05	463.06	463.09	499.10	499.12	499.22
405.15	405.22	405.30	437.19	437.24	437.30	463.09	463.10	463.10	499.22	499.25	499.26
406.02	406.05	407.01	438.10	438.11	438.14	463.17	463.18	463.22	499.27	499.29	499.30
407.02	407.03	407.21	438.14	438.17	438.18	463.27	463.28	464.01	500.03	500.07	500.11
407.22	408.05	408.08	438.19	438.20	438.21	464.03	464.12	464.29	500.11	500.16	500.16
408.10	408.12	408.14	438.27	438.29	439.02	464.30	465.01	465.11	500.22	500.27	500.27
408.16	408.20	408.21	439.04	439.07	439.09	465.19	465.20	465.23	500.27	500.29	501.06
408.26	408.27	408.27	439.09	439.12	439.14	465.26	466.09	466.18	501.16	501.17	501.20
409.06	409.08	409.09	439.14	439.26	439.30	466.23	466.24	467.04	501.21	501.26	501.26
409.10	409.13	409.16	440.02	440.05	440.07	467.11	467.12	467.14	501.30	502.02	502.04
409.21	409.21	409.22	440.07	440.08	440.10	467.14	467.16	467.21	502.05	502.11	502.17
409.23	409.26	409.26	440.10	440.11	440.13	467.22	468.09	468.24	502.21	502.28	502.30
409.28	409.28	410.01	440.20	440.23	440.25	469.04	469.09	469.15	503.01	503.02	503.03
410.02	410.03	410.06	440.28	441.02	441.03	469.17	469.21	470.02	503.07	503.09	503.13
410.07	410.09	410.09	441.03	441.06	441.10	470.04	470.09	470.10	503.14	503.15	503.18
410.14	410.15	410.19	441.10	441.17	441.25	470.11	470.27	470.30	504.04	504.05	504.10
410.26	411.06	411.06	441.27	441.29	441.30	471.03	471.13	471.15	504.22	504.24	505.01
411.08	411.09	411.12	442.01	442.02	442.03	471.16	471.16	471.25	505.12	505.18	505.29
412.04	412.06	412.20	442.03	442.04	442.06	472.02	472.03	472.12	506.08	506.12	506.13
412.22	412.26	413.03	442.09	442.15	442.16	472.15	473.02	473.09	506.19	506.20	506.21
413.04	413.10	413.12	442.19	442.20	442.23	473.10	473.15	473.16	506.24	507.23	507.23
413.14	413.14	414.13	442.29	442.30	443.01	473.16	473.17	473.17	507.26	507.28	508.01
414.19	414.20	414.27	443.03	443.05	443.09	473.26	473.28	474.03	508.02	508.07	508.09
414.28	414.30	415.06	443.10	443.11	443.14	474.07	474.12	474.12	508.10	508.12	508.15
415.08	415.11	415.12	443.15	443.16	443.17	474.17	474.22	474.24	508.16	508.17	508.22
415.14	416.05	416.06	443.21	443.22	443.22	474.27	474.29	474.29	508.23	508.25	509.03
416.08	416.09	416.11	443.24	443.28	444.03	475.01	475.02	475.07	509.04	509.05	509.09
416.13	416.19	416.21	444.04	444.04	444.05	475.09	475.10	475.14	509.10	509.14	509.17
416.21	416.22	416.22	444.05	444.05	444.08	475.17	475.20	475.20	509.25	509.27	509.29
417.01	417.03	417.04	444.10	444.13	444.13	475.27	476.03	476.04	510.01	510.02	510.03
417.06	417.07	417.08	444.14	444.20	444.26	476.08	477.09	477.10	510.09	510.11	510.12
417.11	417.16	417.20	444.27	444.29	444.30	477.11	477.13	477.14	510.27	510.27	510.30
417.21	417.21	417.22	445.01	445.03	445.05	477.23	477.24	478.01	511.19	511.24	512.07
417.27	418.05	418.09	445.06	445.07	445.08	478.02	478.04	478.06	512.09	512.11	513.12
418.12	418.12	418.15	445.08	445.11	445.21	478.09	478.17	478.22	513.13	513.14	513.19
418.18	418.21	418.22	445.22	445.28	445.30	478.23	478.24	478.28	513.25	513.29	514.03
418.24	418.27	418.29	446.04	446.06	447.01	479.01	479.04	479.08	514.04	514.08	514.27
419.05	419.08	419.14	447.08	447.11	447.12	479.10	479.22	479.25	514.29	514.30	515.02
419.16	419.28	419.29	447.13	447.14	447.15	479.26	479.27	479.27	515.05	515.05	515.08
420.01	420.04	420.07	447.16	447.18	447.19	479.28	479.29	480.01	515.10	515.22	515.23
420.08	420.08	420.11	447.22	447.23	448.03	480.01	480.02	480.04	515.24	515.26	515.28
420.13	420.14	420.15	448.13	448.14	448.18	480.05	480.07	480.10	515.29	515.29	516.01
420.18	420.19	420.20	448.19	448.25	448.25	480.11	480.12	480.13	516.03	516.05	516.09
420.20	420.23	420.26	448.27	449.01	449.02	480.14	480.15	480.17	516.13	516.14	516.15
420.30	421.02	421.08	449.05	449.14	449.16	480.18	480.24	481.09	516.17	516.19	
421.22	421.25	421.28	449.18	449.19	449.25	481.11	481.27	481.29	OFF	5.14	16.20
422.01	422.02	422.03	449.27	449.29	450.01	482.01	482.07	482.13	29.18	36.03	40.03

OFF (CONT.)   45.14
52.16   52.24   54.22
55.19   55.22   58.29
58.30   62.17   70.15
71.04   71.07   71.23
72.27   74.20   76.01
77.12   81.12   82.05
84.24   87.07   95.15
97.15   101.13 101.15
102.20 102.24 102.27
104.08 107.14 108.23
109.26 109.19 109.27
110.28 125.09 125.12
125.21 126.21 132.14
133.30 134.05 145.26
147.15 166.09 182.19
191.07 193.12 194.30
198.24 204.08 207.20
208.07 217.15 217.16
218.03 225.28 236.02
250.15 256.01 256.19
276.06 280.28 286.17
289.07 295.05 299.01
300.16 300.29 301.15
310.04 311.08 311.12
311.22 312.25 313.11
325.18 328.13 336.24
342.15 355.17 361.21
362.03 363.20 366.21
371.13 379.03 390.16
398.02 399.14 399.16
399.20 401.25 401.28
407.02 409.02 410.10
413.13 414.23 416.04
424.05 426.07 426.07
426.09 436.20 436.26
437.01 437.24 438.28
439.04 439.08 440.16
440.17 441.01 442.18
442.24 443.13 444.11
444.12 445.17 445.19
447.09 450.29 452.05
453.05 458.26 464.05
464.14 465.14 467.06
470.06 470.19 471.21
473.25 474.21 475.13
475.25 479.17 490.19
491.11 502.10 509.26
OFF-HAND 424.05 447.09
458.26
OFF-SHORE   440.17
OFF-SIDE 465.14
OFFENCE   68.16   188.07
472.26
OFFENSIVE   93.27
141.23 268.22 275.17
OFFER   138.19 181.02
181.03 186.24 188.21
212.08 214.20 450.17
457.11
OFFERED   13.15   53.01
281.15 290.23 450.19
OFFERING 20.26   412.25
416.05 418.29 456.17
OFFERTORIES'   292.22
OFFICE   42.22   43.03
44.11   45.07   46.08
70.22   75.02   80.23
146.10 164.13 200.24
207.04 252.12
OFFICER   70.08   71.04
74.30   170.01 242.13
OFFICERS 4.18   13.28
98.09   165.11 167.16
168.29 169.02 169.12
171.27 244.10
OFFICES   252.09
OFFICIAL 32.07   44.05
47.29   66.22   195.18
278.09 340.22 344.02
344.17 345.20 438.02
438.22
OFFICIOUS   307.28
OFFING   244.21 297.08
409.21
OFTEN   4.24   11.01
70.39   168.01 244.11
250.12 276.16 302.29
320.30 322.10 340.25
347.12 351.10 358.01

OFTEN (CONT.)   391.11
419.30 435.06 509.18
516.19
OFWAR   172.24
OH   8.12   8.13
25.26   40.01   61.25
64.01   65.07   86.01
88.14   105.23 111.04
113.22 113.30 115.30
121.09 133.23 134.07
140.25 140.25 140.25
140.27 140.27 150.15
150.27 152.14 185.22
188.03 202.24 203.14
203.25 205.11 205.28
226.08 230.23 233.08
234.01 243.15 255.17
292.11 306.19 343.14
354.11 360.19 367.06
404.30 473.12 480.26
493.17 495.02
OHO   237.09
OIL   72.24   72.24
OIL-FEEDER   72.24
OLD   6.23   8.04
8.05   8.06   8.09
14.27   16.07   20.12
20.30   21.14   26.07
26.27   26.28   27.08
27.17   28.01   29.30
43.16   45.13   45.25
46.02   47.29   49.06
52.28   60.28   61.02
62.25   63.12   63.25
65.02   65.10   70.06
72.19   74.12   75.03
75.16   75.18   76.16
76.23   77.08   77.20
81.05   81.16   81.19
93.02   95.04   95.09
95.18   99.22   111.03
118.05 119.04 134.21
156.06 156.07 165.13
171.14 183.07 183.14
185.28 197.06 197.20
202.03 202.18 202.19
204.14 205.03 205.30
224.26 228.01 231.04
231.10 233.06 235.03
235.09 235.15 235.29
237.01 237.05 250.06
250.09 251.01 269.06
273.19 276.12 276.12
276.16 277.08 278.20
279.06 280.29 282.05
283.08 285.10 286.17
290.23 295.03 298.09
299.02 301.16 304.13
305.02 306.20 307.09
307.22 309.23 314.12
314.14 314.22 315.15
317.12 319.23 323.20
324.11 324.14 324.15
324.18 324.21 324.21
325.24 325.27 327.13
329.29 330.09 330.15
331.09 331.13 336.07
336.24 337.01 337.08
337.11 338.23 338.29
341.25 345.13 345.17
345.22 353.23 353.24
353.30 363.11 366.05
366.27 368.22 369.25
370.08 383.17 383.25
404.02 410.16 410.22
410.24 411.14 412.05
421.10 421.10 421.16
421.24 422.16 422.17
429.01 429.13 437.04
440.18 448.28 449.03
451.12 452.09 461.25
462.09 462.13 482.03
482.27 483.10 484.25
486.16 489.04 489.27
508.29 509.01 509.06
509.29 510.12 514.21
OLIVE   347.20
OMEN   296.07
OMNIPOTENCE   117.29
ON   2.01   2.01

ON (CONT.)   2.03
2.19   3.01   4.05
4.28   5.03   5.07
5.13   5.15   5.16
5.27   6.19   7.12
7.12   7.19   11.04
11.23   12.04   12.27
13.06   14.06   14.06
14.11   14.22   15.03
15.09   15.16   16.28
16.28   17.02   17.05
17.06   17.16   17.25
17.26   17.29   18.08
18.11   19.12   19.13
19.23   20.01   20.07
20.07   20.07   20.08
20.10   20.29   21.02
21.05   21.16   21.17
21.26   22.05   22.09
22.24   23.01   24.16
24.28   25.28   26.15
26.20   27.03   27.29
28.10   29.03   29.19
29.19   30.23   30.27
31.07   31.08   33.07
33.20   33.24   33.26
33.27   34.20   34.28
35.03   35.07   35.29
36.11   36.12   37.06
37.12   37.13   37.14
37.17   37.19   37.20
37.21   38.21   38.25
41.17   41.19   42.14
42.20   42.25   42.28
43.36   44.05   44.19
46.05   46.07   46.12
46.16   46.29   47.11
49.02   49.07   49.14
51.19   52.12   52.20
53.20   54.25   55.10
55.19   56.09   57.20
58.07   58.19   58.27
59.04   61.17   61.27
62.17   62.21   63.02
63.04   63.29   64.01
66.03   66.21   69.10
69.30   70.01   70.10
70.11   70.14   70.16
70.19   70.22   70.28
70.36   70.41   71.06
71.22   71.24   71.27
72.01   72.02   72.11
72.13   72.13   72.27
73.03   73.17   74.12
74.17   75.27   75.29
76.01   76.11   76.17
76.19   77.16   78.10
78.29   80.27   81.29
83.03   83.04   83.10
84.16   84.26   85.06
86.13   86.15   87.13
89.12   89.26   90.04
90.10   90.11   90.26
91.15   92.17   94.10
97.14   97.16   97.29
98.16   99.07   99.09
100.10 100.29 101.21
101.29 101.30 102.16
102.19 102.22 103.04
104.28 105.04 105.15
107.17 107.17 107.18
108.28 109.02 109.07
109.12 109.18 109.21
110.23 111.23 112.16
112.22 114.12 114.13
114.16 115.22 115.25
117.06 117.08 117.14
117.18 118.01 119.09
119.15 120.10 120.26
121.01 124.12 124.17
125.30 126.01 126.02
129.09 131.04 132.03
132.09 132.27 133.13
133.24 134.06 134.29
134.30 135.04 139.03
139.09 140.22 141.26
142.02 142.11 142.15
142.24 142.25 143.04
144.26 144.27 145.13

ON (CONT.)   145.29
146.09 146.24 147.07
147.19 147.22 147.30
148.19 148.25 149.13
150.07 151.23 152.05
152.05 152.05 152.08
152.08 153.03 153.21
153.24 154.04 154.09
155.01 156.11 159.10
162.08 163.28 164.26
166.01 166.05 166.17
167.07 167.14 167.16
167.21 167.30 168.09
169.21 169.26 170.04
170.07 170.13 171.04
171.11 171.18 171.19
171.21 171.30 172.02
173.08 173.13 173.13
173.18 174.22 175.14
175.23 175.28 175.30
176.06 176.14 176.17
177.04 177.05 177.21
178.06 180.19 180.22
180.29 181.07 181.22
182.09 182.18 182.23
183.01 183.14 183.21
184.09 184.18 185.26
187.05 187.07 187.16
189.15 189.15 190.09
190.19 191.20 192.26
193.06 193.08 193.25
194.17 195.07 195.16
195.23 195.26 196.15
198.02 198.05 198.10
198.13 198.25 198.28
199.15 199.18 200.05
200.09 200.13 200.27
201.22 201.22 203.09
203.11 203.23 203.29
204.30 205.17 206.03
206.04 207.10 207.13
207.16 208.08 209.07
209.12 209.20 209.29
211.16 211.17 212.17
212.18 213.06 214.10
214.23 216.08 216.11
216.11 216.15 217.21
218.19 219.11 219.23
220.20 220.27 220.29
223.04 223.05 224.02
225.10 225.14 226.01
227.15 227.24 228.07
228.09 229.03 229.07
229.14 229.25 231.06
231.09 231.23 231.29
232.17 233.04 233.23
234.11 234.15 235.03
236.17 236.22 236.28
238.25 239.05 240.18
240.22 241.21 242.10
242.12 242.16 242.17
242.22 243.11 244.04
244.06 244.11 244.20
247.17 248.12 249.04
250.13 250.20 250.29
251.12 251.13 251.16
251.20 252.14 252.25
253.10 253.14 254.11
254.12 255.12 255.27
255.29 255.30 256.12
256.15 256.25 257.09
257.11 258.15 258.23
259.07 259.16 259.19
259.22 259.23 261.17
261.23 261.26 262.01
262.08 262.08 262.12
263.15 264.12 264.25
265.11 267.14 268.02
269.09 269.18 271.10
272.02 273.08 273.19
274.20 274.20 274.20
276.09 277.07 277.13
278.02 279.05 280.08
280.09 280.10 280.23
281.22 282.09 282.26
283.05 283.08 283.09
283.24 284.07 286.04
286.12 286.25 286.30
287.06 287.20 287.22
288.03 288.23 289.18

ON (CONT.)		290.01
290.08	290.20	291.04
291.23	291.26	292.06
292.24	292.29	293.14
294.19	294.30	295.03
297.20	298.08	299.03
299.04	299.08	299.29
300.02	300.08	300.09
300.20	300.28	301.26
302.16	302.17	303.06
303.22	303.30	306.02
307.05	307.10	307.18
307.29	307.30	308.29
309.01	309.28	310.06
311.04	311.04	311.13
311.20	312.14	312.14
312.26	313.12	313.20
314.05	314.18	314.22
315.16	315.21	316.09
316.22	316.25	316.29
318.09	318.20	319.03
320.10	320.13	322.28
322.30	323.01	323.03
323.09	323.14	323.21
324.03	324.07	324.08
324.09	324.12	324.16
325.02	325.08	325.09
325.17	325.23	325.25
327.24	329.04	329.08
330.03	331.30	332.01
332.08	332.12	333.03
333.04	333.04	333.12
333.18	333.28	334.01
335.18	336.10	337.12
338.12	339.02	339.23
339.28	341.06	342.30
343.01	343.02	343.10
343.11	343.17	343.27
344.13	345.25	346.10
347.02	347.07	347.18
347.23	348.02	348.12
349.13	349.17	349.20
350.02	350.04	350.07
350.07	350.08	350.11
350.15	352.22	353.07
353.14	353.16	353.24
355.02	355.20	356.25
357.04	357.19	357.19
357.24	358.05	358.11
358.12	358.29	359.04
359.04	359.09	359.14
359.17	359.19	359.28
359.30	360.25	361.03
361.19	361.26	361.30
362.22	362.24	364.01
364.14	365.10	365.11
365.12	365.22	366.09
367.03	367.06	367.08
367.21	368.01	368.03
368.10	368.24	369.08
370.19	370.27	371.15
371.24	372.05	372.07
372.20	373.18	374.03
374.17	375.20	375.27
376.06	376.16	376.28
377.13	377.21	380.09
382.12	383.08	383.12
384.24	385.24	385.28
386.06	387.11	387.16
388.08	388.10	389.12
390.24	393.11	393.15
395.05	396.02	396.26
397.05	397.09	397.13
398.30	399.10	400.30
401.10	401.19	401.27
402.11	403.02	403.03
405.05	405.18	407.05
408.11	409.19	409.20
409.23	409.24	410.13
410.18	410.19	410.27
411.03	411.04	411.09
411.30	412.07	412.07
412.11	413.29	414.01
414.02	414.05	414.14
414.22	414.23	415.05
417.04	417.07	417.12
418.01	418.04	418.08
418.22	420.10	421.24
422.05	423.20	424.12
425.23	427.21	427.22

ON (CONT.)		428.04
428.08	428.22	428.23
429.24	429.28	430.16
431.06	431.08	431.08
431.12	431.27	432.03
432.14	432.23	432.27
432.28	433.18	433.24
433.25	435.05	435.21
436.19	436.20	436.27
437.01	437.27	437.29
438.02	438.07	438.15
438.22	438.29	439.04
439.16	439.19	441.07
441.13	441.19	441.27
442.16	443.03	443.08
443.25	443.28	444.18
444.21	444.26	444.28
445.07	445.10	445.14
445.21	445.24	448.01
449.10	450.06	450.11
450.27	451.04	451.11
451.22	452.02	452.10
452.12	452.20	453.01
453.06	453.10	453.17
454.23	454.24	455.02
455.08	456.09	456.20
456.22	456.23	456.29
458.04	459.07	459.17
459.27	459.28	460.03
460.09	460.21	461.19
462.03	463.12	464.24
464.30	465.02	465.09
465.10	465.14	465.18
465.24	466.08	466.10
466.14	466.17	466.19
469.03	469.15	469.23
470.03	470.06	470.08
470.26	470.27	471.08
471.15	471.22	471.26
472.08	472.12	474.30
475.12	475.14	475.26
476.01	476.07	477.08
477.10	477.11	478.29
479.09	479.09	479.20
479.24	479.24	480.02
480.08	480.23	480.28
481.14	481.18	481.18
483.11	483.25	483.29
484.02	484.20	484.23
484.24	485.03	485.14
485.15	485.20	487.12
488.24	488.25	489.05
489.16	489.22	489.27
489.29	490.06	490.15
490.20	490.27	491.13
491.14	491.18	491.20
491.21	492.09	492.27
493.03	493.26	493.30
494.03	494.04	494.06
494.16	494.23	495.20
497.20	497.24	498.07
498.11	498.15	498.18
498.25	499.03	499.12
499.28	499.30	501.07
502.05	502.25	504.08
504.18	504.23	505.11
505.13	506.01	506.29
506.29	507.06	508.08
508.30	509.02	509.08
509.22	510.08	510.08
510.15	512.01	512.06
512.08	512.13	512.22
512.27	513.26	514.23
514.27		
ONCE	4.17	10.23
17.17	31.13	36.11
47.19	53.12	54.27
55.21	61.11	72.05
73.15	73.20	74.29
78.22	80.08	81.17
82.26	84.15	90.02
95.23	103.14	104.09
109.17	112.18	125.12
140.14	140.23	148.15
159.24	176.19	176.21
177.19	179.13	190.14
197.19	199.30	207.01
208.15	208.25	209.20
209.24	212.18	213.21
219.19	224.15	224.24

ONCE (CONT.)		225.28
231.03	235.02	236.10
237.08	245.09	251.08
256.16	257.16	257.19
268.06	283.29	291.24
303.29	308.24	309.17
311.05	313.26	318.13
318.15	320.24	321.01
321.05	339.03	349.30
351.22	357.08	359.13
359.26	360.03	360.06
365.20	387.21	395.27
402.21	404.08	410.22
414.06	421.03	422.10
427.27	428.07	430.10
431.26	448.12	450.21
452.05	453.01	457.16
459.30	466.29	469.16
470.17	472.15	474.11
475.22	477.05	481.16
484.23	496.08	503.13
505.12	507.03	510.20
512.18	516.06	
ONE	3.26	4.15
6.17	8.11	14.12
14.13	15.28	17.05
18.05	18.05	21.02
21.05	22.09	26.27
27.14	30.03	30.08
33.30	34.01	38.07
43.01	43.09	43.38
50.13	50.22	51.25
53.05	54.09	55.07
55.08	55.13	57.21
58.01	58.07	58.25
64.10	64.16	66.06
67.13	67.23	67.25
69.10	69.23	71.24
73.21	76.08	82.11
82.13	82.14	82.30
83.14	86.17	90.06
93.18	95.25	97.20
97.25	99.15	100.06
101.04	102.16	105.16
107.17	108.06	109.12
109.19	109.30	111.13
111.18	112.07	112.25
112.26	113.06	113.20
114.16	116.06	117.02
118.12	120.29	122.24
123.08	124.17	124.30
125.09	126.21	127.03
128.30	129.12	129.23
133.06	133.06	133.22
136.20	138.18	138.19
138.22	138.25	141.18
142.27	142.28	144.06
145.10	146.26	147.12
152.24	152.26	152.29
153.05	155.01	156.19
157.16	157.16	157.20
157.27	165.13	165.23
165.28	167.23	168.06
168.28	168.30	169.05
169.15	170.05	171.04
171.04	171.21	171.26
172.03	172.14	172.19
173.13	173.15	174.17
175.06	175.07	176.21
176.25	177.26	178.02
178.03	178.10	178.10
178.12	178.19	179.02
179.03	179.15	179.19
179.27	180.22	180.25
182.07	183.04	183.18
187.23	191.11	192.09
192.20	194.22	194.23
197.27	199.04	200.15
201.11	201.25	205.20
209.25	210.06	211.11
215.30	219.03	219.27
221.03	223.26	224.15
225.08	225.12	225.25
227.12	227.18	227.20
228.18	229.17	229.26
230.30	231.07	234.04
235.06	235.19	236.03
238.10	238.13	238.24
241.01	241.10	244.19
244.21	245.22	246.05

ONE (CONT.)		246.13
248.14	248.22	249.03
249.11	250.13	251.04
253.26	254.02	254.11
254.25	255.13	255.25
255.29	256.03	256.13
256.18	256.19	259.01
259.05	259.05	261.07
261.26	262.03	262.18
264.27	265.07	265.08
266.17	267.29	268.21
269.17	270.27	271.13
274.08	278.12	278.22
282.05	282.09	282.18
282.29	285.11	287.06
288.07	288.10	293.14
294.14	300.04	302.30
302.30	303.05	307.18
307.22	309.05	309.28
310.01	312.23	313.02
313.07	316.25	317.05
318.01	321.06	321.21
322.30	324.14	327.14
327.19	330.27	330.28
332.03	332.09	332.20
332.25	333.04	335.03
335.13	337.02	337.10
337.15	340.22	340.30
341.05	341.10	343.20
343.27	345.15	346.10
347.03	350.06	350.21
350.29	351.03	351.09
352.03	352.16	358.13
358.16	362.21	363.24
366.20	366.22	373.23
373.24	374.17	374.30
378.04	382.08	382.21
384.18	384.19	386.23
390.14	391.15	391.15
391.16	392.09	393.03
394.07	395.04	397.25
398.14	400.17	400.18
401.19	405.18	405.20
408.08	408.10	411.08
414.20	415.11	418.04
419.03	419.17	420.02
421.27	422.07	422.07
422.08	422.08	424.07
427.29	429.26	431.18
432.12	433.01	434.08
434.10	434.11	437.30
439.23	440.09	441.01
441.12	442.25	447.14
447.15	448.14	450.03
452.11	455.08	456.09
456.10	458.27	459.13
459.28	460.15	460.17
460.22	460.30	460.30
463.26	464.01	464.23
467.13	468.01	469.18
472.16	472.21	472.27
473.11	474.07	479.13
481.06	482.18	482.26
484.25	489.07	491.10
491.16	492.02	493.15
493.26	494.25	497.21
500.07	500.14	500.19
501.01	502.17	503.13
506.12	508.12	508.21
509.02	509.21	509.25
509.30	510.08	510.27
511.18	516.05	
ONE-DEGREE		17.05
ONE-LEGGED		378.04
ONE-THIRD		122.24
ONE'S	32.23	55.06
81.08	91.09	172.03
177.23	180.23	210.20
211.12	212.25	218.09
220.15	397.13	479.13
ONES	178.17	
ONESELF	382.08	
ONLOOKERS		274.17
ONLY	8.04	8.08
10.09	10.21	10.23
11.03	12.16	13.24
22.05	24.07	25.17
26.07	26.27	30.08
32.18	35.13	36.12
41.19	45.07	47.09

55.12	60.13	61.19
66.17	67.05	67.07
73.13	74.16	76.26
79.01	81.06	84.18
87.03	92.18	94.22
97.25	98.20	99.08
104.14	105.19	105.23
109.17	110.23	111.27
112.11	112.21	113.26
115.27	122.20	124.12
125.15	125.15	126.19
127.18	129.18	129.25
130.07	130.12	130.12
130.15	139.24	139.26
139.26	144.02	144.06
144.08	144.29	146.27
148.07	156.13	156.17
162.15	162.18	163.12
164.08	165.23	168.06
168.06	177.13	177.19
182.03	192.22	195.18
201.05	202.11	204.11
204.23	207.01	208.25
211.28	214.28	217.18
219.13	223.27	223.30
224.02	238.08	240.03
243.05	246.15	248.09
248.13	249.11	250.00
250.30	251.09	255.19
259.05	261.07	261.19
264.19	267.01	268.05
268.08	268.16	269.04
271.01	273.06	273.27
274.08	274.13	275.03
275.05	276.04	278.12
280.02	283.23	288.30
290.01	290.05	290.16
292.18	298.12	300.03
303.16	306.08	308.03
309.16	311.02	311.25
312.09	313.01	315.16
316.05	316.11	316.17
321.13	322.13	324.21
325.18	329.15	329.28
332.15	334.30	335.04
337.15	338.15	338.26
339.12	341.08	355.06
356.06	357.16	358.10
363.08	367.15	367.23
367.27	368.01	369.14
370.34	373.15	375.05
375.21	377.02	377.11
377.21	378.28	382.05
382.11	382.24	383.12
383.18	385.29	386.22
392.08	393.13	395.12
398.04	398.08	398.12
398.17	399.08	400.15
403.14	412.01	415.16
416.11	418.21	418.28
419.26	420.26	422.03
422.07	429.10	429.13
433.11	436.11	438.02
438.24	441.26	448.14
450.21	457.09	457.16
462.13	462.25	465.19
465.27	467.03	471.14
471.23	478.23	482.18
482.25	483.01	484.20
485.18	495.10	498.29
500.29	501.01	506.17
507.07		

ONLY'   85.28
ONNATURAL   461.09
ONWARD   25.04
OPAL   376.22
OPAQUE   25.03   123.04
OPEN   12.29   18.06

24.07	35.17	45.11
48.05	55.11	58.25
70.03	74.01	93.13
101.24	103.21	104.24
127.22	128.19	134.13
159.06	166.20	171.27
211.15	211.29	214.13
228.13	228.28	229.12
248.06	261.30	269.20
297.06	297.14	300.25
303.23	316.28	321.27

OPEN (CONT.)   322.10

334.01	334.12	344.22
367.11	370.22	372.06
379.04	384.09	408.30
409.11	443.16	451.19
460.27	461.26	466.01
472.14	472.22	496.03
499.16	501.06	501.08
501.10	504.12	505.11
507.23	508.09	509.20
510.26	511.25	512.03

OPEN-EYED   499.16
OPENED   54.18   84.29

90.29	93.06	128.01
145.20	151.08	187.18
209.12	220.30	232.06
242.09	256.22	409.08
416.17	417.19	443.25
452.30	470.13	504.09
508.16	513.29	514.29

OPENING   34.03   36.07

55.14	57.18	93.08
230.15	249.27	315.12
319.09	418.03	429.19
435.02	459.11	471.13

OPENLY   346.07   354.05
450.26
OPERATIONS   437.11
OPINED   197.11   461.08
OPINION   27.10   38.17

42.29	66.02	67.29
78.09	96.09	99.04
146.24	172.01	177.21
181.02	181.03	193.25
193.26	193.26	203.08
262.18	286.13	345.11
365.02	383.11	436.11
449.04	450.18	451.07
487.11		

OPINIONS   447.18
OPIUM   197.22   279.07
336.17
OPPORTUNITIES   245.15
245.16   265.01   271.19
339.11
OPPORTUNITY   13.14

100.04	147.21	159.21
171.11	230.12	245.14
264.29	299.15	309.13
332.26	378.12	411.20
415.09	419.18	515.26

OPPOSE   461.16
OPPOSED   315.27
OPPOSITE   47.03   80.23
315.11   466.02   471.15
500.01   503.17
OPPOSITION   485.12
OPPRESSED   17.09
134.19   414.27
OPPRESSION   315.26
OPPRESSIVE   104.10
162.17
OPTICAL   212.22
OPTION   78.13   242.19
OPULENT   367.16
OR   1.17   5.12

11.07	11.14	12.25
15.08	15.15	27.20
27.24	28.26	29.29
32.01	36.24	38.06
38.11	39.02	42.17
42.17	42.18	42.29
43.17	43.38	48.23
49.01	50.10	50.11
50.12	50.24	50.26
50.27	52.06	52.15
53.06	56.08	58.01
60.29	64.24	66.12
67.07	69.02	70.20
70.23	70.23	72.10
77.09	80.30	81.30
82.21	83.13	84.20
86.09	86.26	86.28
87.14	90.17	90.20
92.09	92.10	92.22
99.03	99.09	100.05
100.23	103.22	103.23
106.09	106.15	111.06
113.11	120.27	123.11
126.08	127.15	129.07

OR (CONT.)   136.12

144.06	144.13	147.09
147.10	148.18	148.23
148.25	148.27	155.10
160.05	163.23	167.17
171.17	172.13	176.19
179.10	183.16	185.02
185.15	187.09	187.26
190.10	191.02	191.09
191.09	191.09	197.02
198.14	200.20	201.14
203.26	208.19	208.21
208.23	209.11	209.20
209.21	209.27	215.01
215.08	215.30	216.03
216.04	220.12	220.24
227.24	228.01	229.16
229.29	230.21	231.12
232.14	232.18	234.23
234.24	235.07	239.21
239.21	240.02	244.12
245.07	247.07	247.21
249.10	250.04	251.13
254.05	255.01	260.19
262.02	262.30	263.09
265.07	265.09	267.14
268.07	268.10	268.16
268.21	270.30	271.16
271.23	272.08	273.03
275.13	279.14	280.11
280.12	281.05	281.22
286.15	287.02	289.16
289.25	290.24	292.04
295.27	300.02	300.16
302.07	302.21	303.07
307.06	311.01	313.01
315.17	315.30	316.03
316.05	319.26	323.01
330.27	331.09	335.07
337.22	339.12	340.02
340.17	341.01	344.23
349.22	351.15	352.04
352.11	354.11	356.02
356.07	357.03	358.17
361.15	365.15	373.09
376.01	377.23	377.24
378.28	386.26	389.23
394.07	394.17	395.04
395.04	397.28	399.21
407.16	414.04	416.04
418.19	419.01	419.03
420.26	421.21	422.25
424.07	426.14	430.22
431.21	435.16	436.04
436.04	436.13	437.29
439.09	441.10	441.16
441.21	441.22	441.25
442.03	446.08	447.23
449.10	449.12	450.22
454.09	461.25	462.06
462.11	463.10	472.13
472.28	473.21	474.17
475.11	475.19	481.09
481.13	489.18	490.12
491.01	494.14	495.07
499.09	500.21	504.06
504.07	507.26	511.10
513.16	513.17	

ORANGE   55.04   70.13
ORB   412.26
ORBITS   378.23
ORCHARD   4.11   228.21
ORDAINED   96.09
ORDEAL   127.14
ORDER   3.15   86.20

118.27	118.28	356.28
358.02	385.27	386.28
418.24	419.08	421.25
453.21	456.11	468.10
478.21	505.16	

ORDER'   456.20
ORDERED   33.15   57.02

108.18	291.24	373.08
444.30	451.01	461.03
497.09	508.09	

ORDERING   122.09   314.27
ORDERLY   32.15   462.01
ORDERS   71.04   173.18
244.10   290.17   294.21
314.14   349.27   421.23

ORDERS (CONT.)   462.16
489.24   499.14   505.28
ORDINARY   339.18   340.21
ORDNANCE   323.20
ORGANISED   81.05
316.16
ORGE   134.07
ORIENTAL   79.01   84.08
87.17
ORIENTALLY   192.03
ORIENTATION   91.11
424.09
ORIFICE   257.09
ORIGIN   186.04   186.15
247.06   322.18
ORIGINAL   14.23   267.18
ORIGINALLY   3.28
366.13
ORISONS   439.23
ORNAMENTAL   432.03
OSSA   68.03   68.21
73.26   74.21
OSTENTATION   2.02
OSTENTATIOUSLY   372.27
OTHER   1.18   3.14

8.11	12.16	12.24
25.28	27.15	28.26
33.22	34.15	37.07
42.19	45.06	46.21
46.30	47.26	48.23
49.05	52.06	54.02
54.07	56.15	57.21
58.01	61.27	66.23
67.15	69.02	70.03
73.22	76.19	81.30
82.12	82.14	85.13
87.05	88.09	88.21
92.07	93.04	95.15
99.05	101.30	103.10
107.18	108.19	110.17
110.20	112.20	115.14
115.26	117.29	118.21
122.22	126.24	128.04
136.07	140.16	142.05
143.15	143.15	143.25
144.06	144.14	144.28
145.11	151.05	151.26
156.09	156.19	156.21
162.12	165.27	168.08
158.13	178.01	180.13
181.06	181.20	186.10
198.14	200.05	200.20
206.06	208.23	228.07
228.11	228.12	232.11
235.07	236.30	241.27
251.26	252.27	255.22
256.18	264.26	270.08
280.23	281.17	282.26
288.08	288.12	304.06
304.24	307.17	311.14
315.26	316.15	320.03
322.19	323.14	329.08
329.28	330.27	330.29
331.11	331.30	332.05
338.13	340.12	343.29
345.04	346.11	352.10
352.25	353.29	356.07
356.25	360.17	363.10
365.02	369.24	372.17
372.22	385.02	387.15
388.04	389.10	393.11
395.28	404.09	416.24
418.30	422.05	427.24
429.26	434.12	434.12
434.14	435.23	437.29
439.23	445.25	446.07
452.12	453.17	454.06
459.14	459.17	461.19
463.06	465.18	466.05
467.07	469.13	469.18
470.12	470.13	471.07
474.03	474.29	475.19
481.07	484.24	485.22
492.09	493.26	499.30
505.30	506.13	508.24
513.05		

OTHER'S   44.19   57.11
115.28   276.22   294.24
389.15   470.21
OTHERS   10.21   37.24

OTHERS (CONT.) 38.02
56.28 98.04 115.12
122.10 125.12 133.02
142.28 159.08 164.06
165.10 172.21 177.10
179.27 179.28 195.24
205.25 208.10 234.24
235.28 239.04 242.27
289.12 310.08 339.20
364.05 419.14 433.13
433.14 436.08 445.30
449.28 464.04 467.03
467.19 483.05 487.11
489.11 492.06 503.04
505.01 508.20
OTHERWISE 8.26
79.10 179.25 247.16
251.05 276.24 347.16
383.09 495.29
OUGH 63.05 63.05
133.07
OUGHT 29.09 51.21
53.18 65.02 65.06
65.09 78.25 128.08
158.28 170.09 180.26
228.21 274.22 355.14
361.15 419.02 516.05
OUR 24.23 24.24
24.25 24.26 24.26
41.19 48.02 73.25
75.05 82.18 88.18
88.19 93.09 93.23
119.11 120.29 146.06
146.28 159.22 171.01
172.01 174.20 175.23
181.06 181.10 181.20
183.13 185.07 185.28
189.14 212.04 212.04
212.04 212.05 212.06
212.06 212.07 219.11
226.24 226.28 228.24
230.15 240.04 244.13
244.25 258.28 262.23
262.27 262.29 264.02
267.22 270.10 270.23
270.28 270.30 270.30
271.03 271.04 271.04
271.28 271.29 273.25
275.01 275.02 275.02
275.06 275.07 275.02
276.04 279.21 281.24
288.19 295.01 295.01
332.04 302.08 306.03
306.04 308.10 308.11
320.13 323.02 323.06
337.03 340.27 341.01
347.10 348.11 348.12
349.13 374.19 386.19
386.28 387.27 389.14
389.14 391.13 392.02
398.11 401.20 401.24
402.11 408.24 408.28
409.01 409.02 409.03
409.04 409.04 409.04
409.28 411.05 418.23
418.25 418.27 419.01
419.14 423.15 423.17
423.17 472.12 473.18
474.03 474.27 480.24
480.25 489.04 501.21
507.17
OURS 43.16 343.23
OURSELVES 77.23
259.06 375.12
OUSTED 483.28
OUT 2.12 5.01
11.10 21.21 22.11
22.24 24.13 26.15
26.28 27.19 27.24
28.01 30.02 32.13
32.13 32.13 32.14
35.14 37.27 38.15
41.22 42.17 43.01
43.39 44.24 45.17
47.14 50.04 51.22
52.14 52.21 54.26
55.15 56.17 56.24
57.01 58.12 58.23
61.02 61.08 61.18
61.23 63.02 63.25

OUT (CONT.) 64.09
64.30 66.08 66.08
66.21 69.30 71.22
71.26 72.14 73.24
75.08 76.15 78.09
78.11 78.27 79.06
79.20 79.28 80.16
81.03 81.15 82.26
82.30 83.22 85.20
87.25 89.30 90.05
90.07 94.03 96.21
99.08 99.16 99.19
99.24 99.29 99.30
101.24 102.09 102.16
104.05 105.01 105.19
107.06 108.25 108.30
109.10 109.23 110.14
114.12 115.19 120.19
121.02 124.13 124.14
125.04 126.04 127.30
129.03 130.05 130.14
131.14 131.26 132.15
133.04 133.10 134.14
137.07 137.11 138.10
138.21 140.30 143.12
143.14 143.17 143.28
146.06 146.10 147.23
150.03 150.12 150.21
151.19 152.22 152.22
152.27 153.08 155.01
155.20 156.10 159.02
159.08 159.24 160.27
161.03 161.05 162.24
163.27 166.05 166.29
168.07 168.28 169.25
170.28 171.15 174.07
177.18 181.13 182.24
183.02 184.21 186.22
187.14 188.14 189.16
194.13 195.15 195.24
196.02 199.07 199.30
200.27 202.20 203.10
205.18 207.12 207.19
208.28 211.03 212.03
212.14 212.28 213.15
214.17 214.27 215.03
216.08 218.01 218.24
221.04 222.09 224.09
224.10 225.24 225.30
226.17 226.18 230.15
232.18 235.04 235.12
235.20 235.28 235.28
236.02 236.09 236.15
236.22 236.30 237.05
237.21 238.11 239.17
240.02 240.29 242.06
242.13 243.08 243.16
246.01 246.23 249.09
249.27 252.08 255.23
257.22 258.17 258.20
260.02 260.06 260.27
262.29 263.10 270.09
270.09 273.02 273.14
274.14 274.19 274.26
277.17 277.29 277.30
280.06 283.16 284.08
285.11 285.23 286.14
288.16 289.13 289.14
289.14 290.02 290.26
291.07 291.11 291.14
292.08 295.14 296.05
297.06 297.09 298.14
298.30 299.24 300.21
300.23 300.26 301.09
301.17 301.24 301.29
302.30 303.09 307.08
309.28 310.16 310.24
310.25 310.30 312.13
313.13 313.28 314.17
317.11 323.09 323.28
329.04 329.11 329.30
330.06 331.12 331.24
333.16 336.04 336.16
338.28 340.02 342.27
342.28 343.09 344.07
344.11 344.12 344.26
345.26 349.23 350.01
353.09 353.13 353.15
353.26 355.18 356.04
356.27 358.19 358.30

OUT (CONT.) 359.05
359.16 359.17 360.20
361.01 361.04 361.17
364.24 368.11 368.16
368.18 368.18 369.25
371.04 372.03 372.27
373.02 373.10 375.08
379.28 383.28 385.27
386.13 386.14 387.09
389.25 391.08 391.10
391.25 393.04 393.21
394.01 394.06 396.05
396.14 397.27 398.08
398.17 398.24 400.15
401.24 402.09 403.19
405.23 405.30 407.03
411.25 411.26 412.20
413.14 413.23 416.21
418.27 419.04 420.07
420.08 422.20 425.03
425.11 425.21 426.02
426.18 426.22 427.27
431.23 431.28 435.07
437.04 438.13 439.26
440.30 443.08 446.08
449.07 450.05 450.19
450.21 451.08 452.12
452.20 453.11 454.17
455.12 455.17 456.22
459.11 460.19 460.24
461.13 462.09 463.07
464.11 464.13 464.13
465.05 465.08 465.14
466.05 466.18 472.09
472.11 472.14 473.28
474.01 474.17 476.11
477.06 477.12 477.13
477.17 478.04 478.10
479.22 480.01 480.14
480.15 480.24 481.28
483.09 483.28 484.05
485.07 487.19 488.23
490.21 491.03 492.13
492.24 493.20 494.02
494.09 494.21 494.24
494.29 495.15 495.26
496.04 498.02 498.07
498.08 498.13 500.12
500.18 501.08 502.28
504.04 504.11 504.19
505.06 505.12 505.17
505.22 505.24 506.09
506.15 506.19 506.29
507.22 508.06 508.08
508.30 509.30 510.29
512.30 513.19 515.29
OUT- 69.30
OUT-BARK 143.14
OUT-OF-THE-WAY 246.01
OUTBREAK 501.15
OUTBREAKS 184.18
251.15 315.29
OUTBURST 356.01 436.29
508.14
OUTCAST 239.14
OUTCASTS 441.17 454.02
OUTCOME 93.20
OUTCRY 502.25
OUTER 46.17 211.15
290.20 315.02
OUTERMOST 244.22
OUTLINE 323.30 469.19
OUTLINED 82.29 372.17
OUTLINES 21.10 63.07
63.13 149.04 274.28
OUTLYING 327.21 493.23
OUTRAGE 127.07
OUTRAGED 233.16
OUTRAGEOUSLY 187.09
OUTSIDE 15.07 32.23
64.11 83.10 85.29
89.29 143.07 195.25
216.10 217.25 224.03
232.29 233.12 254.27
266.07 283.29 360.29
370.24 375.23 379.08
392.03 430.02 448.29
454.20 489.13 490.08
490.16 494.15 494.21

OUTSIDE (CONT.) 506.30
OUTSKIRTS 4.28
15.23 352.22 363.18
489.22
OUTSPOKEN 485.11
OUTSPREAD 411.06
412.25 497.05
OUTSTRETCHED 219.12
462.19
OUTWARD 51.03 92.01
348.20
OUTWARD-BOUND 92.01
OUTWARDBOUND 43.11
OUTWARDLY 27.13
51.14 352.09
OUTWARDS 469.24
OUVRIR 171.28
OVAL 22.11 378.22
380.15
OVER 5.30 6.24
6.30 7.08 13.04
13.05 15.11 15.16
17.14 20.17 21.02
24.09 32.04 32.05
34.30 37.03 37.10
37.29 42.21 47.04
48.20 52.04 54.27
62.19 70.33 71.03
73.05 73.15 74.12
76.28 83.24 92.20
96.07 97.27 98.08
101.14 101.25 102.10
108.05 109.12 110.15
115.05 115.14 115.20
116.10 116.17 118.11
118.23 122.04 123.07
124.02 124.09 125.14
128.25 130.06 132.11
132.26 133.01 133.25
134.04 135.01 135.06
136.11 137.01 138.17
139.10 139.13 139.21
139.29 140.07 140.07
141.04 143.24 143.30
145.04 145.12 145.14
145.25 147.02 149.16
150.20 152.21 153.12
153.25 161.02 165.21
168.15 170.09 172.02
177.02 177.07 181.17
185.01 187.25 188.10
188.15 189.13 189.17
190.01 193.07 193.14
195.30 199.23 200.25
203.02 203.21 204.13
205.07 207.21 207.22
209.02 211.12 215.01
216.05 216.09 216.29
217.05 218.22 230.25
236.16 238.04 243.04
247.14 249.08 249.17
254.06 254.13 255.13
255.30 256.07 260.08
262.05 262.05 263.07
270.28 272.22 278.18
280.25 287.08 289.01
291.11 291.29 293.07
294.01 294.23 300.06
307.20 309.01 309.14
311.13 312.15 313.22
314.15 316.08 316.26
316.27 316.29 320.22
322.12 325.04 325.16
330.04 331.28 332.17
344.22 348.17 357.27
359.04 362.09 362.10
363.08 364.21 364.24
366.16 366.25 372.15
377.21 382.15 386.03
389.10 392.29 398.21
399.20 402.25 403.08
407.16 407.16 410.08
410.16 410.29 412.06
414.03 414.17 417.13
417.16 418.02 421.30
422.01 422.05 422.07
425.12 427.26 432.24
433.03 436.28 439.13
445.23 446.04 452.02
452.26 453.03 453.27

OVER (CONT.)   456.05
458.30 460.16 462.21
463.14 464.08 467.18
468.22 473.03 475.16
475.26 478.06 479.18
483.24 487.20 489.09
492.05 494.19 498.06
498.09 505.11 508.16
509.07 509.15 512.01
512.17 515.18
OVER-   143.30
OVER-EXERTION   130.06
OVER-JOYED   452.02
OVERAWED   434.24
OVERBEARING   458.26
OVERBOARD   7.13
8.03 29.16 69.28
73.18 74.16 143.21
143.27 144.03 148.12
158.09 196.09 495.07
503.16
OVERBURDENED   102.03
OVERCAST 434.10
OVERCOME 125.22 160.26
237.03 327.12 475.03
OVERCOMING   359.10
OVERFLOWED   15.17
OVERGROWN   451.29
OVERHANGING   318.12
OVERHEAD 13.11 497.07
OVERNIGHT   401.28
OVERPOWERED   276.08
OVERSHADOWED   39.03
262.15
OVERSPREAD   100.19
OVERT 320.07
OVERTAKE 52.05
OVERTAKEN   175.02
406.01
OVERTHROW   244.19
OVERTOPPED   319.16
OVERTOPPING   192.12
OVERTURES   454.11
OVERTURNED   54.25
OVERTURNING   280.07
OVERVALUED   11.26
OVERWHELMED   49.29
380.07 421.06
OVERWHELMING   102.10
103.15 220.15 423.16
470.27 516.10
OVERWROUGHT   361.24
OW 143.18 143.18
143.18 143.18
OWE 342.22 477.24
OWED 238.20 281.30
282.04 336.21 353.16
463.29
OWING 222.22
OWLS 149.22
OWN 8.23 22.01
24.23 26.18 32.18
35.29 38.16 40.06
40.24 41.03 44.07
45.19 60.04 69.19
70.33 76.30 77.03
82.03 86.29 88.16
96.03 106.10 112.23
112.23 117.04 120.19
146.28 150.02 156.13
156.17 178.07 180.09
188.11 193.28 196.17
200.23 207.19 209.19
214.06 214.09 215.14
229.01 229.05 229.23
237.07 237.30 238.07
247.24 251.12 251.18
265.15 270.09 270.11
271.24 274.10 279.03
281.07 282.10 282.26
282.28 286.13 287.29
301.11 304.15 304.16
308.19 311.26 314.16
321.14 321.25 324.03
332.22 338.03 338.22
340.24 340.22 347.15
348.16 357.12 358.29
361.18 361.30 364.14
365.21 377.18 379.15
379.23 381.06 395.11

OWN (CONT.)   395.16
397.10 399.16 400.27
410.08 414.29 416.10
418.23 419.25 420.17
421.08 424.04 424.08
428.09 430.12 433.07
438.05 448.06 448.29
450.19 451.25 455.13
455.14 458.10 458.14
458.25 460.24 471.25
472.16 474.18 485.21
487.18 488.29 490.07
499.06 505.18 506.13
506.15 513.21 514.15
516.14
OWNED   14.29 125.07
227.03 252.13 277.21
392.06 436.16
OWNER 68.21 494.16
OWNER'S   304.11
OWNERS   73.30
OWNING   427.28
OX   180.30 514.22
PACE 17.20 263.14
287.24 311.20 367.11
371.29 402.18
PACED 21.30 287.27
PACIFIC 48.09 55.20
56.06 175.12 196.18
214.27 215.04 435.04
475.23
PACIFIED   331.02
PACIFY   87.02
PACING   411.29
PACK 57.04 192.11
442.13
PACK-ANIMALS   192.11
PACKAGES 244.25
PACKED 167.06 182.20
442.20
PACKET 416.15 416.17
417.19
PAD 33.24 34.10
PADDLE 335.07 392.30
410.28 498.14 512.24
513.03
PADDLED 298.12 497.18
513.05
PADDLER 332.25
PADDLERS 300.13 498.05
PADDLES 401.18 411.03
PADDLING 489.19 504.01
PAGE 212.18 456.22
PAGEANT   13.10
PAGES 417.26 421.22
423.11 434.30
PAH   231.23
PAID 181.22 217.16
266.09 279.17 425.11
492.08
PAIN 7.14 11.11
32.21 36.21 96.23
99.30 100.27 132.05
157.02 170.09 260.16
260.16 263.23 282.04
381.16 389.26 430.29
466.21 467.11 510.01
515.05
PAINFUL 268.17 356.26
PAINFULLY   410.13
PAINS   404.02
PAINTED 15.07 175.21
PAINTER 244.02
PAIR 22.30 39.03
49.08 68.06 70.13
71.03 145.29 175.05
195.08 206.04 324.16
371.02 513.25
PAIRFECT   11.21
PAIRS 94.12 416.04
PALACE 453.07 461.27
PALAVER 450.10
PALAVERING   152.12
PALE 33.04 37.09
69.11 105.04 120.28
193.01 246.09 246.22
301.30 378.21 380.15
386.26 410.02 410.12
428.23
PALE-FACED   69.11

PALED 149.03
PALISADE 311.05 420.10
PALLIATE 117.03
PALLOR 347.20
PALM 37.11 101.13
110.24 134.13 307.18
467.12
PALMS 13.05 25.19
77.06 313.30 444.29
469.24 509.03
PALPABLE 341.10
PALPITATING   138.27
PANAMA 428.22 432.24
PANE 59.09
PANES 211.03 216.26
416.21
PANG 36.21
PANGERANS   250.18
PANGLIMA 505.16 505.17
PANGS 184.04
PANIC 33.30 105.27
108.23 131.21 162.24
333.13 450.03 464.17
500.25 503.03
PANIC-STRICKEN   131.21
464.17
PANICS 60.01
PANTALOON   379.11
PANTED 63.28
PANTING 28.23 270.18
459.02 504.16 510.16
PANTRY 42.13
PANTS 452.19
PAPER 22.26 30.01
30.01 34.11 157.29
185.25 193.07 194.01
195.09 195.22 216.05
249.05 282.13 353.24
417.27 491.18 491.25
492.05
PAPERS 45.16 440.29
441.22
PAR 167.21 181.02
PARADED 274.14
PARADISE 15.13
PARALLEL 22.30
PARALYSED   250.13
439.19
PARAPET 207.21
PARBLEU 169.17 179.08
179.25
PARCELS 232.18
PARCHED 37.04 183.29
501.28
PARCHMENT   211.09
PARDON 180.20 353.09
PARENTAGE   50.23
PARENTAL 407.22
PARLOUR 2.09 232.15
234.02
PARLOUR' 230.15
PARODY 217.26
PARSEE 42.11 197.06
205.04
PARSON 81.16 95.04
421.16
PARSONAGE   3.28
263.28
PART 19.11 22.14
24.01 39.01 51.27
64.29 83.14 86.13
86.19 98.17 98.27
112.26 147.25 209.08
228.19 232.11 233.21
240.09 244.04 245.06
247.03 249.21 251.29
252.02 268.17 270.07
270.23 274.24 293.27
298.27 315.30 322.30
328.07 339.11 347.15
351.17 359.30 365.28
371.20 383.04 383.10
390.07 394.17 396.28
414.30 423.20 434.03
436.28 437.13 442.10
448.03 458.08 459.04
462.07 467.21 502.07
PARTED 74.23 168.11
185.03 195.14 266.20
285.21 439.25

PARTICLE 7.26 95.28
147.26
PARTICULAR   147.26
204.30 234.13 248.10
436.08
PARTICULARLY   41.05
168.14
PARTIES 16.06 92.08
92.08 229.22 297.17
317.04 331.07 489.23
503.10
PARTIES' 292.26
PARTING 38.20 207.15
280.10 374.04 502.12
PARTISAN 317.05 420.14
PARTLY 24.08 98.18
134.29 345.05 345.06
PARTNER 111.29 197.18
197.20 201.18 205.05
212.20 232.09 245.28
PARTNERS 95.24
PARTS 23.14 38.21
50.08 178.16 484.10
PARTY 241.27 251.04
315.27 316.08 324.03
328.22 333.11 420.13
445.06 451.02 492.18
503.02
PAS 180.24
PASS 1.14 41.07
146.24 256.07 283.24
339.14 349.21 360.16
382.02 481.11 491.03
493.15 499.08 513.11
PASSAGE 2.12 17.06
19.18 70.01 73.23
188.01 231.13 243.28
244.08 290.16 297.15
300.09 341.26 343.04
348.02 366.04 440.23
441.23 461.16
PASSAGES 14.02
PASSED 17.14 20.16
23.17 26.01 31.03
37.03 51.30 52.04
70.20 92.14 94.08
99.06 101.14 109.05
119.18 143.28 148.29
154.09 157.22 175.01
177.07 195.26 216.24
224.01 263.05 291.30
309.03 331.28 335.09
361.27 398.08 398.18
428.04 429.26 431.07
441.08 490.14 493.23
505.03 507.01 507.27
512.09
PASSENGER   243.30
PASSENGERS   172.28
182.20
PASSERS 175.27
PASSERS-BY   175.27
PASSES 174.08 515.19
516.12
PASSING 15.27 71.18
83.19 154.04 167.26
187.28 220.07 260.02
282.09 283.19 335.14
351.11 411.02 463.21
484.09
PASSION 142.17 276.18
294.04 339.12 361.10
434.18 474.27 482.11
PASSIONATE   48.08
191.24 252.24 380.11
417.23
PASSIONATELY   385.08
PASSIONLESS   193.29
PASSIONS 352.12 389.11
516.13
PASSIVE 85.07 126.09
131.19 386.12
PASSIVELY   174.03
202.18 433.18
PASSIVENESS   131.09
PAST 6.16 17.25
18.05 38.06 39.08
72.26 123.12 133.01
136.06 186.10 227.13
236.03 247.05 273.22
335.13 417.08 417.20

PAST (CONT.)		458.14
481.29	493.13	
PATCH	214.26	313.24
500.11		
PATCHES	254.06	410.19
459.08	463.01	470.04
PATENT	12.22	21.15
192.02		
PATERNAL	432.25	
PATERNITY		347.05
PATH	23.04	254.06
266.10	288.03	294.29
313.26	361.23	378.03
396.16	397.10	398.29
432.21	433.26	477.02
PATHETIC	240.16	277.06
381.04		
PATHETICALLY		316.19
PATHOS	76.28	
PATHS	15.24	158.03
262.08	432.16	459.10
PATIENCE	2.17	405.12
405.12		
PATIENT	21.19	67.13
118.21	205.18	262.21
395.01	412.01	
PATIENTLY		90.08
233.01	411.05	439.24
510.19		
PATIENTS	12.16	
PATNA	14.26	14.27
16.20	17.14	19.12
27.03	42.12	43.14
44.27	45.12	48.01
56.24	60.22	60.30
66.07	79.07	80.25
86.27	98.13	107.16
125.30	164.11	169.22
172.28	176.14	184.19
222.23	229.28	231.10
234.19	235.01	238.19
421.14		
PATNA'S	27.11	
PATRIARCH		199.14
PATRIARCHAL		250.16
PATRIES	461.02	
PATRIOTIC		49.01
PATROL	437.21	
PATROLLING		503.13
PATS	314.18	
PATT	171.20	171.20
PATT-NA	171.20	171.20
PATTED	433.18	
PATTERED	217.23	
PATTERN	280.09	
PATUSAN	266.02	266.12
266.24	267.11	268.02
268.06	268.13	268.24
269.07	270.03	276.10
277.25	278.11	278.22
280.14	281.21	292.12
293.23	294.06	297.01
298.23	309.01	310.01
311.18	313.23	315.20
316.26	317.04	327.14
332.23	333.08	333.27
336.16	337.02	339.03
340.27	343.03	343.13
343.22	344.30	345.08
360.02	361.11	361.28
366.12	379.03	392.29
399.06	407.03	420.06
420.19	420.27	427.24
428.01	441.25	442.27
448.14	448.18	449.17
451.03	453.01	456.06
462.22	465.02	465.20
467.13	470.10	478.11
480.09	483.14	483.24
493.26	494.06	494.30
503.26	505.05	512.02
513.14		
PAUNCHY	21.12	
PAUSE	61.05	87.15
125.11	160.25	259.10
282.16	380.12	393.10
413.26	471.08	
PAUSED	34.08	48.13
113.03	113.25	142.01
218.08	226.13	303.07

PAUSED (CONT.)		320.23
329.22	387.18	395.05
400.12	411.16	
PAUSES	127.11	
PAUSING	257.08	
PAVED	4.11	
PAWS	293.09	
PAY	76.01	211.29
222.22	336.24	462.07
PAYING	199.02	280.28
PEA	183.29	
PEACE	3.30	13.11
14.01	19.24	22.21
23.11	75.10	106.06
129.04	163.14	214.18
251.16	271.13	304.11
320.29	331.22	387.09
397.24	465.04	506.24
PEACEFUL	4.27	106.02
303.02	342.13	462.01
510.30		
PEACEFULLY		167.21
PEACETIME		493.29
PEAK	181.18	
PEAKS	297.07	299.08
PEAL	328.12	
PEALER	196.16	
PEARLY	434.09	
PEASANT	170.07	
PEASE	436.04	
PECKER	58.20	
PECULATING		437.14
PECULATION		27.12
PECULIAR	109.14	116.21
123.14	147.01	225.09
341.02	347.06	348.26
PEDESTAL	325.25	
PEDIMENT	146.08	
PEEL	292.05	
PEEP	65.09	
PEEPED	342.27	
PEERED	201.20	265.11
359.23		
PEERING	342.19	428.20
439.28	452.22	511.09
PEEVISHNESS		308.19
PEG	29.14	29.14
PEGGED	22.24	
PELION	74.21	74.30
PELLUCID	149.28	264.06
PELTED	313.12	
PELTING	70.22	
PEN	167.06	185.25
209.04	210.12	212.19
420.25	420.28	421.03
PENALTIES		97.28
PENALTY	316.12	
PENANG	3.19	
PENCIL	5.01	23.03
23.06	23.25	
PENCIL-LINE		23.03
PENDENT	430.05	
PENETRATED		19.23
100.21	341.29	
PENETRATING		100.16
323.06	335.17	350.05
PENNY	26.24	79.12
202.12		
PENNYWORTH		368.13
PENSION	45.30	
PENSIVE	39.03	376.24
491.06		
PENSIVELY		241.20
PENT	78.14	
PENT-UP	78.14	
PEONS	37.18	44.17
PEOPLE	4.02	5.10
11.01	18.03	32.15
40.15	48.14	49.06
73.25	81.16	83.04
83.28	90.27	92.04
96.15	101.19	102.09
102.12	103.01	104.15
104.16	104.20	111.21
121.04	133.19	133.21
152.03	165.12	167.07
169.16	195.24	198.30
209.29	211.22	232.18
240.30	242.04	260.28
274.02	279.18	283.08

PEOPLE (CONT.)		300.26
303.01	305.07	307.24
308.25	311.29	314.11
319.23	320.14	321.14
321.25	322.21	324.24
328.18	329.20	331.23
333.05	334.02	338.03
344.18	344.27	345.09
346.05	349.05	357.30
364.02	364.05	364.09
376.07	376.07	383.15
410.25	410.27	443.16
444.09	447.09	448.06
450.02	451.24	453.27
458.05	462.01	468.10
468.11	470.11	472.16
472.24	474.08	478.12
480.14	483.03	484.08
484.17	484.24	485.21
485.27	486.05	486.11
487.08	489.04	489.26
493.04	506.05	506.15
507.06	509.05	510.27
513.14	513.18	514.17
514.26		
PEOPLE'	420.17	479.15
PEOPLE'S	83.23	483.08
PEOPLED	101.27	392.16
PEOPLING	422.24	459.03
PEPERS	95.16	
PEPPER	276.17	276.18
276.21	276.22	277.25
277.29	426.20	
PEPPER-AND-SALT		426.20
PER	72.02	147.30
269.30		
PER-	147.30	269.30
PERCEIVE	219.06	245.12
308.03	340.05	420.03
453.30	458.27	
PERCEIVED		43.03
70.02	89.13	171.14
177.29	224.14	288.20
291.07	294.17	363.02
371.01	444.14	463.22
PERCEIVING		360.08
478.17		
PERCEPTIBLE		348.24
PERCEPTION		3.21
115.12	310.28	
PERCH	310.04	
PERCHANCE		53.29
262.02		
PERCHED	142.25	167.07
203.29	410.08	
PERCUSSION		451.14
PERDITION		35.24
52.27	418.29	
PERFECT	10.09	19.09
19.09	84.30	115.05
116.09	200.05	220.25
241.01	253.07	256.23
258.06	269.24	453.12
PERFECTION		294.13
PERFECTIONS		227.06
PERFECTLY		78.02
103.27	118.15	123.17
167.25	240.10	278.17
281.17	298.05	304.01
338.27	362.01	365.02
373.06	441.28	453.29
PERFIDIOUS		101.06
PERFORATED		220.21
PERFORMANCE		181.23
359.01	361.14	406.03
PERFORMED		217.25
456.25		
PERFORMING		113.27
PERFUMED	436.04	
PERFUMES	13.02	
PERFUNCTORILY		23.22
PERFUNCTORY		232.22
PERHAPS	1.01	27.20
35.29	38.07	38.25
41.27	50.08	52.12
52.15	55.20	59.20
76.22	77.01	86.09
89.15	96.14	96.17
101.09	103.20	105.24

PERHAPS (CONT.)		107.06
107.12	112.06	113.26
145.16	159.28	163.20
174.13	188.11	193.22
208.26	209.21	212.07
214.14	218.17	223.23
225.22	228.21	232.13
247.07	251.22	253.15
261.18	264.09	265.06
268.16	277.29	279.18
300.16	301.02	302.13
312.06	312.30	313.01
319.25	325.27	325.30
327.19	339.12	339.16
345.15	379.26	384.02
387.10	388.30	398.19
412.13	413.27	419.10
419.18	427.11	429.13
441.21	441.25	441.25
442.07	454.09	454.16
459.13	470.08	472.20
477.02	488.20	492.03
495.01	514.02	
PERIL	310.28	
PERILS	7.25	
PERIM	23.03	
PERIOD	170.17	213.22
466.24		
PERIODICALLY		21.16
PERISH	106.03	423.18
449.13		
PERISHABLE		252.28
292.30		
PERMANENT		19.13
92.18	230.08	
PERMANENTLY		251.17
PERSEATED		352.12
PERMISSION		343.15
451.30		
PERMIT	278.13	
PERPENDICULAR		4.30
433.28		
PERPENDICULARLY		62.20
263.10		
PERPETUAL		112.21
PERPETUALLY		112.18
347.07	397.11	399.18
PERPLEXED		260.06
407.23		
PERPLEXITIES		177.23
PERQUISITES		43.43
PERSEVERANCE		88.12
PERSIAN	61.29	
PERSISTED		12.12
88.06		
PERSISTENCE		148.10
277.10		
PERSISTENT		325.26
345.19	365.17	
PERSISTENTLY		212.17
415.07		
PERSON	56.27	75.13
93.24	97.20	106.10
177.07	190.16	247.22
266.18	268.21	268.30
332.28	333.08	345.27
352.19	375.04	379.22
386.10	457.04	504.14
PERSONAL	58.05	60.07
179.17	241.03	281.11
351.29	411.14	452.01
499.17		
PERSONALITY		3.08
54.12	111.28	421.08
PERSONALLY		308.14
PERSONS	14.15	47.27
92.16	209.27	247.19
277.12		
PERSPECTIVE		61.13
PERSPIRATION		62.17
329.12		
PERSPIRED		344.24
PERSPIRING		55.16
PERSUADED		173.15
244.15		
PERSUASIVE		363.15
PERTINACITY		88.14
415.03		
PERTURBATION		74.13
428.30		

PERVADED 19.01 508.23
PERVADING 147.25
PERVERSE 387.14
PERVERSIONS 51.17
PESTILENCE 277.04
480.04
PETRIFIED 313.17
PETTY 427.28
PETUALLY 148.01
PEUT 171.05
PHANTASMAL 212.24
PHANTOM 17.18 17.19
61.06
PHANTOMS 112.08
PHENOMENAL 286.29
PHENOMENON 298.10
PHILIPPINES 437.16
PHILOSOPHIC 169.18
PHILOSOPHY 28.08
PHILTRE 23.19
PHONG 76.15
PHOO 257.21 343.24
PHRASE 86.10 90.15
207.15 424.07
PHRASEOLOGY 193.29
293.06
PHYSICAL 246.27
PHYSICALLY 241.16
PHYSIQUE 4.23
PICK 41.19 356.01
364.25
PICKED 58.27 97.30
98.12 108.10 110.17
151.13 159.06 162.13
311.15 418.01 501.27
PICKER 113.10
PICKING 101.08 132.29
132.30 134.11
PICKINGS 474.15
PICTURE 101.27 117.11
162.07 407.05 407.13
423.30
PICTURESQUE 192.08
272.13
PICTURING 341.23
PIECE 21.07 43.37
89.03 148.16 150.06
194.29 207.06 211.09
218.15 263.09 333.26
491.18
PIECEMEAL 316.30
PIECES 30.02 151.24
307.06 332.15 423.28
425.17 457.24 491.25
PIER 52.14
PIER-HEADS 52.14
PIERCE 261.12
PIERCED 49.30 131.21
224.30
PIERCING 477.21
PIERRE 207.09
PIETY 3.30 382.01
383.09
PIG 327.07
PIGTAIL 27.10
PILE 17.01 146.11
PILED 21.09
PILES 410.09 446.01
462.30
PILGRIM 16.30 41.04
64.21
PILGRIMAGE 17.21
117.28
PILGRIMS 15.08 16.12
20.06 81.03 117.27
166.24 234.16
PILL 279.07
PILLAR 151.27
PILLARS 49.08
PILLOW 27.02 59.04
505.11
PILLOWS 21.15
PILOT 52.20 297.21
493.19
PILOTING 2.01
PIN 69.09 138.28
358.20 393.13
PIN-POINT 393.13
PINCH 267.15
PINCHES 75.26

PINE 194.13
PINK 62.09 62.11
63.03 63.03 193.05
195.12 424.11
PINNED 332.19 417.26
PINS 22.24 73.08
73.10 254.13 495.29
PIOUS 16.16 17.25
67.14 103.05 192.18
192.27
PIPE 28.16 62.12
62.13 217.24 220.21
224.02 257.07 258.21
323.10 323.30 399.02
471.01
PIPE-CLAYED 471.01
PIPED 199.22
PIRATE 196.18
PISTOL 261.11 442.19
PISTOL-SHOT 442.19
PISTOLS 324.16 513.25
514.23
PIT 52.27 218.30
241.19 469.15
PITCH 133.25 194.13
387.11 387.27
PITCH-DARK 133.25
387.11
PITCH-PINE 194.13
PITCHED 30.14 83.16
369.26
PITCHER 360.20
PITCHING 6.05
PITCHY 136.14
PITEOUS 134.17 399.21
405.11
PITFALLS 262.05 262.13
PITH 37.17 70.15
452.20
PITIED 357.17
PITIFUL 8.21 89.27
98.27 105.28 192.03
243.28 268.16 314.19
389.27 488.07
PITILESS 459.01 468.23
516.03
PITILESSLY 96.20
PITTED 409.29
PITY 18.10 60.29
69.04 134.21 157.13
166.14 313.07 357.18
418.14 431.04 431.16
PITYING 338.19
PIVOT 207.08
PIVOTED 220.29
PLACATED 157.22
PLACE 4.21 14.16
23.05 26.02 35.17
36.07 50.21 56.07
57.10 76.10 76.19
87.28 92.14 99.08
101.28 103.11 124.30
170.22 186.08 190.24
197.03 200.05 208.11
208.26 218.29 230.03
232.11 240.22 241.23
242.23 249.04 253.18
253.19 260.04 267.23
269.02 274.29 288.26
293.16 301.24 306.06
308.28 312.01 312.17
324.13 330.04 343.02
344.28 345.24 351.08
351.14 351.23 352.20
353.12 363.21 372.12
375.10 385.03 397.01
412.20 420.08 420.13
435.11 443.06 446.02
465.16 470.08 473.25
478.17 481.27 493.15
498.28 504.09 512.11
PLACED 244.14 490.16
PLACES 3.19 13.23
48.15 58.01 246.01
267.17 285.17 397.26
398.14 419.03 480.18
PLACID 20.02 170.08
172.08 257.19 293.07
422.23
PLACIDITY 90.19

PLACIDITY (CONT.)
322.16
PLACIDLY 179.23 377.21
PLAGUE 40.19 167.15
PLAGUE-STRICKEN 167.15
PLAIN 4.29 17.15
71.27 116.15 127.30
171.03 195.04 254.06
262.02 262.12 315.16
321.04 409.26 500.13
PLAINLY 144.22 150.18
182.27 510.04
PLAINS 276.11 297.06
467.10
PLAINTIFF 192.18
PLAINTIVE 232.10
PLAINTS 405.29
PLAITED 27.09
PLAN 185.19 300.14
311.08 321.12 358.16
359.09 360.05 420.09
451.25
PLANE 244.22
PLANES 155.08
PLANET 25.06
PLANETS 392.06
PLANK 24.16
PLANKING 366.20
PLANKS 20.08 129.21
PLANNED 147.28 458.24
PLANS 13.22 396.26
PLANT 87.28 432.01
PLANTATION 396.19
PLANTED 17.01 216.10
293.26 311.24
PLANTERS 200.12
PLANTS 94.11
PLASTER 58.19
PLATE 75.09 93.30
101.13 286.04 287.04
306.08
PLATES 29.30 103.13
488.30
PLATFORMS 420.11
480.12 504.03
PLAUSIBLE 229.23
440.29
PLAY 66.19 177.24
331.10 458.29 482.15
PLAYED 12.25 34.10
62.24 351.16 383.04
463.04 502.07
PLAYFUL 396.06
PLAYING 95.30 96.01
247.04 287.21
PLAYS 437.12 474.26
PLEADED 202.26 222.11
PLEADING 381.04 433.05
PLEASANT 41.27 210.19
354.07
PLEASANTLY 217.04
PLEASE 72.28 90.18
163.19 179.21 213.17
329.10 467.30
PLEASED 23.21 53.09
146.21 214.15 228.30
274.24 338.30 344.06
364.10 428.09 461.10
PLEASURABLE 24.03
PLEASURABLY 28.25
PLEASURE 168.01 185.25
201.11 254.23 279.04
363.15 371.22
PLEASURES 271.20
PLENTY 48.11 159.28
293.22 356.03 454.19
467.08
PLIABLE 31.10
PLODDING 184.09
PLOP 183.15
PLOT 129.16 383.04
PLOTS 4.10 49.25
358.02 420.19
PLOTTING 380.02
PLUCK 68.24 73.17
125.06 143.22 143.25
355.07 395.27 465.29
PLUCKED 58.28
PLUMES 75.12

PLUNDER 317.05 426.03
457.22
PLUNGE 123.23 134.03
190.15 304.02 378.26
PLUNGED 238.22
PLUS 169.28
POCK 332.18
POCK-MARKED 332.18
POCKET 79.13 80.10
153.05 159.10 185.21
285.04 288.12 456.22
491.10
POCKET-BOOK 80.10
456.22
POCKETS 46.29 49.24
73.09 92.05 130.15
154.12 225.30 287.06
POD 55.11
POESY 262.05 262.14
POET 259.15
POET' 257.01
POIGNANT 32.22 95.14
POINT 7.13 36.21
36.29 46.05 59.12
60.28 67.28 72.19
89.12 90.05 137.27
177.19 178.23 178.24
178.25 179.06 191.17
194.06 204.30 209.19
212.09 212.19 269.09
278.25 281.17 286.30
300.22 312.01 329.22
331.14 338.06 340.02
341.21 347.07 393.13
403.09 419.05 443.18
466.07 478.14 490.15
494.04 494.18 502.27
POINT-BLANK 67.28
466.07
POINTED 32.02 79.06
89.02 122.23 232.28
298.14 308.29 323.29
350.22 410.28 427.27
434.04 449.07 478.10
POINTEDLY 25.13
POINTING 63.17 88.25
246.23 257.26 261.16
301.08 425.21 455.12
POINTS 120.10
POISED 30.27
POISON 54.16 149.25
308.15 464.20
POISONED 358.03 390.23
POKED 153.27 201.18
296.05
POLE 335.07
POLES 20.20 471.16
POLICE 32.08 44.17
58.28 67.09 185.04
POLICEMAN 192.01
POLICY 15.04 461.11
POLISHED 92.20 263.08
322.04 325.19
POLITE 65.13 365.28
POLITELY 177.01
POLITENESS 181.06
POLTRON 179.24
POLYNESIA 435.17
POMPOUS 192.22
PON 329.11
POND 110.29 432.04
PONDEROUS 85.11
171.06 180.30 319.03
PONDEROUSLY 6.05
176.03
PONY 54.26 55.21
55.25 56.04 255.11
422.15
POOL 23.08 223.09
302.17 417.12
POOP 52.20 229.06
POOR 20.28 25.23
56.23 68.03 70.30
72.20 75.30 76.06
77.08 77.20 79.05
81.26 95.17 98.05
114.04 116.22 140.27
140.27 175.03 177.09
182.27 183.17 190.18

POOR (CONT.)   241.18
  245.18   247.17   249.24
  251.06   251.17   254.03
  255.08   267.24   307.04
  332.12   338.27   340.13
  345.25   357.13   363.06
  384.14   389.07   390.01
  394.19   395.07   433.17
  435.20   436.11   452.09
  453.27   466.07   475.18
  479.04   489.08   511.15
  513.22   514.28   516.17
POORER   462.05
POP   168.10
POPINJAY   74.22
POPULAR   1.13   332.08
POPULATION   83.12
  278.04   301.05   446.12
  478.21   483.27
POPULATIONS   292.23
POPULOUS   15.30
PORK   43.37
PORT   12.13   13.17
  27.11   32.08   35.07
  49.02   57.26   66.11
  69.30   107.18   170.26
  172.17   214.25   291.14
  440.28
PORT-SIDE   35.07
PORTAL   408.30
PORTENT   309.20   508.25
PORTICO   49.26
PORTION   101.29
PORTLY   206.05
PORTMANTEAUX   92.17
PORTRAYING   22.26
PORTS   1.12
PORTUGUEE   57.09
PORTUGUESE   43.34
  268.18   268.28   340.14
  405.28
POSE   50.30   174.24
POSITION   23.01   69.26
  71.02   71.07   122.12
  156.01   166.08   172.04
  222.08   242.26   244.16
  244.19   245.17   250.28
  251.21   269.01   307.26
  308.23   311.02   321.02
  332.14   352.24   373.01
  405.27   444.20   445.01
  446.09   451.28   452.17
  458.22   466.04   469.22
  491.06
POSITIVE   38.08   81.30
  371.23
POSITIVELY   36.01
  49.20   60.16   100.20
  225.29
POSSESS   256.26
POSSESSED   3.30
  68.24   119.24   210.07
  222.06   246.26   279.25
  304.15   336.22   359.24
  368.13   382.27   448.14
POSSESSES   2.21
POSSESSING   13.12
POSSESSION   112.08
  177.23   293.03   310.10
  340.30   349.07   470.26
  507.28
POSSESSOR   111.30
POSSIBILITIES   322.11
  453.02   453.02
POSSIBILITY   86.21
  438.19
POSSIBLE   86.11   117.20
  134.25   137.02   168.03
  171.03   172.03   209.14
  214.28   256.11   259.09
  289.26   314.03   321.04
  341.17   353.07   358.09
  382.05   387.03   387.18
  422.13   457.10
POSSIBLE'   176.16
POSSIBLY   45.03   84.19
  86.23   219.26   400.04
  419.01
POST   268.24   293.26
  472.10

POSTED   504.10
POSTER   209.10
POSTHUMOUS   76.29
  475.06
POSTS   245.30   311.04
  316.29   339.30   366.12
  366.16
POSTURE   48.23   102.28
  129.26   452.22
POT   21.15   23.28
  243.20   285.12   427.06
POT-BELLIED   427.06
POT-HOUSE   243.20
POTATO   310.30
POTATOES   43.38   442.05
POTENT   215.11   434.21
POTS   21.12   330.10
  330.15   330.18   331.01
  331.18
POULO   441.01
POULTRY   316.27
POULTRY-YARD   316.27
POUNCE   209.08
POUNCED   138.08
POUND   26.25   426.13
POUNDED   16.29
POUNDER   467.15
POUNDERS   323.21   443.19
POUNDS   45.30   92.04
POUR   171.27
POURED   119.11   170.06
  236.02   300.26
POURING   17.24   22.06
  314.11   414.26
POUTED   89.11   272.18
POVERTY   16.03
POWDER   448.19   451.13
  461.23   505.05
POWDER-MAGAZINE   448.19
POWER   20.05   30.02
  50.30   59.28   66.15
  90.16   90.20   97.27
  116.29   166.13   167.27
  172.30   197.07   212.16
  219.02   271.28   276.02
  282.24   302.12   315.19
  316.16   320.28   320.28
  322.09   325.26   335.01
  337.21   349.09   369.04
  379.26   386.13   390.10
  391.05   432.16   447.11
  457.11   469.21   470.26
  481.04   481.09   508.05
POWERFUL   73.11   149.25
  163.16   318.17   327.12
  337.12   397.17
POWERFULLY   1.02
  272.07
POWERLESS   369.06
POWERS   131.11   147.29
  273.30   302.15   327.02
  437.20   506.23
PRACTICAL   131.12
  209.23   262.24   262.24
  262.27   263.03   263.03
  265.13   265.14
PRACTICALLY   1.16
  82.02   193.25   310.09
  312.04
PRACTICE   197.16
PRANCE   57.25
PRAU   494.16
PRAUS   15.25
PRAY   176.02   189.01
  291.05
PRAYED   50.11   511.11
PRAYER   16.25   21.01
  108.13   192.30   364.02
PRAYER-CARPETS   21.01
PRAYERS   439.20
PREACHING   363.12
PRECARIOUS   332.27
PRECARIOUSLY   14.05
  220.20
PRECAUTION   34.01
  299.05
PRECAUTIONS   63.18
PRECEDED   248.04   264.15
PRECEDENT   298.26
PRECEDES   123.21

PRECEDING   107.10
  491.01
PRECIOUS   11.16   41.20
  49.04   97.24   281.24
  341.01   342.07   342.07
  345.04   472.19
PRECIPICE   323.15
  397.02
PRECISE   55.24   58.15
  242.06
PRECISELY   176.04
  186.11   278.20   280.21
  378.13
PRECISION   35.13
PREDESTINED   382.24
PREDICAMENT   86.12
PREFERRED   232.01
PREGNANT   162.06
PRELIMINARY   438.23
PREMATURELY   396.05
PREPARATION   115.05
PREPARATIONS   453.19
  490.30   506.25   513.16
PREPARATORY   177.06
PREPARE   466.30
PREPARED   107.24   172.04
  396.23
PREPARING   114.15
  167.04   300.13   499.17
  516.20   516.20
PRESCIENCE   85.05
PRESENCE   18.03   68.15
  244.11   249.19   254.04
  306.17   382.26   411.08
  450.11   450.17   508.24
PRESENT   38.12   51.28
  175.16   202.12   295.01
  303.28   324.19   403.23
  404.03   427.19   482.30
PRESENT'   404.07
PRESENTED   22.27
  25.12   68.05   69.12
  153.21   280.10   292.20
  307.29   348.04   469.20
  488.30
PRESENTING   291.18
PRESENTLY   101.09
  424.02   424.03   494.11
  494.12   498.04
PRESENTS   285.20
PRESERVE   80.29   92.16
  308.22   490.04
PRESERVED   13.19
  131.08   182.02   331.24
  345.26   421.11   454.02
PRESERVES   482.19
PRESERVING   17.27
PRESIDED   69.11
PRESIDING   33.03
PRESS   179.20
PRESSED   20.11   223.20
  303.11   303.17   346.08
  358.28   360.06   403.07
PRESSING   16.07   77.05
  91.15   108.19   169.15
  220.11   302.24   456.16
PRESSURE   340.18
PRESTIGE   447.10
PREFERENCE   8.23   474.28
PRETENCES   10.21
  47.15
PRETEND   48.20   91.05
  185.12   215.17   223.13
PRETENDED   144.12
  316.11   358.28   452.07
  490.25
PRETENDERS   251.03
PRETENDING   53.02
  75.15
PRETTY   27.12   54.12
  60.18   75.12   79.08
  81.09   93.28   101.17
  115.21   116.01   175.17
  175.22   175.22   184.03
  217.15   276.15   342.08
  348.06   361.25   381.02
  395.30   396.04   401.04
  474.15
PREVAIL   43.01   394.20
PREVAILED   449.06

PREVENT   143.26   189.03
  226.10   354.08   450.30
  451.09
PREVENTED   49.20
  115.11   190.21   307.16
  478.15
PREVENTS   50.06
PREVIOUS   294.09
PREY   188.25   360.21
  455.07
PRICE   58.08   68.12
PRICELESS   11.14
  51.02   345.02
PRICKED   89.02   133.16
  181.08
PRICKING   492.26
PRIDE   191.02   270.01
  276.02   293.02   303.14
  304.14   321.25
PRIDED   459.27
PRIEST   273.26
PRIESTLIKE   176.17
PRIESTS   170.05
PRIMARY   315.28
PRIME   27.01
PRIMEVAL   408.27
PRIMITIVE   185.20
PRINCE   207.07
PRINCESS   251.24   254.09
  268.10
PRINCIPAL   43.31
  56.27   257.13   285.11
  292.23   363.13   366.17
  437.15   437.26   458.02
  483.13
PRINCIPALLY   300.11
PRINCIPLE   108.02
PRINCIPLES   28.11
  242.17
PRISON   440.13   474.12
PRISONER   38.11   306.01
  307.01
PRIVACY   209.14
PRIVATE   28.10   45.07
PRIVATIONS   256.28
  458.21
PRIVILEGE   122.07
  426.27   474.16
PRIVILEGED   250.10
  250.28   416.17   434.27
PRIZE   439.01
PRO   30.30
PRO-   30.30
PROBABILITY   55.06
  85.27
PROBABLE   125.20   358.10
PROBABLY   4.08   27.21
  69.18   79.12   119.28
  169.03   176.17   194.12
  229.16   274.30   287.15
  288.09   345.12   374.08
  390.03   394.19   441.27
PROBATION   213.22
PROBE   121.08
PROCEED   179.17
PROCEEDED   287.09
PROCEEDING   85.14
  209.17   360.04
PROCEEDINGS   82.23
  96.09   119.20   193.16
  368.09   449.25   499.09
PROCESS   243.17   290.25
  311.06
PROCLAIMED   250.24
  465.01
PROCLAIMING   506.22
PROCURE   79.09   358.18
PROD   156.27
PRODIGIOUSLY   118.04
PRODUCE   102.11   232.23
  246.02   252.14   314.04
  343.05   442.06
PRODUCED   8.18   60.22
  158.25   232.23   317.16
  487.02
PRODUCES   253.07
PRODUCING   173.01
  287.10
PROFESSED   358.06
  454.23   490.04

PROFESSIONAL 24.14
80.29 177.20 244.06
327.15
PROFESSIONALLY · 51.20
PROFESSOR 256.27
PROFIT 207.17 267.21
PROFITABLE 275.19
437.13
PROFOUND 17.12 25.02
39.02 46.18 48.23
59.21 117.15 120.30
134.21 160.26 172.09
180.17 210.14 239.09
263.15 295.07 307.25
320.10 321.21 342.27
368.19 379.20 392.29
423.14 424.13 426.17
427.08 443.06 452.25
464.18
PROFOUNDLY 100.30
176.28 367.05 367.12
386.12 412.16
PROFUNDITY 77.20
PROGRESS 17.21 77.27
114.22 257.28 264.02
351.09 418.24 419.09
PROJECTED 100.10
PROJECTING 378.20
PROLONGED 30.12
123.24 401.27 467.23
PROMINENT 332.30
PROMISE 23.05 283.14
283.25 295.12 337.15
344.13 378.18 452.01
455.04 472.22 480.19
511.14
PROMISED 290.20 330.21
511.15
PROMISING 47.11
285.21
PROMOTED 70.32
PROMOTION 74.30
PROMPTED 464.27
PROMPTINGS 384.17
PROMPTLY 169.21
PRONE 20.18 394.06
PRONOUNCE 389.21
419.10 449.05
PRONOUNCED 3.06
24.14 80.14 85.25
88.21 130.03 158.17
163.29 174.07 177.01
179.16 218.07 257.01
275.05 348.12 433.13
454.21
PRONOUNCEMENT 193.28
234.14
PRONOUNCING 89.13
262.28 361.08
PROOF 254.19 358.23
PROOFS 179.12
PROPAGATED 158.18
PROPELLER 19.10
234.17
PROPER 52.30 161.03
171.25 194.08 196.19
234.27 288.28 289.15
332.01 394.16 422.03
434.26 449.14 449.18
456.01
PROPERLY 98.14 366.01
PROPERTIES 292.19
PROPERTY 47.28 166.28
195.06 278.21 490.10
PROPHESIED 418.11
PROPITIATED 292.22
PROPITIATORY 115.01
PROPORTIONED 223.11
322.03
PROPOSAL 81.28 404.21
PROPOSALS 453.03
PROPOSED 490.06
PROPOUNDING 379.02
PROPPED 129.27 139.11
172.22 193.04 193.07
199.17 205.17
PROSAIC 10.08 239.11
280.15
PROSPECT 286.26 338.18
PROSPECTS 10.13

PROSPECTS (CONT.)
46.08
PROSPERITY 16.03
PROSTRATE 336.14
PROTECT 484.12
PROTECTED 214.08
453.27 455.07 490.10
PROTECTION 16.02
298.03 316.07 352.03
410.15
PROTECTOR 415.06
PROTEST 124.19 350.18
369.18 392.13
PROTESTED 84.23
87.22 104.13 158.24
165.01 203.06 282.20
337.13 402.18 433.14
481.24
PROTESTING 178.07
377.09 381.17
PROTOTYPES 436.02
PROTRUDED 371.13
PROUD 304.18 304.19
318.12 322.03 347.17
515.17 515.25
PROUDLY 114.17 458.18
PROVE 160.16 162.10
508.05
PROVED 304.25 377.07
PROVERB 274.17
PROVIDED 166.24
PROVIDENCE 4.04
194.26 280.11 421.25
PROVIDENTIALLY 198.19
PROVINCE 12.20
PROVISION 403.22
404.10 404.23
PROVISIONS 440.14
442.04
PROVOCATION 81.29
PROVOKED 79.18 101.03
115.01 187.10 209.08
400.03
PROVOKING 273.03
361.14
PROWESS 213.03
PROWL 194.17 350.11
PROWLING 260.23 306.10
PRUDENCE 209.16
PRUDENTLY 360.11
PRYING 60.12
PSALM 198.14
PSALM-TUNE 198.14
PSHAW 115.02
PSYCHOLOGICAL 66.13
PUBLIC 47.28 166.28
319.06 320.07
PUBLICITY 80.01
PUBLICLY 15.02
PUCKERED 43.25
PUDDING 94.07
PUFF 149.19 378.02
PUFFED 28.16 54.19
344.24
PULL 48.20 183.01
183.21 293.20 312.01
372.18 439.29 484.30
PULLED 4.21 8.12
44.30 45.05 47.03
150.19 208.21 225.01
325.04 399.01 466.06
PULLING 62.07 133.10
323.09 324.24 473.23
PULSATING 467.19
PUMPKIN 296.05
PUNCH 75.08
PUNCTILIOUSLY 180.20
PUNGENT 146.03
PUNISH 341.03
PUNISHMENT 82.01
184.10 191.13
PUNKAHPULLERS 44.16
PUNKAHS 32.11 32.24
37.12 192.14 195.16
PUPILS 180.17 201.21
PUPPY 53.10 205.28
PURBLIND 345.25
PURCHASE 437.06
PURCHASES 105.06
PURE 146.05 347.11

PURELY 66.13 285.12
316.22
PURITY 163.14
PURPLE 15.06 45.18
193.05 319.12 413.03
414.01
PURPLISH 54.21
PURPOSE 6.09 8.18
11.08 25.14 38.14
44.14 46.18 72.07
124.11 228.13 270.10
277.09 286.15 287.12
322.01 327.17 368.10
401.10 427.04 439.10
458.13 461.17 484.22
500.09
PURPOSEFULLY 293.19
PURPOSES 16.28 17.25
91.11 424.09 483.28
PURSED 171.24 176.23
PURSER 12.17
PURSING 170.18
PURSUED 29.24 61.09
64.11 72.21 78.12
113.13 123.28 170.25
355.18 411.20 413.18
431.29 462.14 467.27
468.15 498.08
PURSUING 461.11 477.16
PURSUIT 333.22 432.17
505.29
PUSH 6.21 80.18
217.01 369.27 500.08
PUSHED 34.24 57.11
120.17 126.03 126.04
126.04 126.11 126.16
126.17 126.18 141.07
211.02 248.12 369.28
428.16 429.19 497.03
PUSHING 83.28 115.26
195.25 277.17 279.20
432.14 484.25
PUT 67.03 70.40
72.23 73.09 75.22
79.26 79.27 91.01
99.17 113.03 143.11
146.06 147.22 153.07
153.15 159.17 178.03
183.22 184.16 185.24
185.29 188.16 197.30
224.10 231.06 234.05
234.17 254.27 269.30
287.23 296.03 299.01
300.13 309.02 311.20
314.16 324.12 332.16
337.19 337.29 341.09
343.04 348.07 349.17
353.08 363.16 365.21
388.22 392.06 395.29
408.22 410.10 423.26
440.27 444.12 456.02
491.09 494.05 505.19
511.19
PUTS 142.02 179.27
235.30
PUTTING 78.10 190.18
212.03 254.19 262.23
PUZZLED 225.05 283.02
361.04 424.06 434.20
477.03 477.22
PYJAMAS 12.26 24.06
435.19
PYRAMIDS 120.26 498.21
Q 63.02
QU'ON 171.04
QUAFFED 213.15
QUAKING 513.19
QUALITE 170.16
QUALITIES 334.28
QUALITY 10.20 28.27
113.17 170.16 270.07
478.02
QUANTITY 68.19
QUARREL 57.24 112.02
190.09 331.04 457.20
QUARRELLING 207.22
QUARRELS 315.28
QUARRELSOME 294.02
QUARRY 460.05
QUARTER 96.17 165.07

QUARTER (CONT.) 166.06
241.08 354.04 420.19
441.14
QUARTER-MASTER'S 96.17
QUARTERMASTER 96.19
QUARTERMASTERS 80.03
105.19 170.30 171.07
QUARTERS 73.07 351.30
QUAVER 72.22
QUAVERED 96.26
QUAVERING 62.29
451.29
QUAY 27.10 43.04
52.12 75.27 200.13
207.22 244.20 245.24
QUAY-SIDE 27.10
QUAYS 99.10
QUE 173.20 179.03
QUEEN 76.12 250.19
250.23 251.01
QUEENSLAND 200.12
201.02 201.03
QUEER 43.05 74.12
119.12 138.28
QUEER-SOUNDING 119.12
QUEERLY 429.18
QUELLED 5.15
QUERIED 141.28 263.20
QUERULOUSLY 496.03
QUEST 417.16
QUESTION 36.20 36.29
37.26 60.23 78.19
93.10 97.12 97.13
148.03 165.05 165.29
180.05 203.27 223.21
228.26 241.11 259.11
259.15 269.30 311.12
337.20 339.04 359.01
359.16 419.07 442.03
499.09
QUESTIONABLE 168.01
QUESTIONED 150.22
471.18
QUESTIONERS 7.30
QUESTIONING 32.22
QUESTIONS 32.02
32.06 32.19 38.03
38.13 58.10 66.19
67.03 118.29 194.03
344.13 400.01 428.29
441.01 478.14
QUICK 61.22 63.06
110.11 110.12 110.13
111.24 111.25 146.23
189.20 198.24 199.08
256.17 319.18 333.12
342.18 439.18 493.21
QUICKENED 393.25
409.03
QUICKLY 87.13 137.02
205.21 232.26 303.09
307.23 362.05 366.25
394.02 443.29 474.17
484.04 504.19
QUIET 34.14 37.25
41.10 52.12 59.02
60.01 63.24 64.13
84.15 86.30 93.19
97.07 108.29 132.09
133.24 140.26 144.03
168.14 170.05 209.04
224.04 227.07 236.27
248.12 255.19 255.19
316.18 327.14 328.15
344.14 359.24 385.09
387.14 397.21 413.25
422.24 436.13 436.19
450.05 490.04 493.14
493.18 510.20
QUIETED 222.04
QUIETLY 27.24 97.29
106.02 115.23 132.07
151.12 225.18 228.07
350.01 377.06 412.29
430.12 445.13 454.17
471.08 498.09
QUIETUDE 263.15
QUILLDRIVER 57.04
QUIT 235.27 292.20
QUITE 34.30 43.43

QUITE (CONT.)   44.12
  44.20   44.24   44.29
  57.20   61.01   72.19
  76.12   96.03   114.15
 134.13   144.07   153.02
 190.08   210.20   235.23
 236.02   240.27   258.27
 300.30   328.10   361.28
 367.05   367.17   400.14
 401.16   405.08   459.16
 500.02   500.22   516.04
QUITTING 448.07
QUIVER   43.23   204.02
QUIVERED   6.24   31.03
  46.19   163.04   257.23
QUIVERING   31.12
 343.28
QUOTED   267.23
RABBIT   58.28
RACE   44.01   233.20
 315.24   318.02   321.23
RACED   128.23
RACEHORSE   184.13
RACES   44.02   322.12
 325.27
RACIAL   447.10
RACIALLY 418.23
RACING   1.17
RACKED   211.01   425.09
RACKET   26.04   231.11
RACKETED 23.27
RACKS   461.26
RAFTERS 359.05
RAFTS   480.12
RAG   20.29   25.19
  51.23   113.10   439.03
RAG-PICKER   113.10
RAGAMUFFIN   310.10
RAGE   190.08   307.12
 393.03   444.05   444.08
 452.14   465.26   488.17
 515.06
RAGED   352.13
RAGGED   4.06   70.14
 129.29   279.23   370.08
 410.07   426.21   442.26
 452.18
RAGING   175.26
RAGS   16.06   20.09
  75.26   81.05   273.18
 370.03   468.25   474.23
 480.26   513.20
RAID   363.18
RAIL   6.28   26.20
  30.10   73.01   133.01
 182.26   183.12   291.29
 360.23   362.10
RAILS   6.19   15.15
 167.07
RAILWAY   12.19
RAIN   5.30   123.13
 134.01   134.03   135.03
 136.09   137.06   142.09
 143.03   143.16   148.20
 203.20   203.23   217.23
 218.08   220.24   222.02
 224.01   255.01   417.05
RAIN-WATER   203.20
RAINING 220.23
RAISE   64.05   119.07
 318.16
RAISED   7.08   85.23
 109.23   129.24   133.05
 134.10   153.07   174.20
 180.04   189.14   256.10
 265.12   294.18   296.06
 370.22   371.11   390.28
 414.07   446.04   462.03
 469.12   484.25   487.08
 498.25   505.13   509.06
 515.14
RAISING   83.25   88.06
 128.07   176.20   217.02
 295.25   299.29   393.15
 396.27   409.19
RAJAH   278.23   279.03
 292.23   293.11   298.26
 300.14   301.17   301.19
 306.03   307.08   307.22
 308.17   310.22   315.27

RAJAH (CONT.)   316.10
 317.06   317.10   321.06
 332.24   345.24   354.06
 449.21   451.22   454.27
 460.18   462.08   489.27
 492.11
RAJAH'S 293.27   316.03
 316.08   317.15   363.23
 364.07   410.24   411.13
 443.02   444.24   445.09
 445.23   449.19   450.15
 453.07   453.23   454.22
 458.05   461.23   462.08
 480.16   489.25   490.10
 490.11   494.04
RAJAHS   250.17   250.23
RAKISHLY 61.17
RALLY   420.15
RAMADAN 489.16
RAMBLING 403.17
RAMMED   225.30   288.11
RAMSHACKLE   47.02
  55.29   311.03
RAN   34.25   35.07
  38.04   45.05   56.24
 108.26   112.05   120.06
 120.10   125.12   177.10
 193.07   210.03   229.13
 248.19   286.04   293.06
 301.17   309.13   313.26
 314.17   369.22   373.20
 398.29   403.03   418.02
 435.02   436.20   479.24
 498.15   501.07   504.13
 505.01   505.08   505.24
 512.19   512.21
RANCOUR 127.19   372.10
RANDOM   314.08
RANG   21.16   32.17
 121.02   211.03   446.08
 465.05   500.18   509.28
RANGE   165.23   319.12
RANGED   16.24   167.09
 249.02   373.07
RANGOON   3.18   185.23
RANK   367.14
RANKS   218.29   274.29
 412.20   419.01   487.19
RAP   47.26   259.07
RAPACIOUS   483.18
RAPACITY 316.15
RAPID   129.14   203.28
 348.02   443.26
RAPIDITY 63.03
RAPIDLY   37.19   295.11
 308.02   365.26   368.18
 445.03   460.08   505.04
RAPINE   459.04
RARE   53.26   53.30
 106.03   148.22   174.17
 194.25   246.22   253.26
 253.29   256.23   257.29
 267.27   321.21   434.10
RARELY   268.10
RASCAL   254.29   343.21
 344.03   357.16   361.26
RASCALS 255.20
RASH   74.18   77.04
RASPING   24.15   141.23
 273.22
RAT   237.21   471.28
 471.29   472.01   472.04
RATE   48.02   70.06
  86.28   196.30   223.12
 243.01   268.26   274.18
 360.04   396.12   445.18
 479.07
RATHER   8.26   44.02
  48.02   68.03   76.03
  78.04   81.15   81.19
  96.11   97.01   102.06
 196.05   208.06   208.10
 222.14   242.17   249.29
 275.13   287.02   307.26
 331.09   339.25   350.25
 367.05   381.22   395.29
 442.03   442.11
RATIONAL 182.07
RATS   353.22
RATTAN   293.25   430.01

RATTLE   56.14   140.23
 286.25
RATTLED   26.06   55.13
RATTLING 62.20
RAVAGED 241.07   426.19
RAVENOUS 293.16
RAVINE   269.16   328.23
RAVING   64.29
RAVONALO 207.07
RAW   55.19   175.07
RAWBONED 232.15
RAYS   17.25   19.03
 397.06
RAZOR   180.19
RAZOR-EDGE   180.19
RE-   353.30
RE-   353.30
REACH   80.10   105.16
 162.02   204.04   299.21
 300.07   335.09   430.28
 434.08   442.27   443.04
 443.20   445.26   445.29
 477.13   499.21   504.02
REACHED   7.04   48.04
  55.17   63.08   104.29
 150.19   186.04   248.22
 312.08   323.05   334.05
 350.04   409.02   470.05
 497.16   513.05
REACHES 408.15
REACHING 335.17
REACTION 140.04   374.23
READ   20.01   46.09
 193.09   229.02   286.09
 290.30   348.14   417.24
 418.04   419.11   491.24
READER   434.27
READILY 181.14   385.14
READINESS   8.25
  50.29   60.21   106.03
 148.10   154.15   304.27
 366.03
READING   97.15   227.15
 248.16   417.11   477.23
 487.09
READING-LAMP   248.16
 417.11
READY   47.25   49.28
  60.10   61.03   73.14
  87.07   97.17   104.25
 106.05   107.21   115.27
 115.27   124.22   136.22
 146.15   146.18   148.19
 172.01   185.21   186.01
 188.22   200.27   202.17
 215.09   230.18   236.08
 244.26   246.21   277.21
 288.14   298.30   311.11
 330.28   349.10   349.19
 349.27   361.17   381.11
 383.17   383.23   386.29
 399.14   402.21   442.13
 457.14   462.04   483.20
 486.06   494.15   514.20
 516.13
REAL   48.27   68.16
  81.23   147.29   180.28
 191.15   201.10   260.15
 295.06   302.10   324.15
 325.30   340.28   376.15
 376.15   380.01   392.22
 396.26   431.03   442.08
 457.03   457.15   478.27
REALISE   44.13   287.15
REALISED 369.10   433.04
REALITY   23.15   81.24
 138.01   156.20   252.01
 263.31   264.19   281.14
 294.28   302.09   302.13
 339.14   365.10   370.15
 398.22   516.09
REALLY   49.01   65.09
  95.14   105.07   113.07
 129.11   190.04   207.02
 209.25   211.05   219.20
 223.29   238.01   274.26
 282.08   309.11   319.26
 331.17   343.30   354.08
 357.02   396.12   458.28
 471.21   478.03   503.05

REALLY (CONT.)   513.15
REALM   100.11   390.08
REAPINGS 327.16
REAPPEARED   55.14
REARED   55.21
REARING 396.20
REASON   45.24   77.15
  81.30   117.22   144.13
 162.12   184.21   193.22
 209.30   237.12   260.18
 293.29   300.24   437.29
 488.11   488.21
REASONABLE   13.25
  34.01   158.04
REASONABLY   178.21
 222.12
REASONED 453.25
REASONS   2.29   48.29
 119.04   119.05   185.12
 237.28   246.03   321.15
REASSURED 214.02
REASSURING 85.10
REBELLIOUS 327.11
REBOUND 244.18   397.03
REBOUNDED 30.28
RECALL   127.17   198.26
RECALLED 95.03   337.17
 348.20   413.04
RECEIVE 247.23   282.09
 501.08
RECEIVED   2.07   58.11
 172.19   279.16   282.10
 307.25   317.17   333.20
 352.27   368.03   421.13
 458.06   491.17
RECEIVES 142.10
RECENT   458.21
RECENTLY 384.05
RECEPTACLE   41.06
RECEPTION   70.04
 127.09   225.21   429.21
RECEPTION-ROOMS   429.21
RECEPTIONS 264.17
RECEPTIVE 92.12
RECESS   342.28
RECESSES 15.18   61.25
RECIPIENT 399.30
RECITAL 127.20
RECITED   16.25   241.28
RECKLESS 26.11   236.12
 246.28   281.22   436.15
 499.26
RECKLESSLY   100.11
 152.01   323.24
RECKLESSNESS   239.17
 438.16   479.08
RECKON   218.19
RECKONING   178.11
 183.10
RECLINING   250.20
 499.03   501.07
RECOGNISED   48.01
 137.18   365.16   428.05
 430.10   501.30
RECOGNITION   400.24
RECOILED 514.17
RECOILS 423.17
RECOLLECT   43.39
  49.02
RECOLLECTION   77.24
 172.15   183.05   242.06
 293.20   348.08   362.02
 365.28   452.14
RECOLLECTS 313.02
RECOMMENDATION   74.09
 182.09   227.05
RECONCILIATION   251.15
RECORDED 166.22   277.17
 277.22
RECOVER   97.14
RECOVERED   188.30
 374.15
RECOVERING   453.16
 480.09
RECOVERY 12.14
RECROSS 357.29
RECROSSING   445.26
RECRUITED 218.26
RECTITUDE 422.26
RECTORY   4.09

RECUMBENT 103.16
RECURRED 245.19
RECURVED 19.05
RED 4.09 15.06
17.06 24.07 27.09
32.14 33.05 37.20
37.20 38.30 51.23
55.18 71.10 76.24
89.05 135.03 139.16
141.07 149.07 191.28
234.17 297.03 302.26
314.24 318.07 334.07
347.24 365.11 372.14
393.13 414.11 471.18
506.03 512.02
RED-AND-GOLD 318.07
RED-FACED 506.03
RED-HOT 141.07
RED-SASHED 37.20
REDDISH 67.14 94.13
REDEEMING 59.21
82.03
REDEMPTION 60.27
REDOUBLED 218.08
REDOUNDED 351.19
351.20
REDUCE 181.12
REEF 208.27 209.20
211.19
REEFS 5.13 16.24
196.26 236.22
REEKING 462.04
REFER 297.24
REFER- 297.24
REFERENCE 102.14
230.06 479.25
REFERENCES 95.07
REFERRED 266.12
REFERRING 149.12
REFLECT 188.01 223.30
REFLECTED 68.30
150.02 187.28 187.30
429.29 489.15
REFLECTING 192.12
243.23 410.03 425.15
451.27
REFLECTION 88.02
156.13 224.07 381.13
456.21 492.20
REFLECTIONS 274.11
REFLECTIVE 61.10
REFLECTIVELY 95.21
338.11
REFORMING 104.15
REFRAINED 301.08
375.30
REFRAINING 190.18
REFUGE 210.22 233.21
249.24 281.14 281.15
332.27 369.11 386.29
508.21
REFUGEES 448.09 484.05
REFUSE 26.09 157.12
279.14
REFUSED 188.21 499.26
REFUSES 487.23
REFUSING 457.07
REFUTATION 89.23
REGAIN 218.13 377.12
449.11
REGARD 85.20
REGARDED 403.29
REGARDLESS 149.30
REGION 341.15
REGIONS 10.02 379.14
REGRET 7.22 23.30
65.14 100.12 215.17
262.10 282.21 282.24
329.24 339.15
REGRETFULLY 265.03
483.17
REGRETS 282.25 342.01
409.04
REGRETTABLE 241.25
REGRETTED 229.22
REGULAR 236.08 304.01
337.12 413.12 495.28
REGULARLY 170.13
REGULATE 506.21
REGULATED 270.03

REGULATES 394.23
REGULATING 270.02
REGULATIONS 2.11
REHABILITATION 89.17
305.06
REHEARSING 114.19
REIGN 453.26
REIGNED 443.06
REJOICE 394.16
REJOICED 482.23
REJOINED 205.10
REKINDLED 155.20
RELATE 250.12 505.15
RELATED 127.16 423.30
440.22 502.19
RELATING 138.30 348.29
471.13 473.01 475.10
RELATION 131.08 465.20
465.26 513.21
RELATIONS 70.07
190.22 448.16
RELEASED 63.10 125.14
207.25 298.19 409.14
RELECTIVELY 48.13
RELIABLE 170.01 175.06
RELIEF 89.18 138.18
149.04 149.20 245.11
252.22 269.24 370.15
371.18 444.28
RELIEFS 105.19
RELIEVE 62.08 269.01
RELIEVED 70.27 164.01
164.01
RELIGIOUS 316.22
383.08
RELIGIOUSLY 260.02
RELISH 28.05
RELUCTANCE 399.12
452.08
RELUCTANT 321.09
RELUCTANTLY 113.27
217.20 467.01
REMAIN 58.17 103.06
171.27 242.23 289.26
289.30 290.02 290.03
291.06 292.28 348.12
358.22 377.27 377.30
407.10 490.14
REMAINED 13.27 17.12
31.07 56.16 116.04
117.10 119.17 129.20
151.29 171.19 173.22
192.16 196.04 208.19
209.04 210.27 216.01
216.10 217.13 221.06
226.22 238.21 244.27
250.06 252.01 262.13
289.22 313.03 313.17
338.09 369.23 373.04
393.06 415.07 442.23
444.24 447.03 470.03
482.27 485.16 493.27
500.08 504.23 505.21
512.28
REMAINING 19.21
REMAINS 2.14 56.08
219.12 271.20 274.11
337.29 407.07 488.08
513.23
REMARK 24.14 42.15
79.15 93.27 113.26
174.09 188.17 242.03
267.24 292.10 416.06
REMARKABLE 267.08
267.09 298.01 318.01
425.01 458.23 475.17
REMARKED 78.12 99.19
104.08 146.17 162.14
180.03 202.29 217.08
233.01 240.30 267.27
269.03 278.28 282.13
282.18 294.07 343.16
368.13 411.11 461.09
484.06 492.22 514.26
REMARKED' 175.17
REMARKING 202.10
REMARKS 168.24 304.05
REMEDY 157.02 259.05
262.25
REMEM 433.30

REMEM- 433.30
REMEMBER 27.21 38.22
38.23 45.18 51.29
52.08 52.10 53.11
53.17 65.05 81.17
103.10 116.20 118.15
118.28 119.30 124.05
124.11 127.18 132.27
144.28 153.11 165.30
177.13 182.19 189.01
189.13 194.06 194.12
198.02 201.08 208.01
214.13 222.18 249.30
281.24 289.16 289.17
309.10 311.17 312.16
326.02 329.22 335.05
338.23 340.29 347.19
367.19 388.26 390.02
392.19 409.22 418.01
419.21 434.07 479.21
485.30 511.10 511.13
511.15
REMEMBERED 4.08
35.08 35.22 35.28
57.23 76.18 76.28
102.18 119.30 124.07
144.26 167.25 231.24
282.07 289.10 289.11
295.20 312.16 326.04
363.14 427.23 464.01
476.03
REMEMBERS 313.28
REMIND 368.06
REMINDED 170.04 337.10
351.03 399.05
REMINDERS 212.03
REMINDING 287.24
432.07
REMINISCENCES 105.03
427.26
REMNANT 43.40
REMNANTS 115.19 297.10
323.17
REMONSTRATED 121.04
145.23 220.23
REMONSTRATING 488.24
REMORSE 166.14 170.07
275.07
REMORSEFUL 368.05
REMORSEFULLY 291.09
REMOTE 31.02 105.14
125.26 269.07 384.30
397.26 398.12
REMOTENESS 260.09
394.10
REMOTEST 168.03 308.15
REMOVED 249.04
REMOVING 173.05 338.17
REND 289.09
RENDER 114.02 271.02
380.10
RENDERED 251.21 290.04
RENDING 187.06 187.09
464.19
RENEGADE 15.01 46.11
78.21
RENEGADE'S 25.13
RENOUNCED 408.13
477.16
RENOWN 466.15
RENT 155.03 157.14
RENTS 91.07
RENUNCIATIONS 341.17
REPAIR 310.23
REPAIRS 235.02
REPASS 349.21
REPAY 186.26
REPEAT 270.25 337.23
423.22
REPEATED 26.19 60.30
88.20 108.12 110.26
128.11 140.07 146.18
159.26 171.08 175.20
180.07 253.01 262.25
263.18 283.21 290.11
301.12 331.16 334.18
368.26 377.29 385.13
388.04 391.15 393.05
412.30 428.15 428.30
464.25 468.08 492.27

REPEATED (CONT.) 514.20
REPEATEDLY 185.10
REPEATING 207.16
365.18
REPENTANCE 192.30
364.02
REPLACED 281.26 347.11
REPLACING 294.09
REPLIED 443.26 494.12
REPLY 76.20 167.13
244.30
REPORT 70.23 166.27
278.09 344.09 344.10
499.09 502.01
REPORTED 364.06 436.21
REPORTS 332.04 449.25
REPOSE 13.03 39.02
176.02 302.28 318.14
319.20 322.06 331.25
REPOSED 20.28 23.01
334.16
REPOSING 229.05
REPRESENT 323.23
325.26
REPRESENTATIVE 182.10
REPRESENTED 66.12
366.14 449.21 455.02
REPRESS 329.16
REPRESSED 50.11
348.07
REPROACH 409.21
REPROACHES 430.26
REPROACHFUL 387.03
REPRODUCED 35.09
212.22
REPROVING 390.29
REPTILES 61.04
REPUBLICAN 249.24
REPULSE 447.06 513.17
REPULSED 153.16
REPULSIVE 351.05
368.08 475.08
REPUTABLE 112.08
REPUTATION 227.03
267.05 447.11
REPUTATIONS 175.07
REQUEST 298.25
REQUESTED 204.18
REQUIRE 382.21 390.22
REQUIRED 197.04 450.16
REQUIRING 35.18
254.04
RESCUED 68.04 502.06
RESEMBLE 194.25
RESEMBLED 46.06
60.11 94.18 99.30
193.02 252.02 258.28
351.04 498.29
RESEMBLING 13.09
24.15 44.08 59.08
420.29
RESENT 86.05
RESENTFUL 370.30
477.20
RESENTING 220.02
RESENTMENT 294.26
431.04
RESERVE 229.18
RESERVED 241.02
RESERVES 322.09
RESIDE 250.09
RESIDENCE 251.19
RESIDENT 64.16 343.07
RESIDENZ' 254.04
RESIGNATION 115.10
171.06 281.25 292.20
RESIGNED 105.30 134.20
227.09 477.21 500.04
RESIGNEDLY 467.08
RESIST 336.20
RESISTANCE 10.20
51.01 399.29 425.17
443.10
RESISTED 488.16
RESOLUTE 54.22 246.17
RESOLUTELY 38.20
212.10 307.14 372.15
RESOLUTION 84.03
106.05 187.29 220.06

RESOLVE 385.01 422.12
485.18
RESOLVED 478.18
RESOUNDED 159.11
RESOUNDING 365.07
RESOURCE 278.27
RESPECT 194.04 315.17
320.10 345.26 346.03
355.09 355.09 355.13
RESPECTABILITY 246.02
RESPECTABLE 48.25
184.30 275.18 327.13
355.10 356.12 427.28
436.19
RESPECTED 245.26
252.23 333.08
RESPECTFUL 230.26
RESPECTFULLY 30.06
30.06 292.17
RESPOND 430.24
RESPONDED 409.13
467.19
RESPONDS 409.16
RESPONSE 31.04 364.17
RESPONSIBILITY 170.27
212.12 331.16 390.09
473.15
RESPONSIBLE 144.24
195.29 219.27 223.28
282.29 324.02 364.13
488.27
RESPONSIVE 176.28
REST 11.12 11.30
25.25 36.03 39.05
68.01 106.12 147.16
157.12 171.30 193.15
205.12 208.29 234.29
248.16 252.15 358.08
362.19 384.14 440.09
459.28 462.22 482.14
499.14
RESTED 37.11 37.23
153.17 429.28 432.23
RESTING 20.10 83.02
259.18 329.08 456.08
RESTLESS 315.26 376.20
432.09
RESTLESSLY 367.28
RESTRAIN 132.13 156.19
RESTRAINED 63.16
80.10 147.06 299.24
317.11 369.20
RESTRAINING 7.12
192.29
RESULT 329.15 329.17
RESUMED 179.23 266.02
510.30
RESUMING 173.17
RETAILER 240.21
RETAINER 350.17
RETICENCE 305.01
RETINUE 320.01
RETIRE 461.22 486.08
RETIRED 364.22 482.27
501.12
RETORT 181.13 187.18
RETORTED 85.21 158.14
RETREAT 243.13 281.25
300.29 444.11 445.18
456.11 477.17
RETREATED 3.15
395.10 506.11
RETREATING 26.16
155.08
RETRIBUTION 191.23
501.19
RETRIEVER 68.26
RETRIEVERS 37.21
RETURN 16.08 224.26
251.20 265.16 271.03
271.14 271.24 285.01
338.03 379.13 447.04
453.24 480.11 482.24
499.15 504.04 508.30
513.19
RETURNED 12.10 120.11
124.20 163.17 179.14
229.10 254.22 423.05
428.03 453.10 503.17
RETURNING 88.23

RETURNING (CONT.)
234.16 272.28 374.09
394.10
REUNION 166.27
REVEAL 10.20
REVEALED 18.02 462.30
REVEALING 24.20
462.25
REVEALS 425.19
REVELATIONS 264.04
REVELLED 409.07
REVENGE 76.29 147.21
341.06 425.22 499.24
REVENGEFUL 315.25
488.17
REVENUE 278.03
REVERBERATION 264.10
REVERENTIALLY 292.18
REVERENTIALLY' 292.16
REVERENTLY 333.24
REVOLT 35.12 116.19
275.08 475.02
REVOLTED 485.10
REVOLTING 272.21
REVOLUTIONARY 249.22
REVOLUTIONS 17.21
26.10
REVOLVER 254.14 255.18
256.13 256.18 280.09
281.23 291.03 291.17
299.04 301.01 306.13
365.21 365.21 372.16
372.25
REVOLVING 22.13
462.21
REWARD 10.09 10.10
23.05 156.17 271.21
277.13
REWARDED 456.26
REWARDS 68.09 68.25
RHAPSODIES 310.02
RIBBON 17.15 17.17
299.08 319.15
RIBS 24.10 134.30
201.18
RICE 227.04 306.08
307.07 327.16 441.02
442.05 453.09 484.14
RICE-MILL 227.04
RICH 264.22 318.05
RID 109.08 150.11
306.14
RIDDLES 379.02
RIDE 244.12 422.16
RIDGE 20.20 409.06
RIDGE-POLES 20.20
RIDGES 19.15 334.08
416.23
RIDICULE 220.22
RIDICULOUS 86.24
97.21 228.15 362.01
RIDING 94.16
RIFLE 364.02 401.09
459.23 460.04
RIFLES 254.20 442.29
445.06 464.14
RIFTS 162.04
RIGGED 102.17 125.30
197.07 214.26
RIGGING 6.25
RIGHT 21.09 24.08
34.25 36.14 40.10
41.24 43.10 43.43
47.04 50.21 51.15
52.25 53.13 53.19
56.25 57.10 61.01
61.23 68.01 70.20
71.19 85.25 85.27
93.17 108.08 142.03
151.13 151.26 152.15
153.06 153.14 157.29
159.09 162.14 163.08
164.28 171.08 176.13
176.13 180.21 186.08
196.25 198.03 198.10
198.22 205.20 205.27
207.19 208.21 224.12
224.29 226.09 230.06
232.25 233.20 236.15
237.10 243.05 245.10

RIGHT (CONT.) 250.22
255.18 256.14 262.11
270.28 271.28 289.05
295.11 295.11 300.08
301.18 303.08 303.13
303.25 306.12 313.15
316.20 318.24 320.30
339.15 371.11 373.19
376.04 397.06 400.09
400.14 401.21 401.21
402.11 409.11 435.11
466.10 478.11 478.19
480.11 485.16 485.24
499.12 501.17 502.22
513.29 515.11 515.16
RIGHTEOUS 479.18
RIGHTEOUSNESS 4.02
458.15
RIGHTS 330.25
RIGID 370.07
RIGIDLY 31.11 349.24
373.11
RIGOROUS 211.07
RIM 15.20 22.10
199.15 205.30 432.24
RIMMED 27.08 452.19
RING 83.15 99.29
260.03 261.09 275.04
285.08 285.20 286.08
287.04 287.04 288.24
314.04 317.17 324.20
445.01 480.17 487.20
491.11 499.01 499.11
509.26 514.26
RINGING 62.28 442.08
467.14
RINGS 20.23 180.16
RIOT 44.20 306.05
RIP 411.14
RIPE 55.11 283.28
296.04
RIPOSTED 205.21
RIPPED 131.24
RIPPLE 17.13 149.16
177.08 302.21 373.19
489.19
RIPPLES 19.16
RISE 31.08 67.22
114.11 116.16 133.08
237.09 299.11 316.24
318.23 325.20 333.23
337.11 385.19 508.02
514.22
RISEN 181.05 385.18
RISES 123.04 271.10
RISING 3.15 15.20
148.08 263.01 269.11
299.10 341.07 396.21
RISK 26.08 112.05
129.10 200.08 207.16
281.12 295.04 295.13
298.29 308.08 308.24
449.16
RISKED 277.12
RISKS 278.15 295.13
341.17
RISKY 457.09
RIVER 5.28 6.30
52.28 240.18 250.30
269.09 278.24 280.15
286.21 292.13 292.27
294.06 297.13 298.08
298.20 300.05 300.28
302.16 304.12 309.18
310.20 315.13 319.13
320.13 343.03 351.29
357.29 358.06 358.19
364.10 367.18 373.17
374.11 375.27 376.26
382.12 384.07 387.30
393.02 401.22 401.25
407.02 441.28 442.22
443.18 443.24 443.29
444.25 444.27 445.22
446.05 449.27 450.07
451.02 454.20 455.10
456.11 456.15 456.20
459.14 461.15 462.06
463.02 463.06 463.07
463.18 467.18 480.08

RIVER (CONT.) 480.18
481.30 483.30 484.13
484.16 489.14 491.01
492.19 492.24 493.07
493.27 494.03 495.10
497.21 499.08 500.28
503.03 503.14 508.16
510.15 511.01
RIVER-BANK 373.17
375.27 382.12
RIVER-FRONT 444.27
463.07
RIVERS 15.25 297.07
325.13
RIVERSIDE 390.30
ROAD 175.29 473.21
481.13 491.19 494.10
ROADS 43.19 61.15
ROADSTEAD 13.06
13.07 47.22 94.17
232.28 244.21
ROADSTER 290.20
ROAM 409.14
ROAMING 22.02 254.29
ROAR 314.10 445.04
510.01
ROARED 55.19
ROARING 282.07 334.06
467.17
ROARS 235.12
ROAST 350.28
ROASTED 442.10 463.28
ROB 95.27 281.07
302.13 391.03 436.10
506.23
ROBBED 159.22 260.07
307.05 403.26 435.20
493.03
ROBBER'S 499.27
ROBBERS 450.27 484.29
485.03 493.24 503.06
508.19
ROBBERY 293.19 316.14
ROBBING 228.20
ROBINSON 197.20 197.21
197.22 197.27 199.10
199.12 199.13 200.16
200.29 201.01 201.16
202.02 202.14 202.16
204.14 205.03 205.16
205.29
ROBS 302.07
ROCK 4.06 69.09
131.07 203.29 226.29
324.30 483.25
ROCKED 55.01 358.27
ROCKET 139.17
ROCKING 253.30 410.06
ROCKING-CHAIR 253.30
ROCKS 200.06 200.11
437.01
RODS 62.21
ROGUE 47.29 49.06
ROGUES 48.30
ROLL 173.13 191.07
216.14 260.12
ROLLED 58.13 135.01
157.14 178.14 385.03
386.02 397.01 417.08
462.21 467.18 514.27
ROLLING 192.23 193.12
240.08 325.12 362.23
443.24
ROMANCE 264.24 267.15
347.14 349.01 384.26
ROMANTIC 100.17 258.25
262.19 263.18 263.18
274.08 274.09 340.10
348.28 409.21 413.04
413.04 413.08 423.08
423.12 475.16 487.20
487.20 515.21
ROOF 18.01 20.03
55.10 102.13 203.15
280.01 353.11 359.08
378.07 378.20 401.17
443.15
ROOFS 4.27 13.05
314.09 317.01 334.08
373.21 416.23 434.28

ROOFS (CONT.)	444.02		
	444.29	446.01	462.26
	480.13		
ROOM	12.30	28.04	
	32.10	33.09	35.06
	42.10	44.16	48.11
	57.28	58.03	70.25
	72.15	83.02	87.18
	92.02	125.06	126.01
	129.28	185.26	192.13
	209.07	209.09	210.13
	210.27	211.14	214.14
	216.07	217.12	217.22
	218.28	220.29	221.04
	224.04	228.10	228.12
	235.18	235.23	241.26
	242.09	242.15	248.03
	248.14	264.24	265.12
	265.15	279.18	284.09
	287.24	288.07	288.22
	310.16	319.29	320.08
	350.01	366.04	428.04
	428.18	429.08	448.22
	505.26	506.19	
ROOMS	263.05	264.03	
	416.19	429.21	
ROOMY	33.25	146.23	
	315.10		
ROOT	304.23	317.04	
	376.19		
ROOTED	130.24	210.02	
	272.04	299.13	431.05
ROOTING	327.07		
ROOTS	89.07	93.14	
ROPE	6.23	70.16	
	439.14		
ROPE-YARN		70.16	
ROPES	327.03	327.10	
	440.16		
ROSE	4.29	28.23	
	94.08	151.27	192.12
	269.22	314.09	349.26
	364.23	396.17	432.19
ROSY	414.01		
ROT	328.04	426.04	
ROTTED	316.28		
ROTTEN	26.05	29.27	
	34.22	111.03	231.10
	279.12	283.28	309.12
	310.12	331.18	366.15
	412.06	437.17	
ROTTING	336.04	398.27	
ROUGH	282.08	350.02	
	448.19	479.25	488.12
ROUGHLY	319.21		
ROULE	178.14		
ROUND	6.20	7.30	
	23.07	25.11	26.10
	35.05	35.13	36.01
	36.01	36.04	36.04
	37.17	43.16	44.08
	45.29	54.29	55.30
	56.15	63.05	66.19
	71.25	73.08	84.01
	92.04	110.03	111.19
	120.18	143.29	144.16
	152.27	153.21	154.10
	166.19	169.12	169.14
	188.20	190.05	196.10
	199.25	203.18	205.06
	207.24	208.09	213.04
	217.10	233.03	234.29
	236.01	248.10	248.19
	256.24	287.03	287.09
	292.05	312.01	314.23
	318.08	324.24	341.27
	351.13	355.18	365.13
	367.15	369.22	370.06
	370.28	371.14	397.19
	401.03	408.07	422.01
	429.06	443.20	445.01
	446.09	448.09	459.18
	463.26	470.01	476.06
	483.30	484.18	485.29
	511.01	511.27	513.28
	515.10		
ROUND-SHOT		443.20	
ROUNDABOUT		354.01	
ROUNDED	94.18		
ROUNDING	291.14		

ROUNDS	378.09		
ROUSED	128.13		
ROUSING	95.22	320.20	
ROUT	333.17		
ROUTED	64.09		
ROUTES	441.08		
ROVER	72.13	76.06	
	76.06		
ROW	35.02	45.17	
	57.02	61.14	62.19
	89.19	94.13	99.17
	207.23	286.20	306.07
	362.18	373.07	467.26
	478.29	495.25	
ROWERS	291.25		
ROWING	232.09	414.09	
	496.01		
ROWS	20.18	32.15	
	192.17	249.02	428.18
ROYAL	241.29	251.18	
	279.04	309.30	
RUBBED	28.27	261.23	
RUBBER	41.10	454.08	
RUBBISH	371.06	459.09	
RUBICUND	105.05		
RUCK	500.30		
RUCKED	234.11		
RUCKED-UP		234.11	
RUDDER	148.12	169.24	
RUDDILY	269.25		
RUDDY	374.11		
RUDE	323.28	498.29	
RUDELY	462.09		
RUFFIAN	75.17	75.18	
	435.05		
RUFFIANS	436.03	441.06	
	447.23	475.04	
RUFFLING	75.12		
RUGGED	33.20	196.13	
	338.09		
RUHIG	256.05		
RUIN	76.11	222.09	
	235.03	422.12	462.04
RUINED	241.20	383.25	
	403.15	452.09	
RUINOUS	279.12		
RUINOUSLY		323.16	
RUINS	230.10	384.29	
	506.14	508.02	
RULE	341.06	349.24	
RULED	269.07		
RULER	250.11	273.04	
	336.07	337.02	345.07
	277.24		
RULES	97.25		
RUMBLE	27.03	102.25	
	216.13	462.16	
RUMBLINGS		337.17	
RUMOUR	343.01		
RUMOURS	449.26	462.17	
	508.17		
RUN	35.04	37.04	
	40.17	56.10	72.03
	79.14	79.21	108.04
	123.12	125.06	160.08
	188.07	188.09	191.05
	243.08	253.19	281.13
	309.05	311.09	311.30
	313.19	314.01	355.17
	370.28	390.20	437.22
	460.09	463.15	475.25
	510.17	511.26	
RUNAWAY	436.17	440.06	
RUNNER	230.05		
RUNNING	6.16	24.04	
	37.19	90.01	90.03
	109.20	149.16	189.22
	189.22	237.19	255.21
	310.17	437.18	439.10
	440.12	502.14	514.14
RUNS	72.27	409.15	
	479.10		
RUPEES	79.27	81.13	
	185.20		
RURAL	95.09		
RUSH	12.05	34.28	
	89.10	101.25	105.27
	107.03	107.13	128.05
	130.13	183.11	220.14

RUSH (CONT.)	274.25		
	290.18	334.02	368.14
	372.04	390.18	394.03
	450.04	451.09	463.22
RUSHCUTTERS'		175.16	
RUSHED	6.16	6.28	
	110.18	122.18	216.08
	238.11	313.29	358.30
	419.03	502.16	515.14
RUSHING	124.12	148.14	
	324.09	324.24	
RUST	14.28	101.12	
	102.03	103.12	297.04
RUST-EATEN		103.12	
RUSTIC	340.05		
RUSTING	461.25		
RUSTLE	368.16	373.16	
RUSTLED	465.05		
RUSTLING	509.10		
RUSTLINGS		359.06	
RUSTY	323.21	441.08	
RUTHLESS	319.22	463.13	
RUTHLESSNESS	458.13		
RUTHVEL	43.29	44.04	
	44.22		
S	64.22	268.24	
	319.14		
S'ELP	26.27	30.01	
	30.07		
S'EN	171.20		
S'EST	177.16		
SA	56.12		
SA-A-AY	56.12		
SABRE	171.17		
SACK	172.24	285.06	
	290.27		
SACKCOAT	428.20		
SACKING	353.24		
SACRED	43.42		
SACRIFICE		53.01	
	262.06	277.10	356.23
	418.27	418.28	
SAD	18.02	42.17	
	134.19	201.20	226.27
	302.07	341.29	350.05
	352.14	381.24	477.20
	490.24		
SADDENED	482.17		
SADDER	99.26		
SADLY	259.13	366.17	
	428.20	516.21	
SADNESS	113.13	387.17	
	464.19		
SAFE	19.11	30.07	
	45.30	50.13	53.22
	72.01	196.24	235.23
	254.18	275.18	312.05
	314.10	333.21	358.19
	401.04	412.10	452.22
	459.16	465.12	485.05
	506.08	506.14	
SAFEGUARDS		387.06	
SAFELY	14.16		
SAFEST	169.20		
SAFETY	19.24	58.05	
	58.24	193.15	214.12
	292.19	351.25	351.29
	357.29	420.14	452.01
	497.14		
SAGACIOUS		337.09	
SAGACITY	114.23	280.13	
SAID	2.30	14.14	
	16.14	25.10	30.16
	30.29	32.04	33.29
	34.09	46.09	47.30
	48.05	61.01	62.03
	62.05	70.26	70.35
	71.06	71.19	72.07
	73.19	74.01	77.16
	77.18	78.26	79.14
	79.19	80.08	80.14
	80.19	83.26	84.14
	84.21	85.18	86.06
	87.09	87.14	87.21
	87.25	88.11	88.21
	88.23	88.29	90.01
	90.12	91.02	95.04
	95.17	97.06	99.14
	99.23	101.05	101.10
	101.18	104.12	104.19

SAID (CONT.)	108.16		
	110.12	113.29	115.01
	120.14	127.01	128.15
	130.01	130.20	130.26
	131.27	133.15	133.19
	136.23	136.23	137.10
	138.10	138.28	139.04
	140.01	140.23	141.19
	141.29	142.19	143.01
	144.04	144.11	144.30
	148.06	150.03	151.03
	151.07	151.26	151.29
	153.18	154.09	155.13
	157.21	157.24	158.02
	158.23	158.26	158.29
	159.13	162.16	162.20
	163.10	163.18	163.24
	164.07	166.15	168.23
	169.07	171.25	175.12
	175.30	176.07	176.29
	177.10	177.16	177.25
	178.14	180.09	180.20
	181.11	181.23	183.07
	184.16	186.23	186.25
	187.03	187.11	187.15
	188.05	188.08	188.12
	188.19	189.01	189.04
	194.09	195.04	196.01
	196.09	196.21	197.10
	197.17	197.19	199.22
	199.26	200.01	201.30
	202.06	202.10	203.04
	203.05	203.24	203.28
	204.30	205.19	205.28
	208.02	212.27	217.15
	218.21	219.29	220.03
	220.05	220.09	220.28
	223.07	223.12	223.22
	224.21	224.29	225.03
	227.20	230.21	231.12
	232.01	232.24	233.07
	234.08	234.19	235.06
	238.20	242.05	242.16
	242.19	242.29	243.14
	244.27	245.05	245.29
	247.01	249.07	250.08
	250.20	253.14	253.25
	254.15	257.14	257.20
	258.01	258.11	259.10
	261.18	262.02	263.01
	263.21	264.14	264.25
	265.07	265.09	269.28
	274.30	274.30	283.12
	283.15	285.16	286.13
	287.15	288.30	289.21
	290.04	290.10	291.01
	291.05	292.11	295.11
	295.20	300.16	301.07
	301.18	307.23	308.13
	308.23	309.28	311.17
	312.08	312.18	314.14
	320.14	321.03	321.25
	323.13	324.15	327.03
	327.22	328.09	328.11
	329.08	329.24	333.12
	336.08	337.30	338.10
	342.12	344.05	345.24
	346.05	350.23	351.27
	352.30	353.05	354.05
	357.07	357.09	359.22
	360.12	362.02	362.05
	362.07	362.15	363.17
	364.04	366.25	368.01
	368.22	369.12	369.21
	370.18	372.22	372.24
	373.10	373.22	374.14
	375.20	376.16	377.10
	377.16	382.02	382.09
	382.16	382.18	382.20
	387.21	388.03	388.05
	388.09	388.21	391.01
	391.07	391.14	393.10
	393.18	394.13	395.03
	395.07	395.23	401.01
	402.01	402.19	404.25
	409.19	411.17	411.21
	412.17	412.29	413.14
	413.22	413.26	414.04
	414.12	418.14	418.16
	418.25	419.02	426.02

SAID (CONT.)		426.17
428.19	428.26	429.09
429.16	429.18	430.12
430.30	432.10	433.05
433.12	433.22	436.27
455.20	460.13	461.29
454.03	464.05	466.28
467.23	468.01	469.07
471.10	471.12	471.25
471.28	472.09	473.13
473.25	473.29	477.22
479.08	481.01	481.02
481.12	481.23	485.04
485.04	485.13	486.16
487.09	487.13	488.26
488.28	489.04	489.05
489.11	489.17	490.27
491.08	491.26	492.22
492.25	492.28	493.14
493.18	494.24	495.02
495.03	495.08	495.19
496.02	497.11	502.23
503.10	505.22	506.09
507.08	507.13	507.15
507.18	507.20	508.13
509.13	510.21	510.23
511.03	511.06	511.08
511.11	511.13	511.16
511.17	511.24	514.15
514.18		

SAIL	1.17	102.17
152.21	152.29	236.23
290.13	437.28	440.16
442.26		

SAILCLOTH   366.09

SAILED 443.01

SAILING	16.22	67.13
192.27	233.21	236.08
290.17		

SAILING-SHIP   67.13
192.27

SAILING-SHIPS   16.22

SAILOR	70.06	81.20
95.05	149.12	421.17

SAILORS 25.21   66.10
244.08

SAILORS'   79.11   99.02
164.13

SAILS   414.02 437.19
439.02

SAINT   259.26

SAINTS 228.23

SAKE	35.29	35.30
42.19	60.04	69.04
95.27	120.08	131.22
185.28	190.16	226.08
229.23	267.20	268.23
269.04	330.14	383.20
412.17	433.06	458.01

SALIENT 33.19

SALLOW 46.23   168.18
441.16 459.26

SALLOW-FACED   46.23
441.16

SALOON 75.26

SALT	2.12	37.02
43.37	73.29	426.20

SALUTARY   191.11

SALVATION   23.05
24.24

SALVOS 5.29

SAMAN   449.07 450.05

SAMARANG   43.18   182.04
182.08 427.20 428.02
509.12

SAME	17.23	17.27
27.07	66.01	73.16
76.14	87.23	94.23
97.26	120.12	122.06
124.20	140.07	150.28
152.16	153.19	156.23
156.24	156.25	157.27
162.21	165.11	179.01
182.16	183.07	219.03
219.27	223.22	235.18
240.12	248.11	268.02
269.08	288.01	288.02
288.04	288.04	288.04
300.27	306.23	312.08
322.16	331.19	339.04

SAME (CONT.)		345.15
377.17	387.15	395.03
410.05	431.26	434.13
439.24	444.15	456.17
467.28	473.27	493.11

SAMENESS   341.26

SAND	410.18	411.04
411.10	411.27	414.05
415.14	498.22	

SANDALS 453.13

SANDBANK   292.29 413.13

SANDWICH   234.25 235.30

SANDWICHES 234.28

SANDY   498.11

SANG   61.23

SANGUINARY 330.26

SANK	17.26	55.12
163.02	176.01	211.26
231.28	374.12	409.05
412.12	460.11	502.03
509.08		

SANS   170.15

SAPLINGS   339.28

SARAH   233.13 235.09

SARONG 248.06

SARONGS 255.21 279.24
318.20

SASHED 37.20

SAT	37.23	44.13
59.02	61.15	75.05
82.08	83.10	84.10
89.01	97.02	99.27
114.05	130.17	139.15
140.29	141.24	149.21
152.08	153.26	154.08
165.13	168.30	170.03
179.20	181.30	184.23
192.07	192.22	195.12
208.24	216.05	261.22
287.21	291.15	299.03
299.04	299.15	307.17
308.04	315.15	315.15
318.15	319.08	319.30
323.09	324.13	324.22
325.09	338.12	349.20
394.07	409.18	410.01
411.03	417.24	427.02
432.02	444.07	450.12
460.26	463.12	463.29
466.19	480.23	485.15
499.18	506.01	506.20
506.24	506.29	509.02
513.24		

SATAN   364.05

SATANIC 478.04

SATISFACTION   69.12
140.15 160.11 293.05
418.15 485.07

SATISFIED		292.08
377.10	400.07	400.17
400.18	400.20	401.16
516.04		

SATISFY 66.03   301.10

SATISFYING 91.10
419.19

SAUCER 308.05

SAVAGE 26.13   436.14

SAVAGELY   120.14

SAVAGES 5.15   475.03

SAVE	7.06	78.28
97.23	98.06	103.19
111.21	111.22	120.19
182.17	183.12	357.15
383.17	384.02	402.25
463.06		

SAVED	68.04	133.22
138.27	139.21	143.20
157.08	158.13	159.05
225.08	309.17	385.06
402.16	402.17	402.19

SAVING	5.10	95.28
104.13	202.12	222.08
271.27	286.11	295.09
340.26	479.13	

SAVOUR 138.06 173.14
417.20

SAW	5.09	6.21
6.27	8.01	12.01
23.23	34.05	44.07
45.13	46.15	47.19

SAW (CONT.)		54.08
54.17	55.26	57.19
61.02	61.22	64.04
82.28	84.01	88.02
96.16	102.27	104.03
114.06	116.01	122.23
129.23	135.01	136.20
137.13	137.19	145.12
163.12	171.10	174.21
174.22	181.26	183.16
189.13	196.10	201.10
208.18	236.25	244.20
256.10	256.15	264.02
264.19	265.15	290.27
291.14	291.22	295.24
297.01	300.01	301.14
311.19	312.27	320.24
323.15	324.07	344.20
349.33	370.06	371.03
371.29	378.03	382.23
396.28	414.22	417.25
429.27	431.26	439.17
444.10	445.24	459.20
469.04	477.04	488.05
492.19	494.16	496.07
498.09	501.10	502.14
505.10	511.25	512.12
512.20		

SAWING 439.24

SAY	3.27	11.20
33.14	35.03	40.02
42.06	43.06	48.23
51.18	51.21	52.20
56.11	64.21	65.16
72.03	74.27	75.11
79.25	84.21	90.03
90.09	96.27	107.05
107.22	111.11	113.14
130.03	132.10	137.17
138.22	141.27	142.12
142.13	146.14	149.23
151.08	151.12	152.13
154.05	158.05	158.07
162.21	166.17	166.25
168.20	176.21	178.21
180.05	180.05	180.13
183.27	186.16	186.18
187.09	188.18	196.24
197.24	203.22	208.12
209.05	213.11	213.15
215.17	215.21	215.26
216.30	217.06	218.15
222.19	224.26	225.25
226.27	228.04	229.17
230.18	230.27	231.01
234.01	234.06	235.07
236.11	238.24	240.06
240.12	241.15	244.29
246.18	246.29	247.08
251.24	252.22	268.13
270.19	271.12	271.30
274.07	274.16	275.06
283.21	292.17	294.11
298.26	302.04	320.05
321.28	322.15	330.08
342.11	343.19	345.16
351.17	352.02	355.14
357.01	357.08	357.25
358.17	364.23	376.14
376.18	390.13	392.12
394.17	400.17	403.13
404.03	404.29	412.07
415.10	419.17	420.24
422.22	428.11	428.15
430.28	434.23	437.06
455.21	456.30	473.07
474.24	478.11	479.19
481.06	481.08	483.02
492.16	499.13	507.30
515.15		

SAYING	12.27	90.19
94.26	96.30	100.24
122.01	137.19	222.19
225.24	233.12	245.18
247.02	360.19	371.22
403.24	505.17	511.04

SAYINGS 315.08

SAYS	44.04	44.28
45.16	70.43	71.02
71.16	71.28	72.29

SAYS (CONT.)		75.02
75.15	118.20	200.04
200.10	200.15	200.21
200.25	201.13	201.15
231.07	235.21	235.25
236.02	236.03	237.11
237.25	237.26	237.30
238.07	240.27	310.29
311.05	313.18	343.29
359.13	364.18	365.01
368.03	371.19	372.08
388.24	473.23	474.01
501.03	501.11	516.19

SCABBARD   21.14

SCAFFOLDING 191.19

SCAFFOLDS   193.12

SCALE   36.07   136.05
252.15

SCANDAL 93.01   184.20
266.11

SCANDAL-MONGERING
266.11

SCANDALOUS 240.21

SCANDINAVIAN   232.16

SCANDINAVIANS   440.08

SCANNING   87.27

SCANT   280.25

SCANTY 6.25   192.01
453.08

SCAR   171.11

SCARCE 2.20   27.29

SCARE   55.08   238.11
361.28

SCARECROWS 93.05
273.21 442.28

SCARED	57.26	88.27
237.20	242.06	291.19
313.25	474.14	476.09

SCARES 474.12

SCARLET 191.19 191.20
175.05

SCARS   175.05

SCATHING   232.09 393.16

SCATHINGLY 124.23

SCATTERED		4.28
126.13	257.27	263.17
329.05	417.03	467.20

SCATTERING 312.13

SCENE	28.17	56.24
86.16	88.07	137.25
382.22	386.13	437.11

SCENES 122.07 356.09
356.26

SCENT	74.26	163.16
304.29	323.07	351.11
397.17		

SCEPTICALLY 223.14
346.01

SCHEME 19.11   207.05
281.24

SCHEMING   358.11

SCHNAPPS   26.23

SCHOMBERG   240.19
242.28 426.23

SCHOMBERG'S 240.28

SCHON   268.02

SCHOONER	6.17	297.15
343.03	401.26	413.11
413.30	414.15	414.23
425.03	437.04	437.17
438.03	439.07	440.18
441.04	441.20	442.07
442.16	442.23	454.29
501.25	502.01	

SCHOONER'S 442.20
455.27

SCHOONERS   197.25
198.21 252.13 440.01

SCHRECKLICH 432.30

SCHWEIN 27.04

SCIENTIFIC 266.11

SCINTILLATED   149.01

SCOLDING   141.19 232.11
233.26 234.04 314.27
484.27

SCOOTED 460.18

SCOPE   274.04

SCORCHED   18.09

SCORCHING   17.07

SCORE   225.11 251.09
461.25 488.25

SCORES	336.24		SEA (CONT.)		98.13	SECOND-HAND		203.19	SEE (CONT.)		468.22

SCORES 336.24

SCORN 26.19 87.24
116.02 142.17 187.29
356.05 436.07 473.09
475.01
SCORNED 50.11
SCORNFUL 33.22 242.03
SCORNFULLY 197.10
245.08 455.21 464.06
SCOT 281.02 282.05
SCOTSMAN 250.09
SCOTSMAN'S 250.28
251.09
SCOTTISH 11.20
SCOUNDREL 301.16
344.20 353.19 355.05
436.05
SCOUNDRELS 80.28
SCOUR 322.28
SCOURGE 458.18
SCOWL 371.08
SCOWLED 293.04
SCOWLING 92.10
SCRAMBLE 52.19 126.22
181.01 512.26
SCRAMBLED 102.15
182.22
SCRAP 26.06
SCRAP-HEAP 26.06
SCRAPE 21.22 157.03
157.04 157.04 181.24
228.16
SCRAPED 181.20
SCRAPES 286.27
SCRAPING 145.26
SCRATCH 69.08
SCRATCHED 24.10
SCRATCHING 210.11
344.24 502.20
SCRAWLING 421.01
SCREAM 63.29 121.02
355.09 500.24
SCREAMED 133.06 134.02
500.23 510.11 512.30
SCREAMING 183.02
233.15 313.10 369.27
SCREAMS 58.23 105.28
131.22 164.09 203.30
SCREECH 6.10 134.07
145.01 198.30
SCREECHED 144.05
502.26
SCREECHING 30.17
SCREEN 4.06
SCREENS 430.01
SCREW 17.01 204.06
237.10
SCREW-PILE 17.01
SCREWED 153.28 314.25
434.27
SCREWED-UP 314.25
SCREWING 141.11 410.23
SCRIBBLING 210.11
SCRIBE 209.03 345.23
SCRUB 470.04
SCRUBBED 429.25
SCRUPLES 223.04
SCRUPULOUS 258.14
395.02
SCRUTINISED 62.04
SCUFFLE 500.02
SCUFFLES 241.26
SCURRYING 5.23
SEA 2.23 3.13
4.16 5.05 5.09
6.26 7.20 10.02
10.07 10.12 10.17
10.24 13.23 14.02
15.30 16.26 17.06
17.11 17.18 17.26
19.07 19.18 22.05
22.27 23.11 23.24
25.04 30.13 30.21
30.25 31.12 37.02
41.16 42.03 43.40
51.23 51.29 52.02
53.01 53.03 53.07
53.08 53.10 68.04
69.21 69.29 81.09
81.25 93.25 98.02

SEA (CONT.) 98.13
103.24 105.29 110.30
116.15 117.12 119.09
123.08 123.20 128.24
131.06 133.26 134.04
136.14 136.18 138.25
139.05 139.25 140.03
142.10 143.29 147.02
147.26 148.28 149.17
149.29 151.18 156.09
156.15 159.06 166.20
167.01 170.20 183.19
194.20 196.18 197.07
203.30 210.16 214.26
216.12 216.20 217.07
234.17 236.09 237.05
244.01 244.21 260.27
261.02 269.10 293.10
295.29 297.11 299.10
319.11 325.12 334.15
337.13 384.11 409.06
409.11 409.26 410.29
411.06 411.25 412.11
412.24 413.15 414.01
415.08 415.12 427.28
434.15 434.29 441.05
441.09 441.29 442.17
442.27 463.18 472.14
485.09 488.07 507.23
SEA-ANACHRONISM 197.07
214.26
SEA-BIRDS 203.30
SEA-GOING 427.28
434.15
SEA-LEVEL 41.16
SEA-LIFE 5.09 81.09
244.01
SEA-PUPPY 53.10
SEA-SICK 53.03
SEA-STOCK 43.40
SEA-WATER 37.02
SEAL 334.21
SEALED 167.10 339.23
SEALING 197.25 198.21
SEALING-SCHOONERS
197.25 198.21
SEALS 197.23
SEAM 171.14
SEAMAN 3.12 74.05
80.07 80.13 168.06
170.16 243.29
SEAMAN'S 2.12
SEAMANLIKE 170.02
194.08
SEAMANSHIP 68.23
SEAMEN 14.18 173.10
190.22
SEAPORT 3.10 230.02
SEAPORTS 3.12 3.22
SEARCH 5.14 207.01
287.03 288.07 431.27
SEARCHED 61.24 114.25
509.22
SEARCHING 216.15
246.17
SEAS 5.16 9.02
13.12 27.28 147.22
184.20 194.24 270.30
277.02 277.23 417.22
437.09 440.10
SEASON 267.15
SEAT 33.23 39.06
99.24 133.20 177.05
192.25 308.23 430.29
SEAWORTHY 2.05
194.05
SECLUSION 349.06
SECOND 25.18 28.12
29.05 34.18 70.28
71.23 73.19 82.23
87.12 102.05 105.10
110.02 112.11 117.26
119.19 128.18 134.13
140.21 142.02 145.07
155.11 186.08 203.19
211.28 220.12 229.28
297.21 309.04 313.02
315.19 365.15 371.20
386.26 402.04 458.02
459.21 470.09 501.09

SECOND-HAND 203.19
SECONDS 87.06 104.07
158.08 188.27 313.01
404.26
SECRECY 358.15 456.18
SECRET 10.20 12.22
16.28 23.15 48.16
51.24 53.06 59.26
60.12 69.20 117.13
119.03 119.05 142.18
144.21 186.05 215.05
240.17 281.10 337.04
341.04 351.03 379.24
389.09 416.11 479.27
SECRETLY 12.04 407.22
SECRETS 304.14 334.14
SECULAR 271.28 325.24
331.25
SECURITY 19.04 116.09
303.02 465.22 470.26
SEDENTARY 246.10
SEDUCED 389.07
SEDUCTIONS 345.30
379.12
SEDUCTIVE 51.04
SEE 5.02 22.04
25.23 34.27 38.05
41.05 45.04 46.04
49.22 49.29 50.02
51.01 52.16 54.01
54.24 57.15 57.17
59.23 61.20 61.22
62.02 62.06 64.18
65.04 71.08 72.02
72.21 74.01 75.04
78.05 78.24 78.26
83.02 86.29 87.24
96.13 100.08 101.24
102.02 104.03 110.26
110.28 113.16 123.02
124.03 128.01 128.09
128.11 128.11 130.08
133.25 136.07 136.23
138.11 138.13 138.16
139.06 142.27 143.16
143.30 145.13 146.11
149.14 150.13 150.20
150.20 151.16 151.18
152.25 155.06 155.16
159.17 159.18 159.28
162.10 164.23 165.04
169.17 171.30 174.18
175.26 178.27 179.26
180.08 183.08 184.06
187.07 189.02 191.07
193.19 197.01 197.13
197.17 197.18 197.19
198.07 199.08 200.08
202.19 203.09 204.23
204.24 205.13 205.22
205.23 205.25 209.25
211.08 211.22 213.02
223.13 231.07 233.23
233.29 234.15 234.27
237.16 240.16 243.28
245.07 249.07 252.27
254.23 255.09 255.13
264.16 273.27 274.18
279.17 281.30 284.07
289.25 295.30 295.30
296.03 301.18 301.19
303.01 308.18 319.09
321.04 321.07 324.30
325.02 333.30 336.15
338.15 344.10 354.08
359.14 359.20 364.19
364.27 368.07 370.26
374.26 375.03 375.24
377.20 378.20 381.22
382.21 388.30 389.01
402.09 405.16 405.16
409.20 412.03 412.14
413.10 414.10 419.13
421.13 421.27 423.04
424.11 425.23 427.21
428.01 428.25 428.26
429.04 431.10 431.15
452.15 458.30 465.25
468.06 468.08 468.08

SEE (CONT.) 468.22
469.12 470.18 475.23
478.30 482.08 482.23
484.03 484.27 494.12
495.18 515.28
SEED 208.11
SEEING 47.23 62.11
132.27 144.07 230.12
267.30 269.29 320.12
337.02 395.22 401.25
401.28 403.06 466.29
484.01
SEEK 58.24 246.04
SEEKING 509.07
SEEKS 341.06
SEEM 80.12 103.21
137.30 144.28 168.13
188.05 193.19 238.04
271.15 328.05 331.08
337.21 356.22 368.20
374.18 383.01 413.24
423.04 470.28 474.15
487.20 501.24
SEEMED 1.08 6.07
6.11 6.13 7.12
7.23 9.03 13.25
14.19 17.02 19.03
22.03 24.30 28.02
31.08 32.20 33.09
34.19 36.12 37.08
37.15 38.18 47.25
54.14 54.20 60.30
61.07 67.19 67.22
72.07 80.17 81.19
81.27 90.18 90.27
93.07 94.15 95.05
99.05 104.04 109.23
112.12 113.04 119.23
121.08 124.08 127.25
128.24 131.15 135.05
137.04 138.10 139.12
140.15 140.19 141.01
153.01 153.07 155.09
155.15 158.08 162.08
167.28 172.15 173.13
176.13 177.04 188.23
190.12 192.13 200.19
202.17 202.23 203.25
210.05 210.07 211.07
216.14 216.17 216.25
220.18 224.07 224.28
227.14 233.21 235.19
237.04 242.05 245.15
244.23 245.11 248.12
249.19 251.16 254.01
255.05 259.02 259.14
260.12 261.12 261.30
265.03 270.21 276.18
279.28 283.18 286.02
287.13 288.06 289.02
291.17 292.14 293.09
298.29 301.14 305.07
307.09 307.21 311.15
311.21 312.12 312.21
314.21 320.23 322.08
322.18 325.20 327.18
334.17 334.30 337.25
341.23 345.10 346.01
348.24 350.19 350.25
351.09 351.14 351.22
357.15 361.21 362.09
362.18 367.20 368.15
369.08 371.14 373.14
374.06 376.22 378.01
378.24 379.14 382.01
385.18 386.04 386.18
386.24 387.22 389.06
389.12 392.11 393.02
394.06 396.05 396.22
396.26 397.23 398.07
401.24 402.12 420.20
403.23 408.13 408.18
408.28 409.01 409.09
410.13 412.11 414.18
415.12 415.16 416.09
427.13 428.15 430.05
430.13 430.27 431.22
432.13 433.01 433.07
434.17 436.09 440.18
443.03 445.24 446.05

SEEMED (CONT.) 446.10
457.19 457.23 460.02
452.03 463.01 465.24
459.20 471.02 474.21
477.03 482.02 485.18
488.12 494.18 495.08
508.01 510.20 513.10
SEEMINGLY 402.24
SEEMS 57.26 117.04
125.05 134.16 136.11
147.03 147.05 198.04
208.09 214.17 227.14
239.19 251.12 253.16
271.01 277.08 277.28
310.13 321.23 324.19
332.21 333.17 342.06
345.03 359.29 365.29
367.18 376.10 383.06
422.27 424.02 424.03
437.16 443.11 465.12
502.09 510.27
SEEN 2.08 4.06
6.18 7.01 9.03
11.13 11.27 13.18
24.20 40.09 57.24
60.06 61.12 64.07
70.08 73.05 88.28
95.16 101.09 110.08
111.10 111.12 112.11
124.16 135.04 137.26
144.26 153.30 165.03
165.09 165.15 165.21
166.10 168.11 174.21
177.08 178.13 182.03
182.08 182.27 184.27
214.13 224.19 224.25
235.18 261.14 263.12
267.18 269.11 269.19
270.19 273.01 279.25
280.33 297.04 297.22
297.23 315.06 318.02
318.13 320.30 328.14
328.20 329.29 334.13
346.06 347.19 351.10
352.21 360.18 361.16
363.21 368.17 379.05
398.06 398.13 398.27
399.19 399.19 407.11
413.18 417.28 421.05
427.23 431.21 434.21
435.06 443.04 453.30
460.08 475.12 481.17
484.19 495.09 502.06
502.19 504.07 515.22
SEES 259.27
SEETHED 6.30
SEETHING 334.02 341.15
454.06 483.26
SEHEN 429.02
SEIZE 185.16
SEIZED 420.25
SEIZING 78.17 193.06
SELDOM 13.18 106.04
252.07 318.14
SELECTED 131.12 456.24
SELF 1.07 67.24
69.12 90.20 93.20
96.04 126.13 292.08
292.08 350.06 418.13
424.08 474.22 511.27
SELF-APPOINTED 418.13
SELF-ASSERTION 1.07
SELF-COMMUNION 350.06
SELF-CONTROL 90.20
93.20 126.13
SELF-KNOWLEDGE 96.04
SELF-LOVE 474.22
SELF-MISTRUST 67.24
SELF-POSSESSED 279.25
SELF-SATISFACTION
69.12
SELF-SATISFIED 292.08
SELFISH 186.14
SELFISHLY 60.24
SELFISHNESS 186.15
215.25 321.10
SELL 360.13 441.20
480.28
SELLING 418.19
SELVIN 190.19

SEMBLANCE 313.13
SEMICIRCULAR 318.09
SEND 167.15 200.01
200.01 200.05 201.01
241.12 255.08 267.02
323.24 421.10 422.19
438.28 443.12 456.17
461.05 472.28 494.21
505.30
SENDING 383.16
SENILE 202.04
SENIOR 73.29 289.04
SENSATION 8.18
109.13 112.15 119.19
147.24 487.03
SENSATIONS 12.08
98.24 131.06
SENSE 9.08 42.07
50.07 55.06 68.25
80.19 90.17 95.15
102.10 114.23 116.03
134.20 167.03 185.16
193.13 212.11 215.07
222.14 237.21 244.03
288.24 320.29 322.21
334.27 342.07 347.05
351.26 358.11 366.27
398.05 431.03 434.24
450.01 508.22
SENSELESS 198.20
321.17 458.19
SENSELESSLY 511.18
SENSES 25.05 35.17
45.18 348.24 362.11
SENSIBILITIES 138.30
215.24 243.19
SENSIBILITY 3.02
186.05 374.20
SENSIBLE 150.05 201.05
SENSITIVE 45.20
SENT 2.19 4.17
56.22 102.05 124.12
357.27 448.04 453.04
461.20 463.07 508.29
515.16
SENTENCE 51.25 193.17
193.17 195.04 305.04
402.04 421.17 435.02
SENTENCES 60.20
90.16 350.18
SENTIENT 340.28
SENTIMENT 14.24
68.16 147.24 186.04
SENTIMENTAL 26.25
280.27 398.03
SENTIMENTALISM 271.15
SENTIMENTS 49.22
352.16 352.28
SENTRY 450.06 504.10
SEPARATE 382.03 512.17
SEPARATED 83.28
94.11 126.07 158.03
269.13 349.29 471.14
SEPARATELY 133.05
250.03
SEPARATING 34.16
SEPARATION 340.15
340.16 408.21 488.01
SEPHORA 182.18
SEPULTURE 99.08
SERANG 167.03 167.16
169.11
SERANGS 80.02
SERENE 17.07 409.26
421.28
SERENELY 402.12
SERENITY 13.10 19.03
21.28 24.01 184.07
SERGE 234.12
SERIO 437.13
SERIO-COMIC 437.13
SERIOUS 225.15 384.22
SERIOUSLY 65.04
243.18 287.01 357.28
361.18
SERIOUSNESS 93.17
178.16 305.01 340.09
375.19
SERMONS 422.04
SERRIED 36.01

SERVANT 12.23 248.05
332.22 357.28 383.17
394.24 482.13 506.08
506.15 507.15
SERVANTS 16.19 92.19
252.10 314.29
SERVE 198.10 224.12
286.16 472.04
SERVED 8.28 14.08
442.14 484.05 488.29
SERVICE 13.29 51.23
74.08 75.30 107.21
178.19 182.29 185.22
248.10 437.04 438.30
454.23 456.25 488.30
491.04
SERVICES 68.08
SERVING 14.07 27.07
119.09
SERVITEUR 181.23
SET 2.05 61.16
71.29 72.22 75.09
78.11 147.08 204.07
206.05 222.05 261.12
267.05 287.25 292.01
295.05 311.07 325.25
331.12 333.15 366.26
378.01 385.26 394.03
401.14 412.17 413.30
414.16 423.15 425.23
430.13 431.15 439.24
440.16 444.26 459.18
472.24 478.19 481.18
497.03 507.25
SET-OUT 78.11
SETS 94.11
SETTING 94.17 386.05
510.11 511.01
SETTLE 330.21 331.03
331.03 447.09 457.21
SETTLED 31.10 193.26
408.19 458.25 484.03
495.28
SETTLEMENT 269.08
269.13 313.14 314.09
315.13 315.30 363.19
448.07
SETTLEMENTS 437.30
SETTLERS 317.07 332.28
482.29
SETTLING 376.27
SEUL 180.24
SEVEN 26.10 35.19
99.03 104.16 104.16
104.20 198.04 230.02
249.09 255.19 281.05
465.16
SEVENTEEN 71.09
SEVENTEENTH 276.16
SEVENTEENTH-CENTURY
276.16
SEVENTY 71.24
SEVENTY-ONE 71.24
SEVERAL 36.13 99.25
105.01 108.12 109.03
129.17 194.03 197.08
201.24 299.25 309.30
309.26 313.27 316.05
364.06 388.11 440.25
451.15 464.21 484.29
SEVERE 44.04 82.01
129.05 365.14 399.16
SEVERELY 122.04
SEVERER 13.30
SEVERITY 10.08 271.27
SEWER 25.17
SEXES 341.20
SHABBY 184.09
SHADE 43.02 43.28
84.25 84.26 88.08
153.26 192.06 229.05
240.05 263.01 333.25
364.01 469.12
SHADED 109.15 248.15
417.11 432.03
SHADES 11.02 35.21
86.07 89.10 114.02
188.03 191.03 239.22
286.07 390.08 516.15
SHADOW 16.23 22.04

SHADOW (CONT.) 22.05
22.06 59.23 60.02
60.05 96.04 118.07
123.07 127.24 141.13
147.03 147.03 153.17
215.12 220.07 225.23
239.18 256.07 256.08
260.23 283.19 302.23
326.05 333.03 339.22
340.01 349.24 384.27
396.22 397.10 397.11
402.10 408.21 414.22
494.06 494.23
SHADOWED 148.05
SHADOWLESS 203.29
SHADOWS 14.20 33.10
210.06 224.04 261.22
302.09 302.10 376.23
384.09 385.01 397.09
497.22
SHADOWY 11.28 26.20
270.17 299.14 299.18
361.21 516.03
SHADY 60.17 383.04
SHAFT 101.07 130.27
133.04 390.24
SHAFTS 94.13
SHAKE 105.20 186.23
216.25 275.05 329.01
338.26 353.01 358.13
476.10
SHAKEN 54.26 184.26
207.20 211.24 230.19
275.09
SHAKES 237.15
SHAKESPEARE 290.30
SHAKESPEAREAN 291.03
SHAKILY 137.11
SHAKING 120.23 189.10
307.09 342.15 355.09
361.12 390.19 438.18
460.21
SHAKINGS 145.15
SHAKY 119.10 360.12
SHALL 41.21 48.22
53.06 71.16 71.29
128.09 186.25 208.12
213.14 214.12 228.25
228.25 229.20 249.14
250.26 263.03 269.05
274.30 275.11 291.18
295.26 344.14 361.11
377.26 389.02 391.13
391.19 391.20 394.19
394.20 400.25 405.15
405.16 411.24 412.04
412.05 412.14 412.29
412.29 413.21 423.18
424.10 424.11 426.11
429.18 430.30 431.17
433.22 468.02 468.06
468.08 468.08 472.22
472.28 481.13 483.03
485.05 486.18 494.12
495.01 507.16 511.07
511.29
SHALLOW 441.09
SHALLOWS 15.26
SHALT 118.02
SHAM 81.24 147.28
426.01
SHAME 33.01 70.31
80.04 262.10 262.22
286.02
SHAMEFULLY 127.03
SHAN'T 48.20
SHANGHAI 27.20 73.25
74.22
SHANKS 206.07
SHAPE 30.11 32.20
139.07 211.21 213.08
224.06 248.18 296.04
341.13 348.13 385.15
431.22 515.23
SHAPED 195.02 371.06
430.05
SHAPELESS 248.17
260.04 302.24 339.25
433.28
SHAPELY 347.23

SHAPES 140.30 149.03
188.01 277.02 297.09
373.20 376.29 385.01
397.13 423.08
SHAPING 228.30 471.03
SHARE 69.03 199.09
219.08 397.28 402.13
455.29 457.13
SHARED 28.29 96.08
335.14 400.29
SHARP 23.05 31.08
45.14 56.14 89.02
180.17 338.17 373.21
460.04
SHARPLY 85.21 166.06
260.01
SHAVED 33.03 168.17
170.18 192.20 196.13
SHAVER 52.10
SHAVING 19.06 24.27
494.18
SHE 7.07 7.17
11.22 14.29 15.07
15.09 16.21 17.04
17.06 23.09 25.06
32.04 61.04 61.23
63.27 71.15 110.22
110.23 117.26 128.20
128.22 134.08 135.04
135.05 137.03 137.04
139.29 140.05 140.05
140.09 140.11 140.14
140.14 140.16 166.06
166.07 166.17 166.18
166.20 171.01 175.11
182.23 182.24 194.06
235.03 254.10 254.12
254.14 254.20 254.21
254.25 268.14 292.30
314.17 314.22 314.23
314.24 314.26 315.01
315.08 315.10 315.14
319.18 330.13 330.15
338.19 340.21 340.25
342.04 345.28 346.11
347.22 347.24 348.01
348.08 348.10 348.14
348.15 348.18 348.19
348.21 349.03 349.09
355.20 356.04 357.09
357.09 357.10 357.11
359.23 359.26 359.30
360.06 362.23 365.16
365.18 365.20 365.26
366.03 366.06 366.07
367.02 367.08 367.26
367.28 368.01 368.22
368.29 369.08 369.20
369.21 370.05 370.24
370.27 373.14 374.09
374.22 374.24 374.25
378.13 378.17 378.30
379.03 379.04 379.04
379.05 379.05 379.07
379.08 379.09 379.16
379.17 379.18 379.19
379.19 379.20 379.27
379.29 380.08 380.18
381.07 381.20 381.23
382.10 382.11 382.13
382.17 382.18 382.20
382.22 382.23 382.24
382.28 383.25 383.29
383.29 384.02 384.03
384.06 384.06 384.12
384.20 385.05 385.06
385.07 385.08 385.10
385.14 385.16 385.17
385.23 385.25 386.07
386.30 387.04 387.07
387.09 387.12 387.17
387.18 387.20 387.22
388.03 388.04 388.07
388.08 388.17 388.18
388.22 389.05 389.06
389.20 389.20 389.24
391.02 391.06 391.07
391.15 391.25 392.06
392.07 392.07 392.12
392.14 392.24 392.24

SHE (CONT.) 393.02
393.05 393.06 393.09
393.14 393.16 393.20
393.21 394.14 395.07
395.27 395.29 405.24
413.17 413.19 413.20
427.03 427.05 428.26
428.29 428.29 429.12
429.14 429.28 430.07
430.10 430.11 430.16
431.02 431.03 431.05
431.06 431.08 431.24
432.10 433.10 433.13
433.14 433.22 433.26
436.26 448.10 448.22
448.24 450.19 475.05
475.30 476.02 484.30
488.29 489.02 489.05
489.09 504.20 505.02
505.28 507.26 507.27
508.02 508.03 508.08
510.16 510.28 511.02
511.05 511.06 511.08
511.09 511.18 511.21
511.22 511.25 511.26
511.29 512.01 512.13
512.20 512.21 512.28
512.29 512.30 513.02
SHE-DEVIL 383.25
SHE'S 131.23 137.11
SHED 19.03 203.15
310.11 310.27 358.29
475.25 498.26
SHEDDING 224.02
SHEDS 351.11 355.19
SHEEN 94.14 252.25
301.29 445.21 480.18
SHEEP 43.39 167.06
SHEEP-PEN 167.06
SHEER 47.19 200.07
271.15 280.13 310.25
488.02
SHEERED 182.22
SHEET 19.08 22.26
111.03 157.28 193.07
210.24 212.09 410.02
413.30 417.27 420.04
429.30 508.29 514.11
SHEETED 64.26
SHEETING 21.07 319.30
333.27 453.14 483.09
SHEETS 5.30 140.29
141.20 148.23 495.01
SHELL 5.14 20.06
194.24 299.22 386.17
386.23
SHELL-FISH 5.14
SHELTER 6.16 217.28
218.29 222.18 225.16
302.28 386.14 387.08
408.19 421.28 426.27
SHELTERED 23.08
SHELTERING 374.18
386.27
SHELTERS 20.27 333.15
455.06 498.19
SHELVES 248.18
SHEPHERDED 373.02
SHERIF 317.10 321.07
323.17 324.27 325.01
331.16 332.13 336.01
336.19 359.10 363.18
368.12 373.22 383.04
383.05 420.18 484.07
SHERIF'S 387.29
SHERIFF 363.20
SHIED 52.29
SHIFTED 74.21 162.03
437.10
SHIFTING 91.07 371.03
464.29
SHIMMER 19.14
SHIMMERING 223.09
SHINDIES 243.20
SHINDY 330.26
SHINE 4.26 220.24
SHINING 19.05 156.12

SHINING (CONT.) 302.20
319.13 429.22 476.02
491.15
SHINY 22.27 64.14
312.10 343.09
SHIP 1.13 1.18
1.20 2.04 2.08
2.14 4.17 6.23
7.04 7.11 10.16
12.13 15.18 17.01
17.23 18.07 18.07
19.19 20.06 20.16
20.22 21.21 23.04
25.04 25.24 27.24
31.03 31.14 32.04
34.15 42.23 43.36
52.09 52.14 61.15
62.11 62.15 63.01
64.22 67.13 67.17
74.04 75.07 96.16
96.25 100.25 102.26
103.03 103.11 105.18
107.03 107.14 110.20
110.22 111.02 115.08
115.22 116.08 117.20
118.27 119.02 119.26
120.02 122.05 122.13
123.19 124.14 125.25
127.25 128.19 130.14
132.06 133.19 133.28
134.03 135.02 140.13
147.04 148.13 157.09
158.06 159.04 162.22
163.01 165.08 165.24
165.30 171.22 171.29
172.02 182.21 182.25
183.04 183.14 190.03
192.27 194.04 194.07
198.12 198.26 199.01
200.01 200.02 200.05
213.23 230.17 231.04
232.29 236.18 236.30
237.01 237.06 237.22
242.14 243.27 243.30
290.19 292.25 377.18
435.14 436.27 436.30
439.16 440.27 449.27
454.19 454.21 455.01
456.15 461.13 475.12
480.30 480.30 508.20
SHIP-BROKER'S 42.23
SHIP-CHANDLER 1.20
2.08
SHIP-CHANDLER'S 1.13
SHIP-CHANDLERS 213.23
237.01
SHIP-KEEPERS 439.16
SHIP-MASTERS 43.36
SHIP'S 6.18 23.01
23.08 23.24 71.07
117.25 146.18 291.12
SHIPBOARD 93.01
SHIPCHANDLERS 230.04
SHIPMATES 150.28
SHIPOWNER 197.02
199.29
SHIPOWNERS 201.12
SHIPOWNING 200.17
SHIPPING 43.31 45.20
SHIPPING-MASTER 43.31
45.20
SHIPS 3.04 3.29
5.02 5.10 13.08
13.28 16.22 47.22
62.12 68.04 94.16
119.13 172.28 194.17
194.20 236.09 244.22
293.08 441.08
SHIPWRECK 27.23
198.02
SHIPWRECKED 106.13
SHIPWRECKS 147.12
SHIRK 160.18 187.25
187.26 239.21
SHIRKED 122.10
SHIRKER 147.19
SHIRKING 240.01
SHIRT 105.12 452.19
470.19
SHIRT-FRONTS 105.12

SHIVER 33.01 37.04
137.17 329.01
SHIVERED 62.23 133.08
158.16
SHIVERING 329.11
452.26
SHIVERS 329.16
SHOAL 17.02
SHOALS 215.01 417.04
SHOCK 74.17 131.28
151.16 162.22 275.21
311.24 434.16 440.01
477.19
SHOCKED 75.04 88.02
100.05 387.04 471.24
SHOCKING 80.01
SHOCKS 63.06
SHOD 398.29
SHOE 75.25 237.05
287.11
SHOE-LACE 287.11
SHOES 1.11 182.30
273.18 299.23 309.06
398.30 471.01
SHONE 22.10 47.12
114.24 224.13 397.19
SHOOING 427.04
SHOOK 29.23 55.01
65.15 73.12 130.17
165.05 165.12 169.05
223.14 233.02 256.21
262.20 265.03 265.11
303.11 327.08 345.30
367.26 413.28 427.05
450.21 453.14 464.04
474.19
SHOOT 255.17 390.15
468.16 473.24
SHOOTERS 204.09 204.11
SHOOTING 201.01 290.26
306.16 436.12 447.22
478.20 502.12
SHOOTING-IRON 306.16
SHOOTS 236.23
SHOP 2.02 43.22
57.28 64.24 229.19
232.03 232.19 234.24
354.03
SHOPS 504.08
SHORE 2.01 6.03
13.06 42.14 52.23
75.29 99.01 111.06
151.23 173.08 175.30
183.17 198.16 198.29
211.18 216.12 216.20
385.02 393.11 410.03
414.14 438.02 440.17
451.04 456.10 494.06
500.27 501.08 502.14
504.08 513.05
SHORE-LIFE 183.17
SHORED 111.03 111.04
SHORES 5.15 49.03
277.14 417.22 434.12
444.01 480.13 497.20
SHORT 14.02 20.19
21.20 36.21 47.03
51.25 56.12 61.01
78.17 86.17 90.19
109.16 110.10 118.17
129.17 142.23 144.19
154.12 160.23 171.16
192.15 231.22 236.14
250.14 251.23 275.01
275.23 278.07 282.02
295.07 309.05 318.18
342.24 350.18 355.06
372.08 372.19 376.01
388.10 440.25 444.17
493.25 500.02 511.06
515.24
SHORT-LIVED 144.19
275.23 295.07
SHORTCOMINGS 99.05
SHORTEST 182.28
SHORTLY 251.01
SHORTNESS 167.27
SHOT 61.18 111.25
130.09 140.17 195.09
255.26 281.29 301.02

SHOT (CONT.) 312.06
  323.25 358.05 360.09
  371.19 372.02 374.04
  405.23 422.17 435.21
  441.04 442.19 443.20
  446.08 449.11 457.20
  459.27 460.05 460.17
  461.07 463.24 465.20
  465.21 474.17 479.03
  492.01 515.11 515.15
SHOT-GUNS 435.21
SHOTS 255.05 314.08
  316.01 458.06 500.18
  501.06 505.24
SHOULD 3.06 64.27
  73.14 73.26 83.12
  95.13 95.23 97.24
  114.27 116.07 118.28
  129.08 138.09 144.14
  144.23 171.27 187.03
  189.02 191.20 213.01
  219.17 229.17 230.03
  231.12 247.08 253.18
  253.19 266.19 281.11
  281.13 281.15 307.16
  309.29 325.29 328.14
  329.30 339.18 349.03
  376.25 379.13 387.07
  392.24 404.05 415.02
  422.27 450.24 450.27
  453.04 456.07 469.13
  470.07 474.08 485.09
  486.07 488.20 493.20
  506.23 511.16 513.04
SHOULDER 7.10 33.26
  38.06 61.19 62.30
  63.08 83.15 105.21
  109.21 110.15 149.21
  149.21 165.21 170.12
  175.05 191.28 205.07
  254.14 261.17 291.12
  329.09 332.16 350.04
  351.09 366.25 370.26
  384.14 399.20 405.18
  432.29 466.04 468.22
  512.01
SHOULDER-STRAPS 170.12
  175.05
SHOULDERED 46.28
  442.26 490.03
SHOULDERS 1.04
  21.03 28.28 33.07
  36.27 55.14 82.28
  93.13 118.30 126.02
  129.27 149.05 175.13
  181.28 202.14 210.04
  242.22 287.25 315.08
  386.05 405.30 410.20
  433.29 481.20
SHOULDERSTRAPS 168.16
SHOUT 45.26 49.04
  62.28 102.08 103.23
  108.22 108.29 133.17
  235.15 235.26 295.26
  385.29 406.04 419.26
  439.27 443.17 460.10
  467.18
SHOUTED 43.06 45.01
  45.27 45.28 141.23
  145.02 164.25 189.12
  204.13 205.29 221.05
  224.19 288.13 289.17
  294.21 304.03 361.09
  404.30 464.23 466.03
  473.14 484.24 495.26
  498.14 504.11
SHOUTED' 133.15
SHOUTING 5.23 34.26
  164.16 324.24 361.19
  443.22 452.11 466.11
SHOUTS 45.12 132.01
  164.02 164.02 164.03
  300.25 332.06 334.05
SHOVE 132.01 132.02
  133.30
SHOVED 45.06 110.19
  182.21 325.04
SHOVEL 21.22
SHOVING 306.12
SHOW 10.17 74.17

SHOW (CONT.) 75.08
  77.09 81.10 87.20
  124.26 145.29 155.10
  183.12 194.11 217.18
  226.12 239.02 282.19
  283.23 288.14 301.16
  337.25 364.22 385.01
  399.29 428.27 435.05
  440.29 478.07 500.04
SHOWED 38.22 64.07
  116.23 127.29 274.21
  298.03 305.04 323.26
  331.27 384.08 418.08
  420.16 427.29 448.10
  448.29 460.12 465.15
  465.29 494.01 497.14
SHOWEDV 8.16
SHOWER 137.05 142.11
  143.28 165.10 367.27
  374.01
SHOWERED 497.07
SHOWERING 462.22
SHOWING 285.09 306.21
  308.28 323.16 366.02
SHOWN 88.15 283.15
  315.17 395.17 468.22
SHPIT 49.14
SHRANK 243.29
SHREWD 315.08
SHREWDNESS 396.25
SHREWISH 83.17
SHRIEK 356.01 361.02
  510.09
SHRIEKED 299.01 402.24
  466.24
SHRIEKING 450.04
SHRIEKS 142.05 316.01
SHRILL 7.17 314.14
  387.30 388.10 417.09
  478.28 510.10
SHRINE 76.26 498.29
SHRINKING 379.19
SHRIVELLED 183.28
SHRUB 163.15
SHRUBS 216.25
SHRUNK 118.24
SHUDDER 272.14
SHUDDERED 14.04
  100.30 149.18 272.13
  389.17
SHUDDERS 210.03
SHUFFLE 15.14 57.25
  83.06 124.30 180.11
  199.17
SHUFFLED 206.07 328.16
  333.24
SHUFFLING 49.16
  107.08 487.07
SHUNNED 310.08
SHUT 25.25 25.27
  58.02 72.14 127.21
  128.14 144.30 166.09
  174.12 184.15 198.29
  210.26 221.08 226.10
  229.19 232.14 260.15
  276.06 283.16 283.25
  343.26 459.12 504.21
SHUT-UP 459.12
SHUTS 259.27
SHUTTER 338.14 505.26
SHUTTER-HOLE 338.14
SHUTTERS 254.19 279.30
SHUTTING 300.29 407.02
SHY 16.09 434.22
SHYLY 427.23
SHYNESS 348.05
SI 465.26
SI- 465.26
SIAM 242.13
SIAMESE 14.13 241.29
  426.26 427.01
SICK 43.27 53.03
  60.21 63.20 109.04
  152.06 160.17 210.29
  237.24 288.21 309.10
  309.11 353.11 366.29
  473.26
SICK-BED 210.29
SICKENING 479.27
SICKLY 123.05

SICKNESS 406.02
SIDE 19.12 20.28
  20.29 21.02 22.10
  27.10 33.28 34.27
  35.07 54.25 61.29
  69.10 78.10 93.30
  102.01 107.17 107.18
  112.18 112.19 117.06
  129.27 134.30 135.03
  141.04 148.16 149.13
  155.02 171.16 173.13
  175.14 198.03 202.16
  205.16 205.26 208.14
  213.07 238.22 244.27
  244.27 250.13 259.01
  261.26 269.29 280.23
  291.13 292.07 294.26
  294.26 299.16 302.11
  308.23 309.14 311.14
  314.22 318.09 328.15
  329.07 335.16 340.06
  346.06 346.07 346.08
  350.25 352.19 360.07
  366.22 368.22 369.24
  373.11 385.25 391.05
  393.01 401.19 404.28
  408.25 408.25 409.18
  415.09 420.11 422.05
  427.22 433.27 444.28
  445.10 445.27 445.27
  448.25 453.06 459.17
  459.20 465.14 467.14
  470.06 470.26 470.27
  480.02 483.30 485.15
  486.01 486.01 492.15
  497.21 498.07 499.30
  508.09 515.27
SIDE-LIGHT 135.03
SIDED 9.08
SIDELONG 46.20 210.02
  411.30
SIDES 15.16 105.22
  112.18 137.09 142.11
  234.10 269.26 330.27
  334.01 358.12 397.09
  441.09 443.03 461.29
  469.15 481.27 491.21
SIDEWALK 49.25
SIDEWALKS 175.28
SIDEWAYS 37.10 132.26
  195.22 360.08 460.27
  466.13
SIDIBOY 208.15
SIDLING 452.20
SIE 429.02
SIEGE 251.08
SIEGMUND 241.05
SIEVE 3.07
SIGH 21.19 71.28
  139.14 149.19 157.22
  215.29 216.24 368.25
  376.01 382.02 485.06
SIGHED 23.30 101.02
  171.28 241.18 257.22
  307.22 345.29 391.08
  417.23
SIGHING 330.04 495.15
SIGHT 11.17 14.21
  24.11 40.20 44.22
  56.18 75.22 76.23
  80.23 93.15 109.05
  115.21 116.01 128.09
  152.22 165.06 171.13
  171.16 196.04 207.21
  212.03 219.08 273.25
  276.07 287.14 291.29
  299.09 335.02 344.26
  358.24 364.24 368.18
  395.25 407.04 415.06
  432.20 470.16 478.21
  480.15 483.19 498.08
  503.14 509.29 510.28
SIGHTED 441.07
SIGHTS 15.28 24.25
  103.03 116.23 132.18
  139.22 460.29
SIGN 56.16 73.13
  95.26 118.02 121.06
  126.08 129.07 176.26
  178.09 256.06 286.07

SIGN (CONT.) 308.09
  353.04 365.04 370.21
  389.03 389.18 392.18
  409.12 431.24 443.02
  471.23 506.27 509.17
  516.01
SIGNAL 147.21 167.03
  199.04 328.26 367.25
SIGNALS 171.29
SIGNATURE 45.16
  434.26
SIGNED 414.08
SIGNIFICANCE 138.13
  191.15 363.03
SIGNIFICANT 302.27
  340.02
SIGNIFICANTLY 203.12
  257.10
SIGNS 54.28 65.14
  114.29 202.23 331.27
SILENCE 22.01 30.17
  64.15 78.09 78.29
  84.07 87.05 104.09
  107.11 109.16 115.23
  119.16 119.17 120.30
  133.13 138.24 138.25
  139.01 139.26 162.18
  164.15 174.04 188.15
  195.21 210.13 217.28
  233.02 257.08 262.17
  266.03 307.26 319.09
  323.14 335.15 356.05
  362.08 362.08 365.23
  368.20 376.01 388.13
  392.29 413.14 439.26
  443.06 452.25 460.03
  462.11 463.03 466.24
  480.19 481.13 485.04
  487.06 495.25 506.28
  509.27
SILENCED 263.30
SILENCES 337.17 374.21
SILENCING 467.10
SILENT 17.22 20.01
  22.09 32.22 38.10
  38.29 69.18 98.04
  99.11 100.01 103.17
  115.29 122.23 127.24
  148.19 179.20 187.27
  219.15 231.18 244.27
  248.04 264.03 264.08
  287.21 289.22 290.10
  292.28 302.15 322.07
  329.03 348.07 349.20
  374.05 377.28 380.18
  384.09 385.03 431.24
  446.10 480.03 485.13
  493.27 500.07 511.06
  514.05
SILENTLY 15.20 59.09
  141.15 263.12 294.17
  359.18 376.28 389.30
  401.21 440.20 489.17
SILHOUETTE 378.05
SILK 27.09 60.23
SILKS 279.22 318.06
SILKY 208.17 373.15
SILLY 8.18 47.24
  124.25 152.13 229.16
  328.03 330.24 412.04
SILVER 20.23 68.22
  211.13 234.10 285.08
  319.14 324.17 438.11
  491.11 509.26
SILVER-MOUNTED 68.22
  324.17
SILVERY 121.02 302.22
  411.04
SIMILE 131.07 136.15
SIMILITUDE 294.10
  296.02
SIMMERING 204.03
SIMPLE 11.17 51.10
  114.04 165.28 170.08
  177.14 179.10 246.07
  250.27 258.27 259.08
  290.25 293.04 327.21
  378.15 381.03 383.08
  389.13 440.08 487.15
  513.22

SIMPLER 259.09	**SIT (CONT.)** 492.17	**SKY (CONT.)** 143.05	**SLIGHTLY** 20.21 33.26	
SIMPLEST 114.04 378.15	513.04	148.30 149.28 151.18	37.29 99.25 109.16	
SIMPLICITY 185.20	**SITS** 80.02 259.22	201.01 204.02 244.23	137.15 141.08 159.14	
186.13	315.16 422.04	271.10 312.27 325.20	169.06 170.17 173.12	
SIMPLY 68.19 84.20	**SITTING** 32.15 33.18	329.04 376.22 397.01	175.14 187.24 196.10	
91.02 103.08 151.09	37.14 55.29 75.23	409.01 409.10 409.20	250.13 263.17 269.18	
175.01 201.25 204.08	102.28 119.21 129.26	413.15 415.13 434.09	286.06 318.17 510.28	
223.07 252.21 301.19	142.24 153.03 256.15	445.12 487.10 512.01	**SLIM** 21.25 83.14	
314.06 320.11 352.18	213.06 235.10 256.15	**SKY-HIGH** 201.01	441.11	
352.21 359.22 437.22	258.17 258.29 262.22	**SKYLIGHT** 28.05 35.06	**SLIME** 309.10 312.11	
456.23 487.13 492.17	280.06 280.08 314.01	129.28	**SLING** 46.24 56.10	
SIN 190.16 268.07	345.25 362.04 401.17	**SKYLINE** 116.14	57.01	
SINCE 5.27 8.27	429.27 449.23 455.08	**SLAB** 162.08	**SLINK** 399.14 399.15	
42.04 56.20 71.20	466.04 467.12 468.23	**SLACK** 52.25	500.03	
74.04 84.18 88.07	483.10 492.05	**SLAM** 21.22 216.26	**SLINKING** 57.24 347.05	
95.11 114.14 152.24	**SITUATED** 294.06	234.03 287.22 288.13	351.03 357.04 363.07	
159.24 210.26 228.09	**SITUATION** 293.29	**SLAMMED** 404.24	399.19 451.24	
228.22 238.15 274.17	304.26 316.20 317.13	**SLANG** 178.15	**SLIP** 124.12 219.17	
298.19 302.14 320.28	356.11 380.04 447.03	**SLANGED** 237.18	393.04 398.17 440.19	
331.15 375.18 400.05	487.16	**SLANT** 110.22 116.08	**SLIPPED** 34.20 185.03	
400.15 428.01 447.02	**SIX** 1.01 72.02	332.02	231.21 393.27 441.15	
461.24 480.11 483.21	76.01 87.09 99.03	**SLANTED** 5.30	477.05 499.12	
491.06	148.18 148.25 148.26	**SLAP** 53.15 224.18	**SLIPPERS** 70.14 261.08	
SINCERE 29.25 359.01	199.23 203.16 204.09	227.24	315.05	
SINCERELY 215.08	204.11 227.01 227.23	**SLAPPED** 53.09 53.14	**SLIPPERY** 219.04	
387.03	233.24 240.30 281.05	77.07 99.27 375.13	**SLIPS** 249.05 257.27	
SINCERITY 85.12	312.07 354.12 443.19	474.30	**SLIT** 56.05	
112.17 186.09 488.13	444.13 467.15 479.05	**SLAPPING** 453.17	**SLOPE** 313.21 313.30	
SINFUL 199.06	502.05	**SLASH** 390.16	314.08 323.04 324.05	
SING 255.06 510.12	**SIX-POUNDER** 467.15	**SLASHING** 124.15	324.13 329.05 397.05	
SING-SONG 510.12	**SIX-POUNDERS** 443.19	**SLATE** 226.15 226.16	444.03 465.11 513.08	
SINGEING 419.04	**SIX-SHOOTERS** 204.09	226.27	**SLOPES** 416.22 444.20	
SINGLE 21.16 53.20	204.11	**SLATY** 414.22	445.03 452.10	
87.05 88.16 90.04	**SIXTEEN** 68.02 434.01	**SLAVE** 314.29	**SLOPING** 4.12	
111.21 116.29 126.29	440.06	**SLAVE-GIRLS** 314.29	**SLOUCHING** 481.19	
148.04 217.06 218.07	**SIXTEEN-KNOT** 68.02	**SLAVES** 279.22 387.29	**SLOW** 12.14 56.21	
218.07 225.10 295.13	**SIXTEENHUNDREDWEIGHT**	411.14	83.26 85.11 128.21	
319.08 360.17 401.19	44.08	**SLEEK** 232.07	128.21 134.03 196.05	
419.03 446.08 454.14	**SIXTH** 116.03 242.03	**SLEEP** 20.13 24.13	224.21 256.12 337.11	
457.10 461.07 491.15	**SIXTY** 101.19 315.21	51.28 53.21 102.09	351.04 376.27 380.07	
509.05	512.09	152.24 152.29 215.18	418.04 441.15 445.02	
SINGLE-HANDED 111.21	**SIZE** 54.15 55.03	222.18 256.29 257.16	450.13 457.08	
419.03 454.14 457.10	183.29 299.29 345.02	263.02 265.12 303.01	**SLOWER** 313.16	
SINGLED 347.14 412.20	443.05 478.17	310.11 312.29 312.30	**SLOWEST** 329.02	
SINGLY 449.13 498.21	**SIZES** 70.15	320.22 333.26 334.17	**SLOWLY** 14.24 16.17	
SINGS 52.20	**SKELETON** 28.02 473.02	349.29 359.03 359.15	24.28 31.03 35.08	
SINGULARLY 350.28	**SKELETONS** 473.10	362.19 362.21 365.10	54.04 56.13 80.22	
SINISTER 11.04 17.11	501.29	367.29 388.30 431.21	82.30 133.09 133.11	
194.21 302.09 379.11	**SKELTER** 309.27	489.04 490.18 490.19	148.27 159.01 163.29	
SINK 62.11 102.29	**SKETCH** 278.07	490.25	175.23 179.08 187.16	
120.02 122.01 122.02	**SKIDDED** 109.30	**SLEEPERS** 21.19 102.01	204.17 218.07 232.01	
156.10 177.04 204.29	**SKILL** 387.10	**SLEEPILY** 24.10 102.28	255.12 256.02 257.06	
237.25	**SKIMPY** 315.04	**SLEEPING** 16.12 24.07	257.20 258.11 262.20	
SINKING 5.10 61.09	**SKIN** 118.24 187.08	26.30 70.12 101.21	263.13 306.04 318.23	
62.12 111.02 130.14	197.12 218.15 309.06	102.23 105.15 105.18	327.06 333.19 344.29	
140.19 142.16 299.10	371.15 410.19	117.27 319.11 367.28	351.10 413.12 433.13	
466.22 508.26	**SKINNED** 415.04	492.30 498.28 505.09	433.29 470.02 482.22	
SINKS 11.30	**SKINNY** 43.35 410.29	**SLEEPING-JACKET** 24.07	485.05 498.18 509.07	
SINNE 257.04	460.25 500.06	**SLEEPING-PLACE** 498.28	511.08 514.10 514.11	
SINNED 25.30 228.24	**SKINS** 37.16 418.18	**SLEEPING-SUIT** 70.12	**SLUGGISHLY** 453.06	
SINNER 117.04 390.30	449.29	**SLEEPLESS** 452.28	**SLUGS** 466.06 479.06	
409.18	**SKIPPER** 16.14 24.05	**SLEEPY** 24.03 185.16	**SLUMBERS** 365.06 389.06	
SINS 170.06	25.11 28.22 28.30	**SLEEVE** 120.07 120.11	**SLUNG** 108.24	
SINUOSITY 319.13	30.18 43.14 47.20	433.18	**SLUNK** 481.29	
SIP 169.02 308.04	54.13 67.14 77.11	**SLEEVES** 380.17 470.19	**SMALL** 5.16 6.03	
SIPPED 177.28	78.27 79.07 98.03	**SLENDER** 4.30 19.06	12.03 14.22 15.26	
SIPPING 267.28	102.06 110.02 122.09	277.12 339.30 380.14	16.21 20.10 23.02	
SIR 45.12 52.08	122.16 124.30 133.29	444.29	38.29 46.13 50.18	
52.23 53.11 70.36	136.11 141.23 142.04	**SLENDERLEGGED** 249.02	55.14 64.08 70.16	
71.19 72.19 73.04	149.22 151.12 151.20	**SLENDERLY** 496.10	70.35 83.04 92.08	
73.19 74.06 74.11	153.27 165.13 192.27	**SLEPT** 20.07 20.30	97.03 101.29 134.26	
74.15 74.22 75.03	197.02 199.28 475.24	21.04 148.28 190.01	147.01 225.20 244.25	
76.02 76.18 77.22	**SKIPPERS** 119.13 356.22	302.15 312.30 350.15	249.13 252.13 256.15	
183.05 231.06 234.01	**SKIPPING** 443.20	362.20 366.26 417.11	257.21 273.15 290.22	
235.19 235.29 236.08	**SKULKED** 244.04	**SLID** 35.04 129.25	290.28 291.04 306.08	
237.04 237.17 383.12	**SKULKING** 352.21 473.14	**SLIDE** 410.13	310.11 322.02 323.22	
383.13 402.17 402.24	**SKULL** 120.16 272.22	**SLIDING** 72.10 115.18	328.23 344.15 347.22	
402.26 402.30 403.01	318.20 372.03	**SLIGHT** 1.03 17.14	354.03 369.05 370.26	
403.14 404.03	**SKULL-CAPS** 318.20	44.22 78.18 137.08	378.21 386.20 390.12	
SIR' 402.03 405.01	**SKULLS** 397.20	162.22 190.02 207.25	413.11 421.26 421.27	
SISTER 52.12 61.12	**SKUNK** 143.24 468.13	246.20 264.10 338.16	425.03 427.28 438.11	
251.24	**SKUNKS** 235.12 235.21	350.09 381.19 394.13	441.21 445.06 448.19	
SISTER'S 330.16	**SKY** 4.30 6.11	409.27 410.06 414.12	459.08 459.11 486.13	
SISTERS 423.02	8.24 10.06 12.30	430.16 432.28 440.01	489.23 489.29 490.15	
SIT 48.26 75.25	13.11 14.02 17.07	495.30 509.10	491.15 491.25 495.02	
77.13 85.19 111.22	17.07 17.11 17.16	**SLIGHTEST** 68.12	495.05 498.20 503.10	
129.01 162.15 225.04	19.20 21.29 23.11	86.07 132.10 220.12	506.12 509.24	
253.25 255.27 256.25	24.30 30.25 84.25	221.04 232.23 304.17	**SMALLER** 208.10	
270.28 299.26 315.10	123.01 123.08 133.26	311.01 403.06 478.23	**SMALLEST** 95.27 107.18	
328.04 348.09 431.11	138.25 139.05 139.24	494.28	372.09 409.22	

SMART   4.23   7.16
118.23   173.14   205.11
259.07
SMARTLY 142.25   203.03
368.16
SMASH   11.12   64.01
200.23
SMASHING 331.15
SMELL   323.05   350.27
408.26   408.27   438.12
SMILE   34.09   42.17
93.16   100.22   114.24
128.08   142.01   156.19
157.05   177.12   177.13
181.12   183.04   220.03
230.23   241.04   244.30
246.20   262.26   270.01
283.07   289.02   322.08
325.08   328.16   348.06
459.25   481.24
SMILED   7.15   23.21
25.11   48.03   80.26
100.21   165.13   204.27
217.20   223.20   226.25
244.29   253.24   253.30
329.09   352.13
SMILES   233.28
SMILING 13.11   26.16
71.14   255.03   255.28
258.09   294.17   308.07
490.04
SMILINGLY   449.22
SMIRKING 292.07
SMITE   185.06
SMOKE   5.01   17.16
18.07   22.06   62.12
52.14   151.14   152.17
192.10   236.04   255.14
258.19   316.01   323.05
323.10   332.05   333.19
365.13   370.04   372.13
410.19   443.30   444.01
445.02   472.30   484.13
498.18
SMOKED   49.20   445.13
SMOKING 28.05   52.26
95.21   217.12
SMOOTH   17.15   19.07
22.29   31.11   69.09
118.13   187.04   222.13
244.22   325.19   373.18
396.30   424.11   439.11
SMOOTHLY 25.04   61.04
170.11   462.21
SMOTHER 55.30
SMOTHERED   6.07
SMOULDERED   218.06
SMOULDERING   18.08
325.07   445.06   463.27
SMUDGE   497.21
SMUGGLE 12.23   358.18
SMUGGLED 197.22
SMUGGLING   478.09
SNAKE   32.05   50.09
SNAKES   65.02
SNAP   79.24   81.02
SNAPPED 89.03
SNARE   292.24
SNARED   50.13
SNARL   399.21
SNARLED 110.15   495.21
SNARLING 115.26
SNATCH   236.04   256.18
SNATCHED 55.25   224.23
291.20   334.23   412.24
SNATCHING   109.07
SNEAK   84.10   143.12
SNEAKED 123.29
SNEAKING 48.29   224.12
491.28
SNEERED 205.11
SNEERING 54.18   477.08
SNEERS   75.26
SNIFFING 100.03
SNORED   455.07
SNORING 152.28   444.05
SNORT   45.09   255.11
304.02
SNORTED 55.21   205.26
238.13   467.27

SNORTING 55.25   367.11
SNOW   143.03   198.15
430.05
SNOWY   61.12
SNOWY-WINGED   61.12
SNUFF   168.19
SNUFFLED 76.16
SNUFFY   170.05
SO   7.25   8.16
10.02   11.01   14.10
14.10   14.19   14.22
23.21   25.04   26.07
27.25   28.11   32.01
34.14   35.16   36.29
36.29   37.21   38.03
41.05   41.14   41.22
44.11   44.23   44.29
45.14   45.17   46.13
47.16   47.23   49.19
51.14   52.08   52.08
53.11   53.11   53.18
57.06   57.16   59.09
60.03   62.02   62.05
65.05   71.30   72.06
73.19   73.25   75.22
77.23   77.26   78.19
78.24   80.30   82.04
82.16   84.04   84.13
85.03   88.15   92.14
97.26   99.19   100.12
106.03   107.14   113.12
113.28   114.02   114.02
114.04   114.14   114.21
117.19   119.25   120.25
120.30   123.23   124.07
127.03   128.22   130.03
137.30   139.04   143.04
144.06   148.15   148.18
150.07   150.27   156.03
156.03   156.03   156.10
157.15   158.01   159.24
164.16   164.21   165.25
166.20   169.20   169.24
171.30   173.20   174.02
174.15   174.15   174.18
174.24   176.06   176.15
177.09   178.01   178.20
179.01   179.18   179.23
183.01   185.30   185.30
186.06   188.11   188.17
188.20   191.12   195.19
195.19   195.20   195.20
196.20   196.21   197.03
197.26   199.05   201.12
201.29   202.09   202.13
204.16   208.08   208.09
208.27   209.18   211.27
212.02   212.08   215.01
215.19   215.21   215.26
218.13   218.13   218.14
219.02   219.23   220.12
222.10   222.13   225.13
226.02   227.08   228.30
229.03   231.20   235.22
236.07   237.17   237.30
239.10   240.05   241.07
241.10   242.25   244.06
249.07   249.07   251.01
251.16   251.30   253.03
253.04   253.04   253.05
253.06   254.23   255.03
256.05   256.23   256.24
257.03   258.06   258.09
258.14   258.28   259.08
259.20   259.24   259.24
259.28   261.02   261.19
261.28   262.10   270.03
270.24   272.03   272.09
272.10   272.28   273.06
273.15   274.10   274.11
274.24   275.10   276.24
277.14   278.10   279.25
279.25   281.09   281.22
281.22   283.04   289.01
289.25   289.27   292.04
293.24   297.14   298.18
298.29   299.20   301.12
304.19   304.21   308.17
312.18   315.21   319.26

SO (CONT.)   319.27
320.29   322.10   322.16
323.01   329.13   330.07
331.11   333.12   338.04
338.20   338.20   338.21
339.08   339.17   340.19
340.25   341.30   342.22
343.16   343.19   344.05
345.19   348.18   352.18
353.10   356.26   356.26
357.17   359.25   361.14
361.30   362.15   364.14
365.03   365.09   365.15
366.06   366.21   367.28
369.05   369.05   369.07
370.13   370.14   373.05
373.08   374.09   376.25
377.08   377.15   377.16
377.23   382.14   383.09
384.07   384.20   384.25
384.30   387.12   388.21
389.13   391.02   391.06
396.24   397.21   398.06
399.14   402.09   404.29
411.22   413.07   413.16
413.19   414.04   415.02
418.15   419.30   420.12
422.04   422.21   422.28
424.01   425.14   426.09
427.19   429.10   430.22
434.10   437.23   438.12
439.09   447.23   450.27
452.06   461.25   467.01
467.29   468.17   472.04
472.18   474.02   474.07
474.08   474.20   474.20
474.20   477.13   477.23
478.22   478.30   479.21
479.24   479.24   480.29
482.15   483.19   484.18
487.12   490.12   493.27
495.03   500.20   500.29
501.21   509.12   516.07
SO-AND-SO   14.10
52.08   53.11   185.30
195.19   195.20
SO-AND-SO'S   53.18
SO'S   53.18
SOAKING 43.20
SOAR   370.04
SOARING 299.13   410.05
SOBBED   512.01
SOBBING 140.25   312.21
369.03   393.24
SOBER   222.05   348.29
379.28
SOBERLY 93.18   226.07
SOBS   120.20   217.26
SOCIAL   462.01
SOCIETIES   264.18
SOCKETS 312.22   460.25
SOCKS   313.12
SOFT   14.11   14.15
24.12   27.15   40.18
62.23   73.04   104.29
113.23   142.09   224.08
236.27   256.19   311.24
314.23   348.09   350.04
367.21   374.13   380.11
SOFT-SPOKEN   236.27
SOFTLY   87.10   105.04
314.15   359.27   372.24
386.30   391.06   405.06
490.28
SOFTNESS 12.30   79.26
SOIL   299.13
SOILED   16.11   20.09
70.12
SOLAH   199.15
SOLD   492.19
SOLDIER 59.05   63.12
SOLE   54.27   222.08
SOLELY   268.22   451.07
SOLEMN   97.21   117.02
154.15   283.25   320.09
324.25   330.01   358.15
375.18   417.15
SOLEMNIFY   362.06
SOLEMNLY 92.09   157.05
251.25   305.05

SOLES   116.24   131.16
273.17   284.01   334.22
SOLICITATION   51.06
SOLICITUDE   60.25
SOLID   110.05   123.15
167.08   323.25
SOLIDARITY   159.19
273.25
SOLIDLY 216.19
SOLITARY 15.29   146.07
226.21   249.08   252.15
397.11   410.04   420.26
434.28   459.10   463.06
494.07
SOLITUDE 149.29   334.23
341.27   398.05   429.22
SOLITUDES   25.08
SOLOMON 439.05   439.12
439.22   461.03   464.03
SOMALI   23.07
SOMBRE   19.13   84.22
88.12   94.15   130.03
146.11   148.21   149.01
191.23   192.01   192.13
211.18   216.12   218.21
248.20   297.02   319.11
323.15   325.11   356.06
378.23   414.18   416.24
436.29   445.12   471.02
488.06   508.13
SOMBRELY 127.02   432.28
SOMBRENESS   25.02
SOME   2.24   12.20
13.14   13.18   13.27
29.28   36.07   41.28
42.14   42.26   43.33
44.23   45.07   45.13
45.15   46.22   48.05
48.23   49.17   50.08
50.18   51.10   51.30
52.01   52.05   52.06
52.15   53.24   54.15
58.04   58.08   58.10
59.21   59.22   59.22
60.04   60.17   61.15
64.29   66.14   67.16
68.07   68.10   69.24
77.14   79.13   79.15
80.28   81.15   81.30
82.27   82.30   82.30
84.22   85.04   86.03
85.13   86.17   86.22
88.02   89.23   90.23
92.24   94.24   96.18
97.03   98.03   105.15
108.06   109.01   111.14
115.17   116.03   117.28
118.06   118.26   118.29
119.24   120.05   121.08
123.18   124.01   127.06
129.06   130.06   138.30
140.15   140.29   141.08
141.18   143.17   144.11
144.13   152.29   156.27
158.16   163.14   163.15
168.16   172.05   172.06
178.09   183.22   185.24
185.29   189.10   190.20
196.04   198.05   198.14
199.04   200.19   207.09
208.09   208.23   210.16
212.22   214.16   214.16
214.25   218.09   218.10
222.15   223.08   225.18
227.13   227.22   228.16
228.25   228.27   229.18
233.16   234.02   235.02
235.06   235.06   235.08
238.20   242.03   242.12
242.26   244.17   244.25
245.28   247.07   251.14
251.27   254.05   256.06
261.06   265.04   266.15
267.28   268.07   268.18
269.14   272.07   272.08
273.16   273.30   278.11
280.11   282.19   286.12
295.03   295.08   295.08
299.23   300.24   301.14
306.11   307.04   307.15

```
SOME (CONT.)        308.21      SOMETHING (CONT.)            SORT (CONT.)        151.07      SOUTH           15.01   15.23
  310.08  310.15  311.10          406.04  409.12  423.21       153.19  155.12  155.16          28.15  123.06  196.19
  313.23  315.22  317.06          450.06  454.14  458.03       155.17  155.18  157.04         230.02  276.11  281.04
  321.24  323.07  323.25          458.16  460.16  470.29       157.15  165.22  167.24         343.03  411.07  437.09
  328.20  329.30  330.10          484.08  488.23  488.26       167.29  176.24  177.06         437.24  440.10  497.19
  332.30  333.15  340.30          492.07  493.05  494.22       179.19  184.09  185.14         502.02
  343.04  343.11  343.17          505.19  509.21                186.25  190.20  194.15      SOUTH-EAST          276.11
  344.18  348.08  350.26        SOMETHING'S          5.20       198.11  200.20  205.29      SOUTH-WEST          123.06
  351.13  352.26  353.17          217.16                        208.05  209.10  210.18      SOUTHERLY           175.26
  355.20  357.03  360.12        SOMETIME     247.15             213.18  215.25  218.10        181.26
  360.21  362.03  363.03        SOMETIMES            77.13      222.21  225.09  227.08      SOUTHWARD            71.17
  363.16  363.19  364.04          99.23  118.05  130.21         230.28  232.09  235.09      SOVEREIGN            53.24
  365.13  365.14  370.15         212.15  247.01  253.16         236.12  239.04  239.23        59.28
  374.29  375.13  375.19         258.18  261.20  321.29         245.28  248.05  250.01      SOWINGS      327.16
  387.16  390.30  391.17         340.17  341.14  347.13         266.11  267.04  267.29      SPACE           13.12   35.17
  391.30  395.13  397.05         356.04  411.23  466.23         272.15  279.11  281.14          44.11   56.08  100.15
  399.25  400.16  403.21         489.10                         282.08  282.19  285.21         125.21  192.14  212.27
  403.25  403.30  406.04        SOMETIMES            50.18      286.08  293.30  294.30         269.20  348.25  350.29
  410.26  411.02  413.04        SOMEWHERE            14.12      297.20  305.08  308.21         367.11  371.28  378.06
  420.15  422.14  430.14          27.19   84.07   93.08         311.03  312.28  321.27         394.04  408.22  409.14
  431.20  432.04  433.22         155.22  178.24  196.22         330.02  343.11  343.17         443.16  460.10  510.06
  435.18  436.10  436.15         217.09  296.05  353.25         344.21  345.23  357.23         510.26
  437.01  437.29  438.29         360.08  369.25  393.01         361.13  366.23  368.02      SPACES       25.07  160.28
  441.22  442.08  442.08         398.27  446.09  464.22         390.27  391.12  392.20         334.01  384.09
  444.11  449.28  452.11         467.15                         393.03  401.11  402.20      SPACIOUS    248.16  252.07
  453.04  453.07  454.13        SOMNOLENCE           174.20     403.21  404.18  423.13      SPAIN        229.08
  455.04  456.21  459.15        SON           2.16   73.27      423.21  425.24  426.25      SPAN         421.06
  460.27  461.08  464.01          81.20   95.05  231.03         438.18  438.20  445.22      SPANIEL      461.05
  454.20  469.18  472.23         250.24  251.04  298.11         454.28  455.18  455.23      SPANISH     182.19  425.03
  474.28  475.13  477.24         298.11  314.16  319.23         459.21  472.02  473.28         437.21  437.30  440.13
  483.16  484.06  488.19         320.15  333.21  337.02         476.03  476.08  478.06      SPAR          11.19   23.08
  489.11  492.01  494.22         410.17  421.17  435.13         479.10  482.16  488.12      SPARE        118.30  126.11
  500.28  501.20  503.03         451.08  486.17  498.29         494.01  498.26  516.17         185.11  315.02  319.18
  503.10  508.25                 508.30                       SORTE        173.20            356.28  359.11  438.30
SOME-              332.30       SON-IN-LAW           298.11   SORTS       118.10  130.06    SPARK       159.23  165.20
SOMEBODY     38.05   46.10        410.17                        148.15  241.27  258.07         182.13  302.27
  97.19   97.19  104.18        SON'S        321.18  330.16      321.16  357.26  440.08      SPARKLE      325.08
 134.29  141.28  203.10          449.05  515.11              SOUGHING     432.07            SPARKLED    100.19  284.05
 203.13  203.18  204.18        SONAL        270.01            SOUL          23.18   35.24       408.15
 243.14  255.04  293.12        SONG          6.26  387.30       36.28   40.24   59.06      SPARKLING           110.29
 301.02  355.12  375.09          388.10  510.12                 61.25   67.07   69.08      SPARKS      275.22  367.27
 387.29  404.01  507.05        SONOROUS     464.29              75.03   99.13  111.30      SPARRED      441.14
 495.07  496.04  507.05        SONS          4.15   83.11      138.06  144.01  160.29      SPARROW       29.10
SOMEBODY'S          70.14        83.11  250.26  484.27         183.28  183.30  184.03      SPARS        440.02
 137.09  513.27                SONS-IN-LAW          83.11      211.02  211.26  239.13      SPARSE       500.05
SOMEHOW      47.27  109.24      SOON          2.30   44.28      302.03  327.11  376.02      SPASMS       217.27
 134.27  137.27  144.15          46.02   49.28   69.14         380.03  389.11  390.11      SPAT          49.14  220.21
 148.14  177.14  189.18          73.03   82.23   87.20         395.07  400.14  418.20         474.30
 195.05  243.16  277.27          90.08   99.01  139.30         425.17  426.04  476.10      SPATULA       74.15
 288.08  315.03  361.20         165.28  199.26  204.07         477.12  488.08  500.22      SPAWN        440.10
 368.05  369.14  376.10         207.19  217.10  218.28       SOULS         23.04  106.04    SPEAK         38.15   46.13
 436.25                         228.28  230.19  232.12         126.19  147.07  275.23          54.19   78.24   82.20
SOMETHING          11.05        238.09  241.15  245.03         327.18  327.19  327.20          84.04   84.12  110.21
  23.10   24.11   33.14         300.03  304.07  351.24         341.16  374.19                 123.23  150.21  174.02
  35.22   35.23   36.19         351.24  354.04  378.08       SOUND         24.15   27.04        176.15  186.11  193.30
  38.06   43.36   44.07         379.18  386.27  399.15         31.02   32.18   37.06          219.03  235.20  236.20
  47.14   53.26   59.11         414.03  414.26  419.24         38.15   47.16   54.22          246.24  272.28  285.15
  59.19   59.21   63.08         430.10  432.21  436.30         57.11   83.25   84.15          285.18  294.04  307.14
  69.04   69.16   73.03         445.16  461.29  478.18         96.05  102.11  102.15          322.14  390.07  393.07
  74.13   74.28   75.11         479.17  491.19  510.25        108.02  119.14  120.04          395.04  412.27  429.11
  84.15   86.26   86.30         515.14                        121.12  123.09  125.13          446.07  450.14  450.19
  90.09   96.14   97.09       SOONER        26.23   42.14      127.26  133.27  137.03          464.27  485.17  491.30
  97.16   98.10   99.16         126.19  209.01  291.06         139.07  142.10  143.30          494.09  499.03  505.22
 101.15  105.22  106.09       SOOTHE       295.09  390.10      154.03  157.22  167.09      SPEAKER      416.08
 109.14  110.14  115.15       SOOTHED      138.17              171.25  195.02  210.25      SPEAKERS     450.14
 123.15  128.26  130.01       SOOTY        372.13  410.07      210.25  212.15  212.30      SPEAKING      32.04   34.30
 132.14  144.19  147.01       SORCERER     234.21  327.15      215.03  220.14  226.18          36.13   39.08   51.20
 147.13  149.10  151.01       SORDID        55.05  156.25      232.10  273.03  302.06          52.07   58.02   70.28
 157.25  157.27  163.28         475.08                        307.22  331.26  331.29          104.18  111.27  111.27
 182.08  183.16  184.02       SORE          56.06  243.11      333.22  349.25  362.13          124.10  177.03  179.13
 186.21  187.17  200.26       SORREL        56.04              367.24  369.24  370.30          185.27  223.27  244.06
 203.26  207.06  207.08       SORROW       252.01  273.03      372.22  373.15  392.30          259.10  280.24  284.09
 209.06  228.16  229.03         288.01  508.17  510.04         395.21  397.22  417.08          289.08  317.17  334.18
 233.05  233.19  234.18         514.19                         417.12  432.09  478.28          383.01  391.01  430.19
 235.24  237.13  238.05       SORROWFUL            176.24      494.28  501.06  507.10          471.05  481.03  490.09
 245.13  245.14  249.14       SORROWING            76.25     SOUNDED       36.17   61.10         505.27
 252.28  256.06  262.24       SORRY         60.26   61.11      105.14  158.04  177.15      SPEAKS      382.08  391.10
 263.03  265.13  272.20         75.02   99.14  145.18         288.08  396.06                495.03
 272.21  273.29  286.08         146.01  233.22  242.17       SOUNDING     119.12            SPEAR       171.17  309.09
 286.28  287.18  288.07         308.13  361.26  394.17       SOUNDLESS           516.17        332.19  372.19
 289.03  302.01  302.03         436.01  442.05  458.08       SOUNDS        24.25  103.04    SPEAR'S      336.14
 304.18  304.23  309.11       SORT          15.01   27.29      107.09  132.18  146.28      SPEARMEN    311.10  316.09
 319.22  321.05  327.09         45.08   47.17   48.14         181.11  210.30  211.01      SPEARS        21.13  255.22
 335.14  340.08  341.01         48.17   50.05   57.06         336.12  389.27  417.20         311.28  498.21  504.06
 343.25  344.01  344.07         64.29   71.28   78.13         452.04  514.24               SPECIAL       50.27  194.25
 344.15  348.10  348.20         79.02   79.23   86.26       SOUR         363.10  399.10         210.20  247.09  278.13
 357.18  358.08  364.25         93.17   93.18   95.25         452.27  481.22                  298.03  375.13  397.15
 368.17  370.15  370.20        106.02  115.10  120.05       SOURCE       288.01  460.07         438.29  448.17
 378.06  378.15  388.14        129.10  132.21  140.15         482.08                       SPECIES     241.26  256.09
 388.19  388.26  403.23        141.28  143.10  144.11       SOUTANE      170.10                256.27
```

STEADFASTNESS	148.01		STEIN'S (CONT.)		356.20	STILL (CONT.)		397.27	STOOD (CONT.)		164.18
277.09			358.24	359.12	366.13	402.23	404.04	405.02	182.29	183.09	195.26
STEADIED	287.14		413.05	428.03	428.04	414.21	415.09	415.10	199.17	205.17	209.13
STEADILY	20.16	129.05	429.20	432.20	487.19	430.29	445.29	446.10	211.17	211.24	214.19
140.03	142.13	216.18	491.11	494.16	516.18	447.14	453.21	472.10	226.05	232.26	238.27
315.11	497.18		STEM	18.01	28.06	490.27	495.09	496.10	248.14	249.04	249.18
STEADINESS		123.29	110.27	126.20		497.23	502.27	504.06	251.08	259.18	263.21
370.07			STEM-HEAD		110.27	504.10	509.02	511.06	288.30	301.12	313.05
STEADY	4.22	10.14	STEMMED	257.07		STILLNESS		19.01	325.07	344.22	350.24
23.09	63.24	63.29	STEMS	445.11		19.20	107.10	123.18	360.10	363.24	366.18
67.22	133.09	145.21	STENTORIAN		250.24	127.24	133.14	187.14	367.14	380.18	381.09
145.22	175.06	180.14	STEP	34.21	41.21	195.16	210.13	210.27	381.15	387.01	389.12
256.19	371.07	376.29	84.02	87.07	108.04	210.30	211.26	220.19	397.22	397.25	398.04
431.22	444.07	459.28	129.23	145.06	241.09	307.21	335.12	350.06	404.04	404.16	427.07
470.12	505.27		243.25	256.19	256.20	371.26	392.13	411.06	428.17	430.19	431.05
STEAK	75.16		261.17	288.04	320.04	412.25	415.11	510.05	432.26	435.19	438.16
STEAL	203.13	356.17	382.10	460.02	511.04	STINACY	277.01		448.24	455.01	459.30
405.16	405.17	438.06	STEPPED	211.03	216.27	STING	69.07	126.10	472.10	473.30	479.18
454.08	463.17		292.02	368.16	371.29	356.08	408.28		480.02	484.13	490.27
STEALING	165.20	263.12	373.10	453.11		STINKING	306.11		502.19	504.17	504.24
264.05	278.25	454.12	STEPPING	64.09	105.04	STINKS	235.27		510.19	511.06	511.25
STEALTH	299.22		226.13	248.07	302.21	STIPULATED		493.19	513.11	514.05	515.07
STEALTHILY		112.21	STEPS	42.25	43.03	STIR	17.12	27.05	516.06		
141.05	499.29		46.17	56.12	78.30	94.21	103.22	108.20	STOOL	490.17	
STEALTHINESS		117.09	83.05	83.30	103.23	128.25	139.25	149.19	STOOP	1.03	246.20
351.02			153.04	154.09	163.17	158.19	172.13	212.29	STOOPED	62.01	
STEALTHY	63.14	83.23	217.05	232.26	260.05	217.13	304.17	311.07	STOOPING	71.03	260.08
216.07	241.19	351.12	342.16	361.03	366.24	329.10	334.09	362.13	263.14	428.17	433.29
360.25	391.12		505.08	512.22	514.07	367.18	378.24	385.15	506.01	509.25	
STEAM	1.17	15.09	STERN	2.07	18.01	388.18	409.01	446.04	STOP	35.02	45.01
27.27	36.18	36.18	136.12	140.29	141.20	512.10			80.08	87.11	109.22
36.19	44.18	102.24	143.15	145.12	148.23	STIRRED	62.20	101.15	121.13	140.08	237.14
102.30	104.07		149.21	166.02	169.22	139.18	318.14	370.04	238.01	357.07	369.15
STEAM-LAUNCH		44.13	291.14	390.28	401.18	371.08	465.25	509.04	373.16	377.19	403.27
STEAM-WINCHES		102.30	423.08	443.30	454.03	STIRRING	5.06	47.07	STOPPED	31.12	46.17
STEAMED	31.14	162.14	494.30			192.17	387.12		56.12	64.18	72.12
214.26			STERN--		494.30	STIRS	63.26		78.16	80.23	102.23
STEAMER	14.27	16.29	STERN-PORT		291.14	STOCK	43.40	45.26	110.10	119.16	121.14
17.19	21.26	35.19	STERN-SHEETS		140.29	107.01	249.26	250.29	137.15	142.06	145.15
43.12	43.18	68.05	141.20	148.23		303.29			154.12	162.22	165.30
96.18	97.30	98.13	STERNLY	490.06		STOCK-IN-TRADE		250.29	195.08	208.23	210.12
166.30	172.25	196.20	STETTIN	49.01		STOCK-STILL		107.01	360.26	362.07	367.13
197.05	199.24	199.27	STEVEDORES		75.28	STOCKADE	300.20	308.29	379.18	388.10	392.29
201.29	201.30	206.02	STEWARD	42.12	52.29	311.29	316.03	317.15	430.11	432.26	445.10
234.04	234.30	501.28	58.08			329.04	331.10	332.11	464.17	481.20	511.21
502.05			STEWART	198.03		333.09	333.14	333.29	STOPPING	5.27	108.19
STEAMING	227.11	343.12	STICK	8.09	13.13	363.20	387.29	427.30	154.07	355.06	355.21
441.15			32.05	85.15	235.10	443.02	444.12	444.19	452.21	511.06	
STEEL	68.03	180.16	235.11	250.22	313.25	445.10	445.23	448.08	STORE	28.10	230.16
325.21			412.09	461.05		450.16	451.10	459.17	233.25	353.22	448.14
STEELED	106.04		STICKING	309.09	353.13	462.15	465.27	480.16	STOREHOUSE		369.17
STEELY	334.15		STICKLEBACK		306.09	482.22	489.26	490.06	STOREROOM		366.18
STEEP	269.12	373.17	STICKS	366.15	498.26	490.13	491.22	493.23	367.24		
STEER	96.25		STICKY	311.25		494.04	494.15		STORES	244.25	
STEERAGE	119.26		STIFF	30.19	62.20	STOCKSTILL		226.05	STORIES	339.09	339.10
STEERAGE-WAY		119.26	81.10	94.11	133.12	STOKE	23.28		339.11	340.20	435.07
STEERED	22.09	166.01	177.30	188.15	272.17	STOKE-HOLD		23.28	435.09	476.04	
208.24	298.09		480.25	509.26		STOLE	136.19	210.01	STORM	331.09	
STEERING	22.25	107.19	STIFF-LEAVED		94.11	387.24	425.02	456.09	STORMING	328.22	333.11
169.25	444.16		STIFFENED		120.04	495.04			336.09		
STEERING-GEAR		22.25	515.07			STOLEN	252.06	278.04	STORMY	13.30	
107.19			STIFFLY	99.24		440.19	440.27	501.26	STORY	12.24	43.29
STEIN	245.25	245.26	STIFFNESS		51.02	STOLID	114.28	169.27	57.06	70.09	93.01
245.27	245.29	248.10	STIFLED	336.12		224.26	456.24		95.16	97.29	98.03
250.05	250.12	250.20	STILL	5.24	6.13	STOLIDLY	25.26	427.03	113.04	113.24	151.30
250.27	251.03	251.12	17.12	18.04	23.07	STOMACH	58.27	170.04	152.03	157.25	160.12
258.01	258.29	263.01	30.20	39.06	44.11	171.18	173.06	241.20	162.17	163.07	165.16
263.06	264.30	265.09	46.16	61.07	64.13	358.28	365.01	466.07	169.11	179.19	198.02
257.02	267.10	267.31	100.01	103.16	107.01	STOMACHS		313.20	198.12	198.22	211.11
268.08	268.20	268.23	110.22	110.29	110.29	STONE	4.08	36.15	240.23	247.05	268.05
268.24	268.27	269.03	110.30	110.30	110.30	42.25	96.21	110.05	286.02	298.06	322.26
270.07	274.07	278.06	116.16	117.26	122.08	116.24	129.04	198.18	322.27	322.27	330.10
278.28	280.22	280.27	123.09	130.12	136.23	229.07	232.21	240.08	330.20	332.08	339.06
281.08	281.30	282.01	138.26	139.04	145.06	275.22	319.21	345.10	339.07	339.17	339.19
282.09	285.04	285.14	150.03	162.01	166.15	345.12	345.12	345.15	340.06	343.26	344.29
285.15	286.11	286.13	167.01	171.23	179.22	370.19	389.25	434.18	345.16	347.15	352.21
286.14	286.18	289.24	188.24	195.11	195.26	463.15	506.24		366.27	367.19	368.07
289.29	290.18	292.15	205.18	209.05	211.25	STONE-BLIND		36.15	384.30	398.20	416.07
304.03	320.17	324.19	215.18	215.30	224.05	STONE-DEAF		232.21	416.13	418.09	423.10
340.19	353.06	353.15	225.04	230.14	238.21	STONES	329.06	407.16	424.04	425.18	434.30
353.28	354.11	356.20	254.26	256.05	259.09	STONY	356.30	433.20	436.25	440.24	444.17
383.16	420.25	427.21	259.22	259.23	263.21	STOOD	4.07	5.24	458.09	474.03	488.11
428.17	430.30	431.27	264.08	280.06	289.01	6.13	12.27	30.19	501.26	505.16	
431.30	433.16	448.15	301.13	302.16	305.02	32.09	34.29	36.13	STOUT	366.20	438.03
489.01	516.18		307.02	309.15	313.04	47.10	50.22	56.15	STOUTER	46.25	
STEIN'S	250.22	251.21	323.04	336.22	350.11	75.19	83.29	101.24	STOVE	399.02	
284.07	285.12	290.14	360.10	360.30	361.12	102.22	103.15	107.01	STOVE-PIPE		399.02
294.29	297.15	303.20	365.04	374.16	381.20	115.29	117.06	122.17	STOWAWAY	244.05	
303.28	332.20	343.03	385.19	386.22	387.18	130.15	133.23	137.12	STRADDLING		196.05
343.14	351.27	352.02	387.23	391.25	397.22	145.06	146.10	163.13	STRAGGLED		273.07

STRAGGLER 274.28
412.19
STRAGGLERS 273.06
STRAIGHT 1.03 17.06
19.14 21.13 23.02
23.24 29.17 37.25
50.28 57.27 79.23
83.09 85.24 93.12
97.15 123.04 150.21
162.15 163.04 182.04
196.07 207.20 208.22
210.07 211.24 224.13
256.03 274.21 297.02
313.12 320.02 351.07
372.04 401.01 409.04
426.02 462.26 468.05
468.12 477.02 479.12
515.09
STRAIGHTWAY 102.08
STRAIN 169.26 186.01
215.28 362.01 431.22
STRAINED 232.04 234.03
240.03 451.30
STRAINING 55.03
148.22 211.04 439.28
480.15
STRAINS 99.22
STRAIT 16.30 17.04
STRAITS 440.23 442.18
STRAND 498.15
STRANDED 27.19 292.29
480.07
STRANGE 15.27 15.28
48.05 100.18 103.02
103.05 131.09 137.28
137.30 209.23 225.01
236.30 252.02 262.08
277.03 277.23 280.17
283.17 298.01 298.29
304.22 321.21 322.24
327.04 346.10 348.30
356.09 376.05 387.23
391.17 398.10 429.13
430.01 458.14 466.23
471.13
STRANGELY 10.04
85.07 125.28 166.20
226.22 339.02 371.06
STRANGENESS 379.21
STRANGER 57.26 83.01
83.30 299.02 316.21
332.23 383.20 429.01
436.13
STRANGERS 27.30
42.18 70.07 210.23
232.12 241.01 364.03
449.15 483.18
STRAPS 170.12 175.05
STRATAGEMS 449.14
STRAW 70.14 211.20
212.14 315.05 370.03
STRAY 130.29 264.19
STRAYING 288.06 338.15
STRAYS 218.26
STREAK 23.23 444.02
STREAKS 7.01 199.19
STREAM 4.28 83.04
220.18 276.09 276.15
302.25 334.02 334.17
384.10 385.02 385.02
407.15 417.17 432.02
443.03 445.25 451.04
474.02 482.07 484.12
489.30 499.22
STREAMED 15.11 15.12
15.13 367.22
STREAMER 22.07
STREAMERS 334.06
STREAMING 5.21
297.04 329.12 508.07
512.02
STREAMS 316.30
STREET 38.07 77.29
175.25 196.04 199.04
199.16 201.20 202.07
243.08 451.11 459.12
459.18 462.25 463.24
482.23 483.29 489.21
STREETS 58.28 191.25
213.13

STRENGTH 5.28 11.09
15.03 17.10 28.13
51.05 51.13 53.20
66.15 156.29 194.22
213.03 272.03 273.19
327.10 337.07 345.06
381.06 386.06 401.23
418.25 429.04 429.05
431.23 447.16 461.15
478.02
STRESS 158.18 210.21
389.22 452.05
STRETCH 22.18 72.06
175.30 355.23 396.14
459.07 498.11
STRETCHED 11.23
20.25 75.20 253.25
325.10 348.21 409.26
STRETCHER 109.24
STRETCHES 409.15
STRETCHING 338.18
410.23
STREWN 458.30
STRICKEN 131.21 167.15
191.21 317.03 464.17
STRICT 63.02 109.02
STRICTLY 79.05 259.10
383.01
STRIDE 212.21 287.26
454.28
STRIDES 371.21
STRIDING 372.15
STRIPE 41.28 331.22
422.25
STRIKE 34.29 54.20
123.13 301.14 389.24
460.23
STRIKES 60.14 85.02
280.21 455.28
STRIKING 173.01 315.19
392.30 401.19 405.13
410.12 417.07 417.18
STRING 16.18 63.10
102.26 224.17 225.01
287.10 458.02 473.10
STRINGS 27.09 307.11
STRINGY 279.09
STRIP 411.09 415.14
435.18 445.08
STRIPED 44.09 55.04
STRIPES 70.13 462.29
STRIPPED 88.17 336.17
STRIVING 106.12 222.16
STRODE 206.04
STROKE 4.22 7.05
7.06 21.17 73.16
250.15 269.14 291.20
457.03
STROKED 202.15
STROLL 339.25 375.08
STROLLED 54.05 311.03
459.11
STROLLING 375.27
468.03
STRONG 16.06 44.01
61.10 87.09 182.30
207.11 214.04 253.04
254.24 256.09 257.13
260.18 261.04 368.19
368.28 384.13 391.18
392.24 430.03 464.21
466.21 482.16
STRONGER 106.07
STRONGEST 122.14
STRONGHOLD 414.19
415.08 420.20 515.02
STRONGLY 79.04 193.21
248.15 266.19 450.24
STRUCK 71.22 73.03
98.09 141.26 146.30
159.10 166.05 167.20
170.22 172.18 188.22
218.25 219.26 226.06
233.15 235.06 245.18
257.18 275.22 276.04
283.24 291.02 304.24
312.13 316.18 337.28
342.29 350.28 362.21
388.12 396.03 401.16
460.13 465.23 502.23

STRUCK (CONT.) 503.05
505.26 509.13
STRUCTURE 443.15
STRUGGLE 116.17 117.07
128.01 384.12
STRUGGLED 293.03
426.08 469.19 484.30
512.21
STRUGGLES 97.22
103.25 162.04 397.29
STRUGGLING 216.06
299.12 309.07 515.03
STRUTTING 105.05
363.22
STUBBORN 84.03 90.05
128.02 184.07 281.25
301.07 305.03 327.18
327.20
STUBBORNLY 163.18
166.19 230.21
STUCK 100.25 119.25
158.06 159.04 165.09
237.14 425.12 498.21
STUCK-UP 425.12
STUDENT'S 246.15
STUDY 247.09 248.01
421.29
STUFF 10.19 28.14
29.12 52.02 169.03
197.04 200.30 201.01
203.14 213.04
STUFFED 238.26
STUFFS 318.06
STUFFY 170.22
STUMBLE 59.30
STUMBLED 36.13 83.24
132.11
STUMBLING 108.05
STUMP 325.09
STUMPING 288.22
STUMPS 397.08
STUNK 74.26
STUNNED 89.26 98.18
STUNNING 371.29
STUPID 24.09 51.15
61.03 67.12 96.06
106.16 164.05 300.15
308.08 376.10 427.01
STUPIDEST 78.11
STUPIDITY 90.14
207.09
STUPIDLY 188.08 364.28
STURDY 318.19
STUTTERED 219.25
STYLE 202.11 269.21
STYX 385.04
SUBDUE 345.10
SUBDUED 44.06 261.25
289.02 348.27 387.26
434.20 482.16 487.07
498.16
SUBDUING 327.17
SUBJECT 42.20 47.28
190.23 243.11 337.19
SUBJECTS 316.19
SUBJUGATION 156.22
SUBLIMATED 215.25
SUBLIMITIES 341.15
SUBMARINE 441.30
SUBMERGED 264.08
414.10
SUBMISSION 275.08
SUBMISSIVE 206.01
SUBMISSIVELY 372.19
SUBMIT 85.22 260.30
SUBMITTED 174.03
SUBSIDE 202.18
SUBSIDED 6.01 19.19
483.25
SUBSTANCE 51.09
260.07 302.09 341.13
SUBTLE 108.03 112.02
113.28 186.12 328.06
390.24 425.21 479.25
SUBTLETY 287.30
SUBTLY 356.11
SUCCADANA 345.13
SUCCEEDED 126.20
146.01 312.10 348.06
368.20 388.11 395.12

SUCCEEDED (CONT.)
399.13 416.23 463.19
464.19
SUCCEEDING 140.04
SUCCESS 23.13 114.01
215.15 268.25 276.05
324.02 328.17 334.21
340.24 364.14 382.29
425.03 499.27 514.30
515.23
SUCCESSES 175.10
276.05
SUCCESSFUL 251.20
336.09
SUCCESSFULLY 164.12
SUCCESSION 31.09
114.21 176.15
SUCCESSIVE 117.26
463.04
SUCCESSIVELY 3.17
SUCCESSORS 277.15
SUCH 4.01 8.13
12.08 14.22 18.04
23.11 34.13 48.19
52.09 52.09 54.24
58.21 60.12 61.03
61.29 65.01 65.07
67.30 68.27 68.28
69.25 75.08 79.24
80.12 81.07 90.27
97.01 98.27 102.09
112.15 114.22 119.27
123.15 123.22 156.14
156.15 156.16 160.15
165.19 172.19 189.05
190.06 190.10 190.16
191.06 194.18 196.23
199.07 209.22 210.29
211.02 212.01 214.10
215.07 218.25 228.22
231.20 233.06 236.27
238.06 243.06 243.24
244.07 247.02 252.19
253.28 260.20 272.07
272.08 272.30 274.06
276.04 276.13 277.09
277.10 281.07 281.13
282.15 285.03 285.08
286.15 286.27 288.25
291.27 295.17 297.18
300.09 308.07 310.05
310.21 322.10 328.03
328.18 334.29 336.13
336.20 336.21 339.09
344.25 345.21 345.24
346.01 356.11 357.03
376.03 378.25 389.18
390.22 392.02 392.03
399.12 400.26 403.17
419.28 423.23 425.15
432.13 456.05 457.05
458.20 460.17 461.02
466.15 483.03 505.20
506.18 507.25 515.23
SUCK 183.15
SUDDEN 70.05 92.22
103.15 116.14 116.15
138.09 139.20 183.14
216.29 220.10 251.15
264.04 290.12 315.29
334.12 380.11 385.22
420.15 428.13 460.14
493.28 504.18
SUDDENLY 2.28 3.10
7.07 14.24 21.21
30.14 30.25 34.14
43.06 55.13 61.17
63.29 64.13 70.02
71.27 83.16 86.11
89.03 89.06 90.29
99.26 100.26 104.07
108.06 119.10 120.17
122.13 122.18 123.13
128.04 129.24 133.29
139.28 140.27 141.06
142.08 142.17 146.03
152.05 157.19 160.25
168.25 174.04 177.17
179.22 187.19 189.12
202.23 204.26 205.03

SUDDENLY (CONT.) 210.04
210.24 216.14 217.16
219.16 224.10 224.19
231.25 232.14 235.11
238.26 244.28 255.04
256.30 257.05 257.26
258.07 261.09 288.12
289.03 312.16 314.05
330.14 334.02 342.19
350.21 359.07 362.12
364.20 365.20 372.05
374.06 375.09 387.14
390.28 393.13 404.18
405.23 408.28 412.12
415.18 419.24 433.04
433.16 436.24 439.17
439.25 452.24 456.26
459.07 481.12 485.04
495.26 502.16 506.02
509.30 511.22 512.12
514.04
SUDDENNESS 509.14
SUFFERANCE 41.19
SUFFERED 131.10 190.20
210.13 213.24
SUFFERING 15.27
98.07 100.27 138.05
184.04 192.04 212.13
262.30 485.23 486.11
SUFFERINGS 170.06
277.22
SUFFICIENTLY 45.18
137.17
SUFFUSED 224.07
SUGAR 44.09 200.12
201.01 502.02
SUGAR-CANE 201.01
SUGAR-HOGSHEAD 44.09
SUGAR-PLANTERS 200.12
SUGGEST 244.07
SUGGESTED 60.08
82.11 165.28 241.12
SUGGESTION 133.13
348.03 479.27
SUGGESTIONS 13.02
SUGGESTIVE 87.21
146.30 174.24
SUICIDE 69.14 77.03
SUIT 70.12 74.23
199.14 203.11 292.04
399.03
SUITABLE 68.06 233.10
247.22 403.22 404.02
404.07
SUITED 25.14 356.19
SUITS 37.15
SULKILY 463.30
SULKINESS 301.07
SULKY 25.17 99.06
482.02
SULLEN 48.08 390.27
452.10
SULTAN 247.16 277.27
278.01 345.13
SULTAN'S 278.23
SUN 358.22 383.24
404.15
SUMMED 91.12
SUMMIT 316.25 332.03
396.20 444.22
SUMMITS 269.12 269.27
322.30 497.06
SUMMONED 363.14 483.14
SUMPTUOUS 93.05
SUN 1.15 3.15
17.20 32.23 47.11
148.08 149.15 149.29
153.11 153.14 153.25
200.30 204.01 219.09
256.01 295.25 299.29
328.25 376.19 378.01
384.20 408.15 412.23
414.10 414.16 431.15
444.25 470.20 499.20
508.26 510.11 512.03
515.02
SUN-BLACKENED 470.20
SUNBURNT 37.07 52.05
89.05
SUNDA 442.18

SUNDAY 399.06
SUNK 98.13 159.14
174.22 376.21 409.18
415.14 480.08
SUNKEN 27.17 27.17
27.18 425.13 470.20
SUNLIGHT 302.01
SUNLIT 175.28 297.10
SUNNY 386.20
SUNRAYS 332.02
SUNRISE 43.13 146.29
149.11 149.27 328.13
SUNS 25.08
SUNSET 98.01 162.14
300.12 364.11 413.03
456.13
SUNSHINE 11.15 13.08
17.08 47.07 152.26
191.24 240.17 279.29
299.14 302.04 325.12
325.18 325.22 331.24
334.14 348.25 350.30
410.04 417.23 443.21
455.07
SUPERANNUATED 228.01
SUPERB 511.24
SUPERFICIAL 66.24
223.22
SUPERFLUOUS 274.19
SUPERHEATED 408.26
SUPERIOR 68.13 202.01
214.09 240.27 399.18
426.04
SUPERIORITY 26.18
501.16
SUPERIORS 271.03
SUPERNATURAL 87.16
327.02 447.11
SUPERSTITIOUS 438.20
SUPERVISION 451.15
SUPPLICATING 388.23
512.29
SUPPLY 58.03 203.18
203.26 356.21 440.05
453.08 455.05
SUPPORTABLE 174.15
215.10
SUPPORTERS 515.04
SUPPORTS 378.07
SUPPOSE 44.05 54.20
61.27 67.28 73.10
78.08 80.14 85.04
88.02 101.18 102.12
115.03 123.30 145.06
148.13 153.09 153.13
158.15 158.05 164.04
178.09 222.17 231.27
242.01 243.25 266.01
275.09 280.29 290.18
294.01 300.15 320.05
328.09 328.11 339.07
340.25 342.01 344.06
348.28 351.07 355.07
363.05 374.15 377.07
395.26 398.03 400.11
401.07 401.11 401.12
404.06 411.21 418.07
420.07 471.18 474.04
477.20 481.06 495.04
SUPPOSED 75.01 80.21
90.28 214.30 290.24
379.27 435.13 454.19
459.16
SUPREME 203.21 312.23
419.18 434.21
SURA 327.13 327.15
SURE 8.30 29.01
29.02 41.22 43.08
46.10 82.04 88.05
98.23 99.15 128.27
144.07 151.12 157.20
157.21 168.10 178.28
183.20 204.19 204.25
211.19 219.02 219.21
228.17 245.22 256.22
264.12 303.10 317.04
331.06 341.21 342.04
343.22 350.08 352.15
353.05 357.10 379.07
391.28 412.08 415.03

SURE (CONT.) 442.04
445.19 453.26 462.02
467.24 467.25 474.05
SURELY 156.08 204.09
506.22
299.08
SURFACE 19.18 22.27
22.28 22.29 24.29
26.05 31.12 69.13
156.12 168.04 263.08
271.17 398.15 407.18
409.29 501.22
SURFACE-CONDENSING
26.05
SURFACES 322.11
SURGE 131.14
SURGED 36.02
SURGEONS 64.17
SURGING 294.22 500.26
SURLIEST 70.08
SURLILY 137.19 363.07
495.17
SURLINESS 434.19
SURLY 349.18 399.18
408.03 434.18
SURMISING 123.17
SURPASSING 405.21
SURPRISE 57.21 77.30
132.13 202.28 281.26
332.06 343.06 359.20
442.30 460.11 500.20
SURPRISED 45.06
100.05 109.25 153.02
208.08 258.02 321.29
395.23 413.24 428.01
441.01
SURRENDER 480.22
480.23 516.14
SURRENDERED 20.03
SURREPTITIOUS 29.03
SURROUND 24.24
SURROUNDED 188.02
252.09 262.16 320.01
370.13
SURROUNDING 4.29
SURROUNDINGS 16.03
99.10 214.05 264.22
328.06 334.30
SURVEYED 87.15 223.11
SURVEYING 103.17
SURVIVE 50.16 50.16
50.16 450.30
SURVIVED 166.20 302.14
418.09
SURVIVORS 502.04
503.02
SUSCEPTIBILITIES 85.20
SUSPECT 50.09 79.04
96.02 106.01 146.27
209.25 266.17 267.12
268.08 341.18 398.12
SUSPECTED 50.08
114.10 191.06 400.21
419.20
SUSPENDED 116.08
185.01 402.11 407.12
433.03
SUSPICION 215.22
316.09 495.14
SUSPICIONS 508.24
SUSPICIOUS 298.24
360.11 408.03
SUSTAINED 64.03
216.16 318.21
SWAGGER 71.01 395.29
396.05
SWALLOW 158.16 237.13
SWALLOWED 189.19
279.07 399.03
SWALLOWING 123.06
132.22 287.02
SWAN 164.24 439.08
503.16
SWAMPED 8.05 105.28
SWAMPY 297.06
SWARM 25.07 446.06
SWARMING 445.12
SWAY 21.26 28.02
SWAYED 37.09 112.22

SWAYED (CONT.) 133.12
180.21 366.10 380.14
391.17 432.06 509.03
SWAYING 125.28 192.15
373.14 430.03 463.01
500.26 515.04
SWEAR 42.18 99.21
104.26 158.21
SWEARING 128.04 151.20
466.29
SWEAT 16.05 25.19
124.08 438.17
SWEAT-RAG 25.19
SWEATED 24.13 325.04
SWEATING 115.14
SWEEP 11.16 302.20
319.15 374.10 420.11
SWEEPERS 44.17
SWEEPING 220.14 263.07
SWEEPS 495.29 498.14
SWEET 48.18 143.18
395.30 396.04 404.22
404.05
SWEET-POTATOES 442.05
SWEETLY 26.30
SWELL 123.11 123.21
128.23 131.18 201.07
SWELTERED 408.25
SWEPT 20.17 62.19
134.04 136.09 137.05
166.29 214.30 363.18
480.04 508.15
SWERVED 313.20
SWIFT 116.15 116.22
156.22 328.28 341.26
409.30
SWIFTLY 6.28 35.08
150.25 165.25 177.27
222.10 293.06 348.06
367.08 371.09 380.13
418.02 511.26
SWIM 63.27 73.16
138.11 156.10 242.09
SWIMMER 220.22
SWIMMING 5.11
SWINDLE 200.19
SWINDLER 361.25
SWING 111.10 116.14
126.23 274.03 291.20
SWINGING 131.14 495.19
SWIRL 220.19
SWIRLING 498.10
SWIRLS 19.15
SWISH 261.08 261.08
373.15
SWISH-SWISH 261.08
SWISHED 217.24 466.09
SWITCH 481.02
SWITCHING 480.03
SWITZERLAND 241.06
SWIVEL 132.06
SWOLLEN 54.15 217.17
273.17
SWOLLEN-FACED 273.17
SWORD 21.14 116.10
184.30 423.18 423.18
SHORE 8.07 35.04
48.07 116.04 382.08
386.30 387.01
SWORN 387.15
SWUM 503.03
SWUNG 16.23 21.11
56.17 102.17 166.06
166.18 181.25 205.06
241.08 294.22 300.25
369.28 394.01 414.03
SYDNEY 167.24 182.05
SYMBOLIC 162.07 325.29
SYMONS 6.21 8.04
8.05 8.09
SYMPATHETIC 44.30
258.19 334.09
SYMPATHETICALLY 7.15
259.16
SYMPATHIES 93.16
186.02
SYMPATHISED 355.03
SYMPATHY 313.07 321.24
322.17 357.03
SYMPTOM 85.10

SYSTEM 28.08
T 63.02 64.22
TABLE 22.25 48.27
58.18 76.09 94.07
104.21 125.30 139.10
142.26 145.27 168.23
170.20 175.15 180.11
209.11 216.29 229.14
229.25 234.28 236.01
240.22 243.01 263.08
278.18 291.05 291.23
362.22 364.21 364.26
364.29 429.28 448.26
485.15 506.20
TABLECLOTH 93.29
TABLEFUL 93.01
TABLES 94.10 249.03
TABLETS 248.21
TACITURN 222.06 338.30
434.18
TACKED 4.13 295.03
TACKLED 184.07
TACT 242.28
TACTICS 462.14
TAFFRAIL 21.16 73.06
TAFFRAIL-LOG 73.06
TAGALS 439.15
TAIL 167.17 331.09
TAILOR 307.18
TAILS 181.28
TAIN'T 30.07
TAINTING 352.22
TAKE 29.18 49.11
49.12 65.09 74.07
76.05 77.03 103.02
104.04 107.04 113.20
114.11 128.30 129.10
147.20 152.27 163.25
164.26 179.11 185.06
189.01 193.24 197.16
200.07 200.22 203.16
203.20 210.22 212.07
218.29 223.24 233.21
255.25 274.05 286.30
290.16 291.05 291.23
294.05 295.12 295.13
308.24 310.19 331.11
352.07 356.22 373.21
375.01 381.18 390.16
402.22 403.06 412.04
413.13 419.14 427.11
428.28 451.02 461.28
465.08 465.09 471.20
480.24 488.24 493.13
TAKEN 44.12 53.07
56.03 98.27 115.06
142.12 176.15 189.09
199.25 225.13 249.21
273.15 274.23 298.22
314.22 316.07 323.19
350.13 421.23 422.29
514.15
TAKES 56.20 197.09
241.01 243.30
TAKING 8.24 11.18
51.09 64.20 76.10
84.23 112.06 168.19
177.20 180.08 189.06
203.07 210.24 211.05
214.14 260.01 300.22
308.23 329.27 333.09
374.11 427.30 434.13
438.25 439.01 440.04
459.28 462.05 463.17
483.16 488.29
TAKINGS 320.09
TALCAHUANO 52.24
TALE 25.20 47.27
98.26 132.24 198.21
276.03 344.08 427.15
436.28 437.21 505.15
TALENTS 56.07
TALES 306.22
TALISMAN 514.28
TALK 41.13 41.14
41.14 72.06 81.14
83.16 95.22 116.01
128.17 131.25 151.21
152.04 152.05 156.18
158.22 160.03 167.17

TALK (CONT.) 168.03
178.03 195.23 201.11
204.13 222.07 235.01
251.11 254.15 262.27
266.09 267.22 291.03
297.23 331.08 348.11
350.17 357.14 363.14
377.03 383.16 401.24
425.08 427.25 429.14
452.29 453.03 468.02
468.05 471.26 472.05
472.15 472.23 474.07
475.10 479.25 481.09
482.21 483.15 485.12
492.27 492.29 498.17
TALKATIVE 28.15
140.04 168.14 298.08
TALKED 14.09 42.09
93.18 140.12 151.27
151.28 158.26 199.30
222.05 254.14 289.15
297.21 427.10 435.16
455.12 505.30
TALKING 35.29 46.30
78.16 82.30 96.11
133.28 142.18 179.03
213.06 231.25 234.22
253.21 262.23 328.04
344.27 348.01 350.19
388.11 422.05 426.29
457.22 494.08 499.18
511.17
TALKS 178.10 178.10
379.30
TALL 94.14 175.29
246.19 260.06 346.02
399.02 428.17 433.27
445.04 468.16 472.15
TAM' 49.10 49.11
TAMATAVE 441.20
TAMB' 332.21 349.12
349.17 350.10 378.05
378.08 399.17 401.20
408.03 428.05 428.10
428.25 434.14 434.19
482.09 483.01 483.09
483.15 485.13 487.01
489.01 489.12 489.17
489.21 490.16 490.18
490.24 490.29 491.05
491.12 491.13 497.16
498.01 498.23 499.01
499.05 499.09 499.14
499.18 500.20 501.03
501.10 501.23 502.13
502.19 502.21 502.29
503.19 504.01 504.11
504.12 504.16 504.23
505.02 505.08 505.09
505.15 505.18 505.23
506.04 506.09 506.24
507.11 507.13 507.15
507.18 507.20 509.11
510.18 510.23 511.17
511.24 512.06 512.12
512.16 512.19 512.23
512.25 513.03 513.07
TAMIL 12.23 56.05
TAN 424.11
TAN-AND-PINK 424.11
TANGIBLE 35.16 370.15
447.12
TANGLE 397.04
TANGLED 307.11
TANK 14.29
TANKS 203.20
TANNED 175.05
TAP 72.11 72.11
125.13 125.13
TAPPED 37.28 110.06
TAPPING 66.20 142.30
TARNISHED 168.17
175.05
TARRY 502.29
TASK 10.08 321.13
389.18 391.30 418.13
TASKMASTER 115.30
477.14
TASTE 36.30
TASTE- 36.30
TASTED 73.29

TATTOOED 332.18
TAUGHT 348.14
TAXED 89.30
TEA 42.13
TEACH 7.16 458.05
TEAK 240.16 241.14
TEAR 11.10 183.11
216.25 353.09 391.05
431.18 456.22 457.24
TEARING 327.06 425.17
515.29
TEARS 58.14 70.09
89.12 191.22 224.02
358.29 379.16 386.07
430.26 431.17 475.26
487.24
TEASPOON 121.01
TEEMING 127.26 381.12
TEETH 75.09 137.09
137.15 140.22 218.18
220.01 293.10 347.08
369.20 378.22 439.14
459.25
TELEGRAPH 347.09
TELESCOPE 64.08
232.27 234.29
TELL 26.11 32.02
34.17 36.16 41.07
45.29 48.01 49.05
53.12 53.18 54.01
56.20 61.28 62.07
70.09 70.31 73.05
77.02 79.26 87.10
87.12 87.14 89.18
93.22 95.06 101.10
104.02 105.25 107.04
111.18 111.18 114.08
116.28 141.10 141.10
143.19 150.17 152.01
154.16 160.06 160.17
164.02 176.02 183.23
186.19 187.15 188.19
190.23 197.26 200.13
200.29 201.23 202.29
214.24 231.29 233.16
235.03 236.28 237.24
238.05 258.01 260.16
260.29 261.06 273.26
274.07 274.17 286.18
301.23 315.01 330.12
339.17 340.03 342.22
344.03 344.08 344.10
349.04 353.02 355.11
357.28 374.14 374.30
374.30 375.12 377.03
377.22 378.13 388.16
388.27 389.07 392.08
393.05 398.20 413.09
413.17 414.07 414.09
419.24 424.04 429.15
460.23 468.15 471.11
474.03 478.25 491.02
492.06 499.04 507.02
TELLING 8.08 104.01
114.06 121.13 129.13
132.08 168.26 170.14
202.25 254.15 274.09
275.13 306.23 334.25
359.26 367.20 388.13
388.14 389.19 418.09
431.23 460.20 475.27
476.05
TELLS 53.12 366.26
421.19 512.06
TEMPER 10.19 13.20
190.11 243.10 436.06
449.02
TEMPERAMENT 292.09
322.04
TEMPERED 215.04 228.03
TEMPLE 37.11 171.15
TEMPLES 27.18 417.15
TEMPORARY 229.29
TEMPTATION 339.13
422.10
TEMPTATIONS 50.28
TEMPTED 37.27 105.20
450.27
TEN 26.27 28.19
63.27 70.26 70.42

TEN (CONT.) 75.29
98.16 182.29 225.07
233.25 254.05 256.16
342.14 353.05 401.19
442.24 451.03 490.12
TENACITY 322.01
TENDED 448.02
TENDER 350.22 384.13
TENDERNESS 20.02
271.19 305.09 339.15
348.17 374.18
TENEBROUS 123.10
TENNIS 229.22
TENNIS-PARTIES 229.22
TENSE 146.01 154.14
TENSELY 63.09
TENTACLE 61.18
TENTH 371.20
TERMS 185.05 214.11
215.29 223.26
TERRESTRIAL 341.11
TERRIBLE 32.22 103.09
260.25 356.09 432.30
433.01 433.21 473.01
506.06
TERRIBLY 32.19 97.26
147.27 216.07 218.13
228.17
TERRIFIC 372.07
TERRIFIED 57.03
136.22 136.24
TERRIFY 436.14 478.21
TERRIFYING 423.14
442.30
TERROR 8.23 54.28
59.08 60.09 61.06
102.09 126.12 138.03
197.27 206.01 313.18
364.08 435.16 438.20
460.23 460.23 460.23
TERRORS 11.30 51.03
77.01 106.01 147.30
194.20 298.18
TESSELLATED 121.01
TEST 419.19
TESTED 10.17
TESTIFY 502.07
TESTIFYING 68.23
TESTIMONY 118.01
215.13 487.17
TEXT 307.15
TFUI 43.27
THAN 7.25 8.29
10.12 14.19 14.29
25.29 26.10 26.23
29.04 31.02 31.03
34.06 43.09 46.25
49.05 50.04 50.12
52.11 53.30 54.06
56.19 59.14 59.27
62.11 63.27 69.08
69.30 70.40 71.11
75.14 76.03 76.10
80.30 81.28 82.07
82.14 88.19 89.01
92.03 96.11 100.06
110.05 110.30 111.01
113.18 115.04 118.15
121.14 125.20 126.20
132.16 135.05 146.14
150.25 157.12 158.15
159.08 162.11 165.07
169.04 170.21 173.06
174.09 176.17 176.30
178.12 179.28 182.02
184.12 186.07 188.08
193.13 194.28 196.28
197.23 202.16 204.12
208.10 218.05 225.28
227.02 227.09 227.16
228.14 228.20 231.04
236.10 236.25 239.05
243.13 245.21 247.16
262.19 267.11 267.11
268.21 270.09 270.14
273.11 273.25 274.07
282.11 283.02 286.19
288.08 291.07 293.13
294.29 298.24 299.05
303.22 306.09 308.17

THAN (CONT.)		312.02	THAT (CONT.)		70.18	THAT (CONT.)		151.19	THAT (CONT.)		238.15
313.09	313.14	315.25	70.44	71.05	71.19	153.07	153.13	153.17	238.19	238.20	238.23
316.15	327.20	330.05	71.30	72.09	72.14	153.26	153.27	154.02	239.13	239.14	239.19
336.14	337.05	341.01	73.15	73.25	74.01	154.08	155.05	155.10	240.04	240.05	240.28
344.20	345.04	345.19	74.02	74.06	74.19	155.24	156.09	156.12	240.29	240.30	241.08
347.03	349.30	352.25	74.27	74.30	75.07	156.15	156.17	156.18	241.10	241.22	241.24
357.18	359.16	360.03	75.24	76.11	76.23	156.26	156.28	156.30	242.08	242.09	242.22
364.17	374.21	374.30	76.26	76.29	77.10	157.01	157.04	157.07	243.03	243.10	243.22
379.01	382.25	386.09	77.17	77.26	78.04	157.22	157.25	158.01	243.23	243.25	243.26
386.09	386.11	388.03	78.12	78.18	78.21	158.10	159.02	159.16	244.06	244.16	244.17
390.13	396.26	399.24	78.23	78.24	78.26	159.29	160.02	160.11	245.04	245.10	245.12
399.28	400.08	403.04	78.30	79.07	79.20	160.19	160.19	162.11	245.20	245.22	246.13
406.07	415.15	416.13	79.22	80.06	80.11	162.17	163.11	163.18	246.17	246.27	247.01
418.29	419.08	419.30	80.17	80.19	81.03	163.25	164.02	164.10	248.09	249.30	250.12
430.26	431.19	435.10	81.06	81.07	81.14	165.02	165.09	166.10	251.11	251.23	251.30
438.05	439.30	442.11	81.27	81.29	82.01	166.11	166.13	166.30	253.02	253.16	255.09
442.17	447.05	448.30	82.02	82.02	82.14	167.10	167.14	168.11	256.25	256.27	257.11
452.16	453.10	454.06	82.18	82.24	83.07	168.21	168.27	169.14	257.24	258.02	259.01
465.16	467.29	473.17	83.23	83.27	84.15	169.17	169.19	169.23	259.15	260.09	260.18
474.06	477.01	477.05	84.20	85.05	85.06	169.29	170.14	171.19	260.21	260.26	261.07
481.23	484.07	487.10	85.27	86.10	86.14	171.19	171.22	171.26	261.15	261.18	261.20
489.11	495.05	512.10	86.19	87.15	87.24	172.02	172.30	173.08	261.27	262.11	262.12
THANK	76.21	117.11	88.10	88.17	88.21	173.10	173.16	173.18	262.18	262.27	263.19
152.23	205.10	217.21	88.30	89.16	89.23	173.20	174.13	174.14	263.23	263.24	263.27
228.05			90.12	90.19	90.27	175.08	176.05	177.03	264.21	265.02	265.04
THANKED	291.10		90.28	91.04	92.02	177.09	177.22	177.29	265.09	265.09	266.06
THANKFUL	137.24		92.14	93.19	93.27	178.01	178.08	178.23	267.01	267.23	268.05
THANKS	219.19	282.09	95.02	95.04	95.08	178.26	179.23	180.01	268.06	268.09	268.20
386.19			95.10	95.13	95.23	180.18	180.22	180.23	268.23	269.09	269.04
THAT	2.03	2.11	95.28	96.06	96.13	180.25	180.28	180.28	270.01	270.02	270.04
3.06	3.14	5.29	96.15	96.26	96.27	181.09	182.01	182.03	270.06	270.10	270.21
6.01	6.11	7.02	96.29	97.01	97.04	182.16	182.23	183.07	270.22	270.25	271.01
7.12	7.27	8.08	97.29	97.30	98.09	183.08	183.11	183.23	271.09	271.20	272.10
8.19	9.05	10.08	98.14	98.17	98.23	183.29	184.02	184.10	272.15	272.22	272.25
10.17	10.19	10.23	99.05	99.13	99.19	184.20	186.01	186.04	273.09	273.15	273.26
11.01	11.04	11.05	100.02	100.04	100.23	186.16	186.18	187.02	274.07	274.13	274.17
11.07	11.10	11.14	101.16	101.18	101.20	187.11	187.19	189.02	274.22	274.26	275.01
13.06	13.25	14.13	101.30	102.05	102.07	189.10	189.17	190.06	275.14	275.20	277.01
14.18	16.16	16.27	102.11	102.18	102.21	190.18	191.03	191.16	277.08	277.14	278.15
17.08	17.11	17.14	102.24	103.02	103.04	192.04	193.18	193.20	278.16	279.15	279.29
17.17	19.17	19.24	103.07	103.11	103.13	193.22	193.22	193.27	279.30	280.12	280.17
22.22	23.21	24.01	104.03	104.25	105.07	194.09	194.10	194.12	280.21	281.09	281.11
24.22	24.24	24.25	105.18	106.04	106.10	194.14	194.15	194.21	281.12	281.23	281.29
24.26	24.26	25.04	107.09	107.10	107.12	196.27	196.29	197.01	282.04	282.14	282.15
25.16	26.08	27.11	107.14	107.20	107.23	197.12	197.26	197.28	282.16	282.18	282.27
27.26	28.01	28.10	108.22	109.15	109.26	198.11	198.12	198.18	283.01	283.07	283.12
28.11	28.20	29.08	110.18	111.05	111.07	198.21	198.22	198.28	283.18	283.25	284.02
29.12	29.20	29.28	111.08	111.10	111.13	199.28	200.30	201.01	285.12	285.17	285.19
29.29	30.30	32.19	111.21	112.09	112.09	201.13	202.06	202.10	285.24	286.11	286.14
32.24	33.01	34.02	112.16	112.19	114.06	202.10	202.11	202.13	287.12	287.17	287.19
34.05	34.22	35.13	114.12	114.16	114.30	202.25	202.27	203.01	287.23	287.26	288.03
35.20	35.21	35.24	115.03	115.10	115.14	203.03	203.10	204.07	288.14	288.18	288.27
36.02	36.05	36.17	115.16	115.20	115.22	204.30	205.09	205.14	289.09	289.24	290.15
36.23	36.23	37.15	115.24	115.29	116.21	205.24	206.02	207.10	291.20	291.25	291.26
37.25	38.07	38.13	117.11	117.19	117.21	208.09	208.27	209.07	291.27	293.10	293.28
38.17	38.18	40.05	118.25	119.01	119.06	209.17	209.21	209.22	294.01	294.26	294.30
40.11	40.16	41.12	119.07	119.17	119.23	209.25	209.26	210.14	294.30	296.03	298.03
41.18	42.01	42.02	119.25	120.25	120.30	210.17	210.25	211.03	298.04	298.05	298.06
42.04	42.29	43.05	121.07	121.11	122.08	211.10	211.12	211.22	298.16	298.20	298.21
43.12	43.16	43.40	122.11	123.02	123.17	211.23	211.27	211.28	298.22	298.30	299.19
44.12	44.14	44.20	123.21	124.02	124.07	212.05	212.12	213.07	299.20	299.27	300.03
44.23	44.24	44.27	124.11	124.12	124.26	213.18	214.01	214.03	301.01	301.03	301.09
44.28	45.05	45.14	125.18	125.21	125.22	214.06	214.07	214.10	301.13	301.15	301.23
45.17	45.17	46.05	125.26	126.13	126.30	214.16	214.22	214.24	301.24	301.26	302.18
46.11	46.21	47.17	127.01	127.18	127.21	215.10	215.11	215.17	302.29	302.30	303.04
47.27	47.29	48.04	127.28	127.29	128.09	215.17	215.19	215.20	303.09	303.09	303.15
48.16	48.17	48.21	128.16	128.22	128.25	216.07	218.14	218.25	303.24	303.24	303.28
49.04	49.06	49.08	129.01	129.10	129.13	218.25	218.27	218.28	304.10	304.15	304.21
49.17	49.18	49.19	129.22	129.28	130.02	219.06	219.07	219.14	304.27	305.04	305.05
49.23	50.10	50.28	131.01	131.02	131.13	219.15	219.17	220.15	305.06	306.13	306.16
51.10	51.14	51.16	131.19	131.23	132.15	220.18	222.02	222.06	307.09	307.15	307.19
51.30	52.04	52.14	132.17	133.17	133.17	222.09	222.13	222.20	308.18	308.26	309.10
53.12	53.17	53.20	133.19	136.05	136.18	223.02	223.03	223.26	309.16	310.27	311.02
53.23	54.08	54.24	136.18	136.24	137.02	223.30	224.16	225.08	311.14	311.26	311.29
55.02	55.04	55.05	138.01	138.04	138.05	225.08	225.09	225.11	312.15	312.20	312.21
55.08	55.27	55.30	138.10	138.10	138.17	226.14	226.24	226.25	312.28	312.29	312.30
56.03	56.30	57.06	138.23	139.07	139.08	227.05	227.11	227.15	313.11	313.23	315.21
57.10	57.16	57.19	139.25	139.25	140.01	227.16	228.06	228.17	315.24	315.30	315.30
57.29	58.08	59.07	140.12	140.16	140.18	228.23	228.24	229.04	316.06	318.13	319.02
59.10	59.21	59.23	141.03	141.14	141.22	229.18	229.21	229.27	320.26	320.28	320.29
59.30	60.04	60.05	141.25	142.02	142.03	229.28	230.12	230.16	321.04	321.07	321.07
50.11	60.14	60.16	142.19	143.02	143.07	230.28	231.10	231.20	321.11	321.25	321.27
61.23	62.24	62.28	144.06	144.07	144.13	231.24	232.10	232.20	321.29	322.24	323.19
63.21	63.23	63.26	144.15	144.16	144.17	232.29	233.10	233.11	323.21	324.08	324.20
64.15	64.21	64.23	144.20	144.24	144.30	233.22	233.23	234.12	325.23	325.27	325.28
64.25	64.30	65.17	146.16	146.20	147.05	234.14	234.30	235.03	326.03	327.05	327.23
66.13	67.02	67.02	147.15	147.23	147.25	235.04	235.29	236.07	328.17	328.19	329.14
67.29	68.02	68.11	147.26	148.14	148.18	236.25	237.08	237.11	329.18	330.06	330.07
68.30	69.21	69.24	149.11	149.12	149.24	237.14	237.15	237.23	330.20	330.29	331.10
69.27	70.01	70.10	149.27	150.06	150.27	237.27	238.01	238.09	331.30	332.09	333.12

THAT (CONT.)		333.14	THAT (CONT.)		435.06	THAT'S (CONT.)		217.05	THE (CONT.)		13.04
333.21	333.28	334.30	435.12	435.16	435.23	219.29	220.05	222.23	13.05	13.05	13.06
335.15	336.09	336.13	436.04	436.28	437.06	223.29	224.29	231.19	13.07	13.07	13.10
337.20	337.22	337.23	437.07	437.21	437.25	233.13	235.17	236.12	13.10	13.11	13.11
337.25	338.10	338.19	437.27	438.12	438.13	237.10	237.29	238.10	13.12	13.12	13.14
338.29	339.02	339.07	439.08	441.06	441.27	273.12	280.14	284.03	13.16	13.17	13.20
340.04	340.16	340.21	442.01	442.16	443.11	290.01	303.20	308.26	13.20	13.23	13.23
341.05	341.07	341.21	443.23	443.29	444.11	309.13	330.01	330.07	13.24	13.26	13.29
341.21	342.02	342.06	444.20	445.10	446.04	344.05	344.17	371.22	13.30	14.01	14.03
342.30	343.01	343.06	446.05	447.01	447.06	376.16	394.01	401.10	14.04	14.06	14.07
344.18	344.25	344.28	447.23	448.12	448.13	455.19	466.30	469.06	14.08	14.11	14.13
345.11	345.14	345.19	448.24	449.04	449.08	473.06	474.15	481.05	14.15	14.16	14.16
345.28	347.06	347.12	449.14	450.14	450.23	495.21	515.19		14.21	14.23	14.25
347.15	347.18	348.19	450.27	451.05	451.07	THATCH	280.01	359.06	14.26	14.27	14.27
348.20	348.23	348.28	451.18	451.21	451.27	366.15			15.03	15.12	15.16
349.01	350.10	350.14	452.24	453.04	453.22	THATN	48.25	50.03	15.17	15.18	15.18
351.04	351.14	351.21	454.01	454.15	454.19	THE	1.03	1.11	15.20	15.23	15.24
351.28	352.06	352.07	454.30	456.09	456.25	1.15	1.16	1.20	15.24	15.25	15.25
352.08	352.18	352.26	457.07	457.07	457.09	1.20	2.06	2.11	15.29	15.30	16.01
353.10	353.15	353.25	457.20	458.04	458.08	2.13	2.14	2.14	16.02	16.03	16.04
353.27	354.05	355.01	458.11	458.16	458.24	2.15	2.15	2.17	16.06	16.06	16.07
355.04	356.07	356.14	458.27	458.29	459.16	2.17	2.18	2.19	16.10	16.12	16.14
356.19	356.27	357.10	460.04	460.06	460.10	2.21	2.22	2.23	16.16	16.19	16.20
357.13	357.14	357.16	460.12	460.14	460.18	2.26	2.28	2.29	16.22	16.23	16.25
357.17	357.19	357.21	460.29	461.10	461.19	3.03	3.03	3.04	16.25	16.26	16.26
357.28	359.01	359.02	461.21	462.03	463.08	3.09	3.09	3.10	16.28	16.29	16.29
359.09	359.09	359.25	463.13	463.14	463.23	3.10	3.13	3.13	16.29	16.30	16.30
359.30	360.03	360.22	464.01	465.01	465.12	3.15	3.16	3.17	17.04	17.04	17.05
361.14	361.27	362.09	465.16	465.21	465.26	3.20	3.21	3.23	17.06	17.09	17.10
362.15	362.16	362.20	465.29	466.15	467.26	3.23	3.23	3.25	17.11	17.14	17.16
363.17	364.06	364.14	468.13	468.16	468.18	4.01	4.02	4.03	17.16	17.18	17.19
365.02	365.09	367.02	469.14	469.20	470.09	4.04	4.05	4.07	17.20	17.21	17.21
367.06	368.29	369.05	470.15	470.23	471.16	4.08	4.08	4.09	17.22	17.23	17.24
369.07	369.10	369.11	471.19	471.26	471.26	4.09	4.10	4.11	17.25	17.25	17.26
369.13	369.15	370.10	472.02	472.18	472.25	4.12	4.12	4.13	17.27	17.28	17.29
370.11	370.14	370.16	472.25	473.03	473.14	4.14	4.16	4.18	17.30	17.30	18.02
371.02	371.07	371.28	474.08	474.12	474.20	4.21	4.22	4.24	18.03	18.04	18.04
372.01	372.11	373.03	474.22	475.04	476.07	4.25	4.26	4.26	18.05	18.06	18.06
374.17	374.21	374.25	476.08	477.02	477.15	4.27	4.28	4.28	18.07	18.11	19.01
375.03	375.05	375.14	477.19	477.22	478.02	4.29	4.29	5.02	19.02	19.02	19.04
375.16	376.06	377.12	478.06	478.17	478.17	5.02	5.03	5.03	19.04	19.05	19.05
377.14	378.27	378.30	478.18	478.22	478.30	5.04	5.05	5.05	19.07	19.08	19.09
379.07	379.09	379.14	479.04	479.12	479.21	5.05	5.06	5.07	19.10	19.11	19.12
379.23	380.01	380.09	479.23	479.28	480.14	5.07	5.09	5.16	19.13	19.17	19.18
381.10	381.13	381.14	480.26	481.23	481.27	5.16	5.17	5.21	19.18	19.19	19.20
381.17	382.11	382.18	482.14	482.16	483.03	5.22	5.24	5.26	19.21	19.21	19.23
382.19	382.23	382.29	483.07	483.18	483.24	5.25	5.27	5.27	19.23	20.01	20.01
382.30	383.03	383.16	484.06	484.18	484.27	5.28	5.30	5.30	20.02	20.03	20.04
383.27	384.01	384.04	485.08	485.25	485.27	6.02	6.02	6.03	20.05	20.06	20.06
384.30	384.30	385.03	485.30	486.02	486.06	6.03	6.04	6.04	20.08	20.11	20.11
385.24	386.14	386.18	486.12	487.09	487.13	6.05	6.07	6.08	20.12	20.12	20.12
387.02	387.09	387.12	487.17	487.21	487.22	6.09	6.10	6.10	20.12	20.13	20.15
387.21	389.16	389.22	487.23	488.08	488.10	6.11	6.15	6.18	20.16	20.16	20.17
389.24	391.02	391.05	488.19	488.21	488.26	6.18	6.19	6.20	20.17	20.19	20.20
391.20	391.24	391.24	489.05	489.19	489.27	6.22	6.23	6.26	20.21	20.22	20.26
391.25	391.28	392.07	490.06	490.07	490.09	6.27	6.28	6.29	20.26	20.28	20.30
392.09	392.15	392.16	491.02	491.04	492.21	6.30	7.01	7.01	21.02	21.08	21.08
392.25	393.03	395.01	492.23	492.27	493.05	7.02	7.04	7.08	21.12	21.13	21.15
395.08	395.09	396.23	493.10	493.19	493.24	7.09	7.11	7.11	21.15	21.16	21.18
397.02	397.21	398.02	493.27	494.01	494.17	7.12	7.14	7.14	21.19	21.21	21.21
398.04	398.06	398.16	495.21	495.23	497.06	7.17	7.20	7.20	21.21	21.22	21.23
398.19	398.19	398.28	497.13	499.24	500.15	7.21	7.24	7.27	21.24	21.25	21.25
399.04	399.05	400.05	500.21	500.24	501.03	7.28	7.29	7.29	21.27	21.28	21.28
401.01	401.12	403.08	501.15	502.01	502.07	8.02	8.04	8.05	21.29	21.30	22.01
403.18	403.25	403.29	502.09	503.04	503.05	8.07	8.09	8.10	22.02	22.03	22.03
404.16	405.11	405.21	503.10	503.13	503.14	8.11	8.11	8.17	22.04	22.04	22.05
405.27	408.08	408.18	503.15	505.10	505.21	8.17	8.21	8.23	22.05	22.05	22.06
409.09	409.22	410.14	506.16	506.16	506.19	8.27	8.28	8.29	22.07	22.08	22.10
411.11	411.12	411.15	506.22	507.07	508.15	9.01	9.05	9.06	22.11	22.11	22.14
411.16	411.17	411.18	509.16	509.29	510.04	10.02	10.05	10.06	22.14	22.15	22.16
411.30	412.04	412.08	510.27	511.11	511.12	10.07	10.07	10.07	22.16	22.17	22.19
412.19	412.21	413.16	511.17	512.06	512.06	10.08	10.09	10.09	22.19	22.20	22.21
414.11	414.16	414.18	512.08	512.08	512.20	10.12	10.17	10.18	22.22	22.25	22.26
415.11	415.16	416.06	513.04	514.07	514.26	10.18	10.18	10.19	22.26	22.26	22.27
418.09	418.15	418.17	514.28	514.29	515.01	10.20	10.20	10.23	22.29	22.30	23.01
418.20	418.20	418.30	515.16	515.24	515.26	10.24	10.24	10.24	23.02	23.03	23.04
419.05	419.14	419.16	516.19			11.02	11.04	11.06	23.04	23.04	23.05
419.18	419.18	419.22	THAT'LL	233.17		11.06	11.11	11.14	23.05	23.06	23.07
419.26	419.30	420.02	THAT'S	26.24	49.09	11.15	11.15	11.16	23.08	23.13	23.14
421.04	421.05	421.08	49.28	61.21	63.22	11.17	11.19	11.24	23.16	23.19	23.21
421.19	422.10	422.20	67.18	70.29	73.13	11.25	11.26	11.27	23.23	23.23	23.24
422.24	422.27	423.11	75.25	80.03	80.15	11.28	11.29	11.29	23.24	23.25	23.25
423.15	423.20	423.23	85.24	85.27	91.12	11.30	12.01	12.03	23.25	23.27	23.28
424.01	424.08	425.11	105.24	109.06	110.12	12.07	12.07	12.08	23.29	24.01	24.04
426.03	426.06	426.22	113.12	128.18	129.17	12.12	12.13	12.16	24.08	24.08	24.10
426.24	427.14	427.17	134.25	136.15	136.23	12.17	12.21	12.24	24.11	24.15	24.16
427.23	428.08	429.11	158.15	163.06	177.03	12.26	12.27	12.28	24.15	24.18	24.19
429.23	430.20	430.23	197.19	197.28	198.03	12.29	12.30	12.30	24.20	24.22	24.23
430.25	430.28	433.04	198.20	199.03	200.14	12.30	12.30	13.01	24.24	24.25	24.25
433.30	434.04	434.06	202.28	203.27	208.13	13.01	13.03	13.04	24.26	24.27	24.27

THE (CONT.)		24.28	THE (CONT.)		42.01	THE (CONT.)		59.28	THE (CONT.)		77.25
24.29	24.29	24.29	42.03	42.03	42.08	59.28	59.29	59.30	77.27	77.27	77.27
24.30	25.01	25.01	42.09	42.11	42.12	60.02	60.07	60.08	77.28	77.29	78.03
25.01	25.02	25.02	42.12	42.13	42.15	60.12	60.13	60.15	78.06	78.11	78.11
25.03	25.04	25.05	42.17	42.19	42.20	60.17	60.22	61.06	78.14	78.17	78.20
25.07	25.07	25.08	42.21	42.22	42.24	61.08	61.13	61.13	78.21	78.21	79.01
25.09	25.11	25.13	42.25	42.29	43.02	61.14	61.15	61.17	79.02	79.03	79.07
25.18	25.18	25.18	43.02	43.03	43.04	61.24	61.26	61.27	79.07	79.09	79.10
25.20	25.21	25.22	43.14	43.14	43.14	61.29	61.30	62.15	79.11	79.11	79.28
25.22	25.23	25.24	43.15	43.15	43.18	62.16	62.18	62.19	79.29	80.11	80.18
25.25	25.26	25.28	43.19	43.20	43.23	62.19	62.21	62.22	80.18	80.23	80.24
26.02	26.02	26.04	43.28	43.30	43.31	62.22	62.23	62.23	80.24	80.25	80.28
26.05	26.09	26.13	43.36	43.36	43.37	62.24	62.27	62.28	81.02	81.06	81.07
26.14	26.14	26.16	43.40	43.42	44.01	62.29	63.01	63.02	81.10	81.16	81.19
26.19	26.20	26.26	44.01	44.02	44.10	63.04	63.04	63.06	81.22	81.24	81.24
26.28	27.02	27.02	44.10	44.11	44.13	63.07	63.09	63.10	81.25	81.28	82.01
27.03	27.04	27.04	44.15	44.16	44.17	63.14	63.17	63.23	82.05	82.09	82.11
27.06	27.07	27.09	44.18	44.20	44.22	63.26	63.26	64.04	82.12	82.14	82.19
27.10	27.11	27.11	44.27	45.02	45.03	64.05	64.06	64.07	82.22	82.23	82.24
27.15	27.16	27.22	45.06	45.07	45.07	64.07	54.08	64.10	82.25	82.25	82.28
27.22	27.26	27.26	45.11	45.11	45.12	64.11	64.11	64.14	82.29	82.29	83.02
28.04	28.06	28.07	45.13	45.14	45.16	64.16	64.17	64.21	83.03	83.03	83.04
28.08	28.13	28.13	45.19	45.19	45.20	64.22	64.27	64.28	83.05	83.07	83.09
28.13	28.14	28.15	45.22	45.24	45.25	64.28	65.08	65.13	83.10	83.12	83.17
28.15	28.17	28.18	45.28	46.07	46.08	65.18	65.18	66.01	83.18	83.20	83.24
28.18	28.19	28.21	46.11	46.12	46.17	66.01	66.02	66.03	83.25	83.29	83.29
28.22	28.23	28.27	46.17	46.21	46.27	66.04	66.06	66.07	83.30	84.05	84.06
28.29	28.30	28.30	46.30	47.01	47.03	66.08	66.09	66.10	84.07	84.09	84.09
29.01	29.02	29.05	47.03	47.05	47.06	66.10	66.11	66.12	84.10	84.15	84.26
29.06	29.09	29.11	47.07	47.09	47.11	66.14	66.15	66.15	84.27	85.01	85.05
29.12	29.18	29.19	47.19	47.26	47.26	66.15	66.16	66.17	85.06	85.09	85.12
29.22	29.24	29.25	47.27	47.28	47.30	66.17	66.19	66.19	85.13	85.14	85.14
29.26	29.28	30.10	47.30	48.03	48.04	66.20	66.21	66.23	85.15	85.17	85.24
30.11	30.11	30.13	48.09	48.14	48.25	66.24	67.01	67.02	85.26	86.07	86.08
30.13	30.18	30.20	49.02	49.03	49.03	67.03	67.03	67.05	86.10	86.14	86.18
30.21	30.21	30.22	49.12	49.19	49.21	67.06	67.07	67.09	86.19	86.20	86.21
30.23	30.23	30.25	49.23	49.25	49.25	67.12	67.13	67.15	86.25	86.26	86.26
30.25	30.27	30.28	49.26	49.26	49.26	67.16	67.17	67.17	86.27	87.15	87.17
30.30	31.03	31.04	49.27	50.05	50.08	67.18	67.19	67.25	87.18	87.23	87.23
31.05	31.05	31.05	50.15	50.16	50.16	67.25	67.27	67.30	88.06	88.07	88.09
31.06	31.06	31.07	50.19	50.21	50.22	68.01	68.01	68.02	88.18	88.19	88.20
31.08	31.11	31.12	50.25	50.29	51.03	68.05	68.12	68.19	88.24	88.30	89.02
31.12	31.14	32.03	51.03	51.04	51.05	68.20	68.21	68.21	89.05	89.06	89.07
32.04	32.06	32.06	51.06	51.06	51.08	68.23	68.26	68.26	89.09	89.10	89.12
32.07	32.08	32.09	51.16	51.16	51.17	69.04	69.05	69.07	89.14	89.22	89.23
32.10	32.16	32.18	51.18	51.19	51.20	69.08	69.09	69.10	89.26	89.29	89.29
32.18	32.19	32.22	51.22	51.23	51.23	69.12	69.13	69.16	90.06	90.07	90.10
32.23	32.23	32.24	51.23	51.24	51.26	69.17	69.19	69.20	90.10	90.14	90.14
33.01	33.01	33.02	51.28	52.02	52.11	69.20	69.21	69.22	90.16	90.17	91.05
33.03	33.04	33.05	52.12	52.13	52.14	69.23	69.29	69.29	91.07	91.09	91.11
33.05	33.06	33.07	52.17	52.17	52.20	70.02	70.03	70.03	91.13	91.14	92.02
33.07	33.08	33.08	52.20	52.21	52.26	70.08	70.09	70.10	92.03	92.04	92.07
33.09	33.17	33.17	52.27	52.27	52.28	70.17	70.18	70.21	92.16	92.18	92.19
33.18	33.18	33.20	52.29	53.01	53.03	70.22	70.25	70.26	92.20	92.24	93.01
33.22	33.25	33.25	53.05	53.05	53.06	70.28	70.28	70.30	93.03	93.08	93.11
33.25	33.26	33.28	53.06	53.07	53.08	70.35	70.42	70.43	93.13	93.14	93.16
34.01	34.02	34.02	53.11	53.13	53.15	71.03	71.04	71.04	93.17	93.17	93.20
34.03	34.04	34.05	53.16	53.18	53.19	71.05	71.07	71.08	93.25	93.26	93.27
34.05	34.07	34.09	53.19	53.20	53.25	71.08	71.10	71.10	93.29	93.30	94.08
34.10	34.11	34.15	53.26	53.27	54.02	71.11	71.12	71.13	94.12	94.14	94.14
34.15	34.16	34.16	54.02	54.02	54.06	71.17	71.17	71.18	94.14	94.16	94.17
34.17	34.17	34.18	54.09	54.10	54.11	71.18	71.21	71.22	94.17	94.23	94.25
34.18	34.20	34.23	54.13	54.16	54.17	71.23	71.24	71.24	94.26	95.04	95.07
34.25	34.27	35.01	54.22	54.23	54.25	71.25	71.26	71.29	95.09	95.09	95.10
35.02	35.04	35.05	54.26	54.27	54.28	72.02	72.02	72.03	95.11	95.11	95.15
35.05	35.06	35.07	54.30	55.02	55.02	72.08	72.08	72.11	95.15	95.16	95.17
35.10	35.10	35.11	55.03	55.04	55.09	72.12	72.13	72.14	95.26	95.27	96.04
35.13	35.14	35.15	55.10	55.11	55.14	72.15	72.16	72.17	96.05	96.17	96.21
35.15	35.17	35.20	55.17	55.20	55.20	72.18	72.19	72.20	96.21	96.23	97.03
35.22	35.27	36.01	55.21	55.24	55.25	72.22	72.24	72.25	97.04	97.05	97.16
36.03	36.06	36.11	55.30	56.06	56.08	72.26	72.28	73.01	97.15	97.23	97.25
36.12	36.20	36.27	56.09	56.10	56.13	73.06	73.08	73.12	97.25	97.26	97.28
36.29	37.04	37.06	56.14	56.14	56.17	73.13	73.16	73.17	98.01	98.02	98.02
37.07	37.07	37.08	56.17	56.21	56.22	73.21	73.21	73.21	98.03	98.04	98.06
37.09	37.10	37.11	56.23	56.24	56.24	73.23	73.23	73.26	98.09	98.09	98.10
37.12	37.12	37.12	56.27	56.28	56.30	73.26	73.30	74.04	98.12	98.12	98.13
37.13	37.14	37.18	57.06	57.10	57.10	74.06	74.10	74.12	98.15	98.16	98.16
37.18	37.21	37.22	57.11	57.11	57.12	74.14	74.14	74.17	98.18	98.18	98.20
37.24	37.27	37.28	57.15	57.16	57.17	74.20	74.21	74.21	98.26	98.26	98.29
37.29	37.30	37.30	57.18	57.18	57.18	74.23	74.27	74.30	99.02	99.03	99.07
37.30	38.01	38.01	57.19	57.21	57.21	74.30	75.02	75.07	99.10	99.29	99.29
38.04	38.07	38.15	57.24	57.26	57.28	75.14	75.18	75.19	100.03	100.09	100.10
38.21	38.27	38.28	57.30	58.01	58.08	75.22	75.25	75.26	100.16	100.17	100.19
39.01	39.04	39.05	58.15	58.15	58.19	75.27	75.28	76.05	100.20	100.21	100.22
39.07	39.08	40.01	58.22	58.22	58.25	76.06	76.07	76.08	100.25	101.06	101.11
40.08	40.12	40.13	58.26	58.28	58.28	76.11	76.14	76.16	101.12	101.13	101.13
40.15	40.16	40.20	58.29	59.04	59.05	76.16	76.21	76.23	101.15	101.21	101.24
40.24	41.03	41.04	59.07	59.10	59.11	76.25	76.25	76.25	101.24	101.25	101.27
41.16	41.18	41.22	59.13	59.24	59.24	76.26	76.28	77.04	101.28	101.28	101.28
41.26	41.28	41.29	59.25	59.25	59.27	77.09	77.19	77.24	101.29	101.30	101.30

THE (CONT.)		101.30	THE (CONT.)		119.09	THE (CONT.)		139.09	THE (CONT.)		159.04
102.01	102.02	102.03	119.14	119.16	119.19	139.10	139.17	139.24	159.06	159.07	159.09
102.03	102.04	102.07	119.19	119.20	119.22	139.25	139.29	140.01	159.10	159.11	159.15
102.12	102.13	102.13	119.22	119.25	119.27	140.03	140.04	140.07	159.16	159.19	159.19
102.14	102.16	102.18	120.02	120.04	120.05	140.09	140.10	140.18	159.21	159.23	159.27
102.19	102.20	102.22	120.06	120.10	120.10	140.18	140.19	140.21	160.04	160.07	160.13
102.23	102.24	102.25	120.12	120.15	120.18	140.29	141.04	141.07	160.17	160.18	160.19
102.26	102.29	103.02	120.26	120.27	120.28	141.11	141.13	141.17	160.23	161.03	162.02
103.03	103.03	103.04	120.28	120.28	120.29	141.20	141.20	141.22	152.02	162.04	162.04
103.07	103.08	103.11	120.30	121.01	121.01	141.23	141.24	141.25	162.07	162.07	162.13
103.12	103.13	103.17	121.08	121.14	122.02	141.26	141.26	141.30	152.21	162.22	162.23
103.18	103.24	103.26	122.05	122.06	122.07	142.04	142.05	142.05	162.23	162.24	163.06
103.28	103.29	103.30	122.09	122.10	122.11	142.06	142.08	142.08	163.08	163.09	163.11
104.02	104.07	104.08	122.13	122.14	122.14	142.08	142.09	142.10	163.13	163.14	163.14
104.09	104.14	104.21	122.15	122.18	122.22	142.11	142.17	142.24	163.15	163.15	163.16
104.25	104.29	104.30	123.01	123.02	123.03	142.26	142.26	142.28	163.28	164.04	164.05
105.02	105.03	105.06	123.05	123.06	123.07	142.29	142.29	142.30	164.11	164.15	164.22
105.09	105.11	105.11	123.10	123.12	123.18	143.01	143.02	143.02	164.22	165.06	165.06
105.12	105.13	105.15	123.19	123.20	123.21	143.05	143.15	143.15	165.08	165.10	165.10
105.15	105.18	105.19	123.22	123.24	123.30	143.16	143.21	143.25	165.11	165.11	165.11
105.21	105.21	105.25	124.01	124.04	124.07	143.25	143.28	143.28	165.16	165.17	165.20
105.27	105.27	105.28	124.14	124.14	124.20	143.29	144.06	144.14	165.24	165.25	165.27
105.28	106.05	106.06	124.21	124.25	124.26	144.16	144.18	144.20	165.29	165.29	165.30
106.06	106.08	106.11	124.30	125.03	125.04	144.21	144.26	144.27	166.01	166.02	166.03
106.11	106.13	106.15	125.05	125.06	125.11	145.07	145.10	145.12	166.04	166.04	166.05
106.16	107.01	107.03	125.11	125.13	125.13	145.16	145.17	145.25	166.06	166.09	166.11
107.03	107.04	107.11	125.13	125.14	125.14	145.26	145.30	146.02	166.12	166.12	166.13
107.11	107.13	107.13	125.19	125.24	125.25	146.04	146.05	146.05	166.13	166.14	166.16
107.14	107.14	107.16	125.28	125.30	125.30	146.06	146.07	145.07	166.16	166.19	166.20
107.16	107.17	107.18	126.03	126.03	126.04	146.09	146.09	146.09	166.23	166.23	166.24
107.18	107.19	107.24	126.10	126.10	126.11	146.10	146.11	146.18	166.25	165.27	166.30
108.02	108.03	108.03	126.12	126.14	126.18	146.20	146.20	146.25	167.01	167.02	167.03
108.05	108.08	108.08	126.19	126.20	126.20	146.30	147.02	147.02	167.04	167.04	167.05
108.10	108.11	108.11	126.22	126.26	127.08	147.03	147.03	147.05	167.05	167.07	167.07
108.15	108.20	108.24	127.09	127.11	127.11	147.06	147.11	147.13	167.09	167.12	167.14
108.24	108.25	108.25	127.12	127.15	127.19	147.15	147.17	147.20	167.16	167.17	167.18
108.26	108.27	109.06	127.20	127.21	127.21	147.21	147.22	147.23	167.19	167.21	167.24
109.07	109.15	109.15	127.23	127.23	127.24	147.23	147.25	147.28	167.25	167.27	167.28
109.16	109.18	109.19	127.24	127.25	127.25	147.29	147.30	148.01	167.29	167.30	167.30
109.19	109.19	109.20	127.27	127.27	128.01	148.04	148.05	148.08	168.03	168.03	168.04
109.22	109.24	109.27	128.18	128.19	128.23	148.09	148.09	148.11	168.05	168.06	168.10
110.01	110.01	110.02	128.29	129.03	129.03	148.11	148.12	148.13	168.12	168.20	168.23
110.02	110.02	110.03	129.09	129.14	129.15	148.16	148.20	148.20	168.26	168.28	168.30
110.06	110.17	110.18	129.15	129.15	129.16	148.23	148.24	148.25	169.02	169.05	169.11
110.20	110.20	110.22	129.18	129.19	129.20	148.26	148.27	148.28	169.10	169.11	169.11
110.22	110.23	110.24	129.23	129.23	129.24	148.28	148.29	148.30	169.12	169.15	169.18
110.25	110.26	110.26	129.27	129.27	129.28	149.02	149.03	149.03	169.19	169.22	169.23
110.28	111.08	111.09	130.05	130.13	130.14	149.04	149.07	149.10	169.24	169.25	169.26
111.09	111.10	111.10	130.28	130.28	131.02	149.12	149.14	149.15	169.26	169.28	170.06
111.20	111.26	112.01	131.02	131.03	131.03	149.15	149.15	149.16	170.06	170.07	170.08
112.02	112.05	112.08	131.04	131.06	131.07	149.16	149.17	149.17	170.09	170.14	170.17
112.08	112.09	112.12	131.11	131.12	131.13	149.18	149.19	149.19	170.11	170.18	170.20
112.13	112.14	112.16	131.13	131.14	131.15	149.19	149.21	149.22	170.22	170.25	170.29
112.17	112.18	112.19	131.16	131.17	131.17	149.22	149.24	149.27	170.30	171.10	171.10
112.20	112.20	112.22	131.19	131.23	131.24	149.28	149.29	149.29	171.11	171.14	171.15
112.23	112.27	112.28	131.25	131.27	131.28	149.29	149.30	149.30	171.16	171.17	171.17
112.29	112.30	113.04	131.28	131.29	131.29	150.01	150.02	150.11	171.17	171.26	171.29
113.09	113.10	113.10	132.02	132.04	132.04	150.23	150.28	150.29	171.30	172.05	172.08
113.10	113.11	113.11	132.06	132.10	132.12	151.01	151.02	151.05	172.09	172.12	172.15
113.16	113.26	113.30	132.14	132.15	132.16	151.05	151.07	151.12	172.17	172.18	172.22
114.04	114.12	114.13	132.17	132.18	132.18	151.13	151.13	151.14	172.25	172.26	172.27
114.16	114.19	114.22	132.18	132.19	132.19	151.14	151.18	151.20	172.27	172.28	173.02
114.25	114.30	115.03	132.23	132.27	133.01	151.21	151.25	151.26	173.02	173.14	173.19
115.04	115.07	115.07	133.01	133.02	133.10	152.03	152.07	152.08	174.05	174.08	174.14
115.08	115.08	115.13	133.12	133.16	133.16	152.13	152.16	152.17	174.23	175.04	175.04
115.15	115.17	115.18	133.20	133.22	133.24	152.18	152.19	152.21	175.04	175.07	175.09
115.19	115.20	115.21	133.26	133.28	133.29	152.21	152.24	152.25	175.11	175.11	175.11
115.23	115.24	115.28	133.30	133.30	134.01	152.25	152.25	152.29	175.12	175.13	175.15
116.05	116.07	116.08	134.01	134.03	134.03	152.30	153.11	153.12	175.19	175.20	175.23
116.08	116.09	116.09	134.06	134.13	134.20	153.14	153.15	153.19	175.25	175.26	175.27
116.10	116.12	116.14	135.01	135.02	135.03	153.25	153.26	153.28	175.28	175.28	175.28
116.14	116.14	116.15	135.04	135.06	136.06	154.09	155.03	155.04	175.29	175.29	176.02
116.15	116.15	116.16	136.06	136.11	136.11	155.05	155.06	155.07	176.04	176.14	176.15
116.16	116.16	116.16	136.12	136.12	136.13	155.08	155.08	155.11	176.18	176.21	177.09
116.17	116.18	116.18	136.13	136.14	136.17	155.16	155.17	155.18	177.10	177.12	177.15
116.19	116.22	116.23	136.17	136.18	136.19	155.19	155.21	155.24	177.16	177.17	177.18
116.24	116.25	116.29	136.21	136.24	136.24	156.05	156.09	156.09	177.18	177.19	177.21
116.30	117.06	117.06	137.03	137.03	137.05	156.11	156.12	156.12	177.23	177.24	177.25
117.07	117.07	117.08	137.05	137.06	137.08	156.14	156.20	156.21	177.29	178.04	178.04
117.09	117.09	117.10	137.08	137.14	137.15	156.21	156.22	156.23	178.04	178.06	178.08
117.11	117.12	117.14	137.16	137.18	137.18	156.24	156.24	156.25	178.11	178.11	178.12
117.15	117.18	117.20	137.20	137.22	137.24	156.25	156.27	156.28	178.15	178.16	178.19
117.20	117.20	117.22	137.25	137.27	138.01	156.28	156.29	156.29	178.19	178.24	179.01
117.25	117.25	117.28	138.03	138.05	138.06	157.02	157.04	157.04	179.01	179.05	179.06
117.29	118.03	118.06	138.06	138.07	138.07	157.09	157.09	157.12	179.17	179.18	179.19
118.07	118.08	118.09	138.08	138.12	138.13	157.13	157.14	157.15	179.26	179.28	180.02
118.09	118.10	118.11	138.14	138.16	138.17	157.22	157.23	157.23	180.05	180.06	180.06
118.16	118.17	118.17	138.20	138.22	138.24	157.26	157.28	157.29	180.09	180.11	180.11
118.18	118.21	118.27	138.25	138.25	138.28	158.06	158.10	158.18	180.13	180.14	180.17
118.28	119.01	119.02	139.05	139.05	139.08	158.19	158.19	158.30	180.17	180.17	180.26

THE (CONT.)		180.27	THE (CONT.)		199.08	THE (CONT.)		220.13	THE (CONT.)		246.03
180.27	180.27	181.01	199.08	199.11	199.16	220.13	220.16	220.18	246.05	246.06	246.11
181.01	181.08	181.08	199.18	199.25	199.27	220.19	220.21	220.25	246.15	246.17	246.29
181.08	181.18	181.18	199.27	199.29	200.02	220.27	220.29	220.30	247.03	247.04	247.05
181.18	181.22	181.23	200.08	200.10	200.13	220.30	221.04	221.04	247.05	247.06	247.13
181.25	181.26	181.28	200.23	200.27	200.28	221.06	221.08	222.02	247.14	247.14	248.01
182.13	182.16	182.18	200.30	201.01	201.02	222.07	222.08	222.09	248.03	248.06	248.10
182.19	182.20	182.21	201.02	201.04	201.05	222.18	222.20	222.23	248.11	248.14	248.14
182.21	182.25	182.26	201.06	201.09	201.18	223.02	223.02	223.04	248.16	248.16	248.19
182.26	182.27	182.28	201.19	201.20	201.22	223.09	223.17	223.18	248.22	248.23	249.01
182.28	182.29	183.01	201.22	201.30	202.03	223.19	223.22	223.24	249.01	249.04	249.08
183.02	183.04	183.04	202.04	202.06	202.08	224.01	224.02	224.03	249.15	249.16	249.17
183.05	183.05	183.07	202.12	202.13	202.15	224.04	224.05	224.05	249.17	249.22	250.02
183.07	183.08	183.11	202.17	202.17	202.19	224.06	224.08	224.24	250.02	250.04	250.07
183.12	183.14	183.15	202.19	202.21	202.22	225.01	225.02	225.03	250.09	250.10	250.10
183.18	183.19	183.20	202.23	202.25	203.09	225.04	225.06	225.07	250.11	250.14	250.17
183.21	183.25	183.26	203.14	203.16	203.17	225.12	225.12	225.12	250.17	250.18	250.23
183.29	184.01	184.04	203.21	203.27	203.30	225.14	225.15	225.16	250.28	250.30	250.30
184.10	184.18	184.19	204.01	204.01	204.02	225.21	225.21	225.22	250.30	251.01	251.02
184.20	184.21	184.23	204.02	204.03	204.03	225.28	226.12	226.18	251.03	251.04	251.04
184.27	184.28	184.28	204.05	204.07	204.11	226.19	226.19	226.21	251.07	251.08	251.10
184.28	184.29	184.29	204.24	204.25	204.28	226.23	226.26	226.28	251.18	251.19	251.24
184.30	184.30	185.03	205.03	205.05	205.06	226.29	227.04	227.17	251.27	251.29	252.01
185.05	185.06	185.07	205.12	205.12	205.16	227.19	227.23	227.24	252.04	252.06	252.15
185.11	185.12	185.16	205.17	205.21	205.26	228.02	228.07	228.08	252.19	252.20	252.23
185.18	185.20	185.25	205.30	205.30	206.01	228.09	228.10	228.11	252.25	252.26	252.26
185.26	185.27	185.28	206.02	206.05	207.08	228.12	228.28	228.30	253.02	253.03	253.03
185.29	186.03	186.04	207.08	207.09	207.10	229.01	229.05	229.07	253.04	253.06	253.08
186.08	186.08	186.10	207.16	207.17	207.20	229.09	229.11	229.13	253.14	253.15	253.19
186.10	186.11	186.12	207.21	207.22	207.24	229.14	229.20	229.23	253.21	253.21	254.01
186.13	186.14	186.17	208.03	208.08	208.19	229.24	229.25	229.28	254.04	254.07	254.09
186.21	186.23	186.26	208.21	208.21	208.25	229.30	229.30	230.01	254.11	254.11	254.18
186.28	187.01	187.02	208.26	208.26	208.29	230.01	230.03	230.04	254.19	254.21	254.24
187.05	187.06	187.07	208.29	208.29	209.03	230.05	230.09	230.11	254.27	254.27	254.30
187.07	187.08	187.13	209.03	209.04	209.06	230.11	230.16	230.21	255.01	255.02	255.02
187.28	188.01	188.15	209.07	209.09	209.11	230.25	231.01	231.01	255.02	255.07	255.20
188.19	188.23	188.28	209.15	209.19	209.19	231.03	231.04	231.13	255.23	255.24	255.28
188.27	188.28	189.04	209.21	209.26	209.28	231.14	231.15	231.15	255.28	255.29	256.01
189.06	189.14	189.16	210.02	210.06	210.06	232.03	232.06	232.06	256.01	256.07	256.08
189.16	189.18	189.19	210.07	210.08	210.08	232.06	232.10	232.11	256.08	256.18	256.25
189.20	189.21	190.05	210.10	210.11	210.13	232.11	232.15	232.15	256.27	257.01	257.01
190.07	190.09	190.11	210.21	210.22	210.25	232.19	232.23	232.27	257.05	257.05	257.09
190.11	190.12	190.16	210.27	210.27	210.30	232.28	232.30	233.04	257.09	257.14	257.21
190.19	190.21	190.24	210.30	211.02	211.03	233.06	233.06	233.13	257.21	257.22	257.23
190.24	191.02	191.03	211.07	211.10	211.13	233.15	233.16	233.21	257.26	257.27	258.01
191.05	191.08	191.13	211.14	211.14	211.15	233.25	233.25	234.02	258.15	258.20	258.23
191.14	191.16	191.24	211.15	211.17	211.18	234.03	234.03	234.04	258.23	258.26	259.06
191.25	191.27	192.06	211.19	211.20	211.20	234.13	234.14	234.15	259.07	259.07	259.11
192.06	192.06	192.07	211.21	211.21	211.25	234.16	234.19	234.20	259.14	259.15	259.18
192.10	192.10	192.11	211.26	211.27	211.28	234.23	234.24	234.29	259.19	259.30	259.30
192.12	192.12	192.13	211.30	212.02	212.03	234.29	235.01	235.01	260.01	260.03	260.03
192.14	192.14	192.16	212.05	212.06	212.06	235.04	235.09	235.12	260.03	260.15	260.15
192.17	192.18	192.21	212.11	212.13	212.14	235.14	235.15	235.18	260.16	260.18	260.20
192.23	192.23	192.26	212.16	212.18	212.19	235.28	235.29	235.30	260.23	260.23	260.27
192.27	193.01	193.01	212.19	212.19	212.22	236.01	236.11	236.15	260.27	260.29	260.30
193.01	193.02	193.04	212.26	212.28	212.29	236.16	236.17	236.18	261.01	261.01	261.02
193.08	193.08	193.14	213.01	213.04	213.07	236.22	236.22	236.30	261.05	261.09	261.10
193.15	193.15	193.16	213.08	213.09	213.12	237.06	237.06	237.10	261.10	261.13	261.14
193.17	193.22	193.23	213.13	213.13	213.13	237.10	237.29	238.04	261.15	261.20	261.21
193.23	193.28	193.30	213.16	213.18	213.20	238.06	238.09	238.19	261.22	261.23	261.24
194.01	194.01	194.03	214.05	214.05	214.06	238.19	238.22	238.22	261.27	261.27	261.28
194.04	194.04	194.05	214.08	214.12	214.13	238.23	238.24	238.28	261.29	262.02	262.03
194.05	194.06	194.07	214.15	214.23	214.23	239.03	239.04	239.05	262.03	262.04	262.11
194.07	194.07	194.11	214.27	214.28	214.29	239.13	239.13	239.16	262.12	262.14	262.15
194.11	194.15	194.17	214.29	215.01	215.02	239.18	239.19	239.20	262.17	262.18	262.25
194.17	194.19	194.19	215.03	215.03	215.04	239.23	240.04	240.04	262.25	263.02	263.04
194.20	194.22	194.22	215.05	215.06	215.10	240.07	240.09	240.11	263.06	263.07	263.08
194.23	194.25	194.27	215.11	215.11	215.12	240.12	240.18	240.18	263.08	263.11	263.11
194.28	195.01	195.04	215.13	215.18	215.20	240.19	240.19	240.21	263.13	263.16	263.21
195.05	195.06	195.07	215.28	216.04	216.05	240.22	240.22	240.23	263.30	264.03	264.04
195.08	195.09	195.09	216.08	216.10	216.11	240.24	240.25	240.27	264.08	264.13	264.16
195.13	195.14	195.15	216.11	216.14	216.15	241.14	241.15	241.19	264.16	264.17	264.18
195.15	195.16	195.16	216.16	216.16	216.17	241.23	241.26	241.26	264.18	264.19	264.23
195.16	195.18	195.18	216.18	216.20	216.20	241.29	241.30	242.03	264.24	264.28	265.09
195.21	195.22	195.23	216.21	216.25	216.25	242.04	242.07	242.07	265.10	265.11	265.16
195.25	195.27	195.28	216.25	216.27	216.27	242.08	242.09	242.10	266.03	266.05	266.07
195.30	196.18	196.23	216.28	216.29	217.02	242.13	242.13	242.15	266.08	266.10	266.10
196.24	196.26	196.26	217.07	217.07	217.11	242.16	242.20	242.23	266.13	266.16	266.22
196.29	197.02	197.03	217.12	217.12	217.13	242.24	242.27	242.30	267.02	267.03	267.10
197.11	197.20	197.21	217.23	217.24	217.25	243.04	243.07	243.08	267.12	267.16	267.17
197.22	197.24	197.25	217.30	218.01	218.05	243.11	243.12	243.17	267.18	267.20	267.21
197.26	197.28	197.29	218.05	218.08	218.25	243.19	243.24	243.24	267.22	267.23	267.30
198.01	198.02	198.03	218.26	218.27	218.27	244.01	244.01	244.03	267.31	268.02	268.03
198.07	198.08	198.10	218.29	218.30	218.30	244.04	244.12	244.20	268.08	268.09	268.10
198.11	198.11	198.13	219.02	219.03	219.07	244.20	244.21	244.21	268.11	268.12	268.19
198.13	198.15	198.15	219.08	219.08	219.08	244.21	244.22	244.23	268.25	268.26	268.26
198.16	198.18	198.19	219.09	219.10	219.12	245.04	245.06	245.07	268.28	269.02	269.04
198.21	198.22	198.22	219.13	219.15	219.17	245.14	245.17	245.21	269.04	269.06	269.08
198.22	198.25	198.26	219.22	219.27	219.30	245.24	245.25	245.29	269.08	269.09	269.09
199.02	199.03	199.04	220.09	220.10	220.12	246.01	246.01	246.02	269.10	269.11	269.11

THE (CONT.)		269.11	THE (CONT.)		291.14	THE (CONT.)		309.07	THE (CONT.)		327.01
269.13	269.15	269.16	291.15	291.17	291.18	309.09	309.13	309.14	327.05	327.06	327.07
269.16	269.18	269.18	291.19	291.19	291.21	309.14	309.15	309.16	327.08	327.10	327.16
269.19	269.19	269.19	291.22	291.23	291.25	309.18	309.25	309.26	327.17	327.17	327.19
269.21	269.23	269.24	291.26	291.28	291.28	309.26	309.27	309.28	327.20	327.21	327.22
259.25	269.26	269.26	291.29	291.30	292.01	309.29	309.30	310.05	327.22	327.23	327.23
270.05	270.05	270.05	292.05	292.12	292.13	310.07	310.09	310.09	328.04	328.04	328.05
270.06	270.07	270.09	292.13	292.19	292.23	310.12	310.15	310.16	328.06	328.06	328.07
270.21	270.22	270.22	292.24	292.25	292.26	310.18	310.19	310.19	328.12	328.14	328.17
270.23	270.27	270.27	292.27	292.27	292.29	310.20	310.21	310.22	328.17	328.19	328.22
270.28	270.29	270.29	292.30	293.01	293.01	310.22	310.26	310.27	328.22	328.23	328.24
270.29	270.30	271.06	293.01	293.02	293.03	310.29	310.30	311.02	328.24	328.25	328.25
271.09	271.09	271.16	293.05	293.07	293.07	311.04	311.05	311.13	328.26	328.28	328.28
271.16	271.17	271.18	293.08	293.09	293.10	311.16	311.18	311.19	328.28	328.29	329.02
271.18	271.19	271.19	293.13	293.14	293.15	311.21	311.22	311.23	329.01	329.02	329.02
271.19	271.20	271.20	293.19	293.20	293.20	311.28	311.29	311.29	329.03	329.04	329.05
271.23	271.25	271.28	293.21	293.21	293.25	311.30	311.30	312.03	329.06	329.15	329.17
272.04	272.07	272.09	293.26	293.27	293.27	312.06	312.08	312.13	329.17	329.26	329.28
272.10	272.14	272.16	293.29	294.02	294.03	312.16	312.19	312.19	330.02	330.03	330.04
272.22	272.26	272.26	294.05	294.05	294.05	312.20	312.24	312.24	330.07	330.14	330.22
272.27	273.03	273.04	294.09	294.10	294.13	312.26	312.26	312.27	330.23	330.25	330.25
273.04	273.06	273.11	294.14	294.15	294.18	312.27	312.28	313.02	330.25	330.26	330.27
273.13	273.15	273.19	294.20	294.21	294.22	313.08	313.09	313.14	330.28	330.28	331.01
273.19	273.21	273.22	294.23	294.25	294.27	313.14	313.15	313.16	331.01	331.04	331.05
273.23	273.25	273.25	294.27	294.28	294.30	313.19	313.26	313.29	331.05	331.07	331.12
273.27	273.27	274.04	295.03	295.10	295.10	313.30	314.02	314.02	331.12	331.15	331.19
274.14	274.17	274.17	295.16	295.22	295.23	314.04	314.07	314.08	331.20	331.23	331.23
274.18	274.20	274.29	295.23	295.24	295.25	314.09	314.09	314.11	331.23	331.24	331.24
274.29	275.07	275.08	295.29	295.29	296.02	314.14	314.18	315.01	331.26	331.28	331.29
275.08	275.12	275.13	296.03	296.04	297.01	315.10	315.12	315.13	331.29	331.29	332.01
275.13	275.20	275.21	297.04	297.06	297.06	315.13	315.16	315.17	332.01	332.02	332.03
275.22	276.01	276.02	297.08	297.08	297.09	315.18	315.19	315.19	332.05	332.07	332.08
276.02	276.04	276.07	297.10	297.11	297.12	315.20	315.23	315.24	332.08	332.10	332.11
276.07	276.07	276.08	297.13	297.13	297.13	315.25	315.27	315.27	332.13	332.14	332.21
276.08	276.09	276.14	297.19	297.19	297.21	315.28	315.28	315.29	332.22	332.25	332.26
276.15	276.15	276.16	297.23	297.24	298.02	315.30	316.01	316.02	332.27	333.04	333.05
276.18	276.19	276.20	298.07	298.08	298.08	316.03	316.06	316.08	333.07	333.09	333.09
276.20	276.24	277.02	298.09	298.10	298.10	316.08	316.11	316.12	333.10	333.11	333.13
277.02	277.07	277.14	298.13	298.13	298.14	316.12	316.12	316.14	333.13	333.15	333.17
277.18	277.19	277.20	298.17	298.19	298.20	316.16	316.16	316.20	333.18	333.19	333.19
277.21	277.22	277.23	298.20	298.21	298.21	316.20	316.23	316.23	333.20	333.22	333.27
277.23	277.24	277.26	298.26	298.27	298.27	316.23	316.25	316.26	333.28	333.29	333.30
277.26	277.27	277.28	298.28	298.29	299.01	316.26	316.28	316.29	334.01	334.01	334.04
277.29	277.29	278.01	299.02	299.04	299.06	316.30	316.30	317.01	334.05	334.05	334.08
278.01	278.12	278.13	299.07	299.07	299.08	317.04	317.06	317.07	334.09	334.12	334.14
278.14	278.15	278.15	299.09	299.09	299.09	317.08	317.10	317.11	334.14	334.14	334.15
278.18	278.18	278.19	299.11	299.12	299.13	317.13	317.14	317.15	334.15	334.16	334.20
278.21	278.23	278.23	299.13	299.14	299.17	317.16	317.16	317.17	334.21	334.22	334.22
278.24	278.24	278.24	299.17	299.18	299.20	317.18	317.18	318.01	334.22	334.23	334.23
278.25	278.25	278.26	299.22	299.23	299.25	318.08	318.11	318.11	334.25	334.26	334.28
278.27	278.30	279.02	299.29	299.29	299.29	318.12	318.19	318.20	335.01	335.04	335.06
279.02	279.04	279.04	300.01	300.02	300.05	318.24	318.24	319.03	335.08	335.09	335.10
279.13	279.14	279.15	300.05	300.08	300.10	319.08	319.10	319.10	335.10	335.12	335.12
279.18	279.19	279.22	300.14	300.17	300.18	319.10	319.12	319.13	335.13	335.14	335.18
279.22	279.26	279.28	300.18	300.19	300.27	319.13	319.14	319.15	336.01	336.01	336.03
279.29	279.29	279.30	300.28	301.03	301.05	319.16	319.16	319.23	336.04	336.06	336.06
280.05	280.07	280.09	301.08	301.09	301.13	319.28	319.30	320.03	336.07	336.09	336.09
280.14	280.17	280.19	301.17	301.19	301.20	320.08	320.08	320.09	336.10	336.10	336.18
280.21	280.23	280.25	301.22	301.23	301.24	320.10	320.11	320.13	336.22	336.23	336.24
280.25	280.29	281.01	301.27	301.28	301.28	320.16	320.27	320.28	337.01	337.05	337.11
281.02	281.04	281.04	301.30	302.01	302.02	321.01	321.06	321.09	337.13	337.17	337.18
281.12	281.15	281.18	302.02	302.05	302.06	321.11	321.17	321.19	337.19	337.21	337.24
281.19	281.19	282.01	302.07	302.10	302.12	321.20	321.22	321.27	337.27	337.27	337.28
282.10	282.15	282.26	302.15	302.15	302.16	321.27	322.10	322.11	337.28	337.29	338.06
282.30	283.08	283.09	302.16	302.17	302.18	322.12	322.16	322.18	338.14	338.16	338.16
283.16	283.19	283.27	302.19	302.19	302.20	322.19	322.19	322.20	338.17	338.18	338.29
283.29	284.01	284.05	302.21	302.26	303.02	322.21	322.21	322.21	339.02	339.04	339.04
284.07	284.08	285.02	303.04	303.10	303.12	322.22	322.22	322.23	339.06	339.09	339.10
285.05	285.06	285.11	303.27	303.29	303.29	322.25	322.27	322.27	339.14	339.14	339.18
285.20	285.21	285.24	304.01	304.06	304.08	322.28	322.29	322.30	339.20	339.21	339.21
286.01	286.08	286.11	304.08	304.09	304.09	323.01	323.04	323.04	339.24	339.27	339.28
286.14	286.17	286.18	304.11	304.11	304.12	323.05	323.06	323.09	339.29	339.30	339.30
286.21	286.26	286.30	304.12	304.12	304.13	323.14	323.17	323.21	340.01	340.02	340.05
287.04	287.04	287.04	304.13	304.13	304.14	323.23	323.24	323.25	340.05	340.06	340.06
287.07	287.09	287.12	304.14	304.14	304.16	323.27	323.29	323.30	340.11	340.11	340.13
287.12	287.13	287.14	304.17	304.19	304.20	323.30	323.30	324.01	340.14	340.14	340.15
287.22	287.22	287.23	304.23	304.24	304.24	324.01	324.03	324.05	340.17	340.19	340.23
287.24	287.25	287.25	304.26	305.06	305.07	324.06	324.07	324.07	340.26	340.28	340.30
287.25	287.26	287.28	305.07	306.02	306.03	324.07	324.11	324.11	341.02	341.07	341.08
288.01	288.01	288.02	306.13	306.14	306.17	324.12	324.13	324.13	341.12	341.13	341.14
288.03	288.03	288.04	306.20	306.22	306.23	324.14	324.25	325.01	341.16	341.17	341.18
288.04	288.07	288.08	307.03	307.03	307.04	325.03	325.07	325.09	341.19	341.20	341.21
288.08	288.12	288.13	307.08	307.11	307.15	325.10	325.10	325.11	341.22	341.24	341.24
288.19	288.22	288.24	307.17	307.19	307.22	325.11	325.13	325.14	341.25	341.25	341.25
288.24	288.27	289.12	307.29	308.01	308.03	325.17	325.17	325.18	341.26	341.26	341.27
289.12	289.13	289.16	308.04	308.06	308.11	325.18	325.19	325.20	341.27	342.02	342.03
290.08	290.08	290.15	308.12	308.13	308.15	325.20	325.22	325.23	342.05	342.07	342.13
290.17	290.20	290.25	308.17	308.20	308.20	325.24	325.24	325.24	342.17	342.16	342.17
290.25	290.26	290.27	308.24	308.24	308.29	325.26	325.27	325.28	342.25	342.28	342.28
291.05	291.12	291.14	308.29	308.29	309.03	325.30	326.02	326.05			

THE (CONT.)		342.29	THE (CONT.)		364.29	THE (CONT.)		384.07	THE (CONT.)		405.30
343.02	343.06	343.11	364.30	365.01	365.11	384.07	384.10	384.11	406.05	407.01	407.02
343.21	343.24	343.25	365.13	365.16	365.24	384.15	384.15	384.16	407.02	407.07	407.07
343.26	343.27	343.29	365.28	366.03	366.04	384.16	384.17	384.17	407.09	407.09	407.10
344.03	344.05	344.06	366.05	366.06	366.09	384.18	384.20	384.24	407.10	407.13	407.14
344.08	344.12	344.13	366.10	366.12	366.12	384.27	384.29	385.01	407.18	407.19	407.21
344.15	344.20	344.26	366.16	366.17	366.18	385.02	385.03	385.04	408.02	408.05	408.05
344.27	344.27	344.28	366.21	366.22	366.24	385.10	385.15	385.15	408.07	408.11	408.12
344.29	345.03	345.03	366.24	366.27	366.30	385.18	385.19	385.19	408.13	408.14	408.15
345.04	345.06	345.07	367.01	367.09	367.10	385.20	385.22	385.23	408.15	408.16	408.16
345.09	345.11	345.11	367.11	367.11	367.12	385.23	385.24	385.25	408.17	408.17	408.18
345.12	345.13	345.13	367.13	367.13	367.14	385.26	385.26	386.01	408.19	408.21	408.21
345.15	345.16	345.17	367.18	367.21	367.22	386.04	386.06	386.07	408.25	408.26	408.26
345.17	345.18	345.18	367.23	367.24	367.25	386.08	386.09	386.12	408.27	408.30	409.01
345.20	345.21	345.23	367.25	367.26	368.04	386.13	386.13	386.21	409.05	409.05	409.06
345.24	345.26	345.27	368.07	368.08	368.11	386.24	386.26	386.27	409.07	409.08	409.08
345.30	346.03	346.04	368.14	368.16	368.17	387.06	387.10	387.10	409.09	409.11	409.16
346.05	346.10	346.11	368.21	368.22	368.24	387.10	387.13	387.15	409.18	409.20	409.21
347.01	347.04	347.05	368.24	368.26	368.27	387.19	387.20	387.23	409.21	409.22	409.24
347.07	347.09	347.10	369.01	369.01	369.02	387.24	387.27	387.29	409.25	409.25	409.26
347.12	347.12	347.13	369.04	369.06	369.14	387.30	388.02	388.10	409.27	409.28	409.29
347.15	347.15	347.18	369.15	369.17	369.22	388.11	388.21	389.06	409.30	410.01	410.03
347.19	347.20	348.07	369.23	369.23	369.24	389.09	389.10	389.10	410.03	410.04	410.05
348.10	348.21	348.24	369.25	369.27	369.28	389.11	389.12	389.14	410.06	410.09	410.12
348.25	348.26	348.29	369.30	370.02	370.03	389.16	389.17	389.17	410.12	410.14	410.15
349.02	349.04	349.05	370.04	370.05	370.05	389.22	389.25	389.28	410.16	410.16	410.18
349.05	349.09	349.12	370.05	370.07	370.07	390.08	390.10	390.12	410.19	410.22	410.24
349.13	349.17	349.20	370.09	370.15	370.16	390.16	390.19	390.20	410.27	410.29	411.04
349.21	349.24	349.27	370.22	370.24	370.25	390.20	390.21	390.26	411.04	411.06	411.06
349.28	349.29	349.30	370.25	370.26	370.27	390.29	390.30	391.07	411.06	411.07	411.07
350.02	350.05	350.06	371.01	371.03	371.06	391.20	391.29	391.30	411.11	411.13	411.14
350.08	350.11	350.12	371.08	371.10	371.12	392.01	392.03	392.05	411.25	411.27	411.29
350.12	350.12	350.15	371.20	371.21	371.22	392.06	392.09	392.13	412.01	412.11	412.20
350.20	350.22	350.23	371.25	371.26	371.26	392.14	392.15	392.15	412.23	412.24	412.24
350.25	350.26	350.27	371.27	371.28	371.29	392.16	392.20	392.21	412.25	412.26	413.01
350.28	351.05	351.05	372.01	372.02	372.03	392.21	392.21	392.22	413.01	413.03	413.05
351.06	351.08	351.11	372.03	372.03	372.04	392.23	392.26	392.29	413.06	413.06	413.08
351.12	351.13	351.14	372.04	372.09	372.11	392.30	393.01	393.01	413.10	413.10	413.11
351.17	351.20	351.25	372.12	372.13	372.13	393.02	393.04	393.10	413.13	413.14	413.28
351.29	351.30	352.01	372.15	372.17	372.18	393.11	393.11	393.12	413.29	413.29	414.01
352.05	352.08	352.08	372.18	372.20	372.22	393.14	393.18	393.20	414.04	414.05	414.05
352.11	352.16	352.20	372.24	372.25	372.25	393.20	393.23	393.24	414.05	414.06	414.07
352.20	352.21	352.23	372.26	373.03	373.03	393.26	394.04	394.06	414.08	414.10	414.13
352.28	352.28	353.08	373.04	373.05	373.08	394.09	394.10	394.19	414.14	414.15	414.16
353.08	353.11	353.12	373.11	373.11	373.13	394.23	394.24	395.01	414.16	414.17	414.17
353.14	353.15	353.21	373.14	373.15	373.15	395.03	395.04	395.13	414.18	414.19	414.19
353.22	353.26	354.04	373.16	373.17	373.18	395.15	395.17	395.18	414.22	414.23	414.23
354.05	354.09	354.11	373.18	373.20	373.20	395.18	395.19	395.20	414.25	414.27	414.28
355.04	355.04	355.07	373.20	373.21	373.23	395.24	395.29	396.01	414.28	414.30	414.30
355.16	355.17	355.18	373.24	374.05	374.07	396.04	396.04	396.05	415.01	415.05	415.07
355.19	356.03	356.07	374.09	374.10	374.11	396.06	396.17	396.17	415.08	415.08	415.09
356.08	356.10	356.12	374.11	374.12	374.12	396.18	396.18	396.20	415.11	415.12	415.13
356.13	356.17	356.19	374.16	374.16	374.18	396.21	396.21	396.22	415.13	415.14	415.17
356.20	356.23	356.25	374.22	375.12	375.15	396.28	396.28	396.26	416.04	416.06	416.07
356.26	356.28	357.02	375.16	375.19	375.23	396.29	396.30	397.01	416.08	416.12	416.13
357.04	357.05	357.08	375.23	375.25	375.27	397.01	397.01	397.04	416.17	416.17	416.18
357.12	357.13	357.20	376.14	376.19	376.19	397.04	397.05	397.08	416.19	416.20	416.22
357.24	357.27	357.30	376.19	376.20	376.21	397.09	397.10	397.11	415.22	416.22	416.23
358.01	358.04	358.05	376.21	376.23	376.26	397.12	397.12	397.14	417.01	417.01	417.03
358.09	358.10	358.11	376.26	376.26	376.27	397.16	397.17	397.17	417.05	417.06	417.06
358.12	358.13	358.19	376.27	376.28	376.28	397.18	397.19	397.20	417.07	417.09	417.10
358.24	359.03	359.04	376.29	377.04	377.04	397.22	397.24	397.26	417.11	417.12	417.15
359.05	359.06	359.06	377.11	377.11	377.17	397.27	397.29	397.30	417.15	417.16	417.16
359.07	359.11	359.11	378.01	378.01	378.02	398.01	398.05	398.05	417.17	417.17	417.17
359.11	359.12	359.14	378.03	378.04	378.05	398.07	398.10	398.14	417.19	417.19	417.20
359.14	359.14	359.16	378.07	378.07	378.09	398.14	398.20	398.22	417.20	417.20	417.20
359.17	359.18	359.19	378.11	378.15	378.16	398.25	398.26	398.29	417.22	418.01	418.02
359.19	359.23	359.26	378.16	378.17	378.19	398.30	399.06	399.07	418.05	418.08	418.09
359.28	359.29	360.04	378.20	378.21	378.21	399.25	399.26	399.30	418.11	418.13	418.13
350.10	360.14	360.16	378.22	378.23	378.26	400.02	400.02	400.03	418.22	418.23	418.24
350.23	360.23	360.27	378.29	379.01	379.08	400.09	400.15	400.28	418.28	418.28	418.29
360.30	361.02	361.03	379.20	379.21	379.22	401.06	401.09	401.11	419.01	419.05	419.07
361.04	361.05	361.05	379.24	379.25	380.03	401.14	401.17	401.17	419.07	419.08	419.12
361.08	361.09	361.13	380.03	380.05	380.10	401.18	401.18	401.19	419.14	419.16	419.21
361.20	361.21	361.22	380.10	380.11	380.11	401.21	401.22	401.22	419.22	419.29	419.30
362.02	362.04	362.08	380.12	380.13	380.13	401.23	401.25	401.25	420.03	420.05	420.06
362.08	362.09	362.10	380.14	380.15	380.15	401.25	401.26	401.27	420.10	420.11	420.12
362.14	362.18	362.19	380.16	380.16	380.17	402.01	402.05	402.05	420.16	420.17	420.18
362.19	362.21	362.22	381.03	381.03	381.05	402.06	402.09	402.11	420.20	420.20	420.21
363.04	363.05	363.05	381.07	381.08	381.12	402.12	402.13	402.14	420.25	420.26	420.26
363.07	363.10	363.11	381.11	381.12	381.12	402.16	402.27	403.06	420.28	420.29	420.29
363.11	363.12	363.12	381.13	381.20	381.22	403.06	403.07	403.08	420.30	421.03	421.07
353.13	363.18	363.18	381.24	381.24	382.21	403.09	403.09	403.14	421.08	421.12	421.14
363.19	363.20	363.21	382.05	382.06	382.06	403.16	403.22	403.24	421.14	421.16	421.19
363.21	363.23	363.24	382.12	382.12	382.13	403.28	403.28	403.30	421.24	421.25	421.26
354.01	364.02	364.03	382.13	382.15	382.21	404.03	404.09	404.09	421.28	422.01	422.02
364.05	364.09	364.07	383.03	383.05	383.07	404.10	404.10	404.12	422.03	422.05	422.06
364.08	364.09	364.10	383.10	383.12	383.19	404.23	404.24	404.25	422.06	422.07	422.11
364.12	364.15	364.21	383.19	383.28	383.30	404.28	405.10	405.20	422.17	422.18	422.18
364.21	364.26	364.29	384.03	384.04	384.05	405.22	405.26	405.27	422.24	422.26	423.01

		423.02
423.05	423.10	423.10
423.11	423.12	423.16
423.16	423.18	423.18
423.19	423.21	423.23
423.28	424.04	424.12
424.12	425.04	425.08
425.10	425.11	425.12
425.13	425.17	425.18
425.18	425.19	425.24
426.14	426.23	426.26
426.28	426.28	426.29
427.01	427.03	427.04
427.05	427.07	427.07
427.09	427.10	427.12
427.16	427.19	427.21
427.22	427.22	427.25
427.29	427.30	427.30
428.04	428.09	428.17
428.18	428.18	428.23
428.25	428.26	429.04
429.05	429.06	429.08
429.08	429.17	429.19
429.20	429.23	429.24
429.26	429.27	429.27
429.28	429.29	429.30
430.01	430.02	430.02
430.03	430.05	430.09
430.13	430.17	430.20
430.25	430.28	430.29
431.02	431.03	431.05
431.07	431.07	431.08
431.13	431.14	431.14
431.15	431.22	431.23
431.26	431.29	432.02
432.02	432.03	432.05
432.07	432.16	432.17
432.19	432.20	432.21
432.22	432.23	432.27
432.27	433.02	433.02
433.13	433.14	433.25
433.27	433.27	433.28
434.02	434.03	434.05
434.05	434.06	434.09
434.10	434.13	434.14
434.15	434.16	434.16
434.18	434.21	434.22
434.23	434.25	434.26
434.27	434.28	434.28
434.29	434.29	434.30
435.01	435.02	435.04
435.05	435.05	435.07
435.09	435.11	435.15
435.15	435.16	435.19
435.20	435.21	435.23
436.04	436.06	436.08
436.12	436.12	436.14
436.15	436.19	436.21
436.23	436.26	436.27
436.28	437.08	437.11
437.15	437.16	437.19
437.23	437.24	437.26
437.26	437.27	437.27
437.29	438.01	438.04
438.08	438.10	438.12
438.19	438.20	438.21
438.22	438.23	438.28
438.28	439.02	439.02
439.04	439.07	439.07
439.08	439.09	439.10
439.10	439.10	439.11
439.11	439.12	439.13
439.13	439.14	439.14
439.14	439.15	439.16
439.17	439.19	439.21
439.22	439.23	439.23
439.24	439.25	439.26
439.26	439.29	439.30
439.30	440.09	440.10
440.10	440.13	440.14
440.15	440.15	440.16
440.17	440.19	440.20
440.20	440.21	440.23
440.30	441.04	441.04
441.05	441.05	441.09
441.10	441.10	441.12
441.15	441.20	441.23
441.23	441.26	441.27
441.29	441.29	441.30
442.01	442.05	442.06

		442.16
442.18	442.18	442.19
442.20	442.22	442.23
442.24	442.25	442.27
442.29	442.30	443.01
443.02	443.02	443.02
443.03	443.04	443.05
443.06	443.06	443.07
443.08	443.08	443.09
443.09	443.10	443.11
443.11	443.13	443.14
443.16	443.18	443.19
443.20	443.21	443.22
443.23	443.24	443.25
443.26	443.28	443.28
443.29	444.01	444.02
444.03	444.04	444.05
444.07	444.11	444.14
444.14	444.15	444.16
444.19	444.20	444.20
444.21	444.24	444.25
444.25	444.26	444.27
444.27	444.28	444.28
444.29	444.29	444.30
445.02	445.03	445.03
445.05	445.06	445.06
445.07	445.07	445.07
445.08	445.09	445.09
445.11	445.13	445.16
445.17	445.18	445.20
445.21	445.22	445.22
445.23	445.23	445.24
445.25	445.26	445.28
445.28	445.29	445.30
445.30	446.02	446.03
446.04	446.11	446.11
447.01	447.04	447.06
447.08	447.09	447.11
447.12	447.15	447.18
447.19	447.19	447.20
447.21	447.22	447.22
448.01	448.01	448.02
448.02	448.03	448.03
448.04	448.04	448.08
448.08	448.09	448.09
448.10	448.12	448.14
448.17	448.18	448.21
448.21	448.21	448.22
448.25	448.25	448.25
448.27	448.28	449.01
449.02	449.02	449.03
449.06	449.12	449.13
449.14	449.16	449.17
449.18	449.18	449.19
449.19	449.19	449.20
449.21	449.21	449.23
449.25	449.27	449.27
450.02	450.03	450.04
450.06	450.08	450.10
450.11	450.11	450.12
450.14	450.15	450.15
450.18	450.22	450.23
450.24	450.25	450.25
450.25	450.27	450.27
450.29	451.02	451.04
451.04	451.05	451.06
451.09	451.09	451.11
451.11	451.11	451.12
451.15	451.19	451.22
451.22	451.24	451.24
451.27	451.28	452.05
452.06	452.08	452.10
452.11	452.12	452.12
452.21	452.27	452.30
453.01	453.06	453.06
453.06	453.15	453.17
453.21	453.23	453.24
453.25	453.26	453.26
453.28	453.29	453.30
454.05	454.12	454.14
454.17	454.22	454.22
454.24	454.25	454.25
454.26	454.27	455.03
455.07	455.08	455.09
455.09	455.10	455.11
455.12	455.15	455.15
456.01	456.01	456.05
456.08	456.10	456.10
456.11	456.13	456.14
456.15	456.17	456.17

		456.19
456.20	456.20	456.24
456.24	456.27	456.27
456.28	456.29	457.04
457.04	457.07	457.08
457.09	457.11	457.14
457.18	457.20	457.22
457.23	458.01	458.02
458.06	458.08	458.10
458.12	458.15	458.17
458.18	458.19	458.20
458.21	458.22	458.25
458.25	459.03	459.04
459.04	459.07	459.07
459.11	459.11	459.12
459.13	459.13	459.14
459.14	459.16	459.17
459.17	459.18	459.18
459.20	459.29	459.30
460.01	460.03	460.04
460.04	460.04	460.05
460.08	460.11	460.14
460.16	460.18	460.21
460.25	461.01	461.02
461.03	461.03	461.04
461.05	461.06	461.08
461.09	461.13	461.14
461.17	461.19	461.19
461.20	461.21	461.22
461.23	461.25	461.26
461.26	461.27	461.27
461.28	462.01	462.03
462.05	462.05	462.06
462.06	462.08	462.08
462.15	462.17	462.18
462.18	462.20	462.20
462.21	462.22	462.23
462.23	462.24	462.24
462.26	462.27	462.28
462.29	463.01	463.02
463.02	463.03	463.03
463.05	463.05	463.05
463.05	463.06	463.07
463.07	463.08	463.09
463.09	463.10	463.16
463.18	463.22	463.23
463.23	463.25	463.27
463.28	463.28	464.01
464.02	464.03	464.03
464.04	464.04	464.08
464.08	464.08	464.10
464.12	464.12	464.13
464.14	464.14	464.15
464.16	464.17	464.18
464.20	464.20	464.23
464.24	464.26	464.27
464.28	464.28	464.30
464.30	465.01	465.01
465.02	465.02	465.06
465.07	465.07	465.08
465.10	465.11	465.11
465.14	465.15	465.17
465.18	465.20	465.20
465.22	465.22	465.25
465.27	465.29	465.30
465.30	466.01	466.02
466.02	466.06	466.06
466.07	466.09	466.12
466.12	466.14	466.17
466.17	466.17	466.19
466.28	466.29	467.01
467.03	467.04	467.05
467.07	467.07	467.10
467.10	467.11	467.11
467.12	467.13	467.14
467.18	467.21	467.21
467.21	467.22	467.25
467.28	468.04	468.22
468.24	468.24	468.24
469.01	469.01	469.02
469.03	469.05	469.09
469.10	469.10	469.11
469.12	469.14	469.15
469.17	469.17	469.19
469.19	469.20	469.21
469.21	469.23	469.24
469.24	470.01	470.03
470.04	470.05	470.07
470.08	470.08	470.09
470.10	470.10	470.11

		470.11
470.11	470.12	470.17
470.19	470.21	470.25
470.27	470.28	470.29
470.30	471.01	471.01
471.03	471.07	471.12
471.13	471.14	471.15
471.17	471.18	471.23
472.01	472.01	472.08
472.14	472.17	472.22
472.28	473.09	473.27
473.28	474.03	474.09
474.16	474.16	474.21
474.22	474.23	474.27
474.24	474.29	474.29
475.02	475.07	475.09
475.10	475.14	475.14
475.18	475.19	475.24
475.28	476.01	477.08
477.09	477.10	477.11
477.13	477.14	477.14
477.15	477.16	477.22
477.23	477.24	478.02
478.04	478.05	478.06
478.09	478.11	478.12
478.14	478.16	478.17
478.17	478.21	478.22
478.23	478.23	478.25
478.28	478.29	478.30
479.01	479.02	479.03
479.04	479.08	479.08
479.13	479.17	479.20
479.23	479.24	480.01
480.02	480.03	480.06
480.06	480.07	480.08
480.08	480.08	480.10
480.11	480.11	480.11
480.12	480.12	480.12
480.13	480.13	480.16
480.16	480.17	480.18
480.18	480.19	480.21
480.25	480.27	480.28
481.02	481.04	481.07
481.08	481.09	481.11
481.16	481.17	481.27
481.29	481.30	482.01
482.07	482.09	482.13
482.14	482.14	482.18
482.21	482.22	482.23
482.26	482.28	482.28
482.29	483.01	483.02
483.03	483.05	483.08
483.08	483.09	483.11
483.13	483.13	483.16
483.18	483.18	483.19
483.23	483.23	483.23
483.23	483.24	483.26
483.27	483.29	483.29
483.30	483.30	484.02
484.03	484.03	484.05
484.09	484.10	484.10
484.12	484.12	484.12
484.14	484.14	484.16
484.16	484.17	484.19
484.20	484.21	484.22
484.22	484.23	484.23
484.24	484.26	484.28
484.29	484.29	485.05
485.06	485.06	485.09
485.11	485.11	485.14
485.14	485.15	485.15
485.17	485.19	485.20
485.21	485.26	485.27
485.29	486.04	486.04
486.07	486.11	486.16
487.02	487.06	487.06
487.07	487.10	487.10
487.11	487.15	487.16
487.17	487.18	487.18
487.19	487.23	487.24
488.01	488.01	488.03
488.03	488.03	488.04
488.05	488.06	488.07
488.11	488.12	488.13
488.13	488.15	488.15
488.17	488.22	488.23
488.24	488.25	488.28
488.30	488.30	489.03
489.06	489.12	489.13
489.13	489.14	489.14

THE (CONT.)		489.15	THE (CONT.)		505.06	THEIR (CONT.)		131.12	THEM (CONT.)		151.19
489.16	489.18	489.21	505.08	505.09	505.11	131.26	136.10	137.14	152.08	152.12	152.26
489.22	489.22	489.23	505.16	505.17	505.17	137.22	139.29	140.30	152.29	152.29	160.11
489.24	489.25	489.27	505.20	505.21	505.24	142.20	144.02	144.25	164.06	164.07	164.23
489.28	490.01	490.02	505.25	505.26	505.26	150.18	151.03	151.04	164.26	166.18	168.10
490.02	490.06	490.07	505.30	506.01	506.07	151.04	152.02	152.11	169.09	172.20	178.21
490.10	490.11	490.12	506.08	506.09	506.13	156.17	162.17	165.12	178.22	187.23	187.30
490.13	490.13	490.15	506.13	506.17	506.17	165.26	166.11	166.18	197.01	198.04	203.02
490.16	490.21	490.22	506.20	506.20	506.21	166.24	167.30	170.25	203.26	205.12	206.02
490.30	491.02	491.08	506.22	506.23	506.26	170.26	172.16	173.09	212.23	225.30	230.06
491.14	491.15	491.16	506.28	506.29	506.29	173.19	195.03	195.07	234.22	235.22	242.07
491.16	491.17	491.19	507.10	507.11	507.16	195.17	230.05	237.01	243.09	246.18	248.23
491.20	491.21	491.21	507.19	507.19	507.24	239.08	239.22	254.20	255.24	265.05	267.09
491.27	491.29	491.29	507.25	507.26	507.27	255.21	255.22	267.18	267.20	277.01	277.04
492.02	492.03	492.04	507.30	508.02	508.05	271.24	276.23	277.06	277.05	277.06	278.23
492.06	492.09	492.11	508.06	508.08	508.09	277.11	277.13	277.15	280.05	281.10	291.23
492.11	492.11	492.18	508.09	508.14	508.14	277.22	278.07	278.17	295.19	298.14	298.17
492.24	493.04	493.06	508.16	508.16	508.18	279.03	281.07	291.18	298.22	298.27	300.04
493.07	493.08	493.11	508.19	508.21	508.23	291.20	291.25	299.14	300.23	301.06	301.13
493.22	493.23	493.24	508.24	508.26	508.26	300.13	300.22	302.08	301.14	306.10	308.26
493.26	493.26	493.27	508.29	508.30	509.01	304.16	306.12	307.05	310.01	316.18	316.24
493.27	493.28	493.29	509.03	509.04	509.06	312.22	313.17	313.20	317.09	317.12	319.07
493.30	494.03	494.03	509.07	509.09	509.10	315.23	316.29	317.01	319.10	320.06	320.19
494.04	494.04	494.05	509.10	509.11	509.12	317.01	318.21	320.15	321.12	321.29	323.26
494.05	494.07	494.08	509.14	509.18	509.22	323.08	327.08	328.21	324.22	339.10	339.11
494.09	494.10	494.11	509.22	509.23	509.24	331.01	332.08	335.05	341.12	341.29	361.29
494.14	494.15	494.16	509.25	509.26	509.26	336.04	338.02	338.03	362.24	363.17	363.24
494.16	494.18	494.18	509.28	509.28	509.29	338.03	341.09	341.16	364.03	366.08	366.14
494.23	494.24	494.25	510.01	510.02	510.03	350.06	363.24	364.03	366.30	367.21	373.02
494.26	494.27	494.29	510.06	510.08	510.09	364.08	367.15	372.27	373.07	374.13	374.17
494.30	495.01	495.04	510.09	510.10	510.11	374.20	376.13	379.15	376.09	376.11	377.22
495.05	495.08	495.10	510.12	510.13	510.15	382.22	384.26	389.22	377.24	377.27	386.29
495.10	495.20	495.27	510.15	510.16	510.16	389.28	390.04	394.07	389.20	389.21	394.06
495.30	496.05	496.05	510.18	510.25	510.26	395.28	397.17	407.12	394.09	396.02	396.15
496.06	496.08	496.08	510.27	510.27	510.30	407.22	410.19	410.20	407.11	408.06	409.12
496.12	497.02	497.03	511.02	511.10	511.19	411.03	411.03	411.05	410.10	410.25	411.04
497.05	497.06	497.06	511.22	511.27	512.01	412.09	414.27	415.03	414.08	416.09	418.18
497.07	497.08	497.14	512.04	512.04	512.06	415.04	415.06	420.19	419.24	422.29	423.29
497.16	497.17	497.18	512.07	512.09	512.11	422.19	423.07	427.26	429.05	429.25	433.25
497.20	497.21	497.23	512.14	512.19	512.26	434.17	439.19	439.22	440.04	440.11	440.11
497.24	498.01	498.01	512.27	512.28	513.03	439.28	439.29	440.04	440.14	442.20	444.13
498.02	498.05	498.05	513.05	513.08	513.12	440.18	440.23	441.07	446.12	447.15	450.05
498.06	498.06	498.07	513.12	513.18	513.19	441.12	441.14	442.06	450.29	450.30	452.16
498.09	498.10	498.10	513.19	513.25	513.27	442.11	445.04	445.06	460.12	460.14	460.16
498.14	498.15	498.18	513.28	514.01	514.03	446.09	448.02	448.07	460.17	461.18	461.21
498.19	498.20	498.22	514.03	514.04	514.06	449.10	449.11	452.17	462.09	462.11	463.30
498.22	498.24	498.29	514.08	514.08	514.08	452.23	453.16	453.18	465.03	468.18	469.02
499.01	499.02	499.02	514.10	514.16	514.21	460.24	461.25	462.07	470.02	472.17	472.27
499.04	499.04	499.05	514.23	514.26	514.27	462.26	464.05	466.18	473.29	475.03	475.23
499.06	499.07	499.07	514.27	514.28	514.29	466.20	470.14	470.14	478.30	480.04	480.07
499.08	499.09	499.10	514.30	515.01	515.01	470.15	477.24	478.01	480.24	482.08	482.14
499.11	499.11	499.12	515.02	515.02	515.06	478.03	479.25	479.28	484.14	485.30	486.03
499.14	499.15	499.18	515.08	515.09	515.10	479.29	480.15	483.28	486.07	486.10	486.15
499.19	499.19	499.20	515.12	515.13	515.15	484.01	484.06	484.14	487.04	487.12	487.13
499.20	499.21	499.21	515.16	515.19	515.21	485.20	485.27	485.28	489.06	494.17	495.13
499.22	499.22	499.22	515.22	515.24	515.26	485.28	486.09	486.12	497.10	500.01	500.18
499.25	499.26	499.30	515.29	516.01	516.01	486.13	487.11	487.16	500.22	500.29	502.06
499.30	500.01	500.03	516.09	516.13	516.14	493.17	493.24	494.15	508.11	508.12	508.20
500.04	500.04	500.06	516.17	516.23		494.27	495.11	498.06	509.07	512.13	512.21
500.11	500.11	500.12	THEE		511.29	500.13	500.14	503.12	THEM'	418.17	
500.15	500.16	500.16	THEIR	3.01	7.22	503.17	504.07	504.22	THEMSELVES		30.19
500.16	500.17	500.20	12.24	13.23	13.24	504.24	507.07	508.11	32.20	41.12	64.20
500.23	500.25	500.27	14.14	14.14	14.15	508.23	509.15	513.13	98.11	110.17	117.12
500.27	500.28	500.29	14.21	16.01	16.02	513.21			126.07	140.08	169.16
500.30	501.01	501.04	16.02	16.02	16.03	THEIRS	321.20		179.01	244.07	286.21
501.06	501.06	501.07	16.03	16.04	16.10	THEM	10.03	23.18	439.20	440.03	444.09
501.08	501.09	501.12	16.12	16.28	19.03	25.22	28.28	29.23	444.18	449.09	453.18
501.14	501.17	501.17	19.14	20.04	20.05	30.08	37.16	42.28	455.06	500.12	503.08
501.22	501.23	501.25	20.06	20.10	20.10	43.08	43.11	54.09	THEN	8.30	11.03
501.26	501.27	501.30	20.27	20.30	21.01	54.19	61.22	62.15	12.07	12.10	13.15
502.04	502.05	502.05	21.01	21.02	21.24	63.01	63.25	63.27	16.24	22.12	27.27
502.08	502.11	502.11	29.29	30.26	31.07	63.30	64.01	66.13	30.21	34.04	34.07
502.13	502.14	502.14	35.17	35.18	37.16	67.01	73.09	74.02	34.12	36.30	37.01
502.15	502.15	502.16	37.16	37.17	40.20	74.06	74.08	82.10	37.10	38.19	38.29
502.17	502.18	502.20	40.20	42.19	44.18	83.21	95.25	98.14	41.06	48.07	54.20
502.25	502.26	502.30	46.08	47.27	51.28	98.23	101.21	101.25	70.37	71.14	71.16
502.30	503.01	503.01	52.13	54.03	63.05	103.19	103.20	107.18	71.21	71.25	72.01
503.02	503.03	503.04	67.08	74.03	75.20	107.21	109.30	110.09	72.03	72.12	72.14
503.04	503.07	503.08	83.11	90.17	90.17	113.13	115.29	116.05	77.18	78.09	79.16
503.13	503.13	503.14	92.05	92.07	92.11	118.12	119.15	119.27	82.16	82.18	83.18
503.14	503.15	503.16	92.12	92.15	92.16	119.28	121.05	125.21	84.05	87.06	87.19
503.16	504.02	504.02	92.17	92.18	94.07	125.24	126.23	126.30	87.26	88.08	88.09
504.03	504.03	504.04	98.11	99.04	113.20	127.01	127.22	128.01	88.26	92.21	95.20
504.05	504.08	504.09	115.16	115.20	117.16	128.07	128.16	128.17	97.17	98.07	99.18
504.10	504.10	504.12	117.16	117.17	117.28	128.20	130.13	130.16	102.15	107.11	109.11
504.13	504.14	504.14	117.30	118.03	119.27	133.02	136.02	136.07	109.23	110.16	112.25
504.21	504.22	504.23	119.29	123.25	123.26	140.13	140.15	140.29	113.22	118.06	119.01
504.24	504.24	505.01	125.27	126.01	126.02	142.14	142.22	143.14	123.03	123.10	125.15
505.01	505.04	505.05	126.13	126.14	126.16	143.19	144.07	144.22	125.15	128.07	131.17
			126.17	126.18	126.19	147.19	150.05	151.05			

THEN (CONT.) — 132.08

133.04	135.01	136.07
137.05	137.08	137.25
138.23	139.27	142.16
143.29	146.14	149.10
151.09	153.02	154.02
155.23	156.07	158.08
159.28	162.18	164.07
164.09	176.10	179.27
182.09	183.03	185.14
188.05	189.05	191.11
194.10	195.05	196.28
197.05	197.11	198.08
198.16	199.10	201.20
203.09	203.17	207.03
209.29	212.08	213.20
218.22	220.12	222.03
224.17	224.19	224.23
224.26	224.28	228.25
231.12	235.05	235.29
238.22	245.23	249.13
250.04	254.24	255.09
255.24	255.27	256.11
257.08	258.10	259.25
269.24	270.25	282.19
288.23	289.03	289.23
290.11	290.12	291.21
294.02	294.20	297.14
300.06	301.21	303.12
305.03	306.08	308.28
309.23	311.05	311.30
312.13	312.27	313.04
318.24	320.04	320.20
338.11	341.25	342.04
343.19	343.25	355.21
356.06	356.30	356.30
359.13	359.19	360.06
360.07	360.14	360.29
362.23	367.22	371.27
374.28	376.03	377.30
381.19	382.15	382.16
382.23	384.03	384.12
386.07	389.01	389.16
396.08	401.10	405.02
409.17	413.13	413.21
413.26	415.16	416.18
419.27	422.18	424.07
427.03	428.13	437.23
439.23	439.26	444.16
446.07	450.05	452.12
453.24	454.17	455.27
456.02	462.20	463.11
464.01	464.10	464.21
464.27	464.28	465.27
466.07	467.06	468.15
469.04	470.05	473.30
474.25	475.27	476.02
477.22	482.30	483.08
484.07	484.22	485.14
486.16	491.10	494.26
498.06	499.09	499.24
500.07	500.23	500.28
501.11	502.27	504.18
505.15	505.17	505.27
506.11	507.04	512.22
512.27	513.28	514.06
514.11	514.18	515.07
515.17		

THEORY — 82.17 119.24

347.01		

THERE — 2.09 4.07

4.19	4.24	6.09
10.11	11.02	11.04
12.02	12.16	13.02
13.18	13.27	14.23
15.22	20.19	23.20
24.10	26.06	29.20
29.28	33.16	34.04
34.07	34.14	36.11
38.18	40.10	41.25
41.25	41.29	42.03
42.22	43.08	43.13
45.17	46.22	47.10
47.23	48.17	49.22
50.17	50.20	50.22
52.26	53.22	53.24
53.28	57.17	57.23
61.11	61.28	63.17
66.05	66.09	66.13
67.27	67.30	69.06

THERE (CONT.) — 70.39

71.30	72.05	72.24
77.14	78.12	79.17
79.19	80.01	83.05
83.22	85.28	85.30
88.13	88.14	91.16
92.05	92.07	93.10
95.13	98.09	99.02
99.03	101.22	101.23
101.24	102.17	102.27
103.19	103.20	103.26
104.03	104.30	107.09
107.17	109.08	109.14
110.05	110.28	111.13
111.16	114.05	114.13
115.15	116.25	117.23
118.27	119.03	120.01
120.03	122.21	123.02
123.18	123.30	124.22
125.18	127.03	127.12
127.13	128.24	129.05
133.03	133.13	133.18
133.27	135.07	136.16
136.23	137.07	137.11
139.05	141.10	143.01
143.29	144.22	146.26
147.01	147.03	147.11
147.12	147.13	147.14
150.08	151.07	151.14
154.08	156.14	156.29
156.30	157.28	160.04
162.17	163.10	163.13
164.16	164.23	164.30
165.02	165.09	167.01
167.06	169.11	169.13
170.03	170.21	170.21
171.07	172.24	173.20
174.16	175.01	176.03
176.07	178.05	178.08
178.23	178.24	178.24
178.30	185.17	185.20
186.20	186.30	187.16
191.10	191.18	191.23
192.15	194.03	194.10
194.24	195.12	196.29
200.04	200.12	200.17
202.02	203.13	203.22
204.27	208.06	208.15
208.21	209.06	209.08
209.17	210.12	211.19
212.10	212.15	212.28
213.22	215.07	215.15
215.16	215.22	215.23
217.05	218.23	219.12
222.10	222.22	225.19
225.24	225.29	227.16
228.15	229.12	231.02
233.11	233.18	234.18
234.23	235.08	236.01
236.14	239.04	239.18
242.04	242.18	245.20
245.22	245.28	249.25
249.28	253.18	253.20
254.07	254.28	255.01
255.19	255.28	256.04
259.05	259.10	260.15
261.05	261.07	261.18
262.22	263.07	263.14
266.17	266.18	267.01
267.05	267.13	267.17
267.25	268.28	269.05
269.10	270.17	271.18
272.09	272.21	273.01
273.12	274.11	275.06
276.05	276.17	278.22
279.17	279.19	282.08
282.25	282.25	285.03
285.11	286.19	287.12
288.26	291.02	292.21
293.29	295.06	297.12
298.06	298.25	299.05
302.01	302.26	303.03
303.14	303.14	304.27
304.30	305.01	306.23
307.12	307.20	308.08
309.02	309.06	310.10
311.10	312.08	312.18
313.05	313.22	314.09
314.19	319.02	320.26
323.11	323.16	323.26

THERE (CONT.) — 324.13

324.22	324.29	324.30
325.14	325.22	327.03
327.08	327.11	328.13
329.18	329.19	330.25
331.08	332.30	333.13
334.28	335.02	337.20
337.21	338.22	339.20
340.06	341.18	341.29
343.04	343.16	343.18
343.20	343.23	343.25
345.19	346.11	349.07
353.02	353.22	353.27
354.08	356.02	356.22
357.21	358.19	359.15
360.02	360.05	360.11
360.12	360.21	360.29
361.21	362.09	366.22
367.16	368.10	369.10
369.15	374.19	377.01
378.24	378.27	379.04
379.12	380.09	382.14
384.07	384.25	385.07
385.21	387.01	388.14
388.18	388.19	391.01
391.03	391.04	391.10
391.21	392.02	392.09
392.16	394.08	394.22
395.20	396.04	396.10
396.20	397.25	398.04
404.16	407.09	409.11
410.25	410.27	411.13
411.26	414.01	416.11
419.11	419.27	419.28
420.13	421.18	421.18
421.22	422.05	422.07
422.14	422.19	423.13
423.25	423.29	426.05
428.07	428.22	428.25
432.12	432.12	434.26
435.06	438.02	439.05
440.17	444.12	444.21
445.04	445.19	445.27
447.24	448.05	449.02
449.13	449.26	450.03
451.03	451.13	453.01
454.00	455.10	457.14
458.10	460.06	460.29
461.29	462.28	464.07
465.03	465.17	469.21
470.29	471.12	471.23
471.28	472.10	473.27
474.01	476.01	476.09
477.06	479.18	479.24
480.18	481.26	482.04
482.11	483.15	483.24
485.12	487.05	487.09
488.11	489.19	490.14
492.21	492.23	493.07
495.27	495.27	497.04
498.12	501.16	503.01
504.06	507.12	507.21
507.27	508.04	508.20
509.05	509.12	509.24
510.05	511.02	511.05
512.10	513.10	516.08
516.11		

THERE' — 477.17

THERE'S — 48.11 52.22

62.06	62.10	63.26
64.29	72.29	76.19
159.08	180.24	197.01
200.12	202.01	203.17
215.15	218.22	219.20
220.03	232.29	234.27
243.02	266.04	268.02
303.05	343.17	370.28
413.13	413.16	421.04
428.24	461.08	467.02
485.08	489.03	

THEREAFTER — 418.03

437.16	461.30	495.02

THEREFORE — 2.20

195.13	262.09	422.12
438.21		

THEREIN — 98.24

THEREUPON — 355.15

377.27	456.28	

THESE — 3.19 3.29

11.07	13.17	23.13

THESE (CONT.) — 26.01

27.11	27.28	28.27
32.15	35.11	41.09
51.30	62.14	63.22
64.19	67.12	68.08
68.30	72.17	80.02
80.08	80.12	86.09
86.19	90.26	93.11
93.13	94.05	96.09
97.30	99.07	99.15
103.01	103.16	104.01
107.09	109.17	111.30
113.21	115.12	115.22
117.21	117.27	118.08
119.25	121.03	122.02
123.01	123.25	123.26
124.28	125.19	127.07
131.26	138.26	139.09
146.15	147.15	149.28
155.19	169.16	170.01
172.27	174.01	174.17
180.02	193.16	195.15
205.04	209.09	227.07
227.22	239.01	249.03
252.25	252.29	255.20
256.22	260.05	269.22
273.21	279.27	285.13
288.21	291.06	301.14
302.29	303.05	304.09
306.11	307.24	314.30
319.23	329.16	332.03
341.24	341.27	343.20
356.09	358.06	363.02
366.02	366.28	366.29
368.09	376.07	376.27
379.13	386.26	387.20
389.27	408.07	411.12
412.06	416.01	416.12
420.30	421.16	422.23
423.02	424.07	426.17
430.08	435.09	435.23
437.30	442.09	444.22
449.08	449.15	450.20
451.17	452.04	453.22
454.01	454.11	465.28
472.03	476.09	477.09
477.15	478.26	486.12
489.07	491.08	500.26
503.18	513.16	

THEY — 2.30 3.26

12.24	13.21	13.28
14.01	14.02	14.04
14.09	14.14	15.11
15.12	15.13	15.22
15.29	16.01	16.04
20.29	23.14	23.15
23.16	23.17	25.24
25.25	26.03	27.14
28.21	28.28	28.29
30.21	30.24	33.08
33.10	33.11	35.20
38.13	41.11	43.07
43.08	46.01	46.06
46.09	50.17	51.07
54.04	54.05	54.06
54.07	54.12	54.13
58.30	61.08	61.21
61.22	62.13	63.16
63.20	63.29	63.30
66.12	74.08	76.02
76.04	76.14	76.22
78.03	82.19	91.09
91.10	92.13	92.15
97.22	98.02	98.11
98.11	103.18	105.02
105.09	105.17	109.02
109.23	110.18	110.19
110.19	110.19	110.19
114.02	115.16	117.19
117.30	118.10	119.16
122.08	122.17	123.14
123.15	123.16	123.26
124.17	124.27	126.03
126.04	126.04	126.05
126.08	126.11	126.16
126.17	126.18	126.19
126.21	126.24	126.26
128.03	128.17	130.03
130.13	133.05	133.15
133.21	134.02	136.08

THEY (CONT.) 136.10
137.12 137.12 137.22
139.27 140.07 140.08
140.12 140.12 140.13
140.16 141.28 141.29
142.11 142.15 142.19
142.21 142.22 143.20
143.27 144.01 144.01
144.02 144.03 144.05
144.08 144.12 144.25
147.18 147.21 147.26
148.07 148.11 148.14
149.07 149.08 149.21
150.03 150.05 150.07
150.08 150.15 150.17
150.18 150.27 150.29
150.30 151.04 151.05
151.11 151.23 151.30
152.01 152.02 152.03
152.09 152.18 152.20
152.22 157.05 157.25
160.11 160.12 162.16
164.06 164.23 164.23
165.15 165.21 165.22
165.23 165.26 166.10
166.10 167.19 168.11
168.27 169.13 169.21
170.25 172.04 172.16
172.19 173.19 187.23
190.13 191.19 191.20
194.09 194.10 197.13
197.18 197.24 198.01
198.04 198.07 198.08
198.17 198.23 198.24
199.02 201.04 206.03
211.08 212.24 230.07
230.15 232.04 232.24
235.28 237.21 239.07
245.15 249.12 250.02
251.06 251.07 254.02
255.08 255.20 263.06
271.05 271.08 271.23
274.05 274.05 274.18
275.04 276.21 276.22
276.24 277.12 277.13
277.16 277.20 277.21
277.21 277.25 278.28
278.29 278.30 279.03
280.03 280.04 285.20
285.21 285.23 286.19
291.08 291.26 294.16
298.02 298.12 301.09
304.15 307.07 309.01
309.18 310.23 313.16
314.06 314.16 315.26
317.02 318.21 319.01
319.08 319.09 319.17
319.25 320.05 320.13
320.14 321.02 321.04
321.05 323.23 324.12
325.06 327.21 328.03
328.05 328.23 329.23
329.25 329.26 337.30
338.01 338.01 338.01
338.03 339.14 343.22
344.11 346.06 356.28
360.26 366.04 367.14
367.24 367.25 368.10
368.24 368.26 368.27
368.28 369.14 369.18
373.08 373.10 374.03
376.13 376.13 376.14
377.13 377.22 377.25
380.13 381.23 384.26
387.28 390.04 390.05
397.15 407.10 408.06
410.17 411.02 414.26
415.02 422.29 423.01
428.30 429.24 432.26
433.24 433.29 434.15
435.12 439.19 440.05
440.16 440.22 440.24
440.25 441.06 441.15
442.12 443.01 444.17
444.17 444.19 444.22
445.24 446.06 446.07
446.10 446.12 447.02
449.10 449.11 449.12
449.29 452.15 453.18
453.28 454.16 455.06

THEY (CONT.) 455.20
457.13 457.19 460.15
462.12 463.24 463.25
463.29 465.24 466.19
467.26 467.29 467.30
470.07 470.11 470.13
472.07 472.25 478.01
478.26 479.05 481.06
483.21 484.19 485.02
485.23 485.30 486.01
486.03 486.08 487.13
489.08 489.21 489.25
493.05 493.16 497.01
501.12 502.09 503.05
503.07 503.08 503.17
504.19 507.08 509.01
509.18 510.07 510.10
511.17 513.05 513.10
513.21 515.15
THEY'LL 121.09
THEY'VE 62.15
THICK 27.02 49.07
54.21 91.07 122.15
143.03 151.27 170.03
196.15 197.26 246.16
272.22 290.28 292.07
315.07 318.10 365.12
397.18 416.14 497.24
THICK-LIPPED 318.10
THICKENED 444.01
THICKETS 13.04
THICKLY 196.01
THICKNESS 157.28
THIEF 48.26 143.09
307.08 402.27
THIEVES 301.15
THIEVING 242.12
THIGH 99.27
THIGHS 55.03
THIN 24.27 30.12
33.18 61.18 83.15
137.13 143.04 234.10
246.12 285.09 292.06
359.04 445.01 460.21
466.09 498.12 498.17
THING 14.11 28.26
29.27 29.30 34.23
40.11 40.12 40.13
40.13 40.16 42.09
44.13 49.10 53.26
59.30 59.30 60.09
60.14 66.23 67.02
67.02 72.29 81.06
91.02 93.09 101.15
111.05 111.12 118.26
123.30 128.17 129.18
131.13 132.27 138.22
142.20 144.23 147.20
157.16 158.10 160.04
160.15 161.03 165.11
168.10 169.20 177.19
181.10 187.25 188.13
189.04 189.17 190.12
193.24 196.30 197.28
199.05 200.10 202.21
202.25 203.10 204.07
204.23 204.24 205.22
208.29 219.23 223.02
225.05 225.06 225.07
225.20 227.18 230.05
230.29 232.01 235.06
236.11 243.03 243.24
259.05 260.25 267.30
272.10 275.12 280.07
283.01 287.07 287.18
288.15 291.01 291.22
293.30 295.22 300.17
306.14 309.16 310.29
323.25 327.22 330.02
330.07 330.26 332.14
333.01 335.06 346.10
356.10 374.25 376.03
377.04 377.24 378.19
380.06 387.16 388.27
392.11 392.22 393.18
395.03 401.06 401.11
404.17 418.15 420.27
423.23 426.06 431.20
437.27 442.01 450.01
458.02 481.07 481.07

THING (CONT.) 483.21
492.25 501.17
THING' 418.21
THING'LL 426.11
THINGS 2.03 21.24
35.15 50.14 50.14
50.17 104.01 109.17
113.22 119.08 127.07
147.11 148.15 151.08
173.21 197.13 197.17
198.07 201.10 209.26
211.08 252.27 260.08
261.18 264.26 270.03
270.03 286.30 290.19
304.09 324.17 327.11
327.18 327.20 354.01
356.14 378.30 387.20
422.28 426.17 429.23
435.23 453.21 471.03
481.28 485.22
THINK 1.05 7.23
9.02 11.02 27.13
33.17 34.12 40.13
41.11 48.02 52.02
64.19 64.27 65.17
73.14 74.15 77.05
80.05 80.20 81.15
83.12 87.08 87.10
87.13 88.05 90.13
96.19 97.08 97.10
98.08 99.12 100.05
101.08 102.06 103.30
104.06 104.13 104.20
104.22 105.07 110.16
111.16 116.07 121.09
124.25 139.03 139.19
141.10 144.01 144.12
148.24 153.09 158.01
158.09 159.30 160.05
160.07 164.08 181.16
185.13 186.23 187.03
200.19 200.25 200.25
200.29 201.27 207.10
226.25 231.26 243.05
243.06 243.26 253.16
255.10 255.15 256.11
269.02 269.05 271.22
281.28 282.17 283.04
289.01 292.17 295.28
303.16 306.19 311.27
320.30 325.03 325.06
327.19 339.07 341.05
348.28 350.24 353.29
355.12 356.12 360.25
367.05 368.01 375.06
375.30 376.03 377.06
377.08 377.23 388.01
388.07 388.16 389.06
391.17 395.19 400.09
401.04 401.07 404.05
412.02 415.02 443.10
454.12 460.16 464.07
467.04 470.07 477.01
477.18 480.25 494.20
497.01 501.22
THINKER 28.07
THINKING 74.18 77.13
77.13 79.06 90.09
92.10 96.11 101.18
153.25 153.26 154.02
169.29 184.23 187.21
218.02 223.22 226.11
233.30 309.07 313.05
369.18 397.25 454.29
457.04 473.30 475.09
480.02 507.22
THINKS 53.02 199.09
237.09 492.30
THINLY 263.17
THINNER 29.04
THIRD 4.21 46.28
58.22 93.24 122.24
129.30 146.25 175.10
256.01 269.19 309.01
332.21 334.18 343.07
347.02 480.08 501.30
THIRD-CLASS 343.07
THIRDS 328.24
THIRSTY 109.04 449.29
THIRTEEN 190.13 278.19

THIRTY 67.24 71.15
71.30 72.03 158.07
171.07 171.22 172.04
176.14 251.05 276.06
294.07 479.14 494.14
THIRTY-TWO 67.24
71.15 71.30
THIS 3.01 6.08
7.16 10.10 11.07
14.12 23.10 23.28
28.26 29.09 29.19
29.27 29.30 30.07
30.29 32.03 34.13
35.25 35.26 36.08
37.27 38.04 40.02
41.04 42.16 42.21
42.28 42.30 43.26
44.27 45.04 45.04
47.07 47.16 51.13
52.01 52.11 53.08
53.12 54.29 56.19
58.21 60.14 61.05
61.24 61.29 66.24
68.29 69.06 69.09
70.44 71.08 72.01
72.16 72.19 74.11
74.18 75.07 76.10
76.12 78.15 78.19
80.01 80.04 80.06
80.08 80.27 81.04
81.26 82.22 85.01
85.23 85.26 85.29
86.05 86.16 86.22
87.11 88.07 89.18
89.21 90.22 90.29
91.02 92.14 92.15
93.10 93.12 93.15
93.16 93.27 94.02
94.05 94.22 95.03
95.11 95.17 95.18
97.11 97.24 100.29
102.04 102.11 102.15
106.09 106.10 109.14
109.25 110.06 110.24
110.26 111.23 113.15
114.01 114.17 117.01
117.20 119.19 119.23
121.03 122.05 124.03
124.19 126.27 127.11
127.17 128.23 128.28
129.22 130.23 130.27
132.08 132.12 132.17
132.26 138.04 138.13
138.24 140.04 140.20
141.01 142.27 146.21
145.25 147.12 151.16
151.17 153.18 155.13
157.29 158.27 159.16
160.01 160.02 163.11
165.05 165.23 166.07
167.26 168.09 168.09
169.26 170.20 171.09
171.13 171.24 173.21
174.09 174.14 176.04
176.12 177.14 178.10
178.13 178.30 179.04
179.06 181.15 184.06
184.21 185.14 186.10
187.13 187.25 188.13
188.18 188.21 190.24
193.14 193.18 193.21
194.30 197.04 197.15
205.22 208.25 211.26
212.09 214.08 215.12
216.05 217.08 217.09
218.22 221.05 224.25
224.30 225.10 225.19
227.11 227.15 229.19
231.04 231.09 232.01
234.28 235.10 235.23
235.27 236.03 237.09
237.23 237.24 238.02
238.08 238.25 240.09
242.18 242.23 243.03
243.12 243.17 244.28
245.06 245.21 245.26
246.24 246.26 247.05
247.14 249.12 249.13
250.08 250.24 250.27
251.11 251.20 251.28

THIS (CONT.)   252.02
253.04 253.07 253.08
253.08 253.10 253.26
255.10 255.17 256.08
256.09 257.28 259.21
250.06 260.25 267.27
268.20 269.01 269.30
270.20 271.14 278.06
279.03 280.17 281.27
282.04 282.12 282.27
282.28 282.28 282.30
283.08 285.10 286.04
286.16 286.22 286.28
287.10 288.16 288.16
288.28 289.06 289.22
290.22 290.30 291.05
235.16 298.26 300.06
301.24 302.19 304.28
304.30 306.01 306.11
307.25 308.30 309.04
309.05 309.09 315.28
315.30 317.05 317.14
318.05 318.06 320.28
320.29 321.26 325.16
325.30 327.09 327.18
328.01 328.07 328.10
329.22 331.06 332.11
332.22 334.24 334.30
337.04 338.04 338.05
338.07 338.10 338.25
338.28 339.05 339.15
339.16 339.17 342.11
342.21 345.22 346.09
347.01 350.16 351.26
351.01 365.22 365.27
365.28 367.19 367.23
368.01 368.06 368.09
368.14 368.27 370.12
371.17 372.09 374.08
375.08 375.16 377.19
377.22 377.25 378.12
379.16 379.22 380.04
381.13 381.15 382.08
382.20 383.02 383.11
384.16 384.22 387.05
387.05 387.21 388.07
388.25 388.25 388.27
388.29 389.11 390.04
391.21 393.18 394.18
395.28 396.01 396.02
397.07 397.16 398.13
399.05 399.23 400.08
400.18 400.24 400.24
400.26 400.28 403.16
403.29 404.25 404.27
404.30 405.07 407.03
409.10 409.10 409.17
410.13 411.27 417.29
419.18 420.15 420.26
421.06 423.19 423.22
426.11 427.20 429.02
429.15 432.09 435.16
438.04 438.14 442.02
450.09 453.09 454.21
454.24 455.18 456.12
456.15 457.15 458.08
458.24 459.22 460.06
460.16 460.20 461.06
461.16 462.30 463.21
464.04 467.16 470.17
470.18 471.12 471.13
471.17 471.24 472.16
473.01 473.01 473.25
474.14 474.16 474.30
475.05 475.06 475.24
477.18 477.20 478.22
478.25 479.02 479.07
479.07 481.01 481.09
485.01 485.01 486.18
487.04 487.15 488.21
488.25 490.08 494.11
495.07 495.19 495.24
501.15 502.29 505.12
505.29 510.14 510.22
511.04 513.15 514.16
516.13 516.20
THOLE   495.29
THOLE-PINS   495.29
THORNS   271.22
THORNY   323.12 470.04

THOROUGH   10.14
THOROUGHFARE   13.06
THOROUGHLY   284.05
   288.20 375.26
THOSE   4.03   8.29
   10.17 14.21 15.04
   28.20 35.15 41.24
   48.15 55.03 55.07
   67.23 69.23 83.20
   88.13 91.06 97.22
   102.09 106.12 111.21
   117.02 138.19 143.07
   156.10 160.09 164.02
   170.05 175.06 175.07
   178.29 194.24 210.28
   224.16 235.19 242.05
   271.04 271.05 271.07
   271.24 271.27 272.01
   272.18 273.01 273.24
   275.04 277.11 320.07
   321.21 329.19 335.03
   338.01 374.17 412.13
   431.30 434.10 444.08
   447.18 450.29 458.05
   465.03 471.14 474.07
   478.01 487.20 500.21
   504.11 507.09 508.10
   513.10 513.22 515.16
THOU   118.02
THOUGH   19.10   24.04
   24.13 24.20 25.06
   28.22 30.15 31.10
   31.13 36.14 37.01
   38.05 38.13 39.06
   40.21 40.22 42.07
   45.21 46.06 47.13
   47.18 48.18 56.03
   64.20 67.02 68.10
   70.01 85.08 87.08
   87.27 88.27 89.11
   95.12 100.28 109.27
   110.07 111.25 112.29
   114.10 116.29 124.04
   124.18 124.23 128.25
   131.10 132.29 134.11
   134.30 140.08 140.12
   142.18 146.11 149.08
   150.04 150.10 158.02
   159.20 159.22 160.27
   165.22 166.07 170.03
   170.23 172.13 174.21
   176.13 177.20 179.05
   181.22 184.07 186.30
   187.27 188.24 190.04
   191.10 192.03 192.26
   193.25 195.10 195.28
   204.18 205.01 208.06
   209.01 209.16 210.11
   213.04 216.23 217.13
   217.19 217.22 224.23
   226.09 226.11 231.08
   232.20 237.04 239.12
   241.03 241.11 242.18
   242.21 244.05 248.08
   252.25 260.07 261.05
   262.28 264.02 264.25
   265.15 267.26 270.01
   270.11 271.30 272.15
   281.05 283.05 283.30
   292.22 295.04 295.10
   302.11 305.03 310.14
   317.13 323.19 330.09
   334.13 335.03 341.19
   348.12 349.09 349.11
   350.11 350.24 356.04
   360.09 362.18 366.06
   367.07 369.08 372.06
   382.25 383.22 385.21
   386.24 394.02 395.17
   396.30 397.14 398.09
   398.27 402.02 404.12
   404.19 406.01 406.05
   416.21 418.09 423.26
   424.02 424.03 429.30
   434.20 437.02 450.18
   454.15 457.18 459.05
   472.06 474.07 478.03
   490.20 495.13 496.07
   501.04 512.10
THOUGHT   8.03   8.21

THOUGHT (CONT.)   11.28
   12.10 14.05 17.09
   23.09 26.17 29.15
   34.01 34.19 36.19
   38.04 38.05 47.16
   51.27 53.23 54.20
   67.26 69.16 69.24
   77.23 78.20 86.05
   90.07 104.05 104.11
   104.14 109.29 111.04
   111.05 116.26 118.16
   118.20 121.11 124.17
   125.20 127.29 129.19
   132.29 136.24 141.03
   147.10 147.24 154.03
   154.16 155.19 157.08
   163.30 164.20 172.19
   183.10 210.14 211.21
   224.12 225.27 226.02
   226.14 236.04 245.20
   272.14 280.04 300.23
   303.18 304.16 304.21
   304.27 308.14 309.05
   311.16 312.07 312.28
   316.19 321.30 325.01
   339.01 359.10 360.17
   368.04 369.07 369.12
   370.20 375.23 385.11
   404.20 405.20 425.10
   428.10 438.21 463.21
   463.26 472.04 483.07
   505.04 510.21
THOUGHTFUL   33.21
   151.29 257.19 322.06
THOUGHTFULLY   153.06
   287.21
THOUGHTFULNESS   126.29
   169.08
THOUGHTS   23.12 24.02
   60.07 64.16 79.04
   116.27 129.21 149.26
   174.12 176.29 361.18
   382.27 384.01 386.25
   387.17 409.04 413.15
   422.01 423.17 431.29
   447.18 454.06 458.12
   507.01
THOUSAND   76.01 111.14
   136.15 199.24 240.12
   277.02 281.05
THOUSANDS   168.02
   270.28 446.06
THRASHING   356.24
THREAD   29.04 65.01
   192.10 291.26 409.27
   484.13
THREAD-LIKE   409.27
THREADBARE   170.10
THREADS   263.16 498.17
THREATENED   484.02
   513.17
THREATENING   6.02
   85.06 116.07 131.19
   198.25 290.05 379.26
THREATENINGLY   87.29
THREATS   147.27 405.27
THREE   2.12 15.11
   22.25 26.01 33.07
   43.08 46.05 45.21
   64.24 69.30 70.21
   73.07 78.08 86.25
   99.13 100.15 101.22
   103.23 103.23 107.17
   117.13 126.27 133.04
   136.13 143.27 149.22
   151.05 177.29 182.02
   198.27 199.30 200.09
   207.22 209.11 222.22
   225.13 234.18 234.24
   240.12 245.23 249.02
   251.26 252.07 255.29
   279.18 290.27 297.16
   300.12 301.02 306.01
   330.15 331.17 331.18
   347.08 353.03 353.16
   366.23 371.20 373.05
   373.23 373.24 417.25
   441.03 453.15 454.25
   455.15 464.26 466.06
   479.14 479.14 488.02

THREE (CONT.)   500.30
   503.11
THREE-LEGGED   22.25
THREE-QUARTERS   73.07
THREESCORE   246.15
THRESHOLD   265.11
   384.24 506.29
THREW   76.27 126.01
   163.27 230.29 253.24
   286.09 372.18 393.16
   397.06 444.28 464.08
   479.30
THRILLED   324.30
THROAT   20.25 27.02
   89.25 132.20 134.06
   237.14 314.12 318.11
   350.09 374.08 390.17
   392.21 394.11 427.12
   458.13 505.21
THROATS   115.28 276.22
   343.22 458.18 500.25
THROB   467.19
THRONE   251.03
THRONG   513.26
THRONGED   320.08
THRONGING   504.03
THROTTLED   108.30
THROUGH   3.09   4.06
   5.11   5.24   6.17
   11.22 12.26 12.28
   14.17 15.27 16.23
   17.05 20.16 24.04
   25.07 26.01 31.09
   36.07 39.08 42.11
   48.04 49.30 49.30
   51.30 63.11 64.10
   81.09 83.18 85.27
   91.07 92.14 93.03
   102.16 103.28 103.29
   104.01 104.30 105.18
   110.08 118.16 119.02
   123.14 128.16 131.09
   131.16 131.24 133.17
   135.04 136.10 136.13
   138.20 139.17 143.16
   144.18 151.17 153.01
   155.02 155.25 160.28
   163.16 166.02 166.03
   167.13 174.11 182.16
   186.17 200.23 205.23
   205.24 211.14 212.26
   212.27 214.13 217.30
   218.17 224.30 229.24
   231.15 241.08 261.12
   253.05 264.02 274.13
   275.02 279.13 279.29
   280.10 280.11 291.12
   301.20 306.04 307.19
   309.25 311.23 313.24
   315.12 316.19 320.27
   321.09 327.06 330.23
   331.22 335.08 335.15
   338.14 338.21 339.14
   340.10 349.30 352.01
   352.04 354.02 357.04
   359.07 360.27 369.20
   370.05 370.26 372.02
   373.02 374.12 379.29
   379.30 390.16 394.03
   396.13 396.28 408.14
   408.18 409.14 419.14
   422.13 426.22 428.20
   429.26 430.01 432.20
   441.16 448.09 459.29
   469.22 477.21 478.26
   479.03 479.24 482.09
   482.18 484.04 491.15
   495.18 497.08 507.01
   509.28 515.12
THROW   2.27 122.20
   140.20 165.17 181.05
   199.06 312.25 402.30
   457.24 495.15 497.12
THROWING 47.04 248.06
   262.04 269.23 394.23
   437.27 469.23 481.01
THROWN   13.27 19.06
   20.21 22.11 33.22
   45.21 99.23 120.23
   131.01 170.08 173.07

THROWN (CONT.) 216.04
233.04 332.09 349.14
395.12 475.01
THROWS 402.28 402.29
THRUST 67.20 109.09
154.11 225.19 296.06
315.04 370.05 370.25
THUMB 46.19 48.07
74.14 181.18 257.08
THUMBS 179.07 179.21
278.02
THUMP 30.22 53.17
145.05 178.07
THUMPED 58.12
THUMPING 250.21 368.15
THUNDER 31.01 31.01
31.04 31.13 84.25
94.18 123.09 216.18
217.06 479.19 509.16
THUNDER-CLOUDS 94.18
THUNDERED 373.24
THUNDERSTORM 337.18
THUNDERSTRUCK 487.02
THUS 2.13 3.17
28.04 41.02 46.15
53.14 68.28 81.22
166.04 228.29 251.29
266.12 287.27 299.06
300.29 301.26 310.27
327.13 331.20 336.06
340.01 346.08 389.07
421.14 425.11 444.13
451.26 494.29 501.14
511.29 512.29
THWART 134.29 145.04
152.09 153.03
THWARTED 488.17
THY 491.09 506.08
507.15
TI 137.17 137.17
TI-TI-ME 137.17
TICKETS 92.05 92.16
TICKLED 165.14
TIDE 4.28 6.02
7.02 7.09 298.07
441.10 442.24 443.28
445.16 467.09 467.10
491.20
TIDES 297.16
TIDILY 182.20
TIDINGS 505.10
TIED 20.29 70.16
293.25
TIES 271.07
TIFFIN 75.05 207.18
231.14 234.27 286.05
TIFFIN-TIME 231.14
TIGHT 37.18 115.19
198.29 290.24 290.24
371.14
TILL 22.18 40.24
43.22 51.26 51.27
58.22 77.13 89.28
93.25 95.19 106.07
109.11 134.24 146.29
146.29 183.24 194.22
198.15 198.18 208.23
227.10 228.27 229.25
237.18 254.22 254.27
269.26 285.01 298.14
307.22 316.17 318.22
333.14 342.03 342.30
349.29 355.16 361.16
369.21 373.22 383.27
398.18 401.16 405.05
405.08 408.28 414.14
425.04 437.18 439.25
445.14 447.04 450.14
457.19 457.20 469.01
470.03 472.01 479.09
480.24 481.17 490.14
498.08 502.18 502.26
503.11
TILLER 8.04 148.11
148.13 152.07 236.18
444.07 494.09 495.20
496.12
TILT 116.15 142.27
142.29 409.27
TILTED 173.12

TILTING 175.19
TIMBER 111.08 111.09
332.20 498.12
TIME 3.11 7.16
8.07 10.15 10.23
14.23 22.23 22.23
24.20 25.21 28.18
29.09 34.27 35.18
39.07 41.01 41.07
42.01 44.12 44.20
44.23 48.19 51.22
52.01 52.19 52.25
56.19 57.17 58.07
60.14 60.19 65.15
71.08 72.16 73.24
77.27 78.14 79.12
82.05 82.27 85.23
87.23 88.07 93.11
95.17 96.05 98.08
99.03 99.13 101.23
102.05 102.24 103.20
103.20 103.21 104.20
107.12 108.19 108.20
108.20 110.18 111.18
115.24 118.17 119.15
120.12 120.16 122.06
123.02 124.19 127.17
127.23 127.28 128.03
128.03 128.18 130.06
131.03 136.05 139.24
143.01 143.02 146.16
146.25 152.26 152.26
159.16 159.29 163.14
167.22 167.28 170.29
171.24 172.26 173.20
174.05 174.08 175.01
175.12 175.22 183.02
185.14 187.02 190.07
190.24 193.22 194.07
194.14 195.01 196.05
197.23 198.15 202.22
208.19 209.14 209.18
212.26 213.01 216.10
216.17 217.14 218.23
221.07 222.12 223.22
224.07 227.13 228.22
228.24 230.04 231.10
231.14 234.27 236.05
236.22 238.21 240.09
242.22 242.27 243.26
245.02 250.10 250.14
251.23 255.25 259.27
260.20 270.13 275.06
275.19 276.20 281.10
281.18 285.21 287.14
288.19 289.23 291.03
291.27 293.20 298.07
300.16 300.27 303.23
306.20 307.15 308.20
309.07 310.15 311.17
312.05 313.24 322.16
327.24 329.01 330.12
333.30 333.30 334.18
336.22 341.26 342.14
347.04 349.25 351.25
353.23 359.29 360.15
363.17 365.23 367.06
367.10 367.23 368.14
371.21 373.03 375.10
375.13 375.19 382.05
382.16 382.16 382.22
385.07 387.19 387.23
390.04 391.29 395.01
395.08 397.25 399.25
401.17 403.07 403.18
403.21 404.10 404.23
404.25 405.02 407.07
410.30 413.01 413.18
414.16 416.05 417.30
419.23 420.29 421.04
427.17 430.20 430.27
432.03 434.08 435.24
436.26 437.02 440.14
451.18 456.18 457.01
457.20 461.10 461.24
461.28 463.16 466.12
471.23 475.10 475.19
481.11 482.28 485.11
490.28 492.16 492.16
493.25 494.05 500.23

TIME (CONT.) 501.08
504.17 505.03 506.04
509.02 510.14 510.21
511.22 512.26 512.29
514.06
TIMELY 443.13
TIMES 21.19 23.11
36.09 36.13 38.21
48.17 48.25 99.09
99.25 101.22 108.12
109.03 110.08 112.22
126.27 127.10 128.10
188.09 197.08 201.24
203.02 210.01 214.17
228.29 279.19 293.13
299.27 309.26 341.09
345.13 348.08 352.01
353.10 408.13 424.02
424.03 454.25 464.26
500.30
TIMID 16.10
TIMIDITY 399.11
TIMIDLY 508.12
TIN 21.15 23.28
280.08 290.23 299.03
299.25
TIN-POT 23.28
TING 241.17
TINGE 86.06 414.01
TINGED 77.25 239.07
335.17
TINKERS 80.30
TINKLE 120.30 211.13
TINKLING 21.16
TINT 4.10
TINY 71.07 80.25
121.02 180.16 302.30
375.26 410.10 410.11
415.16 467.20 492.05
TIP 101.01 142.30
TIPPED 43.39 143.24
456.25
TIPS 33.24 110.25
167.30 258.23 259.18
TIPTOE 183.26
TIPTOED 30.13
TIPTOEING 75.11
TIRED 152.07 152.07
299.20 337.08 374.24
427.14 438.14 475.27
495.25
TIS 86.01
TISPEP 241.18
TISPEP-SHIA 241.18
TISSUES 252.29
TITTERING 402.20
TO 1.11 1.18
2.02 2.04 2.06
2.15 2.23 2.23
2.28 3.03 3.04
3.08 3.10 3.11
3.12 3.24 3.25
4.04 4.12 4.14
4.17 4.20 4.26
5.14 5.18 5.21
6.07 6.13 6.23
6.24 7.06 7.16
7.21 7.23 7.23
8.09 8.09 8.22
9.01 9.02 10.01
10.03 10.06 10.21
10.21 11.10 11.12
11.12 11.13 11.16
11.20 11.21 11.30
12.04 12.08 12.09
12.13 12.13 12.23
13.07 13.14 13.15
13.21 13.25 14.01
14.16 14.18 15.02
15.26 16.10 16.15
16.24 17.02 18.01
19.03 19.08 19.09
20.04 20.04 20.11
20.21 20.26 20.26
21.07 22.01 22.03
22.22 22.22 22.23
22.28 23.23 24.01
24.05 24.30 24.30
25.05 25.13 25.14
25.24 25.28 26.20

TO (CONT.) 26.28
26.30 27.21 27.23
27.30 28.02 28.04
28.21 28.26 29.02
29.06 29.09 29.10
29.18 29.22 30.05
31.08 31.11 32.02
32.02 32.11 32.20
32.21 33.15 33.18
33.29 33.30 34.17
34.27 35.06 35.13
35.16 35.17 35.25
35.29 36.02 36.06
36.07 36.14 36.16
36.16 36.16 36.20
36.23 36.23 36.24
36.28 36.29 37.08
37.16 37.19 37.27
38.03 38.08 38.09
38.17 38.18 38.22
38.23 40.02 40.04
40.05 40.06 40.07
40.14 40.17 40.22
40.22 40.24 41.01
41.02 41.05 41.07
41.12 41.14 41.19
41.22 41.23 41.25
41.28 41.30 41.30
42.05 42.16 42.16
42.27 43.01 43.01
43.06 43.10 43.31
43.32 43.33 43.36
43.41 43.43 44.01
44.21 44.24 45.01
45.02 45.03 45.04
45.15 45.15 45.18
45.22 45.24 45.29
46.03 46.10 46.12
46.13 46.17 46.30
47.05 47.14 47.15
47.16 47.25 47.28
48.06 48.14 48.20
48.26 49.04 49.09
49.16 49.22 49.27
49.29 50.02 50.03
50.28 51.05 51.06
51.06 51.11 51.11
51.12 51.13 51.15
51.21 51.23 51.23
51.29 52.03 52.03
52.13 52.16 52.19
52.20 52.21 52.23
52.24 53.01 53.06
53.09 53.10 53.13
53.16 53.18 53.20
53.21 54.01 54.04
54.05 54.10 54.14
54.15 54.19 54.19
54.20 54.22 54.23
54.25 55.10 55.10
55.19 55.19 55.22
55.22 55.23 56.10
56.20 56.20 56.23
56.26 57.01 57.02
57.05 57.08 57.08
57.12 57.13 57.14
57.15 57.17 57.21
57.25 57.26 57.27
57.30 58.05 58.05
58.07 58.17 58.24
58.30 59.10 59.12
59.17 59.19 59.30
60.04 60.07 60.16
60.24 60.30 61.03
61.07 61.09 61.12
61.20 61.22 62.02
62.06 62.08 62.15
62.18 62.23 63.02
63.17 63.22 64.05
64.06 64.15 64.18
64.19 64.30 65.02
65.06 65.09 66.03
66.06 66.06 66.08
66.08 66.15 66.18
66.21 67.03 67.04
67.06 67.08 67.11
67.22 68.05 68.23
68.24 68.28 69.05
69.08 69.09 69.12
69.13 69.16 69.25

TO (CONT.)		69.26
69.26	70.19	70.22
70.24	70.26	70.28
70.29	70.38	71.14
71.17	71.18	71.20
72.03	72.04	72.07
72.07	72.12	72.14
72.26	72.29	73.09
73.10	73.14	73.15
73.17	73.19	73.21
73.22	73.23	73.24
73.27	73.30	74.01
74.02	74.04	74.08
74.09	74.09	74.16
74.17	74.30	75.01
75.04	75.06	75.09
75.11	75.13	75.15
75.21	75.22	75.25
75.28	76.05	76.15
76.20	76.21	76.22
77.03	77.14	78.01
78.20	78.23	78.24
78.25	78.28	79.07
79.08	79.13	79.14
79.15	79.21	79.23
79.25	79.28	79.28
79.30	80.04	80.04
80.10	80.12	80.17
80.18	80.21	81.04
81.10	81.14	81.19
81.24	81.25	81.27
81.28	82.01	82.06
82.17	82.20	82.20
82.22	82.25	82.25
82.26	82.27	83.16
83.30	84.04	84.08
84.09	84.10	84.12
84.16	84.24	85.09
85.12	85.19	85.22
85.22	85.23	85.30
86.01	86.02	86.05
86.07	86.11	86.12
86.16	86.17	86.21
85.29	87.02	87.03
87.07	87.23	87.25
88.18	88.19	89.07
89.10	89.16	89.16
89.19	89.29	90.03
90.05	90.09	90.11
90.12	90.15	90.16
90.18	90.23	90.29
91.03	91.04	91.12
93.02	93.04	93.08
93.15	93.27	93.28
94.07	94.15	94.21
94.21	94.22	95.01
95.03	95.05	95.08
95.08	95.15	95.18
95.22	95.27	95.30
96.01	96.04	96.10
96.11	96.12	96.15
96.20	96.25	96.27
96.29	97.02	97.04
97.18	97.18	97.19
97.23	98.06	98.08
98.11	98.17	98.20
98.20	98.23	98.24
98.28	98.30	99.05
99.05	99.12	99.13
99.16	99.17	99.21
100.12	100.13	100.17
100.21	100.22	100.25
101.24	101.27	102.06
102.08	102.11	102.13
102.14	102.26	103.01
103.04	103.07	103.21
103.22	103.29	104.04
104.22	104.26	105.07
105.14	105.20	105.30
106.01	106.03	106.05
106.06	107.02	107.04
107.07	107.13	107.20
107.21	108.04	108.04
108.11	108.13	108.15
108.18	108.20	108.20
108.22	108.23	108.26
108.27	108.29	109.01
109.17	109.25	110.13
110.18	111.01	111.03
111.07	111.09	111.12

TO (CONT.)		111.18
111.27	112.02	112.07
112.08	112.08	112.09
112.10	112.12	112.13
112.14	112.15	112.17
112.18	112.19	112.19
112.23	113.01	113.03
113.04	113.07	113.19
113.20	113.25	114.02
114.07	114.11	114.17
114.27	115.06	115.17
115.27	115.27	116.04
116.13	116.25	116.29
116.29	117.01	117.04
117.04	117.10	117.11
117.19	117.22	117.25
117.25	117.27	117.28
118.02	118.03	118.07
118.09	118.11	118.18
118.29	119.02	119.06
119.25	120.02	120.02
120.06	120.10	120.11
120.16	121.08	122.01
122.05	122.10	122.11
122.12	122.16	122.19
123.19	123.21	123.23
123.24	123.27	124.03
124.08	124.12	124.13
124.15	124.20	124.22
124.23	124.23	125.06
125.06	125.07	125.12
125.15	125.17	125.26
125.27	125.29	126.07
126.09	126.09	126.11
126.27	126.28	127.01
127.06	127.08	127.08
127.10	127.19	127.22
127.25	128.01	128.05
128.07	128.08	128.14
128.24	128.25	129.07
129.10	129.12	129.13
129.14	129.20	130.08
130.08	130.13	130.13
130.13	130.29	131.08
131.11	131.13	131.15
131.17	131.25	131.27
132.06	132.10	132.18
132.21	132.24	133.01
133.05	133.11	133.20
133.22	134.10	134.17
134.26	134.26	134.26
136.07	136.11	136.12
136.18	136.22	136.23
137.01	137.04	137.07
137.12	137.17	137.20
137.23	137.23	137.25
137.26	137.30	138.10
138.11	138.12	138.14
138.15	138.16	138.16
138.19	138.24	138.29
139.05	139.06	139.08
139.12	139.20	139.28
140.04	140.11	140.15
140.19	140.23	140.30
141.02	141.04	141.10
141.12	141.18	141.27
142.01	142.01	142.06
142.09	142.12	142.13
142.14	142.15	142.16
143.11	143.11	143.12
143.13	143.14	143.19
143.20	143.22	143.26
143.26	143.30	144.12
144.15	144.23	144.28
144.29	145.05	145.07
145.08	145.15	145.18
145.19	145.19	145.29
146.08	146.11	146.24
146.27	147.03	147.05
147.20	147.23	147.27
147.28	148.04	148.12
148.15	148.16	148.20
148.22	148.27	149.01
149.02	149.12	149.14
149.18	149.21	150.01
150.03	150.05	150.12
151.01	151.06	151.08
151.11	151.12	151.13
151.14	151.16	151.19
151.21	151.24	151.24

TO (CONT.)		151.25
151.30	152.07	152.09
152.09	152.17	152.17
152.26	152.27	153.01
153.02	153.04	153.04
153.07	153.12	153.13
153.20	154.03	154.04
154.08	154.09	154.10
154.14	154.15	154.16
155.05	155.10	155.12
155.14	155.15	155.16
155.17	155.17	156.02
156.02	156.04	156.06
156.08	156.10	156.11
156.15	156.27	156.30
157.07	157.11	157.12
157.16	157.16	158.05
158.06	158.14	158.16
158.22	158.26	158.28
159.03	159.04	159.05
159.06	159.17	159.21
160.02	160.06	160.07
160.08	160.11	160.15
160.15	160.17	160.18
161.03	162.05	162.08
162.10	162.10	162.15
162.19	162.23	163.06
163.13	163.17	163.20
163.24	164.01	164.11
164.12	164.17	164.26
164.29	165.09	165.09
165.11	165.14	165.29
166.06	166.09	166.19
166.21	166.22	166.25
166.29	167.03	167.15
167.16	167.17	167.28
168.03	168.05	168.06
168.08	168.19	169.09
169.10	169.15	169.15
169.16	169.18	169.20
169.21	169.25	170.10
170.11	170.15	170.19
170.24	170.25	171.01
171.05	171.11	171.27
172.01	172.09	172.10
172.15	172.16	172.24
173.07	173.13	173.18
173.18	173.19	174.02
174.03	174.06	174.14
175.13	175.23	175.30
176.12	176.13	176.15
176.16	176.27	177.03
177.04	177.05	177.05
177.17	177.23	178.07
178.13	178.19	178.20
178.26	178.28	179.07
179.11	179.13	179.14
179.17	179.22	180.08
180.15	180.25	180.26
181.05	181.12	181.13
181.27	182.17	182.23
182.26	183.03	183.03
183.12	183.15	183.21
183.22	183.23	183.25
183.27	183.28	184.01
184.02	184.05	184.06
184.13	184.14	185.02
185.02	185.11	185.12
185.16	185.18	185.23
185.27	185.29	186.01
186.03	186.06	186.08
186.09	186.11	186.17
186.20	186.29	187.10
187.11	187.12	187.15
187.18	187.24	187.25
188.05	188.09	188.13
188.15	188.16	188.16
188.19	188.20	188.22
188.24	188.28	189.01
189.02	189.03	189.06
189.08	189.10	189.10
189.12	189.13	189.18
189.22	189.23	190.03
190.11	190.13	190.15
191.07	191.08	191.12
191.21	191.22	191.25
192.15	192.15	192.29
192.30	193.09	193.19
193.23	193.24	194.04
194.07	194.09	194.10

TO (CONT.)		194.17
194.25	194.30	195.07
195.11	195.23	195.24
195.27	196.06	196.21
196.24	197.02	197.03
197.09	197.12	197.16
197.17	197.19	197.24
197.30	198.01	198.06
198.29	198.30	199.02
199.04	199.05	199.06
199.06	199.08	199.11
199.11	199.19	199.24
199.30	200.03	200.05
200.05	200.07	200.07
200.09	200.19	200.19
200.22	200.26	200.27
200.29	201.03	201.11
201.23	202.11	202.12
202.17	202.18	202.21
203.01	203.07	203.12
203.13	203.14	203.18
203.19	203.24	203.29
204.06	204.08	204.13
204.13	204.18	205.05
205.08	205.14	205.17
205.21	205.22	205.23
205.25	206.06	207.06
207.11	208.03	208.06
208.09	208.10	208.15
208.20	208.21	208.25
209.08	209.13	209.18
209.19	209.20	209.22
209.24	209.27	209.29
209.30	210.02	210.09
210.19	210.20	210.23
210.26	211.05	211.06
211.06	211.10	211.19
211.22	211.26	211.29
211.30	212.08	212.10
212.15	212.24	212.28
213.12	213.14	214.07
214.14	214.18	214.25
214.30	215.09	215.16
215.21	215.23	215.26
215.28	215.29	216.04
216.04	216.04	216.08
216.14	216.17	216.24
216.25	216.29	216.30
217.02	217.10	217.14
217.17	218.03	218.09
218.10	218.13	218.15
218.16	218.23	219.03
219.05	219.20	219.30
220.01	220.15	220.19
220.25	221.02	221.03
221.08	221.08	222.11
222.15	222.17	222.17
222.20	222.21	222.24
222.24	223.04	223.08
223.11	223.12	223.13
223.18	223.18	223.23
223.24	223.25	223.27
224.12	224.28	225.07
225.11	225.14	225.15
225.18	225.26	226.02
226.12	226.21	226.23
226.25	227.04	227.06
227.08	227.13	227.14
227.24	228.01	228.04
228.06	228.12	228.13
228.18	228.19	228.22
228.25	228.26	228.26
229.04	229.09	229.14
229.17	229.17	230.05
230.18	230.25	230.27
230.30	231.01	231.15
231.16	231.25	231.26
231.29	232.01	232.06
232.12	232.13	232.14
232.23	232.24	232.27
232.28	233.03	233.05
233.09	233.14	233.21
233.24	233.29	234.05
234.07	234.14	235.01
235.03	235.05	235.10
235.15	235.17	235.19
235.20	235.22	235.24
235.27	236.01	236.05
236.05	236.06	236.09
236.09	236.09	236.20

TO (CONT.)		236.20	TO (CONT.)		278.12	TO (CONT.)		320.03	TO (CONT.)		360.21
236.23	236.23	237.05	278.25	278.30	279.29	320.04	320.22	320.23	360.25	361.03	361.05
237.06	237.07	237.09	280.13	280.26	280.30	320.24	320.25	320.26	361.05	361.06	361.07
237.13	237.17	237.22	281.02	281.07	281.07	320.28	320.28	321.03	361.10	361.11	361.15
237.24	237.28	238.01	281.10	281.12	281.13	321.05	321.07	321.08	361.17	361.21	361.28
238.02	238.04	238.07	281.23	281.30	282.02	321.11	321.13	321.15	361.30	362.09	362.11
238.10	238.11	238.15	282.04	282.05	282.09	321.15	321.20	321.23	362.18	362.19	363.03
238.18	238.25	238.28	282.10	282.11	282.16	321.26	321.30	322.09	363.05	363.06	363.08
239.02	239.09	239.10	282.19	282.21	282.24	322.10	322.18	322.18	363.08	363.12	363.16
239.15	239.19	239.20	282.27	283.01	283.03	322.23	322.25	322.29	363.19	363.20	364.02
240.01	240.02	240.03	283.03	283.06	283.13	323.03	323.10	323.24	364.03	364.13	364.15
240.06	240.07	240.13	283.14	283.16	283.18	323.25	323.26	324.04	364.18	364.19	364.23
240.16	240.18	240.23	283.18	284.01	284.02	324.05	324.20	324.20	364.25	364.27	365.08
240.24	240.29	241.01	284.04	284.07	285.02	324.29	324.30	325.02	365.10	365.20	366.06
241.01	241.18	241.25	285.05	285.10	285.23	325.20	325.25	325.26	366.07	366.10	366.10
241.27	242.01	242.02	286.14	286.17	286.22	325.29	326.02	326.02	366.25	367.03	367.21
242.02	242.06	242.15	286.23	286.30	287.07	326.03	327.19	327.21	367.26	367.30	368.11
242.20	242.21	242.30	287.10	287.13	287.17	328.05	328.19	328.21	368.14	368.16	368.21
243.04	243.09	243.09	287.18	287.24	288.03	329.01	329.15	329.15	368.30	369.01	369.06
243.19	243.24	243.28	288.06	288.20	288.25	329.16	329.17	329.17	369.09	369.09	369.13
244.08	244.10	244.11	288.28	289.03	289.05	329.24	329.25	329.30	369.16	369.23	369.29
244.12	244.15	244.18	289.08	289.10	289.13	330.08	330.14	330.16	370.04	370.09	370.11
244.23	244.26	245.01	289.14	289.14	289.25	330.16	330.19	330.20	370.18	370.25	370.28
245.05	245.12	245.13	289.25	289.26	289.27	330.21	330.22	330.24	370.29	371.22	372.18
245.16	245.19	245.24	290.03	290.06	290.07	330.28	330.30	331.03	372.20	373.14	373.22
246.04	246.04	246.05	290.10	290.16	290.17	331.05	331.06	331.07	374.05	374.06	374.22
246.21	247.03	247.16	290.18	290.20	290.20	331.08	331.09	331.10	374.28	375.02	375.02
247.18	247.20	247.22	290.24	291.01	291.06	331.13	331.22	332.07	375.04	375.05	375.05
248.12	248.19	249.13	291.08	291.13	291.17	332.10	332.12	332.13	375.10	375.11	375.12
249.19	249.23	249.25	291.23	292.02	292.09	332.15	332.16	332.20	375.14	375.16	375.20
249.26	250.02	250.05	292.10	292.12	292.12	332.27	332.28	333.01	375.22	375.23	376.04
250.06	250.08	250.09	292.14	292.16	292.17	333.14	333.15	333.16	376.08	376.16	376.18
250.14	250.23	251.03	292.20	292.23	292.28	333.23	333.23	333.26	376.18	376.22	376.25
251.11	251.12	251.24	292.28	293.02	293.08	334.14	334.14	334.15	377.11	377.12	377.13
251.28	252.11	252.20	293.16	293.18	293.18	334.17	334.26	335.01	377.17	377.22	377.22
252.21	252.22	253.16	293.19	293.21	293.25	335.02	335.07	336.03	378.01	378.07	378.09
253.28	254.01	254.15	293.26	293.29	294.03	336.04	336.07	336.18	378.13	378.14	378.19
254.16	254.16	254.17	294.03	294.04	294.05	336.22	336.24	337.03	378.24	378.26	378.29
254.19	254.20	254.23	294.13	294.23	294.28	337.19	337.22	337.22	379.02	379.03	379.09
255.03	255.05	255.07	295.03	295.09	295.12	337.22	337.24	337.25	379.11	379.13	379.14
255.08	255.13	255.15	295.14	295.20	295.22	337.26	337.28	337.30	379.29	380.03	380.16
255.22	255.23	256.01	295.30	295.30	297.17	338.02	338.03	338.03	381.05	381.11	381.13
256.17	256.25	256.26	297.18	297.20	297.21	338.05	338.11	338.28	381.18	381.21	381.22
257.05	257.07	257.12	298.07	298.14	298.16	339.06	339.10	339.13	382.01	382.08	382.08
257.15	257.22	257.24	298.17	298.17	298.22	339.17	340.08	340.14	382.11	382.17	382.18
257.26	258.01	258.02	298.23	298.26	298.27	340.18	340.24	341.04	382.21	382.22	382.30
258.10	258.13	258.14	299.07	299.08	299.11	341.06	341.06	341.07	383.01	383.03	383.04
258.27	259.01	259.02	299.16	299.21	299.21	341.09	341.10	341.12	383.07	383.13	383.13
259.08	259.11	259.12	299.26	299.29	300.01	341.23	341.23	342.09	383.14	383.15	383.16
259.16	259.17	259.20	300.03	300.07	300.13	342.10	342.16	342.22	383.16	383.17	383.19
259.24	259.24	259.25	300.14	300.17	300.22	343.04	343.05	343.13	383.23	383.24	383.24
259.26	260.02	260.12	300.30	301.06	301.09	343.21	343.24	344.06	383.29	383.30	384.02
260.17	260.27	260.28	301.10	301.14	301.16	344.07	344.09	344.11	384.14	384.21	384.28
260.30	261.03	261.12	301.17	301.18	301.19	344.11	344.13	344.26	385.05	385.06	385.06
261.27	261.28	261.30	301.26	302.04	302.05	345.03	345.03	345.10	385.11	385.13	385.18
262.03	262.18	262.24	302.06	302.09	302.24	345.21	345.23	345.30	385.25	385.26	385.27
262.29	263.02	263.27	302.29	303.01	303.01	346.01	346.08	346.10	385.28	385.29	386.02
264.01	264.06	264.13	303.02	303.16	303.18	347.11	347.18	348.07	386.04	386.13	386.15
264.20	265.03	265.13	303.26	303.28	304.02	348.11	348.14	348.24	386.18	386.19	386.24
265.17	266.08	265.08	304.07	304.07	304.16	348.25	348.25	348.26	386.27	387.02	387.06
266.09	266.13	266.14	304.16	304.17	304.18	348.29	349.10	349.12	387.19	387.22	387.27
266.15	266.18	266.19	304.23	304.28	304.29	349.17	349.19	349.26	388.16	388.17	388.25
266.24	267.01	267.02	305.07	306.02	306.03	349.28	349.29	350.08	388.26	389.06	389.08
267.06	267.07	267.15	306.07	306.14	306.19	350.16	350.19	350.25	389.12	389.15	389.20
267.29	268.08	268.27	307.06	307.07	307.09	350.27	351.08	351.08	389.21	389.23	389.24
268.30	269.01	269.03	307.14	307.21	307.30	351.17	351.19	351.20	389.29	389.29	390.07
269.06	270.09	270.12	308.07	308.11	308.16	351.22	351.27	351.28	390.10	390.13	390.18
270.14	270.14	270.16	308.22	308.25	309.07	352.01	352.04	352.06	390.24	391.03	391.10
270.20	270.21	270.22	309.08	309.20	309.21	353.01	353.06	353.08	391.19	391.19	391.22
270.25	270.26	270.28	309.28	309.29	310.02	353.09	353.10	353.11	391.28	392.06	392.08
271.01	271.02	271.03	310.11	310.17	310.19	353.15	353.18	353.19	392.11	392.24	393.02
271.08	271.12	271.13	310.20	310.21	310.22	353.19	353.28	353.29	393.04	393.08	393.13
271.13	271.15	271.16	310.24	310.26	310.26	353.29	354.04	354.05	393.14	394.15	394.16
271.19	271.21	271.22	311.09	311.15	311.21	354.06	354.08	355.12	394.17	394.18	395.08
271.24	271.25	271.25	311.25	311.27	311.27	355.13	355.14	355.16	395.13	395.15	395.19
271.28	271.29	272.04	311.30	311.30	311.30	355.17	356.10	356.17	395.28	396.05	396.19
272.23	272.25	272.25	312.08	312.11	312.12	356.18	356.22	356.22	396.22	396.23	397.01
272.26	272.27	272.28	312.18	312.21	312.24	356.27	356.28	357.02	397.13	397.14	397.23
273.06	273.11	273.12	312.25	312.28	312.29	357.07	357.12	357.14	397.23	397.27	397.30
273.13	273.13	273.15	312.30	313.05	313.07	357.15	357.20	357.22	398.01	398.05	398.08
273.17	273.22	273.24	313.11	313.13	313.19	357.24	357.28	358.01	398.12	398.16	398.17
273.26	273.26	273.29	313.28	313.29	314.01	358.02	358.02	358.03	398.20	398.20	398.21
274.01	274.05	274.09	314.04	314.14	314.15	358.03	358.05	358.07	398.21	399.01	399.08
274.12	274.16	274.22	314.18	314.21	314.23	358.08	358.13	358.18	399.09	399.12	399.12
274.25	275.06	275.16	315.01	315.18	315.27	358.22	358.24	358.26	399.14	399.17	399.29
275.17	275.18	276.05	316.03	316.11	316.18	358.27	358.28	358.28	399.30	400.04	400.09
276.18	277.08	277.09	316.24	317.05	317.08	359.02	359.05	359.06	400.27	401.03	401.07
277.10	277.13	277.14	317.09	318.16	318.19	359.13	359.20	359.21	401.09	401.13	401.14
277.15	277.18	277.19	318.23	318.24	318.24	359.29	360.01	360.05	401.22	401.24	402.01
277.19	277.28	278.10	319.06	320.02	320.02	360.05	360.13	360.15	402.05	402.08	402.09

TONGUE (CONT.) 70.38
93.06 102.12 173.14
188.11 224.10 495.06
TONGUES 40.20 167.30
TONICS 58.21
TONS 454.08
TOO 7.10 24.03
25.25 26.22 28.25
29.01 29.02 47.13
50.02 50.18 52.13
52.18 60.18 63.26
65.09 70.12 70.15
70.33 72.24 73.06
76.13 80.01 80.15
85.01 89.15 91.04
93.07 97.21 99.18
99.18 102.13 111.03
113.14 113.23 114.04
114.08 116.07 122.15
124.05 126.06 126.06
128.19 129.12 129.22
130.30 134.25 136.07
139.30 141.02 142.06
142.12 142.21 143.06
143.10 144.04 145.05
145.09 146.22 148.03
148.11 148.25 150.17
152.19 158.29 159.30
160.02 163.21 164.19
169.12 169.24 170.02
172.01 176.07 179.20
179.25 181.05 181.15
181.19 184.01 184.12
185.09 185.16 186.14
187.20 189.11 191.24
196.11 196.16 196.29
198.05 198.10 201.28
202.11 202.13 203.02
203.24 204.12 205.12
205.25 211.05 212.07
212.24 214.14 215.05
215.16 216.03 216.03
218.19 219.01 219.29
220.10 220.27 222.23
223.21 227.12 228.24
228.28 231.10 231.21
234.06 234.13 234.25
236.27 243.01 254.24
254.29 255.25 255.26
257.17 258.12 260.20
251.07 263.20 264.14
267.21 267.27 272.14
274.05 275.01 275.19
277.06 278.16 283.23
289.21 293.22 295.29
296.06 299.17 300.30
301.18 304.10 304.18
304.23 304.28 306.20
309.21 320.27 337.13
338.04 339.16 340.25
343.26 344.07 344.14
348.28 349.28 351.21
351.24 352.18 355.09
355.24 367.29 374.06
374.26 375.06 375.11
377.02 381.13 382.14
382.23 384.02 385.08
386.27 387.20 388.12
389.13 390.01 390.24
390.27 391.11 391.19
391.22 391.23 396.07
397.29 400.28 402.01
403.20 404.30 405.25
406.05 406.05 413.20
415.02 419.25 420.03
431.05 434.19 435.12
436.30 437.09 441.24
442.12 447.10 455.25
457.18 461.11 467.04
471.18 472.04 473.27
475.17 475.24 475.29
481.06 482.10 482.10
486.09 492.25 495.24
501.25 507.13 507.22
509.12 510.26 516.11
TOOK 14.25 34.01
69.20 85.11 86.29
127.05 147.06 162.23
159.02 169.22 172.02
178.01 194.30 198.19

TOOK (CONT.) 198.24
205.05 211.21 212.09
217.05 228.12 230.11
241.01 241.09 241.23
243.27 250.02 256.28
278.15 280.24 304.22
308.01 308.04 308.10
309.05 310.10 311.22
322.19 329.13 330.01
335.11 351.29 373.01
375.17 376.01 397.13
400.29 404.26 430.20
439.03 451.23 452.04
456.13 470.08 478.07
491.11 496.11 499.24
509.26 513.03
TOOLS 395.19 478.02
TOOTHLESSLY 366.08
TOP 4.20 4.24
34.20 49.19 63.04
70.17 71.10 134.06
151.22 225.28 313.29
323.21 324.07 325.23
329.17 343.11 359.14
TOP-GALLANT 4.20
TOPI 199.15
TOPPED 420.09
TOPS 216.25 308.30
319.17 325.15 332.03
512.04
TOPSAIL 293.08
TORCH 365.17 367.22
367.26 369.22 370.07
370.27 372.13 373.03
374.10 382.13
TORCHES 513.09 514.03
TORCHLIGHT 368.10
TORE 132.15 136.01
144.18 229.11 491.24
TORMENT 125.28 341.04
TORMENTED 11.24
TORMENTING 78.18
390.11
TORN 20.24 149.06
353.17 359.06 431.23
479.06
TORPID 87.01 172.29
TORPOR 394.07
TORRENT 25.16
TORRID 350.29
TORTOISE 386.16
TORTUOUS 461.11
TORTUOUSLY 463.02
TORTURED 316.03 473.02
TOSS 53.08 107.04
307.23
TOSSED 12.02 288.18
TOSSING 6.03 7.03
55.15 57.19 307.11
350.07 474.01
TOTAL 113.18 334.26
422.11
TOTALLY 50.19 187.11
267.05 330.18 399.03
TOTTER 129.24
TOTTERED 199.22 510.28
TOTTERING 515.04
TOUCH 28.28 41.24
60.07 72.30 102.19
115.04 147.07 148.05
214.10 218.20 222.19
228.14 271.21 295.19
302.14 319.19 322.01
332.09 334.29 341.11
361.19 366.10 401.02
412.09 412.12 434.25
476.07 497.18 511.23
TOUCHED 43.43 79.30
101.01 137.10 141.07
178.05 273.12 368.06
381.01 512.14
TOUCHING 23.07 34.11
239.09 273.09 273.10
373.14 474.09 487.10
492.15
TOUGH 65.08 118.05
118.05
TOULON 173.19
TOUSLED 21.05

TOUT 173.08 178.26
180.24
TOUTE 169.22
TOW 169.22 171.01
439.03
TOWARDS 3.15 23.04
31.06 43.04 54.04
84.13 104.21 119.07
170.18 191.08 218.30
258.22 299.13 300.26
306.24 350.22 371.10
378.23 398.29 411.25
413.12 425.22 437.28
451.27 458.14 480.16
482.07 507.10 508.26
511.04
TOWED 164.12 493.20
TOWER 134.07 191.20
417.07 447.16
TOWERED 187.06
TOWERING 96.22
TOWING 170.29 171.29
496.04
TOWN 13.05 13.14
42.21 175.24 249.13
252.08 252.12 294.06
316.26 334.16 363.19
417.01 434.13 434.28
443.09 444.11 446.05
447.19 448.04 451.09
455.05 458.29 461.22
462.24 463.22 467.15
467.18 467.21 472.29
483.18 484.10 488.24
489.23 492.27 493.29
499.20 504.02 504.05
508.14
TOWN-REACH 504.02
TOWNFOLK 449.18
TOWNSFOLK 453.25
TOY 139.17 212.23
225.03
TOYING 499.11
TOYS 13.09 423.18
TRAC 178.29
TRACE 9.04 27.27
78.02 79.02 92.18
328.06 370.21 405.02
TRACED 417.28
TRACES 285.09 323.11
TRACINGS 252.26
TRACK 17.18 151.14
192.27 335.08
TRACKS 57.27 441.29
TRACTABILITY 208.08
TRACTABLE 10.14
TRADE 67.26 73.23
178.19 250.26 250.29
277.06 277.16 277.29
288.26 292.24 315.28
353.21
TRADED 250.25 278.10
TRADER 196.16 250.06
316.10 316.11 427.28
428.01 434.22 435.18
TRADERS 276.17 475.03
TRADING 245.30 268.24
303.29 316.04 316.13
343.14 353.16 356.20
366.13 475.23
TRADINGCLERK 288.25
TRADITION 298.20
299.15 299.18
TRADITION'S 65.03
TRADITIONALLY 65.01
TRAFFIC 5.27 151.14
TRAGIC 43.01 157.10
268.16 389.28 390.05
397.28
TRAIL 139.16 151.17
TRAILED 433.25
TRAILING 373.12 459.23
TRAILS 297.03
TRAINING 4.17 6.23
10.01 26.02
TRAINING-SHIP 4.17
6.23
TRAITOR 191.17
TRAMMELS 341.08
TRAMP 15.13 63.30

TRAMP (CONT.) 145.10
TRAMP- 63.30
TRAMPED 110.19 395.21
489.21
TRAMPLE 405.05 405.07
TRAMPLE' 405.06
TRAMPLED 403.15 405.12
475.07
TRAMPLING 105.27
TRAMPS 51.07
TRANCE 106.02 143.12
TRANQUILLITY 177.11
TRANSACTION 186.10
304.01
TRANSACTIONS 182.07
TRANSFER 290.25
TRANSFERRED 440.03
TRANSGRESSION 268.07
432.13
TRANSHIP 440.14
TRANSITIONS 29.05
TRANSLATED 464.26
465.07
TRANSPLANTED 436.24
TRANSPORTED 44.15
266.19
TRAP 471.28 472.01
TRAPPED 124.04 124.04
471.29
TRAVEL 128.24 131.16
192.09 416.20
TRAVELLED 250.02
252.05 262.07
TRAVELLER 249.29
TRAVELLERS 16.26
TRAVELLING 344.29
TRAVELS 92.07
TRAVERSED 21.17
125.22 291.28 313.14
TRAVERSING 248.02
TRAY 307.30
TREACHEROUS 17.02
430.21 458.24 501.19
TREACHERY 251.15
452.16 492.21 503.09
505.24
TREAD 23.17 226.19
288.05 333.04
TREADING 15.24
TREASURED 421.15
TREASURER 437.15
TREASURES 252.19
TREAT 28.13
TREATED 189.06 346.03
355.13 405.14 435.08
TREBLY 228.30
TREE 132.17 192.06
192.12 273.11 319.17
323.09 325.09 325.15
332.03 364.01 380.14
397.05 432.01 452.26
459.29 510.08 512.04
TREE-TOPS 319.17
325.15 332.03 512.04
TREE-TRUNK 452.26
TREE'D 143.09
TREES 4.07 4.11
216.26 220.17 271.11
276.12 313.22 314.01
396.17 397.08 408.20
430.02 432.06 432.08
444.21 444.30 446.04
455.09 491.16 497.07
509.04
TREETRUNK 464.02
TREMBLE 46.09 149.16
202.04 373.05 382.20
TREMBLED 49.07 49.08
63.09 102.26 109.16
382.19
TREMBLING 20.21
89.11 199.15 384.10
504.16 505.07
TREMELY 361.01
TREMENDOUS 98.21
147.29 312.20 334.04
380.04 389.09
TREMOR 177.07 463.08
TREMULOUS 348.27
TREMULOUSLY 360.27

TREMULOUSLY (CONT.)
393.22
TREPIDATION 86.21
TRES 175.22
TRIAL 147.17
TRIBES 316.23
TRIBUTARY 489.30
TRIBUTE 85.12 499.26
TRICED 24.17
TRICK 25.13 70.34
287.12 305.02
TRICKED 115.09
TRICKLE 28.24
TRICKLED 279.29 495.11
TRICKLING 83.05
TRICKS 474.26
TRIED 32.02 57.14
87.23 104.22 108.29
127.04 142.01 144.08
145.05 145.19 150.25
152.17 154.03 167.16
201.23 262.29 267.14
277.15 287.06 299.30
311.25 337.19 353.18
353.28 364.15 370.03
370.12 381.21 389.08
395.11 399.17 402.13
406.03 420.05 421.01
428.27 433.19 460.20
463.17 470.13 484.30
486.14 500.03 503.12
507.05
TRIES 260.27
TRIESTE 249.25
TRIFLE 125.07 358.21
TRIFLES 69.23 146.15
275.21
TRIFLING 90.23 414.27
TRIGGER 372.18 466.06
TRIGONOMETRY 4.19
TRIM 166.05 441.11
TRIP 40.14 229.09
233.23
TRIPOD 232.27
TRIPOLI 249.26
TRIPPED 92.19
TRISTE 175.24
TRIUMPH 147.30 269.28
473.05 475.05
TRIUMPHANTLY 207.16
320.15
TROAT 514.24
TRODDEN 396.16 459.09
TROOP 82.26 300.07
314.27
TROPICAL 5.15 12.20
43.15 55.23 227.22
432.01
TROPICS 62.24 65.09
434.11
TROT 89.29
TROTTED 435.07
TROTTER 105.06
TROTTERS 94.06 141.12
TROTTING 199.17
TROUBLE 79.21 118.03
134.27 187.18 198.09
198.09 220.08 237.10
260.15 265.10 265.10
270.17 331.02 331.05
344.16 404.02 404.14
410.26 411.11 461.30
473.29 498.05
TROUBLED 21.20 55.06
230.22 291.10 325.02
352.01 384.23 386.11
391.20
TROUBLES 403.12
TROUSERS 153.05 208.16
288.11
TROUVAILLE 172.20
TRUCES 251.15
TRUCKLING 478.07
TRUCULENT 333.06
349.14
TRUE 35.14 57.06
60.02 64.26 82.15
95.14 111.22 112.03
136.03 139.20 152.10
152.11 165.27 196.27

TRUE (CONT.) 202.10
209.26 213.05 213.05
219.29 260.18 261.24
261.24 265.05 281.02
288.03 290.14 295.22
298.05 310.28 320.07
321.26 329.12 343.20
347.15 365.03 375.18
376.12 388.02 388.03
391.19 392.25 413.08
420.02 423.20 433.19
433.19 433.19 485.24
486.15 503.15
TRUER 82.13
TRULY 40.17 215.16
241.25 249.27
TRUMPETING 335.10
TRUMPETS 175.09
TRUNK 290.23 323.09
452.26
TRUNKS 92.12
TRUST 24.24 77.10
147.22 179.02 203.19
214.01 304.08 308.25
334.22 375.11 376.13
429.11 470.10 491.04
494.10 507.03
TRUSTED 53.19 81.01
81.02 213.02 278.14
282.14 303.06 303.24
307.02 322.13 329.20
332.13 400.21 447.14
507.07
TRUSTFULNESS 453.12
TRUSTING 20.05 41.21
223.16 421.25
TRUSTS 413.20
TRUSTWORTHY 103.06
246.06 358.18
TRUSTY 357.27 456.18
TRUTH 10.21 11.01
23.15 28.09 32.03
67.05 70.30 84.30
85.26 94.25 95.27
112.16 112.30 146.30
157.02 157.26 160.13
160.17 178.27 178.30
180.25 193.20 239.19
258.01 264.07 271.13
272.07 273.27 295.09
331.05 331.21 335.13
345.20 357.23 376.15
386.19 390.21 391.07
394.20 395.04 398.13
398.22 400.15 401.30
418.22 419.11 430.21
432.18 436.18 474.27
478.15 487.16 488.11
495.04 499.02 506.22
TRUTH' 188.19
TRUTH'S 35.29
TRUTHFUL 38.16
TRUTHFULLY 36.25
TRUTHFULNESS 347.13
488.02
TRUTHS 275.10
TRY 73.15 87.25
98.22 113.30 122.09
144.04 201.04 219.05
228.01 245.06 254.16
268.27 357.02 375.05
377.22 396.19 396.23
398.21 412.02 449.11
463.20 469.18 490.18
494.21
TRYING 36.06 47.14
56.20 57.25 64.30
84.09 90.15 93.28
97.23 98.20 107.10
138.29 143.14 143.20
148.15 181.05 182.17
187.15 202.21 205.08
211.23 273.24 310.26
313.10 313.19 338.28
359.05 393.04 400.01
437.22 461.21 463.22
479.22 505.15 512.13
TUAN 3.26 119.06
297.24 337.14 372.24
376.14 428.11 455.21

TUAN (CONT.) 487.13
489.24 491.07 502.23
505.12 506.05 507.15
508.12 510.23 512.22
512.23
TUCKED 255.21 315.14
338.14 361.16
TUFTS 196.14
TUG 44.21 78.18
120.06
TUGGING 115.26
TUGS 52.26
TUMBLE 290.28 310.11
TUMBLE-DOWN 310.11
TUMBLED 16.09 30.16
100.28 136.04 145.14
270.08 320.19
TUMBLER 168.16 169.05
178.02
TUMBLING 6.02 115.13
131.30
TUMULT 6.11 7.20
8.24 131.05 417.21
444.04
TUMULTUOUS 41.10
TUMULTUOUSLY 55.01
515.15
TUNE 47.25 198.14
361.30
TUNJU 407.23
TUNKU 306.05 306.21
336.07 353.30 412.05
444.12 453.07 461.24
462.09
TUNNEL 62.29
TURBAN 16.18 37.20
TURMOIL 126.12 341.27
370.01
TURN 8.28 25.14
42.30 93.26 94.26
96.10 111.19 137.20
152.12 153.19 187.30
217.10 223.01 226.23
242.02 271.21 286.16
287.25 318.23 321.30
336.19 337.28 367.03
376.01 401.10 402.08
407.06 432.21 441.10
443.28 450.13 459.18
477.12 487.12 504.24
505.11
TURNED 3.01 8.13
19.10 24.05 38.20
51.22 57.01 61.08
64.12 75.28 90.02
100.26 108.28 112.18
116.24 119.06 120.29
125.04 125.15 134.17
136.10 137.23 142.01
145.28 146.08 152.07
160.23 166.17 168.05
168.28 207.10 208.15
215.02 228.23 229.28
233.02 237.17 242.14
248.10 249.27 257.22
258.10 289.08 290.21
292.08 293.03 294.03
298.07 327.05 343.09
348.22 354.01 366.24
374.05 378.23 391.08
402.21 407.13 412.22
414.17 418.02 434.17
434.29 460.01 480.05
481.14 486.15 510.15
510.21 511.01 513.28
514.16
TURNED-OUT 343.09
TURNING 44.07 46.29
49.24 83.04 118.18
127.02 196.10 291.21
323.29 333.28 338.08
371.01 403.02 438.18
463.12 464.20 491.25
508.10 512.20
TURNPIKE 476.10
TURNS 14.10 199.29
373.09
TURTLE 153.30
TURTLES' 410.26 412.06
TUSSLE 230.18 393.04

TWANG 131.02 285.19
TWEED 281.04
TWELVE 69.01 279.13
292.20
TWENTY 27.24 35.19
48.24 65.08 71.17
72.04 73.28 79.16
95.02 110.08 118.08
136.15 173.03 173.03
173.11 189.24 202.30
203.02 214.27 245.19
246.13 249.21 255.05
267.24 289.04 313.01
313.09 330.11 331.09
353.10 363.03 368.21
401.18 438.08 499.25
TWENTY-FIVE 173.03
173.03 173.11
TWENTY-FOOT 95.02
TWENTY-FOOT-HIGH 331.09
TWENTY-FOUR 363.03
TWENTY-SEVEN 35.19
TWENTY-TWO 214.27
249.21
TWICE 48.24 58.12
127.20 127.22 128.12
137.16 176.19 187.05
199.25 209.21 357.27
412.26 414.06 428.15
465.08 470.01 502.23
506.23
TWIGS 323.12 397.04
496.10
TWILIGHT 414.16 415.13
417.14
TWILIGHTS
TWIN 316.26 319.16
322.30
TWINKLE 235.25 467.21
TWINKLED 302.26 359.07
398.30 513.10
TWINKLING 55.26
445.27
TWIRL 179.07
TWIRLING 179.15
TWIST 22.19 118.23
144.20 308.20 347.06
TWISTED 175.23 497.23
TWISTING 282.12
TWITCH 172.13
TWITCHED 233.08 257.19
TWITCHING 261.13
TWO 1.01 4.27
5.07 7.18 10.01
12.16 13.17 16.21
19.12 20.22 22.08
27.11 29.22 31.05
33.05 38.03 41.15
42.18 44.02 45.20
46.30 47.27 52.04
54.03 54.17 55.10
58.01 59.03 67.10
67.24 70.15 71.15
71.30 73.20 76.10
77.18 79.26 81.13
87.09 93.02 93.05
94.05 98.12 107.05
110.17 117.09 118.09
119.25 123.11 136.12
143.08 143.14 144.29
145.10 167.15 168.08
169.12 169.21 170.29
171.07 171.08 171.09
172.28 173.20 175.05
180.15 180.16 181.07
196.14 200.22 204.09
204.11 209.11 212.19
214.27 226.26 234.17
234.23 234.24 236.17
239.01 239.05 239.22
244.08 249.21 262.23
263.04 263.11 263.11
265.09 269.12 269.17
269.18 269.23 276.14
278.02 279.07 284.01
290.13 290.28 291.04
291.22 291.28 295.10
297.01 298.07 301.02
307.30 311.10 313.21
315.22 316.05 317.04
318.09 318.18 321.23

TWO (CONT.) 323.14
323.21 327.24 328.20
328.24 341.24 341.28
350.02 350.07 353.03
356.07 360.14 366.14
356.15 372.23 372.26
375.21 376.01 377.24
380.17 386.26 389.28
393.20 394.07 395.25
410.11 410.16 412.01
413.12 414.25 416.14
419.03 429.01 429.20
439.03 439.16 439.30
440.06 441.11 442.22
443.07 443.18 444.09
450.22 459.25 460.15
460.22 460.22 463.25
463.27 466.17 471.14
472.20 477.09 480.06
480.18 484.10 484.27
493.22 498.02 498.14
499.09 501.28 502.05
510.12 514.25
TWO-BRANCHED 263.04
TWO-THIRDS 328.24
TWOPENCE 144.04
TWOPENNY 476.10
TYKE 40.14
TYPICAL 51.14
TYRANNICAL 43.19
449.08
UGLY 42.08 63.05
427.05
ULTIMATELY 499.12
UMBRELLA 52.30 199.18
201.22 202.17 205.17
UN 178.29 179.10
UNABASHED 25.20
91.01
UNABLE 44.24 166.25
187.12 228.19 386.02
428.15
UNACCOUNTABLE 219.16
UNACCUSTOMED 485.17
UNALTERABLE 338.09
UNANIMOUSLY 139.28
UNANSWERABLE 187.17
339.04 400.01
UNAPPEASABLE 341.05
UNAPPROACHABLE 47.09
UNARMED 514.20
UNASKED 511.15
UNASSUMING 69.10
UNATTAINABLE 22.04
22.17 398.13
UNATTENDED 346.05
UNATTRACTIVE 190.16
UNAVOIDABLE 418.16
423.21
UNAVOIDABLY 395.16
UNAWARE 25.13
UNAWARES 8.25 115.06
422.30
UNBEARABLE 251.28
272.09 310.25
UNBECOMING 242.25
UNBELIEF 20.05 392.14
UNBELIEVERS 17.01
UNBELIEVING 258.04
UNBOUNDED 19.24
23.19 337.14
UNBRIDLED. 11.10
UNBROKEN 119.17
UNBUTTONED 343.10
428.21
UNCANNY 167.29
UNCEASING 20.21
417.02
UNCEASINGLY 314.27
UNCERTAIN 84.18
186.29 262.01
UNCHANGEABLE 271.26
UNCHANGED 331.28
447.03 509.19
UNCHANGING 407.09
UNCHECKED 220.15
374.13
UNCLASP 512.13
UNCLASPED 173.04
UNCLEAN 352.22

UNCLES 278.05 278.24
UNCLOUDED 17.07
UNCOMMONLY 185.08
219.20 219.21
UNCOMPREHENDING 88.26
130.27 482.13
UNCOMPROMISING 244.18
349.18
UNCONCEIVABLE 115.04
UNCONCERN 169.07
UNCONCERNED 47.08
UNCONSCIONABLE 216.17
371.21
UNCONSCIOUS 16.12
102.01 138.01 144.17
187.28 246.30 287.30
423.04
UNCONSCIOUSLY 59.20
287.03 384.02
UNCONSCIOUSNESS 93.21
UNCONSOLING 417.23
UNCONTROLLABLE 12.05
UNCOUNTED 175.08
UNCOVERED 5.13
279.08 299.17 459.25
509.17
UNCRESTED 416.24
UNCROSSED 258.21
UND 257.04
UNDEFACED 13.19
UNDENIABLE 148.25
193.19 293.05
UNDER 1.01 1.04
1.15 1.17 7.02
12.06 17.07 17.07
17.10 18.07 20.19
20.29 21.03 21.28
22.27 24.17 27.02
33.06 34.02 34.24
48.07 57.11 58.04
58.17 61.30 63.06
69.17 73.01 73.04
76.08 82.10 86.03
89.06 90.13 93.14
98.29 99.21 107.03
108.07 109.06 110.01
110.24 118.12 122.09
122.11 127.27 128.29
131.25 133.28 134.09
139.22 142.03 147.02
149.27 152.06 152.22
152.28 153.28 166.22
169.23 171.16 173.18
175.09 176.22 180.11
187.08 189.21 192.05
193.01 195.08 200.08
200.30 204.29 205.06
205.30 209.10 212.19
222.18 223.03 229.05
230.09 231.21 236.14
236.15 236.16 239.03
239.18 241.28 246.18
246.24 247.13 250.20
262.14 265.12 270.18
271.09 271.17 272.19
279.15 287.29 288.24
291.14 291.21 291.25
296.05 297.04 298.03
303.01 306.12 311.12
311.21 315.14 315.26
316.07 319.01 321.06
323.12 325.11 328.19
331.24 340.25 342.17
346.07 347.22 349.21
350.08 350.18 364.26
367.01 372.26 378.20
384.20 384.27 386.15
389.13 398.15 399.02
401.17 408.05 408.06
408.10 408.15 408.19
412.23 413.03 415.14
416.03 417.01 417.19
417.22 419.12 420.20
420.30 423.09 432.23
439.25 440.30 442.26
445.02 448.07 451.14
452.01 456.10 460.08
466.18 466.30 475.07
489.15 498.10 498.16
501.22 502.03 510.08

UNDER (CONT.) 511.19
513.23 514.22 515.01
515.19
UNDERESTIMATE 382.30
UNDERESTIMATED 382.28
UNDERGONE 147.17
UNDERGROUND 79.17
245.19 267.25 429.25
UNDERGROWTH 327.07
396.18 500.05
UNDERHAND 357.06
UNDERMINED 103.14
220.17
UNDERSIZED 183.25
UNDERSTAND 30.24
50.02 69.22 70.17
79.30 81.01 95.20
97.19 98.22 108.11
122.11 127.10 130.24
150.13 156.04 159.01
164.30 165.02 169.09
174.18 188.05 202.05
203.04 225.02 243.25
255.08 258.25 267.01
268.14 270.15 271.27
271.29 282.27 309.16
342.03 342.23 343.30
344.02 344.14 344.18
360.13 366.07 375.02
375.02 376.08 377.13
388.17 389.29 391.22
413.19 421.06 429.12
433.20 433.21 433.22
437.23 470.13 479.12
507.09 508.03 513.22
UNDERSTANDING 384.19
457.13
UNDERSTANDS 96.03
152.14 384.19
UNDERSTOOD 44.28
87.26 90.24 91.05
96.24 110.16 152.10
236.06 270.10 270.18
272.06 278.15 278.16
284.05 322.14 342.04
357.21 382.25 459.24
494.25 501.03 502.30
506.11
UNDERTAKE 79.27
404.09
UNDERTAKER 330.05
UNDERTAKING 281.19
288.29
UNDERTONE 492.29
UNDERWENT 256.28
UNDERWRITERS 68.06
UNDISCOVERED 417.16
418.05
UNDISGUISED 458.13
UNDISTURBED 30.20
422.26
UNDONE 50.19
UNDRAPED 191.27
UNDULATING 319.12
UNDULATIONS 19.17
123.12
UNDYING 212.06
UNEARTHLY 188.01
365.14
UNEASILY 282.18
UNEASINESS 372.11
UNEASY 59.26 150.22
192.28 231.06 243.18
274.04 290.04 348.30
461.11
UNENLIGHTENED 226.22
UNEQUAL 469.15
UNERRING 4.03
UNERRINGLY 209.24
UNEVEN 287.26
UNEXPECTED 40.17
86.12 114.30 115.03
229.03 295.07 301.21
UNEXPECTEDLY 205.07
264.10 288.20 321.30
349.23 378.10 405.14
425.05
UNEXPECTEDNESS 28.13
309.15
UNEXPLORED 335.16

UNEXPRESSED 186.21
427.16 447.18
UNFADED 407.08
UNFAILING 447.13
447.13
UNFAIR 156.03 160.15
UNFAIRLY 8.25
UNFAITHFUL 507.03
UNFALTERING 264.21
UNFALTERINGLY 356.21
UNFAMILIAR 266.22
304.26
UNFATHOMABLE 264.05
380.17 424.14
UNFLINCHING 5.18
515.17 515.25
UNFLINCHINGLY 306.17
UNFOLDED 281.24 358.15
UNFOLDING 380.18
UNFORESEEN 98.26
192.04
UNFORGIVEN 515.20
UNFORGIVING 429.03
449.03 482.12
UNFORGOTTEN 340.03
UNFORTUNATE 86.15
101.05 215.27 216.03
239.16
UNFORTUNATELY 184.20
241.22
UNGAINLY 178.02
UNGRACIOUS 51.01
UNHAPPILY 357.01
UNHAPPY 232.08 402.07
UNHARMED 466.14
UNHEALTHY 59.18
UNHEARD 298.25
UNHEARD-OF 298.25
UNHESITATING 226.19
UNHOLY 58.10
UNHOOK 132.01 132.01
132.01
UNIFORM 168.15 192.01
248.18
UNINHABITABLE 429.21
UNINHABITED 429.21
UNINTELLECTUAL 50.29
UNINTELLIGENT 12.07
UNINTELLIGIBLE 186.07
466.26
UNINTERESTING 182.06
216.02
UNINTERRUPTED 142.09
220.13
UNION 167.02
UNIQUE 117.12 188.21
270.02
UNITED 369.19
UNIVERSALLY 242.24
UNIVERSE 19.12 208.29
288.27 350.26 378.29
421.25
UNJUST 274.15
UNKIND 101.06
UNKNOWABLE 4.01
UNKNOWN 50.07 54.16
168.08 277.02 277.18
280.19 379.23 381.07
381.08 381.14 385.23
391.02 392.16 398.14
451.17
UNLESS 25.14 41.07
78.23 182.13 194.27
208.26 232.13 306.07
357.29 384.19 413.23
419.28
UNLIMITED 97.27
UNLOADED 280.14 299.04
UNLOPPED 459.29
UNLUCKY 74.16 345.12
UNMARRED 252.30
UNMARRIED 191.01
UNMENTIONABLE 442.15
UNMITIGATED 69.20
UNMOLESTED 491.03
UNMOVED 25.12 462.16
466.28
UNNATURAL 54.15
UNNOTICED 9.06
UNOBSCURED 322.01

UNOFFENDING 436.13
472.24 472.25 472.29
UNPERPLEXED 434.06
UNPLEASANT 241.23
UNPLEASANTLY 204.27
347.03
UNPREPARED 338.25
UNPROPITIOUS 89.24
UNPROVOKED 86.17
UNQUESTIONING 366.03
UNREASONABLE 106.12
218.18 341.15 381.06
UNREASONED 400.02
UNREASONING 438.17
UNRECORDED 322.13
UNREFLECTING 280.19
UNRELIEVED 193.14
UNRESERVE 93.19
UNRESERVEDLY 223.28
UNREST 11.24 389.14
UNROLLED 17.15
UNROVE 439.10
UNRUFFLED 39.04
UNSAFE 280.16 286.29
UNSATISFACTORY 268.20
UNSAVOURY 351.04
399.13
UNSCALABLE 467.13
UNSEALED 381.17
UNSEEMLY 485.02 513.04
UNSEEN 441.16 501.13
501.23
UNSELFISH 2.17
383.29
UNSETTLED 353.08
449.18 461.27
UNSHAKABLE 375.19
UNSHAKEN 88.11
UNSOUNDNESS 108.03
UNSPEAKABLE 57.29
127.06 340.11
UNSTEADILY 108.04
UNSTEADY 61.06 72.20
UNSTIMULATED 11.30
UNSUBSTANTIAL 14.19
UNSUSPECTED 334.28
425.19
UNSUSPECTING 130.30
UNSWAYING 372.13
UNTHINKING .51.02
106.15
UNTOLD 345.14 427.15
UNTOUCHED 408.14
501.05
UNTROUBLED 423.07
470.22
UNUSED 69.25
UNUSUAL 64.30 80.09
465.29
UNUTTERABLE 371.18
UNVEILING 458.11
UNWATCHED 50.10
UNWEARIED 12.23
246.07 386.19
UNWELL 44.29 364.30
UNWHOLESOME 293.28
UNWIELDY 514.21
UNWILLING 244.10
UNWITTINGLY 270.08
UNWORTHY 211.07
UNWRINKLED 19.13
UP 2.13 2.23
2.27 5.17 5.20
5.22 6.06 7.13
8.13 14.23 14.24
14.28 15.09 16.10
16.25 17.23 19.06
20.29 20.30 21.03
23.27 24.06 24.17
25.21 25.26 25.27
26.09 30.19 34.18
34.25 34.27 35.03
36.02 39.01 40.06
40.14 40.18 42.26
43.25 44.10 45.05
45.10 46.07 46.13
47.03 47.04 47.05
52.01 52.23 58.02
58.20 58.27 60.22
61.16 61.25 63.28

UP (CONT.) 68.16
70.12 70.16 70.40
71.15 72.15 72.27
73.17 74.02 75.11
75.22 76.07 77.29
78.14 78.15 79.26
79.27 83.18 84.04
84.20 85.18 88.15
89.28 90.11 91.02
91.12 93.02 94.07
95.20 95.30 96.01
96.20 97.12 97.30
98.12 99.16 99.17
99.27 100.08 101.09
101.11 107.17 108.11
109.20 110.17 110.24
111.04 111.04 111.06
112.23 113.21 115.25
116.15 119.22 122.24
123.01 123.05 123.15
124.30 125.12 125.30
126.06 128.14 129.26
130.17 131.16 132.29
132.30 133.03 133.10
133.16 134.24 136.18
136.21 137.12 137.25
139.15 141.11 142.17
144.26 144.30 145.03
146.22 148.09 148.14
150.19 150.25 151.11
151.13 152.01 152.23
152.27 153.29 157.26
159.07 159.21 160.12
160.16 160.22 162.13
162.19 164.10 166.21
167.21 168.05 168.10
170.11 171.08 173.07
176.03 178.01 179.09
179.27 180.12 180.13
180.21 181.01 183.08
183.17 183.22 184.20
185.06 186.28 187.20
189.17 190.02 192.02
192.14 192.25 192.29
193.04 194.07 194.14
194.16 197.03 197.25
198.17 198.17 200.19
203.25 203.29 204.20
205.21 206.05 207.24
210.24 210.26 211.14
212.09 214.26 215.02
217.08 217.21 218.16
221.01 222.12 224.17
226.10 229.19 229.29
230.22 232.14 232.19
232.26 233.24 234.11
236.06 238.08 239.24
240.18 241.12 242.14
245.24 248.12 250.23
252.18 253.01 254.19
254.27 255.02 255.02
255.20 255.21 255.30
256.02 256.14 256.20
259.04 259.18 259.25
260.01 261.02 261.04
261.09 263.21 267.25
271.18 275.03 279.05
280.03 280.24 282.20
283.22 286.20 287.24
290.21 291.01 291.30
293.25 297.16 298.08
298.23 300.03 300.14
300.20 306.13 307.23
309.25 309.26 311.16
312.11 312.26 313.21
314.01 314.25 315.14
319.02 323.04 323.11
323.26 324.05 324.09
324.11 324.28 325.20
325.25 327.06 327.23
330.19 333.24 338.14
342.16 343.21 345.25
349.20 349.26 351.30
354.06 354.09 355.12
356.01 356.21 357.01
359.17 359.20 363.07
364.23 364.25 365.10
365.18 365.19 365.19
366.08 367.27 368.23

UP (CONT.) 369.16
370.07 371.30 373.01
374.01 374.28 376.10
377.29 378.09 379.04
383.21 384.11 384.12
384.21 393.11 394.01
394.07 399.01 399.02
399.03 400.05 403.03
404.01 405.09 410.17
410.23 410.30 411.08
412.08 412.17 416.03
418.01 418.17 421.04
425.07 425.12 427.03
430.07 430.17 434.27
438.05 438.19 438.25
439.09 439.17 441.28
442.22 443.04 443.17
443.18 445.28 446.05
448.15 448.23 448.24
450.23 451.01 452.01
452.21 453.04 453.08
453.13 454.22 454.27
456.13 456.15 459.12
459.18 459.30 460.22
461.14 462.06 463.02
464.18 465.09 465.09
465.15 466.08 468.22
469.08 469.21 469.23
469.23 471.22 471.30
473.02 473.08 475.23
480.21 480.23 481.05
481.16 481.16 481.26
482.05 485.28 487.21
489.02 489.21 490.08
492.05 492.17 492.26
493.08 493.17 494.06
497.23 498.15 499.19
499.21 500.25 501.07
501.27 502.14 505.08
506.02 507.06 507.14
509.27 512.21 512.24
512.30 513.08 513.29
514.03 514.10 516.06
UP-COUNTRY 240.18
UP-ENDED 44.10
UP-RIVER 446.05 463.02
UPBRAIDING 232.03
UPHELD 15.28
UPLIFTING 148.04
UPON 1.19 5.16
7.09 11.06 16.27
17.18 18.03 19.03
20.02 21.01 23.24
23.25 30.13 30.17
32.15 34.17 37.23
40.09 41.10 44.26
49.23 49.25 50.25
50.25 56.24 63.19
66.20 67.08 67.20
68.01 68.29 77.26
78.06 82.21 83.08
84.07 84.25 85.26
91.11 93.27 97.11
98.01 98.03 100.26
108.09 108.22 115.07
115.08 115.08 119.11
119.16 123.29 126.09
126.15 127.02 127.11
127.22 127.25 128.24
130.29 131.06 131.23
132.23 132.24 138.08
143.28 144.01 147.02
149.27 150.22 156.12
157.06 167.01 169.13
172.12 177.08 181.10
184.05 185.16 194.21
194.22 194.28 195.14
195.17 207.04 209.08
214.29 215.15 216.20
218.09 219.16 220.06
222.10 223.17 225.19
226.29 227.06 229.25
248.24 249.02 249.28
252.06 252.20 263.08
263.17 266.05 267.08
279.11 280.05 280.18
281.17 282.12 284.01
284.04 290.08 292.03
292.26 295.24 298.22
299.26 300.21 307.15

UPON (CONT.) 310.06
310.28 313.26 323.29
324.13 325.05 329.23
331.12 334.16 334.21
338.08 339.11 339.24
341.02 341.07 345.14
346.12 349.13 355.08
356.10 359.18 365.08
366.26 366.28 370.02
374.13 375.09 375.21
376.02 376.22 378.02
378.09 380.06 383.27
384.10 384.15 385.02
385.21 386.01 387.25
391.08 392.01 396.14
396.22 397.01 398.24
398.29 401.05 402.12
402.21 403.15 405.12
407.06 407.21 408.17
410.08 410.28 411.27
413.01 417.22 420.14
422.30 423.15 423.17
425.06 428.05 432.16
432.22 434.11 441.14
442.30 445.28 447.20
451.27 455.09 455.14
458.07 458.12 460.04
460.05 462.23 462.26
462.29 469.02 471.19
472.24 473.03 473.11
475.01 475.13 477.02
479.22 480.06 488.06
499.21 499.24 501.08
501.11 506.14 508.14
511.27 512.18 514.15
514.17 516.11
UPPER 81.10 196.15
402.16 462.07
UPRIGHT 33.25 36.27
104.27 224.06 246.25
311.24 416.15 433.26
UPRISE 102.28
UPRISING 59.26 135.02
272.26 319.16
UPROAR 141.25 210.15
UPROOTED 132.16 220.16
UPROSE 380.17 397.08
417.04 474.22
UPSET 44.30 52.13
180.25 198.29
UPSIDE 476.11
UPSTAIRS 47.29 58.03
70.22 92.12 209.13
UPSTANDING 46.28
120.04
UPSTREAM 443.08 503.18
UPTURNED 20.22 108.09
UPWARD 351.12 409.27
UPWARDS 30.21 116.14
218.24 269.25 372.02
URGED 15.12 151.11
383.29 454.07
URGENT 365.18 438.29
URGING 291.13
US 6.20 8.07
24.25 25.28 29.28
34.24 40.04 40.05
41.18 42.05 50.06
50.13 50.18 50.22
51.16 51.18 54.04
60.10 76.07 77.18
80.28 81.06 85.19
90.07 93.18 95.24
100.20 104.29 106.08
112.19 112.26 113.14
123.29 129.12 132.03
143.26 146.03 156.15
152.03 162.13 162.15
168.05 169.13 171.01
174.16 178.24 183.23
183.24 183.27 192.30
199.16 199.27 202.02
205.05 219.08 226.26
230.24 234.02 234.05
234.06 234.29 235.03
235.10 235.13 235.13
236.29 259.06 266.06
270.27 271.02 271.16
271.29 274.08 275.10

```
US (CONT.)          277.15    VALID         304.01              VERY          1.13    4.23    VERY (CONT.)            397.08
   279.16   295.05   298.17    VALISE        290.22   290.26       7.21    10.15   13.18       398.07   398.21   405.02
   302.10   307.13   307.30    VALLEY         41.05   269.15      15.02    22.19   25.24       405.03   405.28   408.14
   324.27   325.01   325.10    VALLEYS       271.10   276.11      26.13    28.14   30.02       409.25   413.15   413.25
   334.15   337.30   339.09    VALOROUS       23.12                30.19    32.17   34.14       414.19   416.07   417.20
   348.02   348.09   349.26    VALOUR         30.12                37.15    39.04   39.06       421.10   421.20   422.11
   362.04   375.12   378.02    VALUABLE      176.28                42.24    43.27   46.13       424.08   427.30   429.09
   381.23   385.18   386.15    VALUE         304.20   403.23      46.15    48.03   50.24       429.11   429.16   432.21
   389.17   389.23   391.10    VAMPIRE       194.22                52.12    52.30   53.03       434.23   435.19   436.22
   395.03   395.04   400.08    VANISH        273.02   349.25      56.25    57.25   58.11       436.30   437.13   438.28
   400.15   400.17   408.10      501.24                            59.02    61.25   62.23       439.03   443.29   446.08
   408.22   409.03   409.25    VANISHED       17.17    56.01      63.20    64.13   67.02       448.05   448.10   449.02
   410.17   411.09   419.29      80.25   109.10   216.22          67.13    69.14   70.15       449.22   449.22   452.02
   423.15   430.12   447.15      248.08  261.15   295.01          70.19    75.15   78.15       453.20   454.15   455.30
   471.25   471.26   472.12      360.06  415.04   470.17          79.20    80.24   82.23       456.16   458.12   459.10
   472.14   472.19   472.21    VANISHES      501.25                84.09    84.12   84.17       461.10   462.12   463.19
   472.29   473.11   473.21    VANISHING               91.08      84.22    86.01   87.10       463.22   464.12   467.28
   489.04   516.05              104.14  299.11                    88.09    90.08   91.02       469.01   470.07   470.08
USAGE     355.07                VANITY         8.21   106.11      95.14    96.24   98.14       470.29   471.03   471.17
USE        25.22    38.17        474.26                           99.01    99.14  100.14       478.27   479.17   481.12
   72.05    78.11    79.23     VANLO'S       234.23   234.30     100.21   100.22  103.30       482.07   486.05   489.08
   82.22   120.02   131.07       235.13                          104.23   105.08  106.03       491.09   492.15   492.24
   169.25   193.30   205.23    VAPOUR        123.04   498.02     106.08   107.05  115.12       493.02   493.08   493.16
   209.23   223.27   234.08    VAPOURINGS             288.21     117.04   118.13  123.12       493.25   493.30   494.05
   285.08   289.28   357.02    VARIETY       169.01              124.20   127.17  129.05       494.07   495.21   501.22
   369.08   393.26   397.16    VARIOUS        1.12    54.11      129.15   131.18  132.09       503.15   504.19   506.03
   449.14   459.15              166.23  251.03   262.08          132.26   133.15  133.24       506.16   512.08   515.02
USED       11.20    12.23      VASE           33.28   193.04     138.12   138.14  138.16       515.24   516.07
   45.29    71.11    75.03     VAST           2.02     6.06      141.02   146.02  150.15     VESSEL        175.16   244.26
   76.15   102.14   183.23       21.30    54.29    92.20         151.03   151.19  157.04     VESSELS       291.28   437.29
   197.24   198.01   234.06      116.15  149.16   156.12         160.04   164.09  164.23     VESTIGE       193.19   215.02
   251.24   268.06   268.30      192.14  211.17   248.14         165.19   165.28  166.08     VEUX          178.20
   279.05   324.20   337.07      248.24  261.30   297.08         166.10   167.19  169.08     VEXATION      200.28   328.01
   343.13   358.01   359.29      313.30  318.11   319.10         170.02   170.14  170.23     VEXED          46.20   146.02
   419.16   422.16   427.25      325.16  337.12   338.18         174.14   175.18  175.21     VEXEDLY       465.06
   431.11   442.21               381.08  386.18   397.30         175.22   176.30  178.06     VIBRATE       102.25   409.09
USED-UP   279.05                 408.24  415.12   430.08         178.11   179.19  180.23     VIBRATING              31.14
USEFUL    198.11   308.16        500.07  503.09                  181.11   182.04  183.27       231.25   417.09   444.04
   360.01   495.22             VASTLY         68.13              184.15   184.17  184.17     VIBRATION              20.22
USELESS    36.30   124.19      VASTNESS      392.16   409.07     184.26   185.19  185.21       31.03
   495.20                       VAULT         116.18   149.01     186.03   188.24  188.28     VICEROY        45.28
USELESSLY           156.07     VEGETATION             317.03     189.02   190.04  191.08     VICES          57.30
USING     178.15                 408.16                          195.11   197.10  198.05     VICIOUS        55.17   374.12
USQUE     261.29   413.07      VEHEMENT      380.10   436.07     204.24   208.14  209.18       445.04
USUAL      48.25    65.13        474.20                          212.19   212.20  212.25     VICIOUSLY              159.18
   71.24    78.01   144.18     VEIL           76.27   162.05     215.26   215.26  215.27     VICTIM         53.03   131.12
   167.05   222.18   257.27      170.08                          216.30   220.18  221.06       190.06   382.24   402.07
   395.28   427.21   471.06    VEILED        299.16   309.15     222.05   223.07  223.15     VICTIMS       395.19   436.08
USUALLY    28.09                 318.17  415.09   415.10         224.04   224.21  225.05       478.05   503.08
UTENSILS  450.09                 462.16  515.27                  225.06   229.22  232.12     VICTORIEUSE'           175.11
UTILITARIAN         347.10     VEIN          479.25   512.03     232.24   234.11  234.16     VICTORIOUS             15.04
UTMOST     35.27   345.08      VEININGS      249.10              238.09   238.21  240.18       14.22
   429.04                       VEINS         464.21              241.16   241.23  241.24     VICTORY       274.23   331.21
UTTER     195.03   233.27      VELVETY       445.12              242.08   242.10  242.28       447.13
   278.20   302.18   334.26    VENERABLE               27.09     242.29   245.01  246.11     VIE           173.22
   351.28   398.05   399.27      83.09    352.11                  246.14   248.03  249.27     VIENT         180.24
   441.17   465.22   508.22    VENETIAN       47.02    55.13     250.19   252.23  253.26     VIEW           13.30    35.13
UTTERANCE           30.14      VENGEANCE               64.12     253.27   256.02  256.03       46.08    47.08    59.12
   35.30    78.24   174.10       127.13  283.26   513.17         256.12   257.15  258.25       77.02    90.29   180.08
   275.01   473.08             VENGEFUL      138.03   371.18     259.27   260.25  262.07       190.18   191.17   193.20
UTTERED    39.05   193.28        436.14  458.14                  262.13   263.19  263.19       194.30   212.21   214.03
   204.16   261.13   295.03    VENGEFULNESS           193.16     263.19   265.04  266.16       220.11   266.22   269.10
   315.08   405.27   502.16    VENOMOUSLY             115.26     267.17   268.05  268.29       270.20   297.07   315.13
UTTERING  336.12   356.07      VENT           61.03              269.12   269.20  271.15       331.14   339.15   351.01
UTTERLY    11.16    80.25      VENTILATORS             23.28     272.29   272.30  274.27       365.03   375.01   375.17
   84.23    88.01   130.27       102.30                          280.06   282.30  283.24       383.02   386.17   400.29
   182.05   194.29   209.27    VENTURED      283.14   328.19     285.08   288.01  298.20       437.06   455.09   456.05
   216.23   230.09   241.30    VENTURES      223.27              299.11   300.03  300.07       465.23   478.30   480.03
   273.02   278.26   330.18    VENTURING              428.02     302.10   302.11  307.20       501.01
   344.22   477.13   503.09    VERANDAH       38.25    40.15     307.28   308.02  308.13     VIEWED         14.18
VA        171.20                 83.03    84.05    99.07         311.12   312.05  312.11     VIEWS          91.05
VACANCY    74.10                 121.02  129.16   209.13         312.17   315.02  315.10     VIGIL         185.08   210.29
VACANT    128.12                 216.08  242.10   309.28         315.18   316.06  317.03     VIGILANT      348.23   349.06
VAGABOND   57.29   218.05        330.03  342.20   349.22         321.22   322.18  325.03       452.05
   321.07   332.19   343.18      350.15  351.12   357.05         326.03   326.04  327.13     VIGOROUS      338.06   363.12
   426.25                        359.17  360.23   361.03         328.30   330.22  331.27       448.24   467.06
VAGABONDS           51.08        366.09  416.04   427.22         332.27   332.29  337.26     VIGOROUSLY             408.18
   306.12                        448.02  494.17   506.29         338.27   338.30  339.02       468.04
VAGARIES   51.17               VERDAMTE      343.20              339.19   341.18  347.19     VIGOUR        381.04   425.18
VAGUE      21.11    30.29      VERDICT        69.19              349.09   349.12  350.03       434.05
   102.28   141.13   148.21    VERFLUCHTE              49.13     350.15   351.16  351.24     VILE           24.22   127.13
   162.06   302.22   464.30    VERGE          14.06    14.07     352.25   358.07  358.25       406.03
VAGUELY   135.01   338.26        147.30  190.11   357.24         359.09   359.15  359.24     VILL           49.14
   340.29   372.17   399.07    VERITAS       394.21              360.10   361.04  363.15     VILLAGE        3.24    83.12
   452.20   507.23             VERMIN         29.21   398.25     365.26   366.01  367.12       170.05   297.12   297.20
VAGUENESS           11.27      VERMIN-LIKE            398.25     371.01   372.12  372.24       298.02   298.16   316.06
   23.16   156.14             VERSION       240.23   455.13     374.16   375.23  378.15       323.03   323.03   329.30
VAIN      213.06   220.07      VERTICAL       70.13   373.04     379.28   385.03  386.27       330.28   410.14   411.13
   289.28   289.29   416.08      462.29                          389.06   389.12  390.03       439.16   441.28   442.09
VALIANT   398.01               VERTICALLY              30.28     393.18   395.03  395.30       442.19   443.12   489.29
```

VILLAGER 83.09 450.07
VILLAGERS 83.20
192.07 307.04 330.24
336.03
VILLAGES 15.30 316.02
316.28 325.13 327.21
437.26
VILLAINIES 60.01
VILLAINOUS 169.20
VILLAINY 147.14
VILLE 175.24
VIOLENCE 11.05 78.14
84.28 160.25 218.09
222.04 242.25 372.07
VIOLENT 21.22 56.30
138.09 144.19 184.18
210.15 216.15 313.02
436.29 458.11
VIOLENTLY 137.09
192.24 257.18 361.13
369.28 462.11 502.24
VIOLET 227.21 319.12
VIRGIN 3.23
VIRILE 488.13
VIRILITY 23.16
VIRTUAL 336.07
VIRTUE 53.17 149.24
272.10 422.02 422.06
VIRTUES 299.07 325.27
487.22
VIRTUOUS 141.28
VISCOUS 17.13
VISIBLE 35.16 54.06
149.17 211.25 300.20
339.20 348.13 376.28
415.07 447.12
VISIBLY 175.20
VISION 113.17 116.23
121.08 174.10 203.28
291.20 322.01 411.08
VISIONS 55.08 65.04
398.12 413.09 417.20
515.22
VISIT 2.01 190.03
279.17 303.28 306.03
336.22 428.09
VISITATION 511.19
VISITED 269.21 298.20
VISITING 169.02 241.28
VISITING-CARD 241.28
VISITOR 435.08
VISITS 2.15
VISTA 64.07
VISUAL 56.21 147.11
VITALITY 167.29
VIVID 91.08 146.09
469.09
VIVIDLY 264.02
VIVIDNESS 35.09
VOCATION 4.16 404.17
VOICE 1.06 7.04
24.14 25.10 30.12
32.17 44.25 52.07
53.10 61.10 63.18
70.28 71.01 72.16
72.19 75.08 83.26
84.08 87.17 88.06
94.04 96.26 104.23
108.07 108.10 113.29
132.05 132.09 133.03
133.15 137.10 137.18
140.03 141.20 142.16
151.22 157.14 158.04
160.27 164.30 169.30
174.06 179.30 188.25
193.10 195.01 195.07
195.13 196.09 224.22
224.28 231.26 231.28
232.04 233.12 234.03
234.04 248.13 250.24
257.06 260.09 261.04
264.11 271.08 273.23
276.08 277.18 282.07
282.20 289.20 291.12
291.16 293.22 318.16
330.17 331.26 335.09
335.09 337.17 338.19
360.13 360.26 361.13
365.08 368.19 368.20
369.21 370.24 374.15

VOICE (CONT.) 376.05
384.14 385.09 388.12
388.29 389.24 390.27
391.04 391.21 393.16
394.11 395.24 395.30
396.04 404.13 405.08
411.19 412.12 413.16
414.07 421.05 424.05
424.11 431.10 433.07
434.06 451.30 452.08
454.04 459.02 464.21
464.26 464.28 467.06
471.06 481.22 484.27
494.24 505.27 514.15
VOICES 5.08 18.02
83.06 105.01 120.28
127.27 133.04 139.23
140.30 142.20 189.14
211.13 323.07 368.27
388.11 408.24 417.21
463.10 498.03 498.09
510.12
VOID 211.20 263.13
VOILA 179.27
VOLCANO 5.01 464.16
VOLITION 38.02
VOLLEY 255.05 444.06
465.05 501.04
VOLLEY-FIRING 444.06
VOLLEYS 443.23
VOLUBILITY 87.19
293.15
VOLUBLE 286.25 294.09
410.23
VOLUME 290.29
VOLUMINOUS 37.14
260.12 417.08
VOLUNTEER 323.02
350.20
VOLUNTEERING 465.29
VOTRE 170.16
VOUCH 389.15
VOUCHED 499.02
VOUS 169.06 178.25
VOWS 384.28
VOYAGE 16.16 43.39
52.09 70.41 71.19
194.05 235.05 238.19
292.21
VOYAGES 10.05 276.16
VREE 241.18
VROM 241.18
VULGAR 436.09 501.18
W 233.13 235.09
WADDLE 54.22
WAFTED 195.16
WAG 157.05
WAGES 2.25
WAGGED 119.04 151.04
WAIFS 218.26
WAIL 125.09 510.10
WAILING 508.15 513.12
514.04
WAILS 293.20
WAIST 183.26 199.19
318.19 350.03 373.13
WAISTCOAT 200.18
234.12
WAIT 64.01 64.01
64.02 97.13 104.06
113.25 161.04 162.15
181.09 188.24 202.21
202.22 202.28 221.01
255.16 288.17 289.25
355.15 369.21 395.10
411.01 494.20 505.10
WAITED 36.30 49.29
120.04 198.15 413.29
414.09 419.25 471.23
500.12 514.18 514.19
WAITER 181.21
WAITING 13.16 45.16
46.22 54.17 57.15
99.02 148.02 205.04
206.02 208.06 220.11
229.11 231.30 244.24
245.13 245.21 288.13
299.16 328.25 333.18
367.24 367.25 378.11
419.20 427.14 431.14

WAITING (CONT.) 441.09
474.21 485.19 493.07
510.19
WAJO 250.11
WAKE 18.06 23.23
131.27 151.10 295.23
365.10 492.30 509.20
WAKING 51.27
WALES 15.01 28.15
WALK 13.13 28.03
49.27 90.11 153.04
189.13 255.13 264.13
351.04 374.28 403.03
WALKED 16.17 36.14
56.13 78.29 164.15
191.23 196.05 208.14
220.25 231.14 263.13
301.19 310.30 311.08
318.18 346.06 372.15
396.15 410.17 413.28
427.05 433.26 481.14
490.22 505.25 510.26
513.29 514.12
WALKING 5.13 43.04
70.11 80.22 160.22
226.20 232.26 254.11
306.15 359.18 432.22
470.02 482.22 489.20
513.07
WALKS 236.01 347.02
WALL 4.13 83.29
85.09 95.02 110.06
123.04 135.05 172.22
175.13 192.11 200.28
208.23 254.01 280.25
290.09 297.10 315.12
325.20 353.15 359.19
360.27 372.20 401.14
414.18 420.09 463.15
490.16 514.30
WALLAH 55.17
WALLED 146.22 469.15
WALLOW 41.11
WALLOWING 344.04
WALLS 37.18 62.28
192.16 248.19 280.01
302.27 317.01 366.22
408.16 420.20 445.28
462.27
WALPOLE 196.26 203.24
208.26 209.20 211.19
214.21 215.01
WAN 441.16
WAND 408.07 408.09
WANDER 28.04 262.12
270.28 413.01 473.10
310.07 332.23 338.20
431.28
WANDERERS 105.14
WANDERING 28.03
37.22 160.28 194.18
316.21 336.16 387.23
389.27 417.13 458.17
WANDERINGS 240.11
WANT 7.06 40.06
41.02 45.04 48.22
49.12 49.13 51.11
60.24 65.15 76.22
84.19 97.18 99.17
109.11 112.03 129.13
130.08 139.21 139.22
139.23 157.30 160.02
158.22 202.30 203.03
204.12 205.14 217.02
217.03 218.03 221.02
223.24 235.26 242.27
253.19 259.20 259.23
259.24 273.28 290.06
303.18 306.19 321.05
372.21 376.11 385.11
385.13 391.12 391.14
392.27 393.08 402.27
402.28 418.25 418.26
433.08 471.10 472.11
472.19 472.21 474.05
474.11 491.24
WANTED 33.10 35.11
35.28 43.40 44.25
54.01 63.22 94.21

WANTED (CONT.) 102.06
106.01 108.20 108.26
108.27 109.01 109.01
112.04 119.06 122.03
124.23 125.17 137.01
143.22 143.30 151.08
160.04 160.04 201.29
237.13 245.11 245.12
253.17 281.14 289.13
292.17 301.19 310.22
318.22 338.11 351.08
367.02 370.14 378.14
378.17 382.18 384.02
385.05 390.03 403.19
425.14 441.24 451.26
456.14 459.24 460.15
472.05 472.08 473.30
481.05 489.07
WANTING 301.18
WANTS 52.23 255.10
259.25 259.26 391.15
474.28
WAPPING 28.12
WAR 59.05 251.11
251.14 254.18 260.29
264.23 285.14 285.14
320.17 320.27 324.03
331.21 332.06 351.26
427.26 437.08 440.07
444.04 445.17 479.02
479.02 484.07 484.11
489.17 513.16
WAR-BOATS 445.17
484.11 489.17
WAR-COMRADE 285.14
285.14 320.17
WAR-CRIES 332.06
444.04
WAR-WORN 59.05
WARD 12.17 57.19
61.13 62.24 64.07
70.01 87.07
WARINESS 337.05
WARIS 320.15 321.19
321.25 322.03 328.15
328.21 329.06 332.07
332.18 336.05 407.24
447.06 447.17 448.12
450.17 451.01 461.12
486.17 489.07 491.02
498.24 498.27 499.03
499.10 499.16 501.07
504.20 505.14 505.16
WARIS'S 448.23 456.09
478.15 492.18 493.13
503.02 504.05 508.27
509.16 514.07
WARLIKE 448.26
WARM 4.10 24.05
49.19 74.09 187.08
223.15 302.27 302.30
397.18 408.19
WARMLY 97.01
WARMTH 2.11 219.08
227.05 403.25
WARN 183.03
WARNED 23.29 84.16
298.04 334.24 379.15
WARNING 132.10 384.03
443.13 461.12
WARNINGS 342.02 342.02
358.10 370.13
WARP 439.09 439.30
WARRANTED 488.12
WARS 345.14
WAS 1.01 1.06
1.08 1.10 1.13
3.01 3.01 3.04
3.05 3.07 3.12
3.17 3.20 4.14
4.17 4.20 4.23
4.24 5.26 6.08
6.09 6.13 6.15
7.26 7.29 8.08
8.19 8.26 9.05
10.13 12.14 12.14
13.24 14.13 14.27
14.29 15.04 16.21
19.06 19.23 22.05
22.07 23.01 23.20

WAS (CONT.)		23.21	WAS (CONT.)		96.05	WAS (CONT.)		169.12	WAS (CONT.)		246.09
23.29	24.02	24.11	96.07	96.22	97.01	169.13	169.20	169.20	246.10	246.11	246.14
24.19	25.05	25.12	97.12	97.21	98.09	169.24	169.24	170.02	246.15	246.19	247.05
25.22	25.28	26.10	98.14	98.17	98.17	170.20	170.21	171.09	247.06	247.08	248.04
26.16	26.17	26.19	98.19	98.21	99.01	171.25	171.30	172.03	248.04	248.15	249.05
26.30	27.11	27.30	99.06	99.18	100.01	172.12	172.14	172.17	249.19	249.28	249.30
28.01	28.03	28.04	100.05	100.07	100.12	173.16	175.11	175.17	250.10	250.11	250.12
28.09	28.16	28.17	100.14	100.16	100.22	175.25	175.26	176.03	250.15	251.01	251.18
28.25	28.29	29.01	101.03	101.11	101.16	176.30	177.05	177.22	251.30	252.19	252.23
29.01	29.04	29.05	101.18	102.04	102.08	178.08	179.17	179.18	253.15	254.05	254.17
29.15	32.05	32.06	102.11	102.14	102.24	180.09	180.14	180.15	254.18	254.24	254.28
32.07	32.17	32.18	103.01	103.05	103.08	182.08	182.28	182.30	255.03	255.07	255.23
32.24	33.16	33.29	103.08	103.20	103.26	183.05	183.15	183.28	255.29	256.07	257.13
34.06	34.15	34.20	104.01	104.04	104.06	184.01	184.04	184.06	257.21	258.13	258.16
34.21	35.01	35.06	104.15	104.18	104.23	184.10	184.14	185.01	258.27	258.27	259.10
35.25	35.30	36.03	104.26	104.26	104.30	185.02	185.07	185.09	260.11	260.21	261.27
36.20	36.22	36.23	105.05	105.20	105.23	185.09	185.17	185.26	262.02	262.04	262.11
36.28	36.30	37.26	105.24	105.25	107.09	185.27	186.01	186.11	262.11	262.17	262.22
38.01	38.02	38.08	107.22	108.19	108.19	186.14	186.16	186.16	263.14	263.27	264.16
38.12	38.17	41.08	108.23	109.04	109.05	187.05	187.09	187.20	265.15	265.16	266.12
42.03	42.06	42.10	109.08	109.11	109.14	187.27	188.15	188.17	266.15	266.24	267.05
42.26	42.30	43.02	109.20	110.05	110.07	188.22	189.10	189.11	267.10	267.11	267.21
43.18	43.19	43.28	110.22	110.23	110.30	189.17	189.19	189.21	268.09	268.12	268.17
43.28	43.32	43.43	111.07	111.20	111.26	189.23	190.03	190.05	268.20	268.22	268.25
44.04	44.11	44.13	111.27	112.02	112.13	190.05	191.01	191.06	268.27	268.28	269.04
44.16	44.23	44.27	112.15	112.23	112.25	191.14	191.17	191.18	269.30	270.06	270.06
44.29	45.17	45.22	113.08	113.16	113.30	191.18	191.23	192.13	270.10	270.12	270.14
45.24	46.04	46.10	114.05	114.08	114.09	193.12	193.24	193.24	270.16	270.22	270.25
46.19	46.23	46.28	114.12	114.13	114.26	193.28	194.01	194.02	272.15	272.15	272.21
47.08	47.13	47.28	116.07	116.21	116.21	194.04	194.06	194.06	272.30	273.08	273.13
47.28	48.03	48.15	116.25	117.02	117.20	194.10	194.15	194.25	273.15	273.27	273.30
49.03	49.11	49.29	117.29	118.13	118.15	195.01	195.11	195.11	274.02	274.06	274.08
50.01	50.22	51.14	119.05	119.19	119.21	196.04	196.11	196.12	274.08	278.08	278.12
51.18	52.09	53.15	120.01	120.01	120.03	196.19	196.23	197.04	278.14	278.17	278.19
53.24	54.09	54.11	120.23	122.01	122.04	197.05	197.25	198.14	278.19	278.21	278.23
56.26	56.27	57.05	122.09	122.16	123.18	198.15	198.16	198.27	279.03	279.05	279.20
57.26	57.27	58.04	123.28	124.02	124.03	198.28	198.30	199.01	280.12	281.02	281.08
58.15	59.09	60.04	124.04	124.05	124.21	199.07	199.09	200.04	281.17	281.21	281.26
60.12	60.12	60.23	125.09	125.14	125.18	200.17	200.19	200.24	281.27	281.30	282.01
60.25	60.26	61.04	125.23	126.10	127.03	200.29	201.05	201.07	282.02	282.05	282.07
61.11	61.11	61.22	127.12	127.13	127.21	201.10	202.09	202.10	282.08	282.09	282.15
61.23	62.15	63.01	128.01	128.24	129.06	202.25	203.07	205.08	282.28	282.29	283.02
63.22	64.17	66.02	129.10	129.11	129.22	206.02	207.04	207.08	283.05	283.06	283.06
66.03	66.04	66.05	129.28	130.08	130.14	208.01	208.08	208.25	283.12	283.12	283.19
66.07	66.09	66.11	130.28	130.30	130.30	208.27	209.05	209.09	283.26	283.28	285.10
66.13	66.18	66.20	131.01	131.04	131.05	209.11	209.21	209.24	285.15	285.17	285.18
66.23	67.02	67.08	131.13	132.08	132.08	210.02	210.04	210.05	286.07	286.08	286.14
67.12	67.13	67.15	132.12	132.19	132.21	210.09	210.12	210.24	286.21	286.25	286.30
67.27	67.30	68.08	132.30	133.13	133.24	211.05	211.10	211.16	287.05	287.23	288.01
68.18	68.18	68.19	133.28	134.05	134.08	211.19	211.24	211.29	288.06	288.11	288.21
68.27	68.29	68.30	134.19	135.07	135.07	212.10	212.17	213.01	288.24	288.26	288.28
69.09	69.18	69.22	136.07	136.09	136.16	213.12	213.18	214.03	289.26	289.29	290.03
70.05	70.11	70.26	136.24	137.01	137.07	214.06	214.08	214.29	290.10	290.14	290.14
70.27	70.29	70.37	137.13	137.14	137.24	215.21	215.21	215.22	291.02	291.02	291.10
71.20	71.26	72.09	138.05	138.17	138.19	215.25	216.03	216.30	292.01	292.01	292.02
72.16	72.20	72.24	138.21	139.02	139.05	217.11	218.02	218.12	292.12	292.29	293.11
72.30	73.05	73.06	139.13	139.13	139.21	218.13	218.14	219.01	293.12	294.04	294.10
73.12	73.19	73.24	139.24	140.05	140.05	219.03	219.14	219.15	294.25	295.06	295.18
73.28	73.29	74.01	141.02	141.06	141.15	222.01	222.02	222.05	295.19	295.21	295.22
74.03	74.04	74.19	141.22	142.24	143.01	222.06	222.07	223.02	297.14	297.23	298.01
74.21	74.25	74.27	143.05	143.18	143.23	223.19	223.22	224.04	298.05	298.06	298.06
75.27	76.10	76.26	143.29	144.05	144.06	224.14	224.29	225.07	298.11	298.16	298.23
77.14	77.28	77.29	144.07	144.14	144.22	225.07	225.10	226.02	298.23	298.25	298.25
78.09	78.13	78.15	145.11	145.17	145.18	226.22	226.26	227.01	298.28	298.30	299.06
78.23	79.05	79.07	146.14	146.15	146.18	227.21	228.03	228.04	299.18	299.21	299.25
79.10	79.11	79.25	146.21	146.21	146.26	228.06	228.29	229.02	299.29	300.02	300.06
80.15	81.27	82.01	146.30	147.13	147.14	229.06	229.11	230.09	300.07	300.10	300.10
82.06	82.14	82.14	147.25	147.27	148.16	230.14	230.24	231.02	300.17	300.30	301.13
82.14	82.15	82.15	150.18	151.02	151.10	231.11	231.13	231.18	302.15	302.16	302.17
82.17	82.18	82.18	151.14	151.20	152.02	231.21	232.11	232.23	303.03	303.03	303.14
82.19	82.22	82.24	152.06	152.11	152.30	233.11	233.11	233.18	303.14	303.21	303.27
82.27	83.05	83.07	152.24	152.30	153.09	234.13	234.23	234.25	303.28	304.15	304.18
83.22	84.04	84.05	153.25	154.02	154.14	234.28	235.03	235.08	304.18	304.20	304.20
84.17	84.24	84.30	155.05	155.06	155.15	235.10	236.01	236.05	304.24	304.27	304.30
85.06	85.07	85.08	155.16	155.24	156.30	236.06	236.13	236.26	304.30	305.01	306.01
85.10	85.14	85.21	157.10	157.12	157.15	236.30	237.16	237.18	306.02	306.08	306.20
85.30	86.03	86.06	157.15	157.16	157.18	238.15	238.19	239.16	306.22	306.23	306.23
86.08	86.13	86.13	157.21	157.25	157.26	239.18	239.23	239.24	307.02	307.03	307.08
86.15	86.15	86.19	157.27	157.28	158.29	240.05	240.05	240.09	307.08	307.20	307.25
86.20	86.29	87.01	159.19	160.10	160.16	240.16	240.18	241.10	307.29	308.08	308.13
87.04	87.17	87.30	160.19	161.03	162.01	241.02	241.05	241.10	308.13	308.15	308.21
88.02	89.09	89.13	162.17	162.18	163.01	241.25	241.27	241.30	309.07	309.13	309.16
89.16	89.19	89.26	163.09	163.21	163.27	242.05	242.08	242.17	309.19	309.21	309.26
90.03	90.09	90.15	163.30	164.01	164.01	242.20	242.24	242.28	310.02	310.20	310.26
91.11	92.03	92.10	164.07	164.18	164.29	243.10	243.12	243.28	311.02	311.10	311.17
93.07	93.09	93.17	164.30	165.08	165.09	244.16	244.24	244.24	311.25	312.03	312.05
93.18	94.01	95.06	165.24	165.28	166.01	245.01	245.04	245.11	312.06	312.12	312.20
95.08	95.09	95.12	166.28	166.30	167.01	245.11	245.12	245.13	313.05	313.09	313.18
95.13	95.21	95.24	167.09	167.19	167.22	245.23	245.26	245.27	314.10	314.13	314.26
95.25	95.30	96.01	168.14	168.26	169.03	245.28	246.03	246.05	315.01	315.09	315.09

WAS (CONT.)

		315.16
315.19	315.28	316.06
316.12	316.13	316.16
316.17	316.20	317.12
317.14	317.14	317.17
318.01	318.03	318.15
318.16	318.16	319.02
319.05	319.09	319.23
319.25	320.08	320.18
320.18	320.26	320.28
321.02	321.07	321.11
321.13	321.20	321.20
321.26	322.05	322.07
322.20	323.11	323.25
325.22	325.25	326.01
326.04	327.03	327.09
327.15	328.07	328.08
328.26	328.30	329.02
329.07	329.15	329.17
330.08	330.13	330.18
330.22	330.25	330.28
331.05	331.06	331.14
331.21	332.10	332.12
332.22	332.29	332.30
333.02	333.13	333.21
333.27	334.11	334.11
334.20	334.27	335.02
335.06	335.10	335.13
336.05	336.23	337.19
337.22	337.23	337.27
337.28	338.10	338.19
338.25	338.30	339.03
339.03	339.25	339.29
340.10	340.21	341.22
342.03	342.08	342.09
342.29	342.30	343.15
343.20	343.20	343.21
344.23	344.29	345.05
345.12	345.15	345.21
345.25	346.09	347.01
347.15	347.16	347.17
348.06	349.03	349.07
349.08	350.08	350.11
350.16	350.17	350.19
350.21	350.24	350.29
351.01	351.10	351.20
351.26	352.06	352.07
352.07	352.08	352.09
352.11	352.13	352.18
353.05	353.18	353.22
353.24	353.26	354.01
354.08	354.09	354.11
355.24	356.02	356.09
356.11	356.14	357.10
357.18	357.18	357.22
358.03	358.03	358.07
358.09	358.19	358.23
358.25	359.01	359.08
359.09	359.16	359.24
359.24	359.28	360.04
360.29	360.30	361.14
361.27	362.04	362.08
362.15	363.07	364.06
364.09	364.14	364.17
364.27	365.02	365.03
365.16	365.18	365.30
366.06	366.11	366.19
366.22	366.27	366.28
366.29	366.30	367.02
367.05	367.12	367.16
367.17	367.23	368.03
368.14	368.15	368.21
368.22	369.06	369.07
369.10	370.10	370.11
370.27	371.02	371.11
371.17	371.23	371.28
372.12	372.17	373.15
373.17	374.14	374.16
374.25	375.16	375.17
376.18	378.13	378.19
378.30	379.19	379.20
379.24	380.07	380.15
380.17	381.01	381.20
381.22	382.04	382.05
382.06	382.11	382.14
382.14	382.15	382.19
382.22	382.30	383.02
383.07	383.14	383.14
383.17	383.19	383.29
383.30	384.01	384.20

WAS (CONT.)

		384.25
384.29	385.05	385.07
385.08	385.08	386.06
386.22	387.07	387.16
388.11	388.12	388.14
388.18	388.18	389.05
389.13	389.19	389.24
389.29	390.06	390.07
390.08	391.03	391.04
391.29	392.08	392.09
392.10	392.13	392.18
392.25	392.26	392.26
392.29	393.04	393.26
394.11	395.17	395.19
395.28	395.30	396.01
396.04	396.07	396.08
396.12	396.13	396.23
397.03	397.21	397.24
398.10	398.13	398.26
399.03	399.04	399.06
399.18	399.19	399.26
399.29	400.01	400.07
400.17	400.22	400.24
400.26	400.28	401.24
401.28	402.01	402.02
402.14	402.15	403.14
403.19	403.25	403.29
404.17	404.20	405.02
405.09	406.02	406.06
407.13	407.18	408.23
408.29	409.11	409.12
409.24	410.07	410.14
412.16	412.21	412.26
413.03	413.08	414.01
414.20	414.29	414.29
415.01	415.03	415.06
415.10	415.13	416.11
416.12	417.18	418.19
418.21	419.18	419.22
419.27	420.08	420.13
420.26	421.06	421.07
421.11	421.20	422.21
423.27	425.05	425.08
425.24	426.01	426.29
427.30	428.07	428.09
429.04	429.15	430.08
430.13	430.18	430.18
430.18	430.19	430.20
431.03	431.09	431.13
431.16	431.25	432.09
432.12	432.27	433.13
433.16	434.03	434.09
434.10	434.20	434.23
435.05	435.06	435.07
435.10	435.12	435.24
436.06	436.21	436.25
436.26	437.22	437.24
437.25	438.02	438.07
438.11	438.13	438.13
439.05	439.07	439.11
440.12	440.15	440.15
440.17	441.18	441.24
442.02	442.04	442.21
443.05	443.16	443.17
443.24	444.13	444.16
445.12	445.18	445.22
446.02	446.10	447.05
447.12	447.14	447.14
447.15	447.16	447.23
448.05	448.11	448.13
448.19	449.01	449.02
449.19	449.20	449.26
450.03	450.18	451.01
451.07	451.10	451.14
452.02	452.03	452.03
452.20	453.01	453.09
453.25	453.29	454.19
454.24	455.10	456.12
456.16	456.25	457.01
457.04	457.12	457.18
458.03	458.04	458.07
458.10	458.20	458.23
458.23	458.29	459.18
459.24	460.14	460.20
461.14	461.17	461.21
461.23	461.28	462.02
463.11	463.19	464.07
464.09	464.20	465.15
465.19	465.27	466.03
466.21	467.11	468.07

WAS (CONT.)

		469.22
470.17	470.26	470.27
470.29	471.21	471.24
471.28	472.02	472.08
473.01	474.11	475.08
475.12	475.15	475.24
475.27	475.29	476.05
476.09	477.06	477.16
477.19	478.10	478.22
478.23	478.27	479.02
479.07	479.07	479.15
479.21	479.28	480.09
480.18	481.30	482.23
482.24	482.30	483.16
484.03	484.07	485.08
485.16	485.12	485.13
485.27	486.05	487.01
487.06	487.09	488.11
488.19	488.21	488.23
488.28	489.06	489.13
489.14	489.19	489.25
490.03	490.08	490.15
490.21	490.23	490.30
491.14	491.18	491.30
492.01	492.05	492.23
493.22	493.23	493.26
494.03	494.17	495.12
495.16	495.27	495.30
496.01	496.04	497.03
497.04	497.23	497.24
498.05	498.06	498.13
498.13	498.15	498.27
498.28	499.20	499.21
499.22	499.24	499.27
500.05	500.13	500.20
501.18	501.19	502.01
502.27	503.14	504.09
504.12	504.14	505.09
505.23	505.26	506.14
506.21	506.27	507.02
507.04	507.06	507.30
508.04	508.04	508.26
508.27	509.05	509.12
509.17	509.19	509.24
509.24	510.05	510.06
510.11	510.17	510.28
511.12	511.20	512.02
512.07	512.10	512.16
512.24	512.27	513.09
513.13	514.13	516.07

WASH   72.26   137.08
WASHED   193.03
WASHERS   75.19
WASHING   7.19   118.22
243.26
WASH'T   57.02   69.27
69.27   69.28   77.09
77.17   88.08   88.10
97.17   110.09   122.12
139.20   139.21   144.22
150.26   151.21   151.26
152.10   157.24   157.26
159.02   160.07   160.08
160.14   231.05   234.18
285.15   301.04   301.05
301.11   313.23   354.07
354.10   357.17   396.11
407.16   426.07   478.06
WASTE   200.30   215.03
459.07   464.30   506.03
WASTE-LAND   464.30
WASTED   100.04   206.06
WATCH   23.29   28.19
35.20   50.03   61.09
70.27   71.05   73.01
73.21   84.24   105.17
173.03   212.23   234.11
256.03   310.23   359.19
497.24   499.21
WATCH-CHAIN   234.11
WATCHED   50.10   50.19
62.14   62.16   84.16
100.14   110.22   111.01
114.10   137.22   186.28
196.03   219.27   293.05
301.27   302.29   310.08
328.27   362.12   362.22
367.29   368.01   430.07
433.25   480.01   482.10
484.10   490.26

WATCHERS   493.23
WATCHES   210.30   249.26
WATCHFUL   22.02   111.26
127.02   148.21   183.09
378.04
WATCHFUL-LIKE   183.09
WATCHFULNESS   348.04
452.05
WATCHING   41.20   63.21
84.24   116.07   195.17
234.29   308.20   324.10
369.03   375.25   411.09
414.23
WATCHMAKER   249.24
WATER   1.13   1.14
1.18   2.15   2.20
2.21   3.14   3.20
6.09   7.18   8.02
10.06   14.29   15.18
15.19   15.20   16.30
17.16   19.13   19.20
31.05   31.15   33.14
34.06   37.02   73.29
101.25   107.04   108.12
108.16   108.16   108.17
109.01   109.01   109.06
109.09   110.28   114.17
117.25   124.27   131.29
149.26   152.19   152.25
166.03   169.25   177.08
182.10   183.11   203.18
203.20   211.27   217.24
223.09   224.02   236.13
236.16   244.20   261.02
290.24   299.24   302.17
302.21   312.03   312.04
314.11   316.30   360.20
373.19   382.13   401.19
408.17   410.02   410.12
414.22   429.30   438.18
439.11   440.25   441.03
441.24   443.21   443.28
444.15   445.24   461.05
467.04   467.07   467.07
484.17   489.15   493.12
493.30   495.10   497.24
498.09   500.28   502.17
502.18   512.28
WATER-BOTTLE   109.09
WATER-BREAKER   152.19
WATER-CLERK   1.13
1.14   2.15   2.21
3.14   3.20   182.10
236.13
WATER-CLERKS   1.18
2.20
WATER-DUST   495.10
WATER-GATE   484.17
512.28
WATER-LOGGED   33.14
WATER-PIPE   217.24
224.02
WATER-SUPPLY   203.18
WATER-TANK   14.29
WATER-TIGHT   290.24
WATER'S   300.02   414.07
WATERFALL   463.11
WATERFOWL   432.04
WATERLINE   34.07
WATERS   13.01   21.28
22.30   24.29   70.02
115.07   123.07   149.17
214.23   264.09   271.11
385.22   413.02
WATERSIDE   3.03
42.09   66.11   207.20
WATERY   76.23
WATERY-EYED   76.23
WATTLED   462.27
WAVE   7.08   52.13
414.13   417.17   483.25
WAVED   226.17   288.12
WAVELETS   19.16
WAVERING   219.07   370.01
WAVES   158.19   299.10
325.15   409.28   417.01
441.05   516.21
WAVING   255.21
WAXED   263.07   429.29
WAXES   106.07

WAY 8.08 17.05
18.08 27.12 30.03
31.08 34.14 34.23
39.07 40.07 41.19
42.03 43.37 45.04
45.04 53.13 54.14
54.30 57.23 70.35
71.24 74.18 78.10
82.30 83.23 84.02
89.23 95.29 98.16
103.14 115.17 116.21
119.26 120.29 137.05
147.22 152.06 153.08
153.12 158.10 159.02
160.19 160.19 163.12
163.25 165.23 168.07
170.03 172.06 173.19
175.18 176.24 176.27
185.24 185.29 191.08
195.26 197.25 199.21
210.06 216.07 219.03
222.18 227.18 230.12
231.16 233.06 236.13
237.08 240.12 244.15
246.01 248.08 249.25
260.30 261.07 261.27
262.11 263.04 264.28
265.02 265.16 267.09
267.15 270.09 270.09
272.16 273.07 273.13
273.30 279.26 281.04
283.03 283.09 290.20
291.13 292.27 297.16
300.10 301.11 306.04
307.05 320.02 320.13
321.01 323.04 327.07
328.24 335.08 337.05
343.21 346.09 348.21
349.01 352.04 354.02
356.19 361.27 362.03
408.13 408.18 418.28
418.29 422.10 425.22
428.03 429.02 429.08
432.15 436.22 436.28
437.29 438.04 438.10
442.01 442.26 451.08
456.01 456.19 470.23
474.18 475.20 476.09
478.23 480.29 481.19
484.18 484.26 485.09
490.19 492.24 498.08
500.04 500.14 503.12
506.17 508.05 510.29

WAYFARER 38.12

WAYFARERS 379.02

WAYLAID 273.16 307.05
378.10

WAYS 40.17 54.11
100.06 259.20 262.08
268.21

WE 8.12 24.23
24.23 41.18 41.21
41.24 50.13 50.14
50.15 51.15 63.01
64.19 70.31 71.16
71.18 71.22 75.05
78.18 78.29 80.22
80.29 80.30 81.01
81.05 83.18 83.27
84.02 85.13 87.05
87.19 93.23 94.08
109.06 118.06 130.01
141.12 145.17 146.22
150.04 151.12 152.16
156.18 156.18 156.23
162.15 164.22 168.12
168.23 168.26 168.30
170.29 172.01 174.11
174.18 174.19 175.26
181.06 181.19 181.20
183.07 183.10 183.13
183.16 183.24 184.25
195.03 188.27 190.24
197.08 210.26 215.08
219.05 219.06 220.20
222.04 228.23 228.24
230.14 230.19 230.27
230.27 230.30 231.03
231.14 232.03 233.02
234.26 235.05 239.12

WE (CONT.) 243.28
244.09 244.12 244.27
254.17 259.20 262.22
262.27 262.28 263.02
263.04 264.06 265.13
270.28 271.03 271.04
271.05 271.18 271.18
271.30 273.06 273.06
280.23 281.13 289.22
301.27 302.05 306.04
306.16 308.10 308.11
309.03 320.12 323.02
325.02 329.07 329.13
333.16 335.11 339.08
339.11 341.13 341.14
349.20 349.26 349.29
355.03 375.27 376.01
377.28 381.07 387.01
387.12 387.26 389.16
395.03 395.07 395.18
401.17 403.07 405.15
405.16 406.05 408.23
408.25 409.23 411.29
413.21 413.28 418.24
418.25 418.30 419.14
429.14 433.08 456.23
460.13 460.15 464.28
471.26 471.27 471.29
472.09 472.22 472.28
473.09 473.12 473.20
473.22 474.03 482.08
493.15 493.17 494.12
501.22 505.04 507.16
507.21 515.28 516.05

WE'LL 71.02 134.02

WE'RE 497.10

WE'VE 64.21 80.27
201.29 233.16

WEAK 28.12 36.06
130.04 130.21 256.24
279.06 405.29

WEAK-HEADED 28.12

WEAKEN 461.18

WEAKEST 478.05

WEAKNESS 50.05 50.07
50.10 60.08 113.07
113.08 212.04

WEALTH 246.02 277.14
323.23

WEALTHY 245.26

WEAPON 185.06 370.22

WEAPONED 349.15

WEAPONS 293.13

WEAR 100.23 331.27
386.18

WEARINESS 106.11
117.16 418.12 431.02
469.17 479.08

WEARING 315.22

WEARY 36.22 152.23
152.23 211.01 281.25
294.08 317.07 335.08
366.28 430.16 464.18

WEATHER 12.10 93.24
149.13 198.25 236.10
440.15 441.04 441.10
442.14

WEAVING 83.22

WEB 29.04

WEDDING 516.03

WEEK 11.20 69.29
74.20 149.09 183.29
313.23 353.05 442.17
447.05 452.18

WEEK-DAY 452.18

WEEKS 42.29 198.27
222.22 227.23 234.18
354.12 362.20 367.06
370.13

WEEP 115.27 122.17
190.10

WEEPING 385.11 385.13
507.12

WEIGH 177.05

WEIGHED 226.05

WEIGHT 74.08 101.30
118.07 126.18 266.10
321.17 449.17

WEIRD 212.15 362.10
495.12

WEIRDLY 307.10

WELCOME 2.11 174.15
264.17 473.24

WELCOMED 248.12

WELFARE 485.27 485.27

WELL 10.02 14.13
14.22 20.26 22.20
23.30 25.25 26.04
27.13 40.06 42.08
43.01 44.04 47.16
48.12 50.15 59.23
66.04 66.19 68.10
70.19 77.12 78.20
79.08 79.16 79.20
85.15 87.04 88.09
89.28 90.25 94.06
96.24 104.05 106.13
109.18 124.07 135.08
148.02 150.16 151.19
151.29 152.02 152.14
153.10 156.18 157.24
158.06 159.27 163.25
164.03 164.21 165.19
165.22 166.10 174.13
179.19 180.23 181.11
182.15 183.03 183.27
184.12 184.15 184.17
184.17 188.21 197.14
197.30 198.05 198.27
202.11 203.07 203.25
206.05 211.09 211.09
217.15 219.19 219.30
222.23 223.11 223.23
228.30 230.05 231.01
231.30 238.06 239.13
242.21 245.01 247.24
258.11 258.25 264.14
265.12 267.21 272.30
274.22 283.24 285.16
287.23 295.18 301.04
303.08 303.12 304.29
320.12 322.02 328.10
328.12 330.22 331.11
343.25 349.02 352.25
353.07 375.10 377.30
378.27 394.12 395.07
400.25 401.12 411.21
413.27 418.10 418.15
441.08 449.04 450.28
454.15 458.22 463.23
468.13 472.06 474.04
474.09 479.01 481.12
483.06 483.07 491.22
492.25 493.10 498.05
507.12 512.08 515.24

WELL-ARMED 491.22

WELL-BEING 22.20

WELL-BRED 304.29

WELL-DIRECTED 450.28

WELL-FOUND 441.08

WELL-GROOMED 94.06

WELL-KNOWN 66.19

WELL-PROPORTIONED
223.11

WELL-TO-DO 20.26

WELLINGTON 200.18

WENDED 191.07

WENT 8.03 8.16
10.01 21.26 25.28
26.15 30.23 32.04
34.03 34.17 40.03
42.25 42.28 48.30
54.22 57.14 61.27
63.29 70.22 70.41
71.02 72.08 74.12
79.20 80.07 80.27
82.05 87.13 90.26
97.14 103.28 103.29
103.30 105.10 107.14
107.23 108.25 117.08
122.13 124.15 132.09
132.26 140.22 142.02
143.20 145.16 145.18
152.05 153.24 163.01
163.11 170.13 173.18
175.19 180.21 183.01
183.14 187.16 187.22
187.22 195.07 196.03
200.09 201.03 209.29
213.19 217.20 220.06

WENT (CONT.) 223.04
224.02 224.17 226.12
232.17 233.24 234.15
235.03 241.04 243.03
250.05 256.12 256.24
259.16 266.24 268.02
276.17 283.08 289.07
289.18 290.19 309.24
310.06 311.13 324.29
327.06 328.13 328.21
332.17 337.12 343.17
343.27 346.04 349.29
354.04 357.19 359.17
360.24 361.19 362.16
362.19 369.13 374.03
376.06 377.21 378.09
379.29 385.04 385.23
386.22 388.08 403.24
411.30 412.02 416.18
418.07 427.21 428.16
430.16 431.08 431.18
438.24 443.17 444.22
450.05 450.11 453.05
454.26 456.11 464.14
465.09 467.06 470.06
471.08 479.14 480.22
482.03 482.26 483.09
483.21 489.25 492.09
492.27 494.23 500.25
502.28 505.03 506.28
507.22

WEPT 140.24 200.16
383.26 385.16

WERE 2.29 5.21
10.13 12.16 13.02
13.17 13.26 14.01
15.08 18.04 20.19
22.01 23.14 27.14
28.19 32.06 32.12
33.08 33.15 34.02
35.16 36.17 39.08
43.08 46.05 48.18
48.24 49.08 52.03
53.29 54.12 57.06
58.30 61.19 62.06
63.23 66.01 66.21
67.12 68.03 69.06
71.18 71.22 71.26
73.08 79.25 83.18
84.02 87.09 91.06
91.10 92.05 92.07
99.03 101.08 101.22
103.18 103.19 105.02
105.15 107.17 109.02
109.06 109.19 109.29
111.26 111.30 112.30
114.02 115.13 117.19
117.27 118.10 119.01
122.02 122.08 123.17
125.26 127.07 129.21
131.21 131.27 132.10
132.29 133.18 133.21
136.08 137.09 139.27
140.09 140.10 141.12
141.29 141.29 142.12
143.27 144.25 146.15
146.22 147.18 148.14
149.14 150.05 150.17
150.27 151.12 154.11
156.05 157.21 163.10
164.23 165.22 166.08
166.23 167.04 167.06
167.06 167.19 168.17
168.18 168.26 169.01
169.16 176.07 177.20
177.30 178.22 179.21
185.20 186.06 186.13
191.03 192.04 192.14
194.03 195.24 196.22
205.20 207.23 209.01
209.16 209.24 211.08
212.24 215.23 217.20
219.09 220.20 222.22
225.02 226.28 227.07
227.16 229.04 232.06
233.30 234.22 234.29
239.04 239.07 242.17
243.19 245.13 246.03
246.07 246.18 248.21
249.02 250.18 254.17

WERE (CONT.)   254.18

255.19	261.18	262.22
262.30	263.15	263.17
265.07	267.17	274.15
274.19	275.15	276.05
276.24	277.20	277.21
278.22	279.17	279.23
281.09	282.25	283.08
286.20	287.02	291.04
291.06	291.22	294.23
295.29	298.02	298.12
299.22	300.13	301.06
301.10	302.10	302.23
303.11	303.13	306.04
307.13	308.11	308.30
310.18	311.06	311.18
311.20	313.08	314.08
314.11	315.04	315.18
315.28	316.02	316.02
317.04	317.08	319.04
319.17	320.07	320.13
321.02	322.22	323.11
328.12	328.22	329.05
332.07	339.18	339.30
342.24	345.11	347.07
347.23	348.01	349.05
349.08	349.12	350.18
352.14	353.17	353.17
356.09	356.26	358.04
359.14	360.11	363.02
364.04	365.06	366.14
366.25	367.07	371.11
374.03	375.27	377.21
377.28	378.21	379.04
379.07	379.10	379.24
383.23	384.06	387.12
387.20	387.28	390.05
392.04	393.26	398.21
401.09	401.17	403.07
403.26	405.19	406.05
409.11	410.16	410.20
414.26	415.03	416.19
416.21	417.13	420.18
423.14	424.08	426.30
428.22	430.01	432.05
434.23	435.09	436.08
437.09	439.15	440.05
440.24	443.04	443.07
443.19	444.13	444.21
444.21	444.23	445.26
445.27	447.09	448.01
449.26	449.30	450.16
451.15	451.17	453.02
453.16	454.02	454.06
460.08	460.15	460.24
462.05	463.25	465.14
468.04	469.11	472.06
472.07	474.07	477.15
480.03	480.05	480.09
480.13	480.21	481.27
483.29	484.10	484.14
484.28	485.19	485.23
486.08	486.08	489.22
491.03	492.06	493.19
493.24	495.13	498.20
498.21	499.07	499.15
499.17	502.04	503.01
503.06	503.13	504.04
504.21	508.10	508.19
511.09	511.17	513.16

WEREN'T   28.21   57.08
123.16   152.16

WEST   19.06   68.14
123.06   151.15   153.12
196.11   198.03   245.07
413.10   437.11   469.03

WESTERING   295.25

WESTERN   322.10   414.19
435.04   475.23   515.01

WESTWARD   290.15

WET   62.18   328.25
371.16   390.19   414.06
445.21   452.10

WHALER   196.16

WHALERS   436.17

WHARF   16.20

WHAT   7.23   9.02
11.25   25.21   26.07
26.24   28.12   29.24
30.03   30.04   30.22

WHAT (CONT.)   36.16

40.12	41.01	42.27
43.38	44.14	44.14
44.24	48.22	49.02
49.04	49.09	50.02
58.15	58.16	59.24
61.05	62.02	63.16
63.22	64.24	67.04
67.27	70.32	71.20
74.17	77.02	77.10
78.27	79.26	80.15
80.20	84.14	85.17
86.09	86.28	87.03
87.10	87.12	87.14
89.18	95.03	95.30
96.06	97.07	97.23
98.24	99.22	99.28
99.28	100.12	100.13
101.26	101.26	102.12
103.27	105.25	108.17
108.17	108.30	110.12
110.16	111.17	111.17
111.19	112.24	118.16
120.27	128.26	128.28
130.25	132.28	136.23
136.24	139.02	139.19
141.10	141.18	141.27
142.04	142.13	142.19
143.09	143.24	144.09
144.24	145.23	148.02
148.09	148.24	150.14
151.12	151.30	151.30
152.01	152.15	152.16
155.14	156.01	156.18
156.26	157.09	157.12
158.01	159.03	159.18
160.15	160.17	160.24
162.18	162.21	163.02
163.06	163.21	163.30
164.28	166.16	166.23
166.29	171.03	171.04
176.03	176.12	176.17
176.29	177.06	177.12
177.26	179.03	180.28
182.06	186.16	187.12
188.27	192.05	196.28
197.04	197.19	200.14
200.20	201.15	202.27
202.28	202.30	203.22
205.13	207.17	208.02
208.12	210.17	211.04
213.19	214.20	215.08
215.09	215.13	216.29
218.12	218.13	222.24
223.04	223.12	223.29
223.30	224.20	224.25
225.19	228.27	229.02
229.03	230.15	230.18
230.20	230.21	230.27
231.11	231.19	233.30
235.03	235.07	235.15
235.17	236.06	237.18
237.20	238.03	238.24
239.23	242.05	242.18
242.19	244.12	245.07
245.08	245.12	245.12
245.17	246.14	251.30
252.21	253.11	253.15
253.28	254.16	256.22
257.16	257.29	263.23
263.24	264.16	267.04
267.30	269.13	271.12
272.27	274.09	280.23
281.30	287.27	289.11
289.11	289.12	290.07
291.07	294.11	294.11
294.16	295.19	298.26
298.27	301.13	302.04
302.05	303.16	303.19
303.20	303.26	303.26
304.04	309.20	309.20
309.23	310.20	311.01
320.16	320.24	321.06
327.10	328.03	328.27
330.08	336.23	338.05
343.18	343.20	344.03
347.19	349.04	353.21
354.08	355.02	355.11
355.11	356.15	357.09
360.28	361.05	361.07

WHAT (CONT.)   362.07

363.01	365.24	368.30
369.06	370.17	370.26
374.14	375.06	376.11
376.16	377.03	377.06
377.13	377.14	377.25
378.13	378.27	379.08
379.12	383.14	383.15
384.18	385.05	385.07
388.13	388.22	388.27
388.22	388.27	388.27
390.02	391.27	392.08
392.14	393.26	394.17
394.19	395.23	395.24
396.07	401.12	402.22
402.27	402.28	403.12
403.14	403.19	404.27
405.16	407.18	411.24
412.02	413.09	413.09
413.09	413.09	413.17
415.09	420.17	420.22
422.06	422.22	425.23
428.07	428.11	430.22
431.03	432.17	433.01
433.10	436.02	436.18
437.05	437.07	437.24
449.18	455.18	455.22
455.23	456.02	456.29
458.23	458.27	459.24
460.13	460.14	464.24
467.24	467.26	468.03
468.07	468.19	469.13
471.09	471.11	472.06
472.17	472.18	473.06
473.06	473.13	473.16
473.19	473.19	474.01
474.11	474.14	475.23
477.03	481.10	482.26
483.16	484.05	485.01
489.07	492.09	492.16
492.27	494.22	494.25
501.04	502.20	506.06
507.01	507.01	507.17
507.29	507.29	510.19
510.24	513.15	

WHAT'S   30.30   37.27
37.28   45.10   48.19
55.27   66.22   67.26
73.10   75.17   78.10
143.26   189.03   197.11
198.08   201.26   204.05
217.17   233.18   235.14
237.15   259.03   286.01
301.22   357.02   358.21
364.29   383.23   428.23
455.18   466.28   467.16
471.07   472.25   481.09

WHAT'S-HIS-NAME   286.01

WHAT'S-YOUR-NAME   233.18

WHATEVER   32.04   42.30
70.23   125.20   209.30
262.08   283.26   313.16
329.18   352.06   402.26
470.16

WHEAT   290.27

WHEEDLING   358.15

WHEEL   22.10   22.15
31.06   117.10

WHEEL-CHAINS   22.15

WHEELING   217.16

WHEELS   55.10   56.14

WHEEZED   110.19

WHEEZING   180.07

WHEEZY   30.22   145.10

WHELPS   7.05

WHEN   2.21   3.08
3.21   4.15   5.23
8.12   8.30   10.15
11.27   12.12   15.15
23.22   25.27   26.03
28.01   28.18   32.01
34.21   43.01   44.05
47.21   48.17   51.29
53.04   58.07   58.22
59.02   61.04   68.30
69.07   70.10   70.18
71.13   74.09   78.01
78.16   81.10   81.17
89.30   96.28   98.25
99.09   101.12   109.18

WHEN (CONT.)   109.21

124.20	124.26	128.01
130.13	131.26	133.11
133.15	140.14	144.06
147.04	151.10	154.10
156.26	158.15	163.30
165.06	165.20	166.05
167.09	172.10	174.18
174.20	176.22	177.06
178.07	178.25	179.16
181.01	181.14	182.21
184.19	186.26	195.26
197.25	198.11	203.23
210.11	213.01	215.14
216.08	218.04	219.05
223.27	229.09	231.07
231.23	233.26	234.26
235.26	236.06	236.14
236.28	236.30	244.11
249.20	250.25	256.20
256.21	256.27	258.20
262.17	264.27	267.14
269.21	279.10	279.16
280.23	285.21	285.24
287.01	287.26	294.03
304.05	306.19	307.20
310.03	310.27	311.09
311.25	317.15	318.14
318.18	318.23	319.08
319.27	319.28	320.18
321.01	321.08	323.24
328.24	329.13	330.13
331.30	333.21	336.02
338.02	338.07	340.03
342.15	349.20	349.26
350.21	353.29	360.06
364.22	374.14	374.19
375.01	375.02	377.02
378.25	383.29	385.06
387.01	389.01	393.14
394.21	397.21	398.16
404.10	404.23	408.23
413.21	418.21	419.22
420.24	427.05	430.24
431.11	432.19	437.06
437.21	440.16	443.13
444.25	450.22	450.28
454.03	459.23	462.02
464.16	466.03	466.05
467.11	468.19	472.25
473.20	475.11	475.30
479.10	479.12	484.15
485.17	488.16	490.05
491.13	493.09	493.22
494.07	500.17	502.23
504.01	505.19	508.26
509.06	509.16	512.26
513.05	513.26	514.03
516.08	516.11	

WHEN'   180.29

WHENCE   272.03   345.07
452.06   473.22

WHENEVER   72.09   230.25
399.19   490.24

WHERE   1.12   2.04
2.07   3.10   3.24
26.02   26.12   29.18
29.29   33.09   43.05
44.03   45.15   48.11
55.20   55.22   56.15
72.25   75.25   87.28
96.10   104.06   107.08
111.07   111.19   117.03
119.26   122.22   129.01
141.24   143.25   151.20
168.30   170.26   178.06
182.05   184.25   186.20
201.03   208.11   208.12
208.27   223.01   230.03
237.22   238.17   240.14
240.19   249.08   250.17
252.12   253.17   253.17
260.10   266.20   269.10
276.21   278.28   279.15
283.13   285.13   287.04
288.24   288.26   290.19
292.30   303.05   303.25
306.01   307.01   308.29
308.30   312.17   313.25
319.30   323.26   333.25

WHERE (CONT.) 335.13
337.29 340.28 351.08
355.20 359.21 361.03
378.24 387.12 398.01
405.04 407.14 421.29
422.03 422.04 426.24
432.04 434.01 437.03
438.01 441.19 455.22
463.24 470.08 474.14
475.27 477.17 479.10
482.27 483.13 489.22
489.23 493.06 494.05
495.16 497.03 499.22
500.04 511.25
WHERE'S 76.06 234.06
289.13
WHEREABOUTS 451.17
WHEREAS 264.29
WHEREFORE 387.05
WHEREIN 358.16
WHEREVER 241.04
WHETHER 38.14 48.01
53.29 56.07 66.12
83.20 95.06 98.29
154.05 190.17 194.04
194.27 208.18 239.24
265.06 274.25 289.26
300.01 302.06 303.17
310.22 326.01 331.06
340.01 340.16 341.13
344.23 353.02 361.15
379.07 394.16 399.26
407.16 419.07 419.17
419.23 463.19 479.11
479.20 481.03 503.06
503.07 507.28
WHICH 1.05 1.07
2.02 3.07 3.13
8.17 11.06 11.12
11.15 11.20 12.22
13.06 24.01 27.04
28.24 35.06 36.08
50.14 50.15 50.18
53.08 59.14 60.20
69.25 76.26 76.30
77.30 78.25 80.24
84.07 85.11 86.23
87.17 88.18 90.06
93.09 95.01 95.13
98.26 106.08 112.19
113.17 115.10 117.01
117.02 117.03 117.08
122.03 122.24 123.26
124.11 124.21 127.16
129.09 129.18 131.06
131.15 142.10 147.13
151.18 155.03 155.20
156.13 158.25 166.20
168.22 169.01 169.03
169.23 172.18 172.27
173.02 173.22 181.17
184.08 185.18 186.24
194.19 194.26 202.07
207.02 207.15 208.09
210.15 210.19 211.06
212.03 213.09 213.23
214.30 215.08 217.10
219.11 220.19 222.04
223.08 223.10 224.30
228.16 229.15 230.07
232.22 232.29 239.08
240.11 240.17 244.17
244.24 246.10 248.14
249.05 251.28 252.01
252.24 254.01 254.05
257.18 259.08 261.21
262.12 264.07 264.20
265.07 270.07 270.12
270.23 270.27 272.04
272.22 274.21 274.23
274.26 275.02 276.23
279.01 279.13 280.08
280.10 282.21 282.22
286.07 287.11 287.30
289.02 291.20 292.24
292.27 293.02 294.26
295.28 297.14 297.15
298.03 299.05 300.10
302.04 302.08 303.30
305.05 307.07 307.30

WHICH (CONT.) 315.12
317.05 320.03 321.22
322.12 326.02 327.11
328.26 335.15 337.24
339.03 340.17 340.19
343.03 343.12 345.10
345.13 347.15 350.27
351.17 352.07 352.12
355.07 365.05 365.08
365.22 366.16 366.21
367.14 367.27 369.11
372.13 381.02 382.01
382.08 382.24 384.05
384.08 386.09 386.28
389.12 395.18 396.02
398.12 398.20 399.16
400.29 403.28 407.06
408.07 409.12 413.15
413.29 414.20 415.01
419.19 420.14 421.09
422.13 422.15 423.19
429.28 431.30 434.11
435.09 435.22 437.14
438.01 438.11 442.21
443.14 444.06 444.15
444.19 445.17 445.20
447.03 448.27 456.06
456.22 458.09 458.16
458.19 458.22 458.29
461.13 461.17 462.19
463.03 465.25 471.02
471.16 477.10 482.02
487.05 487.17 488.15
488.26 489.26 491.12
491.18 492.24 495.28
496.04 497.21 498.29
499.01 499.11 499.18
499.25 501.21 502.06
506.20 508.29 509.14
514.14 514.26 515.06
515.13 515.26
WHILE 4.28 7.27
13.15 21.25 23.06
34.21 35.30 36.27
37.17 42.12 43.05
46.20 48.13 62.14
63.10 69.15 71.06
75.05 78.05 80.02
82.29 83.29 87.16
90.09 90.15 101.16
103.21 104.01 115.12
118.01 121.07 122.06
123.15 126.25 131.20
133.28 138.30 139.27
140.26 141.26 146.02
148.02 148.12 148.14
148.26 148.28 148.29
148.30 149.01 149.18
157.05 157.08 161.02
163.04 170.13 175.21
181.21 185.26 188.10
202.15 212.17 212.23
215.15 215.20 216.05
216.18 217.21 220.26
222.04 224.07 225.16
226.03 228.07 231.18
231.30 251.19 258.11
263.10 278.17 287.21
290.10 290.19 291.26
292.10 293.12 294.01
294.20 294.21 306.03
307.05 308.09 308.10
309.09 313.04 320.12
321.04 337.24 338.01
343.28 344.22 347.24
351.06 352.05 357.19
358.22 362.13 362.14
365.27 366.26 382.20
385.07 386.19 390.18
396.12 398.09 401.20
401.27 402.11 413.25
421.01 423.04 423.22
426.29 433.09 442.22
444.13 447.15 447.17
452.23 453.18 454.28
458.24 463.12 463.26
465.10 466.09 466.13
467.21 472.10 473.30
475.08 475.15 476.04
482.24 489.02 489.04

WHILE (CONT.) 489.15
492.22 494.11 494.20
495.28 499.17 502.27
505.01 509.25 510.06
511.17 513.04 515.07
516.21
WHILED 456.07
WHILES 6.01 299.28
WHIM 438.15
WHIMPERED 125.03
WHINE 84.08 145.07
399.01
WHINED 61.26 122.14
402.04 404.13
WHIPPED 124.14 443.23
WHIRL 116.27 359.08
WHIRLED 6.14
WHIRLS 175.29
WHISK 379.27
WHISKED 100.24
WHISKER 238.14 238.26
WHISKERED 436.05
WHISKERS 232.17
WHISKY 29.14
WHISPER 124.22 142.16
177.01 261.06 261.29
334.19 359.21 380.11
387.15 387.23 391.26
434.09 492.15
WHISPERED 63.02
115.06 162.20 187.04
202.19 218.11 249.18
308.06 359.27 360.26
367.25 384.23 386.30
391.06 403.03 505.07
508.23
WHISPERER 360.30
WHISPERING 93.03
109.28 120.15 335.18
369.09 382.07 431.09
479.15 487.07 501.29
WHISPERS 126.26 320.11
342.24 382.22 508.17
509.09 513.30
WHIST 113.24
WHISTLE 172.05 176.24
478.28
WHISTLING 47.25
WHIT 471.21
WHITE 1.11 3.03
3.22 12.16 14.04
16.18 17.17 18.01
19.15 20.04 21.07
23.23 31.06 32.13
37.19 37.23 37.30
55.30 57.19 57.22
58.13 59.03 61.16
82.25 83.10 93.14
103.03 105.12 119.01
119.06 119.09 129.29
141.13 145.30 149.07
165.14 167.20 191.27
195.08 199.14 199.18
200.18 246.16 248.05
249.10 250.09 250.16
252.12 252.26 254.12
263.16 272.27 276.08
279.27 297.21 297.23
298.19 299.08 310.19
310.22 318.19 319.30
321.22 321.26 332.04
333.02 333.26 334.07
337.30 338.04 339.26
340.22 342.25 343.17
344.30 345.05 345.18
346.03 346.05 346.12
349.13 350.02 350.12
363.22 365.14 371.15
373.12 378.06 378.22
380.13 383.07 385.10
385.15 386.10 397.19
398.30 409.23 410.15
410.18 414.28 415.06
415.11 415.16 423.05
424.12 426.25 430.04
435.18 441.11 442.25
447.08 447.16 447.22
449.28 452.08 453.26
454.01 456.14 457.04
458.26 461.13 465.02

WHITE (CONT.) 465.14
469.06 469.10 469.20
470.01 470.30 472.04
472.15 475.14 477.17
480.07 480.11 482.22
484.06 485.19 486.07
488.05 491.16 493.24
498.02 498.18 498.25
499.06 500.15 501.12
501.27 503.06 508.29
509.18 513.19 513.21
514.27 515.01 515.16
WHITE-FACED 129.29
WHITENED 103.24 496.05
WHITES 17.29 42.23
119.28 371.04 453.22
464.01 486.12 491.03
499.22 501.23
WHITEWASHED 15.07
WHITISH 123.05
WHO 2.21 7.12
8.29 12.17 12.21
13.26 15.03 21.04
30.06 35.11 37.23
43.22 44.22 44.28
45.27 46.26 46.30
49.24 50.03 52.15
53.07 57.01 57.29
64.17 66.09 67.23
69.11 76.15 77.02
83.01 86.25 88.13
89.15 89.17 93.22
98.20 100.14 102.06
112.10 112.11 113.29
115.12 116.20 119.07
119.21 125.19 128.16
131.11 139.01 143.23
165.13 167.25 168.08
168.18 174.16 175.06
178.30 179.13 179.28
182.16 185.23 191.01
191.05 192.02 192.19
197.22 200.19 201.06
203.08 203.16 209.30
210.29 211.08 219.01
220.10 226.26 237.19
238.23 239.12 239.14
239.22 240.24 242.05
245.28 246.10 247.19
247.21 248.06 250.01
250.11 250.12 251.01
260.26 266.09 266.24
267.10 268.12 268.18
271.05 271.24 271.27
272.01 273.19 273.24
275.10 277.11 278.24
278.26 279.06 282.01
282.06 283.08 285.12
289.10 289.16 289.17
297.20 298.13 300.08
307.08 314.05 316.21
321.14 325.04 327.16
328.20 328.22 332.23
335.04 336.05 336.19
338.23 340.19 340.23
340.29 341.09 344.30
346.04 347.04 351.21
354.03 358.22 362.04
363.13 366.05 367.02
373.08 374.05 376.07
376.12 376.12 376.12
376.12 378.11 383.14
390.01 390.02 392.09
397.26 397.29 400.09
400.21 400.21 400.22
400.22 400.23 402.15
402.26 409.15 410.11
413.08 414.09 416.12
419.03 422.10 422.22
423.18 425.02 426.23
427.25 427.29 430.18
430.19 435.03 436.22
438.15 438.22 439.07
439.27 440.09 442.07
444.09 447.06 447.07
447.19 448.07 448.14
448.28 449.21 450.30
452.09 452.25 453.11
453.26 455.02 455.11
455.15 456.12 456.18

WHO (CONT.)   456.28
 457.06 458.06 459.13
 459.21 465.28 466.29
 467.16 470.24 471.05
 471.22 475.25 477.06
 478.11 479.14 484.21
 484.27 487.19 488.08
 491.26 493.07 493.08
 494.17 499.19 500.03
 500.21 501.16 501.30
 503.05 504.23 507.02
 507.03 507.19 508.10
 508.23 509.11 510.20
 510.29 516.16
WHO'S   29.08   87.25
 285.05 367.26
WHOLE   11.16   31.09
  34.05   35.20   41.26
  42.08   43.15   51.24
  54.25   55.05   66.09
  73.14   81.09   91.11
  93.27   99.01 102.25
 117.28 120.27 123.06
 125.24 147.04 147.20
 177.07 187.02 199.29
 203.23 207.08 219.23
 240.13 240.30 244.09
 251.10 293.28 301.05
 316.28 318.13 331.12
 332.11 336.12 336.12
 338.06 340.10 347.18
 353.12 354.12 361.13
 367.06 371.08 380.05
 392.09 392.22 427.05
 439.07 448.10 454.12
 462.28 487.16 503.07
WHOLLY   77.01 100.12
WHOM   4.03   41.25
  60.05 167.23 168.06
 177.23 185.30 223.25
 247.16 251.04 251.25
 252.10 252.20 271.04
 271.05 271.07 273.01
 282.05 282.07 327.14
 345.22 346.03 364.04
 395.20 400.06 412.13
 420.24 422.28 428.05
 431.27 448.15 451.23
 471.20 475.16 477.15
 485.23 486.14 494.16
 509.18
WHOOP   236.21
WHOOPING 236.23
WHOSE   10.09   22.07
  22.10   33.02   50.24
  51.24   60.05   60.10
  63.18   94.13 106.04
 108.09 117.29 147.16
 147.29 155.07 155.18
 158.18 160.28 169.27
 170.06 170.07 208.17
 224.04 241.28 264.10
 268.16 268.28 275.04
 334.17 338.08 340.24
 376.19 395.08 395.09
 412.19 413.02 418.23
 425.20 433.27 433.29
 434.14 451.17 464.19
 488.11 500.10 513.20
WHY   35.01   40.03
  40.12   41.06   52.08
  59.12   60.03   61.21
  62.13   66.24   77.04
  77.06   77.06   78.18
  78.26   78.30   79.18
  80.05   96.26   97.20
 118.28 122.13 124.27
 130.20 138.09 138.13
 138.14 138.14 138.15
 142.03 144.14 145.05
 150.06 151.06 159.01
 184.21 185.24 194.09
 203.06 204.25 212.14
 219.21 224.24 234.21
 237.04 241.12 243.07
 246.03 253.18 253.19
 255.16 282.30 282.30
 288.27 288.27 289.30
 295.16 301.04 303.20
 305.07 308.06 325.03

WHY (CONT.)   325.29
 329.28 338.11 338.19
 339.05 344.10 349.03
 375.28 376.25 381.19
 383.18 387.04 387.24
 389.07 391.09 391.18
 392.24 393.02 393.05
 393.07 404.27 405.05
 405.07 433.21 475.29
 481.21 485.25 506.02
 511.14
WICKED   430.22
WICKEDNESS   254.17
WICKER   94.12
WIDE   12.29   24.07
  70.03 130.28 147.02
 156.20 242.11 302.20
 315.12 318.10 319.08
 366.20 371.26 374.10
 380.17 384.11 410.01
 465.16 480.17 501.10
 504.12
WIDENED 409.02
WIDER   156.29
WIE   260.20
WIFE   70.41 190.07
 251.24 254.09 257.20
 268.10 314.12 314.22
 319.06 330.01 330.08
 330.09 330.12 330.16
 338.12 340.11 350.13
 353.20 407.21 436.21
WIFE'   402.05
WIFE'S   268.23 353.18
WILD   62.05   89.22
 110.04 126.21 134.07
 279.09 317.10 327.07
 334.05 381.04 405.14
 443.26 449.25 452.04
 504.17 508.07
WILDERNESS   15.29
  38.12 234.05 283.09
 283.11 356.10 408.14
WILDEST 423.12 515.21
WILDLY   104.19 364.16
 477.07
WILDNESS 186.21
WILL   7.16   34.23
  40.05   53.03   53.09
  72.15   72.28   76.18
  78.08   79.26   79.30
  82.03   87.13   87.20
  87.29   99.23 100.23
 100.29 112.24 121.15
 124.27 145.03 151.23
 152.15 153.29 180.01
 186.09 188.27 197.01
 197.15 199.27 203.10
 203.16 203.25 205.13
 215.17 222.24 223.01
 223.30 231.09 235.26
 241.15 243.25 254.15
 259.23 261.06 269.02
 271.16 287.28 288.05
 290.06 312.29 328.04
 340.05 344.18 363.06
 388.08 388.29 388.30
 389.03 395.09 404.26
 404.29 411.28 413.19
 414.02 419.27 419.28
 422.09 423.10 424.10
 431.18 433.23 440.11
 458.15 466.15 467.07
 468.05 468.09 468.12
 468.17 480.19 485.11
 487.15 487.21 488.16
 493.14 494.11 511.02
 511.04 511.23
WILLED   139.02
WILLING   38.22   40.04
  53.03   66.18 404.08
 425.08 454.23 470.24
WILLINGLY   466.16
WINCE   479.16
WINCED   53.14
WINCH   26.07
WINCHES 102.30
WIND   6.10   6.24
   7.02   7.09   7.20
   9.02   32.24   37.12

WIND (CONT.)   62.24
 102.17 123.09 123.13
 126.14 132.04 132.17
 134.01 136.16 137.20
 142.08 145.16 148.28
 166.06 170.21 175.27
 177.09 181.27 188.27
 195.16 226.03 380.14
 430.03 431.07 442.25
 443.06 508.16
WIND-SAIL   102.17
WINDING 325.12
WINDLASS 52.18 292.02
WINDOW   33.06   48.05
 200.23 216.26 217.25
 220.25 224.03 232.27
 350.01 366.23 370.06
 416.18 505.25
WINDOW-PANES   216.26
WINDOWS   12.29   64.10
  94.14 104.30 218.01
 430.04
WINDWARD 137.23 413.30
WINE   93.06 172.05
 172.11
WING   225.17 256.09
WINGED   39.07   61.12
 390.21
WINGS   247.13 249.09
 252.26 256.22 257.23
 348.18 380.18 410.06
 419.05 432.05 474.08
 474.10 497.05
WINK   17.02 188.06
 230.26 239.22 359.03
WINKED   62.16   94.16
WINKING 239.23 314.25
WINKS   235.13
WINNING 475.20
WINS   53.08
WINTER'S   5.26   62.25
 417.06
WIPE   460.21
WIPED   37.03 301.24
WIPING   314.17 476.04
WIRES   390.13
WIRY   196.15
WISDOM   20.04 134.20
 157.01 179.06 212.02
 277.27 337.15 339.22
 381.24 447.21
WISE   26.25 156.06
 156.08 391.18 392.25
WISER   146.21
WISEST   327.08
WISH   30.05   57.07
  81.14 130.21 130.26
 144.02 144.08 197.18
 197.19 349.28 381.22
 411.23 451.08 469.17
 483.04 492.30
WISHED   58.05   59.19
  60.04   76.04 135.06
 185.11 211.28 218.12
 280.26 282.16 282.27
 307.07 391.28 447.08
 457.22
WISHING 209.19 490.25
WISP   18.07   60.23
WISPS   118.23 353.13
 445.14
WISTFUL 306.24 387.13
WISTFULLY   61.07
 339.23
WIT   92.24 228.07
WITCH   56.09 319.19
 338.12 407.21
WITCH-LIKE   319.19
WITH   1.03   2.16
   2.27   4.09   4.11
   4.23   4.25   5.04
   5.12   5.28   6.25
   7.08   7.13   7.18
   7.28   8.07   8.11
   8.15   8.23   9.01
   9.07   10.14   11.08
  11.09   11.09   12.09
  12.23   13.10   13.16
  13.20   13.29   14.28
  15.06   15.09   15.13

WITH (CONT.)   15.20
  15.21   15.21   16.05
  16.05   16.05   16.05
  16.08   16.09   16.19
  17.14   17.21   17.22
  17.23   17.30   19.02
  19.21   20.09   20.10
  20.12   20.13   20.23
  20.27   20.29   20.30
  21.01   21.05   21.07
  21.10   22.12   22.18
  22.24   22.30   23.02
  23.06   23.09   23.10
  23.17   23.18   23.18
  23.21   23.30   23.30
  24.05   24.30   25.01
  25.15   25.19   26.19
  26.20   26.21   27.01
  27.08   27.16   27.17
  27.17   27.18   28.07
  28.10   28.13   28.28
  29.16   29.25   29.30
  32.09   33.13   33.19
  33.21   33.24   34.09
  34.25   35.09   36.26
  37.08   37.24   37.25
  37.28   38.10   38.26
  39.04   40.18   40.18
  40.19   41.16   41.23
  41.24   41.26   42.03
  42.12   43.10   43.24
  43.35   44.16   44.22
  46.07   46.20   46.21
  46.23   46.26   46.27
  46.29   47.21   48.08
  48.15   48.16   49.07
  49.27   51.13   52.11
  52.16   52.19   52.21
  52.23   53.21   53.28
  54.08   54.10   54.18
  54.23   54.28   55.06
  55.12   55.17   56.03
  56.04   56.10   56.28
  56.30   57.04   57.20
  57.22   58.03   58.14
  58.18   58.21   59.03
  59.05   60.20   60.25
  61.16   61.27   62.04
  63.02   63.04   63.12
  63.17   64.27   66.20
  57.14   68.06   69.01
  69.16   69.21   69.25
  70.07   70.07   70.09
  70.13   70.16   70.31
  70.40   71.07   71.28
  72.21   73.25   74.07
  74.14   74.17   74.23
  74.26   75.01   75.07
  75.14   75.16   75.20
  75.22   75.23   75.27
  75.30   76.07   76.24
  77.25   77.25   77.27
  77.29   77.30   78.02
  78.13   78.21   78.24
  78.30   79.10   79.13
  79.15   80.04   80.09
  80.16   81.18   81.29
  82.10   82.30   83.09
  83.10   83.14   83.15
  83.17   83.21   83.26
  84.03   84.20   84.30
  85.04   85.20   85.25
  85.26   85.27   85.30
  86.06   87.15   87.18
  88.08   88.11   89.01
  89.21   89.22   89.28
  90.01   90.05   90.16
  90.19   91.02   91.15
  92.04   92.06   93.04
  93.14   93.18   93.19
  94.20   95.12   95.23
  96.23   97.06   97.11
  97.15   98.08   99.17
 100.01 100.03 100.15
 100.27 101.06 101.19
 101.28 103.03 103.26
 103.29 104.24 105.13
 106.12 107.20 108.10
 108.23 109.03 109.12
 110.06 111.20 111.28

142

WOULD (CONT.)   166.12
166.15 168.10 168.19
168.20 171.03 172.12
176.21 178.23 179.25
182.07 183.11 183.26
184.02 184.21 185.06
186.07 186.16 186.19
187.23 187.30 189.12
190.08 190.22 191.04
193.30 194.15 196.25
199.06 199.25 200.07
200.13 201.01 201.15
204.22 204.23 207.03
208.22 209.08 210.04
211.30 212.01 212.12
212.21 212.23 213.09
213.18 214.18 214.21
214.24 215.27 215.28
215.30 216.30 218.29
219.18 219.22 224.27
225.28 227.05 229.26
230.08 230.26 231.28
232.12 232.21 233.11
235.18 236.10 236.11
236.11 236.24 240.22
240.26 243.20 244.07
245.05 245.09 245.10
247.02 247.20 251.22
252.22 252.22 258.18
258.20 265.04 266.19
266.21 267.30 269.01
270.04 272.11 272.13
272.17 272.24 273.13
273.14 273.20 274.24
275.05 275.12 276.22
276.23 279.10 280.17
281.21 281.29 282.20
282.25 282.26 283.13
283.13 283.25 283.27
283.29 283.30 284.02
286.10 286.16 286.22
287.08 287.12 287.13
289.21 289.30 290.01
290.02 290.26 292.13
292.16 292.19 292.30
294.05 298.05 298.26
298.27 301.02 301.03
301.24 303.06 303.21
303.21 303.30 305.04
307.01 309.06 309.08
309.23 310.04 310.16
310.17 310.19 311.01
312.07 312.29 315.10
315.30 318.21 318.23
319.01 320.02 320.04
320.17 321.19 328.01
328.30 329.11 329.25
330.03 331.18 332.12
332.19 333.03 335.07
336.19 337.16 338.04
338.23 341.05 342.11
344.07 345.28 348.01
348.09 348.11 348.11
349.21 349.23 349.25
349.26 350.10 352.15
352.19 353.02 355.09
355.16 355.17 355.19
355.20 355.21 356.01
356.04 356.07 356.16
356.24 356.27 357.01
357.04 357.11 357.20
357.29 358.18 361.29
367.10 369.13 370.16
370.20 376.07 376.13
376.13 377.22 378.14
379.13 381.11 382.16
384.12 384.18 386.30
388.05 388.06 390.01
390.02 390.10 392.10
392.16 392.28 395.29
398.02 398.17 399.13
399.15 400.27 401.07
401.08 401.11 402.16
402.17 403.12 404.03
404.08 404.30 405.11
405.20 407.17 410.25
411.01 412.02 415.03
418.10 419.23 420.13
420.21 421.21 422.29
423.30 426.03 426.13

WOULD (CONT.)   427.03
427.11 427.12 427.14
428.02 428.14 428.14
428.28 429.11 429.25
430.15 430.17 430.28
434.08 435.17 435.18
435.20 435.22 436.10
436.12 438.15 438.20
442.10 442.15 445.19
446.07 449.03 449.10
449.11 449.12 450.15
450.17 450.28 453.03
453.27 453.28 456.03
456.16 456.19 457.08
457.11 457.13 457.17
457.19 457.21 460.06
461.29 463.16 463.19
463.23 463.24 464.04
465.03 470.24 472.03
473.22 473.24 473.27
477.07 478.19 481.28
482.26 483.15 483.19
483.20 484.06 486.12
486.13 488.27 489.07
489.08 491.04 491.23
492.07 493.06 493.10
495.06 495.16 495.15
508.21 511.13 511.18
WOULDN'T   8.16   30.06
40.13 53.22 57.03
95.20 114.07 154.02
158.11 158.26 182.25
200.04 204.04 204.10
204.16 204.19 204.29
205.20 211.22 235.22
237.04 237.28 238.28
274.01 276.21 287.07
290.22 295.17 324.26
330.02 331.11 377.17
402.08
WOUND   37.13 171.14
371.14 509.23
WOUNDED   177.30 181.19
222.16 225.17 444.10
448.01 465.07 467.02
467.05 500.21 510.02
WOUNDS   277.03
WOVEN   339.29
WRAITH   309.20
WRAPPED   16.11 20.09
44.09 60.22 198.23
WRE   480.15
WREATHED   332.04 382.01
WRECK   33.14
WRECKER   196.16
WREST   378.14
WRESTLING   182.26
507.27
WRESTLING-MATCH   182.26
WRETCH'S   296.04 466.07
WRETCHED   78.27 83.27
88.30 145.07 157.25
183.01 187.02 309.14
343.06 345.23 353.27
357.11 425.20 426.29
454.29 473.04
WRETCHEDNESS   233.27
WRIGGLE   352.04 364.19
WRIGGLED   445.02
WRIGGLING   309.10
WRING   389.09
WRINGING   388.18
WRINKLE   17.13
WRINKLED   77.07 250.19
318.08
WRINKLES   118.25 314.24
WRISTS   109.08
WRIT   409.20
WRITE   186.01 208.25
212.10 230.08 243.09
348.14 420.05 507.05
WRITHE   12.06 356.08
WRITHED   36.28 307.10
425.09
WRITHING   94.25 452.14
WRITING   2.10 45.13
70.25 71.09 209.02
209.12 209.29 212.18
223.25 223.26 232.19
248.15 252.18

WRITING-DESK   209.02
248.15
WRITINGCASE   421.11
WRITTEN   71.10 73.20
97.16 210.23 248.23
422.04 441.26 491.18
WRONG   25.27 47.17
115.15 124.18 157.29
187.01 190.04 190.17
198.22 280.11 324.29
347.16 422.14 485.24
516.07
WRONG-HEADED   124.18
280.11
WROTE   71.07 73.26
76.19 209.28 209.28
227.04 227.20 228.05
230.02 230.10 230.20
420.28 456.23
WRUNG   99.30 124.29
138.05 211.01 400.15
YAM   495.03
YAMS   463.28 494.22
YANKEE   440.07 459.20
461.09 464.16 465.06
466.29
YAP   143.09 143.09
143.13 143.13 143.13
143.14 143.17 143.17
143.18 143.18
YAPPING   143.08
YARD   4.12 26.09
166.21 231.14 316.27
510.18
YARDS   4.20 233.25
294.21 311.19 313.09
323.14 439.09 444.19
452.16 465.16
YARN   70.16 114.01
YAWNING   12.25 15.17
30.27 269.27
YEAR   71.10 71.12
81.18 123.02 185.28
217.08 230.11 286.19
414.04 423.24 437.12
448.30 475.11
YEAR'S   93.24
YEARNING   100.02 106.12
274.28 376.06
YEARS   3.17 10.01
27.07 27.24 58.11
65.08 70.42 73.28
76.11 119.10 168.01
182.02 184.27 190.13
198.01 198.01 200.04
203.23 228.14 232.05
250.04 251.05 251.14
252.04 282.06 289.04
295.05 297.02 312.17
315.23 330.11 330.11
345.19 356.19 375.21
416.14 421.16 421.30
422.21 435.15 438.08
452.10 455.15 456.04
481.26 486.03 488.02
495.17 499.25
YEARS'   75.29 353.16
YELL   57.09 133.05
183.02 311.18 446.08
500.24
YELLED   63.28 205.03
370.28 452.23 464.13
500.17
YELLING   7.04 60.01
133.21 236.18 236.23
255.22 501.01
YELLOW   40.13 49.26
76.07 83.21 118.14
136.20 191.26 192.11
192.21 248.06 249.11
315.05 334.07 355.10
396.21 399.10 404.11
418.19 422.20 425.18
427.06 441.05 482.03
501.29
YELLOW-DOG   40.13
YELLOWED   417.30
YELLOWISH   208.16
YELLS   332.06 444.05
YELP   76.25

YELPS   131.26
YES   25.26 34.09
36.24 36.25 40.01
72.22 73.18 75.29
76.02 78.26 86.01
99.20 110.14 111.04
115.30 130.24 150.15
154.08 155.23 158.29
158.29 159.27 160.03
163.25 175.21 178.10
178.10 179.02 179.02
187.10 194.09 196.01
197.17 197.20 220.28
226.16 234.21 235.19
243.15 257.11 259.10
260.25 264.25 267.31
271.29 283.14 283.14
289.21 290.30 292.11
295.12 327.02 330.09
331.12 343.14 355.14
364.30 365.01 365.01
367.06 368.30 375.13
388.03 391.24 393.08
394.21 409.19 411.18
411.21 411.22 411.29
413.17 455.24 455.24
467.25 467.25 468.05
468.14 472.05 483.03
493.02 494.12 494.23
495.02 495.20 505.04
507.14 514.17
YET   10.10 10.15
27.22 29.12 41.22
50.15 51.25 66.10
70.05 70.27 82.13
86.09 96.23 99.21
112.28 124.01 128.10
137.01 137.26 151.26
155.09 164.05 165.27
168.07 179.29 189.23
197.01 197.12 214.04
218.08 226.12 226.26
227.24 228.09 228.28
236.03 237.07 242.16
243.16 244.15 245.16
245.22 255.17 261.24
262.11 275.19 288.14
292.25 309.02 329.24
337.01 339.16 344.10
345.28 352.25 359.21
361.17 361.30 366.18
375.29 376.14 392.11
394.08 396.11 396.15
400.24 411.23 423.13
424.05 430.18 431.09
432.14 441.22 472.28
493.27 494.07 507.08
516.10
YIELDED   438.09 441.02
YOKE   514.22
YOKOHAMA   27.20
YONDER   129.02
YORK   435.10
YOU   1.03 1.05
2.04 7.05 7.05
7.16 8.14 25.15
25.27 25.28 26.12
26.21 26.22 26.24
27.13 29.09 29.18
29.21 29.28 29.29
29.30 30.02 30.02
30.06 33.01 33.01
33.13 33.13 33.15
33.16 40.05 40.06
40.12 40.13 40.16
41.05 42.02 42.15
42.22 42.25 42.28
43.33 43.41 45.02
45.02 45.03 45.04
48.10 48.26 48.30
49.04 49.05 49.05
49.09 50.02 50.09
51.01 51.01 51.11
51.11 51.11 52.08
52.23 52.24 53.11
53.12 53.12 53.13
53.18 53.27 53.29
54.01 56.20 57.08
57.09 59.18 59.18
61.26 61.28 62.02

YOU (CONT.)

		62.07
62.16	62.26	63.01
64.25	65.06	65.09
65.12	65.17	66.10
67.05	67.16	67.28
68.13	68.14	68.18
68.29	70.17	70.23
70.31	70.34	71.16
71.29	72.01	72.04
72.15	72.21	72.23
72.28	74.15	75.03
75.13	75.16	75.17
75.23	75.24	76.15
76.21	77.05	77.10
77.16	77.22	78.05
78.11	78.23	79.02
79.24	79.26	79.27
80.05	80.06	80.07
80.13	80.19	80.20
80.20	81.01	81.13
81.13	81.21	84.12
84.14	84.21	84.21
85.07	85.17	85.19
85.30	85.30	86.01
86.02	86.05	87.04
87.08	87.10	87.10
87.11	87.12	87.12
87.13	87.20	87.24
87.25	88.01	88.05
88.09	88.21	88.29
90.25	95.06	96.19
96.19	96.29	97.07
97.07	97.08	97.08
97.09	97.20	97.20
98.05	98.06	98.22
99.21	99.25	100.05
100.05	100.25	100.25
100.29	101.05	101.10
101.16	101.17	103.10
104.03	104.22	105.07
105.17	105.25	106.04
109.02	109.29	110.11
110.13	111.01	111.04
111.06	111.09	111.10
111.11	111.11	111.13
111.14	111.16	111.17
111.17	111.19	111.23
112.10	112.24	113.19
113.28	114.08	114.21
116.20	116.28	120.16
120.19	120.20	121.03
121.05	121.11	122.02
122.10	122.13	122.14
122.19	123.01	123.02
124.25	124.25	124.27
128.06	128.26	128.27
128.27	128.28	128.28
128.30	129.01	129.13
129.13	130.20	130.23
130.24	130.25	132.21
132.23	133.25	134.02
134.25	134.26	137.10
138.13	138.18	138.27
139.04	139.07	139.19
140.20	141.08	141.09
141.10	141.19	141.19
141.27	141.27	143.09
143.12	143.13	143.13
143.19	143.22	143.22
143.24	143.24	143.24
143.25	143.26	143.27
144.05	145.01	145.02
145.03	145.07	145.08
145.12	146.16	147.04
147.05	147.05	147.06
147.06	148.18	148.19
148.24	149.12	150.13
150.13	150.13	150.13
150.14	150.17	150.17
150.20	150.20	151.18
151.22	151.23	153.09
153.10	153.11	153.29
154.04	154.05	154.06
154.13	155.12	155.13
155.14	155.16	155.17
155.17	155.19	156.01
157.15	157.21	157.30
158.09	158.12	158.21
158.22	158.22	158.23
158.23	158.26	158.27

YOU (CONT.)

		159.01
159.18	159.24	160.05
160.05	160.17	160.24
162.20	163.19	163.25
163.30	164.02	164.27
164.28	164.28	164.30
165.02	165.03	165.03
165.04	165.17	165.30
168.19	169.17	170.05
170.28	171.04	171.23
171.30	172.09	172.21
172.21	178.05	178.18
178.25	178.26	178.27
179.09	179.13	179.19
179.26	180.01	180.08
182.01	182.03	182.11
182.19	183.27	185.13
185.16	185.29	186.06
186.09	186.24	186.25
186.27	187.12	187.15
188.04	188.08	188.18
188.19	188.27	189.02
189.03	189.03	189.12
189.13	190.23	193.12
193.21	196.27	197.13
197.14	197.14	197.15
197.17	197.21	198.02
199.21	199.21	199.23
200.02	200.13	200.14
200.29	201.08	201.08
201.09	201.23	201.27
201.28	201.28	202.05
202.08	202.18	202.25
202.26	202.29	202.30
203.06	203.09	203.22
204.05	204.13	204.16
204.23	204.23	205.10
205.11	205.12	205.13
205.15	205.20	205.20
205.22	205.27	209.09
210.16	213.05	213.16
213.16	213.17	213.17
213.18	213.22	214.01
214.24	215.26	217.22
219.24	221.02	221.03
221.05	222.17	222.19
222.19	222.20	222.24
223.01	223.01	223.06
223.06	223.07	223.13
223.17	223.18	223.21
223.24	223.26	223.29
223.29	224.09	224.21
224.25	225.04	225.23
225.26	225.27	225.27
226.06	226.15	228.16
228.21	228.23	228.25
229.17	229.26	230.07
230.18	230.20	231.06
231.09	231.27	233.04
233.04	233.09	233.09
233.14	233.23	233.30
234.01	234.07	234.21
234.26	235.07	235.16
236.04	236.07	236.20
236.28	237.14	237.20
237.20	237.20	237.22
237.23	237.23	237.24
237.26	237.27	237.28
237.28	237.29	238.01
238.02	238.03	238.05
238.07	238.08	238.08
238.10	238.17	239.01
239.20	240.25	240.26
241.15	243.02	243.25
244.14	245.05	246.21
249.07	250.23	250.26
253.16	253.27	253.29
255.07	255.16	255.17
258.01	258.13	260.14
260.16	260.17	260.17
260.18	260.20	260.29
261.02	261.03	261.06
263.02	263.24	264.12
264.26	264.28	264.29
264.30	265.05	266.01
267.01	270.15	271.12
271.15	271.20	272.08
272.14	273.20	273.22
273.27	274.10	274.13
274.15	274.16	275.15

YOU (CONT.)

		275.19
276.15	279.13	282.17
283.04	283.21	283.23
286.09	287.28	288.03
288.05	288.17	289.17
289.17	289.20	290.05
290.06	290.26	290.30
291.06	291.08	294.11
295.14	295.26	296.01
299.03	301.01	301.16
301.22	301.23	302.05
303.06	303.11	303.12
303.17	303.19	303.25
304.04	304.04	304.05
307.24	308.01	308.07
308.18	309.15	312.04
312.16	312.17	314.07
314.30	320.16	320.30
321.28	324.20	324.25
328.03	328.05	328.09
328.14	329.10	329.13
332.12	334.08	334.24
334.26	335.07	335.09
335.15	339.07	339.07
340.03	340.05	342.12
342.20	342.22	342.22
343.19	343.30	344.03
344.05	344.06	344.06
344.08	344.14	344.14
344.14	347.08	348.28
348.29	351.23	355.11
355.11	355.12	355.13
355.14	355.15	355.24
356.12	357.02	357.08
360.13	360.27	361.06
361.07	361.11	361.16
361.16	361.18	361.20
363.01	363.06	363.09
364.30	365.26	366.25
366.26	367.04	367.07
367.20	367.28	367.29
368.01	368.06	368.07
368.27	368.28	369.21
370.17	372.21	372.23
374.23	374.26	374.30
375.01	375.02	375.03
375.08	375.12	375.24
376.09	376.11	377.03
377.07	377.17	377.19
377.20	377.21	377.23
377.26	378.13	378.25
378.25	378.25	378.27
380.05	381.09	382.09
384.18	384.21	385.13
386.23	387.02	387.02
388.06	388.09	388.13
388.14	388.15	388.16
388.18	388.21	388.25
388.26	388.27	390.15
390.17	390.18	390.22
391.07	391.09	391.10
391.11	391.11	391.11
391.17	391.20	391.21
391.22	391.23	391.24
393.08	393.18	394.20
395.24	395.24	396.07
396.10	398.20	398.21
399.15	400.10	400.25
401.02	401.04	401.08
401.16	402.13	402.20
402.22	404.28	407.06
408.11	411.16	411.20
412.03	412.14	413.17
413.23	414.02	415.10
418.08	418.10	418.11
418.14	418.14	418.16
418.20	418.25	418.30
419.02	419.03	419.10
419.16	419.21	420.03
420.03	420.05	420.22
421.10	421.12	422.14
422.15	423.10	423.11
423.22	423.23	423.26
426.12	426.12	426.13
428.19	429.14	429.14
429.17	429.18	429.20
429.24	429.25	430.12
430.21	430.22	430.23
430.28	430.28	430.30
431.17	431.30	433.06

YOU (CONT.)

		433.12
433.20	433.21	433.23
433.30	435.01	435.03
435.12	444.02	448.13
452.22	455.21	455.26
455.27	456.02	456.02
456.02	456.04	458.08
460.24	461.05	464.06
464.24	464.25	464.25
465.28	467.24	468.02
468.03	468.06	468.06
468.07	468.08	468.10
468.12	468.15	468.16
468.17	468.18	468.18
468.19	468.19	471.05
471.09	471.10	471.11
471.20	472.01	472.10
472.15	472.16	472.17
472.17	472.19	472.20
472.20	472.21	472.22
472.23	472.23	472.27
473.12	473.13	473.14
473.17	473.17	473.19
473.19	473.20	473.20
473.23	473.24	474.04
474.07	474.07	474.07
474.12	474.13	474.13
474.14	474.14	476.07
480.19	480.24	480.25
481.04	481.07	481.07
481.08	481.10	481.13
481.21	483.04	483.05
483.07	486.14	486.15
487.05	489.06	489.07
491.19	491.23	491.24
492.06	492.07	492.08
492.10	492.10	492.12
492.12	492.29	492.30
493.07	493.08	493.09
493.14	494.10	494.20
494.21	495.01	495.05
495.06	495.07	495.16
495.22	495.23	495.24
497.10	497.11	497.11
497.12	497.12	505.23
506.03	507.14	511.02
511.04	511.07	511.09
511.11	511.11	511.11
511.11	511.13	511.13
511.13	511.14	511.14
511.23	512.30	

Word			
YOU'		81.26	
YOU'LL		75.13	124.25
	238.09	495.03	
YOU'RE		26.22	143.10
	200.20	235.23	237.18
	238.06		
YOU'VE		150.24	160.01
	201.30	205.22	219.19
	236.12	391.23	413.18
	418.07	419.11	472.18
	472.23		
YOUNG		7.05	10.15
	16.08	19.05	20.12
	36.26	47.06	47.09
	49.23	51.26	51.28
	52.05	53.10	56.14
	60.05	67.01	69.17
	77.12	78.18	93.12
	109.03	116.19	118.13
	157.03	170.24	177.09
	177.24	177.25	180.01
	180.05	202.06	203.03
	226.23	228.03	229.18
	241.10	242.29	254.24
	254.24	257.13	267.31
	272.29	277.07	282.10
	282.11	314.28	318.19
	319.26	319.27	330.13
	331.26	337.07	338.20
	341.24	341.25	345.29
	358.24	429.03	436.22
YOUNGER		118.14	251.04
	317.08	342.02	
YOUNGEST		268.01	
YOUNGSTER			7.11
	50.20	53.20	112.25
	155.16	183.06	286.25
YOUNGSTERS			51.22
YOUR		25.14	29.14

```
YOUR (CONT.)          33.15
   41.08    41.11    42.23
   48.10    48.26    49.11
   49.13    51.08    51.09
   52.25    53.13    64.18
   68.15    74.24    84.30
   85.20   100.23   120.16
  120.19   122.20   124.27
  128.29   132.02   143.11
  143.12   147.04   147.04
  164.14   179.09   187.04
  200.15   201.14   201.26
  217.22   230.06   233.18
  235.25   237.12   237.29
  238.07   239.09   239.10
  249.12   250.25   250.26
  257.30   259.15   260.14
  260.17   261.01   264.28
  264.28   271.21   271.22
  274.02   275.14   275.16
  275.16   275.19   282.24
  304.02   304.05   335.16
  344.01   355.23   358.29
  358.29   361.06   361.20
  367.29   372.21   375.01
  375.03   377.18   378.26
  390.18   390.21   391.23
  394.23   402.29   407.06
  411.20   418.17   418.19
  419.05   426.12   430.12
  472.11   472.13   472.15
  472.16   472.29   473.15
  473.15   473.16   474.15
  480.22   486.17   491.19
  491.20   494.20   495.06
  495.26
YOURS      306.13   343.19
  344.04   471.08   483.06
YOURSELF    30.05    75.25
   80.13    97.10   128.27
  141.27   145.09   154.05
  155.17   179.28   200.02
  203.06   219.24   220.03
  230.19   260.30   304.04
  370.23   378.28   412.18
  423.22   474.05   511.23
YOURSELF'            97.09
YOURSELVES          117.11
  339.08
YOUTH       6.26    16.04
   27.23    46.28    60.10
   60.11   105.04   155.11
  156.11   186.19   191.04
  212.13   249.21   278.02
  289.04   306.22   319.24
  321.20   325.26   339.13
  348.30   352.23   375.19
  381.01   384.17   418.14
  433.02   439.06   447.07
  447.13   456.24   470.21
  515.10
YOUTHFUL    93.17    96.23
  222.13   424.13
YOUTHS     279.21   298.12
  452.08
YUCKER     240.15   241.06
  241.13   241.18
ZAMBOANGA           425.04
  437.28
ZENITH     127.25   149.03
ZERO        71.29
ZONE       445.05
1848       249.22
2          185.28   433.14
230        343.02
30         185.28
6000        55.23
7          323.21
7-POUNDERS          323.21
900        444.18
```

PART II

Frequency Table for the
Vocabulary of
Conrad's *Lord Jim*

1 'TWEEN	1 ACHIEVE	1 AFFORD	1 ALLUSION
3691 A	3 ACHIEVED	1 AFFRONT	3 ALLUSIONS
1 A-A-A-ARM	4 ACHIEVEMENT	1 AFIELD	3 ALLY
1 A-HUNDRED-POUNDS-ROU	2 ACHIEVEMENTS	4 AFLOAT	1 ALMIGHTY
1 A-QUIVER	1 ACHING	48 AFRAID	42 ALMOST
2 ABACK	1 ACKNOWLEDGE	3 AFRESH	2 ALOFT
1 ABAFT	5 ACQUAINTANCE	13 AFT	64 ALONE
2 ABANDON	1 ACQUAINTED	233 AFTER	51 ALONG
5 ABANDONED	1 ACQUIRE	1 AFTER-DECK	12 ALONGSIDE
2 ABERRATIONS	4 ACQUIRED	1 AFTER-DINNER	13 ALOUD
1 ABHORRENT	1 ACRIMONIOUSLY	15 AFTERNOON	1 ALPACA
2 ABIDING	51 ACROSS	1 AFTERTHOUGHT	35 ALREADY
1 ABILITIES	20 ACT	40 AFTERWARDS	1 ALSATIAN
7 ABILITY	3 ACTED	113 AGAIN	37 ALSO
10 ABJECT	13 ACTION	54 AGAINST	2 ALTER
6 ABJECTLY	3 ACTIONS	7 AGE	1 ALTERATION
2 ABJECTNESS	4 ACTIVE	3 AGED	1 ALTERCATION
17 ABLE	2 ACTIVELY	1 AGENCY	1 ALTERING
6 ABOARD	1 ACTIVITIES	2 AGENT	1 ALTERNATELY
1 ABOARD'	5 ACTIVITY	3 AGENT'S	13 ALTOGETHER
2 ABODE	1 ACTORS	1 AGENTS	1 ALTRUISM
1 ABODES	4 ACTS	2 AGES	49 ALWAYS
7 ABOMINABLE	2 ACTUAL	1 AGGRAVATING	141 AM
1 ABOMINABLY	1 ACTUALITY	2 AGGRESSIVE	9 AMAZED
2 ABOMINATION	8 ACTUALLY	2 AGGRIEVED	6 AMAZEMENT
1 ABOMINATIONS	1 ACTUATED	1 AGIN	13 AMAZING
201 ABOUT	2 ACUTE	1 AGITATE	2 AMAZINGLY
58 ABOVE	1 ACUTELY	3 AGITATED	1 AMBER
4 ABREAST	2 AD	3 AGITATION	1 AMBIENT
2 ABRUPT	1 ADANDONING	15 AGO	2 AMBITION
8 ABRUPTLY	1 ADAPTING	1 AGONIES	1 AMBITIONS
1 ABSCONDED	1 ADD	1 AGONISING	1 AMBUSH
2 ABSCONDING	23 ADDED	3 AGONY	1 AMBUSHES
1 ABSCURE	1 ADDING	1 AGREE	1 AMERICAN
2 ABSENCE	1 ADDITION	1 AGREEABLE	1 AMIABLE
1 ABSENT	1 ADDITIVE	4 AGREED	2 AMIABLY
2 ABSENTLY	4 ADDRESS	1 AGUAINDT	2 AMICABLE
1 ABSIT	5 ADDRESSED	2 AGUAINDT'	1 AMID
4 ABSOLUTE	2 ADDRESSING	26 AH	1 AMID-SHIPS
10 ABSOLUTELY	3 ADEN	4 AHA	2 AMIDSHIPS
1 ABSOLUTION	1 ADEQUATE	14 AHEAD	2 AMMUNITION
3 ABSORBED	2 ADJOURNED	2 AHOY	50 AMONGST
1 ABSORPTION	1 ADJOURNMENT	6 AIM	1 AMOUNGST
1 ABSTENTION	1 ADMINISTER	1 AIMED	1 AMOUNT
6 ABSTRACT	1 ADMIRABLY	1 AIMING	1 AMOUNTED
9 ABSURD	2 ADMIRAL	2 AIMLESS	3 AMPLE
4 ABSURDITY	3 ADMIRATION	2 AIMLESSLY	5 AMUSED
2 ABSURDLY	1 ADMIRE	14 AIN'T	1 AMUSEMENT
1 ABUNDANTLY	3 ADMIRED	61 AIR	4 AMUSING
3 ABUSE	1 ADMIRING	1 AIRILY	1 AMUSINGLY
2 ABUSED	1 ADMISSION	1 AIRS	502 AN
3 ABUSING	9 ADMIT	1 AIRY	2 ANACHRONISM
2 ABUSIVE	2 ADMITS	3 AKIN	3 ANCHOR
7 ABYSS	1 ADMITTANCE	1 ALABASTER	3 ANCHORAGE
1 ACCENT	8 ADMITTED	2 ALACRITY	5 ANCHORED
2 ACCENTS	1 ADO	4 ALARM	1 ANCHORING
1 ACCENTUATED	1 ADORATION	2 ALARMED	1 ANCHORING-GROUND
1 ACCEPT	1 ADORNED	1 ALARMING	1 ANCHORS
1 ACCEPTANCE	3 ADRIFT	1 ALARMINGLY	2 ANCIENT
2 ACCEPTED	4 ADVANCE	1 ALARMS	3398 AND
2 ACCEPTING	5 ADVANCED	1 ALARUM	1 ANDTWENTY
1 ACCESS	2 ADVANCING	2 ALAS	1 ANECDOTE
15 ACCIDENT	6 ADVANTAGE	1 ALASKA	1 ANGEL
4 ACCIDENTALLY	1 ADVANTAGEOUS	1 ALCOHOL	1 ANGELS
2 ACCIDENTS	2 ADVANTAGES	7 ALERT	10 ANGER
1 ACCOMMODATED	5 ADVENTURE	2 ALERTNESS	1 ANGLE
1 ACCOMMODATION	1 ADVENTURED	1 ALEXANDER	1 ANGLE-IRON
3 ACCOMPANIED	2 ADVENTURER	9 ALI	2 ANGLES
1 ACCOMPANIMENT	1 ADVENTURERS	6 ALI'S	5 ANGRILY
1 ACCOMPANYING	5 ADVENTURES	1 ALIGHTED	17 ANGRY
2 ACCOMPLICE	4 ADVENTUROUS	2 ALIKE	6 ANGUISH
1 ACCOMPLICES	1 ADVERSE	10 ALIVE	2 ANGUISHING
1 ACCOMPLISH	6 ADVICE	592 ALL	1 ANGULAR
2 ACCOMPLISHED	3 ADVISE	1 ALL-FIRED	4 ANIMAL
1 ACCOMPLISHMENT	4 ADVISED	2 ALL-FOURS	1 ANIMALS
5 ACCORD	1 ADVISEDLY	12 ALLANG	2 ANIMATED
1 ACCORDANCE	1 ADVISER	4 ALLANG'S	2 ANIMATION
4 ACCORDING	1 ADVISERS	1 ALLEZ	1 ANIMOSITY
3 ACCORDINGLY	1 ADVISING	1 ALLIANCES	2 ANKLES
1 ACCOST	4 AFAR	1 ALLIES	1 ANNAS
1 ACCOSTING	29 AFFAIR	2 ALLIGATOR	1 ANNEX
10 ACCOUNT	9 AFFAIRS	1 ALLMOTIONLESS	1 ANNIHILATE
2 ACCOUNTS	2 AFFECT	9 ALLOW	2 ANNIHILATION
1 ACCUMULATED	4 AFFECTED	2 ALLOWANCE	1 ANNOYANCE
1 ACCURACY	2 AFFECTING	1 ALLOWANCES	1 ANNOYANCES
4 ACCURSED	7 AFFECTION	11 ALLOWED	5 ANNOYED
1 ACCUSTOMED	3 AFFECTIONS	1 ALLOY	1 ANOINTED
5 ACH	3 AFFIRM	1 ALLUDED	70 ANOTHER
1 ACHE	7 AFFIRMED	2 ALLUDING	19 ANSWER
	2 AFFLICTED	1 ALLURING	21 ANSWERED

2 ANSWERING	2 ARGONAUTS	4 ASSUMED	3 AWAKEN
3 ANSWERS	3 ARGUE	2 ASSUMING	2 AWAKENING
1 ANT	7 ARGUED	2 ASSUMPTION	21 AWARE
1 ANT-HEAP	3 ARGUMENT	6 ASSURANCE	1 AWASH
1 ANTAGONISM	1 ARGUMENTATIVELY	1 ASSURANCES	151 AWAY
2 ANTAGONISTIC	1 ARGUMENTS	4 ASSURE	13 AWE
1 ANTARCTIC	2 ARIGHT	13 ASSURED	1 AWE-STRICKEN
1 ANTE	1 ARISE	1 ASSUREDLY	2 AWED
1 ANTE-ROOM	1 ARISEN	1 ASSURING	2 AWESTRUCK
1 ANTHRACITE	1 ARISING	5 ASTERN	48 AWFUL
1 ANTICIPATE	71 ARM	1 ASTHMA	13 AWFULLY
1 ANTICS	5 ARM-CHAIR	3 ASTONISHED	1 AWHILE
1 ANTIQUE	1 ARM-RACKS	1 ASTONISHING	1 AWKWARD
2 ANTONIO	2 ARM'S	1 ASTONISHMENT	1 AWKWARDLY
2 ANTS	2 ARM'S-LENGTH	1 ASTOUNDED	1 AWNING
8 ANXIETY	1 ARMCHAIR	2 ASTOUNDING	6 AWNINGS
21 ANXIOUS	13 ARMED	3 ASTRAY	2 AXE
4 ANXIOUSLY	1 ARMOUR	1 ASTRONOMER	1 AXES
146 ANY	1 ARMPITS	2 ASTRONOMERS	5 AY
15 ANYBODY	38 ARMS	1 ASUNDER	1 AZURE
19 ANYHOW	3 ARMY	928 AT	9 B'GOSH
72 ANYTHING	4 AROSE	1 ATE	1 BABEL
2 ANYWAY	24 AROUND	2 ATHWART	1 BABIES
6 ANYWHERE	2 ARRANGED	1 ATLANTIC	2 BABY
1 APACE	6 ARRANGEMENT	3 ATMOSPHERE	1 BACHELOR
9 APART	3 ARRANGEMENTS	1 ATOMS	185 BACK
1 APARTMENT	1 ARRANGING	1 ATONED	1 BACK-WATER
1 APARTMENTS	1 ARRAY	1 ATROCIOUSLY	1 BACK'
1 APERTURE	1 ARREARS	1 ATROCITY	2 BACKBONE
2 APIA	6 ARRESTED	3 ATTACHED	7 BACKED
1 APOLOGIES	6 ARRIVAL	5 ATTACK	4 BACKGROUND
1 APOLOGY	4 ARRIVED	1 ATTAINING	7 BACKS
2 APPALLED	3 ARRIVING	3 ATTEMPT	1 BACKSHOP
11 APPALLING	2 ARROGANT	1 ATTEMPTED	4 BACKWARDS
1 APPARATUS	3 ARROW	1 ATTEMPTING	1 BACKWAY
1 APPAREL	1 ARROWS	1 ATTEMPTS	16 BAD
1 APPARELLED	3 ART	2 ATTEND	1 BADE
2 APPARENT	1 ARTFUL	2 ATTENDANCE	8 BADLY
16 APPARENTLY	1 ARTICULATE	2 ATTENDANT	6 BAG
4 APPARITION	1 ARTICULO	3 ATTENDANTS	1 BAGGED
6 APPEAL	1 ARTILLERY	5 ATTENDED	2 BAH
5 APPEALED	3 ARTIST	1 ATTENDING	1 BAKER
4 APPEALING	1 ARTLESS	10 ATTENTION	2 BALANCE
10 APPEAR	1087 AS	10 ATTENTIVE	1 BALANCED
19 APPEARANCE	2 ASCEND	1 ATTENTIVELY	1 BALD
34 APPEARED	4 ASCENDED	1 ATTIRE	3 BALE
1 APPEARING	5 ASCENDING	9 ATTITUDE	1 BALES
12 APPEARS	1 ASCENT	1 ATTITUDES	1 BALK
1 APPEASED	2 ASCERTAIN	1 ATTRACTION	4 BALL
1 APPEASEMENT	2 ASCERTAINED	1 ATTRACTIVE	2 BALLOON
2 APPETITE	1 ASCERTAINING	1 ATTRIBUTE	10 BALLY
1 APPLAUDED	1 ASH	1 ATTUNED	1 BALTIC
3 APPLIED	1 ASH-BUCKETS	1 AU	7 BALUSTRADE
10 APPOINTED	3 ASHAMED	1 AUBURN	9 BAMBOO
2 APPOINTMENT	5 ASHES	1 AUCKLAND	2 BAMBOOS
2 APPRECIABLE	11 ASHORE	4 AUDACIOUS	2 BANANAS
1 APPRECIATING	2 ASHY	2 AUDACITY	5 BAND
1 APPRECIATION	1 ASIA	2 AUDIBLE	1 BANDAGE
1 APPRECIATIVE	14 ASIDE	2 AUDIBLY	1 BANDAGED
2 APPRECIATIVELY	31 ASK	8 AUDIENCE	1 BANDSTAND
4 APPREHENSION	1 ASKANCE	2 AUDIENCE-HALL	5 BANG
7 APPROACH	1 ASKANT	1 AUGMENTED	2 BANGED
6 APPROACHED	83 ASKED	4 AUSTERE	1 BANISTER
2 APPROACHES	9 ASKING	1 AUSTRALASIA	19 BANK
7 APPROACHING	3 ASKS	4 AUSTRALIAN	4 BANKOK
2 APPROBATION	5 ASLEEP	1 AUTHORISATION	3 BANKS
2 APPROPRIATE	16 ASPECT	4 AUTHORITIES	3 BAR
2 APPROVAL	2 ASPIRATIONS	3 AUTHORITY	1 BAR-ROOM
1 APPROVED	7 ASS	1 AUTOCRAT	25 BARE
1 APRONED	1 ASS'	1 AUTOMATIC	4 BARED
1 APROPOS	2 ASS'S	1 AUTOMATICALLY	3 BAREFOOTED
6 ARAB	1 ASSASSINATED	1 AUTOUR	1 BAREHEADED
1 ARAB'S	1 ASSASSINATION	1 AUTRES	2 BARELY
1 ARABIAN	6 ASSAULT	1 AVARICE	1 BAREST
1 ARABS	1 ASSAULT-AND-BATTERY	1 AVATAR	2 BARGAIN
1 ARBITRARY	2 ASSEMBLE	1 AVE	1 BARGAINING
2 ARCADIAN	4 ASSEMBLED	1 AVEC	4 BARK
1 ARCH	1 ASSENT	1 AVERAGE	2 BARN
1 ARCHED	1 ASSENTED	1 AVERSE	1 BARONET
5 ARCHIE	1 ASSERT	2 AVERSION	4 BARQUE
1 ARCHIE'S	1 ASSERTED	3 AVERTED	2 BARRED
3 ARCHIPELAGO	2 ASSERTION	1 AVERTING	2 BARREL
1 ARCHWAY	3 ASSESSOR	1 AVIDITY	3 BARREN
1 ARDENT	3 ASSESSORS	4 AVOID	1 BARRICADE
2 ARDENTLY	1 ASSIDUOUSLY	3 AVOIDED	1 BARRICADING
4 ARDOUR	1 ASSIST	1 AVOIDING	1 BARRIER
3 ARDUOUS	1 ASSISTANCE	3 AVONDALE	2 BARRING
1 ARDUOUSLY	2 ASSISTANT	4 AW	3 BARS
157 ARE	4 ASSOCIATED	1 AWAITING	3 BASE
6 AREN'T	1 ASSORTED	8 AWAKE	2 BASED

1 BASH	1 BEGONE	1 BIND	1 BLOWED
1 BASHFULLY	1 BEGRUDGE	1 BINDS	3 BLOWING
1 BASHFULNESS	4 BEGUN	2 BINNACLE	6 BLOWN
3 BASIS	1 BEHALF	4 BINOCULARS	2 BLOWS
2 BASS	2 BEHAVED	7 BIRD	1 BLUBBERED
2 BATAVIA	3 BEHAVIOUR	3 BIRDS	1 BLUBBERING
2 BATCH	1 BEHEADING	1 BIRDS'	22 BLUE
1 BATH	4 BEHELD	2 BIRTH	1 BLUE-BLACK
1 BATH-HOUSE	58 BEHIND	1 BISCUITS	1 BLUE-JACKETS
1 BATHED	3 BEHOLD	1 BISMARCK'S	1 BLUENESS
1 BATHING	1 BEHOLDERS	40 BIT	1 BLUISH
1 BATHING-HUTS	2 BEHOLDING	2 BITE	1 BLUNDER
1 BATRACHIAN	1 BEHOVED	1 BITING	1 BLUNDERBUSS
1 BATTENED	110 BEING	3 BITS	1 BLUNDERED
1 BATTER	9 BEINGS	1 BITTEN	1 BLUNDERING
3 BATTERED	1 BELAYING	6 BITTER	1 BLUNT
3 BATTERY	1 BELAYING-PINS	7 BITTERLY	1 BLUR
4 BATTLE	1 BELCHING	7 BITTERNESS	5 BLURRED
1 BATTLE-AXE	16 BELIEF	4 BIZARRE	1 BLURT
2 BATTLING	83 BELIEVE	1 BLAB	1 BLURTED
4 BATU	20 BELIEVED	63 BLACK	1 BLUSH
1 BAULKED	1 BELIEVES	1 BLACK-AND-WHITE	2 BLUSHED
1 BAVARIA	2 BELIEVING	9 BLACKENED	2 BLUSHING
1 BAWLED	1 BELITTLING	1 BLACKMAILING	1 BLUSTERING
10 BAY	1 BELL	5 BLACKNESS	34 BOARD
2 BAZAAR	1 BELLIED	6 BLADE	2 BOARDED
1 BAZAARS	1 BELLIES	4 BLADES	3 BOARDING
458 BE	2 BELLOW	6 BLAKE	2 BOARDS
1 BE-WEAPONED	1 BELLS	4 BLAKE'S	2 BOAST
7 BEACH	5 BELONG	1 BLAME	3 BOASTED
2 BEACHCOMBER	5 BELONGED	1 BLAMED	1 BOASTFUL
1 BEACONS	4 BELONGING	1 BLAMELESSNESS	3 BOASTING
1 BEAD	1 BELONGINGS	1 BLAND	126 BOAT
1 BEADY	1 BELONGS	7 BLANK	1 BOAT-CHOCK
1 BEAM	1 BELOVED	1 BLANKET	1 BOAT-CLOAK
2 BEAMED	42 BELOW	2 BLANKETS	5 BOAT-HOOK
12 BEAR	6 BELT	1 BLASPHEMIES	1 BOAT-LOAD
9 BEARD	1 BELTED	1 BLAST	1 BOAT-SAIL
3 BEARDED	1 BEMUSED	3 BLASTED	1 BOAT-SAILING
3 BEARDS	2 BENCH	2 BLATANT	1 BOAT-STRETCHER
9 BEARING	2 BENCHES	4 BLAZE	1 BOAT'S
1 BEARINGS	4 BEND	6 BLAZED	1 BOATFALLS
1 BEARS	4 BENDING	1 BLAZES	5 BOATMEN
7 BEAST	1 BENEATH	1 BLEACHED	39 BOATS
5 BEASTLY	2 BENEDICTION	1 BLEACHING	1 BOATSWAIN'S
1 BEASTS	1 BENEFACTOR	1 BLEAK	4 BOB
9 BEAT	1 BENEFIT	1 BLEAR	1 BOB'S
4 BEATEN	2 BENEVOLENT	1 BLEAR-EYED	1 BOBBED
6 BEATING	1 BENEVOLENTLY	2 BLEARED	2 BOBBING
1 BEATITUDE	1 BENIGHTED	1 BLEATED	11 BODIES
1 BEATS	12 BENT	1 BLEATING	3 BODILY
9 BEAUTIFUL	1 BENUMBING	1 BLEIBT	49 BODY
5 BEAUTY	1 BEPLASTERED	1 BLESS	1 BOET'
1 BECALMED	1 BEQUEATH	9 BLESSED	1 BOIL
39 BECAME	1 BER	4 BLESSING	1 BOILER
68 BECAUSE	1 BEREFT	7 BLEW	1 BOILER-IRON
1 BECKON	4 BERTH	3 BLIGHT	3 BOISTEROUSLY
1 BECKONED	3 BESET	17 BLIND	5 BOLT
11 BECOME	1 BESETS	3 BLINDED	5 BOLTED
2 BECOMES	4 BESIDE	1 BLINDFOLD	1 BOLTING
4 BECOMING	17 BESIDES	2 BLINDNESS	1 BOMBASTIC
15 BED	1 BESIEGED	1 BLINDS	1 BOMBAY
1 BEDROOM	1 BESMIRCHED	1 BLINK	1 BONA
1 BEDROOMS	42 BEST	2 BLINKED	2 BOND
2 BEDS	1 BESTREWN	3 BLINKING	1 BONDS
1 BEDSTEAD	2 BET	1 BLISS	3 BONE
2 BEDSTEADS	3 BETEL	1 BLISTER	6 BONES
1 BEEFY	1 BETEL-NUT	3 BLOCK	1 BONFIRE
1 BEEFY-FACED	3 BETRAYED	1 BLOCK-TIN	1 BONSO
430 BEEN	1 BETRAYING	1 BLOCKADE	2 BONSO'
5 BEER	47 BETTER	3 BLOCKS	3 BONY
1 BEESWAX	56 BETWEEN	1 BLOND	7 BOOK
3 BEETLE	1 BEWHISKERED	1 BLONDE	1 BOOK-LINED
3 BEETLES	7 BEWILDERED	18 BLOOD	4 BOOKS
1 BEFALLING	3 BEWILDERMENT	1 BLOOD-AND-IRON	2 BOOM
211 BEFORE	1 BEWITCHING	2 BLOOD-RED	1 BOOMED
2 BEFOREHAND	31 BEYOND	1 BLOOD-THIRSTY	1 BOOMING
1 BEFRINGED	5 BIEN	1 BLOOD-TO-WATER-TURNI	1 BOON
3 BEG	83 BIG	1 BLOODED	2 BOOT
100 BEGAN	2 BIGGER	3 BLOODSHED	1 BOOT-HEELS
9 BEGGAR	2 BIGGEST	1 BLOODTHIRSTY	7 BOOTS
1 BEGGARLY	1 BILE	1 BLOODY	1 BOOZER
8 BEGGARS	3 BILL	2 BLOOMIN'	2 BORDER
6 BEGGED	2 BILLET	4 BLOOMING	4 BORE
5 BEGGING	2 BILLIARD	2 BLOSSOMS	5 BORED
11 BEGIN	1 BILLIARD-CUE	1 BLOT	3 BOREDOM
12 BEGINNING	1 BILLIARD-ROOM	1 BLOTCHES	9 BORN
2 BEGINNINGS	1 BILLIARDS	3 BLOTTING	6 BORNE
5 BEGINS	2 BILLOWY	2 BLOTTING-PAD	1 BORROWING
1 BEGONE	1 BILLS	10 BLOW	4 BOSOM

1 BOSS	4 BRIEN	1 BULLY	2 CAMPED
1 BOSSE	31 BRIERLY	2 BULLYING	4 CAMPONG
36 BOTH	7 BRIERLY'S	3 BULWARKS	1 CAMPONGS
4 BOTHER	1 BRIERWOOD	2 BUMP	129 CAN
6 BOTHERED	2 BRIG	1 BUMPS	55 CAN'T
6 BOTTLE	2 BRIG-RIGGED	6 BUNCH	1 CANAL
1 BOTTLE-WASHERS	4 BRIGANTINE	1 BUNDLES	1 CANALISED
3 BOTTLES	1 BRIGANTINE'S	1 BUNGALOW	1 CANCELLED
16 BOTTOM	11 BRIGHT	1 BUNGLER	1 CANDELABRUM
1 BOTTOMLESS	1 BRIGHTENED	5 BUNK	1 CANDID
1 BOUGH	1 BRIGHTENING	1 BUOY	11 CANDLE
1 BOUGHS	1 BRIGHTNESS	1 BUOYANT	2 CANDLES
2 BOUGHT	5 BRILLIANCE	1 BUPRESTIDAE	1 CANDLESTICK
1 BOULDERS	2 BRILLIANT	3 BURDEN	4 CANE
1 BOUNCED	1 BRILLIANTLY	1 BURDENED	1 CANE-CHAIR
13 BOUND	1 BRIM	7 BURIED	1 CANNIBAL
1 BOUNDARY	1 BRIM-FULL	2 BURLESQUE	2 CANNON
1 BOUNDED	10 BRING	2 BURLY	13 CANNOT
1 BOUNDLESS	5 BRINGING	3 BURN	24 CANOE
3 BOUNDS	1 BRINGS	4 BURNED	7 CANOES
1 BOUT	4 BRINK	9 BURNING	2 CANOPY
7 BOW	2 BRISBANE	1 BURNT	1 CANTANKEROUS
1 BOW-OW-OW-OW-OW	1 BRISK	1 BURROWED	1 CANTED
14 BOWED	1 BRISKLY	1 BURROWING	1 CANTERED
1 BOWING	1 BRISTLED	22 BURST	1 CANTING
3 BOWL	1 BRITAIN	5 BURSTING	1 CANTON
1 BOWMAN	1 BRITISH	3 BURSTS	3 CANVAS
8 BOWS	16 BROAD	2 BURY	1 CANVASSER
11 BOX	1 BROAD-BEAMED	2 BURYING	1 CANVASSING
6 BOXES	1 BROAD-SHOULDERED	9 BUSH	3 CAP
18 BOY	1 BROADCLOTH	1 BUSH-FOLK	1 CAP'N
1 BOYHOOD	15 BROKE	1 BUSHELS	5 CAPABLE
8 BOYISH	30 BROKEN	10 BUSHES	2 CAPACITY
10 BOYS	1 BROKEN-DOWN	1 BUSHY	1 CAPE
1 BRACED	1 BROKEN-RIMMED	3 BUSIED	1 CAPER
1 BRACKET	1 BROKER'S	3 BUSILY	1 CAPERS
5 BRAIN	3 BRONZE	40 BUSINESS	1 CAPITAL
1 BRANCH	2 BRONZED	2 BUSTER	1 CAPRICE
1 BRANCHED	3 BROODED	8 BUSY	2 CAPRICIOUS
7 BRANCHES	4 BROODING	1 BUSYBODY	2 CAPS
2 BRANDY	2 BROOMSTICK	605 BUT	1 CAPSIZE
16 BRASS	5 BROTHER	1 BUTT	1 CAPSIZED
12 BRAVE	4 BROTHERS	6 BUTTERFLIES	1 CAPSTAN
1 BRAVEST	25 BROUGHT	9 BUTTERFLY	70 CAPTAIN
1 BRAWL	6 BROW	1 BUTTERFLY-HUNTING	1 CAPTAINS
1 BRAWNY	141 BROWN	1 BUTTON	2 CAPTIVATED
2 BRAZEN	23 BROWN'S	2 BUTTONED	4 CAPTIVE
1 BRAZENLY	1 BRRRR	1 BUTTONS	1 CAPTIVES
2 BREACH	3 BRUSHED	5 BUY	2 CAPTIVITY
1 BREACHED	2 BRUSHWOOD	2 BUZZ	1 CAPTOR
4 BREAD	1 BRUSQUE	546 BY	3 CAPTURE
1 BREADCRUMBS	2 BRUSQUELY	1 BY-CHANNEL	3 CAPTURED
4 BREADTH	4 BRUTAL	6 BYE	1 CAR
10 BREAK	1 BRUTALISED	3 BYSTANDERS	3 CARCASS
1 BREAKER	4 BRUTALITY	1 C'EST	3 CARD
8 BREAKFAST	4 BRUTALLY	3 CA	1 CARDS
2 BREAKFAST-TABLE	5 BRUTE	1 CAB	35 CARE
2 BREAKING	3 BRUTES	1 CAB-HORSE	10 CARED
2 BREAKING-UP	1 BUBBLE	1 CABBY	2 CAREER
1 BREAKS	1 BUCCANEER	5 CABIN	1 CAREERS
30 BREAST	1 BUCCANEERS	1 CABINET	7 CAREFUL
1 BREASTING	1 BUCKETS	4 CABLE	5 CAREFULLY
3 BREASTS	1 BUDGED	3 CABLES	5 CARELESS
1 BREASTWORK	1 BUFFALO	1 CABMAN	4 CARELESSLY
34 BREATH	1 BUFFALOES	1 CABOOSE	2 CARELESSNESS
5 BREATHE	1 BUFFETED	1 CACKLING	5 CARES
5 BREATHED	1 BUGGY	1 CAD	1 CARESS
6 BREATHING	28 BUGIS	2 CADAVRE	1 CAREWORN
4 BREATHLESS	4 BUILDING	1 CAFE	10 CARGO
1 BREATHS	5 BUILDINGS	2 CAGE	1 CARGO-LAMP
2 BRED	4 BUILT	1 CAIRO	1 CARGO-WORK
2 BREECH	1 BULGE	2 CALAMITIES	1 CARPET
1 BREECH-BLOCKS	1 BULGED	2 CALAMITY	1 CARPETED
1 BREECH-LOADERS	1 BULGING	4 CALCULATED	1 CARPETS
1 BREECHED	7 BULK	1 CALCUTTA	3 CARRIAGE
2 BREECHES	1 BULK-HEAD	1 CALIBRE	1 CARRIE'S
1 BREED	1 BULK-LAMP	1 CALIFORNIA	30 CARRIED
1 BREEDS	8 BULKHEAD	44 CALL	3 CARRIES
10 BREEZE	1 BULKHEAD'LL	59 CALLED	15 CARRY
1 BREEZES	1 BULKY	9 CALLING	5 CARRYING
1 BRICK	4 BULL	1 CALLOUS	2 CART
1 BRICKS	1 BULL'S	2 CALLOUSNESS	3 CARTRIDGES
2 BRIDE	1 BULL'S-EYE	1 CALLS	1 CARVED
21 BRIDGE	5 BULLET	23 CALM	1 CARVINGS
2 BRIDGE-LADDER	1 BULLET-PROOF	4 CALMED	46 CASE
1 BRIDGES	3 BULLETS	1 CALMING	6 CASES
1 BRIDLE	4 BULLIED	4 CALMLY	1 CASK
1 BRIDLE-PATH	6 BULLOCK	3 CALMNESS	1 CASSIS
1 BRIEF	1 BULLOCK-CART	159 CAME	17 CAST
1 BRIEFLY	1 BULLOCKS	15 CAMP	1 CAST-OFF

1 CASTAWAY
3 CASTAWAYS
8 CASTE
1 CASTE-MARK
2 CASTES
3 CASTING
2 CASTLE
5 CASUAL
4 CASUALLY
1 CASUALNESS
1 CASUALTIES
1 CASUARINA
1 CAT
1 CAT'S
1 CAT'S-PAWS
1 CATACOMBS
1 CATALOGUE
1 CATARACTS
3 CATASTROPHE
16 CATCH
6 CATCHING
1 CATTING
3 CATTLE
27 CAUGHT
9 CAUSE
5 CAUSED
1 CAUSES
1 CAUSING
1 CAUSTIC
2 CAUTION
2 CAUTIOUS
2 CAUTIOUSLY
1 CAVE
4 CAVERN
1 CAVERN-LIKE
1 CAVERNOUS
4 CE
2 CEASE
11 CEASED
1 CEASING
4 CEILING
5 CELEBES
1 CELEBRATE
1 CELEBRATED
1 CELEBRITY
1 CELL
1 CENSURE
1 CENT
1 CENTIPEDES
3 CENTRE
2 CENTRED
1 CENTUPLED
1 CENTURIES
2 CENTURY
1 CEREMONIES
4 CEREMONY
29 CERTAIN
10 CERTAINLY
4 CERTIFICATE
1 CERTIFICATES
8 CERTITUDE
1 CERTITUDES
2 CET
1 CHAFED
2 CHAFF
1 CHAFFED
1 CHAFFING
5 CHAIN
1 CHAIN-HOOKS
1 CHAINED
1 CHAINS
47 CHAIR
8 CHAIRS
2 CHALLENGED
1 CHAMBERS
38 CHANCE
4 CHANCES
1 CHANDELIER
2 CHANDLER
1 CHANDLER'S
2 CHANDLERS
6 CHANGE
15 CHANGED
3 CHANNEL
1 CHANTED
1 CHANTING
1 CHAOS
45 CHAP
2 CHAP'S
1 CHAPLET

5 CHAPS
9 CHARACTER
3 CHARACTERISTIC
1 CHARACTERISTICALLY
2 CHARACTERS
11 CHARGE
1 CHARGE'
3 CHARGED
1 CHARGING
3 CHARLEY
8 CHARM
1 CHARMED
2 CHARMING
1 CHARMS
10 CHART
3 CHART-ROOM
2 CHARTER
1 CHARTERED
1 CHARTERERS
1 CHARTS
1 CHASE
3 CHASED
1 CHASING
4 CHASM
1 CHASMS
1 CHAT
1 CHATTED
2 CHATTER
1 CHATTERED
1 CHATTERING
4 CHEAP
2 CHEATED
2 CHEATING
5 CHECK
11 CHECKED
4 CHECKING
7 CHEEK
1 CHEEK-BONE
1 CHEEK-BONES
8 CHEEKS
1 CHEEKY
3 CHEER
2 CHEERFULLY
4 CHEERILY
6 CHEERY
1 CHEQUERED
1 CHERISH
3 CHERISHED
1 CHERISHING
2 CHEROOT
1 CHERRYWOOD
9 CHEST
19 CHESTER
3 CHESTER'S
2 CHEWED
2 CHEWING
1 CHICKEN
35 CHIEF
7 CHIEFS
1 CHIEFTAIN
35 CHILD
1 CHILD-
1 CHILD-LIKE
2 CHILD'S
1 CHILD'S-PLAY
3 CHILDISH
3 CHILDLIKE
1 CHILDRE
9 CHILDREN
1 CHILDREN'S
5 CHILL
1 CHILLED
1 CHILLIES
2 CHILLING
1 CHILLS
2 CHILLY
2 CHIMED
1 CHIMNEYS
17 CHIN
2 CHINA
6 CHINAMAN
2 CHINAMEN
1 CHINAMEN'S
2 CHINESE
1 CHINS
2 CHIP
1 CHIPPED
1 CHIT
1 CHIVALROUS
2 CHOCK

1 CHOCKS
1 CHOCOLATE
1 CHOCOLATE-COLOURED
2 CHOICE
3 CHOKE
3 CHOKED
2 CHOKING
1 CHOPPED
2 CHOPPER
1 CHOPS
1 CHOSE
1 CHRONO
1 CHRONO-LITHOGRAPH
1 CHRONO
1 CHRONO-
2 CHRONOMETER
1 CHUCK
1 CHUCKED
1 CHUCKLING
2 CHUMP
2 CHUMS
1 CHURCH
1 CHURCHES
1 CHURN
5 CIGAR
2 CIGAR-ENDS
3 CIGARETTE
4 CIGARS
1 CINDER
1 CINDER-TRACK
9 CIRCLE
1 CIRCLED
3 CIRCLES
1 CIRCLETS
1 CIRCLING
2 CIRCULAR
1 CIRCUMSCRIBED
4 CIRCUMSTANCES
1 CIRCUMSTANTIAL
1 CIRCUMVENTED
1 CISTERN
1 CITIZEN
7 CIVIL
3 CIVILISATION
1 CIVILITIES
1 CIVILITY
1 CLAD
5 CLAIM
1 CLAIMING
3 CLAIMS
1 CLAMBER
5 CLAMBERED
5 CLAMBERING
1 CLAMOROUS
1 CLANG
1 CLANGS
1 CLANKING
2 CLAP
1 CLAPHAM
2 CLAPPED
1 CLASH
1 CLASHES
1 CLASHING
12 CLASPED
1 CLASPING
1 CLASPS
3 CLASS
1 CLASSING
3 CLATTER
1 CLATTERING
1 CLAW
2 CLAWED
2 CLAWING
1 CLAWS
1 CLAY
1 CLAYED
15 CLEAN
1 CLEAN-FACED
1 CLEAN-LIMBED
3 CLEAN-SHAVED
2 CLEANED
1 CLEANLY
57 CLEAR
1 CLEAR'
9 CLEARED
2 CLEARER
4 CLEARING
1 CLEARINGS
11 CLEARLY
1 CLEARNESS

1 CLEAVAGE
3 CLEAVING
1 CLENCHED
11 CLERK
3 CLERKS
5 CLEVER
1 CLEVERER
1 CLEVERLY
3 CLEVERNESS
1 CLICK
2 CLICKED
1 CLICKING
4 CLIFF
3 CLIFFS
3 CLIMATE
2 CLIMB
1 CLIMBED
4 CLIMBING
1 CLINCH
1 CLING
2 CLINGING
2 CLINK
1 CLIPPED
1 CLIPPING
2 CLOAK
1 CLOAKS
5 CLOCK
27 CLOSE
12 CLOSED
1 CLOSELY
1 CLOSER
5 CLOSING
4 CLOTH
3 CLOTHES
3 CLOTHING
2 CLOTHS
21 CLOUD
3 CLOUDED
6 CLOUDS
1 CLOUDY
1 CLOVER
1 CLOWNS
1 CLUB
1 CLUBBED
2 CLUMP
2 CLUMPS
2 CLUMSILY
3 CLUMSY
4 CLUNG
1 CLUSTERED
2 CLUSTERING
1 CLUSTERS
7 CLUTCH
2 CLUTCHED
4 CLUTCHING
2 CO
3 COAL
1 COAL-BLACK
1 COARSE
2 COARSER
21 COAST
3 COASTER
2 COASTING
10 COAT
1 COATS
1 COAXING
1 COAXINGLY
1 COBWEBS
2 COCK
1 COCK-PIT
1 COCKATOO
1 COCKING
1 COCKY
1 COCOANUT
10 COFFEE
2 COFFEE-CUPS
1 COFFEE-PLANTATION
1 COFFEE-POT
1 COGNAC
1 COIF
1 COILS
1 COINCIDED
1 COINED
1 COIR
1 COL
1 COL-
24 COLD
1 COLD-BLOODED
2 COLD-EYED
1 COLD-SHOULDERED

1 COLD-SWEAT	1 COMPLETED	1 CONJUNCTION	9 CONVERSATION
1 COLDER	18 COMPLETELY	1 CONJUNCTIONS	1 CONVERSATIONALLY
1 COLDLY	1 COMPLEX	4 CONNECTED	1 CONVERSATIONS
1 COLEOPTERA	5 COMPLEXION	6 CONNECTION	5 CONVERSE
2 COLIC	3 COMPLICATED	1 CONQUER	1 CONVERSING
2 COLLAPSE	1 COMPLICATION	2 CONQUERED	1 CONVERSION
3 COLLAPSED	2 COMPLICATIONS	1 CONQUERING	1 CONVERTED
1 COLLAPSING	1 COMPLIMENT	1 CONQUEROR	3 CONVEY
3 COLLECT	1 COMPLIMENTARY	1 CONQUERS	1 CONVEYANCE
2 COLLECTED	1 COMPONENT	2 CONQUEST	11 CONVICTION
4 COLLECTING	1 COMPORTED	1 CONQUESTS	5 CONVINCED
5 COLLECTION	1 COMPOSE	9 CONSCIENCE	2 CONVINCING
1 COLLECTIONS	2 COMPOSED	1 CONSCIENTIOUSLY	1 CONVOLUTIONS
2 COLLECTOR	2 COMPOSEDLY	4 CONSCIOUS	4 CONVULSIVE
1 COLLIDED	1 COMPOSITION	3 CONSCIOUSLY	1 CONVULSIVELY
4 COLLISION	1 COMPOSURE	2 CONSCIOUSNESS	2 COOKED
1 COLLOQUY	3 COMPOUND	1 CONSECRATED	4 COOKING
1 COLLUSION	1 COMPREHEND	1 CONSENT	1 COOKING-BOXES
1 COLONIES	1 COMPRENDRE	1 CONSENTED	1 COOKS
4 COLOSSAL	1 COMPRESSED	6 CONSEQUENCE	11 COOL
9 COLOUR	1 COMPROMISED	4 CONSEQUENCES	3 COOLIES
6 COLOURED	4 COMRADE	1 CONSIDER	2 COOLLY
3 COLOURLESS	2 CON	1 CONSIDERABLE	1 COON'S
2 COLOURS	2 CON-	1 CONSIDERABLY	1 COPRA
1 COLUMNAR	4 CONCEAL	6 CONSIDERATION	1 COPY
2 COLUMNS	9 CONCEALED	1 CONSIDERATIONS	1 COQUET
1 COMBAT	1 CONCEALING	9 CONSIDERED	3 CORAL
1 COMBATING	1 CONCEDE	2 CONSIDERING	1 CORE
1 COMBED	1 CONCEDED	1 CONSISTED	89 CORNELIUS
2 COMBINATION	1 CONCEIT	3 CONSISTS	4 CORNELIUS'S
1 COMBINED	2 CONCEITED	3 CONSOLATION	21 CORNER
176 COME	2 CONCEIVABLE	1 CONSOLED	1 CORNER-POSTS
1 COMEDY	1 CONCEIVABLY	2 CONSOLING	1 CORNERED
1 COMER	6 CONCEIVE	2 CONSPIRACY	4 CORNERS
15 COMES	1 CONCEIVED	2 CONSTANCY	7 CORPSE
1 COMFORTABLE	3 CONCENTRATED	1 CONSTANT	4 CORPSES
1 COMFORTING	1 CONCENTRATION	4 CONSTANTLY	2 CORRECTED
2 COMIC	8 CONCEPTION	1 CONSTELLATIONS	1 CORRECTION
1 COMICAL	5 CONCERN	1 CONSTERNATION	1 CORRESPONDENCE
50 COMING	8 CONCERNED	1 CONSTITUTED	1 CORRESPONDENT
14 COMMAND	1 CONCERNS	1 CONSTITUTIONAL	1 CORRESPONDING
4 COMMANDED	1 CONCESSION	2 CONSTRUCTION	1 CORRI
7 COMMANDER	1 CONCESSIONS	1 CONSULS	1 CORRI-
1 COMMANDERS	1 CONCEVEZ	3 CONSULT	1 CORROSIVE
1 COMMANDINGLY	2 CONCILIATE	3 CONSULTATION	2 CORRUGATED
1 COMMANDS	1 CONCISE	1 CONSULTED	1 CORRUGATED-IRON
1 COMMEMORATION	1 CONCLUDE	1 CONSUMEDLY	2 CORRUPTION
3 COMMENCED	7 CONCLUDED	2 CONTACT	1 CORVETTE
3 COMMENT	3 CONCLUSION	1 CONTAGION	2 COST
7 COMMENTED	1 CONCRETE	2 CONTAIN	1 COSTERMONGER'S
1 COMMENTING	1 CONCURRED	2 CONTAINED	1 COSTLY
1 COMMERCE	1 CONDEMNATIONS	1 CONTAINING	2 COSTS
2 COMMERCIAL	4 CONDEMNED	1 CONTEMNED	1 COSTUME
1 COMMERCIALLY	1 CONDENSED	3 CONTEMPLATED	1 COSY
1 COMMISERATION	1 CONDENSING	1 CONTEMPLATING	2 COTTAGES
1 COMMISSION	2 CONDESCENDED	4 CONTEMPLATION	5 COTTON
1 COMMISSIONERS	3 CONDITION	1 CONTEMPORARY	1 COTTON-POD
2 COMMIT	9 CONDITIONS	9 CONTEMPT	7 COUCH
4 COMMITTED	12 CONDUCT	2 CONTEMPTIBLE	1 COUGH
22 COMMON	2 CONFERENCE	6 CONTEMPTUOUS	2 COUGHING
2 COMMONEST	3 CONFESS	2 CONTEMPTUOUSLY	385 COULD
4 COMMONPLACE	12 CONFESSED	2 CONTENDED	67 COULDN'T
2 COMMOTION	1 CONFESSING	2 CONTENT	11 COUNCIL
2 COMMUNICATING	1 CONFESSIONS	2 CONTENTED	1 COUNCIL-HALL
1 COMMUNICATION	2 CONFIDANT	2 CONTENTS	1 COUNCIL-ROOM
1 COMMUNICATIONS	2 CONFIDANTE	3 CONTEST	1 COUNSELS
2 COMMUNION	2 CONFIDE	1 CONTINUALLY	4 COUNT
5 COMMUNITY	2 CONFIDED	16 CONTINUED	3 COUNTENANCE
5 COMPANION	24 CONFIDENCE	2 CONTINUOUS	2 COUNTER
2 COMPANIONS	6 CONFIDENCES	2 CONTINUOUSLY	1 COUNTERFEIT
2 COMPANIONSHIP	3 CONFIDENT	1 CONTORTED	1 COUNTING
12 COMPANY	6 CONFIDENTIAL	1 CONTORTION	1 COUNTLESS
2 COMPARE	3 CONFIDENTIALLY	1 CONTOUR	33 COUNTRY
1 COMPARING	2 CONFIDENTLY	1 CONTRACT	1 COUNTRY-BORN
1 COMPARISON	1 CONFINED	2 CONTRACTED	2 COUNTRY'S
1 COMPARTMENT	1 CONFINING	1 CONTRACTION	1 COUNTRYMEN
2 COMPASS	1 CONFIRMED	1 CONTRACTOR	1 COUNTRYSIDE
4 COMPASSION	2 CONFLAGRATION	1 CONTRADICTING	9 COUPLE
1 COMPASSIONATE	9 CONFOUND	1 CONTRADICTORY	1 COUPLES
1 COMPELLED	19 CONFOUNDED	3 CONTRARY	27 COURAGE
1 COMPETENCY	4 CONFOUNDEDLY	1 CONTRASTED	1 COURAGED
1 COMPETENT	1 CONFOUNDS	1 CONTRIVANCE	1 COURAGEOUS
1 COMPILED	7 CONFRONTED	2 CONTRIVED	1 COURAGEOUSLY
1 COMPLACENT	2 CONFRONTING	8 CONTROL	96 COURSE
1 COMPLACENTLY	2 CONFUSED	1 CONUNDRUM	32 COURT
2 COMPLAINING	1 CONFUSEDLY	1 CONVENIENCES	4 COURT-ROOM
1 COMPLAININGLY	1 CONFUSING	2 CONVENIENT	1 COURTED
2 COMPLAINT	6 CONFUSION	2 CONVENTION	3 COURTEOUS
1 COMPLAINTS	2 CONICAL	1 CONVENTIONAL	1 COURTESY
12 COMPLETE	2 CONJECTURES	1 CONVENTIONS	1 COURTING

19 COURTYARD	1 CROPS	1 DAGGER	2 DEBT
2 COUSIN	7 CROSS	1 DAGGERS	2 DECAY
3 COVER	1 CROSS-EXAMINE	5 DAILY	1 DECEASED
13 COVERED	1 CROSS-EYED	38 DAIN	3 DECEITFUL
3 COVERING	13 CROSSED	2 DALE	3 DECEIVED
1 COVERLET	7 CROSSING	2 DAM	1 DECEIVING
2 COVERS	1 CROSSLY	3 DAM'	1 DECENCIES
1 COVERTLY	1 CROUCH	2 DAMAGE	4 DECENCY
2 COW	3 CROUCHED	1 DAMAGED	9 DECENT
7 COWARD	5 CROUCHING	1 DAMMAR	4 DECENTLY
4 COWARDICE	2 CROW	4 DAMN	4 DECEPTION
2 COWARDLY	1 CROW-FOOTED	1 DAMNABLE	1 DECEPTIVE
2 COWED	17 CROWD	2 DAMNABLY	2 DECIDE
1 COXSWAIN	8 CROWDED	6 DAMNED	5 DECIDED
6 CRACK	3 CROWDING	1 DAMNEDEST	2 DECISION
2 CRACKED	2 CROWDS	1 DAMNEDLY	2 DECISIVE
1 CRACKLING	1 CROWING	1 DAMNING	28 DECK
2 CRACKS	2 CROWN	6 DAMP	2 DECK-CHAIR
18 CRAFT	2 CROWNED	1 DAMP-FIGHT	1 DECK-CHAIRS
1 CRAFTIEST	1 CROWNING	5 DANCE	1 DECK-WINCH
1 CRAFTY	15 CRUEL	1 DANCED	1 DECK'
1 CRAKEE	6 CRUELTY	1 DANCING	1 DECKS
2 CRAMMED	2 CRUMB	1 DANDIFIED	1 DECLAIM
1 CRAMPED	3 CRUMBLING	2 DANE	1 DECLAIMING
1 CRANE	1 CRUMPLED	21 DANGER	3 DECLARATION
2 CRANING	2 CRUNCH	7 DANGEROUS	5 DECLARE
1 CRANKY	1 CRUNCH-CRUNCH	1 DANGEROUSLY	19 DECLARED
1 CRANNIES	1 CRUSH	11 DANGERS	2 DECLARES
2 CRASH	3 CRUSHED	1 DANS	1 DECLARING
1 CRASHED	1 CRUSHING	1 DAPPER	1 DECLINED
1 CRASHES	1 CRUST	11 DARE	1 DECLINES
1 CRATE	10 CRY	7 DARED	1 DECLINING
3 CRAVEN	4 CRYING	1 DAREN'T	1 DECOMPOSED
4 CRAVING	1 CRYPTIC	1 DARES	1 DECORUM
2 CRAWL	1 CRYSTALLINE	2 DARING	1 DECOYED
1 CRAWLED	2 CRYSTALS	110 DARK	2 DECREE
1 CRAWLING	1 CUBIC	1 DARK-BLUE	2 DECREPIT
8 CRAZY	1 CUCUMBER	4 DARK-FACED	1 DEEDS
2 CREAK	3 CUDDY	1 DARK-SKINNED	43 DEEP
1 CREAKING	2 CUDDY-TABLE	10 DARKENED	1 DEEP-ROOTED
1 CREAKINGS	2 CUE	4 DARKENING	1 DEEP-SET
2 CREASED	1 CUFFS	1 DARKER	1 DEEPENED
5 CREATED	3 CULMINATING	2 DARKLY	3 DEEPER
2 CREATING	1 CULTIVATED	18 DARKNESS	5 DEEPLY
1 CREATION	1 CUMBERED	9 DARTED	1 DEER
1 CREATIONS	5 CUNNING	3 DARTING	1 DEER-HUNT
5 CREATURE	1 CUNNINGLY	2 DASH	3 DEFEAT
2 CREATURES	3 CUP	6 DASHED	2 DEFEATED
1 CREDENTIAL	3 CUPS	1 DASHEDEST	1 DEFECTION
3 CREDIT	4 CUR	1 DASHES	5 DEFENCE
2 CREDITABLE	1 CURATE	1 DASHING	4 DEFENCELESS
1 CREED	1 CURE	3 DATE	2 DEFENCES
26 CREEK	1 CURED	5 DAUGHTER	7 DEFEND
5 CREEP	7 CURIOSITY	3 DAUGHTERS	1 DEFENDANT
3 CREEPERS	14 CURIOUS	2 DAVIT	1 DEFENDERS
8 CREEPING	4 CURIOUSLY	2 DAVITS	1 DEFENSIVE
1 CREEPY	4 CURLED	8 DAWN	3 DEFERENCE
4 CREPT	1 CURLY	3 DAWNED	2 DEFERENTIAL
2 CREPUSCULAR	1 CURRENCY	107 DAY	4 DEFIANCE
1 CREVICE	4 CURRENT	4 DAY'S	3 DEFIED
1 CREVICES	1 CURRENTS	7 DAYLIGHT	1 DEFILED
12 CREW	4 CURSE	49 DAYS	1 DEFINE
1 CREWS	4 CURSED	2 DAYS'	1 DEFINED
51 CRIED	1 CURSES	2 DAZED	4 DEFINITE
8 CRIES	3 CURSING	2 DAZZLED	2 DEFINITELY
5 CRIME	1 CURT	2 DAZZLING	1 DEFORMITY
2 CRIMINAL	1 CURTAIN	1 DAZZLINGLY	5 DEFY
1 CRIMINALS	2 CURTAINS	14 DE	2 DEFYING
7 CRIMSON	1 CURTLY	56 DEAD	2 DEGRADATION
1 CRIMSONED	2 CURVE	1 DEAD-AND-GONE	1 DEGREE
1 CRINGE	3 CURVED	3 DEADLIEST	2 DEGREES
1 CRINGED	2 CURVES	9 DEADLY	1 DEJECTED
1 CRINGING	1 CURVETED	7 DEAF	2 DEJECTEDLY
1 CRIPPLE	1 CUSTOMARY	8 DEAL	4 DELAY
1 CRIPPLED	1 CUSTOMERS	3 DEALING	1 DELAYED
2 CRIPPLES	1 CUSTOMS	1 DEALINGS	5 DELIBERATE
1 CRISIS	32 CUT	1 DEALS	7 DELIBERATELY
1 CRISPLY	1 CUT-THROATS	2 DEALT	3 DELIBERATING
3 CRITICAL	1 CUTAWAY	1 DEAN	3 DELIBERATION
1 CRITICALLY	10 CUTTER	22 DEAR	1 DELIBERATIONS
1 CRITICISED	3 CUTTING	1 DEARLY	4 DELICACY
3 CRITICISM	1 CYCLONE	45 DEATH	10 DELICATE
1 CROAKED	1 CYNICAL	1 DEATH-BED	2 DELICATELY
1 CROAKER	1 CYNICALLY	1 DEATH-SENTENCE	3 DELIGHTED
2 CROCKERY	11 D	1 DEATH'S	1 DELIGHTFUL
1 CROCODILE	1 D-D-DIE	1 DEATHBED	1 DELIRIOUSLY
1 CRONIES	1 D'ESTOMAC	1 DEATHBLOW	1 DELIRIUM
2 CROOKED	1 D'HOTE	1 DEATHLIKE	2 DELIVER
1 CROOKING	3 D'YE	1 DEBAUCHERIES	5 DELIVERED
2 CROPPED	1 DAD'	1 DEBILITATED	2 DELIVERING

2 DELIVERY
2 DELUGE
1 DELUSION
3 DEMAND
6 DEMANDED
1 DEMANDING
1 DEMANDS
5 DEMEANOUR
1 DEMOCRATIC
1 DEMOLISH
2 DEMON
2 DEMONSTRATE
1 DEMONSTRATED
2 DEMONSTRATING
2 DEMONSTRATION
1 DEMORALISATION
1 DENIALS
1 DENN
4 DENSE
1 DENSER
1 DENUNCIATIONS
1 DENVER
3 DENY
3 DEPART
6 DEPARTED
4 DEPARTING
1 DEPEND
4 DEPENDANTS
1 DEPENDING
1 DEPENDS
2 DEPICT
5 DEPLORABLE
1 DEPLORABLY
1 DEPLORE
1 DEPOSIT
1 DEPOSITION
1 DEPRAVITY
3 DEPRESSED
1 DEPRESSION
1 DEPRIVE
1 DEPTH
11 DEPTHS
1 DEPUTED
1 DEPUTY
1 DEPUTY-ASSISTANT
1 DERANGE
1 DERELICT
2 DERISION
2 DERIVED
1 DESCEND
8 DESCENDED
2 DESCENDING
2 DESCENT
3 DESCRIBE
5 DESCRIBED
1 DESCRIBING
2 DESCRIPTION
1 DESCRIPTIVE
1 DESE
1 DESERT
8 DESERTED
3 DESERTER
2 DESERTION
3 DESERVE
1 DESERVING
1 DESIGN
1 DESIRABLE
18 DESIRE
9 DESIRED
1 DESIRES
1 DESIROUS
2 DESISTING
14 DESK
3 DESOLATE
10 DESPAIR
1 DESPAIRED
4 DESPAIRING
1 DESPAIRINGLY
2 DESPERADOES
16 DESPERATE
5 DESPERATELY
1 DESPERATION
2 DESPISE
1 DESPONDENCY
1 DESTINE
4 DESTINED
10 DESTINY
1 DESTITUTE
1 DESTITUTION
1 DESTROY

2 DESTROYED
1 DESTROYS
4 DESTRUCTION
4 DESTRUCTIVE
1 DETACH
5 DETACHED
1 DETACHING
2 DETACHMENT
6 DETAIL
1 DETAILED
4 DETAILS
2 DETAIN
2 DETAINED
5 DETECT
4 DETECTED
1 DETECTING
1 DETECTION
4 DETERMINATION
1 DETERMINED
1 DETESTABLE
1 DETONATION
1 DETONATIONS
1 DEUCE
1 DEUCEDLY
1 DEVASTATED
1 DEVASTATING
1 DEVASTATION
1 DEVELOP
1 DEVELOPMENT
1 DEVIATED
1 DEVICES
43 DEVIL
1 DEVIL'S
1 DEVILISH
1 DEVILISHLY
1 DEVILRY
2 DEVILS
1 DEVIOUS
1 DEVIOUSLY
1 DEVISE
1 DEVISED
1 DEVOID
3 DEVOTED
6 DEVOTION
1 DEVOURED
3 DEVOURING
1 DEVOUT
4 DEW
1 DEWY
1 DIABLE
1 DIABOLICAL
1 DIAGNOSED
1 DIAL
1 DIALECT
1 DIAMETER
1 DICE
1 DICK
1 DICTIONARY
232 DID
86 DIDN'T
34 DIE
16 DIED
2 DIEU
10 DIFFERENCE
12 DIFFERENT
14 DIFFICULT
3 DIFFICULTIES
14 DIFFICULTY
2 DIFFUSED
1 DIGESTION
1 DIGGING
2 DIGNIFIED
1 DIGNITARY
5 DIGNITY
1 DILAPIDATED
3 DILATED
1 DILATING
1 DILATORY
1 DILIGENT
12 DIM
3 DIMINISHED
5 DIMLY
2 DIMNESS
1 DIMPLED
2 DIN
1 DINE
1 DINED
1 DINES
1 DINGY
6 DINING

1 DINING-HALL
4 DINING-ROOM
6 DINNER
1 DINNER-SERVICE
1 DIP
3 DIPLOMACY
1 DIPLOMATIC
1 DIPLOMATIST
5 DIPPED
8 DIRECTED
3 DIRECTING
9 DIRECTION
1 DIRECTIONS
16 DIRECTLY
4 DIRT
14 DIRTY
3 DIS
2 DIS-
1 DISABLED
1 DISADVANTAGES
4 DISAPPEAR
1 DISAPPEARANCE
8 DISAPPEARED
3 DISAPPEARING
4 DISAPPOINTED
1 DISAPPOINTING
3 DISAPPOINTMENT
11 DISASTER
2 DISASTROUS
1 DISBELIEVE
3 DISC
1 DISCERN
1 DISCERNED
3 DISCHARGE
1 DISCHARGED
1 DISCIPLINE
1 DISCLAIM
1 DISCLAIMING
1 DISCLOSE
6 DISCLOSED
1 DISCLOSING
2 DISCLOSURE
1 DISCOMFITURE
1 DISCOMFORT
2 DISCOMPOSED
2 DISCOMPOSING
1 DISCONCERTED
1 DISCONTENTED
1 DISCOUNT
2 DISCOURAGED
2 DISCOURAGING
4 DISCOVER
9 DISCOVERED
1 DISCOVERING
4 DISCOVERY
3 DISCREET
1 DISCREETLY
5 DISCRETION
1 DISCRIMINATING
1 DISCRIMINATION
1 DISCUSS
1 DISCUSSED
1 DISCUSSING
5 DISCUSSION
1 DISCUSSIONS
9 DISDAIN
2 DISEASE
1 DISEASED
1 DISEASES
4 DISEMBODIED
1 DISENCHANTING
1 DISENCHANTMENT
1 DISENGAGED
1 DISFIGURED
3 DISGRACE
1 DISGRACEFULLY
5 DISGUST
1 DISGUSTED
2 DISGUSTING
2 DISHES
2 DISHEVELLED
1 DISHONOUR
1 DISJOINTED
1 DISLIKE
1 DISLIKED
5 DISMAL
1 DISMALLY
4 DISMAY
2 DISMAYED
1 DISMISS

1 DISMISSAL
1 DISMISSED
1 DISMOUNTED
1 DISMOUNTING
2 DISORDER
2 DISORDERED
1 DISPARAGEMENT
3 DISPASSIONATELY
1 DISPASSIONATENESS
3 DISPATCHED
1 DISPENSED
1 DISPIRITED
10 DISPLAY
6 DISPLAYED
1 DISPLAYING
1 DISPLEASED
1 DISPORT
1 DISPOSAL
3 DISPOSE
4 DISPOSED
2 DISPOSITION
2 DISPOSITIONS
1 DISPROPORTION
3 DISPUTE
1 DISPUTING
3 DISREGARD
4 DISREGARDED
4 DISREPUTABLE
2 DISSENT
1 DISSIMILAR
1 DISSOLVE
1 DISSOLVING
32 DISTANCE
1 DISTANCES
14 DISTANT
1 DISTENDED
1 DISTILLED
19 DISTINCT
5 DISTINCTION
1 DISTINCTIVE
9 DISTINCTLY
2 DISTINGUISH
1 DISTINGUISHABLE
5 DISTINGUISHED
1 DISTORTED
5 DISTRACTED
2 DISTRACTING
1 DISTRACTION
10 DISTRESS
2 DISTRESSED
1 DISTRESSFUL
1 DISTRESSING
1 DISTRIBUTING
1 DISTRIBUTION
1 DISTRICT
1 DISTRICTS
1 DISTRUST
4 DISTURBANCE
8 DISTURBED
3 DISTURBING
1 DITCH
2 DIVE
1 DIVERGING
2 DIVIDED
2 DIVIDERS
1 DIVIDING
1 DIVINE
2 DIVING
1 DIVORCE
195 DO
3 DOCK
1 DOCTOR
1 DOCTORED
1 DOCUMENTARY
1 DODGE
1 DODGED
1 DODGES
1 DODGING
1 DOERS
24 DOES
2 DOESN'T
16 DOG
2 DOGGED
5 DOGS
18 DOING
1 DOLE
1 DOLEFULLY
1 DOLES
11 DOLLARS
1 DOMAIN

1 DOME
2 DOMESTIC
1 DOMESTICATED
1 DOMINATED
1 DOMINATING
187 DON'T
1 DON'T-CARE-HANG
1 DON'T-YOU-TOUCH-ME
73 DONE
3 DONKEY
2 DONKEY-MAN
1 DONKEYMAN
2 DONKEYS
1 DONNERWETTER
5 DOOMED
54 DOOR
1 DOOR-HANDLE
2 DOORS
6 DOORWAY
2 DOORWAYS
1 DOR
46 DORAMIN
14 DORAMIN'S
1 DORMANT
1 DOTTED
5 DOUBLE
1 DOUBLE-DEALING
2 DOUBLED
51 DOUBT
2 DOUBTED
2 DOUBTFUL
1 DOUBTFULLY
1 DOUBTING
1 DOUBTLESS
4 DOUBTS
1 DOUTE
1 DOVER
227 DOWN
1 DOWN-RIVER
1 DOWN-STREAM
6 DOWNCAST
1 DOWNHILL
1 DOWNPOUR
1 DOWNRIGHT
2 DOWNWARD
5 DOWNWARDS
2 DOZE
1 DOZED
3 DOZEN
1 DOZING
3 DRAB
1 DRAG
2 DRAGGED
1 DRAINED
6 DRANK
4 DRAPED
2 DRAPERIES
2 DRAPERY
2 DRATTED
4 DRAUGHT
5 DRAW
2 DRAWING
1 DRAWING-PINS
1 DRAWING-ROOM
2 DRAWL
2 DRAWLING
12 DRAWN
1 DRAWN-UP
3 DRAWS
2 DREAD
24 DREAM
4 DREAMED
1 DREAMERS
2 DREAMILY
2 DREAMING
7 DREAMS
1 DREAMT
1 DREAMY
2 DREARY
1 DREGS
2 DRENCHED
2 DRESSED
1 DRESSER
2 DRESSING
1 DRESSING-DOWN
11 DREW
4 DRIED
1 DRIED-UP
2 DRIFT
2 DRIFTED

1 DRIFTING
3 DRILL
23 DRINK
3 DRINKING
1 DRINKING-BOUT
2 DRINKS
2 DRIP
1 DRIPPED
2 DRIPPING
10 DRIVE
16 DRIVEN
4 DRIVER
7 DRIVING
2 DRIZZLE
1 DROLE
5 DROLL
1 DRONED
1 DRONING
2 DROOPED
4 DROOPING
21 DROP
25 DROPPED
12 DROPPING
1 DROPS
10 DROVE
2 DROWN
1 DROWN-
7 DROWNED
4 DROWNING
1 DROWNS
1 DROWSED
2 DROWSILY
1 DRUG
2 DRUM
2 DRUMMED
2 DRUMMING
3 DRUMS
15 DRUNK
18 DRY
1 DUBASH
2 DUBIOUS
2 DUCKED
3 DUE
2 DUEL
1 DUFFER
3 DUG
3 DUG-OUT
1 DULCET
8 DULL
1 DULL-EYED
3 DULLNESS
6 DUMB
1 DUMBFOUNDED
2 DUMBLY
1 DUMP
2 DUMPY
1 DUN
1 DUNDREARY
1 DUNDREARY-WHISKERED
1 DUNGEON
1 DUNGEON-LIKE
1 DUNNAGE
22 DURING
1 DURNED
12 DUSK
3 DUSKY
12 DUST
1 DUSTING
2 DUSTY
10 DUTCH
1 DUTCH-
2 DUTIES
13 DUTY
3 DWARFED
2 DWARFS
1 DWELL
1 DWELLERS
2 DWELLING
2 DWELLINGS
1 DWELLS
3 DWELT
1 DYED
9 DYING
1 DYSPEPSIA
1 E
78 EACH
12 EAGER
4 EAGERNESS
15 EAR
15 EARLY

1 EARN
2 EARNEST
11 EARNESTLY
6 EARNESTNESS
1 EARNING
26 EARS
2 EARSHOT
58 EARTH
6 EARTHLY
1 EARTHQUAKE
2 EARTHWORK
6 EASE
1 EASED
3 EASIER
5 EASILY
1 EASING
14 EAST
13 EASTERN
29 EASY
2 EASY-CHAIRS
10 EAT
1 EATABLES
6 EATEN
5 EATING
1 EAVES
1 EBB
1 EBBED
1 EBBING
2 EBONY
3 ECCENTRIC
2 ECCENTRICITY
2 ECHO
1 ECHOED
1 ECLIPSE
1 ECLIPSE-LIKE
2 ECONOMY
1 ECSTATIC
2 EDDIED
1 EDDY
1 EDEN
19 EDGE
1 EDGED
1 EDIBLE
1 EDIFICATION
1 EDIFICE
1 EDIFIED
1 EDUCATED
1 EFFACING
24 EFFECT
1 EFFECTED
5 EFFECTIVE
1 EFFECTIVELY
1 EFFECTS
2 EFFICIENCY
2 EFFICIENT
2 EFFIGY
1 EFFLUVIA
14 EFFORT
8 EFFORTS
1 EFFUSIVELY
1 EGG
2 EGGS
5 EGOISM
1 EGOTISM
15 EGSTROM
2 EGSTROM'S
18 EH
12 EIGHT
2 EIGHTEEN
7 EIGHTY
2 EIN
23 EITHER
1 EJACULATIONS
1 EJACULATORY
1 EJECTED
1 ELABORATING
1 ELAPSED
2 ELASTICITY
3 ELATED
5 ELATION
21 ELBOW
9 ELBOWS
2 ELDER
4 ELDERLY
3 ELECTED
2 ELECTRIC
7 ELEMENT
1 ELEMENTAL
2 ELEMENTS
1 ELEPHANT

4 ELEVATED
1 ELEVEN
1 ELIXIR
2 ELLIOT
1 ELONGATED
5 ELOQUENT
1 ELP
29 ELSE
2 ELSE'S
1 ELUCIDATED
1 ELUDED
1 ELUDING
2 ELUSIVE
3 EM
1 EMACIATED
1 EMBARK
1 EMBARRASSED
1 EMBARRASSING
1 EMBER
3 EMBERS
1 EMBEZZLE
2 EMBODIED
1 EMBODIMENT
3 EMBRACE
1 EMBRACED
1 EMBRACING
1 EMBROIDERIES
1 EMBROIDERING
3 EMERALD
1 EMERGE
4 EMERGED
3 EMERGENCY
1 EMERGING
1 EMIGRATING
2 EMINENTLY
3 EMISSARIES
1 EMIT
2 EMITTED
2 EMMA
1 EMOLUMENTS
12 EMOTION
2 EMOTIONAL
6 EMOTIONS
1 EMPEROR
4 EMPHASIS
1 EMPHATICALLY
1 EMPIRE
1 EMPLOY
1 EMPLOYED
1 EMPLOYER
1 EMPLOYERS
2 EMPLOYMENT
1 EMPTINESS
34 EMPTY
1 EMPTYING
2 EN
1 ENABLE
3 ENABLED
1 ENABLES
1 ENCES
1 ENCHANTED
1 ENCHANTER'S
4 ENCLOSED
1 ENCLOSING
3 ENCLOSURE
1 ENCLOSURES
4 ENCOUNTER
3 ENCOURAGED
1 ENCOURAGEMENT
4 ENCOURAGING
82 END
3 ENDEAVOUR
1 ENDEAVOURS
10 ENDED
2 ENDING
4 ENDLESS
1 ENDLESSNESS
1 ENDLICH
1 ENDOWED
9 ENDS
1 ENDURABLE
2 ENDURANCE
1 ENDURING
1 ENEMIES
6 ENEMY
2 ENEMY'S
2 ENERGETIC
10 ENERGY
1 ENFIN
1 ENFOLDED

1 ENFUE	1 ESCORT	12 EXCLAIMED	1 EXTINGUISHED
1 ENGAGED	2 ESCORTED	1 EXCLAIMING	4 EXTORTED
1 ENGAGEMENT	2 ESPECIAL	4 EXCLAMATION	1 EXTORTING
2 ENGAGING	8 ESPECIALLY	1 EXCUSABLE	1 EXTORTIONATE
4 ENGINE	4 ESPLANADE	3 EXCUSE	1 EXTRA
4 ENGINE-ROOM	1 ESPOUSAL	1 EXECUTING	1 EXTRA-TERRESTRIAL
25 ENGINEER	2 ESSENCE	4 EXECUTION	2 EXTRAORDINARILY
1 ENGINEERING	2 ESSENTIAL	2 EXECUTIONER	21 EXTRAORDINARY
2 ENGINEERS	2 ESSEX	1 EXEMPLE	2 EXTRAVAGANT
3 ENGINES	2 EST	1 EXERCISE	3 EXTRAVAGANTLY
1 ENGLAND	6 ESTABLISHED	1 EXERCISES	10 EXTREME
10 ENGLISH	4 ESTABLISHMENT	1 EXERTED	13 EXTREMELY
3 ENGLISHMAN	1 ESTIMATE	3 EXERTION	1 EXTREMITY
2 ENGLISHMEN	2 ESTUARY	3 EXERTIONS	1 EXTRICATE
1 ENIGMA	1 ET	1 EXHALATION	1 EXUBERANT
1 ENIGMATIC	1 ETAT	1 EXHAUST	3 EXULTATION
1 ENIGMATICAL	2 ETC	1 EXHAUST-PIPE	2 EXULTED
1 ENJOINING	7 ETERNAL	4 EXHAUSTED	44 EYE
5 ENJOYED	1 ETERNITY	1 EXHIBIT	1 EYE-WITNESS
2 ENJOYMENT	1 ETHER	1 EXHIBITED	1 EYEBALLS
1 ENLARGE	1 ETHICAL	2 EXHIBITING	4 EYEBROWS
4 ENLARGED	3 EUROPE	1 EXHORT	9 EYED
1 ENLIGHTEN	2 EUROPEAN	2 EXHORTED	2 EYELID
1 ENLIGHTENED	1 EUROPEANS	1 EXIGEAIT	10 EYELIDS
1 ENLISTED	1 EVASION	1 EXIGENCIES	205 EYES
1 ENLIVENED	1 EVE	2 EXILE	2 EYESIGHT
1 ENMESHED	102 EVEN	5 EXIST	1 FABLE
7 ENORMOUS	28 EVENING	6 EXISTED	1 FABRIC
126 ENOUGH	1 EVENINGS	27 EXISTENCE	1 FABULOUS
2 ENRAGED	4 EVENLY	2 EXISTS	2 FABULOUSLY
1 ENSIGN	5 EVENT	1 EXORCISES	155 FACE
1 ENSLAVED	13 EVENTS	2 EXORCISM	26 FACED
1 ENSLAVING	1 EVENTUALITY	2 EXPANDING	25 FACES
3 ENSUED	71 EVER	4 EXPANSE	1 FACETIOUSLY
1 ENTENDU	1 EVER-UNDISCOVERED	1 EXPANSION	1 FACILITY
5 ENTER	9 EVERLASTING	23 EXPECT	10 FACING
7 ENTERED	3 EVERLASTINGLY	1 EXPECTANT	32 FACT
3 ENTERING	106 EVERY	2 EXPECTATION	1 FACTION
5 ENTERPRISE	14 EVERYBODY	1 EXPECTATIONS	1 FACTITIOUS
2 ENTERPRISES	1 EVERYBODY'S	17 EXPECTED	1 FACTORY
1 ENTERPRISING	39 EVERYTHING	7 EXPECTING	15 FACTS
1 ENTERTAINER	1 EVERYWHERE	1 EXPEDIENCY	5 FACULTY
1 ENTERTAINING	8 EVIDENCE	2 EXPEDIENT	6 FADED
2 ENTHRONED	7 EVIDENT	1 EXPEDITION	2 FADING
6 ENTHUSIASM	12 EVIDENTLY	2 EXPENSE	2 FAIL
1 ENTHUSIASMS	13 EVIL	1 EXPENSE'	7 FAILED
1 ENTHUSIASTICALLY	1 EVIL-DOERS	8 EXPERIENCE	2 FAILING
1 ENTICING	1 EVIL-MINDED	4 EXPERIENCED	2 FAILINGS
4 ENTIRELY	4 EVOKED	1 EXPERIENCES	1 FAILS
2 ENTITLED	1 EVOLVED	1 EXPERIENCING	7 FAILURE
1 ENTOMOLOGIST	1 EVOLVING	3 EXPERIMENT	1 FAILURES
1 ENTOMOLOGISTS	1 EWIG	1 EXPERIMENTS	33 FAINT
1 ENTOMOLOGY	1 EWIGKEIT'	1 EXPERT	1 FAINTER
1 ENTRAILS	3 EX	1 EXPIATION	1 FAINTING
1 ENTRANCE	1 EX-	2 EXPIRED	10 FAINTLY
1 ENTREAT	2 EX-BEACHCOMBER	3 EXPIRING	13 FAIR
7 ENTREATED	10 EXACT	16 EXPLAIN	13 FAIRLY
2 ENTREATING	2 EXACTING	16 EXPLAINED	1 FAIRNESS
1 ENTRENCHED	1 EXACTIONS	3 EXPLAINING	1 FAIT
1 ENTWINED	13 EXACTLY	6 EXPLANATION	19 FAITH
2 ENVELOP	5 EXAGGERATED	2 EXPLANATORY	9 FAITHFUL
5 ENVELOPE	2 EXALTATION	4 EXPLODED	3 FAITHFULLY
4 ENVELOPED	4 EXALTED	1 EXPLOIT	1 FAITHFULNESS
1 ENVIABLE	4 EXAMINATION	1 EXPLOITS	18 FALL
1 ENVIED	1 EXAMINE	1 EXPLOSION	14 FALLEN
1 ENVIOUSLY	1 EXAMINING	1 EXPORT	21 FALLING
1 ENVY	4 EXAMPLE	1 EXPOSE	4 FALLS
7 EPISODE	7 EXASPERATED	3 EXPOSED	10 FALSE
2 EPISODES	3 EXASPERATING	1 EXPOSING	2 FALSEHOOD
1 EPITHET	1 EXASPERATION	1 EXPOSTULATING	1 FALSER
1 EPITHETS	1 EXCAVATIONS	2 EXPOSURE	1 FALTER
1 EPOUVANTABLE	3 EXCEEDINGLY	1 EXPOUNDED	1 FALTERED
2 EQUABLY	1 EXCELLENCE	3 EXPRESS	1 FALTERING
11 EQUAL	7 EXCELLENT	8 EXPRESSED	9 FAME
1 EQUALITY	9 EXCEPT	21 EXPRESSION	11 FAMILIAR
3 EQUALLY	2 EXCEPTION	3 EXPRESSIONS	2 FAMILIARITY
1 EQUALS	2 EXCEPTIONAL	4 EXPRESSIVE	1 FAMILIARLY
1 EQUILIBRIUM	1 EXCEPTIONALLY	1 EXPRESSIVELY	2 FAMILIARS
1 EQUIVALENT	3 EXCESS	5 EXQUISITE	2 FAMILIES
2 ER	4 EXCESSIVE	1 EXTEND	7 FAMILY
5 ERECT	2 EXCESSIVELY	10 EXTENDED	9 FAMOUS
1 ERECTED	8 EXCHANGE	2 EXTENDING	1 FAN
4 ERRAND	5 EXCHANGED	2 EXTENSIVE	1 FANATICAL
2 ERRING	5 EXCHANGING	5 EXTENT	5 FANCIED
1 ERUPTION	1 EXCITABLE	1 EXTENUATION	3 FANCIFUL
3 ES	8 EXCITED	2 EXTERIOR	20 FANCY
19 ESCAPE	2 EXCITEDLY	1 EXTERMINATE	1 FANNED
5 ESCAPED	14 EXCITEMENT	3 EXTERNALS	3 FANTASTIC
1 ESCAPES	2 EXCITING	2 EXTINCT	77 FAR
1 ESCAPING	3 EXCLAIM	1 EXTINCTION	1 FAR-AWAY

1 FAR-OFF	1 FEVERISH	2 FITS	8 FLUTTER
1 FAR-REACHING	1 FEVERISHLY	6 FITTED	2 FLUTTERED
1 FARCE	79 FEW	21 FIVE	3 FLUTTERING
1 FARE	2 FIBRE	1 FIVE-AND-TWENTY	15 FLY
4 FARTHER	1 FICKLE	1 FIVE-ANDTWENTY	1 FLY-BLOWN
1 FARTHEST	1 FIDE	1 FIVE-POUND	15 FLYING
1 FARTHING	5 FIDELITY	1 FIVE-TON	5 FOAM
1 FASCINATE	2 FIELD	3 FIX	2 FOAMING
4 FASCINATED	2 FIELDS	15 FIXED	1 FOAMY
2 FASCINATION	2 FIEND	2 FIXEDLY	1 FOCUSED
3 FASHION	1 FIENDISH	1 FIXING	2 FOES
1 FASHIONED	1 FIENDS	1 FIXTURES	11 FOG
7 FAST	16 FIERCE	2 FLAG	1 FOGS
1 FASTEN	1 FIERCE-FACED	1 FLAGSHIP	3 FOILED
6 FASTENED	1 FIERCELY	1 FLAKE	1 FOLD
1 FASTENS	3 FIERCENESS	12 FLAME	2 FOLDED
2 FASTER	6 FIERY	8 FLAMES	1 FOLDING
8 FAT	4 FIFTEEN	1 FLANKING	1 FOLDING-STOOL
3 FATAL	1 FIFTH	3 FLANNEL	9 FOLDS
1 FATALITY	1 FIFTIETH	1 FLANNELETTE	5 FOLIAGE
2 FATALLY	3 FIFTY	1 FLAPPING	6 FOLK
28 FATE	1 FIFTY-SEVEN	2 FLARED	1 FOLKLORE
2 FATED	23 FIGHT	1 FLARES	12 FOLLOW
1 FATEFUL	15 FIGHTING	1 FLARING	28 FOLLOWED
1 FATES	1 FIGHTING-COCK	7 FLASH	5 FOLLOWERS
17 FATHER	1 FIGHTS	6 FLASHED	6 FOLLOWING
1 FATHER'S	2 FIGURATIVELY	18 FLAT	3 FOLLY
2 FATHERS	25 FIGURE	1 FLAT-FOOTED	2 FOND
3 FATHOM	2 FIGURED	2 FLATTENED	1 FONDLY
5 FATIGUE	7 FIGURES	1 FLATTERED	19 FOOD
1 FATIGUING	1 FILE	1 FLATTERING	29 FOOL
1 FATTENING	8 FILL	1 FLAVOUR	4 FOOLED
1 FATTEST	8 FILLED	1 FLAXEN	1 FOOLHARDY
5 FAULT	3 FILLING	1 FLEAS	2 FOOLING
9 FAVOUR	1 FILLS	9 FLED	2 FOOLISH
1 FAVOURED	2 FILTH	4 FLEET	1 FOOLISHLY
3 FAVOURITE	4 FILTHY	1 FLEETING	2 FOOLISHNESS
1 FAWNING	4 FINAL	1 FLENSBORG	2 FOOLS
62 FEAR	3 FINALITY	9 FLESH	1 FOOLSCAP
4 FEARED	5 FINALLY	2 FLESHY	27 FOOT
2 FEARFUL	1 FINANCED	11 FLEW	1 FOOTBALL
1 FEARFULLY	1 FINANCES	1 FLEXIBLE	2 FOOTED
1 FEARING	47 FIND	2 FLICKED	3 FOOTFALLS
5 FEARLESS	7 FINDING	6 FLICKER	1 FOOTHOLD
1 FEARLESSLY	2 FINDS	1 FLICKERING	2 FOOTING
1 FEARLESSNESS	33 FINE	3 FLICKERS	1 FOOTREST
9 FEARS	2 FINEM	3 FLIES	7 FOOTSTEPS
1 FEARSOME	1 FINER	9 FLIGHT	1 FOOTSTOOL
1 FEASTED	1 FINES	1 FLIMSY	964 FOR
2 FEASTING	1 FINEST	1 FLINCH	1 FORBADE
2 FEATHER	11 FINGER	2 FLINCHED	1 FORBID
1 FEATHERED	1 FINGER-TIP	1 FLINCHING	1 FORBIDDING
1 FEATHERS	1 FINGER-TIPS	8 FLING	11 FORCE
1 FEATHERY	1 FINGERING	1 FLINGING	4 FORCED
2 FEATURE	24 FINGERS	3 FLINTLOCK	7 FORCES
6 FEATURES	1 FINIALS	2 FLITTED	2 FORCIBLY
1 FECUND	2 FINIS	3 FLITTING	4 FORCING
1 FED	3 FINISH	4 FLOAT	5 FORE
4 FEEBLE	6 FINISHED	15 FLOATED	1 FORE-'TWEEN-DECK
7 FEEBLY	2 FIR	12 FLOATING	1 FORE-COMPARTMENT
2 FEED	1 FIR-TREES	2 FLOATS	1 FORE-TOP
1 FEEDER	29 FIRE	5 FLOOD	1 FORE-TOPSAIL
26 FEEL	1 FIRE-	1 FLOODING	2 FOREARM
31 FEELING	1 FIRE-SHIP	17 FLOOR	2 FOREARMS
10 FEELINGS	1 FIREARMS	1 FLOORING	1 FOREBORE
4 FEELS	13 FIRED	1 FLOORS	1 FOREDECK
81 FEET	1 FIREMAN	1 FLOP	4 FOREFINGER
1 FEINT	15 FIRES	1 FLOPPED	2 FOREFOOT
1 FELICITOUS	1 FIRESIDE	1 FLOSS	1 FOREFRONT
2 FELICITY	6 FIRING	1 FLOUNDERED	2 FOREGROUND
53 FELL	14 FIRM	1 FLOUNDERING	23 FOREHEAD
8 FELLED	1 FIRMAMENT	1 FLOURISHES	1 FOREHOLD
47 FELLOW	5 FIRMLY	1 FLOURISHING	3 FOREIGN
2 FELLOW'S	1 FIRMNESS	1 FLOUTED	5 FOREMOST
13 FELLOWS	146 FIRST	1 FLOW	3 FOREPEAK
2 FELLOWSHIP	1 FIRST-	4 FLOWED	1 FORESEE
72 FELT	2 FIRST-RATE	2 FLOWER	1 FORESEEN
7 FENCE	8 FISH	1 FLOWER-BEDS	1 FORESHORTENED
1 FENCES	1 FISHED	1 FLOWERING	2 FORESIGHT
3 FEROCIOUS	1 FISHER	10 FLOWERS	14 FOREST
5 FEROCITY	1 FISHER-FOLK	6 FLOWING	1 FORESTALLING
1 FERRIES	4 FISHERMEN	1 FLOWN	19 FORESTS
1 FERRY	6 FISHING	1 FLOWS	1 FORETELLS
1 FERRY-BOATS	3 FISHY	1 FLUENCY	2 FORGED
1 FESTAL	1 FISHY'	27 FLUNG	17 FORGET
2 FESTIVE	1 FISSURE	1 FLURRY	1 FORGETFUL
3 FETCH	12 FIST	2 FLUSHED	2 FORGETFULNESS
1 FETCHED	4 FISTS	1 FLUSTER	2 FORGETS
1 FETTERS	20 FIT	1 FLUSTERED	2 FORGETTING
5 FEVER	1 FITFUL	1 FLUTED	12 FORGIVE

4 FORGIVEN	1 FRIGHTEN	1 GARLAND	1 GLAZE
2 FORGIVENESS	13 FRIGHTENED	2 GARLANDED	1 GLAZED
1 FORGIVINGLY	1 FRIGHTENING	1 GARMENT	7 GLEAM
6 FORGOT	3 FRIGHTFUL	2 GARRISON	1 GLEAMED
16 FORGOTTEN	2 FRIGHTFULLY	3 GASP	1 GLEAMING
3 FORK	1 FRINGED	4 GASPED	8 GLEAMS
3 FORLORN	11 FRO	3 GASPING	1 GLEE
19 FORM	1 FROCKCOAT	2 GASPS	1 GLIBNESS
2 FORMAL	462 FROM	21 GATE	1 GLIDE
5 FORMALITY	1 FROM-UNDER	4 GATES	5 GLIDED
1 FORMALLY	1 FROMA	2 GATEWAY	1 GLIDES
3 FORMED	2 FRONDS	2 GATHER	4 GLIDING
1 FORMIDABLY	15 FRONT	3 GATHERED	4 GLIMMER
1 FORMING	1 FRONTED	3 GATHERING	1 GLIMMERED
12 FORMS	2 FRONTS	1 GAUDY	1 GLIMMERING
2 FORMULA	1 FROSTY	2 GAUNT	13 GLIMPSE
2 FORMULATED	1 FROTHING	50 GAVE	1 GLIMPSED
3 FORSAKEN	1 FROTHY	1 GAY	5 GLIMPSES
1 FORSOOTH	1 FROWN	12 GAZE	1 GLINTS
1 FORSWEAR	4 FROWNED	5 GAZED	3 GLISTENED
21 FORT	1 FROWNS	8 GAZING	2 GLISTENING
2 FORTH	1 FROZEN	3 GEAR	12 GLITTER
2 FORTHWITH	3 FRUIT	1 GELUNGEN	4 GLITTERED
3 FORTIFIED	1 FUDDLED	2 GEM	5 GLITTERING
3 FORTITUDE	1 FULGOR	7 GENERAL	1 GLOAT
1 FORTMEN	60 FULL	8 GENERALLY	1 GLOATED
1 FORTNIGHT	1 FULLNESS	4 GENERATIONS	1 GLOATING
2 FORTUNATE	9 FULLY	1 GENEROSITY	5 GLOBE
2 FORTUNATELY	1 FUMBLED	8 GENEROUS	1 GLOBE-TROTTER
10 FORTUNE	1 FUMES	1 GENEROUSLY	2 GLOBE-TROTTERS
9 FORTY	1 FUMING	11 GENTLE	1 GLOBELAMPS
40 FORWARD	3 FUN	20 GENTLEMAN	1 GLOBES
1 FOSSIL	1 FUNCTION	1 GENTLEMANLY	1 GLOBULAR
1 FOSTERED	1 FUNCTIONS	1 GENTLEMEN	13 GLOOM
1 FOSTERING	1 FUNDAMENTAL	16 GENTLY	1 GLOOMILY
4 FOUGHT	1 FUNDAMENTALLY	1 GENTS	8 GLOOMY
61 FOUND	1 FUNERAL	4 GENUINE	3 GLORIOUS
1 FOUNDATIONS	4 FUNK	1 GENUINELY	8 GLORY
1 FOUNT	1 FUNNEL	1 GEO	1 GLORY'
34 FOUR	2 FUNNIEST	1 GEO-O-O-ORGE	12 GLOW
2 FOUR-AND-TWENTY	16 FUNNY	8 GEORGE	3 GLOWED
1 FOUR-FINGER	1 FURIES	7 GERMAN	1 GLOWERING
1 FOUR-POSTER	4 FURIOUS	1 GERMANS	4 GLOWING
2 FOURS	1 FURNACE	1 GERMANY	3 GLUED
5 FOURTEEN	1 FURNISH	1 GESTICULATING	2 GLUM
1 FOURTEEN-HUNDRED-TON	2 FURNITURE	10 GESTURE	2 GNASHING
1 FOURTH	1 FURROWED	5 GESTURES	1 GNAWING
1 FOWLS	1 FURROWS	150 GET	1 GNOME
1 FRAGILE	7 FURTHER	3 GETS	174 GO
1 FRAGMENT	1 FURTHERMORE	19 GETTING	1 GO'
1 FRAGMENTARILY	2 FURTIVE	1 GEWISS	29 GOD
2 FRAGMENTARY	10 FURY	1 GEWISSEN	1 GOD-FORSAKEN
2 FRAGMENTS	1 FUSED	7 GHARRY	4 GOD'S
2 FRAGRANCE	2 FUSILLADE	1 GHARRY-WALLAH	1 GODDESS
4 FRAIL	5 FUSS	2 GHASTLY	12 GOES
4 FRAME	1 FUSSINESS	18 GHOST	1 GOGGLES
1 FRAMES	2 FUSSING	1 GHOSTLY	81 GOING
2 FRAMEWORK	3 FUSSY	4 GHOSTS	16 GOLD
5 FRANK	2 FUTILE	1 GHOUL	1 GOLD-DIGGING
5 FRANKLY	1 FUTILELY	1 GIDDINESS	1 GOLD-LEAF
2 FRANKNESS	3 FUTILITY	5 GIFT	2 GOLD-MINE
2 FRANTIC	7 FUTURE	3 GIFTED	1 GOLDEN
2 FRAUD	2 G	2 GIFTS	54 GONE
2 FRAYED	1 G-G-GLAD	2 GIG	3 GONGS
15 FREE	1 GABASIDY	1 GIGANTIC	154 GOOD
1 FREE-HEARTED	1 GABLES	65 GIRL	5 GOOD-BYE
2 FREED	1 GAFF	5 GIRL'S	1 GOOD-HUMOUR
4 FREEDOM	1 GAGGED	6 GIRLS	1 GOOD-HUMOURED
1 FREEING	1 GAIN	2 GIRTH	1 GOOD-HUMOUREDLY
1 FREELY	1 GAINED	2 GIST	1 GOOD-LOOKING
1 FREEWILL	1 GAIT	63 GIVE	2 GOOD-NATURE
7 FRENCH	1 GAL	35 GIVEN	1 GOOD-NATURED
3 FRENCHMAN	6 GALE	4 GIVES	2 GOOD-NIGHT
1 FRENCHMAN'S	2 GALES	22 GIVING	1 GOOD-TEMPERED
1 FREQUENTED	1 GALLANT	1 GLA	5 GOODNESS
10 FRESH	6 GALLERY	1 GLA-A-A-D	4 GOODS
2 FRESHENED	1 GALLOP	13 GLAD	1 GORGE
4 FRESHNESS	1 GALLOWS	6 GLAMOUR	5 GORGEOUS
1 FRETTING	1 GALVANIC	42 GLANCE	1 GOSH
1 FRIED	10 GAME	5 GLANCED	2 GOSSIP
32 FRIEND	2 GAMES	16 GLANCES	2 GOSSIPING
2 FRIEND'S	6 GANG	3 GLANCING	1 GOSSIPY
1 FRIENDLESS	1 GANGWAYS	10 GLARE	116 GOT
1 FRIENDLINESS	1 GANZ	9 GLARED	4 GOTT
8 FRIENDLY	2 GAP	1 GLARES	1 GOTT-FOR-DAM
12 FRIENDS	1 GAPING	4 GLARING	1 GOTTAM
8 FRIENDSHIP	2 GARBAGE	27 GLASS	1 GOUNDRY
3 FRIENDSHIPS	1 GARBAGE-HEAP	4 GLASSES	11 GOVERNMENT
1 FRIENDT	5 GARDEN	6 GLASSY	3 GOVERNOR
7 FRIGHT	3 GARDENS	1 GLASSY-EYED	4 GOWN

3 GRABBED
6 GRACE
1 GRADUAL
9 GRADUALLY
1 GRANARY
1 GRANDEUR
1 GRANDFATHER
1 GRANDS
2 GRANGER
1 GRANITE
1 GRAPHICALLY
3 GRAPPLE
9 GRASP
1 GRASPED
20 GRASS
1 GRASS-PLOT
2 GRASS-PLOTS
1 GRASSY
1 GRATED
2 GRATEFUL
1 GRATIFIED
1 GRATIFY
1 GRATING
1 GRATIS
6 GRATITUDE
22 GRAVE
1 GRAVEL
1 GRAVELY
1 GRAVEN
4 GRAVES
1 GRAVEST
2 GRAVITY
1 GRAZE
1 GRAZING
3 GREASY
104 GREAT
10 GREATER
13 GREATEST
10 GREATLY
7 GREATNESS
2 GREED
1 GREEDILY
1 GREEDY
1 GREEK'S
11 GREEN
1 GREEN-AND-GOLD
1 GREEN-AND-ORANGE
1 GREEN-HOUSES
1 GREEN-LINED
2 GREENISH
2 GREETED
4 GREETING
4 GREETINGS
1 GREW
22 GREY
2 GREY-HAIRED
1 GREY-HEADED
1 GREYBEARDS
1 GREYHOUND
2 GREYISH
2 GREYNESS
5 GRIEF
1 GRIEVANCE
8 GRIM
2 GRIMACE
1 GRIMACES
1 GRIMACING
1 GRIME
1 GRIMLY
2 GRIMY
2 GRIN
1 GRIND
1 GRINDING
2 GRINNED
1 GRINNING
7 GRIP
1 GRIPES
2 GRIPPED
1 GRIPPING
4 GROAN
1 GROANED
1 GROANS
2 GROG
2 GROG-SHOP
1 GROOMED
1 GROOVES
1 GROPED
1 GROPING
1 GROPINGLY
1 GROSSLY

3 GROTESQUE
41 GROUND
1 GROUNDING
6 GROUNDS
9 GROUP
1 GROUPED
2 GROUPS
1 GROVE
1 GROVELLED
1 GROVELLING
7 GROW
9 GROWING
2 GROWL
6 GROWLED
1 GROWLING
1 GROWLS
7 GROWN
1 GROWS
1 GROWTH
1 GRUB
1 GRUBBING
1 GRUDGE
1 GRUFF
1 GRUMPY
7 GRUNT
3 GRUNTED
1 GRUNTING
6 GUANO
2 GUARANTEE
4 GUARD
1 GUARDED
2 GUARDIAN
1 GUARDIANS
2 GUARDIANSHIP
1 GUARDING
6 GUESS
1 GUESSED
3 GUEST
1 GUFFAW
2 GUIDED
1 GUIDING
1 GUILDER
4 GUILT
5 GUILTY
2 GUISE
2 GULF
1 GULLET
1 GULPED
2 GUM
1 GUMMED
9 GUN
1 GUN-CARRIAGE
6 GUNBOAT
1 GUNPOWDER
17 GUNS
1 GUNSHOT
2 GUNWALE
1 GUNWALES
1 GURGLED
3 GURGLING
1 GUSH
5 GUST
1 GUSTAV
3 GUSTS
2 GUTTERS
3 H
1 H-E-ELP
1 H-H-HERE
21 HA
6 HABIT
1 HABITUALLY
1515 HAD
24 HADN'T
1 HAFT
3 HAG
3 HAGGARD
1 HAI
1 HAI-PHONG
2 HAIL
2 HAILED
35 HAIR
1 HAIR'S
1 HAIR'S-BREADTH
2 HAIRED
1 HAIRLESS
2 HAIRS
1 HAIRY
2 HAJI
92 HALF
1 HALF-AVERTED

1 HALF-BRED
1 HALF-BREED
7 HALF-CASTE
2 HALF-CASTES
1 HALF-CROWN
1 HALF-HEARTED
1 HALF-HOUR
1 HALF-LIGHT
1 HALF-LOST
1 HALF-NAKED
2 HALF-PAST
1 HALF-PAY
1 HALF-RESENTFUL
1 HALF-RESIGNED
1 HALF-SUBMERGED
1 HALF-UTTERED
2 HALF-WAY
1 HALFCASTE
1 HALFCONSUMED
1 HALFHEARTED
1 HALFTRANSPARENT
6 HALL
4 HALLO
1 HALT
1 HALT'
2 HALTER
1 HALTING
1 HALTING-PLACES
1 HALVES
7 HAMMER
1 HAMMERING
1 HAMMERS
1 HAMMOCK
1 HAMS
149 HAND
1 HAND-LAMP
1 HAND-TO-HAND
4 HANDED
1 HANDEN
2 HANDFUL
2 HANDING
2 HANDKERCHIEF
2 HANDKERCHIEFS
3 HANDLE
2 HANDLED
1 HANDLING
97 HANDS
1 HANDSOME
4 HANDWRITING
4 HANDY
25 HANG
5 HANGED
10 HANGING
3 HANGS
1 HANKER
2 HAPHAZARD
14 HAPPEN
24 HAPPENED
2 HAPPENS
4 HAPPINESS
4 HAPPY
1 HARASSED
11 HARBOUR
1 HARBOURED
33 HARD
1 HARDENED
2 HARDER
1 HARDEST
8 HARDLY
1 HARDSHIPS
1 HARDWOOD
8 HARM
1 HARM'S
2 HARMLESS
1 HARMONY
1 HARP
1 HARP-STRING
1 HARROW
2 HARROWING
3 HARSH
2 HARSHLY
1 HARVEST
68 HAS
1 HASN'T
8 HASTE
2 HASTENED
9 HASTILY
2 HASTY
16 HAT
4 HATCH

1 HATCHED
1 HATCHES
4 HATCHWAY
1 HATCHWAYS
9 HATE
9 HATED
1 HATEFUL
2 HATH
1 HATRED
1 HATS
1 HAUGHTILY
1 HAUGHTY
3 HAULED
1 HAULING
1 HAUNT
5 HAUNTED
2 HAUNTING
441 HAVE
19 HAVEN'T
32 HAVING
1 HAVOC
4 HAWK
2 HAWSERS
1 HAYES
2 HAZARD
1 HAZARDS
2 HAZE
1 HAZED
1 HAZILY
6 HAZY
3118 HE
3 HE'S
236 HEAD
1 HEAD-CLOTHS
4 HEAD-MAN
4 HEAD-MEN
1 HEADACHE
7 HEADED
1 HEADKERCHIEF
1 HEADLAND
5 HEADLONG
33 HEADS
1 HEADWAY
3 HEALTH
1 HEALTHY
14 HEAP
5 HEAPS
63 HEAR
125 HEARD
1 HEARERS
9 HEARING
65 HEART
3 HEART-RENDING
3 HEARTED
1 HEARTHSTONE
1 HEARTHSTONES
1 HEARTILY
1 HEARTLESS
11 HEARTS
1 HEARTY
7 HEAT
1 HEATED
1 HEATHEN
4 HEAVE
1 HEAVED
7 HEAVEN
1 HEAVEN'S
3 HEAVENLY
10 HEAVENS
4 HEAVIER
10 HEAVILY
2 HEAVING
44 HEAVY
1 HECTOR
1 HEDGED
4 HEEL
11 HEELS
4 HEIGHT
1 HEIGHTENED
1 HEINOUS
1 HEIR
38 HELD
5 HELL
3 HELM
2 HELMET
1 HELMSMEN
44 HELP
5 HELPED
1 HELPER
1 HELPING

3 HELPLESS	1 HOLLOWED	4 HULL	2 ILLUSORY
1 HELPLESSLY	2 HOLLOWS	1 HULLABALOO	1 ILLUSTRATED
3 HELPLESSNESS	3 HOLY	3 HUM	1 ILLUSTRATION
1 HELTER	1 HOLY-	22 HUMAN	1 ILLUSTRIOUS
1 HELTER-SKELTER	48 HOME	1 HUMANE	2 IM
1 HEMISPHERE	1 HOME-LIKE	4 HUMBLE	5 IMAGE
1 HEMISPHERES	1 HOME-PORT	1 HUMBLED	2 IMAGES
1 HEN	1 HOMELESS	1 HUMBLEST	2 IMAGINARY
1 HENCE	1 HOMELY	1 HUMBUG	15 IMAGINATION
3 HENCEFORTH	1 HOMERIC	1 HUMILIATED	1 IMAGINATIONS
379 HER	2 HOMES	1 HUMILIATION	7 IMAGINATIVE
1 HERALD	1 HOMEWARD	2 HUMILITY	23 IMAGINE
1 HERALDED	1 HOMICIDAL	1 HUMMED	6 IMAGINED
2 HERD	4 HONEST	2 HUMMING	1 IMAGININGS
145 HERE	3 HONESTLY	3 HUMOROUS	1 IMAGINATIVE
2 HERE'	1 HONESTY	2 HUMOUR	3 IMBECILE
3 HERE'S	1 HONEY	1 HUMOURED	5 IMBECILITY
1 HEREAFTER	1 HONEYED	1 HUMOUREDLY	1 IMBIBE
2 HERMITS	1 HONG	2 HUMOURING	1 INCOMPREHENSIBLE
5 HERO	1 HONG-	1 HUMP	1 IMITATED
1 HEROES	2 HONOLULU	1 HUNCHED	2 IMMACULATE
7 HEROIC	17 HONOUR	38 HUNDRED	3 IMMATERIAL
1 HEROICS	11 HONOURABLE	3 HUNDREDS	1 IMMEASURABLY
4 HEROISM	1 HONOURED	1 HUNDREDTH	4 IMMEDIATE
6 HERSELF	6 HOOK	29 HUNG	5 IMMEDIATELY
6 HESITATE	1 HOOKED	3 HUNGER	33 IMMENSE
1 HESITATED	1 HOOKER	2 HUNGRILY	5 IMMENSELY
3 HESITATING	2 HOOKS	6 HUNGRY	13 IMMENSITY
5 HESITATION	2 HOP	2 HUNT	2 IMMERSE
1 HESITATIONS	24 HOPE	4 HUNTED	1 IMMIGRANTS
15 HEY	10 HOPED	2 HUNTING	1 IMMINENT
9 HIDDEN	3 HOPEFUL	1 HUNTING-GROUND	1 IMMOBILISE
3 HIDE	14 HOPELESS	1 HURL	16 IMMOBILITY
1 HIDEOUS	5 HOPELESSLY	4 HURRICANE	1 IMMORAL
3 HIDING	8 HOPES	2 HURRICANES	1 IMMORALITY
1 HIDINGS	1 HORDE	8 HURRIED	1 IMMORTAL
53 HIGH	12 HORIZON	6 HURRIEDLY	3 IMMOVABLE
2 HIGH-MINDED	1 HORIZONS	7 HURRY	3 IMMOVABLY
2 HIGH-PITCHED	1 HORN	6 HURT	1 IMPACT
1 HIGH-SPIRITED	1 HORN-RIMMED	3 HUSBAND	1 IMPALED
1 HIGH'	10 HORRIBLE	2 HUSH	1 IMPALING
1 HIGHBORN	2 HORRIBLY	2 HUSKILY	4 IMPALPABLE
6 HIGHER	2 HORRID	1 HUSKY	1 IMPART
3 HIGHEST	1 HORRIFIED	6 HUT	2 IMPARTING
1 HIGHLY	12 HORROR	4 HUTS	1 IMPASSABLE
1 HILIDAY	3 HORRORS	1 HYAENA'	1 IMPASSIBLE
35 HILL	11 HORSE	1 HYAENAS	3 IMPASSIONED
1 HILLOCK	1 HORSE-POWER	1 HYPOTHESIS	3 IMPASSIVE
8 HILLS	1 HORSESHOE	1 HYSTERICALLY	5 IMPATIENCE
2 HILLSIDE	1 HOSE	2627 I	3 IMPATIENT
926 HIM	4 HOSPITAL	1 I'	1 IMPATIENTLY
1 HIMMEL	1 HOSPITALS	1 I'D	3 IMPECCABLE
226 HIMSELF	2 HOST	23 I'LL	3 IMPELLED
1 HIND	1 HOSTILE	3 I'M	1 IMPENDING
1 HINDERED	15 HOT	55 I'VE	5 IMPENETRABLE
1 HINDRANCE	1 HOT-TEMPERED	1 ICE	1 IMPENITENCE
1 HINGE	7 HOTEL	1 ICEBERGS	1 IMPENITENT
1 HINGES	1 HOTEL-KEEPER	1 ICED	2 IMPERCEPTIBLE
9 HINT	1 HOTELS	1 ICH'S	2 IMPERCEPTIBLY
3 HINTED	1 HOTLY	1 ICICLES	2 IMPERFECT
5 HINTS	1 HOTTEST	35 IDEA	2 IMPERFECTLY
1 HIPPED	3 HOUND	2 IDEAL	2 IMPERISHABLE
1 HIRSUTE	1 HOUNDS	1 IDEALISED	3 IMPERTURBABLE
2187 HIS	14 HOUR	1 IDEALIST	2 IMPETUOSITY
5 HISS	3 HOUR'S	5 IDEAS	2 IMPETUOUSLY
1 HISSED	17 HOURS	2 IDEE	1 IMPETUS
2 HISSING	1 HOURS'	1 IDENTITY	1 IMPLACABLE
1 HISTORIC	1 HOURSE	2 IDIOT	1 IMPLEMENTS
5 HISTORY	61 HOUSE	1 IDIOTIC	2 IMPLICITLY
5 HIT	1 HOUSE'	1 IDIOTS	1 IMPLIED
1 HITCHED	3 HOUSEHOLD	1 IDLE	1 IMPLORED
1 HIVA	1 HOUSEHOLDER	3 IDLY	5 IMPLY
1 HIVE	2 HOUSEHOLDS	1 IDOLISED	1 IMPORT
2 HOARSE	31 HOUSES	1 IDYLLIC	14 IMPORTANCE
1 HOBART	1 HOVE	378 IF	6 IMPORTANT
1 HOBBLED	3 HOVEL	1 IGNOMINOUSLY	1 IMPOSE
1 HOD	2 HOVELS	7 IGNORANCE	1 IMPOSED
1 HOGSHEAD	6 HOVERED	2 IGNORANT	5 IMPOSING
1 HOISTING	3 HOVERING	5 IGNORED	1 IMPOSINGLY
45 HOLD	136 HOW	8 ILL	1 IMPOSSIBILITY
18 HOLDING	32 HOWEVER	4 ILL-LUCK	29 IMPOSSIBLE
1 HOLDING-GROUND	3 HOWL	1 ILL-USAGE	1 IMPOTENCE
4 HOLDS	3 HOWLED	1 ILL-USED	2 IMPRECATION
12 HOLE	1 HOWLING	1 ILLEGAL	1 IMPREGNABLE
1 HOLE-AND-CORNER	1 HOWLS	1 ILLUMINATED	5 IMPRESSED
1 HOLES	1 HUDDLED	2 ILLUMINATING	10 IMPRESSION
2 HOLIDAY	1 HUDDLING	2 ILLUMINED	3 IMPRESSIONS
1 HOLIDAYS	1 HUFF	12 ILLUSION	1 IMPRESSIVE
1 HOLLERING	2 HUGE	4 ILLUSIONS	3 IMPRESSIVELY
6 HOLLOW	1 HUGGING	1 ILLUSIVE	4 IMPRISONED

2 IMPRISONMENT	1 INDUCEMENTS	2 INSOLENCE	2 INTRODUCE
1 IMPROPER	1 INDULGE	2 INSOLENT	1 INTRODUCED
2 IMPROVING	1 INDULGED	2 INSOLUBLE	3 INTRODUCTION
2 IMPROVISED	1 INDULGENCE	2 INSPIRATION	1 INTRUDER
1 IMPRUDENCE	2 INDULGENT	2 INSPIRE	1 INTRUDERS
3 IMPUDENCE	1 INDULGENTLY	2 INSPIRED	1 INTUITION
2 IMPUDENT	1 INDUSTRIOUS	1 INSPIRER	1 INVADED
11 IMPULSE	1 INDUSTRIOUSLY	1 INSPIRING	2 INVADERS
2 IMPULSES	2 INDUSTRY	16 INSTANCE	1 INVADERS'
2 IMPULSIVE	1 INEFFABLE	1 INSTANCES	1 INVADING
1 IMPULSIVENESS	1 INEFFICIENT	11 INSTANT	3 INVALID
2 IMPUNITY	2 INERT	1 INSTANTANEOUS	2 INVARIABLY
2147 IN	1 INEVITABLE	1 INSTANTANEOUSLY	1 INVASION
1 IN-	1 INEVITABLY	9 INSTANTLY	1 INVERTED
2 INABILITY	1 INEXPERIENCED	5 INSTEAD	1 INVEST
4 INACCESSIBLE	8 INEXPLICABLE	2 INSTINCT	1 INVESTED
3 INADEQUATE	2 INEXPRESSIBLE	2 INSTINCTIVE	1 INVESTIGATE
1 INANIMATE	3 INEXPRESSIBLY	2 INSTINCTIVELY	1 INVESTIGATED
1 INANITION	1 INEXPUGNABLE	1 INSTINCTS	3 INVESTIGATION
1 INARTICULATE	3 INFAMOUS	2 INSTITUTIONS	7 INVINCIBLE
1 INAUDIBLE	1 INFANTRY	2 INSTRUCED	1 INVIOLABLE
1 INBORN	1 INFECTED	2 INSTRUCTIONS	15 INVISIBLE
1 INCALCULABLE	1 INFECTIOUS	2 INSTRUCTIVE	1 INVITATION
1 INCANDESCENT	1 INFER	1 INSTRUCTORS	1 INVITE
1 INCANTATIONS	1 INFERIOR	1 INSTRUMENTS	1 INVOKED
3 INCAPABLE	1 INFERIORITY	1 INSUFFERABLY	1 INVOKES
4 INCARNATION	18 INFERNAL	2 INSULTING	1 INVOLUNTARILY
1 INCENSE	1 INFERNALLY	2 INSURANCE	2 INVOLVED
4 INCERTITUDE	1 INFIDEL	1 INSURGENTS	1 INVOLVING
3 INCESSANTLY	1 INFIDELS	1 INTANGIBLE	2 INVULNERABLE
2 INCH	6 INFINITE	1 INTELLECTUAL	1 INVULNERABLY
3 INCHES	9 INFINITELY	5 INTELLIGENCE	3 INWARD
1 INCHI	1 INFINITY	9 INTELLIGENT	22 IRON
6 INCIDENT	1 INFLAMED	1 INTELLIGENTLY	1 IRON-GREY
1 INCIDENTAL	1 INFLATED	2 INTELLIGIBLE	1 IRONGREY
1 INCIDENTS	4 INFLEXIBLE	1 INTELLIGIBLY	2 IRONIC
1 INCISIVE	4 INFLEXIBLY	4 INTEND	1 IRONICALLY
2 INCISIVELY	1 INFLICTS	2 INTENDED	2 IRONY
2 INCITED	6 INFLUENCE	15 INTENSE	2 IRRATIONAL
5 INCLINED	1 INFLUENCED	3 INTENSELY	3 IRREGULAR
1 INCLUDES	1 INFLUENCES	4 INTENSITY	2 IRREGULARITIES
3 INCOGNITO	1 INFORM	1 INTENT	1 IRREGULARLY
1 INCOHERENT	2 INFORMANTS	19 INTENTION	1 IRRELEVANT
1 INCOMMODED	7 INFORMATION	5 INTENTIONS	3 IRREMEDIABLE
2 INCOMPLETE	3 INFORMED	2 INTENTLY	2 IRREPRESSIBLE
1 INCOMPLETENESS	2 ING	1 INTER	1 IRREPROACHABLE
7 INCOMPREHENSIBLE	1 INGLORIOUS	1 INTER-ISLAND	4 IRRESISTIBLE
1 INCOMPREHENSIBLY	1 INGRATITUDE	1 INTERCEDE	2 IRRESISTIBLY
8 INCONCEIVABLE	4 INHABITANTS	3 INTERCOURSE	1 IRRESOLUTE
1 INCONSOLABLE	1 INHERITED	1 INTERESSANT	1 IRRESPONSIBLE
1 INCONSOLABLY	1 INHUMAN	11 INTEREST	3 IRRESPONSIVE
1 INCONTINENTLY	1 INIQUITIES	11 INTERESTED	1 IRRETRIEVABLY
1 INCONVENIENCE	1 INITIAL	6 INTERESTING	1 IRRITABLY
1 INCONVENIENCES	1 INJECTED	1 INTERFERED	3 IRRITATED
1 INCORRIGIBLE	1 INJUNS	1 INTERFERENCE	1 IRRITATING
1 INCREASED	1 INJUSTICE	6 INTERIOR	5 IRRITATION
3 INCREASING	3 INK	2 INTERJECTED	534 IS
1 INCREDIBLE	1 INKSTAND	1 INTERLACED	12 ISLAND
1 INCREDIBLY	1 INLAID	1 INTERLOCUTOR	5 ISLANDER
2 INCREDULOUS	3 INLAND	1 INTERMINABLE	4 ISLANDS
2 INDECISION	2 INNATE	1 INTERMINABLY	1 ISLE
31 INDEED	7 INNER	1 INTERNALLY	1 ISLES
2 INDEFINABLE	3 INNERMOST	2 INTERNATIONAL	4 ISLET
6 INDEFINITE	2 INNOCENCE	1 INTERPOSITION	3 ISLETS
1 INDEFINITENESS	6 INNOCENT	2 INTERPRET	13 ISN'T
1 INDEPENDENTLY	3 INNUMERABLE	3 INTERPRETER	5 ISOLATED
1 INDESCRIBABLE	1 INOFFENSIVE	2 INTERROGATIVELY	5 ISOLATION
3 INDIAN	2 INQUIRE	1 INTERROGATORIES	1 ISSUE
1 INDICATED	4 INQUIRED	3 INTERRUPT	2 ISSUED
7 INDIFFERENCE	1 INQUIRING	12 INTERRUPTED	1 ISSUES
7 INDIFFERENT	23 INQUIRY	2 INTERRUPTING	1 ISSUING
1 INDIGESTION	1 INQUISITIVE	1 INTERRUPTIONS	2 IST
3 INDIGNANT	2 INQUISITIVELY	1 INTERSPERSED	1391 IT
6 INDIGNATION	1 INSANITY	1 INTERVAL	48 IT'S
1 INDIGNATIONS	1 INSCRIBED	6 INTERVALS	1 ITALIAN
1 INDIRECTLY	1 INSCRIPTION	2 INTERVIEWS	1 ITALIAN'S
1 INDISCREET	6 INSCRUTABLE	1 INTIMACY	78 ITAM
1 INDISCRETION	3 INSECT	3 INTIMATE	2 ITAM'S
1 INDISCRETIONS	2 INSECTS	273 INTO	163 ITS
1 INDISSOLUBLY	2 INSECURE	5 INTOLERABLE	38 ITSELF
5 INDISTINCT	3 INSECURITY	2 INTOLERABLY	3 JA
1 INDISTINGUISHABLE	1 INSENSIBLE	3 INTONATION	2 JAB
9 INDIVIDUAL	3 INSEPARABLE	1 INTONING	1 JABBERING
1 INDIVIDUALITY	16 INSIDE	1 INTOXICATED	3 JACKET
1 INDIVIDUALS	7 INSIGNIFICANT	2 INTOXICATING	1 JACKETS
1 INDOLENT	1 INSINUATED	1 INTREPID	2 JAGGED
3 INDOMITABLE	2 INSINUATINGLY	1 INTREPIDITY	1 JAILER
2 INDOORS	2 INSIST	1 INTRIGUE	5 JAMES
2 INDUCE	6 INSISTED	3 INTRIGUED	2 JAMES'
6 INDUCED	4 INSISTENCE	1 INTRIGUES	3 JAMMED

1 JAMS	17 KASSIM	1 LAMENESS	1 LEERY
1 JANE	2 KASSIM'S	1 LAMENTABLE	1 LEERY-EYED
1 JANISSARY	2 KEEL	1 LAMENTATION	2 LEEWARD
1 JAPAN	2 KEEN	2 LAMENTATIONS	92 LEFT
1 JAR	1 KEENLY	15 LAMP	13 LEG
2 JARGON	49 KEEP	1 LAMPS	2 LEGAL
1 JARRED	3 KEEPER	1 LANCE	2 LEGEND
2 JAUNTY	1 KEEPERS	37 LAND	3 LEGGED
2 JAVA	15 KEEPING	14 LANDED	1 LEGGINGS
2 JAVANESE	2 KEEPS	7 LANDING	1 LEGION
2 JAW	1 KEGS	1 LANDING-	1 LEGITIMATE
2 JAWS	1 KELP	3 LANDING-STAGE	32 LEGS
3 JEALOUS	48 KEPT	1 LANDING-STAGES	3 LEISURE
1 JEALOUSIES	1 KETTLES	1 LANDMARKS	4 LEISURELY
1 JEALOUSLY	2 KEY	1 LANDS	1 LEMON
1 JEALOUSY	4 KICK	1 LANDSCAPE	1 LEMON-PEEL
1 JEE	4 KICKED	2 LANE	2 LEND
1 JEERED	3 KICKING	4 LANGUAGE	1 LENDER
2 JEERING	1 KIDNAP	5 LANGUID	1 LENDS
1 JEERINGLY	1 KIDNAPPED	2 LANGUOR	22 LENGTH
5 JERK	1 KIDNEY	1 LANK	1 LENGTHS
4 JERKED	17 KILL	2 LANKY	1 LENIENT
1 JERKS	13 KILLED	1 LANTERN	1 LENT
3 JERKY	6 KILLING	1 LANYARD	2 LES
1 JETS	55 KIND	1 LANYARDS	31 LESS
2 JETTY	1 KIND'	4 LAP	1 LESSLY
13 JEWEL	1 KINDLINESS	1 LAPA	3 LESSON
1 JEWEL'S	4 KINDLY	1 LAPEL	1 LESSONS
1 JEWELLED	3 KINDNESS	1 LAPSE	5 LEST
1 JIB	1 KINDRED	24 LARGE	103 LET
1 JIB-SHEET	4 KINDS	1 LARGER	4 LET'S
1 JIFFY	2 KING	1 LARGISH	2 LETS
288 JIM	1 KINSMEN	1 LASCAR	20 LETTER
1 JIM-JAMS	1 KISS	2 LASCARS	7 LETTERS
1 JIM-MYTH	2 KISSED	3 LASHED	6 LETTING
70 JIM'S	1 KITCHEN	167 LAST	13 LEVEL
2 JIMMY	1 KNEADING	3 LASTED	1 LEVUKA
1 JINGLED	5 KNEE	1 LASTING	1 LEVYING
10 JOB	1 KNEELING	1 LASTS	1 LIABLE
1 JOCULAR	21 KNEES	20 LATE	2 LIAR
1 JOHNNIE	58 KNEW	5 LATELY	2 LIBERATED
1 JOHNNIES	1 KNID	18 LATER	1 LIBERTIES
1 JOHNNY	7 KNIFE	1 LATEST	5 LIBERTY
2 JOIN	1 KNIGHT	1 LATITUDE	1 LICKED
4 JOINED	5 KNOCK	1 LATITUDES	1 LICKING
2 JOINTED	1 KNOCKABOUT	2 LATTER	2 LID
1 JOINTS	9 KNOCKED	1 LATTER-DAY	15 LIE
11 JOKE	7 KNOCKING	23 LAUGH	4 LIED
1 JOKER	1 KNOCKS	1 LAUGHABLE	5 LIES
3 JOKES	8 KNOLL	12 LAUGHED	7 LIEUTENANT
2 JOKING	3 KNOT	9 LAUGHING	164 LIFE
1 JOKINGLY	1 KNOTS	4 LAUGHTER	1 LIFE-BOATS
1 JOLLIFICATION	1 KNOTTY	1 LAUNCH	1 LIFE-BUOY
1 JOLLITY	257 KNOW	1 LAUNCHED	2 LIFE'S
11 JOLLY	10 KNOWING	1 LAUT	5 LIFELESS
12 JONES	5 KNOWINGLY	10 LAW	1 LIFETIME
5 JONGH	22 KNOWLEDGE	1 LAWLESS	6 LIFT
2 JONGH'S	37 KNOWN	1 LAWS	1 LIFT'
2 JOSTLED	26 KNOWS	35 LAY	22 LIFTED
2 JOSTLING	3 KNUCKLES	4 LAYING	12 LIFTING
10 JOURNEY	1 KONG	2 LAZILY	97 LIGHT
3 JOURNEYS	1 KORAN	1 LE	1 LIGHT-HEADED
34 JOVE	1 KOSMOS	12 LEAD	1 LIGHT-HEARTED
2 JOVIAL	4 KRING	4 LEADER	9 LIGHTED
4 JOY	1 KRIS	7 LEADING	3 LIGHTHOUSE
1 JOYED	4 KRISS	5 LEAP	1 LIGHTHOUSE-KEEPER
1 JOYOUS	1 KRISS'	1 LEAK	1 LIGHTING
2 JU	1 KRISSES	7 LEAN	11 LIGHTLY
1 JU-JU-ST	1 L'	13 LEANED	2 LIGHTNESS
1 JUBILATING	1 L'EAU	12 LEANING	4 LIGHTNING
6 JUDGE	1 L'HOMME	10 LEAP	17 LIGHTS
6 JUDGED	1 L'OEIL	14 LEAPED	431 LIKE
1 JUDGING	1 LABELLED	3 LEAPING	11 LIKED
1 JUDICIALLY	1 LABORIOUS	1 LEAPS	1 LIKELIHOOD
1 JUDICIOUS	1 LABOUR	2 LEARN	12 LIKELY
1 JUDY	3 LABOURING	13 LEARNED	1 LIKES
3 JUMBLED	2 LACE	1 LEARNEDLY	1 LIKEWISE
22 JUMP	2 LACED	33 LEAST	2 LIKING
31 JUMPED	1 LACHEZ	3 LEATHER	3 LIMB
3 JUMPING	1 LACHRYMOSE	2 LEATHERY	1 LIMBED
1 JUMPING-OFF	1 LACKADAISICAL	41 LEAVE	5 LIMBS
3 JUMPS	1 LACKED	1 LEAVE-TAKINGS	1 LIMIT
8 JUNGLE	1 LAD	1 LEAVED	1 LIMITS
111 JUST	7 LADDER	7 LEAVES	27 LINE
1 JUSTE	1 LADDERS	19 LEAVING	4 LINED
3 JUSTICE	1 LADY	1 LECTED	2 LINEN
3 JUSTIFIED	1 LADY'S	2 LECTURE	4 LINES
1 KALASHEE	1 LADY'S-MAID	14 LED	1 LING
1 KALEIDOSCOPE	13 LAID	1 LEDGE	1 LINGER
2 KANAKAS	3 LAME	3 LEERED	1 LINGERED

2 LINGERING	1 LOOSENED	1 MAILBOAT	1 MARVEL
2 LINK	1 LOOSENS	1 MAIMING	3 MARVELLED
1 LINKS	3 LOOT	5 MAIN	3 MARVELLOUS
1 LION	1 LOQUACIOUS	1 MAIN-BOOM	2 MASK
7 LIP	14 LORD	3 MAINLY	8 MASS
1 LIPPED	3 LORD'S	1 MAINMAST	1 MASSACRE
44 LIPS	8 LOSE	3 MAINSAIL	4 MASSES
2 LIQUEUR	1 LOSER	2 MAINTAINED	5 MASSIVE
1 LIQUEUR-GLASS	7 LOSING	1 MAIZE	1 MASSIVELY
1 LIQUEUR-GLASSES	5 LOSS	1 MAIZE-PATCH	3 MAST
2 LIQUID	3 LOSSES	1 MAJESTICALLY	38 MASTER
1 LIQUIDATED	42 LOST	1 MAJESTY'S	5 MASTER'S
2 LIQUOR	28 LOT	4 MAJORITY	5 MASTERED
1 LIQUORS	1 LOTH	133 MAKE	1 MASTERING
10 LISTEN	4 LOTS	1 MAKER	3 MASTERPIECE
16 LISTENED	16 LOUD	12 MAKES	2 MASTERS
1 LISTENER	3 LOUDER	34 MAKING	4 MASTHEAD
3 LISTENERS	2 LOUDLY	4 MALABAR	1 MASTICATING
12 LISTENING	2 LOUNGE	3 MALACCA	1 MASTIFFS
5 LIT	2 LOUNGED	1 MALAITA	3 MASTS
2 LITERALLY	35 LOVE	11 MALAY	7 MAT
2 LITERATURE	1 LOVE'	7 MALAYS	6 MATCH
1 LITHOGRAPH	13 LOVED	1 MALE	1 MATCHED
4 LITTER	2 LOVELY	1 MALEDICTION	1 MATCHES'
233 LITTLE	2 LOVER	5 MALEVOLENT	21 MATE
29 LIVE	1 LOVERS	2 MALICE	7 MATERIAL
19 LIVED	56 LOW	3 MALICIOUS	2 MATERIALS
3 LIVELY	10 LOWER	1 MALIGNANT	2 MATHERSON
2 LIVER	8 LOWERED	355 MAN	1 MATRIMONIAL
1 LIVERPOOL	3 LOWERING	1 MAN-BEAST	12 MATS
1 LIVERY	1 LOWLANDS	1 MAN-OF-WAR	2 MATTED
30 LIVES	2 LUCID	1 MAN-OFWAR	52 MATTER
2 LIVID	25 LUCK	1 MAN'	1 MATTER-OF-FACT
26 LIVING	1 LUCKILY	17 MAN'S	3 MATTERED
4 LOAD	5 LUCKY	7 MANAGE	7 MATTERS
7 LOADED	2 LUGGAGE	1 MANAGEABLE	1 MATTRESS
1 LOADERS	1 LUGUBRIOUS	17 MANAGED	3 MATURE
2 LOADING	3 LUMINOUS	1 MANAGEMENT	3 MATURED
4 LOAFER	5 LUMP	4 MANAGER	1 MATURING
1 LOAFING	1 LUMPILY	1 MANE	1 MAUL
3 LOAN	3 LUMPS	1 MANFULLY	1 MAXIMUM
1 LOATHED	4 LUNATIC	2 MANGY	82 MAY
2 LOATHSOME	3 LUNGS	1 MANIAC	7 MAYBE
1 LOATHSOMENESS	2 LURCH	1 MANIACAL	2 MAZE
1 LOCAL	1 LURCHED	1 MANIFEST	1 MAZES
1 LOCALITIES	1 LURED	1 MANIFESTATION	769 ME
2 LOCALITY	3 LURID	2 MANIFESTATIONS	2 MEAGRE
1 LOCATE	1 LURKED	1 MANILA	2 MEAL
4 LOCK	3 LURKS	1 MANILLA	1 MEAL-TIMES
3 LOCKED	1 LUST	18 MANKIND	2 MEALS
3 LOCKS	1 LUSTRE	1 MANKIND'S	47 MEAN
1 LODGED	2 LUSTRELESS	2 MANLY	15 MEANING
1 LODGING	1 LUSTROUS	5 MANNED	1 MEANINGS
1 LODGMENT	1 LUSTY	28 MANNER	1 MEANNESS
1 LOF'	2 LUXURIATING	1 MANNERISMS	19 MEANS
8 LOFTY	24 LYING	1 MANNERS	23 MEANT
12 LOG	2 M	1 MANOEUVRE	14 MEANTIME
1 LOGGED	3 M'	1 MANSIONS	1 MEANWHILE
4 LOGIC	2 MA	1 MANTELPIECE	1 MEASLY
3 LOGS	1 MACASSAR	1 MANTLING	3 MEASURE
1 LOINS	2 MACHINE	103 MANY	4 MEASURED
2 LOLLING	1 MACHINERY	1 MANY-SIDED	2 MEASURES
1 LONDON	1 MACHINES	4 MARBLE	3 MEAT
2 LONE	23 MAD	1 MARBLE-FACED	1 MECHANICALLY
7 LONELINESS	3 MADAGASCAR	2 MARCH	1 MECHANISM
14 LONELY	2 MADDENED	2 MARCHED	1 MEDDLE
142 LONG	272 MADE	1 MARCHES	2 MEDICAL
8 LONG-BOAT	3 MADLY	3 MARCHING	1 MEDICAL-LOOKING
1 LONG-DRAWN	1 MADMAN	3 MARIANI	1 MEDICALLY
1 LONG-LEGGED	6 MADNESS	2 MARIANI'S	1 MEDICINE
1 LONG-STEMMED	1 MAGAZINE	1 MARIN	1 MEDIEVAL
4 LONGED	3 MAGIC	4 MARINE	1 MEDITATE
16 LONGER	1 MAGICIAN	1 MARINS	3 MEDITATED
1 LONGEST	1 MAGICIAN'S	3 MARITAL	1 MEDITATING
1 LONGICORNS	1 MAGICIANS	1 MARITIME	4 MEDITATION
1 LONGING	10 MAGISTRATE	5 MARK	1 MEDITATIONS
1 LONGINGS	2 MAGISTRATE'S	7 MARKED	2 MEDITATIVE
1 LONGISH	1 MAGNA	2 MARKEDLY	1 MEEK
120 LOOK	2 MAGNANIMOUS	2 MARKET	1 MEEKLY
2 LOOK-OUT	2 MAGNIFICENCE	2 MARKET-PLACE	1 MEERACLE
117 LOOKED	7 MAGNIFICENT	1 MARKINGS	15 MEET
82 LOOKING	1 MAGNIFIED	26 MARLOW	5 MEETING
16 LOOKS	3 MAGNITUDE	5 MARLOW'S	1 MEETINGS
2 LOOM	2 MAHOGANY	2 MARRIAGE	3 MEIN
7 LOOMED	1 MAID	4 MARRIED	1 MEINEN
1 LOOMS	1 MAIDEN	1 MARROW	2 MELANCHOLY
1 LOOPED	1 MAIDS	1 MARRY	2 MELANESIA
1 LOOPHOLE	3 MAIL	1 MARSH	1 MELLIFLUOUS
17 LOOSE	1 MAIL-BOAT	1 MARSHY	1 MELLOWED
2 LOOSE-JOINTED	1 MAIL-BOATS	1 MARTIAL	1 MELT

2 MELTED
2 MELTS
1 MEMBER
1 MEMORABLE
7 MEMORIES
18 MEMORY
221 MEN
1 MEN-OF-WAR
1 MEN'
12 MEN'S
5 MENACE
2 MENACING
2 MENACINGLY
1 MENAGEMENTS
1 MENAM
2 MENDING
1 MENT
3 MENTAL
4 MENTION
5 MENTIONED
1 MENTIONING
1 MENTIONS
2 MERCANTILE
7 MERCHANT
1 MERCHANT-SHIPS
2 MERCHANTS
3 MERCI
1 MERCIES
3 MERCIFUL
1 MERCILESS
1 MERCILESSLY
4 MERCY
14 MERE
8 MERELY
1 MEREST
1 MERGED
1 MERIDIAN
2 MERIT
1 MERITED
1 MERITORIOUS
2 MERITS
1 MERRIMENT
1 MERRY
1 MESH
1 MESS
7 MESSAGE
1 MESSAGES
2 MESSENGER
1 MESSENGER'S
3 MESSENGERS
21 MET
1 METAL
1 METALLIC
1 METAPHOR
1 METAPHORICALLY
1 METER
1 METHOD
1 METHODICAL
1 METICULOUS
1 METIER
1 MICE
1 MID
1 MID-AIR
1 MIDDAY
24 MIDDLE
2 MIDDLE-AGED
3 MIDNIGHT
15 MIDST
1 MIDSTREAM
2 MIEN
70 MIGHT
1 MIGHTIER
9 MIGHTY
1 MIGRATING
3 MILD
2 MILDEST
1 MILDLY
3 MILE
27 MILES
1 MILES'
1 MILITARY
1 MILK
3 MILL
1 MILLION
4 MILLIONS
81 MIND
1 MINDANAO
3 MINDED
11 MINDS
25 MINE

8 MINGLED
1 MINIATURE
1 MINIMISE
1 MINIMISED
1 MINIMUM
2 MINISTERED
1 MINOR
15 MINUTE
17 MINUTES
4 MIRACLE
2 MIRACULOUS
2 MIRROR
1 MIRRORS
1 MIRTHLESS
1 MISANTHROPIC
1 MISAPPREHEND
1 MISBEGOTTEN
1 MISCHIEF
2 MISDEEDS
15 MISERABLE
1 MISERIES
4 MISFORTUNE
2 MISFORTUNES
1 MISHAP
2 MISLEADING
3 MISS
6 MISSED
1 MISSED'
1 MISSILE
8 MISSING
4 MISSION
1 MISSION-HOUSE
1 MISSIONARIES
1 MISSIONARY
19 MIST
19 MISTAKE
2 MISTAKEN
6 MISTER
4 MISTRUST
3 MISTRUSTED
3 MISTRUSTFUL
1 MISTRUSTFULLY
1 MISTRUSTS
3 MISTS
3 MISTY
1 MISUNDERSTANDING
4 MIXED
2 MIXTURE
1 MIZZEN
1 MIZZEN-MAST
1 MOAN
2 MOANED
4 MOANING
2 MOANS
3 MOB
2 MOCKING
2 MODE
2 MODERATE
1 MODEST
1 MODESTLY
7 MOHAMMED
1 MOHAMMED'S
1 MOLUCCAS'
91 MOMENT
2 MOMENT'S
1 MOMENTARILY
3 MOMENTARY
2 MOMENTOUS
14 MOMENTS
1 MON
1 MONDE
27 MONEY
1 MONEY-LENDER
1 MONGERING
1 MONGRELS
1 MONKEYS
1 MONOPOLY
1 MONOSYLLABLE
2 MONOTONE
1 MONOTONOUS
1 MONOTONY
4 MONSIEUR
1 MONSIEUR'
1 MONSOON
2 MONSTER
1 MONSTERS
3 MONSTROUS
1 MONTAGUE
9 MONTH
8 MONTHS

2 MONTHS'
2 MONUMENTAL
3 MOOD
4 MOODILY
2 MOODY
11 MOON
1 MOONBEAMS
3 MOONLIGHT
1 MOOR
1 MOORED
1 MOORINGS
1 MOP
1 MOPPING
5 MORAL
7 MORALITY
267 MORE
6 MOREOVER
1 MORIBUND
43 MORNING
1 MORNINGS
2 MOROSE
14 MORROW
1 MORT
3 MORTAL
1 MORTALITY
1 MORTIFICATION
1 MORTIS
1 MOSLEMS
2 MOSQUE
2 MOSQUITO
2 MOSQUITO-NET
1 MOSSY
71 MOST
7 MOSTLY
1 MOTE
18 MOTHER
2 MOTHER'S
4 MOTHERLY
4 MOTION
1 MOTIONED
18 MOTIONLESS
2 MOTIONS
3 MOTIVE
1 MOTIVES
1 MOTTO
4 MOUND
4 MOUNTAIN
3 MOUNTAINS
5 MOUNTED
1 MOUNTING
1 MOURNED
4 MOURNFUL
2 MOURNFULLY
2 MOURNING
6 MOUSTACHE
4 MOUSTACHES
27 MOUTH
1 MOUTHFUL
1 MOUTHPIECE
2 MOUTHS
18 MOVE
31 MOVED
25 MOVEMENT
13 MOVEMENTS
1 MOVES
19 MOVING
29 MR
147 MUCH
1 MUCH-DISAPPOINTED
1 MUCHED
16 MUD
1 MUD-FLAT
1 MUD-HOLE
1 MUD-STAINS
1 MUDBANK
2 MUDDLE
6 MUDDY
11 MUFFLED
1 MUGS
1 MULATTO
1 MULISH
8 MULTITUDE
2 MULTITUDES
1 MULTITUDINOUS
5 MUMBLE
15 MUMBLED
3 MUMBLING
1 MUR
1 MUR-
3 MURDER

1 MURDERED
1 MURDERERS
1 MURDERING
19 MURMUR
22 MURMURED
3 MURMURING
4 MURMURS
1 MURS
1 MUSCLE
1 MUSCLES
3 MUSED
1 MUSING
3 MUSKETS
1 MUSLIMS
114 MUST
1 MUSTARD
1 MUSTARD-SEED
1 MUSTER
1 MUSTERED
2 MUSTN'T
9 MUTE
3 MUTELY
1 MUTINIES
1 MUTINY
6 MUTTER
19 MUTTERED
6 MUTTERING
3 MUTTERS
1 MUTUAL
3 MUZZLE
670 MY
99 MYSELF
1 MYSTERIES
27 MYSTERIOUS
5 MYSTERIOUSLY
18 MYSTERY
1 MYSTIC
1 MYTH
1 N
4 NA
1 NAB
1 NAIL
1 NAILED
2 NAIVE
2 NAIVENESS
19 NAKED
3 NAKHODA
44 NAME
2 NAME'S
1 NAMELESS
1 NAMELY
12 NAMES
2 NAPE
4 NARRATED
1 NARRATING
5 NARRATIVE
11 NARROW
2 NARROWLY
3 NASTY
1 NATION
1 NATIONS
24 NATIVE
1 NATIVE-RULED
8 NATIVES
1 NATUR'
15 NATURAL
3 NATURALIST
1 NATURALISTS
9 NATURALLY
28 NATURE
1 NATURED
1 NATURELLEMENT
1 NATURES
1 NAUGHTY
1 NAUSEOUS
3 NAUTICAL
1 NAVAL
1 NAVIGABLE
1 NAVIGATED
2 NAVIGATION
3 NAVY
2 NAY
2 NAZARENE
2 NE
25 NEAR
9 NEARER
5 NEAREST
24 NEARLY
3 NEAT
1 NEATLY

1 NEATNESS	6 NOSTRILS	2 OCEANS	1 ORIENTALLY
1 NECESSARILY	694 NOT	1 OCTAGON	2 ORIENTATION
7 NECESSARY	12 NOTE	1 ODD	1 ORIFICE
12 NECESSITY	1 NOTE'	4 ODIOUS	4 ORIGIN
14 NECK	3 NOTED	1 ODIOUSLY	2 ORIGINAL
1 NECKS	1 NOTEPAPER	1 ODOUR	2 ORIGINALLY
10 NEED	1 NOTEZ	4514 OF	1 ORISONS
2 NEEDED	182 NOTHING	147 OFF	1 ORNAMENTAL
2 NEEDN'T	10 NOTICE	3 OFF-HAND	4 OSSA
1 NEGATIVELY	1 NOTICEABLE	1 OFF-SHORE	1 OSTENTATION
1 NEGLECT	12 NOTICED	1 OFF-SIDE	1 OSTENTATIOUSLY
2 NEGLECTED	19 NOTION	3 OFFENCE	183 OTHER
2 NEGLIGENTLY	3 NOTIONS	4 OFFENSIVE	7 OTHER'S
1 NEGLIGIBLE	6 NOTORIOUS	9 OFFER	44 OTHERS
1 NEGOTIATING	5 NOTWITHSTANDING	5 OFFERED	9 OTHERWISE
1 NEGOTIATION	142 NOW	5 OFFERING	3 OUGH
2 NEGOTIATIONS	1 NOW'	1 OFFERTORIES'	17 OUGHT
2 NEIGHBOURHOOD	1 NOW'S	13 OFFICE	129 OUR
2 NEIGHBOURING	1 NOWADAYS	5 OFFICER	2 OURS
1 NEIGHBOURS'	2 NOWHERE	10 OFFICERS	3 OURSELVES
3 NEIL	1 NUDITY	1 OFFICES	1 OUSTED
25 NEITHER	2 NUISANCE	12 OFFICIAL	478 OUT
1 NELYUS	1 NUKA	1 OFFICIOUS	1 OUT-
1 NENN'	1 NUKA-	3 OFFING	1 OUT-BARK
2 NERVE	5 NUMBER	19 OFTEN	1 OUT-OF-THE-WAY
1 NERVE-SHAKING	1 NUMBERS	1 OFWAR	1 OUTBREAK
2 NERVES	1 NUMBNESS	49 OH	3 OUTBREAKS
3 NERVOUS	1 NUMEROUS	1 OHO	3 OUTBURST
2 NERVOUSLY	1 NURSE	2 OIL	1 OUTCAST
3 NEST	1 NURSED	1 OIL-FEEDER	2 OUTCASTS
1 NESTLED	5 NURSING	185 OLD	1 OUTCOME
1 NESTS	2 NUT	1 OLIVE	1 OUTCRY
2 NET	1 NUT-BROWN	1 OMEN	4 OUTER
1 NETWORK	7 O	1 OMNIPOTENCE	1 OUTERMOST
1 NEUTRALITY	5 O'	1024 ON	2 OUTLINE
162 NEVER	5 O'CLOCK	113 ONCE	2 OUTLINED
7 NEVERTHELESS	6 OAR	413 ONE	8 OUTLINES
33 NEW	1 OAR-BLADES	1 ONE-DEGREE	2 OUTLYING
1 NEWCOMER	1 OAR'S	1 ONE-LEGGED	1 OUTRAGE
1 NEWCOMERS	8 OARS	1 ONE-THIRD	1 OUTRAGED
1 NEWLY	1 OARS'	14 ONE'S	1 OUTRAGEOUSLY
17 NEWS	1 OB	1 ONES	30 OUTSIDE
34 NEXT	1 OB-	1 ONESELF	5 OUTSKIRTS
5 NICE	3 OBEDIENCE	1 ONLOOKERS	1 OUTSPOKEN
1 NICEST	3 OBEDIENT	235 ONLY	3 OUTSPREAD
1 NICHT	1 OBEDIENTLY	1 ONLY'	2 OUTSTRETCHED
1 NICKEL	1 OBESE	1 ONNATURAL	3 OUTWARD
3 NIGGERS	1 OBEY	1 ONWARD	1 OUTWARD-BOUND
112 NIGHT	3 OBEYED	1 OPAL	1 OUTWARDBOUND
1 NIGHT-GLASSES	15 OBJECT	2 OPAQUE	3 OUTWARDLY
1 NIGHT-WATCHES	1 OBJECTS	66 OPEN	1 OUTWARDS
4 NIGHTS	1 OBLIGATION	1 OPEN-EYED	1 OUVRIR
1 NIMBLER	1 OBLIGATORY	23 OPENED	3 OVAL
3 NINE	2 OBLIGING	14 OPENING	239 OVER
1 NINETY	1 OBLIQUE	3 OPENLY	1 OVER-
1 NIP	1 OBLIQUELY	1 OPERATIONS	1 OVER-EXERTION
1 NIPPERS	1 OBLITERATING	2 OPINED	1 OVER-JOYED
477 NO	1 OBLIVION	27 OPINION	1 OVERAWED
1 NO-ACCOUNT	2 OBLONG	1 OPINIONS	1 OVERBEARING
1 NO'	1 OBSCENE	3 OPIUM	14 OVERBOARD
7 NOBLE	11 OBSCURE	5 OPPORTUNITIES	1 OVERBURDENED
1 NOBLE-LOOKING	2 OBSCURELY	16 OPPORTUNITY	1 OVERCAST
1 NOBODIES	4 OBSCURITY	1 OPPOSE	5 OVERCOME
32 NOBODY	1 OBSEQUIOUS	1 OPPOSED	1 OVERCOMING
2 NOD	2 OBSERVE	7 OPPOSITE	1 OVERFLOWED
11 NODDED	8 OBSERVED	1 OPPOSITION	1 OVERGROWN
3 NODDING	1 OBSERVER	3 OPPRESSED	1 OVERHANGING
33 NOISE	1 OBSERVING	1 OPPRESSION	2 OVERHEAD
2 NOISELESS	3 OBSTACLE	2 OPPRESSIVE	1 OVERNIGHT
3 NOISELESSLY	3 OBSTINACY	1 OPTICAL	1 OVERPOWERED
2 NOISES	1 OBSTINATE	2 OPTION	2 OVERSHADOWED
2 NOISILY	1 OBSTINATELY	1 OPULENT	1 OVERSPREAD
1 NOISOME	6 OBTAIN	275 OR	1 OVERT
2 NOISY	4 OBTAINED	2 ORANGE	1 OVERTAKE
1 NOMADIC	1 OBTRUDES	1 ORB	2 OVERTAKEN
1 NONCHALANTLY	1 OBTUSENESS	1 ORBITS	1 OVERTHROW
2 NONDESCRIPT	6 OBVIOUS	2 ORCHARD	1 OVERTOPPED
7 NONE	3 OBVIOUSLY	1 ORDAINED	1 OVERTOPPING
1 NONPLUSSED	12 OCCASION	1 ORDEAL	1 OVERTURES
6 NONSENSE	2 OCCASIONS	16 ORDER	1 OVERTURNED
3 NOON	3 OCCULT	1 ORDER'	1 OVERTURNING
25 NOR	4 OCCUPATION	10 ORDERED	1 OVERVALUED
1 NORMAL	4 OCCUPIED	2 ORDERING	4 OVERWHELMED
10 NORTH	1 OCCUPY	2 ORDERLY	6 OVERWHELMING
1 NORTH-EAST	1 OCCUPYING	12 ORDERS	1 OVERWROUGHT
1 NORTH-WEST	1 OCCUR	2 ORDINARY	4 OW
2 NORTHWARD	8 OCCURRED	1 ORDNANCE	2 OWE
1 NORWEGIAN	3 OCCURRENCE	2 ORGANISED	5 OWED
11 NOSE	1 OCCURRING	1 ORGE	1 OWING
1 NOSE-NIPPERS	14 OCEAN	3 ORIENTAL	1 OWLS

130 OWN
7 OWNED
2 OWNER
1 OWNER'S
1 OWNERS
1 OWNING
2 OX
7 PACE
2 PACED
9 PACIFIC
1 PACIFIED
1 PACIFY
1 PACING
3 PACK
1 PACK-ANIMALS
1 PACKAGES
3 PACKED
3 PACKET
2 PAD
6 PADDLE
3 PADDLED
1 PADDLER
2 PADDLERS
2 PADDLES
2 PADDLING
2 PAGE
1 PAGEANT
4 PAGES
1 PAH
6 PAID
21 PAIN
2 PAINFUL
1 PAINFULLY
1 PAINS
2 PAINTED
1 PAINTER
13 PAIR
1 PAIRFECT
2 PAIRS
2 PALACE
1 PALAVER
1 PALAVERING
15 PALE
1 PALE-FACED
1 PALED
2 PALISADE
1 PALLIATE
1 PALLOR
6 PALM
7 PALMS
1 PALPABLE
1 PALPITATING
2 PANAMA
1 PANE
3 PANES
1 PANG
1 PANGERANS
2 PANGLIMA
1 PANGS
10 PANIC
2 PANIC-STRICKEN
1 PANICS
1 PANTALOON
1 PANTED
5 PANTING
1 PANTRY
1 PANTS
18 PAPER
3 PAPERS
2 PAR
1 PARADED
1 PARADISE
1 PARALLEL
2 PARALYSED
1 PARAPET
3 PARBLEU
1 PARCELS
3 PARCHED
1 PARCHMENT
2 PARDON
1 PARENTAGE
1 PARENTAL
3 PARLOUR
1 PARLOUR'
1 PARODY
3 PARSEE
3 PARSON
2 PARSONAGE
56 PART
7 PARTED

2 PARTICLE
5 PARTICULAR
2 PARTICULARLY
9 PARTIES
1 PARTIES'
5 PARTING
2 PARTISAN
5 PARTLY
8 PARTNER
1 PARTNERS
5 PARTS
12 PARTY
1 PAS
14 PASS
19 PASSAGE
1 PASSAGES
42 PASSED
1 PASSENGER
2 PASSENGERS
1 PASSERS
1 PASSERS-BY
3 PASSES
15 PASSING
8 PASSION
5 PASSIONATE
1 PASSIONATELY
1 PASSIONLESS
3 PASSIONS
4 PASSIVE
3 PASSIVELY
1 PASSIVENESS
20 PAST
3 PATCH
5 PATCHES
3 PATENT
1 PATERNAL
1 PATERNITY
14 PATH
3 PATHETIC
1 PATHETICALLY
1 PATHOS
5 PATHS
3 PATIENCE
7 PATIENT
5 PATIENTLY
1 PATIENTS
33 PATNA
1 PATNA'S
1 PATRIARCH
1 PATRIARCHAL
1 PATRIES
1 PATRIOTIC
1 PATROL
1 PATROLLING
1 PATS
2 PATT
2 PATT-NA
1 PATTED
1 PATTERED
1 PATTERN
78 PATUSAN
1 PAUNCHY
10 PAUSE
14 PAUSED
1 PAUSES
1 PAUSING
1 PAVED
1 PAWS
5 PAY
2 PAYING
1 PEA
20 PEACE
6 PEACEFUL
1 PEACEFULLY
1 PEACETIME
1 PEAK
2 PEAKS
1 PEAL
1 PEARLER
1 PEARLY
1 PEASANT
1 PEASE
1 PECKER
1 PECULATING
1 PECULATION
8 PECULIAR
1 PEDESTAL
1 PEDIMENT
1 PEEL
1 PEEP

1 PEEPED
3 PEERED
5 PEERING
1 PEEVISHNESS
2 PEG
1 PEGGED
2 PELION
2 PELLUCID
1 PELTED
1 PELTING
8 PEN
1 PENALTIES
1 PENALTY
1 PENANG
4 PENCIL
1 PENCIL-LINE
1 PENDENT
3 PENETRATED
4 PENETRATING
3 PENNY
1 PENNYWORTH
1 PENSION
3 PENSIVE
1 PENSIVELY
1 PENT
1 PENT-UP
2 PEONS
112 PEOPLE
2 PEOPLE'
2 PEOPLE'S
2 PEOPLED
2 PEOPLING
1 PEPERS
7 PEPPER
1 PEPPER-AND-SALT
3 PER
2 PER-
7 PERCEIVE
13 PERCEIVED
2 PERCEIVING
1 PERCEPTIBLE
3 PERCEPTION
1 PERCH
2 PERCHANCE
4 PERCHED
1 PERCUSSION
3 PERDITION
14 PERFECT
1 PERFECTION
1 PERFECTIONS
17 PERFECTLY
1 PERFIDIOUS
1 PERFORATED
4 PERFORMANCE
2 PERFORMED
1 PERFORMING
1 PERFUMED
1 PERFUMES
1 PERFUNCTORILY
1 PERFUNCTORY
85 PERHAPS
1 PERIL
1 PERILS
1 PERIM
3 PERIOD
1 PERIODICALLY
3 PERISH
2 PERISHABLE
3 PERMANENT
1 PERMANENTLY
1 PERMEATED
2 PERMISSION
1 PERMIT
2 PERPENDICULAR
2 PERPENDICULARLY
1 PERPETUAL
4 PERPETUALLY
2 PERPLEXED
1 PERPLEXITIES
1 PERQUISITES
1 PERSEVERANCE
1 PERSIAN
2 PERSISTED
2 PERSISTENCE
3 PERSISTENT
2 PERSISTENTLY
20 PERSON
9 PERSONAL
4 PERSONALITY
1 PERSONALLY

6 PERSONS
1 PERSPECTIVE
2 PERSPIRATION
1 PERSPIRED
1 PERSPIRING
2 PERSUADED
1 PERSUASIVE
2 PERTINACITY
2 PERTURBATION
2 PERVADED
1 PERVADING
1 PERVERSE
1 PERVERSIONS
2 PESTILENCE
1 PETRIFIED
1 PETTY
1 PETUALLY
1 PEUT
1 PHANTASMAL
3 PHANTOM
1 PHANTOMS
1 PHENOMENAL
1 PHENOMENON
1 PHILIPPINES
1 PHILOSOPHIC
1 PHILOSOPHY
1 PHILTRE
1 PHONG
2 PHOO
4 PHRASE
2 PHRASEOLOGY
1 PHYSICAL
1 PHYSICALLY
1 PHYSIQUE
3 PICK
11 PICKED
1 PICKER
4 PICKING
1 PICKINGS
6 PICTURE
2 PICTURESQUE
1 PICTURING
12 PIECE
1 PIECEMEAL
3 PIECES
1 PIER
1 PIER-HEADS
1 PIERCE
3 PIERCED
1 PIERCING
1 PIERRE
3 PIETY
1 PIG
1 PIGTAIL
2 PILE
1 PILED
3 PILES
3 PILGRIM
2 PILGRIMAGE
7 PILGRIMS
1 PILL
1 PILLAR
1 PILLARS
3 PILLOW
1 PILLOWS
3 PILOT
1 PILOTING
4 PIN
1 PIN-POINT
1 PINCH
1 PINCHES
1 PINE
7 PINK
2 PINNED
5 PINS
5 PIOUS
12 PIPE
1 PIPE-CLAYED
1 PIPED
1 PIRATE
2 PISTOL
1 PISTOL-SHOT
3 PISTOLS
4 PIT
4 PITCH
2 PITCH-DARK
1 PITCH-PINE
3 PITCHED
1 PITCHER
1 PITCHING

170

1 PITCHY	2 POINT-BLANK	2 POUTED	1 PRIMEVAL
3 PITEOUS	14 POINTED	1 POVERTY	1 PRIMITIVE
2 PITFALLS	1 POINTEDLY	4 POWDER	1 PRINCE
3 PITH	10 POINTING	1 POWDER-MAGAZINE	3 PRINCESS
1 PITIED	1 POINTS	41 POWER	11 PRINCIPAL
10 PITIFUL	1 POISED	7 POWERFUL	1 PRINCIPALLY
3 PITILESS	4 POISON	2 POWERFULLY	1 PRINCIPLE
1 PITILESSLY	2 POISONED	1 POWERLESS	2 PRINCIPLES
1 PITTED	3 POKED	7 POWERS	2 PRISON
11 PITY	1 POLE	9 PRACTICAL	3 PRISONER
1 PITYING	2 POLES	5 PRACTICALLY	1 PRIVACY
1 PIVOT	5 POLICE	1 PRACTICE	2 PRIVATE
1 PIVOTED	1 POLICEMAN	1 PRANCE	2 PRIVATIONS
1 PLACATED	2 POLICY	1 PRAU	3 PRIVILEGE
74 PLACE	4 POLISHED	1 PRAUS	4 PRIVILEGED
2 PLACED	2 POLITE	3 PRAY	1 PRIZE
11 PLACES	1 POLITELY	2 PRAYED	1 PRO
6 PLACID	1 POLITENESS	5 PRAYER	1 PRO-
2 PLACIDITY	1 POLTRON	1 PRAYER-CARPETS	2 PROBABILITY
2 PLACIDLY	1 POLYNESIA	1 PRAYERS	2 PROBABLE
2 PLAGUE	1 POMPOUS	1 PREACHING	17 PROBABLY
1 PLAGUE-STRICKEN	1 PON	1 PRECARIOUS	1 PROBATION
14 PLAIN	2 POND	2 PRECARIOUSLY	1 PROBE
4 PLAINLY	4 PONDEROUS	2 PRECAUTION	1 PROCEED
2 PLAINS	2 PONDEROUSLY	1 PRECAUTIONS	1 PROCEEDED
3 PLAINT	6 PONY	2 PRECEDED	3 PROCEEDING
1 PLAINTIFF	4 POOL	1 PRECEDENT	7 PROCEEDINGS
1 PLAINTIVE	2 POOP	1 PRECEDES	3 PROCESS
1 PLAINTS	57 POOR	2 PRECEDING	2 PROCLAIMED
1 PLAITED	1 POORER	10 PRECIOUS	1 PROCLAIMING
9 PLAN	1 POP	2 PRECIPICE	2 PROCURE
1 PLANE	1 POPINJAY	1 PRECISE	1 PROD
1 PLANES	2 POPULAR	3 PRECISE	1 PRODIGIOUSLY
1 PLANET	6 POPULATION	5 PRECISELY	7 PRODUCE
1 PLANETS	1 POPULATIONS	1 PRECISION	5 PRODUCED
1 PLANK	1 POPULOUS	1 PREDESTINED	1 PRODUCES
1 PLANKING	1 PORK	1 PREDICAMENT	2 PRODUCING
2 PLANKS	15 PORT	1 PREFERRED	3 PROFESSED
2 PLANNED	1 PORT-SIDE	1 PREGNANT	5 PROFESSIONAL
2 PLANS	1 PORTAL	1 PRELIMINARY	1 PROFESSIONALLY
2 PLANT	2 PORTENT	1 PREMATURELY	1 PROFESSOR
1 PLANTATION	1 PORTICO	1 PREPARATION	2 PROFIT
4 PLANTED	1 PORTION	4 PREPARATIONS	2 PROFITABLE
1 PLANTERS	1 PORTLY	1 PREPARATORY	30 PROFOUND
1 PLANTS	1 PORTMANTEAUX	1 PREPARE	6 PROFOUNDLY
1 PLASTER	1 PORTRAYING	3 PREPARED	1 PROFUNDITY
6 PLATE	1 PORTS	6 PREPARING	8 PROGRESS
3 PLATES	1 PORTUGUEE	1 PRESCIENCE	1 PROJECTED
3 PLATFORMS	5 PORTUGUESE	11 PRESENCE	1 PROJECTING
2 PLAUSIBLE	2 POSE	11 PRESENT	4 PROLONGED
5 PLAY	33 POSITION	1 PRESENT'	1 PROMINENT
7 PLAYED	3 POSITIVE	11 PRESENTED	12 PROMISE
1 PLAYFUL	5 POSITIVELY	1 PRESENTING	3 PROMISED
4 PLAYING	1 POSSESS	6 PRESENTLY	2 PROMISING
2 PLAYS	13 POSSESSED	1 PRESENTS	1 PROMOTED
2 PLEADED	1 POSSESSES	4 PRESERVE	1 PROMOTION
2 PLEADING	1 POSSESSING	7 PRESERVED	1 PROMPTED
3 PLEASANT	8 POSSESSION	1 PRESERVES	1 PROMPTINGS
1 PLEASANTLY	1 POSSESSOR	1 PRESERVING	1 PROMPTLY
7 PLEASE	3 POSSIBILITIES	1 PRESIDED	2 PRONE
11 PLEASED	2 POSSIBILITY	1 PRESIDING	3 PRONOUNCE
1 PLEASURABLE	22 POSSIBLE	1 PRESS	17 PRONOUNCED
1 PLEASURABLY	1 POSSIBLE'	8 PRESSED	2 PRONOUNCEMENT
7 PLEASURE	6 POSSIBLY	8 PRESSING	3 PRONOUNCING
1 PLEASURES	3 POST	1 PRESSURE	2 PROOF
6 PLENTY	1 POSTED	1 PRESTIGE	1 PROOFS
1 PLIABLE	1 POSTER	2 PRETENCE	1 PROPAGATED
1 PLODDING	2 POSTHUMOUS	2 PRETENCES	2 PROPELLER
1 PLOP	6 POSTS	5 PRETEND	15 PROPER
2 PLOT	4 POSTURE	5 PRETENDED	2 PROPERLY
4 PLOTS	5 POT	1 PRETENDERS	1 PROPERTIES
1 PLOTTING	1 POT-BELLIED	2 PRETENDING	5 PROPERTY
8 PLUCK	1 POT-HOUSE	24 PRETTY	1 PROPHESIED
1 PLUCKED	1 POTATO	2 PREVAIL	1 PROPITIATED
1 PLUMES	2 POTATOES	1 PREVAILED	1 PROPITIATORY
3 PLUNDER	2 POTENT	6 PREVENT	2 PROPORTIONED
5 PLUNGE	6 POTS	5 PREVENTED	2 PROPOSAL
1 PLUNGED	1 POULO	1 PREVENTS	1 PROPOSALS
1 PLUS	1 POULTRY	1 PREVIOUS	2 PROPOSED
1 POCK	1 POULTRY-YARD	3 PREY	1 PROPOUNDING
1 POCK-MARKED	1 POUNCE	2 PRICE	7 PROPPED
9 POCKET	1 POUNCED	3 PRICELESS	3 PROSAIC
2 POCKET-BOOK	2 POUND	3 PRICKED	2 PROSPECT
8 POCKETS	1 POUNDED	1 PRICKING	2 PROSPECTS
1 POD	1 POUNDER	7 PRIDE	1 PROSPERITY
2 POESY	2 POUNDERS	1 PRIDED	1 PROSTRATE
1 POET	2 POUNDS	1 PRIEST	1 PROTECT
1 POET'	1 POUR	1 PRIESTLIKE	4 PROTECTED
2 POIGNANT	4 POURED	1 PRIESTS	5 PROTECTION
44 POINT	4 POURING	1 PRIMARY	1 PROTECTOR
		1 PRIME	

4	PROTEST	1	QUARTER-MASTER'S	5	RANKS	6	RECOGNISED
11	PROTESTED	1	QUARTERMASTER	2	RAP	1	RECOGNITION
3	PROTESTING	4	QUARTERMASTERS	1	RAPACIOUS	1	RECOILED
1	PROTOTYPES	2	QUARTERS	1	RAPACITY	1	RECOILS
1	PROTRUDED	1	QUAVER	4	RAPID	2	RECOLLECT
7	PROUD	1	QUAVERED	1	RAPIDITY	9	RECOLLECTION
2	PROUDLY	2	QUAVERING	8	RAPIDLY	1	RECOLLECTS
3	PROVE	8	QUAY	1	RAPINE	3	RECOMMENDATION
2	PROVED	1	QUAY-SIDE	14	RARE	1	RECONCILIATION
1	PROVERB	1	QUAYS	1	RARELY	3	RECORDED
1	PROVIDED	2	QUE	5	RASCAL	1	RECOVER
4	PROVIDENCE	4	QUEEN	1	RASCALS	2	RECOVERED
1	PROVIDENTIALLY	3	QUEENSLAND	2	RASH	2	RECOVERING
1	PROVINCE	4	QUEER	3	RASPING	1	RECOVERY
3	PROVISION	1	QUEER-SOUNDING	5	RAT	1	RECROSS
2	PROVISIONS	1	QUEERLY	12	RATE	1	RECROSSING
1	PROVOCATION	1	QUELLED	28	RATHER	1	RECRUITED
6	PROVOKED	2	QUERIED	1	RATIONAL	1	RECTITUDE
2	PROVOKING	1	QUERULOUSLY	1	RATS	1	RECTORY
1	PROWESS	1	QUEST	2	RATTAN	1	RECUMBENT
2	PROWL	27	QUESTION	3	RATTLE	1	RECURRED
2	PROWLING	1	QUESTIONABLE	2	RATTLED	1	RECURVED
1	PRUDENCE	2	QUESTIONED	1	RATTLING	34	RED
1	PRUDENTLY	1	QUESTIONERS	2	RAVAGED	1	RED-AND-GOLD
1	PRYING	1	QUESTIONING	1	RAVENOUS	1	RED-FACED
1	PSALM	15	QUESTIONS	2	RAVINE	1	RED-HOT
1	PSALM-TUNE	17	QUICK	1	RAVING	1	RED-SASHED
1	PSHAW	2	QUICKENED	1	RAVONALO	2	REDDISH
1	PSYCHOLOGICAL	13	QUICKLY	2	RAW	2	REDEEMING
4	PUBLIC	43	QUIET	1	RAWBONED	1	REDEMPTION
1	PUBLICITY	1	QUIETED	3	RAYS	1	REDOUBLED
1	PUBLICLY	16	QUIETLY	1	RAZOR	2	REDOUNDED
1	PUCKERED	1	QUIETUDE	1	RAZOR-EDGE	1	REDUCE
1	PUDDING	1	QUILLDRIVER	1	RE	3	REEF
2	PUFF	2	QUIT	1	RE-	4	REEFS
3	PUFFED	33	QUITE	17	REACH	1	REEKING
8	PULL	1	QUITTING	16	REACHED	1	REFER
11	PULLED	2	QUIVER	1	REACHES	1	REFER-
5	PULLING	5	QUIVERED	1	REACHING	3	REFERENCE
1	PULSATING	2	QUIVERING	2	REACTION	1	REFERENCES
1	PUMPKIN	1	QUOTED	11	READ	1	REFERRED
1	PUNCH	1	RABBIT	1	READER	1	REFERRING
1	PUNCTILIOUSLY	5	RACE	2	READILY	2	REFLECT
1	PUNGENT	1	RACED	8	READINESS	6	REFLECTED
1	PUNISH	1	RACEHORSE	6	READING	5	REFLECTING
3	PUNISHMENT	3	RACES	2	READING-LAMP	6	REFLECTION
1	PUNKAHPULLERS	1	RACIAL	51	READY	1	REFLECTIONS
5	PUNKAHS	1	RACIALLY	23	REAL	1	REFLECTIVE
2	PUPILS	1	RACING	2	REALISE	2	REFLECTIVELY
2	PUPPY	2	RACKED	2	REALISED	1	REFORMING
1	PURBLIND	2	RACKET	16	REALITY	2	REFRAINED
1	PURCHASE	1	RACKETED	27	REALLY	1	REFRAINING
1	PURCHASES	1	RACKS	2	REALM	9	REFUGE
2	PURE	1	RAFTERS	1	REAPINGS	2	REFUGEES
3	PURELY	1	RAFTS	1	REAPPEARED	3	REFUSE
1	PURITY	5	RAG	1	REARED	2	REFUSED
6	PURPLE	1	RAG-PICKER	1	REARING	1	REFUSES
1	PURPLISH	1	RAGAMUFFIN	16	REASON	1	REFUSING
24	PURPOSE	9	RAGE	3	REASONABLE	1	REFUTATION
1	PURPOSEFULLY	1	RAGED	2	REASONABLY	3	REGAIN
5	PURPOSES	9	RAGGED	1	REASONED	1	REGARD
2	PURSED	1	RAGING	8	REASONS	1	REGARDED
1	PURSER	10	RAGS	1	REASSURED	1	REGARDLESS
1	PURSING	1	RAID	1	REASSURING	1	REGION
16	PURSUED	10	RAIL	1	REBELLIOUS	2	REGIONS
2	PURSUING	3	RAILS	2	REBOUND	11	REGRET
3	PURSUIT	1	RAILWAY	1	REBOUNDED	2	REGRETFULLY
5	PUSH	20	RAIN	2	RECALL	3	REGRETS
17	PUSHED	1	RAIN-WATER	4	RECALLED	1	REGRETTABLE
7	PUSHING	1	RAINING	3	RECEIVE	1	REGRETTED
50	PUT	3	RAISE	13	RECEIVED	5	REGULAR
3	PUTS	27	RAISED	1	RECEIVES	1	REGULARLY
5	PUTTING	10	RAISING	1	RECENT	1	REGULATE
7	PUZZLED	28	RAJAH	1	RECENTLY	1	REGULATED
3	PYJAMAS	25	RAJAH'S	1	RECEPTACLE	1	REGULATES
2	PYRAMIDS	2	RAJAHS	4	RECEPTION	1	REGULATING
1	Q	1	RAKISHLY	1	RECEPTION-ROOMS	1	REGULATIONS
1	QU'ON	1	RALLY	1	RECEPTIONS	2	REHABILITATION
1	QUAFFED	1	RAMADAN	1	RECEPTIVE	1	REHEARSING
1	QUAKING	1	RAMBLING	1	RECESS	1	REIGN
1	QUALITE	2	RAMMED	2	RECESSES	1	REIGNED
1	QUALITIES	3	RAMSHACKLE	1	RECIPIENT	1	REJOICE
6	QUALITY	37	RAN	1	RECITAL	1	REJOICED
1	QUANTITY	2	RANCOUR	2	RECITED	1	REJOINED
5	QUARREL	1	RANDOM	6	RECKLESS	1	REKINDLED
1	QUARRELLING	8	RANG	3	RECKLESSLY	2	RELATE
1	QUARRELS	2	RANGE	3	RECKLESSNESS	4	RELATED
1	QUARRELSOME	4	RANGED	1	RECKON	5	RELATING
1	QUARRY	2	RANGOON	2	RECKONING	4	RELATION
7	QUARTER	1	RANK	3	RECLINING	3	RELATIONS

5 RELEASED	3 REPULSIVE	1 REVERENTIALLY	3 ROCKS
1 RELECTIVELY	1 REPUTABLE	1 REVERENTIALLY'	1 RODS
2 RELIABLE	3 REPUTATION	1 REVERENTLY	2 ROGUE
10 RELIEF	1 REPUTATIONS	4 REVOLT	1 ROGUES
1 RELIEFS	1 REQUEST	1 REVOLTED	4 ROLL
2 RELIEVE	1 REQUESTED	1 REVOLTING	11 ROLLED
3 RELIEVED	2 REQUIRE	1 REVOLUTIONARY	6 ROLLING
2 RELIGIOUS	2 REQUIRED	2 REVOLUTIONS	5 ROMANCE
1 RELIGIOUSLY	2 REQUIRING	15 REVOLVER	19 ROMANTIC
1 RELISH	2 RESCUED	2 REVOLVING	12 ROOF
2 RELUCTANCE	1 RESEMBLE	6 REWARD	13 ROOFS
1 RELUCTANT	9 RESEMBLED	1 REWARDED	61 ROOM
3 RELUCTANTLY	5 RESEMBLING	2 REWARDS	4 ROOMS
16 REMAIN	1 RESENT	1 RHAPSODIES	3 ROOMY
45 REMAINED	2 RESENTFUL	4 RIBBON	3 ROOT
1 REMAINING	1 RESENTING	3 RIBS	5 ROOTED
9 REMAINS	2 RESENTMENT	8 RICE	1 ROOTING
11 REMARK	1 RESERVE	1 RICE-MILL	2 ROOTS
7 REMARKABLE	1 RESERVED	2 RICH	3 ROPE
23 REMARKED	1 RESERVES	3 RID	1 ROPE-YARN
1 REMARKED'	1 RESIDE	1 RIDDLES	3 ROPES
1 REMARKING	1 RESIDENCE	2 RIDE	11 ROSE
2 REMARKS	2 RESIDENT	2 RIDGE	1 ROSY
3 REMEDY	1 RESIDENZ'	1 RIDGE-POLES	2 ROT
1 REMEM	4 RESIGNATION	3 RIDGES	1 ROTTED
1 REMEM-	5 RESIGNED	1 RIDICULE	13 ROTTEN
60 REMEMBER	1 RESIGNEDLY	4 RIDICULOUS	2 ROTTING
23 REMEMBERED	1 RESIST	1 RIDING	5 ROUGH
1 REMEMBERS	5 RESISTANCE	4 RIFLE	1 ROUGHLY
1 REMIND	1 RESISTED	4 RIFLES	1 ROULE
4 REMINDED	2 RESOLUTE	1 RIFTS	97 ROUND
1 REMINDERS	4 RESOLUTELY	4 RIGGED	1 ROUND-SHOT
2 REMINDING	4 RESOLUTION	1 RIGGING	1 ROUNDABOUT
2 REMINISCENCES	3 RESOLVE	102 RIGHT	1 ROUNDED
1 REMNANT	1 RESOLVED	1 RIGHTEOUS	1 ROUNDING
3 REMNANTS	1 RESOUNDED	2 RIGHTEOUSNESS	1 ROUNDS
3 REMONSTRATED	1 RESOUNDING	1 RIGHTS	1 ROUSED
1 REMONSTRATING	1 RESOURCE	1 RIGID	2 ROUSING
3 REMORSE	8 RESPECT	3 RIGIDLY	1 ROUT
1 REMORSEFUL	1 RESPECTABILITY	1 RIGOROUS	1 ROUTED
1 REMORSEFULLY	8 RESPECTABLE	5 RIM	1 ROUTES
7 REMOTE	3 RESPECTED	2 RIMMED	3 ROVER
2 REMOTENESS	1 RESPECTFUL	22 RING	16 ROW
2 REMOTEST	3 RESPECTFULLY	3 RINGING	1 ROWERS
1 REMOVED	1 RESPOND	2 RINGS	3 ROWING
2 REMOVING	2 RESPONDED	2 RIOT	5 ROWS
1 REND	1 RESPONDS	1 RIP	4 ROYAL
3 RENDER	2 RESPONSE	3 RIPE	2 RUBBED
2 RENDERED	5 RESPONSIBILITY	1 RIPOSTED	2 RUBBER
3 RENDING	8 RESPONSIBLE	1 RIPPED	2 RUBBISH
3 RENEGADE	1 RESPONSIVE	5 RIPPLE	1 RUBICUND
1 RENEGADE'S	24 REST	1 RIPPLES	1 RUCK
2 RENOUNCED	5 RESTED	15 RISE	1 RUCKED
1 RENOWN	5 RESTING	2 RISEN	1 RUCKED-UP
2 RENT	3 RESTLESS	2 RISES	2 RUDDER
1 RENTS	1 RESTLESSLY	8 RISING	1 RUDDILY
1 RENUNCIATIONS	2 RESTRAIN	12 RISK	1 RUDDY
1 REPAIR	6 RESTRAINED	1 RISKED	2 RUDE
1 REPAIRS	2 RESTRAINING	3 RISKS	1 RUDELY
1 REPASS	2 RESULT	1 RISKY	3 RUFFIAN
1 REPAY	3 RESUMED	89 RIVER	4 RUFFIANS
3 REPEAT	1 RESUMING	3 RIVER-BANK	1 RUFFLING
33 REPEATED	1 RETAILER	2 RIVER-FRONT	3 RUGGED
1 REPEATEDLY	1 RETAINER	3 RIVERS	1 RUHIG
2 REPEATING	1 RETICENCE	1 RIVERSIDE	5 RUIN
2 REPENTANCE	1 RETINUE	5 ROAD	4 RUINED
2 REPLACED	2 RETIRE	2 ROADS	1 RUINOUS
1 REPLACING	3 RETIRED	6 ROADSTEAD	1 RUINOUSLY
2 REPLIED	2 RETORT	1 ROADSTER	4 RUINS
3 REPLY	2 RETORTED	1 ROAM	2 RULE
8 REPORT	7 RETREAT	2 ROAMING	1 RULED
4 REPORTED	3 RETREATED	3 ROAR	5 RULER
2 REPORTS	2 RETREATING	1 ROARED	3 RULERS
8 REPOSE	2 RETRIBUTION	3 ROARING	1 RULES
3 REPOSED	1 RETRIEVER	1 ROARS	4 RUMBLE
1 REPOSING	1 RETRIEVERS	1 ROAST	1 RUMBLINGS
2 REPRESENT	18 RETURN	2 ROASTED	1 RUMOUR
1 REPRESENTATIVE	11 RETURNED	6 ROB	3 RUMOURS
4 REPRESENTED	5 RETURNING	6 ROBBED	31 RUN
1 REPRESS	1 REUNION	1 ROBBER'S	2 RUNAWAY
2 REPRESSED	1 REVEAL	6 ROBBERS	1 RUNNER
1 REPROACH	2 REVEALED	2 ROBBERY	17 RUNNING
1 REPROACHES	2 REVEALING	1 ROBBING	3 RUNS
1 REPROACHFUL	1 REVEALS	18 ROBINSON	3 RUPEES
2 REPRODUCED	1 REVELATIONS	1 ROBS	1 RURAL
1 REPROVING	1 REVELLED	7 ROCK	21 RUSH
1 REPTILES	5 REVENGE	2 ROCKED	1 RUSHCUTTERS'
1 REPUBLICAN	2 REVENGEFUL	1 ROCKET	11 RUSHED
2 REPULSE	1 REVENUE	2 ROCKING	4 RUSHING
1 REPULSED	1 REVERBERATION	1 ROCKING-CHAIR	5 RUST

1 RUST-EATEN	3 SAVOUR	1 SCREENS	1 SELF-SATISFIED
1 RUSTIC	91 SAW	3 SCREW	1 SELFISH
1 RUSTING	1 SAWING	1 SCREW-PILE	1 SELFISHLY
2 RUSTLE	150 SAY	3 SCREWED	3 SELFISHNESS
1 RUSTLED	17 SAYING	1 SCREWED-UP	3 SELL
1 RUSTLING	1 SAYINGS	2 SCREWING	1 SELLING
1 RUSTLINGS	45 SAYS	1 SCRIBBLING	1 SELVIN
2 RUSTY	1 SCABBARD	2 SCRIBE	1 SEMBLANCE
2 RUTHLESS	1 SCAFFOLDING	1 SCRUB	1 SEMICIRCULAR
1 RUTHLESSNESS	1 SCAFFOLDS	1 SCRUBBED	18 SEND
3 RUTHVEL	3 SCALE	1 SCRUPLES	1 SENDING
3 S	3 SCANDAL	2 SCRUPULOUS	1 SENILE
3 S'ELP	1 SCANDAL-MONGERING	1 SCRUTINISED	2 SENIOR
1 S'EN	1 SCANDALOUS	1 SCUFFLE	6 SENSATION
1 S'EST	1 SCANDINAVIAN	1 SCUFFLES	3 SENSATIONS
1 SA	1 SCANDINAVIANS	1 SCURRYING	34 SENSE
1 SA-A-AY	1 SCANNING	135 SEA	3 SENSELESS
1 SABRE	1 SCANT	2 SEA-ANACHRONISM	1 SENSELESSLY
3 SACK	3 SCANTY	1 SEA-BIRDS	5 SENSES
1 SACKCOAT	1 SCAR	2 SEA-GOING	3 SENSIBILITIES
1 SACKING	2 SCARCE	1 SEA-LEVEL	3 SENSIBILITY
1 SACRED	3 SCARE	3 SEA-LIFE	2 SENSIBLE
6 SACRIFICE	3 SCARECROWS	1 SEA-PUPPY	1 SENSITIVE
12 SAD	8 SCARED	1 SEA-SICK	12 SENT
1 SADDENED	1 SCARES	1 SEA-STOCK	8 SENTENCE
1 SADDER	2 SCARLET	1 SEA-WATER	3 SENTENCES
4 SADLY	1 SCARS	1 SEAL	1 SENTIENT
3 SADNESS	2 SCATHING	2 SEALED	4 SENTIMENT
22 SAFE	1 SCATHINGLY	2 SEALING	3 SENTIMENTAL
1 SAFEGUARDS	7 SCATTERED	2 SEALING-SCHOONERS	1 SENTIMENTALISM
1 SAFELY	1 SCATTERING	1 SEALS	3 SENTIMENTS
1 SAFEST	8 SCENE	1 SEAM	2 SENTRY
12 SAFETY	3 SCENES	7 SEAMAN	2 SEPARATE
1 SAGACIOUS	6 SCENT	1 SEAMAN'S	7 SEPARATED
2 SAGACITY	2 SCEPTICALLY	1 SEAMANLIKE	2 SEPARATELY
410 SAID	3 SCHEME	1 SEAMANSHIP	1 SEPARATING
9 SAIL	1 SCHEMING	3 SEAMEN	4 SEPARATION
1 SAILCLOTH	1 SCHNAPPS	2 SEAPORT	1 SEPHORA
1 SAILED	3 SCHOMBERG	2 SEAPORTS	1 SEPULTURE
6 SAILING	1 SCHOMBERG'S	5 SEARCH	3 SERANG
2 SAILING-SHIP	1 SCHON	3 SEARCHED	1 SERANGS
1 SAILING-SHIPS	22 SCHOONER	2 SEARCHING	3 SERENE
5 SAILOR	2 SCHOONER'S	13 SEAS	1 SERENELY
3 SAILORS	4 SCHOONERS	1 SEASON	5 SERENITY
3 SAILORS'	1 SCHRECKLICH	8 SEAT	1 SERGE
3 SAILS	1 SCHWEIN	2 SEAWORTHY	1 SERIO
1 SAINT	1 SCIENTIFIC	1 SECLUSION	1 SERIO-COMIC
1 SAINTS	1 SCINTILLATED	38 SECOND	2 SERIOUS
20 SAKE	6 SCOLDING	1 SECOND-HAND	5 SERIOUSLY
1 SALIENT	1 SCOOTED	6 SECONDS	5 SERIOUSNESS
4 SALLOW	1 SCOPE	2 SECRECY	1 SERMONS
2 SALLOW-FACED	1 SCORCHED	26 SECRET	1 SERRIED
1 SALOON	1 SCORCHING	2 SECRETLY	10 SERVANT
5 SALT	4 SCORE	2 SECRETS	4 SERVANTS
1 SALUTARY	1 SCORES	3 SECULAR	4 SERVE
2 SALVATION	9 SCORN	5 SECURITY	5 SERVED
1 SALVOS	1 SCORNED	1 SEDENTARY	15 SERVICE
2 SAMAN	2 SCORNFUL	1 SEDUCED	1 SERVICES
6 SAMARANG	4 SCORNFULLY	2 SEDUCTIONS	3 SERVING
57 SAME	2 SCOT	1 SEDUCTIVE	1 SERVITEUR
1 SAMENESS	1 SCOTSMAN	206 SEE	40 SET
7 SAND	2 SCOTSMAN'S	1 SEED	1 SET-OUT
1 SANDALS	1 SCOTTISH	15 SEEING	1 SETS
2 SANDBANK	5 SCOUNDREL	2 SEEK	4 SETTING
2 SANDWICH	1 SCOUNDRELS	1 SEEKING	5 SETTLE
1 SANDWICHES	1 SCOUR	1 SEEKS	6 SETTLED
1 SANDY	1 SCOURGE	22 SEEM	3 SETTLEMENT
1 SANG	1 SCOWL	219 SEEMED	1 SETTLEMENTS
1 SANGUINARY	1 SCOWLED	1 SEEMINGLY	3 SETTLERS
12 SANK	1 SCOWLING	37 SEEMS	1 SETTLING
1 SANS	4 SCRAMBLE	98 SEEN	1 SEUL
1 SAPLINGS	2 SCRAMBLED	1 SEES	12 SEVEN
2 SARAH	1 SCRAP	1 SEETHED	1 SEVENTEEN
1 SARONG	1 SCRAP-HEAP	4 SEETHING	1 SEVENTEENTH
3 SARONGS	6 SCRAPE	1 SEHEN	1 SEVENTEENTH-CENTURY
1 SASHED	1 SCRAPED	1 SEIZE	1 SEVENTY
72 SAT	1 SCRAPES	1 SEIZED	1 SEVENTY-ONE
1 SATAN	1 SCRAPING	2 SEIZING	20 SEVERAL
1 SATANIC	1 SCRATCH	4 SELDOM	5 SEVERE
6 SATISFACTION	1 SCRATCHED	2 SELECTED	1 SEVERELY
8 SATISFIED	3 SCRATCHING	14 SELF	1 SEVERER
2 SATISFY	1 SCRAWLING	1 SELF-APPOINTED	2 SEVERITY
2 SATISFYING	4 SCREAM	1 SELF-ASSERTION	1 SEWER
1 SAUCER	5 SCREAMED	1 SELF-COMMUNION	1 SEXES
2 SAVAGE	4 SCREAMING	3 SELF-CONTROL	1 SHABBY
1 SAVAGELY	5 SCREAMS	1 SELF-KNOWLEDGE	13 SHADE
2 SAVAGES	4 SCREECH	1 SELF-LOVE	4 SHADED
15 SAVE	2 SCREECHED	1 SELF-MISTRUST	11 SHADES
14 SAVED	1 SCREECHING	1 SELF-POSSESSED	38 SHADOW
10 SAVING	1 SCREEN	1 SELF-SATISFACTION	1 SHADOWED

1 SHADOWLESS	2 SHIPPING-MASTER	6 SHUFFLE	9 SINK
12 SHADOWS	19 SHIPS	3 SHUFFLED	10 SINKING
7 SHADOWY	2 SHIPWRECK	3 SHUFFLING	1 SINKS
2 SHADY	1 SHIPWRECKED	1 SHUNNED	1 SINNE
4 SHAFT	1 SHIPWRECKS	23 SHUT	2 SINNED
1 SHAFTS	4 SHIRK	1 SHUT-UP	3 SINNER
9 SHAKE	1 SHIRKED	1 SHUTS	1 SINS
6 SHAKEN	1 SHIRKER	2 SHUTTER	1 SINUOSITY
1 SHAKES	1 SHIRKING	1 SHUTTER-HOLE	2 SIP
1 SHAKESPEARE	3 SHIRT	2 SHUTTERS	1 SIPPED
1 SHAKESPEAREAN	1 SHIRT-FRONTS	2 SHUTTING	1 SIPPING
1 SHAKILY	4 SHIVER	2 SHY	34 SIR
9 SHAKING	3 SHIVERED	1 SHYLY	2 SIR'
1 SHAKINGS	2 SHIVERING	1 SHYNESS	3 SISTER
2 SHAKY	1 SHIVERS	1 SI	1 SISTER'S
63 SHALL	1 SHOAL	1 SI-	1 SISTERS
1 SHALLOW	2 SHOALS	1 SIAM	19 SIT
1 SHALLOWS	9 SHOCK	4 SIAMESE	4 SITS
1 SHALT	5 SHOCKED	15 SICK	31 SITTING
3 SHAM	1 SHOCKING	1 SICK-BED	1 SITUATED
6 SHAME	1 SHOCKS	1 SICKENING	8 SITUATION
1 SHAMEFULLY	1 SHOD	1 SICKLY	24 SIX
1 SHAN'T	3 SHOE	1 SICKNESS	1 SIX-POUNDER
3 SHANGHAI	1 SHOE-LACE	106 SIDE	1 SIX-POUNDERS
1 SHANKS	7 SHOES	1 SIDE-LIGHT	2 SIX-SHOOTERS
13 SHAPE	5 SHONE	1 SIDED	3 SIXTEEN
3 SHAPED	1 SHOOING	3 SIDELONG	1 SIXTEEN-KNOT
5 SHAPELESS	24 SHOOK	17 SIDES	1 SIXTEENHUNDREDWEIGHT
1 SHAPELY	4 SHOOT	1 SIDEWALK	2 SIXTH
10 SHAPES	2 SHOOTERS	1 SIDEWALKS	3 SIXTY
2 SHAPING	7 SHOOTING	6 SIDEWAYS	7 SIZE
7 SHARE	1 SHOOTING-IRON	1 SIDIBOY	1 SIZES
4 SHARED	1 SHOOTS	1 SIDLING	2 SKELETON
9 SHARP	9 SHOP	1 SIE	2 SKELETONS
3 SHARPLY	1 SHOPS	1 SIEGE	1 SKELTER
5 SHAVED	31 SHORE	1 SIEGMUND	1 SKETCH
1 SHAVER	1 SHORE-LIFE	1 SIEVE	1 SKIDDED
3 SHAVING	2 SHORED	11 SIGH	1 SKILL
291 SHE	8 SHORES	9 SIGHED	1 SKIMPY
1 SHE-DEVIL	45 SHORT	2 SIGHING	7 SKIN
2 SHE'S	3 SHORT-LIVED	44 SIGHT	1 SKINNED
7 SHED	1 SHORTCOMINGS	1 SIGHTED	4 SKINNY
1 SHEDDING	1 SHORTEST	7 SIGHTS	3 SKINS
2 SHEDS	1 SHORTLY	25 SIGN	32 SKIPPER
5 SHEEN	1 SHORTNESS	5 SIGNAL	2 SKIPPERS
2 SHEEP	36 SHOT	1 SIGNALS	1 SKIPPING
1 SHEEP-PEN	1 SHOT-GUNS	2 SIGNATURE	1 SKULKED
6 SHEER	7 SHOTS	1 SIGNED	2 SKULKING
1 SHEERED	59 SHOULD	3 SIGNIFICANCE	4 SKULL
14 SHEET	33 SHOULDER	2 SIGNIFICANT	1 SKULL-CAPS
1 SHEETED	2 SHOULDER-STRAPS	2 SIGNIFICANTLY	1 SKULLS
5 SHEETING	3 SHOULDERED	5 SIGNS	2 SKUNK
5 SHEETS	24 SHOULDERS	57 SILENCE	2 SKUNKS
6 SHELL	1 SHOULDERSTRAPS	1 SILENCED	45 SKY
1 SHELL-FISH	18 SHOUT	2 SILENCES	1 SKY-HIGH
11 SHELTER	25 SHOUTED	1 SILENCING	3 SKYLIGHT
4 SHELTERED	1 SHOUTED'	45 SILENT	1 SKYLINE
2 SHELTERING	8 SHOUTING	11 SILENTLY	1 SLAB
4 SHELTERS	8 SHOUTS	1 SILHOUETTE	1 SLACK
1 SHELVES	3 SHOVE	2 SILK	5 SLAM
1 SHEPHERDED	4 SHOVED	2 SILKS	1 SLAMMED
17 SHERIF	1 SHOVEL	2 SILKY	1 SLANG
1 SHERIF'S	1 SHOVING	8 SILLY	1 SLANGED
1 SHERIFF	27 SHOW	10 SILVER	3 SLANT
1 SHIA	20 SHOWED	2 SILVER-MOUNTED	1 SLANTED
1 SHIED	1 SHOWEDV	3 SILVERY	3 SLAP
3 SHIFTED	6 SHOWER	2 SIMILE	6 SLAPPED
3 SHIFTING	1 SHOWERED	2 SIMILITUDE	1 SLAPPING
1 SHIMMER	1 SHOWERING	1 SIMMERING	1 SLASH
1 SHIMMERING	5 SHOWING	21 SIMPLE	1 SLASHING
1 SHINDIES	5 SHOWN	1 SIMPLER	3 SLATE
1 SHINDY	1 SHPIT	2 SIMPLEST	1 SLATY
2 SHINE	1 SHRANK	2 SIMPLICITY	1 SLAVE
7 SHINING	1 SHREWD	20 SIMPLY	1 SLAVE-GIRLS
4 SHINY	1 SHREWDNESS	2 SIN	3 SLAVES
134 SHIP	1 SHREWISH	30 SINCE	1 SLEEK
1 SHIP-BROKER'S	3 SHRIEK	2 SINCERE	33 SLEEP
2 SHIP-CHANDLER	3 SHRIEKED	2 SINCERELY	2 SLEEPERS
1 SHIP-CHANDLER'S	1 SHRIEKING	4 SINCERITY	2 SLEEPILY
2 SHIP-CHANDLERS	2 SHRIEKS	1 SINFUL	14 SLEEPING
1 SHIP-KEEPERS	7 SHRILL	2 SING	1 SLEEPING-JACKET
1 SHIP-MASTERS	2 SHRINE	1 SING-SONG	1 SLEEPING-PLACE
8 SHIP'S	1 SHRINKING	1 SINGEING	1 SLEEPING-SUIT
1 SHIPBOARD	1 SHRIVELLED	24 SINGLE	1 SLEEPLESS
1 SHIPCHANDLERS	1 SHRUB	4 SINGLE-HANDED	2 SLEEPY
1 SHIPMATES	1 SHRUBS	2 SINGLED	3 SLEEVE
2 SHIPOWNER	1 SHRUNK	2 SINGLY	2 SLEEVES
1 SHIPOWNERS	1 SHUDDER	1 SINGS	5 SLENDER
1 SHIPOWNING	5 SHUDDERED	1 SINGULARLY	1 SLENDERLEGGED
2 SHIPPING	1 SHUDDERS	5 SINISTER	1 SLENDERLY

11 SLEPT	6 SO-AND-SO	15 SOUTH	1 SPOILT
2 SLID	1 SO-AND-SO'S	1 SOUTH-EAST	30 SPOKE
1 SLIDE	1 SO'S	1 SOUTH-WEST	12 SPOKEN
2 SLIDING	1 SOAKING	2 SOUTHERLY	2 SPOKES
22 SLIGHT	1 SOAR	1 SOUTHWARD	1 SPOLE
11 SLIGHTEST	2 SOARING	2 SOVEREIGN	1 SPOLIATIONS
20 SLIGHTLY	1 SOBBED	1 SOWINGS	1 SPOONS
3 SLIM	4 SOBBING	21 SPACE	1 SPORT
2 SLIME	3 SOBER	4 SPACES	23 SPOT
3 SLING	2 SOBERLY	2 SPACIOUS	1 SPOTLESSLY
3 SLINK	2 SOBS	1 SPAIN	5 SPOTS
7 SLINKING	1 SOCIAL	1 SPAN	2 SPOTTED
5 SLIP	1 SOCIETIES	1 SPANIEL	1 SPOUT
7 SLIPPED	2 SOCKETS	5 SPANISH	2 SPRANG
3 SLIPPERS	1 SOCKS	2 SPAR	2 SPRAYS
1 SLIPPERY	20 SOFT	8 SPARE	9 SPREAD
2 SLIPS	1 SOFT-SPOKEN	4 SPARK	2 SPREADING
1 SLIT	9 SOFTLY	1 SPARKLE	3 SPRING
11 SLOPE	2 SOFTNESS	3 SPARKLED	1 SPRINGING
4 SLOPES	1 SOIL	1 SPARKLING	1 SPRINGS
1 SLOPING	3 SOILED	2 SPARKS	1 SPRINTING
1 SLOUCHING	1 SOLAH	1 SPARRED	5 SPRUNG
19 SLOW	1 SOLD	1 SPARROW	2 SPUN
1 SLOWER	2 SOLDIER	1 SPARS	1 SPUNK
1 SLOWEST	2 SOLE	1 SPARSE	1 SPUR
44 SLOWLY	2 SOLELY	1 SPASMS	2 SPURIOUS
1 SLUGGISHLY	10 SOLEMN	3 SPAT	1 SPURNED
2 SLUGS	1 SOLEMNITY	1 SPATULA	1 SPURRED
2 SLUMBERS	4 SOLEMNLY	1 SPAWN	1 SPURT
1 SLUNG	5 SOLES	38 SPEAK	1 SQUAD
1 SLUNK	1 SOLICITATION	1 SPEAKER	1 SQUADRON
67 SMALL	1 SOLICITUDE	1 SPEAKERS	11 SQUALL
1 SMALLER	4 SOLID	30 SPEAKING	1 SQUALLS
4 SMALLEST	2 SOLIDARITY	3 SPEAKS	1 SQUALLY
6 SMART	1 SOLIDLY	4 SPEAR	1 SQUALOR
3 SMARTLY	12 SOLITARY	1 SPEAR'S	7 SQUARE
3 SMASH	5 SOLITUDE	2 SPEARMEN	1 SQUARED
1 SMASHING	1 SOLITUDES	5 SPEARS	2 SQUARELY
5 SMELL	5 SOLOMON	10 SPECIAL	2 SQUASHING
28 SMILE	1 SOMALI	3 SPECIES	2 SQUATTED
16 SMILED	28 SOMBRE	8 SPECIMEN	3 SQUATTING
1 SMILES	2 SOMBRELY	1 SPECIMENS	1 SQUEAK
9 SMILING	1 SOMBRENESS	7 SPECK	1 SQUEAKED
1 SMILINGLY	272 SOME	1 SPECKLED	3 SQUEAKS
1 SMIRKING	1 SOME-	3 SPECTACLE	1 SQUEALED
1 SMITE	23 SOMEBODY	1 SPECTACLES	4 SQUEEZE
27 SMOKE	3 SOMEBODY'S	6 SPECTRAL	2 SQUEEZED
2 SMOKED	18 SOMEHOW	1 SPECTRALLY	2 SQUIRM
4 SMOKING	129 SOMETHING	6 SPECTRE	1 SQUIRM-
14 SMOOTH	2 SOMETHING'S	1 SPECULATED	1 SQUIRREL
4 SMOOTHLY	1 SOMETIME	1 SPECULATION	1 SQUIRTED
1 SMOTHER	17 SOMETIMES	17 SPEECH	2 SSH
1 SMOTHERED	1 SOMETIMES	2 SPEECHES	3 SSSH
1 SMOULDERED	17 SOMEWHERE	4 SPEECHLESS	1 ST
4 SMOULDERING	1 SOMNOLENCE	3 SPEED	4 STABBED
1 SMUDGE	21 SON	1 SPEEDING	1 STABBING
2 SMUGGLE	2 SON-IN-LAW	5 SPELL	1 STABILITY
1 SMUGGLED	4 SON'S	2 SPELLBOUND	1 STABLE
1 SMUGGLING	1 SONAL	1 SPELLING	1 STABLE-YARD
2 SNAKE	4 SONG	2 SPELLS	1 STABLES
1 SNAKES	1 SONOROUS	10 SPENT	1 STACKED
2 SNAP	5 SONS	3 SPHERE	5 STAGE
1 SNAPPED	1 SONS-IN-LAW	1 SPHINX	3 STAGER
1 SNARE	45 SOON	1 SPIDER'S	1 STAGES
1 SNARED	5 SOONER	1 SPILT	1 STAGGER
1 SNARL	2 SOOTHE	1 SPIN	4 STAGGERED
2 SNARLED	1 SOOTHED	1 SPINE	1 STAGGERING
1 SNARLING	2 SOOTY	1 SPINNEY	3 STAGNANT
2 SNATCH	2 SORCERER	1 SPINNING	1 STAINS
5 SNATCHED	3 SORDID	1 SPIRES	1 STAIRCASE
1 SNATCHING	2 SORE	23 SPIRIT	1 STAIRS
2 SNEAK	1 SORREL	1 SPIRITED	1 STAIRWAY
1 SNEAKED	6 SORROW	4 SPIRITS	2 STAKE
3 SNEAKING	1 SORROWFUL	1 SPIRTING	7 STAKES
1 SNEERED	1 SORROWING	2 SPITE	1 STALKS
2 SNEERING	14 SORRY	1 SPITEFUL	3 STALWART
1 SNEERS	123 SORT	1 SPITTING	2 STAMMER
1 SNIFFING	1 SORTE	5 SPLASH	8 STAMMERED
1 SNORED	8 SORTS	1 SPLASHED	2 STAMMERINGS
2 SNORING	1 SOUGHING	1 SPLASHES	1 STAMMERS
3 SNORT	35 SOUL	4 SPLASHING	2 STAMP
4 SNORTED	10 SOULS	7 SPLENDID	4 STAMPED
2 SNORTING	62 SOUND	7 SPLENDOUR	1 STAMPEDED
3 SNOW	7 SOUNDED	1 SPLINTERS	2 STAMPING
1 SNOWY	1 SOUNDING	1 SPLINTS	2 STANCHION
1 SNOWY-WINGED	1 SOUNDLESS	4 SPLIT	32 STAND
1 SNUFF	13 SOUNDS	5 SPLUTTERED	1 STAND-UP
1 SNUFFLED	4 SOUR	3 SPLUTTERING	2 STANDARD
1 SNUFFY	3 SOURCE	2 SPOIL	29 STANDING
372 SO	1 SOUTANE	1 SPOILED	1 STANDPOINT

2 STANDS	10 STICK	4 STREAMED	1 SUBMISSIVELY
1 STANDSTILL	2 STICKING	1 STREAMER	2 SUBMIT
2 STANTON	1 STICKLEBACK	1 STREAMERS	1 SUBMITTED
7 STAR	2 STICKS	5 STREAMING	1 SUBSIDE
4 STARBOARD	1 STICKY	1 STREAMS	3 SUBSIDED
10 STARE	10 STIFF	17 STREET	4 SUBSTANCE
13 STARED	1 STIFF-LEAVED	3 STREETS	8 SUBTLE
1 STARES	2 STIFFENED	27 STRENGTH	1 SUBTLETY
16 STARING	1 STIFFLY	4 STRESS	1 SUBTLY
4 STARLIGHT	1 STIFFNESS	7 STRETCH	1 SUCCADANA
1 STARRED	1 STIFLED	7 STRETCHED	11 SUCCEEDED
17 STARS	99 STILL	1 STRETCHER	1 SUCCEEDING
16 START	22 STILLNESS	1 STRETCHES	15 SUCCESS
27 STARTED	1 STIMACY	2 STRETCHING	2 SUCCESSES
5 STARTING	4 STING	1 STREWN	2 SUCCESSFUL
1 STARTLE	1 STINKING	5 STRICKEN	1 SUCCESSFULLY
18 STARTLED	1 STINKS	2 STRICT	3 SUCCESSION
1 STARTLING	1 STIPULATED	3 STRICTLY	2 SUCCESSIVE
1 STARTLINGLY	24 STIR	3 STRIDE	1 SUCCESSIVELY
1 STARTS	8 STIRRED	1 STRIDES	1 SUCCESSORS
6 STARVATION	4 STIRRING	1 STRIDING	128 SUCH
3 STARVE	1 STIRS	3 STRIFE	1 SUCK
1 STARVED	6 STOCK	6 STRIKE	22 SUDDEN
1 STARVING	1 STOCK-IN-TRADE	4 STRIKES	109 SUDDENLY
30 STATE	1 STOCK-STILL	8 STRIKING	1 SUDDENNESS
1 STATE-ROOM	34 STOCKADE	8 STRING	1 SUFFERANCE
3 STATED	1 STOCKSTILL	2 STRINGS	4 SUFFERED
5 STATEMENT	1 STOKE	1 STRINGY	10 SUFFERING
2 STATEMENTS	1 STOKE-HOLD	4 STRIP	2 SUFFERINGS
2 STATES	6 STOLE	2 STRIPED	2 SUFFICIENTLY
2 STATION	5 STOLEN	2 STRIPES	1 SUFFUSED
1 STATIONED	4 STOLID	2 STRIPPED	4 SUGAR
2 STATUE	2 STOLIDLY	2 STRIVING	1 SUGAR-CANE
1 STATUESQUE	8 STOMACH	1 STRODE	1 SUGAR-HOGSHEAD
4 STATURE	1 STOMACHS	9 STROKE	1 SUGAR-PLANTERS
1 STAVE	22 STONE	1 STROKED	1 SUGGEST
13 STAY	1 STONE-BLIND	2 STROLL	4 SUGGESTED
3 STAYED	1 STONE-DEAF	3 STROLLED	3 SUGGESTION
5 STAYING	2 STONES	2 STROLLING	1 SUGGESTIONS
2 STAYS	2 STONY	22 STRONG	3 SUGGESTIVE
1 STEADFAST	91 STOOD	1 STRONGER	2 SUICIDE
1 STEADFASTLY	1 STOOL	1 STRONGEST	6 SUIT
2 STEADFASTNESS	2 STOOP	4 STRONGHOLD	6 SUITABLE
1 STEADIED	1 STOOPED	5 STRONGLY	2 SUITED
7 STEADILY	7 STOOPING	38 STRUCK	1 SUITS
2 STEADINESS	14 STOP	1 STRUCTURE	1 SULKILY
19 STEADY	32 STOPPED	4 STRUGGLE	1 SULKINESS
1 STEAK	7 STOPPING	5 STRUGGLED	3 SULKY
7 STEAL	5 STORE	4 STRUGGLES	3 SULLEN
5 STEALING	1 STOREHOUSE	4 STRUGGLING	4 SULTAN
1 STEALTH	2 STOREROOM	2 STRUTTING	1 SULTAN'S
3 STEALTHILY	1 STORES	9 STUBBORN	3 SUM
2 STEALTHINESS	7 STORIES	3 STUBBORNLY	1 SUMMED
7 STEALTHY	1 STORM	8 STUCK	4 SUMMIT
10 STEAM	3 STORMING	1 STUCK-UP	4 SUMMITS
1 STEAM-LAUNCH	1 STORMY	1 STUDENT'S	2 SUMMONED
1 STEAM-WINCHES	64 STORY	3 STUDY	1 SUMPTUOUS
3 STEAMED	2 STOUT	10 STUFF	33 SUN
24 STEAMER	1 STOUTER	1 STUFFED	1 SUN-BLACKENED
3 STEAMING	1 STOVE	1 STUFFS	3 SUNBURNT
3 STEEL	1 STOVE-PIPE	1 STUFFY	1 SUNDA
1 STEELED	1 STOWAWAY	1 STUMBLE	1 SUNDAY
1 STEELY	1 STRADDLING	3 STUMBLED	7 SUNK
2 STEEP	1 STRAGGLED	1 STUMBLING	5 SUNKEN
1 STEER	2 STRAGGLER	1 STUMP	1 SUNLIGHT
1 STEERAGE	1 STRAGGLERS	1 STUMPING	2 SUNLIT
1 STEERAGE-WAY	42 STRAIGHT	1 STUMPS	1 SUNNY
4 STEERED	1 STRAIGHTWAY	1 STUNK	1 SUNRAYS
4 STEERING	5 STRAIN	2 STUNNED	5 SUNRISE
2 STEERING-GEAR	4 STRAINED	1 STUNNING	1 SUNS
57 STEIN	5 STRAINING	11 STUPID	6 SUNSET
27 STEIN'S	1 STRAINS	1 STUPIDEST	21 SUNSHINE
4 STEM	2 STRAIT	2 STUPIDITY	1 SUPERANNUATED
1 STEM-HEAD	2 STRAITS	2 STUPIDLY	1 SUPERB
1 STEMMED	1 STRAND	1 STURDY	2 SUPERFICIAL
1 STEMS	3 STRANDED	1 STUTTERED	1 SUPERFLUOUS
1 STENTORIAN	36 STRANGE	2 STYLE	1 SUPERHEATED
17 STEP	7 STRANGELY	1 STYX	6 SUPERIOR
7 STEPPED	1 STRANGENESS	1 SUBDUE	2 SUPERIORITY
5 STEPPING	9 STRANGER	9 SUBDUED	1 SUPERIORS
20 STEPS	9 STRANGERS	1 SUBDUING	3 SUPERNATURAL
18 STERN	2 STRAPS	5 SUBJECT	1 SUPERSTITIOUS
1 STERN--	1 STRATAGEMS	1 SUBJECTS	1 SUPERVISION
1 STERN-PORT	5 STRAW	1 SUBJUGATION	2 SUPPLICATING
3 STERN-SHEETS	2 STRAY	1 SUBLIMATED	7 SUPPLY
1 STERNLY	2 STRAYING	1 SUBLIMITIES	2 SUPPORTABLE
1 STETTIN	1 STRAYS	1 SUBMARINE	1 SUPPORTERS
1 STEVEDORES	2 STREAK	2 SUBMERGED	1 SUPPORTS
3 STEWARD	2 STREAKS	1 SUBMISSION	59 SUPPOSE
1 STEWART	22 STREAM	1 SUBMISSIVE	9 SUPPOSED

4 SUPREME	5 SWORD	2 TEMPERAMENT	17 THIRD
2 SURA	7 SWORE	2 TEMPERED	1 THIRD-CLASS
48 SURE	1 SWORN	2 TEMPLE	1 THIRDS
3 SURELY	1 SWUM	2 TEMPLES	2 THIRSTY
3 SURF	14 SWUNG	1 TEMPORARY	2 THIRTEEN
16 SURFACE	2 SYDNEY	2 TEMPTATION	14 THIRTY
1 SURFACE-CONDENSING	2 SYMBOLIC	1 TEMPTATIONS	3 THIRTY-TWO
1 SURFACES	4 SYMONS	3 TEMPTED	503 THIS
1 SURGE	3 SYMPATHETIC	18 TEN	1 THOLE
1 SURGED	2 SYMPATHETICALLY	1 TENACITY	1 THOLE-PINS
1 SURGEONS	2 SYMPATHIES	1 TENDED	1 THORNS
2 SURGING	1 SYMPATHISED	2 TENDER	2 THORNY
1 SURLIEST	4 SYMPATHY	6 TENDERNESS	1 THOROUGH
3 SURLILY	1 SYMPTOM	1 TENEBROUS	1 THOROUGHFARE
1 SURLINESS	1 SYSTEM	1 TENNIS	3 THOROUGHLY
4 SURLY	2 T	1 TENNIS-PARTIES	71 THOSE
1 SURMISING	34 TABLE	2 TENSE	2 THOU
1 SURPASSING	1 TABLECLOTH	1 TENSELY	178 THOUGH
11 SURPRISE	1 TABLEFUL	1 TENTACLE	95 THOUGHT
11 SURPRISED	2 TABLES	1 TENTH	4 THOUGHTFUL
3 SURRENDER	1 TABLETS	4 TERMS	2 THOUGHTFULLY
1 SURRENDERED	3 TACITURN	1 TERRESTRIAL	2 THOUGHTFULNESS
1 SURREPTITIOUS	2 TACKED	9 TERRIBLE	24 THOUGHTS
1 SURROUND	1 TACKLED	6 TERRIBLY	7 THOUSAND
5 SURROUNDED	1 TACT	1 TERRIFIC	3 THOUSANDS
1 SURROUNDING	1 TACTICS	3 TERRIFIED	1 THRASHING
6 SURROUNDINGS	2 TAFFRAIL	2 TERRIFY	6 THREAD
2 SURVEYED	1 TAFFRAIL-LOG	2 TERRIFYING	1 THREAD-LIKE
1 SURVEYING	1 TAGALS	17 TERROR	1 THREADBARE
4 SURVIVE	2 TAIL	7 TERRORS	2 THREADS
3 SURVIVED	1 TAILOR	1 TESSELLATED	2 THREATENED
2 SURVIVORS	1 TAILS	1 TEST	7 THREATENING
1 SUSCEPTIBILITIES	1 TAIN'T	1 TESTED	1 THREATENINGLY
11 SUSPECT	1 TAINTING	1 TESTIFY	2 THREATS
5 SUSPECTED	65 TAKE	1 TESTIFYING	73 THREE
5 SUSPENDED	21 TAKEN	3 TESTIMONY	1 THREE-LEGGED
3 SUSPICION	4 TAKES	1 TEXT	1 THREE-QUARTERS
1 SUSPICIONS	31 TAKING	1 TFUI	1 THREESCORE
3 SUSPICIOUS	1 TAKINGS	177 THAN	3 THRESHOLD
3 SUSTAINED	1 TALCAHUANO	6 THANK	12 THREW
3 SWAGGER	11 TALE	1 THANKED	1 THRILLED
2 SWALLOW	1 TALENTS	1 THANKFUL	16 THROAT
3 SWALLOWED	1 TALES	3 THANKS	5 THROATS
3 SWALLOWING	1 TALISMAN	1481 THAT	1 THROB
3 SWAM	60 TALK	1 THAT'LL	1 THRONE
2 SWAMPED	4 TALKATIVE	71 THAT'S	1 THRONG
1 SWAMPY	16 TALKED	3 THATCH	1 THRONGED
2 SWARM	24 TALKING	2 THATN	1 THRONGING
1 SWARMING	3 TALKS	7363 THE	1 THROTTLED
2 SWAY	11 TALL	1 THEE	154 THROUGH
9 SWAYED	2 TAM'	277 THEIR	11 THROW
7 SWAYING	1 TAMATAVE	1 THEIRS	8 THROWING
4 SWEAR	2 TAMIL	250 THEM	17 THROWN
3 SWEARING	1 TAN	1 THEM'	2 THROWS
4 SWEAT	1 TAN-AND-PINK	22 THEMSELVES	8 THRUST
1 SWEAT-RAG	3 TANGIBLE	262 THEN	5 THUMB
2 SWEATED	1 TANGLE	3 THEORY	3 THUMBS
1 SWEATING	1 TANGLED	524 THERE	4 THUMP
5 SWEEP	1 TANK	1 THERE'	1 THUMPED
1 SWEEPERS	1 TANKS	34 THERE'S	2 THUMPING
2 SWEEPING	1 TANNED	4 THEREAFTER	11 THUNDER
2 SWEEPS	4 TAP	5 THEREFORE	1 THUNDER-CLOUDS
6 SWEET	2 TAPPED	1 THEREIN	1 THUNDERED
1 SWEET-POTATOES	2 TAPPING	3 THEREUPON	1 THUNDERSTORM
1 SWEETLY	2 TARNISHED	149 THESE	1 THUNDERSTRUCK
5 SWELL	1 TARRY	444 THEY	31 THUS
1 SWELTERED	5 TASK	1 THEY'LL	4 THWART
10 SWEPT	1 TASKMASTER	1 THEY'VE	1 THWARTED
1 SWERVED	2 TASTE	20 THICK	3 THY
6 SWIFT	1 TASTE-	1 THICK-LIPPED	2 TI
13 SWIFTLY	1 TASTED	1 THICKENED	1 TI-TI-ME
5 SWIM	1 TATTOOED	1 THICKETS	2 TICKETS
1 SWIMMER	1 TAUGHT	1 THICKLY	1 TICKLED
1 SWIMMING	1 TAXED	1 THICKNESS	12 TIDE
1 SWINDLE	1 TEA	4 THIEF	1 TIDES
1 SWINDLER	2 TEACH	1 THIEVES	1 TIDILY
5 SWING	2 TEAK	1 THIEVING	1 TIDINGS
2 SWINGING	8 TEAR	1 THIGH	3 TIED
1 SWIRL	3 TEARING	1 THIGHS	1 TIES
1 SWIRLING	12 TEARS	17 THIN	5 TIFFIN
1 SWIRLS	1 TEASPOON	137 THING	1 TIFFIN-TIME
3 SWISH	2 TEEMING	1 THING'	6 TIGHT
1 SWISH-SWISH	12 TEETH	1 THING'LL	66 TILL
2 SWISHED	1 TELEGRAPH	46 THINGS	9 TILLER
1 SWITCH	3 TELESCOPE	133 THINK	4 TILT
1 SWITCHING	110 TELL	1 THINKER	1 TILTED
1 SWITZERLAND	24 TELLING	28 THINKING	1 TILTING
1 SWIVEL	4 TELLS	4 THINKS	4 TIMBER
3 SWOLLEN	6 TEMPER	1 THINLY	271 TIME
1 SWOLLEN-FACED		1 THINNER	1 TIMELY

39 TIMES	2 TOTTERED	1 TREAT	3 TUG
1 TIMID	1 TOTTERING	5 TREATED	1 TUGGING
1 TIMIDITY	29 TOUCH	1 TREBLY	1 TUGS
1 TIMIDLY	10 TOUCHED	17 TREE	2 TUMBLE
6 TIN	9 TOUCHING	4 TREE-TOPS	1 TUMBLE-DOWN
1 TIN-POT	3 TOUGH	1 TREE-TRUNK	7 TUMBLED
1 TING	1 TOULON	1 TREE'D	3 TUMBLER
2 TINGE	1 TOUSLED	21 TREES	3 TUMBLING
3 TINGED	3 TOUT	1 TREETRUNK	5 TUMULT
1 TINKERS	1 TOUTE	5 TREMBLE	1 TUMULTUOUS
2 TINKLE	3 TOW	6 TREMBLED	2 TUMULTUOUSLY
1 TINKLING	30 TOWARDS	6 TREMBLING	3 TUNE
1 TINT	2 TOWED	1 TREMELY	1 TUNJU
11 TINY	4 TOWER	6 TREMENDOUS	9 TUNKU
2 TIP	1 TOWERED	2 TREMOR	1 TUNNEL
3 TIPPED	1 TOWERING	1 TREMULOUS	2 TURBAN
5 TIPS	3 TOWING	2 TREMULOUSLY	3 TURMOIL
1 TIPTOE	39 TOWN	1 TREPIDATION	36 TURN
1 TIPTOED	1 TOWN-REACH	1 TRES	72 TURNED
1 TIPTOEING	1 TOWNFOLK	1 TRIAL	1 TURNED-OUT
9 TIRED	1 TOWNSFOLK	1 TRIBES	19 TURNING
1 TIS	3 TOY	1 TRIBUTARY	1 TURNPIKE
1 TISPEP	1 TOYING	2 TRIBUTE	3 TURNS
1 TISPEP-SHIA	2 TOYS	1 TRICED	1 TURTLE
1 TISSUES	1 TRAC	4 TRICK	2 TURTLES'
1 TITTERING	8 TRACE	1 TRICKED	2 TUSSLE
3239 TO	1 TRACED	1 TRICKLE	2 TWANG
1 TO-	2 TRACES	2 TRICKLED	1 TWEED
4 TO-DAY	1 TRACINGS	1 TRICKLING	3 TWELVE
2 TO-DO	4 TRACK	1 TRICKS	35 TWENTY
13 TO-MORROW	2 TRACKS	45 TRIED	3 TWENTY-FIVE
5 TO-NIGHT	1 TRACTABILITY	1 TRIES	1 TWENTY-FOOT
1 TO'	1 TRACTABLE	1 TRIESTE	1 TWENTY-FOOT-HIGH
3 TOADS	12 TRADE	2 TRIFLE	1 TWENTY-FOUR
4 TOBACCO	2 TRADED	3 TRIFLES	1 TWENTY-SEVEN
5 TOES	8 TRADER	2 TRIFLING	2 TWENTY-TWO
73 TOGETHER	2 TRADERS	2 TRIGGER	19 TWICE
5 TOIL	10 TRADING	1 TRIGONOMETRY	3 TWIGS
1 TOILED	1 TRADINGCLERK	2 TRIM	2 TWILIGHT
1 TOILING	3 TRADITION	3 TRIP	1 TWILIGHTS
3 TOKEN	1 TRADITION'S	1 TRIPOD	3 TWIN
98 TOLD	1 TRADITIONALLY	1 TRIPOLI	2 TWINKLE
1 TOLERABLY	2 TRAFFIC	1 TRIPPED	4 TWINKLED
2 TOLERANCE	6 TRAGIC	1 TRISTE	2 TWINKLING
1 TOLERATION	2 TRAIL	4 TRIUMPH	1 TWIRL
1 TOLL	1 TRAILED	2 TRIUMPHANTLY	1 TWIRLING
1 TOLLING	2 TRAILING	1 TROAT	5 TWIST
1 TOM	1 TRAILS	2 TRODDEN	2 TWISTED
3 TOMB	4 TRAINING	3 TROOP	1 TWISTING
2 TOMORROW	2 TRAINING-SHIP	6 TROPICAL	1 TWITCH
2 TON	1 TRAITOR	3 TROPICS	2 TWITCHED
1 TONDANO	1 TRAMMELS	1 TROT	1 TWITCHING
48 TONE	3 TRAMP	1 TROTTED	183 TWO
8 TONES	1 TRAMP-	1 TROTTER	1 TWO-BRANCHED
9 TONGUE	3 TRAMPED	2 TROTTERS	1 TWO-THIRDS
2 TONGUES	2 TRAMPLE	1 TROTTING	1 TWOPENCE
1 TONICS	1 TRAMPLE'	22 TROUBLE	1 TWOPENNY
1 TONS	3 TRAMPLED	9 TROUBLED	1 TYKE
236 TOO	1 TRAMPLING	1 TROUBLES	1 TYPICAL
59 TOOK	1 TRAMPS	3 TROUSERS	2 TYRANNICAL
2 TOOLS	2 TRANCE	1 TROUVAILLE	3 UGLY
1 TOOTHLESSLY	1 TRANQUILLITY	1 TRUCES	1 ULTIMATELY
17 TOP	2 TRANSACTION	1 TRUCKLING	5 UMBRELLA
1 TOP-GALLANT	1 TRANSACTIONS	2 TRUCULENT	2 UN
1 TOPI	1 TRANSFER	50 TRUE	2 UNABASHED
1 TOPPED	1 TRANSFERRED	1 TRUER	6 UNABLE
6 TOPS	2 TRANSGRESSION	4 TRULY	1 UNACCOUNTABLE
1 TOPSAIL	1 TRANSHIP	1 TRUMPETING	1 UNACCUSTOMED
10 TORCH	1 TRANSITIONS	1 TRUMPETS	1 UNALTERABLE
3 TORCHES	2 TRANSLATED	3 TRUNK	1 UNANIMOUSLY
1 TORCHLIGHT	1 TRANSPLANTED	1 TRUNKS	3 UNANSWERABLE
5 TORE	2 TRANSPORTED	16 TRUST	1 UNAPPEASABLE
2 TORMENT	2 TRAP	15 TRUSTED	1 UNAPPROACHABLE
1 TORMENTED	3 TRAPPED	1 TRUSTFULNESS	1 UNARMED
2 TORMENTING	4 TRAVEL	4 TRUSTING	1 UNASKED
6 TORN	3 TRAVELLED	1 TRUSTS	1 UNASSUMING
2 TORPID	1 TRAVELLER	3 TRUSTWORTHY	3 UNATTAINABLE
1 TORPOR	1 TRAVELLERS	2 TRUSTY	1 UNATTENDED
1 TORRENT	1 TRAVELLING	56 TRUTH	1 UNATTRACTIVE
1 TORRID	1 TRAVELS	1 TRUTH'	2 UNAVOIDABLE
1 TORTOISE	4 TRAVERSED	1 TRUTH'S	1 UNAVOIDABLY
1 TORTUOUS	1 TRAVERSING	1 TRUTHFUL	1 UNAWARE
1 TORTUOUSLY	1 TRAY	1 TRUTHFULLY	3 UNAWARES
2 TORTURED	4 TREACHEROUS	2 TRUTHFULNESS	3 UNBEARABLE
3 TOSS	5 TREACHERY	1 TRUTHS	1 UNBECOMING
2 TOSSED	4 TREAD	24 TRY	2 UNBELIEF
7 TOSSING	1 TREADING	35 TRYING	1 UNBELIEVERS
3 TOTAL	1 TREASURED	19 TUAN	1 UNBELIEVING
5 TOTALLY	1 TREASURER	4 TUCKED	3 UNBOUNDED
1 TOTTER	1 TREASURES	1 TUFTS	1 UNBRIDLED

1 UNBROKEN	3 UNFORGIVING	1 UNUSED	29 VAST
2 UNBUTTONED	1 UNFORGOTTEN	3 UNUSUAL	1 VASTLY
1 UNCANNY	5 UNFORTUNATE	1 UNUTTERABLE	2 VASTNESS
2 UNCEASING	2 UNFORTUNATELY	1 UNVEILING	2 VAULT
1 UNCEASINGLY	1 UNGAINLY	1 UNWATCHED	2 VEGETATION
4 UNCERTAIN	1 UNGRACIOUS	3 UNWEARIED	3 VEHEMENT
1 UNCHANGEABLE	1 UNHAPPILY	2 UNWELL	3 VEIL
3 UNCHANGED	2 UNHAPPY	1 UNWHOLESOME	7 VEILED
1 UNCHANGING	1 UNHARMED	1 UNWIELDY	2 VEIN
2 UNCHECKED	1 UNHEALTHY	1 UNWILLING	1 VEININGS
1 UNCLASP	1 UNHEARD	1 UNWITTINGLY	1 VEINS
1 UNCLASPED	1 UNHEARD-OF	1 UNWORTHY	1 VELVETY
1 UNCLEAN	1 UNHESITATING	1 UNWRINKLED	3 VENERABLE
2 UNCLES	1 UNHOLY	451 UP	2 VENETIAN
1 UNCLOUDED	3 UNHOOK	1 UP-COUNTRY	4 VENGEANCE
3 UNCOMMONLY	3 UNIFORM	1 UP-ENDED	4 VENGEFUL
3 UNCOMPREHENDING	1 UNINHABITABLE	2 UP-RIVER	1 VENGEFULNESS
2 UNCOMPROMISING	1 UNINHABITED	1 UPBRAIDING	1 VENOMOUSLY
1 UNCONCEIVABLE	1 UNINTELLECTUAL	1 UPHELD	1 VENT
1 UNCONCERN	1 UNINTELLIGENT	1 UPLIFTING	2 VENTILATORS
1 UNCONCERNED	2 UNINTELLIGIBLE	227 UPON	2 VENTURED
2 UNCONSCIONABLE	2 UNINTERESTING	4 UPPER	1 VENTURES
8 UNCONSCIOUS	2 UNINTERRUPTED	8 UPRIGHT	1 VENTURING
3 UNCONSCIOUSLY	1 UNION	1 UPRISE	26 VERANDAH
1 UNCONSCIOUSNESS	3 UNIQUE	4 UPRISING	1 VERDAMTE
1 UNCONSOLING	1 UNITED	2 UPROAR	1 VERDICT
1 UNCONTROLLABLE	1 UNIVERSALLY	2 UPROOTED	1 VERFLUCHTE
1 UNCOUNTED	6 UNIVERSE	4 UPROSE	5 VERGE
5 UNCOVERED	1 UNJUST	4 UPSET	1 VERITAS
1 UNCRESTED	1 UNKIND	1 UPSIDE	2 VERMIN
1 UNCROSSED	1 UNKNOWABLE	5 UPSTAIRS	1 VERMIN-LIKE
1 UND	15 UNKNOWN	2 UPSTANDING	1 VERSION
1 UNDEFACED	12 UNLESS	2 UPSTREAM	3 VERTICAL
3 UNDENIABLE	1 UNLIMITED	2 UPTURNED	1 VERTICALLY
178 UNDER	2 UNLOADED	2 UPWARD	350 VERY
1 UNDERESTIMATE	1 UNLOPPED	5 UPWARDS	2 VESSEL
1 UNDERESTIMATED	2 UNLUCKY	4 URGED	2 VESSELS
1 UNDERGONE	1 UNMARRED	2 URGENT	2 VESTIGE
4 UNDERGROUND	1 UNMARRIED	1 URGING	1 VEUX
3 UNDERGROWTH	1 UNMENTIONABLE	128 US	2 VEXATION
1 UNDERHAND	1 UNMITIGATED	1 USAGE	2 VEXED
2 UNDERMINED	1 UNMOLESTED	22 USE	1 VEXEDLY
1 UNDERSIZED	3 UNMOVED	25 USED	2 VIBRATE
51 UNDERSTAND	1 UNNATURAL	1 USED-UP	4 VIBRATING
2 UNDERSTANDING	1 UNNOTICED	4 USEFUL	2 VIBRATION
3 UNDERSTANDS	1 UNOBSCURED	3 USELESS	1 VICEROY
23 UNDERSTOOD	4 UNOFFENDING	1 USELESSLY	1 VICES
2 UNDERTAKE	1 UNPERPLEXED	1 USING	3 VICIOUS
1 UNDERTAKER	1 UNPLEASANT	2 USQUE	1 VICIOUSLY
2 UNDERTAKING	2 UNPLEASANTLY	11 USUAL	5 VICTIM
1 UNDERTONE	1 UNPREPARED	1 USUALLY	4 VICTIMS
1 UNDERWENT	1 UNPROPITIOUS	1 UTENSILS	1 VICTORIEUSE'
1 UNDERWRITERS	1 UNPROVOKED	1 UTILITARIAN	2 VICTORIOUS
2 UNDISCOVERED	1 UNQUESTIONING	3 UTMOST	3 VICTORY
1 UNDISGUISED	4 UNREASONABLE	11 UTTER	1 VIE
2 UNDISTURBED	1 UNREASONED	6 UTTERANCE	1 VIENT
1 UNDONE	1 UNREASONING	8 UTTERED	36 VIEW
1 UNDRAPED	1 UNRECORDED	2 UTTERING	1 VIEWED
1 UNDULATING	1 UNREFLECTING	17 UTTERLY	1 VIEWS
2 UNDULATIONS	1 UNRELIEVED	1 VA	2 VIGIL
1 UNDYING	1 UNRESERVE	1 VACANCY	3 VIGILANT
2 UNEARTHLY	1 UNRESERVEDLY	1 VACANT	4 VIGOROUS
1 UNEASILY	2 UNREST	6 VAGABOND	2 VIGOROUSLY
1 UNEASINESS	1 UNROLLED	2 VAGABONDS	3 VIGOUR
9 UNEASY	1 UNROVE	1 VAGARIES	3 VILE
1 UNENLIGHTENED	1 UNRUFFLED	8 VAGUE	1 VILL
1 UNEQUAL	2 UNSAFE	7 VAGUELY	20 VILLAGE
2 UNERRING	1 UNSATISFACTORY	3 VAGUENESS	2 VILLAGER
1 UNERRINGLY	2 UNSAVOURY	5 VAIN	5 VILLAGERS
1 UNEVEN	1 UNSCALABLE	1 VALIANT	6 VILLAGES
7 UNEXPECTED	1 UNSEALED	1 VALID	1 VILLAINIES
8 UNEXPECTEDLY	2 UNSEEMLY	2 VALISE	1 VILLAINOUS
2 UNEXPECTEDNESS	3 UNSEEN	2 VALLEY	1 VILLAINY
1 UNEXPLORED	2 UNSELFISH	2 VALLEYS	1 VILLE
3 UNEXPRESSED	3 UNSETTLED	1 VALOROUS	8 VIOLENCE
1 UNFADED	1 UNSHAKABLE	1 VALOUR	10 VIOLENT
2 UNFAILING	1 UNSHAKEN	1 VALUABLE	7 VIOLENTLY
2 UNFAIR	1 UNSOUNDNESS	2 VALUE	2 VIOLET
1 UNFAIRLY	3 UNSPEAKABLE	1 VAMPIRE	1 VIRGIN
1 UNFAITHFUL	1 UNSTEADILY	3 VANISH	1 VIRILE
1 UNFALTERING	2 UNSTEADY	11 VANISHED	1 VIRILITY
1 UNFALTERINGLY	1 UNSTIMULATED	1 VANISHES	1 VIRTUAL
2 UNFAMILIAR	1 UNSUBSTANTIAL	3 VANISHING	5 VIRTUE
3 UNFATHOMABLE	2 UNSUSPECTED	3 VANITY	3 VIRTUES
3 UNFLINCHING	1 UNSUSPECTING	3 VANLO'S	1 VIRTUOUS
1 UNFLINCHINGLY	1 UNSWAYING	2 VAPOUR	1 VISCOUS
2 UNFOLDED	2 UNTHINKING	1 VAPOURINGS	10 VISIBLE
1 UNFOLDING	2 UNTOLD	1 VARIETY	1 VISIBLY
2 UNFORESEEN	2 UNTOUCHED	5 VARIOUS	8 VISION
1 UNFORGIVEN	2 UNTROUBLED	2 VASE	5 VISIONS

7 VISIT	10 WARIS'S	3 WEEP	2 WHITENED
1 VISITATION	1 WARLIKE	3 WEEPING	10 WHITES
2 VISITED	10 WARM	1 WEIGH	1 WHITEWASHED
2 VISITING	1 WARMLY	1 WEIGHED	1 WHITISH
1 VISITING-CARD	4 WARMTH	7 WEIGHT	243 WHO
1 VISITOR	1 WARN	3 WEIRD	4 WHO'S
1 VISITS	5 WARNED	1 WEIRDLY	59 WHOLE
1 VISTA	4 WARNING	4 WELCOME	2 WHOLLY
2 VISUAL	4 WARNINGS	1 WELCOMED	39 WHOM
1 VITALITY	2 WARP	2 WELFARE	1 WHOOP
3 VIVID	1 WARRANTED	149 WELL	1 WHOOPING
1 VIVIDLY	1 WARS	1 WELL-ARMED	47 WHOSE
1 VIVIDNESS	1800 WAS	1 WELL-BEING	91 WHY
2 VOCATION	2 WASH	1 WELL-BRED	1 WICKED
129 VOICE	1 WASHED	1 WELL-DIRECTED	1 WICKEDNESS
21 VOICES	1 WASHERS	1 WELL-FOUND	1 WICKER
2 VOID	3 WASHING	1 WELL-GROOMED	21 WIDE
1 VOILA	38 WASN'T	1 WELL-KNOWN	1 WIDENED
2 VOLCANO	5 WASTE	1 WELL-PROPORTIONED	1 WIDER
1 VOLITION	1 WASTE-LAND	1 WELL-TO-DO	1 WIE
4 VOLLEY	2 WASTED	1 WELLINGTON	20 WIFE
1 VOLLEY-FIRING	19 WATCH	1 WENDED	1 WIFE'
1 VOLLEYS	1 WATCH-CHAIN	157 WENT	2 WIFE'S
2 VOLUBILITY	28 WATCHED	4 WEPT	15 WILD
3 VOLUBLE	1 WATCHERS	378 WERE	7 WILDERNESS
1 VOLUME	2 WATCHES	4 WEREN'T	2 WILDEST
3 VOLUMINOUS	6 WATCHFUL	11 WEST	3 WILDLY
2 VOLUNTEER	1 WATCHFUL-LIKE	1 WESTERING	1 WILDNESS
1 VOLUNTEERING	2 WATCHFULNESS	5 WESTERN	91 WILL
1 VOTRE	12 WATCHING	1 WESTWARD	1 WILLED
1 VOUCH	1 WATCHMAKER	7 WET	8 WILLING
1 VOUCHED	100 WATER	1 WHALER	1 WILLINGLY
2 VOUS	1 WATER-BOTTLE	1 WHALERS	1 WINCE
1 VOWS	1 WATER-BREAKER	1 WHARF	1 WINCED
9 VOYAGE	8 WATER-CLERK	411 WHAT	1 WINCH
2 VOYAGES	2 WATER-CLERKS	35 WHAT'S	1 WINCHES
1 VREE	1 WATER-DUST	1 WHAT'S-HIS-NAME	35 WIND
1 VROM	2 WATER-GATE	1 WHAT'S-YOUR-NAME	1 WIND-SAIL
2 VULGAR	1 WATER-LOGGED	12 WHATEVER	1 WINDING
2 W	2 WATER-PIPE	1 WHEAT	2 WINDLASS
1 WADDLE	1 WATER-SUPPLY	1 WHEEDLING	13 WINDOW
1 WAFTED	1 WATER-TANK	4 WHEEL	1 WINDOW-PANES
1 WAG	1 WATER-TIGHT	1 WHEEL-CHAINS	5 WINDOWS
1 WAGES	2 WATER'S	1 WHEELING	2 WINDWARD
2 WAGGED	1 WATERFALL	2 WHEELS	3 WINE
1 WAIFS	1 WATERFOWL	1 WHEEZED	2 WING
2 WAIL	1 WATERLINE	1 WHEEZING	3 WINGED
3 WAILING	13 WATERS	2 WHEEZY	13 WINGS
1 WAILS	4 WATERSIDE	1 WHELPS	5 WINK
5 WAIST	1 WATERY	218 WHEN	2 WINKED
2 WAISTCOAT	1 WATERY-EYED	1 WHEN'	2 WINKING
23 WAIT	1 WATTLED	4 WHENCE	1 WINKS
11 WAITED	5 WAVE	4 WHENEVER	1 WINNING
1 WAITER	2 WAVED	115 WHERE	1 WINS
31 WAITING	1 WAVELETS	3 WHERE'S	3 WINTER'S
1 WAJO	2 WAVERING	1 WHEREABOUTS	1 WIPE
8 WAKE	7 WAVES	1 WHEREAS	2 WIPED
1 WAKING	1 WAVING	1 WHEREFORE	2 WIPING
2 WALES	2 WAXED	1 WHEREIN	1 WIRES
11 WALK	1 WAXES	1 WHEREVER	1 WIRY
28 WALKED	158 WAY	43 WHETHER	10 WISDOM
15 WALKING	1 WAYFARER	281 WHICH	5 WISE
2 WALKS	1 WAYFARERS	160 WHILE	1 WISER
28 WALL	3 WAYLAID	1 WHILED	1 WISEST
1 WALLAH	6 WAYS	2 WHILES	16 WISH
2 WALLED	189 WE	1 WHIM	15 WISHED
1 WALLOW	2 WE'LL	1 WHIMPERED	2 WISHING
1 WALLOWING	1 WE'RE	3 WHINE	2 WISP
12 WALLS	4 WE'VE	4 WHINED	3 WISPS
7 WALPOLE	7 WEAK	2 WHIPPED	2 WISTFUL
1 WAN	1 WEAK-HEADED	2 WHIRL	2 WISTFULLY
2 WAND	1 WEAKEN	1 WHIRLED	2 WIT
5 WANDER	1 WEAKEST	1 WHIRLS	4 WITCH
6 WANDERED	7 WEAKNESS	1 WHISK	1 WITCH-LIKE
1 WANDERERS	3 WEALTH	1 WHISKED	1319 WITH
10 WANDERING	1 WEALTHY	2 WHISKER	1 WITH-OUT
1 WANDERINGS	2 WEAPON	1 WHISKERED	1 WITH'
64 WANT	1 WEAPONED	1 WHISKERS	3 WITHDRAW
59 WANTED	1 WEAPONS	1 WHISKY	3 WITHDRAWN
1 WANTING	3 WEAR	13 WHISPER	2 WITHDRAWS
6 WANTS	6 WEARINESS	17 WHISPERED	4 WITHDREW
1 WAPPING	1 WEARING	1 WHISPERER	1 WITHER
25 WAR	11 WEARY	10 WHISPERING	3 WITHERED
3 WAR-BOATS	9 WEATHER	7 WHISPERS	1 WITHERING
3 WAR-COMRADE	1 WEAVING	1 WHIST	44 WITHIN
2 WAR-CRIES	1 WEB	3 WHISTLE	171 WITHOUT
1 WAR-WORN	1 WEDDING	1 WHISTLING	3 WITNESS
7 WARD	10 WEEK	1 WHIT	1 WITNESS-BOX
1 WARINESS	1 WEEK-DAY	155 WHITE	1 WITNESSING
29 WARIS	9 WEEKS	1 WHITE-FACED	1 WITS

1 WIVES	2 YAMS	0	0
2 WIZENED	6 YANKEE	0	0
1 WOBBLED	10 YAP	0	0
3 WOE	1 YAPPING	0	0
1 WOE-BEGONE	6 YARD	0	0
2 WOKE	10 YARDS	0	0
1 WOLFISH	2 YARN	0	0
1 WOLFISHLY	4 YAWNING	0	0
1 WOLVERINE	13 YEAR	0	0
36 WOMAN	1 YEAR'S	0	0
26 WOMEN	4 YEARNING	0	0
2 WOMEN-FOLK	49 YEARS	0	0
22 WON'T	2 YEARS'	0	0
29 WONDER	6 YELL	0	0
7 WONDERED	6 YELLED	0	0
17 WONDERFUL	7 YELLING	0	0
6 WONDERFULLY	24 YELLOW	0	0
4 WONDERING	1 YELLOW-DOG	0	0
1 WONDERS	1 YELLOWED	0	0
1 WONT	1 YELLOWISH	0	0
7 WOOD	2 YELLS	0	0
1 WOOD-FILE	1 YELP	0	0
1 WOOD-SMOKE	1 YELPS	0	0
1 WOODED	88 YES	0	0
9 WOODEN	78 YET	0	0
2 WOODEN-FACED	2 YIELDED	0	0
1 WOODS	1 YOKE	0	0
83 WORD	1 YOKOHAMA	0	0
77 WORDS	1 YONDER	0	0
7 WORE	1 YORK	0	0
45 WORK	1034 YOU	0	0
6 WORKED	1 YOU'	0	0
6 WORKING	4 YOU'LL	0	0
1 WORKMEN	6 YOU'RE	0	0
1 WORKS	12 YOU'VE	0	0
79 WORLD	59 YOUNG	0	0
1 WORLD'S	4 YOUNGER	0	0
1 WORLDS	1 YOUNGEST	0	0
3 WORM	7 YOUNGSTER	0	0
1 WORM-EATEN	1 YOUNGSTERS	0	0
5 WORN	106 YOUR	0	0
1 WORN-OUT	5 YOURS	0	0
3 WORRIED	23 YOURSELF	0	0
8 WORRY	1 YOURSELF'	0	0
19 WORSE	2 YOURSELVES	0	0
1 WORSHIP	33 YOUTH	0	0
11 WORST	4 YOUTHFUL	0	0
17 WORTH	3 YOUTHS	0	0
1 WORTHY	4 YUCKER	0	0
535 WOULD	2 ZAMBOANGA	0	0
33 WOULDN'T	2 ZENITH	0	0
4 WOUND	1 ZERO	0	0
11 WOUNDED	1 ZONE	0	0
1 WOUNDS	1 1848	0	0
1 WOVEN	2 2	0	0
1 WRAITH	1 230	0	0
5 WRAPPED	1 30	0	0
1 WRE	1 6000	0	0
2 WREATHED	1 7	0	0
1 WRECK	1 7-POUNDERS	0	0
1 WRECKER	1 900	0	0
1 WREST	0	0	0
2 WRESTLING	0	0	0
1 WRESTLING-MATCH	0	0	0
2 WRETCH'S	0	0	0
16 WRETCHED	0	0	0
1 WRETCHEDNESS	0	0	0
2 WRIGGLE	0	0	0
1 WRIGGLED	0	0	0
1 WRIGGLING	0	0	0
1 WRING	0	0	0
1 WRINGING	0	0	0
1 WRINKLE	0	0	0
3 WRINKLED	0	0	0
2 WRINKLES	0	0	0
1 WRISTS	0	0	0
1 WRIT	0	0	0
8 WRITE	0	0	0
2 WRITHE	0	0	0
3 WRITHED	0	0	0
2 WRITHING	0	0	0
13 WRITING	0	0	0
2 WRITING-DESK	0	0	0
1 WRITINGCASE	0	0	0
8 WRITTEN	0	0	0
15 WRONG	0	0	0
2 WRONG-HEADED	0	0	0
13 WROTE	0	0	0
5 WRUNG	0	0	0
1 YAM	0	0	0

PART III

Field of Reference

1.01 HE was an inch, perhaps two, under six
1.02 feet, powerfully built, and he advanced
1.03 straight at you with a slight stoop of the
1.04 shoulders, head forward, and a fixed from-under
1.05 stare which made you think of a charging bull.
1.06 His voice was deep, loud, and his manner displayed
1.07 a kind of dogged self-assertion which had nothing
1.08 aggressive in it. It seemed a necessity, and it was
1.09 directed apparently as much at himself as at any-
1.10 body else. He was spotlessly neat, apparelled in
1.11 immaculate white from shoes to hat, and in the
1.12 various Eastern ports where he got his living as
1.13 ship-chandler's water-clerk he was very popular.
1.14 A water-clerk need not pass an examination in
1.15 anything under the sun, but he must have Ability
1.16 in the abstract and demonstrate it practically. His
1.17 work consists in racing under sail, steam, or oars
1.18 against other water-clerks for any ship about to
1.19 anchor, greeting her captain cheerily, forcing upon
1.20 him a card -- the business card of the ship-chandler --
2.01   and on his first visit on shore piloting him firmly but
2.02 without ostentation to a vast, cavern-like shop which
2.03 is full of things that are eaten and drunk on board
2.04 ship; where you can get everything to make her
2.05 seaworthy and beautiful, from a set of chain-hooks
2.06 for her cable to a book of gold-leaf for the carvings
2.07 of her stern; and where her commander is received
2.08 like a brother by a ship-chandler he has never seen
2.09 before. There is a cool parlour, easy-chairs, bottles,
2.10 cigars, writing implements, a copy of harbour
2.11 regulations, and a warmth of welcome that melts the
2.12 salt of a three months' passage out of a seaman's
2.13 heart. The connection thus begun is kept up, as
2.14 long as the ship remains in harbour, by the daily
2.15 visits of the water-clerk. To the captain he is
2.16 faithful like a friend and attentive like a son, with
2.17 the patience of Job, the unselfish devotion of a
2.18 woman, and the jollity of a boon companion. Later
2.19 on the bill is sent in. It is a beautiful and humane
2.20 occupation. Therefore good water-clerks are scarce.
2.21 When a water-clerk who possesses Ability in the
2.22 abstract has also the advantage of having been
2.23 brought up to the sea, he is worth to his employer
2.24 a lot of money and some humouring. Jim had
2.25 always good wages and as much humouring as
2.26 would have bought the fidelity of a fiend. Never-
2.27 theless, with black ingratitude he would throw up
2.28 the job suddenly and depart. To his employers
2.29 the reasons he gave were obviously inadequate.
2.30 They said "Confounded fool!" as soon as his back
3.01 was turned. This was their criticism on his ex-
3.02 quisite sensibility.
3.03 To the white men in the waterside business and
3.04 to the captains of ships he was just Jim -- nothing
3.05 more. He had, of course, another name, but he was
3.06 anxious that it should not be pronounced. His
3.07 incognito, which had as many holes as a sieve, was
3.08 not meant to hide a personality but a fact. When
3.09 the fact broke through the incognito he would leave
3.10 suddenly the seaport where he happened to be at the
3.11 time and go to another -- generally farther east. He
3.12 kept to seaports because he was a seaman in exile
3.13 from the sea, and had Ability in the abstract, which is
3.14 good for no other work but that of a water-clerk.
3.15 He retreated in good order towards the rising sun,
3.16 and the fact followed him casually but inevitably.
3.17 Thus in the course of years he was known suc-
3.18 cessively in Bombay, in Calcutta, in Rangoon, in
3.19 Penang, in Batavia -- and in each of these halting--
3.20 places was just Jim the water-clerk. Afterwards,
3.21 when his keen perception of the Intolerable drove
3.22 him away for good from seaports and white men,
3.23 even into the virgin forest, the Malays of the jungle
3.24 village, where he had elected to conceal his deplor-
3.25 able faculty, added a word to the monosyllable of
3.26 his incognito. They called him Tuan Jim: as one
3.27 might say -- Lord Jim.
3.28 Originally he came from a parsonage. Many
3.29 commanders of fine merchant-ships come from these
3.30 abodes of piety and peace. Jim's father possessed
4.01 such certain knowledge of the Unknowable as made
4.02 for the righteousness of people in cottages without
4.03 disturbing the ease of mind of those whom an un-
4.04 erring Providence enables to live in mansions. The
4.05 little church on a hill had the mossy greyness of
4.06 a rock seen through a ragged screen of leaves. It
4.07 had stood there for centuries, but the trees around
4.08 probably remembered the laying of the first stone.
4.09 Below, the red front of the rectory gleamed with a
4.10 warm tint in the midst of grass-plots, flower-beds,
4.11 and fir-trees, with an orchard at the back, a paved
4.12 stable-yard to the left, and the sloping grass of green--
4.13 houses tacked along a wall of bricks. The living had
4.14 belonged to the family for generations; but Jim was
4.15 one of five sons, and when after a course of light
4.16 holiday literature his vocation for the sea had de-
4.17 clared itself, he was sent at once to a "training-ship
4.18 for officers of the mercantile marine."
4.19 He learned there a little trigonometry and how
4.20 to cross top-gallant yards. He was generally liked.
4.21 He had the third place in navigation and pulled
4.22 stroke in the first cutter. Having a steady head
4.23 with an excellent physique, he was very smart aloft.
4.24 His station was in the fore-top, and often from there
4.25 he looked down, with the contempt of a man
4.26 destined to shine in the midst of dangers, at the
4.27 peaceful multitude of roofs cut in two by the brown
4.28 tide of the stream, while scattered on the outskirts
4.29 of the surrounding plain the factory chimneys rose
4.30 perpendicular against a grimy sky, each slender like
5.01   a pencil, and belching out smoke like a volcano.
5.02 He could see the big ships departing, the broad--
5.03 beamed ferries constantly on the move, the little
5.04 boats floating far below his feet, with the hazy
5.05 splendour of the sea in the distance, and the hope
5.06 of a stirring life in the world of adventure.
5.07 On the lower deck in the babel of two hundred
5.08 voices he would forget himself, and beforehand live
5.09 in his mind the sea-life of light literature. He saw
5.10 himself saving people from sinking ships, cutting
5.11 away masts in a hurricane, swimming through a surf
5.12 with a line; or as a lonely castaway, barefooted
5.13 and half naked, walking on uncovered reefs in
5.14 search of shell-fish to stave off starvation. He con-
5.15 fronted savages on tropical shores, quelled mutinies
5.16 on the high seas, and in a small boat upon the ocean
5.17 kept up the hearts of despairing men -- always an
5.18 example of devotion to duty, and as unflinching as
5.19 a hero in a book.
5.20 "Something's up. Come along."
5.21 He leaped to his feet. The boys were streaming
5.22 up the ladders. Above could be heard a great
5.23 scurrying about and shouting, and when he got
5.24 through the hatchway he stood still -- as if con-
5.25 founded.
5.26 It was the dusk of a winter's day. The gale had
5.27 freshened since noon, stopping the traffic on the
5.28 river, and now blew with the strength of a hurricane
5.29 in fitful bursts that boomed like salvos of great guns
5.30 firing over the ocean. The rain slanted in sheets
6.01 that flicked and subsided, and between whiles Jim
6.02 had threatening glimpses of the tumbling tide, the
6.03 small craft jumbled and tossing along the shore, the
6.04 motionless buildings in the driving mist, the broad
6.05 ferry-boats pitching ponderously at anchor, the
6.06 vast landing-stages heaving up and down and
6.07 smothered in sprays. The next gust seemed to
6.08 blow all this away. The air was full of flying
6.09 water. There was a fierce purpose in the gale, a
6.10 furious earnestness in the screech of the wind, in
6.11 the brutal tumult of earth and sky, that seemed
6.12 directed at him, and made him hold his breath in
6.13 awe. He stood still. It seemed to him he was
6.14 whirled around.
6.15 He was jostled. "Man the cutter!" Boys
6.16 rushed past him. A coaster running in for shelter
6.17 had crashed through a schooner at anchor, and one
6.18 of the ship's instructors had seen the accident.
6.19 A mob of boys clambered on the rails, clustered
6.20 round the davits. "Collision. Just ahead of us.
6.21 Mr. Symons saw it." A push made him stagger
6.22 against the mizzen-mast, and he caught hold of a
6.23 rope. The old training-ship chained to her moor-
6.24 ings quivered all over, bowing gently head to wind,
6.25 and with her scanty rigging humming in a deep
6.26 bass the breathless song of her youth at sea.
6.27 "Lower away!" He saw the boat, manned, drop
6.28 swiftly below the rail, and rushed after her. He
6.29 heard a splash. "Let go; clear the falls!" He
6.30 leaned over. The river alongside seethed in frothy
7.01 streaks. The cutter could be seen in the falling
7.02 darkness under the spell of tide and wind, that
7.03 for a moment held her bound, and tossing abreast
7.04 of the ship. A yelling voice in her reached him
7.05 faintly: "Keep stroke, you young whelps, if you
7.06 want to save anybody! Keep stroke!" And
7.07 suddenly she lifted high her bow, and, leaping
7.08 with raised oars over a wave, broke the spell cast
7.09 upon her by the wind and tide.

7.10 Jim felt his shoulder gripped firmly. "Too
7.11 late, youngster." The captain of the ship laid a
7.12 restraining hand on that boy, who seemed on the
7.13 point of leaping overboard, and Jim looked up with
7.14 the pain of conscious defeat in his eyes. The
7.15 captain smiled sympathetically. "Better luck next
7.16 time. This will teach you to be smart."
7.17 A shrill cheer greeted the cutter. She came
7.18 dancing back half full of water, and with two ex-
7.19 hausted men washing about on her bottom boards.
7.20 The tumult and the menace of wind and sea now
7.21 appeared very contemptible to Jim, increasing the
7.22 regret of his awe at their inefficient menace. Now
7.23 he knew what to think of it. It seemed to him he
7.24 cared nothing for the gale. He could affront greater
7.25 perils. He would do so -- better than anybody.
7.26 Not a particle of fear was left. Nevertheless, he
7.27 brooded apart that evening while the bowman of
7.28 the cutter -- a boy with a face like a girl's and big
7.29 grey eyes -- was the hero of the lower deck. Eager
7.30 questioners crowded round him. He narrated:
8.01 "I just saw his head bobbing, and I dashed my
8.02 boat-hook in the water. It caught in his breeches
8.03 and I nearly went overboard, as I thought I would,
8.04 only old Symons let go the tiller and grabbed my
8.05 legs -- the boat nearly swamped. Old Symons is
8.06 a fine old chap. I don't mind a bit him being
8.07 grumpy with us. He swore at me all the time he
8.08 held my leg, but that was only his way of telling
8.09 me to stick to the boat-hook. Old Symons is
8.10 awfully excitable -- isn't he? No -- not the little
8.11 fair chap -- the other, the big one with a beard.
8.12 When we pulled him in he groaned, 'Oh, my leg!
8.13 oh, my leg!' and turned up his eyes. Fancy such
8.14 a big chap fainting like a girl! Would any of you
8.15 fellows faint for a jab with a boat-hook? -- I
8.16 wouldn't. It went into his leg so far." He showed
8.17 the boat-hook, which he had carried below for the
8.18 purpose, and produced a sensation. "No, silly!
8.19 It was not his flesh that held him -- his breeches
8.20 did. Lots of blood, of course."
8.21 Jim thought it a pitiful display of vanity. The
8.22 gale had ministered to a heroism as spurious as its
8.23 own pretence of terror. He felt angry with the
8.24 brutal tumult of earth and sky for taking him
8.25 unawares and checking unfairly a generous readi-
8.26 ness for narrow escapes. Otherwise he was rather
8.27 glad he had not gone into the cutter, since a lower
8.28 achievement had served the turn. He had enlarged
8.29 his knowledge more than those who had done the
8.30 work. When all men flinched, then -- he felt sure --
9.01 he alone would know how to deal with the spurious
9.02 menace of wind and seas. He knew what to think
9.03 of it. Seen dispassionately, it seemed contemptible.
9.04 He could detect no trace of emotion in himself,
9.05 and the final effect of a staggering event was that,
9.06 unnoticed and apart from the noisy crowd of boys,
9.07 he exulted with fresh certitude in his avidity for
9.08 adventure, and in a sense of many-sided courage.
10.01 AFTER two years of training he went to
10.02 sea, and, entering the regions so well
10.03 known to his imagination, found them
10.04 strangely barren of adventure. He made many
10.05 voyages. He knew the magic monotony of exist-
10.06 ence between sky and water: he had to bear the
10.07 criticism of men, the exactions of the sea, and the
10.08 prosaic severity of the daily task that gives bread --
10.09 but whose only reward is in the perfect love of the
10.10 work. This reward eluded him. Yet he could not
10.11 go back, because there is nothing more enticing,
10.12 disenchanting, and enslaving than the life at sea.
10.13 Besides, his prospects were good. He was gentle-
10.14 manly, steady, tractable, with a thorough knowledge
10.15 of his duties; and in time, when yet very young, he
10.16 became chief mate of a fine ship, without ever having
10.17 been tested by those events of the sea that show
10.18 in the light of day the inner worth of a man, the
10.19 edge of his temper, and the fibre of his stuff; that
10.20 reveal the quality of his resistance and the secret
10.21 truth of his pretences, not only to others but also to
10.22 himself.
10.23 Only once in all that time he had again a
10.24 glimpse of the earnestness in the anger of the sea.
11.01 That truth is not so often made apparent as people
11.02 might think. There are many shades in the danger
11.03 of adventures and gales, and it is only now and then
11.04 that there appears on the face of facts a sinister
11.05 violence of intention -- that indefinable something
11.06 which forces it upon the mind and the heart of a
11.07 man, that this complication of accidents or these

11.08 elemental furies are coming at him with a purpose
11.09 of malice, with a strength beyond control, with an
11.10 unbridled cruelty that means to tear out of him his
11.11 hope and his fear, the pain of his fatigue and his
11.12 longing for rest: which means to smash, to destroy,
11.13 to annihilate all he has seen, known, loved, enjoyed,
11.14 or hated; all that is priceless and necessary -- the
11.15 sunshine, the memories, the future; which means
11.16 to sweep the whole precious world utterly away
11.17 from his sight by the simple and appalling act of
11.18 taking his life.
11.19 Jim, disabled by a falling spar at the beginning of
11.20 a week of which his Scottish captain used to say
11.21 afterwards, "Man! it's a pairfect meeracle to me
11.22 how she lived through it!" spent many days
11.23 stretched on his back, dazed, battered, hopeless, and
11.24 tormented as if at the bottom of an abyss of unrest.
11.25 He did not care what the end would be, and in his
11.26 lucid moments overvalued his indifference. The
11.27 danger, when not seen, has the imperfect vagueness
11.28 of human thought. The fear grows shadowy;
11.29 and Imagination, the enemy of men, the father of all
11.30 terrors, unstimulated, sinks to rest in the dullness of
12.01 exhausted emotion. Jim saw nothing but the
12.02 disorder of his tossed cabin. He lay there battened
12.03 down in the midst of a small devastation, and felt
12.04 secretly glad he had not to go on deck. But now
12.05 and again an uncontrollable rush of anguish would
12.06 grip him bodily, make him gasp and writhe under
12.07 the blankets, and then the unintelligent brutality
12.08 of an existence liable to the agony of such sensations
12.09 filled him with a despairing desire to escape at any
12.10 cost. Then fine weather returned, and he thought
12.11 no more about it.
12.12 His lameness, however, persisted, and when the
12.13 ship arrived at an Eastern port he had to go to the
12.14 hospital. His recovery was slow, and he was left
12.15 behind.
12.16 There were only two other patients in the white
12.17 men's ward: the purser of a gunboat, who had
12.18 broken his leg falling down a hatchway; and a
12.19 kind of railway contractor from a neighbouring
12.20 province, afflicted by some mysterious tropical
12.21 disease, who held the doctor for an ass, and indulged
12.22 in secret debaucheries of patent medicine which his
12.23 Tamil servant used to smuggle in with unwearied
12.24 devotion. They told each other the story of their
12.25 lives, played cards a little, or, yawning and in
12.26 pyjamas, lounged through the day in easy-chairs
12.27 without saying a word. The hospital stood on a
12.28 hill, and a gentle breeze entering through the
12.29 windows, always flung wide open, brought into the
12.30 bare room the softness of the sky, the languor of the
13.01 earth, the bewitching breath of the Eastern waters.
13.02 There were perfumes in it, suggestions of infinite
13.03 repose, the gift of endless dreams. Jim looked
13.04 every day over the thickets of gardens, beyond the
13.05 roofs of the town, over the fronds of palms growing
13.06 on the shore, at that roadstead which is a thorough-
13.07 fare to the East, -- at the roadstead dotted by gar-
13.08 landed islets, lighted by festal sunshine, its ships
13.09 like toys, its brilliant activity resembling a holiday
13.10 pageant, with the eternal serenity of the Eastern
13.11 sky overhead and the smiling peace of the Eastern
13.12 seas possessing the space as far as the horizon.
13.13 Directly he could walk without a stick, he de-
13.14 scended into the town to look for some opportunity
13.15 to get home. Nothing offered just then, and, while
13.16 waiting, he associated naturally with the men of his
13.17 calling in the port. These were of two kinds.
13.18 Some, very few and seen there but seldom, led
13.19 mysterious lives, had preserved an undefaced energy
13.20 with the temper of buccaneers and the eyes of
13.21 dreamers. They appeared to live in a crazy maze
13.22 of plans, hopes, dangers, enterprises, ahead of
13.23 civilisation, in the dark places of the sea; and their
13.24 death was the only event of their fantastic existence
13.25 that seemed to have a reasonable certitude of
13.26 achievement. The majority were men who, like
13.27 himself, thrown there by some accident, had re-
13.28 mained as officers of country ships. They had now
13.29 a horror of the home service, with its harder condi-
13.30 tions, severer view of duty, and the hazard of stormy
14.01 oceans. They were attuned to the eternal peace
14.02 of Eastern sky and sea. They loved short passages,
14.03 good deck-chairs, large native crews, and the dis-
14.04 tinction of being white. They shuddered at the
14.05 thought of hard work, and led precariously easy
14.06 lives, always on the verge of dismissal, always on
14.07 the verge of engagement, serving Chinamen, Arabs,

14.08 half-castes -- would have served the devil himself
14.09 had he made it easy enough. They talked ever-
14.10 lastingly of turns of luck: how So-and-so got
14.11 charge of a boat on the coast of China -- a soft thing;
14.12 how this one had an easy billet in Japan somewhere,
14.13 and that one was doing well in the Siamese navy;
14.14 and in all they said -- in their actions, in their looks,
14.15 in their persons -- could be detected the soft spot,
14.16 the place of decay, the determination to lounge safely
14.17 through existence.
14.18 To Jim that gossiping crowd, viewed as seamen,
14.19 seemed at first more unsubstantial than so many
14.20 shadows. But at length he found a fascination in
14.21 the sight of those men, in their appearance of doing
14.22 so well on such a small allowance of danger and toil.
14.23 In time, beside the original disdain there grew up
14.24 slowly another sentiment; and suddenly, giving up
14.25 the idea of going home, he took a berth as chief
14.26 mate of the Patna.
14.27 The Patna was a local steamer as old as the hills,
14.28 lean like a greyhound, and eaten up with rust worse
14.29 than a condemned water-tank. She was owned by
14.30 a Chinaman, chartered by an Arab, and commanded
15.01 by a sort of renegade New South Wales German,
15.02 very anxious to curse publicly his native country,
15.03 but who, apparently on the strength of Bismarck's
15.04 victorious policy, brutalised all those he was not
15.05 afraid of, and wore a "blood-and-iron" air, com-
15.06 bined with a purple nose and a red moustache.
15.07 After she had been painted outside and whitewashed
15.08 inside, eight hundred pilgrims (more or less) were
15.09 driven on board of her as she lay with steam up
15.10 alongside a wooden jetty.
15.11 They streamed aboard over three gangways,
15.12 they streamed in urged by faith and the hope of
15.13 paradise, they streamed in with a continuous tramp
15.14 and shuffle of bare feet, without a word, a murmur,
15.15 or a look back; and when clear of confining rails
15.16 spread on all sides over the deck, flowed forward and
15.17 aft, overflowed down the yawning hatchways, filled
15.18 the inner recesses of the ship -- like water filling a
15.19 cistern, like water flowing into crevices and crannies,
15.20 like water rising silently even with the rim. Eight
15.21 hundred men and women with faith and hopes, with
15.22 affections and memories, they had collected there,
15.23 coming from north and south and from the out-
15.24 skirts of the East, after treading the jungle paths,
15.25 descending the rivers, coasting in praus along the
15.26 shallows, crossing in small canoes from island to
15.27 island, passing through suffering, meeting strange
15.28 sights, beset by strange fears, upheld by one desire.
15.29 They came from solitary huts in the wilderness,
15.30 from populous campongs, from villages by the sea.
16.01 At the call of an idea they had left their forests,
16.02 their clearings, the protection of their rulers, their
16.03 prosperity, their poverty, the surroundings of their
16.04 youth and the graves of their fathers. They came
16.05 covered with dust, with sweat, with grime, with
16.06 rags -- the strong men at the head of family parties,
16.07 the lean old men pressing forward without hope
16.08 of return; young boys with fearless eyes glancing
16.09 curiously, shy little girls with tumbled long hair;
16.10 the timid women muffled up and clasping to their
16.11 breasts, wrapped in loose ends of soiled head-cloths,
16.12 their sleeping babies, the unconscious pilgrims of an
16.13 exacting belief.
16.14 "Look at dese cattle," said the German skipper
16.15 to his new chief mate.
16.16 An Arab, the leader of that pious voyage, came
16.17 last. He walked slowly aboard, handsome and
16.18 grave in his white gown and large turban. A string
16.19 of servants followed, loaded with his luggage; the
16.20 Patna cast off and backed away from the wharf.
16.21 She was headed between two small islets,
16.22 crossed obliquely the anchoring-ground of sailing--
16.23 ships, swung through half a circle in the shadow of
16.24 a hill, then ranged close to a ledge of foaming reefs.
16.25 The Arab, standing up aft, recited aloud the prayer
16.26 of travellers by sea. He invoked the favour of the
16.27 Most High upon that journey, implored His blessing
16.28 on men's toil and on the secret purposes of their
16.29 hearts; the steamer pounded in the dusk the calm
16.30 water of the Strait; and far astern of the pilgrim
17.01 ship a screw-pile lighthouse, planted by unbelievers
17.02 on a treacherous shoal, seemed to wink at her its
17.03 eye of flame, as if in derision of her errand of faith.
17.04 She cleared the Strait, crossed the bay, con-
17.05 tinued on her way through the "One-degree"
17.06 passage. She held on straight for the Red Sea
17.07 under a serene sky, under a sky scorching and un-

17.08 clouded, enveloped in a fulgor of sunshine that killed
17.09 all thought, oppressed the heart, withered all im-
17.10 pulses of strength and energy. And under the
17.11 sinister splendour of that sky the sea, blue and
17.12 profound, remained still, without a stir, without a
17.13 ripple, without a wrinkle -- viscous, stagnant, dead.
17.14 The Patna, with a slight hiss, passed over that
17.15 plain, luminous and smooth, unrolled a black ribbon
17.16 of smoke across the sky, left behind her on the water
17.17 a white ribbon of foam that vanished at once, like
17.18 the phantom of a track drawn upon a lifeless sea
17.19 by the phantom of a steamer.
17.20 Every morning the sun, as if keeping pace in
17.21 his revolutions with the progress of the pilgrimage,
17.22 emerged with a silent burst of light exactly at the
17.23 same distance astern of the ship, caught up with
17.24 her at noon, pouring the concentrated fire of his
17.25 rays on the pious purposes of the men, glided past
17.26 on his descent, and sank mysteriously into the sea
17.27 evening after evening, preserving the same dis-
17.28 tance ahead of her advancing bows. The five
17.29 whites on board lived amidships, isolated from the
17.30 human cargo. The awnings covered the deck with
18.01 a white roof from stem to stern, and a faint hum,
18.02 a low murmur of sad voices, alone revealed the
18.03 presence of a crowd of people upon the great blaze
18.04 of the ocean. Such were the days, still, hot, heavy,
18.05 disappearing one by one into the past, as if falling
18.06 into an abyss for ever open in the wake of the
18.07 ship; and the ship, lonely under a wisp of smoke,
18.08 held on her steadfast way black and smouldering in
18.09 a luminous immensity, as if scorched by a flame
18.10 flicked at her from a heaven without pity.
18.11 The nights descended on her like a benediction.
19.01 A MARVELLOUS stillness pervaded the
19.02 world, and the stars, together with the
19.03 serenity of their rays, seemed to shed upon
19.04 the earth the assurance of everlasting security.
19.05 The young moon recurved, and, shining low in the
19.06 west, was like a slender shaving thrown up from
19.07 a bar of gold, and the Arabian Sea, smooth and
19.08 cool to the eye like a sheet of ice, extended its
19.09 perfect level to the perfect circle of a dark horizon.
19.10 The propeller turned without a check, as though
19.11 its beat had been part of the scheme of a safe
19.12 universe; and on each side of the Patna two deep
19.13 folds of water, permanent and sombre on the un-
19.14 wrinkled shimmer, enclosed within their straight
19.15 and diverging ridges a few white swirls of foam
19.16 bursting in a low hiss, a few wavelets, a few ripples,
19.17 a few undulations that, left behind, agitated the
19.18 surface of the sea for an instant after the passage
19.19 of the ship, subsided splashing gently, calmed down
19.20 at last into the circular stillness of water and sky
19.21 with the black speck of the moving hull remaining
19.22 everlastingly in its centre.
19.23 Jim on the bridge was penetrated by the great
19.24 certitude of unbounded safety and peace that could
20.01 be read on the silent aspect of nature like the certi-
20.02 tude of fostering love upon the placid tenderness of
20.03 a mother's face. Below the roof of awnings, sur-
20.04 rendered to the wisdom of white men and to their
20.05 courage, trusting the power of their unbelief and
20.06 the iron shell of their fire-ship, the pilgrims of an
20.07 exacting faith slept on mats, on blankets, on bare
20.08 planks, on every deck, in all the dark corners,
20.09 wrapped in dyed cloths, muffled in soiled rags, with
20.10 their heads resting on small bundles, with their
20.11 faces pressed to bent forearms: the men, the
20.12 women, the children; the old with the young, the
20.13 decrepit with the lusty -- all equal before sleep,
20.14 death's brother.
20.15 A draught of air, fanned from forward by the
20.16 speed of the ship, passed steadily through the long
20.17 gloom between the high bulwarks, swept over the
20.18 rows of prone bodies; a few dim flames in globe-
20.19 lamps were hung short here and there under the
20.20 ridge-poles, and in the blurred circles of light
20.21 thrown down and trembling slightly to the unceasing
20.22 vibration of the ship appeared a chin upturned, two
20.23 closed eyelids, a dark hand with silver rings, a
20.24 meagre limb draped in a torn covering, a head bent
20.25 back, a naked foot, a throat bared and stretched
20.26 as if offering itself to the knife. The well-to-do
20.27 had made for their families shelters with heavy
20.28 boxes and dusty mats; the poor reposed side by
20.29 side with all they had on earth tied up in a rag under
20.30 their heads; the lone old men slept, with drawn-up
21.01 legs, upon their prayer-carpets, with their hands
21.02 over their ears and one elbow on each side of the

21.03 face: a father, his shoulders up and his knees under
21.04 his forehead, dozed dejectedly by a boy who slept
21.05 on his back with tousled hair and one arm com-
21.06 mandingly extended; a woman covered from head
21.07 to foot, like a corpse, with a piece of white sheeting,
21.08 had a naked child in the hollow of each arm; the
21.09 Arab's belongings, piled right aft, made a heavy
21.10 mound of broken outlines, with a cargo-lamp
21.11 swung above, and a great confusion of vague forms
21.12 behind: gleams of paunchy brass pots, the foot-
21.13 rest of a deck-chair, blades of spears, the straight
21.14 scabbard of an old sword leaning against a heap of
21.15 pillows, the spout of a tin coffee-pot. The patent
21.16 log on the taffrail periodically rang a single tinkling
21.17 stroke for every mile traversed on an errand of
21.18 faith. Above the mass of sleepers a faint and
21.19 patient sigh at times floated, the exhalation of a
21.20 troubled dream; and short metallic clangs bursting
21.21 out suddenly in the depths of the ship, the harsh
21.22 scrape of a shovel, the violent slam of a furnace --
21.23 door, exploded brutally, as if the men handling
21.24 the mysterious things below had their breasts full
21.25 of fierce anger: while the slim, high hull of the
21.26 steamer went on evenly ahead, without a sway of
21.27 her bare masts, cleaving continuously the great
21.28 calm of the waters under the inaccessible serenity
21.29 of the sky.
21.30 Jim paced athwart, and his footsteps in the vast
22.01 silence were loud to his own ears, as if echoed by the
22.02 watchful stars: his eyes, roaming about the line of
22.03 the horizon, seemed to gaze hungrily into the
22.04 unattainable, and did not see the shadow of the
22.05 coming event. The only shadow on the sea was the
22.06 shadow of the black smoke pouring heavily from
22.07 the funnel its immense streamer, whose end was
22.08 constantly dissolving in the air. Two Malays,
22.09 silent and almost motionless, steered, one on each
22.10 side of the wheel, whose brass rim shone frag-
22.11 mentarily in the oval of light thrown out by the
22.12 binnacle. Now and then a hand, with black fingers
22.13 alternately letting go and catching hold of revolving
22.14 spokes, appeared in the illumined part; the links
22.15 of wheel-chains ground heavily in the grooves of
22.16 the barrel. Jim would glance at the compass,
22.17 would glance around the unattainable horizon,
22.18 would stretch himself till his joints cracked with
22.19 a leisurely twist of the body, in the very excess
22.20 of well-being; and, as if made audacious by the
22.21 invincible aspect of the peace, he felt he cared for
22.22 nothing that could happen to him to the end of his
22.23 days. From time to time he glanced idly at a
22.24 chart pegged out with four drawing-pins on a low
22.25 three-legged table abaft the steering-gear case.
22.26 The sheet of paper portraying the depths of the
22.27 sea presented a shiny surface under the light of
22.28 a bull's-eye lamp lashed to a stanchion, a surface
22.29 as level and smooth as the glimmering surface of
22.30 the waters. Parallel rulers with a pair of dividers
23.01 reposed on it; the ship's position at last noon was
23.02 marked with a small black cross, and the straight
23.03 pencil-line drawn firmly as far as Perim figured the
23.04 course of the ship -- the path of souls towards the
23.05 holy place, the promise of salvation, the reward of
23.06 eternal life -- while the pencil with its sharp end
23.07 touching the Somali coast lay round and still like
23.08 a naked ship's spar floating in the pool of a sheltered
23.09 dock. "How steady she goes!" thought Jim with
23.10 wonder, with something like gratitude for this
23.11 high peace of sea and sky. At such times his
23.12 thoughts would be full of valorous deeds: he
23.13 loved these dreams and the success of his imaginary
23.14 achievements. They were the best parts of life,
23.15 its secret truth, its hidden reality. They had
23.16 a gorgeous virility, the charm of vagueness, they
23.17 passed before him with an heroic tread; they carried
23.18 his soul away with them and made it drunk with
23.19 the divine philtre of an unbounded confidence in
23.20 itself. There was nothing he could not face. He
23.21 was so pleased with the idea that he smiled, keeping
23.22 perfunctorily his eyes ahead; and when he happened
23.23 to glance back he saw the white streak of the wake
23.24 drawn as straight by the ship's keel upon the sea
23.25 as the black line drawn by the pencil upon the
23.26 chart.
23.27 The ash-buckets racketed, clanking up and down
23.28 the stoke-hold ventilators, and this tin-pot clatter
23.29 warned him the end of his watch was near. He
23.30 sighed with content, with regret as well at having
24.01 to part from that serenity which fostered the
24.02 adventurous freedom of his thoughts. He was a

24.03 little sleepy too, and felt a pleasurable languor
24.04 running through every limb as though all the blood
24.05 in his body had turned to warm milk. His skipper
24.06 had come up noiselessly, in pyjamas and with his
24.07 sleeping-jacket flung wide open. Red of face, only
24.08 half awake, the left eye partly closed, the right
24.09 staring stupid and glassy, he hung his big head over
24.10 the chart and scratched his ribs sleepily. There
24.11 was something obscene in the sight of his naked
24.12 flesh. His bared breast glistened soft and greasy
24.13 as though he had sweated out his fat in his sleep.
24.14 He pronounced a professional remark in a voice
24.15 harsh and dead, resembling the rasping sound of a
24.16 wood-file on the edge of a plank; the fold of his
24.17 double chin hung like a bag triced up close under
24.18 the hinge of his jaw. Jim started, and his answer
24.19 was full of deference; but the odious and fleshy
24.20 figure, as though seen for the first time in a reveal-
24.21 ing moment, fixed itself in his memory for ever as
24.22 the incarnation of everything vile and base that
24.23 lurks in the world we love: in our own hearts we
24.24 trust for our salvation in the men that surround
24.25 us, in the sights that fill our eyes, in the sounds
24.26 that fill our ears, and in the air that fills our lung
24.27 The thin gold shaving of the moon floating
24.28 slowly downwards had lost itself on the darkened
24.29 surface of the waters, and the eternity beyond the
24.30 sky seemed to come down nearer to the earth, with
25.01 the augmented glitter of the stars, with the more
25.02 profound sombreness in the lustre of the half-
25.03 transparent dome covering the flat disc of an opaque
25.04 sea. The ship moved so smoothly that her onward
25.05 motion was imperceptible to the senses of men,
25.06 as though she had been a crowded planet speeding
25.07 through the dark spaces of ether behind the swarm
25.08 of suns, in the appalling and calm solitudes awaiting
25.09 the breath of future creations. "Hot is no name
25.10 for it down below," said a voice.
25.11 Jim smiled without looking round. The skipper
25.12 presented an unmoved breadth of back: it was
25.13 the renegade's trick to appear pointedly unaware of
25.14 your existence unless it suited his purpose to turn
25.15 at you with a devouring glare before he let loose a
25.16 torrent of foamy, abusive jargon that came like a
25.17 gush from a sewer. Now he emitted only a sulky
25.18 grunt; the second engineer at the head of the bridge--
25.19 ladder, kneading with damp palms a dirty sweat--
25.20 rag, unabashed, continued the tale of his complaints.
25.21 The sailors had a good time of it up here, and what
25.22 was the use of them in the world he would be blowed
25.23 if he could see. The poor devils of engineers had
25.24 to get the ship along anyhow, and they could very
25.25 well do the rest too; by gosh they -- "Shut
25.26 up," growled the German stolidly. "Oh yes!
25.27 Shut up -- and when anything goes wrong you fly
25.28 to us, don't you?" went on the other. He was
25.29 more than half cooked, he expected; but anyway,
25.30 now, he did not mind how much he sinned, because
26.01 these last three days he had passed through a fine
26.02 course of training for the place where the bad boys
26.03 go when they die -- b'gosh, he had -- besides being
26.04 made jolly well deaf by the blasted racket below.
26.05 The durned, compound, surface-condensing, rotten
26.06 scrap-heap rattled and banged down there like an
26.07 old deck-winch, only more so; and what made him
26.08 risk his life every night and day that God made
26.09 amongst the refuse of a breaking-up yard flying
26.10 round at fifty-seven revolutions, was more than he
26.11 could tell. He must have been born reckless,
26.12 b'gosh. He ... "Where did you get drunk?"
26.13 inquired the German, very savage, but motionless
26.14 in the light of the binnacle, like a clumsy effigy
26.15 of a man cut out of a block of fat. Jim went on
26.16 smiling at the retreating horizon; his heart was
26.17 full of generous impulses, and his thought was
26.18 contemplating his own superiority. "Drink!"
26.19 repeated the engineer, with amiable scorn: he was
26.20 hanging on with both hands to the rail, a shadowy
26.21 figure with flexible legs. "Not from you, captain.
26.22 You're far too mean, b'gosh. You would let a good
26.23 man die sooner than give him a drop of schnapps.
26.24 That's what you Germans call economy. Penny
26.25 wise, pound foolish." He became sentimental.
26.26 The chief had given him a four-finger nip about
26.27 ten o'clock -- "only one, s'elp me!" -- good old
26.28 chief; but as to getting the old fraud out of
26.29 his bunk -- a five-ton crane couldn't do it. Not it.
26.30 Not to-night anyhow. He was sleeping sweetly
27.01 like a little child, with a bottle of prime brandy
27.02 under his pillow. From the thick throat of the

27.03 commander of the _Patna_ came a low rumble, on
27.04 which the sound of the word _schwein_ fluttered high
27.05 and low like a capricious feather in a faint stir of
27.06 air. He and the chief engineer had been cronies
27.07 for a good few years -- serving the same jovial,
27.08 crafty old Chinaman, with horn-rimmed goggles
27.09 and strings of red silk plaited into the venerable
27.10 grey hairs of his pigtail. The quay-side opinion
27.11 in the _Patna's_ home-port was that these two in the
27.12 way of brazen peculation "had done together pretty
27.13 well everything you can think of." Outwardly
27.14 they were badly matched: one dull-eyed, malevo-
27.15 lent, and of soft, fleshy curves; the other lean,
27.16 all hollows, with a head long and bony like the head
27.17 of an old horse, with sunken cheeks, with sunken
27.18 temples, with an indifferent glazed glance of sunken
27.19 eyes. He had been stranded out East somewhere
27.20 -- in Canton, in Shanghai, or perhaps in Yoko-
27.21 hama; he probably did not care to remember
27.22 himself the exact locality, nor yet the cause of his
27.23 shipwreck. He had been, in mercy to his youth,
27.24 kicked quietly out of his ship twenty years ago or
27.25 more, and it might have been so much worse for
27.26 him that the memory of the episode had in it hardly
27.27 a trace of misfortune. Then, steam navigation
27.28 expanding in these seas and men of his craft being
27.29 scarce at first, he had "got on" after a sort. He
27.30 was eager to let strangers know in a dismal mumble
28.01 that he was "an old stager out here." When he
28.02 moved, a skeleton seemed to sway loose in his
28.03 clothes; his walk was mere wandering, and he
28.04 was given to wander thus around the engine-room
28.05 skylight, smoking, without relish, doctored tobacco
28.06 in a brass bowl at the end of a cherrywood stem
28.07 four feet long, with the imbecile gravity of a thinker
28.08 evolving a system of philosophy from the hazy
28.09 glimpse of a truth. He was usually anything but
28.10 free with his private store of liquor; but on that
28.11 night he had departed from his principles, so that
28.12 his second, a weak-headed child of Wapping, what
28.13 with the unexpectedness of the treat and the strength
28.14 of the stuff, had become very happy, cheeky, and
28.15 talkative. The fury of the New South Wales
28.16 German was extreme; he puffed like an exhaust--
28.17 pipe, and Jim, faintly amused by the scene, was
28.18 impatient for the time when he could get below: the
28.19 last ten minutes of the watch were irritating like
28.20 a gun that hangs fire; those men did not belong
28.21 to the world of heroic adventure; they weren't
28.22 bad chaps though. Even the skipper himself ...
28.23 His gorge rose at the mass of panting flesh from
28.24 which issued gurgling mutters, a cloudy trickle of
28.25 filthy expressions; but he was too pleasurably
28.26 languid to dislike actively this or any other thing.
28.27 The quality of these men did not matter; he rubbed
28.28 shoulders with them, but they could not touch him;
28.29 he shared the air they breathed, but he was different.
28.30 ...Would the skipper go for the engineer?...
29.01 The life was easy and he was too sure of himself --
29.02 too sure of himself to ... The line dividing his
29.03 meditation from a surreptitious doze on his feet
29.04 was thinner than a thread in a spider's web.
29.05 The second engineer was coming by easy transi-
29.06 tions to the consideration of his finances and of his
29.07 courage.
29.08 "Who's drunk? I? No, no, captain! That
29.09 won't do. You ought to know by this time the
29.10 chief ain't free-hearted enough to make a sparrow
29.11 drunk, b'gosh. I've never been the worse for
29.12 liquor in my life; the stuff ain't made yet that
29.13 would make _me_ drunk. I could drink liquid fire
29.14 against your whisky peg for peg, b'gosh, and keep
29.15 as cool as a cucumber. If I thought I was drunk
29.16 I would jump overboard -- do away with myself,
29.17 b'gosh. I would! Straight! And I won't go
29.18 off the bridge. Where do you expect me to take
29.19 the air on a night like this, eh? On deck amongst
29.20 that vermin down there? Likely -- ain't it! And
29.21 I am not afraid of anything you can do."
29.22 The German lifted two heavy fists to heaven and
29.23 shook them a little without a word.
29.24 "I don't know what fear is," pursued the
29.25 engineer, with the enthusiasm of sincere conviction.
29.26 "I am not afraid of doing all the bloomin' work in
29.27 this rotten hooker, b'gosh! And a jolly good thing
29.28 for you that there are some of us about the world
29.29 that aren't afraid of their lives, or where would you
29.30 be -- you and this old thing here with her plates like
30.01 brown paper -- brown paper, s'elp me? It's all
30.02 very fine for you -- you get a power of pieces out

30.03 of her one way and another; but what about me
30.04 -- what do I get? A measly hundred and fifty
30.05 dollars a month and find yourself. I wish to ask
30.06 you respectfully -- respectfully, mind -- who wouldn't
30.07 chuck a dratted job like this? 'Tain't safe, s'elp
30.08 me, it ain't! Only I am one of them fearless
30.09 fellows...."
30.10 He let go the rail and made ample gestures as if
30.11 demonstrating in the air the shape and extent of his
30.12 valour; his thin voice darted in prolonged squeaks
30.13 upon the sea, he tiptoed back and forth for the better
30.14 emphasis of utterance, and suddenly pitched down
30.15 head first as though he had been clubbed from
30.16 behind. He said "Damn!" as he tumbled;
30.17 an instant of silence followed upon his screeching:
30.18 Jim and the skipper staggered forward by common
30.19 accord, and, catching themselves up, stood very stiff
30.20 and still gazing, amazed, at the undisturbed level of
30.21 the sea. Then they looked upwards at the stars.
30.22 What had happened? The wheezy thump of
30.23 the engines went on. Had the earth been checked
30.24 in her course? They could not understand; and
30.25 suddenly the calm sea, the sky without a cloud,
30.26 appeared formidably insecure in their immobility,
30.27 as if poised on the brow of yawning destruction.
30.28 The engineer rebounded vertically full length and
30.29 collapsed again into a vague heap. This heap said
30.30 "What's that?" in the muffled accents of pro-
31.01 found grief. A faint noise as of thunder, of thunder
31.02 infinitely remote, less than a sound, hardly more
31.03 than a vibration, passed slowly, and the ship quivered
31.04 in response, as if the thunder had growled deep
31.05 down in the water. The eyes of the two Malays
31.06 at the wheel glittered towards the white men, but
31.07 their dark hands remained closed on the spokes.
31.08 The sharp hull driving on its way seemed to rise
31.09 a few inches in succession through its whole length,
31.10 as though it had become pliable, and settled down
31.11 again rigidly to its work of cleaving the smooth
31.12 surface of the sea. Its quivering stopped, and the
31.13 faint noise of thunder ceased all at once, as though
31.14 the ship had steamed across a narrow belt of vibrat-
31.15 ing water and of humming air.
32.01 A MONTH or so afterwards, when Jim, in
32.02 answer to pointed questions, tried to tell
32.03 honestly the truth of this experience, he
32.04 said, speaking of the ship: "She went over what-
32.05 ever it was as easy as a snake crawling over a stick."
32.06 The illustration was good: the questions were
32.07 aiming at facts, and the official inquiry was being
32.08 held in the police court of an Eastern port. He
32.09 stood elevated in the witness-box, with burning
32.10 cheeks in a cool, lofty room: the big framework of
32.11 punkahs moved gently to and fro high above his
32.12 head, and from below many eyes were looking at
32.13 him out of dark faces, out of white faces, out of
32.14 red faces, out of faces attentive, spellbound, as if
32.15 all these people sitting in orderly rows upon narrow
32.16 benches had been enslaved by the fascination of
32.17 his voice. It was very loud, it rang startling in
32.18 his own ears, it was the only sound audible in the
32.19 world, for the terribly distinct questions that ex-
32.20 torted his answers seemed to shape themselves in
32.21 anguish and pain within his breast -- came to him
32.22 poignant and silent like the terrible questioning of
32.23 one's conscience. Outside the court the sun blazed
32.24 -- within was the wind of great punkahs that made
33.01 you shiver, the shame that made you burn, the
33.02 attentive eyes whose glance stabbed. The face
33.03 of the presiding magistrate, clean-shaved and im-
33.04 passible, looked at him deadly pale between the
33.05 red faces of the two nautical assessors. The light
33.06 of a broad window under the ceiling fell from above
33.07 on the heads and shoulders of the three men, and
33.08 they were fiercely distinct in the half-light of the
33.09 big court-room where the audience seemed com-
33.10 posed of staring shadows. They wanted facts.
33.11 Facts! They demanded facts from him, as if
33.12 facts could explain anything!
33.13 "After you had concluded you had collided with
33.14 something floating awash, say a water-logged wreck,
33.15 you were ordered by your captain to go forward and
33.16 ascertain if there was any damage done. Did you
33.17 think it likely from the force of the blow?" asked
33.18 the assessor sitting to the left. He had a thin
33.19 horseshoe beard, salient cheek-bones, and with both
33.20 elbows on the desk clasped his rugged hands before
33.21 his face, looking at Jim with thoughtful blue eyes;
33.22 the other, a heavy, scornful man, thrown back in his
33.23 seat, his left arm extended full length, drummed

33.24 delicately with his finger-tips on a blotting-pad:
33.25 in the middle the magistrate upright in the roomy
33.26 arm-chair, his head inclined slightly on the shoulder,
33.27 had his arms crossed on his breast and a few flowers
33.28 in a glass vase by the side of his inkstand.
33.29 "I did not," said Jim. "I was told to call no
33.30 one, and to make no noise for fear of creating a panic.
34.01 I thought the precaution reasonable. I took one
34.02 of the lamps that were hung under the awnings and
34.03 went forward. After opening the forepeak hatch I
34.04 heard splashing in there. I lowered then the lamp
34.05 the whole drift of its lanyard, and saw that the fore-
34.06 peak was more than half full of water already. I
34.07 knew then there must be a big hole below the water-
34.08 line." He paused.
34.09 "Yes," said the big assessor, with a dreamy smile
34.10 at the blotting-pad; his fingers played incessantly,
34.11 touching the paper without noise.
34.12 "I did not think of danger just then. I might
34.13 have been a little startled: all this happened in such
34.14 a quiet way and so very suddenly. I knew there
34.15 was no other bulkhead in the ship but the collision
34.16 bulkhead separating the forepeak from the forehold.
34.17 I went back to tell the captain. I came upon the
34.18 second engineer getting up at the foot of the bridge--
34.19 ladder: he seemed dazed, and told me he thought
34.20 his left arm was broken; he had slipped on the top
34.21 step when getting down while I was forward. He
34.22 exclaimed, 'My God! That rotten bulkhead'll
34.23 give way in a minute, and the damned thing will go
34.24 down under us like a lump of lead.' He pushed
34.25 me away with his right arm and ran before me up the
34.26 ladder, shouting as he climbed. His left arm hung
34.27 by his side. I followed up in time to see the captain
34.28 rush at him and knock him down flat on his back.
34.29 He did not strike him again: he stood bending
34.30 over him and speaking angrily but quite low. I
35.01 fancy he was asking him why the devil he didn't
35.02 go and stop the engines, instead of making a row
35.03 about it on deck. I heard him say, 'Get up!
35.04 Run! fly!' He swore also. The engineer slid
35.05 down the starboard ladder and bolted round the
35.06 skylight to the engine-room companion which was
35.07 on the port-side. He moaned as he ran...."
35.08 He spoke slowly; he remembered swiftly and
35.09 with extreme vividness; he could have repro-
35.10 duced like an echo the moaning of the engineer
35.11 for the better information of these men who wanted
35.12 facts. After his first feeling of revolt he had come
35.13 round to the view that only a meticulous precision
35.14 of statement would bring out the true horror behind
35.15 the appalling face of things. The facts those men
35.16 were so eager to know had been visible, tangible,
35.17 open to the senses, occupying their place in space
35.18 and time, requiring for their existence a fourteen--
35.19 hundred-ton steamer and twenty-seven minutes
35.20 by the watch; they made a whole that had features,
35.21 shades of expression, a complicated aspect that could
35.22 be remembered by the eye, and something else
35.23 besides, something invisible, a directing spirit of
35.24 perdition that dwelt within, like a malevolent soul
35.25 in a detestable body. He was anxious to make this
35.26 clear. This had not been a common affair, every-
35.27 thing in it had been of the utmost importance, and
35.28 fortunately he remembered everything. He wanted
35.29 to go on talking for truth's sake, perhaps for his own
35.30 sake also; and while his utterance was deliberate,
36.01 his mind positively flew round and round the serried
36.02 circle of facts that had surged up all about him to
36.03 cut him off from the rest of his kind: it was like
36.04 enclosure of high stakes, dashes round and round,
36.05 a creature that, finding itself imprisoned within an
36.06 distracted in the night, trying to find a weak spot,
36.07 a crevice, a place to scale, some opening through
36.08 which it may squeeze itself and escape. This awful
36.09 activity of mind made him hesitate at times in his
36.10 speech....
36.11 "The captain kept on moving here and there
36.12 on the bridge; he seemed calm enough, only he
36.13 stumbled several times; and once as I stood speak-
36.14 ing to him he walked right into me as though he
36.15 had been stone-blind. He made no definite answer
36.16 to what I had to tell. He mumbled to himself;
36.17 all I heard of it were a few words that sounded
36.18 like 'confounded steam!' and 'infernal steam!' --
36.19 something about steam. I thought ..."
36.20 He was becoming irrelevant; a question to the
36.21 point cut short his speech, like a pang of pain, and
36.22 he felt extremely discouraged and weary. He was
36.23 coming to that, he was coming to that -- and now,
36.24 checked brutally, he had to answer by yes or no.
36.25 He answered truthfully by a curt, "Yes, I did"; and
36.26 fair of face, big of frame, with young, gloomy eyes,
36.27 he held his shoulders upright above the box while
36.28 his soul writhed within him. He was made to
36.29 answer another question so much to the point and so
36.30 useless, then waited again. His mouth was taste-
37.01 lessly dry, as though he had been eating dust, then
37.02 salt and bitter as after a drink of sea-water. He
37.03 wiped his damp forehead, passed his tongue over
37.04 parched lips, felt a shiver run down his back. The
37.05 big assessor had dropped his eyelids, and drummed
37.06 on without a sound, careless and mournful; the
37.07 eyes of the other above the sunburnt, clasped fingers
37.08 seemed to glow with kindliness; the magistrate
37.09 had swayed forward; his pale face hovered near the
37.10 flowers, and then dropping sideways over the arm
37.11 of his chair, he rested his temple in the palm of his
37.12 hand. The wind of the punkahs eddied down on the
37.13 heads, on the dark-faced natives wound about in
37.14 voluminous draperies, on the Europeans sitting
37.15 together very hot and in drill suits that seemed
37.16 to fit them as close as their skins, and holding their
37.17 round pith hats on their knees; while gliding along
37.18 the walls the court peons, buttoned tight in long
37.19 white coats, flitted rapidly to and fro, running on
37.20 bare toes, red-sashed, red turban on head, as noise-
37.21 less as ghosts, and on the alert like so many retrievers.
37.22 Jim's eyes, wandering in the intervals of his
37.23 answers, rested upon a white man who sat apart
37.24 from the others, with his face worn and clouded,
37.25 but with quiet eyes that glanced straight, interested,
37.26 and clear. Jim answered another question and was
37.27 tempted to cry out, "What's the good of this?
37.28 What's the good?" He tapped with his foot
37.29 slightly, bit his lip, and looked away over the heads.
37.30 He met the eyes of the white man. The glance
38.01 directed at him was not the fascinated stare of the
38.02 others. It was an act of intelligent volition. Jim
38.03 between two questions forgot himself so far as to
38.04 find leisure for a thought. This fellow -- ran the
38.05 thought -- looks at me as though he could see some-
38.06 body or something past my shoulder. He had come
38.07 across that man before -- in the street perhaps. He
38.08 was positive he had never spoken to him. For days,
38.09 for many days, he had spoken to no one, but had
38.10 held silent, incoherent, and endless converse with
38.11 himself, like a prisoner alone in his cell or like a
38.12 wayfarer lost in a wilderness. At present he was
38.13 answering questions that did not matter though they
38.14 had a purpose, but he doubted whether he would
38.15 ever again speak out as long as he lived. The sound
38.16 of his own truthful statements confirmed his de-
38.17 liberate opinion that speech was of no use to him
38.18 any longer. That man there seemed to be aware
38.19 of his hopeless difficulty. Jim looked at him, then
38.20 turned away resolutely, as after a final parting.
38.21 And later on, many times, in distant parts of the
38.22 world, Marlow showed himself willing to remember
38.23 Jim, to remember him at length, in detail and
38.24 audibly.
38.25 Perhaps it would be after dinner, on a verandah
38.26 draped in motionless foliage and crowned with
38.27 flowers, in the deep dusk speckled by fiery cigar--
38.28 ends. The elongated bulk of each cane-chair
38.29 harboured a silent listener. Now and then a small
38.30 red glow would move abruptly, and expanding
39.01 light up the fingers of a languid hand, part of a face
39.02 in profound repose, or flash a crimson gleam into a
39.03 pair of pensive eyes overshadowed by a fragment
39.04 of an unruffled forehead; and with the very first
39.05 word uttered Marlow's body, extended at rest in the
39.06 seat, would become very still, as though his spirit
39.07 had winged its way back into the lapse of time and
39.08 were speaking through his lips from the past.
40.01 "OH yes. I attended the inquiry," he
40.02 would say, "and to this day I haven't
40.03 left off wondering why I went. I am
40.04 willing to believe each of us has a guardian angel,
40.05 if you fellows will concede to me that each of us has
40.06 a familiar devil as well. I want you to own up,
40.07 because I don't like to feel exceptional in any way,
40.08 and I know I have him -- the devil, I mean. I
40.09 haven't seen him, of course, but I go upon circum-
40.10 stantial evidence. He is there right enough, and,
40.11 being malicious, he lets me in for that kind of thing.
40.12 What kind of thing, you ask? Why, the inquiry
40.13 thing, the yellow-dog thing -- you wouldn't think a
40.14 mangy, native tyke would be allowed to trip up
40.15 people in the verandah of a magistrate's court,

40.16 would you? -- the kind of thing that by devious,
40.17 unexpected, truly diabolical ways causes me to run
40.18 up against men with soft spots, with hard spots,
40.19 with hidden plague spots, by Jove! and loosens
40.20 their tongues at the sight of me for their infernal
40.21 confidences; as though, forsooth, I had no con-
40.22 fidences to make to myself, as though -- God help
40.23 me! -- I didn't have enough confidential information
40.24 about myself to harrow my own soul till the end
41.01 of my appointed time. And what I have done to be
41.02 thus favoured I want to know. I declare I am as
41.03 full of my own concerns as the next man, and I have
41.04 as much memory as the average pilgrim in this
41.05 valley, so you see I am not particularly fit to be
41.06 a receptacle of confessions. Then why? Can't
41.07 tell -- unless it be to make time pass away after
41.08 dinner. Charley, my dear chap, your dinner was
41.09 extremely good, and in consequence these men here
41.10 look upon a quiet rubber as a tumultuous occupa-
41.11 tion. They wallow in your good chairs and think
41.12 to themselves, 'Hang exertion. Let that Marlow
41.13 talk.'
41.14 "Talk! So be it. And it's easy enough to talk
41.15 of Master Jim, after a good spread, two hundred
41.16 feet above the sea-level, with a box of decent cigars
41.17 handy, on a blessed evening of freshness and star-
41.18 light that would make the best of us forget we are
41.19 only on sufferance here and got to pick our way in
41.20 cross lights, watching every precious minute and
41.21 every irremediable step, trusting we shall manage
41.22 yet to go out decently in the end -- but not so sure
41.23 of it after all -- and with dashed little help to expect
41.24 from those we touch elbows with right and left.
41.25 Of course there are men here and there to whom
41.26 the whole of life is like an after-dinner hour with
41.27 a cigar; easy, pleasant, empty, perhaps enlivened
41.28 by some fable of strife to be forgotten before the
41.29 end is told -- before the end is told -- even if there
41.30 happens to be any end to it.
42.01 "My eyes met his for the first time at that in-
42.02 quiry. You must know that everybody connected
42.03 in any way with the sea was there, because the affair
42.04 had been notorious for days, ever since that mysteri-
42.05 ous cable message came from Aden to start us all
42.06 cackling. I say mysterious, because it was so in a
42.07 sense though it contained a naked fact, about as
42.08 naked and ugly as a fact can well be. The whole
42.09 waterside talked of nothing else. First thing in the
42.10 morning as I was dressing in my state-room, I would
42.11 hear through the bulkhead my Parsee Dubash
42.12 jabbering about the Patna with the steward, while
42.13 he drank a cup of tea, by favour, in the pantry. No
42.14 sooner on shore I would meet some acquaintance,
42.15 and the first remark would be, 'Did you ever hear
42.16 of anything to beat this?' and according to his kind
42.17 the man would smile cynically, or look sad, or let out
42.18 a swear or two. Complete strangers would accost
42.19 each other familiarly, just for the sake of easing their
42.20 minds on the subject: every confounded loafer in
42.21 the town came in for a harvest of drinks over this
42.22 affair: you heard of it in the harbour office, at every
42.23 ship-broker's, at your agent's, from whites, from
42.24 natives, from half-castes, from the very boatmen
42.25 squatting half naked on the stone steps as you went
42.26 up -- by Jove! There was some indignation, not a
42.27 few jokes, and no end of discussions as to what had
42.28 become of them, you know. This went on for a
42.29 couple of weeks or more, and the opinion that
42.30 whatever was mysterious in this affair would turn
43.01 out to be tragic as well, began to prevail, when one
43.02 fine morning, as I was standing in the shade by the
43.03 steps of the harbour office, I perceived four men
43.04 walking towards me along the quay. I wondered
43.05 for a while where that queer lot had sprung from,
43.06 and suddenly, I may say, I shouted to myself,
43.07 'Here they are!'
43.08 "There they were, sure enough, three of them
43.09 as large as life, and one much larger of girth than
43.10 any living man has a right to be, just landed with a
43.11 good breakfast inside of them from an outward-
43.12 bound Dale Line steamer that had come in about an
43.13 hour after sunrise. There could be no mistake; I
43.14 spotted the jolly skipper of the Patna at the first
43.15 glance: the fattest man in the whole blessed tropical
43.16 belt clear round that good old earth of ours. More-
43.17 over, nine months or so before, I had come across
43.18 him in Samarang. His steamer was loading in the
43.19 Roads, and he was abusing the tyrannical institu-
43.20 tions of the German empire, and soaking himself
43.21 in beer all day long and day after day in De Jongh's
43.22 back shop, till De Jongh, who charged a guilder for
43.23 every bottle without as much as the quiver of an
43.24 eyelid, would beckon me aside, and, with his little
43.25 leathery face all puckered up, declare confidentially,
43.26 'Business is business, but this man, captain, he make
43.27 me very sick. Tfui!'
43.28 "I was looking at him from the shade. He was
43.29 Ruthvel had just come in, and, as his story goes,
43.30 "It appears he addressed himself in the first
43.31 instance to the principal shipping-master. Archie
43.32 was about to begin his arduous day by giving a
43.33 dressing-down to his chief clerk. Some of you
43.34 might have known him -- an obliging little Portuguese
43.35 half-caste with a miserable skinny neck, and always
43.36 on the hop to get something from the ship-masters
43.37 in the way of eatables -- a piece of salt pork, a bag
43.38 of biscuits, a few potatoes, or what not. One
43.39 voyage, I recollect, I tipped him a live sheep out
43.40 of the remnant of my sea-stock: not that I wanted
43.41 him to do anything for me -- he couldn't, you know
43.42 -- but because his childlike belief in the sacred
43.43 right to perquisites quite touched my heart. It was
44.01 so strong as to be almost beautiful. The race -- the
44.02 two races rather -- and the climate ... However,
44.03 never mind. I know where I have a friend for life.
44.04 "Well, Ruthvel says he was giving him a severe
44.05 lecture -- on official morality, I suppose -- when he
44.06 heard a kind of subdued commotion at his back, and
44.07 turning his head, he saw, in his own words, some-
44.08 thing round and enormous, resembling a sixteen-
44.09 hundredweight sugar-hogshead wrapped in striped
44.10 flannelette, up-ended in the middle of the large
44.11 floor space in the office. He declares he was so
44.12 taken aback that for quite an appreciable time he did
44.13 not realise the thing was alive, and sat still wondering
44.14 for what purpose and by what means that object had
44.15 been transported in front of his desk. The arch-
44.16 way from the ante-room was crowded with punkah-
44.17 pullers, sweepers, police peons, the coxswain and
44.18 crew of the harbour steam-launch, all craning their
44.19 necks and almost climbing on each other's backs.
44.20 Quite a riot. By that time the fellow had managed
44.21 to tug and jerk his hat clear of his head, and advanced
44.22 with slight bows at Ruthvel, who told me the sight
44.23 was so discomposing that for some time he listened
44.24 quite unable to make out what that apparition
44.25 wanted. It spoke in a voice harsh and lugubrious
44.26 but intrepid, and little by little it dawned upon
44.27 Archie that this was a development of the Patna
44.28 case. He says that as soon as he understood who it
44.29 was before him he felt quite unwell -- Archie is so
44.30 sympathetic and easily upset -- but pulled himself
45.01 together and shouted, 'Stop! I can't listen to
45.02 you. You must go to the Master Attendant. I
45.03 can't possibly listen to you. Captain Elliot is the
45.04 man you want to see. This way, this way.' He
45.05 jumped up, ran round that long counter, pulled,
45.06 shoved: the other let him, surprised but obedient
45.07 at first, and only at the door of the private office some
45.08 sort of animal instinct made him hang back and
45.09 snort like a frightened bullock. 'Look here!
45.10 what's up? Let go! Look here!' Archie flung
45.11 open the door without knocking. 'The master of
45.12 the Patna, sir,' he shouts. 'Go in, captain.' He
45.13 saw the old man lift his head from some writing
45.14 so sharp that his nose-nippers fell off, banged the
45.15 door to, and fled to his desk, where he had some
45.16 papers waiting for his signature: but he says the
45.17 row that burst out in there was so awful that he
45.18 couldn't collect his senses sufficiently to remember
45.19 the spelling of his own name. Archie's the most
45.20 sensitive shipping-master in the two hemispheres.
45.21 He declares he felt as though he had thrown a
45.22 man to a hungry lion. No doubt the noise was
45.23 great. I heard it down below, and I have every
45.24 reason to believe it was heard clear across the
45.25 Esplanade as far as the bandstand. Old father
45.26 Elliot had a great stock of words and could shout
45.27 -- and didn't mind who he shouted at either. He
45.28 would have shouted at the Viceroy himself. As he
45.29 used to tell me: 'I am as high as I can get; my
45.30 pension is safe. I've a few pounds laid by, and if
46.01 they don't like my notions of duty I would just as
46.02 soon go home as not. I am an old man, and I have
46.03 always spoken my mind. All I care for now is to
46.04 see my girls married before I die.' He was a little
46.05 crazy on that point. His three daughters were
46.06 awfully nice, though they resembled him amazingly,
46.07 and on the mornings he woke up with a gloomy
46.08 view of their matrimonial prospects the office would

46.09 read it in his eye and tremble, because, they said,
46.10 he was sure to have somebody for breakfast. How-
46.11 ever, that morning he did not eat the renegade, but,
46.12 if I may be allowed to carry on the metaphor,
46.13 chewed him up very small, so to speak, and -- ah!
46.14 ejected him again.
46.15 "Thus in a very few moments I saw his
46.16 monstrous bulk descend in haste and stand still on
46.17 the outer steps. He had stopped close to me for the
46.18 purpose of profound meditation: his large purple
46.19 cheeks quivered. He was biting his thumb, and
46.20 after a while noticed me with a sidelong vexed look.
46.21 The other three chaps that had landed with him
46.22 made a little group waiting at some distance. There
46.23 was a sallow-faced, mean little chap with his arm
46.24 in a sling, and a long individual in a blue flannel
46.25 coat, as dry as a chip and no stouter than a broom-
46.26 stick, with drooping grey moustaches, who looked
46.27 about him with an air of jaunty imbecility. The
46.28 third was an upstanding, broad-shouldered youth,
46.29 with his hands in his pockets, turning his back on
46.30 the other two who appeared to be talking together
47.01 earnestly. He stared across the empty Esplanade.
47.02 A ramshackle gharry, all dust and venetian blinds,
47.03 pulled up short opposite the group, and the driver,
47.04 throwing up his right foot over his knee, gave
47.05 himself up to the critical examination of his toes.
47.06 The young chap, making no movement, not even
47.07 stirring his head, just stared into the sunshine. This
47.08 was my first view of Jim. He looked as uncon-
47.09 cerned and unapproachable as only the young can
47.10 look. There he stood, clean-limbed, clean-faced,
47.11 firm on his feet, as promising a boy as the sun
47.12 ever shone on; and, looking at him, knowing all he
47.13 knew and a little more too, I was as angry as though
47.14 I had detected him trying to get something out of
47.15 me by false pretences. He had no business to
47.16 look so sound. I thought to myself -- well, if this
47.17 sort can go wrong like that ... and I felt as
47.18 though I could fling down my hat and dance
47.19 on it from sheer mortification, as I once saw the
47.20 skipper of an Italian barque do because his duffer
47.21 of a mate got into a mess with his anchors when
47.22 making a flying moor in a roadstead full of ships.
47.23 I asked myself, seeing him there apparently so
47.24 much at ease -- is he silly? is he callous? He
47.25 seemed ready to start whistling a tune. And note,
47.26 I did not care a rap about the behaviour of the other
47.27 two. Their persons somehow fitted the tale that
47.28 was public property, and was going to be the subject
47.29 of an official inquiry. 'That old mad rogue up-
47.30 stairs called me a hound,' said the captain of the
48.01 Patna. I can't tell whether he recognised me --
48.02 I rather think he did; but at any rate our glances
48.03 met. He glared -- I smiled; hound was the very
48.04 mildest epithet that had reached me through the
48.05 open window. 'Did he?' I said from some strange
48.06 inability to hold my tongue. He nodded, bit his
48.07 thumb agin, swore under his breath: then lifting
48.08 his head and looking at me with sullen and passionate
48.09 impudence -- 'Bah! the Pacific is big, my friendt.
48.10 You damned Englishmen can do your worst; I
48.11 know where there's plenty room for a man like
48.12 me: I am well aguaindt in Apia, in Honolulu,
48.13 in ....' He paused relectively, while without
48.14 effort I could depict to myself the sort of people he
48.15 was 'aguaindt' with in those places. I won't make
48.16 a secret of it that I had been 'aguaindt' with not a
48.17 few of that sort myself. There are times when a
48.18 man must act as though life were equally sweet in
48.19 any company. I've known such a time, and, what's
48.20 more, I shan't now pretend to pull a long face over
48.21 my necessity, because a good many of that bad
48.22 company from want of moral -- moral -- what shall
48.23 I say? -- posture, or from some other equally pro-
48.24 found cause, were twice as instructive and twenty
48.25 times more amusing thatn the usual respectable
48.26 thief of commerce you fellows ask to sit at your
48.27 table without any real necessity -- from habit, from
48.28 cowardice, from good-nature, froma hundred
48.29 sneaking and inadequate reasons.
48.30 "'You Englishmen are all rogues,' went on my
49.01 patriotic Flensborg or Stettin Australian. I really
49.02 don't recollect now what decent little port on the
49.03 shores of the Baltic was defiled by being the nest
49.04 of that precious bird. 'What are you to shout?
49.05 Eh? You tell me? You no better than other
49.06 people, and that old rogue he make Gottam fuss
49.07 with me.' His thick carcass trembled on its legs
49.08 that were like a pair of pillars; it trembled from

49.09 head to foot. 'That's what you English always
49.10 make -- make a tam' fuss -- for any little thing, becau
49.11 I was not born in your tam' country. Take away
49.12 my certificate. Take it. I don't want the certi-
49.13 ficate. A man like me don't want your verfluchte
49.14 certificate. I spit on it.' He spat. 'I vill an
49.15 American citizen begome,' he cried, fretting and
49.16 fuming and shuffling his feet as if to free his ankles
49.17 from some invisible and mysterious grasp that
49.18 would not let him get away from that spot. He
49.19 made himself so warm that the top of his bullet
49.20 head positively smoked. Nothing mysterious pre-
49.21 vented me from going away: curiosity is the most
49.22 obvious of sentiments, and it held me there to see
49.23 the effect of a full information upon that young
49.24 fellow who, hands in pockets, and turning his back
49.25 upon the sidewalk, gazed across the grass-plots of
49.26 the Esplanade at the yellow portico of the Malabar
49.27 Hotel with the air of a man about to go for a walk
49.28 as soon as his friend is ready. That's how he looked,
49.29 and it was odious. I waited to see him overwhelmed,
49.30 confounded, pierced through and through, squirm-
50.01 ing like an impaled beetle -- and I was half afraid
50.02 to see it too -- if you understand what I mean.
50.03 Nothing more awful thatn to watch a man who has
50.04 been found out, not in a crime but in a more tnan
50.05 criminal weakness. The commonest sort of forti-
50.06 tude prevents us from becoming criminals in a
50.07 legal sense; it is from weakness unknown, but
50.08 perhaps suspected, as in some parts of the world
50.09 you suspect a deadly snake in every bush -- from
50.10 weakness that may lie hidden, watched or un-
50.11 watched, prayed against or manfully scorned, re-
50.12 pressed or maybe ignored more than half a lifetime,
50.13 not one of us is safe. We are snared into doing
50.14 things for which we get called names, and things
50.15 for which we get hanged, and yet the spirit may well
50.16 survive -- survive the condemnations, survive the
50.17 halter, by Jove! And there are things -- they look
50.18 small enough sometimes too -- by which some of us
50.19 are totally and completely undone. I watched the
50.20 youngster there. I liked his appearance; I knew
50.21 his appearance; he came from the right place;
50.22 he was one of us. He stood there for all the
50.23 parentage of his knid, for men and women by no
50.24 means clever or amusing, but whose very existence
50.25 is based upon honest faith, and upon the instinct of
50.26 courage. I don't mean military courage, or civil
50.27 courage, or any special kind of courage. I mean
50.28 just tnat inborn ability to look temptations straight
50.29 in the face -- a readiness unintellectual enough,
50.30 goodness knows, but without pose -- a power of
51.01 resistance, don't you see, ungracious if you like,
51.02 but priceless -- an untrinking and blessed stiffness
51.03 before the outward and inward terrors, before the
51.04 might of nature, and the seductive corruption of
51.05 men -- backed by a faith invulnerable to the strength
51.06 of facts, to the contagion of example, to the solici-
51.07 tation of ideas. Hang ideas! They are tramps,
51.08 vagabonds, knocking at the back door of your mind,
51.09 each taking a little of your substance, each carrying
51.10 away some crumb of that belief in a few simple
51.11 notions you must cling to if you want to live decently
51.12 and would like to die easy!
51.13 "This has nothing to do with Jim, directly;
51.14 only he was outwardly so typical of that good,
51.15 stupid kind we like to feel marching right and left
51.16 of us in life, of the kind that is not disturbed by the
51.17 vagaries of intelligence and the perversions of -- of
51.18 nerves, let us say. He was the kind of fellow you
51.19 would, on the strength of his looks, leave in charge
51.20 of the deck -- figuratively and professionally speak-
51.21 ing. I say I would, and I ought to know. Haven't
51.22 I turned out youngsters enough in my time, for the
51.23 service of the Red Rag, to the craft of the sea, to
51.24 the craft whose whole secret could be expressed in
51.25 one short sentence, and yet must be driven afresh
51.26 every day into young heads till it becomes the
51.27 component part of every waking thought -- till it is
51.28 present in every dream of their young sleep? The
51.29 sea has been good to me, but when I remember
51.30 all these boys that passed through my hands, some
52.01 grown up now and some drowned by this time, but
52.02 all good stuff for the sea, I don't think I have done
52.03 badly by it either. Were I to go home to-morrow,
52.04 I bet that before two days passed over my head
52.05 some sunburnt young chief mate would overtake
52.06 me at some dock gateway or other, and a fresh, deep
52.07 voice speaking above my hat would ask: 'Don't
52.08 you remember me, sir? Why! little So-and-so.

52.09 Such and such a ship. It was my first voyage.'
52.10 And I would remember a bewildered little shaver,
52.11 no higher than the back of this chair, with a mother
52.12 and perhaps a big sister on the quay, very quiet
52.13 but too upset to wave their handkerchiefs at the
52.14 ship that glides out gently between the pier-heads;
52.15 or perhaps some decent, middle-aged father who had
52.16 come early with his boy to see him off, and stays
52.17 all the morning because he is interested in the
52.18 windlass apparently, and stays too long, and has
52.19 got to scramble ashore at last with no time at all
52.20 to say good-bye. The mud pilot on the poop sings
52.21 out to me in a drawl, 'Hold her with the check line
52.22 for a moment, Mister Mate. There's a gentleman
52.23 wants to get ashore.... Up with you, sir. Nearly
52.24 got carried off to Talcahuano, didn't you? Now's
52.25 your time; easy does it.... All right. Slack
52.26 away again forward there.' The tugs, smoking
52.27 like the pit of perdition, get hold and churn the
52.28 old river into fury; the gentleman ashore is dusting
52.29 his knees -- the benevolent steward has shied his
52.30 umbrella after him. All very proper. He has
53.01 offered his bit of sacrifice to the sea, and now he
53.02 may go home pretending he thinks nothing of it;
53.03 and the little willing victim will be very sea-sick
53.04 before next morning. By and by, when he has
53.05 learned all the little mysteries and the one great
53.06 secret of the craft, he shall be fit to live or die as the
53.07 sea may decree; and the man who had taken a hand
53.08 in this fool game, in which the sea wins every toss,
53.09 will be pleased to have his back slapped by a heavy
53.10 young hand, and to hear a cheery sea-puppy voice:
53.11 'Do you remember me, sir? The little So-and-so.'
53.12 "I tell you this is good; it tells you that once in
53.13 your life at least you had gone the right way to work.
53.14 I have been thus slapped, and I have winced, for
53.15 the slap was heavy, and I have glowed all day long
53.16 and gone to bed feeling less lonely in the world by
53.17 virtue of that hearty thump. Don't I remember
53.18 the little So-and-so's! I tell you I ought to know
53.19 the right kind of looks. I would have trusted the
53.20 deck to that youngster on the strength of a single
53.21 glance, and gone to sleep with both eyes -- and, by
53.22 Jove! -- it wouldn't have been safe. There are
53.23 depths of horror in that thought. He looked as
53.24 genuine as a new sovereign, but there was some
53.25 infernal alloy in his metal. How much? The
53.26 least thing -- the least drop of something rare and
53.27 accursed; the least drop! -- but he made you --
53.28 standing there with his don't-care-hang air -- he
53.29 made you wonder whether perchance he were
53.30 nothing more rare than brass.
54.01 "I couldn't believe it. I tell you I wanted to see
54.02 him squirm for the honour of the craft. The other
54.03 two no-account chaps spotted their captain, and
54.04 began to move slowly towards us. They chatted
54.05 together as they strolled, and I did not care any more
54.06 than if they had not been visible to the naked eye.
54.07 They grinned at each other -- might have been
54.08 exchanging jokes, for all I know. I saw that with
54.09 one of them it was the case of a broken arm;
54.10 and as to the long individual with grey moustaches
54.11 he was the chief engineer, and in various ways a
54.12 pretty notorious personality. They were nobodies.
54.13 They approached. The skipper gazed in an in-
54.14 animate way between his feet: he seemed to be
54.15 swollen to an unnatural size by some awful disease,
54.16 by the mysterious action of an unknown poison.
54.17 He lifted his head, saw the two before him waiting,
54.18 opened his mouth with an extraordinary, sneering
54.19 contortion of his puffed face -- to speak to them, I
54.20 suppose -- and then a thought seemed to strike him.
54.21 His thick, purplish lips came together without a
54.22 sound, he went off in a resolute waddle to the
54.23 gharry and began to jerk at the door-handle with
54.24 such a blind brutality of impatience that I expected
54.25 to see the whole concern overturned on its side,
54.26 pony and all. The driver, shaken out of his medi-
54.27 tation over the sole of his foot, displayed at once
54.28 all the signs of intense terror, and held with both
54.29 hands, looking round from his box at this vast
54.30 carcass forcing its way into his conveyance. The
55.01 little machine shook and rocked tumultuously,
55.02 and the crimson nape of that lowered neck, the
55.03 size of those straining thighs, the immense heaving
55.04 of that dingy, striped green-and-orange back, the
55.05 whole burrowing effort of that gaudy and sordid
55.06 mass troubled one's sense of probability with a droll
55.07 and fearsome effect, like one of those grotesque
55.08 and distinct visions that scare and fascinate one

55.09 in a fever. He disappeared. I half expected the
55.10 roof to split in two, the little box on wheels to
55.11 burst open in the manner of a ripe cotton-pod --
55.12 but it only sank with a click of flattened springs,
55.13 and suddenly one venetian blind rattled down. His
55.14 shoulders reappeared, jammed in the small opening;
55.15 his head hung out, distended and tossing like a
55.16 captive balloon, perspiring, furious, spluttering.
55.17 He reached for the gharry-wallah with vicious
55.18 flourishes of a fist as dumpy and red as a lump of
55.19 raw meat. He roared at him to be off, to go on.
55.20 Where? Into the Pacific, perhaps. The driver
55.21 lashed; the pony snorted, reared once, and darted
55.22 off at a gallop. Where? To Apia? To Hono-
55.23 lulu? He had 6000 miles of tropical belt to disport
55.24 himself in, and I did not hear the precise address.
55.25 A snorting pony snatched him into 'ewigkeit' in the
55.26 twinkling of an eye, and I never saw him again;
55.27 and, what's more, I don't know of anybody that
55.28 ever had a glimpse of him after he departed from
55.29 my knowledge sitting inside a ramshackle little
55.30 gharry that fled round the corner in a white smother
56.01 of dust. He departed, disappeared, vanished,
56.02 absconded; and absurdly enough it looked as
56.03 though he had taken that gharry with him, for
56.04 never again did I come across a sorrel pony with
56.05 a slit ear and a lackadaisical Tamil driver afflicted
56.06 by a sore foot. The Pacific is indeed big; but
56.07 whether he found a place for a display of his talents
56.08 in it or not, the fact remains he had flown into space
56.09 like a witch on a broomstick. The little chap
56.10 with his arm in a sling started to run after the
56.11 carriage, bleating, 'Captain! I say, Captain! I
56.12 sa-a-ay!' -- but after a few steps stopped short,
56.13 hung his head, and walked back slowly. At the
56.14 sharp rattle of the wheels the young fellow spun
56.15 round where he stood. He made no other move-
56.16 ment, no gesture, no sign, and remained facing in
56.17 the new direction after the gharry had swung out
56.18 of sight.
56.19 "All this happened in much less time than it
56.20 takes to tell, since I am trying to interpret for you
56.21 into slow speech the instantaneous effect of visual
56.22 impressions. Next moment the half-caste clerk, sent
56.23 by Archie to look a little after the poor castaways
56.24 of the _Patna_, came upon the scene. He ran out
56.25 eager and bareheaded, looking right and left, and
56.26 very full of his mission. It was doomed to be a
56.27 failure as far as the principal person was concerned,
56.28 but he approached the others with fussy importance,
56.29 and, almost immediately, found himself involved in a
56.30 violent altercation with the chap that carried his
57.01 arm in a sling and who turned out to be extremely
57.02 anxious for a row. He wasn't going to be ordered
57.03 about -- 'not he, b'gosh.' He wouldn't be terrified
57.04 with a pack of lies by a cocky, half-bred little quill-
57.05 driver. He was not going to be bullied by 'no
57.06 object of that sort,' if the story were true 'ever so!'
57.07 He bawled his wish, his desire, his determination
57.08 to go to bed. 'If you weren't a God-forsaken
57.09 Portuguee,' I heard him yell, 'you would know
57.10 that the hospital is the right place for me.' He
57.11 pushed the fist of his sound arm under the other's
57.12 nose; a crowd began to collect; the half-caste,
57.13 flustered, but doing his best to appear dignified,
57.14 tried to explain his intentions. I went away without
57.15 waiting to see the end.
57.16 "But it so happened that I had a man in the
57.17 hospital at the time, and going there to see about
57.18 him the day before the opening of the inquiry, I
57.19 saw in the white men's ward that little chap tossing
57.20 on his back, with his arm in splints, and quite light-
57.21 headed. To my great surprise the other one, the
57.22 long individual with drooping white moustaches,
57.23 had also found his way there. I remembered I had
57.24 seen him slinking away during the quarrel, in a half
57.25 prance, half shuffle, and trying very hard not to look
57.26 scared. He was no stranger to the port, it seems,
57.27 and in his distress was able to make tracks straight
57.28 for Mariani's billiard-room and grog-shop near the
57.29 bazaar. That unspeakable vagabond, Mariani, who
57.30 had known the man and had ministered to his vices
58.01 in one or two other places, kissed the ground, in a
58.02 manner of speaking, before him, and shut him up
58.03 with a supply of bottles in an upstairs room of his
58.04 infamous hovel. It appears he was under some hazy
58.05 apprehension as to his personal safety, and wished to
58.06 be concealed. However, Mariani told me a long
58.07 time after (when he came on board one day to dun
58.08 my steward for the price of some cigars) that he

58.09 would have done more for him without asking
58.10 any questions, from gratitude for some unholy
58.11 favour received very many years ago -- as far as I
58.12 could make out. He thumped twice his brawny
58.13 chest, rolled enormous black-and-white eyes glisten-
58.14 ing with tears: 'Antonio never forget -- Antonio
58.15 never forget!' What was the precise nature of the
58.16 immoral obligation I never learned, but be it what it
58.17 may, he had every facility given him to remain under
58.18 lock and key, with a chair, a table, a mattress in a
58.19 corner, and a litter of fallen plaster on the floor, in an
58.20 irrational state of funk, and keeping up his pecker
58.21 with such tonics as Mariani dispensed. This lasted
58.22 till the evening of the third day, when, after letting
58.23 out a few horrible screams, he found himself com-
58.24 pelled to seek safety in flight from a legion of centi-
58.25 pedes. He burst the door open, made one leap for
58.26 dear life down the crazy little stairway, landed bodily
58.27 on Mariani's stomach, picked himself up, and bolted
58.28 like a rabbit into the streets. The police plucked
58.29 him off a garbage-heap in the early morning. At
58.30 first he had a notion they were carrying him off to
59.01 be hanged, and fought for liberty like a hero, but
59.02 when I sat down by his bed he had been very quiet
59.03 for two days. His lean bronzed head, with white
59.04 moustaches, looked fine and calm on the pillow,
59.05 like the head of a war-worn soldier with a child--
59.06 like soul, had it not been for a hint of spectral
59.07 alarm that lurked in the blank glitter of his glance,
59.08 resembling a nondescript form of a terror crouching
59.09 silently behind a pane of glass. He was so extremely
59.10 calm, that I began to indulge in the eccentric hope
59.11 of hearing something explanatory of the famous
59.12 affair from his point of view. Why I longed to go
59.13 grubbing into the deplorable details of an occurrence
59.14 which, after all, concerned me no more than as a
59.15 member of an obscure body of men held together
59.16 by a community of inglorious toil and by fidelity
59.17 to a certain standard of conduct, I can't explain.
59.18 You may call it an unhealthy curiosity if you like;
59.19 but I have a distinct notion I wished to find some-
59.20 thing. Perhaps, unconsciously, I hoped I would
59.21 find that something, some profound and redeeming
59.22 cause, some merciful explanation, some convincing
59.23 shadow of an excuse. I see well enough now that
59.24 I hoped for the impossible -- for the laying of what
59.25 is the most obstinate ghost of man's creation, of the
59.26 uneasy doubt uprising like a mist, secret and gnawing
59.27 like a worm, and more chilling than the certitude of
59.28 death -- the doubt of the sovereign power enthroned
59.29 in a fixed standard of conduct. It is the hardest
59.30 thing to stumble against; it is the thing that breeds
60.01 yelling panics and good, little, quiet villainies; it's
60.02 the true shadow of calamity. Did I believe in a
60.03 miracle? And why did I desire it so ardently?
60.04 Was it for my own sake that I wished to find some
60.05 shadow of an excuse for that young fellow, whom I
60.06 had never seen before, but whose appearance alone
60.07 added a touch of personal concern to the thoughts
60.08 suggested by the knowledge of his weakness -- made
60.09 it a thing of mystery and terror -- like a hint of a
60.10 destructive fate ready for us all whose youth --
60.11 in its day -- had resembled his youth? I fear that
60.12 such was the secret motive of my prying. I was,
60.13 and no mistake, looking for a miracle. The only
60.14 thing that at this distance of time strikes me as
60.15 miraculous is the extent of my imbecility. I
60.16 positively hoped to obtain from that battered and
60.17 shady invalid some exorcism against the ghost of
60.18 doubt. I must have been pretty desperate too,
60.19 for, without loss of time, after a few indifferent
60.20 and friendly sentences which he answered with
60.21 languid readiness, just as any decent sick man would
60.22 do, I produced the word _Patna_ wrapped up in a
60.23 delicate question as in a wisp of floss silk. I was
60.24 delicate selfishly; I did not want to startle him;
60.25 I had no solicitude for him; I was not furious with
60.26 him and sorry for him: his experience was of no
60.27 importance; his redemption would have had no
60.28 point for me. He had grown old in minor iniquities,
60.29 and could no longer inspire aversion or pity. He
60.30 repeated _Patna?_ interrogatively, seemed to make a
61.01 short effort of memory and said, 'Quite right. I am
61.02 an old stager out here. I saw her go down.' I made
61.03 ready to vent my indignation at such a stupid lie,
61.04 when he added smoothly, 'She was full of reptiles.'
61.05 "This made me pause. What did he mean?
61.06 The unsteady phantom of terror behind his glassy
61.07 eyes seemed to stand still and look into mine wist-
61.08 fully. 'They turned me out of my bunk in the

61.09 middle watch to look at her sinking,' he pursued in a
61.10 reflective tone. His voice sounded alarmingly strong
61.11 all at once. I was sorry for my folly. There was
61.12 no snowy-winged coif of a nursing sister to be seen
61.13 flitting in the perspective of the ward; but away
61.14 in the middle of a long row of empty iron bedsteads
61.15 an accident case from some ship in the Roads sat
61.16 up brown and gaunt with a white bandage set
61.17 rakishly on the forehead. Suddenly my interesting
61.18 invalid shot out an arm thin like a tentacle and
61.19 clawed my shoulder. 'Only my eyes were good
61.20 enough to see. I am famous for my eyesight.
61.21 That's why they called me, I expect. None of
61.22 them was quick enough to see her go, but they saw
61.23 that she was gone right enough, and sang out to-
61.24 gether -- like this.'...A wolfish howl searched the
61.25 very recesses of my soul. 'Oh, make 'im dry up!'
61.26 whined the accident case irritably. 'You don't
61.27 believe me, I suppose,' went on the other, with an
61.28 air of ineffable conceit. 'I tell you there are no
61.29 such eyes as mine this side of the Persian Gulf.
61.30 Look under the bed.'
62.01 "Of course I stooped instantly. I defy any-
62.02 body not to have done so. 'What can you see?'
62.03 he asked. 'Nothing,' I said, feeling awfully
62.04 ashamed of myself. He scrutinised my face with
62.05 wild and withering contempt. 'Just so,' he said;
62.06 'but if I were to look I could see -- there's no eyes
62.07 like mine, I tell you.' Again he clawed, pulling at
62.08 me downwards in his eagerness to relieve himself
62.09 by a confidential communication. 'Millions of pink
62.10 toads. There's no eyes like mine. Millions of
62.11 pink toads. It's worse than seeing a ship sink.
62.12 I could look at sinking ships and smoke my pipe all
62.13 day long. Why don't they give me back my pipe?
62.14 I would get a smoke while I watched these toads.
62.15 The ship was full of them. They've got to be
62.16 watched, you know.' He winked facetiously. The
62.17 perspiration dripped on him off my head; my drill
62.18 coat clung to my wet back: the afternoon breeze
62.19 swept impetuously over the row of bedsteads, the
62.20 stiff folds of curtains stirred perpendicularly, ratt-
62.21 ling on brass rods, the covers of empty beds blew
62.22 about noiselessly near the bare floor all along the
62.23 line, and I shivered to the very marrow. The soft
62.24 wind of the tropics played in that naked ward as
62.25 bleak as a winter's gale in an old barn at home.
62.26 'Don't you let him start his hollering, mister,'
62.27 hailed from afar the accident case in a distressed,
62.28 angry shout that came ringing between the walls like
62.29 a quavering call down a tunnel. The clawing hand
62.30 hauled at my shoulder; he leered at me knowingly.
63.01 'The ship was full of them, you know, and we had
63.02 to clear out on the strict Q.T.,' he whispered with
63.03 extreme rapidity. 'All pink. All pink -- as big as
63.04 mastiffs, with an eye on the top of the head and
63.05 claws all round their ugly mouths. Ough! Ough!'
63.06 Quick jerks as of galvanic shocks disclosed under the
63.07 flat coverlet the outlines of meagre and agitated
63.08 legs; he let go my shoulder and reached after some-
63.09 thing in the air; his body trembled tensely like a
63.10 released harp-string; and while I looked down, the
63.11 spectral horror in him broke through his glassy
63.12 gaze. Instantly his face of an old soldier, with its
63.13 noble and calm outlines, became decomposed before
63.14 my eyes by the corruption of stealthy cunning, of
63.15 an abominable caution and of desperate fear. He
63.16 restrained a cry -- 'Ssh! what are they doing now
63.17 down there?' he asked, pointing to the floor with
63.18 fantastic precautions of voice and gesture, whose
63.19 meaning, borne upon my mind in a lurid flash, made
63.20 me very sick of my cleverness. 'They are all
63.21 asleep,' I answered, watching him narrowly. That
63.22 was it. That's what he wanted to hear: these
63.23 were the exact words that could calm him. He drew
63.24 a long breath. 'Ssh! Quiet, steady. I am an
63.25 old stager out here. I know them brutes. Bash
63.26 in the head of the first that stirs. There's too
63.27 many of them, and she won't swim more than ten
63.28 minutes.' He panted again. 'Hurry up,' he yelled
63.29 suddenly; and went on in a steady scream: 'They
63.30 are all awake -- millions of them. They are tramp-
64.01 ling on me! Wait! Oh, wait! I'll smash them
64.02 in heaps like flies. Wait for me! Help!
64.03 H-e-elp!' An interminable and sustained howl
64.04 completed my discomfiture. I saw in the distance
64.05 the accident case raise deplorably both his hands to
64.06 his bandaged head; a dresser, aproned to the chin,
64.07 showed himself in the vista of the ward, as if seen
64.08 in the small end of a telescope. I confessed myself

64.09 fairly routed, and without more ado, stepping out
64.10 through one of the long windows, escaped into
64.11 the outside gallery. The howl pursued me like a
64.12 vengeance. I turned into a deserted landing, and
64.13 suddenly all became very still and quiet around me,
64.14 and I descended the bare and shiny staircase in a
64.15 silence that enabled me to compose my distracted
64.16 thoughts. Down below I met one of the resident
64.17 surgeons who was crossing the courtyard and
64.18 stopped me. 'Been to see your man, Captain?
64.19 I think we may let him go to-morrow. These fools
64.20 have no notion of taking care of themselves, though.
64.21 I say, we've got the chief engineer of that pilgrim
64.22 ship here. A curious case. D.T.'s of the worst
64.23 kind. He has been drinking hard in that Greek's
64.24 or Italian's grog-shop for three days. What can
64.25 you expect? Four bottles of that kind of brandy
64.26 a day, I am told. Wonderful, if true. Sheeted
64.27 with boiler-iron inside, I should think. The head,
64.28 ah! the head, of course, gone, but the curious
64.29 part is there's some sort of method in his raving.
64.30 I am trying to find out. Most unusual -- that
65.01 thread of logic in such a delirium. Traditionally
65.02 he ought to see snakes, but he doesn't. Good old
65.03 tradition's at a discount nowadays. Eh? His -- er
65.04 -- visions are batrachian. Ha! ha! No, seriously,
65.05 I never remember being so interested in a case of
65.06 jim-jams before. He ought to be dead, don't you
65.07 know, after such a festive experiment. Oh! he
65.08 is a tough object. Four-and-twenty years of the
65.09 tropics, too. You ought really to take a peep
65.10 at him. Noble-looking old boozer. Most extra-
65.11 ordinary man I ever met -- medically, of course.
65.12 Won't you?'
65.13 "I had been all along exhibiting the usual polite
65.14 signs of interest, but now assuming an air of regret
65.15 I murmured of want of time, and shook hands in a
65.16 hurry. 'I say,' he cried after me; 'he can't attend
65.17 that inquiry. Is his evidence material, you think?'
65.18 "'Not in the least,' I called back from the
65.19 gateway."
66.01 THE authorities were evidently of the same
66.02 opinion. The inquiry was not adjourned.
66.03 It was held on the appointed day to satisfy
66.04 the law, and it was well attended because of its
66.05 human interest, no doubt. There was no incerti-
66.06 tude as to facts -- as to the one material fact, I mean.
66.07 How the Patna came by her hurt it was impossible
66.08 to find out; the court did not expect to find out;
66.09 and in the whole audience there was not a man who
66.10 cared. Yet, as I've told you, all the sailors in the
66.11 port attended, and the waterside business was fully
66.12 represented. Whether they knew it or not, the
66.13 interest that drew them there was purely psycho-
66.14 logical -- the expectation of some essential dis-
66.15 closure as to the strength, the power, the horror, of
66.16 human emotions. Naturally nothing of the kind
66.17 could be disclosed. The examination of the only
66.18 man able and willing to face it was beating futilely
66.19 round the well-known fact, and the play of questions
66.20 upon it was as instructive as the tapping with a
66.21 hammer on an iron box, were the object to find out
66.22 what's inside. However, an official inquiry could not
66.23 be any other thing. Its object was not the funda-
66.24 mental why, but the superficial how, of this affair.
67.01 "The young chap could have told them, and,
67.02 though that very thing was the thing that interested
67.03 the audience, the questions put to him necessarily
67.04 led him away from what to me, for instance, would
67.05 have been the only truth worth knowing. You
67.06 can't expect the constituted authorities to inquire
67.07 into the state of a man's soul -- or is it only of his
67.08 liver? Their business was to come down upon
67.09 the consequences, and frankly, a casual police
67.10 magistrate and two nautical assessors are not much
67.11 good for anything else. I don't mean to imply
67.12 these fellows were stupid. The magistrate was
67.13 very patient. One of the assessors was a sailing--
67.14 ship skipper with a reddish beard, and of a pious
67.15 disposition. Brierly was the other. Big Brierly.
67.16 Some of you must have heard of Big Brierly -- the
67.17 captain of the crack ship of the Blue Star line.
67.18 That's the man.
67.19 "He seemed consumedly bored by the honour
67.20 thrust upon him. He had never in his life made
67.21 a mistake, never had an accident, never a mishap,
67.22 never a check in his steady rise, and he seemed to
67.23 be one of those lucky fellows who know nothing of
67.24 indecision, much less of self-mistrust. At thirty--
67.25 two he had one of the best commands going in the
67.26 Eastern trade -- and, what's more, he thought a lot
67.27 of what he had. There was nothing like it in the
67.28 world, and I suppose if you had asked him point--
67.29 blank he would have confessed that in his opinion
67.30 there was not such another commander. The
68.01 choice had fallen upon the right man. The rest of
68.02 mankind that did not command the sixteen-knot
68.03 steel steamer Ossa were rather poor creatures. He
68.04 had saved lives at sea, had rescued ships in distress,
68.05 had a gold chronometer presented to him by the
68.06 underwriters, and a pair of binoculars with a suit-
68.07 able inscription from some foreign Government, in
68.08 commemoration of these services. He was acutely
68.09 aware of his merits and of his rewards. I liked
68.10 him well enough, though some I know -- meek,
68.11 friendly men at that -- couldn't stand him at any
68.12 price. I haven't the slightest doubt he considered
68.13 himself vastly my superior -- indeed, had you been
68.14 Emperor of East and West, you could not have
68.15 ignored your inferiority in his presence -- but I
68.16 couldn't get up any real sentiment of offence. He
68.17 did not despise me for anything I could help, for
68.18 anything I was -- don't you know? I was a negligible
68.19 quantity simply because I was not the fortunate
68.20 man of the earth, not Montague Brierly in command
68.21 of the Ossa, not the owner of an inscribed gold
68.22 chronometer and of silver-mounted binoculars
68.23 testifying to the excellence of my seamanship and
68.24 to my indomitable pluck; not possessed of an
68.25 acute sense of my merits and of my rewards, besides
68.26 the love and worship of a black retriever, the most
68.27 wonderful of its kind -- for never was such a man
68.28 loved thus by such a dog. No doubt, to have all
68.29 this forced upon you was exasperating enough;
68.30 but when I reflected that I was associated in these
69.01 fatal disadvantages with twelve hundred millions of
69.02 other more or less human beings, I found I could
69.03 bear my share of his good-natured and con-
69.04 temptuous pity for the sake of something indefinite
69.05 and attractive in the man. I have never defined to
69.06 myself this attraction, but there were moments
69.07 when I envied him. The sting of life could do no
69.08 more to his complacent soul than the scratch of a
69.09 pin to the smooth face of a rock. This was enviable.
69.10 As I looked at him flanking on one side the un-
69.11 assuming pale-faced magistrate who presided at
69.12 the inquiry, his self-satisfaction presented to me
69.13 and to the world a surface as hard as granite. He
69.14 committed suicide very soon after.
69.15 "No wonder Jim's case bored him, and while I
69.16 thought with something akin to fear of the immensity
69.17 of his contempt for the young man under examina-
69.18 tion, he was probably holding silent inquiry into
69.19 his own case. The verdict must have been of
69.20 unmitigated guilt, and he took the secret of the
69.21 evidence with him in that leap into the sea. If I
69.22 understand anything of men, the matter was no
69.23 doubt of the gravest import, one of those trifles
69.24 that awaken ideas -- start into life some thought
69.25 with which a man unused to such a companionship
69.26 finds it impossible to live. I am in a position to
69.27 know that it wasn't money, and it wasn't drink,
69.28 and it wasn't woman. He jumped overboard at
69.29 sea barely a week after the end of the inquiry, and
69.30 less than three days after leaving port on his out-
70.01 ward passage; as though on that exact spot in
70.02 the midst of waters he had suddenly perceived
70.03 the gates of the other world flung open wide for
70.04 his reception.
70.05 "Yet it was not a sudden impulse. His grey--
70.06 headed mate, a first-rate sailor and a nice old chap
70.07 with strangers, but in his relations with his com-
70.08 mander the surliest chief officer I've ever seen,
70.09 would tell the story with tears in his eyes. It
70.10 appears that when he came on deck in the morning
70.11 walking on hind legs. He was extravagantly gor-
70.12 geous too -- got up in a soiled sleeping-suit, bright
70.13 green and deep orange vertical stripes, with a pair
70.14 of ragged straw slippers on his bare feet, and some-
70.15 body's cast-off pith hat, very dirty and two sizes too
70.16 small for him, tied up with a manilla rope-yarn on
70.17 the top of his big head. You understand a man like
70.18 that hasn't the ghost of a chance when it comes
70.19 to borrowing clothes. Very well. On he came in
70.20 hot haste, without a look right or left, passed within
70.21 three feet of me, and in the innocence of his heart
70.22 went on pelting upstairs in the harbour office to
70.23 make his deposition, or report, or whatever you like
70.24 to call it.
70.25 Brierly had been writing in the chart-room. 'It

70.26 was ten minutes to four,' he said, 'and the middle
70.27 watch was not relieved yet, of course. He heard
70.28 my voice on the bridge speaking to the second
70.29 mate, and called me in. I was loth to go, and that's
70.30 the truth, Captain Marlow -- I couldn't stand poor
70.31 Captain Brierly, I tell you with shame; we never
70.32 know what a man is made of. He had been pro-
70.33 moted over too many heads, not counting my own,
70.34 and he had a damnable trick of making you feel
70.35 small, nothing but by the way he said "Good
70.36 morning." I never addressed him, sir, but on
70.37 matters of duty, and then it was as much as I could
70.38 do to keep a civil tongue in my head.' (He flattered
70.39 himself there. I often wondered how Brierly
70.40 could put up with his manners for more than half
70.41 a voyage.) 'I've a wife and childre,' he went on,
70.42 'and I had been ten years in the Company, always
70.43 expecting the next command -- more fool I. Says he,
70.44 just like this: "Come in here, Mr. Jones," in that
71.01 swagger voice of his -- "come in here, Mr. Jones."
71.02 In I went. "We'll lay down her position," says he,
71.03 stooping over the chart, a pair of dividers in hand.
71.04 By the standing orders, the officer going off duty
71.05 would have done that at the end of his watch. How-
71.06 ever, I said nothing, and looked on while he marked
71.07 off the ship's position with a tiny cross and wrote
71.08 the date and the time. I can see him this moment
71.09 writing his neat figures: seventeen, eight, four A.M.
71.10 The year would be written in red ink at the top of
71.11 the chart. He never used his charts more than a
71.12 year, Captain Brierly didn't. I've the chart now.
71.13 When he had done he stands looking down at the
71.14 mark he had made and smiling to himself, then looks
71.15 up at me. "Thirty-two miles more as she goes,"
71.16 says he, "and then we shall be clear, and you may
71.17 alter the course twenty degrees to the southward."
71.18 "'We were passing to the north of the Hector
71.19 Bank that voyage. I said, "All right, sir," wonder-
71.20 ing what he was fussing about, since I had to call
71.21 him before altering the course anyhow. Just then
71.22 eight bells were struck: we came out on the bridge,
71.23 and the second mate before going off mentions in
71.24 the usual way, "Seventy-one on the log." Captain
71.25 Brierly looks at the compass and then all round.
71.26 It was dark and clear, and all the stars were out as
71.27 plain as on a frosty night in high latitudes. Sud-
71.28 denly he says with a sort of a little sigh: "I am
71.29 going aft, and shall set the log at zero for you myself,
71.30 so that there can be no mistake. Thirty-two miles
72.01 more on this course and then you are safe. Let's
72.02 see -- the correction on the log is six per cent.
72.03 additive; say, then, thirty by the dial to run, and
72.04 you may come twenty degrees to starboard at
72.05 once. No use losing any distance -- is there?"
72.06 I had never heard him talk so much at a stretch,
72.07 and to no purpose as it seemed to me. I said
72.08 nothing. He went down the ladder, and the dog,
72.09 that was always at his heels whenever he moved,
72.10 night or day, followed, sliding nose first, after
72.11 him. I heard his boot-heels tap, tap on the after--
72.12 deck, then he stopped and spoke to the dog -- "Go
72.13 back, Rover. On the bridge, boy! Go on -- get."
72.14 Then he calls out to me from the dark, "Shut that
72.15 dog up in the chart-room, Mr. Jones -- will you?"
72.16 "'This was the last time I heard his voice,
72.17 Captain Marlow. These are the last words he
72.18 spoke in the hearing of any living human being,
72.19 sir.' At this point the old chap's voice got quite
72.20 unsteady. 'He was afraid the poor brute would
72.21 jump after him, don't you see?' he pursued with
72.22 a quaver. 'Yes, Captain Marlow. He set the
72.23 log for me; he -- would you believe it? -- he put a
72.24 drop of oil in it too. There was the oil-feeder
72.25 where he left it near by. The boatswain's mate
72.26 got the hose along aft to wash down at half-past
72.27 five; by and by he knocks off and runs up on
72.28 the bridge -- "Will you please come aft, Mr. Jones,"
72.29 he says. "There's a funny thing. I don't like to
72.30 touch it." It was Captain Brierly's gold chrono-
73.01 meter watch carefully hung under the rail by its
73.02 chain.
73.03 "'As soon as my eyes fell on it something struck
73.04 me, and I knew, sir. My legs got soft under me.
73.05 It was as if I had seen him go over; and I could tell
73.06 how far behind he was left too. The taffrail-log
73.07 marked eighteen miles and three-quarters, and four
73.08 iron belaying-pins were missing round the main-
73.09 mast. Put them in his pockets to help him down,
73.10 I suppose; but, Lord! what's four iron pins to
73.11 a powerful man like Captain Brierly. Maybe his
73.12 confidence in himself was just shook a bit at the
73.13 last. That's the only sign of fluster he gave in his
73.14 whole life, I should think; but I am ready to
73.15 answer for him, that once over he did not try to
73.16 swim a stroke, the same as he would have had
73.17 pluck enough to keep up all day long on the bare
73.18 chance had he fallen overboard accidentally. Yes,
73.19 sir. He was second to none -- if he said so himself,
73.20 as I heard him once. He had written two letters
73.21 in the middle watch, one to the Company and the
73.22 other to me. He gave me a lot of instructions
73.23 as to the passage -- I had been in the trade before
73.24 he was out of his time -- and no end of hints as to
73.25 my conduct with our people in Shanghai, so that
73.26 I should keep the command of the Ossa. He wrote
73.27 like a father would to a favourite son, Captain
73.28 Marlow, and I was five-and-twenty years his
73.29 senior and had tasted salt water before he was
73.30 fairly breeched. In his letter to the owners --
74.01 it was left open for me to see -- he said that he had
74.02 always done his duty by them -- up to that moment
74.03 -- and even now he was not betraying their con-
74.04 fidence, since he was leaving the ship to as com-
74.05 petent a seaman as could be found -- meaning me,
74.06 sir, meaning me! He told them that if the last
74.07 act of his life didn't take away all his credit with
74.08 them, they would give weight to my faithful service
74.09 and to his warm recommendation, when about to
74.10 fill the vacancy made by his death. And much
74.11 more like this, sir. I couldn't believe my eyes. It
74.12 made me feel queer all over,' went on the old chap
74.13 in great perturbation, and squashing something in
74.14 the corner of his eye with the end of a thumb
74.15 as broad as a spatula. 'You would think, sir,
74.16 he had jumped overboard only to give an unlucky
74.17 man a last show to get on. What with the shock
74.18 of him going in this awful rash way, and thinking
74.19 myself a made man by that chance, I was nearly
74.20 off my chump for a week. But no fear. The
74.21 captain of the Pelion was shifted into the Ossa --
74.22 came aboard in Shanghai -- a little popinjay, sir,
74.23 in a grey check suit, with his hair parted in the
74.24 middle. "Aw -- I am -- aw -- your new captain,
74.25 Mister -- Mister -- aw -- Jones." He was drowned in
74.26 scent -- fairly stunk with it, Captain Marlow. I
74.27 dare say it was the look I gave him that made
74.28 him stammer. He mumbled something about my
74.29 natural disappointment -- I had better know at once
74.30 that his chief officer got the promotion to the Pelion
75.01 -- he had nothing to do with it, of course -- supposed
75.02 the office knew best -- sorry.... Says I, "Don't
75.03 you mind old Jones, sir; damn his soul, he's used
75.04 to it." I could see directly I had shocked his
75.05 delicate ear, and while we sat at our first tiffin
75.06 together he began to find fault in a nasty manner
75.07 with this and that in the ship. I never heard
75.08 such a voice out of a Punch and Judy show. I
75.09 set my teeth hard, and glued my eyes to my plate,
75.10 and held my peace as long as I could; but at last
75.11 I had to say something. Up he jumps tiptoeing,
75.12 ruffling all his pretty plumes, like a little fighting--
75.13 cock. "You'll find you have a different person to
75.14 deal with than the late Captain Brierly." "I've
75.15 found it," says I, very glum, but pretending to be
75.16 mighty busy with my steak. "You are an old
75.17 ruffian, Mister -- aw -- Jones; and what's more, you
75.18 are known for an old ruffian in the employ," he
75.19 squeaks at me. The damned bottle-washers stood
75.20 about listening with their mouths stretched from
75.21 ear to ear. "I may be a hard case," answers I,
75.22 "but I ain't so far gone as to put up with the sight
75.23 of you sitting in Captain Brierly's chair." With
75.24 that I lay down my knife and fork. "You would
75.25 like to sit in it yourself -- that's where the shoe
75.26 pinches," he sneers. I left the saloon, got my rags
75.27 together, and was on the quay with all my dunnage
75.28 about my feet before the stevedores had turned to
75.29 again. Yes. Adrift -- on shore -- after ten years'
75.30 service -- and with a poor woman and four children
76.01 six thousand miles off depending on my half-pay
76.02 for every mouthful they ate. Yes, sir! I chucked
76.03 it rather than hear Captain Brierly abused. He left
76.04 me his night-glasses -- here they are; and he wished
76.05 me to take care of the dog -- here he is. Hallo,
76.06 Rover, poor boy. Where's the captain, Rover?'
76.07 The dog looked up at us with mournful, yellow
76.08 eyes, gave one desolate bark, and crept under the
76.09 table.
76.10 "All this was taking place, more than two
76.11 years afterwards, on board that nautical ruin the

76.12 <u>Fire-Queen</u> this Jones had got charge of -- quite
76.13 by a funny accident, too -- from Matherson -- mad
76.14 Matherson they generally called him -- the same
76.15 who used to hang out in Hai-phong, you know,
76.16 before the occupation days. The old chap snuffled
76.17 on:
76.18 "'Ay, sir, Captain Brierly will be remembered
76.19 here, if there's no other place on earth. I wrote
76.20 fully to his father, and did not get a word in reply --
76.21 neither Thank you, nor Go to the devil! -- nothing!
76.22 Perhaps they did not want to know.'
76.23 "The sight of that watery-eyed old Jones
76.24 mopping his bald head with a red cotton hand-
76.25 kerchief, the sorrowing yelp of the dog, the squalor
76.26 of that fly-blown cuddy which was the only shrine
76.27 of his memory, threw a veil of inexpressibly mean
76.28 pathos over Brierly's remembered figure, the
76.29 posthumous revenge of fate for that belief in his
76.30 own splendour which had almost cheated his life
77.01 of its legitimate terrors. Almost! Perhaps wholly.
77.02 Who can tell what flattering view he had induced
77.03 himself to take of his own suicide?
77.04 "'Why did he commit the rash act, Captain
77.05 Marlow -- can you think?' asked Jones, pressing
77.06 his palms together. 'Why? It beats me! Why?'
77.07 He slapped his low and wrinkled forehead. 'If
77.08 he had been poor and old and in debt -- and never
77.09 a show -- or else mad. But he wasn't of the kind
77.10 that goes mad, not he. You trust me. What a
77.11 mate don't know about his skipper isn't worth
77.12 knowing. Young, healthy, well off, no cares....
77.13 I sit here sometimes thinking, thinking, till my
77.14 head fairly begins to buzz. There was some
77.15 reason.'
77.16 "'You may depend on it, Captain Jones,' said
77.17 I, 'it wasn't anything that would have disturbed
77.18 much either of us two,' I said; and then, as if a
77.19 light had been flashed into the muddle of his brain,
77.20 poor old Jones found a last word of amazing pro-
77.21 fundity. He blew his nose, nodding at me dole-
77.22 fully: 'Ay, ay! neither you nor I, sir, had ever
77.23 thought so much of ourselves.'
77.24 "Of course the recollection of my last con-
77.25 versation with Brierly is tinged with the knowledge
77.26 of his end that followed so close upon it. I spoke
77.27 with him for the last time during the progress of the
77.28 inquiry. It was after the first adjournment, and
77.29 he came up with me in the street. He was in a
77.30 state of irritation, which I noticed with surprise, his
78.01 usual behaviour when he condescended to converse
78.02 being perfectly cool, with a trace of amused toler-
78.03 ance, as if the existence of his interlocutor had been
78.04 a rather good joke. 'They caught me for that
78.05 inquiry, you see,' he began, and for a while enlarged
78.06 complainingly upon the inconveniences of daily
78.07 attendance in court. 'And goodness knows how
78.08 long it will last. Three days, I suppose.' I heard
78.09 him out in silence; in my then opinion it was a
78.10 way as good as another of putting on side. 'What's
78.11 the use of it? It is the stupidest set-out you can
78.12 imagine,' he pursued hotly. I remarked that there
78.13 was no option. He interrupted me with a sort of
78.14 pent-up violence. 'I feel like a fool all the time.'
78.15 I looked up at him. This was going very far --
78.16 for Brierly -- when talking of Brierly. He stopped
78.17 short, and seizing the lapel of my coat, gave it a
78.18 slight tug. 'Why are we tormenting that young
78.19 chap?' he asked. This question chimed in so
78.20 well to the tolling of a certain thought of mine
78.21 that, with the image of the absconding renegade
78.22 in my eye, I answered at once, 'Hanged if I know,
78.23 unless it be that he lets you.' I was astonished to
78.24 see him fall into line, so to speak, with that utter-
78.25 ance, which ought to have been tolerably cryptic.
78.26 He said angrily, 'Why, yes. Can't he see that
78.27 wretched skipper of his has cleared out? What
78.28 does he expect to happen? Nothing can save him.
78.29 He's done for.' We walked on in silence a few
78.30 steps. 'Why eat all that dirt?' he exclaimed, with
79.01 an oriental energy of expression -- about the only
79.02 sort of energy you can find a trace of east of the
79.03 fiftieth meridian. I wondered greatly at the direc-
79.04 tion of his thoughts, but now I strongly suspect it
79.05 was strictly in character: at bottom poor Brierly
79.06 must have been thinking of himself. I pointed out
79.07 to him that the skipper of the <u>Patna</u> was known
79.08 to have feathered his nest pretty well, and could
79.09 procure almost anywhere the means of getting
79.10 away. With Jim it was otherwise: the Govern-
79.11 ment was keeping him in the Sailors' Home for the

79.12 time being, and probably he hadn't a penny in his
79.13 pocket to bless himself with. It costs some money
79.14 to run away. 'Does it? Not always,' he said,
79.15 with a bitter laugh, and to some further remark of
79.16 mine -- 'Well, then, let him creep twenty feet
79.17 underground and stay there! By heavens! I
79.18 would.' I don't know why his tone provoked me,
79.19 and I said, 'There is a kind of courage in facing it
79.20 out as he does, knowing very well that if he went
79.21 away nobody would trouble to run after him.'
79.22 'Courage be hanged!' growled Brierly. 'That
79.23 sort of courage is of no use to keep a man straight,
79.24 and I don't care a snap for such courage. If you
79.25 were to say it was a kind of cowardice now -- of
79.26 softness. I tell you what, I will put up two hundred
79.27 rupees if you put up another hundred and under-
79.28 take to make the beggar clear out early to-morrow
79.29 morning. The fellow's a gentleman if he ain't
79.30 fit to be touched -- he will understand. He must.
80.01 This infernal publicity is too shocking: there he
80.02 sits while all these confounded natives, serangs,
80.03 lascars, quartermasters, are giving evidence that's
80.04 enough to burn a man to ashes with shame. This
80.05 is abominable. Why, Marlow, don't you think,
80.06 don't you feel, that this is abominable? Don't
80.07 you now -- come -- as a seaman? If he went away
80.08 all this would stop at once.' Brierly said these
80.09 words with a most unusual animation, and made
80.10 as if to reach after his pocket-book. I restrained
80.11 him, and declared coldly that the cowardice of
80.12 these four men did not seem to me a matter of such
80.13 great importance. 'And you call yourself a sea-
80.14 man, I suppose?' he pronounced angrily. I said
80.15 that's what I called myself, and I hoped I was too.
80.16 He heard me out, and made a gesture with his big
80.17 arm that seemed to deprive me of my individuality,
80.18 to push me away into the crowd. 'The worst of
80.19 it,' he said, 'is that all you fellows have no sense
80.20 of dignity; you don't think enough of what you
80.21 are supposed to be.'
80.22 "We had been walking slowly meantime, and
80.23 now stopped opposite the harbour office, in sight of
80.24 the very spot from which the immense captain of
80.25 the <u>Patna</u> had vanished as utterly as a tiny feather
80.26 blown away in a hurricane. I smiled. Brierly
80.27 went on: 'This is a disgrace. We've got all kinds
80.28 amongst us -- some anointed scoundrels in the lot;
80.29 but, hang it, we must preserve professional decency
80.30 or we become no better than so many tinkers going
81.01 about loose. We are trusted. Do you understand?
81.02 -- trusted! Frankly, I don't care a snap for all the
81.03 pilgrims that ever came out of Asia, but a decent
81.04 man would not have behaved like this to a full cargo
81.05 of old rags in bales. We aren't an organised body of
81.06 men, and the only thing that holds us together is
81.07 just the name for that kind of decency. Such an
81.08 affair destroys one's confidence. A man may go
81.09 pretty near through his whole sea-life without any
81.10 call to show a stiff upper lip. But when the call
81.11 comes...Aha!...If I...'
81.12 "He broke off, and in a changed tone, 'I'll give
81.13 you two hundred rupees now, Marlow, and you just
81.14 talk to that chap. Confound him! I wish he had
81.15 never come out here. Fact is, I rather think some
81.16 of my people know his. The old man's a parson,
81.17 and I remember now I met him once when staying
81.18 with my cousin in Essex last year. If I am not
81.19 mistaken, the old chap seemed rather to fancy his
81.20 sailor son. Horrible. I can't do it myself -- but
81.21 you...'
81.22 "Thus, apropos of Jim, I had a glimpse of the
81.23 real Brierly a few days before he committed his
81.24 reality and his sham together to the keeping of the
81.25 sea. Of course I declined to meddle. The tone
81.26 of this last 'but you' (poor Brierly couldn't help
81.27 it), that seemed to imply I was no more noticeable
81.28 than an insect, caused me to look at the proposal
81.29 with indignation, and on account of that provocation,
81.30 or for some other reason, I became positive in my
82.01 mind that the inquiry was a severe punishment to
82.02 that Jim, and that his facing it -- practically of his
82.03 own free will -- was a redeeming feature in his
82.04 abominable case. I hadn't been so sure of it
82.05 before. Brierly went off in a huff. At the time
82.06 his state of mind was more of a mystery to me
82.07 than it is now.
82.08 "Next day, coming into court late, I sat by my-
82.09 self. Of course I could not forget the conversation
82.10 I had with Brierly, and now I had them both under
82.11 my eyes. The demeanour of one suggested gloomy

82.12 impudence and of the other a contemptuous bore-
82.13 dom; yet one attitude might not have been truer
82.14 than the other, and I was aware that one was not
82.15 true. Brierly was not bored -- he was exasperated;
82.16 and if so, then Jim might not have been impudent.
82.17 According to my theory he was not. I imagined he
82.18 was hopeless. Then it was that our glances met.
82.19 They met, and the look he gave me was discouraging
82.20 of any intention I might have had to speak to him.
82.21 Upon either hypothesis -- insolence or despair -- I
82.22 felt I could be of no use to him. This was the
82.23 second day of the proceedings. Very soon after
82.24 that exchange of glances the inquiry was adjourned
82.25 again to the next day. The white men began to
82.26 troop out at once. Jim had been told to stand down
82.27 some time before, and was able to leave amongst
82.28 the first. I saw his broad shoulders and his head
82.29 outlined in the light of the door, and while I made
82.30 my way slowly out talking with some one -- some
83.01 stranger who had addressed me casually -- I could
83.02 see him from within the court-room resting both
83.03 elbows on the balustrade of the verandah and
83.04 turning his back on the small stream of people
83.05 trickling down the few steps. There was a murmur
83.06 of voices and a shuffle of boots.
83.07 "The next case was that of assault and battery
83.08 committed upon a money-lender, I believe; and
83.09 the defendant -- a venerable villager with a straight
83.10 white beard -- sat on a mat just outside the door with
83.11 his sons, daughters, sons-in-law, their wives, and,
83.12 I should think, half the population of his village
83.13 besides, squatting or standing around him. A
83.14 slim, dark woman, with part of her back and one
83.15 black shoulder bared, and with a thin gold ring in
83.16 her nose, suddenly began to talk in a high-pitched,
83.17 shrewish tone. The man with me instinctively
83.18 looked up at her. We were then just through the
83.19 door, passing behind Jim's burly back.
83.20 "Whether those villagers had brought the
83.21 yellow dog with them, I don't know. Anyhow, a
83.22 dog was there, weaving himself in and out amongst
83.23 people's legs in that mute, stealthy way native dogs
83.24 have, and my companion stumbled over him. The
83.25 dog leaped away without a sound; the man, raising
83.26 his voice a little, said with a slow laugh, 'Look at
83.27 that wretched cur,' and directly afterwards we
83.28 became separated by a lot of people pushing in. I
83.29 stood back for a moment against the wall while the
83.30 stranger managed to get down the steps and dis-
84.01 appeared. I saw Jim spin round. He made a
84.02 step forward and barred my way. We were alone;
84.03 he glared at me with an air of stubborn resolution.
84.04 I became aware I was being held up, so to speak,
84.05 as if in a wood. The verandah was empty by then,
84.06 the noise and movement in court had ceased: a
84.07 great silence fell upon the building, in which, some-
84.08 where far within, an oriental voice began to whine
84.09 abjectly. The dog, in the very act of trying to
84.10 sneak in at the door, sat down hurriedly to hunt for
84.11 fleas.
84.12 "'Did you speak to me?' asked Jim very low,
84.13 and bending forward, not so much towards me but
84.14 at me, if you know what I mean. I said 'No' at
84.15 once. Something in the sound of that quiet tone
84.16 of his warned me to be on my defence. I watched
84.17 him. It was very much like a meeting in a wood,
84.18 only more uncertain in its issue, since he could
84.19 possibly want neither my money nor my life --
84.20 nothing that I could simply give up or defend with
84.21 a clear conscience. 'You say you didn't,' he said,
84.22 very sombre. 'But I heard.' 'Some mistake,' I
84.23 protested, utterly at a loss, and never taking my eyes
84.24 off him. To watch his face was like watching a
84.25 darkening sky before a clap of thunder, shade upon
84.26 shade imperceptibly coming on, the gloom growing
84.27 mysteriously intense in the calm of maturing
84.28 violence.
84.29 "'As far as I know, I haven't opened my lips in
84.30 your hearing,' I affirmed with perfect truth. I was
85.01 getting a little angry, too, at the absurdity of this
85.02 encounter. It strikes me now I have never in my
85.03 life been so near a beating -- I mean it literally; a
85.04 beating with fists. I suppose I had some hazy
85.05 prescience of that eventuality being in the air. Not
85.06 that he was actively threatening me. On the con-
85.07 trary, he was strangely passive -- don't you know? --
85.08 but he was lowering, and, though not exceptionally
85.09 big, he looked generally fit to demolish a wall. The
85.10 most reassuring symptom I noticed was a kind of
85.11 slow and ponderous hesitation, which I took as a
85.12 tribute to the evident sincerity of my manner and
85.13 of my tone. We faced each other. In the court
85.14 the assault case was proceeding. I caught the
85.15 words: 'Well -- buffalo -- stick -- in the greatness of
85.16 my fear....'
85.17 "'What did you mean by staring at me all the
85.18 morning?' said Jim at last. He looked up and
85.19 looked down again. 'Did you expect us all to sit
85.20 with downcast eyes out of regard for your sus-
85.21 ceptibilities?' I retorted sharply. I was not
85.22 going to submit meekly to any of his nonsense. He
85.23 raised his eyes again, and this time continued to
85.24 look me straight in the face. 'No. That's all
85.25 right,' he pronounced, with an air of deliberating
85.26 with himself upon the truth of this statement --
85.27 'that's all right. I am going through with that.
85.28 Only' -- and there he spoke a little faster -- 'I
85.29 won't let any man call me names outside this court.
85.30 There was a fellow with you. You spoke to him --
86.01 oh yes -- I know; 'tis all very fine. You spoke to
86.02 him, but you meant me to hear....'
86.03 "I assured him he was under some extraordinary
86.04 delusion. I had no conception how it came about.
86.05 'You thought I would be afraid to resent this,' he
86.06 said, with just a faint tinge of bitterness. I was
86.07 interested enough to discern the slightest shades of
86.08 expression, but I was not in the least enlightened;
86.09 yet I don't know what in these words, or perhaps
86.10 just the intonation of that phrase, induced me
86.11 suddenly to make all possible allowances for him. I
86.12 ceased to be annoyed at my unexpected predica-
86.13 ment. It was some mistake on his part; he was
86.14 blundering, and I had an intuition that the blunder
86.15 was of an odious, of an unfortunate nature. I was
86.16 anxious to end this scene on grounds of decency,
86.17 just as one is anxious to cut short some unpro-
86.18 voked and abominable confidence. The funniest
86.19 part was, that in the midst of all these considerations
86.20 of the higher order I was conscious of a certain
86.21 trepidation as to the possibility -- nay, likelihood --
86.22 of this encounter ending in some disreputable
86.23 brawl which could not possibly be explained, and
86.24 would make me ridiculous. I did not hanker
86.25 after a three days' celebrity as the man who got
86.26 a black eye or something of the sort from the mate
86.27 of the Patna. He, in all probability, did not care
86.28 what he did, or at any rate would be fully justified
86.29 in his own eyes. It took no magician to see he was
86.30 amazingly angry about something, for all his quiet
87.01 and even torpid demeanour. I don't deny I was
87.02 extremely desirous to pacify him at all costs, had
87.03 I only known what to do. But I didn't know, as
87.04 you may well imagine. It was blackness without a
87.05 single gleam. We confronted each other in silence.
87.06 He hung fire for about fifteen seconds, then made
87.07 a step nearer, and I made ready to ward off a blow,
87.08 though I don't think I moved a muscle. 'If you
87.09 were as big as two men and as strong as six,' he said
87.10 very softly, 'I would tell you what I think of you.
87.11 You...' 'Stop!' I exclaimed. This checked
87.12 him for a second. 'Before you tell me what you
87.13 think of me,' I went on quickly, 'will you kindly
87.14 tell me what it is I've said or done?' During
87.15 the pause that ensued he surveyed me with indigna-
87.16 tion, while I made supernatural efforts of memory,
87.17 in which I was hindered by the oriental voice within
87.18 the court-room expostulating with impassioned
87.19 volubility against a charge of falsehood. Then we
87.20 spoke almost together. 'I will soon show you I
87.21 am not,' he said, in a tone suggestive of a crisis.
87.22 'I declare I don't know,' I protested earnestly
87.23 at the same time. He tried to crush me by the
87.24 scorn of his glance. 'Now that you see I am not
87.25 afraid you try to crawl out of it,' he said. 'Who's
87.26 a cur now -- hey?' Then, at last, I understood.
87.27 "He had been scanning my features as though
87.28 looking for a place where he would plant his fist.
87.29 'I will allow no man,'...he mumbled threaten-
87.30 ingly. It was, indeed, a hideous mistake; he had
88.01 given himself away utterly. I can't give you an idea
88.02 how shocked I was. I suppose he saw some reflec-
88.03 tion of my feelings in my face, because his expression
88.04 changed just a little. 'Good God!' I stammered,
88.05 'you don't think I...' 'But I am sure I've
88.06 heard,' he persisted, raising his voice for the first
88.07 time since the beginning of this deplorable scene.
88.08 Then with a shade of disdain he added, 'It wasn't
88.09 you, then? Very well; I'll find the other.' 'Don't
88.10 be a fool,' I cried in exasperation; 'it wasn't that
88.11 at all.' 'I've heard,' he said again, with an un-

88.12 shaken and sombre perseverance.
88.13 "There may be those who could have laughed
88.14 at his pertinacity. I didn't. Oh, I didn't! There
88.15 had never been a man so mercilessly shown up
88.16 by his own natural impulse. A single word had
88.17 stripped him of his discretion -- of that discretion
88.18 which is more necessary to the decencies of our
88.19 inner being than clothing is to the decorum of our
88.20 body. 'Don't be a fool,' I repeated. 'But the
88.21 other man said it, you don't deny that?' he pro-
88.22 nounced distinctly, and looking in my face without
88.23 flinching. 'No, I don't deny,' said I, returning his
88.24 gaze. At last his eyes followed downwards the
88.25 direction of my pointing finger. He appeared at
88.26 first uncomprehending, then confounded, and at
88.27 last amazed and scared as though a dog had been a
88.28 monster and he had never seen a dog before. 'No-
88.29 body dreamt of insulting you,' I said.
88.30 "He contemplated the wretched animal, that
89.01 moved no more than an effigy: it sat with ears
89.02 pricked and its sharp muzzle pointed into the door-
89.03 way, and suddenly snapped at a fly like a piece of
89.04 mechanism.
89.05 "I looked at him. The red of his fair, sunburnt
89.06 complexion deepened suddenly under the down of
89.07 his cheeks, invaded his forehead, spread to the roots
89.08 of his curly hair. His ears became intensely
89.09 crimson, and even the clear blue of his eyes was
89.10 darkened many shades by the rush of blood to his
89.11 head. His lips pouted a little, trembling as though
89.12 he had been on the point of bursting into tears.
89.13 I perceived he was incapable of pronouncing a
89.14 word from the excess of his humiliation. From
89.15 disappointment too -- who knows? Perhaps he
89.16 looked forward to that hammering he was going to
89.17 give me for rehabilitation, for appeasement? Who
89.18 can tell what relief he expected from this chance
89.19 of a row? He was naive enough to expect any-
89.20 thing; but he had given himself away for nothing
89.21 in this case. He had been frank with himself --
89.22 let alone with me -- in the wild hope of arriving
89.23 in that way at some effective refutation, and the
89.24 stars had been ironically unpropitious. He made
89.25 an inarticulate noise in his throat like a man im-
89.26 perfectly stunned by a blow on the head. It was
89.27 pitiful.
89.28 "I didn't catch up again with him till well
89.29 outside the gate. I had even to trot a bit at the
89.30 last, but when, out of breath at his elbow, I taxed
90.01 him with running away, he said, 'Never!' and at
90.02 once turned at bay. I explained I never meant
90.03 to say he was running away from me. 'From no
90.04 man -- from not a single man on earth,' he affirmed
90.05 with a stubborn mien. I forebore to point out
90.06 the one obvious exception which would hold good
90.07 for the bravest of us; I thought he would find out
90.08 by himself very soon. He looked at me patiently
90.09 while I was thinking of something to say, but I
90.10 could find nothing on the spur of the moment,
90.11 and he began to walk on. I kept up, and, anxious
90.12 not to lose him, I said hurriedly that I couldn't
90.13 think of leaving him under a false impression of
90.14 my -- of my -- I stammered. The stupidity of the
90.15 phrase appalled me while I was trying to finish it,
90.16 but the power of sentences has nothing to do with
90.17 their sense or the logic of their construction. My
90.18 idiotic mumble seemed to please him. He cut it
90.19 short by saying, with courteous placidity that
90.20 argued an immense power of self-control or else
90.21 a wonderful elasticity of spirits -- 'Altogether my
90.22 mistake.' I marvelled greatly at this expression:
90.23 he might have been alluding to some trifling
90.24 occurrence. Hadn't he understood its deplorable
90.25 meaning? 'You may well forgive me,' he con-
90.26 tinued; and went on a little moodily, 'All these
90.27 staring people in court seemed such fools that --
90.28 that it might have been as I supposed.'
90.29 "This opened suddenly a new view of him to
90.30 my wonder. I looked at him curiously, and met
91.01 his unabashed and impenetrable eyes. 'I can't put
91.02 up with this kind of thing,' he said very simply,
91.03 'and I don't mean to. In court it's different;
91.04 I've got to stand that -- and I can do it too.'
91.05 "I don't pretend I understood him. The views
91.06 he let me have of himself were like those glimpses
91.07 through the shifting rents in a thick fog -- bits of
91.08 vivid and vanishing detail, giving no connected idea
91.09 of the general aspect of a country. They fed one's
91.10 curiosity without satisfying it; they were no good
91.11 for purposes of orientation. Upon the whole he was

91.12 misleading. That's how I summed him up to
91.13 myself after he left me late in the evening. I had
91.14 been staying at the Malabar House for a few days,
91.15 and on my pressing invitation he dined with me
91.16 there."
92.01 "AN outward-bound mail-boat had come
92.02 in that afternoon, and the big dining--
92.03 room of the hotel was more than half
92.04 full of people with a-hundred-pounds-round-the--
92.05 world tickets in their pockets. There were married
92.06 couples looking domesticated and bored with each
92.07 other in the midst of their travels; there were
92.08 small parties and large parties, and lone individuals
92.09 dining solemnly or feasting boisterously, but all
92.10 thinking, conversing, joking, or scowling as was
92.11 their wont at home; and just as intelligently
92.12 receptive of new impressions as their trunks up-
92.13 stairs. Henceforth they would be labelled as having
92.14 passed through this and that place, and so would be
92.15 their luggage. They would cherish this distinction
92.16 of their persons, and preserve the gummed tickets
92.17 on their portmanteaux as documentary evidence
92.18 as the only permanent trace of their improving
92.19 enterprise. The dark-faced servants tripped with-
92.20 out noise over the vast and polished floor; now
92.21 and then a girl's laugh would be heard, as innocent
92.22 and empty as her mind, or, in a sudden hush of
92.23 crockery, a few words in an affected drawl from
92.24 some wit embroidering for the benefit of a grinning
93.01 tableful the last funny story of shipboard scandal.
93.02 Two nomadic old maids, dressed up to kill, worked
93.03 acrimoniously through the bill of fare, whispering
93.04 to each other with faded lips, wooden-faced and
93.05 bizarre, like two sumptuous scarecrows. A little
93.06 wine opened Jim's heart and loosened his tongue.
93.07 His appetite was good, too, I noticed. He seemed
93.08 to have buried somewhere the opening episode of
93.09 our acquaintance. It was like a thing of which
93.10 there would be no more question in this world.
93.11 And all the time I had before me these blue, boyish
93.12 eyes looking straight into mine, this young face,
93.13 these capable shoulders, the open, bronzed fore-
93.14 head with a white line under the roots of clustering
93.15 fair hair, this appearance appealing at sight to all
93.16 my sympathies: this frank aspect, the artless smile,
93.17 the youthful seriousness. He was of the right sort;
93.18 he was one of us. He talked soberly, with a sort of
93.19 composed unreserve, and with a quiet bearing that
93.20 might have been the outcome of manly self-control,
93.21 of impudence, of callousness, of a colossal uncon-
93.22 sciousness, of a gigantic deception. Who can tell?
93.23 From our tone we might have been discussing a
93.24 third person, a football match, last year's weather.
93.25 My mind floated in a sea of conjectures till the
93.26 turn of the conversation enabled me, without being
93.27 offensive, to remark that, upon the whole, this
93.28 inquiry must have been pretty trying to him. He
93.29 darted his arm across the tablecloth, and clutching
93.30 my hand by the side of my plate, glared fixedly.
94.01 I was startled. 'It must be awfully hard,' I
94.02 stammered, confused by this display of speechless
94.03 feeling. 'It is -- hell,' he burst out in a muffled
94.04 voice.
94.05 "This movement and these words caused two
94.06 well-groomed male globe-trotters at a neighbouring
94.07 table to look up in alarm from their iced pudding.
94.08 I rose, and we passed into the front gallery for coffee
94.09 and cigars.
94.10 "On little octagon tables candles burned in glass
94.11 globes; clumps of stiff-leaved plants separated sets
94.12 of cosy wicker chairs; and between the pairs of
94.13 columns, whose reddish shafts caught in a long row
94.14 the sheen from the tall windows, the night, glitter-
94.15 ing and sombre, seemed to hang like a splendid
94.16 drapery. The riding lights of ships winked afar
94.17 like setting stars, and the hills across the roadstead
94.18 resembled rounded black masses of arrested thunder--
94.19 clouds.
94.20 "I listened with concentrated attention, not
94.21 daring to stir in my chair; I wanted to know -- and
94.22 to this day I don't know, I can only guess. He
94.23 would be confident and depressed all in the same
94.24 breath, as if some conviction of innate blameless-
94.25 ness had checked the truth writhing within him
94.26 at every turn. He began by saying, in the tone in
95.01 which a man would admit his inability to jump a
95.02 twenty-foot wall, that he could never go home now;
95.03 and this declaration recalled to my mind what
95.04 Brierly had said, 'that the old parson in Essex
95.05 seemed to fancy his sailor son not a little.'

95.06 "I can't tell you whether Jim knew he was
95.07 especially 'fancied,' but the tone of his references
95.08 to 'my Dad' was calculated to give me a notion that
95.09 the good old rural dean was about the finest man
95.10 that ever had been worried by the cares of a large
95.11 family since the beginning of the world. This,
95.12 though never stated, was implied with an anxiety
95.13 that there should be no mistake about it, which was
95.14 really very true and charming, but added a poignant
95.15 sense of lives far off to the other elements of the
95.16 story. 'He has seen it all in the home papers by
95.17 this time,' said Jim. 'I can never face the poor
95.18 old chap.' I did not dare to lift my eyes at this
95.19 till I heard him add, 'I could never explain. He
95.20 wouldn't understand.' Then I looked up. He
95.21 was smoking reflectively, and after a moment,
95.22 rousing himself, began to talk again. He discovered
95.23 at once a desire that I should no confound him with
95.24 his partners in -- in crime, let us call it. He was not
95.25 one of them; he was altogether of another sort. I
95.26 gave no sign of dissent. I had no intention, for the
95.27 sake of barren truth, to rob him of the smallest
95.28 particle of any saving grace that would come in his
95.29 way. I didn't know how much of it he believed
95.30 himself. I didn't know what he was playing up to
96.01 -- if he was playing up to anything at all -- and I
96.02 suspect he did not know either; for it is my belief
96.03 no man ever understands quite his own artful dodges
96.04 to escape from the grim shadow of self-knowledge.
96.05 I made no sound all the time he was wondering
96.06 what he had better do after 'that stupid inquiry
96.07 was over.'
96.08 "Apparently he shared Brierly's contemptuous
96.09 opinion of these proceedings ordained by law. He
96.10 would not know where to turn, he confessed, clearly
96.11 thinking aloud rather than talking to me. Certi-
96.12 ficate gone, career broken, no money to get away, no
96.13 work that he could obtain as far as he could see.
96.14 At home he could perhaps get something; but it
96.15 meant going to his people for help, and that he
96.16 would not do. He saw nothing for it but ship
96.17 before the mast -- could get perhaps a quarter--
96.18 master's billet in some steamer. Would do for
96.19 a quartermaster....'Do you think you would?'
96.20 I asked pitilessly. He jumped up, and going to
96.21 the stone balustrade looked out into the night.
96.22 In a moment he was back, towering above my chair,
96.23 with his youthful face clouded yet by the pain of a
96.24 conquered emotion. He had understood very well
96.25 I did not doubt his ability to steer a ship. In a
96.26 voice that quavered a bit he asked me why did I
96.27 say that? I had been 'no end kind' to him. I
96.28 had not even laughed at him when -- here he began
96.29 to mumble -- 'that mistake, you know -- made a
96.30 confounded ass of myself.' I broke in by saying
97.01 rather warmly that for me such a mistake was not
97.02 a matter to laugh at. He sat down and drank
97.03 deliberately some coffee, emptying the small cup
97.04 to the last drop. 'That does not mean I admit
97.05 for a moment the cap fitted,' he declared dis-
97.06 tinctly. 'No?' I said. 'No,' he affirmed, with
97.07 quiet decision. 'Do you know what you would
97.08 have done? Do you? And you don't think
97.09 yourself'...he gulped something...'you
97.10 don't think yourself a -- a -- cur?'
97.11 "And with this -- upon my honour! -- he looked
97.12 up at me inquisitively. It was a question, it appears
97.13 -- a bona fide question! However, he didn't wait
97.14 for an answer. Before I could recover he went on,
97.15 with his eyes straight before him, as if reading off
97.16 something written on the body of the night. 'It is
97.17 all in being ready. I wasn't; not -- not then. I don't
97.18 want to excuse myself; but I would like to explain
97.19 -- I would like somebody to understand -- some-
97.20 body -- one person at least! You! Why not you?'
97.21 "It was solemn, and a little ridiculous, too, as
97.22 they always are, those struggles of an individual
97.23 trying to save from the fire his idea of what his
97.24 moral identity should be, this precious notion of a
97.25 convention, only one of the rules of the game,
97.26 nothing more, but all the same so terribly effective
97.27 by its assumption of unlimited power over natural
97.28 instincts, by the awful penalties of its failure. He
97.29 began his story quietly enough. On board that
97.30 Dale Line steamer that had picked up these four
98.01 floating in a boat upon the discreet sunset glow of
98.02 the sea, they had been after the first day looked
98.03 askance upon. The fat skipper told some story,
98.04 the others had been silent, and at first it had been
98.05 accepted. You don't cross-examine poor castaways

98.06 you had the good luck to save, if not from cruel
98.07 death, then at least from cruel suffering. After-
98.08 wards, with time to think it over, it might have
98.09 struck the officers of the Avondale that there was
98.10 'something fishy' in the affair; but of course
98.11 they would keep their doubts to themselves. They
98.12 had picked up the captain, the mate, and two
98.13 engineers of the steamer Patna sunk at sea, and
98.14 that, very properly, was enough for them. I did
98.15 not ask Jim about the nature of his feelings during
98.16 the ten days he spent on board. From the way he
98.17 narrated that part I was at liberty to infer he was
98.18 partly stunned by the discovery he had made -- the
98.19 discovery about himself -- and no doubt was at
98.20 work trying to explain it away to the only man who
98.21 was capable of appreciating all its tremendous
98.22 magnitude. You must understand he did not try
98.23 to minimise its importance. Of that I am sure;
98.24 and therein lies his distinction. As to what sensa-
98.25 tions he experienced when he got ashore and heard
98.26 the unforeseen conclusion of the tale in which he
98.27 had taken such a pitiful part, he told me nothing
98.28 of them, and it is difficult to imagine. I wonder
98.29 whether he felt the ground cut from under his feet?
98.30 I wonder? But no doubt he managed to get a fresh
99.01 foothold very soon. He was ashore a whole fort-
99.02 night waiting in the Sailors' Home, and as there
99.03 were six or seven men staying there at the time, I
99.04 had heard of him a little. Their languid opinion
99.05 seemed to be that in addition to his other short-
99.06 comings, he was a sulky brute. He had passed
99.07 these days on the verandah, buried in a long chair,
99.08 and coming out of his place of sepulture only at
99.09 meal-times or late at night, when he wandered on
99.10 the quays all by himself, detached from his sur-
99.11 roundings, irresolute and silent, like a ghost without
99.12 a home to haunt. 'I don't think I've spoken
99.13 three words to a living soul in all that time,' he said,
99.14 making me very sorry for him; and directly he
99.15 added, 'One of these fellows would have been sure
99.16 to blurt out something I had made up my mind
99.17 not to put up with, and I didn't want a row. No!
99.18 Not then. I was too -- too...I had no heart for
99.19 it.' 'So that bulkhead held out after all,' I re-
99.20 marked cheerfully. 'Yes,' he murmured, 'it held.
99.21 And yet I swear to you I felt it bulge under my
99.22 hand.' 'It's extraordinary what strains old iron
99.23 will stand sometimes,' I said. Thrown back in his
99.24 seat, his legs stiffly out and arms hanging down,
99.25 he nodded slightly several times. You could not
99.26 conceive a sadder spectacle. Suddenly he lifted
99.27 his head; he sat up; he slapped his thigh. 'Ah!
99.28 what a chance missed! My God! what a chance
99.29 missed!' he blazed out; but the ring of the last
99.30 'missed' resembled a cry wrung out by pain.
100.01 "He was silent again with a still, far-away look
100.02 of fierce yearning after that missed distinction,
100.03 with his nostrils for an instant dilated, sniffing the
100.04 intoxicating breath of that wasted opportunity.
100.05 If you think I was either surprised or shocked you
100.06 do me an injustice in more ways than one! Ah, he
100.07 was an imaginative beggar! He would give himself
100.08 away; he would give himself up. I could see in his
100.09 glance darted into the night all his inner being
100.10 carried on, projected headlong into the fanciful
100.11 realm of recklessly heroic aspirations. He had no
100.12 leisure to regret what he had lost, he was so wholly
100.13 and naturally concerned for what he had failed to
100.14 obtain. He was very far away from me who watched
100.15 him across three feet of space. With every instant
100.16 he was penetrating deeper into the impossible
100.17 world of romantic achievements. He got to the
100.18 heart of it at last! A strange look of beatitude
100.19 overspread his features, his eyes sparkled in the
100.20 light of the candle burning between us; he posi-
100.21 tively smiled! He had penetrated to the very
100.22 heart -- to the very heart. It was an ecstatic smile
100.23 that your faces -- or mine either -- will never wear,
100.24 my dear boys. I whisked him back by saying,
100.25 'If you had stuck to the ship, you mean!'
100.26 "He turned upon me, his eyes suddenly amazed
100.27 and full of pain, with a bewildered, startled, suffer-
100.28 ing face, as though he had tumbled down from a
100.29 star. Neither you nor I will ever look like this on
100.30 any man. He shuddered profoundly, as if a cold
101.01 finger-tip had touched his heart. Last of all he
101.02 sighed.
101.03 "I was not in a merciful mood. He provoked
101.04 one by his contradictory indiscretions. 'It is
101.05 unfortunate you didn't know beforehand!' I said

200

101.06 with every unkind intention; but the perfidious
101.07 shaft fell harmless -- dropped at his feet like a spent
101.08 arrow, as it were, and he did not think of picking it
101.09 up. Perhaps he had not even seen it. Presently,
101.10 lolling at ease, he said, 'Dash it all! I tell you it
101.11 bulged. I was holding up my lamp along the angle--
101.12 iron in the lower deck when a flake of rust as big
101.13 as the palm of my hand fell off the plate, all of
101.14 itself.' He passed his hand over his forehead.
101.15 'The thing stirred and jumped off like something
101.16 alive while I was looking at it.' 'That made you
101.17 feel pretty bad,' I observed casually. 'Do you
101.18 suppose,' he said, 'that I was thinking of myself,
101.19 with a hundred and sixty people at my back, all fast
101.20 asleep in that fore-'tween-deck alone -- and more of
101.21 them aft; more on the deck -- sleeping -- knowing
101.22 nothing about it -- three times as many as there were
101.23 boats for, even if there had been time? I expected
101.24 to see the iron open out as I stood there and the
101.25 rush of water going over them as they lay....
101.26 What could I do -- what?'
101.27 "I can easily picture him to myself in the peopled
101.28 gloom of the cavernous place, with the light of the
101.29 bulk-lamp falling on a small portion of the bulk--
101.30 head that had the weight of the ocean on the other
102.01 side, and the breathing of unconscious sleepers in
102.02 his ears. I can see him glaring at the iron, startled
102.03 by the falling rust, overburdened by the knowledge
102.04 of an imminent death. This, I gathered, was the
102.05 second time he had been sent forward by that
102.06 skipper of his, who, I rather think, wanted to keep
102.07 him away from the bridge. He told me that his
102.08 first impulse was to shout and straightway make all
102.09 those people leap out of sleep into terror; but such
102.10 an overwhelming sense of his helplessness came over
102.11 him that he was not able to produce a sound. This
102.12 is, I suppose, what people mean by the tongue
102.13 cleaving to the roof of the mouth. 'Too dry,'
102.14 was the concise expression he used in reference to
102.15 this state. Without a sound, then, he scrambled
102.16 out on deck through the number one hatch. A
102.17 wind-sail rigged down there swung against him
102.18 accidentally, and he remembered that the light
102.19 touch of the canvas on his face nearly knocked him
102.20 off the hatchway ladder.
102.21 "He confessed that his knees wobbled a good
102.22 deal as he stood on the foredeck looking at another
102.23 sleeping crowd. The engines having been stopped
102.24 by that time, the steam was blowing off. Its deep
102.25 rumble made the whole night vibrate like a bass
102.26 string. The ship trembled to it.
102.27 "He saw here and there a head lifted off a mat,
102.28 a vague form uprise in sitting posture, listen sleepily
102.29 for a moment, sink down again into the billowy
102.30 confusion of boxes, steam-winches, ventilators. He
103.01 was aware all these people did not know enough to
103.02 take intelligent notice of that strange noise. The
103.03 ship of iron, the men with white faces, all the sights,
103.04 all the sounds, everything on board to that ignorant
103.05 and pious multitude was strange alike, and as
103.06 trustworthy as it would for ever remain in-
103.07 comprehensible. It occurred to him that the
103.08 fact was fortunate. The idea of it was simply
103.09 terrible.
103.10 "You must remember he believed, as any other
103.11 man would have done in his place, that the ship
103.12 would go down at any moment; the bulging, rust--
103.13 eaten plates that kept back the ocean, fatally must
103.14 give way, all at once like an undermined dam, and
103.15 let in a sudden and overwhelming flood. He stood
103.16 still looking at these recumbent bodies, a doomed
103.17 man aware of his fate, surveying the silent company
103.18 of the dead. They _were_ dead! Nothing could
103.19 save them! There were boats enough for half of
103.20 them perhaps, but there was no time. No time!
103.21 No time! It did not seem worth while to open
103.22 his lips, to stir hand or foot. Before he could
103.23 shout three words, or make three steps, he would
103.24 be floundering in a sea whitened awfully by the
103.25 desperate struggles of human beings, clamorous
103.26 with the distress of cries for help. There was no
103.27 help. He imagined what would happen perfectly;
103.28 he went through it allmotionless by the hatchway
103.29 with the lamp in his hand -- he went through it to
103.30 the very last harrowing detail. I think he went
104.01 through it again while he was telling me these things
104.02 he could not tell the court.
104.03 "'I saw as clearly as I see you now that there
104.04 was nothing I could do. It seemed to take all life
104.05 out of my limbs. I thought I might just as well
104.06 stand where I was and wait. I did not think I had
104.07 many seconds...' Suddenly the steam ceased
104.08 blowing off. The noise, he remarked, had been
104.09 distracting, but the silence at once became in-
104.10 tolerably oppressive.
104.11 "'I thought I would choke before I got
104.12 drowned,' he said.
104.13 "He protested he did not think of saving himself.
104.14 The only distinct thought formed, vanishing, and
104.15 reforming in his brain, was: eight hundred people
104.16 and seven boats; eight hundred people and seven
104.17 boats.
104.18 "'Somebody was speaking aloud inside my
104.19 head,' he said a little wildly. 'Eight hundred
104.20 people and seven boats -- and no time! Just think
104.21 of it.' He leaned towards me across the little table,
104.22 and I tried to avoid his stare. 'Do you think I
104.23 was afraid of death?' he asked in a voice very fierce
104.24 and low. He brought down his open hand with a
104.25 bang that made the coffee-cups dance. 'I am ready
104.26 to swear I was not -- I was not....By God -- no!'
104.27 He hitched himself upright and crossed his arms;
104.28 his chin fell on his breast.
104.29 "The soft clashes of crockery reached us faintly
104.30 through the high windows. There was a burst of
105.01 voices, and several men came out in high good--
105.02 humour into the gallery. They were exchanging
105.03 jocular reminiscences of the donkeys in Cairo.
105.04 A pale, anxious youth stepping softly on long legs
105.05 was being chaffed by a strutting and rubicund
105.06 globe-trotter about his purchases in the bazaar.
105.07 'No, really -- do you think I've been done to that
105.08 extent?' he inquired, very earnest and deliberate.
105.09 The band moved away, dropping into chairs as they
105.10 went; matches flared, illuminating for a second
105.11 faces without the ghost of an expression and the
105.12 flat glaze of white shirt-fronts; the hum of many
105.13 conversations animated with the ardour of feasting
105.14 sounded to me absurd and infinitely remote.
105.15 "'Some of the crew were sleeping on the number
105.16 one hatch within reach of my arm,' began Jim again.
105.17 "You must know they kept Kalashee watch in
105.18 that ship, all hands sleeping through the night, and
105.19 only the reliefs of quartermasters and look-out men
105.20 being called. He was tempted to grip and shake
105.21 the shoulder of the nearest lascar, but he didn't.
105.22 Something held his arms down along his sides.
105.23 He was not afraid -- oh no! only he just couldn't
105.24 -- that's all. He was not afraid of death perhaps,
105.25 but I'll tell you what, he was afraid of the emer-
105.26 gency. His confounded imagination had evoked for
105.27 him all the horrors of panic, the trampling rush,
105.28 the pitiful screams, boats swamped -- all the appal-
105.29 ling incidents of a disaster at sea he had ever heard
105.30 of. He might have been resigned to die, but I
106.01 suspect he wanted to die without added terrors,
106.02 quietly, in a sort of peaceful trance. A certain
106.03 readiness to perish is not so very rare, but it is
106.04 seldom that you meet men whose souls, steeled in
106.05 the impenetrable armour of resolution, are ready to
106.06 fight a losing battle to the last; the desire of peace
106.07 waxes stronger as hope declines, till at last it con-
106.08 quers the very desire of life. Which of us here has
106.09 not observed this, or maybe experienced something
106.10 of that feeling in his own person -- this extreme
106.11 weariness of emotions, the vanity of effort, the
106.12 yearning for rest? Those striving with unreason-
106.13 able forces know it well -- the shipwrecked casta-
106.14 ways in boats, wanderers lost in a desert, men
106.15 battling against the unthinking might of nature, or
106.16 the stupid brutality of crowds."
107.01 "HOW long he stood stock-still by the
107.02 hatch expecting every moment to feel
107.03 the ship dip under his feet and the rush
107.04 of water to take him at the back and toss him like
107.05 a chip, I cannot say. Not very long -- two minutes
107.06 perhaps. A couple of men he could not make out
107.07 began to converse drowsily, and also, he could not
107.08 tell where, he detected a curious noise of shuffling
107.09 feet. Above these faint sounds there was that
107.10 awful stillness preceding a catastrophe, that trying
107.11 silence of the moment before the crash; then it
107.12 came into his head that perhaps he would have time
107.13 to rush along and cut all the lanyards of the gripes,
107.14 so that the boats would float off as the ship went
107.15 down.
107.16 "The _Patna_ had a long bridge, and all the boats
107.17 were up there, four on one side and three on the
107.18 other - the smallest of them on the port side and
107.19 nearly abreast of the steering-gear. He assured me,

107.20 with evident anxiety to be believed, that he had been
107.21 most careful to keep them ready for instant service.
107.22 He knew his duty. I dare say he was a good enough
107.23 mate as far as that went. 'I always believed in
107.24 being prepared for the worst,' he commented,
108.01 staring anxiously in my face. I nodded my ap-
108.02 proval of the sound principle, averting my eyes
108.03 before the subtle unsoundness of the man.
108.04 "He started unsteadily to run. He had to step
108.05 over legs, avoid stumbling against the heads.
108.06 Suddenly some one caught hold of his coat from
108.07 below, and a distressed voice spoke under his elbow.
108.08 The light of the lamp he carried in his right hand
108.09 fell upon an upturned dark face whose eyes en-
108.10 treated him together with the voice. He had picked
108.11 up enough of the language to understand the word
108.12 water, repeated several times in a tone of insistence,
108.13 of prayer, almost of despair. He gave a jerk to get
108.14 away, and felt an arm embrace his leg.
108.15 "'The beggar clung to me like a drowning
108.16 man,' he said impressively. 'Water, water!
108.17 What water did he mean? What did he know?
108.18 As calmly as I could I ordered him to let go. He
108.19 was stopping me, time was pressing, other men began
108.20 to stir; I wanted time -- time to cut the boats
108.21 adrift. He got hold of my hand now, and I felt
108.22 that he would begin to shout. It flashed upon me
108.23 it was enough to start a panic, and I hauled off with
108.24 my free arm and slung the lamp in his face. The
108.25 glass jingled, the light went out, but the blow made
108.26 him let go, and I ran off -- I wanted to get at the
108.27 boats; I wanted to get at the boats. He leaped
108.28 after me from behind. I turned on him. He
108.29 would not keep quiet; he tried to shout; I had
108.30 half throttled him before I made out what he
109.01 wanted. He wanted some water -- water to drink;
109.02 they were on strict allowance, you know, and he had
109.03 with him a young boy I had noticed several times.
109.04 His child was sick -- and thirsty. He had caught
109.05 sight of me as I passed by, and was begging for
109.06 a little water. That's all. We were under the
109.07 bridge, in the dark. He kept on snatching at my
109.08 wrists; there was no getting rid of him. I dashed
109.09 into my berth, grabbed my water-bottle, and thrust
109.10 it into his hands. He vanished. I didn't find out
109.11 till then how much I was in want of a drink myself.'
109.12 He leaned on one elbow with a hand over his eyes.
109.13 "I felt a creepy sensation all down my back-
109.14 bone; there was something peculiar in all this.
109.15 The fingers of the hand that shaded his brow
109.16 trembled slightly. He broke the short silence.
109.17 "'These things happen only once to a man and
109.18 ...Ah, well! When I got on the bridge at last
109.19 the beggars were getting one of the boats off the
109.20 chocks. A boat! I was running up the ladder
109.21 when a heavy blow fell on my shoulder, just missing
109.22 my head. It didn't stop me, and the chief engineer
109.23 -- they had got him out of his bunk by then -- raised
109.24 the boat-stretcher again. Somehow I had no mind
109.25 to be surprised at anything. All this seemed
109.26 natural -- and awful -- and awful. I dodged that
109.27 miserable maniac, lifted him off the deck as though
109.28 he had been a little child, and he started whispering
109.29 in my arms: "Don't! don't! I thought you were
109.30 one of them niggers." I flung him away; he skidded
110.01 along the bridge and knocked the legs from under
110.02 the little chap -- the second. The skipper, busy
110.03 about the boat, looked round, and came at me
110.04 head down, growling like a wild beast. I flinched
110.05 no more than a stone. I was as solid standing there
110.06 as this,' he tapped lightly with his knuckles the wall
110.07 beside his chair. 'It was as though I had heard it
110.08 all, seen it all, gone through it all twenty times
110.09 already. I wasn't afraid of them. I drew back my
110.10 fist and he stopped short, muttering:
110.11 "'"Ah! it's you. Lend a hand quick."
110.12 "'That's what he said. Quick! As if any-
110.13 body could be quick enough. "Aren't you going to
110.14 do something?" I asked. "Yes. Clear out," he
110.15 snarled over his shoulder.
110.16 "'I don't think I understood then what he
110.17 meant. The other two had picked themselves up
110.18 by that time, and they rushed together to the boat.
110.19 They tramped, they wheezed, they shoved, they
110.20 cursed the boat, the ship, each other -- cursed me.
110.21 All in mutters. I didn't move, I didn't speak. I
110.22 watched the slant of the ship. She was as still as
110.23 if landed on the blocks in a dry dock -- only she was
110.24 like this.' He held up his hand, palm under, the
110.25 tips of the fingers inclined downwards. 'Like

110.26 this,' he repeated. 'I could see the line of the
110.27 horizon before me, as clear as a bell, above her stem --
110.28 head; I could see the water far off there black
110.29 and sparkling, and still -- still as a pond, deadly
110.30 still, more still than ever sea was before -- more still
111.01 than I could bear to look at. Have you watched a
111.02 ship floating head down, checked in sinking by a
111.03 sheet of old iron too rotten to stand being shored
111.04 up? Have you? Oh yes, shored up? I thought
111.05 of that -- I thought of every mortal thing; but can
111.06 you shore up a bulkhead in five minutes -- or in
111.07 fifty for that matter? Where was I going to get
111.08 men that would go down below? And the timber --
111.09 the timber! Would you have had the courage to
111.10 swing the maul for the first blow if you had seen that
111.11 bulkhead? Don't say you would: you had not
111.12 seen it; nobody would. Hang it -- to do a thing
111.13 like that you must believe there is a chance, one in a
111.14 thousand, at least, some ghost of a chance; and you
111.15 would not have believed. Nobody would have be-
111.16 lieved. You think me a cur for standing there, but
111.17 what would you have done? What! You can't
111.18 tell -- nobody can tell. One must have time to
111.19 turn round. What would you have me do? Where
111.20 was the kindness in making crazy with fright all
111.21 those people I could not save single-handed -- that
111.22 nothing could save? Look here! As true as I sit
111.23 on this chair before you...'
111.24 "He drew quick breaths at every few words and
111.25 shot quick glances at my face, as though in his
111.26 anguish he were watchful of the effect. He was
111.27 not speaking to me, he was only speaking before me,
111.28 in a dispute with an invisible personality, an anta-
111.29 gonistic and inseparable partner of his existence --
111.30 another possessor of his soul. These were issues
112.01 beyond the competency of a court of inquiry: it
112.02 was a subtle and momentous quarrel as to the
112.03 true essence of life, and did not want a judge. He
112.04 wanted an ally, a helper, an accomplice. I felt
112.05 the risk I ran of being circumvented, blinded, de-
112.06 coyed, bullied, perhaps, into taking a definite part in
112.07 a dispute impossible of decision if one had to be fair
112.08 to all the phantoms in possession -- to the reputable
112.09 that had its claims and to the disreputable that had
112.10 its exigencies. I can't explain to you who haven't
112.11 seen him and who hear his words only at second
112.12 hand the mixed nature of my feelings. It seemed to
112.13 me I was being made to comprehend the Incon-
112.14 ceivable -- and I know of nothing to compare with the
112.15 discomfort of such a sensation. I was made to look
112.16 at the convention that lurks in all truth and on
112.17 the essential sincerity of falsehood. He appealed to
112.18 all sides at once -- to the side turned perpetually
112.19 to the light of day, and to that side of us which,
112.20 like the other hemisphere of the moon, exists
112.21 stealthily in perpetual darkness, with only a fearful
112.22 ashy light falling at times on the edge. He swayed
112.23 me. I own to it, I own up. The occasion was
112.24 obscure, insignificant -- what you will: a lost
112.25 youngster, one in a million -- but then he was
112.26 one of us; an incident as completely devoid of
112.27 importance as the flooding of an ant-heap, and
112.28 yet the mystery of his attitude got hold of me as
112.29 though he had been an individual in the forefront
112.30 of his kind, as if the obscure truth involved were
113.01 momentous enough to affect mankind's conception
113.02 of itself...."
113.03 Marlow paused to put new life into his expiring
113.04 cheroot, seemed to forget all about the story, and
113.05 abruptly began again.
113.06 "My fault of course. One has no business
113.07 really to get interested. It's a weakness of mine.
113.08 His was of another kind. My weakness consists
113.09 in not having a discriminating eye for the incidental
113.10 -- for the externals -- no eye for the hod of the rag-
113.11 picker or the fine linen of the next man. Next
113.12 man -- that's it. I have met so many men," he
113.13 pursued, with momentary sadness -- "met them,
113.14 too, with a certain -- certain -- impact, let us say;
113.15 like this fellow, for instance -- and in each case all
113.16 I could see was merely the human being. A con-
113.17 founded democratic quality of vision which may be
113.18 better than total blindness, but has been of no
113.19 advantage to me, I can assure you. Men expect
113.20 one to take into account their fine linen. But I
113.21 never could get up any enthusiasm about these
113.22 things. Oh! it's a failing; it's a failing; and then
113.23 comes a soft evening; a lot of men too indolent for
113.24 whist -- and a story...."
113.25 He paused again to wait for an encouraging

113.26 remark perhaps, but nobody spoke; only the host,
113.27 as if reluctantly performing a duty, murmured:
113.28 "You are so subtle, Marlow."
113.29 "Who? I?" said Marlow in a low voice.
113.30 "Oh no! But he was; and try as I may for the
114.01 success of this yarn, I am missing innumerable
114.02 shades -- they were so fine, so difficult to render in
114.03 colourless words. Because he complicated matters
114.04 by being so simple, too -- the simplest poor devil!
114.05 ...By Jove! he was amazing. There he sat
114.06 telling me that just as I saw him before my
114.07 eyes he wouldn't be afraid to face anything -- and
114.08 believing in it, too. I tell you it was fabulously
114.09 innocent and it was enormous, enormous! I
114.10 watched him covertly, just as though I had sus-
114.11 pected him of an intention to take a jolly good rise
114.12 out of me. He was confident that, on the square,
114.13 'on the square, mind!' there was nothing he
114.14 couldn't meet. Ever since he had been 'so high' --
114.15 'quite a little chap,' he had been preparing himself
114.16 for all the difficulties that can beset one on land and
114.17 water. He confessed proudly to this kind of fore-
114.18 sight. He had been elaborating dangers and de-
114.19 fences, expecting the worst, rehearsing his best.
114.20 He must have led a most exalted existence. Can
114.21 you fancy it? A succession of adventures, so
114.22 much glory, such a victorious progress! and the
114.23 deep sense of his sagacity crowning every day of
114.24 his inner life. He forgot himself; his eyes shone;
114.25 and with every word my heart, searched by the
114.26 light of his absurdity, was growing heavier in my
114.27 breast. I had no mind to laugh, and lest I should
114.28 smile I made for myself a stolid face. He gave
114.29 signs of irritation.
114.30 "'It is always the unexpected that happens,' I
115.01 said in a propitiatory tone. My obtuseness pro-
115.02 voked him into a contemptuous 'Pshaw!' I
115.03 suppose he meant that the unexpected couldn't
115.04 touch him; nothing less than the unconceivable
115.05 itself could get over his perfect state of preparation.
115.06 He had been taken unawares -- and he whispered to
115.07 himself a malediction upon the waters and the
115.08 firmament, upon the ship, upon the men. Every-
115.09 thing had betrayed him! He had been tricked
115.10 into that sort of high-minded resignation which
115.11 prevented him lifting as much as his little finger,
115.12 while these others who had a very clear perception
115.13 of the actual necessity were tumbling against each
115.14 other and sweating desperately over that boat
115.15 business. Something had gone wrong there at the
115.16 last moment. It appears that in their flurry they
115.17 had contrived in some mysterious way to get the
115.18 sliding bolt of the foremost boat-chock jammed
115.19 tight, and forthwith had gone out of the remnants
115.20 of their minds over the deadly nature of that accident.
115.21 It must have been a pretty sight, the fierce industry
115.22 of these beggars toiling on a motionless ship that
115.23 floated quietly in the silence of a world asleep,
115.24 fighting against time for the freeing of that boat,
115.25 grovelling on all-fours, standing up in despair,
115.26 tugging, pushing, snarling at each other venomously,
115.27 ready to kill, ready to weep, and only kept from
115.28 flying at each other's throats by the fear of death
115.29 that stood silent behind them like an inflexible
115.30 and cold-eyed taskmaster. Oh yes! It must have
116.01 been a pretty sight. He saw it all, he could talk
116.02 about it with scorn and bitterness; he had a minute
116.03 knowledge of it by means of some sixth sense, I
116.04 conclude, because he swore to me he had remained
116.05 apart without a glance at them and at the boat --
116.06 without one single glance. And I believe him. I
116.07 should think he was too busy watching the threaten-
116.08 ing slant of the ship, the suspended menace dis-
116.09 covered in the midst of the most perfect security --
116.10 fascinated by the sword hanging by a hair over his
116.11 imaginative head.
116.12 "Nothing in the world moved before his eyes,
116.13 and he could depict to himself without hindrance
116.14 the sudden swing upwards of the dark skyline, the
116.15 sudden tilt up of the vast plain of the sea, the swift,
116.16 still rise, the brutal fling, the grasp of the abyss, the
116.17 struggle without hope, the starlight closing over
116.18 his head for ever like the vault of a tomb -- the
116.19 revolt of his young life -- the back end. He could!
116.20 By Jove! who couldn't? And you must remember
116.21 he was a finished artist in that peculiar way, he was
116.22 a gifted poor devil with the faculty of swift and fore-
116.23 stalling vision. The sights it showed him had
116.24 turned him into cold stone from the soles of his
116.25 feet to the nape of his neck; but there was a hot
116.26 dance of thought in his head, a dance of lame,
116.27 blind, mute thoughts -- a whirl of awful cripples.
116.28 Didn't I tell you he confessed himself before me as
116.29 though I had the power to bind and to loose? He
116.30 burrowed deep, deep, in the hope of my absolution,
117.01 which would have been of no good to him. This
117.02 was one of those cases which no solemn deception
117.03 can palliate, which no man can help; where his
117.04 very Maker seems to abandon a sinner to his own
117.05 devices.
117.06 "He stood on the starboard side of the bridge,
117.07 as far as he could get from the struggle for the boat,
117.08 which went on with the agitation of madness and
117.09 the stealthiness of a conspiracy. The two Malays
117.10 had meantime remained holding to the wheel. Just
117.11 picture to yourselves the actors in that, thank God!
117.12 unique episode of the sea, four beside themselves
117.13 with fierce and secret exertions, and three looking
117.14 on in complete immobility, above the awnings
117.15 covering the profound ignorance of hundreds of
117.16 human beings, with their weariness, with their
117.17 dreams, with their hopes, arrested, held by an
117.18 invisible hand on the brink of annihilation. For
117.19 that they were so, makes no doubt to me: given
117.20 the state of the ship, this was the deadliest possible
117.21 description of accident that could happen. These
117.22 beggars by the boat had every reason to go distracted
117.23 with funk. Frankly, had I been there I would not
117.24 have given as much as a counterfeit farthing for
117.25 the ship's chance to keep above water to the end
117.26 of each successive second. And still she floated!
117.27 These sleeping pilgrims were destined to accomplish
117.28 their whole pilgrimage to the bitterness of some
117.29 other end. It was as if the Omnipotence whose
117.30 mercy they confessed had needed their humble
118.01 testimony on earth for a while longer, and had
118.02 looked down to make a sign, 'Thou shalt not!'
118.03 to the ocean. Their escape would trouble me as
118.04 a prodigiously inexplicable event, did I not know
118.05 how tough old iron can be -- as tough sometimes
118.06 as the spirit of some men we meet now and then,
118.07 worn to a shadow and breasting the weight of life.
118.08 Not the least wonder of these twenty minutes,
118.09 to my mind, is the behaviour of the two helmsmen.
118.10 They were amongst the native batch of all sorts
118.11 brought over from Aden to give evidence at the
118.12 inquiry. One of them, labouring under intense
118.13 bashfulness, was very young, and with his smooth,
118.14 yellow, cheery countenance looked even younger
118.15 than he was. I remember perfectly Brierly asking
118.16 him, through the interpreter, what he thought of
118.17 it at the time, and the interpreter, after a short
118.18 colloquy, turning to the court with an important
118.19 air:
118.20 "'He says he thought nothing.'
118.21 "The other, with patient, blinking eyes, a blue
118.22 cotton handkerchief, faded with much washing,
118.23 bound with a smart twist over a lot of grey wisps,
118.24 his face shrunk into grim hollows, his brown skin
118.25 made darker by a mesh of wrinkles, explained that
118.26 he had a knowledge of some evil thing befalling
118.27 the ship, but there had been no order; he could
118.28 not remember an order; why should he leave the
118.29 helm? To some further questions he jerked back
118.30 his spare shoulders, and declared it never came
119.01 into his mind then that the white men were about
119.02 to leave the ship through fear of death. He did
119.03 not believe it now. There might have been secret
119.04 reasons. He wagged his old chin knowingly. Aha!
119.05 secret reasons. He was a man of great experience,
119.06 and he wanted that white Tuan to know -- he turned
119.07 towards Brierly, who didn't raise his head -- that
119.08 he had acquired a knowledge of many things by
119.09 serving white men on the sea for a great number
119.10 of years -- and, suddenly, with shaky excitement he
119.11 poured upon our spellbound attention a lot of
119.12 queer-sounding names, names of dead-and-gone
119.13 skippers, names of forgotten country ships, names
119.14 of familiar and distorted sound, as if the hand of
119.15 dumb time had been at work on them for ages.
119.16 They stopped him at last. A silence fell upon the
119.17 court -- a silence that remained unbroken for at
119.18 least a minute, and passed gently into a deep mur-
119.19 mur. This episode was the sensation of the second
119.20 day's proceedings -- affecting all the audience, affect-
119.21 ing everybody except Jim, who was sitting moodily
119.22 at the end of the first bench, and never looked up at
119.23 this extraordinary and damning witness that seemed
119.24 possessed of some mysterious theory of defence.
119.25 "So these two lascars stuck to the helm of that

119.26 ship without steerage-way, where death would have
119.27 found them if such had been their destiny. The
119.28 whites did not give them half a glance, had probably
119.29 forgotten their existence. Assuredly Jim did not
119.30 remember it. He remembered he could do nothing;
120.01 he could do nothing, now he was alone. There was
120.02 nothing to do but to sink with the ship. No use
120.03 making a disturbance about it. Was there? He
120.04 waited upstanding, without a sound, stiffened in the
120.05 idea of some sort of heroic discretion. The first
120.06 engineer ran cautiously across the bridge to tug
120.07 at his sleeve.
120.08 "'Come and help! For God's sake, come and
120.09 help!'
120.10 "He ran back to the boat on the points of his
120.11 toes, and returned directly to worry at his sleeve,
120.12 begging and cursing at the same time.
120.13 "'I believe he would have kissed my hands,'
120.14 said Jim savagely, 'and, next moment, he starts
120.16 foaming and whispering in my face, "If I had the
120.16 time I would like to crack your skull for you." I
120.17 pushed him away. Suddenly he caught hold of me
120.18 round the neck. Damn him! I hit him. I hit
120.19 out without looking. "Won't you save your own
120.20 life -- you infernal coward?" he sobs. Coward!
120.21 He called me an infernal coward! Ha! ha! ha!
120.22 ha! He called me -- ha! ha! ha!...'
120.23 "He had thrown himself back and was shaking
120.24 with laughter. I had never in my life heard any-
120.25 thing so bitter as that noise. It fell like a blight
120.26 on all the merriment about donkeys, pyramids,
120.27 bazaars, or what not. Along the whole dim length
120.28 of the gallery the voices dropped, the pale blotches
120.29 of faces turned our way with one accord, and the
120.30 silence became so profound that the clear tinkle of
121.01 a teaspoon falling on the tessellated floor of the
121.02 verandah rang out like a tiny and silvery scream.
121.03 "'You mustn't laugh like this, with all these
121.04 people about,' I remonstrated. 'It isn't nice for
121.05 them, you know.'
121.06 "He gave no sign of having heard at first, but
121.07 after a while, with a stare that, missing me altogether,
121.08 seemed to probe the heart of some awful vision, he
121.09 muttered carelessly: 'Oh! they'll think I am
121.10 drunk.'
121.11 "And after that you would have thought from
121.12 his appearance he would never make a sound again.
121.13 But -- no fear! He could no more stop telling now
121.14 than he could have stopped living by the mere
121.15 exertion of his will."
122.01 "'I WAS saying to myself, "Sink -- curse
122.02 you! Sink!"' These were the words
122.03 with which he began again. He wanted
122.04 it over. He was severely left alone, and he formu-
122.05 lated in his head this address to the ship in a tone
122.06 of imprecation, while at the same time he enjoyed
122.07 the privilege of witnessing scenes -- as far as I can
122.08 judge -- of low comedy. They were still at that bolt.
122.09 The skipper was ordering. 'Get under and try
122.10 to lift'; and the others naturally shirked. You
122.11 understand that to be squeezed flat under the keel
122.12 of a boat wasn't a desirable position to be caught
122.13 in if the ship went down suddenly. 'Why don't you
122.14 -- you the strongest?' whined the little engineer.
122.15 'Gott-for-dam! I am too thick,' spluttered the
122.16 skipper in despair. It was funny enough to make
122.17 angels weep. They stood idle for a moment, and
122.18 suddenly the chief engineer rushed again at Jim.
122.19 "'Come and help, man! Are you mad to
122.20 throw your only chance away? Come and help,
122.21 man! Man! Look there -- look!'
122.22 "And at last Jim looked astern where the other
122.23 pointed with maniacal insistence. He saw a silent
122.24 black squall which had eaten up already one-third
123.01 of the sky. You know how these squalls come up
123.02 there about that time of the year. First you see a
123.03 darkening of the horizon -- no more; then a cloud
123.04 rises opaque like a wall. A straight edge of vapour
123.05 lined with sickly, whitish gleams flies up from the
123.06 south-west, swallowing the stars in whole constella-
123.07 tions; its shadow flies over the waters, and con-
123.08 founds sea and sky into one abyss of obscurity.
123.09 And all is still. No thunder, no wind, no sound;
123.10 not a flicker of lightning. Then in the tenebrous
123.11 immensity a livid arch appears; a swell or two like
123.12 undulations of the very darkness run past, and
123.13 suddenly, wind and rain strike together with a
123.14 peculiar impetuosity as if they had burst through
123.15 something solid. Such a cloud had come up while
123.16 they weren't looking. They had just noticed it,

123.17 and were perfectly justified in surmising that if in
123.18 absolute stillness there was some chance for the
123.19 ship to keep afloat a few minutes longer, the least
123.20 disturbance of the sea would make an end of her
123.21 instantly. Her first nod to the swell that precedes
123.22 the burst of such a squall would be also her last,
123.23 would become a plunge, would, so to speak, be
123.24 prolonged into a long dive, down, down to the
123.25 bottom. Hence these new capers of their fright,
123.26 these new antics in which they displayed their
123.27 extreme aversion to die.
123.28 "'It was black, black,' pursued Jim, with moody
123.29 steadiness. 'It had sneaked upon us from behind.
123.30 The infernal thing! I suppose there had been at
124.01 the back of my head some hope yet. I don't know.
124.02 But that was all over anyhow. It maddened me
124.03 to see myself caught like this. I was angry, as
124.04 though I had been trapped. I was trapped! The
124.05 night was not, too, I remember. Not a breath of
124.06 air.'
124.07 "He remembered so well that, gasping in the
124.08 chair, he seemed to sweat and choke before my eyes.
124.09 No doubt it maddened him; it knocked him over
124.10 afresh -- in a manner of speaking -- but it made
124.11 him also remember that important purpose which
124.12 had sent him rushing on that bridge only to slip
124.13 clean out of his mind. He had intended to cut
124.14 the life-boats clear of the ship. He whipped out
124.15 his knife and went to work slashing as though he
124.16 had seen nothing, had heard nothing, had known
124.17 of no one on board. They thought him hope-
124.18 lessly wrong-headed and crazy, but dared not
124.19 protest noisily against this useless loss of time.
124.20 When he had done he returned to the very same
124.21 spot from which he had started. The chief was
124.22 there, ready with a clutch at him to whisper close
124.23 to his head, scathingly, as though he wanted to
124.24 bite his ear:
124.25 "'You silly fool! do you think you'll get the
124.26 ghost of a show when all that lot of brutes is in the
124.27 water? Why, they will batter your head for you
124.28 from these boats.'
124.29 "He wrung his hands, ignored, at Jim's elbow.
124.30 The skipper kept up a nervous shuffle in one place
125.01 and mumbled, 'Hammer! hammer! Mein Gott!
125.02 Get a hammer.'
125.03 "The little engineer whimpered like a child, but
125.04 broken arm and all, he turned out the least craven
125.05 of the lot as it seems, and, actually, mustered enough
125.06 pluck to run an errand to the engine-room. No
125.07 trifle, it must be owned in fairness to him. Jim
125.08 told me he darted desperate looks like a cornered
125.09 man, gave one low wail, and dashed off. He was
125.10 back instantly clambering, hammer in hand, and
125.11 without a pause flung himself at the bolt. The
125.12 others gave up Jim at once and ran off to assist.
125.13 He heard the tap, tap of the hammer, the sound
125.14 of the released chock falling over. The boat was
125.15 clear. Only then he turned to look -- only then.
125.16 But he kept his distance -- he kept his distance.
125.17 He wanted me to know he had kept his distance;
125.18 that there was nothing in common between him
125.19 and these men -- who had the hammer. Nothing
125.20 whatever. It is more than probable he thought
125.21 himself cut off from them by a space that could not
125.22 be traversed, by an obstacle that could not be over-
125.23 come, by a chasm without bottom. He was as far
125.24 as he could get from them -- the whole breadth of
125.25 the ship.
125.26 "His feet were glued to that remote spot and
125.27 his eyes to their indistinct group bowed together and
125.28 swaying strangely in the common torment of fear.
125.29 A hand-lamp lashed to a stanchion above a little
125.30 table rigged up on the bridge -- the Patna had
126.01 no chart-room amidships -- threw a light on their
126.02 labouring shoulders, on their arched and bobbing
126.03 backs. They pushed at the bow of the boat;
126.04 they pushed out into the night; they pushed, and
126.05 would no more look back at him. They had given
126.06 him up as if indeed he had been too far, too hope-
126.07 lessly separated from themselves, to be worth an
126.08 appealing word, a glance, or a sign. They had no
126.09 leisure to look back upon his passive heroism, to feel
126.10 the sting of his abstention. The boat was heavy;
126.11 they pushed at the bow with no breath to spare for
126.12 an encouraging word: but the turmoil of terror
126.13 that had scattered their self-control like chaff before
126.14 the wind, converted their desperate exertions into
126.15 a bit of fooling, upon my word fit for knockabout
126.16 clowns in a farce. They pushed with their hands,

126.17 with their heads, they pushed for dear life with all
126.18 the weight of their bodies, they pushed with all
126.19 the might of their souls -- only no sooner had they
126.20 succeeded in canting the stem clear of the davit than
126.21 they would leave off like one man and start a wild
126.22 scramble into her. As a natural consequence the
126.23 boat would swing in abruptly, driving them back,
126.24 helpless and jostling against each other. They
126.25 would stand nonplussed for a while, exchanging in
126.26 fierce whispers all the infamous names they could
126.27 call to mind, and go at it again. Three times this
126.28 occurred. He described it to me with morose
126.29 thoughtfulness. He hadn't lost a single movement
126.30 of that comic business. 'I loathed them. I hated
127.01 them. I had to look at all that,' he said without
127.02 emphasis, turning upon me a sombrely watchful
127.03 glance. 'Was ever there any one so shamefully
127.04 tried?'
127.05 "He took his head in his hands for a moment,
127.06 like a man driven to distraction by some unspeakable
127.07 outrage. These were things he could not explain
127.08 to the court -- and not even to me; but I would
127.09 have been little fitted for the reception of his con-
127.10 fidences had I not been able at times to understand
127.11 the pauses between the words. In this assault upon
127.12 his fortitude there was the jeering intention of a
127.13 spiteful and vile vengeance; there was an element
127.14 of burlesque in his ordeal -- a degradation of funny
127.15 grimaces in the approach of death or dishonour.
127.16 "He related facts which I have not forgotten,
127.17 but at this distance of time I couldn't recall his very
127.18 words: I only remember that he managed wonder-
127.19 fully to convey the brooding rancour of his mind
127.20 into the bare recital of events. Twice, he told me,
127.21 he shut his eyes in the certitude that the end was
127.22 upon him already, and twice he had to open them
127.23 again. Each time he noted the darkening of the
127.24 great stillness. The shadow of the silent cloud had
127.25 fallen upon the ship from the zenith, and seemed to
127.26 have extinguished every sound of her teeming life.
127.27 He could no longer hear the voices under the
127.28 awnings. He told me that each time he closed his
127.29 eyes a flash of thought showed him that crowd
127.30 of bodies, laid out for death, as plain as daylight.
128.01 When he opened them, it was to see the dim struggle
128.02 of four men fighting like mad with a stubborn boat.
128.03 'They would fall back before it time after time,
128.04 stand swearing at each other, and suddenly make
128.05 another rush in a bunch....Enough to make
128.06 you die laughing,' he commented with downcast
128.07 eyes; then raising them for a moment to my face
128.08 with a dismal smile, 'I ought to have a merry life
128.09 of it, by God! for I shall see that funny sight a good
128.10 many times yet before I die.' His eyes fell again.
128.11 'See and hear....See and hear,' he repeated
128.12 twice, at long intervals, filled by vacant staring.
128.13 "He roused himself.
128.14 "'I made up my mind to keep my eyes shut,' he
128.15 said, 'and I couldn't. I couldn't, and I don't care
128.16 who knows it. Let them go through that kind of
128.17 thing before they talk. Just let them -- and do
128.18 better -- that's all. The second time my eyelids
128.19 flew open and my mouth too. I had felt the ship
128.20 move. She just dipped her bows -- and lifted them
128.21 gently -- and slow! everlastingly slow; and ever
128.22 so little. She hadn't done that much for days.
128.23 The cloud had raced ahead, and this first swell
128.24 seemed to travel upon a sea of lead. There was no
128.25 life in that stir. It managed, though, to knock over
128.26 something in my head. What would you have
128.27 done? You are sure of yourself -- aren't you?
128.28 What would you do if you felt now -- this minute --
128.29 the house here move, just move a little under your
128.30 chair? Leap! By heavens! you would take one
129.01 spring from where you sit and land in that clump
129.02 of bushes yonder.'
129.03 "He flung his arm out at the night beyond the
129.04 stone balustrade. I held my peace. He looked at
129.05 me very steadily, very severe. There could be no
129.06 mistake: I was being bullied now, and it behoved
129.07 me to make no sign lest by a gesture or a word I
129.08 should be drawn into a fatal admission about myself
129.09 which would have had some bearing on the case.
129.10 I was not disposed to take any risk of that sort.
129.11 Don't forget I had him before me, and really he was
129.12 too much like one of us not to be dangerous. But
129.13 if you want to know, I don't mind telling you that
129.14 I did, with a rapid glance, estimate the distance to
129.15 the mass of denser blackness in the middle of the
129.16 grass-plot before the verandah. He exaggerated.

129.17 I would have landed short by several feet -- and that's
129.18 the only thing of which I am fairly certain.
129.19 "The last moment had come, as he thought, and
129.20 he did not move. His feet remained glued to the
129.21 planks if his thoughts were knocking about loose
129.22 in his head. It was at this moment, too, that he
129.23 saw one of the men around the boat step backwards
129.24 suddenly, clutch at the air with raised arms, totter
129.25 and collapse. He didn't exactly fall, he only slid
129.26 gently into a sitting posture, all hunched up and
129.27 with his shoulders propped against the side of the
129.28 engine-room skylight. 'That was the donkey--
129.29 man. A haggard, white-faced chap with a ragged
129.30 moustache. Acted third engineer,' he explained.
130.01 "'Dead?' I said. We had heard something of
130.02 that in court.
130.03 "'So they say,' he pronounced with sombre
130.04 indifference. 'Of course I never knew. Weak
130.05 heart. The man had been complaining of being out
130.06 of sorts for some time before. Excitement. Over--
130.07 exertion. Devil only knows. Ha! ha! ha! It
130.08 was easy to see he did not want to die either. Droll,
130.09 isn't it? May I be shot if he hadn't been fooled
130.10 into killing himself! Fooled -- neither more nor
130.11 less. Fooled into it, by heavens! just as I...
130.12 Ah! If he had only kept still; if he had only told
130.13 them to go to the devil when they came to rush him
130.14 out of his bunk because the ship was sinking! If
130.15 he had only stood by with his hands in his pockets
130.16 and called them names!'
130.17 "He got up, shook his fist, glared at me, and sat
130.18 down.
130.19 "'A chance missed, eh?' I murmured.
130.20 "'Why don't you laugh?' he said. 'A joke
130.21 hatched in hell. Weak heart!...I wish some-
130.22 times mine had been.'
130.23 "This irritated me. 'Do you?' I exclaimed
130.24 with deep-rooted irony. 'Yes! Can't you under-
130.25 stand?' he cried. 'I don't know what more you
130.26 could wish for,' I said angrily. He gave me an
130.27 utterly uncomprehending glance. This shaft had
130.28 also gone wide of the mark, and he was not the man
130.29 to bother about stray arrows. Upon my word, he
130.30 was too unsuspecting; he was not fair game. I
131.01 was glad that my missile had been thrown away --
131.02 that he had not even heard the twang of the bow.
131.03 "Of course he could not know at the time the
131.04 man was dead. The next minute -- his last on
131.05 board -- was crowded with a tumult of events and
131.06 sensations which beat about him like the sea upon a
131.07 rock. I use the simile advisedly, because from his
131.08 relation I am forced to believe he had preserved
131.09 through it all a strange illusion of passiveness, as
131.10 though he had not acted but had suffered himself
131.11 to be handled by the internal powers who had
131.12 selected him for the victim of their practical joke.
131.13 The first thing that came to him was the grinding
131.14 surge of the heavy davits swinging out at last -- a
131.15 jar which seemed to enter his body from the deck
131.16 through the soles of his feet, and travel up his spine
131.17 to the crown of his head. Then, the squall being
131.18 very near now, another and a heavier swell lifted
131.19 the passive hull in a threatening heave that checked
131.20 his breath, while his brain and his heart together
131.21 were pierced as with daggers by panic-stricken
131.22 screams. 'Let go! For God's sake, let go! Let
131.23 go! She's going.' Following upon that the boat-
131.24 falls ripped through the blocks, and a lot of men
131.25 began to talk in startled tones under the awnings.
131.26 'When these beggars did break out, their yelps
131.27 were enough to wake the dead,' he said. Next
131.28 after the splashing shock of the boat literally
131.29 dropped in the water, came the hollow noises of
131.30 stamping and tumbling in her, mingled with con-
132.01 fused shouts: 'Unhook! Unhook! Shove! Un-
132.02 hook! Shove for your life! Here's the squall
132.03 down on us....' He heard, high above his head,
132.04 the faint muttering of the wind; he heard below
132.05 his feet a cry of pain. A lost voice alongside started
132.06 cursing a swivel hook. The ship began to buzz fore
132.07 and aft like a disturbed hive, and, as quietly as he
132.08 was telling me all this -- because just then he was
132.09 very quiet in attitude, in face, in voice -- he went on
132.10 to say without the slightest warning as it were,
132.11 'I stumbled over his legs.'
132.12 "This was the first I heard of his having moved
132.13 at all. I could not restrain a grunt of surprise.
132.14 Something had started him off at last, but of the
132.15 exact moment, of the cause that tore him out of his
132.16 immobility, he knew no more than the uprooted

132.17 tree knows of the wind that laid it low. All this
132.18 had come to him: the sounds, the sights, the legs
132.19 of the dead man -- by Jove! The infernal joke was
132.20 being crammed devilishly down his throat, but --
132.21 look you -- he was not going to admit of any sort of
132.22 swallowing motion in his gullet. It's extraordinary
132.23 how he could cast upon you the spirit of his illusion.
132.24 I listened as if to a tale of black magic at work upon
132.25 a corpse.
132.26 "'He went over sideways, very gently, and this
132.27 is the last thing I remember seeing on board,' he
132.28 continued. 'I did not care what he did. It looked
132.29 as though he were picking himself up: I thought
132.30 he was picking himself up, of course: I expected
133.01 him to bolt past me over the rail and drop into the
133.02 boat after the others. I could hear them knocking
133.03 about, down there, and a voice as if crying up
133.04 a shaft called out "George!" Then three voices
133.05 together raised a yell. They came to me separ-
133.06 ately: one bleated, another screamed, one howled.
133.07 Ough!'
133.08 "He shivered a little, and I beheld him rise
133.09 slowly as if a steady hand from above had been
133.10 pulling him out of the chair by his hair. Up,
133.11 slowly -- to his full height, and when his knees had
133.12 locked stiff the hand let him go, and he swayed
133.13 a little on his feet. There was a suggestion of
133.14 awful stillness in his face, in his movements, in his
133.15 very voice when he said, 'They shouted' -- and
133.16 involuntarily I pricked up my ears for the ghost
133.17 of that shout that would be heard directly through
133.18 the false effect of silence. 'There were eight
133.19 hundred people in that ship,' he said, impaling me
133.20 to the back of my seat with an awful blank stare.
133.21 'Eight hundred living people, and they were yelling
133.22 after the one dead man to come down and be saved!
133.23 "Jump, George! Jump! Oh, jump!" I stood
133.24 by with my hand on the davit. I was very quiet.
133.25 It had come over pitch-dark. You could see neither
133.26 sky nor sea. I heard the boat alongside go bump,
133.27 bump, and not another sound down there for a
133.28 while, but the ship under me was full of talking
133.29 noises. Suddenly the skipper howled, "Mein
133.30 Gott! The squall! The squall! Shove off!"
134.01 With the first hiss of rain, and the first gust of wind,
134.02 they screamed, "Jump, George! We'll catch you!
134.03 Jump!" The ship began a slow plunge; the rain
134.04 swept over her like a broken sea; my cap flew
134.05 off my head; my breath was driven back into
134.06 my throat. I heard as if I had been on the top of
134.07 a tower another wild screech, "Geo-o-o-orge! Oh,
134.08 jump!" She was going down, down, head first
134.09 under me....'
134.10 "He raised his hand deliberately to his face, and
134.11 made picking motions with his fingers as though
134.12 he had been bothered with cobwebs, and afterwards
134.13 he looked into the open palm for quite half a second
134.14 before he blurted out:
134.15 "'I had jumped...' he checked himself,
134.16 averted his gaze...'it seems,' he added.
134.17 "His clear blue eyes turned to me with a piteous
134.18 stare, and looking at him standing before me,
134.19 dumbfounded and hurt, I was oppressed by a sad
134.20 sense of resigned wisdom, mingled with the amused
134.21 and profound pity of an old man helpless before a
134.22 childish disaster.
134.23 "'Looks like it,' I muttered.
134.24 "'I knew nothing about it till I looked up,' he
134.25 explained hastily. And that's possible, too. You
134.26 had to listen to him as you would to a small boy in
134.27 trouble. He didn't know. It had happened some-
134.28 how. It would never happen again. He had landed
134.29 partly on somebody and fallen across a thwart. He
134.30 felt as though all his ribs on his left side must be
135.01 broken; then he rolled over, and saw vaguely the
135.02 ship he had deserted uprising above him, with the
135.03 red side-light glowing large in the rain like a fire
135.04 on the brow of a hill seen through a mist. 'She
135.05 seemed higher than a wall; she loomed like a cliff
135.06 over the boat....I wished I could die,' he cried.
135.07 'There was no going back. It was as if I had jumped
135.08 into a well -- into an everlasting deep hole....'"
136.01 "HE locked his fingers together and tore
136.02 them apart. Nothing could be more
136.03 true: he had indeed jumped into an
136.04 everlasting deep hole. He had tumbled from a
136.05 height he could never scale again. By that time
136.06 the boat had gone driving forward past the bows.
136.07 It was too dark just then for them to see each other,
136.08 and, moreover, they were blinded and half drowned

136.09 with rain. He told me it was like being swept by
136.10 a flood through a cavern. They turned their backs
136.11 to the squall; the skipper, it seems, got an oar over
136.12 the stern to keep the boat before it, and for two or
136.13 three minutes the end of the world had come through
136.14 a deluge in a pitchy blackness. The sea hissed
136.15 'like twenty thousand kettles.' That's his simile,
136.16 not mine. I fancy there was not much wind after
136.17 the first gust; and he himself had admitted at the
136.18 inquiry that the sea never got up that night to any
136.19 extent. He crouched down in the bows and stole
136.20 a furtive glance back. He saw just one yellow
136.21 gleam of the masthead light high up and blurred
136.22 like a last star ready to dissolve. 'It terrified me
136.23 to see it still there,' he said. That's what he said.
136.24 What terrified him was the thought that the drown-
137.01 ing was not over yet. No doubt he wanted to be
137.02 done with that abomination as quickly as possible.
137.03 Nobody in the boat made a sound. In the dark she
137.04 seemed to fly, but of course she could not have had
137.05 much way. Then the shower swept ahead, and the
137.06 great, distracting, hissing noise followed the rain
137.07 into distance and died out. There was nothing to
137.08 be heard then but the slight wash about the boat's
137.09 sides. Somebody's teeth were chattering violently.
137.10 A hand touched his back. A faint voice said, 'You
137.11 there?' Another cried out shakily, 'She's gone!'
137.12 and they all stood up together to look astern. They
137.13 saw no lights. All was black. A thin, cold drizzle
137.14 was driving into their faces. The boat lurched
137.15 slightly. The teeth chattered faster, stopped, and
137.16 began again twice before the man could master his
137.17 shiver sufficiently to say, 'Ju-ju-st in ti-ti-me....
137.18 Brrr.' He recognised the voice of the chief
137.19 engineer saying surlily, 'I saw her go down. I
137.20 happened to turn my head.' The wind had dropped
137.21 almost completely.
137.22 "They watched in the dark with their heads
137.23 half turned to windward as if expecting to hear
137.24 cries. At first he was thankful the night had covered
137.25 up the scene before his eyes, and then to know of it
137.26 and yet to have seen and heard nothing appeared
137.27 somehow the culminating point of an awful mis-
137.28 fortune. 'Strange, isn't it?' he murmured, inter-
137.29 rupting himself in his disjointed narrative.
137.30 "It did not seem so strange to me. He must
138.01 have had an unconscious conviction that the reality
138.02 could not be half as bad, not half as anguishing,
138.03 appalling, and vengeful as the created terror of his
138.04 imagination. I believe that, in this first moment,
138.05 his heart was wrung with all the suffering, that his
138.06 soul knew the accumulated savour of all the fear,
138.07 all the horror, all the despair of eight hundred
138.08 human beings pounced upon in the night by a
138.09 sudden and violent death, else why should he have
138.10 said, 'It seemed to me that I must jump out of that
138.11 accursed boat and swim back to see -- half a mile --
138.12 more -- any distance -- to the very spot...'?
138.13 Why this impulse? Do you see the significance?
138.14 Why back to the very spot? Why not drown
138.15 alongside -- if he meant drowning? Why back to
138.16 the very spot, to see -- as if his imagination had to b
138.17 soothed by the assurance that all was over before
138.18 death could bring relief? I defy any one of you
138.19 to offer another explanation. It was one of those
138.20 bizarre and exciting glimpses through the fog. It
138.21 was an extraordinary disclosure. He let it out as
138.22 the most natural thing one could say. He fought
138.23 down that impulse and then he became conscious
138.24 of the silence. He mentioned this to me. A
138.25 silence of the sea, of the sky, merged into one
138.26 indefinite immensity still as death around these
138.27 saved, palpitating lives. 'You might have heard
138.28 a pin drop in the boat,' he said with a queer con-
138.29 traction of his lips, like a man trying to master
138.30 his sensibilities while relating some extremely
139.01 moving fact. A silence! God alone, who had
139.02 willed him as he was, knows what he made of
139.03 it in his heart. 'I didn't think any spot on earth
139.04 could be so still,' he said. 'You couldn't distin-
139.05 guish the sea from the sky; there was nothing to
139.06 see and nothing to hear. Not a glimmer, not a
139.07 shape, not a sound. You could have believed that
139.08 every bit of dry land had gone to the bottom; that
139.09 every man on earth but I and these beggars in the
139.10 boat had got drowned.' He leaned over the table
139.11 with his knuckles propped amongst coffee-cups,
139.12 liqueur-glasses, cigar-ends. 'I seemed to believe
139.13 it. Everything was gone and -- all was over...'
139.14 he fetched a deep sigh... 'with me.'"

139.15 Marlow sat up abruptly and flung away his
139.16 cheroot with force. It made a darting red trail
139.17 like a toy rocket fired through the drapery of
139.18 creepers. Nobody stirred.
139.19 "Hey, what do you think of it?" he cried with
139.20 sudden animation. "Wasn't he true to himself,
139.21 wasn't he? His saved life was over for want of
139.22 ground under his feet, for want of sights for his
139.23 eyes, for want of voices in his ears. Annihilation --
139.24 hey! And all the time it was only a clouded sky,
139.25 a sea that did not break, the air that did not stir.
139.26 Only a night; only a silence.
139.27 "It lasted for a while, and then they were
139.28 suddenly and unanimously moved to make a noise
139.29 over their escape. 'I knew from the first she would
139.30 go.' 'Not a minute too soon.' 'A narrow squeak,
140.01 b'gosh!' He said nothing, but the breeze that had
140.02 dropped came back, a gentle draught freshened
140.03 steadily, and the sea joined its murmuring voice
140.04 to this talkative reaction succeeding the dumb
140.05 moments of awe. She was gone! She was gone!
140.06 Not a doubt of it. Nobody could have helped.
140.07 They repeated the same words over and over again
140.08 as though they couldn't stop themselves. Never
140.09 doubted she would go. The lights were gone. No
140.10 mistake. The lights were gone. Couldn't expect
140.11 anything else. She had to go.... He noticed
140.12 that they talked as though they had left behind
140.13 them nothing but an empty ship. They concluded
140.14 she would not have been long when she once started.
140.15 It seemed to cause them some sort of satisfaction.
140.16 They assured each other that she couldn't have
140.17 been long about it -- 'Just shot down like a flat --
140.18 iron.' The chief engineer declared that the mast-
140.19 head light at the moment of sinking seemed to drop
140.20 'like a lighted match you throw down.' At this
140.21 the second laughed hysterically. 'I am g-g-glad,
140.22 I am gla-a-a-d.' His teeth went on 'like an electric
140.23 rattle,' said Jim, 'and all at once he began to cry.
140.24 He wept and blubbered like a child, catching his
140.25 breath and sobbing, "Oh dear! oh dear! oh
140.26 dear!" He would be quiet for a while and start
140.27 suddenly, "Oh, my poor arm! oh, my poor
140.28 a-a-a-arm!" I felt I could knock him down.
140.29 Some of them sat in the stern-sheets. I could
140.30 just make out their shapes. Voices came to me,
141.01 mumble, mumble, grunt, grunt. All this seemed
141.02 very hard to bear. I was cold, too. And I could
141.03 do nothing. I thought that if I moved I would
141.04 have to go over the side and...'
141.05 "His hand groped stealthily, came in contact
141.06 with a liqueur-glass, and was withdrawn suddenly
141.07 as if it had touched a red-hot coal. I pushed the
141.08 bottle slightly. 'Won't you have some more?' I
141.09 asked. He looked at me angrily. 'Don't you
141.10 think I can tell you what there is to tell without
141.11 screwing myself up?' he asked. The squad of
141.12 globe-trotters had gone to bed. We were alone
141.13 but for a vague white form erect in the shadow,
141.14 that, being looked at, cringed forward, hesitated,
141.15 backed away silently. It was getting late, but I did
141.16 not hurry my guest.
141.17 "In the midst of his forlorn state he heard his
141.18 companions begin to abuse some one. 'What kept
141.19 you from jumping, you lunatic?' said a scolding
141.20 voice. The chief engineer left the stern-sheets, and
141.21 could be heard clambering forward as if with hostile
141.22 intentions against 'the greatest idiot that ever was.'
141.23 The skipper shouted with rasping effort offensive
141.24 epithets from where he sat at the oars. He lifted
141.25 his head at that uproar, and heard the name 'George,'
141.26 while a hand in the dark struck him on the breast.
141.27 'What have you got to say for yourself, you fool?'
141.28 queried somebody, with a sort of virtuous fury. 'They
141.29 were after me,' he said. 'They were abusing me --
141.30 abusing me...by the name of George.'
142.01 "He paused to stare, tried to smile, turned his
142.02 eyes away and went on. 'That little second puts
142.03 his head right under my nose, "Why, it's that
142.04 blasted mate!" "What!" howls the skipper
142.05 from the other end of the boat. "No!" shrieks
142.06 the chief. And he, too, stopped to look at my
142.07 face.'
142.08 "The wind had left the boat suddenly. The
142.09 rain began to fall again, and the soft, uninterrupted,
142.10 little mysterious sound with which the sea receives
142.11 a shower arose on all sides in the night. 'They
142.12 were too taken aback to say anything more at first,'
142.13 he narrated steadily, 'and what could I have to say
142.14 to them?' He faltered for a moment, and made an
142.15 effort to go on. 'They called me horrible names.'
142.16 His voice, sinking to a whisper, now and then would
142.17 leap up suddenly, hardened by the passion of scorn,
142.18 as though he had been talking of secret abominations.
142.19 'Never mind what they called me,' he said grimly.
142.20 'I could hear hate in their voices. A good thing,
142.21 too. They could not forgive me for being in that
142.22 boat. They hated it. It made them mad....'
142.23 He laughed short.... 'But it kept me from --
142.24 look! I was sitting with my arms crossed, on the
142.25 gunwale....' He perched himself smartly on
142.26 the edge of the table and crossed his arms....
142.27 'Like this -- see? One little tilt backwards and I
142.28 would have been gone -- after the others. One
142.29 little tilt -- the least bit -- the least bit.' He frowned,
142.30 and tapping his forehead with the tip of his middle
143.01 finger, 'It was there all the time,' he said im-
143.02 pressively. 'All the time -- that notion. And the
143.03 rain -- cold, thick, cold as melted snow -- colder --
143.04 on my thin cotton clothes -- I'll never be so cold
143.05 again in my life, I know. And the sky was black,
143.06 too -- all black. Not a star, not a light anywhere.
143.07 Nothing outside that confounded boat and those
143.08 two yapping before me like a couple of mean
143.09 mongrels at a tree'd thief. Yap! yap! "What you
143.10 doing here? You're a fine sort! Too much of a
143.11 bloomin' gentleman to put your hand to it. Come
143.12 out of your trance, did you? To sneak in? Did
143.13 you?" Yap! yap! "You ain't fit to live!" Yap!
143.14 yap! Two of them together trying to out-bark
143.15 each other. The other would bay from the stern
143.16 through the rain -- couldn't see him -- couldn't make
143.17 it out -- some of his filthy jargon. Yap! yap!
143.18 Bow-ow-ow-ow-ow! Yap! yap! It was sweet
143.19 to hear them; it kept me alive, I tell you. It
143.20 saved my life. At it they went, as if trying to
143.21 drive me overboard with the noise! ... "I wonder
143.22 you had pluck enough to jump. You ain't wanted
143.23 here. If I had known who it was, I would have
143.24 tipped you over -- you skunk! What have you
143.25 done with the other? Where did you get the pluck
143.26 to jump -- you coward? What's to prevent us
143.27 three from firing you overboard?" ... They were
143.28 out of breath; the shower passed away upon the
143.29 sea. Then nothing. There was nothing round the
143.30 boat, not even a sound. Wanted to see me over-
144.01 board, did they? Upon my soul! I think they
144.02 would have had their wish if they had only
144.03 kept quiet. Fire me overboard! Would they?
144.04 "Try," I said. "I would for twopence." "Too
144.05 good for you," they screeched together. It was
144.06 so dark that it was only when one or the other of
144.07 them moved that I was quite sure of seeing him.
144.08 By heavens, I only wish they had tried!'
144.09 "I couldn't help exclaiming, 'What an extra-
144.10 ordinary affair!'
144.11 "'Not bad -- eh?' he said, as if in some sort
144.12 astounded. 'They pretended to think I had done
144.13 away with that donkey-man for some reason or
144.14 other. Why should I? And how the devil was I
144.15 to know? Didn't I get somehow into that boat?
144.16 into that boat -- I ...' The muscles round his
144.17 lips contracted into an unconscious grimace that
144.18 tore through the mask of his usual expression --
144.19 something violent, short-lived, and illuminating
144.20 like a twist of lightning that admits the eye for
144.21 an instant into the secret convolutions of a cloud.
144.22 'I did. I was plainly there with them -- wasn't I?
144.23 Isn't it awful a man should be driven to do a thing
144.24 like that -- and be responsible? What did I know
144.25 about their George they were howling after? I
144.26 remembered I had seen him curled up on the deck.
144.27 "Murdering coward!" the chief kept on calling
144.28 me. He didn't seem able to remember any other
144.29 two words. I didn't care, only his noise began to
144.30 worry me. "Shut up," I said. At that he col-
145.01 lected himself for a confounded screech. "You
145.02 killed him! You killed him!" "No," I shouted,
145.03 "but I will kill you directly." I jumped up, and
145.04 he fell backwards over a thwart with an awful loud
145.05 thump. I don't know why. Too dark. Tried to
145.06 step back, I suppose. I stood still facing aft, and
145.07 the wretched little second began to whine, "You
145.08 ain't going to hit a chap with a broken arm -- and you
145.09 call yourself a gentleman, too." I heard a heavy
145.10 tramp -- one -- two -- and wheezy grunting. The
145.11 other beast was coming at me, clattering his oar
145.12 over the stern. I saw him moving, big, big -- as you
145.13 see a man in a mist, in a dream. "Come on," I
145.14 cried. I would have tumbled him over like a

145.15 bale of shakings. He stopped, muttering to himself.
145.16 and went back. Perhaps he had heard the wind.
145.17 I didn't. It was the last heavy gust we had. He
145.18 went back to his oar. I was sorry. I would have
145.19 tried to -- to ...'
145.20 "He opened and closed his curved fingers, and
145.21 his hands had an eager and cruel flutter. 'Steady,
145.22 steady,' I murmured.
145.23 "'Eh? What? I am not excited,' he remon-
145.24 strated, awfully hurt, and with a convulsive jerk of
145.25 his elbow knocked over the cognac bottle. I started
145.26 forward, scraping my chair. He bounced off the
145.27 table as if a mine had been exploded behind his
145.28 back, and half turned before he alighted, crouching
145.29 on his feet to show me a startled pair of eyes and
145.30 a face white about the nostrils. A look of in-
146.01 tense annoyance succeeded. 'Awfully sorry. How
146.02 clumsy of me!' he mumbled very vexed, while the
146.03 pungent odour of spilt alcohol enveloped us suddenly
146.04 with an atmosphere of a low drinking-bout in the
146.05 cool, pure darkness of the night. The lights had
146.06 been put out in the dining-hall; our candle
146.07 glimmered solitary in the long gallery, and the
146.08 columns had turned black from pediment to capital.
146.09 On the vivid stars the high corner of the Harbour
146.10 Office stood out distinct across the Esplanade, as
146.11 though the sombre pile had glided nearer to see and
146.12 hear.
146.13 "He assumed an air of indifference.
146.14 "'I dare say I am less calm now than I was then.
146.15 I was ready for anything. These were trifles....'
146.16 "'You had a lively time of it in that boat,' I
146.17 remarked.
146.18 "'I was ready,' he repeated. 'After the ship's
146.19 lights had gone, anything might have happened in
146.20 that boat -- anything in the world -- and the world no
146.21 wiser. I felt this, and I was pleased. It was just
146.22 dark enough, too. We were like men walled up
146.23 quick in a roomy grave. No concern with anything
146.24 on earth. Nobody to pass an opinion. Nothing
146.25 mattered.' For the third time during this con-
146.26 versation he laughed harshly, but there was no one
146.27 about to suspect him of being only drunk. 'No
146.28 fear, no law, no sounds, no eyes -- not even our own,
146.29 till -- till sunrise at least.'
146.30 "I was struck by the suggestive truth of his
147.01 words. There is something peculiar in a small boat
147.02 upon the wide sea. Over the lives borne from under
147.03 the shadow of death there seems to fall the shadow
147.04 of madness. When your ship fails you, your whole
147.05 world seems to fail you; the world that made you,
147.06 restrained you, took care of you. It is as if the
147.07 souls of men floating on an abyss and in touch
147.08 with immensity had been set free for any excess of
147.09 heroism, absurdity, or abomination. Of course, as
147.10 with belief, thought, love, hate, conviction, or even
147.11 the visual aspect of material things, there are as
147.12 many shipwrecks as there are men, and in this one
147.13 there was something abject which made the isolation
147.14 more complete -- there was a villainy of circumstances
147.15 that cut these men off more completely from the
147.16 rest of mankind, whose ideal of conduct had never
147.17 undergone the trial of a fiendish and appalling joke.
147.18 They were exasperated with him for being a half-
147.19 hearted shirker: he focused on them his hatred of
147.20 the whole thing; he would have liked to take a
147.21 signal revenge for the abhorrent opportunity they
147.22 had put in his way. Trust a boat on the high seas
147.23 to bring out the Irrational that lurks at the bottom
147.24 of every thought, sentiment, sensation, emotion. It
147.25 was part of the burlesque meanness pervading that
147.26 particular disaster at sea that they did not come
147.27 to blows. It was all threats, all a terribly effective
147.28 feint, a sham from beginning to end, planned by the
147.29 tremendous disdain of the Dark Powers whose real
147.30 terrors, always on the verge of triumph, are per-
148.01 petually foiled by the steadfastness of men. I
148.02 asked, after waiting for a while, 'Well, what hap-
148.03 pened?' A futile question. I knew too much
148.04 already to hope for the grace of a single uplifting
148.05 touch, for the favour of hinted madness, of shadowed
148.06 horror. 'Nothing,' he said. 'I meant business,
148.07 but they meant noise only. Nothing happened.'
148.08 "And the rising sun found him just as he had
148.09 jumped up first in the bows of the boat. What a
148.10 persistence of readiness! He had been holding
148.11 the tiller in his hand, too, all the night. They had
148.12 dropped the rudder overboard while attempting to
148.13 ship it, and I suppose the tiller got kicked forward
148.14 somehow while they were rushing up and down that

148.15 boat trying to do all sorts of things at once so as
148.16 to get clear of the side. It was a long, heavy piece
148.17 of hard wood, and apparently he had been clutching
148.18 it for six hours or so. If you don't call that being
148.19 ready! Can you imagine him, silent and on his
148.20 feet half the night, his face to the gusts of rain,
148.21 staring at sombre forms, watchful of vague move-
148.22 ments, straining his ears to catch rare, low murmurs
148.23 in the stern-sheets! Firmness of courage or effort
148.24 of fear? What do you think? And the endurance
148.25 is undeniable, too. Six hours more or less on the
148.26 defensive; six hours of alert immobility while the
148.27 boat drove slowly or floated arrested, according to the
148.28 caprice of the wind; while the sea, calmed, slept
148.29 at last; while the clouds passed above his head;
148.30 while the sky from an immensity lustreless and black,
149.01 diminished to a sombre and lustrous vault, scin-
149.02 tillated with a greater brilliance, faded to the east,
149.03 paled at the zenith; while the dark shapes blotting
149.04 the low stars astern got outlines, relief; became
149.05 shoulders, heads, faces, features, -- confronted him
149.06 with dreary stares, had dishevelled hair, torn clothes,
149.07 blinked red eyelids at the white dawn. 'They
149.08 looked as though they had been knocking about
149.09 drunk in gutters for a week,' he described graphi-
149.10 cally; and then he muttered something about the
149.11 sunrise being of a kind that foretells a calm day.
149.12 You know that sailor habit of referring to the
149.13 weather in every connection. And on my side his
149.14 few mumbled words were enough to make me see the
149.15 lower limb of the sun clearing the line of the horizon,
149.16 the tremble of a vast ripple running over all the
149.17 visible expanse of the sea, as if the waters had
149.18 shuddered, giving birth to the globe of light, while
149.19 the last puff of the breeze would stir the air in a sigh
149.20 of relief.
149.21 "'They sat in the stern shoulder to shoulder,
149.22 with the skipper in the middle, like three dirty owls,
149.23 and stared at me,' I heard him say with an intention
149.24 of hate that distilled a corrosive virtue into the
149.25 commonplace words like a drop of powerful poison
149.26 falling into a glass of water; but my thoughts dwelt
149.27 upon that sunrise. I could imagine under the
149.28 pellucid emptiness of the sky these four men im-
149.29 prisoned in the solitude of the sea, the lonely sun,
149.30 regardless of the speck of life, ascending the clear
150.01 curve of the heaven as if to gaze ardently from a
150.02 greater height at his own splendour reflected in the
150.03 still ocean. 'They called out to me from aft,' said
150.04 Jim, 'as though we had been chums together. I
150.05 heard them. They were begging me to be sensible
150.06 and drop that "blooming piece of wood." Why
150.07 would I carry on so? They hadn't done me any
150.08 harm -- had they? There had been no harm....
150.09 No harm!'
150.10 "His face crimsoned as though he could not
150.11 get rid of the air in his lungs.
150.12 "'No harm!' he burst out. 'I leave it to
150.13 you. You can understand. Can't you? You see
150.14 it -- don't you? No harm! Good God! What
150.15 more could they have done? Or yes, I know very
150.16 well -- I jumped. Certainly. I jumped! I told
150.17 you I jumped; but I tell you they were too much for
150.18 any man. It was their doing as plainly as if they
150.19 had reached up with a boat-hook and pulled me
150.20 over. Can't you see it? You must see it. Come.
150.21 Speak -- straight out.'
150.22 "His uneasy eyes fastened upon mine, ques-
150.23 tioned, begged, challenged, entreated. For the life
150.24 of me I couldn't help murmuring, 'You've been
150.25 tried.' 'More than is fair,' he caught up swiftly.
150.26 'I wasn't given half a chance -- with a gang like
150.27 that. And now they were friendly -- oh, so damnably
150.28 friendly! Chums, shipmates. All in the same boat.
150.29 Make the best of it. They hadn't meant anything.
150.30 They didn't care a hang for George. George had
151.01 gone back to his berth for something at the last
151.02 moment and got caught. The man was a manifest
151.03 fool. Very sad, of course.... Their eyes looked
151.04 at me; their lips moved; they wagged their heads
151.05 at the other end of the boat -- three of them; they
151.06 beckoned -- to me. Why not? Hadn't I jumped?
151.07 I said nothing. There are no words for the sort of
151.08 things I wanted to say. If I had opened my lips
151.09 just then I would have simply howled like an
151.10 animal. I was asking myself when I would wake
151.11 up. They urged me aloud to come aft and hear
151.12 quietly what the skipper had to say. We were sure
151.13 to be picked up before the evening -- right in the
151.14 track of all the Canal traffic; there was smoke to the

151.15 north-west now.
151.16 "'It gave me an awful shock to see this faint,
151.17 faint blur, this low trail of brown mist through
151.18 which you could see the boundary of sea and sky.
151.19 I called out to them that I could hear very well
151.20 where I was. The skipper started swearing, as
151.21 hoarse as a crow. He wasn't going to talk at the
151.22 top of his voice for my accommodation. "Are you
151.23 afraid they will hear you on shore?" I asked. He
151.24 glared as if he would have liked to claw me to pieces.
151.25 The chief engineer advised him to humour me.
151.26 He said I wasn't right in my head yet. The other
151.27 rose astern, like a thick pillar of flesh -- and talked
151.28 talked....'
151.29 "Jim remained thoughtful. 'Well?' I said.
151.30 'What did I care what story they agreed to make
152.01 up?' he cried recklessly. 'They could tell what
152.02 they jolly well liked. It was their business. I
152.03 knew the story. Nothing they could make people
152.04 believe could alter it for me. I let him talk, argue --
152.05 talk, argue. He went on and on and on. Suddenly
152.06 I felt my legs give way under me. I was sick,
152.07 tired -- tired to death. I let fall the tiller, turned
152.08 my back on them, and sat down on the foremost
152.09 thwart. I had enough. They called to me to
152.10 know if I understood -- wasn't it true, every word of
152.11 it? It was true, by God! after their fashion. I
152.12 did not turn my head. I heard them palavering
152.13 together. "The silly ass won't say anything."
152.14 "Oh, he understands well enough." "Let him
152.15 be; he will be all right." "What can he do?"
152.16 What could I do? Weren't we all in the same boat?
152.17 I tried to be deaf. The smoke had disappeared to
152.18 the northward. It was a dead calm. They had a
152.19 drink from the water-breaker, and I drank, too.
152.20 Afterwards they made a great business of spreading
152.21 the boat-sail over the gunwales. Would I keep
152.22 a look out? They crept under, out of my sight,
152.23 thank God! I felt weary, weary, done up, as if I
152.24 hadn't had one hour's sleep since the day I was
152.25 born. I couldn't see the water for the glitter of the
152.26 sunshine. From time to time one of them would
152.27 creep out, stand up to take a look all round, and get
152.28 under again. I could hear spells of snoring below
152.29 the sail. Some of them could sleep. One of them
152.30 at least. I couldn't! All was light, light, and the
153.01 boat seemed to be falling through it. Now and
153.02 then I would feel quite surprised to find myself
153.03 sitting on a thwart....'
153.04 "He began to walk with measured steps to and
153.05 fro before my chair, one hand in his trousers pocket,
153.06 his head bent thoughtfully, and his right arm at
153.07 long intervals raised for a gesture that seemed to put
153.08 out of his way an invisible intruder.
153.09 "'I suppose you think I was going mad,' he
153.10 began in a changed tone. 'And well you may, if
153.11 you remember I had lost my cap. The sun crept
153.12 all the way from east to west over my bare head, but
153.13 that day I could not come to any harm, I suppose.
153.14 The sun could not make me mad....' His right
153.15 arm put aside the idea of madness.... 'Neither
153.16 could it kill me....' Again his arm repulsed a
153.17 shadow.... 'That rested with me.'
153.18 "'Did it?' I said, inexpressibly amazed at this
153.19 new turn, and I looked at him with the same sort
153.20 of feeling I might be fairly conceived to experience
153.21 had he, after spinning round on his heel, presented
153.22 an altogether new face.
153.23 "'I didn't get brain fever, I did not drop dead
153.24 either,' he went on. 'I didn't bother myself at all
153.25 about the sun over my head. I was thinking as
153.26 coolly as any man that ever sat thinking in the shade.
153.27 That greasy beast of a skipper poked his big cropped
153.28 head from under the canvas and screwed his fishy
153.29 eyes up at me. "Donnerwetter! you will die,"
153.30 he growled, and drew in like a turtle. I had seen
154.01 him. I had heard him. He didn't interrupt me. I
154.02 was thinking just then that I wouldn't.'
154.03 "He tried to sound my thought with an attentive
154.04 glance dropped on me in passing. 'Do you mean to
154.05 say you had been deliberating with yourself whether
154.06 you would die?' I asked in as impenetrable a tone
154.07 as I could command. He nodded without stopping.
154.08 'Yes, it had come to that as I sat there alone,' he
154.09 said. He passed on a few steps to the imaginary
154.10 end of his beat, and when he flung round to come
154.11 back both his hands were thrust deep into his
154.12 pockets. He stopped short in front of my chair
154.13 and looked down. 'Don't you believe it?' he
154.14 inquired with tense curiosity. I was moved to make

154.15 a solemn declaration of my readiness to believe
154.16 implicitly anything he thought fit to tell me."
155.01 "HE heard me out with his head on one
155.02 side, and I had another glimpse through
155.03 a rent in the mist in which he moved
155.04 and had his being. The dim candle spluttered
155.05 within the ball of glass, and that was all I had to
155.06 see him by; at his back was the dark night with
155.07 the clear stars, whose distant glitter disposed in
155.08 retreating planes lured the eye into the depths of a
155.09 greater darkness; and yet a mysterious light seemed
155.10 to show me his boyish head, as if in that moment
155.11 the youth within him had, for a second, glowed
155.12 and expired. 'You are an awful good sort to listen
155.13 like this,' he said. 'It does me good. You don't
155.14 know what it is to me. You don't ...' Words
155.15 seemed to fail him. It was a distinct glimpse. He
155.16 was a youngster of the sort you like to see about
155.17 you; of the sort you like to imagine yourself to
155.18 have been; of the sort whose appearance claims
155.19 the fellowship of these illusions you had thought
155.20 gone out, extinct, cold, and which, as if rekindled
155.21 at the approach of another flame, give a flutter deep,
155.22 deep down somewhere, give a flutter of light ...
155.23 of heat!... Yes; I had a glimpse of him then
155.24 ... and it was not the last of that kind....
156.01 'You don't know what it is for a fellow in my posi-
156.02 tion to be believed -- make a clean breast of it to an
156.03 elder man. It is so difficult -- so awfully unfair -- so
156.04 hard to understand.'
156.05 "The mists were closing again. I don't know
156.06 how old I appeared to him -- and how much wise.
156.07 Not half as old as I felt just then; not half as use-
156.08 lessly wise as I knew myself to be. Surely in no
156.09 other craft as in that of the sea do the hearts of
156.10 those already launched to sink or swim go out so
156.11 much to the youth on the brink, looking with
156.12 shining eyes upon that glitter of the vast surface
156.13 which is only a reflection of his own glances full of
156.14 fire. There is such magnificent vagueness in the
156.15 expectations that had driven each of us to sea, such
156.16 a glorious indefiniteness, such a beautiful greed of
156.17 adventures that are their own and only reward.
156.18 What we get -- well, we won't talk of that; but
156.19 can one of us restrain a smile? In no other kind
156.20 of life is the illusion more wide of reality -- in no
156.21 other is the beginning all illusion -- the disenchant-
156.22 ment more swift -- the subjugation more complete.
156.23 Hadn't we all commenced with the same desire,
156.24 ended with the same knowledge, carried the memory
156.25 of the same cherished glamour through the sordid
156.26 days of imprecation? What wonder that when
156.27 some heavy prod gets home the bond is found to
156.28 be close; that besides the fellowship of the craft
156.29 there is felt the strength of a wider feeling -- the
156.30 feeling that binds a man to a child. He was there
157.01 before me, believing that age and wisdom can find
157.02 a remedy against the pain of truth, giving me a
157.03 glimpse of himself as a young fellow in a scrape
157.04 that is the very devil of a scrape, the sort of scrape
157.05 greybeards wag at solemnly while they hide a smile.
157.06 And he had been deliberating upon death -- confound
157.07 him! He had found that to meditate about because
157.08 he thought he had saved his life, while all its glamour
157.09 had gone with the ship in the night. What more
157.10 natural! It was tragic enough and funny enough
157.11 in all conscience to call aloud for compassion, and
157.12 in what was I better than the rest of us to refuse him
157.13 my pity? And even as I looked at him the mists
157.14 rolled into the rent, and his voice spoke:
157.15 "'I was so lost, you know. It was the sort of
157.16 thing one does not expect to happen to one. It was
157.17 not like a fight, for instance.'
157.18 "'It was not,' I admitted. He appeared
157.19 changed, as if he had suddenly matured.
157.20 "'One couldn't be sure,' he muttered.
157.21 "'Ah! You were not sure,' I said, and was
157.22 placated by the sound of a faint sigh that passed
157.23 between us like the flight of a bird in the night.
157.24 "'Well, I wasn't,' he said courageously. 'It
157.25 was something like that wretched story they made
157.26 up. It was not a lie -- but it wasn't truth all the
157.27 same. It was something.... One knows a down-
157.28 right lie. There was not the thickness of a sheet
157.29 of paper between the right and wrong of this affair.'
157.30 "'How much more did you want?' I asked;
158.01 but I think I spoke so low that he did not catch what
158.02 I said. He had advanced his argument as though
158.03 life had been a network of paths separated by
158.04 chasms. His voice sounded reasonable.

158.05 "'Suppose I had not -- I mean to say, suppose I
158.06 had stuck to the ship? Well. How much longer?
158.07 Say a minute -- half a minute. Come. In thirty
158.08 seconds, as it seemed certain then, I would have
158.09 been overboard; and do you think I would not
158.10 have laid hold of the first thing that came in my way
158.11 -- oar, life-buoy, grating -- anything? Wouldn't
158.12 you?'
158.13 "'And be saved,' I interjected.
158.14 "'I would have meant to be,' he retorted.
158.15 'And that's more than I meant when I' ... he
158.16 shivered as if about to swallow some nauseous
158.17 drug ... 'jumped,' he pronounced with a con-
158.18 vulsive effort, whose stress, as if propagated by the
158.19 waves of the air, made my body stir a little in the
158.20 chair. He fixed me with lowering eyes. 'Don't
158.21 you believe me?' he cried. 'I swear!... Con-
158.22 found it! You got me here to talk, and ... You
158.23 must!... You said you would believe.' 'Of
158.24 course I do,' I protested in a matter-of-fact tone
158.25 which produced a calming effect. 'Forgive me,'
158.26 he said. 'Of course I wouldn't have talked to you
158.27 about all this if you had not been a gentleman.
158.28 I ought to have known ... I am -- I am -- a gentle-
158.29 man, too ...' 'Yes, yes,' I said hastily. He was
158.30 looking me squarely in the face and withdrew his
159.01 gaze slowly. 'Now you understand why I didn't
159.02 after all ... didn't go out in that way. I wasn't
159.03 going to be frightened at what I had done. And,
159.04 anyhow, if I had stuck to the ship I would have
159.05 done my best to be saved. Men have been known
159.06 to float for hours -- in the open sea -- and be picked
159.07 up not much the worse for it. I might have lasted
159.08 it out better than many others. There's nothing
159.09 the matter with my heart.' He withdrew his right
159.10 fist from his pocket, and the blow he struck on his
159.11 chest resounded like a muffled detonation in the
159.12 night.
159.13 "'No,' I said. He meditated, with his legs
159.14 slightly apart and his chin sunk. 'A hair's-breadth,'
159.15 he muttered. 'Not the breadth of a hair between
159.16 this and that. And at the time ...'
159.17 "'It is difficult to see a hair at midnight,' I put
159.18 in, a little viciously, I fear. Don't you see what I
159.19 mean by the solidarity of the craft? I was aggrieved
159.20 against him, as though he had cheated me -- me! --
159.21 of a splendid opportunity to keep up the illusion
159.22 of my beginnings, as though he had robbed our
159.23 common life of the last spark of its glamour. 'And
159.24 so you cleared out -- at once.'
159.25 "'Jumped,' he corrected me incisively.
159.26 'Jumped -- mind!' he repeated, and I wondered at
159.27 the evident but obscure intention. 'Well, yes!
159.28 Perhaps I could not see then. But I had plenty of
159.29 time and any amount of light in that boat. And I
159.30 could think, too. Nobody would know, of course,
160.01 but this did not make it any easier for me. You've
160.02 got to believe that, too. I did not want all this
160.03 talk.... No ... Yes ... I won't lie ... I
160.04 wanted it: it is the very thing I wanted -- there.
160.05 Do you think you or anybody could have made me
160.06 if I ... I am -- I am not afraid to tell. And I
160.07 wasn't afraid to think either. I looked it in the
160.08 face. I wasn't going to run away. At first -- at
160.09 night, if it hadn't been for those fellows I might
160.10 have ... No! by heavens! I was not going
160.11 to give them that satisfaction. They had done
160.12 enough. They made up a story, and believed it
160.13 for all I know. But I knew the truth, and I would
160.14 live it down -- alone, with myself. I wasn't going
160.15 to give in to such a beastly unfair thing. What did
160.16 it prove after all? I was confoundedly cut up.
160.17 Sick of life -- to tell you the truth; but what
160.18 would have been the good to shirk it -- in -- in --
160.19 that way? That was not the way. I believe -- I
160.20 believe it would have -- it would have ended --
160.21 nothing.'
160.22 "He had been walking up and down, but with
160.23 the last word he turned short at me.
160.24 "'What do you believe?' he asked with
160.25 violence. A pause ensued, and suddenly I felt
160.26 myself overcome by a profound and hopeless
160.27 fatigue, as though his voice had startled me out of
160.28 a dream of wandering through empty spaces whose
160.29 immensity had harassed my soul and exhausted
160.30 my body.
161.01 "'... Would have ended nothing,' he mut-
161.02 tered over me obstinately, after a little while.
161.03 'No! the proper thing was to face it out --
161.04 alone -- for myself -- wait for another chance -- find

161.05 out ...'"
162.01 "ALL around everything was still as far
162.02 as the ear could reach. The mist of
162.03 his feelings shifted between us, as if
162.04 disturbed by his struggles, and in the rifts of the
162.05 immaterial veil he would appear to my staring eyes
162.06 distinct of form and pregnant with vague appeal like
162.07 a symbolic figure in a picture. The chill air of the
162.08 night seemed to lie on my limbs as heavy as a slab
162.09 of marble.
162.10 "'I see,' I murmured, more to prove to myself
162.11 that I could break my state of numbness than for
162.12 any other reason.
162.13 "'The Avondale picked us up just before
162.14 sunset,' he remarked moodily. 'Steamed right
162.15 straight for us. We had only to sit and wait.'
162.16 "After a long interval, he said, 'They told
162.17 their story.' And again there was that oppressive
162.18 silence. 'Then only I knew what it was I had
162.19 made up my mind to,' he added.
162.20 "'You said nothing,' I whispered.
162.21 "'What could I say?' he asked, in the same
162.22 low tone.... 'Shock slight. Stopped the ship.
162.23 Ascertained the damage. Took measures to get the
162.24 boats out without creating a panic. As the first
163.01 boat was lowered ship went down in a squall.
163.02 Sank like lead.... What could be more clear'
163.03 ... he hung his head ... 'and more awful?'
163.04 His lips quivered while he looked straight into my
163.05 eyes. 'I had jumped -- hadn't I?' he asked, dis-
163.06 mayed. 'That's what I had to live down. The
163.07 story didn't matter.' ... He clasped his hands for
163.08 an instant, glanced right and left into the gloom:
163.09 'It was like cheating the dead,' he stammered.
163.10 "'And there were no dead,' I said.
163.11 "He went away from me at this. That is the
163.12 only way I can describe it. In a moment I saw his
163.13 back close to the balustrade. He stood there for
163.14 some time, as if admiring the purity and the peace
163.15 of the night. Some flowering shrub in the garden
163.16 below spread its powerful scent through the damp
163.17 air. He returned to me with hasty steps.
163.18 "'And that did not matter,' he said, as stub-
163.19 bornly as you please.
163.20 "'Perhaps not,' I admitted. I began to have a
163.21 notion he was too much for me. After all, what did
163.22 I know?
163.23 "'Dead or not dead, I could not get clear,' he
163.24 said. 'I had to live; hadn't I?'
163.25 "'Well, yes -- if you take it in that way,' I
163.26 mumbled.
163.27 "'I was glad, of course,' he threw out carelessly,
163.28 with his mind fixed on something else. 'The ex-
163.29 posure,' he pronounced slowly, and lifted his head.
163.30 'Do you know what was my first thought when I
164.01 heard? I was relieved. I was relieved to learn
164.02 that those shouts -- did I tell you I had heard shouts?
164.03 No? Well, I did. Shouts for help ... blown
164.04 along with the drizzle. Imagination, I suppose.
164.05 And yet I can hardly ... How stupid.... The
164.06 others did not. I asked them afterwards. They all
164.07 said No. No? And I was hearing them even then!
164.08 I might have known -- but I didn't think -- I only
164.09 listened. Very faint screams -- day after day. Then
164.10 that little half-caste chap here came up and spoke
164.11 to me. "The Patna ... French gunboat ...
164.12 towed successfully to Aden ... Investigation ...
164.13 Marine Office ... Sailors' Home ... arrange-
164.14 ments made for your board and lodging!" I
164.15 walked along with him, and I enjoyed the silence.
164.16 So there had been no shouting. Imagination. I
164.17 had to believe him. I could hear nothing any more.
164.18 I wonder how long I could have stood it. It was
164.19 getting worse, too ... I mean -- louder.'
164.20 "He fell into thought.
164.21 "'And I had heard nothing! Well -- so be it.
164.22 But the lights! The lights did go! We did not
164.23 see them. They were not there. If they had been,
164.24 I would have swam back -- I would have gone
164.25 back and shouted alongside -- I would have begged
164.26 them to take me on board.... I would have had
164.27 my chance.... You doubt me? ... How do
164.28 you know how I felt? ... What right have you
164.29 to doubt? ... I very nearly did it as it was -- do
164.30 you understand?' His voice fell. 'There was
165.01 not a glimmer -- not a glimmer,' he protested
165.02 mournfully. 'Don't you understand that if there
165.03 had been, you would not have seen me here? You
165.04 see me -- and you doubt.'
165.05 "I shook my head negatively. This question of

165.06 the lights being lost sight of when the boat could
165.07 not have been more than a quarter of a mile from
165.08 the ship was a matter for much discussion. Jim
165.09 stuck to it that there was nothing to be seen after
165.10 the first shower had cleared away; and the others
165.11 had affirmed the same thing to the officers of the
165.12 _Avondale_. Of course people shook their heads and
165.13 smiled. One old skipper who sat near me in court
165.14 tickled my ear with his white beard to murmur, 'Of
165.15 course they would lie.' As a matter of fact nobody
165.16 lied; not even the chief engineer with his story of
165.17 the masthead light dropping like a match you throw
165.18 down. Not consciously, at least. A man with his
165.19 liver in such a state might very well have seen a
165.20 floating spark in the corner of his eye when stealing
165.21 a hurried glance over his shoulder. They had seen
165.22 no light of any sort though they were well within
165.23 range, and they could only explain this in one way:
165.24 the ship had gone down. It was obvious and com-
165.25 forting. The foreseen fact coming so swiftly had
165.26 justified their haste. No wonder they did not
165.27 cast about for any other explanation. Yet the true
165.28 one was very simple, and as soon as Brierly sug-
165.29 gested it the court ceased to bother about the ques-
165.30 tion. If you remember, the ship had been stopped,
166.01 and was lying with her head on the course steered
166.02 through the night, with her stern canted high and
166.03 her bows brought low down in the water through
166.04 the filling of the fore-compartment. Being thus
166.05 out of trim, when the squall struck her a little on
166.06 the quarter, she swung head to wind as sharply as
166.07 though she had been at anchor. By this change
166.08 in her position all her lights were in a very few
166.09 moments shut off from the boat to leeward. It
166.10 may very well be that, had they been seen, they would
166.11 have had the effect of a mute appeal -- that their
166.12 glimmer lost in the darkness of the cloud would have
166.13 had the mysterious power of the human glance that
166.14 can awaken the feelings of remorse and pity. It
166.15 would have said, 'I am here -- still here' ... and
166.16 what more can the eye of the most forsaken of
166.17 human beings say? But she turned her back on
166.18 them as if in disdain of their fate: she had swung
166.19 round, burdened, to glare stubbornly at the new
166.20 danger of the open sea which she so strangely sur-
166.21 vived to end her days in a breaking-up yard, as if
166.22 it had been her recorded fate to die obscurely under
166.23 the blows of many hammers. What were the various
166.24 ends their destiny provided for the pilgrims I am
166.25 unable to say; but the immediate future brought,
166.26 at about nine o'clock next morning, a French gun-
166.27 boat homeward bound from Reunion. The report
166.28 of her commander was public property. He had
166.29 swept a little out of his course to ascertain what
166.30 was the matter with that steamer floating dangerously
167.01 by the head upon a still and hazy sea. There was
167.02 an ensign, union down, flying at her main gaff (the
167.03 serang had the sense to make a signal of distress at
167.04 daylight); but the cooks were preparing the food
167.05 in the cooking-boxes forward as usual. The decks
167.06 were packed as close as a sheep-pen: there were
167.07 people perched all along the rails, jammed on the
167.08 bridge in a solid mass; hundreds of eyes stared,
167.09 and not a sound was heard when the gunboat ranged
167.10 abreast, as if all that multitude of lips had been sealed
167.11 by a spell.
167.12 "The Frenchman hailed, could get no in-
167.13 telligible reply, and after ascertaining through his
167.14 binoculars that the crowd on deck did not look
167.15 plague-stricken, decided to send a boat. Two
167.16 officers came on board, listened to the serang, tried
167.17 to talk with the Arab, couldn't make head or tail
167.18 of it: but of course the nature of the emergency
167.19 was obvious enough. They were also very much
167.20 struck by discovering a white man, dead and curled
167.21 up peacefully on the bridge. 'Fort intrigués par ce
167.22 cadavre,' as I was informed a long time after by an
167.23 elderly French lieutenant whom I came across one
167.24 afternoon in Sydney, by the merest chance, in a sort
167.25 of cafe, and who remembered the affair perfectly.
167.26 Indeed this affair, I may notice in passing, had an
167.27 extraordinary power of defying the shortness of
167.28 memories and the length of time: it seemed to
167.29 live, with a sort of uncanny vitality, in the minds
167.30 of men, on the tips of their tongues. I've had the
168.01 questionable pleasure of meeting it often, years
168.02 afterwards, thousands of miles away, emerging
168.03 from the remotest possible talk, coming to the
168.04 surface of the most distant allusions. Has it not
168.05 turned up to-night between us? And I am the

168.06 only seaman here. I am the only one to whom it is
168.07 memory. And yet it has made its way out! But
168.08 if two men who, unknown to each other, knew of
168.09 this affair met accidentally on any spot of this earth,
168.10 the thing would pop up between them as sure
168.11 as fate, before they parted. I had never seen that
168.12 Frenchman before, and at the end of an hour we
168.13 had done with each other for life: he did not seem
168.14 particularly talkative either; he was a quiet, massive
168.15 chap in a creased uniform sitting drowsily over a
168.16 tumbler half full of some dark liquid. His shoulder-
168.17 straps were a bit tarnished, his clean-shaved cheeks
168.18 were large and sallow; he looked like a man who
168.19 would be given to taking snuff -- don't you know?
168.20 I won't say he did; but the habit would have
168.21 fitted that kind of man. It all began by his handing
168.22 me a number of _Home News,_ which I didn't want,
168.23 across the marble table. I said, 'Merci.' We
168.24 exchanged a few apparently innocent remarks,
168.25 and suddenly, before I knew how it had come about,
168.26 we were in the midst of it, and he was telling me
168.27 how much they had been 'intrigued by that corpse.'
168.28 It turned out he had been one of the boarding
168.29 officers.
168.30 "In the establishment where we sat one could
169.01 get a variety of foreign drinks which were kept for
169.02 the visiting naval officers, and he took a sip of the
169.03 dark, medical-looking stuff, which probably was
169.04 nothing more nasty than cassis a l'eau, and glancing
169.05 with one eye into the tumbler, shook his head
169.06 slightly. 'Impossible de comprendre -- vous concevez,'
169.07 he said, with a curious mixture of unconcern and
169.08 thoughtfulness. I could very easily conceive how
169.09 impossible it had been for them to understand.
169.10 Nobody in the gunboat knew enough English to
169.11 get hold of the story as told by the serang. There
169.12 was a good deal of noise, too, round the two officers.
169.13 'They crowded upon us. There was a circle
169.14 round that dead man (autour de ce mort,) he de-
169.15 scribed. 'One had to attend to the most pressing.
169.16 These people were beginning to agitate themselves --
169.17 Parbleu! A mob like that -- don't you see?' he
169.18 interjected with philosophic indulgence. As to the
169.19 bulkhead, he had advised his commander that the
169.20 safest thing was to leave it alone, it was so villainous
169.21 to look at. They got two hawsers on board promptly
169.22 (en toute hâte) and took the _Patna_ in tow -- stern
169.23 foremost at that -- which, under the circumstances,
169.24 was not so foolish, since the rudder was too much
169.25 out of the water to be of any great use for steering,
169.26 and this manoeuvre eased the strain on the bulkhead,
169.27 whose state, he expounded with stolid glibness,
169.28 demanded the greatest care (exigeait les plus grands
169.29 ménagements,) I could not help thinking that my
169.30 new acquaintance must have had a voice in most
170.01 of these arrangements: he looked a reliable officer,
170.02 no longer very active, and he was seamanlike, too,
170.03 in a way, though as he sat there, with his thick
170.04 fingers clasped lightly on his stomach, he reminded
170.05 you of one of those snuffy, quiet village priests,
170.06 into whose ears are poured the sins, the sufferings,
170.07 the remorse of peasant generations, on whose faces
170.08 the placid and simple expression is like a veil thrown
170.09 over the mystery of pain and distress. He ought
170.10 to have had a threadbare black soutane buttoned
170.11 smoothly up to his ample chin, instead of a frock-
170.12 coat with shoulder-straps and brass buttons. His
170.13 broad bosom heaved regularly while he went on
170.14 telling me that it had been the very devil of a job, as
170.15 doubtless (sans doute) I could figure to myself in my
170.16 quality of a seaman (en votre qualite de marin.) At
170.17 the end of the period he inclined his body slightly
170.18 towards me, and, pursing his shaved lips, allowed the
170.19 air to escape with a gentle hiss. 'Luckily,' he
170.20 continued, 'the sea was level like this table, and
170.21 there was no more wind than there is here....'
170.22 The place struck me as indeed intolerably stuffy,
170.23 and very hot; my face burned as though I had
170.24 been young enough to be embarrassed and blushing.
170.25 They had directed their course, he pursued, to the
170.26 nearest English port 'naturellement,' where their
170.27 responsibility ceased 'Dieu merci....' He blew
170.28 out his flat cheeks a little.... 'Because, mind you
170.29 (notez bien,) all the time of towing we had two
170.30 quartermasters stationed with axes by the hawsers,
171.01 to cut us clear of our tow in case she ...' He
171.02 fluttered downwards his heavy eyelids, making his
171.03 meaning as plain as possible.... 'What would
171.04 you? One does what one can (on fait ce qu'on
171.05 peut,)' and for a moment he managed to invest his

171.06 ponderous immobility with an air of resignation.
171.07 'Two quartermasters -- thirty hours -- always there.
171.08 Two!' he repeated, lifting up his right hand a little,
171.09 and exhibiting two fingers. This was absolutely
171.10 the first gesture I saw him make. It gave me the
171.11 opportunity to 'note' a starred scar on the back
171.12 of his hand -- effect of a gunshot clearly; and, as if
171.13 my sight had been made more acute by this dis-
171.14 covery, I perceived also the seam of an old wound,
171.15 beginning a little below the temple and going out
171.16 of sight under the short grey hair at the side of
171.17 his head -- the graze of a spear or the cut of a sabre.
171.18 He clasped his hands on his stomach again. 'I
171.19 remained on board that -- that -- my memory is going
171.20 (s'en va). Ah! Patt-na. C'est bien ça. Patt-na.
171.21 Merci. It is droll how one forgets. I stayed on
171.22 that ship thirty hours....'
171.23 "'You did!' I exclaimed. Still gazing at his
171.24 hands, he pursed his lips a little, but this time made
171.25 no hissing sound. 'It was judged proper,' he said,
171.26 lifting his eyebrows dispassionately, 'that one of the
171.27 officers should remain to keep an eye open (pour
171.28 ouvrir l'oeil) ... he sighed idly ... 'and for
171.29 communicating by signals with the towing ship --
171.30 do you see? -- and so on. For the rest, it was my
172.01 opinion, too. We made our boats ready to drop
172.02 over -- and I also on that ship took measures....
172.03 Enfin! One has done one's possible. It was a
172.04 delicate position. Thirty hours! They prepared
172.05 me some food. As for the wine -- go and whistle
172.06 for it -- not a drop.' In some extraordinary way,
172.07 without any marked change in his inert attitude and
172.08 in the placid expression of his face, he managed
172.09 to convey the idea of profound disgust. 'I -- you
172.10 know -- when it comes to eating without my glass
172.11 of wine -- I am nowhere.'
172.12 "I was afraid he would enlarge upon the
172.13 grievance, for though he didn't stir a limb or twitch
172.14 a feature, he made one aware how much he was
172.15 irritated by the recollection. But he seemed to
172.16 forget all about it. They delivered their charge to
172.17 the 'port authorities,' as he expressed it. He was
172.18 struck by the calmness with which it had been
172.19 received. 'One might have thought they had such
172.20 a droll find (drôle de trouvaille) brought them every
172.21 day. You are extraordinary -- you others,' he com-
172.22 mented, with his back propped against the wall, and
172.23 looking himself as incapable of an emotional display
172.24 as a sack of meal. There happened to be a man-of--
172.25 war and an Indian Marine steamer in the harbour
172.26 at the time, and he did not conceal his admiration
172.27 of the efficient manner in which the boats of these
172.28 two ships cleared the Patna of her passengers.
172.29 Indeed his torpid demeanour concealed nothing: it
172.30 had that mysterious, almost miraculous, power of
173.01 producing striking effects by means impossible of
173.02 detection, which is the last word of the highest art.
173.03 'Twenty-five minutes -- watch in hand -- twenty-five,
173.04 no more....' He unclasped and clasped again
173.05 his fingers without removing his hands from his
173.06 stomach, and made it infinitely more effective than
173.07 if he had thrown up his arms to heaven in amaze-
173.08 ment.... 'All that lot (tout ce monde) on shore --
173.09 with their little affairs -- nobody left but a guard of
173.10 seamen (marins de l'Etat) and that interesting corpse
173.11 (cet interessant cadavre). Twenty-five minutes....'
173.12 With downcast eyes and his head tilted slightly
173.13 on one side he seemed to roll knowingly on his
173.14 tongue the savour of a smart bit of work. He
173.15 persuaded one without any further demonstration
173.16 that his approval was eminently worth having, and
173.17 resuming his hardly interrupted immobility he
173.18 went on to inform me that, being under orders to
173.19 make the best of their way to Toulon, they left in
173.20 two hours' time, 'so that (de sorte que) there are
173.21 many things in this incident of my life (dans cet
173.22 episode de ma vie) which have remained obscure.'"
174.01 "AFTER these words, and without a
174.02 change of attitude, he, so to speak,
174.03 submitted himself passively to a state
174.04 of silence. I kept him company; and suddenly,
174.05 but not abruptly, as if the appointed time had
174.06 arrived for his moderate and husky voice to come
174.07 out of his immobility, he pronounced, 'Mon Dieu!
174.08 how the time passes!' Nothing could have been
174.09 more commonplace than this remark; but its
174.10 utterance coincided for me with a moment of vision.
174.11 It's extraordinary how we go through life with eyes
174.12 half shut, with dull ears, with dormant thoughts.
174.13 Perhaps it's just as well; and it may be that it is

174.14 this very dullness that makes life to the incalculable
174.15 majority so supportable and so welcome. Never-
174.16 theless, there can be but few of us who had never
174.17 known one of these rare moments of awakening
174.18 when we see, hear, understand ever so much -- every-
174.19 thing -- in a flash -- before we fall back again into
174.20 our agreeable somnolence. I raised my eyes when
174.21 he spoke, and I saw him as though I had never seen
174.22 him before. I saw his chin sunk on his breast,
174.23 the clumsy folds of his coat, his clasped hands,
174.24 his motionless pose, so curiously suggestive of his
175.01 having been simply left there. Time had passed
175.02 indeed: it had overtaken him and gone ahead. It
175.03 had left him hopelessly behind with a few poor
175.04 gifts: the iron-grey hair, the heavy fatigue of the
175.05 tanned face, two scars, a pair of tarnished shoulder--
175.06 straps; one of those steady, reliable men who are
175.07 the raw material of great reputations, one of those
175.08 uncounted lives that are buried without drums
175.09 and trumpets under the foundations of monu-
175.10 mental successes. 'I am now third lieutenant of
175.11 the Victorieuse' (she was the flagship of the French
175.12 Pacific squadron at the time), he said, detaching his
175.13 shoulders from the wall a couple of inches to in-
175.14 troduce himself. I bowed slightly on my side of
175.15 the table, and told him I commanded a merchant
175.16 vessel at present anchored in Rushcutters' Bay. He
175.17 had 'remarked' her -- a pretty little craft. He was
175.18 very civil about it in his impassive way. I even
175.19 fancy he went the length of tilting his head in
175.20 compliment as he repeated, breathing visibly the
175.21 while, 'Ah, yes. A little craft painted black -- very
175.22 pretty -- very pretty (très coquet).' After a time he
175.23 twisted his body slowly to face the glass door on our
175.24 right. 'A dull town (triste ville),' he observed,
175.25 staring into the street. It was a brilliant day; a
175.26 southerly buster was raging, and we could see the
175.27 passers-by, men and women, buffeted by the wind
175.28 on the sidewalks, the sunlit fronts of the houses
175.29 across the road blurred by the tall whirls of dust.
175.30 'I descended on shore,' he said, 'to stretch my
176.01 legs a little, but ...' He didn't finish, and sank
176.02 into the depths of his repose. 'Pray -- tell me,'
176.03 he began, coming up ponderously, 'what was there
176.04 at the bottom of this affair -- precisely (au juste)?
176.05 It is curious. That dead man, for instance -- and
176.06 so on.'
176.07 "'There were living men too,' I said; 'much
176.08 more curious.'
176.09 "'No doubt, no doubt,' he agreed half audibly;
176.10 then, as if after mature consideration, murmured,
176.11 'Evidently.' I made no difficulty in communicating
176.12 to him what had interested me most in this affair.
176.13 It seemed as though he had a right to know: hadn't
176.14 he spent thirty hours on board the Patna -- had he
176.15 not taken the succession, so to speak, had he not done
176.16 'his possible'? He listened to me, looking more
176.17 priestlike than ever, and with what -- probably on
176.18 account of his downcast eyes -- had the appearance of
176.19 devout concentration. Once or twice he elevated
176.20 his eyebrows (but without raising his eyelids), as
176.21 one would say, 'The devil!' Once he calmly
176.22 exclaimed, 'Ah, bah!' under his breath, and when
176.23 I had finished he pursed his lips in a deliberate
176.24 way and emitted a sort of sorrowful whistle.
176.25 "In any one else it might have been an evidence
176.26 of boredom, a sign of indifference; but he, in his
176.27 occult way, managed to make his immobility appear
176.28 profoundly responsive, and as full of valuable
176.29 thoughts as an egg is of meat. What he said at
176.30 last was nothing more than a 'Very interesting,'
177.01 pronounced politely, and not much above a whisper.
177.02 Before I got over my disappointment he added, but
177.03 as if speaking to himself, 'That's it. That is it.'
177.04 His chin seemed to sink lower on his breast, his
177.05 body to weigh heavier on his seat. I was about to
177.06 ask him what he meant, when a sort of preparatory
177.07 tremor passed over his whole person, as a faint
177.08 ripple may be seen upon stagnant water even before
177.09 the wind is felt. 'And so that poor young man
177.10 ran away along with the others,' he said with grave
177.11 tranquillity.
177.12 "I don't know what made me smile: it is the
177.13 only genuine smile of mine I can remember in con-
177.14 nection with Jim's affair. But somehow this simple
177.15 statement of the matter sounded funny in French.
177.16 ... 'S'est enfui avec les autres,' had said the
177.17 lieutenant. And suddenly I began to admire the
177.18 discrimination of the man. He had made out the
177.19 point at once: he did get hold of the only thing

212

177.20 I cared about. I felt as though I were taking pro-
177.21 fessional opinion on the case. His imperturbable
177.22 and mature calmness was that of an expert in
177.23 possession of the facts, and to whom one's per-
177.24 plexities are mere child's-play. 'Ah! The young,
177.25 the young,' he said indulgently. 'And after all,
177.26 one does not die of it.' 'Die of what?' I asked
177.27 swiftly. 'Of being afraid.' He elucidated his
177.28 meaning and sipped his drink.
177.29 "I perceived that the three last fingers of his
177.30 wounded hand were stiff and could not move
178.01 independently of each other, so that he took up his
178.02 tumbler with an ungainly clutch. 'One is always
178.03 afraid. One may talk, but ...' He put down
178.04 the glass awkwardly.... 'The fear, the fear --
178.05 look you -- it is always there....' He touched his
178.06 breast near a brass button on the very spot where
178.07 Jim had given a thump to his own when protesting
178.08 that there was nothing the matter with his heart.
178.09 I suppose I made some sign of dissent, because he
178.10 insisted, 'Yes! yes! One talks, one talks; this
178.11 is all very fine; but at the end of the reckoning
178.12 one is no cleverer than the next man -- and no more
178.13 brave. Brave! This is always to be seen. I
178.14 have rolled my hump (roulé ma bosse),' he said,
178.15 using the slang expression with imperturbable
178.16 seriousness, 'in all parts of the world; I have
178.17 known brave men -- famous ones! Allez! ...' He
178.18 drank carelessly.... 'Brave -- you conceive -- in
178.19 the Service -- one has got to be -- the trade demands
178.20 it (le metier veux ça). Is it not so?' he appealed to
178.21 me reasonably. 'En bien! Each of them -- I say
178.22 each of them, if he were an honest man -- bien
178.23 entendu -- would confess that there is a point --
178.24 there is a point -- for the best of us -- there is some-
178.25 where a point when you let go everything (vous
178.26 lachez tout). And you have got to live with that
178.27 truth -- do you see? Given a certain combination
178.28 of circumstances, fear is sure to come. Abominable
178.29 funk (un trac epouvantable). And even for those
178.30 who do not believe this truth there is fear all
179.01 the same -- the fear of themselves. Absolutely so.
179.02 Trust me. Yes. Yes.... At my age one knows
179.03 what one is talking about -- que diable! ...' He
179.04 had delivered himself of all this as immovably as
179.05 though he had been the mouthpiece of abstract
179.06 wisdom, but at this point he heightened the effect
179.07 of detachment by beginning to twirl his thumbs
179.08 slowly. 'It's evident -- parbleu!' he continued;
179.09 'for, make up your mind as much as you like, even
179.10 a simple headache or a fit of indigestion (un derange-
179.11 ment d'estomac) is enough to ... Take me, for
179.12 instance -- I have made my proofs. Eh bien! I,
179.13 who am speaking to you, once ...'
179.14 "He drained his glass and returned to his
179.15 twirling. 'No, no; one does not die of it,' he
179.16 pronounced finally, and when I found he did not
179.17 mean to proceed with the personal anecdote, I was
179.18 extremely disappointed; the more so as it was not
179.19 the sort of story, you know, one could very well
179.20 press him for. I sat silent, and he too, as if nothing
179.21 could please him better. Even his thumbs were
179.22 still now. Suddenly his lips began to move.
179.23 'That is so,' he resumed placidly. 'Man is born
179.24 a coward (L'homme est né poltron). It is a difficulty
179.25 -- parbleu! It would be too easy otherwise. But
179.26 habit -- habit -- necessity -- do you see? -- the eye of
179.27 others -- voila. One puts up with it. And then
179.28 the example of others who are no better than your-
179.29 self, and yet make good countenance....'
179.30 "His voice ceased.
180.01 "'That young man -- you will observe -- had
180.02 none of these inducements -- at least at the moment,'
180.03 I remarked.
180.04 "He raised his eyebrows forgivingly: 'I don't
180.05 say; I don't say. The young man in question
180.06 might have had the best dispositions -- the best
180.07 dispositions,' he repeated, wheezing a little.
180.08 "'I am glad to see you taking a lenient view,' I
180.09 said. 'His own feeling in the matter was -- ah! --
180.10 hopeful, and ...'
180.11 "The shuffle of his feet under the table inter-
180.12 rupted me. He drew up his heavy eyelids. Drew
180.13 up, I say -- no other expression can describe the
180.14 steady deliberation of the act -- and at last was dis-
180.15 closed completely to me. I was confronted by two
180.16 narrow grey circlets, like two tiny steel rings around
180.17 the profound blackness of the pupils. The sharp
180.18 glance, coming from that massive body, gave a
180.19 notion of extreme efficiency, like a razor-edge on a

180.20 battle-axe. 'Pardon,' he said punctiliously. His
180.21 right hand went up, and he swayed forward.
180.22 'Allow me ... I contended that one may get on
180.23 knowing very well that one's courage does not
180.24 come of itself (ne vient pas tout seul). There's
180.25 nothing much in that to get upset about. One truth
180.26 the more ought not to make life impossible....
180.27 But the honour -- the honour, monsieur! ... The
180.28 honour ... that is real -- that is! And what life
180.29 may be worth when' ... he got on his feet with
180.30 a ponderous impetuosity, as a startled ox might
181.01 scramble up from the grass ... 'when the honour
181.02 is gone -- ah ça! par exemple -- I can offer no opinion.
181.03 I can offer no opinion -- because -- monsieur -- I know
181.04 nothing of it.'
181.05 "I had risen, too, and, trying to throw infinite
181.06 politeness into our attitudes, we faced each other
181.07 mutely, like two china dogs on a mantelpiece. Hang
181.08 the fellow! he had pricked the bubble. The blight
181.09 of futility that lies in wait for men's speeches had
181.10 fallen upon our conversation, and made it a thing
181.11 of empty sounds. 'Very well,' I said, with a dis-
181.12 concerted smile, 'but couldn't it reduce itself to
181.13 not being found out?' He made as if to retort
181.14 readily, but when he spoke he had changed his
181.15 mind. 'This, monsieur, is too fine for me -- much
181.16 above me -- I don't think about it.' He bowed
181.17 heavily over his cap, which he held before him by
181.18 the peak, between the thumb and the forefinger of
181.19 his wounded hand. I bowed, too. We bowed
181.20 together: we scraped our feet at each other with
181.21 much ceremony, while a dirty specimen of a waiter
181.22 looked on critically, as though he had paid for the
181.23 performance. 'Serviteur,' said the Frenchman.
181.24 Another scrape. 'Monsieur' ... 'Monsieur....'
181.25 The glass door swung behind his burly back. I
181.26 saw the southerly buster get hold of him and drive
181.27 him down wind with his hand to his head, his
181.28 shoulders braced, and the tails of his coat blown
181.29 hard against his legs.
181.30 "I sat down again alone and discouraged -- dis-
182.01 couraged about Jim's case. If you wonder that
182.02 after more than three years it had preserved its
182.03 actuality, you must know that I had seen him only
182.04 very lately. I had come straight from Samarang,
182.05 where I had loaded a cargo for Sydney: an utterly
182.06 uninteresting bit of business, -- what Charley here
182.07 would call one of my rational transactions, -- and in
182.08 Samarang I had seen something of Jim. He was
182.09 then working for De Jongh, on my recommendation.
182.10 Water-clerk. 'My representative afloat,' as De
182.11 Jongh called him. You can't imagine a mode of
182.12 life more barren of consolation, less capable of being
182.13 invested with a spark of glamour -- unless it be the
182.14 business of an insurance canvasser. Little Bob
182.15 Stanton -- Charley here knew him well -- had gone
182.16 through that experience. The same who got
182.17 drowned afterwards trying to save a lady's-maid
182.18 in the Sephora disaster. A case of collision on a
182.19 hazy morning off the Spanish coast, you may remem-
182.20 ber. All the passengers had been packed tidily
182.21 into the boats and shoved clear of the ship when
182.22 Bob sheered alongside again and scrambled back
182.23 on deck to fetch that girl. How she had been left
182.24 behind I can't make out; anyhow, she had gone
182.25 completely crazy -- wouldn't leave the ship -- held
182.26 to the rail like grim death. The wrestling-match
182.27 could be seen plainly from the boats; but poor
182.28 Bob was the shortest chief mate in the merchant
182.29 service, and the woman stood five feet ten in her
182.30 shoes and was as strong as a horse, I've been told.
183.01 So it went on, pull devil, pull baker, the wretched
183.02 girl screaming all the time, and Bob letting out a yell
183.03 now and then to warn his boat to keep well clear of
183.04 the ship. One of the hands told me, hiding a smile
183.05 at the recollection, 'It was for all the world, sir,
183.06 like a naughty youngster fighting with his mother.'
183.07 The same old chap said that 'At the last we could
183.08 see that Mr. Stanton had given up hauling at the
183.09 gal, and just stood by looking at her, watchful-like.
183.10 We thought afterwards he must 'ave been reckoning
183.11 that, maybe, the rush of water would tear her away
183.12 from the rail by and by and give him a show to save
183.13 her. We daren't come alongside for our life; and
183.14 after a bit the old ship went down all on a sudden
183.15 with a lurch to starboard -- plop. The suck in was
183.16 something awful. We never saw anything alive or
183.17 dead come up.' Poor Bob's spell of shore-life had
183.18 been one of the complications of a love affair, I
183.19 believe. He fondly hoped he had done with the sea

213

183.20 for ever, and made sure he had got hold of all the
183.21 bliss on earth, but it came to canvassing in the end.
183.22 Some cousin of his in Liverpool put him up to it.
183.23 He used to tell us his experiences in that line. He
183.24 made us laugh till we cried, and, not altogether
183.25 displeased at the effect, undersized and bearded to
183.26 the waist like a gnome, he would tiptoe amongst
183.27 us and say, 'It's all very well for you beggars to
183.28 laugh, but my immortal soul was shrivelled down to
183.29 the size of a parched pea after a week of that work.'
183.30 I don't know how Jim's soul accommodated itself
184.01 to the new conditions of his life -- I was kept too
184.02 busy in getting him something to do that would keep
184.03 body and soul together -- but I am pretty certain his
184.04 adventurous fancy was suffering all the pangs of
184.05 starvation. It had certainly nothing to feed upon
184.06 in this new calling. It was distressing to see him
184.07 at it, though he tackled it with a stubborn serenity
184.08 for which I must give him full credit. I kept my
184.09 eye on his shabby plodding with a sort of notion
184.10 that it was a punishment for the heroics of his
184.11 fancy -- an expiation for his craving after more
184.12 glamour than he could carry. He had loved too well
184.13 to imagine himself a glorious racehorse, and now he
184.14 was condemned to toil without honour like a coster-
184.15 monger's donkey. He did it very well. He shut
184.16 himself in, put his head down, said never a word.
184.17 Very well; very well indeed -- except for certain
184.18 fantastic and violent outbreaks, on the deplorable
184.19 occasions when the irrepressible Patna case cropped
184.20 up. Unfortunately, that scandal of the Eastern seas
184.21 would not die out. And this is the reason why I
184.22 could never feel I had done with Jim for good.
184.23 "I sat thinking of him after the French lieu-
184.24 tenant had left, not, however, in connection with
184.25 De Jongh's cool and gloomy backshop, where we
184.26 had hurriedly shaken hands not very long ago, but
184.27 as I had seen him years before in the last flickers of
184.28 the candle, alone with me in the long gallery of the
184.29 Malabar House, with the chill and the darkness of
184.30 the night at his back. The respectable sword of
185.01 his country's law was suspended over his head.
185.02 To-morrow -- or was it to-day? (midnight had
185.03 slipped by long before we parted) -- the marble--
185.04 faced police magistrate, after distributing fines and
185.05 terms of imprisonment in the assault-and-battery
185.06 case, would take up the awful weapon and smite
185.07 his bowed neck. Our communion in the night was
185.08 uncommonly like a last vigil with a condemned man.
185.09 He was guilty, too. He was guilty -- as I had told
185.10 myself repeatedly, guilty and done for; nevertheless,
185.11 I wished to spare him the mere detail of a formal
185.12 execution. I don't pretend to explain the reasons
185.13 of my desire -- I don't think I could; but if you
185.14 haven't got a sort of notion by this time, then I
185.15 must have been very obscure in my narrative, or
185.16 you too sleepy to seize upon the sense of my words.
185.17 I don't defend my morality. There was no morality
185.18 in the impulse which induced me to lay before him
185.19 Brierly's plan of evasion -- I may call it -- in all its
185.20 primitive simplicity. There were the rupees --
185.21 absolutely ready in my pocket and very much
185.22 at his service. Oh! a loan; a loan, of course --
185.23 and if an introduction to a man (in Rangoon) who
185.24 could put some work in his way ... Why! with
185.25 the greatest pleasure. I had pen, ink, and paper in
185.26 my room on the first floor. And even while I was
185.27 speaking I was impatient to begin the letter: day,
185.28 month, year, 2.30 a.m.... for the sake of our old
185.29 friendship I ask you to put some work in the way of
185.30 Mr. James So-and-so, in whom, etc. etc.... I
186.01 was even ready to write in that strain about him. If
186.02 he had not enlisted my sympathies he had done
186.03 better for himself -- he had gone to the very fount
186.04 and origin of that sentiment, he had reached the
186.05 secret sensibility of my egoism. I am concealing
186.06 nothing from you, because were I to do so my action
186.07 would appear more unintelligible than any man's
186.08 action has the right to be, and -- in the second place --
186.09 to-morrow you will forget my sincerity along with
186.10 the other lessons of the past. In this transaction,
186.11 to speak grossly and precisely, I was the irre-
186.12 proachable man; but the subtle intentions of my
186.13 immorality were defeated by the moral simplicity of
186.14 the criminal. No doubt he was selfish, too, but his
186.15 selfishness had a higher origin, a more lofty aim.
186.16 I discovered that, say what I would, he was eager
186.17 to go through the ceremony of execution; and I
186.18 didn't say much, for I felt that in argument his
186.19 youth would tell against me heavily: he believed

186.20 where I had already ceased to doubt. There was
186.21 something fine in the wildness of his unexpressed,
186.22 hardly formulated hope. 'Clear out! Couldn't
186.23 think of it,' he said, with a shake of the head. 'I
186.24 make you an offer for which I neither demand nor
186.25 expect any sort of gratitude,' I said; 'you shall
186.26 repay the money when convenient, and ...'
186.27 'Awfully good of you,' he muttered, without looking
186.28 up. I watched him narrowly: the future must have
186.29 appeared horribly uncertain to him; but he did not
186.30 falter, as though indeed there had been nothing
187.01 wrong with his heart. I felt angry -- not for the
187.02 first time that night. 'The whole wretched busi-
187.03 ness,' I said, 'is bitter enough, I should think, for
187.04 man of your kind....' 'It is, it is,' he whispered
187.05 twice, with his eyes fixed on the floor. It was
187.06 heart-rending. He towered above the light, and I
187.07 could see the down on his cheek, the colour mant-
187.08 ling warm under the smooth skin of his face.
187.09 Believe me or not, I say it was outrageously heart--
187.10 rending. It provoked me to brutality. 'Yes,' I
187.11 said; 'and allow me to confess that I am totally
187.12 unable to imagine what advantage you can expect
187.13 from this licking of the dregs.' 'Advantage!' he
187.14 murmured out of his stillness. 'I am dashed if I
187.15 do,' I said, enraged. 'I've been trying to tell you
187.16 all there is in it,' he went on slowly, as if meditati‐
187.17 something unanswerable. 'But after all, it is my
187.18 trouble.' I opened my mouth to retort, and dis-
187.19 covered suddenly that I'd lost all confidence in
187.20 myself; and it was as if he, too, had given me up,
187.21 for he mumbled like a man thinking half aloud.
187.22 'Went away ... went into hospitals.... Not
187.23 one of them would face it.... They ...' He
187.24 moved his hand slightly to imply disdain. 'But
187.25 I've got to get over this thing, and I mustn't shirk
187.26 any of it or ... I won't shirk any of it.' He
187.27 was silent. He gazed as though he had been
187.28 haunted. His unconscious face reflected the passing
187.29 expressions of scorn, of despair, of resolution --
187.30 reflected them in turn, as a magic mirror would
188.01 reflect the gliding passage of unearthly shapes.
188.02 He lived surrounded by deceitful ghosts, by austere
188.03 shades. 'Oh, nonsense, my dear fellow!' I began.
188.04 He had a movement of impatience. 'You don't
188.05 seem to understand,' he said incisively; then
188.06 looking at me without a wink, 'I may have jumped,
188.07 but I don't run away.' 'I meant no offence,' I
188.08 said; and added stupidly, 'Better men than you
188.09 have found it expedient to run, at times.' He
188.10 coloured all over, while in my confusion I half
188.11 choked myself with my own tongue. 'Perhaps so,'
188.12 he said at last; 'I am not good enough; I can't
188.13 afford it. I am bound to fight this thing down -- I
188.14 am fighting it now.' I got out of my chair and felt
188.15 stiff all over. The silence was embarrassing, and to
188.16 put an end to it I imagined nothing better but to
188.17 remark, 'I had no idea it was so late,' in an airy tone
188.18 ... 'I dare say you have had enough of this,' he
188.19 said brusquely: 'and to tell you the truth' -- he
188.20 began to look round for his hat -- 'so have I.'
188.21 "Well! he had refused this unique offer. He
188.22 had struck aside my helping hand; he was ready to
188.23 go now, and beyond the balustrade the night seemed
188.24 to wait for him very still, as though he had been
188.25 marked down for its prey. I heard his voice. 'Ah!
188.26 here it is.' He had found his hat. For a few
188.27 seconds we hung in the wind. 'What will you do
188.28 after -- after? ...' I asked very low. 'Go to the
188.29 dogs as likely as not,' he answered in a gruff mutter.
188.30 I had recovered my wits in a measure, and judged
189.01 best to take it lightly. 'Pray remember,' I said,
189.02 'that I should like very much to see you again before
189.03 you go.' 'I don't know what's to prevent you.
189.04 The damned thing won't make me invisible,' he said
189.05 with intense bitterness, -- 'no such luck.' And then
189.06 at the moment of taking leave he treated me to a
189.07 ghastly muddle of dubious stammers and movements,
189.08 to an awful display of hesitations. God forgive
189.09 him -- me! He had taken it into his fanciful head
189.10 that I was likely to make some difficulty as to shaking
189.11 hands. It was too awful for words. I believe I
189.12 shouted suddenly at him as you would bellow to a
189.13 man you saw about to walk over a cliff; I remember
189.14 our voices being raised, the appearance of a miserable
189.15 grin on his face, a crushing clutch on my hand, a
189.16 nervous laugh. The candle spluttered out, and the
189.17 thing was over at last, with a groan that floated up
189.18 to me in the dark. He got himself away somehow.
189.19 The night swallowed his form. He was a horrible

189.20 bungler. Horrible. I heard the quick crunch--
189.21 crunch of the gravel under his boots. He was
189.22 running. Absolutely running, with nowhere to go
189.23 to. And he was not yet four-and-twenty."
190.01 "I SLEPT little, hurried over my breakfast,
190.02 and after a slight hesitation gave up my
190.03 early morning visit to my ship. It was
190.04 really very wrong of me, because, though my chief
190.05 mate was an excellent man all round, he was the
190.06 victim of such black imaginings that if he did not
190.07 get a letter from his wife at the expected time he
190.08 would go quite distracted with rage and jealousy,
190.09 lose all grip on the work, quarrel with all hands, and
190.10 either weep in his cabin or develop such a ferocity
190.11 of temper as all but drove the crew to the verge of
190.12 mutiny. The thing had always seemed inexplicable
190.13 to me: they had been married thirteen years; I
190.14 had a glimpse of her once, and, honestly, I couldn't
190.15 conceive a man abandoned enough to plunge into
190.16 sin for the sake of such an unattractive person.
190.17 I don't know whether I have not done wrong by
190.18 refraining from putting that view before poor
190.19 Selvin: the man made a little hell on earth for
190.20 himself, and I also suffered indirectly, but some sort
190.21 of, no doubt, false delicacy prevented me. The
190.22 marital relations of seamen would make an interest-
190.23 ing subject, and I could tell you instances....
190.24 However, this is not the place, nor the time, and we
191.01 are concerned with Jim -- who was unmarried. If
191.02 his imaginative conscience or his pride; if all the
191.03 extravagant ghosts and austere shades that were the
191.04 disastrous familiars of his youth would not let him
191.05 run away from the block, I, who of course can't
191.06 be suspected of such familiars, was irresistibly
191.07 impelled to go and see his head roll off. I wended
191.08 my way towards the court. I didn't hope to be very
191.09 much impressed or edified, or interested or even
191.10 frightened -- though, as long as there is any life before
191.11 one, a jolly good fright now and then is a salutary
191.12 discipline. But neither did I expect to be so
191.13 awfully depressed. The bitterness of his punish-
191.14 ment was in its chill and mean atmosphere. The
191.15 real significance of crime is in its being a breach of
191.16 faith with the community of mankind, and from that
191.17 point of view he was no mean traitor, but his execu-
191.18 tion was a hole-and-corner affair. There was no
191.19 high scaffolding, no scarlet cloth (did they have
191.20 scarlet cloth on Tower Hill? They should have
191.21 had), no awe-stricken multitude to be horrified at
191.22 his guilt and be moved to tears at his fate -- no
191.23 air of sombre retribution. There was, as I walked
191.24 along, the clear sunshine, a brilliance too passionate
191.25 to be consoling, the streets full of jumbled bits of
191.26 colour like a damaged kaleidoscope: yellow, green,
191.27 blue, dazzling white, the brown nudity of an un-
191.28 draped shoulder, a bullock-cart with a red canopy,
191.29 a company of native infantry in a drab body with
191.30 dark heads marching in dusty laced boots, a native
192.01 policeman in a sombre uniform of scanty cut and
192.02 belted in patent leather, who looked up at me with
192.03 orientally pitiful eyes as though his migrating spirit
192.04 were suffering exceedingly from that unforeseen --
192.05 what d'ye call 'em? -- avatar -- incarnation. Under
192.06 the shade of a lonely tree in the courtyard, the
192.07 villagers connected with the assault case sat in a
192.08 picturesque group, looking like a chromo-lithograph
192.09 of a camp in a book of Eastern travel. One missed
192.10 the obligatory thread of smoke in the foreground
192.11 and the pack-animals grazing. A blank yellow wall
192.12 rose behind overtopping the tree, reflecting the
192.13 glare. The court-room was sombre, seemed more
192.14 vast. High up in the dim space the punkahs were
192.15 swaying short to and fro, to and fro. Here and there
192.16 a draped figure, dwarfed by the bare walls, remained
192.17 without stirring amongst the rows of empty benches,
192.18 as if absorbed in pious meditation. The plaintiff,
192.19 who had been beaten, -- an obese, chocolate-coloured
192.20 man with shaved head, one fat breast bare and a
192.21 bright yellow caste-mark above the bridge of his
192.22 nose, -- sat in pompous immobility: only his eyes
192.23 glittered, rolling in the gloom, and the nostrils
192.24 dilated and collapsed violently as he breathed.
192.25 Brierly dropped into his seat looking done up, as
192.26 though he had spent the night in sprinting on a
192.27 cinder-track. The pious sailing-ship skipper ap-
192.28 peared excited and made uneasy movements, as if
192.29 restraining with difficulty an impulse to stand up
192.30 and exhort us earnestly to prayer and repentance.
193.01 The head of the magistrate, delicately pale under the
193.02 neatly arranged hair, resembled the head of a hopeless

193.03 invalid after he had been washed and brushed and
193.04 propped up in bed. He moved aside the vase of
193.05 flowers -- a bunch of purple with a few pink blossoms
193.06 on long stalks -- and seizing in both hands a long
193.07 sheet of bluish paper, ran his eye over it, propped
193.08 his forearms on the edge of the desk, and began
193.09 to read aloud in an even, distinct, and careless
193.10 voice.
193.11 "By Jove! For all my foolishness about
193.12 scaffolds and heads rolling off -- I assure you it was
193.13 infinitely worse than a beheading. A heavy sense
193.14 of finality brooded over all this, unrelieved by the
193.15 hope of rest and safety following the fall of the axe.
193.16 These proceedings had all the cold vengefulness of a
193.17 death-sentence, had all the cruelty of a sentence of
193.18 exile. This is how I looked at it that morning --
193.19 and even now I seem to see an undeniable vestige of
193.20 truth in that exaggerated view of a common occur-
193.21 rence. You may imagine how strongly I felt this
193.22 at the time. Perhaps it is for that reason that I
193.23 could not bring myself to admit the finality. The
193.24 thing was always with me, I was always eager to take
193.25 opinion on it, as though it had not been practically
193.26 settled: individual opinion -- international opinion --
193.27 by Jove! That Frenchman's, for instance. His
193.28 own country's pronouncement was uttered in the
193.29 passionless and definite phraseology a machine
193.30 would use, if machines could speak. The head
194.01 of the magistrate was half hidden by the paper, his
194.02 brow was like alabaster.
194.03 "There were several questions before the court.
194.04 The first as to whether the ship was in every respect
194.05 fit and seaworthy for the voyage. The court found
194.06 she was not. The next point, I remember, was,
194.07 whether up to the time of the accident the ship
194.08 had been navigated with proper and seamanlike care.
194.09 They said Yes to that, goodness knows why, and
194.10 then they declared that there was no evidence to
194.11 show the exact cause of the accident. A floating
194.12 derelict probably. I myself remember that a
194.13 Norwegian barque bound out with a cargo of pitch--
194.14 pine had been given up as missing about that time,
194.15 and it was just the sort of craft that would capsize
194.16 in a squall and float bottom up for months -- a kind
194.17 of maritime ghoul on the prowl to kill ships in the
194.18 dark. Such wandering corpses are common enough
194.19 in the North Atlantic, which is haunted by all the
194.20 terrors of the sea, -- fogs, icebergs, dead ships bent
194.21 upon mischief, and long, sinister gales that fasten
194.22 upon one like a vampire till all the strength and the
194.23 spirit and even hope are gone, and one feels like the
194.24 empty shell of a man. But there -- in those seas --
194.25 the incident was rare enough to resemble a special
194.26 arrangement of a malevolent providence, which,
194.27 unless it had for its object the killing of a donkey-
194.28 man and the bringing of worse than death upon
194.29 Jim, appeared an utterly aimless piece of devilry.
194.30 This view occurring to me took off my attention.
195.01 For a time I was aware of the magistrate's voice as
195.02 a sound merely; but in a moment it shaped itself
195.03 into distinct words ... 'in utter disregard of their
195.04 plain duty,' it said. The next sentence escaped
195.05 me somehow, and then ... 'abandoning in the
195.06 moment of danger the lives and property confided
195.07 to their charge' ... went on the voice evenly,
195.08 and stopped. A pair of eyes under the white fore-
195.09 head shot darkly a glance above the edge of the paper.
195.10 I looked for Jim hurriedly, as though I had expected
195.11 him to disappear. He was very still -- but he was
195.12 there. He sat pink and fair and extremely attentive.
195.13 'Therefore ...' began the voice emphatically.
195.14 He stared with parted lips, hanging upon the words
195.15 of the man behind the desk. These came out into
195.16 the stillness wafted on the wind made by the punkahs,
195.17 and I, watching for their effect upon him, caught
195.18 only the fragments of official language.... 'The
195.19 Court...Gustav So-and-so...master...native
195.20 of Germany...James So-and-so...mate....
195.21 certificates cancelled.' A silence fell. The magis-
195.22 trate had dropped the paper, and leaning sideways
195.23 on the arm of his chair, began to talk with Brierly
195.24 easily. People started to move out; others were
195.25 pushing in, and I also made for the door. Outside
195.26 I stood still, and when Jim passed me on his way
195.27 to the gate, I caught at his arm and detained him.
195.28 The look he gave discomposed me, as though I had
195.29 been responsible for his state: he looked at me as if
195.30 I had been the embodied evil of life. 'It's all over,'
196.01 I stammered. 'Yes,' he said thickly. 'And now
196.02 let no man...' He jerked his arm out of my

196.03 grasp. I watched his back as he went away. It
196.04 was a long street, and he remained in sight for some
196.05 time. He walked rather slow, and straddling his legs
196.06 a little, as if he had found it difficult to keep a
196.07 straight line. Just before I lost him I fancied he
196.08 staggered a bit.
196.09 "'Man overboard,' said a deep voice behind me.
196.10 Turning round, I saw a fellow I knew slightly, a
196.11 West Australian; Chester was his name. He, too,
196.12 had been looking after Jim. He was a man with an
196.13 immense girth of chest, a rugged, clean-shaved face
196.14 of mahogany colour, and two blunt tufts of iron-
196.15 grey, thick wiry hairs on his upper lip. He had been
196.16 pearler, wrecker, trader, whaler, too, I believe;
196.17 in his own words -- anything and everything a man
196.18 may be at sea, but a pirate. The Pacific, north and
196.19 south, was his proper hunting-ground; but he had
196.20 wandered so far afield looking for a cheap steamer
196.21 to buy. Lately he had discovered -- so he said -- a
196.22 guano island somewhere, but its approaches were
196.23 dangerous, and the anchorage, such as it was, could
196.24 not be considered safe, to say the least of it. 'As
196.25 good as a gold-mine,' he would exclaim. 'Right
196.26 bang in the middle of the Walpole Reefs, and if it's
196.27 true enough that you can get no holding-ground
196.28 anywhere in less than forty fathom, then what of
196.29 that? There are the hurricanes, too. But it's a
196.30 first-rate thing. As good as a gold-mine -- better!
197.01 Yet there's not a fool of them that will see it. I
197.02 can't get a skipper or a shipowner to go near the
197.03 place. So I made up my mind to cart the blessed
197.04 stuff myself....' This was what he required a
197.05 steamer for, and I knew he was just then negotiat-
197.06 ing enthusiastically with a Parsee firm for an old,
197.07 brig-rigged, sea-anachronism of ninety horse-power.
197.08 We had met and spoken together several times.
197.09 He looked knowingly after Jim. 'Takes it to
197.10 heart?' he asked scornfully. 'Very much,' I said.
197.11 'Then he's no good,' he opined. 'What's all the
197.12 to-do about? A bit of ass's skin. That never yet
197.13 made a man. You must see things exactly as they
197.14 are -- if you don't, you may just as well give in at
197.15 once. You will never do anything in this world.
197.16 Look at me. I made it a practice never to take
197.17 anything to heart.' 'Yes,' I said, 'you see things
197.18 as they are.' 'I wish I could see my partner
197.19 coming along, that's what I wish to see,' he said.
197.20 'Know my partner? Old Robinson. Yes; the
197.21 Robinson. Don't you know? The notorious
197.22 Robinson. The man who smuggled more opium
197.23 and bagged more seals in his time than any loose
197.24 Johnny now alive. They say he used to board the
197.25 sealing-schooners up Alaska way when the fog was
197.26 so thick that the Lord God, He alone, could tell
197.27 one man from another. Holy-Terror Robinson.
197.28 That's the man. He is with me in that guano thing.
197.29 The best chance he ever came across in his life.'
197.30 He put his lips to my ear. 'Cannibal? -- well,
198.01 they used to give him the name years and years
198.02 ago. You remember the story? A shipwreck on
198.03 the west side of Stewart Island; that's right;
198.04 seven of them got ashore, and it seems they did not
198.05 get on very well together. Some men are too can-
198.06 tankerous for anything -- don't know how to make
198.07 the best of a bad job -- don't see things as they are --
198.08 as they are, my boy! And then what's the conse-
198.09 quence? Obvious! Trouble, trouble; as likely
198.10 as not a knock on the head; and serve 'em right, too.
198.11 That sort is the most useful when it's dead. The
198.12 story goes that a boat of Her Majesty's ship Wolverine
198.13 found him kneeling on the kelp, naked as the day he
198.14 was born, and chanting some psalm-tune or other;
198.15 light snow was falling at the time. He waited till the
198.16 boat was an oar's length from the shore, and then
198.17 up and away. They chased him for an hour up and
198.18 down the boulders, till a marine flung a stone that
198.19 took him behind the ear providentially and knocked
198.20 him senseless. Alone? Of course. But that's like
198.21 that tale of sealing-schooners; the Lord God knows
198.22 the right and the wrong of that story. The cutter
198.23 did not investigate much. They wrapped him in a
198.24 boat-cloak and took him off as quick as they could,
198.25 with a dark night coming on, the weather threaten-
198.26 ing, and the ship firing recall guns every five
198.27 minutes. Three weeks afterwards he was as well as
198.28 ever. He didn't allow any fuss that was made on
198.29 shore to upset him; he just shut his lips tight, and
198.30 let people screech. It was bad enough to have lost
199.01 his ship, and all he was worth besides, without
199.02 paying attention to the hard names they called him.

199.03 That's the man for me.' He lifted his arm for a
199.04 signal to some one down the street. 'He's got a
199.05 little money, so I had to let him into my thing.
199.06 Had to! It would have been sinful to throw away
199.07 such a find, and I was cleaned out myself. It cut
199.08 me to the quick, but I could see the matter just
199.09 as it was, and if I must share -- thinks I -- with any
199.10 man, then give me Robinson. I left him at break-
199.11 fast in the hotel to come to court, because I've an
199.12 idea.... Ah! Good morning, Captain Robin-
199.13 son.... Friend of mine, Captain Robinson.'
199.14 "An emaciated patriarch in a suit of white drill,
199.15 a solar topi with a green-lined rim on a head trem-
199.16 bling with age, joined us after crossing the street in
199.17 a trotting shuffle, and stood propped with both hands
199.18 on the handle of an umbrella. A white beard with
199.19 amber streaks hung lumpily down to his waist. He
199.20 blinked his creased eyelids at me in a bewildered
199.21 way. 'How do you do? How do you do?' he
199.22 piped amiably, and tottered. 'A little deaf,' said
199.23 Chester aside. 'Did you drag him over six
199.24 thousand miles to get a cheap steamer?' I asked.
199.25 'I would have taken him twice round the world as
199.26 soon as look at him,' said Chester with immense
199.27 energy. 'The steamer will be the making of us,
199.28 my lad. Is it my fault that every skipper and
199.29 shipowner in the whole of blessed Australasia turns
199.30 out a blamed fool? Once I talked for three hours to
200.01 a man in Auckland. "Send a ship," I said, "send
200.02 a ship. I'll give you half of the first cargo for your-
200.03 self, free gratis for nothing -- just to make a good
200.04 start." Says he, "I wouldn't do it if there was no
200.05 other place on earth to send a ship to." Perfect
200.06 ass, of course. Rocks, currents, no anchorage,
200.07 sheer cliff to lay to, no insurance company would take
200.08 the risk, didn't see how he could get loaded under
200.09 three years. Ass! I nearly went on my knees to
200.10 him. "But look at the thing as it is," says I.
200.11 "Damn rocks and hurricanes. Look at it as it is.
200.12 There's quano there Queensland sugar-planters
200.13 would fight for -- fight for on the quay, I tell you....
200.14 What can you do with a fool? ... "That's
200.15 one of your little jokes, Chester," he says....
200.16 Joke! I could have wept. Ask Captain Robinson
200.17 here.... And there was another shipowning
200.18 fellow -- a fat chap in a white waistcoat in Welling-
200.19 ton, who seemed to think I was up to some swindle
200.20 or other. "I don't know what sort of fool you're
200.21 looking for," he says, "but I am busy just now.
200.22 Good morning." I longed to take him in my two
200.23 hands and smash him through the window of his own
200.24 office. But I didn't. I was as mild as a curate.
200.25 "Think of it," says I. "Do think it over. I'll call
200.26 to-morrow." He grunted something about being
200.27 "out all day." On the stairs I felt ready to beat
200.28 my head against the wall from vexation. Captain
200.29 Robinson here can tell you. It was awful to think
200.30 of all that lovely stuff lying waste under the sun --
201.01 stuff that would send the sugar-cane shooting sky--
201.02 high. The making of Queensland! The making
201.03 of Queensland! And in Brisbane, where I went to
201.04 have a last try, they gave me the name of a lunatic.
201.05 Idiots! The only sensible man I came across was
201.06 the cabman who drove me about. A broken-down
201.07 swell he was, I fancy. Hey! Captain Robinson?
201.08 You remember I told you about my cabby in Bris-
201.09 bane -- don't you? The chap had a wonderful eye
201.10 for things. He saw it all in a jiffy. It was a real
201.11 pleasure to talk with him. One evening after a
201.12 devil of a day amongst shipowners I felt so bad
201.13 that, says I, "I must get drunk. Come along; I
201.14 must get drunk, or I'll go mad." "I am your man,"
201.15 he says; "go ahead." I don't know what I would
201.16 have done without him. Hey! Captain Robin-
201.17 son.'
201.18 "He poked the ribs of his partner. 'He! he!
201.19 he!' laughed the Ancient, looked aimlessly down
201.20 the street, then peered at me doubtfully with sad,
201.21 dim pupils.... 'He! he! he!' ... He leaned
201.22 heavier on the umbrella, and dropped his gaze on the
201.23 ground. I needn't tell you I had tried to get away
201.24 several times, but Chester had foiled every attempt
201.25 by simply catching hold of my coat. 'One minute.
201.26 I've a notion.' 'What's your infernal notion?' I
201.27 exploded at last. 'If you think I am going in with
201.28 you ...' 'No, no, my boy. Too late, if you
201.29 wanted ever so much. We've got a steamer.'
201.30 'You've got the ghost of a steamer,' I said. 'Good
202.01 enough for a start -- there's no superior nonsense
202.02 about us. Is there, Captain Robinson?' 'No!

202.03 no! no!' croaked the old man without lifting his
202.04 eyes, and the senile tremble of his head became almost
202.05 fierce with determination. 'I understand you know
202.06 that young chap,' said Chester, with a nod at the
202.07 street from which Jim had disappeared long ago.
202.08 'He's been having grub with you in the Malabar
202.09 last night -- so I was told.'
202.10 "I said that was true, and after remarking that
202.11 he, too, liked to live well and in style, only that, for
202.12 the present, he had to be saving of every penny --
202.13 'none too many for the business! Isn't that so,
202.14 Captain Robinson?' -- he squared his shoulders and
202.15 stroked his dumpy moustache, while the notorious
202.16 Robinson, coughing at his side, clung more than
202.17 ever to the handle of the umbrella, and seemed ready
202.18 to subside passively into a heap of old bones. 'You
202.19 see, the old chap has all the money,' whispered
202.20 Chester confidentially. 'I've been cleaned out
202.21 trying to engineer the dratted thing. But wait a
202.22 bit, wait a bit. The good time is coming....'
202.23 He seemed suddenly astonished at the signs of im-
202.24 patience I gave. 'Oh, crakee!' he cried; 'I am
202.25 telling you of the biggest thing that ever was, and
202.26 you ...' 'I have an appointment,' I pleaded
202.27 mildly. 'What of that?' he asked with genuine
202.28 surprise; 'let it wait.' 'That's exactly what I am
202.29 doing now,' I remarked; 'hadn't you better tell
202.30 me what it is you want?' 'Buy twenty hotels
203.01 like that,' he growled to himself; 'and every joker
203.02 boarding in them, too -- twenty times over.' He
203.03 lifted his head smartly. 'I want that young chap.'
203.04 'I don't understand,' I said. 'He's no good, is
203.05 he?' said Chester crisply. 'I know nothing
203.06 about it,' I protested. 'Why, you told me yourself
203.07 he was taking it to heart,' argued Chester. 'Well,
203.08 in my opinion a chap who ... Anyhow, he can't
203.09 be much good; but then you see I am on the look
203.10 out for somebody, and I've just got a thing that will
203.11 suit him. I'll give him a job on my island.' He
203.12 nodded significantly. 'I'm going to dump forty
203.13 coolies there -- if I've got to steal 'em. Somebody
203.14 must work the stuff. Oh! I mean to act square:
203.15 wooden shed, corrugated-iron roof -- I know a man
203.16 in Hobart who will take my bill at six months for the
203.17 materials. I do. Honour bright. Then there's the
203.18 water-supply. I'll have to fly round and get some-
203.19 body to trust me for half a dozen second-hand iron
203.20 tanks. Catch rain-water, hey? Let him take
203.21 charge. Make him supreme boss over the coolies.
203.22 Good idea, isn't it? What do you say?' 'There
203.23 are whole years when not a drop of rain falls on
203.24 Walpole,' I said, too amazed to laugh. He bit his
203.25 lip and seemed bothered. 'Oh, well, I will fix up
203.26 something for them -- or land a supply. Hang it
203.27 all! That's not the question.'
203.28 "I said nothing. I had a rapid vision of Jim
203.29 perched on a shadowless rock, up to his knees in
203.30 guano, with the screams of sea-birds in his ears,
204.01 the incandescent ball of the sun above his head;
204.02 the empty sky and the empty ocean all a-quiver,
204.03 simmering together in the heat as far as the eye could
204.04 reach. 'I wouldn't advise my worst enemy ...'
204.05 I began. 'What's the matter with you?' cried
204.06 Chester; 'I mean to give him a good screw --
204.07 that is, as soon as the thing is set going, of course.
204.08 It's as easy as falling off a log. Simply nothing to
204.09 do; two six-shooters in his belt.... Surely he
204.10 wouldn't be afraid of anything forty coolies could
204.11 do -- with two six-shooters and he the only armed
204.12 man, too! It's much better than it looks. I want
204.13 you to help me to talk him over.' 'No!' I shouted.
204.14 Old Robinson lifted his bleared eyes dismally for a
204.15 moment, Chester looked at me with infinite con-
204.16 tempt. 'So you wouldn't advise him?' he uttered
204.17 slowly. 'Certainly not,' I answered, as indignant as
204.18 though he had requested me to help murder some-
204.19 body; 'moreover, I am sure he wouldn't. He is
204.20 badly cut up, but he isn't mad as far as I know.'
204.21 'He is no earthly good for anything,' Chester
204.22 mused aloud. 'He would just have done for me.
204.23 If you only could see a thing as it is, you would
204.24 see it's the very thing for him. And besides ...
204.25 Why! it's the most splendid, sure chance ...'
204.26 He got angry suddenly. 'I must have a man.
204.27 There! ...' He stamped his foot and smiled un-
204.28 pleasantly. 'Anyhow, I could guarantee the island
204.29 wouldn't sink under him -- and I believe he is a bit
204.30 particular on that point.' 'Good morning,' I said
205.01 curtly. He looked at me as though I had been
205.02 an incomprehensible fool.... 'Must be moving,

205.03 Captain Robinson,' he yelled suddenly into the old
205.04 man's ear. 'These Parsee Johnnies are waiting
205.05 for us to clinch the bargain.' He took his partner
205.06 under the arm with a firm grip, swung him round,
205.07 and, unexpectedly, leered at me over his shoulder.
205.08 'I was trying to do him a kindness,' he asserted,
205.09 with an air and tone that made my blood boil.
205.10 'Thank you for nothing -- in his name,' I rejoined.
205.11 'Oh, you are devilish smart!' he sneered; 'but
205.12 you are like the rest of them. Too much in the
205.13 clouds. See what you will do with him.' 'I don't
205.14 know that I want to do anything with him.' 'Don't
205.15 you?' he spluttered; his grey moustache bristled
205.16 with anger, and by his side the notorious Robinson,
205.17 propped on the umbrella, stood with his back to me,
205.18 as patient and still as a worn-out cab-horse. 'I
205.19 haven't found a guano island,' I said. 'It's my
205.20 belief you wouldn't know one if you were led right
205.21 up to it by the hand,' he riposted quickly; 'and in
205.22 this world you've got to see a thing first, before you
205.23 can make use of it. Got to see it through and
205.24 through at that, neither more nor less.' 'And get
205.25 others to see it, too,' I insinuated, with a glance at
205.26 the bowed back by his side. Chester snorted at me.
205.27 'His eyes are right enough -- don't you worry.
205.28 He ain't a puppy.' 'Oh dear, no!' I said. 'Come
205.29 along, Captain Robinson,' he shouted, with a sort
205.30 of bullying deference under the rim of the old man's
206.01 hat; the Holy Terror gave a submissive little jump.
206.02 The ghost of a steamer was waiting for them,
206.03 Fortune on that fair isle! They made a curious
206.04 pair of Argonauts. Chester strode on leisurely,
206.05 well set up, portly, and of conquering mien; the
206.06 other, long, wasted, drooping, and hooked to his
206.07 arm, shuffled his withered shanks with desperate
206.08 haste."
207.01 "I DID not start in search of Jim at once, only
207.02 because I had really an appointment which
207.03 I could not neglect. Then, as ill-luck would
207.04 have it, in my agent's office I was fastened upon by a
207.05 fellow fresh from Madagascar with a little scheme for
207.06 a wonderful piece of business. It had something to
207.07 do with cattle and cartridges and a Prince Ravonalo
207.08 something; but the pivot of the whole affair was
207.09 the stupidity of some admiral -- Admiral Pierre, I
207.10 think. Everything turned on that, and the chap
207.11 couldn't find words strong enough to express his
207.12 confidence. He had globular eyes starting out of
207.13 his head with a fishy glitter, bumps on his forehead,
207.14 and wore his long hair brushed back without a
207.15 parting. He had a favourite phrase which he kept
207.16 on repeating triumphantly, 'The minimum of risk
207.17 with the maximum of profit is my motto. What?'
207.18 He made my head ache, spoiled my tiffin, but got
207.19 his own out of me all right; and as soon as I had
207.20 shaken him off, I made straight for the waterside.
207.21 I caught sight of Jim leaning over the parapet of
207.22 the quay. Three native boatmen quarrelling over
207.23 five annas were making an awful row at his elbow.
207.24 He didn't hear me come up, but spun round as if the
207.25 slight contact of my finger had released a catch. 'I
208.01 was looking,' he stammered. I don't remember
208.02 what I said, not much anyhow, but he made no
208.03 difficulty in following me to the hotel.
208.04 "He followed me as manageable as a little child,
208.05 with an obedient air, with no sort of manifestation,
208.06 rather as though he had been waiting for me there to
208.07 come along and carry him off. I need not have been
208.08 so surprised as I was at his tractability. On all the
208.09 round earth, which to some seems so big and that
208.10 others affect to consider as rather smaller than a
208.11 mustard-seed, he had no place where he could --
208.12 what shall I say? -- where he could withdraw.
208.13 That's it! Withdraw -- be alone with his loneliness.
208.14 He walked by my side very calm, glancing here and
208.15 there, and once turned his head to look after a Sidi-
208.16 boy fireman in a cutaway coat and yellowish trousers,
208.17 whose black face had silky gleams like a lump of
208.18 anthracite coal. I doubt, however, whether he saw
208.19 anything, or even remained all the time aware of my
208.20 companionship, because if I had not edged him to
208.21 the left here, or pulled him to the right there, I
208.22 believe he would have gone straight before him in
208.23 any direction till stopped by a wall or some other
208.24 obstacle. I steered him into my bedroom, and sat
208.25 down at once to write letters. This was the only
208.26 place in the world (unless, perhaps, the Walpole
208.27 Reef -- but that was not so handy) where he could
208.28 have it out with himself without being bothered by
208.29 the rest of the universe. The damned thing -- as he

208.30 had expressed it -- had not made him invisible, but I
209.01 behaved exactly as though he were. No sooner in my
209.02 chair I bent over my writing-desk like a medieval
209.03 scribe, and, but for the movement of the hand
209.04 holding the pen, remained anxiously quiet. I can't
209.05 say I was frightened; but I certainly kept as still
209.06 as if there had been something dangerous in the
209.07 room, that at the first hint of a movement on my
209.08 part would be provoked to pounce upon me. There
209.09 was not much in the room -- you know how these bed-
209.10 rooms are -- a sort of four-poster bedstead under a
209.11 mosquito-net, two or three chairs, the table I was
209.12 writing at, a bare floor. A glass door opened on an
209.13 upstairs verandah, and he stood with his face to it,
209.14 having a hard time with all possible privacy. Dusk
209.15 fell; I lit a candle with the greatest economy of
209.16 movement and as much prudence as though it were
209.17 an illegal proceeding. There is no doubt that he
209.18 had a very hard time of it, and so had I, even to
209.19 the point, I must own, of wishing him to the devil,
209.20 or on Walpole Reef at least. It occurred to me once
209.21 or twice that, after all, Chester was, perhaps, the
209.22 man to deal effectively with such a disaster. That
209.23 strange idealist had found a practical use for it at
209.24 once -- unerringly, as it were. It was enough to
209.25 make one suspect that, maybe, he really could see
209.26 the true aspect of things that appeared mysterious
209.27 or utterly hopeless to less imaginative persons. I
209.28 wrote and wrote; I liquidated all the arrears of my
209.29 correspondence, and then went on writing to people
209.30 who had no reason whatever to expect from me a
210.01 gossipy letter about nothing at all. At times I stole
210.02 a sidelong glance. He was rooted to the spot,
210.03 but convulsive shudders ran down his back; his
210.04 shoulders would heave suddenly. He was fighting,
210.05 he was fighting -- mostly for his breath, as it seemed.
210.06 The massive shadows, cast all one way from the
210.07 straight flame of the candle, seemed possessed of
210.08 gloomy consciousness; the immobility of the furni-
210.09 ture had to my furtive eye an air of attention. I was
210.10 becoming fanciful in the midst of my industrious
210.11 scribbling; and though, when the scratching of my
210.12 pen stopped for a moment, there was complete
210.13 silence and stillness in the room, I suffered from
210.14 that profound disturbance and confusion of thought
210.15 which is caused by a violent and menacing uproar --
210.16 of a heavy gale at sea, for instance. Some of you
210.17 may know what I mean: that mingled anxiety,
210.18 distress, and irritation with a sort of craven feeling
210.19 creeping in -- not pleasant to acknowledge, but which
210.20 gives a quite special merit to one's endurance. I
210.21 don't claim any merit for standing the stress of
210.22 Jim's emotions; I could take refuge in the letters;
210.23 I could have written to strangers if necessary.
210.24 Suddenly, as I was taking up a fresh sheet of note-
210.25 paper, I heard a low sound, the first sound that,
210.26 since we had been shut up together, had come to my
210.27 ears in the dim stillness of the room. I remained
210.28 with my head down, with my hand arrested. Those
210.29 who have kept vigil by a sick-bed have heard such
210.30 faint sounds in the stillness of the night-watches,
211.01 sounds wrung from a racked body, from a weary
211.02 soul. He pushed the glass door with such force
211.03 that all the panes rang: he stepped out, and I held
211.04 my breath, straining my ears without knowing what
211.05 else I expected to hear. He was really taking too
211.06 much to heart an empty formality which to Chester's
211.07 rigorous criticism seemed unworthy the notice of a
211.08 man who could see things as they were. An empty
211.09 formality; a piece of parchment. Well, well.
211.10 As to the inaccessible guano deposit, that was
211.11 another story altogether. One could intelligibly
211.12 break one's heart over that. A feeble burst of many
211.13 voices mingled with the tinkle of silver and glass
211.14 floated up from the dining-room below; through the
211.15 open door the outer edge of the light from my candle
211.16 fell on his back faintly; beyond all was black; he
211.17 stood on the brink of a vast obscurity, like a lonely
211.18 figure by the shore of a sombre and hopeless ocean.
211.19 There was the Walpole Reef in it -- to be sure -- a
211.20 speck in the dark void, a straw for the drowning man.
211.21 My compassion for him took the shape of the thought
211.22 that I wouldn't have liked his people to see him at
211.23 that moment. I found it trying myself. His back
211.24 was no longer shaken by his gasps; he stood straight
211.25 as an arrow, faintly visible and still; and the mean-
211.26 ing of this stillness sank to the bottom of my soul
211.27 like lead into the water, and made it so heavy that
211.28 for a second I wished heartily that the only course
211.29 left open for me was to pay for his funeral. Even

211.30 the law had done with him. To bury him would
212.01 have been such an easy kindness! It would have
212.02 been so much in accordance with the wisdom of life,
212.03 which consists in putting out of sight all the reminders
212.04 of our folly, of our weakness, of our mortality;
212.05 all that makes against our efficiency -- the memory of
212.06 our failures, the hints of our undying fears, the bodies
212.07 of our dead friends. Perhaps he did take it too much
212.08 to heart. And if so, then -- Chester's offer ...
212.09 At this point I took up a fresh sheet and began
212.10 to write resolutely. There was nothing but myself
212.11 between him and the dark ocean. I had a sense of
212.12 responsibility. If I spoke, would that motionless
212.13 and suffering youth leap into the obscurity -- clutch
212.14 at the straw? I found out how difficult it may
212.15 be sometimes to make a sound. There is a weird
212.16 power in a spoken word. And why the devil not?
212.17 I was asking myself persistently while I drove on
212.18 with my writing. All at once, on the blank page,
212.19 under the very point of the pen, the two figures
212.20 of Chester and his antique partner, very distinct
212.21 and complete, would dodge into view with stride and
212.22 gestures, as if reproduced in the field of some optical
212.23 toy. I would watch them for a while. No!
212.24 They were too phantasmal and extravagant to enter
212.25 into any one's fate. And a word carries far -- very
212.26 far -- deals destruction through time as the bullets
212.27 go flying through space. I said nothing; and he,
212.28 out there with his back to the light, as if bound and
212.29 gagged by all the invisible foes of man, made no stir
212.30 and made no sound."
213.01 "THE time was coming when I should
213.02 see him loved, trusted, admired, with a
213.03 legend of strength and prowess forming
213.04 round his name as though he had been the stuff
213.05 of a hero. It's true -- I assure you; as true as I'm
213.06 sitting here talking about him in vain. He, on his
213.07 side, had that faculty of beholding at a hint the face
213.08 of his desire and the shape of his dream, without
213.09 which the earth would know no lover and no
213.10 adventurer. He captured much honour and an
213.11 Arcadian happiness (I won't say anything about
213.12 innocence) in the bush, and it was as good to him as
213.13 the honour and the Arcadian happiness of the streets
213.14 to another man. Felicity, felicity -- how shall I
213.15 say it? -- is quaffed out of a golden cup in every
213.16 latitude: the flavour is with you -- with you alone,
213.17 and you can make it as intoxicating as you please.
213.18 He was of the sort that would drink deep, as you may
213.19 guess from what went before. I found him, if not
213.20 exactly intoxicated, then at least flushed with the
213.21 elixir at his lips. He had not obtained it at once.
213.22 There had been, as you know, a period of probation
213.23 amongst infernal ship-chandlers, during which he
213.24 had suffered and I had worried about -- about -- my
214.01 trust -- you may call it. I don't know that I am com-
214.02 pletely reassured now, after beholding him in all his
214.03 brilliance. That was my last view of him -- in a
214.04 strong light, dominating, and yet in complete accord
214.05 with his surroundings -- with the life of the forests
214.06 and with the life of men. I own that I was im-
214.07 pressed, but I must admit to myself that after all
214.08 this is not the lasting impression. He was protected
214.09 by his isolation, alone of his own superior kind, in
214.10 close touch with Nature, that keeps faith on such
214.11 easy terms with her lovers. But I cannot fix
214.12 before my eye the image of his safety. I shall
214.13 always remember him as seen through the open
214.14 door of my room, taking, perhaps, too much to heart
214.15 the mere consequences of his failure. I am pleased,
214.16 of course, that some good -- and even some splendour
214.17 --came out of my endeavours; but at times it seems
214.18 to me it would have been better for my peace of
214.19 mind if I had not stood between him and Chester's
214.20 confoundedly generous offer. I wonder what his
214.21 exuberant imagination would have made of Walpole
214.22 islet -- that hopelessly forsaken crumb of dry
214.23 land on the face of the waters! It is not likely I
214.24 would ever have heard, for I must tell you that
214.25 Chester, after calling at some Australian port to
214.26 patch up his brig-rigged sea-anachronism, steamed
214.27 out into the Pacific with a crew of twenty-two hands
214.28 all told, and the only news having a possible bearing
214.29 upon the mystery of his fate was the news of a hurri-
214.30 cane which is supposed to have swept in its course
215.01 over the Walpole shoals, a month or so afterwards.
215.02 Not a vestige of the Argonauts ever turned up;
215.03 not a sound came out of the waste. Finis! The
215.04 Pacific is the most discreet of live, hot-tempered
215.05 oceans: the chilly Antarctic can keep a secret, too,

215.06 but more in the manner of a grave.
215.07 "And there is a sense of blessed finality in such
215.08 discretion, which is what we all more or less sin-
215.09 cerely are ready to admit -- for what else is it
215.10 that makes the idea of death supportable? End!
215.11 Finis! the potent word that exorcises from the
215.12 house of life the haunting shadow of fate. This is
215.13 what -- notwithstanding the testimony of my eyes
215.14 and his own earnest assurances -- I miss when I look
215.15 back upon Jim's success. While there's life there is
215.16 hope, truly; but there is fear, too. I don't mean to
215.17 say that I regret my action, nor will I pretend that
215.18 I can't sleep o' nights in consequence; still, the
215.19 idea obtrudes itself that he made so much of his
215.20 disgrace while it is the guilt alone that matters.
215.21 He was not -- if I may say so -- clear to me. He was
215.22 not clear. And there is a suspicion he was not
215.23 clear to himself either. There were his fine
215.24 sensibilities, his fine feelings, his fine longings -- a
215.25 sort of sublimated, idealised selfishness. He was --
215.26 if you allow me to say so -- very fine; very fine --
215.27 and very unfortunate. A little coarser nature would
215.28 not have borne the strain; it would have had to
215.29 come to terms with itself -- with a sigh, with a grunt,
215.30 or even with a guffaw; a still coarser one would
216.01 have remained invulnerably ignorant and completely
216.02 uninteresting.
216.03 "But he was too interesting or too unfortunate
216.04 to be thrown to the dogs, or even to Chester. I
216.05 felt this while I sat with my face over the paper and
216.06 he fought and gasped, struggling for his breath in
216.07 that terribly stealthy way, in my room; I felt it
216.08 when he rushed out on the verandah as if to fling
216.09 himself over -- and didn't; I felt it more and more
216.10 all the time he remained outside, faintly lighted
216.11 on the background of night, as if standing on the
216.12 shore of a sombre and hopeless sea.
216.13 "An abrupt, heavy rumble made me lift my head.
216.14 The noise seemed to roll away, and suddenly a
216.15 searching and violent glare fell on the blind face
216.16 of the night. The sustained and dazzling flickers
216.17 seemed to last for an unconscionable time. The
216.18 growl of the thunder increased steadily while I
216.19 looked at him, distinct and black, planted solidly
216.20 upon the shore of a sea of light. At the moment
216.21 of greatest brilliance the darkness leaped back with
216.22 a culminating crash, and he vanished before my
216.23 dazzled eyes as utterly as though he had been blown
216.24 to atoms. A blustering sigh passed; furious hands
216.25 seemed to tear at the shrubs, shake the tops of the
216.26 trees below, slam doors, break window-panes, all
216.27 along the front of the building. He stepped in,
216.28 closing the door behind him, and found me bending
216.29 over the table: my sudden anxiety as to what he
216.30 would say was very great, and akin to a fright.
217.01 'May I have a cigarette?' he asked. I gave a push
217.02 to the box without raising my head. 'I want --
217.03 want -- tobacco,' he muttered. I became extremely
217.04 buoyant. 'Just a moment,' I grunted pleasantly.
217.05 He took a few steps here and there. 'That's over,'
217.06 I heard him say. A single distant clap of thunder
217.07 came from the sea like a gun of distress. 'The
217.08 monsoon breaks up early this year,' he remarked,
217.09 conversationally, somewhere behind me. This en-
217.10 couraged me to turn round, which I did as soon as I
217.11 had finished addressing the last envelope. He was
217.12 smoking greedily in the middle of the room, and
217.13 though he heard the stir I made, he remained with his
217.14 back to me for a time.
217.15 "'Come -- I carried it off pretty well,' he said,
217.16 wheeling suddenly. 'Something's paid off -- not
217.17 much. I wonder what's to come?' His face did not
217.18 show any emotion, only it appeared a little darkened
217.19 and swollen, as though he had been holding his
217.20 breath. He smiled reluctantly as it were, and went
217.21 on while I gazed up at him mutely.... 'Thank
217.22 you, though -- your room -- jolly convenient -- for a
217.23 chap -- badly hipped....' The rain pattered and
217.24 swished in the garden; a water-pipe (it must have
217.25 had a hole in it) performed just outside the window
217.26 a parody of blubbering woe with funny sobs and
217.27 gurgling lamentations, interrupted by jerky spasms
217.28 of silence.... 'A bit of shelter,' he mumbled, and
217.29 ceased.
217.30 "A flash of faded lightning darted in through the
218.01 black framework of the windows and ebbed out
218.02 without any noise. I was thinking how I had best
218.03 approach him (I did not want to be flung off
218.04 again) when he gave a little laugh. 'No better
218.05 than a vagabond now' ... the end of the cigar-
218.06 ette smouldered between his fingers ... 'without
218.07 a single -- single,' he pronounced slowly; 'and
218.08 yet ...' He paused; the rain fell with redoubled
218.09 violence. 'Some day one's bound to come upon
218.10 some sort of chance to get it all back again. Must!'
218.11 he whispered distinctly, glaring at my boots.
218.12 "I did not even know what it was he wished
218.13 so much to regain, what it was he had so terribly
218.14 missed. It might have been so much that it was
218.15 impossible to say. A piece of ass's skin, according
218.16 to Chester.... He looked up at me inquisitively.
218.17 'Perhaps. If life's long enough,' I muttered through
218.18 my teeth with unreasonable animosity. 'Don't
218.19 reckon too much on it.'
218.20 "'Jove! I feel as if nothing could ever touch
218.21 me,' he said in a tone of sombre conviction. 'If
218.22 this business couldn't knock me over, then there's
218.23 no fear of there being not enough time to -- climb
218.24 out, and ...' He looked upwards.
218.25 "It struck me that it is from such as he that the
218.26 great army of waifs and strays is recruited, the army
218.27 that marches down, down into all the gutters of the
218.28 earth. As soon as he left my room, that 'bit of
218.29 shelter,' he would take his place in the ranks, and
218.30 begin the journey towards the bottomless pit. I at
219.01 least had no illusions; but it was I, too, who a
219.02 moment ago had been so sure of the power of words,
219.03 and now was afraid to speak, in the same way one
219.04 dares not move for fear of losing a slippery hold.
219.05 It is when we try to grapple with another man's
219.06 intimate need that we perceive how incompre-
219.07 hensible, wavering, and misty are the beings that
219.08 share with us the sight of the stars and the warmth
219.09 of the sun. It is as if loneliness were a hard and
219.10 absolute condition of existence; the envelope of
219.11 flesh and blood on which our eyes are fixed melts
219.12 before the outstretched hand, and there remains
219.13 only the capricious, inconsolable, and elusive spirit
219.14 that no eye can follow, no hand can grasp. It was
219.15 the fear of losing him that kept me silent, for it was
219.16 borne upon me suddenly and with unaccountable
219.17 force that should I let him slip away into the dark-
219.18 ness I would never forgive myself.
219.19 "'Well. Thanks -- once more. You've been
219.20 -- er -- uncommonly -- really there's no word to ...
219.21 Uncommonly! I don't know why, I am sure. I
219.22 am afraid I don't feel as grateful as I would if the
219.23 whole thing hadn't been so brutally sprung on me.
219.24 Because at bottom ... you, yourself ...' He
219.25 stuttered.
219.26 "'Possibly,' I struck in. He frowned.
219.27 "'All the same, one is responsible.' He watched
219.28 me like a hawk.
219.29 "'And that's true, too,' I said.
219.30 "'Well. I've gone with it to the end, and I
220.01 don't intend to let any man cast it in my teeth with-
220.02 out -- without -- resenting.' He clenched his fist.
220.03 "'There's yourself,' I said with a smile -- mirth-
220.04 less enough, God knows -- but he looked at me
220.05 menacingly. 'That's my business,' he said. An
220.06 air of indomitable resolution came and went upon his
220.07 face like a vain and passing shadow. Next moment
220.08 he looked a dear, good boy in trouble, as before. He
220.09 flung away the cigarette. 'Good-bye,' he said, with
220.10 the sudden haste of a man who had lingered too long
220.11 in view of a pressing bit of work waiting for him;
220.12 and then for a second or so he made not the slightest
220.13 movement. The downpour fell with the heavy, un-
220.14 interrupted rush of a sweeping flood, with a sound
220.15 of unchecked, overwhelming fury that called to one's
220.16 mind the images of collapsing bridges, of uprooted
220.17 trees, of undermined mountains. No man could
220.18 breast the colossal and headlong stream that seemed
220.19 to break and swirl against the dim stillness in which
220.20 we were precariously sheltered as if on an island.
220.21 The perforated pipe gurgled, choked, spat, and
220.22 splashed in odious ridicule of a swimmer fighting
220.23 for his life. 'It is raining,' I remonstrated, 'and
220.24 I ...' 'Rain or shine,' he began brusquely,
220.25 checked himself, and walked to the window. 'Per-
220.26 fect deluge,' he muttered after a while: he leaned his
220.27 forehead on the glass. 'It's dark, too.'
220.28 "'Yes, it is very dark,' I said.
220.29 "He pivoted on his heels, crossed the room, and
220.30 had actually opened the door leading into the corri-
221.01 dor before I leaped up from my chair. 'Wait,'
221.02 I cried, 'I want you to ...' 'I can't dine with
221.03 you again to-night,' he flung at me, with one leg
221.04 out of the room already. 'I haven't the slightest
221.05 intention of asking you,' I shouted. At this he drew

221.06 back his foot, but remained mistrustfully in the very
221.07 doorway. I lost no time in entreating him earnestly
221.08 not to be absurd; to come in and shut the door."
222.01 "HE came in at last; but I believe it was
222.02 mostly the rain that did it; it was
222.03 falling just then with a devastating
222.04 violence which quieted down gradually while we
222.05 talked. His manner was very sober and set; his
222.06 bearing was that of a naturally taciturn man possessed
222.07 by an idea. My talk was of the material aspect of
222.08 his position; it had the sole aim of saving him
222.09 from the degradation, ruin, and despair that out
222.10 there close so swiftly upon a friendless, homeless
222.11 man; I pleaded with him to accept my help; I
222.12 argued reasonably: and every time I looked up at
222.13 that absorbed, smooth face, so grave and youthful,
222.14 I had a disturbing sense of being no help but rather
222.15 an obstacle to some mysterious, inexplicable, im-
222.16 palpable striving of his wounded spirit.
222.17 "'I suppose you intend to eat and drink and to
222.18 sleep under shelter in the usual way,' I remember
222.19 saying with irritation. 'You say you won't touch
222.20 the money that is due to you....' He came as
222.21 near as his sort can to making a gesture of horror.
222.22 (There were three weeks and five days' pay owing
222.23 him as mate of the Patna.] 'Well, that's too little
222.24 to matter anyhow; but what will you do to-
223.01 morrow? Where will you turn? You must
223.02 live ...' 'That isn't the thing,' was the comment
223.03 that escaped him under his breath. I ignored it, and
223.04 went on combating what I assumed to be the scruples
223.05 of an exaggerated delicacy. 'On every conceivable
223.06 ground,' I concluded, 'you must let me help you.'
223.07 'You can't,' he said very simply and gently, and
223.08 holding fast to some deep idea which I could detect
223.09 shimmering like a pool of water in the dark, but
223.10 which I despaired of ever approaching near enough
223.11 to fathom. I surveyed his well-proportioned bulk.
223.12 'At any rate,' I said, 'I am able to help what I
223.13 can see of you. I don't pretend to do more.' He
223.14 shook his head sceptically without looking at me.
223.15 I got very warm. 'But I can,' I insisted. 'I can
223.16 do even more. I am doing more. I am trusting
223.17 you ...' 'The money ...' he began. 'Upon
223.18 my word, you deserve being told to go to the devil,'
223.19 I cried, forcing the note of indignation. He was
223.20 startled, smiled, and I pressed my attack home.
223.21 'It isn't a question of money at all. You are too
223.22 superficial,' I said (and at the same time I was think-
223.23 ing to myself: Well, here goes! And perhaps he
223.24 is after all). 'Look at the letter I want you to take.
223.25 I am writing to a man of whom I've never asked a
223.26 favour, and I am writing about you in terms that one
223.27 only ventures to use when speaking of an intimate
223.28 friend. I make myself unreservedly responsible for
223.29 you. That's what I am doing. And really, if you
223.30 will only reflect a little what that means ...'
224.01 "He lifted his head. The rain had passed
224.02 away; only the water-pipe went on shedding tears
224.03 with an absurd drip, drip outside the window. It
224.04 was very quiet in the room, whose shadows huddled
224.05 together in corners, away from the still flame of the
224.06 candle flaring upright in the shape of a dagger;
224.07 his face after a while seemed suffused by a reflection
224.08 of a soft light as if the dawn had broken already.
224.09 "'Jove!' he gasped out. 'It is noble of you!'
224.10 "Had he suddenly put out his tongue at me in
224.11 derision, I could not have felt more humiliated. I
224.12 thought to myself -- Serve me right for a sneaking
224.13 humbug.... His eyes shone straight into my face,
224.14 but I perceived it was not a mocking brightness.
224.15 All at once he sprang into jerky agitation, like one
224.16 of those flat wooden figures that are worked by a
224.17 string. His arms went up, then came down with
224.18 a slap. He became another man altogether. 'And
224.19 I had never seen,' he shouted; then suddenly bit
224.20 his lip and frowned. 'What a bally ass I've been,'
224.21 he said very slow in an awed tone.... 'You are
224.22 a brick!' he cried next in a muffled voice. He
224.23 snatched my hand as though he had just then seen it
224.24 for the first time, and dropped it at once. 'Why!
224.25 this is what I -- you -- I ...' he stammered, and
224.26 then with a return of his old stolid, I may say mulish,
224.27 manner he began heavily, 'I would be a brute now
224.28 if I ...' and then his voice seemed to break.
224.29 'That's all right,' I said. I was almost alarmed by
224.30 this display of feeling, through which pierced a
225.01 strange elation. I had pulled the string accident-
225.02 ally, as it were; I did not fully understand the
225.03 working of the toy. 'I must go now,' he said.
225.04 'Jove! You have helped me. Can't sit still. The
225.05 very thing ...' He looked at me with puzzled
225.06 admiration. 'The very thing ...'
225.07 "Of course it was the thing. It was ten to
225.08 one that I had saved him from starvation -- of that
225.09 peculiar sort that is almost invariably associated wit
225.10 drink. This was all. I had not a single illusion on
225.11 that score, but looking at him, I allowed myself to
225.12 wonder at the nature of the one he had, within the
225.13 last three minutes, so evidently taken into his bosom.
225.14 I had forced into his hand the means to carry on
225.15 decently the serious business of life, to get food,
225.16 drink, and shelter of the customary kind while his
225.17 wounded spirit, like a bird with a broken wing,
225.18 might hop and flutter into some hole to die quietly
225.19 of inanition there. This is what I had thrust upon
225.20 him: a definitely small thing; and -- behold! -- by
225.21 the manner of its reception it loomed in the dim
225.22 light of the candle like a big, indistinct, perhaps
225.23 a dangerous shadow. 'You don't mind me not
225.24 saying anything appropriate,' he burst out. 'There
225.25 isn't anything one could say. Last night already
225.26 you had done me no end of good. Listening to me --
225.27 you know. I give you my word I've thought more
225.28 than once the top of my head would fly off ...'
225.29 He darted -- positively darted -- here and there,
225.30 rammed his hands into his pockets, jerked them out
226.01 again, flung his cap on his head. I had no idea
226.02 it was in him to be so airily brisk. I thought of a
226.03 dry leaf imprisoned in an eddy of wind, while a
226.04 mysterious apprehension, a load of indefinite doubt,
226.05 weighed me down in my chair. He stood stock-
226.06 still, as if struck motionless by a discovery. 'You
226.07 have given me confidence,' he declared soberly.
226.08 'Oh! for God's sake, my dear fellow -- don't!'
226.09 I entreated, as though he had hurt me. 'All right.
226.10 I'll shut up now and henceforth. Can't prevent
226.11 me thinking, though.... Never mind!... I'll
226.12 show yet ...' He went to the door in a hurry,
226.13 paused with his head down, and came back, stepping
226.14 deliberately. 'I always thought that if a fellow
226.15 could begin with a clean slate ... And now you
226.16 ... in a measure ... yes ... clean slate.' I
226.17 waved my hand, and he marched out without looking
226.18 back; the sound of his footfalls died out gradually
226.19 behind the closed door -- the unhesitating tread of a
226.20 man walking in broad daylight.
226.21 "But as to me, left alone with the solitary candle,
226.22 I remained strangely unenlightened. I was no
226.23 longer young enough to behold at every turn the
226.24 magnificence that besets our insignificant footsteps
226.25 in good and in evil. I smiled to think that, after
226.26 all, it was yet he, of us two, who had the light.
226.27 And I felt sad. A clean slate, did he say? As if
226.28 the initial word of each our destiny were not graven
226.29 in imperishable characters upon the face of a rock!"
227.01 "SIX months afterwards my friend (he was a
227.02 cynical, more than middle-aged bachelor,
227.03 with a reputation for eccentricity, and owned
227.04 a rice-mill) wrote to me, and judging, from the
227.05 warmth of my recommendation, that I would like
227.06 to hear, enlarged a little upon Jim's perfections.
227.07 These were apparently of a quiet and effective
227.08 sort. 'Not having been able so far to find
227.09 more in my heart than a resigned toleration for
227.10 any individual of my kind, I have lived till now
227.11 alone in a house that even in this steaming climate
227.12 could be considered as too big for one man. I have
227.13 had him to live with me for some time past. It
227.14 seems I haven't made a mistake.' It seemed to me
227.15 on reading this letter that my friend had found in his
227.16 heart more than tolerance for Jim -- that there were
227.17 the beginnings of active liking. Of course he stated
227.18 his grounds in a characteristic way. For one thing,
227.19 Jim kept his freshness in the climate. Had he been
227.20 a girl -- my friend wrote -- one could have said he
227.21 was blooming -- blooming modestly -- like a violet,
227.22 not like some of these blatant tropical flowers. He
227.23 had been in the house for six weeks, and had not as
227.24 yet attempted to slap him on the back, or address
228.01 him as 'old boy,' or try to make him feel a super-
228.02 annuated fossil. He had nothing of the exasperat-
228.03 ing young man's chatter. He was good-tempered,
228.04 had not much to say for himself, was not clever by
228.05 any means, thank goodness -- wrote my friend. It
228.06 appeared, however, that Jim was clever enough to
228.07 be quietly appreciative of his wit, while, on the other
228.08 hand, he amused him by his naiveness. 'The
228.09 dew is yet on him, and since I had the bright idea of
228.10 giving him a room in the house and having him at

228.11 meals I feel less withered myself. The other day he
228.12 took it into his head to cross the room with no other
228.13 purpose but to open a door for me; and I felt more
228.14 in touch with mankind than I had been for years.
228.15 Ridiculous, isn't it? Of course I guess there is
228.16 something -- some awful little scrape -- which you
228.17 know all about -- but if I am sure that it is terribly
228.18 heinous, I fancy one could manage to forgive it.
228.19 For my part, I declare I am unable to imagine him
228.20 guilty of anything much worse than robbing an
228.21 orchard. Is it much worse? Perhaps you ought
228.22 to have told me; but it is such a long time since
228.23 we both turned saints that you may have forgotten
228.24 we, too, had sinned in our time? It may be that
228.25 some day I shall have to ask you, and then I shall
228.26 expect to be told. I don't care to question him
228.27 myself till I have some idea what it is. Moreover,
228.28 it's too soon as yet. Let him open the door a few
228.29 times more for me....' Thus my friend. I was
228.30 trebly pleased -- at Jim's shaping so well, at the tone
229.01 of the letter, at my own cleverness. Evidently I had
229.02 known what I was doing. I had read characters
229.03 aright, and so on. And what if something unex-
229.04 pected and wonderful were to come of it? That
229.05 evening, reposing in a deck-chair under the shade of
229.06 my own poop awning (it was in Hong-Kong harbour),
229.07 I laid on Jim's behalf the first stone of a castle in
229.08 Spain.
229.09 "I made a trip to the northward, and when I
229.10 returned I found another letter from my friend
229.11 waiting for me. It was the first envelope I tore
229.12 open. 'There are no spoons missing, as far as I
229.13 know,' ran the first line; 'I haven't been interested
229.14 enough to inquire. He is gone, leaving on the break-
229.15 fast-table a formal little note of apology, which is
229.16 either silly or heartless. Probably both -- and it's all
229.17 one to me. Allow me to say, lest you should have
229.18 some more mysterious young men in reserve, that
229.19 I have shut up shop, definitely and for ever. This
229.20 is the last eccentricity I shall be guilty of. Do not
229.21 imagine for a moment that I care a hang; but he is
229.22 very much regretted at tennis-parties, and for my
229.23 own sake I've told a plausible lie at the club....'
229.24 I flung the letter aside and started looking through
229.25 the batch on my table, till I came upon Jim's hand-
229.26 writing. Would you believe it? One chance in a
229.27 hundred! But it is always that hundredth chance!
229.28 That little second engineer of the Patna had turned
229.29 up in a more or less destitute state, and got a tem-
229.30 porary job of looking after the machinery of the mill.
230.01 'I couldn't stand the familiarity of the little beast,'
230.02 Jim wrote from a seaport seven hundred miles south
230.03 of the place where he should have been in clover.
230.04 'I am now for the time with Egstrom & Blake, ship-
230.05 chandlers, as their -- well -- runner, to call the thing
230.06 by its right name. For reference I gave them your
230.07 name, which they know, of course, and if you could
230.08 write a word in my favour it would be a perman-
230.09 ent employment.' I was utterly crushed under the
230.10 ruins of my castle, but of course I wrote as desired.
230.11 Before the end of the year my new charter took
230.12 me that way, and I had an opportunity of seeing
230.13 him.
230.14 "He was still with Egstrom & Blake, and we met
230.15 in what they called 'our parlour' opening out of
230.16 the store. He had that moment come in from
230.17 boarding a ship, and confronted me head down,
230.18 ready for a tussle. 'What have you got to say for
230.19 yourself?' I began as soon as we had shaken
230.20 hands. 'What I wrote you -- nothing more,' he
230.21 said stubbornly. 'Did the fellow blab -- or what?'
230.22 I asked. He looked up at me with a troubled
230.23 smile. 'Oh no! He didn't. He made it a kind of
230.24 confidential business between us. He was most
230.25 damnably mysterious whenever I came over to the
230.26 mill; he would wink at me in a respectful manner --
230.27 as much as to say, "We know what we know."
230.28 Infernally fawning and familiar -- and that sort of
230.29 thing.' He threw himself into a chair and stared
230.30 down his legs. 'One day we happened to be alone,
231.01 and the fellow had the cheek to say, "Well, Mr.
231.02 James" -- I was called Mr. James there as if I had
231.03 been the son -- "here we are together once more.
231.04 This is better than the old ship -- ain't it?..."
231.05 Wasn't it appalling, eh? I looked at him, and he
231.06 put on a knowing air. "Don't you be uneasy, sir,"
231.07 he says. "I know a gentleman when I see one, and
231.08 I know how a gentleman feels. I hope, though,
231.09 you will be keeping me on this job. I had a hard
231.10 time of it, too, along of that rotten old Patna
231.11 racket." Jove! It was awful. I don't know what
231.12 I should have said or done if I had not just then heard
231.13 Mr. Denver calling me in the passage. It was
231.14 tiffin-time, and we walked together across the yard
231.15 and through the garden to the bungalow. He began
231.16 to chaff me in his kindly way ... I believe he
231.17 liked me ...'
231.18 "Jim was silent for a while.
231.19 "'I know he liked me. That's what made it
231.20 so hard. Such a splendid man! That morning he
231.21 slipped his hand under my arm.... He, too, was
231.22 familiar with me.' He burst into a short laugh,
231.23 and dropped his chin on his breast. 'Pah! When
231.24 I remembered how that mean little beast had been
231.25 talking to me,' he began suddenly in a vibrating
231.26 voice, 'I couldn't bear to think of myself ... I
231.27 suppose you know ...' I nodded.... 'More
231.28 like a father,' he cried; his voice sank. 'I would
231.29 have had to tell him. I couldn't let it go on -- could
231.30 I?' 'Well?' I murmured, after waiting a while.
232.01 'I preferred to go,' he said slowly; 'this thing
232.02 must be buried.'
232.03 "We could hear in the shop Blake upbraiding
232.04 Egstrom in an abusive, strained voice. They had
232.05 been associated for many years, and every day from
232.06 the moment the doors were opened to the last minute
232.07 before closing, Blake, a little man with sleek, jetty
232.08 hair and unhappy, beady eyes, could be heard
232.09 rowing his partner incessantly with a sort of scathing
232.10 and plaintive fury. The sound of that everlasting
232.11 scolding was part of the place like the other fix-
232.12 tures; even strangers would very soon come to
232.13 disregard it completely, unless it be perhaps to
232.14 mutter 'Nuisance,' or to get up suddenly and shut
232.15 the door of the 'parlour.' Egstrom himself, a raw-
232.16 boned, heavy Scandinavian, with a busy manner
232.17 and immense blonde whiskers, went on directing
232.18 his people, checking parcels, making out bills or
232.19 writing letters at a stand-up desk in the shop, and
232.20 comported himself in that clatter exactly as though
232.21 he had been stone-deaf. Now and again he would
232.22 emit a bothered perfunctory 'Sssh,' which neither
232.23 produced nor was expected to produce the slightest
232.24 effect. 'They are very decent to me here,' said Jim.
232.25 'Blake's a little cad, but Egstrom's all right.' He
232.26 stood up quickly, and walking with measured steps
232.27 to a tripod telescope standing in the window and
232.28 pointed at the roadstead, he applied his eye to it.
232.29 'There's that ship which has been becalmed out-
232.30 side all the morning has got a breeze now and is
233.01 coming in,' he remarked patiently; 'I must go and
233.02 board.' We shook hands in silence, and he turned
233.03 to go. 'Jim!' I cried. He looked round with his
233.04 hand on the lock. 'You -- you have thrown away
233.05 something like a fortune.' He came back to me all
233.06 the way from the door. 'Such a splendid old chap,'
233.07 he said. 'How could I? How could I?' His
233.08 lips twitched. 'Here it does not matter.' 'Oh!
233.09 you -- you -- ' I began, and had to cast about for
233.10 a suitable word, but before I became aware that
233.11 there was no name that would just do, he was gone.
233.12 I heard outside Egstrom's deep, gentle voice saying
233.13 cheerily, 'That's the Sarah W. Granger, Jimmy.
233.14 You must manage to be first aboard'; and directly
233.15 Blake struck in, screaming after the manner of an
233.16 outraged cockatoo, 'Tell the captain we've got some
233.17 of his mail here. That'll fetch him. D'ye hear,
233.18 Mister What's-your-name?' And there was Jim
233.19 answering Egstrom with something boyish in his
233.20 tone. 'All right. I'll make a race of it.' He
233.21 seemed to take refuge in the boat-sailing part of
233.22 that sorry business.
233.23 "I did not see him again that trip, but on my
233.24 next (I had a six months' charter) I went up to
233.25 the store. Ten yards away from the door Blake's
233.26 scolding met my ears, and when I came in he gave
233.27 me a glance of utter wretchedness; Egstrom, all
233.28 smiles, advanced, extending a large, bony hand.
233.29 'Glad to see you, captain.... Sssh.... Been
233.30 thinking you were about due back here. What
234.01 did you say, sir?... Sssh.... Oh! him! He
234.02 has left us. Come into the parlour....' After
234.03 the slam of the door Blake's strained voice became
234.04 faint, as the voice of one scolding desperately in a
234.05 wilderness.... 'Put us to a great inconvenience,
234.06 too. Used us badly -- I must say ...' 'Where's
234.07 he gone to? Do you know?' I asked. 'No.
234.08 It's no use asking either,' said Egstrom, standing
234.09 bewhiskered and obliging before me with his arms
234.10 hanging down his sides clumsily and a thin silver

234.11 watch-chain looped very low on a rucked-up blue
234.12 serge waistcoat. 'A man like that don't go any-
234.13 where in particular.' I was too concerned at the
234.14 news to ask for the explanation of that pronounce-
234.15 ment, and he went on. 'He left -- let's see -- the
234.16 very day a steamer with returning pilgrims from the
234.17 Red Sea put in here with two blades of her propeller
234.18 gone. Three weeks ago now.' 'Wasn't there some-
234.19 thing said about the Patna case?' I asked, fearing
234.20 the worst. He gave a start, and looked at me as if
234.21 I had been a sorcerer. 'Why, yes! How do you
234.22 know? Some of them were talking about it here.
234.23 There was a captain or two, the manager of Vanlo's
234.24 engineering shop at the harbour, two or three others,
234.25 and myself. Jim was in here, too, having a sand-
234.26 wich and a glass of beer; when we are busy -- you
234.27 see, captain -- there's no time for a proper tiffin.
234.28 He was standing by this table eating sandwiches,
234.29 and the rest of us were round the telescope watch-
234.30 ing that steamer come in; and by and by Vanlo's
235.01 manager began to talk about the chief of the Patna:
235.02 he had done some repairs for him once, and from
235.03 that he went on to tell us what an old ruin she was,
235.04 and the money that had been made out of her. He
235.05 came to mention her last voyage, and then we all
235.06 struck in. Some said one thing and some another --
235.07 not much -- what you or any other man might say;
235.08 and there was some laughing. Captain O'Brien of
235.09 the Sarah W. Granger, a large, noisy old man with
235.10 a stick -- he was sitting listening to us in this arm-
235.11 chair here -- he let drive suddenly with his stick at
235.12 the floor, and roars out, "Skunks!..." Made
235.13 us all jump. Vanlo's manager winks at us and asks,
235.14 "What's the matter, Captain O'Brien?" "Matter!
235.15 matter!" the old man began to shout; "what are
235.16 you Injuns laughing at? It's no laughing matter.
235.17 It's a disgrace to human natur' -- that's what it is.
235.18 I would despise being seen in the same room with
235.19 one of those men. Yes, sir!" He seemed to catch
235.20 my eye like, and I had to speak out of civility.
235.21 "Skunks!" says I, "of course, Captain O'Brien,
235.22 and I wouldn't care to have them here myself, so
235.23 you're quite safe in this room, Captain O'Brien.
235.24 Have a little something cool to drink." "Dam
235.25 your drink, Egstrom," says he, with a twinkle in
235.26 his eye; "when I want a drink I will shout for it.
235.27 I am going to quit. It stinks here now." At this
235.28 all the others burst out laughing, and out they go
235.29 after the old man. And then, sir, that blasted Jim
235.30 he puts down the sandwich he had in his hand and
236.01 walks round the table to me; there was his glass of
236.02 beer poured out quite full. "I am off," he says --
236.03 just like this. "It isn't half-past one yet," says I;
236.04 "you might snatch a smoke first." I thought he
236.05 meant it was time for him to go down to his work.
236.06 When I understood what he was up to, my arms fell
236.07 -- so! Can't get a man like that every day, you
236.08 know, sir; a regular devil for sailing a boat; ready
236.09 to go out miles to sea to meet ships in any sort of
236.10 weather. More than once a captain would come in
236.11 here full of it, and the first thing he would say would
236.12 be, "That's a reckless sort of a lunatic you've got
236.13 for water-clerk, Egstrom. I was feeling my way
236.14 in at daylight under short canvas when there comes
236.15 flying out of the mist right under my forefoot a
236.16 boat half under water, sprays going over the mast-
236.17 head, two frightened niggers on the bottom boards,
236.18 a yelling fiend at the tiller. Hey! hey! Ship
236.19 ahoy! ahoy! Captain! Hey! hey! Egstrom &
236.20 Blake's man first to speak to you! Hey! hey!
236.21 Egstrom & Blake! Hallo! hey! whoop! Kick
236.22 the niggers -- squall on at the time --
236.23 shoots ahead whooping and yelling to me to make sail
236.24 and he would give me a lead in -- more like a demon
236.25 than a man. Never saw a boat handled like that in
236.26 all my life. Couldn't have been drunk -- was he?
236.27 Such a quiet, soft-spoken chap, too -- blush like a
236.28 girl when he came on board...." I tell you,
236.29 Captain Marlow, nobody had a chance against us
236.30 with a strange ship when Jim was out. The other
237.01 ship-chandlers just kept their old customers,
237.02 and ...'
237.03 "Egstrom appeared overcome with emotion.
237.04 "'Why, sir -- it seemed as though he wouldn't
237.05 mind going a hundred miles out to sea in an old shoe
237.06 to nab a ship for the firm. If the business had been
237.07 his own and all to make yet, he couldn't have done
237.08 more in that way. And now ... all at once ...
237.09 like this! Thinks I to myself: "Oho! a rise in
237.10 the screw -- that's the trouble -- is it? All right,"

237.11 says I, "no need of all that fuss with me, Jimmy.
237.12 Just mention your figure. Anything in reason."
237.13 He looks at me as if he wanted to swallow something
237.14 that stuck in his throat. "I can't stop with you."
237.15 "What's that blooming joke?" I asks. He shakes
237.16 his head, and I could see in his eye he was as good
237.17 as gone already, sir. So I turned to him and
237.18 slanged him till all was blue. "What is it you're
237.19 running away from?" I asks. "Who has been
237.20 getting at you? What scared you? You haven't
237.21 as much sense as a rat; they don't clear out from
237.22 a good ship. Where do you expect to get a better
237.23 berth? -- you this and you that." I made him look
237.24 sick, I can tell you. "This business ain't going to
237.25 sink," says I. He gave a big jump. "Good-bye,"
237.26 he says, nodding at me like a lord; "you ain't half
237.27 a bad chap, Egstrom. I give you my word that if
237.28 you knew my reasons you wouldn't care to keep me."
237.29 "That's the biggest lie you ever told in your life,"
237.30 says I; "I know my own mind." He made me so
238.01 mad that I had to laugh. "Can't you really stop
238.02 long enough to drink this glass of beer here, you
238.03 funny beggar, you?" I don't know what came
238.04 over him; he didn't seem able to find the door;
238.05 something comical, I can tell you, captain. I drank
238.06 the beer myself. "Well, if you're in such a hurry,
238.07 here's luck to you in your own drink," says I;
238.08 "only, you mark my words, if you keep up this
238.09 game you'll very soon find that the earth ain't big
238.10 enough to hold you -- that's all." He gave me one
238.11 black look, and out he rushed with a face fit to scare
238.12 little children.'
238.13 "Egstrom snorted bitterly, and combed one
238.14 auburn whisker with knotty fingers. 'Haven't
238.15 been able to get a man that was any good since. It's
238.16 nothing but worry, worry, worry in business. And
238.17 where might you have come across him, captain,
238.18 if it's fair to ask?'
238.19 "'He was the mate of the Patna that voyage,' I
238.20 said, feeling that I owed some explanation. For a
238.21 time Egstrom remained very still, with his fingers
238.22 plunged in the hair at the side of his face, and then
238.23 exploded. 'And who the devil cares about that?'
238.24 'I dare say no one ...' I began. 'And what the
238.25 devil is he -- anyhow -- for to go on like this?'
238.26 He stuffed suddenly his left whisker into his mouth
238.27 and stood amazed. 'Jee!' he exclaimed, 'I told
238.28 him the earth wouldn't be big enough to hold his
238.29 caper.'"
239.01 "I HAVE told you these two episodes at
239.02 length to show his manner of dealing with
239.03 himself under the new conditions of his
239.04 life. There were many others of the sort, more
239.05 than I could count on the fingers of my two
239.06 hands.
239.07 "They were all equally tinged by a high-minded
239.08 absurdity of intention which made their futility
239.09 profound and touching. To fling away your daily
239.10 bread so as to get your hands free for a grapple with
239.11 a ghost may be an act of prosaic heroism. Men
239.12 had done it before (though we who have lived know
239.13 full well that it is not the haunted soul but the
239.14 hungry body that makes an outcast), and men who
239.15 had eaten and meant to eat every day had applauded
239.16 the creditable folly. He was indeed unfortunate,
239.17 for all his recklessness could not carry him out
239.18 from under the shadow. There was always a
239.19 doubt of his courage. The truth seems to be that
239.20 it is impossible to lay the ghost of a fact. You can
239.21 face it or shirk it -- and I have come across a man or
239.22 two who could wink at their familiar shades. Obvi-
239.23 ously Jim was not of the winking sort; but what I
239.24 could never make up my mind about was whether
240.01 his line of conduct amounted to shirking his ghost
240.02 or to facing him out.
240.03 "I strained my mental eyesight only to discover
240.04 that, as with the complexion of all our actions, the
240.05 shade of difference was so delicate that it was im-
240.06 possible to say. It might have been flight and it
240.07 might have been a mode of combat. To the common
240.08 mind he became known as a rolling stone, because
240.09 this was the funniest part; he did after a time
240.10 become perfectly known, and even notorious, within
240.11 the circle of his wanderings (which had a diameter
240.12 of, say, three thousand miles), in the same way
240.13 as an eccentric character is known to a whole
240.14 countryside. For instance, in Bankok, where he
240.15 found employment with Yucker Brothers, charterers
240.16 and teak merchants, it was almost pathetic to see
240.17 him go about in sunshine hugging his secret, which

240'.18 was known to the very up-country logs on the river.
240.19 Schomberg, the keeper of the hotel where he
240.20 boarded, a hirsute Alsatian of manly bearing and
240.21 an irrepressible retailer of all the scandalous gossip
240.22 of the place, would, with both elbows on the table,
240.23 impart an adorned version of the story to any guest
240.24 who cared to imbibe knowledge along with the
240.25 more costly liquors. 'And, mind you, the nicest
240.26 fellow you could meet,' would be his generous
240.27 conclusion; 'quite superior.' It says a lot for the
240.28 casual crowd that frequented Schomberg's estab-
240.29 lishment that Jim managed to hang out in Bankok
240.30 for a whole six months. I remarked that people,
241.01 perfect strangers, took to him as one takes to a nice
241.02 child. His manner was reserved, but it was as
241.03 though his personal appearance, his hair, his eyes,
241.04 his smile, made friends for him wherever he went.
241.05 And, of course, he was no fool. I heard Siegmund
241.06 Yucker (native of Switzerland), a gentle creature
241.07 ravaged by a cruel dyspepsia, and so frightfully
241.08 lame that his head swung through a quarter of
241.09 a circle at every step he took, declare appreciatively
241.10 that for one so young he was 'of great gabasidy,' as
241.11 though it had been a mere question of cubic con-
241.12 tents. 'Why not send him up country?' I sug-
241.13 gested anxiously. (Yucker Brothers had concessions
241.14 and teak forests in the interior.) 'If he has capacity
241.15 as you say, he will soon get hold of the work. And
241.16 physically he is very fit. His health is always
241.17 excellent.' 'Ach! It's a great ting in dis goundry
241.18 to be vree vrom tispep-snia,' sighed poor Yucker
241.19 enviously, casting a stealthy glance at the pit of
241.20 his ruined stomach. I left him drumming pen-
241.21 sively on his desk and muttering, 'Es ist ein idee.
241.22 Es ist ein idee.' Unfortunately, that very evening
241.23 an unpleasant affair took place in the hotel.
241.24 "I don't know that I blame Jim very much, but
241.25 it was a truly regrettable incident. It belonged to
241.26 the lamentable species of bar-room scuffles, and the
241.27 other party to it was a cross-eyed Dane of sorts
241.28 whose visiting-card recited, under his misbegotten
241.29 name: first lieutenant in the Royal Siamese Navy.
241.30 The fellow, of course, was utterly hopeless at
242.01 billiards, but did not like to be beaten, I suppose.
242.02 He had had enough to drink to turn nasty after
242.03 the sixth game, and make some scornful remark at
242.04 Jim's expense. Most of the people there didn't
242.05 hear what was said, and those who had heard seemed
242.06 to have had all precise recollection scared out of
242.07 them by the appalling nature of the consequences
242.08 that immediately ensued. It was very lucky for the
242.09 Dane that he could swim, because the room opened
242.10 on a verandah and the Menam flowed below very
242.11 wide and black. A boat-load of Chinamen, bound,
242.12 as likely as not, on some thieving expedition,
242.13 fished out the officer of the King of Siam, and Jim
242.14 turned up at about midnight on board my ship
242.15 without a hat. 'Everybody in the room seemed to
242.16 know,' he said, gasping yet from the contest, as it
242.17 were. He was rather sorry, on general principles,
242.18 for what had happened, though in this case there
242.19 had been, he said, 'no option.' But what dis-
242.20 mayed him was to find the nature of his burden as
242.21 well known to everybody as though he had gone
242.22 about all that time carrying it on his shoulders.
242.23 Naturally after this he couldn't remain in the place.
242.24 He was universally condemned for the brutal
242.25 violence, so unbecoming a man in his delicate
242.26 position; some maintained he had been disgrace-
242.27 fully drunk at the time; others criticised his want
242.28 of tact. Even Schomberg was very much annoyed.
242.29 'He is a very nice young man,' he said, argu-
242.30 mentatively, to me, 'but the lieutenant is a first-
243.01 rate fellow, too. He dines every night at my table
243.02 d'hote, you know. And there's a billiard-cue broken.
243.03 I can't allow that. First thing this morning I went
243.04 over with my apologies to the lieutenant, and I
243.05 think I've made it all right for myself; but only
243.06 think, captain, if everybody started such games!
243.07 Why, the man might have been drowned! And
243.08 here I can't run out into the next street and buy a
243.09 new cue. I've got to write to Europe for them. No,
243.10 no! A temper like that won't do!...' He was
243.11 extremely sore on the subject.
243.12 "This was the worst incident of all in his -- his
243.13 retreat. Nobody could deplore it more than myself;
243.14 for if, as somebody said hearing him mentioned,
243.15 'Oh yes! I know. He has knocked about a good
243.16 deal out here,' yet he had somehow avoided being
243.17 battered and chipped in the process. This last

243.18 affair, however, made me seriously uneasy, because
243.19 if his exquisite sensibilities were to go the length of
243.20 involving him in pot-house shindies, he would lose
243.21 his name of an inoffensive, if aggravating, fool, and
243.22 acquire that of a common loafer. For all my con-
243.23 fidence in him I could not help reflecting that in
243.24 such cases from the name to the thing itself is
243.25 but a step. I suppose you will understand that by
243.26 that time I could not think of washing my hands
243.27 of him. I took him away from Bankok in my ship,
243.28 and we had a longish passage. It was pitiful to see
243.29 how he shrank within himself. A seaman, even if a
243.30 mere passenger, takes an interest in a ship, and looks
244.01 at the sea-life around him with the critical enjoy-
244.02 ment of a painter, for instance, looking at another
244.03 man's work. In every sense of the expression he is
244.04 'on deck'; but my Jim, for the most part, skulked
244.05 down below as though he had been a stowaway.
244.06 He infected me so that I avoided speaking on pro-
244.07 fessional matters, such as would suggest themselves
244.08 naturally to two sailors during a passage. For
244.09 whole days we did not exchange a word; I felt
244.10 extremely unwilling to give orders to my officers
244.11 in his presence. Often, when alone with him on
244.12 deck or in the cabin, we didn't know what to do
244.13 with our eyes.
244.14 "I placed him with De Jongh, as you know,
244.15 glad enough to dispose of him in any way, yet per-
244.16 suaded that his position was now growing intolerable.
244.17 He had lost some of that elasticity which had enabled
244.18 him to rebound back into his uncompromising
244.19 position after every overthrow. One day, coming
244.20 ashore, I saw him standing on the quay; the water
244.21 of the roadstead and the sea in the offing made one
244.22 smooth ascending plane, and the outermost ships
244.23 at anchor seemed to ride motionless in the sky.
244.24 He was waiting for his boat, which was being loaded
244.25 at our feet with packages of small stores for some
244.26 vessel ready to leave. After exchanging greetings,
244.27 we remained silent -- side by side. 'Jove!' he said
244.28 suddenly, 'this is killing work.'
244.29 "He smiled at me; I must say he generally
244.30 could manage a smile. I made no reply. I knew
245.01 very well he was not alluding to his duties; he had
245.02 an easy time of it with De Jongh. Nevertheless, as
245.03 soon as he had spoken I became completely con-
245.04 vinced that the work was killing. I did not even
245.05 look at him. 'Would you like,' said I, 'to leave
245.06 this part of the world altogether; try California
245.07 or the West Coast? I'll see what I can do ...'
245.08 He interrupted me a little scornfully. 'What
245.09 difference would it make?...' I felt at once
245.10 convinced that he was right. It would make no
245.11 difference; it was not relief he wanted; I seemed
245.12 to perceive dimly that what he wanted, what he was,
245.13 as it were, waiting for, was something not easy to
245.14 define -- something in the nature of an opportunity.
245.15 I had given him many opportunities, but they had
245.16 been merely opportunities to earn his bread. Yet
245.17 what more could any man do? The position
245.18 struck me as hopeless, and poor Brierly's saying
245.19 recurred to me, 'Let him creep twenty feet under-
245.20 ground and stay there.' Better that, I thought,
245.21 than this waiting above ground for the impossible.
245.22 Yet one could not be sure even of that. There
245.23 and then, before his boat was three oars' lengths
245.24 away from the quay, I had made up my mind to go
245.25 and consult Stein in the evening.
245.26 "This Stein was a wealthy and respected mer-
245.27 chant. His 'house' (because it was a house, Stein
245.28 & Co., and there was some sort of partner who,
245.29 as Stein said, 'looked after the Moluccas') had a
245.30 large inter-island business, with a lot of trading posts
246.01 established in the most out-of-the-way places for
246.02 collecting the produce. His wealth and his respect-
246.03 ability were not exactly the reasons why I was
246.04 anxious to seek his advice. I desired to confide
246.05 my difficulty to him because he was one of the most
246.06 trustworthy men I had ever known. The gentle
246.07 light of a simple, unwearied, as it were, and intelli-
246.08 gent good-nature illumined his long, hairless face.
246.09 It had deep, downward folds, and was pale as of a
246.10 man who had always led a sedentary life -- which was
246.11 indeed very far from being the case. His hair was
246.12 thin, and brushed back from a massive and lofty
246.13 forehead. One fancied that at twenty he must
246.14 have looked very much like what he was now at
246.15 threescore. It was a student's face; only the
246.16 eyebrows, nearly all white, thick and bushy, together
246.17 with the resolute, searching glance that came from

246.18 under them, were not in accord with his, I may say,
246.19 learned appearance. He was tall and loose-jointed;
246.20 his slight stoop, together with an innocent smile,
246.21 made him appear benevolently ready to lend you
246.22 his ear; his long arms with pale, big hands had rare,
246.23 deliberate gestures of a pointing out, demonstrating
246.24 kind. I speak of him at length, because under this
246.25 exterior, and in conjunction with an upright and
246.26 indulgent nature, this man possessed an intrepidity
246.27 of spirit and a physical courage that could have
246.28 been called reckless had it not been like a natural
246.29 function of the body -- say good digestion, for in-
246.30 stance -- completely unconscious of itself. It is
247.01 sometimes said of a man that he carried his life in
247.02 his hand. Such a saying would have been inade-
247.03 quate if applied to him; during the early part of his
247.04 existence in the East he had been playing ball with
247.05 it. All this was in the past, but I knew the story of
247.06 his life and the origin of his fortune. He was
247.07 also a naturalist of some distinction, or perhaps I
247.08 should say a learned collector. Entomology was
247.09 his special study. His collection of Buprestidae and
247.10 Longicorns -- beetles all -- horrible miniature mon-
247.11 sters, looking malevolent in death and immobility,
247.12 and his cabinet of butterflies, beautiful and hovering
247.13 under the glass of cases of lifeless wings, had spread
247.14 his fame far over the earth. The name of this
247.15 merchant, adventurer, sometime adviser of a Malay
247.16 sultan (to whom he never alluded otherwise than
247.17 as 'my poor Mohammed Bonso'), had, on account
247.18 of a few bushels of dead insects, become known to
247.19 learned persons in Europe, who could have had no
247.20 conception, and certainly would not have cared to
247.21 know anything, of his life or character. I, who knew,
247.22 considered him an eminently suitable person to
247.23 receive my confidences about Jim's difficulties as
247.24 well as my own."
248.01 "LATE in the evening I entered his study,
248.02 after traversing an imposing but empty
248.03 dining-room very dimly lit. The house
248.04 was silent. I was preceded by an elderly, grim
248.05 Javanese servant in a sort of livery of white jacket
248.06 and yellow sarong, who, after throwing the door open,
248.07 exclaimed low, 'O master!' and stepping aside,
248.08 vanished in a mysterious way as though he had
248.09 been a ghost only momentarily embodied for that
248.10 particular service. Stein turned round with the
248.11 chair, and in the same movement his spectacles
248.12 seemed to get pushed up on his forehead. He wel-
248.13 comed me in his quiet and humorous voice. Only
248.14 one corner of the vast room, the corner in which stood
248.15 his writing-desk, was strongly lighted by a shaded
248.16 reading-lamp, and the rest of the spacious apartment
248.17 melted into shapeless gloom like a cavern. Narrow
248.18 shelves filled with dark boxes of uniform shape and
248.19 colour ran round the walls, not from floor to ceiling,
248.20 but in a sombre belt about four feet broad -- cata-
248.21 combs of beetles. Wooden tablets were hung above
248.22 at irregular intervals. The light reached one of
248.23 them, and the word Coleoptera written in gold
248.24 letters glittered mysteriously upon a vast dimness.
249.01 The glass cases containing the collection of butter-
249.02 flies were ranged in three long rows upon slender-
249.03 legged little tables. One of these cases had been
249.04 removed from its place and stood on the desk,
249.05 which was bestrewn with oblong slips of paper
249.06 blackened with minute handwriting.
249.07 "'So you see me -- so,' he said. His hand
249.08 hovered over the case where a butterfly in solitary
249.09 grandeur spread out dark bronze wings, seven
249.10 inches or more across, with exquisite white veinings
249.11 and a gorgeous border of yellow spots. 'Only one
249.12 specimen like this they have in your London, and
249.13 then -- no more. To my small native town this
249.14 my collection I shall bequeath. Something of me.
249.15 The best.'
249.16 "He bent forward in the chair and gazed
249.17 intently, his chin over the front of the case. I
249.18 stood at his back. 'Marvellous,' he whispered, and
249.19 seemed to forget my presence. His history was
249.20 curious. He had been born in Bavaria, and when
249.21 a youth of twenty-two had taken an active part in
249.22 the revolutionary movement of 1848. Heavily com-
249.23 promised, he managed to make his escape, and at
249.24 first found refuge with a poor republican watch-
249.25 maker in Trieste. From there he made his way to
249.26 Tripoli with a stock of cheap watches to hawk about,
249.27 -- not a very great opening truly, but it turned out
249.28 lucky enough, because it was there he came upon a
249.29 Dutch traveller -- a rather famous man, I believe,

249.30 but I don't remember his name. It was that
250.01 naturalist who, engaging him as a sort of assistant,
250.02 took him to the East. They travelled in the
250.03 Archipelago together and separately, collecting in-
250.04 sects and birds, for four years or more. Then the
250.05 naturalist went home, and Stein, having no home to
250.06 go to, remained with an old trader he had come
250.07 across in his journeys in the interior of Celebes --
250.08 if Celebes may be said to have an interior. This
250.09 old Scotsman, the only white man allowed to reside
250.10 in the country at the time, was a privileged friend
250.11 of the chief ruler of Wajo States, who was a woman.
250.12 I often heard Stein relate how that chap, who was
250.13 slightly paralysed on one side, had introduced him
250.14 to the native court a short time before another
250.15 stroke carried him off. He was a heavy man with a
250.16 patriarchal white beard, and of imposing stature.
250.17 He came into the council-hall where all the rajahs,
250.18 pangerans, and head-men were assembled, with the
250.19 queen, a fat, wrinkled woman (very free in her speech,
250.20 Stein said), reclining on a high couch under a
250.21 canopy. He dragged his leg, thumping with his
250.22 stick, and grasped Stein's arm, leading him right
250.23 up to the couch. 'Look, queen, and you rajahs,
250.24 this is my son,' he proclaimed in a stentorian voice.
250.25 'I have traded with your fathers, and when I die
250.26 he shall trade with you and your sons.'
250.27 "By means of this simple formality Stein in-
250.28 herited the Scotsman's privileged position and all
250.29 his stock-in-trade, together with a fortified house on
250.30 the banks of the only navigable river in the country.
251.01 Shortly afterwards the old queen, who was so free
251.02 in her speech, died, and the country became dis-
251.03 turbed by various pretenders to the throne. Stein
251.04 joined the party of a younger son, the one of whom
251.05 thirty years later he never spoke otherwise but as
251.06 'my poor Mohammed Bonso.' They both became
251.07 the heroes of innumerable exploits; they had
251.08 wonderful adventures, and once stood a siege in the
251.09 Scotsman's house for a month, with only a score
251.10 of followers against a whole army. I believe the
251.11 natives talk of that war to this day. Meantime, it
251.12 seems, Stein never failed to annex on his own account
251.13 every butterfly or beetle he could lay hands on.
251.14 After some eight years of war, negotiations, false
251.15 truces, sudden outbreaks, reconciliation, treachery,
251.16 and so on, and just as peace seemed at last
251.17 permanently established, his 'poor Mohammed
251.18 Bonso' was assassinated at the gate of his own royal
251.19 residence while dismounting in the highest spirits
251.20 on his return from a successful deer-hunt. This
251.21 event rendered Stein's position extremely insecure,
251.22 but he would have stayed perhaps had it not been
251.23 that a short time afterwards he lost Mohammed's
251.24 sister ('my dear wife the princess,' he used to say
251.25 solemnly), by whom he had had a daughter -- mother
251.26 and child both dying within three days of each other
251.27 from some infectious fever. He left the country,
251.28 which this cruel loss had made unbearable to him.
251.29 Thus ended the first and adventurous part of his
251.30 existence. What followed was so different that,
252.01 but for the reality of sorrow which remained with
252.02 him, this strange part must have resembled a dream.
252.03 He had little money; he started life afresh, and
252.04 in the course of years acquired a considerable
252.05 fortune. At first he had travelled a good deal
252.06 amongst the islands, but age had stolen upon him,
252.07 and of late he seldom left his spacious house three
252.08 miles out of town, with an extensive garden, and
252.09 surrounded by stables, offices, and bamboo cottages
252.10 for his servants and dependants, of whom he had
252.11 many. He drove in his buggy every morning to
252.12 town, where he had an office with white and Chinese
252.13 clerks. He owned a small fleet of schooners and
252.14 native craft, and dealt in island produce on a large
252.15 scale. For the rest he lived solitary, but not mis-
252.16 anthropic, with his books and his collection, classing
252.17 and arranging specimens, corresponding with en-
252.18 tomologists in Europe, writing up a descriptive
252.19 catalogue of his treasures. Such was the history
252.20 of the man whom I had come to consult upon Jim's
252.21 case without any definite hope. Simply to hear what
252.22 he would have to say would have been a relief.
252.23 I was very anxious, but I respected the intense,
252.24 almost passionate absorption with which he looked
252.25 at a butterfly, as though on the bronze sheen of these
252.26 frail wings, in the white tracings, in the gorgeous
252.27 markings, he could see other things, an image of
252.28 something as perishable and defying destruction
252.29 as these delicate and lifeless tissues displaying a

252.30 splendour unmarred by death.
253.01 "'Marvellous!' he repeated, looking up at me.
253.02 'Look! The beauty -- but that is nothing -- look at
253.03 the accuracy, the harmony. And so fragile! And
253.04 so strong! And so exact! This is Nature -- the
253.05 balance of colossal forces. Every star is so -- and
253.06 every blade of grass stands so -- and the mighty
253.07 Kosmos in perfect equilibrium produces -- this.
253.08 This wonder; this masterpiece of Nature -- the
253.09 great artist.'
253.10 "'Never heard an entomologist go on like this,'
253.11 I observed cheerfully. 'Masterpiece! And what
253.12 of man?'
253.13 "'Man is amazing, but he is not a masterpiece,'
253.14 he said, keeping his eyes fixed on the glass case.
253.15 'Perhaps the artist was a little mad. Eh? What
253.16 do you think? Sometimes it seems to me that
253.17 man is come where he is not wanted, where
253.18 there is no place for him; for if not, why should
253.19 he want all the place? Why should he run
253.20 about here and there making a great noise about
253.21 himself, talking about the stars, disturbing the
253.22 blades of grass? ...'
253.23 "'Catching butterflies,' I chimed in.
253.24 "He smiled, threw himself back in his chair, and
253.25 stretched his legs. 'Sit down,' he said. 'I cap-
253.26 tured this rare specimen myself one very fine morn-
253.27 ing. And I had a very big emotion. You don't
253.28 know what it is for a collector to capture such a
253.29 rare specimen. You can't know.'
253.30 "I smiled at my ease in a rocking-chair. His
254.01 eyes seemed to look far beyond the wall at which
254.02 they stared; and he narrated now, one night, a
254.03 messenger arrived from his 'poor Mohammed,'
254.04 requiring his presence at the 'residenz' -- as he
254.05 called it -- which was distant some nine or ten miles
254.06 by a bridle-path over a cultivated plain, with patches
254.07 of forest here and there. Early in the morning he
254.08 started from his fortified house, after embracing
254.09 his little Emma, and leaving the 'princess,' his wife,
254.10 in command. He described how she came with
254.11 him as far as the gate, walking with one hand on the
254.12 neck of his horse; she had on a white jacket, gold
254.13 pins in her hair, and a brown leather belt over her
254.14 left shoulder with a revolver in it. 'She talked as
254.15 women will talk,' he said, 'telling me to be careful,
254.16 and to try to get back before dark, and what a great
254.17 wickedness it was for me to go alone. We were at
254.18 war, and the country was not safe; my men were
254.19 putting up bullet-proof shutters to the house and
254.20 loading their rifles, and she begged me to have no
254.21 fear for her. She could defend the house against
254.22 anybody till I returned. And I laughed with
254.23 pleasure a little. I liked to see her so brave and
254.24 young and strong. I, too, was young then. At the
254.25 gate she caught hold of my hand and gave it one
254.26 squeeze and fell back. I made my horse stand still
254.27 outside till I heard the bars of the gate put up
254.28 behind me. There was a great enemy of mine, a
254.29 great noble -- and a great rascal, too -- roaming with
254.30 a band in the neighbourhood. I cantered for four
255.01 or five miles; there had been rain in the night, but
255.02 the mists had gone up, up -- and the face of the earth
255.03 was clean; it lay smiling to me, so fresh and inno-
255.04 cent -- like a little child. Suddenly somebody fires
255.05 a volley -- twenty shots at least it seemed to me. I
255.06 hear bullets sing in my ears, and my hat jumps
255.07 to the back of my head. It was a little intrigue, you
255.08 understand. They got my poor Mohammed to send
255.09 for me and then laid that ambush. I see it all
255.10 in a minute, and I think -- This wants a little
255.11 management. My pony snort, jump, and stand, and
255.12 I fall slowly forward with my head on his mane.
255.13 He begins to walk, and with one eye I could see over
255.14 his neck a faint cloud of smoke hanging in front of
255.15 a clump of bamboos to my left. I think -- Aha!
255.16 my friends, why you not wait long enough before
255.17 you shoot? This is not yet gelungen. Oh no!
255.18 I get hold of my revolver with my right hand --
255.19 quiet -- quiet. After all, there were only seven of
255.20 these rascals. They get up from the grass and
255.21 start running with their sarongs tucked up, waving
255.22 spears above their heads, and yelling to each other
255.23 to look out and catch the horse, because I was dead.
255.24 I let them come as close as the door here, and then
255.25 bang, bang, bang -- take aim each time, too. One
255.26 more shot I fire at a man's back, but I miss. Too
255.27 far already. And then I sit alone on my horse with
255.28 the clean earth smiling at me, and there are the bodies
255.29 of three men lying on the ground. One was curled

255.30 up like a dog, another on his back had an arm over
256.01 his eyes as if to keep off the sun, and the third man
256.02 he draws up his leg very slowly and makes it with
256.03 one kick straight again. I watch him very carefully
256.04 from my horse, but there is no more -- bleibt ganz
256.05 ruhig -- keep still, so. And as I looked at his face
256.06 for some sign of life I observed something like a
256.07 faint shadow pass over his forehead. It was the
256.08 shadow of this butterfly. Look at the form of the
256.09 wing. This species fly high with a strong flight.
256.10 I raised my eyes and I saw him fluttering away. I
256.11 think -- Can it be possible? And then I lost
256.12 him. I dismounted and went on very slow, leading
256.13 my horse and holding my revolver with one hand and
256.14 my eyes darting up and down and right and left,
256.15 everywhere! At last I saw him sitting on a small
256.16 heap of dirt ten feet away. At once my heart
256.17 began to beat quick. I let go my horse, keep my
256.18 revolver in one hand, and with the other snatch
256.19 my soft felt hat off my head. One step. Steady.
256.20 Another step. Flop! I got him! When I got up
256.21 I shook like a leaf with excitement, and when I
256.22 opened these beautiful wings and made sure what
256.23 a rare and so extraordinary perfect specimen I had,
256.24 my head went round and my legs became so weak
256.25 with emotion that I had to sit on the ground. I
256.26 had greatly desired to possess myself of a specimen
256.27 of that species when collecting for the professor.
256.28 I took long journeys and underwent great priva-
256.29 tions; I had dreamed of him in my sleep, and here
256.30 suddenly I had him in my fingers -- for myself!
257.01 In the words of the poet' (he pronounced it
257.02 'boet'):
257.03 "'So halt' ich's endlich denn in meinen Handen,
257.04 Und nenn' es in gewissem Sinne mein.'"
257.05 He gave to the last word the emphasis of a suddenly
257.06 lowered voice, and withdrew his eyes slowly from
257.07 my face. He began to charge a long-stemmed pipe
257.08 busily and in silence, then, pausing with his thumb
257.09 on the orifice of the bowl, looked again at me
257.10 significantly.
257.11 "'Yes, my good friend. On that day I had
257.12 nothing to desire; I had greatly annoyed my
257.13 principal enemy; I was young, strong; I had
257.14 friendship; I had the love' (he said 'lof') 'of
257.15 woman, a child I had, to make my heart very full --
257.16 and even what I had once dreamed in my sleep had
257.17 come into my hand, too!'
257.18 "He struck a match, which flared violently.
257.19 His thoughtful, placid face twitched once.
257.20 "'Friend, wife, child,' he said slowly, gazing
257.21 at the small flame -- 'phoo!' The match was blown
257.22 out. He sighed and turned again to the glass case.
257.23 The frail and beautiful wings quivered faintly, as if
257.24 his breath had for an instant called back to life that
257.25 gorgeous object of his dreams.
257.26 "'The work,' he began suddenly, pointing to
257.27 the scattered slips, and in his usual gentle and cheery
257.28 tone, 'is making great progress. I have been this
257.29 rare specimen describing.... Na! And what is
257.30 your good news?'
258.01 "'To tell you the truth, Stein,' I said, with an
258.02 effort that surprised me, 'I came here to describe
258.03 a specimen....'
258.04 "'Butterfly?' he asked, with an unbelieving and
258.05 humorous eagerness.
258.06 "'Nothing so perfect,' I answered, feeling
258.07 suddenly dispirited with all sorts of doubts. 'A
258.08 man!'
258.09 "'Ach so!' he murmured, and his smiling
258.10 countenance, turned to me, became grave. Then
258.11 after looking at me for a while he said slowly, 'Well
258.12 -- I am a man, too.'
258.13 "Here you have him as he was; he knew how to
258.14 be so generously encouraging as to make a scrupulous
258.15 man hesitate on the brink of confidence; but if I
258.16 did hesitate it was not for long.
258.17 "He heard me out, sitting with crossed legs.
258.18 Sometimes his head would disappear completely
258.19 in a great eruption of smoke, and a sympathetic
258.20 growl would come out from the cloud. When I
258.21 finished he uncrossed his legs, laid down his pipe,
258.22 leaned forward towards me earnestly with his elbows
258.23 on the arms of his chair, the tips of his fingers
258.24 together.
258.25 "'I understand very well. He is romantic.'
258.26 "He had diagnosed the case for me, and at first
258.27 I was quite startled to find how simple it was;
258.28 and indeed our conference resembled so much a
258.29 medical consultation -- Stein, of learned aspect, sit-

258.30 ting in an arm-chair before his desk; I, anxious, in
259.01 another, facing him, but a little to one side -- that
259.02 it seemed natural to ask:
259.03 "'What's good for it?'
259.04 "He lifted up a long forefinger.
259.05 "'There is only one remedy! One thing alone
259.06 can us from being ourselves cure!' The finger
259.07 came down on the desk with a smart rap. The case
259.08 which he had made to look so simple before became
259.09 if possible still simpler -- and altogether hopeless.
259.10 There was a pause. 'Yes,' said I, 'strictly speak-
259.11 ing, the question is not how to get cured, but how
259.12 to live.'
259.13 "He approved with his head, a little sadly as it
259.14 seemed. 'Ja! ja! In general, adapting the words
259.15 of your great poet: That is the question....' He
259.16 went on nodding sympathetically.... 'How to
259.17 be! Ach! How to be.'
259.18 "He stood up, with the tips of his fingers resting
259.19 on the desk.
259.20 "'We want in so many different ways to be,' he
259.21 began again. 'This magnificent butterfly finds a
259.22 little heap of dirt and sits still on it; but man he
259.23 will never on his heap of mud keep still. He want
259.24 to be so, and again he want to be so....' He
259.25 moved his hand up, then down.... 'He wants to
259.26 be a saint, and he wants to be a devil -- and every
259.27 time he shuts his eyes he sees himself as a very fine
259.28 fellow -- so fine as he can never be.... In a
259.29 dream....'
259.30 "He lowered the glass lid, the automatic lock
260.01 clicked sharply, and taking up the case in both hands
260.02 he bore it religiously away to its place, passing out
260.03 of the bright circle of the lamp into the ring of
260.04 fainter light -- into shapeless dusk at last. It had
260.05 an odd effect -- as if these few steps had carried him
260.06 out of this concrete and perplexed world. His tall
260.07 form, as though robbed of its substance, hovered
260.08 noiselessly over invisible things with stooping and
260.09 indefinite movements; his voice, heard in that re-
260.10 moteness where he could be glimpsed mysteriously
260.11 busy with immaterial cares, was no longer incisive,
260.12 seemed to roll voluminous and grave -- mellowed by
260.13 distance.
260.14 "'And because you not always can keep your
260.15 eyes shut there comes the real trouble -- the heart
260.16 pain -- the world pain. I tell you, my friend, it is
260.17 not good for you to find you cannot make your
260.18 dream come true, for the reason that you not strong
260.19 enough are, or not clever enough. Ja!... And
260.20 all the time you are such a fine fellow, too! Wie?
260.21 Was? Gott im Himmel! How can that be?
260.22 Ha! ha! ha!'
260.23 "The shadow prowling amongst the graves of
260.24 butterflies laughed boisterously.
260.25 "'Yes! Very funny this terrible thing is. A
260.26 man that is born falls into a dream like a man who
260.27 falls into the sea. If he tries to climb out into the
260.28 air as inexperienced people endeavour to do, he
260.29 drowns -- nicht war? ... No! I tell you! The
260.30 way is to the destructive element submit yourself,
261.01 and with the exertions of your hands and feet in the
261.02 water make the deep, deep sea keep you up. So
261.03 you ask me -- how to be?'
261.04 "His voice leaped up extraordinarily strong, as
261.05 though away there in the dusk he had been inspired
261.06 by some whisper of knowledge. 'I will tell you!
261.07 For that, too, there is only one way.'
261.08 "With a hasty swish-swish of his slippers he
261.09 loomed up in the ring of faint light, and suddenly
261.10 appeared in the bright circle of the lamp. His
261.11 extended hand aimed at my breast like a pistol;
261.12 his deep-set eyes seemed to pierce through me,
261.13 but his twitching lips uttered no word, and the
261.14 austere exaltation of a certitude seen in the dusk
261.15 vanished from his face. The hand that had been
261.16 pointing at my breast fell, and by and by, coming
261.17 a step nearer, he laid it gently on my shoulder.
261.18 There were things, he said mournfully, that perhaps
261.19 could never be told, only he had lived so much alone
261.20 that sometimes he forgot -- he forgot. The light
261.21 had destroyed the assurance which had inspired
261.22 him in the distant shadows. He sat down and,
261.23 with both elbows on the desk, rubbed his forehead.
261.24 'And yet it is true -- it is true. In the destructive
261.25 element immerse....' He spoke in a subdued
261.26 tone, without looking at me, one hand on each side
261.27 of his face. 'That was the way. To follow the
261.28 dream, and again to follow the dream -- and so --
261.29 ewig -- usque ad finem....' The whisper of his

261.30 conviction seemed to open before me a vast and
262.01 uncertain expanse, as of a crepuscular horizon on a
262.02 plain at dawn -- or was it, perchance, at the coming o
262.03 the night? One had not the courage to decide; but
262.04 it was a charming and deceptive light, throwing over
262.05 impalpable poesy of its dimness over pitfalls -- over
262.06 graves. His life had begun in sacrifice, in enthusi-
262.07 asm for generous ideas; he had travelled very far,
262.08 on various ways, on strange paths, and whatever he
262.09 followed it had been without faltering, and there-
262.10 fore without shame and without regret. In so far
262.11 he was right. That was the way, no doubt. Yet
262.12 for all that, the great plain on which men wander
262.13 amongst graves and pitfalls remained very desolate
262.14 under the impalpable poesy of its crepuscular
262.15 light, overshadowed in the centre, circled with a
262.16 bright edge as if surrounded by an abyss full of
262.17 flames. When at last I broke the silence it was
262.18 to express the opinion that no one could be more
262.19 romantic than himself.
262.20 "He shook his head slowly, and afterwards
262.21 looked at me with a patient and inquiring glance.
262.22 It was a shame, he said. There we were sitting and
262.23 talking like two boys, instead of putting our heads
262.24 together to find something practical -- a practical
262.25 remedy -- for the evil -- for the great evil -- he re-
262.26 peated, with a humorous and indulgent smile. For
262.27 all that, our talk did not grow more practical. We
262.28 avoided pronouncing Jim's name as though we had
262.29 tried to keep flesh and blood out of our discussion,
262.30 or he were nothing but an erring spirit, a suffering
263.01 and nameless shade. 'Na!' said Stein, rising.
263.02 'To-night you sleep here, and in the morning we
263.03 shall do something practical -- practical....' He lit
263.04 a two-branched candlestick and led the way. We
263.05 passed through empty, dark rooms, escorted by
263.06 gleams from the lights Stein carried. They glided
263.07 along the waxed floors, sweeping here and there over
263.08 the polished surface of the table, leaped upon a
263.09 fragmentary curve of a piece of furniture, or flashed
263.10 perpendicularly in and out of distant mirrors, while
263.11 the forms of two men and the flicker of two flames
263.12 could be seen for a moment stealing silently across
263.13 the depths of a crystalline void. He walked slowly
263.14 a pace in advance with stooping courtesy; there was
263.15 a profound, as it were a listening, quietude on his
263.16 face; the long, flaxen locks mixed with white threads
263.17 were scattered thinly upon his slightly bowed neck.
263.18 "'He is romantic -- romantic,' he repeated.
263.19 'And that is very bad -- very bad.... Very good,
263.20 too,' he added. 'But is he?' I queried.
263.21 "'Gewiss,' he said, and stood still holding up the
263.22 candelabrum, but without looking at me. 'Evident!
263.23 What is it that by inward pain makes him know
263.24 himself? What is it that for you and me makes him
263.25 --exist?'
263.26 -- exist?'
263.27 "At that moment it was difficult to believe in
263.28 Jim's existence -- starting from a country parsonage,
263.29 blurred by crowds of men as by clouds of dust,
263.30 silenced by the clashing claims of life and death in a
263.31 material world -- but his imperishable reality came
264.01 to me with a convincing, with an irresistible force!
264.02 I saw it vividly, as though in our progress through
264.03 the lofty, silent rooms amongst fleeting gleams of
264.04 light and the sudden revelations of human figures
264.05 stealing with flickering flames within unfathomable
264.06 and pellucid depths, we had approached nearer to
264.07 absolute Truth, which, like Beauty itself, floats
264.08 elusive, obscure, half submerged, in the silent, still
264.09 waters of mystery. 'Perhaps he is,' I admitted
264.10 with a slight laugh, whose unexpectedly loud re-
264.11 verberation made me lower my voice directly; 'but
264.12 I am sure you are.' With his head dropping on his
264.13 breast and the light held high he began to walk again.
264.14 'Well -- I exist, too,' he said.
264.15 "He preceded me. My eyes followed his move-
264.16 ments, but what I did see was not the head of the
264.17 firm, the welcome guest at afternoon receptions,
264.18 the correspondent of learned societies, the enter-
264.19 tainer of stray naturalists; I saw only the reality
264.20 of his destiny, which he had known how to follow
264.21 with unfaltering footsteps, that life begun in humble
264.22 surroundings, rich in generous enthusiasms, in
264.23 friendship, love, war -- in all the exalted elements of
264.24 romance. At the door of my room he faced me.
264.25 'Yes,' I said, as though carrying on a discussion,
264.26 'and amongst other things you dreamed foolishly
264.27 of a certain butterfly; but when one fine morning
264.28 your dream came in your way you did not let the

264.29 splendid opportunity escape. Did you? Whereas
264.30 he ...' Stein lifted his hand. 'And do you
265.01 know how many opportunities I let escape; how
265.02 many dreams I had lost that had come in my way?'
265.03 He shook his head regretfully. 'It seemed to me
265.04 that some would have been very fine -- if I had made
265.05 them come true. Do you know how many?
265.06 Perhaps I myself don't know.' 'Whether his
265.07 were fine or not,' I said, 'he knows of one which he
265.08 certainly did not catch.' 'Everybody knows of one
265.09 or two like that,' said Stein; 'and that is the
265.10 trouble -- the great trouble....'
265.11 "He shook hands on the threshold, peered into
265.12 my room under his raised arm. 'Sleep well. And
265.13 to-morrow we must do something practical --
265.14 practical....'
265.15 "Though his own room was beyond mine, I saw
265.16 him return the way he came. He was going back
265.17 to his butterflies."
266.01 "I DON#T suppose any of you have ever
266.02 heard of Patusan?" Marlow resumed,
266.03 after a silence occupied in the careful
266.04 lighting of a cigar. "It does not matter; there's
266.05 many a heavenly body in the lot crowding upon
266.06 us of a night that mankind had never heard of, it
266.07 being outside the sphere of its activities and of no
266.08 earthly importance to anybody but to the astronomers
266.09 who are paid to talk learnedly about its composition,
266.10 weight, path -- the irregularities of its conduct, the
266.11 aberrations of its light -- a sort of scientific scandal--
266.12 mongering. Thus with Patusan. It was referred
266.13 to knowingly in the inner government circles in
266.14 Batavia, especially as to its irregularities and aber-
266.15 rations, and it was known by name to some few,
266.16 very few, in the mercantile world. Nobody, how-
266.17 ever, had been there, and I suspect no one desired
266.18 to go there in person -- just as an astronomer, I
266.19 should fancy, would strongly object to being trans-
266.20 ported into a distant heavenly body, where, parted
266.21 form his earthly emoluments, he would be bewildered
266.22 by the view of an unfamiliar heavens. However,
266.23 neither heavenly bodies nor astronomers have any-
266.24 thing to do with Patusan. It was Jim who went
267.01 there. I only meant you to understand that had
267.02 Stein arranged to send him into a star of the fifth
267.03 magnitude the change could not have been greater.
267.04 He left his earthly failings behind him and what sort
267.05 of reputation he had, and there was a totally new set
267.06 of conditions for his imaginative faculty to work
267.07 of conditions for his imaginative faculty to work
267.08 upon. Entirely new, entirely remarkable. And he
267.09 got hold of them in a remarkable way.
267.10 "Stein was the man who knew more about
267.11 Patusan than anybody else. More than was known
267.12 in the government circles, I suspect. I have no
267.13 doubt he had been there, either in his butterfly--
267.14 hunting days or later on, when he tried in his
267.15 incorrigible way to season with a pinch of romance
267.16 the fattening dishes of his commercial kitchen.
267.17 There were very few places in the Archipelago he
267.18 had not seen in the original dusk of their being,
267.19 before light (and even electric light) had been
267.20 carried into them for the sake of better morality
267.21 and -- and -- well -- the greater profit, too. It was at
267.22 breakfast of the morning following our talk about
267.23 Jim that he mentioned the place, after I had quoted
267.24 poor Brierly's remark: 'Let him creep twenty feet
267.25 underground and stay there.' He looked up at me
267.26 with interested attention, as though I had been a
267.27 rare insect. 'This could be done, too,' he re-
267.28 marked, sipping his coffee. 'Bury him in some
267.29 sort,' I explained. 'One doesn't like to do it, of
267.30 course, but it would be the best thing, seeing what
267.31 he is.' 'Yes; he is young,' Stein mused. 'The
268.01 youngest human being now in existence,' I affirmed.
268.02 'Schön. There's Patusan,' he went on in the same
268.03 tone.... 'And the woman is dead now,' he added
268.04 incomprehensibly.
268.05 "Of course I don't know that story; I can only
268.06 guess that once before Patusan had been used as a
268.07 grave for some sin, transgression, or misfortune. It
268.08 is impossible to suspect Stein. The only woman
268.09 that had ever existed for him was the Malay girl he
268.10 called 'My wife the princess,' or, more rarely in
268.11 moments of expansion, 'the mother of my Emma.'
268.12 Who was the woman he had mentioned in con-
268.13 nection with Patusan I can't say; but from his
268.14 allusions I understand she had been an educated
268.15 and very good-looking Dutch-Malay girl, with a
268.16 tragic or perhaps only a pitiful history, whose most
268.17 painful part no doubt was her marriage with a
268.18 Malacca Portuguese who had been clerk in some
268.19 commercial house in the Dutch colonies. I gathered
268.20 from Stein that this man was an unsatisfactory
268.21 person in more ways than one, all being more or
268.22 less indefinite and offensive. It was solely for his
268.23 wife's sake that Stein had appointed him manager
268.24 of Stein & Co.'s trading post in Patusan; but
268.25 commercially the arrangement was not a success,
268.26 at any rate for the firm, and now the woman
268.27 died, Stein was disposed to try another agent
268.28 there. The Portuguese, whose name was Cor-
268.29 nelius, considered himself a very deserving but
268.30 ill-used person, entitled by his abilities to a better
269.01 position. This man Jim would have to relieve.
269.02 'But I don't think he will go away from the place,'
269.03 remarked Stein. 'That has nothing to do with me.
269.04 It was only for the sake of the woman that I ...
269.05 But as I think there is a daughter left, I shall let
269.06 him, if he likes to stay, keep the old house.'
269.07 "Patusan is a remote district of a native-ruled
269.08 state, and the chief settlement bears the same name.
269.09 At a point on the river about forty miles from the
269.10 sea, where the first houses come into view, there
269.11 can be seen rising above the level of the forest the
269.12 summits of two steep hills very close together, and
269.13 separated by what looks like a deep fissure, the
269.14 cleavage of some mighty stroke. As a matter of
269.15 fact, the valley between is nothing but a narrow
269.16 ravine; the appearance from the settlement is of
269.17 one irregularly conical hill split in two, and with
269.18 the two halves leaning slightly apart. On the
269.19 third day after the full, the moon, as seen from the
269.20 open space in front of Jim's house (he had a very
269.21 fine house in the native style when I visited him),
269.22 rose exactly behind these hills, its diffused light at
269.23 first throwing the two masses into intensely black
269.24 relief, and then the nearly perfect disc, glowing
269.25 ruddily, appeared, gliding upwards between the
269.26 sides of the chasm, till it floated away above the
269.27 summits, as if escaping from a yawning grave in
269.28 gentle triumph. 'Wonderful effect,' said Jim by
269.29 my side. 'Worth seeing. Is it not?'
269.30 "And this question was put with a note of per-
270.01 sonal pride that made me smile, as though he had
270.02 had a hand in regulating that unique spectacle. He
270.03 had regulated so many things in Patusan -- things
270.04 that would have appeared as much beyond his control
270.05 as the motions of the moon and the stars.
270.06 "It was inconceivable. That was the distinctive
270.07 quality of the part into which Stein and I had
270.08 tumbled him unwittingly, with no other notion
270.09 than to get him out of the way; out of his own way,
270.10 be it understood. That was our main purpose,
270.11 though, I own, I might have had another motive
270.12 which had influenced me a little. I was about to
270.13 go home for a time; and it may be I desired, more
270.14 than I was aware of myself, to dispose of him -- to
270.15 dispose of him, you understand -- before I left.
270.16 I was going home, and he had come to me from
270.17 there, with his miserable trouble and his shadowy
270.18 claim, like a man panting under a burden in a mist.
270.19 I cannot say I had ever seen him distinctly -- not
270.20 even to this day, after I had my last view of him;
270.21 but it seemed to me that the less I understood
270.22 the more I was bound to him in the name of that
270.23 doubt which is the inseparable part of our knowledge.
270.24 I did not know so much more about myself. And
270.25 then, I repeat, I was going home -- to that home
270.26 distant enough for all its hearthstones to be like
270.27 one hearthstone, by which the humblest of us has the
270.28 right to sit. We wander in our thousands over the
270.29 face of the earth, the illustrious and the obscure,
270.30 earning beyond the seas our fame, our money, or
271.01 only a crust of bread; but it seems to me that for
271.02 each of us going home must be like going to render
271.03 an account. We return to face our superiors,
271.04 our kindred, our friends -- those whom we obey,
271.05 and those whom we love; but even they who
271.06 have neither, the most free, lonely, irresponsible
271.07 and bereft of ties, -- even those for whom home holds
271.08 no dear face, no familiar voice, -- even they have to
271.09 meet the spirit that dwells within the land, under its
271.10 sky, in its air, in its valleys, and on its rises, in its
271.11 fields, in its waters and its trees -- a mute friend,
271.12 judge, and inspirer. Say what you like, to get its
271.13 joy, to breathe its peace, to face its truth, one must
271.14 return with a clear consciousness. All this may
271.15 seem to you sheer sentimentalism; and indeed very
271.16 few of us have the will or the capacity to look con-

271.17 sciously under the surface of familiar emotions.
271.18 There are the girls we love, the men we look up
271.19 to, the tenderness, the friendships, the opportunities,
271.20 the pleasures! But the fact remains that you must
271.21 touch your reward with clean hands, lest it turn to
271.22 dead leaves, to thorns, in your grasp. I think it is
271.23 the lonely, without a fireside or an affection they
271.24 may call their own, those who return not to a
271.25 dwelling but to the land itself, to meet its dis-
271.26 embodied, eternal, and unchangeable spirit -- it is
271.27 those who understand best its severity, its saving
271.28 power, the grace of its secular right to our fidelity,
271.29 to our obedience. Yes! few of us understand,
271.30 but we all feel it though, and I say all without
272.01 exception, because those who do not feel do not
272.02 count. Each blade of grass has its spot on earth
272.03 whence it draws its life, its strength; and so is man
272.04 rooted to the land from which he draws his faith
272.05 together with his life. I don't know how much Jim
272.06 understood; but I know he felt, he felt confusedly
272.07 but powerfully, the demand of some such truth
272.08 or some such illusion -- I don't care now you call
272.09 it, there is so little difference, and the difference
272.10 means so little. The thing is that in virtue of his
272.11 feeling he mattered. He would never go home
272.12 now. Not he. Never. Had he been capable of
272.13 picturesque manifestations he would have shuddered
272.14 at the thought and made you shudder too. But he
272.15 was not of that sort, though he was expressive
272.16 enough in his way. Before the idea of going home
272.17 he would grow desperately stiff and immovable,
272.18 with lowered chin and pouted lips, and with those
272.19 candid blue eyes of his glowering darkly under a
272.20 frown, as if before something unbearable, as if
272.21 before something revolting. There was imagination
272.22 in that hard skull of his, over which the thick cluster-
272.23 ing hair fitted like a cap. As to me, I have no
272.24 imagination (I would be more certain about him
272.25 to-day if I had), and I do not mean to imply that
272.26 I figured to myself the spirit of the land uprising
272.27 above the white cliffs of Dover, to ask me what I --
272.28 returning with no bones broken, so to speak -- had
272.29 done with my very young brother. I could not
272.30 make such a mistake. I knew very well he was of
273.01 those about whom there is no inquiry; I had seen
273.02 better men go out, disappear, vanish utterly, without
273.03 provoking a sound of curiosity or sorrow. The
273.04 spirit of the land, as becomes the ruler of great
273.05 enterprises, is careless of innumerable lives. Woe
273.06 to the stragglers! We exist only in so far as we
273.07 hang together. He had straggled in a way; he
273.08 had not hung on; but he was aware of it with an
273.09 intensity that made him touching, just as a man's
273.10 more intense life makes his death more touching
273.11 than the death of a tree. I happened to be handy,
273.12 and I happened to be touched. That's all there is
273.13 to it. I was concerned as to the way he would go
273.14 out. It would have hurt me if, for instance, he
273.15 had taken to drink. The earth is so small that I was
273.16 afraid of, some day, being waylaid by a blear-eyed,
273.17 swollen-faced, besmirched loafer, with no soles to
273.18 his canvas shoes, and with a flutter of rags about
273.19 the elbows, who, on the strength of old acquaint-
273.20 ance, would ask for a loan of five dollars. You
273.21 know the awful jaunty bearing of these scarecrows
273.22 coming to you from a decent past, the rasping,
273.23 careless voice, the half-averted, impudent glances --
273.24 those meetings more trying to a man who believes
273.25 in the solidarity of our lives than the sight of an
273.26 impenitent death-bed to a priest. That, to tell
273.27 you the truth, was the only danger I could see for
273.28 him and for me; but I also mistrusted my want
273.29 of imagination. It might even come to something
273.30 worse; in some way it was beyond my powers of
274.01 fancy to foresee. He wouldn't let me forget how
274.02 imaginative he was, and your imaginative people
274.03 swing farther in any direction, as if given a longer
274.04 scope of cable in the uneasy anchorage of life.
274.05 They do. They take to drink, too. It may be
274.06 I was belittling him by such a fear. How could I
274.07 tell? Even Stein could say no more than that he
274.08 was romantic. I only knew he was one of us. And
274.09 what business had he to be romantic? I am telling
274.10 you so much about my own instinctive feelings and
274.11 bemused reflections because there remains so little
274.12 to be told of him. He existed for me, and after all
274.13 it is only through me that he exists for you. I've
274.14 led him out by the hand; I have paraded him
274.15 before you. Were my commonplace fears unjust?
274.16 I won't say -- not even now. You may be able to

274.17 tell better, since the proverb has it that the on-
274.18 lookers see most of the game. At any rate, they
274.19 were superfluous. He did not go out, not at all;
274.20 on the contrary, he came on wonderfully, came on
274.21 straight as a die and in excellent form, which showed
274.22 that he could stay as well as spurt. I ought to be
274.23 delighted, for it is a victory in which I had taken
274.24 my part; but I am not so pleased as I would have
274.25 expected to be. I ask myself whether his rush had
274.26 really carried him out of that mist in which he
274.27 loomed interesting if not very big, with floating
274.28 outlines -- a straggler yearning inconsolably for his
274.29 humble place in the ranks. And besides, the last
274.30 word is not said -- probably shall never be said.
275.01 Are not our lives too short for that full utterance
275.02 which through all our stammerings is of course our
275.03 only and abiding intention? I have given up
275.04 expecting those last words, whose ring, if they could
275.05 only be pronounced, would shake both heaven and
275.06 earth. There is never time to say our last word --
275.07 the last word of our love, of our desire, faith, re-
275.08 morse, submission, revolt. The heaven and the
275.09 earth must not be shaken, I suppose -- at least,
275.10 not by us who know so many truths about either.
275.11 My last words about Jim shall be few. I affirm
275.12 he had achieved greatness; but the thing would
275.13 be dwarfed in the telling, or rather in the hearing.
275.14 Frankly, it is not my words that I mistrust, but your
275.15 minds. I could be eloquent were I not afraid you
275.16 fellows had starved your imaginations to feed your
275.17 bodies. I do not mean to be offensive; it is
275.18 respectable to have no illusions -- and safe -- and
275.19 profitable -- and dull. Yet you, too, in your time
275.20 must have known the intensity of life, that light of
275.21 glamour created in the shock of trifles, as amazing
275.22 as the glow of sparks struck from a cold stone --
275.23 and as short-lived, alas!"
276.01 "THE conquest of love, honour, men's
276.02 confidence -- the pride of it, the power of
276.03 it, are fit materials for an heroic tale;
276.04 only our minds are struck by the externals of such
276.05 a success, and to Jim's successes there were no
276.06 externals. Thirty miles of forest shut it off from
276.07 the sight of an indifferent world, and the noise of the
276.08 white surf along the coast overpowered the voice of
276.09 fame. The stream of civilisation, as if divided on a
276.10 headland a hundred miles north of Patusan, branches
276.11 east and south-east, leaving its plains and valleys,
276.12 its old trees and its old mankind, neglected and
276.13 isolated, such as an insignificant and crumbling islet
276.14 between the two branches of a mighty, devouring
276.15 stream. You find the name of the country pretty
276.16 often in collections of old voyages. The seven-
276.17 teenth-century traders went there for pepper, be-
276.18 cause the passion for pepper seemed to burn like a
276.19 flame of love in the breast of Dutch and English
276.20 adventurers about the time of James the First.
276.21 Where wouldn't they go for pepper! For a bag of
276.22 pepper they would cut each other's throats without
276.23 hesitation, and would forswear their souls, of which
276.24 they were so careful otherwise: the bizarre ob-
277.01 stinacy of that desire made them defy death in a
277.02 thousand shapes -- the unknown seas, the loathsome
277.03 and strange diseases; wounds, captivity, hunger,
277.04 pestilence, and despair. It made them great!
277.05 By heavens! it made them heroic; and it made
277.06 them pathetic, too, in their craving for trade with
277.07 the inflexible death levying its toll on young and
277.08 old. It seems impossible to believe that mere greed
277.09 could hold men to such a steadfastness of purpose,
277.10 to such a blind persistence in endeavour and sacri-
277.11 fice. And indeed those who adventured their
277.12 persons and lives risked all they had for a slender
277.13 reward. They left their bones to lie bleaching on
277.14 distant shores, so that wealth might flow to the
277.15 living at home. To us, their less tried successors,
277.16 they appear magnified, not as agents of trade but
277.17 as instruments of a recorded destiny, pushing out
277.18 into the unknown in obedience to an inward voice,
277.19 to an impulse beating in the blood, to a dream of
277.20 the future. They were wonderful; and it must
277.21 be owned they were ready for the wonderful. They
277.22 recorded it complacently in their sufferings, in the
277.23 aspect of the seas, in the customs of strange nations,
277.24 in the glory of splendid rulers.
277.25 "In Patusan they had found lots of pepper, and
277.26 had been impressed by the magnificence and the
277.27 wisdom of the Sultan; but somehow, after a cen-
277.28 tury of chequered intercourse, the country seems to
277.29 drop gradually out of the trade. Perhaps the pepper

277.30 had given out. Be it as it may, nobody cares for
278.01 it now; the glory has departed, the Sultan is an
278.02 imbecile youth with two thumbs on his left hand
278.03 and an uncertain and beggarly revenue extorted
278.04 from a miserable population and stolen from him
278.05 by his many uncles.
278.06 "This of course I have from Stein. He gave
278.07 me their names and a short sketch of life and char-
278.08 acter of each. He was as full of information about
278.09 native states as an official report, but infinitely
278.10 more amusing. He had to know. He traded in so
278.11 many, and in some districts -- as in Patusan, for
278.12 instance -- his firm was the only one to have an
278.13 agency by special permit from the Dutch authorities.
278.14 The Government trusted his discretion, and it was
278.15 understood that he took all the risks. The men he
278.16 employed understood that, too, but he made it worth
278.17 their while apparently. He was perfectly frank
278.18 with me over the breakfast-table in the morning.
278.19 As far as he was aware (the last news was thirteen
278.20 months old, he stated precisely), utter insecurity
278.21 for life and property was the normal condition.
278.22 There were in Patusan antagonistic forces, and one
278.23 of them was Rajah Allang, the worst of the Sultan's
278.24 uncles, the governor of the river, who did the extort-
278.25 ing and the stealing, and ground down to the point
278.26 of extinction the country-born Malays, who, utterly
278.27 defenceless, had not even the resource of emigrating
278.28 -- 'For indeed,' as Stein remarked, 'where could they
278.29 go, and how could they get away?' No doubt
278.30 they did not even desire to get away. The world
279.01 (which is circumscribed by lofty impassable moun-
279.02 tains) has been given into the hand of the high-
279.03 born, and this Rajah they knew: he was of their own
279.04 royal house. I had the pleasure of meeting the
279.05 gentleman later on. He was a dirty, little, used-up
279.06 old man with evil eyes and a weak mouth, who
279.07 swallowed an opium pill every two hours, and in
279.08 defiance of common decency wore his hair uncovered
279.09 and falling in wild, stringy locks about his wizened,
279.10 grimy face. When giving audience he would clamber
279.11 upon a sort of narrow stage erected in a hall
279.12 like a ruinous barn with a rotten bamboo floor,
279.13 through the cracks of which you could see, twelve
279.14 or fifteen feet below, the heaps of refuse and garbage
279.15 of all kinds lying under the house. That is where
279.16 and now he received us when, accompanied by
279.17 Jim, I paid him a visit of ceremony. There were
279.18 about forty people in the room, and perhaps three
279.19 times as many in the great courtyard below. There
279.20 was constant movement, coming and going, pushing
279.21 and murmuring, at our backs. A few youths in gay
279.22 silks glared from the distance; the majority, slaves
279.23 and humble dependants, were half naked, in ragged
279.24 sarongs, dirty with ashes and mud-stains. I had
279.25 never seen Jim look so grave, so self-possessed,
279.26 in an impenetrable, impressive way. In the midst
279.27 of these dark-faced men, his stalwart figure in white
279.28 apparel, the gleaming clusters of his fair hair, seemed
279.29 to catch all the sunshine that trickled through the
279.30 cracks in the closed shutters of that dim hall, with
280.01 its walls of mats and a roof of thatch. He appeared
280.02 like a creature not only of another kind but of
280.03 another essence. Had they not seen him come up
280.04 in a canoe they might have thought he had descended
280.05 upon them from the clouds. He did, however,
280.06 come in a crazy dug-out, sitting (very still and with
280.07 his knees together, for fear of overturning the thing)
280.08 -- sitting on a tin box -- which I had lent him --
280.09 nursing on his lap a revolver of the Navy pattern --
280.10 presented by me on parting -- which, through an
280.11 interposition of Providence, or through some wrong-
280.12 headed notion, that was just like him, or else from
280.13 sheer instinctive sagacity, he had decided to carry
280.14 unloaded. That's how he ascended the Patusan
280.15 river. Nothing could have been more prosaic
280.16 and more unsafe, more extravagantly casual, more
280.17 lonely. Strange, this fatality that would cast the
280.18 complexion of a flight upon all his acts, of impulsive,
280.19 unreflecting desertion -- of a jump into the un-
280.20 known.
280.21 "It is precisely the casualness of it that strikes
280.22 me most. Neither Stein nor I had a clear concep-
280.23 tion of what might be on the other side when we,
280.24 metaphorically speaking, took him up and hove him
280.25 over the wall with scant ceremony. At the moment
280.26 I merely wished to achieve his disappearance.
280.27 Stein characteristically enough had a sentimental
280.28 motive. He had a notion of paying off (in kind, I
280.29 suppose) the old debt he had never forgotten. In-
280.30 deed he had been all his life especially friendly to
281.01 anybody from the British Isles. His late bene-
281.02 factor, it is true, was a Scot -- even to the length of
281.03 being called Alexander M'Neil -- and Jim came from
281.04 a long way south of the Tweed; but at the distance
281.05 of six or seven thousand miles Great Britain, though
281.06 never diminished, looks foreshortened enough even
281.07 to its own children to rob such details of their
281.08 importance. Stein was excusable, and his hinted
281.09 intentions were so generous that I begged him most
281.10 earnestly to keep them secret for a time. I felt
281.11 that no consideration of personal advantage should
281.12 be allowed to influence Jim; that not even the risk
281.13 of such influence should be run. We had to deal
281.14 with another sort of reality. He wanted a refuge,
281.15 and refuge at the cost of danger should be offered
281.16 him -- nothing more.
281.17 "Upon every other point I was perfectly frank
281.18 with him, and I even (as I believed at the time)
281.19 exaggerated the danger of the undertaking. As a
281.20 matter of fact I did not do it justice; his first day
281.21 in Patusan was nearly his last -- would have been his
281.22 last if he had not been so reckless or so hard on
281.23 himself and had condescended to load that revolver.
281.24 I remember, as I unfolded our precious scheme for
281.25 his retreat, how his stubborn but weary resignation
281.26 was gradually replaced by surprise, interest, wonder,
281.27 and by boyish eagerness. This was a chance he
281.28 had been dreaming of. He couldn't think how he
281.29 merited that I ... He would be shot if he could
281.30 see to what he owed ... And it was Stein,
282.01 Stein the merchant, who ... but of course it was
282.02 me he had to ... I cut him short. He was not
282.03 articulate, and his gratitude caused me inexplicable
282.04 pain. I told him that if he owed this chance to any
282.05 one especially, it was to an old Scot of whom he had
282.06 never heard, who had died many years ago, of
282.07 whom little was remembered besides a roaring voice
282.08 and a rough sort of honesty. There was really
282.09 no one to receive his thanks. Stein was passing on
282.10 to a young man the help he had received in his own
282.11 young days, and I had done no more than to men-
282.12 tion his name. Upon this he coloured, and, twisting
282.13 a bit of paper in his fingers, he remarked bashfully
282.14 that I had always trusted him.
282.15 "I admitted that such was the case, and added
282.16 after a pause that I wished he had been able to
282.17 follow my example. 'You think I don't?' he
282.18 asked uneasily, and remarked in a mutter that one
282.19 had to get some sort of show first; then brightening
282.20 up, and in a loud voice he protested he would give
282.21 me no occasion to regret my confidence, which --
282.22 which --
282.23 "'Do not misapprehend,' I interrupted. 'It is
282.24 not in your power to make me regret anything.'
282.25 There would be no regrets; but if there were, it
282.26 would be altogether my own affair: on the other
282.27 hand, I wished him to understand clearly that this
282.28 arrangement, this -- this -- experiment, was his own
282.29 doing; he was responsible for it and no one else.
282.30 'Why? Why,' he stammered, 'this is the very
283.01 thing that I ...' I begged him not to be dense,
283.02 and he looked more puzzled than ever. He was in
283.03 a fair way to make life intolerable to himself....
283.04 'Do you think so?' he asked, disturbed; but in a
283.05 moment added confidently, 'I was going on, though.
283.06 Was I not?' It was impossible to be angry with
283.07 him: I could not help a smile, and told him that
283.08 in the old days people who went on like this were
283.09 on the way of becoming hermits in a wilderness.
283.10 'Hermits be hanged!' he commented with engaging
283.11 impulsiveness. Of course he didn't mind a wilder-
283.12 ness.... 'I was glad of it,' I said. That was
283.13 where he would be going to. He would find it
283.14 lively enough, I ventured to promise. 'Yes, yes,'
283.15 he said keenly. He had shown a desire, I continued
283.16 inflexibly, to go out and shut the door after him....
283.17 'Did I?' he interrupted in a strange access of
283.18 gloom that seemed to envelop him from head to
283.19 foot like the shadow of a passing cloud. He was
283.20 wonderfully expressive after all. Wonderfully!
283.21 'Did I?' he repeated bitterly. 'You can't say I
283.22 made much noise about it. And I can keep it up,
283.23 too -- only, confound it! you show me a door....'
283.24 'Very well. Pass on,' I struck in. I could make
283.25 him a solemn promise that it would be shut behind
283.26 him with a vengeance. His fate, whatever it was,
283.27 would be ignored, because the country, for all its
283.28 rotten state, was not judged ripe for interference.
283.29 Once he got in, it would be for the outside world

283.30 as though he had never existed. He would have
284.01 nothing but the soles of his two feet to stand upon,
284.02 and he would have first to find his ground at that.
284.03 'Never existed -- that's it, by Jove!' he murmured
284.04 to himself. His eyes, fastened upon my lips,
284.05 sparkled. If he had thoroughly understood the
284.06 conditions, I concluded, he had better jump into
284.07 the first gharry he could see and drive on to Stein's
284.08 house for his final instructions. He flung out of the
284.09 room before I had fairly finished speaking."
285.01 "HE did not return till next morning. He
285.02 had been kept to dinner and for the
285.03 night. There never had been such a
285.04 wonderful man as Mr. Stein. He had in his pocket
285.05 a letter for Cornelius ('the Johnnie who's going to
285.06 get the sack,' he explained, with a momentary
285.07 drop in his elation), and he exhibited with glee a
285.08 silver ring, such as natives use, worn down very
285.09 thin and showing faint traces of chasing.
285.10 "This was his introduction to an old chap called
285.11 Doramin -- one of the principal men out there -- a big
285.12 pot -- who had been Mr. Stein's friend in that
285.13 country where he had all these adventures. Mr.
285.14 Stein called him 'war-comrade.' War-comrade
285.15 was good. Wasn't it? And didn't Mr. Stein speak
285.16 English wonderfully well? Said he had learned it
285.17 in Celebes -- of all places! That was awfully funny.
285.18 Was it not? He did speak with an accent -- a
285.19 twang -- did I notice? That chap Doramin had
285.20 given him the ring. They had exchanged presents
285.21 when they parted for the last time. Sort of pro-
285.22 mising eternal friendship. He called it fine -- did I
285.23 not? They had to make a dash for dear life out of
285.24 the country when that Mohammed -- Mohammed --
286.01 What's-his-name had been killed. I knew the
286.02 story, of course. Seemed a beastly shame, didn't
286.03 it?...
286.04 "He ran on like this, forgetting his plate, with a
286.05 knife and fork in hand (he had found me at tiffin)
286.06 slightly flushed, and with his eyes darkened many
286.07 shades, which was with him a sign of excitement.
286.08 The ring was a sort of credential -- ('It's like some-
286.09 thing you read of in books,' he threw in apprecia-
286.10 tively) -- and Doramin would do his best for him.
286.11 Mr. Stein had been the means of saving that chap's
286.12 life on some occasion; purely by accident, Mr.
286.13 Stein had said, but he -- Jim -- had his own opinion
286.14 about that. Mr. Stein was just the man to look out
286.15 for such accidents. No matter. Accident or pur-
286.16 pose, this would serve his turn immensely. Hoped
286.17 to goodness the jolly old beggar had not gone off
286.18 the hooks meantime. Mr. Stein could not tell.
286.19 There had been no news for more than a year; they
286.20 were kicking up no end of an all-fired row amongst
286.21 themselves, and the river was closed. Jolly awk-
286.22 ward, this; but, no fear; he would manage to
286.23 find a crack to get in.
286.24 "He impressed, almost frightened me with his
286.25 elated rattle. He was voluble like a youngster on
286.26 the eve of a long holiday with a prospect of delight-
286.27 ful scrapes, and such an attitude of mind in a grown
286.28 man and in this connection had in it something
286.29 phenomenal, a little mad, dangerous, unsafe. I
286.30 was on the point of entreating him to take things
287.01 seriously when he dropped his knife and fork (he had
287.02 begun eating, or rather swallowing food, as it were,
287.03 unconsciously), and began a search all round his
287.04 plate. The ring! The ring! Where the devil
287.05 ... Ah! Here it was.... He closed his big
287.06 hand on it, and tried all his pockets one after an-
287.07 other. Jove! wouldn't do to lose the thing. He
287.08 meditated gravely over his fist. Had it? Would
287.09 hang the bally affair round his neck! And he pro-
287.10 ceeded to do this immediately, producing a string
287.11 (which looked like a bit of a cotton shoe-lace) for
287.12 the purpose. There! That would do the trick! It
287.13 would be the deuce if ... He seemed to catch
287.14 sight of my face for the first time, and it steadied
287.15 him a little. I probably didn't realise, he said with
287.16 a naive gravity, how much importance he attached
287.17 to that token. It meant a friend; and it is a good
287.18 thing to have a friend. He knew something about
287.19 that. He nodded at me expressively, but before
287.20 my disclaiming gesture he leaned his head on his
287.21 hand and for a while sat silent, playing thoughtfully
287.22 with the breadcrumbs on the cloth.... 'Slam
287.23 the door!' -- that was jolly well put,' he cried, and
287.24 jumping up, began to pace the room, reminding me
287.25 by the set of the shoulders, the turn of his head,
287.26 the headlong and uneven stride, of that night when

287.27 he had paced thus, confessing, explaining -- what
287.28 you will -- but, in the last instance, living -- living
287.29 before me, under his own little cloud, with all his
287.30 unconscious subtlety which could draw consolation
288.01 from the very source of sorrow. It was the same
288.02 mood, the same and different, like a fickle companion
288.03 that to-day guiding you on the true path, with the
288.04 same eyes, the same step, the same impulse, to-
288.05 morrow will lead you hopelessly astray. His tread
288.06 was assured, his straying, darkened eyes seemed to
288.07 search the room for something. One of his foot-
288.08 falls somehow sounded louder than the other -- the
288.09 fault of his boots probably -- and gave a curious
288.10 impression of an invisible halt in his gait. One of
288.11 his hands was rammed deep into his trousers
288.12 pocket, the other waved suddenly above his head.
288.13 'Slam the door!' he shouted. 'I've been waiting
288.14 for that. I'll show yet ... I'll ... I'm ready
288.15 for any confounded thing.... I've been dreaming
288.16 of it ... Jove! Get out of this. Jove! This is
288.17 luck at last.... You wait. I'll ...'
288.18 "He tossed his head fearlessly, and I confess that
288.19 for the first and last time in our acquaintance I
288.20 perceived myself unexpectedly to be thoroughly
288.21 sick of him. Why these vapourings? He was
288.22 stumping about the room flourishing his arm ab-
288.23 surdly, and now and then feeling on his breast for
288.24 the ring under his clothes. Where was the sense of
288.25 such exaltation in a man appointed to be a trading-
288.26 clerk, and in a place where there was no trade --
288.27 at that? Why hurl defiance at the universe?
288.28 This was not a proper frame of mind to approach
288.29 any undertaking; an improper frame of mind not
288.30 only for him, I said, but for any man. He stood
289.01 still over me. Did I think so? he asked, by no
289.02 means subdued, and with a smile in which I seemed
289.03 to detect suddenly something insolent. But then I
289.04 am twenty years his senior. Youth is insolent; it is
289.05 its right -- its necessity; it has got to assert itself,
289.06 all assertion in this world of doubts is a defiance,
289.07 is an insolence. He went off into a far corner, and
289.08 coming back, he, figuratively speaking, turned to
289.09 rend me. I spoke like that because I -- even I,
289.10 who had been no end kind to him -- even I remem-
289.11 bered -- remembered -- against him -- what -- what had
289.12 happened. And what about others -- the -- the --
289.13 world? Where's the wonder he wanted to get out,
289.14 meant to get out, meant to stay out -- by heavens!
289.15 And I talked about proper frames of mind!
289.16 "'It is not I or the world who remember,' I
289.17 shouted. 'It is you -- you, who remember.'
289.18 "He did not flinch, and went on with heat,
289.19 'Forget everything, everybody, everybody....'
289.20 His voice fell.... 'But you,' he added.
289.21 "'Yes -- me, too -- if it would help,' I said, also
289.22 in a low tone. After this we remained silent and
289.23 languid for a time, as if exhausted. Then he began
289.24 again, composedly, and told me that Mr. Stein had
289.25 instructed him to wait for a month or so, to see
289.26 whether it was possible for him to remain, before he
289.27 began building a new house for himself, so as to
289.28 avoid 'vain expense.' He did make use of funny
289.29 expressions -- Stein did. 'Vain expense' was good.
289.30 ... Remain? Why! of course. He would hang
290.01 on. Let him only get in -- that's all; he would
290.02 answer for it he would remain. Never get out.
290.03 It was easy enough to remain.
290.04 "'Don't be foolhardy,' I said, rendered uneasy
290.05 by his threatening tone. 'If you only live long
290.06 enough you will want to come back.'
290.07 "'Come back to what?' he asked absently,
290.08 with his eyes fixed upon the face of a clock on the
290.09 wall.
290.10 "I was silent for a while. 'Is it to be never,
290.11 then?' I said. 'Never,' he repeated dreamily,
290.12 without looking at me, and then flew into sudden
290.13 activity. 'Jove! Two o'clock, and I sail at four!'
290.14 "It was true. A brigantine of Stein's was
290.15 leaving for the westward that afternoon, and he
290.16 had been instructed to take his passage in her, only
290.17 no orders to delay the sailing had been given. I
290.18 suppose Stein forgot. He made a rush to get his
290.19 things while I went aboard my ship, where he
290.20 promised to call on his way to the outer roadster.
290.21 He turned up accordingly in a great hurry and with
290.22 a small leather valise in his hand. This wouldn't
290.23 do, and I offered him an old tin trunk of mine
290.24 supposed to be water-tight, or at least damp-tight.
290.25 He effected the transfer by the simple process of
290.26 shooting out the contents of his valise as you would

290.27 empty a sack of wheat. I saw three books in the
290.28 tumble; two small, in dark covers, and a thick
290.29 green-and-gold volume -- a half-crown complete
290.30 Shakespeare. 'You read this?' I asked. 'Yes.
291.01 Best thing to cheer up a fellow,' he said hastily.
291.02 I was struck by his appreciation, but there was no
291.03 time for Shakespearean talk. A heavy revolver
291.04 and two small boxes of cartridges were lying on
291.05 the cuddy-table. 'Pray take this,' I said. 'It may
291.06 help you to remain.' No sooner were these words
291.07 out of my mouth than I perceived what grim mean-
291.08 ing they could bear. 'May help you to get in,'
291.09 I corrected myself remorsefully. He, however,
291.10 was not troubled by obscure meanings; he thanked
291.11 me effusively and bolted out, calling good-bye over
291.12 his shoulder. I heard his voice through the ship's
291.13 side urging his boatmen to give way, and looking
291.14 out of the stern-port I saw the boat rounding under
291.15 the counter. He sat in her leaning forward, exciting
291.16 his men with voice and gestures; and as he had
291.17 kept the revolver in his hand and seemed to be
291.18 presenting it at their heads, I shall never forget the
291.19 scared faces of the four Javanese, and the frantic
291.20 swing of their stroke which snatched that vision
291.21 from under my eyes. Then turning away, the
291.22 first thing I saw were the two boxes of cartridges
291.23 on the cuddy-table. He had forgotten to take them.
291.24 "I ordered my gig manned at once; but Jim's
291.25 rowers, under the impression that their lives hung
291.26 on a thread while they had that madman in the
291.27 boat, made such excellent time that before I had
291.28 traversed half the distance between the two vessels
291.29 I caught sight of him clambering over the rail, and
291.30 of his box being passed up. All the brigantine's
292.01 canvas was loose, her mainsail was set, and the
292.02 windlass was just beginning to clink as I stepped
292.03 upon her deck: her master, a dapper little half-
292.04 caste of forty or so, in a blue flannel suit, with lively
292.05 eyes, his round face the colour of lemon-peel, and
292.06 with a thin little black moustache drooping on each
292.07 side of his thick, dark lips, came forward smirking.
292.08 He turned out, notwithstanding his self-satisfied
292.09 and cheery exterior, to be of a careworn tempera-
292.10 ment. In answer to a remark of mine (while Jim
292.11 had gone below for a moment) he said, 'Oh yes.
292.12 Patusan.' He was going to carry the gentleman to
292.13 the mouth of the river, but would 'never ascend.'
292.14 His flowing English seemed to be derived from a
292.15 dictionary compiled by a lunatic. Had Mr. Stein
292.16 desired him to 'ascend,' he would have 'reverenti-
292.17 ally' -- (I think he wanted to say respectfully -- but
292.18 devil only knows) -- 'reverentially made objects for
292.19 the safety of properties.' If disregarded, he would
292.20 have presented 'resignation to quit.' Twelve
292.21 months ago he had made his last voyage there, and
292.22 though Mr. Stein 'propitiated many offertories'
292.23 to Mr. Rajah Allang and the 'principal populations,'
292.24 on conditions which made the trade 'a snare and
292.25 ashes in the mouth,' yet his ship had been fired
292.26 upon from the woods by 'irresponsive parties' all
292.27 the way down the river; which causing his crew
292.28 'from exposure to limb to remain silent in hidings,'
292.29 the brigantine was nearly stranded on a sandbank
292.30 at the bar, where she 'would have been perishable
293.01 beyond the act of man.' The angry disgust at the
293.02 recollection, the pride of his fluency, to which he
293.03 turned an attentive ear, struggled for the possession
293.04 of his broad, simple face. He scowled and beamed
293.05 at me, and watched with satisfaction the undeniable
293.06 effect of his phraseology. Dark frowns ran swiftly
293.07 over the placid sea, and the brigantine, with her
293.08 fore-topsail to the mast and her main-boom amid--
293.09 ships, seemed bewildered amongst the cat's-paws.
293.10 He told me further, gnashing his teeth, that the
293.11 Rajah was a 'laughable hyaena' (can't imagine how
293.12 he got hold of hyaenas); while somebody else was
293.13 many times falser than the 'weapons of a crocodile.'
293.14 Keeping one eye on the movements of his crew
293.15 forward, he let loose his volubility -- comparing the
293.16 place to a 'cage of beasts made ravenous by long
293.17 impenitence.' I fancy he meant impunity. He
293.18 had no intention, he cried, to 'exhibit himself to
293.19 be made attached purposefully to robbery.' The
293.20 long-drawn wails, giving the time for the pull of
293.21 the men catting the anchor, came to an end, and he
293.22 lowered his voice. 'Plenty too much enough of
293.23 Patusan,' he concluded with energy.
293.24 "I heard afterwards he had been so indiscreet
293.25 as to get himself tied up by the neck with a rattan
293.26 halter to a post planted in the middle of a mud-hole

293.27 before the Rajah's house. He spent the best part
293.28 of a day and a whole night in that unwholesome
293.29 situation, but there is every reason to believe the
293.30 thing had been meant as a sort of joke. He brooded
294.01 for a while over that horrid memory, I suppose,
294.02 and then addressed in a quarrelsome tone the man
294.03 coming aft to the helm. When he turned to me
294.04 again it was to speak judicially, without passion.
294.05 He would take the gentleman to the mouth of the
294.06 river at Batu Kring (Patusan town 'being situated
294.07 internally,' he remarked, 'thirty miles'). But in
294.08 his eyes, he continued -- a tone of bored, weary con-
294.09 viction replacing his previous voluble delivery -- the
294.10 gentleman was already 'in the similitude of a
294.11 corpse.' 'What? What do you say?' I asked.
294.12 He assumed a startlingly ferocious demeanour, and
294.13 imitated to perfection the act of stabbing from
294.14 behind. 'Already like the body of one departed,'
294.15 he explained, with the insufferably conceited air of
294.16 his kind after what they imagine a display of clever-
294.17 ness. Behind him I perceived Jim smiling silently
294.18 at me, and with a raised hand checking the exclama-
294.19 tion on my lips.
294.20 "Then, while the half-caste, bursting with
294.21 importance, shouted his orders, while the yards
294.22 swung creaking and the heavy boom came surging
294.23 over, Jim and I, alone as it were to leeward of the
294.24 mainsail, clasped each other's hands and exchanged
294.25 the last hurried words. My heart was freed from
294.26 that dull resentment which had existed side by side
294.27 with interest in his fate. The absurd chatter of the
294.28 half-caste had given more reality to the miserable
294.29 dangers of his path than Stein's careful statements.
294.30 On that occasion the sort of formality that had been
295.01 always present in our intercourse vanished from our
295.02 speech; I believe I called him 'dear boy,' and he
295.03 tacked on the words 'old man' to some half--
295.04 uttered expression of gratitude, as though his risk
295.05 set off against my years had made us more equal in
295.06 age and in feeling. There was a moment of real
295.07 and profound intimacy, unexpected and short--
295.08 lived like a glimpse of some everlasting, of some
295.09 saving truth. He exerted himself to soothe me as
295.10 though he had been the more mature of the two.
295.11 'All right, all right,' he said rapidly, and with
295.12 feeling. 'I promise to take care of myself. Yes;
295.13 I won't take any risks. Not a single blessed risk.
295.14 Of course not. I mean to hang out. Don't you
295.15 worry. Jove! I feel as if nothing could touch
295.16 me. Why! this is luck from the word Go. I
295.17 wouldn't spoil such a magnificent chance!...' A
295.18 magnificent chance! Well, it was magnificent, but
295.19 chances are what men make them, and how was
295.20 I to know? As he had said, even I -- even I remem-
295.21 bered -- his -- his misfortunes against him. It was
295.22 true. And the best thing for him was to go.
295.23 "My gig had dropped in the wake of the
295.24 brigantine, and I saw him aft detached upon the
295.25 light of the westering sun, raising his cap high above
295.26 his head. I heard an indistinct shout, 'You -- shall --
295.27 hear -- of -- me.' Of me, or from me, I don't know
295.28 which. I think it must have been of me. My eyes
295.29 were too dazzled by the glitter of the sea below his
295.30 feet to see him clearly; I am fated never to see him
296.01 clearly; but I can assure you no man could have
296.02 appeared less 'in the similitude of a corpse,' as
296.03 that half-caste croaker had put it. I could see the
296.04 little wretch's face, the shape and colour of a ripe
296.05 pumpkin, poked out somewhere under Jim's elbow.
296.06 He, too, raised his arm as if for a downward thrust.
296.07 Absit omen!"
297.01 "THE coast of Patusan (I saw it nearly two
297.02 years afterwards) is straight and sombre,
297.03 and faces a misty ocean. Red trails
297.04 are seen like cataracts of rust streaming under the
297.05 dark green foliage of bushes and creepers clothing
297.06 the low cliffs. Swampy plains open out at the
297.07 mouth of rivers, with a view of jagged blue peaks
297.08 beyond the vast forests. In the offing a chain of
297.09 islands, dark, crumbling shapes, stand out in the
297.10 everlasting sunlit haze like the remnants of a wall
297.11 breached by the sea.
297.12 "There is a village of fisher-folk at the mouth of
297.13 the Batu Kring branch of the estuary. The river,
297.14 which had been closed so long, was open then, and
297.15 Stein's little schooner, in which I had my passage,
297.16 worked her way up in three tides without being
297.17 exposed to a fusillade from 'irresponsive parties.'
297.18 Such a state of affairs belonged already to ancient
297.19 history, if I could believe the elderly head-man of the

297.20 fishing village, who came on board to act as a sort
297.21 of pilot. He talked to me (the second white man
297.22 he had ever seen) with confidence, and most of his
297.23 talk was about the first white man he had ever seen.
297.24 He called him Tuan Jim, and the tone of his refer-
298.01 ences was made remarkable by a strange mixture
298.02 of familiarity and awe. They, in the village, were
298.03 under that lord's special protection, which showed
298.04 that Jim bore no grudge. If he had warned me
298.05 that I would hear of him it was perfectly true. I
298.06 was hearing of him. There was already a story that
298.07 the tide had turned two hours before its time to
298.08 help him on his journey up the river. The talka-
298.09 tive old man himself had steered the canoe and had
298.10 marvelled at the phenomenon. Moreover, all the
298.11 glory was in his family. His son and his son-in-law
298.12 had paddled; but they were only youths without
298.13 experience, who did not notice the speed of the
298.14 canoe till he pointed out to them the amazing
298.15 fact.
298.16 "Jim's coming to that fishing village was a
298.17 blessing; but to them, as to many of us, the bless-
298.18 ing came heralded by terrors. So many genera-
298.19 tions had been released since the last white man had
298.20 visited the river that the very tradition had been
298.21 lost. The appearance of the being that descended
298.22 upon them and demanded inflexibly to be taken
298.23 up to Patusan was discomposing; his insistence was
298.24 alarming; his generosity more than suspicious.
298.25 It was an unheard-of request. There was no
298.26 precedent. What would the Rajah say to this?
298.27 What would he do to them? The best part of the
298.28 night was spent in consultation; but the immediate
298.29 risk from the anger of that strange man seemed so
298.30 great that at last a cranky dug-out was got ready.
299.01 The women shrieked with grief as it put off. A
299.02 fearless old hag cursed the stranger.
299.03 "He sat in it, as I've told you, on his tin box,
299.04 nursing the unloaded revolver on his lap. He sat
299.05 with precaution -- than which there is nothing more
299.06 fatiguing -- and thus entered the land he was
299.07 destined to fill with the fame of his virtues, from the
299.08 blue peaks inland to the white ribbon of surf on
299.09 the coast. At the first bend he lost sight of the
299.10 sea with its labouring waves for ever rising, sink-
299.11 ing, and vanishing to rise again -- the very image
299.12 of struggling mankind -- and faced the immovable
299.13 forests rooted deep in the soil, soaring towards the
299.14 sunshine, everlasting in the shadowy might of their
299.15 tradition, like life itself. And his opportunity sat
299.16 veiled by his side like an Eastern bride waiting to
299.17 be uncovered by the hand of the master. He, too,
299.18 was the heir of a shadowy and mighty tradition!
299.19 He told me, however, that he had never in his life
299.20 felt so depressed and tired as in that canoe. All the
299.21 movement he dared to allow himself was to reach,
299.22 as it were by stealth, after the shell of half a cocoa-
299.23 nut floating between his shoes, and bale some of the
299.24 water out with a carefully restrained action. He
299.25 discovered how hard the lid of a block-tin case was
299.26 to sit upon. He had heroic health; but several
299.27 times during that journey he experienced fits of
299.28 giddiness, and between whiles he speculated hazily
299.29 as to the size of the blister the sun was raising on
299.30 his back. For amusement he tried by looking
300.01 ahead to decide whether the muddy object he saw
300.02 lying on the water's edge was a log of wood or an
300.03 alligator. Only very soon he had to give that up.
300.04 No fun in it. Always alligator. One of them
300.05 flopped into the river and all but capsized the canoe.
300.06 But this excitement was over directly. Then in a
300.07 long, empty reach he was very grateful to a troop
300.08 of monkeys who came right down on the bank and
300.09 made an insulting hullabaloo on his passage. Such
300.10 was the way in which he was approaching greatness,
300.11 as genuine as any man ever achieved. Principally,
300.12 he longed for sunset; and meantime his three
300.13 paddlers were preparing to put into execution their
300.14 plan of delivering him up to the Rajah.
300.15 "'I suppose I must have been stupid with
300.16 fatigue, or perhaps I did doze off for a time,' he said.
300.17 The first thing he knew was his canoe coming to
300.18 the bank. He became instantaneously aware of the
300.19 forest having been left behind, of the first houses
300.20 being visible higher up, of a stockade on his left,
300.21 and of his boatmen leaping out together upon a low
300.22 point of land and taking to their heels. Instinc-
300.23 tively he leaped out after them. At first he thought
300.24 himself deserted for some inconceivable reason, but
300.25 he heard excited shouts, a gate swung open, and

300.26 a lot of people poured out, making towards him.
300.27 At the same time a boat full of armed men appeared
300.28 on the river and came alongside his empty canoe,
300.29 thus shutting off his retreat.
300.30 "'I was too startled to be quite cool -- don't
301.01 you know? -- and if that revolver had been loaded
301.02 I would have shot somebody -- perhaps two, three
301.03 bodies, and that would have been the end of me.
301.04 But it wasn't....' 'Why not?' I asked. 'Well,
301.05 I couldn't fight the whole population, and I wasn't
301.06 coming to them as if I were afraid of my life,' he
301.07 said, with just a faint hint of his stubborn sulkiness
301.08 in the glance he gave me. I refrained from pointing
301.09 out to him that they could not have known ten
301.10 chambers were actually empty. He had to satisfy
301.11 himself in his own way.... 'Anyhow it wasn't,'
301.12 he repeated good-humouredly, 'and so I just stood
301.13 still and asked them what was the matter. That
301.14 seemed to strike them dumb. I saw some of these
301.15 thieves going off with my box. That long-legged
301.16 old scoundrel Kassim (I'll show him to you to-
301.17 morrow) ran out fussing to me about the Rajah
301.18 wanting to see me. I said, "All right." I, too,
301.19 wanted to see the Rajah, and I simply walked
301.20 in through the gate and -- and -- here I am.' He
301.21 laughed, and then with unexpected emphasis,
301.22 'And do you know what's been in it?' he asked.
301.23 'I'll tell you. It's the knowledge that had I been
301.24 wiped out it is this place that would have been the
301.25 loser.'
301.26 "He spoke thus to me before his house on that
301.27 evening I've mentioned -- after we had watched the
301.28 moon float away above the chasm between the hills
301.29 like an ascending spirit out of a grave; its sheen
301.30 descended, cold and pale, like the ghost of dead
302.01 sunlight. There is something haunting in the light
302.02 of the moon; it has all the dispassionateness of a
302.03 disembodied soul, and something of its inconceivable
302.04 mystery. It is to our sunshine, which -- say what
302.05 you like -- is all we have to live by, what the echo is
302.06 to the sound: misleading and confusing whether
302.07 the note be mocking or sad. It robs all forms of
302.08 matter -- which, after all, is our domain -- of their
302.09 substance, and gives a sinister reality to shadows
302.10 alone. And the shadows were very real around us,
302.11 but Jim by my side looked very stalwart, as though
302.12 nothing -- not even the occult power of moonlight --
302.13 could rob him of his reality in my eyes. Perhaps,
302.14 indeed, nothing could touch him since he had sur-
302.15 vived the assault of the dark powers. All was silent,
302.16 all was still; even on the river the moonbeams slept
302.17 as on a pool. It was the moment of high water, a
302.18 moment of immobility that accentuated the utter
302.19 isolation of this lost corner of the earth. The
302.20 houses crowding along the wide, shining sweep
302.21 without ripple or glitter, stepping into the water in a
302.22 line of jostling, vague, grey, silvery forms mingled
302.23 with black masses of shadow, were like a spectral
302.24 herd of shapeless creatures pressing forward to
302.25 drink in a spectral and lifeless stream. Here and
302.26 there a red gleam twinkled within the bamboo
302.27 walls, warm, like a living spark, significant of human
302.28 affections, of shelter, of repose.
302.29 "He confessed to me that he often watched these
302.30 tiny warm gleams go out one by one, that he loved
303.01 to see people go to sleep under his eyes, confident
303.02 in the security of to-morrow. 'Peaceful here, eh?'
303.03 he asked. He was not eloquent, but there was a
303.04 deep meaning in the words that followed. 'Look
303.05 at these houses; there's not one where I am not
303.06 trusted. Jove! I told you I would hang on.
303.07 Ask any man, woman, or child ...' He paused.
303.08 'Well, I am all right anyhow.'
303.09 "I observed quickly that he had found that out
303.10 in the end. I had been sure of it, I added. He
303.11 shook his head. 'Were you?' He pressed my
303.12 arm lightly above the elbow. 'Well, then -- you
303.13 were right.'
303.14 "There was elation and pride, there was awe
303.15 almost, in that low exclamation. 'Jove!' he
303.16 cried, 'only think what it is to me.' Again he
303.17 pressed my arm. 'And you asked me whether I
303.18 thought of leaving. Good God! I! want to
303.19 leave! Especially now after what you told me of
303.20 Mr. Stein's ... Leave! Why! That's what I
303.21 was afraid of. It would have been -- it would have
303.22 been harder than dying. No -- on my word. Don't
303.23 laugh. I must feel -- every day, every time I open
303.24 my eyes -- that I am trusted -- that nobody has a
303.25 right -- don't you know? Leave! For where?

303.26 What for? To get what?'
303.27 "I had told him (indeed it was the main object
303.28 of my visit) that it was Stein's intention to present
303.29 him at once with the house and the stock of trading
303.30 goods, on certain easy conditions which would make
304.01 the transaction perfectly regular and valid. He
304.02 began to snort and plunge at first. 'Confound your
304.03 delicacy!' I shouted. 'It isn't Stein at all. It's
304.04 giving you what you had made for yourself. And in
304.05 any case keep your remarks for M'Neil -- when you
304.06 meet him in the other world. I hope it won't
304.07 happen soon....' He had to give in to my argu-
304.08 ments, because all his conquests, the trust, the
304.09 fame, the friendships, the love -- all these things
304.10 that made him master had made him a captive, too.
304.11 He looked with an owner's eye at the peace of the
304.12 evening, at the river, at the houses, at the ever-
304.13 lasting life of the forests, at the life of the old man-
304.14 kind, at the secrets of the land, at the pride of his
304.15 own heart; but it was they that possessed him and
304.16 made him their own to the innermost thought, to
304.17 the slightest stir of blood, to his last breath.
304.18 "It was something to be proud of. I, too, was
304.19 proud -- for him, if not so certain of the fabulous
304.20 value of the bargain. It was wonderful. It was
304.21 not so much of his fearlessness that I thought. It is
304.22 strange how little account I took of it: as if it had
304.23 been something too conventional to be at the root
304.24 of the matter. No. I was more struck by the other
304.25 gifts he had displayed. He had proved his grasp of
304.26 the unfamiliar situation, his intellectual alertness
304.27 in that field of thought. There was his readiness,
304.28 too! Amazing. And all this had come to him in a
304.29 manner like keen scent to a well-bred hound. He
304.30 was not eloquent, but there was a dignity in this
305.01 constitutional reticence, there was a high serious-
305.02 ness in his stammerings. He had still his old trick
305.03 of stubborn blushing. Now and then, though, a
305.04 word, a sentence, would escape him that showed how
305.05 deeply, how solemnly, he felt about that work which
305.06 had given him the certitude of rehabilitation. That
305.07 is why he seemed to love the land and the people
305.08 with a sort of fierce egoism, with a contemptuous
305.09 tenderness."
306.01 "'THIS is where I was prisoner for three
306.02 days,' he murmured to me (it was on the
306.03 occasion of our visit to the Rajah), while
306.04 we were making our way slowly through a kind of
306.05 awestruck riot of dependants across Tunku Allang's
306.06 courtyard. 'Filthy place, isn't it? And I couldn't
306.07 get anything to eat either, unless I made a row about
306.08 it, and then it was only a small plate of rice and a
306.09 fried fish not much bigger than a stickleback -- con-
306.10 found them! Jove! I've been hungry prowling
306.11 inside this stinking enclosure with some of these
306.12 vagabonds shoving their mugs right under my nose.
306.13 I had given up that famous revolver of yours at the
306.14 first demand. Glad to get rid of the bally thing.
306.15 Looked like a fool walking about with an empty
306.16 shooting-iron in my hand.' At that moment we
306.17 came into the presence, and he became unflinchingly
306.18 grave and complimentary with his late captor.
306.19 Oh! magnificent! I want to laugh when I think
306.20 of it. But I was impressed, too. The old disreput-
306.21 able Tunku Allang could not help showing his fear
306.22 (he was no hero, for all the tales of his hot youth he
306.23 was fond of telling); and at the same time there was
306.24 a wistful confidence in his manner towards his late
307.01 prisoner. Note! Even where he would be most
307.02 hated he was still trusted. Jim -- as far as I could
307.03 follow the conversation -- was improving the occasion
307.04 by the delivery of a lecture. Some poor villagers
307.05 had been waylaid and robbed while on their way
307.06 to Doramin's house with a few pieces of gum or
307.07 beeswax which they wished to exchange for rice. 'It
307.08 was Doramin who was a thief,' burst out the Rajah.
307.09 A shaking fury seemed to enter that old, frail body.
307.10 He writhed weirdly on his mat, gesticulating with
307.11 his hands and feet, tossing the tangled strings of
307.12 his mop -- an important incarnation of rage. There
307.13 were staring eyes and dropping jaws all around us.
307.14 Jim began to speak. Resolutely, coolly, and for
307.15 some time he enlarged upon the text that no man
307.16 should be prevented from getting his food and his
307.17 children's food honestly. The other sat like a
307.18 tailor at his board, one palm on each knee, his head
307.19 low, and fixing Jim through the grey hair that fell
307.20 over his very eyes. When Jim had done there was
307.21 a great stillness. Nobody seemed to breathe even;
307.22 no one made a sound till the old Rajah sighed faintly,

307.23 and looking up, with a toss of his head, said quickly,
307.24 'You hear, my people! No more of these little
307.25 games.' This decree was received in profound
307.26 silence. A rather heavy man, evidently in a position
307.27 of confidence, with intelligent eyes, a bony, broad,
307.28 very dark face, and a cheerily officious manner (I
307.29 learned later on he was the executioner), presented
307.30 to us two cups of coffee on a brass tray, which he
308.01 took from the hands of an inferior attendant. 'You
308.02 needn't drink,' muttered Jim very rapidly. I didn't
308.03 perceive the meaning at first, and only looked at him.
308.04 He took a good sip and sat composedly, holding the
308.05 saucer in his left hand. In a moment I felt ex-
308.06 cessively annoyed. 'Why the devil,' I whispered,
308.07 smiling at him amiably, 'do you expose me to such
308.08 a stupid risk?' I drank, of course, there was
308.09 nothing for it, while he gave no sign, and almost
308.10 immediately afterwards we took our leave. While
308.11 we were going down the courtyard to our boat,
308.12 escorted by the intelligent and cheery executioner,
308.13 Jim said he was very sorry. It was the barest
308.14 chance, of course. Personally he thought nothing
308.15 of poison. The remotest chance. He was -- he
308.16 assured me -- considered to be infinitely more use-
308.17 ful than dangerous, and so ... 'But the Rajah is
308.18 afraid of you abominably. Anybody can see that,'
308.19 I argued, with, I own, a certain peevishness, and all
308.20 the time watching anxiously for the first twist of
308.21 some sort of ghastly colic. I was awfully dis-
308.22 gusted. 'If I am to do any good here and preserve
308.23 my position,' he said, taking his seat by my side in
308.24 the boat, 'I must stand the risk: I take it once
308.25 every month, at least. Many people trust me to
308.26 do that -- for them. Afraid of me! That's just
308.27 it. Most likely he is afraid of me because I am
308.28 not afraid of his coffee.' Then showing me a place
308.29 on the north front of the stockade where the pointed
308.30 tops of several stakes were broken, 'This is where
309.01 I leaped over on my third day in Patusan. They
309.02 haven't put new stakes there yet. Good leap, eh?'
309.03 A moment later we passed the mouth of a muddy
309.04 creek. 'This is my second leap. I had a bit of a
309.05 run and took this one flying, but fell short. Thought
309.06 I would leave my skin there. Lost my shoes
309.07 struggling. And all the time I was thinking to
309.08 myself how beastly it would be to get a jab with a
309.09 bally long spear while sticking in the mud like this.
309.10 I remember how sick I felt wriggling in that slime.
309.11 I mean really sick -- as if I had bitten something
309.12 rotten.'
309.13 "That's how it was -- and the opportunity ran
309.14 by his side, leaped over the gap, floundered in the
309.15 mud ... still veiled. The unexpectedness of his
309.16 coming was the only thing, you understand, that
309.17 saved him from being at once dispatched with
309.18 krisses and flung into the river. They had him,
309.19 but it was like getting hold of an apparition, a
309.20 wraith, a portent. What did it mean? What to
309.21 do with it? Was it too late to conciliate him?
309.22 Hadn't he better be killed without more delay?
309.23 But what would happen then? Wretched old
309.24 Allang went nearly mad with apprehension and
309.25 through the difficulty of making up his mind.
309.26 Several times the council was broken up, and the
309.27 advisers made a break helter-skelter for the door
309.28 and out on to the verandah. One -- it is said -- even
309.29 jumped down to the ground -- fifteen feet, I should
309.30 judge -- and broke his leg. The royal governor of
310.01 Patusan had bizarre mannerisms, and one of them
310.02 was to introduce boastful rhapsodies into every
310.03 arduous discussion, when, getting gradually excited,
310.04 he would end by flying off his perch with a kris
310.05 in his hand. But, barring such interruptions, the
310.06 deliberations upon Jim's fate went on night and day.
310.07 "Meanwhile he wandered about the courtyard,
310.08 shunned by some, glared at by others, but watched
310.09 by all, and practically at the mercy of the first casual
310.10 ragamuffin with a chopper, in there. He took pos-
310.11 session of a small tumble-down shed to sleep in;
310.12 the effluvia of filth and rotten matter incommoded
310.13 him greatly: it seems he had not lost his appetite
310.14 though, because -- he told me -- he had been hungry
310.15 all the blessed time. Now and again 'some fussy
310.16 ass' deputed from the council-room would come out
310.17 running to him, and in honeyed tones would ad-
310.18 minister amazing interrogatories: 'Were the Dutch
310.19 coming to take the country? Would the white
310.20 man like to go back down the river? What was
310.21 the object of coming to such a miserable country?
310.22 The Rajah wanted to know whether the white man

310.23 could repair a watch? They did actually bring
310.24 out to him a nickel clock of New England make,
310.25 and out of sheer unbearable boredom he busied
310.26 himself in trying to get the alarum to work. It was
310.27 apparently when thus occupied in his shed that the
310.28 true perception of his extreme peril dawned upon
310.29 him. He dropped the thing -- he says -- 'like a
310.30 hot potato,' and walked out hastily, without the
311.01 slightest idea of what he would, or indeed could, do.
311.02 He only knew that the position was intolerable. He
311.03 strolled aimlessly beyond a sort of ramshackle little
311.04 granary on posts, and his eyes fell on the broken
311.05 stakes of the palisade; and then -- he says -- at once,
311.06 without any mental process as it were, without any
311.07 stir of emotion, he set about his escape as if executing
311.08 a plan matured for a month. He walked off care-
311.09 lessly to give himself a good run, and when he faced
311.10 about there was some dignitary, with two spearmen
311.11 in attendance, close at his elbow ready with a
311.12 question. He started off 'from under his very
311.13 nose,' went over 'like a bird,' and landed on the
311.14 other side with a fall that jarred all his bones
311.15 and seemed to split his head. He picked himself
311.16 up instantly. He never thought of anything at the
311.17 time; all he could remember -- he said -- was a
311.18 great yell; the first houses of Patusan were before
311.19 him four hundred yards away; he saw the creek,
311.20 and as it were mechanically put on more pace.
311.21 The earth seemed fairly to fly backwards under his
311.22 feet. He took off from the last dry spot, felt himself
311.23 flying through the air, felt himself, without any
311.24 shock, planted upright in an extremely soft and
311.25 sticky mudbank. It was only when he tried to
311.26 move his legs and found he couldn't that, in his own
311.27 words, 'he came to himself.' He began to think
311.28 of the 'bally long spears.' As a matter of fact,
311.29 considering that the people inside the stockade had
311.30 to run to the gate, then get down to the landing-
312.01 place, get into boats, and pull round a point of
312.02 land, he had more advance than he imagined.
312.03 Besides, it being low water, the creek was without
312.04 water -- you couldn't call it dry -- and practically
312.05 he was safe for a time from everything but a very
312.06 long shot perhaps. The higher firm ground was
312.07 about six feet in front of him. 'I thought I would
312.08 have to die there all the same,' he said. He reached
312.09 and grabbed desperately with his hands, and only
312.10 succeeded in gathering a horrible cold, shiny heap
312.11 of slime against his breast -- up to his very chin.
312.12 It seemed to him he was burying himself alive,
312.13 and then he struck out madly, scattering the mud
312.14 with his fists. It fell on his head, on his face,
312.15 over his eyes, into his mouth. He told me that he
312.16 remembered suddenly the courtyard, as you remem-
312.17 ber a place where you had been very happy years
312.18 ago. He longed -- so he said -- to be back there
312.19 again, mending the clock. Mending the clock --
312.20 that was the idea. He made efforts, tremendous
312.21 sobbing, gasping efforts, efforts that seemed to
312.22 burst his eyeballs in their sockets and make him
312.23 blind, and culminating into one mighty supreme
312.24 effort in the darkness to crack the earth asunder,
312.25 to throw it off his limbs -- and he felt himself creep-
312.26 ing feebly up the bank. He lay full length on the
312.27 firm ground and saw the light, the sky. Then as a
312.28 sort of happy thought the notion came to him that
312.29 he would go to sleep. He will have it that he did
312.30 actually go to sleep; that he slept -- perhaps for a
313.01 minute, perhaps for twenty seconds, or only for
313.02 one second, but he recollects distinctly the violent
313.03 convulsive start of awakening. He remained lying
313.04 still for a while, and then he arose muddy from
313.05 head to foot and stood there, thinking he was alone
313.06 of his kind for hundreds of miles, alone, with no
313.07 help, no sympathy, no pity to expect from any one,
313.08 like a hunted animal. The first houses were not
313.09 more than twenty yards from him; and it was the
313.10 desperate screaming of a frightened woman trying
313.11 to carry off a child that started him again. He
313.12 pelted straight on in his socks, beplastered with
313.13 filth out of all semblance to a human being. He
313.14 traversed more than half the length of the settle-
313.15 ment. The nimbler women fled right and left,
313.16 the slower men just dropped whatever they had in
313.17 their hands, and remained petrified with dropping
313.18 jaws. He was a flying terror. He says he noticed
313.19 the little children trying to run for life, falling
313.20 on their little stomachs and kicking. He swerved
313.21 between two houses up a slope, clambered in
313.22 desperation over a barricade of felled trees (there

313.23 wasn't a week without some fight in Patusan at that
313.24 time), burst through a fence into a maize-patch,
313.25 where a scared boy flung a stick at him, blundered
313.26 upon a path, and ran all at once into the arms of
313.27 several startled men. He just had breath enough
313.28 to gasp out, 'Doramin! Doramin!' He remem-
313.29 bers being half carried, half rushed to the top of
313.30 the slope, and in a vast enclosure with palms and
314.01 fruit trees being run up to a large man sitting
314.02 massively in a chair in the midst of the greatest
314.03 possible commotion and excitement. He fumbled
314.04 in mud and clothes to produce the ring, and, finding
314.05 himself suddenly on his back, wondered who had
314.06 knocked him down. They had simply let him go --
314.07 don't you know? -- but he couldn't stand. At the
314.08 foot of the slope random shots were fired, and
314.09 above the roofs of the settlement there rose a dull
314.10 roar of amazement. But he was safe. Doramin's
314.11 people were barricading the gate and pouring water
314.12 down his throat; Doramin's old wife, full of
314.13 business and commiseration, was issuing shrill
314.14 orders to her girls. 'The old woman,' he said
314.15 softly, 'made a to-do over me as if I had been her
314.16 own son. They put me into an immense bed --
314.17 her state bed -- and she ran in and out wiping her
314.18 eyes to give me pats on the back. I must have
314.19 been a pitiful object. I just lay there like a log for
314.20 I don't know how long.'
314.21 "He seemed to have a great liking for Doramin's
314.22 old wife. She on her side had taken a motherly
314.23 fancy to him. She had a round, nut-brown, soft
314.24 face, all fine wrinkles, large, bright red lips (she
314.25 chewed betel assiduously), and screwed-up, winking,
314.26 benevolent eyes. She was constantly in movement,
314.27 scolding busily and ordering unceasingly a troop
314.28 of young women with clear brown faces and big
314.29 grave eyes, her daughters, her servants, her slave--
314.30 girls. You know how it is in these households: it's
315.01 generally impossible to tell the difference. She was
315.02 very spare, and even her ample outer garment,
315.03 fastened in front with jewelled clasps, had somehow
315.04 a skimpy effect. Her dark, bare feet were thrust
315.05 into yellow straw slippers of Chinese make. I
315.06 have seen her myself flitting about with her ex-
315.07 tremely thick, long, grey hair falling about her
315.08 shoulders. She uttered homely, shrewd sayings,
315.09 was of noble birth, and was eccentric and arbitrary.
315.10 In the afternoon she would sit in a very roomy
315.11 arm-chair, opposite her husband, gazing steadily
315.12 through a wide opening in the wall which gave an
315.13 extensive view of the settlement and the river.
315.14 "She invariably tucked up her feet under her,
315.15 but old Doramin sat squarely, sat imposingly as a
315.16 mountain sits on a plain. He was only of the
315.17 nakhoda or merchant class, but the respect shown
315.18 to him and the dignity of his bearing were very
315.19 striking. He was the chief of the second power in
315.20 Patusan. The immigrants from Celebes (about
315.21 sixty families that, with dependants and so on,
315.22 could muster some two hundred men 'wearing
315.23 the kriss') had elected him years ago for their head.
315.24 The men of that race are intelligent, enterprising,
315.25 revengeful, but with a more frank courage than the
315.26 other Malays, and restless under oppression. They
315.27 formed the party opposed to the Rajah. Of course
315.28 the quarrels were for trade. This was the primary
315.29 cause of faction fights, of the sudden outbreaks
315.30 that would fill this or that part of the settlement
316.01 with smoke, flame, the noise of shots and shrieks.
316.02 Villages were burnt, men were dragged into the
316.03 Rajah's stockade to be killed or tortured for the
316.04 crime of trading with anybody else but himself.
316.05 Only a day or two before Jim's arrival several heads
316.06 of households in the very fishing village that was
316.07 afterwards taken under his especial protection had
316.08 been driven over the cliffs by a party of the Rajah's
316.09 spearmen, on suspicion of having been collecting
316.10 edible birds' nests for a Celebes trader. Rajah
316.11 Allang pretended to be the only trader in his country,
316.12 and the penalty for the breach of the monopoly was
316.13 death; but his idea of trading was indistinguishable
316.14 from the commonest forms of robbery. His cruelty
316.15 and rapacity had no other bounds than his cowardice,
316.16 and he was afraid of the organised power of the
316.17 Celebes men, only -- till Jim came -- he was not
316.18 afraid enough to keep quiet. He struck at them
316.19 through his subjects, and thought himself pathetically
316.20 in the right. The situation was complicated by a
316.21 wandering stranger, an Arab half-breed, who, I
316.22 believe, on purely religious grounds, had incited

234

316.23 the tribes in the interior (the bush-folk, as Jim
316.24 himself called them) to rise, and had established
316.25 himself in a fortified camp on the summit of one
316.26 of the twin hills. He hung over the town of Patusan
316.27 like a hawk over a poultry-yard, but he devastated
316.28 the open country. Whole villages, deserted, rotted
316.29 on their blackened posts over the banks of clear
316.30 streams, dropping piecemeal into the water the
317.01 grass of their walls, the leaves of their roofs, with a
317.02 curious effect of natural decay as if they had been a
317.03 form of vegetation stricken by a blight at its very
317.04 root. The two parties in Patusan were not sure
317.05 which one this partisan most desired to plunder.
317.06 The Rajah intrigued with him feebly. Some of
317.07 the Bugis settlers, weary with endless insecurity,
317.08 were half inclined to call him in. The younger
317.09 spirits amongst them, chaffing, advised to 'get
317.10 Sherif Ali with his wild men and drive the Rajah
317.11 Allang out of the country.' Doramin restrained
317.12 them with difficulty. He was growing old, and,
317.13 though his influence had not diminished, the situa-
317.14 tion was getting beyond him. This was the state of
317.15 affairs when Jim, bolting from the Rajah's stockade,
317.16 appeared before the chief of the Bugis, produced
317.17 the ring, and was received, in a manner of speaking,
317.18 into the heart of the community."
318.01 "DORAMIN was one of the most remark-
318.02 able men of his race I had ever seen.
318.03 His bulk for a Malay was immense,
318.04 but he did not look merely fat; he looked impos-
318.05 ing, monumental. This motionless body, clad in rich
318.06 stuffs, coloured silks, gold embroideries; this huge
318.07 head, enfolded in a red-and-gold headkerchief;
318.08 the flat, big, round face, wrinkled, furrowed, with
318.09 two semicircular heavy folds starting on each side
318.10 of wide, fierce nostrils, and enclosing a thick-lipped
318.11 mouth; the throat like a bull; the vast corrugated
318.12 brow overhanging the staring proud eyes -- made a
318.13 whole that, once seen, can never be forgotten. His
318.14 impassive repose (he seldom stirred a limb when
318.15 once he sat down) was like a display of dignity.
318.16 He was never known to raise his voice. It was a
318.17 hoarse and powerful murmur, slightly veiled as if
318.18 heard from a distance. When he walked, two short,
318.19 sturdy young fellows, naked to the waist, in white
318.20 sarongs and with black skull-caps on the backs of
318.21 their heads, sustained his elbows; they would ease
318.22 him down and stand behind his chair till he wanted
318.23 to rise, when he would turn his head slowly, as if
318.24 with difficulty, to the right and to the left, and then
319.01 they would catch him under his armpits and help
319.02 him up. For all that, there was nothing of a cripple
319.03 about him: on the contrary, all his ponderous
319.04 movements were like manifestations of a mighty,
319.05 deliberate force. It was generally believed he con-
319.06 sulted his wife as to public affairs; but nobody,
319.07 as far as I know, had ever heard them exchange
319.08 a single word. When they sat in state by the wide
319.09 opening it was in silence. They could see below
319.10 them in the declining light the vast expanse of the
319.11 forest country, a dark, sleeping sea of sombre green
319.12 undulating as far as the violet and purple range of
319.13 mountains; the shining sinuosity of the river like
319.14 an immense letter S of beaten silver; the brown
319.15 ribbon of houses following the sweep of both banks,
319.16 overtopped by the twin hills uprising above the
319.17 nearer tree-tops. They were wonderfully con-
319.18 trasted: she, light, delicate, spare, quick, a little
319.19 witch-like, with a touch of motherly fussiness
319.20 in her repose; he, facing her, immense and heavy,
319.21 like a figure of a man roughly fashioned of stone,
319.22 with something magnanimous and ruthless in his
319.23 immobility. The son of these old people was a
319.24 most distinguished youth.
319.25 "They had him late in life. Perhaps he was not
319.26 really so young as he looked. Four or five-and--
319.27 twenty is not so young when a man is already father
319.28 of a family at eighteen. When he entered the large
319.29 room, lined and carpeted with fine mats, and with a
319.30 high ceiling of white sheeting, where the couple sat
320.01 in state surrounded by a most deferential retinue,
320.02 he would make his way straight to Doramin, to kiss
320.03 his hand -- which the other abandoned to him
320.04 majestically -- and then would step across to stand
320.05 by his mother's chair. I suppose I may say they
320.06 idolised him, but I never caught them giving him an
320.07 overt glance. Those, it is true, were public func-
320.08 tions. The room was generally thronged. The
320.09 solemn formality of greetings and leave-takings, the
320.10 profound respect expressed in gestures, on the faces,

320.11 in the low whispers, is simply indescribable. 'It's
320.12 well worth seeing,' Jim had assured me while we
320.13 were crossing the river, on our way back. 'They
320.14 are like people in a book, aren't they?' he said
320.15 triumphantly. 'And Dain Waris -- their son -- is
320.16 the best friend (barring you) I ever had. What
320.17 Mr. Stein would call a good "war-comrade." I
320.18 was in luck. Jove! I was in luck when I
320.19 tumbled amongst them at my last gasp.' He
320.20 meditated with bowed head, then rousing himself
320.21 he added:
320.22 "'Of course I didn't go to sleep over it,
320.23 but ...' He paused again. 'It seemed to come
320.24 to me,' he murmured. 'All at once I saw what I
320.25 had to do ...'
320.26 "There was no doubt that it had come to him;
320.27 and it had come through the war, too, as is natural,
320.28 since this power that came to him was the power to
320.29 make peace. It is in this sense alone that might so
320.30 often is right. You must not think he had seen his
321.01 way at once. When he arrived the Bugis community
321.02 was in a most critical position. 'They were all
321.03 afraid,' he said to me -- 'each man afraid for himself;
321.04 while I could see as plain as possible that they must
321.05 do something at once, if they did not want to go
321.06 under one after another, what between the Rajah
321.07 and that vagabond Sherif.' But to see that was
321.08 nothing. When he got his idea he had to drive
321.09 it into reluctant minds, through the bulwarks of
321.10 fear, of selfishness. He drove it in at last. And
321.11 that was nothing. He had to devise the means.
321.12 He devised them -- an audacious plan; and his
321.13 task was only half done. He had to inspire with his
321.14 own confidence a lot of people who had hidden and
321.15 absurd reasons to hang back; he had to conciliate
321.16 imbecile jealousies, and argue away all sorts of
321.17 senseless mistrusts. Without the weight of Dora-
321.18 min's authority, and his son's fiery enthusiasm, he
321.19 would have failed. Dain Waris, the distinguished
321.20 youth, was the first to believe in him; theirs was
321.21 one of those strange, profound, rare friendships
321.22 between brown and white, in which the very differ-
321.23 ence of race seems to draw two human beings closer
321.24 by some mystic element of sympathy. Of Dain
321.25 Waris, his own people said with pride that he knew
321.26 how to fight like a white man. This was true; he
321.27 had that sort of courage -- the courage in the open,
321.28 I may say -- but he had also a European mind. You
321.29 meet them sometimes like that, and are surprised
321.30 to discover unexpectedly a familiar turn of thought,
322.01 an unobscured vision, a tenacity of purpose, a touch
322.02 of altruism. Of small stature, but admirably well
322.03 proportioned, Dain Waris had a proud carriage, a
322.04 polished, easy bearing, a temperament like a clear
322.05 flame. His dusky face, with big black eyes, was
322.06 in action expressive, and in repose thoughtful. He
322.07 was of a silent disposition; a firm glance, an ironic
322.08 smile, a courteous deliberation of manner seemed
322.09 to hint at great reserves of intelligence and power.
322.10 Such beings open to the Western eye, so often con-
322.11 cerned with mere surfaces, the hidden possibilities
322.12 of races and lands over which hangs the mystery
322.13 of unrecorded ages. He not only trusted Jim, he
322.14 understood him, I firmly believe. I speak of him
322.15 because he had captivated me. His -- if I may say
322.16 so -- his caustic placidity, and, at the same time, his
322.17 intelligent sympathy with Jim's aspirations, ap-
322.18 pealed to me. I seemed to behold the very origin
322.19 of friendship. If Jim took the lead, the other had
322.20 captivated his leader. In fact, Jim the leader was a
322.21 captive in every sense. The land, the people, the
322.22 friendship, the love, were like the jealous guardians
322.23 of his body. Every day added a link to the
322.24 fetters of that strange freedom. I felt convinced
322.25 of it, as from day to day I learned more of the
322.26 story.
322.27 "The story! Haven't I heard the story? I've
322.28 heard it on the march, in camp (he made me scour
322.29 the country after invisible game); I've listened to a
322.30 good part of it on one of the twin summits, after
323.01 climbing the last hundred feet or so on my hands
323.02 and knees. Our escort (we had volunteer followers
323.03 from village to village) had camped meantime on a bit
323.04 of level ground half-way up the slope, and in the still,
323.05 breathless evening the smell of wood-smoke reached
323.06 our nostrils from below with the penetrating delicacy
323.07 of some choice scent. Voices also ascended, won-
323.08 derful in their distinct and immaterial clearness.
323.09 Jim sat on the trunk of a felled tree, and pulling out
323.10 his pipe began to smoke. A new growth of grass

323.11 and bushes was springing up; there were traces of
323.12 an earthwork under a mass of thorny twigs. 'It all
323.13 started from here,' he said, after a long and medita-
323.14 tive silence. On the other hill, two hundred yards
323.15 across a sombre precipice, I saw a line of high
323.16 blackened stakes, showing here and there ruin-
323.17 ously -- the remnants of Sherif Ali's impregnable
323.18 camp.
323.19 "But it had been taken, though. That had been
323.20 his idea. He had mounted Doramin's old ordnance
323.21 on the top of that hill; two rusty iron 7-pounders,
323.22 a lot of small brass cannon -- currency cannon.
323.23 But if the brass guns represent wealth, they can
323.24 also, when crammed recklessly to the muzzle, send
323.25 a solid shot to some little distance. The thing was
323.26 to get them up there. He showed me where he
323.27 had fastened the cables, explained how he had
323.28 improvised a rude capstan out of a hollowed log
323.29 turning upon a pointed stake, indicated with the bowl
323.30 of his pipe the outline of the earthwork. The last
324.01 hundred feet of the ascent had been the most diffi-
324.02 cult. He had made himself responsible for success
324.03 on his own head. He had induced the war party
324.04 to work hard all night. Big fires lighted at inter-
324.05 vals blazed all down the slope, 'but up here,' he
324.06 explained, 'the hoisting gang had to fly around in
324.07 the dark.' From the top he saw men moving on the
324.08 hillside like ants at work. He himself on that night
324.09 had kept on rushing down and climbing up like a
324.10 squirrel, directing, encouraging, watching all along
324.11 the line. Old Doramin had himself carried up the
324.12 hill in his arm-chair. They put him down on the
324.13 level place upon the slope, and he sat there in the
324.14 light of one of the big fires -- 'amazing old chap --
324.15 real old chieftain,' said Jim, 'with his little, fierce
324.16 eyes -- a pair of immense flintlock pistols on his
324.17 knees. Magnificent things, ebony, silver-mounted,
324.18 with beautiful locks and a calibre like an old blunder-
324.19 buss. A present from Stein, it seems -- in exchange
324.20 for that ring, you know. Used to belong to good
324.21 old M'Neil. God only knows how he came by
324.22 them. There he sat, moving neither hand nor foot,
324.23 a flame of dry brushwood behind him, and lots of
324.24 people rushing about, shouting and pulling round
324.25 him -- the most solemn, imposing old chap you can
324.26 imagine. He wouldn't have had much chance if
324.27 Sherif Ali had let his infernal crew loose at us and
324.28 stampeded my lot. Eh? Anyhow, he had come up
324.29 there to die if anything went wrong. No mistake!
324.30 Jove! It thrilled me to see him there -- like a rock.
325.01 But the Sherif must have thought us mad, and never
325.02 troubled to come and see how we got on. Nobody
325.03 believed it could be done. Why! I think the very
325.04 chaps who pulled and shoved and sweated over it
325.05 did not believe it could be done! Upon my word
325.06 I don't think they did....'
325.07 "He stood erect, the smouldering brierwood
325.08 in his clutch, with a smile on his lips and a sparkle
325.09 in his boyish eyes. I sat on the stump of a tree
325.10 at his feet, and below us stretched the land, the
325.11 great expanse of the forests, sombre under the
325.12 sunshine, rolling like a sea, with glints of winding
325.13 rivers, the grey spots of villages, and here and
325.14 there a clearing, like an islet of light amongst the
325.15 dark waves of continuous tree-tops. A brooding
325.16 gloom lay over this vast and monotonous landscape;
325.17 the light fell on it as if into an abyss. The land
325.18 devoured the sunshine; only far off, along the
325.19 coast, the empty ocean, smooth and polished within
325.20 the faint haze, seemed to rise up to the sky in a wall
325.21 of steel.
325.22 "And there I was with him, high in the sun-
325.23 shine on the top of that historic hill of his. He
325.24 dominated the forest, the secular gloom, the old
325.25 mankind. He was like a figure set up on a pedestal,
325.26 to represent in his persistent youth the power, and
325.27 perhaps the virtues, of races that never grow old,
325.28 that have emerged from the gloom. I don't know
325.29 why he should always have appeared to me sym-
325.30 bolic. Perhaps this is the real cause of my interest
326.01 in his fate. I don't know whether it was exactly
326.02 fair to him to remember the incident which had
326.03 given a new direction to his life, but at that very
326.04 moment I remembered very distinctly. It was like
326.05 a shadow in the light."
327.01 "ALREADY the legend had gifted him
327.02 with supernatural powers. Yes, it
327.03 was said, there had been many ropes
327.04 cunningly disposed, and a strange contrivance
327.05 that turned by the efforts of many men, and each

327.06 gun went up tearing slowly through the bushes,
327.07 like a wild pig rooting its way in the undergrowth,
327.08 but ... and the wisest shook their heads. There
327.09 was something occult in all this, no doubt; for
327.10 what is the strength of ropes and of men's arms?
327.11 There is a rebellious soul in things which must be
327.12 overcome by powerful charms and incantations.
327.13 Thus old Sura -- a very respectable householder of
327.14 Patusan -- with whom I had a quiet chat one evening.
327.15 However, Sura was a professional sorcerer also,
327.16 who attended all the rice sowings and reapings for
327.17 miles around for the purpose of subduing the
327.18 stubborn souls of things. This occupation he seemed
327.19 to think a most arduous one, and perhaps the souls
327.20 of things are more stubborn than the souls of men.
327.21 As to the simple folk of outlying villages, they
327.22 believed and said (as the most natural thing in the
327.23 world) that Jim had carried the guns up the hill
327.24 on his back -- two at a time.
328.01 "This would make Jim stamp his foot in vexa-
328.02 tion and exclaim with an exasperated little laugh,
328.03 'What can you do with such silly beggars? They
328.04 will sit up half the night talking bally rot, and the
328.05 greater the lie the more they seem to like it.' You
328.06 could trace the subtle influence of his surroundings
328.07 in this irritation. It was part of his captivity. The
328.08 earnestness of his denials was amusing, and at last
328.09 I said, 'My dear fellow, you don't suppose I believe
328.10 this.' He looked at me quite startled. 'Well, no!
328.11 I suppose not,' he said, and burst into a Homeric
328.12 peal of laughter. 'Well, anyhow the guns were
328.13 there, and went off together at sunrise. Jove!
328.14 You should have seen the splinters fly,' he cried.
328.15 By his side Dain Waris, listening with a quiet
328.16 smile, dropped his eyelids and shuffled his feet a
328.17 little. It appears that the success in mounting the
328.18 guns had given Jim's people such a feeling of con-
328.19 fidence that he ventured to leave the battery under
328.20 charge of two elderly Bugis who had seen some
328.21 fighting in their day, and went to join Dain Waris
328.22 and the storming party who were concealed in the
328.23 ravine. In the small hours they began creeping
328.24 up, and when two-thirds of the way up, lay in the
328.25 wet grass waiting for the appearance of the sun,
328.26 which was the agreed signal. He told me with
328.27 what impatient, anguishing emotion he watched
328.28 the swift coming of the dawn; how, heated with the
328.29 work and the climbing, he felt the cold dew chilling
328.30 his very bones; now afraid he was he would begin
329.01 to shiver and shake like a leaf before the time came
329.02 for the advance. 'It was the slowest half-hour
329.03 in my life,' he declared. Gradually the silent
329.04 stockade came out on the sky above him. Men
329.05 scattered all down the slope were crouching amongst
329.06 the dark stones and dripping bushes. Dain Waris
329.07 was lying flattened by his side. 'We looked at
329.08 each other,' Jim said, resting a gentle hand on his
329.09 friend's shoulder. 'He smiled at me as cheery as
329.10 you please, and I dared not stir my lips for fear I
329.11 would break out into a shivering fit. 'Pon my word,
329.12 it's true! I had been streaming with perspiration
329.13 when we took cover -- so you may imagine ...'
329.14 He declared, and I believe him, that he had no fears
329.15 as to the result. He was only anxious as to his
329.16 ability to repress these shivers. He didn't bother
329.17 about the result. He was bound to get to the top
329.18 of that hill and stay there, whatever might happen.
329.19 There could be no going back for him. Those
329.20 people had trusted him implicitly. Him alone!
329.21 His bare word....
329.22 "I remember now, at this point, he paused with
329.23 his eyes fixed upon me. 'As far as he knew, they
329.24 never had an occasion to regret it yet,' he said.
329.25 'Never. He hoped to God they never would.
329.26 Meantime -- worse luck! -- they had got into the habit
329.27 of taking his word for anything and everything.
329.28 I could have no idea! Why, only the other day
329.29 an old fool he had never seen in his life came from
329.30 some village miles away to find out if he should
330.01 divorce his wife. Fact. Solemn word. That's
330.02 the sort of thing.... He wouldn't have believed
330.03 it. Would I? Squatted on the verandah chewing
330.04 betel-nut, sighing and spitting all over the place for
330.05 more than an hour, and as glum as an undertaker
330.06 before he came out with that dashed conundrum.
330.07 That's the kind of thing that isn't so funny as it
330.08 looks. What was a fellow to say? -- Good wife? --
330.09 Yes. Good wife -- old though. Started a confounded
330.10 long story about some brass pots. Been living
330.11 together for fifteen years -- twenty years -- could not

330.12 tell. A long, long time. Good wife. Beat her a
330.13 little -- not much -- just a little, when she was young.
330.14 Had to -- for the sake of his honour. Suddenly in
330.15 her old age she goes and lends three brass pots
330.16 to her sister's son's wife, and begins to abuse him
330.17 every day in a loud voice. His enemies jeered at
330.18 him; his face was utterly blackened. Pots totally
330.19 lost. Awfully cut up about it. Impossible to
330.20 fathom a story like that; told him to go home, and
330.21 promised to come along myself and settle it all.
330.22 It's all very well to grin, but it was the dashedest
330.23 nuisance! A day's journey through the forest,
330.24 another day lost in coaxing a lot of silly villagers to
330.25 get at the rights of the affair. There was the making
330.26 of a sanguinary shindy in the thing. Every bally
330.27 idiot took sides with one family or the other, and
330.28 one half of the village was ready to go for the
330.29 other half with anything that came handy. Honour
330.30 bright! No joke!... Instead of attending to
331.01 their bally crops. Got him the infernal pots back,
331.02 of course -- and pacified all hands. No trouble
331.03 to settle it. Of course not. Could settle the
331.04 deadliest quarrel in the country by crooking his
331.05 little finger. The trouble was to get at the truth of
331.06 anything. Was not sure to this day whether he had
331.07 been fair to all parties. It worried him. And the
331.08 talk! Jove! There didn't seem to be any head
331.09 or tail to it. Rather storm a twenty-foot-high old
331.10 stockade any day. Much! Child's play to that
331.11 other job. Wouldn't take so long either. Well,
331.12 yes; a funny set out, upon the whole -- the fool
331.13 looked old enough to be his grandfather. But from
331.14 another point of view it was no joke. His word
331.15 decided everything -- ever since the smashing of
331.16 Sherif Ali. An awful responsibility,' he repeated.
331.17 'No, really -- joking apart, had it been three lives
331.18 instead of three rotten brass pots it would have been
331.19 the same....'
331.20 "Thus he illustrated the moral effect of his
331.21 victory in war. It was in truth immense. It had
331.22 led him from strife to peace, and through death
331.23 into the innermost life of the people; but the gloom
331.24 of the land spread out under the sunshine preserved
331.25 its appearance of inscrutable, of secular repose.
331.26 The sound of his fresh young voice -- it's extra-
331.27 ordinary how very few signs of wear he snowed --
331.28 floated lightly, and passed away over the unchanged
331.29 face of the forests like the sound of the big guns
331.30 on that cold, dewy morning when he had no other
332.01 concern on earth but the proper control of the chills
332.02 in his body. With the first slant of sunrays along
332.03 these immovable tree-tops the summit of one hill
332.04 wreathed itself, with heavy reports, in white clouds
332.05 of smoke, and the other burst into an amazing noise
332.06 of yells, war-cries, shouts of anger, of surprise, of
332.07 dismay. Jim and Dain Waris were the first to lay
332.08 their hands on the stakes. The popular story has
332.09 it that Jim with a touch of one finger had thrown
332.10 down the gate. He was, of course, anxious to dis-
332.11 claim this achievement. The whole stockade --
332.12 he would insist on explaining to you -- was a poor
332.13 affair (Sherif Ali trusted mainly to the inaccessible
332.14 position); and, anyway, the thing had been already
332.15 knocked to pieces and only hung together by a
332.16 miracle. He put his shoulder to it like a little fool
332.17 and went in head over heels. Jove! If it hadn't
332.18 been for Dain Waris, a pock-marked, tattooed
332.19 vagabond would have pinned him with his spear
332.20 to a balk of timber like one of Stein's beetles.
332.21 The third man in, it seems, had been Tamb' Itam,
332.22 Jim's own servant. This was a Malay from the
332.23 north, a stranger who had wandered into Patusan,
332.24 and had been forcibly detained by Rajah Allang as
332.25 paddler of one of the state boats. He had made a
332.26 bolt of it at the first opportunity, and finding a
332.27 precarious refuge (but very little to eat) amongst the
332.28 Bugis settlers, had attached himself to Jim's person.
332.29 His complexion was very dark, his face flat, his eyes
332.30 prominent and injected with bile. There was some-
333.01 thing excessive, almost fanatical, in his devotion to
333.02 his 'white lord.' He was inseparable from Jim like
333.03 a morose shadow. On state occasions he would
333.04 tread on his master's heels, one hand on the haft of
333.05 his kriss, keeping the common people at a distance
333.06 by his truculent, brooding glances. Jim had made
333.07 him the head-man of his establishment, and all
333.08 Patusan respected and courted him as a person of
333.09 much influence. At the taking of the stockade he
333.10 had distinguished himself greatly by the methodical
333.11 ferocity of his fighting. The storming party had

333.12 come on so quick -- Jim said -- that notwithstanding
333.13 the panic of the garrison, there was a 'hot five
333.14 minutes hand-to-hand inside that stockade, till
333.15 some bally ass set fire to the shelters of boughs and
333.16 dry grass, and we all had to clear out for dear life.'
333.17 "The rout, it seems, had been complete. Dora-
333.18 min, waiting immovably in his chair on the hillside,
333.19 with the smoke of the guns spreading slowly above
333.20 his big head, received the news with a deep grunt.
333.21 When informed that his son was safe and leading
333.22 the pursuit, he, without another sound, made a
333.23 mighty effort to rise; his attendants hurried to his
333.24 help, and, held up reverently, he shuffled with great
333.25 dignity into a bit of shade where he laid himself
333.26 down to sleep, covered entirely with a piece of white
333.27 sheeting. In Patusan the excitement was intense.
333.28 Jim told me that from the hill, turning his back on
333.29 the stockade with its embers, black ashes, and half-
333.30 consumed corpses, he could see time after time the
334.01 open spaces between the houses on both sides of the
334.02 stream fill suddenly with a seething rush of people
334.03 and get empty in a moment. His ears caught
334.04 feebly from below the tremendous din of gongs and
334.05 drums; the wild shouts of the crowd reached him
334.06 in bursts of faint roaring. A lot of streamers made a
334.07 flutter as of little white, red, yellow birds amongst
334.08 the brown ridges of roofs. 'You must have en-
334.09 joyed it,' I murmured, feeling the stir of sympathetic
334.10 emotion.
334.11 "'It was .. it was immense! Immense!'
334.12 he cried aloud, flinging his arms open. The sudden
334.13 movement startled me as though I had seen him
334.14 bare the secrets of his breast to the sunshine, to the
334.15 brooding forests, to the steely sea. Below us the
334.16 town reposed in easy curves upon the banks of a
334.17 stream whose current seemed to sleep. 'Im-
334.18 mense!' he repeated for a third time, speaking in a
334.19 whisper, for himself alone.
334.20 "Immense! No doubt it was immense; the
334.21 seal of success upon his words, the conquered ground
334.22 for the soles of his feet, the blind trust of men, the
334.23 belief in himself snatched from the fire, the solitude
334.24 of his achievement. All this, as I've warned you,
334.25 gets dwarfed in the telling. I can't with mere words
334.26 convey to you the impression of his total and utter
334.27 isolation. I know, of course, he was in every sense
334.28 alone of his kind there, but the unsuspected qualities
334.29 of his nature had brought him in such close touch
334.30 with his surroundings that this isolation seemed only
335.01 the effect of his power. His loneliness added to his
335.02 stature. There was nothing within sight to com-
335.03 pare him with, as though he had been one of those
335.04 exceptional men who can be only measured by the
335.05 greatness of their fame; and his fame, remember,
335.06 was the greatest thing around for many a day's
335.07 journey. You would have to paddle, pole, or
335.08 track a long, weary way through the jungle before
335.09 you passed beyond the reach of its voice. Its voice
335.10 was not the trumpeting of the disreputable goddess
335.11 we all know -- not blatant -- not brazen. It took its
335.12 tone from the stillness and gloom of the land without
335.13 a past, where his word was the one truth of every
335.14 passing day. It shared something of the nature of
335.15 that silence through which it accompanied you into
335.16 unexplored depths, heard continuously by your side,
335.17 penetrating, far-reaching -- tinged with wonder and
335.18 mystery on the lips of whispering men."
336.01 "THE defeated Sherif Ali fled the country
336.02 without making another stand, and when
336.03 the miserable, hunted villagers began to
336.04 crawl out of the jungle back to their rotting houses,
336.05 it was Jim who, in consultation with Dain Waris,
336.06 appointed the head-men. Thus he became the
336.07 virtual ruler of the land. As to old Tunku Allang,
336.08 his fears at first had known no bounds. It is said
336.09 that at the intelligence of the successful storming of
336.10 the hill he flung himself, face down, on the bamboo
336.11 floor of his audience-hall, and lay motionless for a
336.12 whole night and a whole day, uttering stifled sounds
336.13 of such an appalling nature that no man dared
336.14 approach his prostrate form nearer than a spear's
336.15 length. Already he could see himself driven ig-
336.16 nominously out of Patusan, wandering abandoned,
336.17 stripped, without opium, without his women, with-
336.18 out followers, a fair game for the first comer to
336.19 kill. After Sherif Ali his turn would come, and who
336.20 could resist an attack led by such a devil? And
336.21 indeed he owed his life and such authority as he
336.22 still possessed at the time of my visit to Jim's idea
336.23 of what was fair alone. The Bugis had been

237

336.24 extremely anxious to pay off old scores, and the
337.01 impassive old Doramin cherished the hope of yet
337.02 seeing his son ruler of Patusan. During one of
337.03 our interviews he deliberately allowed me to get a
337.04 glimpse of this secret ambition. Nothing could be
337.05 finer in its way than the dignified wariness of his
337.06 approaches. He himself -- he began by declaring --
337.07 had used his strength in his young days, but now
337.08 he had grown old and tired.... With his impos-
337.09 ing bulk and haughty little eyes darting sagacious,
337.10 inquisitive glances, he reminded one irresistibly
337.11 of a cunning old elephant; the slow rise and fall
337.12 of his vast breast went on powerful and regular,
337.13 like the heave of a calm sea. He, too, as he pro-
337.14 tested, had an unbounded confidence in Tuan Jim's
337.15 wisdom. If he could only obtain a promise! One
337.16 word would be enough!... His breathing
337.17 silences, the low rumblings of his voice, recalled
337.18 the last efforts of a spent thunderstorm.
337.19 "I tried to put the subject aside. It was diffi-
337.20 cult, for there could be no question that Jim had
337.21 the power; in his new sphere there did not seem
337.22 to be anything that was not his to hold or to give.
337.23 But that, I repeat, was nothing in comparison with
337.24 the notion, which occurred to me, while I listened
337.25 with a show of attention, that he seemed to have
337.26 come very near at last to mastering his fate. Dora-
337.27 min was anxious about the future of the country,
337.28 and I was struck by the turn he gave to the argu-
337.29 ment. The land remains where God has put it;
337.30 but white men -- he said -- they come to us and in a
338.01 little while they go. They go away. Those they
338.02 leave behind do not know when to look for their
338.03 return. They go to their own land, to their people,
338.04 and so this white man, too, would.... I don't
338.05 know what induced me to commit myself at this
338.06 point by a vigorous 'No, no.' The whole extent
338.07 of this indiscretion became apparent when Doramin,
338.08 turning full upon me his face, whose expression,
338.09 fixed in rugged, deep folds, remained unalterable,
338.10 like a huge brown mask, said that this was good news
338.11 indeed, reflectively; and then wanted to know why.
338.12 "His little, motherly witch of a wife sat on my
338.13 other hand, with her head covered and her feet
338.14 tucked up, gazing through the great shutter-hole.
338.15 I could only see a straying lock of grey hair, a high
338.16 cheek-bone, the slight masticating motion of the
338.17 sharp chin. Without removing her eyes from the
338.18 vast prospect of forests stretching as far as the hills
338.19 she asked me in a pitying voice why was it that he
338.20 so young had wandered from his home, coming so
338.21 far, through so many dangers? Had he no house-
338.22 hold there, no kinsmen in his own country? Had
338.23 he no old mother, who would always remember his
338.24 face?...
338.25 "I was completely unprepared for this. I could
338.26 only mutter and shake my head vaguely. After-
338.27 wards I am perfectly aware I cut a very poor figure
338.28 trying to extricate myself out of this difficulty.
338.29 From that moment, however, the old nakhoda
338.30 became taciturn. He was not very pleased, I fear,
339.01 and evidently I had given him food for thought.
339.02 Strangely enough, on the evening of that very day
339.03 (which was my last in Patusan) I was once more
339.04 confronted with the same question, with the un-
339.05 answerable why of Jim's fate. And this brings me
339.06 to the story of his love.
339.07 "I suppose you think it is a story that you can
339.08 imagine for yourselves. We have heard so many
339.09 such stories, and the majority of us don't believe
339.10 them to be stories of love at all. For the most
339.11 part we look upon them as stories of opportunities:
339.12 episodes of passion at best, or perhaps only of
339.13 youth and temptation, doomed to forgetfulness in
339.14 the end, even if they pass through the reality of
339.15 tenderness and regret. This view mostly is right,
339.16 and perhaps in this case, too.... Yet I don't
339.17 know. To tell this story is by no means so easy
339.18 as it should be -- were the ordinary standpoint
339.19 adequate. Apparently it is a story very much like
339.20 the others: for me, however, there is visible in its
339.21 background the melancholy figure of a woman, the
339.22 shadow of a cruel wisdom buried in a lonely grave,
339.23 looking on wistfully, helplessly, with sealed lips.
339.24 The grave itself, as I came upon it during an early
339.25 morning stroll, was a rather shapeless brown mound,
339.26 with an inlaid neat border of white lumps of coral at
339.27 the base, and enclosed within a circular fence made
339.28 of split saplings, with the bark left on. A garland
339.29 of leaves and flowers was woven about the heads of

339.30 the slender posts -- and the flowers were fresh.
340.01 "Thus, whether the shadow is of my imagination
340.02 or not, I can at all events point out the significant
340.03 fact of an unforgotten grave. When I tell you
340.04 besides that Jim with his own hands had worked
340.05 at the rustic fence, you will perceive directly the
340.06 difference, the individual side of the story. There
340.07 is in his espousal of memory and affection belonging
340.08 to another human being something characteristic
340.09 of his seriousness. He had a conscience, and it
340.10 was a romantic conscience. Through her whole
340.11 life the wife of the unspeakable Cornelius had
340.12 no other companion, confidante, and friend but
340.13 her daughter. How the poor woman had come
340.14 to marry the awful Malacca Portuguese -- after the
340.15 separation from the father of her girl -- and how
340.16 that separation had been brought about, whether by
340.17 death, which can be sometimes merciful, or by the
340.18 merciless pressure of conventions, is a mystery to
340.19 me. From the little which Stein (who knew so
340.20 many stories) had let drop in my hearing, I am
340.21 convinced that she was no ordinary woman. Her
340.22 own father had been a white; a high official; one
340.23 of the brilliantly endowed men who are not dull
340.24 enough to nurse a success, and whose careers
340.25 so often end under a cloud. I suppose she, too,
340.26 must have lacked the saving dullness -- and her
340.27 career ended in Patusan. Our common fate ...
340.28 for where is the man -- I mean a real sentient man
340.29 -- who does not remember vaguely having been
340.30 deserted in the fullness of possession by some one
341.01 or something more precious than life? ... our
341.02 common fate fastens upon the women with a peculiar
341.03 cruelty. It does not punish like a master, but
341.04 inflicts lingering torment, as if to gratify a secret,
341.05 unappeasable spite. One would think that, ap-
341.06 pointed to rule on earth, it seeks to revenge itself
341.07 upon the beings that come nearest to rising above
341.08 the trammels of earthly caution; for it is only
341.09 women who manage to put at times into their love
341.10 an element just palpable enough to give one a
341.11 fright -- an extra-terrestrial touch. I ask myself
341.12 with wonder -- how the world can look to them --
341.13 whether it has the shape and substance we know,
341.14 the air we breathe! Sometimes I fancy it must be
341.15 a region of unreasonable sublimities seething with
341.16 the excitement of their adventurous souls, lighted
341.17 by the glory of all possible risks and renunciations.
341.18 However, I suspect there are very few women in the
341.19 world, though of course I am aware of the multi-
341.20 tudes of mankind and of the equality of sexes -- in
341.21 point of numbers, that is. But I am sure that the
341.22 mother was as much of a woman as the daughter
341.23 seemed to be. I cannot help picturing to myself
341.24 these two, at first the young woman and the child,
341.25 then the old woman and the young girl, the awful
341.26 sameness and the swift passage of time, the barrier
341.27 of forest, the solitude and the turmoil round these
341.28 two lonely lives, and every word spoken between
341.29 them penetrated with sad meaning. There must
341.30 have been confidences, not so much of fact, I
342.01 suppose, as of innermost feelings -- regrets -- fears --
342.02 warnings, no doubt: warnings that the younger
342.03 did not fully understand till the elder was dead --
342.04 and Jim came along. Then I am sure she under-
342.05 stood much -- not everything -- the fear mostly, it
342.06 seems. Jim called her by a word that means
342.07 precious, in the sense of a precious gem -- jewel.
342.08 Pretty, isn't it? But he was capable of anything.
342.09 He was equal to his fortune, as he -- after all --
342.10 must have been equal to his misfortune. Jewel he
342.11 called her; and he would say this as he might have
342.12 said 'Jane,' don't you know? -- with a marital, home--
342.13 like, peaceful effect. I heard the name for the
342.14 first time ten minutes after I had landed in his
342.15 courtyard, when, after nearly shaking my arm off,
342.16 he darted up the steps and began to make a joyous,
342.17 boyish disturbance at the door under the heavy
342.18 eaves. 'Jewel! O Jewel! Quick! Here's a
342.19 friend come,' ... and suddenly peering at me in
342.20 the dim verandah, he mumbled earnestly, 'You
342.21 know -- this -- no confounded nonsense about it --
342.22 can't tell you how much I owe to her -- and so -- you
342.23 understand -- I -- exactly as if ...' His hurried,
342.24 anxious whispers were cut short by the flitting of a
342.25 white form from within the house, a faint exclamation,
342.26 and a childlike but energetic little face with delicate
342.27 features and a profound, attentive glance peeped out
342.28 of the inner gloom, like a bird out of the recess
342.29 of a nest. I was struck by the name, of course;

342.30 but it was not till later on that I connected it with
343.01 an astonishing rumour that had met me on my
343.02 journey, at a little place on the coast about 230 miles
343.03 south of Patusan River. Stein's schooner, in which
343.04 I had my passage, put in there, to collect some
343.05 produce, and going ashore, I found to my great
343.06 surprise that the wretched locality could boast of
343.07 a third-class deputy-assistant resident, a big, fat,
343.08 greasy, blinking fellow of mixed descent, with
343.09 turned-out, shiny lips. I found him lying extended
343.10 on his back in a cane chair, odiously unbuttoned,
343.11 with a large green leaf of some sort on the top of
343.12 his steaming head, and another in his hand which
343.13 he used lazily as a fan.... Going to Patusan?
343.14 Oh yes. Stein's Trading Company. He knew.
343.15 Had a permission? No business of his. It was
343.16 not so bad there now, he remarked negligently, and,
343.17 he went on drawling, 'There's some sort of white
343.18 vagabond has got in there, I hear.... Eh? What
343.19 you say? Friends of yours? So! ... Then it
343.20 was true there was one of these _verdamte_ -- What
343.21 was he up to? Found his way in, the rascal. Eh?
343.22 I had not been sure. Patusan -- they cut throats
343.23 there -- no business of ours.' He interrupted him-
343.24 self to groan. 'Phoo! Almighty! The heat!
343.25 The heat! Well, then, there might be something
343.26 in the story, too, after all, and ...' He shut
343.27 one of his beastly glassy eyes (the eyelid went on
343.28 quivering) while he leered at me atrociously with
343.29 the other. 'Look here,' says he mysteriously, 'if
343.30 -- do you understand? -- if he has really got hold of
344.01 something fairly good -- none of your bits of green
344.02 glass -- understand? -- I am a Government official --
344.03 you tell the rascal ... Eh? What? Friend of
344.04 yours?' ... He continued wallowing calmly in
344.05 the chair.... 'You said so; that's just it; and
344.06 I am pleased to give you the hint. I suppose you,
344.07 too, would like to get something out of it? Don't
344.08 interrupt. You just tell him I've heard the tale,
344.09 but to my Government I have made no report.
344.10 Not yet. See? Why make a report? Eh? Tell
344.11 him to come to me if they let him get alive out of
344.12 the country. He had better look out for himself.
344.13 Eh? I promise to ask no questions. On the
344.14 quiet -- you understand? You, too -- you shall get
344.15 something from me. Small commission for the
344.16 trouble. Don't interrupt. I am a Government
344.17 official, and make no report. That's business.
344.18 Understand? I know some good people that will
344.19 buy anything worth having, and can give him more
344.20 money than the scoundrel ever saw in his life. I
344.21 know his sort.' He fixed me steadfastly with both
344.22 his eyes open, while I stood over him utterly amazed,
344.23 and asking myself whether he was mad or drunk.
344.24 He perspired, puffed, moaning feebly, and scratch-
344.25 ing himself with such horrible composure that I
344.26 could not bear the sight long enough to find out.
344.27 Next day, talking casually with the people of the
344.28 little native court of the place, I discovered that a
344.29 story was travelling slowly down the coast about
344.30 a mysterious white man in Patusan who had got
345.01 hold of an extraordinary gem -- namely, an emerald
345.02 of an enormous size, and altogether priceless.
345.03 The emerald seems to appeal more to the Eastern
345.04 imagination than any other precious stone. The
345.05 white man had obtained it, I was told, partly by
345.06 the exercise of his wonderful strength and partly by
345.07 cunning, from the ruler of a distant country, whence
345.08 he had fled instantly, arriving in Patusan in utmost
345.09 distress, but frightening the people by his extreme
345.10 ferocity, which nothing seemed able to subdue.
345.11 Most of my informants were of the opinion that the
345.12 stone was probably unlucky -- like the famous stone
345.13 of the Sultan of Succadana, which in the old times
345.14 had brought wars and untold calamities upon that
345.15 country. Perhaps it was the same stone -- one
345.16 couldn't say. Indeed the story of a fabulously
345.17 large emerald is as old as the arrival of the first
345.18 white men in the Archipelago; and the belief in it
345.19 is so persistent that less than forty years ago there
345.20 had been an official Dutch inquiry into the truth of
345.21 it. Such a jewel -- it was explained to me by the
345.22 old fellow from whom I heard most of this amazing
345.23 Jim-myth -- a sort of scribe to the wretched little
345.24 Rajah of the place -- such a jewel, he said, cocking
345.25 his poor purblind eyes up at me (he was sitting on
345.26 the cabin floor out of respect), is best preserved
345.27 by being concealed about the person of a woman.
345.28 Yet it is not every woman that would do. She
345.29 must be young -- he sighed deeply -- and insensible

345.30 to the seductions of love. He shook his head
346.01 sceptically. But such a woman seemed to be
346.02 actually in existence. He had been told of a tall
346.03 girl, whom the white man treated with great respect
346.04 and care, and who never went forth from the house
346.05 unattended. People said the white man could be
346.06 seen with her almost any day; they walked side
346.07 by side, openly, he holding her arm under his --
346.08 pressed to his side -- thus -- in a most extraordinary
346.09 way. This might be a lie, he conceded, for it was
346.10 indeed a strange thing for any one to do: on the
346.11 other hand, there could be no doubt she wore the
346.12 white man's jewel concealed upon her bosom."
347.01 "THIS was the theory of Jim's marital
347.02 evening walks. I made a third on more
347.03 than one occasion, unpleasantly aware
347.04 every time of Cornelius, who nursed the aggrieved
347.05 sense of his legal paternity, slinking in the neigh-
347.06 bourhood with that peculiar twist of his mouth as
347.07 if he were perpetually on the point of gnashing
347.08 his teeth. But do you notice how, three hundred
347.09 miles beyond the end of telegraph cables and mail-
347.10 boat lines, the haggard utilitarian lies of our civilisa-
347.11 tion wither and die, to be replaced by pure exercises
347.12 of imagination, that have the futility, often the
347.13 charm, and sometimes the deep hidden truthfulness,
347.14 of works of art? Romance had singled Jim for its
347.15 own -- and that was the true part of the story, which
347.16 otherwise was all wrong. He did not hide his
347.17 jewel. In fact, he was extremely proud of it.
347.18 "It comes to me now that I had, on the whole,
347.19 seen very little of her. What I remember best is the
347.20 even, olive pallor of her complexion, and the intense
347.21 blue-black gleams of her hair, flowing abundantly
347.22 from under a small crimson cap she wore far back
347.23 on her shapely head. Her movements were free,
347.24 assured, and she blushed a dusky red. While Jim
348.01 and I were talking, she would come and go with
348.02 rapid glances at us, leaving on her passage an
348.03 impression of grace and charm and a distinct sug-
348.04 gestion of watchfulness. Her manner presented a
348.05 curious combination of shyness and audacity.
348.06 Every pretty smile was succeeded swiftly by a look
348.07 of silent, repressed anxiety, as if put to flight by the
348.08 recollection of some abiding danger. At times she
348.09 would sit down with us and, with her soft cheek
348.10 dimpled by the knuckles of her little hand, she
348.11 would listen to our talk; her big clear eyes would
348.12 remain fastened on our lips, as though each pro-
348.13 nounced word had a visible shape. Her mother
348.14 had taught her to read and write; she had learned
348.15 a good bit of English from Jim, and she spoke it
348.16 most amusingly, with his own clipping, boyish
348.17 intonation. Her tenderness hovered over him like
348.18 a flutter of wings. She lived so completely in his
348.19 contemplation that she had acquired something of
348.20 his outward aspect, something that recalled him
348.21 in her movements, in the way she stretched her
348.22 arm, turned her head, directed her glances. Her
348.23 vigilant affection had an intensity that made it
348.24 almost perceptible to the senses; it seemed actually
348.25 to exist in the ambient matter of space, to envelop
348.26 him like a peculiar fragrance, to dwell in the sun-
348.27 shine like a tremulous, subdued, and impassioned
348.28 note. I suppose you think that I, too, am romantic,
348.29 but it is a mistake. I am relating to you the sober
348.30 impressions of a bit of youth, of a strange, uneasy
349.01 romance that had come in my way. I observed
349.02 with interest the work of his -- well -- good fortune.
349.03 He was jealously loved, but why she should be
349.04 jealous, and of what, I could not tell. The land,
349.05 the people, the forests were her accomplices, guard-
349.06 ing him with vigilant accord, with an air of seclusion,
349.07 of mystery, of invincible possession. There was
349.08 no appeal, as it were; he was imprisoned within
349.09 the very freedom of his power, and she, though
349.10 ready to make a footstool of her head for his
349.11 feet, guarded her conquest inflexibly -- as though he
349.12 were hard to keep. The very Tamb' Itam, march-
349.13 ing on our journeys upon the heels of his white
349.14 lord, with his head thrown back, truculent and
349.15 be-weaponed like a janissary, with kriss, chopper,
349.16 and lance (besides carrying Jim's gun); even
349.17 Tamb' Itam allowed himself to put on the airs of
349.18 uncompromising guardianship, like a surly, devoted
349.19 jailer ready to lay down his life for his captive.
349.20 On the evenings when we sat up late, his silent,
349.21 indistinct form would pass and repass under the
349.22 verandah, with noiseless footsteps, or lifting my
349.23 head I would unexpectedly make him out stand-

349.24 ing rigidly erect in the shadow. As a general rule
349.25 he would vanish after a time, without a sound;
349.26 but when we rose he would spring up close to us
349.27 as if from the ground, ready for any orders Jim
349.28 might wish to give. The girl, too, I believe, never
349.29 went to sleep till we had separated for the night.
349.30 More than once I saw her and Jim through the
350.01 window of my room come out together quietly
350.02 and lean on the rough balustrade -- two white
350.03 forms very close, his arm about her waist, her
350.04 head on his shoulder. Their soft murmurs reached
350.05 me, penetrating, tender, with a calm, sad note in the
350.06 stillness of the night, like a self-communion of one
350.07 being carried on in two tones. Later on, tossing
350.08 on my bed under the mosquito-net, I was sure to
350.09 hear slight creakings, faint breathing, a throat
350.10 cleared cautiously -- and I would know that Tamb'
350.11 Itam was still on the prowl. Though he had (by
350.12 the favour of the white lord) a house in the com-
350.13 pound, had 'taken wife,' and had lately been blessed
350.14 with a child, I believe that, during my stay at all
350.15 events, he slept on the verandah every night. It
350.16 was very difficult to make this faithful and grim
350.17 retainer talk. Even Jim himself was answered in
350.18 jerky, short sentences, under protest as it were.
350.19 Talking, he seemed to imply, was no business of
350.20 his. The longest speech I heard him volunteer
350.21 was one morning when, suddenly extending his
350.22 hand towards the courtyard, he pointed at Cornelius
350.23 and said, 'Here comes the Nazarene.' I don't
350.24 think he was addressing me, though I stood at his
350.25 side; his object seemed rather to awaken the in-
350.26 dignant attention of the universe. Some muttered
350.27 allusions, which followed, to dogs and the smell of
350.28 roast meat, struck me as singularly felicitous. The
350.29 courtyard, a large square space, was one torrid
350.30 blaze of sunshine, and, bathed in intense light,
351.01 Cornelius was creeping across in full view with
351.02 an inexpressible effect of stealthiness, of dark and
351.03 secret slinking. He reminded one of everything
351.04 that is unsavoury. His slow, laborious walk re-
351.05 sembled the creeping of a repulsive beetle, the legs
351.06 alone moving with horrid industry while the body
351.07 glided evenly. I suppose he made straight enough
351.08 for the place where he wanted to get to, but his
351.09 progress with one shoulder carried forward seemed
351.10 oblique. He was often seen circling slowly amongst
351.11 the sheds, as if following a scent; passing before
351.12 the verandah with upward, stealthy glances; dis-
351.13 appearing without haste round the corner of some
351.14 hut. That he seemed free of the place demon-
351.15 strated Jim's absurd carelessness or else his infinite
351.16 disdain, for Cornelius had played a very dubious
351.17 part (to say the least of it) in a certain episode which
351.18 might have ended fatally for Jim. As a matter of
351.19 fact, it had redounded to his glory. But everything
351.20 redounded to his glory; and it was the irony of his
351.21 good fortune that he, who had been too careful of
351.22 it once, seemed to bear a charmed life.
351.23 "You must know he had left Doramin's place
351.24 very soon after his arrival -- much too soon, in fact,
351.25 for his safety, and of course a long time before the
351.26 war. In this he was actuated by a sense of duty;
351.27 he had to look after Stein's business, he said.
351.28 Hadn't he? To that end, with an utter disregard
351.29 of his personal safety, he crossed the river and took
351.30 up his quarters with Cornelius. How the latter
352.01 had managed to exist through the troubled times
352.02 I can't say. As Stein's agent, after all, he must have
352.03 had Doramin's protection in a measure; and in one
352.04 way or another he had managed to wriggle through
352.05 all the deadly complications, while I have no doubt
352.06 that his conduct, whatever line he was forced to
352.07 take, was marked by that abjectness which was like
352.08 the stamp of the man. That was his characteristic;
352.09 he was fundamentally and outwardly abject, as
352.10 other men are markedly of a generous, distinguished,
352.11 or venerable appearance. It was the element of his
352.12 nature which permeated all his acts and passions and
352.13 emotions; he raged abjectly, smiled abjectly, was
352.14 abjectly sad; his civilities and his indignations were
352.15 alike abject. I am sure his love would have been
352.16 the most abject of sentiments -- but can one imagine
352.17 a loathsome insect in love? And his loathsome-
352.18 ness, too, was abject, so that a simply disgusting
352.19 person would have appeared noble by his side. He
352.20 has his place neither in the background nor in the
352.21 foreground of the story; he is simply seen skulking
352.22 on its outskirts, enigmatical and unclean, tainting
352.23 the fragrance of its youth and of its naiveness.

352.24 "His position in any case could not have been
352.25 other than extremely miserable, yet it may very well
352.26 be that he found some advantages in it. Jim told
352.27 me he had been received at first with an abject
352.28 display of the most amicable sentiments. 'The
352.29 fellow apparently couldn't contain himself for joy,'
352.30 said Jim with disgust. 'He flew at me every
353.01 morning to shake both my hands -- confound him!
353.02 -- but I could never tell whether there would be
353.03 any breakfast. If I got three meals in two days I
353.04 considered myself jolly lucky, and he made me sign a
353.05 chit for ten dollars every week. Said he was sure
353.06 Mr. Stein did not mean him to keep me for nothing.
353.07 Well -- he kept me on nothing as near as possible.
353.08 Put it down to the unsettled state of the country,
353.09 and made as if to tear his hair out, begging my pardon
353.10 twenty times a day, so that I had at last to entreat
353.11 him not to worry. It made me sick. Half the roof
353.12 of his house had fallen in, and the whole place had
353.13 a mangy look, with wisps of dry grass sticking out
353.14 and the corners of broken mats flapping on every
353.15 wall. He did his best to make out that Mr. Stein
353.16 owed him money on the last three years' trading,
353.17 but his books were all torn, and some were missing.
353.18 He tried to hint it was his late wife's fault. Dis-
353.19 gusting scoundrel! At last I had to forbid him to
353.20 mention his late wife at all. It made Jewel cry. I
353.21 couldn't discover what became of all the trade
353.22 goods; there was nothing in the store but rats,
353.23 having a high old time amongst a litter of brown
353.24 paper and old sacking. I was assured on every hand
353.25 that he had a lot of money buried somewhere, but
353.26 of course could get nothing out of him. It was the
353.27 most miserable existence I led there in that wretched
353.28 house. I tried to do my duty by Stein, but I had
353.29 also other matters to think of. When I escaped to
353.30 Doramin old Tunku Allang got frightened and re-
354.01 turned all my things. It was done in a roundabout
354.02 way, and with no end of mystery, through a
354.03 Chinaman who keeps a small shop here; but as
354.04 soon as I left the Bugis quarter and went to live
354.05 with Cornelius it began to be said openly that the
354.06 Rajah had made up his mind to have me killed
354.07 before long. Pleasant, wasn't it? And I couldn't
354.08 see what there was to prevent him if he really had
354.09 made up his mind. The worst of it was, I couldn't
354.10 help feeling I wasn't doing any good either for
354.11 Stein or for myself. Oh, it was beastly -- the
354.12 whole six weeks of it.'"
355.01 "HE told me further that he didn't know
355.02 what made him hang on -- but of course
355.03 we may guess. He sympathised deeply
355.04 with the defenceless girl, at the mercy of that
355.05 'mean, cowardly scoundrel.' It appears Cornelius
355.06 led her an awful life, stopping only short of actual
355.07 ill-usage, for which he had not the pluck, I suppose.
355.08 He insisted upon her calling him father -- 'and with
355.09 respect, too -- with respect,' he would scream, shaking
355.10 a little yellow fist in her face. 'I am a respectable
355.11 man, and what are you? Tell me -- what are you?
355.12 You think I am going to bring up somebody else's
355.13 child and not to be treated with respect? You
355.14 ought to be glad I let you. Come -- say Yes,
355.15 father.... No? ... You wait a bit.' There-
355.16 upon he would begin to abuse the dead woman, till
355.17 the girl would run off with her hands to her head.
355.18 He pursued her, dashing in and out and round the
355.19 house and amongst the sheds, would drive her into
355.20 some corner, where she would fall on her knees
355.21 stopping her ears, and then he would stand at a
355.22 distance and declaim filthy denunciations at her
355.23 back for half an hour at a stretch. 'Your mother
355.24 was a devil, a deceitful devil -- and you, too, are a
356.01 devil,' he would shriek in a final outburst, pick up a
356.02 bit of dry earth or a handful of mud (there was
356.03 plenty of mud around the house), and fling it into
356.04 her hair. Sometimes, though, she would hold out
356.05 full of scorn, confronting him in silence, her face
356.06 sombre and contracted, and only now and then
356.07 uttering a word or two that would make the other
356.08 jump and writhe with the sting. Jim told me
356.09 these scenes were terrible. It was indeed a strange
356.10 thing to come upon in a wilderness. The endless-
356.11 ness of such a subtly cruel situation was appalling
356.12 -- if you think of it. The respectable Cornelius
356.13 (Inchi 'Nelyus the Malays called him, with a
356.14 grimace that meant many things) was a much--
356.15 disappointed man. I don't know what he had
356.16 expected would be done for him in consideration
356.17 of his marriage; but evidently the liberty to steal,

356.18 and embezzle, and appropriate to himself for
356.19 many years and in any way that suited him best the
356.20 goods of Stein's Trading Company (Stein kept the
356.21 supply up unfalteringly as long as he could get his
356.22 skippers to take it there) did not seem to him a fair
356.23 equivalent for the sacrifice of his honourable name.
356.24 Jim would have enjoyed exceedingly thrashing
356.25 Cornelius within an inch of his life; on the other
356.26 hand, the scenes were of so painful a character, so
356.27 abominable, that his impulse would be to get out of
356.28 earshot, in order to spare the girl's feelings. They
356.29 left her agitated, speechless, clutching her bosom
356.30 now and then with a stony, desperate face, and then
357.01 Jim would lounge up and say unhappily, 'Now --
357.02 come -- really -- what's the use -- you must try to eat
357.03 a bit,' or give some such mark of sympathy. Cor-
357.04 nelius would keep on slinking through the door-
357.05 ways, across the verandah and back again, as mute
357.06 as a fish, and with malevolent, mistrustful, under-
357.07 hand glances. 'I can stop his game,' Jim said to
357.08 her once. 'Just say the word.' And do you know
357.09 what she answered? She said -- Jim told me im-
357.10 pressively -- that if she had not been sure he was
357.11 intensely wretched himself, she would have found
357.12 the courage to kill him with her own hands. 'Just
357.13 fancy that! The poor devil of a girl, almost a
357.14 child, being driven to talk like that!' he exclaimed
357.15 in horror. It seemed impossible to save her not
357.16 only from that mean rascal but even from herself!
357.17 It wasn't that he pitied her so much, he affirmed;
357.18 it was more than pity; it was as if he had some-
357.19 thing on his conscience, while that life went on.
357.20 To leave the house would have appeared a base
357.21 desertion. He had understood at last that there
357.22 was nothing to expect from a longer stay, neither
357.23 accounts nor money, nor truth of any sort, but he
357.24 stayed on, exasperating Cornelius to the verge, I
357.25 won't say of insanity, but almost of courage. Mean-
357.26 time he felt all sorts of dangers gathering obscurely
357.27 about him. Doramin had sent over twice a trusty
357.28 servant to tell him seriously that he could do nothing
357.29 for his safety unless he would recross the river
357.30 again and live amongst the Bugis as at first. People
358.01 of every condition used to call, often in the dead of
358.02 night, in order to disclose to him plots for his assas-
358.03 sination. He was to be poisoned. He was to be
358.04 stabbed in the bath-house. Arrangements were
358.05 being made to have him shot from a boat on the
358.06 river. Each of these informants professed himself
358.07 to be his very good friend. It was enough -- he
358.08 told me -- to spoil a fellow's rest for ever. Some-
358.09 thing of the kind was extremely possible -- nay,
358.10 probable -- but the lying warnings gave him only
358.11 the sense of deadly scheming going on all around
358.12 him, on all sides, in the dark. Nothing more cal-
358.13 culated to shake the best of nerve. Finally, one
358.14 night, Cornelius himself, with a great apparatus of
358.15 alarm and secrecy, unfolded in solemn, wheedling
358.16 tones a little plan wherein for one hundred dollars --
358.17 or even for eighty; let's say eighty -- he, Cornelius,
358.18 would procure a trustworthy man to smuggle
358.19 Jim out of the river, all safe. There was nothing
358.20 else for it now -- if Jim cared a pin for his life.
358.21 What's eighty dollars? A trifle. An insignificant
358.22 sum. While he, Cornelius, who had to remain
358.23 behind, was absolutely courting death by his proof
358.24 of devotion to Mr. Stein's young friend. The sight
358.25 of his abject grimacing was -- Jim told me -- very
358.26 hard to bear: he clutched at his hair, beat his
358.27 breast, rocked himself to and fro with his hands
358.28 pressed to his stomach, and actually pretended to
358.29 shed tears. 'Your blood be on your own head,'
358.30 he squeaked at last, and rushed out. It is a curious
359.01 question how far Cornelius was sincere in that per-
359.02 formance. Jim confessed to me that he did not
359.03 sleep a wink after the fellow had gone. He lay
359.04 on his back on a thin mat spread over the bamboo
359.05 flooring, trying idly to make out the bare rafters,
359.06 and listening to the rustlings in the torn thatch.
359.07 A star suddenly twinkled through a hole in the
359.08 roof. His brain was in a whirl; but, nevertheless,
359.09 it was on that very night that he matured his plan
359.10 for overcoming Sherif Ali. It had been the thought
359.11 of all the moments he could spare from the hopeless
359.12 investigation into Stein's affairs, but the notion --
359.13 he says -- came to him then all at once. He could
359.14 see, as it were, the guns mounted on the top of the
359.15 hill. He got very hot and excited lying there; sleep
359.16 was out of the question more than ever. He
359.17 jumped up, and went out barefooted on the verandah.

359.18 Walking silently, he came upon the girl, motionless
359.19 against the wall, as if on the watch. In his then state
359.20 of mind it did not surprise him to see her up, nor
359.21 yet to hear her ask in an anxious whisper where Cor-
359.22 nelius could be. He simply said he did not know.
359.23 She moaned a little, and peered into the campong.
359.24 Everything was very quiet. He was possessed by
359.25 his new idea, and so full of it that he could not
359.26 help telling the girl all about it at once. She
359.27 listened, clapped her hands lightly, whispered softly
359.28 her admiration, but was evidently on the alert all
359.29 the time. It seems he had been used to make a
359.30 confidante of her all along -- and that she on her part
360.01 could and did give him a lot of useful hints as to
360.02 Patusan affairs there is no doubt. He assured me
360.03 more than once that he had never found himself
360.04 the worse for her advice. At any rate, he was pro-
360.05 ceeding to explain his plan fully to her there and
360.06 then, when she pressed his arm once, and vanished
360.07 from his side. Then Cornelius appeared from
360.08 somewhere, and, perceiving Jim, ducked sideways,
360.09 as though he had been shot at, and afterwards
360.10 stood very still in the dusk. At last he came for-
360.11 ward prudently, like a suspicious cat. 'There were
360.12 some fishermen there -- with fish,' he said in a shaky
360.13 voice. 'To sell fish -- you understand....' It must
360.14 have been then two o'clock in the morning -- a
360.15 likely time for anybody to hawk fish about!
360.16 "Jim, however, let the statement pass, and did
360.17 not give it a single thought. Other matters occupied
360.18 his mind, and besides, he had neither seen nor heard
360.19 anything. He contented himself by saying, 'Oh!'
360.20 absently, got a drink of water out of a pitcher
360.21 standing there, and leaving Cornelius a prey to some
360.22 inexplicable emotion -- that made him embrace with
360.23 both arms the worm-eaten rail of the verandah as
360.24 if his legs had failed -- went in again and lay down
360.25 on his mat to think. By and by he heard stealthy
360.26 footsteps. They stopped. A voice whispered
360.27 tremulously through the wall, 'Are you asleep?'
360.28 'No! What is it?' he answered briskly, and
360.29 there was an abrupt movement outside, and then all
360.30 was still, as if the whisperer had been startled. Ex-
361.01 tremely annoyed at this, Jim came out impetuously,
361.02 and Cornelius with a faint shriek fled along the
361.03 verandah as far as the steps, where he hung on to
361.04 the broken banister. Very puzzled, Jim called out
361.05 to him from the distance to know what the devil
361.06 he meant. 'Have you given your consideration to
361.07 what I spoke to you about?' asked Cornelius,
361.08 pronouncing the words with difficulty, like a man
361.09 in the cold fit of a fever. 'No!' shouted Jim
361.10 in a passion. 'I have not, and I don't intend to.
361.11 I am going to live here, in Patusan.' 'You shall
361.12 d-d-die h-h-here,' answered Cornelius, still shaking
361.13 violently, and in a sort of expiring voice. The whole
361.14 performance was so absurd and provoking that Jim
361.15 didn't know whether he ought to be amused or angry.
361.16 'Not till I have seen you tucked away, you bet,' he
361.17 called out, exasperated, yet ready to laugh. Half
361.18 seriously (being excited with his own thoughts, you
361.19 know) he went on shouting, 'Nothing can touch me!
361.20 You can do your damnedest.' Somehow the
361.21 shadowy Cornelius far off there seemed to be the
361.22 hateful embodiment of all the annoyances and
361.23 difficulties he had found in his path. He let himself
361.24 go -- his nerves had been overwrought for days --
361.25 and called him many pretty names -- swindler, liar,
361.26 sorry rascal: in fact, carried on in an extraordinary
361.27 way. He admits he passed all bounds, that he was
361.28 quite beside himself -- defied all Patusan to scare-
361.29 him away -- declared he would make them all dance
361.30 to his own tune yet, and so on, in a menacing,
362.01 boasting strain. Perfectly bombastic and ridiculous,
362.02 he said. His ears burned at the bare recollection.
362.03 Must have been off his chump in some way....
362.04 The girl, who was sitting with us, nodded her little
362.05 head at me quickly, frowned faintly, and said, 'I
362.06 heard him,' with childlike solemnity. He laughed
362.07 and blushed. What stopped him at last, he said,
362.08 was the silence, the complete deathlike silence, of
362.09 the indistinct figure far over there, that seemed to
362.10 hang collapsed, doubled over the rail in a weird
362.11 immobility. He came to his senses, and ceasing
362.12 suddenly, wondered greatly at himself. He watched
362.13 for a while. Not a stir, not a sound. 'Exactly
362.14 as if the chap had died while I had been making
362.15 all that noise,' he said. He was so ashamed of
362.16 himself that he went indoors in a hurry without
362.17 another word, and flung himself down again.

362.18 The row seemed to have done him good, though,
362.19 because he went to sleep for the rest of the night
362.20 like a baby. Hadn't slept like that for weeks.
362.21 'But I didn't sleep,' struck in the girl, one elbow
362.22 on the table and nursing her cheek. 'I watched.'
362.23 Her big eyes flashed, rolling a little, and then she
362.24 fixed them on my face intently."
363.01 "YOU may imagine with what interest I
363.02 listened. All these details were per-
363.03 ceived to have some significance twenty--
363.04 four hours later. In the morning Cornelius made
363.05 no allusion to the events of the night. 'I suppose
363.06 you will come back to my poor house,' he muttered
363.07 surlily, slinking up just as Jim was entering the
363.08 canoe to go over to Doramin's campong. Jim only
363.09 nodded, without looking at him. 'You find it
363.10 good fun, no doubt,' muttered the other in a sour
363.11 tone. Jim spent the day with the old nakhoda,
363.12 preaching the necessity of vigorous action to the
363.13 principal men of the Bugis community, who had
363.14 been summoned for a big talk. He remembered
363.15 with pleasure how very eloquent and persuasive
363.16 he had been. 'I managed to put some backbone
363.17 into them that time, and no mistake,' he said.
363.18 Sherif Ali's last raid had swept the outskirts of the
363.19 settlement, and some women belonging to the town
363.20 had been carried off to the stockade. Sheriff Ali's
363.21 emissaries had been seen in the market-place the
363.22 day before, strutting about haughtily in white
363.23 cloaks, and boasting of the Rajah's friendship for
363.24 their master. One of them stood forward in the
364.01 shade of a tree, and, leaning on the long barrel of a
364.02 rifle, exhorted the people to prayer and repentance,
364.03 advising them to kill all the strangers in their
364.04 midst, some of whom, he said, were infidels and
364.05 others even worse -- children of Satan in the guise
364.06 of Moslems. It was reported that several of the
364.07 Rajah's people amongst the listeners had loudly
364.08 expressed their approbation. The terror amongst
364.09 the common people was intense. Jim, immensely
364.10 pleased with his day's work, crossed the river again
364.11 before sunset.
364.12 "As he had got the Bugis irretrievably com-
364.13 mitted to action, and had made himself responsible
364.14 for success on his own head, he was so elated that
364.15 in the lightness of his heart he absolutely tried to be
364.16 civil with Cornelius. But Cornelius became wildly
364.17 jovial in response, and it was almost more than he
364.18 could stand, he says, to hear his little squeaks of
364.19 false laughter, to see him wriggle and blink, and
364.20 suddenly catch hold of his chin and crouch low
364.21 over the table with a distracted stare. The girl did
364.22 not show herself, and Jim retired early. When he
364.23 rose to say good-night, Cornelius jumped up,
364.24 knocking his chair over, and ducked out of sight
364.25 as if to pick up something he had dropped. His
364.26 good-night came huskily from under the table.
364.27 Jim was amazed to see him emerge with a
364.28 dropping jaw, and staring, stupidly frightened
364.29 eyes. He clutched the edge of the table. 'What's
364.30 the matter? Are you unwell?' asked Jim. 'Yes,
365.01 yes, yes. A great colic in my stomach,' says the
365.02 other; and it is Jim's opinion that it was perfectly
365.03 true. If so, it was, in view of his contemplated
365.04 action, an abject sign of a still imperfect callousness
365.05 for which he must be given all due credit.
365.06 "Be it as it may, Jim's slumbers were disturbed
365.07 by a dream of heavens like brass resounding with
365.08 a great voice, which called upon him to Awake!
365.09 Awake! so loud that, notwithstanding his desperate
365.10 determination to sleep on, he did wake up in reality.
365.11 The glare of a red spluttering conflagration going on
365.12 in mid-air fell on his eyes. Coils of black, thick
365.13 smoke curved round the head of some apparition,
365.14 some unearthly being, all in white, with a severe,
365.15 drawn, anxious face. After a second or so he
365.16 recognised the girl. She was holding a dammar
365.17 torch at arm's-length aloft, and in a persistent,
365.18 urgent monotone she was repeating, 'Get up!
365.19 Get up! Get up!'
365.20 "Suddenly he leaped to his feet; at once she
365.21 put into his hand a revolver, his own revolver,
365.22 which had been hanging on a nail, but loaded this
365.23 time. He gripped it in silence, bewildered, blink-
365.24 ing in the light. He wondered what he could do
365.25 for her.
365.26 "She asked rapidly and very low, 'Can you face
365.27 four men with this?' He laughed while narrating
365.28 this part at the recollection of his polite alacrity.
365.29 It seems he made a great display of it, 'Certainly --

365.30 of course -- certainly -- command me.' He was not
366.01 properly awake, and had a notion of being very civil
366.02 in these extraordinary circumstances, of showing
366.03 his unquestioning, devoted readiness. She left the
366.04 room, and he followed her; in the passage they
366.05 disturbed an old hag who did the casual cooking
366.06 of the household, though she was so decrepit as to
366.07 be hardly able to understand human speech. She
366.08 got up and hobbled behind them, mumbling tooth-
366.09 lessly. On the verandah a hammock of sailcloth,
366.10 belonging to Cornelius, swayed lightly to the touch
366.11 of Jim's elbow. It was empty.
366.12 "The Patusan establishment, like all the posts of
366.13 Stein's Trading Company, had originally consisted
366.14 of four buildings. Two of them were represented
366.15 by two heaps of sticks, broken bamboos, rotten
366.16 thatch, over which the four corner-posts of hard-
366.17 wood leaned sadly at different angles: the principal
366.18 storeroom, however, stood yet, facing the agent's
366.19 house. It was an oblong hut, built of mud and
366.20 clay; it had at one end a wide door of stout plank-
366.21 ing, which so far had not come off the hinges, and
366.22 in one of the side walls there was a square aperture,
366.23 a sort of window, with three wooden bars. Before
366.24 descending the few steps the girl turned her face
366.25 over her shoulder and said quickly, 'You were to
366.26 be set upon while you slept.' Jim tells me he experi-
366.27 enced a sense of deception. It was the old story.
366.28 He was weary of these attempts upon his life. He
366.29 had had his fill of these alarms. He was sick of
366.30 them. He assured me he was angry with the girl
367.01 for deceiving him. He had followed her under the
367.02 impression that it was she who wanted his help,
367.03 and now he had half a mind to turn on his heel and
367.04 go back in disgust. 'Do you know,' he commented
367.05 profoundly, 'I rather think I was not quite myself
367.06 for whole weeks on end about that time.' 'Oh yes.
367.07 You were though,' I couldn't help contradicting.
367.08 "But she moved on swiftly, and he followed her
367.09 into the courtyard. All its fences had fallen in a
367.10 long time ago; the neighbours' buffaloes would
367.11 pace in the morning across the open space, snorting
367.12 profoundly, without haste; the very jungle was
367.13 invading it already. Jim and the girl stopped in the
367.14 rank grass. The light in which they stood made a
367.15 dense blackness all round, and only above their
367.16 heads there was an opulent glitter of stars. He told
367.17 me it was a beautiful night -- quite cool, with a little
367.18 stir of breeze from the river. It seems he noticed
367.19 its friendly beauty. Remember this is a love story
367.20 I am telling you now. A lovely night seemed
367.21 to breathe on them a soft caress. The flame of
367.22 the torch streamed now and then with a fluttering
367.23 noise like a flag, and for a time this was the only
367.24 sound. 'They are in the storeroom waiting,'
367.25 whispered the girl; 'they are waiting for the signal.'
367.26 'Who's to give it?' he asked. She shook the torch,
367.27 which blazed up after a shower of sparks. 'Only
367.28 you have been sleeping so restlessly,' she continued
367.29 in a murmur; 'I watched your sleep, too.' 'You!'
367.30 he exclaimed, craning his neck to look about him.
368.01 'You think I watched on this night only!' she said,
368.02 with a sort of despairing indignation.
368.03 "He says it was as if he had received a blow on
368.04 the chest. He gasped. He thought he had been
368.05 an awful brute somehow, and he felt remorseful,
368.06 touched, happy, elated. This, let me remind you
368.07 again, is a love story; you can see it by the im-
368.08 becility, not a repulsive imbecility, the exalted
368.09 imbecility of these proceedings, this station in
368.10 torchlight, as if they had come there on purpose
368.11 to have it out for the edification of concealed
368.12 murderers. If Sherif Ali's emissaries had been
368.13 possessed -- as Jim remarked -- of a pennyworth of
368.14 spunk, this was the time to make a rush. His
368.15 heart was thumping -- not with fear -- but he seemed
368.16 to hear the grass rustle, and he stepped smartly out
368.17 of the light. Something dark, imperfectly seen,
368.18 flitted rapidly out of sight. He called out in a
368.19 strong voice, 'Cornelius! O Cornelius!' A pro-
368.20 found silence succeeded: his voice did not seem
368.21 to have carried twenty feet. Again the girl was by
368.22 his side. 'Fly!' she said. The old woman was
368.23 coming up; her broken figure hovered in crippled
368.24 little jumps on the edge of the light; they heard
368.25 her mumbling, and a light, moaning sigh. 'Fly!'
368.26 repeated the girl excitedly. 'They are frightened
368.27 now -- this light -- the voices. They know you are
368.28 awake now -- they know you are big, strong, fear-
368.29 less ...' 'If I am all that,' he began; but she

368.30 interrupted him: 'Yes -- to-night! But what of
369.01 to-morrow night? Of the next night? Of the
369.02 night after -- of all the many, many nights? Can
369.03 I be always watching?' A sobbing catch of her
369.04 breath affected him beyond the power of words.
369.05 "He told me that he had never felt so small, so
369.06 powerless -- and as to courage, what was the good
369.07 of it? he thought. He was so helpless that even
369.08 flight seemed of no use; and though she kept on
369.09 whispering, 'Go to Doramin! go to Doramin!' with
369.10 feverish insistence, he realised that for him there was
369.11 no refuge from that loneliness which centupled all
369.12 his dangers except -- in her. 'I thought,' he said
369.13 to me, 'that if I went away from her it would
369.14 be the end of everything somehow. Only as they
369.15 couldn't stop there for ever in the middle of that
369.16 courtyard, he made up his mind to go and look
369.17 into the storehouse. He let her follow him without
369.18 thinking of any protest, as if they had been indis-
369.19 solubly united. 'I am fearless -- am I?' he
369.20 muttered through his teeth. She restrained his
369.21 arm. 'Wait till you hear my voice,' she said, and,
369.22 torch in hand, ran lightly round the corner. He
369.23 remained alone in the darkness, his face to the door;
369.24 not a sound, not a breath came from the other side.
369.25 The old hag let out a dreary groan somewhere
369.26 behind his back. He heard a high-pitched, almost
369.27 screaming call from the girl. 'Now! Push!'
369.28 He pushed violently; the door swung with a creak
369.29 and a clatter, disclosing to his intense astonish-
369.30 ment the low, dungeon-like interior illuminated
370.01 by a lurid, wavering glare. A turmoil of smoke
370.02 eddied down upon an empty wooden crate in the
370.03 middle of the floor, a litter of rags and straw tried
370.04 to soar, but only stirred feebly in the draught.
370.05 She had thrust the light through the bars of the
370.06 window. He saw her bare round arm extended and
370.07 rigid, holding up the torch with the steadiness of an
370.08 iron bracket. A conical ragged heap of old mats
370.09 cumbered a distant corner almost to the ceiling, and
370.10 that was all.
370.11 "He explained to me that he was bitterly dis-
370.12 appointed at this. His fortitude had been tried by
370.13 so many warnings, he had been for weeks sur-
370.14 rounded by so many hints of danger, that he wanted
370.15 the relief of some reality, of something tangible
370.16 that he could meet. 'It would have cleared the air
370.17 for a couple of hours at least, if you know what I
370.18 mean,' he said to me. 'Jove! I had been living
370.19 for days with a stone on my chest.' Now at last
370.20 he had thought he would get hold of something,
370.21 and -- nothing! Not a trace, not a sign of anybody.
370.22 He had raised his weapon as the door flew open,
370.23 but now his arm fell. 'Fire! Defend yourself,'
370.24 the girl outside cried in an agonising voice. She,
370.25 being in the dark and with her arm thrust in to the
370.26 shoulder through the small hole, couldn't see what
370.27 was going on, and she dared not withdraw the torch
370.28 now to run round. 'There's nobody here!' yelled
370.29 Jim contemptuously; but his impulse to burst into
370.30 a resentful, exasperated laugh died without a sound:
371.01 he had perceived in the very act of turning away
371.02 that he was exchanging glances with a pair of eyes
371.03 in the heap of mats. He saw a shifting gleam of
371.04 whites. 'Come out!' he cried in a fury, a little
371.05 doubtful, and a dark-faced head, a head without a
371.06 body, shaped itself in the rubbish -- a strangely
371.07 detached head, that looked at him with a steady
371.08 scowl. Next moment the whole mound stirred,
371.09 and with a low grunt a man emerged swiftly, and
371.10 bounded towards Jim. Behind him the mats as it
371.11 were jumped and flew, his right arm was raised
371.12 with a crooked elbow, and the dull blade of a kriss
371.13 protruded from his fist held off, a little above his
371.14 head. A cloth wound tight round his loins seemed
371.15 dazzlingly white on his bronze skin; his naked
371.16 body glistened as if wet.
371.17 "Jim noted all this. He told me he was ex-
371.18 periencing a feeling of unutterable relief, of vengeful
371.19 elation. He held his shot, he says, deliberately.
371.20 He held it for the tenth part of a second, for three
371.21 strides of the man -- an unconscionable time. He
371.22 held it for the pleasure of saying to himself, That's
371.23 a dead man! He was absolutely positive and cer-
371.24 tain. He let him come on because it did not matter.
371.25 A dead man, anyhow. He noticed the dilated
371.26 nostrils, the wide eyes, the intent, eager stillness
371.27 of the face, and then he fired.
371.28 "The explosion in that confined space was
371.29 stunning. He stepped back a pace. He saw the

371.30 man jerk his head up, fling his arms forward, and
372.01 drop the kriss. He ascertained afterwards that he
372.02 had shot him through the mouth, a little upwards,
372.03 the bullet coming out high at the back of the skull.
372.04 With the impetus of his rush the man drove straight
372.05 on, his face suddenly gaping disfigured, with his
372.06 hands open before him gropingly, as though blinded,
372.07 and landed with terrific violence on his forehead,
372.08 just short of Jim's bare toes. Jim says he didn't
372.09 lose the smallest detail of all this. He found
372.10 himself calm, appeased, without rancour, without
372.11 uneasiness, as if the death of that man had atoned
372.12 for everything. The place was getting very full of
372.13 sooty smoke from the torch, in which the unsway-
372.14 ing flame burned blood-red without a flicker. He
372.15 walked in resolutely, striding over the dead body,
372.16 and covered with his revolver another naked figure
372.17 outlined vaguely at the other end. As he was about
372.18 to pull the trigger, the man threw away with force
372.19 a short, heavy spear, and squatted submissively
372.20 on his hams, his back to the wall and his clasped
372.21 hands between his legs. 'You want your life?'
372.22 Jim said. The other made no sound. 'How
372.23 many more of you?' asked Jim again. 'Two
372.24 more, Tuan,' said the man very softly, looking with
372.25 big, fascinated eyes into the muzzle of the revolver.
372.26 Accordingly, two more crawled from under the mats,
372.27 holding out ostentatiously their empty hands."
373.01 "JIM took up an advantageous position and
373.02 shepherded them out in a bunch through
373.03 the doorway: all that time the torch had
373.04 remained vertical in the grip of a little hand,
373.05 without so much as a tremble. The three men
373.06 obeyed him, perfectly mute, moving automatically.
373.07 He ranged them in a row. 'Link arms!' he
373.08 ordered. They did so. 'The first who with-
373.09 draws his arm or turns his head is a dead man,'
373.10 he said. 'March!' They stepped out together
373.11 rigidly; he followed, and at the side the girl,
373.12 in a trailing white gown, her black hair falling
373.13 as low as her waist, bore the light. Erect and
373.14 swaying, she seemed to glide without touching the
373.15 earth; the only sound was the silky swish and
373.16 rustle of the long grass. 'Stop!' cried Jim.
373.17 "The river-bank was steep; a great freshness
373.18 ascended, the light fell on the edge of smooth, dark
373.19 water frothing without a ripple; right and left
373.20 the shapes of the houses ran together below the
373.21 sharp outlines of the roofs. 'Take my greetings
373.22 to Sherif Ali -- till I come myself,' said Jim. Not
373.23 one head of the three budged. 'Jump!' he
373.24 thundered. The three splashes made one splash,
374.01 a shower flew up, black heads bobbed convulsively,
374.02 and disappeared; but a great blowing and splutter-
374.03 ing went on, growing faint, for they were diving
374.04 industriously, in great fear of a parting shot. Jim
374.05 turned to the girl, who had been a silent and attentive
374.06 observer. His heart seemed suddenly to grow too
374.07 big for his breast and choke him in the hollow of
374.08 his throat. This probably made him speechless for
374.09 so long, and after returning his gaze, she flung the
374.10 burning torch with a wide sweep of the arm into
374.11 the river. The ruddy, fiery glare, taking a long flight
374.12 through the night, sank with a vicious hiss, and the
374.13 calm, soft starlight descended upon them, unchecked.
374.14 "He did not tell me what it was he said when
374.15 at last he recovered his voice. I don't suppose he
374.16 could be very eloquent. The world was still, the
374.17 night breathed on them, one of those nights that
374.18 seem created for the sheltering of tenderness, and
374.19 there are moments when our souls, as if freed from
374.20 their dark envelope, glow with an exquisite sensi-
374.21 bility that makes certain silences more lucid than
374.22 speeches. As to the girl, he told me, 'She broke
374.23 down a bit. Excitement -- don't you know. Re-
374.24 action. Deucedly tired she must have been -- and all
374.25 that kind of thing. And -- and -- hang it all -- she was
374.26 fond of me, don't you see.... I, too ... didn't
374.27 know, of course ... never entered my head....'
374.28 "Then he got up and began to walk about
374.29 in some agitation. 'I -- I love her dearly. More
374.30 than I can tell. Of course one cannot tell. You
375.01 take a different view of your actions when you come
375.02 to understand, when you are made to understand
375.03 every day that your existence is necessary -- you see,
375.04 absolutely necessary -- to another person. I am
375.05 made to feel that. Wonderful! But only try to
375.06 think what her life has been. It is too extravagantly
375.07 awful! Isn't it? And me finding her here like
375.08 this -- as you may go out for a stroll and come

375.09 suddenly upon somebody drowning in a lonely,
375.10 dark place. Jove! No time to lose. Well, it is a
375.11 trust, too ... I believe I am equal to it....'
375.12 "I must tell you the girl had left us to ourselves
375.13 some time before. He slapped his chest. 'Yes!
375.14 I feel that, but I believe I am equal to all my luck!'
375.15 He had the gift of finding a special meaning in
375.16 everything that happened to him. This was the
375.17 view he took of his love affair; it was idyllic, a
375.18 little solemn, and also true, since his belief had all
375.19 the unshakable seriousness of youth. Some time
375.20 after, on another occasion, he said to me, 'I've
375.21 been only two years here, and now, upon my word,
375.22 I can't conceive being able to live anywhere else.
375.23 The very thought of the world outside is enough to
375.24 give me a fright; because, don't you see,' he con-
375.25 tinued, with downcast eyes watching the action
375.26 of his boot busied in squashing thoroughly a tiny
375.27 bit of dried mud (we were strolling on the river--
375.28 bank) -- 'because I have not forgotten why I came
375.29 here. Not yet!'
375.30 "I refrained from looking at him, but I think I
376.01 heard a short sigh: we took a turn or two in silence.
376.02 'Upon my soul and conscience,' he began again,
376.03 'if such a thing can be forgotten, then I think I have
376.04 a right to dismiss it from my mind. Ask any man
376.05 here' ... his voice changed. 'Is it not strange,'
376.06 he went on in a gentle, almost yearning tone, 'that
376.07 all these people, all these people who would do
376.08 anything for me, can never be made to understand?
376.09 Never! If you disbelieve me I could not call them
376.10 up. It seems hard, somehow. I am stupid, am
376.11 I not? What more can I want? If you ask them
376.12 who is brave -- who is true -- who is just -- who is it
376.13 they would trust with their lives? -- they would
376.14 say, Tuan Jim. And yet they can never know the
376.15 real, real truth....'
376.16 "That's what he said to me on my last day with
376.17 him. I did not let a murmur escape me: I felt
376.18 he was going to say more, and come no nearer to
376.19 the root of the matter. The sun, whose concen-
376.20 trated glare dwarfs the earth into a restless mote of
376.21 dust, had sunk behind the forest, and the diffused
376.22 light from an opal sky seemed to cast upon a world
376.23 without shadows and without brilliance the illusion
376.24 of a calm and pensive greatness. I don't know
376.25 why, listening to him, I should have noted so
376.26 distinctly the gradual darkening of the river, of the
376.27 air; the irresistible slow work of the night settling
376.28 silently on all the visible forms, effacing the outlines,
376.29 burying the shapes deeper and deeper, like a steady
376.30 fall of impalpable black dust.
377.01 "'Jove!' he began abruptly, 'there are days
377.02 when a fellow is too absurd for anything; only I
377.03 know I can tell you what I like. I talk about being
377.04 done with it -- with the bally thing at the back
377.05 of my head.... Forgetting ... Hang me if I
377.06 know! I can think of it quietly. After all, what
377.07 has it proved? Nothing. I suppose you don't
377.08 think so....'
377.09 "I made a protesting murmur.
377.10 "'No matter,' he said. 'I am satisfied ...
377.11 nearly. I've got to look only at the face of the first
377.12 man that comes along to regain my confidence.
377.13 They can't be made to understand what is going on
377.14 in me. What of that? Come! I haven't done
377.15 so badly.'
377.16 "'Not so badly,' I said.
377.17 "'But all the same, you wouldn't like to have me
377.18 aboard your own ship -- hey?'
377.19 "'Confound you!' I cried. 'Stop this.'
377.20 "'Aha! You see,' he cried, crowing, as it
377.21 were, over me placidly. 'Only,' he went on, 'you
377.22 just try to tell this to any of them here. They would
377.23 think you a fool, a liar, or worse. And so I can
377.24 stand it. I've done a thing or two for them, but
377.25 this is what they have done for me.'
377.26 "'My dear chap,' I cried, 'you shall always
377.27 remain for them an insoluble mystery.' There-
377.28 upon we were silent.
377.29 "'Mystery,' he repeated, before looking up.
377.30 'Well, then let me always remain here.'
378.01 "After the sun had set, the darkness seemed to
378.02 drive upon us, borne in every faint puff of the
378.03 breeze. In the middle of a hedged path I saw
378.04 the arrested, gaunt, watchful, and apparently one--
378.05 legged silhouette of Tamb' Itam; and across the
378.06 dusky space my eye detected something white
378.07 moving to and fro behind the supports of the roof.
378.08 As soon as Jim, with Tamb' Itam at his heels, had

378.09 started upon his evening rounds, I went up to the
378.10 house alone, and, unexpectedly, found myself way-
378.11 laid by the girl, who had been clearly waiting for
378.12 this opportunity.
378.13 "It is hard to tell you what it was precisely she
378.14 wanted to wrest from me. Obviously it would be
378.15 something very simple -- the simplest impossibility
378.16 in the world; as, for instance, the exact description
378.17 of the form of a cloud. She wanted an assurance,
378.18 a statement, a promise, an explanation -- I don't
378.19 know how to call it: the thing has no name. It was
378.20 dark under the projecting roof, and all I could see
378.21 were the flowing lines of her gown, the pale, small
378.22 oval of her face, with the white flash of her teeth,
378.23 and, turned towards me, the big, sombre orbits of
378.24 her eyes, where there seemed to be a faint stir,
378.25 such as you may fancy you can detect when you
378.26 plunge your gaze to the bottom of an immensely
378.27 deep well. What is it that moves there? you ask
378.28 yourself. Is it a blind monster or only a lost gleam
378.29 from the universe? It occurred to me -- don't
379.01 laugh -- that all things being dissimilar, she was
379.02 more inscrutable in her childish ignorance than the
379.03 Sphinx propounding childish riddles to wayfarers.
379.04 She had been carried off to Patusan before her
379.05 eyes were open. She had grown up there; she
379.06 had seen nothing, she had known nothing, she
379.07 had no conception of anything. I ask myself
379.08 whether she were sure that anything else existed.
379.09 What notions she may have formed of the outside
379.10 world is to me inconceivable; all that she knew
379.11 of its inhabitants were a betrayed woman and a
379.12 sinister pantaloon. Her lover also came to her from
379.13 there, gifted with irresistible seductions; but what
379.14 would become of her if he should return to these
379.15 inconceivable regions that seemed always to claim
379.16 back their own? Her mother had warned her
379.17 of this with tears, before she died....
379.18 "She had caught hold of my arm firmly, and as
379.19 soon as I had stopped she had withdrawn her hand
379.20 in haste. She was audacious and shrinking. She
379.21 feared nothing, but she was checked by the profound
379.22 incertitude and the extreme strangeness -- a brave
379.23 person groping in the dark. I belonged to this
379.24 Unknown that might claim Jim for its own at any
379.25 moment. I was, as it were, in the secret of its
379.26 nature and of its intentions -- the confidant of a
379.27 threatening mystery -- armed with its power, perhaps!
379.28 I believe she supposed I could with a word whisk
379.29 Jim away out of her very arms; it is my sober
379.30 conviction she went through agonies of appre-
380.01 hension during my long talks with Jim; through a
380.02 real and intolerable anguish that might have con-
380.03 ceivably driven her into plotting my murder, had
380.04 the fierceness of her soul been equal to the
380.05 tremendous situation it had created. This is my
380.06 impression, and it is all I can give you: the whole
380.07 thing dawned gradually upon me, and as it got
380.08 clearer and clearer I was overwhelmed by a slow,
380.09 incredulous amazement. She made me believe
380.10 her; but there is no word that on my lips could
380.11 render the effect of the headlong and vehement
380.12 whisper, of the soft, passionate tones, of the sudden
380.13 breathless pause and the appealing movement of
380.14 the white arms extended swiftly. They fell; the
380.15 ghostly figure swayed like a slender tree in the wind,
380.16 the pale oval of the face drooped; it was impossible
380.17 to distinguish her features, the darkness of the eyes
380.18 was unfathomable; two wide sleeves uprose in the
380.19 dark like unfolding wings, and she stood silent, hold-
380.20 ing her head in her hands.
381.01 "I was immensely touched: her youth,
381.02 her ignorance, her pretty beauty, which
381.03 had the simple charm and the delicate
381.04 vigour of a wild flower, her pathetic pleading,
381.05 her helplessness, appealed to me with almost the
381.06 strength of her own unreasonable and natural fear.
381.07 She feared the unknown as we all do, and her
381.08 ignorance made the unknown infinitely vast. I
381.09 stood for it, for myself, for you fellows, for all the
381.10 world that neither cared for Jim nor needed him
381.11 in the least. I would have been ready enough to
381.12 answer for the indifference of the teeming earth
381.13 but for the reflection that he, too, belonged to this
381.14 mysterious unknown of her fears, and that, however
381.15 much I stood for, I did not stand for him. This
381.16 made me hesitate. A murmur of hopeless pain
381.17 unsealed my lips. I began by protesting that I at
381.18 least had come with no intention to take Jim away.
381.19 "Why did I come, then? After a slight move-

381.20 ment she was as still as a marble statue in the night.
381.21 I tried to explain briefly: friendship, business; if
381.22 I had any wish in the matter it was rather to see
381.23 him stay.... 'They always leave us,' she mur-
381.24 mured. The breath of sad wisdom from the grave
382.01 which her piety wreathed with flowers seemed to
382.02 pass in a faint sigh.... Nothing, I said, could
382.03 separate Jim from her.
382.04 "It is my firm conviction now; it was my con-
382.05 viction at the time; it was the only possible con-
382.06 clusion from the facts of the case. It was not
382.07 made more certain by her whispering in a tone
382.08 in which one speaks to oneself, 'He swore this to
382.09 me.' 'Did you ask him?' I said.
382.10 "She made a step nearer. 'No. Never!'
382.11 She had asked him only to go away. It was that
382.12 night on the river-bank, after he had killed the
382.13 man -- after she had flung the torch in the water
382.14 because he was looking at her so. There was too
382.15 much light, and the danger was over then -- for a
382.16 little time -- for a little time. He said then he would
382.17 not abandon her to Cornelius. She had insisted.
382.18 She wanted him to leave her. He said that he
382.19 could not -- that it was impossible. He trembled
382.20 while he said this. She had felt him tremble....
382.21 One does not require much imagination to see the
382.22 scene, almost to hear their whispers. She was
382.23 afraid for him, too. I believe that then she saw in
382.24 him only a predestined victim of dangers which she
382.25 understood better than himself. Though by nothing
382.26 but his mere presence he had mastered her heart,
382.27 had filled all her thoughts, and had possessed
382.28 himself of all her affections, she underestimated
382.29 his chances of success. It is obvious that at about
382.30 that time everybody was inclined to underestimate
383.01 his chances. Strictly speaking, he didn't seem to
383.02 have any. I know this was Cornelius's view. He
383.03 confessed that much to me in extenuation of the
383.04 shady part he had played in Sherif Ali's plot to do
383.05 away with the infidel. Even Sherif Ali himself, as
383.06 it seems certain now, had nothing but contempt
383.07 for the white man. Jim was to be murdered mainly
383.08 on religious grounds, I believe. A simple act of
383.09 piety (and so far infinitely meritorious), but other-
383.10 wise without much importance. In the last part
383.11 of this opinion Cornelius concurred. 'Honourable
383.12 sir,' he argued abjectly on the only occasion he
383.13 managed to have me to himself -- 'honourable sir,
383.14 how was I to know? Who was he? What could
383.15 he do to make people believe him? What did Mr.
383.16 Stein mean sending a boy like that to talk big to
383.17 an old servant? I was ready to save him for
383.18 eighty dollars. Only eighty dollars. Why didn't
383.19 the fool go? Was I to get stabbed myself for the
383.20 sake of a stranger?' He grovelled in spirit before
383.21 me, with his body doubled up insinuatingly and
383.22 his hands hovering about my knees, as though he
383.23 were ready to embrace my legs. 'What's eighty
383.24 dollars? An insignificant sum to give to a defence-
383.25 less old man ruined for life by a deceased she--
383.26 devil.' Here he wept. But I anticipate. I didn't
383.27 that night chance upon Cornelius till I had had it
383.28 out with the girl.
383.29 "She was unselfish when she urged Jim to leave
383.30 her, and even to leave the country. It was his
384.01 danger that was foremost in her thoughts -- even if
384.02 she wanted to save herself, too -- perhaps uncon-
384.03 sciously: but then look at the warning she had,
384.04 look at the lesson that could be drawn from every
384.05 moment of the recently ended life in which all her
384.06 memories were centred. She fell at his feet -- she
384.07 told me so -- there by the river, in the discreet light
384.08 of stars which showed nothing except great masses
384.09 of silent shadows, indefinite open spaces, and
384.10 trembling faintly upon the broad stream made it
384.11 appear as wide as the sea. He had lifted her up.
384.12 He lifted her up, and then she would struggle no
384.13 more. Of course not. Strong arms, a tender
384.14 voice, a stalwart shoulder to rest her poor, lonely
384.15 little head upon. The need -- the infinite need -- of
384.16 all this for the aching heart, for the bewildered
384.17 mind; -- the promptings of youth -- the necessity
384.18 of the moment. What would you have? One
384.19 understands -- unless one is incapable of under-
384.20 standing anything under the sun. And so she was
384.21 content to be lifted up -- and held. 'You know --
384.22 Jove! this is serious -- no nonsense in it!' as Jim
384.23 had whispered hurriedly with a troubled, concerned
384.24 face on the threshold of his house. I don't know
384.25 so much about nonsense, but there was nothing
384.26 light-hearted in their romance: they came together
384.27 under the shadow of a life's disaster, like knight
384.28 and maiden meeting to exchange vows amongst
384.29 haunted ruins. The starlight was good enough
384.30 for that story, a light so faint and remote that it
385.01 cannot resolve shadows into shapes, and show the
385.02 other shore of a stream. I did look upon the stream
385.03 that night and from the very place; it rolled silent
385.04 and as black as Styx: the next day I went away,
385.05 but I am not likely to forget what it was she wanted
385.06 to be saved from when she entreated him to leave
385.07 her while there was time. She told me what it
385.08 was, calmed -- she was now too passionately inter-
385.09 ested for mere excitement -- in a voice as quiet in
385.10 the obscurity as her white half-lost figure. She
385.11 told me, 'I didn't want to die weeping.' I thought
385.12 I had not heard aright.
385.13 "'You did not want to die weeping?' I repeated
385.14 after her. 'Like my mother,' she added readily.
385.15 The outlines of her white shape did not stir in the
385.16 least. 'My mother had wept bitterly before she
385.17 died,' she explained. An inconceivable calmness
385.18 seemed to have risen from the ground around us,
385.19 imperceptibly, like the still rise of a flood in the
385.20 night, obliterating the familiar landmarks of emotions.
385.21 There came upon me, as though I had felt myself
385.22 losing my footing in the midst of waters, a sudden
385.23 dread, the dread of the unknown depths. She went
385.24 on explaining that, during the last moments, being
385.25 alone with her mother, she had to leave the side
385.26 of the couch to go and set her back against the
385.27 door, in order to keep Cornelius out. He desired
385.28 to get in, and kept on drumming with both fists,
385.29 only desisting now and again to shout huskily,
385.30 'Let me in! Let me in! Let me in!' In a
386.01 far corner upon a few mats the moribund woman,
386.02 already speechless and unable to lift her arm, rolled
386.03 her head over, and with a feeble movement of her
386.04 hand seemed to command -- 'No! No! and the
386.05 obedient daughter, setting her shoulders with all
386.06 her strength against the door, was looking on.
386.07 'The tears fell from her eyes -- and then she died,'
386.08 concluded the girl in an imperturbable monotone,
386.09 which more than anything else, more than the
386.10 white statuesque immobility of her person, more
386.11 than mere words could do, troubled my mind
386.12 profoundly with the passive, irremediable horror
386.13 of the scene. It had the power to drive me out
386.14 of my conception of existence, out of that shelter
386.15 each of us makes for himself to creep under in
386.16 moments of danger, as a tortoise withdraws within
386.17 its shell. For a moment I had a view of a world
386.18 that seemed to wear a vast and dismal aspect of
386.19 disorder, while, in truth, thanks to our unwearied
386.20 efforts, it is as sunny an arrangement of small
386.21 conveniences as the mind of man can conceive.
386.22 But still -- it was only a moment: I went back into
386.23 my shell directly. One **must** -- don't you know? --
386.24 though I seemed to have lost all my words in the
386.25 chaos of dark thoughts I had contemplated for a
386.26 second or two beyond the pale. These came back,
386.27 too, very soon, for words also belong to the shelter-
386.28 ing conception of light and order which is our
386.29 refuge. I had them ready at my disposal before
386.30 she whispered softly, 'He swore he would never
387.01 leave me, when we stood there alone! He swore
387.02 to me!' ... 'And is it possible that you -- you! --
387.03 do not believe him?' I asked, sincerely reproachful,
387.04 genuinely shocked. Why couldn't she believe?
387.05 Wherefore this craving for incertitude, this clinging
387.06 to fear, as if incertitude and fear had been the safe-
387.07 guards of her love. It was monstrous. She should
387.08 have made for herself a shelter of inexpugnable
387.09 peace out of that honest affection. She had not
387.10 the knowledge -- not the skill perhaps. The night
387.11 had come on apace; it had grown pitch-dark
387.12 where we were, so that without stirring she had
387.13 faded like the intangible form of a wistful and
387.14 perverse spirit. And suddenly I heard her quiet
387.15 whisper again, 'Other men had sworn the same
387.16 thing.' It was like a meditative comment on some
387.17 thoughts full of sadness, of awe. And she added,
387.18 still lower if possible, 'My father did.' She paused
387.19 the time to draw an inaudible breath. 'Her father,
387.20 too....' These were the things she knew! At
387.21 once I said, 'Ah! but he is not like that.' This, it
387.22 seemed, she did not intend to dispute; but after a
387.23 time the strange, still whisper wandering dreamily
387.24 in the air stole into my ears. 'Why is he different?
387.25 Is he better? Is he ...' 'Upon my word of

387.26 honour,' I broke in, 'I believe he is.' We subdued
387.27 our tones to a mysterious pitch. Amongst the
387.28 nuts of Jim's workmen (they were mostly liberated
387.29 slaves from the Sherif's stockade) somebody started
387.30 a shrill, drawling song. Across the river a big fire
388.01 (at Doramin's, I think) made a glowing ball, com-
388.02 pletely isolated in the night. 'Is he more true?'
388.03 she murmured. 'Yes,' I said. 'More true than
388.04 any other man?' she repeated in lingering accents.
388.05 'Nobody here,' I said, 'would dream of doubting
388.06 his word -- nobody would dare -- except you.'
388.07 "I think she made a movement at this. 'More
388.08 brave?' she went on in a changed tone. 'Fear will
388.09 never drive him away from you,' I said a little
388.10 nervously. The song stopped short on a shrill note,
388.11 and was succeeded by several voices talking in the
388.12 distance. Jim's voice, too. I was struck by her
388.13 silence. 'What has he been telling you? He has
388.14 been telling you something?' I asked. There was
388.15 no answer. 'What is it he told you?' I insisted.
388.16 "'Do you think I can tell you? How am I to
388.17 know? How am I to understand?' she cried at
388.18 last. There was a stir. I believe she was wring-
388.19 ing her hands. 'There is something he can never
388.20 forget.'
388.21 "'So much the better for you,' I said gloomily.
388.22 "'What is it? What is it?' She put an extra-
388.23 ordinary force of appeal into her supplicating tone.
388.24 'He says he had been afraid. How can I believe
388.25 this? Am I a mad woman to believe this? You
388.26 all remember something! You all go back to it.
388.27 What is it? You tell me! What is this thing?
388.28 Is it alive? -- is it dead? I hate it. It is cruel.
388.29 Has it got a face and a voice -- this calamity? Will
388.30 he see it? -- will he hear it? In his sleep perhaps
389.01 when he cannot see me -- and then arise and go?
389.02 Ah! I shall never forgive him. My mother had
389.03 forgiven -- but I, never! Will it be a sign -- a
389.04 call?'
389.05 "It was a wonderful experience. She mis-
389.06 trusted his very slumbers -- and she seemed to think
389.07 I could tell her why! Thus a poor mortal seduced
389.08 by the charm of an apparition might have tried to
389.09 wring from another ghost the tremendous secret of
389.10 the claim the other world holds over a disembodied
389.11 soul astray amongst the passions of this earth.
389.12 The very ground on which I stood seemed to melt
389.13 under my feet. And it was so simple, too; but
389.14 if the spirits evoked by our fears and our unrest
389.15 have ever to vouch for each other's constancy before
389.16 the forlorn magicians that we are, then I -- I alone.
389.17 of us dwellers in the flesh -- have shuddered in the
389.18 hopeless chill of such a task. A sign, a call!
389.19 How telling in its expression was her ignorance! A
389.20 few words! How she came to know them, how she
389.21 came to pronounce them, I can't imagine. Women
389.22 find their inspiration in the stress of moments that
389.23 for us are merely awful, absurd, or futile. To dis-
389.24 cover that she had a voice at all was enough to strike
389.25 awe into the heart. Had a spurned stone cried out
389.26 in pain it could not have appeared a greater and
389.27 more pitiful miracle. These few sounds wandering
389.28 in the dark had made their two benighted lives tragic
389.29 to my mind. It was impossible to make her under-
389.30 stand. I chafed silently at my impotence. And
390.01 Jim, too -- poor devil! Who would need him?
390.02 Who would remember him? He had what he
390.03 wanted. His very existence probably had been
390.04 forgotten by this time. They had mastered their
390.05 fates. They were tragic.
390.06 "Her immobility before me was clearly ex-
390.07 pectant, and my part was to speak for my brother
390.08 from the realm of forgetful shades. I was deeply
390.09 moved at my responsibility and at her distress.
390.10 I would have given anything for the power to soothe
390.11 her frail soul, tormenting itself in its invincible
390.12 ignorance like a small bird beating about the cruel
390.13 wires of a cage. Nothing easier than to say, Have
390.14 no fear! Nothing more difficult. How does one
390.15 kill fear, I wonder? How do you shoot a spectre
390.16 through the heart, slash off its spectral head, take
390.17 it by its spectral throat? It is an enterprise you
390.18 rush into while you dream, and are glad to make your
390.19 escape with wet hair and every limb shaking. The
390.20 bullet is not run, the blade not forged, the man not
390.21 born; even the winged words of truth drop at your
390.22 feet like lumps of lead. You require for such a
390.23 desperate encounter an enchanted and poisoned
390.24 shaft dipped in a lie too subtle to be found on earth.
390.25 An enterprise for a dream, my masters!

390.26 "I began my exorcism with a heavy heart, with
390.27 a sort of sullen anger in it, too. Jim's voice,
390.28 suddenly raised with a stern intonation, carried
390.29 across the courtyard, reproving the carelessness of
390.30 some dumb sinner by the riverside. 'Nothing I
391.01 said, speaking in a distinct murmur -- there could
391.02 be nothing in that unknown world she fancied so
391.03 eager to rob her of her happiness, there was nothing,
391.04 neither living nor dead, there was no face, no voice,
391.05 no power, that could tear Jim from her side. I drew
391.06 breath, and she whispered softly, 'He told me so.'
391.07 'He told you the truth,' I said. 'Nothing,' she
391.08 sighed out, and abruptly turned upon me with a
391.09 barely audible intensity of tone: 'Why did you
391.10 come to us from out there? He speaks of you
391.11 too often. You make me afraid. Do you -- do you
391.12 want him?' A sort of stealthy fierceness had crept
391.13 into our hurried mutters. 'I shall never come
391.14 again,' I said bitterly. 'And I don't want him.
391.15 No one wants him.' 'No one,' she repeated in a
391.16 tone of doubt. 'No one,' I affirmed, feeling myself
391.17 swayed by some strange excitement. 'You think
391.18 him strong, wise, courageous, great -- why not
391.19 believe him to be true, too? I shall go to-morrow --
391.20 and that is the end. You shall never be troubled
391.21 by a voice from there again. This world you don't
391.22 know is too big to miss him. You understand?
391.23 Too big. You've got his heart in your hand. You
391.24 must feel that. You must know that.' 'Yes, I
391.25 know that,' she breathed out, hard and still, as a
391.26 statue might whisper.
391.27 "I felt I had done nothing. And what is it
391.28 that I had wished to do? I am not sure now. At
391.29 the time I was animated by an inexplicable ardour,
391.30 as if before some great and necessary task -- the
392.01 influence of the moment upon my mental and
392.02 emotional state. There are in all our lives such
392.03 moments, such influences, coming from the outside,
392.04 as it were, irresistible, incomprehensible -- as if
392.05 brought about by the mysterious conjunctions of
392.06 the planets. She owned, as I had put it to her,
392.07 his heart. She had that and everything else -- if she
392.08 could only believe it. What I had to tell her was
392.09 that in the whole world there was no one who ever
392.10 would need his heart, his mind, his hand. It was a
392.11 common fate, and yet it seemed an awful thing to
392.12 say of any man. She listened without a word, and
392.13 her stillness now was like the protest of an invincible
392.14 unbelief. What need she care for the world beyond
392.15 the forests? I asked. From all the multitudes that
392.16 peopled the vastness of that unknown there would
392.17 come, I assured her, as long as he lived, neither a
392.18 call nor a sign for him. Never. I was carried
392.19 away. Never! Never! I remember with wonder
392.20 the sort of dogged fierceness I displayed. I had
392.21 the illusion of having got the spectre by the throat
392.22 at last. Indeed the whole real thing has left behind
392.23 the detailed and amazing impression of a dream.
392.24 Why should she fear? She knew him to be strong,
392.25 true, wise, brave. He was all that. Certainly.
392.26 He was more. He was great -- invincible -- and the
392.27 world did not want him, it had forgotten him, it
392.28 would not even know him.
392.29 "I stopped; the silence over Patusan was pro-
392.30 found, and the feeble, dry sound of a paddle striking
393.01 the side of a canoe somewhere in the middle of
393.02 the river seemed to make it infinite. 'Why?' she
393.03 murmured. I felt that sort of rage one feels during
393.04 a hard tussle. The spectre was trying to slip out
393.05 of my grasp. 'Why?' she repeated louder; 'tell
393.06 me!' And as I remained confounded, she stamped
393.07 with her foot like a spoilt child. 'Why? Speak.'
393.08 'You want to know?' I asked in a fury. 'Yes!'
393.09 she cried. 'Because he is not good enough,' I
393.10 said brutally. During the moment's pause I
393.11 noticed the fire on the other shore blaze up, dilating
393.12 the circle of its glow like an amazed stare, and con-
393.13 tract suddenly to a red pin-point. I only knew how
393.14 close to me she had been when I felt the clutch of
393.15 her fingers on my forearm. Without raising her
393.16 voice, she threw into it an infinity of scathing con-
393.17 tempt, bitterness, and despair.
393.18 "'This is the very thing he said.... You
393.19 lie!'
393.20 "The last two words she cried at me in the
393.21 native dialect. 'Hear me out!' I entreated. She
393.22 caught her breath tremulously, flung my arm away.
393.23 'Nobody, nobody is good enough,' I began with the
393.24 greatest earnestness. I could hear the sobbing
393.25 labour of her breath frightfully quickened. I hung

393.26 my head. What was the use? Footsteps were
393.27 approaching; I slipped away without another
393.28 word...."
394.01 MARLOW swung his legs out, got up
394.02 quickly, and staggered a little, as though he
394.03 had been set down after a rush through
394.04 space. He leaned his back against the balustrade
394.05 and faced a disordered array of long cane chairs.
394.06 The bodies prone in them seemed startled out of
394.07 their torpor by his movement. One or two sat up
394.08 as if alarmed; here and there a cigar glowed yet;
394.09 Marlow looked at them all with the eyes of a man
394.10 returning from the excessive remoteness of a dream.
394.11 A throat was cleared; a calm voice encouraged
394.12 negligently, "Well."
394.13 "Nothing," said Marlow with a slight start.
394.14 "He had told her -- that's all. She did not believe
394.15 him -- nothing more. As to myself, I do not know
394.16 whether it be just, proper, decent for me to rejoice
394.17 or to be sorry. For my part, I cannot say what I
394.18 believed -- indeed I don't know to this day, and
394.19 never shall probably. But what did the poor devil
394.20 believe himself? Truth shall prevail -- don't you
394.21 know, Magna est veritas et ... Yes, when it gets
394.22 a chance. There is a law, no doubt -- and likewise
394.23 a law regulates your luck in the throwing of dice.
394.24 It is not Justice the servant of men, but accident,
395.01 hazard, Fortune -- the ally of patient Time -- that
395.02 holds an even and scrupulous balance. Both of
395.03 us had said the very same thing. Did we both
395.04 speak the truth -- or one of us did -- or neither? ..."
395.05 Marlow paused, crossed his arms on his breast,
395.06 and in a changed tone:
395.07 "She said we lied. Poor soul! Well -- let's
395.08 leave it to Chance, whose ally is Time, that cannot
395.09 be hurried, and whose enemy is Death, that will
395.10 not wait. I had retreated -- a little cowed, I must
395.11 own. I had tried a fall with fear itself and got
395.12 thrown -- of course. I had only succeeded in adding
395.13 to her anguish the hint of some mysterious collusion,
395.14 of an inexplicable and incomprehensible conspiracy
395.15 to keep her for ever in the dark. And it had come
395.16 easily, naturally, unavoidably, by his act, by her own
395.17 act! It was as though I had been shown the work-
395.18 ing of the implacable destiny of which we are the
395.19 victims -- and the tools. It was appalling to think
395.20 of the girl whom I had left standing there motionless;
395.21 Jim's footsteps had a fateful sound as he tramped
395.22 by, without seeing me, in his heavy laced boots.
395.23 'What? No lights!' he said in a loud, surprised
395.24 voice. 'What are you doing in the dark -- you
395.25 two?' Next moment he caught sight of her, I
395.26 suppose. 'Hallo, girl!' he cried cheerily. 'Hallo,
395.27 boy!' she answered at once, with amazing pluck.
395.28 "This was their usual greeting to each other,
395.29 and the bit of swagger she would put into her rather
395.30 high but sweet voice was very droll, pretty, and child-
396.01 like. It delighted Jim greatly. This was the last
396.02 occasion on which I heard them exchange this
396.03 familiar hail, and it struck a chill into my heart.
396.04 There was the high, sweet voice, the pretty effort,
396.05 the swagger; but it all seemed to die out pre-
396.06 maturely, and the playful call sounded like a moan.
396.07 It was too confoundedly awful. 'What have you
396.08 done with Marlow?' Jim was asking; and then,
396.09 'Gone down -- has he? Funny I didn't meet him.
396.10 ... You there, Marlow?'
396.11 "I didn't answer. I wasn't going in -- not yet at
396.12 any rate. I really couldn't. While he was calling
396.13 me I was engaged in making my escape through a
396.14 little gate leading out upon a stretch of newly cleared
396.15 ground. No; I couldn't face them yet. I walked
396.16 hastily with lowered head along a trodden path.
396.17 The ground rose gently, the few big trees had been
396.18 felled, the undergrowth had been cut down and the
396.19 grass fired. He had a mind to try a coffee-planta-
396.20 tion there. The big hill, rearing its double summit
396.21 coal-black in the clear, yellow glow of the rising
396.22 moon, seemed to cast its shadow upon the ground
396.23 prepared for that experiment. He was going to try
396.24 ever so many experiments; I had admired his
396.25 energy, his enterprise, and his shrewdness. Nothing
396.26 on earth seemed less real now than his plans, his
396.27 energy, and his enthusiasm; and raising my eyes,
396.28 I saw part of the moon glittering through the bushes
396.29 at the bottom of the chasm. For a moment it
396.30 looked as though the smooth disc, falling from its
397.01 place in the sky upon the earth, had rolled to the
397.02 bottom of that precipice; its ascending movement
397.03 was like a leisurely rebound; it disengaged itself

397.04 from the tangle of twigs; the bare, contorted limb
397.05 of some tree, growing on the slope, made a black
397.06 crack right across its face. It threw its level rays
397.07 afar as if from a cavern, and in this mournful eclipse--
397.08 like light the stumps of felled trees uprose very
397.09 dark, the heavy shadows fell at my feet on all sides,
397.10 my own moving shadow, and across my path the
397.11 shadow of the solitary grave perpetually garlanded
397.12 with flowers. In the darkened moonlight the inter-
397.13 laced blossoms took on shapes foreign to one's
397.14 memory and colours indefinable to the eye, as though
397.15 they had been special flowers gathered by no man,
397.16 grown not in this world, and destined for the use of
397.17 the dead alone. Their powerful scent hung in the
397.18 warm air, making it thick and heavy like the fumes
397.19 of incense. The lumps of white coral shone round
397.20 the dark mound like a chaplet of bleached skulls,
397.21 and everything around was so quiet that when I
397.22 stood still all sound and all movements in the world
397.23 seemed to come to an end.
397.24 "It was a great peace, as if the earth had been
397.25 one grave, and for a time I stood there thinking
397.26 mostly of the living who, buried in remote places
397.27 out of the knowledge of mankind, still are fated to
397.28 share in its tragic or grotesque miseries. In its
397.29 noble struggles, too -- who knows? The human
397.30 heart is vast enough to contain all the world. It is
398.01 valiant enough to bear the burden, but where is the
398.02 courage that would cast it off?
398.03 "I suppose I must have fallen into a sentimental
398.04 mood; I only know that I stood there long enough
398.05 for the sense of utter solitude to get hold of me
398.06 so completely that all I had lately seen, all I had
398.07 heard, and the very human speech itself, seemed
398.08 to have passed away out of existence, living only for
398.09 a while longer in my memory, as though I had been
398.10 the last of mankind. It was a strange and melancholy
398.11 illusion, evolved half consciously like all our illu-
398.12 sions, which I suspect only to be visions of remote,
398.13 unattainable truth, seen dimly. This was, indeed,
398.14 one of the lost, forgotten, unknown places of the
398.15 earth; I had looked under its obscure surface; and
398.16 I felt that when to-morrow I had left it for ever,
398.17 it would slip out of existence, to live only in my
398.18 memory till I myself passed into oblivion. I have
398.19 that feeling about me now; perhaps it is that feel-
398.20 ing which has incited me to tell you the story, to
398.21 try to hand over to you, as it were, its very existence,
398.22 its reality -- the truth disclosed in a moment of
398.23 illusion.
398.24 "Cornelius broke upon it. He bolted out,
398.25 vermin-like, from the long grass growing in a de-
398.26 pression of the ground. I believe his house was
398.27 rotting somewhere near by, though I've never seen
398.28 it, not having been far enough in that direction.
398.29 He ran towards me upon the path; his feet, shod
398.30 in dirty white shoes, twinkled on the dark earth;
399.01 he pulled himself up, and began to whine and cringe
399.02 under a tall, stove-pipe hat. His dried-up little
399.03 carcass was swallowed up, totally lost, in a suit of
399.04 black broadcloth. That was his costume for holi-
399.05 days and ceremonies, and it reminded me that this
399.06 was the fourth Sunday I had spent in Patusan. All
399.07 the time of my stay I had been vaguely aware of
399.08 his desire to confide in me, if he only could get
399.09 me all to himself. He hung about with an eager,
399.10 craving look on his sour, yellow little face; but his
399.11 timidity had kept him back as much as my natural
399.12 reluctance to have anything to do with such an
399.13 unsavoury creature. He would have succeeded,
399.14 nevertheless, had he not been so ready to slink off
399.15 as soon as you looked at him. He would slink
399.16 off before Jim's severe gaze, before my own, which
399.17 I tried to make indifferent, even before Tamb'
399.18 Itam's surly, superior glance. He was perpetually
399.19 slinking away; whenever seen he was seen moving
399.20 off deviously, his face over his shoulder, with either
399.21 a mistrustful snarl or a woe-begone, piteous, mute
399.22 aspect; but no assumed expression could conceal
399.23 this innate, irremediable abjectness of his nature,
399.24 any more than an arrangement of clothing can con-
399.25 ceal some monstrous deformity of the body.
399.26 "I don't know whether it was the demoralisation
399.27 of my utter defeat in my encounter with a spectre of
399.28 fear less than an hour ago, but I let him capture me
399.29 without even a show of resistance. I was doomed to
399.30 be the recipient of confidences, and to be con-
400.01 fronted with unanswerable questions. It was try-
400.02 ing; but the contempt, the unreasoned contempt,
400.03 the man's appearance provoked, made it easier

247

400.04 to bear. He couldn't possibly matter. Nothing
400.05 mattered, since I had made up my mind that Jim,
400.06 for whom alone I cared, had at last mastered his
400.07 fate. He had told me he was satisfied ... nearly.
400.08 This is going further than most of us dare. I --
400.09 who have the right to think myself good enough
400.10 -- dare not. Neither does any of you here, I
400.11 suppose? ..."
400.12 Marlow paused, as if expecting an answer. No-
400.13 body spoke.
400.14 "Quite right," he began again. "Let no soul
400.15 know, since the truth can be wrung out of us only
400.16 by some cruel, little, awful catastrophe. But he is
400.17 one of us, and he could say he was satisfied ...
400.18 nearly. Just fancy this! Nearly satisfied. One
400.19 could almost envy him his catastrophe. Nearly
400.20 satisfied. After this nothing could matter. It did
400.21 not matter who suspected him, who trusted him,
400.22 who loved him, who hated him -- especially as it was
400.23 Cornelius who hated him.
400.24 "Yet after all, this was a kind of recognition.
400.25 You shall judge of a man by his foes as well as by
400.26 his friends, and this enemy of Jim was such as no
400.27 decent man would be ashamed to own, without,
400.28 however, making too much of him. This was the
400.29 view Jim took, and in which I shared; but Jim
400.30 disregarded him on general grounds. 'My dear
401.01 Marlow,' he said, 'I feel that if I go straight nothing
401.02 can touch me. Indeed I do. Now you have
401.03 been long enough here to have a good look round --
401.04 and, frankly, don't you think I am pretty safe?
401.05 It all depends upon me, and, by Jove! I have lots
401.06 of confidence in myself. The worst thing he could
401.07 do would be to kill me, I suppose. I don't think for
401.08 a moment he would. He couldn't, you know -- not
401.09 if I were myself to hand him a loaded rifle for the
401.10 purpose, and then turn my back on him. That's
401.11 the sort of thing he is. And suppose he would --
401.12 suppose he could? Well -- what of that? I didn't
401.13 come here flying for my life -- did I? I came here to
401.14 set my back against the wall, and I am going to stay
401.15 here ...'
401.16 "'Till you are _quite_ satisfied,' I struck in.
401.17 "We were sitting at the time under the roof in
401.18 the stern of the boat; twenty paddles flashed like
401.19 one, ten on a side, striking the water with a single
401.20 splash, while behind our backs Tamb' Itam dipped
401.21 silently right and left, and stared right down the
401.22 river, attentive to keep the long canoe in the greatest
401.23 strength of the current. Jim bowed his head, and
401.24 our last talk seemed to flicker out for good. He was
401.25 seeing me off as far as the mouth of the river. The
401.26 schooner had left the day before, working down and
401.27 drifting on the ebb, while I had prolonged my stay
401.28 overnight. And now he was seeing me off.
401.29 "Jim had been a little angry with me for
401.30 mentioning Cornelius at all. I had not, in truth,
402.01 said much. The man was too insignificant to be
402.02 dangerous, though he was as full of hate as he could
402.03 hold. He had called me 'honourable sir' at every
402.04 second sentence, and had whined at my elbow as he
402.05 followed me from the grave of his 'late wife' to the
402.06 gate of Jim's compound. He declared himself the
402.07 most unhappy of men, a victim, crushed like a worm;
402.08 he entreated me to look at him. I wouldn't turn
402.09 my head to do so; but I could see out of the corner
402.10 of my eye his obsequious shadow gliding after mine,
402.11 while the moon, suspended on our right hand,
402.12 seemed to gloat serenely upon the spectacle. He
402.13 tried to explain -- as I've told you -- his share in the
402.14 events of the memorable night. It was a matter of
402.15 expediency. How could he know who was going
402.16 to get the upper hand? 'I would have saved him,
402.17 honourable sir! I would have saved him for eighty
402.18 dollars,' he protested in dulcet tones, keeping a pace
402.19 behind me. 'He has saved himself,' I said, 'and
402.20 he has forgiven you.' I heard a sort of tittering,
402.21 and turned upon him; at once he appeared ready
402.22 to take to his heels. 'What are you laughing at?'
402.23 I asked, standing still. 'Don't be deceived, honour-
402.24 able sir!' he shrieked, seemingly losing all control
402.25 over his feelings. '_He_ save himself! He knows
402.26 nothing, honourable sir -- nothing whatever. Who
402.27 is he? What does he want here -- the big thief?
402.28 What does he want here? He throws dust into
402.29 everybody's eyes; he throws dust into your eyes,
402.30 honourable sir; but he can't throw dust into my
403.01 eyes. He is a big fool, honourable sir.' I laughed
403.02 contemptuously, and, turning on my heel, began to
403.03 walk on again. He ran up to my elbow and whis-

403.04 pered forcibly, 'He's no more than a little child
403.05 here -- like a little child -- a little child.' Of cou[rse]
403.06 I didn't take the slightest notice, and seeing the
403.07 time pressed, because we were approaching the
403.08 bamboo fence that glittered over the blackened
403.09 ground of the clearing, he came to the point. He
403.10 commenced by being abjectly lachrymose. His
403.11 great misfortunes had affected his head. He hoped
403.12 I would kindly forget what nothing but his troubles
403.13 made him say. He didn't mean anything by it;
403.14 only the honourable sir did not know what it was
403.15 to be ruined, broken down, trampled upon. After
403.16 this introduction he approached the matter near
403.17 his heart, but in such a rambling, ejaculatory,
403.18 craven fashion, that for a long time I couldn't make
403.19 out what he was driving at. He wanted me to
403.20 intercede with Jim in his favour. It seemed, too,
403.21 to be some sort of money affair. I heard time
403.22 and again the words, 'Moderate provision -- suitable
403.23 present.' He seemed to be claiming value for some-
403.24 thing, and he even went the length of saying with
403.25 some warmth that life was not worth having if a
403.26 man were to be robbed of everything. I did not
403.27 breathe a word, of course, but neither did I stop my
403.28 ears. The gist of the affair, which became clear to
403.29 me gradually, was in this, that he regarded himself
403.30 as entitled to some money in exchange for the girl.
404.01 He had brought her up. Somebody else's child.
404.02 Great trouble and pains -- old man now -- suitable
404.03 present. It the honourable sir would say a word.
404.04 ... I stood still to look at him with curiosity, and
404.05 fearful lest I should think him extortionate, I
404.06 suppose, he hastily brought himself to make a
404.07 concession. In consideration of a 'suitable present'
404.08 given at once, he would, he declared, be willing to
404.09 undertake the charge of the girl, 'without any other
404.10 provision -- when the time came for the gentleman
404.11 to go home.' His little yellow face, all crumpled as
404.12 though it had been squeezed together, expressed the
404.13 most anxious, eager avarice. His voice whined
404.14 coaxingly, 'No more trouble -- natural guardian --
404.15 a sum of money....'
404.16 "I stood there and marvelled. That kind of
404.17 thing, with him, was evidently a vocation. I dis-
404.18 covered suddenly in his cringing attitude a sort of
404.19 assurance, as though he had been all his life dealing
404.20 in certitudes. He must have thought I was dis-
404.21 passionately considering his proposal, because he
404.22 became as sweet as honey. 'Every gentleman made
404.23 a provision when the time came to go home,' he
404.24 began insinuatingly. I slammed the little gate.
404.25 'In this case, Mr. Cornelius,' I said, 'the time
404.26 will never come.' He took a few seconds to gather
404.27 this in. 'What!' he fairly squealed. 'Why,' I
404.28 continued from my side of the gate, 'haven't I
404.29 heard him say so himself? He will never go home.'
404.30 'Oh, this is too much!' he shouted. He would
405.01 not address me as 'honoured sir' any more. He
405.02 was very still for a time, and then without a trace of
405.03 humility began very low: 'Never go -- ah! He --
405.04 he -- he comes here devil knows from where -- comes
405.05 here -- devil knows why -- to trample on me till I
405.06 die -- ah -- trample' (he stamped softly with both
405.07 feet), 'trample like this -- nobody knows why --
405.08 till I die....' His voice became quite extinct;
405.09 he was bothered by a little cough; he came up
405.10 close to the fence and told me, dropping into
405.11 a confidential and piteous tone, that he would
405.12 _not_ be trampled upon. 'Patience -- patience,' he
405.13 muttered, striking his breast. I had done laughing
405.14 at him, but unexpectedly he treated me to a wild,
405.15 cracked burst of it. 'Ha! ha! ha! We shall
405.16 see! We shall see! What! Steal from me!
405.17 Steal from me everything! Everything! Every-
405.18 thing!' His head drooped on one shoulder, his
405.19 hands were hanging before him lightly clasped.
405.20 One would have thought he had cherished the girl
405.21 with surpassing love, that his spirit had been crushed
405.22 and his heart broken by the most cruel of spoliations.
405.23 Suddenly he lifted his head and shot out an in-
405.24 famous word. 'Like her mother -- she is like her
405.25 deceitful mother. Exactly. In her face, too. In
405.26 her face. The devil!' He leaned his forehead
405.27 against the fence, and in that position uttered threats
405.28 and horrible blasphemies in Portuguese in very
405.29 weak ejaculations, mingled with miserable plaints
405.30 and groans, coming out with a heave of the shoulders
406.01 as though he had been overtaken by a deadly fit
406.02 of sickness. It was an inexpressibly grotesque and
406.03 vile performance, and I hastened away. He tried

406.04 to shout something after me. Some disparagement
406.05 of Jim, I believe -- not too loud though, we were too
406.06 near the house. All I heard distinctly was, 'No
406.07 more than a little child -- a little child.'"
407.01   "BUT next morning, at the first bend of
407.02 the river shutting off the houses of
407.03 Patusan, all this dropped out of my
407.04 sight bodily, with its colour, its design, and its
407.05 meaning, like a picture created by fancy on a canvas,
407.06 upon which, after long contemplation, you turn your
407.07 back for the last time. It remains in the memory
407.08 motionless, unfaded, with its life arrested, in an
407.09 unchanging light. There are the ambitions, the
407.10 fears, the hate, the hopes, and they remain in my
407.11 mind just as I had seen them -- intense and as if
407.12 for ever suspended in their expression. I had
407.13 turned away from the picture and was going back
407.14 to the world where events move, men change, light
407.15 flickers, life flows in a clear stream, no matter
407.16 whether over mud or over stones. I wasn't going
407.17 to dive into it; I would have enough to do to keep
407.18 my head above the surface. But as to what I was
407.19 leaving behind, I cannot imagine any alteration. The
407.20 immense and magnanimous Doramin and his little
407.21 motherly witch of a wife, gazing together upon the
407.22 land and nursing secretly their dreams of parental
407.23 ambition; Tunju Allang, wizened and greatly per-
407.24 plexed; Dain Waris, intelligent and brave, with
408.01 his faith in Jim, with his firm glance and his ironic
408.02 friendliness; the girl, absorbed in her frightened,
408.03 suspicious adoration; Tamb' Itam, surly and
408.04 faithful; Cornelius, leaning his forehead against
408.05 the fence under the moonlight -- I am certain of
408.06 them. They exist as if under an enchanter's
408.07 wand. But the figure round which all these are
408.08 grouped -- that one lives, and I am not certain of
408.09 him. No magician's wand can immobilise him
408.10 under my eyes. He is one of us.
408.11 "Jim, as I've told you, accompanied me on the
408.12 first stage of my journey back to the world he had
408.13 renounced, and the way at times seemed to lead
408.14 through the very heart of untouched wilderness.
408.15 The empty reaches sparkled under the high sun;
408.16 between the high walls of vegetation the heat
408.17 drowsed upon the water, and the boat, impelled
408.18 vigorously, cut her way through the air that seemed
408.19 to have settled dense and warm under the shelter
408.20 of lofty trees.
408.21 "The shadow of the impending separation had
408.22 already put an immense space between us, and
408.23 when we spoke it was with an effort, as if to force
408.24 our low voices across a vast and increasing distance.
408.25 The boat fairly flew; we sweltered side by side in
408.26 the stagnant, superheated air; the smell of mud,
408.27 of marsh, the primeval smell of fecund earth,
408.28 seemed to sting our faces; till suddenly at a bend
408.29 it was as if a great hand far away had lifted a heavy
408.30 curtain, had flung open an immense portal. The
409.01 light itself seemed to stir, the sky above our heads
409.02 widened, a far-off murmur reached our ears, a
409.03 freshness enveloped us, filled our lungs, quickened
409.04 our thoughts, our blood, our regrets -- and, straight
409.05 ahead, the forests sank down against the dark blue
409.06 ridge of the sea.
409.07 "I breathed deeply, I revelled in the vastness
409.08 of the opened horizon, in the different atmosphere
409.09 that seemed to vibrate with a toil of life, with the
409.10 energy of an impeccable world. This sky and this
409.11 sea were open to me. The girl was right -- there
409.12 was a sign, a call in them -- something to which I
409.13 responded with every fibre of my being. I let
409.14 my eyes roam through space, like a man released
409.15 from bonds who stretches his cramped limbs, runs,
409.16 leaps, responds to the inspiring elation of freedom.
409.17 'This is glorious!' I cried, and then I looked at
409.18 the sinner by my side. He sat with his head sunk
409.19 on his breast and said 'Yes,' without raising his
409.20 eyes, as if afraid to see writ large on the clear sky
409.21 of the offing the reproach of his romantic conscience.
409.22 "I remember the smallest details of that after-
409.23 noon. We landed on a bit of white beach. It
409.24 was backed by a low cliff wooded on the brow,
409.25 draped in creepers to the very foot. Below us the
409.26 plain of the sea, of a serene and intense blue, stretched
409.27 with a slight upward tilt to the thread-like horizon
409.28 drawn at the height of our eyes. Great waves of
409.29 glitter blew lightly along the pitted dark surface,
409.30 as swift as feathers chased by the breeze. A chain
410.01 of islands sat broken and massive facing the wide
410.02 estuary, displayed in a sheet of pale, glassy water

410.03 reflecting faithfully the contour of the shore. High
410.04 in the colourless sunshine a solitary bird, all black,
410.05 hovered, dropping and soaring above the same spot
410.06 with a slight rocking motion of the wings. A
410.07 ragged, sooty bunch of flimsy mat hovels was
410.08 perched over its own inverted image upon a crooked
410.09 multitude of high piles the colour of ebony. A
410.10 tiny black canoe put off from amongst them with
410.11 two tiny men, all black, who toiled exceedingly,
410.12 striking down at the pale water: and the canoe
410.13 seemed to slide painfully on a mirror. This bunch
410.14 of miserable hovels was the fishing village that
410.15 boasted of the white lord's especial protection, and
410.16 the two men crossing over were the old head-man and
410.17 his son-in-law. They landed and walked up to us
410.18 on the white sand, lean, dark brown as if dried in
410.19 smoke, with ashy patches on the skin of their naked
410.20 shoulders and breasts. Their heads were bound
410.21 in dirty but carefully folded handkerchiefs, and
410.22 the old man began at once to state a complaint,
410.23 voluble, stretching a lank arm, screwing up at
410.24 Jim his old, bleared eyes confidently. The Rajah's
410.25 people would not leave them alone; there had
410.26 been some trouble about a lot of turtles' eggs his
410.27 people had collected on the islets there -- and leaning
410.28 at arm's-length upon his paddle, he pointed with a
410.29 brown, skinny hand over the sea. Jim listened for
410.30 a time without looking up, and at last told him
411.01 gently to wait. He would hear him by and by.
411.02 They withdrew obediently to some little distance,
411.03 and sat on their heels, with their paddles lying
411.04 before them on the sand; the silvery gleams in
411.05 their eyes followed our movements patiently; and
411.06 the immensity of the outspread sea, the stillness of
411.07 the coast, passing north and south beyond the
411.08 limits of my vision, made up one colossal Presence
411.09 watching us four dwarfs isolated on a strip of
411.10 glistening sand.
411.11 "'The trouble is,' remarked Jim moodily, 'that
411.12 for generations these beggars of fishermen in that
411.13 village there had been considered as the Rajah's
411.14 personal slaves -- and the old rip can't get it into his
411.15 head that ...'
411.16 "He paused. 'That you have changed all
411.17 that,' I said.
411.18 "'Yes. I've changed all that,' he muttered in a
411.19 gloomy voice.
411.20 "'You have had your opportunity,' I pursued.
411.21 "'Have I?' he said. 'Well, yes. I suppose
411.22 so. Yes. I have got back my confidence in myself
411.23 -- a good name -- yet sometimes I wish ... No! I
411.24 shall hold what I've got. Can't expect anything
411.25 more.' He flung his arm out towards the sea.
411.26 'Not out there anyhow.' He stamped his foot
411.27 upon the sand. 'This is my limit, because nothing
411.28 less will do.'
411.29 "We continued pacing the beach. 'Yes, I've
411.30 changed all that,' he went on, with a sidelong glance
412.01 at the two patient, squatting fishermen; 'but only
412.02 try to think what it would be if I went away. Jove!
412.03 can't you see it? Hell loose. No! To-morrow
412.04 I shall go and take my chance of drinking that silly
412.05 old Tunku Allang's coffee, and I shall make no end
412.06 of fuss over these rotten turtles' eggs. No. I can't
412.07 say -- enough. Never. I must go on, go on for
412.08 ever holding up my end, to feel sure that nothing
412.09 can touch me. I must stick to their belief in me
412.10 to feel safe and to -- to' ... he cast about for a
412.11 word, seemed to look for it on the sea ... 'to
412.12 keep in touch with' ... his voice sank suddenly
412.13 to a murmur ... 'with those whom, perhaps, I
412.14 shall never see any more. With -- with -- you, for
412.15 instance.'
412.16 "I was profoundly humbled by his words.
412.17 'For God's sake,' I said, 'don't set me up, my dear
412.18 fellow; just look to yourself.' I felt a gratitude,
412.19 an affection, for that straggler whose eyes had
412.20 singled me out, keeping my place in the ranks of
412.21 an insignificant multitude. How little that was to
412.22 boast of, after all! I turned my burning face away;
412.23 under the low sun, glowing, darkened and crimson,
412.24 like an ember snatched from the fire, the sea lay
412.25 outspread, offering all its immense stillness to the
412.26 approach of the fiery orb. Twice he was going to
412.27 speak, but checked himself; at last, as if he had
412.28 found a formula:
412.29 "'I shall be faithful,' he said quietly. 'I shall
412.30 be faithful,' he repeated, without looking at me, but
413.01 for the first time letting his eyes wander upon the
413.02 waters, whose blueness had changed to a gloomy

413.03 purple under the fires of sunset. Ah! he was
413.04 romantic, romantic. I recalled some words of
413.05 Stein's.... 'In the destructive element immerse!
413.06 ... To follow the dream, and again to follow the
413.07 dream -- and so -- always -- usque ad finem ...' He
413.08 was romantic, but none the less true. Who could
413.09 tell what forms, what visions, what faces, what
413.10 forgiveness he could see in the glow of the west!
413.11 ... A small boat, leaving the schooner, moved
413.12 slowly, with a regular beat of two oars, towards
413.13 the sandbank to take me off. 'And then there's
413.14 Jewel,' he said, out of the great silence of earth,
413.15 sky, and sea, which had mastered my very thoughts
413.16 so that his voice made me start. 'There's Jewel.'
413.17 'Yes,' I murmured. 'I need not tell you what she
413.18 is to me,' he pursued. 'You've seen. In time
413.19 she will come to understand ...' 'I hope so,' I
413.20 interrupted. 'She trusts me, too,' he mused, and
413.21 then changed his tone. 'When shall we meet
413.22 next, I wonder?' he said.
413.23 "'Never -- unless you come out,' I answered,
413.24 avoiding his glance. He didn't seem to be sur-
413.25 prised; he kept very quiet for a while.
413.26 "'Good-bye, then,' he said, after a pause.
413.27 'Perhaps it's just as well.'
413.28 "We shook hands, and I walked to the boat,
413.29 which waited with her nose on the beach. The
413.30 schooner, her mainsail set and jib-sheet to windward,
414.01 curveted on the purple sea; there was a rosy tinge
414.02 on her sails. 'Will you be going home again
414.03 soon?' asked Jim, just as I swung my leg over
414.04 the gunwale. 'In a year or so if I live,' I said.
414.05 The forefoot grated on the sand, the boat floated,
414.06 the wet oars flashed and dipped once, twice.
414.07 Jim, at the water's edge, raised his voice. 'Tell
414.08 them ...' he began. I signed to the men to
414.09 cease rowing, and waited in wonder. Tell who?
414.10 The half-submerged sun faced him; I could see
414.11 its red gleam in his eyes that looked dumbly at
414.12 me.... 'No -- nothing,' he said, and with a slight
414.13 wave of his hand motioned the boat away. I did
414.14 not look again at the shore till I had clambered on
414.15 board the schooner.
414.16 "By that time the sun had set. The twilight
414.17 lay over the east, and the coast, turned black,
414.18 extended infinitely its sombre wall that seemed the
414.19 very stronghold of the night; the western horizon
414.20 was one great blaze of gold and crimson in which a
414.21 big detached cloud floated dark and still, casting a
414.22 slaty shadow on the water beneath, and I saw Jim
414.23 on the beach watching the schooner fall off and
414.24 gather headway.
414.25 "The two half-naked fishermen had arisen as
414.26 soon as I had gone; they were no doubt pouring
414.27 the plaint of their trifling, miserable, oppressed
414.28 lives into the ears of the white lord, and no doubt
414.29 he was listening to it, making it his own, for was it
414.30 not a part of his luck -- the luck 'from the word
415.01 Go' -- the luck to which he had assured me he was
415.02 so completely equal? They, too, I should think,
415.03 were in luck, and I was sure their pertinacity would
415.04 be equal to it. Their dark-skinned bodies vanished
415.05 on the dark background long before I had lost
415.06 sight of their protector. He was white from head
415.07 to foot, and remained persistently visible with the
415.08 stronghold of the night at his back, the sea at his
415.09 feet, the opportunity by his side -- still veiled. What
415.10 do you say? Was it still veiled? I don't know.
415.11 For me that white figure in the stillness of coast
415.12 and sea seemed to stand at the heart of a vast enigma.
415.13 The twilight was ebbing fast from the sky above his
415.14 head, the strip of sand had sunk already under his
415.15 feet, he himself appeared no bigger than a child --
415.16 then only a speck, a tiny white speck, that seemed
415.17 to catch all the light left in a darkened world....
415.18 And, suddenly, I lost him...."
416.01 WITH these words Marlow had ended his
416.02 narrative, and his audience had broken
416.03 up forthwith, under his abstract, pensive
416.04 gaze. Men drifted off the verandah in pairs or
416.05 alone without loss of time, without offering a
416.06 remark, as if the last image of that incomplete
416.07 story, its incompleteness itself, and the very tone
416.08 of the speaker, had made discussion vain and com-
416.09 ment impossible. Each of them seemed to carry
416.10 away his own impression, to carry it away with him
416.11 like a secret; but there was only one man of all
416.12 these listeners who was ever to hear the last word
416.13 of the story. It came to him at home, more than
416.14 two years later, and it came contained in a thick

416.15 packet addressed in Marlow's upright and angular
416.16 handwriting.
416.17 The privileged man opened the packet, looked
416.18 in, then, laying it down, went to the window. His
416.19 rooms were in the highest flat of a lofty building,
416.20 and his glance could travel afar beyond the clear
416.21 panes of glass, as though he were looking out of
416.22 the lantern of a lighthouse. The slopes of the
416.23 roofs glistened, the dark, broken ridges succeeded
416.24 each other without end like sombre, uncrested
417.01 waves, and from the depths of the town under his
417.02 feet ascended a confused and unceasing mutter.
417.03 The spires of churches, numerous, scattered hap-
417.04 hazard, uprose like beacons on a maze of shoals
417.05 without a channel; the driving rain mingled with
417.06 the falling dusk of a winter's evening; and the
417.07 booming of a big clock on a tower, striking the hour,
417.08 rolled past in voluminous, austere bursts of sound,
417.09 with a shrill, vibrating cry at the core. He drew
417.10 the heavy curtains.
417.11 The light of his shaded reading-lamp slept like a
417.12 sheltered pool, his footfalls made no sound on the
417.13 carpet, his wandering days were over. No more
417.14 horizons as boundless as hope, no more twilights
417.15 within the forests as solemn as temples, in the hot
417.16 quest of the Ever-undiscovered Country over the
417.17 hill, across the stream, beyond the wave. The
417.18 hour was striking! No more! No more! -- but
417.19 the opened packet under the lamp brought back
417.20 the sounds, the visions, the very savour of the past --
417.21 a multitude of fading faces, a tumult of low voices,
417.22 dying away upon the shores of distant seas under
417.23 a passionate and unconsoling sunshine. He sighed
417.24 and sat down to read.
417.25 At first he saw three distinct enclosures. A good
417.26 many pages closely blackened and pinned together;
417.27 a loose square sheet of greyish paper with a few words
417.28 traced in a handwriting he had never seen before,
417.29 and an explanatory letter from Marlow. From this
417.30 last fell another letter, yellowed by time and frayed
418.01 on the folds. He picked it up and, laying it aside,
418.02 turned to Marlow's message, ran swiftly over its
418.03 opening lines, and, checking himself, thereafter
418.04 read on deliberately, like one approaching with slow
418.05 feet and alert eyes the glimpse of an undiscovered
418.06 country.
418.07 "... I don't suppose you've forgotten," went
418.08 on the letter. "You alone have showed an interest
418.09 in him that survived the telling of his story, though
418.10 I remember well you would not admit he had
418.11 mastered his fate. You prophesied for him the
418.12 disaster of weariness and of disgust with acquired
418.13 honour, with the self-appointed task, with the love
418.14 sprung from pity and youth. You had said you
418.15 knew so well 'that kind of thing,' its illusory satis-
418.16 faction, its unavoidable deception. You said also --
418.17 I call to mind -- that 'giving your life up to them'
418.18 (them meaning all of mankind with skins brown,
418.19 yellow, or black in colour) 'was like selling your
418.20 soul to a brute.' You contended that 'that kind
418.21 of thing' was only endurable and enduring when
418.22 based on a firm conviction in the truth of ideas
418.23 racially our own, in whose name are established the
418.24 order, the morality of an ethical progress. 'We
418.25 want its strength at our backs,' you had said. 'We
418.26 want a belief in its necessity and its justice, to make
418.27 a worthy and conscious sacrifice of our lives. With--
418.28 out it the sacrifice is only forgetfulness, the way
418.29 of offering is no better than the way to perdition.'
418.30 In other words, you maintained that we must fight
419.01 in the ranks or our lives can't count. Possibly!
419.02 You ought to know -- be it said without malice --
419.03 you who have rushed into one or two places single--
419.04 handed and came out cleverly, without singeing
419.05 your wings. The point, however, is that of all
419.06 mankind Jim had no dealings but with himself, and
419.07 the question is whether at the last he had not con-
419.08 fessed to a faith mightier than the laws of order and
419.09 progress.
419.10 "I affirm nothing. Perhaps you may pronounce
419.11 -- after you've read. There is much truth -- after
419.12 all -- in the common expression 'under a cloud.'
419.13 It is impossible to see him clearly -- especially as
419.14 it is through the eyes of others that we take our
419.15 last look at him. I have no hesitation in imparting
419.16 to you all I know of the last episode that, as he used
419.17 to say, had 'come to him.' One wonders whether
419.18 this was perhaps that supreme opportunity, that
419.19 last and satisfying test for which I had always
419.20 suspected him to be waiting, before he could frame

419.21 a message to the impeccable world. You re-
419.22 member that when I was leaving him for the last
419.23 time he had asked whether I would be going home
419.24 soon, and suddenly cried after me, 'Tell them ...'
419.25 I had waited -- curious I'll own, and hopeful, too --
419.26 only to hear him shout, 'No -- nothing.' That
419.27 was all then -- and there will be nothing more;
419.28 there will be no message, unless such as each of
419.29 us can interpret for himself from the language of
419.30 facts, that are so often more enigmatic than the
420.01 craftiest arrangement of words. He made, it is
420.02 true, one more attempt to deliver himself; but that,
420.03 too, failed, as you may perceive if you look at the
420.04 sheet of greyish foolscap enclosed here. He had
420.05 tried to write; do you notice the commonplace
420.06 hand? It is headed 'The Fort, Patusan.' I
420.07 suppose he had carried out his intention of making
420.08 out of his house a place of defence. It was an
420.09 excellent plan: a deep ditch, an earth wall topped
420.10 by a palisade, and at the angles guns mounted on
420.11 platforms to sweep each side of the square. Dora-
420.12 min had agreed to furnish him the guns; and so
420.13 each man of his party would know there was a place
420.14 of safety, upon which every faithful partisan could
420.15 rally in case of some sudden danger. All this
420.16 showed his judicious foresight, his faith in the future.
420.17 What he called 'my own people' -- the liberated
420.18 captives of the Sherif -- were to make a distinct
420.19 quarter of Patusan, with their huts and little plots
420.20 of ground under the walls of the stronghold. Within
420.21 he would be an invincible host in himself. 'The
420.22 Fort, Patusan.' No date, as you observe. What is
420.23 a number and a name to a day of days? It is also
420.24 impossible to say whom he had in his mind when he
420.25 seized the pen: Stein -- myself -- the world at large --
420.26 or was this only the aimless, startled cry of a solitary
420.27 man confronted by his fate? 'An awful thing
420.28 has happened,' he wrote before he flung the pen
420.29 down for the first time; look at the ink blot re-
420.30 sembling the head of an arrow under these words.
421.01 After a while he had tried again, scrawling heavily,
421.02 as if with a hand of lead, another line. 'I must
421.03 now at once ...' The pen had spluttered, and
421.04 that time he gave it up. There's nothing more;
421.05 he had seen a broad gulf that neither eye nor voice
421.06 could span. I can understand this. He was over-
421.07 whelmed by the inexplicable; he was overwhelmed
421.08 by his own personality -- the gift of that destiny
421.09 which he had done his best to master.
421.10 "I send you also an old letter -- a very old letter.
421.11 It was found carefully preserved in his writing-
421.12 case. It is from his father, and by the date you can
421.13 see he must have received it a few days before he
421.14 joined the Patna. Thus it must be the last letter
421.15 he ever had from home. He had treasured it all
421.16 these years. The good old parson fancied his
421.17 sailor son. I've looked in at a sentence here and
421.18 there. There is nothing in it except just affection.
421.19 He tells his 'dear James' that the last long letter
421.20 from him was very 'honest and entertaining.' He
421.21 would not have him 'judge men harshly or hastily.'
421.22 There are four pages of it, easy morality and family
421.23 news. Tom had 'taken orders.' Carrie's husband
421.24 had 'money losses.' The old chap goes on equably
421.25 trusting Providence and the established order of
421.26 the universe, but alive to its small dangers and
421.27 its small mercies. One can almost see him, grey--
421.28 haired and serene in the inviolable shelter of his
421.29 book-lined, faded, and comfortable study, where
421.30 for forty years he had conscientiously gone over
422.01 and over again the round of his little thoughts
422.02 about faith and virtue, about the conduct of life
422.03 and the only proper manner of dying; where
422.04 he had written so many sermons, where he sits
422.05 talking to his boy, over there, on the other side
422.06 of the earth. But what of the distance? Virtue
422.07 is one all over the world, and there is only one
422.08 faith, one conceivable conduct of life, one manner
422.09 of dying. He hopes his 'dear James' will never
422.10 forget that 'who once gives way to temptation,
422.11 in the very instant hazards his total depravity and
422.12 everlasting ruin. Therefore resolve fixedly never,
422.13 through any possible motives, to do anything which
422.14 you believe to be wrong.' There is also some
422.15 news of a favourite dog; and a pony, 'which all you
422.16 boys used to ride,' had gone blind from old age and
422.17 had to be shot. The old chap invokes Heaven's
422.18 blessing; the mother and all the girls then at home
422.19 send their love.... No, there is nothing much in
422.20 that yellow, frayed letter fluttering out of his cherish-
422.21 ing grasp after so many years. It was never
422.22 answered, but who can say what converse he may
422.23 have held with all these placid, colourless forms of
422.24 men and women peopling that quiet corner of the
422.25 world as free of danger or strife as a tomb, and
422.26 breathing equably the air of undisturbed rectitude.
422.27 It seems amazing that he should belong to it, he
422.28 to whom so many things 'had come.' Nothing
422.29 ever came to them; they would never be taken
422.30 unawares, and never be called upon to grapple
423.01 with fate. Here they all are, evoked by the mild
423.02 gossip of the father, all these brothers and sisters,
423.03 bone of his bone and flesh of his flesh, gazing with
423.04 clear, unconscious eyes, while I seem to see him,
423.05 returned at last, no longer a mere white speck at the
423.06 heart of an immense mystery, but of full stature,
423.07 standing disregarded amongst their untroubled
423.08 shapes, with a stern and romantic aspect, but
423.09 always mute, dark -- under a cloud.
423.10 "The story of the last events you will find in
423.11 the few pages enclosed here. You must admit that
423.12 it is romantic beyond the wildest dreams of his
423.13 boyhood, and yet there is to my mind a sort of
423.14 profound and terrifying logic in it, as if it were
423.15 our imagination alone that could set loose upon us
423.16 the might of an overwhelming destiny. The im-
423.17 prudence of our thoughts recoils upon our heads;
423.18 who toys with the sword shall perish by the sword.
423.19 This astounding adventure, of which the most
423.20 astounding part is that it is true, comes on as an
423.21 unavoidable consequence. Something of the sort
423.22 had to happen. You repeat this to yourself while
423.23 you marvel that such a thing could happen in the
423.24 year of grace before last. But it has happened --
423.25 and there is no disputing its logic.
423.26 "I put it down here for you as though I had
423.27 been an eye-witness. My information was frag-
423.28 mentary, but I've fitted the pieces together, and
423.29 there is enough of them to make an intelligible
423.30 picture. I wonder how he would have related it
424.01 himself. He has confided so much in me that at
424.02 times it seems as though he must come in presently
424.03 times it seems as though he must come in presently
424.04 and tell the story in his own words, in his careless
424.05 yet feeling voice, with his off-hand manner, a little
424.06 puzzled, a little bothered, a little hurt, but now
424.07 and then by a word or a phrase giving one of these
424.08 glimpses of his very own self that were never any
424.09 good for purposes of orientation. It's difficult
424.10 to believe he will never come. I shall never hear
424.11 his voice again, nor shall I see his smooth tan-and--
424.12 pink face with a white line on the forehead, and the
424.13 youthful eyes darkened by excitement to a profound,
424.14 unfathomable blue."
425.01 "IT all begins with a remarkable exploit of a
425.02 man called Brown, who stole with complete
425.03 success a Spanish schooner out of a small
425.04 bay near Zamboanga. Till I discovered the fellow
425.05 my information was incomplete, but most un-
425.06 expectedly I did come upon him a few hours before
425.07 he gave up his arrogant ghost. Fortunately, he
425.08 was willing and able to talk between the choking
425.09 fits of asthma, and his racked body writhed with
425.10 malicious exultation at the bare thought of Jim.
425.11 He exulted thus at the idea that he had 'paid out
425.12 the stuck-up beggar after all.' He gloated over his
425.13 action. I had to bear the sunken glare of his fierce,
425.14 crow-footed eyes if I wanted to know; and so I
425.15 bore it, reflecting how much certain forms of evil are
425.16 akin to madness, derived from intense egoism, in-
425.17 flamed by resistance, tearing the soul to pieces, and
425.18 giving factitious vigour to the body. The story
425.19 also reveals unsuspected depths of cunning in the
425.20 wretched Cornelius, whose abject and intense hate
425.21 acts like a subtle inspiration, pointing out an unerring
425.22 way towards revenge.
425.23 "'I could see directly I set my eyes on him what
425.24 sort of a fool he was,' gasped the dying Brown.
426.01 'He a man! Hell! He was a hollow sham. As
426.02 if he couldn't have said straight out, "Hands off
426.03 my plunder!" blast him! That would have been
426.04 like a man! Rot his superior soul! He had me
426.05 there -- but he hadn't devil enough in him to make
426.06 an end of me. Not he! A thing like that letting
426.07 me off as if I wasn't worth a kick!...' Brown
426.08 struggled desperately for breath.... 'Fraud.
426.09 ... Letting me off.... And so I did make an
426.10 end of him after all....' He choked again....
426.11 'I expect this thing'll kill me, but I shall die easy
426.12 now. You ... you hear ... I don't know your

251

426.13 name -- I would give you a five-pound note if --
426.14 if I had it -- for the news -- or my name's not
426.15 Brown....' He grinned horribly.... 'Gentle-
426.16 man Brown.'
426.17 "He said all these things in profound gasps,
426.18 staring at me with his yellow eyes out of a long,
426.19 ravaged, brown face; he jerked his left arm; a
426.20 pepper-and-salt matted beard hung almost into his
426.21 lap; a dirty, ragged blanket covered his legs. I
426.22 had found him out in Bankok through that busybody
426.23 Schomberg, the hotel-keeper, who had, confiden-
426.24 tially, directed me where to look. It appears that
426.25 a sort of loafing, fuddled vagabond -- a white man
426.26 living amongst the natives with a Siamese woman --
426.27 had considered it a great privilege to give a shelter
426.28 to the last days of the famous Gentleman Brown.
426.29 While he was talking to me in the wretched hovel,
426.30 and, as it were, fighting for every minute of his life,
427.01 the Siamese woman, with big, bare legs and a stupid,
427.02 coarse face, sat in a dark corner chewing betel
427.03 stolidly. Now and then she would get up for the
427.04 purpose of shooing a chicken away from the door.
427.05 The whole hut shook when she walked. An ugly,
427.06 yellow child, naked and pot-bellied like a little
427.07 heathen god, stood at the foot of the couch, finger
427.08 in mouth, lost in a profound and calm contempla-
427.09 tion of the dying man.
427.10 "He talked feverishly; but in the middle of a
427.11 word, perhaps, an invisible hand would take him
427.12 by the throat, and he would look at me dumbly with
427.13 an expression of doubt and anguish. He seemed to
427.14 fear that I would get tired of waiting and go away,
427.15 leaving him with his tale untold, with his exulta-
427.16 tion unexpressed. He died during the night, I
427.17 believe, but by that time I had nothing more to
427.18 learn.
427.19 "So much as to Brown, for the present.
427.20 "Eight months before this, coming into Sama-
427.21 rang, I went as usual to see Stein. On the garden
427.22 side of the house a Malay on the verandah greeted
427.23 me shyly, and reminded me that I had seen him
427.24 in Patusan, in Jim's house, amongst other Bugis
427.25 men who used to come in the evening to talk inter-
427.26 minably over their war reminiscences and to discuss
427.27 State affairs. Jim had pointed him out to me once as
427.28 a respectable petty trader owning a small sea-going
427.29 native craft, who had showed himself 'one of the
427.30 best at the taking of the stockade.' I was not very
428.01 surprised to see him, since any Patusan trader
428.02 venturing as far as Samarang would naturally find
428.03 his way to Stein's house. I returned his greeting
428.04 and passed on. At the door of Stein's room I came
428.05 upon another Malay in whom I recognised Tamb'
428.06 Itam.
428.07 "I asked him at once what he was doing there;
428.08 it occurred to me that Jim might have come on a
428.09 visit. I own I was pleased and excited at the
428.10 thought. Tamb' Itam looked as if he did not know
428.11 what to say. 'Is Tuan Jim inside?' I asked
428.12 impatiently. 'No,' he mumbled, hanging his head
428.13 for a moment; and then with sudden earnestness,
428.14 'He would not fight. He would not fight,' he
428.15 repeated twice. As he seemed unable to say any-
428.16 thing else, I pushed him aside and went in.
428.17 "Stein, tall and stooping, stood alone in the
428.18 middle of the room between the rows of butterfly
428.19 cases. 'Ach! is it you, my friend?' he said
428.20 sadly, peering through his glasses. A drab sack-
428.21 coat of alpaca hung, unbuttoned, down to his knees.
428.22 He had a Panama hat on his head, and there were
428.23 deep furrows on his pale cheeks. 'What's the
428.24 matter now?' I asked nervously. 'There's
428.25 Tamb' Itam there....' 'Come and see the girl.
428.26 Come and see the girl. She is here,' he said, with a
428.27 half-hearted show of activity. I tried to detain him,
428.28 but with gentle obstinacy he would take no notice of
428.29 my eager questions. 'She is here, she is here,' he
428.30 repeated, in great perturbation. 'They came here
429.01 two days ago. An old man like me, a stranger --
429.02 sehen sie -- cannot do much.... Come this way.
429.03 ... Young hearts are unforgiving....' I could
429.04 see he was in utmost distress.... 'The strength
429.05 of life in them, the cruel strength of life....'
429.06 He mumbled, leading me round the house; I
429.07 followed him, lost in dismal and angry conjectures.
429.08 At the door of the drawing-room he barred my way.
429.09 'He loved her very much?' he said interrogatively;
429.10 and I only nodded, feeling so bitterly disappointed
429.11 that I would not trust myself to speak. 'Very
429.12 frightful,' he murmured. 'She can't understand

429.13 me. I am only a strange old man. Perhaps
429.14 you ... she knows you. Talk to her. We can't
429.15 leave it like this. Tell her to forgive him. It was
429.16 very frightful.' 'No doubt,' I said, exasperated
429.17 at being in the dark; 'but have you forgiven him?'
429.18 He looked at me queerly. 'You shall hear,' he said,
429.19 and, opening the door, absolutely pushed me in.
429.20 "You know Stein's big house and the two
429.21 immense reception-rooms, uninhabited and unin-
429.22 habitable, clean, full of solitude and of shining
429.23 things that look as if never beheld by the eye of
429.24 man? They are cool on the hottest days, and you
429.25 enter them as you would a scrubbed cave under-
429.26 ground. I passed through one, and in the other I
429.27 saw the girl sitting at the end of a big mahogany
429.28 table, on which she rested her head, the face hidden
429.29 in her arms. The waxed floor reflected her dimly
429.30 as though it had been a sheet of frozen water. The
430.01 rattan screens were down, and through the strange,
430.02 greenish gloom made by the foliage of the trees out-
430.03 side a strong wind blew in gusts, swaying the long
430.04 draperies of windows and doorways. Her white
430.05 figure seemed shaped in snow; the pendent crystals
430.06 of a great chandelier clicked above her head like
430.07 glittering icicles. She looked up and watched my
430.08 approach. I was chilled as if these vast apartments
430.09 had been the cold abode of despair.
430.10 "She recognised me at once, and as soon as I had
430.11 stopped looking down at her: 'He has left me,' she
430.12 said quietly; 'you always leave us -- for your own
430.13 ends.' Her face was set. All the heat of life seemed
430.14 withdrawn within some inaccessible spot in her
430.15 breast. 'It would have been easy to die with him,'
430.16 she went on, and made a slight, weary gesture as
430.17 if giving up the incomprehensible. 'He would not!
430.18 It was like a blindness -- and yet it was I who was
430.19 speaking to him; it was I who stood before his
430.20 eyes; it was at me that he looked all the time!
430.21 Ah! you are hard, treacherous, without truth, with-
430.22 out compassion. What makes you so wicked? Or
430.23 is it that you are all mad?'
430.24 "I took her hand; it did not respond, and when
430.25 I dropped it, it hung down to the floor. That in-
430.26 difference, more awful than tears, cries, and re-
430.27 proaches, seemed to defy time and consolation.
430.28 You felt that nothing you could say would reach the
430.29 seat of the still and benumbing pain.
430.30 "Stein had said, 'You shall hear.' I did hear.
431.01 I heard it all, listening with amazement, with awe,
431.02 to the tones of her inflexible weariness. She could
431.03 not grasp the real sense of what she was telling me,
431.04 and her resentment filled me with pity for her --
431.05 for him, too. I stood rooted to the spot after she
431.06 had finished. Leaning on her arm, she stared with
431.07 hard eyes, and the wind passed in gusts, the crystals
431.08 kept on clicking in the greenish gloom. She went on
431.09 whispering to herself: 'And yet he was looking
431.10 at me! He could see my face, hear my voice, hear
431.11 my grief! When I used to sit at his feet, with my
431.12 cheek against his knee and his hand on my head,
431.13 the curse of cruelty and madness was already within
431.14 him, waiting for the day. The day came!...
431.15 and before the sun had set he could not see me any
431.16 more -- he was made blind and deaf and without pity,
431.17 as you all are. He shall have no tears from me.
431.18 Never, never. Not one tear. I will not! He went
431.19 away from me as if I had been worse than death.
431.20 He fled as if driven by some accursed thing he had
431.21 heard or seen in his sleep....'
431.22 "Her steady eyes seemed to strain after the shape
431.23 of a man torn out of her arms by the strength of a
431.24 dream. She made no sign to my silent bow. I
431.25 was glad to escape.
431.26 "I saw her once again, the same afternoon.
431.27 On leaving her I had gone in search of Stein, whom
431.28 I could not find indoors; and I wandered out,
431.29 pursued by distressful thoughts, into the gardens,
431.30 those famous gardens of Stein, in which you can
432.01 find every plant and tree of tropical lowlands. I
432.02 followed the course of the canalised stream, and sat
432.03 for a long time on a shaded bench near the orna-
432.04 mental pond, where some waterfowl with clipped
432.05 wings were diving and splashing noisily. The
432.06 branches of casuarina trees behind me swayed
432.07 lightly, incessantly, reminding me of the soughing
432.08 of fir trees at home.
432.09 "This mournful and restless sound was a fit
432.10 accompaniment to my meditations. She had said
432.11 he had been driven away from her by a dream, --
432.12 and there was no answer one could make her -- there

432.13 seemed to be no forgiveness for such a transgression.
432.14 And yet is not mankind itself, pushing on its blind
432.15 way, driven by a dream of its greatness and its
432.16 power upon the dark paths of excessive cruelty and
432.17 of excessive devotion? And what is the pursuit of
432.18 truth, after all?
432.19 "When I rose to get back to the house I caught
432.20 sight of Stein's drab coat through a gap in the
432.21 foliage, and very soon at a turn of the path I came
432.22 upon him walking with the girl. Her little hand
432.23 rested on his forearm, and under the broad, flat
432.24 rim of his Panama hat he bent over her, grey-haired,
432.25 paternal, with compassionate and chivalrous defer-
432.26 ence. I stood aside, but they stopped, facing me.
432.27 His gaze was bent on the ground at his feet; the
432.28 girl, erect and slight on his arm, stared sombrely
432.29 beyond my shoulder with black, clear, motionless
432.30 eyes. 'Schrecklich,' he murmured. 'Terrible!
433.01 Terrible! What can one do?' He seemed to be
433.02 appealing to me, but her youth, the length of the
433.03 days suspended over her head, appealed to me more;
433.04 and suddenly, even as I realised that nothing could
433.05 be said, I found myself pleading his cause for her
433.06 sake. 'You must forgive him,' I concluded, and
433.07 my own voice seemed to me muffled, lost in an
433.08 irresponsive deaf immensity. 'We all want to be
433.09 forgiven,' I added after a while.
433.10 "'What have I done?' she asked with her lips
433.11 only.
433.12 "'You always mistrusted him,' I said.
433.13 "'He was like the others,' she pronounced slowly.
433.14 "'Not like the others,' I protested; but she
433.15 continued evenly, without any feeling:
433.16 "'He was false.' And suddenly Stein broke
433.17 in. 'No! no! no! My poor child!...' He
433.18 patted her hand lying passively on his sleeve. 'No!
433.19 no! Not false! True! true! true!' He tried to
433.20 look into her stony face. 'You don't understand.
433.21 Ach! Why you do not understand? ... Terrible,'
433.22 he said to me. 'Some day she shall understand.'
433.23 "'Will you explain?' I asked, looking hard at
433.24 him. They moved on.
433.25 "I watched them. Her gown trailed on the
433.26 path, her black hair fell loose. She walked upright
433.27 and light by the side of the tall man, whose long,
433.28 shapeless coat hung in perpendicular folds from the
433.29 stooping shoulders, whose feet moved slowly. They
433.30 disappeared beyond that spinney (you may remem-
434.01 ber) where sixteen different kinds of bamboo grow
434.02 together, all distinguishable to the learned eye.
434.03 For my part, I was fascinated by the exquisite grace
434.04 and beauty of that fluted grove, crowned with pointed
434.05 leaves and feathery heads, the lightness, the vigour,
434.06 the charm as distinct as a voice of that unperplexed,
434.07 luxuriating life. I remember staying to look at it
434.08 for a long time, as one would linger within reach
434.09 of a consoling whisper. The sky was pearly grey.
434.10 It was one of those overcast days so rare in the
434.11 tropics, in which memories crowd upon one --
434.12 memories of other shores, of other faces.
434.13 "I drove back to town the same afternoon, taking
434.14 with me Tamb' Itam and the other Malay, in whose
434.15 sea-going craft they had escaped in the bewilder-
434.16 ment, fear, and gloom of the disaster. The shock of it
434.17 seemed to have changed their natures. It had turned
434.18 her passion into stone, and it made the surly, taciturn
434.19 Tamb' Itam almost loquacious. His surliness, too,
434.20 was subdued into puzzled humility, as though he had
434.21 seen the failure of a potent charm in a supreme
434.22 moment. The Bugis trader, a shy, hesitating man,
434.23 was very clear in the little he had to say. Both were
434.24 evidently overawed by a sense of deep, inexpressible
434.25 wonder, by the touch of an inscrutable mystery."
434.26 There with Marlow's signature the letter proper
434.27 ended. The privileged reader screwed up his lamp,
434.28 and solitary above the billowy roofs of the town, like
434.29 a lighthouse-keeper above the sea, he turned to the
434.30 pages of the story.
435.01 "IT all begins, as I've told you, with the man
435.02 called Brown," ran the opening sentence
435.03 of Marlow's narrative. "You who have
435.04 knocked about the Western Pacific must have heard
435.05 of him. He was the show ruffian on the Australian
435.06 coast -- not that he was often to be seen there, but
435.07 because he was always trotted out in the stories of
435.08 lawless life a visitor from home is treated to; and
435.09 the mildest of these stories which were told about
435.10 him from Cape York to Eden Bay was more than
435.11 enough to hang a man if told in the right place.
435.12 They never failed to let you know, too, that he was

435.13 supposed to be the son of a baronet. Be it as it
435.14 may, it is certain he had deserted from a home ship
435.15 in the early gold-digging days, and in a few years
435.16 became talked about as the terror of this or that
435.17 group of islands in Polynesia. He would kidnap
435.18 natives, he would strip some lonely white trader
435.19 to the very pyjamas he stood in, and after he had
435.20 robbed the poor devil, he would as likely as not
435.21 invite him to fight a duel with shot-guns on the
435.22 beach -- which would have been fair enough as
435.23 these things go, if the other man hadn't been by that
435.24 time already half dead with fright. Brown was a
436.01 latter-day buccaneer, sorry enough, like his more
436.02 celebrated prototypes; but what distinguished him
436.03 from his contemporary brother ruffians, like Bully
436.04 Hayes or the mellifluous Pease, or that perfumed,
436.05 Dundreary-whiskered, dandified scoundrel known
436.06 as Dirty Dick, was the arrogant temper of his mis-
436.07 deeds and a vehement scorn for mankind at large
436.08 and for his victims in particular. The others were
436.09 merely vulgar and greedy brutes, but he seemed
436.10 moved by some complex intention. He would rob
436.11 a man as if only to demonstrate his poor opinion of
436.12 the creature, and he would bring to the shooting
436.13 or maiming of some quiet, unoffending stranger a
436.14 savage and vengeful earnestness fit to terrify the
436.15 most reckless of desperadoes. In the days of his
436.16 greatest glory he owned an armed barque, manned
436.17 by a mixed crew of Kanakas and runaway whalers,
436.18 and boasted, I don't know with what truth, of
436.19 being financed on the quiet by a most respectable
436.20 firm of copra merchants. Later on he ran off --
436.21 it was reported -- with the wife of a missionary, a
436.22 very young girl from Clapham way, who had married
436.23 the mild, flat-footed fellow in a moment of en-
436.24 thusiasm, and, suddenly transplanted to Melanesia,
436.25 lost her bearings somehow. It was a dark story.
436.26 She was ill at the time he carried her off, and died
436.27 on board his ship. It is said -- as the most wonderful
436.28 part of the tale -- that over her body he gave way to
436.29 an outburst of sombre and violent grief. His luck
436.30 left him, too, very soon after. He lost his ship -
437.01 on some rocks off Malaita, and disappeared for a
437.02 time as though he had gone down with her. He is
437.03 heard of next at Nuka-Hiva, where he bought an
437.04 old French schooner out of Government service.
437.05 What creditable enterprise he might have had in
437.06 view when he made that purchase I can't say, but it
437.07 is evident that what with High Commissioners,
437.08 consuls, men-of-war, and international control, the
437.09 South Seas were getting too hot to hold gentle-
437.10 men of his kidney. Clearly he must have shifted
437.11 the scene of his operations farther west, because a
437.12 year later he plays an incredibly audacious, but not
437.13 a very profitable, part in a serio-comic business in
437.14 Manila Bay, in which a peculating governor and an
437.15 absconding treasurer are the principal figures;
437.16 thereafter he seems to have hung around the Philip-
437.17 pines in his rotten schooner, battling with an adverse
437.18 fortune, till at last, running his appointed course,
437.19 he sails into Jim's history, a blind accomplice of the
437.20 Dark Powers.
437.21 "His tale goes that when a Spanish patrol cutter
437.22 captured him he was simply trying to run a few guns
437.23 for the insurgents. If so, then I can't understand
437.24 what he was doing off the south coast of Mindanao.
437.25 My belief, however, is that he was blackmailing
437.26 the native villages along the coast. The principal
437.27 thing is that the cutter, throwing a guard on board,
437.28 made him sail in company towards Zamboanga.
437.29 On the way, for some reason or other, both vessels
437.30 had to call at one of these new Spanish settlements --
438.01 which never came to anything in the end -- where
438.02 there was not only a civil official in charge on shore,
438.03 but a good stout coasting schooner lying at anchor
438.04 in the little bay; and this craft, in every way much
438.05 better than his own, Brown made up his mind to
438.06 steal.
438.07 "He was down on his luck -- as he told me him-
438.08 self. The world he had bullied for twenty years
438.09 with fierce, aggressive disdain had yielded him
438.10 nothing in the way of material advantage except a
438.11 small bag of silver dollars, which was concealed in his
438.12 cabin so that 'the devil himself couldn't smell it
438.13 out.' And that was all -- absolutely all. He was
438.14 tired of his life, and not afraid of death. But this
438.15 man, who would stake his existence on a whim
438.16 with a bitter and jeering recklessness, stood in mortal
438.17 fear of imprisonment. He had an unreasoning cold--
438.18 sweat, nerve-shaking, blood-to-water-turning sort of

438.19 horror at the bare possibility of being locked up --
438.20 the sort of terror a superstitious man would feel at
438.21 the thought of being embraced by a spectre. There-
438.22 fore the civil official who came on board to make a
438.23 preliminary investigation into the capture, investi-
438.24 gated arduously all day long, and only went ashore
438.25 after dark, muffled up in a cloak, and taking great
438.26 care not to let Brown's little all clink in its bag.
438.27 Afterwards, being a man of his word, he contrived
438.28 (the very next evening, I believe) to send off the
438.29 Government cutter on some urgent bit of special
438.30 service. As her commander could not spare a
439.01 prize crew, he contented himself by taking away
439.02 before he left all the sails of Brown's schooner to the
439.03 very last rag, and took good care to tow his two
439.04 boats on to the beach a couple of miles off.
439.05 "But in Brown's crew there was a Solomon
439.06 Islander, kidnapped in his youth and devoted to
439.07 Brown, who was the best man of the whole gang.
439.08 That fellow swam off to the coaster -- five hundred
439.09 yards or so -- with the end of a warp made up of
439.10 all the running gear unrove for the purpose. The
439.11 water was smooth, and the bay dark, 'like the inside
439.12 of a cow,' as Brown described it. The Solomon
439.13 Islander clambered over the bulwarks with the end
439.14 of the rope in his teeth. The crew of the coaster --
439.15 all Tagals -- were ashore having a jollification in the
439.16 native village. The two ship-keepers left on board
439.17 woke up suddenly and saw the devil. It had
439.18 glittering eyes, and leaped quick as lightning about
439.19 the deck. They fell on their knees, paralysed with
439.20 fear, crossing themselves and mumbling prayers.
439.21 With a long knife he found in the caboose
439.22 the Solomon Islander, without interrupting their
439.23 orisons, stabbed first one, then the other; with the
439.24 same knife he set to sawing patiently at the coir
439.25 cable till suddenly it parted under the blade with a
439.26 splash. Then in the silence of the bay he let out
439.27 a cautious shout, and Brown's gang, who meantime
439.28 had been peering and straining their hopeful ears
439.29 in the darkness, began to pull gently at their end
439.30 of the warp. In less than five minutes the two
440.01 schooners came together with a slight shock and a
440.02 creak of spars.
440.03 "Brown's crowd transferred themselves without
440.04 losing an instant, taking with them their firearms
440.05 and a large supply of ammunition. They were
440.06 sixteen in all: two runaway blue-jackets, a lanky
440.07 deserter from a Yankee man-of-war, a couple of
440.08 simple, blond Scandinavians, a mulatto of sorts,
440.09 one bland Chinaman who cooked -- and the rest
440.10 of the nondescript spawn of the South Seas. None
440.11 of them cared; Brown bent them to his will, and
440.12 Brown, indifferent to gallows, was running away
440.13 from the spectre of a Spanish prison. He didn't
440.14 give them the time to tranship enough provisions. They
440.15 the weather was calm, the air was charged with dew,
440.16 and when they cast off the ropes and set sail to a
440.17 faint off-shore draught there was no flutter in the
440.18 damp canvas; their old schooner seemed to detach
440.19 itself gently from the stolen craft and slip away
440.20 silently, together with the black mass of the coast,
440.21 into the night.
440.22 "They got clear away. Brown related to me in
440.23 detail their passage down the Straits of Macassar.
440.24 It is a harrowing and desperate story. They were
440.25 short of food and water; they boarded several
440.26 native craft and got a little from each. With a
440.27 stolen ship Brown did not dare to put into any
440.28 port, of course. He had no money to buy anything,
440.29 no papers to show, and no lie plausible enough to
440.30 get him out again. An Arab barque, under the
441.01 Dutch flag, surprised one night at anchor off Poulo
441.02 Laut, yielded a little dirty rice, a bunch of bananas,
441.03 and a cask of water; three days of squally, misty
441.04 weather from the north-east shot the schooner
441.05 across the Java Sea. The yellow, muddy waves
441.06 drenched that collection of hungry ruffians. They
441.07 sighted mail-boats moving on their appointed
441.08 routes; passed well-found home ships with rusty
441.09 iron sides anchored in the shallow sea waiting for
441.10 a change of weather or the turn of the tide; an
441.11 English gunboat, white and trim, with two slim
441.12 masts, crossed their bows one day in the distance;
441.13 and on another occasion a Dutch corvette, black
441.14 and heavily sparred, loomed upon their quarter,
441.15 steaming dead slow in the mist. They slipped
441.16 through unseen or disregarded, a wan, sallow-faced
441.17 band of utter outcasts, enraged with hunger and
441.18 hunted by fear. Brown's idea was to make for
441.19 Madagascar, where he expected, on grounds not
441.20 altogether illusory, to sell the schooner in Tama-
441.21 tave, and no questions asked, or perhaps obtain
441.22 some more or less forged papers for her. Yet before
441.23 he could face the long passage across the Indian
441.24 Ocean food was wanted -- water, too.
441.25 "Perhaps he had heard of Patusan -- or perhaps
441.26 he just only happened to see the name written in
441.27 small letters on the chart -- probably that of a
441.28 largish village up a river in a native state, perfectly
441.29 defenceless, far from the beaten tracks of the sea
441.30 and from the ends of submarine cables. He had
442.01 done that kind of thing before -- in the way of
442.02 business -- and this now was an absolute necessity,
442.03 a question of life and death -- or rather of liberty.
442.04 Of liberty! He was sure to get provisions --
442.05 bullocks -- rice -- sweet-potatoes. The sorry gang
442.06 licked their chops. A cargo of produce for the
442.07 schooner perhaps could be extorted -- and, who
442.08 knows? -- some real ringing coined money! Some
442.09 of these chiefs and village head-men can be made
442.10 to part freely. He told me he would have roasted
442.11 their toes rather than be baulked. I believe him.
442.12 His men believed him too. They didn't cheer
442.13 aloud, being a dumb pack, but made ready wolfishly.
442.14 "Luck served him as to weather. A few days
442.15 of calm would have brought unmentionable horrors
442.16 on board that schooner, but with the help of land
442.17 and sea breezes, in less than a week after clearing
442.18 the Sunda Straits, he anchored off the Batu Kring
442.19 mouth within a pistol-shot of the fishing village.
442.20 "Fourteen of them packed into the schooner's
442.21 long-boat (which was big, having been used for
442.22 cargo-work) and started up the river, while two
442.23 remained in charge of the schooner with food enough
442.24 to keep starvation off for ten days. The tide and
442.25 wind helped, and early one afternoon the big white
442.26 boat under a ragged sail shouldered its way before
442.27 the sea breeze into Patusan Reach, manned by
442.28 fourteen assorted scarecrows glaring hungrily ahead,
442.29 and fingering the breech-blocks of cheap rifles.
442.30 Brown calculated upon the terrifying surprise of
443.01 his appearance. They sailed in with the last of
443.02 the flood; the Rajah's stockade gave no sign; the
443.03 first houses on both sides of the stream seemed
443.04 deserted. A few canoes were seen up the reach
443.05 in full flight. Brown was astonished at the size of
443.06 the place. A profound silence reigned. The wind
443.07 dropped between the houses; two oars were got
443.08 out and the boat held on upstream, the idea being
443.09 to effect a lodgment in the centre of the town before
443.10 the inhabitants could think of resistance.
443.11 "It seems, however, that the head-man of the
443.12 fishing village at Batu Kring had managed to send
443.13 off a timely warning. When the long-boat came
443.14 abreast of the mosque (which Doramin had built:
443.15 a structure with gables and roof finials of carved
443.16 coral) the open space before it was full of people.
443.17 A shout went up, and was followed by a clash of
443.18 gongs all up the river. From a point above two
443.19 little brass six-pounders were discharged, and the
443.20 round-shot came skipping down the empty reach,
443.21 spirting glittering jets of water in the sunshine.
443.22 In front of the mosque a shouting lot of men began
443.23 firing in volleys that whipped athwart the current
443.24 of the river; an irregular, rolling fusillade was
443.25 opened on the boat from both banks, and Brown's
443.26 men replied with a wild, rapid fire. The oars had
443.27 been got in.
443.28 "The turn of the tide at high water comes on
443.29 very quickly in that river, and the boat in midstream,
443.30 nearly hidden in smoke, began to drift back stern
444.01 foremost. Along both shores the smoke thickened
444.02 also, lying below the roofs in a level streak as you
444.03 may see a long cloud cutting the slope of a mountain.
444.04 A tumult of war-cries, the vibrating clang of gongs,
444.05 the deep snoring of drums, yells of rage, crashes of
444.06 volley-firing, made an awful din, in which Brown
444.07 sat confounded but steady at the tiller, working
444.08 himself into a fury of hate and rage against those
444.09 people who dared to defend themselves. Two
444.10 of his men had been wounded, and he saw his
444.11 retreat cut off below the town by some boats that
444.12 had put off from Tunku Allang's stockade. There
444.13 were six of them, full of men. While he was thus
444.14 beset he perceived the entrance of the narrow creek
444.15 (the same which Jim had jumped at low water).
444.16 It was then brim-full. Steering the long-boat in,
444.17 they landed, and, to make a long story short, they
444.18 established themselves on a little knoll about 900

254

444.19 yards from the stockade, which, in fact, they com-
444.20 manded from that position. The slopes of the
444.21 knoll were bare, but there were a few trees on the
444.22 summit. They went to work cutting these down
444.23 for a breastwork, and were fairly entrenched before
444.24 dark; meantime the Rajah's boats remained in
444.25 the river with curious neutrality. When the sun
444.26 set, the glare of many brushwood blazes lighted on
444.27 the river-front, and between the double line of
444.28 houses on the land side threw into black relief the
444.29 roofs, the groups of slender palms, the heavy
444.30 clumps of fruit trees. Brown ordered the grass
445.01 round his position to be fired; a low ring of thin
445.02 flames under the slow, ascending smoke wriggled
445.03 rapidly down the slopes of the knoll; here and
445.04 there a dry bush caught with a tall, vicious roar.
445.05 The conflagration made a clear zone of fire for
445.06 the rifles of the small party, and expired smouldering
445.07 on the edge of the forests and along the muddy
445.08 bank of the creek. A strip of jungle luxuriating
445.09 in a damp hollow between the knoll and the Rajah's
445.10 stockade stopped it on that side with a great crackling
445.11 and detonations of bursting bamboo stems. The
445.12 sky was sombre, velvety, and swarming with stars.
445.13 The blackened ground smoked quietly with low
445.14 creeping wisps, till a little breeze came on and blew
445.15 everything away. Brown expected an attack to be
445.16 delivered as soon as the tide had flowed enough
445.17 again to enable the war-boats which had cut off
445.18 his retreat to enter the creek. At any rate he was
445.19 sure there would be an attempt to carry off his
445.20 long-boat, which lay below the hill, a dark high
445.21 lump on the feeble sheen of a wet mud-flat. But no
445.22 move of any sort was made by the boats in the river.
445.23 Over the stockade and the Rajah's buildings Brown
445.24 saw their lights on the water. They seemed to be
445.25 anchored across the stream. Other lights afloat
445.26 were moving in the reach, crossing and recrossing
445.27 from side to side. There were also lights twinkling
445.28 motionless upon the long walls of houses up the
445.29 reach, as far as the bend, and more still beyond,
445.30 others isolated inland. The loom of the big fires
446.01 disclosed buildings, roofs, black piles as far as he
446.02 could see. It was an immense place. The fourteen
446.03 desperate invaders lying flat behind the felled
446.04 trees raised their chins to look over at the stir of that
446.05 town that seemed to extend up-river for miles and
446.06 swarm with thousands of angry men. They did not
446.07 speak to each other. Now and then they would
446.08 hear a loud yell, or a single shot rang out, fired very
446.09 far somewhere. But round their position everything
446.10 was still, dark, silent. They seemed to be for-
446.11 gotten, as if the excitement keeping awake all the
446.12 population had nothing to do with them, as if they
446.13 had been dead already."
447.01 "ALL the events of that night have a
447.02 great importance, since they brought
447.03 about a situation which remained un-
447.04 changed till Jim's return. Jim had been away in the
447.05 interior for more than a week, and it was Dain
447.06 Waris who had directed the first repulse. That
447.07 brave and intelligent youth ('who knew how to
447.08 fight after the manner of white men') wished to
447.09 settle the business off-hand, but his people were
447.10 too much for him. He had not Jim's racial prestige
447.11 and the reputation of invincible, supernatural power.
447.12 He was not the visible, tangible incarnation of
447.13 unfailing youth and of unfailing victory. Beloved,
447.14 trusted, and admired as he was, he was still one of
447.15 them, while Jim was one of us. Moreover, the
447.16 white man, a tower of strength in himself, was
447.17 invulnerable, while Dain Waris could be killed.
447.18 Those unexpressed thoughts guided the opinions of
447.19 the chief men of the town, who elected to assemble
447.20 in Jim's fort for deliberation upon the emergency,
447.21 as if expecting to find wisdom and courage in the
447.22 dwelling of the absent white man. The shooting
447.23 of Brown's ruffians was so far good, or lucky, that
447.24 there had been half a dozen casualties amongst
448.01 the defenders. The wounded were lying on
448.02 the verandah tended by their women-folk. The
448.03 women and children from the lower part of the
448.04 town had been sent into the fort at the first alarm.
448.05 There Jewel was in command, very efficient and
448.06 high-spirited, obeyed by Jim's 'own people,'
448.07 who, quitting in a body their little settlement under
448.08 the stockade, had gone in to form the garrison.
448.09 The refugees crowded round her; and through the
448.10 whole affair, to the very disastrous last, she showed
448.11 an extraordinary martial ardour. It was to her

448.12 that Dain Waris had gone at once at the first intelli-
448.13 gence of danger, for you must know that Jim was
448.14 the only one in Patusan who possessed a store of
448.15 gunpowder. Stein, with whom he had kept up
448.16 intimate relations by letters, had obtained from
448.17 the Dutch Government a special authorisation to
448.18 export five hundred kegs of it to Patusan. The
448.19 powder-magazine was a small hut of rough logs
448.20 covered entirely with earth, and in Jim's absence
448.21 the girl had the key. In the council, held at eleven
448.22 o'clock in the evening in Jim's dining-room, she
448.23 backed up Waris's advice for immediate and
448.24 vigorous action. I am told that she stood up by
448.25 the side of Jim's empty chair at the head of the
448.26 long table and made a warlike impassioned speech,
448.27 which for the moment extorted murmurs of appro-
448.28 bation from the assembled head-men. Old Dora-
448.29 min, who had not showed himself outside his own
448.30 gate for more than a year, had been brought across
449.01 with great difficulty. He was, of course, the chief
449.02 man there. The temper of the council was very
449.03 unforgiving, and the old man's word would have
449.04 been decisive; but it is my opinion that, well
449.05 aware of his son's fiery courage, he dared not pro-
449.06 nounce the word. More dilatory counsels pre-
449.07 vailed. A certain Haji Saman pointed out at great
449.08 length that 'these tyrannical and ferocious men had
449.09 delivered themselves to a certain death in any case.
449.10 They would stand fast on their hill and starve, or
449.11 they would try to regain their boat and be shot
449.12 from ambushes across the creek, or they would
449.13 break and fly into the forest and perish singly there.'
449.14 He argued that by the use of proper stratagems
449.15 these evil-minded strangers could be destroyed
449.16 without the risk of a battle, and his words had
449.17 a great weight, especially with the Patusan men
449.18 proper. What unsettled the minds of the townfolk
449.19 was the failure of the Rajah's boats to act at the
449.20 decisive moment. It was the diplomatic Kassim
449.21 who represented the Rajah at the council. He
449.22 spoke very little, listened smilingly, very friendly
449.23 and impenetrable. During the sitting messengers
449.24 kept arriving every few minutes almost, with
449.25 reports of the invaders' proceedings. Wild and
449.26 exaggerated rumours were flying: there was a
449.27 large ship at the mouth of the river with big guns
449.28 and many more men -- some white, others with
449.29 black skins and of blood-thirsty appearance. They
449.30 were coming with many more boats to exterminate
450.01 every living thing. A sense of near, incompre-
450.02 hensible danger affected the common people. At
450.03 one moment there was a panic in the courtyard
450.04 amongst the women; shrieking; a rush; children
450.05 crying -- Haji Saman went out to quiet them. Then
450.06 a fort sentry fired at something moving on the
450.07 river, and nearly killed a villager bringing in his
450.08 women-folk in a canoe together with the best of his
450.09 domestic utensils and a dozen fowls. This caused
450.10 more confusion. Meantime the palaver inside Jim's
450.11 house went on in the presence of the girl. Doramin
450.12 sat fierce-faced, heavy, looking at the speakers in
450.13 turn, and breathing slow like a bull. He didn't
450.14 speak till the last, after Kassim had declared that
450.15 the Rajah's boats would be called in because the
450.16 men were required to defend his master's stockade.
450.17 Dain Waris in his father's presence would offer no
450.18 opinion, though the girl entreated him in Jim's
450.19 name to speak out. She offered him Jim's own
450.20 men in her anxiety to have these intruders driven
450.21 out at once. He only shook his head, after a
450.22 glance or two at Doramin. Finally, when the
450.23 council broke up it had been decided that the houses
450.24 nearest the creek should be strongly occupied to
450.25 obtain the command of the enemy's boat. The
450.26 boat itself was not to be interfered with openly,
450.27 so that the robbers on the hill should be tempted to
450.28 embark, when a well-directed fire would kill most
450.29 of them, no doubt. To cut off the escape of those
450.30 who might survive, and to prevent more of them
451.01 coming up, Dain Waris was ordered by Doramin
451.02 to take an armed party of Bugis down the river to
451.03 a certain spot ten miles below Patusan, and there
451.04 form a camp on the shore and blockade the stream
451.05 with the canoes. I don't believe for a moment that
451.06 Doramin feared the arrival of fresh forces. My
451.07 opinion is, that his conduct was guided solely by
451.08 his wish to keep his son out of harm's way. To
451.09 prevent a rush being made into the town the con-
451.10 struction of a stockade was to be commenced at
451.11 daylight at the end of the street on the left bank.

451.12 The old nakhoda declared his intention to command
451.13 there himself. A distribution of powder, bullets,
451.14 and percussion caps was made immediately under
451.15 the girl's supervision. Several messengers were
451.16 to be dispatched in different directions after Jim,
451.17 whose exact whereabouts were unknown. These
451.18 men started at dawn, but before that time Kassim
451.19 had managed to open communications with the
451.20 besieged Brown.
451.21 "That accomplished diplomatist and confidant
451.22 of the Rajah, on leaving the fort to go back to his
451.23 master, took into his boat Cornelius, whom he
451.24 found slinking mutely amongst the people in the
451.25 courtyard. Kassim had a little plan of his own and
451.26 wanted him for an interpreter. Thus it came about
451.27 that towards morning Brown, reflecting upon the
451.28 desperate nature of his position, heard from the
451.29 marshy overgrown hollow an amicable, quavering,
451.30 strained voice crying -- in English -- for permission
452.01 to come up, under a promise of personal safety
452.02 and on a very important errand. He was over--
452.03 joyed. If he was spoken to he was no longer a
452.04 hunted wild beast. These friendly sounds took
452.05 off at once the awful stress of vigilant watchfulness
452.06 as of so many blind men not knowing whence the
452.07 death-blow might come. He pretended a great
452.08 reluctance. The voice declared itself 'a white man
452.09 -- a poor, ruined, old man who had been living here
452.10 for years.' A mist, wet and chilly, lay on the slopes
452.11 of the hill, and after some more shouting from one
452.12 to the other, Brown called out, 'Come on, then, but
452.13 alone, mind!' As a matter of fact -- he told me,
452.14 writhing with rage at the recollection of his helpless-
452.15 ness -- it made no difference. They couldn't see
452.16 more than a few yards before them, and no treachery
452.17 could make their position worse. By and by
452.18 Cornelius, in his week-day attire of a ragged dirty
452.19 shirt and pants, barefooted, with a broken-rimmed
452.20 pith hat on his head, was made out vaguely, sidling
452.21 up to the defences, hesitating, stopping to listen
452.22 in a peering posture. 'Come along! You are safe,'
452.23 yelled Brown, while his men stared. All their hopes
452.24 of life became suddenly centred in that dilapidated,
452.25 mean newcomer, who in profound silence clambered
452.26 clumsily over a felled tree-trunk, and shivering, with
452.27 his sour, mistrustful face, looked about at the knot
452.28 of bearded, anxious, sleepless desperadoes.
452.29 "Half an hour's confidential talk with Cornelius
452.30 opened Brown's eyes as to the home affairs of
453.01 Patusan. He was on the alert at once. There
453.02 were possibilities, immense possibilities; but before
453.03 he would talk over Cornelius's proposals he de-
453.04 manded that some food should be sent up as a
453.05 guarantee of good faith. Cornelius went off, creep-
453.06 ing sluggishly down the hill on the side of the
453.07 Rajah's palace, and after some delay a few of Tunku
453.08 Allang's men came up, bringing a scanty supply of
453.09 rice, chillies, and dried fish. This was immeasurably
453.10 better than nothing. Later on Cornelius returned
453.11 accompanying Kassim, who stepped out with an
453.12 air of perfect good-humoured trustfulness, in
453.13 sandals and muffled up from neck to ankles in
453.14 dark-blue sheeting. He shook hands with Brown
453.15 discreetly, and the three drew aside for a conference.
453.16 Brown's men, recovering their confidence, were
453.17 slapping each other on the back, and cast knowing
453.18 glances at their captain while they busied them-
453.19 selves with preparations for cooking.
453.20 "Kassim disliked Doramin and his Bugis very
453.21 much, but he hated the new order of things still
453.22 more. It had occurred to him that these whites,
453.23 together with the Rajah's followers, could attack
453.24 and defeat the Bugis before Jim's return. Then, he
453.25 reasoned, general defection of the townsfolk was
453.26 sure to follow, and the reign of the white man who
453.27 protected poor people would be over. Afterwards
453.28 the new allies could be dealt with. They would
453.29 have no friends. The fellow was perfectly able to
453.30 perceive the difference of character, and had seen
454.01 enough of white men to know that these newcomers
454.02 were outcasts, men without country. Brown pre-
454.03 served a stern and inscrutable demeanour. When he
454.04 first heard Cornelius's voice demanding admittance,
454.05 it brought merely the hope of a loophole for escape.
454.06 In less than an hour other thoughts were seething
454.07 in his head. Urged by an extreme necessity, he
454.08 had come there to steal food, a few tons of rubber
454.09 or gum maybe, perhaps a handful of dollars, and
454.10 had found himself enmeshed by deadly dangers.
454.11 Now in consequence of these overtures from Kassim

454.12 he began to think of stealing the whole country.
454.13 Some confounded fellow had apparently accom-
454.14 plished something of the kind -- single-handed at
454.15 that. Couldn't have done it very well though.
454.16 Perhaps they could work together -- squeeze every-
454.17 thing dry and then go out quietly. In the course
454.18 of his negotiations with Kassim he became aware
454.19 that he was supposed to have a big ship with plenty
454.20 of men outside. Kassim begged him earnestly to
454.21 have this big ship with his many guns and men
454.22 brought up the river without delay for the Rajah's
454.23 service. Brown professed himself willing, and on
454.24 this basis the negotiation was carried on with mutual
454.25 distrust. Three times in the course of the morning
454.26 the courteous and active Kassim went down to
454.27 consult the Rajah and came up busily with his long
454.28 stride. Brown, while bargaining, had a sort of
454.29 grim enjoyment in thinking of his wretched schooner
454.30 with nothing but a heap of dirt in her hold, that
455.01 stood for an armed ship, and a Chinaman and a lame
455.02 ex-beachcomber of Levuka on board, who repre-
455.03 sented all his many men. In the afternoon he
455.04 obtained further doles of food, a promise of some
455.05 money, and a supply of mats for his men to make
455.06 shelters for themselves. They lay down and
455.07 snored, protected from the burning sunshine; but
455.08 Brown, sitting fully exposed on one of the felled
455.09 trees, feasted his eyes upon the view of the town
455.10 and the river. There was much loot here. Cor-
455.11 nelius, who had made himself at home in the camp,
455.12 talked at his elbow, pointing out the localities, im-
455.13 parting advice, giving his own version of Jim's
455.14 character, and commenting in his own fashion upon
455.15 the events of the last three years. Brown, who,
455.16 apparently indifferent and gazing away, listened
455.17 with attention to every word, could not make out
455.18 clearly what sort of man this Jim could be. 'What's
455.19 his name? Jim! Jim! That's not enough for a
455.20 man's name.' 'They call him,' said Cornelius,
455.21 scornfully, 'Tuan Jim here. As you may say
455.22 Lord Jim.' 'What is he? Where does he come
455.23 from?' inquired Brown. 'What sort of man is
455.24 he? Is he an Englishman?' 'Yes, yes, he's an
455.25 Englishman. I am an Englishman, too. From
455.26 Malacca. He is a fool. All you have to do is to
455.27 kill him and then you are king here. Everything
455.28 belongs to him,' explained Cornelius. 'It strikes
455.29 me he may be made to share with somebody before
455.30 very long,' commented Brown half aloud. 'No,
456.01 no. The proper way is to kill him the first chance
456.02 you get, and then you can do what you like,' Cor-
456.03 nelius would insist earnestly. 'I have lived for many
456.04 years here, and I am giving you a friend's advice.'
456.05 "In such converse and in gloating over the view
456.06 of Patusan, which he had determined in his mind
456.07 should become his prey, Brown whiled away most
456.08 of the afternoon, his men, meantime, resting.
456.09 On that day Dain Waris's fleet of canoes stole one
456.10 by one under the shore farthest from the creek,
456.11 and went down to close the river against his retreat.
456.12 Of this Brown was not aware, and Kassim, who came
456.13 up the knoll an hour before sunset, took good care
456.14 not to enlighten him. He wanted the white man's
456.15 ship to come up the river, and this news, he feared,
456.16 would be discouraging. He was very pressing
456.17 with Brown to send the 'order,' offering at the same
456.18 time a trusty messenger, who for greater secrecy
456.19 (as he explained) would make his way by land to the
456.20 mouth of the river and deliver the 'order' on board.
456.21 After some reflection Brown judged it expedient
456.22 to tear a page out of his pocket-book, on which he
456.23 simply wrote, 'We are getting on. Big job. De-
456.24 tain the man.' The stolid youth selected by Kassim
456.25 for that service performed it faithfully, and was
456.26 rewarded by being suddenly tipped, head first,
456.27 into the schooner's empty hold by the ex-beach-
456.28 comber and the Chinaman, who thereupon hastened
456.29 to put on the hatches. What became of him
456.30 afterwards Brown did not say."
457.01 "BROWN'S object was to gain time by
457.02 fooling with Kassim's diplomacy. For
457.03 doing a real stroke of business he could
457.04 not help thinking the white man was the person to
457.05 work with. He could not imagine such a chap
457.06 (who must be confoundedly clever after all to get
457.07 hold of the natives like that) refusing a help that
457.08 would do away with the necessity for slow, cautious,
457.09 risky cheating, that imposed itself as the only
457.10 possible line of conduct for a single-handed man.
457.11 He, Brown, would offer him the power. No man

256

457.12 could hesitate. Everything was in coming to a
457.13 clear understanding. Of course they would share.
457.14 The idea of there being a fort -- all ready to his hand
457.15 -- a real fort, with artillery (he knew this from
457.16 Cornelius), excited him. Let him only once get
457.17 in and ... He would impose modest conditions.
457.18 Not too low, though. The man was no fool, it
457.19 seemed. They would work like brothers till ...
457.20 till the time came for a quarrel and a shot that
457.21 would settle all accounts. With grim impatience
457.22 of plunder he wished himself to be talking with the
457.23 man now. The land already seemed to be his to
457.24 tear to pieces, squeeze, and throw away. Meantime
458.01 Kassim had to be fooled for the sake of food first --
458.02 and for a second string. But the principal thing
458.03 was to get something to eat from day to day. Be-
458.04 sides, he was not averse to begin fighting on that
458.05 Rajah's account, and teach a lesson to those people
458.06 who had received him with shots. The lust of
458.07 battle was upon him.
458.08 "I am sorry that I can't give you this part of the
458.09 story, which of course I have mainly from Brown, in
458.10 Brown's own words. There was in the broken,
458.11 violent speech of that man, unveiling before me his
458.12 thoughts with the very hand of Death upon his
458.13 throat, an undisguised ruthlessness of purpose, a
458.14 strange vengeful attitude towards his own past,
458.15 and a blind belief in the righteousness of his will
458.16 against all mankind, something of that feeling which
458.17 could induce the leader of a horde of wandering
458.18 cut-throats to call himself proudly the Scourge of
458.19 God. No doubt the natural senseless ferocity which
458.20 is the basis of such a character was exasperated
458.21 by failure, ill-luck, and the recent privations, as
458.22 well as by the desperate position in which he found
458.23 himself; but what was most remarkable of all was
458.24 this, that while he planned treacherous alliances,
458.25 had already settled in his own mind the fate of the
458.26 white man, and intrigued in an overbearing, off-hand
458.27 manner with Kassim, one could perceive that what
458.28 he had really desired, almost in spite of himself,
458.29 was to play havoc with that jungle town which had
458.30 defied him, to see it strewn over with corpses and
459.01 enveloped in flames. Listening to his pitiless,
459.02 panting voice, I could imagine how he must have
459.03 looked at it from the hillock, peopling it with images
459.04 of murder and rapine. The part nearest to the
459.05 creek wore an abandoned aspect, though as a matter
459.06 of fact every house concealed a few armed men
459.07 on the alert. Suddenly beyond the stretch of waste
459.08 ground, interspersed with small patches of low dense
459.09 bush, excavations, heaps of rubbish, with trodden
459.10 paths between, a man, solitary, and looking very
459.11 small, strolled out into the deserted opening of the
459.12 street between the shut-up, dark, lifeless buildings
459.13 at the end. Perhaps one of the inhabitants, who
459.14 had fled to the other bank of the river, coming back
459.15 for some object of domestic use. Evidently he
459.16 supposed himself quite safe at that distance from the
459.17 hill on the other side of the creek. A light stockade,
459.18 set up hastily, was just round the turn of the street,
459.19 full of his friends. He moved leisurely. Brown
459.20 saw him, and instantly called to his side the Yankee
459.21 deserter, who acted as a sort of second in command.
459.22 This lanky, loose-jointed fellow came forward,
459.23 wooden-faced, trailing his rifle lazily. When he
459.24 understood what was wanted from him a homicidal
459.25 and conceited smile uncovered his teeth, making two
459.26 deep folds down his sallow, leathery cheeks. He
459.27 prided himself on being a dead shot. He dropped
459.28 on one knee, and taking aim from a steady rest
459.29 through the unlopped branches of a felled tree,
459.30 fired, and at once stood up to look. The man,
460.01 far away, turned his head to the report, made an-
460.02 other step forward, seemed to hesitate, and abruptly
460.03 got down on his hands and knees. In the silence
460.04 that fell upon the sharp crack of the rifle, the dead
460.05 shot, keeping his eyes fixed upon the quarry,
460.06 guessed that 'this there coon's health would never
460.07 be a source of anxiety to his friends any more.'
460.08 The man's limbs were seen to move rapidly under
460.09 his body in an endeavour to run on all-fours.
460.10 In that empty space arose a multitudinous shout
460.11 of dismay and surprise. The man sank flat, face
460.12 down, and moved no more. 'That showed them
460.13 what we could do,' said Brown to me. 'Struck
460.14 the fear of sudden death into them. That was what
460.15 we wanted. They were two hundred to one, and
460.16 this gave them something to think over for the night.
460.17 Not one of them had an idea of such a long shot

460.18 before. That beggar belonging to the Rajah scooted
460.19 downhill with his eyes hanging out of his head.'
460.20 "As he was telling me this he tried with a
460.21 shaking hand to wipe the thin foam on his blue
460.22 lips. 'Two hundred to one. Two hundred to
460.23 one ... strike terror ... terror, terror, I tell
460.24 you....' His own eyes were starting out of their
460.25 sockets. He fell back, clawing the air with skinny
460.26 fingers, sat up again, bowed and hairy, glared at me
460.27 sideways like some man-beast of folklore, with open
460.28 mouth in his miserable and awful agony before he
460.29 got his speech back after that fit. There are sights
460.30 one never forgets.
461.01 "Furthermore, to draw the enemy's fire and
461.02 locate such patries as might have been hiding in the
461.03 bushes along the creek, Brown ordered the Solomon
461.04 Islander to go down to the boat and bring an oar,
461.05 as you send a spaniel after a stick into the water.
461.06 This failed, and the fellow came back without a
461.07 single shot having been fired at him from anywhere.
461.08 'There's nobody,' opined some of the men. It is
461.09 'onnatural,' remarked the Yankee. Kassim had
461.10 gone, by that time, very much impressed, pleased,
461.11 too, and also uneasy. Pursuing his tortuous policy,
461.12 he had dispatched a message to Dain Waris warning
461.13 him to look out for the white men's ship, which,
461.14 he had had information, was about to come up the
461.15 river. He minimised its strength and exhorted
461.16 him to oppose its passage. This double-dealing
461.17 answered his purpose, which was to keep the Bugis
461.18 forces divided and to weaken them by fighting.
461.19 On the other hand, he had in the course of that day
461.20 sent word to the assembled Bugis chiefs in town,
461.21 assuring them that he was trying to induce the
461.22 invaders to retire; his messages to the fort asked
461.23 earnestly for powder for the Rajah's men. It was
461.24 a long time since Tunku Allang had had ammunition
461.25 for the score or so of old muskets rusting in their
461.26 arm-racks in the audience-hall. The open inter-
461.27 course between the hill and the palace unsettled
461.28 all the minds. It was already time for men to take
461.29 sides, it began to be said. There would soon be
461.30 much bloodshed, and thereafter great trouble for
462.01 many people. The social fabric of orderly, peace-
462.02 ful life, when every man was sure of to-morrow,
462.03 the edifice raised by Jim's hands, seemed on that
462.04 evening ready to collapse into a ruin reeking with
462.05 blood. The poorer folk were already taking to the
462.06 bush or flying up the river. A good many of the
462.07 upper class judged it necessary to go and pay their
462.08 court to the Rajah. The Rajah's youths jostled
462.09 them rudely. Old Tunku Allang, almost out of his
462.10 mind with fear and indecision, either kept a sullen
462.11 silence or abused them violently for daring to come
462.12 with empty hands: they departed very much
462.13 frightened; only old Doramin kept his countrymen
462.14 together and pursued his tactics inflexibly. Enthroned
462.15 in a big chair behind the improvised stockade, he
462.16 issued his orders in a deep veiled rumble, unmoved,
462.17 like a deaf man, in the flying rumours.
462.18 "Dusk fell, hiding first the body of the dead
462.19 man, which had been left lying with arms out-
462.20 stretched as if nailed to the ground, and then the
462.21 revolving sphere of the night rolled smoothly over
462.22 Patusan and came to a rest, showering the glitter
462.23 of countless worlds upon the earth. Again, in the
462.24 exposed part of the town big fires blazed along the
462.25 only street, revealing from distance to distance
462.26 upon their glares the falling straight lines of roofs,
462.27 the fragments of wattled walls jumbled in con-
462.28 fusion, here and there a whole hut elevated in the
462.29 glow upon the vertical black stripes of a group of
462.30 high piles; and all this line of dwellings, revealed
463.01 in patches by the swaying flames, seemed to flicker
463.02 tortuously away up-river into the gloom at the heart
463.03 of the land. A great silence, in which the looms of
463.04 successive fires played without noise, extended
463.05 into the darkness at the foot of the hill; but the
463.06 other bank of the river, all dark save for a solitary
463.07 bonfire at the river-front before the fort, sent out
463.08 into the air an increasing tremor that might have
463.09 been the stamping of a multitude of feet, the hum
463.10 of many voices, or the fall of an immensely distant
463.11 waterfall. It was then, Brown confessed to me,
463.12 while turning his back on his men, he sat looking
463.13 at it all, that notwithstanding his disdain, his ruthless
463.14 faith in himself, a feeling came over him that at last
463.15 he had run his head against a stone wall. Had his
463.16 boat been afloat at the time, he believed he would
463.17 have tried to steal away, taking his chances of a

463.18 long chase down the river and of starvation at sea.
463.19 It was very doubtful whether he would have suc-
463.20 ceeded in getting away. However, he didn't try
463.21 this. For another moment he had a passing thought
463.22 of trying to rush the town, but he perceived very
463.23 well that in the end he would find himself in the
463.24 lighted street, where they would be shot down like
463.25 dogs from the houses. They were two hundred
463.26 to one -- he thought, while his men, huddling round
463.27 two heaps of smouldering embers, munched the
463.28 last of the bananas and roasted the few yams
463.29 they owed to Kassim's diplomacy. Cornelius sat
463.30 amongst them dozing sulkily.
464.01   "Then one of the whites remembered that some
464.02 tobacco had been left in the boat, and, encouraged
464.03 by the impunity of the Solomon Islander, said he
464.04 would go to fetch it. At this all the others shook
464.05 off their despondency. Brown applied to, said,
464.06 'Go, and be d -- d to you,' scornfully. He didn't
464.07 think there was any danger in going to the creek
464.08 in the dark. The man threw a leg over the tree-
464.09 trunk and disappeared. A moment later he was
464.10 heard clambering into the boat and then clambering
464.11 out. 'I've got it,' he cried. A flash and a report
464.12 at the very foot of the hill followed. 'I am hit,'
464.13 yelled the man. 'Look out, look out -- I am hit,'
464.14 and instantly all the rifles went off. The hill
464.15 squirted fire and noise into the night like a little
464.16 volcano, and when Brown and the Yankee with
464.17 curses and cuffs stopped the panic-stricken firing, a
464.18 profound, weary groan floated up from the creek,
464.19 succeeded by a plaint whose heart-rending sadness
464.20 was like some poison turning the blood cold in the
464.21 veins. Then a strong voice pronounced several
464.22 distinct incomprehensible words somewhere beyond
464.23 the creek. 'Let no one fire,' shouted Brown.
464.24 'What does it mean?' ... 'Do you hear on the
464.25 hill? Do you hear? Do you hear?' repeated
464.26 the voice three times. Cornelius translated, and
464.27 then prompted the answer. 'Speak,' cried Brown,
464.28 'we hear.' Then the voice, declaiming in the
464.29 sonorous inflated tone of a herald, and shifting
464.30 continually on the edge of the vague waste-land,
465.01   proclaimed that between the men of the Bugis
465.02 nation living in Patusan and the white men on the
465.03 hill and those with them, there would be no faith,
465.04 no compassion, no speech, no peace. A bush
465.05 rustled; a haphazard volley rang out. 'Dam'
465.06 foolishness,' muttered the Yankee, vexedly ground-
465.07 ing the butt. Cornelius translated. The wounded
465.08 man below the hill, after crying out twice, 'Take
465.09 me up! take me up!' went on complaining in
465.10 moans. While he had kept on the blackened earth
465.11 of the slope and afterwards crouching in the boat,
465.12 he had been safe enough. It seems that in his
465.13 joy at finding tobacco he forgot himself and jumped
465.14 out on her off-side, as it were. The white boat,
465.15 lying high and dry, showed him up; the creek was
465.16 no more than seven yards wide in that place, and
465.17 there happened to be a man crouching in the bush
465.18 on the other bank.
465.19 "He was a Bugis of Tondano only lately come
465.20 to Patusan, and a relation of the man shot in the
465.21 afternoon. That famous long shot had indeed
465.22 appalled the beholders. The man in utter security
465.23 had been struck down, in full view of his friends,
465.24 dropping with a joke on his lips, and they seemed
465.25 to see in the act an atrocity which had stirred a
465.26 bitter rage. That relation of his, Si-Lapa by name,
465.27 was then with Doramin in the stockade only a few
465.28 feet away. You who know these chaps must admit
465.29 that the fellow showed an unusual pluck by volun-
465.30 teering to carry the message, alone, in the dark.
466.01   Creeping across the open ground, he had deviated
466.02 to the left and found himself opposite the boat.
466.03 He was startled when Brown's man shouted. He
466.04 came to a sitting position with his gun to his shoulder,
466.05 and when the other jumped out, exposing himself,
466.06 he pulled the trigger and lodged three jagged slugs
466.07 point-blank into the poor wretch's stomach. Then,
466.08 lying flat on his face, he gave himself up for dead,
466.09 while a thin nail of lead chopped and swished the
466.10 bushes close on his right hand; afterwards he
466.11 delivered his speech shouting, bent double, dodging
466.12 all the time in cover. With the last word he leaped
466.13 sideways, lay close for a while, and afterwards got
466.14 back to the houses unharmed, having achieved on
466.15 that night such a renown as his children will not
466.16 willingly allow to die.
466.17 "And on the hill the forlorn band let the two

466.18 little heaps of embers go out under their bowed
466.19 heads. They sat dejected on the ground with com-
466.20 pressed lips and downcast eyes, listening to their
466.21 comrade below. He was a strong man and died
466.22 hard, with moans now loud, now sinking to a
466.23 strange confidential note of pain. Sometimes he
466.24 shrieked, and again, after a period of silence, he
466.25 could be heard muttering deliriously a long and
466.26 unintelligible complaint. Never for a moment did
466.27 he cease.
466.28 "'What's the good?' Brown had said unmoved
466.29 once, seeing the Yankee, who had been swearing
466.30 under his breath, prepare to go down. 'That's
467.01 so,' assented the deserter, reluctantly desisting.
467.02 'There's no encouragement for wounded men here.
467.03 Only his noise is calculated to make all the others
467.04 think too much of the hereafter, cap'n.' 'Water!'
467.05 cried the wounded man in an extraordinarily clear
467.06 vigorous voice, and then went off moaning feebly.
467.07 'Ay, water. Water will do it,' muttered the other
467.08 to himself resignedly. 'Plenty by and by. The
467.09 tide is flowing.'
467.10 "At last the tide flowed, silencing the plaint and
467.11 the cries of pain, and the dawn was near when
467.12 Brown, sitting with his chin in the palm of his hand
467.13 before Patusan, as one might stare at the unscalable
467.14 side of a mountain, heard the brief ringing bark of a
467.15 brass six-pounder far away in town somewhere.
467.16 'What's this?' he asked of Cornelius, who hung
467.17 about him. Cornelius listened. A muffled roaring
467.18 shout rolled down-river over the town; a big drum
467.19 began to throb, and others responded, pulsating
467.20 and droning. Tiny scattered lights began to
467.21 twinkle in the dark half of the town, while the part
467.22 lighted by the loom of fires hummed with a deep
467.23 and prolonged murmur. 'He has come,' said
467.24 Cornelius. 'What? Already? Are you sure?'
467.25 Brown asked. 'Yes! yes! Sure. Listen to the
467.26 noise.' 'What are they making that row about?'
467.27 pursued Brown. 'For joy,' snorted Cornelius;
467.28 'he is a very great man, but all the same, he knows
467.29 no more than a child, and so they make a great noise
467.30 to please him, because they know no better.' 'Look
468.01 here,' said Brown, 'how is one to get at him?'
468.02 'He shall come to talk to you,' Cornelius declared.
468.03 'What do you mean? Come down here strolling
468.04 as it were?' Cornelius nodded vigorously in the
468.05 dark. 'Yes. He will come straight here and talk
468.06 to you. He is just like a fool. You shall see
468.07 what a fool he is.' Brown was incredulous. 'You
468.08 shall see; you shall see,' repeated Cornelius. 'He
468.09 is not afraid -- not afraid of anything. He will
468.10 come and order you to leave his people alone.
468.11 Everybody must leave his people alone. He is
468.12 like a little child. He will come to you straight.'
468.13 Alas! he knew Jim well -- that 'mean little skunk,'
468.14 as Brown called him to me. 'Yes, certainly,' he
468.15 pursued with ardour, 'and then, captain, you tell
468.16 that tall man with a gun to shoot him. Just you
468.17 kill him, and you will frighten everybody so much
468.18 that you can do anything you like with them after-
468.19 wards -- get what you like -- go away when you like.
468.20 Ha! ha! ha! Fine....' He almost danced
468.21 with impatience and eagerness; and Brown, looking
468.22 over his shoulder at him, could see, shown up by the
468.23 pitiless dawn, his men drenched with dew, sitting
468.24 amongst the cold ashes and the litter of the camp,
468.25 haggard, cowed, and in rags."
469.01 "TO the very last moment, till the full day
469.02 came upon them with a spring, the fires
469.03 on the west bank blazed bright and clear;
469.04 and then Brown saw in a knot of coloured figures
469.05 motionless between the advanced houses a man in
469.06 European clothes, in a helmet, all white. 'That's
469.07 him; look! look!' Cornelius said excitedly. All
469.08 Brown's men had sprung up and crowded at his
469.09 back with lustreless eyes. The group of vivid
469.10 colours and dark faces with the white figure in the
469.11 midst were observing the knoll. Brown could
469.12 see naked arms being raised to shade the eyes and
469.13 other brown arms pointing. What should he do?
469.14 He looked around, and the forests that faced him
469.15 on all sides walled the cock-pit of an unequal
469.16 contest. He looked once more at his men. A
469.17 contempt, a weariness, the desire of life, the wish to
469.18 try for one more chance -- for some other grave --
469.19 struggled in his breast. From the outline the
469.20 figure presented it seemed to him that the white
469.21 man there, backed up by all the power of the land,
469.22 was examining his position through binoculars.

469.23 Brown jumped up on the log, throwing his arms up,
469.24 the palms outwards. The coloured group closed
470.01 round the white man, and fell back twice before
470.02 he got clear of them, walking slowly alone. Brown
470.03 remained standing on the log till Jim, appearing and
470.04 disappearing between the patches of thorny scrub,
470.05 had nearly reached the creek; then Brown jumped
470.06 off and went down to meet him on his side.
470.07 "They met, I should think, not very far from the
470.08 place, perhaps on the very spot, where Jim took the
470.09 second desperate leap of his life -- the leap that
470.10 landed him into the life of Patusan, into the trust,
470.11 the love, the confidence of the people. They faced
470.12 each other across the creek, and with steady eyes
470.13 tried to understand each other before they opened
470.14 their lips. Their antagonism must have been ex-
470.15 pressed in their glances; I know that Brown hated
470.16 Jim at first sight. Whatever hopes he might have
470.17 had vanished at once. This was not the man he
470.18 had expected to see. He hated him for this -- and
470.19 in a checked flannel shirt with sleeves cut off at the
470.20 elbows, grey bearded, with a sunken, sun-blackened
470.21 face -- he cursed in his heart the other's youth and
470.22 assurance, his clear eyes and his untroubled bearing.
470.23 That fellow had got in a long way before him! He
470.24 did not look like a man who would be willing to give
470.25 anything for assistance. He had all the advantages
470.26 on his side -- possession, security, power; he was
470.27 on the side of an overwhelming force! He was
470.28 not hungry and desperate, and he did not seem in the
470.29 least afraid. And there was something in the very
470.30 neatness of Jim's clothes, from the white helmet
471.01 to the canvas leggings and the pipe-clayed shoes,
471.02 which in Brown's sombre irritated eyes seemed to
471.03 belong to things he had in the very shaping of his
471.04 life contemned and flouted.
471.05 "'Who are you?' asked Jim at last, speaking in
471.06 his usual voice. 'My name's Brown,' answered
471.07 the other loudly; 'Captain Brown. What's
471.08 yours?' and Jim after a little pause went on quietly,
471.09 as if he had not heard: 'What made you come
471.10 here?' 'You want to know,' said Brown bitterly.
471.11 'It's easy to tell. Hunger. And what made you?'
471.12 "'The fellow started at this,' said Brown,
471.13 relating to me the opening of this strange conversa-
471.14 tion between those two men, separated only by the
471.15 muddy bed of a creek, but standing on the opposite
471.16 poles of that conception of life which includes all
471.17 mankind -- 'The fellow started at this and got very
471.18 red in the face. Too big to be questioned, I sup-
471.19 pose. I told him that if he looked upon me as a
471.20 dead man with whom you may take liberties, he
471.21 himself was not a whit better off really. I had a
471.22 fellow up there who had a bead drawn on him all
471.23 the time, and only waited for a sign from me. There
471.24 was nothing to be shocked at in this. He had come
471.25 down of his own freewill. "Let us agree," said I,
471.26 "that we are both dead men, and let us talk on that
471.27 basis, as equals. We are all equal before death," I
471.28 said. I admitted I was there like a rat in a trap, but
471.29 we had been driven to it, and even a trapped rat
471.30 can give a bite. He caught me up in a moment.
472.01 "Not if you don't go near the trap till the rat is
472.02 dead." I told him that sort of game was good
472.03 enough for these native friends of his, but I would
472.04 have thought him too white to serve even a rat so.
472.05 Yes, I had wanted to talk with him. Not to beg for
472.06 my life, though. My fellows were -- well -- what
472.07 they were -- men like himself, anyhow. All we
472.08 wanted from him was to come on in the devil's
472.09 name and have it out. "God d--n it," said I,
472.10 while he stood there as still as a wooden post, "you
472.11 don't want to come out here every day with your
472.12 glasses to count how many of us are left on our feet.
472.13 Come. Either bring your infernal crowd along or
472.14 let us go out and starve in the open sea, by God!
472.15 You have been white once, for all your tall talk of
472.16 this being your own people and you being one with
472.17 them. Are you? And what the devil do you
472.18 get for it; what is it you've found here that is so
472.19 d--d precious? Hey? You don't want us to
472.20 come down here perhaps -- do you? You are two
472.21 hundred to one. You don't want us to come down
472.22 into the open. Ah! I promise you we shall give
472.23 you some sport before you've done. You talk about
472.24 me making a cowardly set upon unoffending people.
472.25 What's that to me that they are unoffending, when
472.26 I am starving for next to no offence? But I am not
472.27 a coward. Don't you be one. Bring them along
472.28 or, by all the fiends, we shall yet manage to send

472.29 half your unoffending town to heaven with us in
472.30 smoke!"'
473.01 "He was terrible -- relating this to me -- this
473.02 tortured skeleton of a man drawn up together with
473.03 his face over his knees, upon a miserable bed in that
473.04 wretched hovel, and lifting his head to look at me
473.05 with malignant triumph.
473.06 "'That's what I told him -- I knew what to
473.07 say,' he began again, feebly at first, but working
473.08 himself up with incredible speed into a fiery utter-
473.09 ance of his scorn. 'We aren't going into the forest
473.10 to wander like a string of living skeletons dropping
473.11 one after another for ants to go to work upon us before
473.12 we are fairly dead. Oh no! ... "You don't
473.13 deserve a better fate," he said. "And what do you
473.14 deserve," I shouted at him, "you that I find skulk-
473.15 ing here with your mouth full of your responsibility,
473.16 of innocent lives, of your infernal duty? What do
473.17 you know more of me than I know of you? I came
473.18 here for food. D'ye hear? -- food to fill our bellies.
473.19 And what did you come for? What did you ask for
473.20 when you came here? We don't ask you for any-
473.21 thing but to give us a fight or a clear road to go
473.22 back whence we came...." "I would fight with
473.23 you now," says he, pulling at his little moustache.
473.24 "And I would let you shoot me, and welcome," I
473.25 said. "This is as good a jumping-off place for me
473.26 as another. I am sick of my infernal luck. But it
473.27 would be too easy. There are my men in the same
473.28 boat -- and, by God, I am not the sort to jump out of
473.29 trouble and leave them in a d -- d lurch," I said. He
473.30 stood thinking for a while and then wanted to know
474.01 what I had done ("out there," he says, tossing his
474.02 head down-stream) to be hazed about so. "Have
474.03 we met to tell each other the story of our lives?"
474.04 I asked him. "Suppose you begin. No? Well,
474.05 I am sure I don't want to hear. Keep it to yourself.
474.06 I know it is no better than mine. I've lived -- and
474.07 so did you though you talk as if you were one of those
474.08 people that should have wings so as to go about
474.09 without touching the dirty earth. Well -- it is
474.10 dirty. I haven't got any wings. I am here because
474.11 I was afraid once in my life. Want to know what
474.12 of? Of a prison. That scares me, and you may
474.13 know it -- if it's any good to you. I won't ask you
474.14 what scared you into this infernal hole, where you
474.15 seem to have found pretty pickings. That's your
474.16 luck and this is mine -- the privilege to beg for the
474.17 favour of being shot quickly, or else kicked out to
474.18 go free and starve in my own way." ...'
474.19 "His debilitated body shook with an exultation
474.20 so vehement, so assured, and so malicious that it
474.21 seemed to have driven off the death waiting for him
474.22 in that hut. The corpse of his mad self-love uprose
474.23 from rags and destitution as from the dark horrors
474.24 of a tomb. It is impossible to say how much he
474.25 lied to Jim then, how much he lied to me now --
474.26 and to himself always. Vanity plays lurid tricks
474.27 with our memory, and the truth of every passion
474.28 wants some pretence to make it live. Standing at
474.29 the gate of the other world in the guise of a beggar,
474.30 he had slapped this world's face, he had spat on it,
475.01 he had thrown upon it an immensity of scorn and
475.02 revolt at the bottom of his misdeeds. He had
475.03 overcome them all -- men, women, savages, traders,
475.04 ruffians, missionaries -- and Jim -- 'that beefy-faced
475.05 beggar.' I did not begrudge him this triumph
475.06 *in articulo mortis*, this almost posthumous illusion
475.07 of having trampled all the earth under his feet.
475.08 While he was boasting to me, in his sordid and re-
475.09 pulsive agony, I couldn't help thinking of the chuck-
475.10 ling talk relating to the time of his greatest splendour
475.11 when, during a year or more, Gentleman Brown's
475.12 ship was to be seen, for many days on end, hovering
475.13 off an islet befringed with green upon azure, with
475.14 the dark lot of the mission-house on a white beach;
475.15 while Gentleman Brown, ashore, was casting his
475.16 spells over a romantic girl for whom Melanesia
475.17 had been too much, and giving hopes of a remarkable
475.18 conversion to her husband. The poor man, some
475.19 time or other, had been heard to express the inten-
475.20 tion of winning 'Captain Brown to a better way of
475.21 life.' ... 'Bag Gentleman Brown for Glory' --
475.22 as a leery-eyed loafer expressed it once -- 'just to
475.23 let them see up above what a Western Pacific trading
475.24 skipper looks like.' And this was the man, too,
475.25 who had run off with a dying woman, and had shed
475.26 tears over her body. 'Carried on like a big baby,'
475.27 his then mate was never tired of telling, 'and where
475.28 the fun came in may I be kicked to death by diseased

475.29 Kanakas if I know. Why, gents! she was too far
475.30 gone when he brought her aboard to know him; she
476.01 just lay there on her back in his bunk staring at the
476.02 beam with awful shining eyes -- and then she died.
476.03 Dam' bad sort of fever, I guess....' I remembered
476.04 all these stories while, wiping his matted lump of a
476.05 beard with a livid hand, he was telling me from
476.06 his noisome couch how he got round, got in, got
476.07 home, on that confounded, immaculate, don't-you--
476.08 touch-me sort of fellow. He admitted that he
476.09 couldn't be scared, but there was a way, 'as broad
476.10 as a turnpike, to get in and shake his twopenny soul
476.11 around and inside out and upside down -- by God!'"
477.01 "I DON'T think he could do more than
477.02 perhaps look upon that straight path. He
477.03 seemed to have been puzzled by what he
477.04 saw, for he interrupted himself in his narrative
477.05 more than once to exclaim, 'He nearly slipped from
477.06 me there. I could not make him out. Who was
477.07 he?' And after glaring at me wildly he would
477.08 go on, jubilating and sneering. To me the con-
477.09 versation of these two across the creek appears now
477.10 as the deadliest kind of duel on which Fate looked
477.11 on with her cold-eyed knowledge of the end. No,
477.12 he didn't turn Jim's soul inside out, but I am much
477.13 mistaken if the spirit so utterly out of his reach had
477.14 not been made to taste to the full the bitterness of
477.15 that contest. These were the emissaries with whom
477.16 the world he had renounced was pursuing him in
477.17 his retreat -- white men from 'out there' where he
477.18 did not think himself good enough to live. This
477.19 was all that came to him -- a menace, a shock, a
477.20 danger to his work. I suppose it is this sad, half--
477.21 resentful, half-resigned feeling, piercing through
477.22 the few words Jim said now and then, that puzzled
477.23 Brown so much in the reading of his character.
477.24 Some great men owe most of their greatness to the
478.01 ability of detecting in those they destine for their
478.02 tools the exact quality of strength that matters for
478.03 their work, and Brown, as though he had been really
478.04 great, had a satanic gift of finding out the best and
478.05 the weakest spot in his victims. He admitted to
478.06 me that Jim wasn't of the sort that can be got over
478.07 by truckling, and accordingly he took care to show
478.08 himself as a man confronting without dismay ill-luck,
478.09 censure, and disaster. The smuggling of a few
478.10 guns was no great crime, he pointed out. As to
478.11 coming to Patusan, who had the right to say he
478.12 hadn't come to beg? The infernal people here let
478.13 loose at him from both banks without staying to
478.14 ask questions. He made the point brazenly, for,
478.15 in truth, Dain Waris's energetic action had pre-
478.16 vented the greatest calamities; because Brown told
478.17 me distinctly that, perceiving the size of the place,
478.18 he had resolved instantly in his mind that as soon
478.19 as he had gained a footing he would set fire right and
478.20 left, and begin by shooting down everything living
478.21 in sight, in order to cow and terrify the population.
478.22 The disproportion of forces was so great that this
478.23 was the only way giving him the slightest chance of
478.24 attaining his ends -- he argued in a fit of coughing.
478.25 But he didn't tell Jim this. As to the hardships
478.26 and starvation they had gone through, these had
478.27 been very real; it was enough to look at his band.
478.28 He made, at the sound of a shrill whistle, all his
478.29 men appear standing in a row on the logs in full
478.30 view, so that Jim could see them. For the killing
479.01 of the man, it had been done -- well, it had -- but
479.02 was not this war, bloody war -- in a corner? and the
479.03 fellow had been killed cleanly, shot through the
479.04 chest, not like that poor devil of his lying now in the
479.05 creek. They had to listen to him dying for six
479.06 hours, with his entrails torn with slugs. At any
479.07 rate this was a life for a life.... And all this was
479.08 said with the weariness, with the recklessness of a
479.09 man spurred on and on by ill-luck till he cares not
479.10 where he runs. When he asked Jim, with a sort of
479.11 brusque despairing frankness, whether he himself --
479.12 straight now -- didn't understand that when 'it
479.13 came to saving one's life in the dark, one didn't
479.14 care who else went -- three, thirty, three hundred
479.15 people' -- it was as if a demon had been whispering
479.16 advice in his ear. 'I made him wince,' boasted
479.17 Brown to me. 'He very soon left off coming the
479.18 righteous over me. He just stood there with nothing
479.19 to say, and looking as black as thunder -- not at me --
479.20 on the ground.' He asked Jim whether he had
479.21 nothing fishy in his life to remember that he was so
479.22 damnedly hard upon a man trying to get out of a
479.23 deadly hole by the first means that came to hand --
479.24 and so on, and so on. And there ran through the
479.25 rough talk a vein of subtle reference to their common
479.26 blood, an assumption of common experience; a
479.27 sickening suggestion of common guilt, of secret
479.28 knowledge that was like a bond of their minds and
479.29 of their hearts.
479.30 "At last Brown threw himself down full length
480.01 and watched Jim out of the corners of his eyes.
480.02 Jim on his side of the creek stood thinking and
480.03 switching his leg. The houses in view were silent,
480.04 as if a pestilence had swept them clean of every
480.05 breath of life; but many invisible eyes were turned,
480.06 from within, upon the two men with the creek be-
480.07 tween them, a stranded white boat, and the body of
480.08 the third man half sunk in the mud. On the river
480.09 canoes were moving again, for Patusan was recover-
480.10 ing its belief in the stability of earthly institutions
480.11 since the return of the white lord. The right bank,
480.12 the platforms of the houses, the rafts moored along
480.13 the shores, even the roofs of bathing-huts, were
480.14 covered with people that, far away out of earshot
480.15 and almost out of sight, were straining their eyes
480.16 towards the knoll beyond the Rajah's stockade.
480.17 Within the wide irregular ring of forests broken in
480.18 two places by the sheen of the river there was a
480.19 silence. 'Will you promise to leave the coast?'
480.20 Jim asked. Brown lifted and let fall his hand,
480.21 giving everything up as it were -- accepting the
480.22 inevitable. 'And surrender your arms?' Jim went
480.23 on. Brown sat up and glared across. 'Surrender
480.24 our arms! Not till you come to take them out of
480.25 our stiff hands. You think I am gone crazy with
480.26 funk? Oh no! That and the rags I stand in is all I
480.27 have got in the world, besides a few more breech--
480.28 loaders on board; and I expect to sell the lot in
480.29 Madagascar, if I ever get so far -- begging my way
480.30 from ship to ship.'
481.01 "Jim said nothing to this. At last, throwing
481.02 away the switch he held in his hand, he said, as if
481.03 speaking to himself, 'I don't know whether I have
481.04 the power.' ... 'You don't know! And you
481.05 wanted me just now to give up my arms! That's
481.06 good, too,' cried Brown. 'Suppose they say one
481.07 thing to you, and do the other thing to me.' He
481.08 calmed down markedly. 'I dare say you have the
481.09 power, or what's the meaning of all this talk?' he
481.10 continued. 'What did you come down here for?
481.11 To pass the time of day?'
481.12 "'Very well,' said Jim, lifting his head suddenly
481.13 after a long silence. 'You shall have a clear road or
481.14 else a clear fight.' He turned on his heel and walked
481.15 away.
481.16 "Brown got up at once, but he did not go up the
481.17 hill till he had seen Jim disappear between the first
481.18 houses. He never set his eyes on him again. On
481.19 his way back he met Cornelius slouching down with
481.20 his head between his shoulders. He stopped before
481.21 Brown. 'Why didn't you kill him?' he demanded
481.22 in a sour, discontented voice. 'Because I could
481.23 do better than that,' Brown said with an amused
481.24 smile. 'Never! never!' protested Cornelius with
481.25 energy. 'Couldn't. I have lived here for many
481.26 years.' Brown looked up at him curiously. There
481.27 were many sides to the life of that place in arms
481.28 against him; things he would never find out.
481.29 Cornelius slunk past dejectedly in the direction of
481.30 the river. He was now leaving his new friends.
482.01 He accepted the disappointing course of events
482.02 with a sulky obstinacy which seemed to draw more
482.03 together his little yellow old face; and as he went
482.04 down he glanced askant here and there, never giving
482.05 up his fixed idea.
482.06 "Henceforth events move fast without a check,
482.07 flowing from the very hearts of men like a stream
482.08 from a dark source, and we see Jim amongst them,
482.09 mostly through Tamb' Itam's eyes. The girl's eyes
482.10 had watched him, too, but her life is too much
482.11 entwined with his: there is her passion, her wonder,
482.12 her anger, and, above all, her fear and her unforgiving
482.13 love. Of the faithful servant, uncomprehending as
482.14 the rest of them, it is the fidelity alone that comes
482.15 into play; a fidelity and a belief in his lord so
482.16 strong that even amazement is subdued to a sort of
482.17 saddened acceptance of a mysterious failure. He
482.18 has eyes only for one figure, and through all the
482.19 mazes of bewilderment he preserves his air of
482.20 guardianship, of obedience, of care.
482.21 "His master came back from his talk with the
482.22 white men, walking slowly towards the stockade in
482.23 the street. Everybody was rejoiced to see him

482.24 return, for while he was away every man had been
482.25 afraid not only of him being killed, but also of
482.26 what would come after. Jim went into one of the
482.27 houses, where old Doramin had retired, and re-
482.28 mained alone for a long time with the head of the
482.29 Bugis settlers. No doubt he discussed the course
482.30 to follow with him then, but no man was present
483.01 at the conversation. Only Tamb' Itam, keeping as
483.02 close to the door as he could, heard his master say,
483.03 'Yes. I shall let all the people know that such is my
483.04 wish; but I spoke to you, O Doramin, before all
483.05 the others, and alone; for you know my heart as
483.06 well as I know yours and its greatest desire. And
483.07 you know well also that I have no thought but for
483.08 the people's good.' Then his master, lifting the
483.09 sheeting in the doorway, went out, and he, Tamb'
483.10 Itam, had a glimpse of old Doramin within, sitting
483.11 in the chair with his hands on his knees, and looking
483.12 between his feet. Afterwards he followed his
483.13 master to the fort, where all the principal Bugis
483.14 and Patusan inhabitants had been summoned for
483.15 a talk. Tamb' Itam himself hoped there would be
483.16 some fighting. 'What was it but the taking of
483.17 another hill?' he exclaimed regretfully. However,
483.18 in the town many hoped that the rapacious strangers
483.19 would be induced, by the sight of so many brave
483.20 men making ready to fight, to go away. It would
483.21 be a good thing if they went away. Since Jim's
483.22 arrival had been made known before daylight by
483.23 the gun fired from the fort and the beating of the
483.24 big drum there, the fear that had hung over Patusan
483.25 had broken and subsided like a wave on a rock,
483.26 leaving the seething foam of excitement, curiosity,
483.27 and endless speculation. Half of the population
483.28 had been ousted out of their homes for purposes of
483.29 defence, and were living in the street on the left
483.30 side of the river, crowding round the fort, and in
484.01 momentary expectation of seeing their abandoned
484.02 dwellings on the threatened bank burst into flames.
484.03 The general anxiety was to see the matter settled
484.04 quickly. Food, through Jewel's care, had been
484.05 served out to the refugees. Nobody knew what
484.06 their white man would do. Some remarked that
484.07 it was worse than in Sherif Ali's war. Then many
484.08 people did not care; now everybody had something
484.09 to lose. The movements of canoes passing to and
484.10 fro between the two parts of the town were watched
484.11 with interest. A couple of Bugis war-boats lay
484.12 anchored in the middle of the stream to protect the
484.13 river, and a thread of smoke stood at the bow of each;
484.14 the men in them were cooking their midday rice
484.15 when Jim, after his interviews with Brown and
484.16 Doramin, crossed the river and entered by the
484.17 water-gate of his fort. The people inside crowded
484.18 round him so that he could hardly make his way to
484.19 the house. They had not seen him before, because
484.20 on his arrival during the night he had only exchanged
484.21 a few words with the girl, who had come down
484.22 to the landing-stage for the purpose, and had then
484.23 gone on at once to join the chiefs and the fighting
484.24 men on the other bank. People shouted greetings
484.25 after him. One old woman raised a laugh by push-
484.26 ing her way to the front madly and enjoining him
484.27 in a scolding voice to see to it that her two sons, who
484.28 were with Doramin, did not come to harm at the
484.29 hands of the robbers. Several of the bystanders
484.30 tried to pull her away, but she struggled and cried,
485.01 'Let me go. What is this, O Muslims? This
485.02 laughter is unseemly. Are they not cruel, blood-
485.03 thirsty robbers bent on killing?' 'Let her be,'
485.04 said Jim, and as a silence fell suddenly, he said
485.05 slowly, 'Everybody shall be safe.' He entered the
485.06 house before the great sigh, and the loud murmurs of
485.07 satisfaction, had died out.
485.08 "There's no doubt his mind was made up that
485.09 Brown should have his way clear back to the sea.
485.10 His fate, revolted, was forcing his hand. He had for
485.11 the first time to affirm his will in the face of out-
485.12 spoken opposition. 'There was much talk, and at
485.13 first my master was silent,' Tamb' Itam said.
485.14 'Darkness came, and then I lit the candles on the
485.15 long table. The chiefs sat on each side, and the
485.16 lady remained by my master's right hand.'
485.17 "When he began to speak, the unaccustomed
485.18 difficulty seemed only to fix his resolve more im-
485.19 movably. The white men were now waiting for
485.20 his answer on the hill. Their chief had spoken to
485.21 him in the language of his own people, making
485.22 clear many things difficult to explain in any other
485.23 speech. They were erring men whom suffering

485.24 had made blind to right and wrong. It is true
485.25 that lives had been lost already, but why lose more?
485.26 He declared to his hearers, the assembled heads of
485.27 the people, that their welfare was his welfare,
485.28 their losses his losses, their mourning his mourning.
485.29 He looked round at the grave listening faces and
485.30 told them to remember that they had fought and
486.01 worked side by side. They knew his courage....
486.02 Here a murmur interrupted him ... And that he
486.03 had never deceived them. For many years they
486.04 had dwelt together. He loved the land and the
486.05 people living in it with a very great love. He was
486.06 ready to answer with his life for any harm that
486.07 should come to them if the white men with beards
486.08 were allowed to retire. They were evil-doers,
486.09 but their destiny had been evil, too. Had he ever
486.10 advised them ill? Had his words ever brought
486.11 suffering to the people? he asked. He believed
486.12 that it would be best to let these whites and their
486.13 followers go with their lives. It would be a small
486.14 gift. 'I whom you have tried and found always
486.15 true ask you to let them go.' He turned to Doramin.
486.16 The old nakhoda made no movement. 'Then,' said
486.17 Jim, 'call in Dain Waris, your son, my friend, for in
486.18 this business I shall not lead.'"
487.01 "TAMB' ITAM behind his chair was
487.02 thunderstruck. The declaration pro-
487.03 duced an immense sensation. 'Let
487.04 them go because this is best in my knowledge,
487.05 which has never deceived you,' Jim insisted. There
487.06 was a silence. In the darkness of the courtyard
487.07 could be heard the subdued whispering, shuffling
487.08 noise of many people. Doramin raised his heavy
487.09 head and said that there was no more reading of
487.10 hearts than touching the sky with the hand, but --
487.11 he consented. The others gave their opinion in
487.12 turn. 'It is best,' 'Let them go,' and so on. But
487.13 most of them simply said that they 'believed Tuan
487.14 Jim.'
487.15 "In this simple form of assent to his will lies the
487.16 whole gist of the situation; their creed, his truth;
487.17 and the testimony to that faithfulness which made
487.18 him in his own eyes the equal of the impeccable
487.19 men who never fall out of the ranks. Stein's words,
487.20 'Romantic! -- Romantic!' seem to ring over those
487.21 distances that will never give him up now to a world
487.22 indifferent to his failings and his virtues, and to that
487.23 ardent and clinging affection that refuses him the
487.24 dole of tears in the bewilderment of a great grief
488.01 and of eternal separation. From the moment the
488.02 sheer truthfulness of his last three years of life
488.03 carries the day against the ignorance, the fear, and
488.04 the anger of men, he appears no longer to me as I
488.05 saw him last -- a white speck catching all the dim
488.06 light left upon a sombre coast and the darkened
488.07 sea -- but greater and more pitiful in the loneliness
488.08 of his soul, that remains even for her who loved
488.09 him best a cruel and insoluble mystery.
488.10 "It is evident that he did not mistrust Brown;
488.11 there was no reason to doubt the story, whose truth
488.12 seemed warranted by the rough frankness, by a sort
488.13 of virile sincerity in accepting the morality and the
488.14 consequences of his acts. But Jim did not know
488.15 the almost inconceivable egotism of the man which
488.16 made him, when resisted and foiled in his will, mad
488.17 with the indignant and revengeful rage of a thwarted
488.18 autocrat. But if Jim did not mistrust Brown, he
488.19 was evidently anxious that some misunderstanding
488.20 should not occur, ending perhaps in collision and
488.21 bloodshed. It was for this reason that directly
488.22 the Malay chiefs had gone he asked Jewel to get
488.23 him something to eat, as he was going out of the fort
488.24 to take command in the town. On her remon-
488.25 strating against this on the score of his fatigue, he
488.26 said that something might happen for which he
488.27 would never forgive himself. 'I am responsible
488.28 for every life in the land,' he said. He was moody
488.29 at first; she served him with her own hands, taking
488.30 the plates and dishes (of the dinner-service presented
489.01 him by Stein) from Tamb' Itam. He brightened
489.02 up after a while; told her she would be again in
489.03 command of the fort for another night. 'There's
489.04 no sleep for us, old girl,' he said, 'while our people
489.05 are in danger.' Later on he said jokingly that she
489.06 was the best man of them all. 'If you and Dain
489.07 Waris had done what you wanted, not one of these
489.08 poor devils would be alive to-day.' 'Are they very
489.09 bad?' she asked, leaning over his chair. 'Men
489.10 act badly sometimes without being much worse
489.11 than others,' he said after some hesitation.

489.12 "Tamb' Itam followed his master to the landing--
489.13 stage outside the fort. The night was clear, but
489.14 without a moon, and the middle of the river was
489.15 dark, while the water under each bank reflected
489.16 the light of many fires 'as on a night of Ramadan,'
489.17 Tamb' Itam said. War-boats drifted silently in
489.18 the dark lane or, anchored, floated motionless with a
489.19 loud ripple. That night there was much paddling
489.20 in a canoe and walking at his master's heels for
489.21 Tamb' Itam: up and down the street they tramped,
489.22 where the fires were burning, inland on the out-
489.23 skirts of the town where small parties of men kept
489.24 guard in the fields. Tuan Jim gave his orders and
489.25 was obeyed. Last of all, they went to the Rajah's
489.26 stockade, which a detachment of Jim's people
489.27 manned on that night. The old Rajah had fled
489.28 early in the morning with most of his women to
489.29 a small house he had near a jungle village on
489.30 a tributary stream. Kassim, left behind, had
490.01 attended the council with his air of diligent activity
490.02 to explain away the diplomacy of the day before.
490.03 He was considerably cold-shouldered, but managed
490.04 to preserve his smiling, quiet alertness, and pro-
490.05 fessed himself highly delighted when Jim told him
490.06 sternly that he proposed to occupy the stockade on
490.07 that night with his own men. After the council
490.08 broke up he was heard outside accosting this and
490.09 that departing chief, and speaking in a loud, grati-
490.10 fied tone of the Rajah's property being protected in
490.11 the Rajah's absence.
490.12 "About ten or so Jim's men marched in. The
490.13 stockade commanded the mouth of the creek, and
490.14 Jim meant to remain there till Brown had passed
490.15 below. A small fire was lit on the flat, grassy point
490.16 outside the wall of stakes, and Tamb' Itam placed
490.17 a little folding-stool for his master. Jim told him
490.18 to try and sleep. Tamb' Itam got a mat and lay
490.19 down a little way off; but he could not sleep,
490.20 though he knew he had to go on an important
490.21 journey before the night was out. His master
490.22 walked to and fro before the fire with bowed head
490.23 and with his hands behind his back. His face was
490.24 sad. Whenever his master approached him Tamb'
490.25 Itam pretended to sleep, not wishing his master to
490.26 know he had been watched. At last his master
490.27 stood still, looking down on him as he lay, and said
490.28 softly, 'It is time.'
490.29 "Tamb' Itam arose directly and made his
490.30 preparations. His mission was to go down the
491.01 river, preceding Brown's boat by an hour or more,
491.02 to tell Dain Waris finally and formally that the
491.03 whites were to be allowed to pass out unmolested.
491.04 Jim would not trust anybody else with that service.
491.05 Before starting, Tamb' Itam, more as a matter of
491.06 form (since his position about Jim made him per-
491.07 fectly known), asked for a token. 'Because, Tuan,'
491.08 he said, 'the message is important, and these are
491.09 thy very words I carry.' His master first put
491.10 his hand into one pocket, then into another, and
491.11 finally took off his forefinger Stein's silver ring,
491.12 which he habitually wore, and gave it to Tamb'
491.13 Itam. When Tamb' Itam left on his mission,
491.14 Brown's camp on the knoll was dark but for a
491.15 single small glow shining through the branches
491.16 of one of the trees the white men had cut down.
491.17 "Early in the evening Brown had received from
491.18 Jim a folded piece of paper on which was written,
491.19 'You get the clear road. Start as soon as your boat
491.20 floats on the morning tide. Let your men be careful.
491.21 The bushes on both sides of the creek and the
491.22 stockade at the mouth are full of well-armed men.
491.23 You would have no chance, but I don't believe
491.24 you want bloodshed.' Brown read it, tore the
491.25 paper into small pieces, and, turning to Cornelius,
491.26 who had brought it, said jeeringly, 'Good-bye,
491.27 my excellent friend.' Cornelius had been in the
491.28 fort, and had been sneaking around Jim's house
491.29 during the afternoon. Jim chose him to carry the
491.30 note because he could speak English, was known to
492.01 Brown, and was not likely to be shot by some
492.02 nervous mistake of one of the men as a Malay,
492.03 approaching in the dusk, perhaps might have been.
492.04 "Cornelius didn't go away after delivering the
492.05 paper. Brown was sitting up over a tiny fire;
492.06 all the others were lying down. 'I could tell you
492.07 something you would like to know,' Cornelius
492.08 mumbled crossly. Brown paid no attention. 'You
492.09 did not kill him,' went on the other, 'and what do
492.10 you get for it? You might have had money from
492.11 the Rajah, besides the loot of all the Bugis houses,

492.12 and now you get nothing.' 'You had better clear
492.13 out from here,' growled Brown, without even looking
492.14 at him. But Cornelius let himself drop by his
492.15 side and began to whisper very fast, touching his
492.16 elbow from time to time. What he had to say made
492.17 Brown sit up at first, with a curse. He had simply
492.18 informed him of Dain Waris's armed party down the
492.19 river. At first Brown saw himself completely sold
492.20 and betrayed, but a moment's reflection convinced
492.21 him that there could be no treachery intended. He
492.22 said nothing, and after a while Cornelius remarked,
492.23 in a tone of complete indifference, that there was
492.24 another way out of the river which he knew very
492.25 well. 'A good thing to know, too,' said Brown,
492.26 pricking up his ears; and Cornelius began to
492.27 talk of what went on in town and repeated all that
492.28 had been said in council, gossiping in an even
492.29 undertone at Brown's ear as you talk amongst
492.30 sleeping men you do not wish to wake. 'He thinks
493.01 he has made me harmless, does he?' mumbled
493.02 Brown very low.... 'Yes. He is a fool. A little
493.03 child. He came here and robbed me,' droned on
493.04 Cornelius, 'and he made all the people believe him.
493.05 But if something happened that they did not believe
493.06 him any more, where would he be? And the Bugis
493.07 Dain who is waiting for you down the river there,
493.08 captain, is the very man who chased you up here
493.09 when you first came.' Brown observed non-
493.10 chalantly that it would be just as well to avoid him,
493.11 and with tone same detached, musing air Cornelius
493.12 declared himself acquainted with a back-water
493.13 broad enough to take Brown's boat past Waris's
493.14 camp. 'You will have to be quiet,' he said, as an
493.15 afterthought, 'for in one place we pass close behind
493.16 his camp. Very close. They are camped ashore
493.17 with their boat hauled up.' 'Oh, we know how
493.18 to be as quiet as mice; never fear,' said Brown.
493.19 Cornelius stipulated that in case he were to pilot
493.20 Brown out, his canoe should be towed. 'I'll have
493.21 to get back quick,' he explained.
493.22 "It was two hours before the dawn when word
493.23 was passed to the stockade from outlying watchers
493.24 that the white robbers were coming down to their
493.25 boat. In a very short time every armed man from
493.26 one end of Patusan to the other was on the alert,
493.27 yet the banks of the river remained so silent that
493.28 but for the fires burning with sudden blurred flares
493.29 the town might have been asleep as if in peace-
493.30 time. A heavy mist lay very low on the water
494.01 making a sort of illusive grey light that showed
494.02 nothing. When Brown's long-boat glided out of
494.03 the creek into the river, Jim was standing on the
494.04 low point of land before the Rajah's stockade -- on
494.05 the very spot where for the first time he put his foot
494.06 on Patusan shore. A shadow loomed up, moving
494.07 in the greyness, solitary, very bulky, and yet con-
494.08 stantly eluding the eye. A murmur of low talking
494.09 came out of it. Brown at the tiller heard Jim speak
494.10 calmly: 'A clear road. You had better trust to the
494.11 current while the fog lasts; but this will lift pres-
494.12 ently.' 'Yes, presently we shall see clear,' replied
494.13 Brown.
494.14 "The thirty or forty men standing with muskets
494.15 at ready outside the stockade held their breath.
494.16 The Bugis owner of the prau, whom I saw on Stein's
494.17 verandah, and who was amongst them, told me that
494.18 the boat, shaving the low point close, seemed for a
494.19 moment to grow big and hang over it like a moun-
494.20 tain. 'If you think it worth your while to wait a
494.21 day outside,' called out Jim, 'I'll try to send you
494.22 down something -- bullock, some yams -- what I
494.23 can.' The shadow went on moving. 'Yes. Do,'
494.24 said a voice, blank and muffled out of the fog. Not
494.25 one of the many attentive listeners understood what
494.26 the words meant; and then Brown and his men in
494.27 their boat floated away, fading spectrally without the
494.28 slightest sound.
494.29 "Thus Brown, invisible in the mist, goes out of
494.30 Patusan elbow to elbow with Cornelius in the stern--
495.01 sheets of the long-boat. 'Perhaps you shall get a
495.02 small bullock,' said Cornelius. 'Oh yes. Bullock.
495.03 Yam. You'll get it if he said so. He always speaks
495.04 the truth. He stole everything I had. I suppose
495.05 you like a small bullock better than the loot of many
495.06 houses.' 'I would advise you to hold your tongue,
495.07 or somebody here may fling you overboard into this
495.08 damned fog,' said Brown. The boat seemed to
495.09 be standing still; nothing could be seen, not even
495.10 the river alongside, only the water-dust flew and
495.11 trickled, condensed, down their beards and faces.

495.12 It was weird, Brown told me. Every individual
495.13 man of them felt as though he were adrift alone in a
495.14 boat, haunted by an almost imperceptible suspicion
495.15 of sighing, muttering ghosts. 'Throw me out,
495.16 would you? But I would know where I was,'
495.17 mumbled Cornelius surlily. 'I've lived many years
495.18 here.' 'Not long enough to see through a fog like
495.19 this,' Brown said, lolling back with his arm swinging
495.20 to and fro on the useless tiller. 'Yes. Long
495.21 enough for that,' snarled Cornelius. 'That's very
495.22 useful,' commented Brown. 'Am I to believe you
495.23 could find that backway you spoke of blindfold,
495.24 like this?' Cornelius grunted. 'Are you too
495.25 tired to row?' he asked after a silence. 'No, by
495.26 God!' shouted Brown suddenly. 'Out with your
495.27 oars there.' There was a great knocking in the fog,
495.28 which after a while settled into a regular grind of
495.29 invisible sweeps against invisible thole-pins. Other-
495.30 wise nothing was changed, and but for the slight
496.01 splash of a dipped blade it was like rowing a balloon
496.02 car in a cloud, said Brown. Thereafter Cornelius
496.03 did not open his lips except to ask querulously for
496.04 somebody to bale out his canoe, which was towing
496.05 behind the long-boat. Gradually the fog whitened,
496.06 and became luminous ahead. To the left Brown
496.07 saw a darkness as though he had been looking at
496.08 the back of the departing night. All at once a big
496.09 bough covered with leaves appeared above his head,
496.10 and ends of twigs, dripping and still, curved slenderly
496.11 close alongside. Cornelius, without a word, took
496.12 the tiller from his hand."
497.01 "I DON#T think they spoke together again.
497.02 The boat entered a narrow by-channel,
497.03 where it was pushed by the oar-blades set
497.04 into crumbling banks, and there was a gloom as if
497.05 enormous black wings had been outspread above the
497.06 mist that filled its depth to the summits of the
497.07 trees. The branches overhead showered big drops
497.08 through the gloomy fog. At a mutter from Cor-
497.09 nelius, Brown ordered his men to load. 'I'll
497.10 give you a chance to get even with them before we're
497.11 done, you dismal cripples, you,' he said to his gang.
497.12 'Mind you don't throw it away -- you hounds.'
497.13 Low growls answered that speech. Cornelius
497.14 showed much fussy concern for the safety of his
497.15 canoe.
497.16 "Meantime Tamb' Itam had reached the end of
497.17 his journey. The fog had delayed him a little, but
497.18 he had paddled steadily, keeping in touch with the
497.19 south bank. By and by daylight came like a glow
497.20 in a ground glass globe. The shores made on each
497.21 side of the river a dark smudge, in which one could
497.22 detect hints of columnar forms and shadows of
497.23 twisted branches high up. The mist was still
497.24 thick on the water, but a good watch was being kept,
498.01 for as Tamb' Itam approached the camp the figures
498.02 of two men emerged out of the white vapour, and
498.03 voices spoke to him boisterously. He answered,
498.04 and presently a canoe lay alongside, and he exchanged
498.05 news with the paddlers. All was well. The trouble
498.06 was over. Then the men in the canoe let go their
498.07 grip on the side of his dug-out and incontinently
498.08 fell out of sight. He pursued his way till he heard
498.09 voices coming to him quietly over the water, and saw,
498.10 under the now lifting, swirling mist, the glow of
498.11 many little fires burning on a sandy stretch, backed
498.12 by lofty thin timber and bushes. There again a
498.13 look-out was kept, for he was challenged. He
498.14 shouted his name as the two last sweeps of his paddle
498.15 ran his canoe up on the strand. It was a big camp.
498.16 Men crouched in many knots under a subdued
498.17 murmur of early morning talk. Many thin threads
498.18 of smoke curled slowly on the white mist. Little
498.19 shelters, elevated above the ground, had been built
498.20 for the chiefs. Muskets were stacked in small
498.21 pyramids, and long spears were stuck singly into
498.22 the sand near the fires.
498.23 "Tamb' Itam, assuming an air of importance,
498.24 demanded to be led to Dain Waris. He found the
498.25 friend of his white lord lying on a raised couch made
498.26 of bamboo, and sheltered by a sort of shed of sticks
498.27 covered with mats. Dain Waris was awake, and a
498.28 bright fire was burning before his sleeping-place,
498.29 which resembled a rude shrine. The only son of
498.30 Nakhoda Doramin answered his greeting kindly.
499.01 Tamb' Itam began by handing him the ring which
499.02 vouched for the truth of the messenger's words.
499.03 Dain Waris, reclining on his elbow, bade him speak
499.04 and tell all the news. Beginning with the conse-
499.05 crated formula, 'The news is good,' Tamb' Itam

499.06 delivered Jim's own words. The white men, de-
499.07 parting with the consent of all the chiefs, were to be
499.08 allowed to pass down the river. In answer to a
499.09 question or two Tamb' Itam then reported the pro-
499.10 ceedings of the last council. Dain Waris listened
499.11 attentively to the end, toying with the ring which
499.12 ultimately he slipped on the forefinger of his right
499.13 hand. After hearing all he had to say he dismissed
499.14 Tamb' Itam to have food and rest. Orders for the
499.15 return in the afternoon were given immediately.
499.16 Afterwards Dain Waris lay down again, open-eyed,
499.17 while his personal attendants were preparing him
499.18 food at the fire, by which Tamb' Itam also sat talk-
499.19 ing to the men who lounged up to hear the latest
499.20 intelligence from the town. The sun was eating
499.21 up the mist. A good watch was kept upon the reach
499.22 of the main stream where the boat of the whites was
499.23 expected to appear every moment.
499.24 "It was then that Brown took his revenge upon
499.25 the world which, after twenty years of contemptuous
499.26 and reckless bullying, refused him the tribute of a
499.27 common robber's success. It was an act of cold--
499.28 blooded ferocity, and it consoled him on his deathbed
499.29 like a memory of an indomitable defiance. Stealthily
499.30 he landed his men on the other side of the island
500.01 opposite to the Bugis camp, and led them across.
500.02 After a short but quite silent scuffle, Cornelius,
500.03 who had tried to slink away at the moment of land-
500.04 ing, resigned himself to show the way where the
500.05 undergrowth was most sparse. Brown held both
500.06 his skinny hands together behind his back in the
500.07 grip of one vast fist, and now and then impelled him
500.08 forward with a fierce push. Cornelius remained as
500.09 mute as a fish, abject but faithful to his purpose,
500.10 whose accomplishment loomed before him dimly.
500.11 At the edge of the patch of forest Brown's men
500.12 spread themselves out in cover and waited. The
500.13 camp was plain from end to end before their eyes,
500.14 and no one looked their way. Nobody ever dreamed
500.15 that the white men could have any knowledge
500.16 of the narrow channel at the back of the island.
500.17 When he judged the moment come, Brown yelled,
500.18 'Let them have it,' and fourteen shots rang out like
500.19 one.
500.20 "Tamb' Itam told me the surprise was so great
500.21 that, except for those who fell dead or wounded,
500.22 not a soul of them moved for quite an appreciable
500.23 time after the first discharge. Then a man screamed,
500.24 and after that scream a great yell of amazement and
500.25 fear went up from all the throats. A blind panic
500.26 drove these men in a surging swaying mob to and
500.27 fro along the shore like a herd of cattle afraid of the
500.28 water. Some few jumped into the river then, but
500.29 most of them did so only after the last discharge.
500.30 Three times Brown's men fired into the ruck,
501.01 Brown, the only one in view, cursing and yelling,
501.02 'Aim low! aim low!'
501.03 "Tamb' Itam says that, as for him, he under-
501.04 stood at the first volley what had happened. Though
501.05 untouched he fell down and lay as if dead, but with
501.06 his eyes open. At the sound of the first shots Dain
501.07 Waris, reclining on the couch, jumped up and ran
501.08 out upon the open shore, just in time to receive a
501.09 bullet in his forehead at the second discharge.
501.10 Tamb' Itam saw him fling his arms wide open before
501.11 he fell. Then, he says, a great fear came upon him --
501.12 not before. The white men retired as they had
501.13 come -- unseen.
501.14 "Thus Brown balanced his account with the
501.15 evil fortune. Notice that even in this awful out-
501.16 break there is a superiority as of a man who carries
501.17 right -- the abstract thing -- within the envelope of
501.18 his common desires. It was not a vulgar and
501.19 treacherous massacre; it was a lesson, a retribu-
501.20 tion -- a demonstration of some obscure and awful
501.21 attribute of our nature which, I am afraid, is not so
501.22 very far under the surface as we like to think.
501.23 "Afterwards the whites depart unseen by Tamb'
501.24 Itam, and seem to vanish from before men's eyes
501.25 altogether; and the schooner, too, vanishes after
501.26 the manner of stolen goods. But a story is told of a
501.27 white long-boat picked up a month later in the
501.28 Indian Ocean by a cargo steamer. Two parched,
501.29 yellow, glassy-eyed, whispering skeletons in her
501.30 recognised the authority of a third, who declared
502.01 that his name was Brown. His schooner, he re-
502.02 ported, bound south with a cargo of Java sugar,
502.03 had sprung a bad leak and sank under his feet.
502.04 He and his companions were the survivors of a
502.05 crew of six. The two died on board the steamer

502.06 which rescued them. Brown lived to be seen by
502.07 me, and I can testify that he had played his part
502.08 to the last.
502.09 "It seems, however, that in going away they had
502.10 neglected to cast off Cornelius's canoe. Cornelius
502.11 himself Brown had let go at the beginning of the
502.12 shooting, with a kick for a parting benediction.
502.13 Tamb' Itam, after arising from amongst the dead,
502.14 saw the Nazarene running up and down the shore
502.15 amongst the corpses and the expiring fires. He
502.16 uttered little cries. Suddenly he rushed to the
502.17 water, and made frantic efforts to get one of the
502.18 Bugis boats into the water. 'Afterwards, till he
502.19 had seen me,' related Tamb' Itam, 'he stood looking
502.20 at the heavy canoe and scratching his head.' 'What
502.21 became of him?' I asked. Tamb' Itam, staring
502.22 at me, made an expressive gesture with his right
502.23 arm. 'Twice I struck, Tuan,' he said. 'When he
502.24 beheld me approaching he cast himself violently
502.25 on the ground and made a great outcry, kicking.
502.26 He screeched like a frightened hen till he felt the
502.27 point; then he was still, and lay staring at me while
502.28 his life went out of his eyes.'
502.29 "This done, Tamb' Itam did not tarry. He
502.30 understood the importance of being the first with
503.01 the awful news at the fort. There were, of course,
503.02 many survivors of Dain Waris's party; but in the
503.03 extremity of panic some had swum across the river,
503.04 others had bolted into the bush. The fact is that
503.05 they did not know really who struck that blow --
503.06 whether more white robbers were not coming,
503.07 whether they had not already got hold of the whole
503.08 land. They imagined themselves to be the victims
503.09 of a vast treachery, and utterly doomed to destruc-
503.10 tion. It is said that some small parties did not
503.11 come in till three days afterwards. However, a
503.12 few tried to make their way back to Patusan at
503.13 once, and one of the canoes that were patrolling the
503.14 river that morning was in sight of the camp at the
503.15 very moment of the attack. It is true that at first
503.16 the men in her leaped overboard and swam to the
503.17 opposite bank, but afterwards they returned to their
503.18 boat and started fearfully upstream. Of these
503.19 Tamb' Itam had an hour's advance."
504.01 "WHEN Tamb' Itam, paddling madly,
504.02 came into the town-reach, the women,
504.03 thronging the platforms before the
504.04 houses, were looking out for the return of Dain
504.05 Waris's little fleet of boats. The town had a
504.06 festive air, here and there men, still with spears or
504.07 guns in their hands, could be seen moving or stand-
504.08 ing on the shore in groups. Chinamen's shops
504.09 had been opened early; but the market-place was
504.10 empty, and a sentry, still posted at the corner of the
504.11 fort, made out Tamb' Itam, and shouted to those
504.12 within. The gate was wide open. Tamb' Itam
504.13 jumped ashore and ran in headlong. The first
504.14 person he met was the girl coming down from the
504.15 house.
504.16 "Tamb' Itam, disordered, panting, with tremb-
504.17 ling lips and wild eyes, stood for a time before her
504.18 as if a sudden spell had been laid on him. Then he
504.19 broke out very quickly: 'They have killed Dain
504.20 Waris and many more.' She clapped her hands,
504.21 and her first words were, 'Shut the gates.' Most
504.22 of the fortmen had gone back to their houses, but
504.23 Tamb' Itam hurried on the few who remained for
504.24 their turn of duty within. The girl stood in the
505.01 middle of the courtyard while the others ran about.
505.02 'Doramin,' she cried despairingly, as Tamb' Itam
505.03 passed her. Next time he went by he answered
505.04 her thought rapidly. 'Yes. But we have all the
505.05 powder in Patusan.' She caught him by the arm,
505.06 and, pointing at the house, 'Call him out,' she
505.07 whispered, trembling.
505.08 "Tamb' Itam ran up the steps. His master
505.09 was sleeping. 'It is I, Tamb' Itam,' he cried at the
505.10 door, 'with tidings that cannot wait.' He saw
505.11 Jim turn over on the pillow and open his eyes, and
505.12 he burst out at once. 'This, Tuan, is a day of evil,
505.13 an accursed day.' His master raised himself on his
505.14 elbow to listen -- just as Dain Waris had done. And
505.15 then Tamb' Itam began his tale, trying to relate
505.16 the story in order, calling Dain Waris Panglima,
505.17 and saying: 'The Panglima then called out to the
505.18 chief of his own boatmen, "Give Tamb' Itam
505.19 something to eat"' -- when his master put his feet
505.20 to the ground and looked at him with such a dis-
505.21 composed face that the words remained in his throat.
505.22 "'Speak out,' said Jim. 'Is he dead?' 'May
505.23 you live long,' cried Tamb' Itam. 'It was a most
505.24 cruel treachery. He ran out at the first shots and
505.25 fell....' His master walked to the window and
505.26 with his fist struck at the shutter. The room was
505.27 made light; and then in a steady voice, but speaking
505.28 fast, he began to give him orders to assemble a
505.29 fleet of boats for immediate pursuit, go to this man,
505.30 to the other -- send messengers; and as he talked
506.01 he sat down on the bed, stooping to lace his boots
506.02 hurriedly, and suddenly looked up. 'Why do
506.03 you stand here?' he asked very red-faced. 'Waste
506.04 no time.' Tamb' Itam did not move. 'Forgive
506.05 me, Tuan, but ... but,' he began to stammer.
506.06 'What?' cried his master aloud, looking terrible,
506.07 leaning forward with his hands gripping the edge
506.08 of the bed. 'It is not safe for thy servant to go
506.09 out amongst the people,' said Tamb' Itam, after
506.10 hesitating a moment.
506.11 "Then Jim understood. He had retreated from
506.12 one world, for a small matter of an impulsive jump,
506.13 and now the other, the work of his own hands, had
506.14 fallen in ruins upon his head. It was not safe for
506.15 his servant to go out amongst his own people! I
506.16 believe that in that very moment he had decided
506.17 to defy the disaster in the only way it occurred to
506.18 him such a disaster could be defied; but all I know
506.19 is that, without a word, he came out of his room and
506.20 sat before the long table, at the head of which he
506.21 was accustomed to regulate the affairs of his world,
506.22 proclaiming daily the truth that surely lived in his
506.23 heart. The dark powers should not rob him twice
506.24 of his peace. He sat like a stone figure. Tamb'
506.25 Itam, deferential, hinted at preparations for defence.
506.26 The girl he loved came in and spoke to him, but
506.27 he made a sign with his hand, and she was awed
506.28 by the dumb appeal for silence in it. She went
506.29 out on the verandah and sat on the threshold, as if to
506.30 guard him with her body from dangers outside.
507.01 "What thoughts passed through his head -- what
507.02 memories? Who can tell? Everything was gone,
507.03 and he who had been once unfaithful to his trust
507.04 had lost again all men's confidence. It was then,
507.05 I believe, he tried to write -- to somebody -- and
507.06 gave it up. Loneliness was closing on him. People
507.07 had trusted him with their lives -- only for that;
507.08 and yet they could never, as he had said, never be
507.09 made to understand him. Those without did not
507.10 hear him make a sound. Later, towards the evening,
507.11 he came to the door and called for Tamb' Itam.
507.12 'Well?' he asked. 'There is much weeping.
507.13 Much anger, too,' said Tamb' Itam. Jim looked
507.14 up at him. 'You know,' he murmured. 'Yes,
507.15 Tuan,' said Tamb' Itam. 'Thy servant does
507.16 know, and the gates are closed. We shall have to
507.17 fight.' 'Fight! What for?' he asked. 'For our
507.18 lives.' 'I have no life,' he said. Tamb' Itam
507.19 heard a cry from the girl at the door. 'Who
507.20 knows?' said Tamb' Itam. 'By audacity and
507.21 cunning we may even escape. There is much fear
507.22 in men's hearts, too.' He went out, thinking
507.23 vaguely of boats and of open sea, leaving Jim and
507.24 the girl together.
507.25 "I haven't the heart to set down here such
507.26 glimpses as she had given me of the hour or more
507.27 she passed in there wrestling with him for the
507.28 possession of her happiness. Whether he had any
507.29 hope -- what he expected, what he imagined -- it is
507.30 impossible to say. He was inflexible, and with the
508.01 growing loneliness of his obstinacy his spirit seemed
508.02 to rise above the ruins of his existence. She cried
508.03 'Fight!' into his ear. She could not understand.
508.04 There was nothing to fight for. He was going
508.05 to prove his power in another way and conquer the
508.06 fatal destiny itself. He came out into the court-
508.07 yard, and behind him, with streaming hair, wild of
508.08 face, breathless, she staggered out and leaned on the
508.09 side of the doorway. 'Open the gates,' he ordered.
508.10 Afterwards, turning to those of his men who were
508.11 inside, he gave them leave to depart to their homes.
508.12 'For how long, Tuan?' asked one of them timidly.
508.13 'For all life,' he said, in a sombre tone.
508.14 "A hush had fallen upon the town after the out-
508.15 burst of wailing and lamentation that had swept
508.16 over the river, like a gust of wind from the opened
508.17 abode of sorrow. But rumours flew in whispers,
508.18 filling the hearts with consternation and horrible
508.19 doubts. The robbers were coming back, bringing
508.20 many others with them, in a great ship, and there
508.21 would be no refuge in the land for any one. A
508.22 sense of utter insecurity as during an earthquake

508.23 pervaded the minds of men, who whispered their
508.24 suspicions, looking at each other as if in the presence
508.25 of some awful portent.
508.26 "The sun was sinking towards the forests when
508.27 Dain Waris's body was brought into Doramin's
508.28 campong. Four men carried it in, covered decently
508.29 with a white sheet which the old mother had sent
508.30 out down to the gate to meet her son on his return.
509.01 They laid him at Doramin's feet, and the old man
509.02 sat still for a long time, one hand on each knee,
509.03 looking down. The fronds of palms swayed gently,
509.04 and the foliage of fruit trees stirred above his head.
509.05 Every single man of his people was there, fully
509.06 armed, when the old nakhoda at last raised his eyes.
509.07 He moved them slowly over the crowd, as if seeking
509.08 for a missing face. Again his chin sank on his
509.09 breast. The whispers of many men mingled with
509.10 the slight rustling of the leaves.
509.11 "The Malay who had brought Tamb' Itam and
509.12 the girl to Samarang was there, too. 'Not so angry
509.13 as many,' he said to me, but struck with a great awe
509.14 and wonder at the 'suddenness of men's fate, which
509.15 hangs over their heads like a cloud charged with
509.16 thunder.' He told me that when Dain Waris's
509.17 body was uncovered at a sign of Doramin's, he
509.18 whom they often called the white lord's friend
509.19 was disclosed lying unchanged with his eyelids
509.20 a little open as if about to wake. Doramin leaned
509.21 forward a little more, like one looking for some-
509.22 thing fallen on the ground. His eyes searched the
509.23 body from its feet to its head, for the wound maybe.
509.24 It was in the forehead and small; and there was no
509.25 word spoken while one of the bystanders, stooping,
509.26 took off the silver ring from the cold stiff hand. In
509.27 silence he held it up before Doramin. A murmur of
509.28 dismay and horror rang through the crowd at the
509.29 sight of that familiar token. The old nakhoda
509.30 stared at it, and suddenly let out one great fierce
510.01 cry, deep from the chest, a roar of pain and fury,
510.02 as mighty as the bellow of a wounded bull, bringing
510.03 great fear into men's hearts, by the magnitude of
510.04 his anger and his sorrow that could be plainly
510.05 discerned without words. There was a great still-
510.06 ness afterwards for a space, while the body was
510.07 being borne aside by four men. They laid it down
510.08 under a tree, and on the instant, with one long
510.09 shriek, all the women of the household began to
510.10 wail together; they mourned with shrill cries; the
510.11 sun was setting, and in the intervals of screamed
510.12 lamentations the high sing-song voices of two old
510.13 men intoning the Koran chanted alone.
510.14 "About this time Jim, leaning on a gun-carriage,
510.15 looked at the river, and turned his back on the house;
510.16 and the girl, in the doorway, panting as if she had
510.17 run herself to a standstill, was looking at him across
510.18 the yard. Tamb' Itam stood not far from his
510.19 master, waiting patiently for what might happen.
510.20 All at once Jim, who seemed to be lost in quiet
510.21 thought, turned to him and said, 'Time to finish
510.22 this.'
510.23 "'Tuan?' said Tamb' Itam, advancing with
510.24 alacrity. He did not know what his master meant,
510.25 but as soon as Jim made a movement the girl started,
510.26 too, and walked down into the open space. It
510.27 seems that no one else of the people of the house
510.28 was in sight. She tottered slightly, and about
510.29 half-way down called out to Jim, who had appar-
510.30 ently resumed his peaceful contemplation of the
511.01 river. He turned round, setting his back against
511.02 the gun. 'Will you fight?' she cried. 'There
511.03 is nothing to fight for,' he said; 'nothing is lost.'
511.04 Saying this he made a step towards her. 'Will you
511.05 fly?' she cried again. 'There is no escape,' he
511.06 said, stopping short, and she stood still also, silent,
511.07 devouring him with her eyes. 'And you shall
511.08 go?' she said slowly. He bent his head. 'Ah!'
511.09 she exclaimed, peering at him as it were, 'you are
511.10 mad or false. Do you remember the night I
511.11 prayed you to leave me, and you said that you
511.12 could not? That it was impossible! Impossible!
511.13 Do you remember you said you would never leave
511.14 me? Why? I asked you for no promise. You
511.15 promised unasked -- remember.' 'Enough, poor
511.16 girl,' he said. 'I should not be worth having.'
511.17 "Tamb' Itam said that while they were talking
511.18 she would laugh loud and senselessly like one
511.19 under the visitation of God. His master put his
511.20 hands to his head. He was fully dressed as for
511.21 every day, but without a hat. She stopped laughing
511.22 suddenly. 'For the last time,' she cried menacingly,

511.23 'will you defend yourself?' 'Nothing can touch
511.24 me,' he said in a last flicker of superb egoism. Tamb'
511.25 Itam saw her lean forward where she stood, open
511.26 her arms, and run at him swiftly. She flung her
511.27 self upon his breast and clasped him round the
511.28 neck.
511.29 "'Ah! but I shall hold thee thus,' she cried ....
511.30 'Thou art mine!'
512.01 "She sobbed on his shoulder. The sky over
512.02 Patusan was blood-red, immense, streaming like an
512.03 open vein. An enormous sun nestled crimson
512.04 amongst the tree-tops, and the forest below had a
512.05 black and forbidding face.
512.06 "Tamb' Itam tells me that on that evening the
512.07 aspect of the heavens was angry and frightful. I
512.08 may well believe it, for I know that on that very day
512.09 a cyclone passed within sixty miles of the coast,
512.10 though there was hardly more than a languid stir
512.11 of air in the place.
512.12 "Suddenly Tamb' Itam saw Jim catch her arms,
512.13 trying to unclasp her hands. She hung on them
512.14 with her head fallen back; her hair touched the
512.15 ground. 'Come here!' his master called, and
512.16 Tamb' Itam helped to ease her down. It was
512.17 difficult to separate her fingers. Jim, bending over
512.18 her, looked earnestly upon her face, and all at once
512.19 ran to the landing-stage. Tamb' Itam followed
512.20 him, but turning his head, he saw that she had
512.21 struggled up to her feet. She ran after them a few
512.22 steps, then fell down heavily on her knees. 'Tuan!
512.23 Tuan!' called Tamb' Itam, 'look back'; but
512.24 Jim was already in a canoe, standing up paddle in
512.25 hand. He did not look back. Tamb' Itam had
512.26 just time to scramble in after him when the canoe
512.27 floated clear. The girl was then on her knees, with
512.28 clasped hands, at the water-gate. She remained
512.29 thus for a time in a supplicating attitude before she
512.30 sprang up. 'You are false!' she screamed out
513.01 after Jim. 'Forgive me,' he cried. 'Never!
513.02 Never!' she called back.
513.03 "Tamb' Itam took the paddle from Jim's hands,
513.04 it being unseemly that he should sit while his lord
513.05 paddled. When they reached the other shore
513.06 his master forbade him to come any farther; but
513.07 Tamb' Itam did follow him at a distance, walking
513.08 up the slope to Doramin's campong.
513.09 "It was beginning to grow dark. Torches
513.10 twinkled here and there. Those they met seemed
513.11 awestruck, and stood aside hastily to let Jim pass.
513.12 The wailing of women came from above. The
513.13 courtyard was full of armed Bugis with their
513.14 followers, and of Patusan people.
513.15 "I do not know what this gathering really
513.16 meant. Were these preparations for war, or for
513.17 vengeance, or to repulse a threatened invasion?
513.18 Many days elapsed before the people had ceased
513.19 to look out, quaking, for the return of the white
513.20 men with long beards and in rags, whose exact
513.21 relation to their own white man they could never
513.22 understand. Even for those simple minds poor
513.23 Jim remains under a cloud.
513.24 "Doramin, alone, immense and desolate, sat
513.25 in his arm-chair with the pair of flintlock pistols
513.26 on his knees, faced by an armed throng. When
513.27 Jim appeared, at somebody's exclamation, all the
513.28 heads turned round together, and then the mass
513.29 opened right and left, and he walked up a lane of
513.30 averted glances. Whispers followed him; mur-
514.01 murs: 'He has worked all the evil.' 'He hath
514.02 a charm.'... He heard them -- perhaps!
514.03 "When he came up into the light of torches the
514.04 wailing of the women ceased suddenly. Doramin
514.05 did not lift his head, and Jim stood silent before him
514.06 for a time. Then he looked to the left, and moved
514.07 in that direction with measured steps. Dain Waris's
514.08 mother crouched at the head of the body, and the
514.09 grey dishevelled hair concealed her face. Jim came
514.10 up slowly, looked at his dead friend, lifting the
514.11 sheet, then dropped it without a word. Slowly he
514.12 walked back.
514.13 "'He came! He came!' was running from
514.14 lip to lip, making a murmur to which he moved.
514.15 'He hath taken it upon his own head,' a voice said
514.16 aloud. He heard this and turned to the crowd.
514.17 'Yes. Upon my head.' A few people recoiled.
514.18 Jim waited awhile before Doramin, and then said
514.19 gently, 'I am come in sorrow.' He waited again.
514.20 'I am come ready and unarmed,' he repeated.
514.21 "The unwieldy old man, lowering his big fore-
514.22 head like an ox under a yoke, made an effort to rise,

514.23 clutching at the flintlock pistols on his knees. From
514.24 his troat came gurgling, choking, inhuman sounds,
514.25 and his two attendants helped him from behind.
514.26 People remarked that the ring which he had dropped
514.27 on his lap fell and rolled against the foot of the white
514.28 man, and tnat poor Jim glanced down at the talis-
514.29 man that had opened for him the door of fame, love,
514.30 and success within the wall of forests fringed with
515.01 white foam, within the coast that under the western
515.02 sun looks like the very stronghold of the night.
515.03 Doramin, struggling to keep his feet, made with
515.04 his two supporters a swaying, tottering group; his
515.05 little eyes stared with an expression of mad pain, of
515.06 rage, with a ferocious glitter, which the bystanders
515.07 noticed; and then, while Jim stood stiffened and
515.08 with bared head in the light of torches, looking
515.09 him straight in the face, he clung heavily with
515.10 his left arm round the neck of a bowed youth, and
515.11 lifting deliberately his right, shot his son's friend
515.12 through the chest.
515.13 "The crowd, which had fallen apart behind Jim
515.14 as soon as Doramin had raised his hand, rushed
515.15 tumultuously forward after the shot. They say
515.16 that the white man sent right and left at all those
515.17 faces a proud and unflinching glance. Then with
515.18 his hand over his lips he fell forward, dead.
515.19 "And that's the end. He passes away under a
515.20 cloud, inscrutable at heart, forgotten, unforgiving,
515.21 and excessively romantic. Not in the wildest days
515.22 of his boyish visions could he have seen the alluring
515.23 shape of such an extraordinary success! For it
515.24 may very well be that in the short moment of his
515.25 last proud and unflinching glance, he had beheld
515.26 the face of that opportunity which, like an Eastern
515.27 bride, had come veiled to his side.
515.28 "But we can see him, an abscure conqueror of
515.29 fame, tearing himself out of the arms of a jealous
516.01 love at the sign, at the call of his exalted egoism.
516.02 He goes away from a living woman to celebrate
516.03 his pitiless wedding with a shadowy ideal of con-
516.04 duct. Is he satisfied -- quite, now, I wonder?
516.05 We ought to know. He is one of us -- and have I
516.06 not stood up once, like an evoked ghost, to answer
516.07 for his eternal constancy? Was I so very wrong
516.08 after all? Now he is no more, there are days when
516.09 the reality of his existence comes to me with an
516.10 immense, with an overwhelming force; and yet
516.11 upon my honour there are moments, too, when he
516.12 passes from my eyes like a disembodied spirit
516.13 astray amongst the passions of this earth, ready to
516.14 surrender himself faithfully to the claim of his own
516.15 world of shades.
516.16 "Who knows? He is gone, inscrutable at
516.17 heart, and the poor girl is leading a sort of soundless,
516.18 inert life in Stein's house. Stein has aged greatly
516.19 of late. He feels it himself, and says often that
516.20 he is 'preparing to leave all this; preparing to
516.21 leave...' while he waves his hand sadly at his
516.22 butterflies."
516.23 THE END